# HERBACEOUS PERENNIAL PLANTS

# HERBACEOUS PERENNIAL PLANTS

## A Treatise on their Identification, Culture, and Garden Attributes

Third Edition

Allan M. Armitage
University of Georgia

**Library of Congress Cataloging in Publication Data**

Armitage, Allan M.
Herbaceous Perennial Plants
A Treatise on their Identification, Culture, and Garden Attributes
Third Edition

Summary: A reference guide to the identification and culture of over 3500 herbaceous perennial plant species, varieties and cultivars. Includes bibliography, common name and scientific indexes.

1. Plant Identification. 2. Plant Culture. 3. Plant Propagation. 4. Encyclopedia of Specific Identification and Cultural Requirements of Herbaceous Perennial Plants.

Paperback ISBN 978-1-58874-775-4
Hardback ISBN 978-158874-776-1



*Front cover photograph by:* Allan M. Armitage

*Cover photograph:* Crocosmia 'Lucifer' and friends at the spectacular Minter Gardens, Chilliwack, British Columbia.

*Back cover photograph by:* Jonathan H. Armitage

## *Dedication*

This book has always been dedicated to my wife, Susan, and our children, Laura, Heather, and Jonathan. However, while I wasn't looking, a few other members arrived since the last edition was published. Today I also dedicate it to Laura's children, Mary Grace and Hampton Yarbrough, and to Heather's children, Drew, Will, Ben and XX Dunagan. They are the future and the future is bright.

# *Acknowledgements*

The book just keeps getting larger, and like a bad penny, will not go away. With the publication of the third edition, there is an entire army I should thank.

Judy Marriott Laushman provided invaluable help with the third edition. She proofread, edited, and consistently corrected my poor spelling and reckless grammar. The refined quality of the writing in this edition is reflective of her editorial abilities. Her sense of humor is boundless, and her encouragement, advice and love of the work are reflected in every page.

Dr. Michael Dirr, whose vast knowledge of plant materials, enthusiasm and encouragement made the first edition (1989) possible.

Bonnie Dirr and Dr. David Sanrock, for the excellent line drawings that bring life to the endless ocean of words.

Laura Ann Segrest, for passing on to me so much of her knowledge of Southern plants and gardens. She is sorely missed.

Stephanie Shelton, who was such a large help in editing the second edition (1997).

Sandy Mackenzie, for sharing her holiday with a computer.

Kate Lee for helping choose the photos for the book, and for spending hours on bringing the common names up to date.

# Some Thoughts of the Author

***On a Third Edition:***

While awash in obscure cultivars of an obscure genus at 5:00 on an obscure morning, I asked myself why I was doing this. In fact, that question arose on many obscure mornings. The reasons are many, but the only one that counts is "Because I want to". I love this book; I love seeing it in peoples' hands, on bookshelves, in retail garden centers, on coffee tables, and worn out and tattered in the garden. As I've wandered around gardens and nurseries since the second edition was published, it was obvious that new cultivars, new genera and new names had to be brought up to date. Books on perennials come and go, but damned if I was going to watch this one end up on the clearance table in some Book Mart. Writing a new edition is not nearly as sexy as writing a new book, but almost as difficult. So, here it is, not because I had to, but because I wanted to.

***On the Internet vs. Books:***

When the first edition was written in 1989, the Internet was in its infancy, crashing around like a drunken sophomore. As I finished the second edition in 1997, far more information was available, and the future of this medium was pretty obvious. In 2008, there is no subject that cannot be searched, found, and occasionally believed on the Internet. Information about plants is everywhere, from catalogs and photos, to personal opinions about every plant (and author) known to man. How many times have I been told that people (especially young people) don't read any more, so why bother with all those printed words when you can find an e-book online? I have been asked "Why write a reference book that will be out of date when the next catalog appears, especially when anyone can find information for free at home?" Perhaps I am an old fogey, but for me, books will never go away, and a good book becomes a friend. I have never felt the same contentment hunched over a laptop wired to God knows where, as I have when curled in a comfy chair with a good book. Never will. Perhaps books will go the way of the VCR, and perhaps Gens X, Y and Z may never read a word I write, but I'll still keep penning away. See you in that comfy chair.

Having said that, the Internet has made buying plants, especially unusual plants, easier than ever before. Specialty nurseries can attract customers from all over the country more efficiently and with less expense than sending out thousands of paper catalogs. If the Internet has changed anything, it is not what we read but how we buy. Today, the successful nurseryman and the inquisitive gardener more frequently meet online in the ether, not in line at the store.

*On the Decline of Gardening:*

If I listened to the plant marketing gurus out there, I would believe that gardening is on its deathbed. According to them, nobody cares about plants, only plant function. Nobody cares about gardens, only lifestyles. Heck, so few people actually garden anymore that it is amazing any plants are sold at all. I have heard so many times that "gardening is work", nobody wants to work, too much time, too much effort, yada, yada, yada, that I am nauseated. I might even believe such drivel if I was a marketing fellow, but those comments aren't at all consistent with my experiences. Perhaps they need to join me for a few weeks when I speak to gardeners and industry people like you. The hundreds and hundreds of "gardeners" who find their way to my talks are not coming to see my pretty face. They are there because they love the subject, and can't get enough. Good grief, look at the catalogs, look at the stores—people would not be spending money on breeding, promotion and distribution of plants if they believed nobody cared. I have no doubt the markets are changing, and no doubt that the data are real, but gardening and gardeners aren't going anywhere for a long time.

That is not to say change has not occurred. One of the disturbing trends has been the closing of some fine nurseries since the last edition was published. Most times, such shut-downs are normal; competition, poor management, or tired owners who want to relax a little more. Online sites and newer ventures have more than made up for the number of nurseries that have been lost; however, when places like Heronswood Nursery in Oregon shutters its northwestern doors, we are all a little wounded.

*On the Meaning of Gardening:*

When gardeners are asked to describe reasons for gardening, three words emerge time and again: therapeutic, creative and exciting. Such words are more often associated with sporting events than gardening, however, therapy, creativity, and excitement are integral parts of gardening.

Therapeutic, because of the feeling that all is well with the world when our hands are in Mother Earth. Therapeutic because when a seed is sown, a cutting rooted, or seedling planted, we have accomplished something important.

Creative, because artistry is an inescapable part of gardening. A swath of *Astilbe* brightens the shade, a grouping of cool-leaved *Artemisia* brings calm to its neighbors, and a half dozen forget-me-nots sing of spring. Each grouping creates vistas of beauty. We do not require a degree in landscape architecture to create such beauty; all we need is the simple love of gardening.

Exciting is a word seldom attributed to gardening. But is it not exciting to watch a garden change with time? To watch *Asarum*, wild ginger, bull through the soil in early spring, anticipate the popping of the buds of balloon flower, and anticipate the magic of the re-emergence of resurrection flower, is truly exciting.

*Voices about Gardening:*

Perhaps a couple of quotes from the past are also appropriate. The first is attributed to the great plant hunter Ernest Henry Wilson, who wrote it just three years before his death in 1930. "There are no happier folk than plant-lovers and none more generous than those who garden. There is a delightful freemasonry about them; they mingle on a common plane, share freely their knowledge and with advice help one over the stepping stones that lead to success. It is truthfully said that a congenial companion doubles the pleasures and halves the discomforts of travel and so it is with the brotherhood who love plants." E. H. Wilson, *Plant Hunting,* v.1, 1927.

A second quote comes from another one of my former students, who wrote an essay on the why people embrace perennials in their gardens. Those who believe our students aren't among the finest in the world need to come and visit my classes.

"Americans, as a rule, live with a certain sense of urgency. Perhaps this is the price we pay for living in such a young country. Why waste time with some fickle plant which will flower only for a few short moments each year when there are countless annuals just begging to bloom all summer long? The commitment perennials require represents the driving force behind gardening as a whole. When someone kills a window box of petunias, there is no love lost. Odds are that a quick trip to Kmart will have the window box blooming again in short order. Let there be no doubt about the glorious beauty of a well-planted annual garden. But, for all their show and eagerness-to-please, annuals provoke no anticipation. To be among an established garden teaches one why we have gardens at all; gardens are our refuge from the irritations of everyday life, a place of peace, serenity and provide the hope and anticipation of good things to come." Ken James, student, 1995. By the way, today, Ken and his wife Leah are proud owners of James Greenhouses in beautiful Colbert, Georgia, and are exceptional growers of perennials.

***On a Garden:***

A garden is a melding of different plants, including trees, shrubs, and herbaceous species. A garden lacks grandeur and grace without the architecture and framework provided by stately trees. A single specimen, such as a cedar of Lebanon, can define an entire garden. Like a snow-capped mountain in the distance, it is never out of sight or out of mind. Shrubs are indispensable for screening, massing, form and texture. From abelia to zenobia, they provide the glue that bonds the trees and herbaceous plants together. Broad sweeps of annuals such as geraniums, celosia and marigolds provide interest through the gardening season and, like magnets, draw the eye to their carpet of color. Herbaceous perennials add a unique charm and flavor to any garden.

There are few times when perennials do not add interest and change. From barren winter ground, through frenzied activity in the spring, until flower buds are visible, perennials are always changing. Finally, the flowers can wait no longer and islands of color blaze like flares in the night. Many have foliage more colorful than flowers, fruits that compete with holly, and fall colors as dramatic as sugar maples. To the connoisseur and amateur, there is nothing more colorful and interesting than a well-conceived perennial border. However, all great borders have backdrops of hedges or tree canopies, and annuals to fill in gaps. Perennials are an important part of the garden but are just that, a part of the garden. Perennials or a perennial border should be woven into a garden, rather than being the garden. Such a garden is much more beautiful than the sum of the beauty of the individual parts.

***On a Gardener:***

Gardening is hard work! Low maintenance does not mean no maintenance. "No maintenance" gardening does not exist, although lower maintenance is possible with proper plant selection. I travel and talk with gardeners of all ages all the time. I have met sore gardeners, tired gardeners and broke gardeners, but I've never met an old gardener. If anything defines a gardener, it is his belief in the future. It is impossible to get old when one is always thinking about the future. Planting bulbs in the fall turns one's thoughts to spring, planting a small tree today transports us to its cool shade tomorrow. Gardening simply does not allow one to be mentally old, because there are too many plants and beauty yet to be realized.

The one absolute of gardeners is faith. Regardless of how bad past gardens have been, every gardener believes that next year's will be better. We even still believe that the descriptions and photos in catalogs are true! Yes, we are a trusting bunch. It is easy to age when there is nothing to believe in, nothing to hope for; gardeners, however, simply refuse to grow up. As Thomas Jefferson so eloquently stated "Though an old man, I am but a young gardener".

***On North and South:***

Many of the same species are cultivated in Montreal, Canada, and Athens, Georgia, areas characterized, as far north and deep south. I have gardened in both places as well as in East Lansing, Michigan and traveled with open eyes throughout the United States, Canada, Australia, New Zealand, the Mideast, South Africa and much of Europe. Certain species may thrive in one area but perform poorly in another. Obvious climatic differences exist among areas in North America, and even subtle differences within a garden influence plant performance. No absolute demarcation exists where North ends and South begins, but in this book the South incorporates zones 7-10 of the United States Department of Agriculture Hardiness Zone Map. Zone 7 (minimum 0-10°F) ranges as far north as Rhode Island, into Virginia, and cuts across Tennessee, Arkansas, central Oklahoma, central Texas, southern New Mexico and into Arizona and California. Many climatic factors interact with the plants' ability to thrive or languish in a given zone, and hardiness ratings must be treated cautiously (see On Hardiness Ratings).

Several differences are obvious between plants of the same species grown in northern and southern locales. In the South, temperate zone plants flower earlier, are taller and may have weaker stems due to the accumulated heat. Tall forms tend to collapse without support and dwarf selections are usually more effective in the southern garden. Fertilizer need not be applied as generously in the South as in the North, particularly on tall cultivars, as additional growth is not the goal. Lanky, leggy growth occurs at the expense of flower production if too much nitrogen is applied. This happens regardless of latitude, but is more prominent in the South. The lack of snow is a major detriment to overwintering perennials anywhere. Snow provides insulation from the cold and plants tucked beneath the protective eiderdown survive cold winters well. That is why my friends in the Gaspe' of Quebec (zone 3) claim that gardening is so easy there.

Where rain replaces snow (as in the South), the major survival problem is inadequate drainage. This is particularly true on heavy clay where cold winter rains result in soggy, water-logged soils and roots, crowns, and bulbs are immersed in free-standing water. Rot organisms proliferate and plants disappear, not because of lack of cold hardiness but because they rotted in the ground. Addition of bark, peat moss or other materials that aid drainage alleviate root rot problems. Summer temperatures and humidity in the South are also detriments to perenniality. Plants not adapted to the South often perform poorly because of high night temperatures. Plants use oxygen and release carbon dioxide (similar to humans) in the process of respiration. Heat significantly affects the rate of plant respiration. In general, for every 16°F rise in temperature, respiration doubles. When night temperatures remain above 70°F the process of respiration continues unabated and competes more aggressively for the carbohydrates produced during the day by photosynthesis. This results in lack of stored carbohydrates, inhibition of chlorophyll synthesis, and lack of secondary cell wall formation. The consequence is reduced vigor, weak stunted plants and small foliage. Species not capable of acclimatization cannot store the reserves necessary to survive the winter. In many cases, death is due not to lack of winter hardiness, but lack of summer tolerance. Many problems may be minimized with fall planting, allowing plants time to build starch reserves and develop an extensive root system prior to the onset of winter. Fall planting is more critical in the South than the North for most temperate species.

Reading all the problems associated with gardening in the South, one would believe that I think southern gardening is more difficult than northern gardening. I do. More difficult, but equally wonderful. I have gardened in Athens for over 25 years now, and I think I am finally getting the hang of it. I have a ball every day.

Regardless of where one gardens, two things become self-evident. The first is that soil preparation is half the battle. The second has to do with the plants one selects. Choosing plants that are adapted to the site and climate makes more sense than constantly trying to grow plants that are doomed to failure within a year or two. This is not to say that we shouldn't experiment with plant selection—half the fun of gardening is to try plants that "are not supposed to grow here". A quick read of good catalogs quickly shows that there is no end to species and cultivars to try, without trying to overwinter a plant native to the tropics.

### *On Hardiness Ratings:*

United States Department of Agriculture (USDA) hardiness zones have been used by commercial growers and gardeners for many years. Zones provide guidelines to measure plants' ability to survive cold temperatures. To be sure, they are imperfect but they are the best we have at present to objectively evaluate geographical limits of adaptability. The USDA hardiness map, published in 1990 (see page xxviii), is based on minimum winter temperatures and must be interpreted cautiously. In fact, with the obvious climate changes occurring today, minimum temperatures will rise and zone designations throughout North America are bound to inch up. Many factors affect plant growth other than average minimum temperatures. For example, zone 7 in Athens, Georgia is a different world from zone 7 in central California. Although minimum temperatures may be similar, summer temperatures during the night, humidity and rainfall are quite different. Valleys and mountains in the same hardiness zone are different climatically and plants that survive in higher elevations may perish when they descend 500 feet. Experienced gardeners will tell you they have multiple zones in their own gardens. Microclimates exist even in a small garden and plants that perform poorly in one location often perk up when moved to a more sheltered environment.

Heat tolerance is more difficult to evaluate than cold tolerance. Plants respond to cold by dying; to heat by languishing. However, heat tolerance or summer hardiness ratings are equally important in predicting plant performance. European garden literature is a rich source of information but descriptions must be taken with a grain of salt. Similarly, descriptions of plant habit in the North and West may not mirror performance in the South or East. This is primarily due to differences in summer hardiness. In this text, I have attempted to provide summer hardiness ratings for all species based on experimentation, observation, existing literature, and discussions with gardeners. The southern hardiness range listed is one in which the species performs well, if other factors such as shade, sun, or proper drainage are provided. Plants may survive south of that rating, but performance is significantly reduced. The ratings must not be considered gospel, but it is hoped they will add to the body of horticultural knowledge. Plants do not read, and testing species where they are not supposed to grow often provides pleasant surprises.

### *On Garden Design:*

Design is an important aspect of gardening. Great garden designers are born, not made, and nurtured through observation and experience. Principles of design abound and even I try to adhere to the basics. Most importantly, the design should be pleasing to the owner and not planned with others in mind. Select one or two dominant colors that appeal and use colors that complement, rather than distract from each other. The aim of color is to tie plants together and then wed the planting to the site. One of the reasons for the popularity of gray and silver foliage, as well as white flowers, is their ability to unite the garden.

However, I am the first to admit that I am a poor designer. To me, the most important part of design is that the plants perform well in the site. I can usually be found with a trowel in one hand and a potted plant in the other, searching for any empty ground in which to place the sucker. Good performance is defined by persistent, fresh foliage, vigorous growth, and copious flower production. Selection on the basis of plant performance is more important than selection based on the color wheel. To totally ignore design, however, is to relegate a garden to a collection of plants.

Water features should be included in every garden. The presence of water, be it a birdbath, fountain, pond, or stream, does more to soften and define a garden than all other features combined. I am always learning about garden design and someday will discourse competently on hues, shapes, feelings, and combinations. Until then, however, I will enjoy the eclectic combination of plant material around my garden pond.

***On Plant Nomenclature:***

Plant names are no different than any other names; some are long and complicated, others are short and sweet. A scientific name defines a single species only, but a common name may describe a dozen or more. A valid scientific name is accepted throughout the world, regardless of language or politics. The science of nomenclature is practiced by taxonomists who attempt to bring order out of chaos. Because one of their goals is to validate current scientific names and replace incorrect ones, scientific names are constantly evolving. Two main problems occur when taxonomist meets gardener. The first occurs when a new scientific name replaces one of long standing. *Chrysanthemum leucanthemum* became *Leucanthemum vulgare; Vinca rosea* is *Catharanthus roseus; Helleborus corsicus* has become *H. argutifolius;* and the entire *Aster* and *Cimicifuga* genera have essentially disappeared. At times, it seems like a change in nomenclature is accomplished just to keep someone busy, however, if the new name is agreed on by taxonomic authorities, it should also be accepted by horticulturists and gardeners.

This brings up the second problem. Taxonomists don't always agree. Names accepted by one authority aren't necessarily accepted by other equally respected authorities due to valid differences of opinion and methodology. That leaves everyone in a muddle, so muddle we do.

Plants are listed by genus, species, variety and cultivar. A genus is a closely related group of plants consisting of one or more species. Species within a genus have more characteristics in common with each other than they do with species in other genera. Often genera are closely related and differences are difficult to discern. *Silene* and *Delphinium* are obviously different but telling the difference between *Silene, Agrostemma* and *Lychnis* is difficult. The genus name begins with an upper case letter and is underlined or written in italics. A species is difficult to define but may be thought of as a type of plant distinct from other types by identifiable features. The unique characteristics are reproducible from one generation to generation through seed. A species name begins with a lower case letter and is underlined or written in italics.

Often, individual plants may be slightly different from other members of the species and the definable characteristic is reproduced each generation. This group of plants is known as a variety and has enough similarities with others to be in the same species but is sufficiently different to be grouped as a separate variety. Often varieties are geographically distinct and have their own range. Varieties breed relatively true from seed, passing on their definable differences from parent to offspring. Varieties are preceded with "var." and underlined or written in italics. For example, *Muscari comosum* var. *monstrosum* infers that a group of plants of *Muscari comosum* differs in some way to be placed in var. *monstrosum,* and reproduces this difference by seed.

A cultivar refers to a cultivated variety and may be the result of hybridization, random mutation, or plant selection. For our purposes, cultivar differs from variety in that the definable factors that make a cultivar unique are not passed on from generation to generation by seed. Cultivars are propagated vegetatively by tissue culture, cuttings, grafting or divisions (although commercial breeders maintain homozygous lines so seed-propagated cultivars may be offered). Cultivars begin with upper case letters and are enclosed by single quotation marks. For example, *Lychnis coronaria* 'Abbotswood Rose' has lighter pink flowers than the species. Seeds produced by plants of 'Abbotswood Rose' do not result in similar plants.

The distinction between variety and cultivar diminishes when varieties are given cultivar names. For example, var. *alba* is a common variety of many species and usually refers to the presence of white flowers. If those plants are marketed under a cultivar name such as 'White Knight' or 'Snow White', it is impossible to know if plants are reproducible sexually or asexually. Unfortunately, in horticultural and gardening circles, the terms cultivar and variety are used interchangeably.

Hybrids are common and characteristics from each parent may be found in the offspring. Interspecific hybrids are designated by an "x" and are usually reproducible only vegetatively. For example, *Polygonatum* x *hybridum* is a hybrid between *P. multiflorum* and *P. odoratum* and is reproduced by division of the rootstock. Intergeneric hybrids occasionally occur and are designated by an uppercase (X) before the name. X *Heucherella alba* is a hybrid between *Heuchera brizoides* and *Tiarella wherryi.* The X is not sounded.

I have attempted to sort out the nomenclature where possible. There is still a long way to go. Comments from readers are welcome.

### *On Common Names:*

I like common names. Names like cardinal flower, resurrection lily, pussytoes, and blackberry lily are far more interesting than *Lobelia cardinalis, Lycoris squamigera, Antennaria dioica,* and *Belamcanda chinensis.* They also bring with them part of the history of discovery and use of the species. Lily-of-the-valley tells me more about the plant I am about to buy than *Convallaria majalis,* while lungwort describes a philosophy of naming plants much better than does *Pulmonaria officinalis.* Common names may describe the flower, such as pincushion flower (*Scabiosa*); leaves, spotted geranium, (*Geranium maculatum*); origin, Persian buttercup (*Ranunculus asiaticus*); medicinal properties, self-heal (*Prunella vulgaris*); or the discoverer, Stokes aster, (*Stokesia*). Unfortunately, the same common name may be used for more than one species or a single species may be known by several common names, depending on area of the country.

I have heard arguments from purists that common names are irrelevant and their use should not be encouraged. What nonsense! If one wants to see the demise of gardening, keep making it complicated. Gardening is way too complicated as it is, what with 30 cultivars of this, 10 of that and names that are unpronounceable even by Professor Higgins. Gardeners and professionals should encourage common names; they make what we do so much more user-friendly.

***On Pronunciation:***

Most people like to pronounce names with some degree of confidence. Scientific names can be intimidating and often we will not say them for fear of sounding ignorant. Like anything else, pronunciation is something that one feels confident with only with continued use. If scientific names are seldom part of one's gardening vocabulary, we will always stumble and stutter. I have provided pronunciation guides for most genera and specific epithets principally based on books and articles but with a definite Armitage bias as well.

However, let's get real. Does it really matter if *paniculata* is pronounced (pa-nik-ew-lah′ ta) or (pa-nik-ew-lay′ ta)? I prefer to pronounce *Stokesia* as (stokes′ ee-a), in recognition of Dr. John Stokes, for whom the genus was named. However (stow-keys′ ee-a) is commonly used.and equally understood. So, here is the important part. Get the syllables in the right order, then fire away. Don't worry about sounding silly, it is only the garden snob who continually tries to correct you. And who needs snobs in a garden?

***On The Most Important Thing:***

The most important thing about gardening is to have fun. There will be aches, frustration, money poorly spent and disappointment, but the pleasure should always outweigh the pain. Don't get serious, ever, about gardening. The worst oxymoron in all of horticulture is "serious gardener". Don't be one; let it wash over you and enjoy the day.

# An Explanation of Plant Headings

Generic entries are provided with a pronunciation guide, common name and family. Each specific epithet (the species term) has a pronunciation guide, common name, and average height and width of mature plants. The height and width are guides to help with placement in the garden. Climate, soils, rainfall, irrigation practices and fertility will influence these guidelines. The next line provides season of flowering (based on zone 5-7), flower color, origin and cold hardiness range, based on the USDA zone hardiness map.

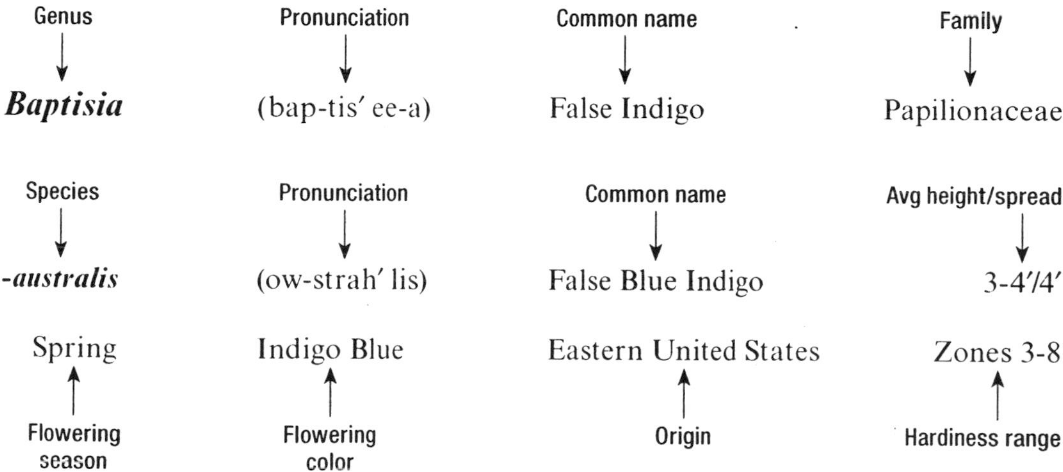


A quick reference table is provided for genera with two or more cultivated species. Easily identifiable differences among species are listed. Descriptions for each species and known cultivars and varieties are also included. Not every cultivar or variety has found its way into the book, but ideally most of available selections are present. Related species and hybrids are then described briefly. In general, related species are not always as available to the gardening public but have worthy garden characteristics.

Descriptions such as flower color and height are based on my experience and travels and they will differ slightly from North to South and East to West. All the bad jokes and opinions are mine, made proudly and without shame. But, regardless of how opined I may be, they are still only opinions. I welcome yours.

# Leaf and Flower Terminology

## Leaves:

***Arrangement:***

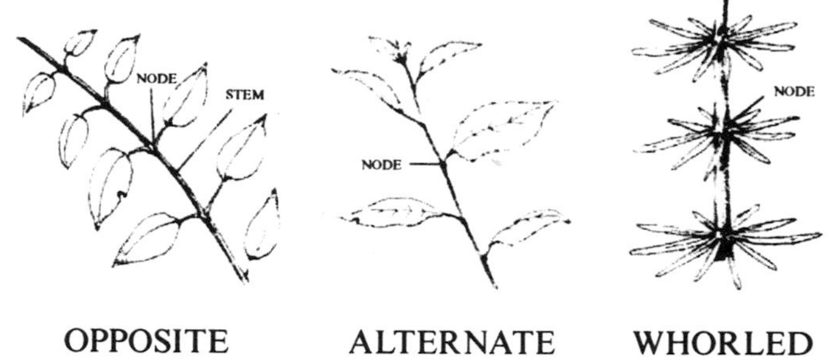


***Simple vs. Compound leaves:***

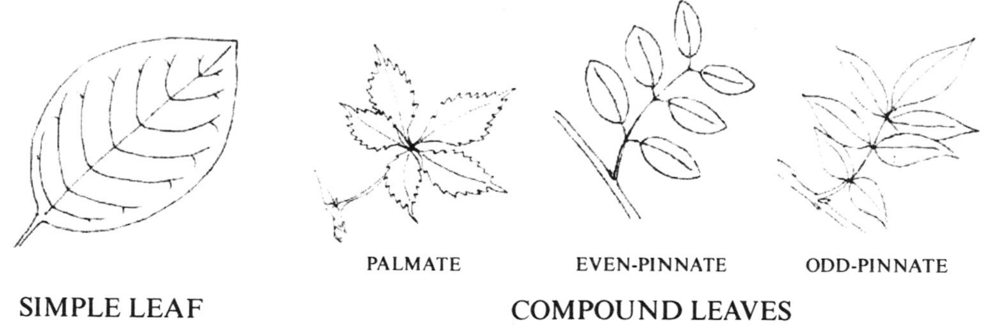

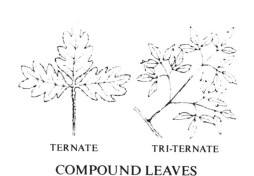


TERNATE TRI-TERNATE

COMPOUND LEAVES

***Shapes:***

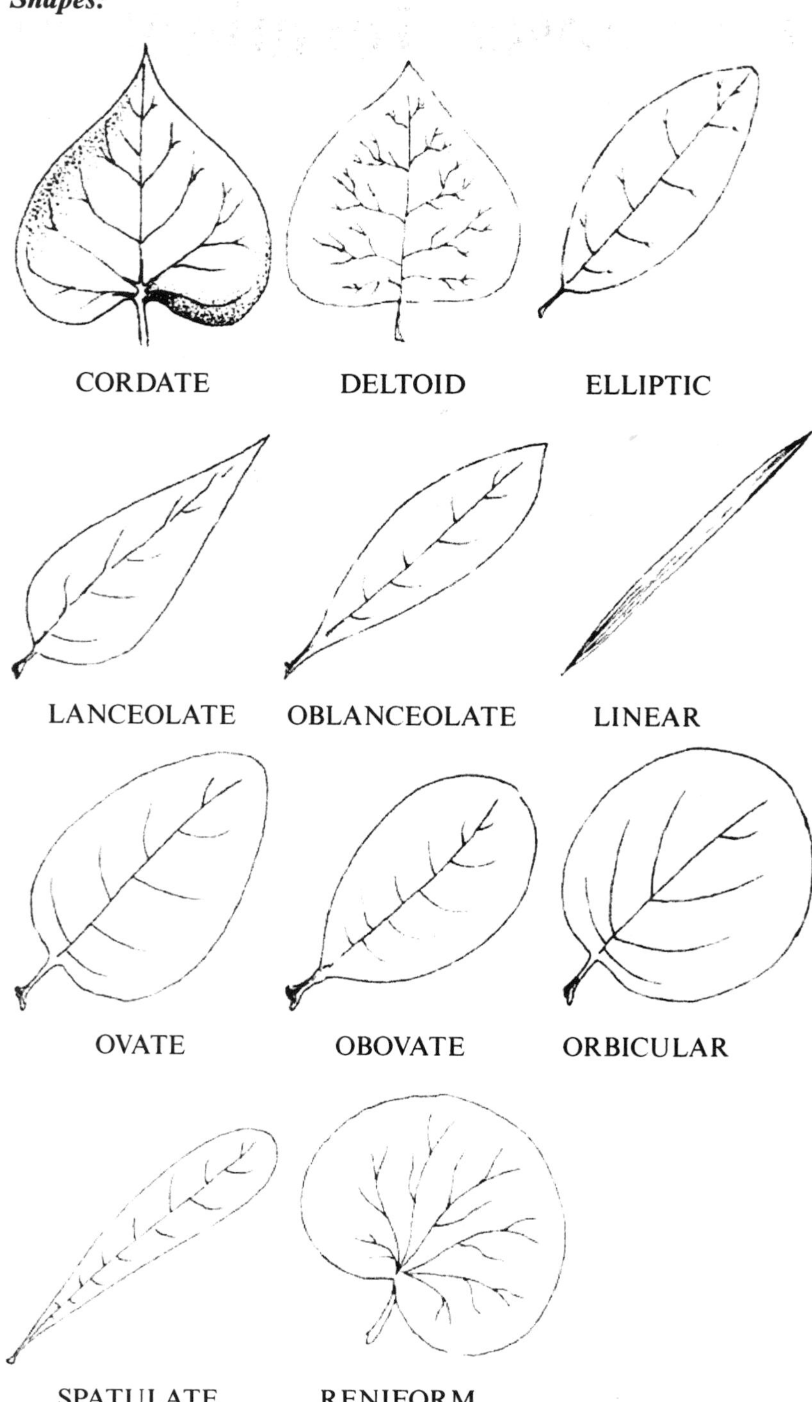
CORDATE
DELTOID
ELLIPTIC
LANCEOLATE
OBLANCEOLATE
LINEAR
OVATE
OBOVATE
ORBICULAR
SPATULATE
RENIFORM

***Margins:***

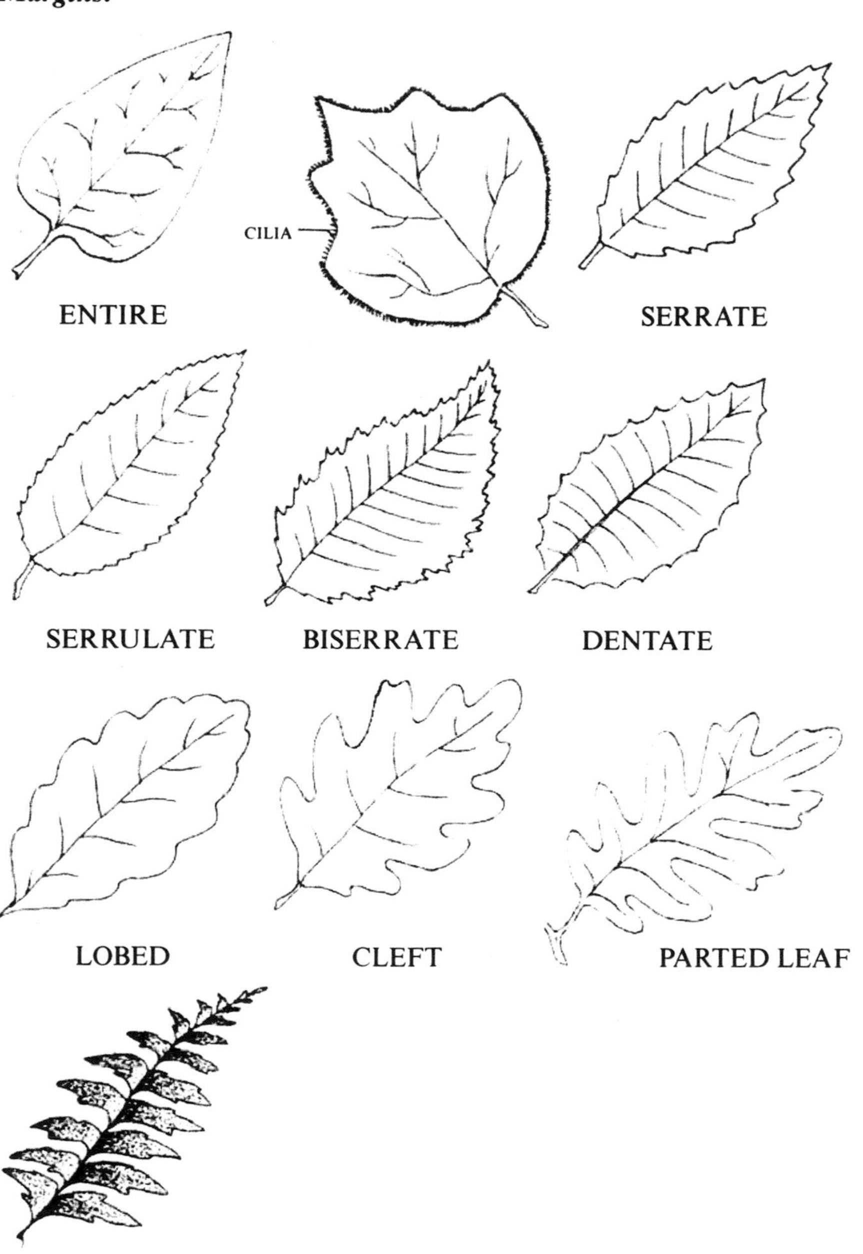
ENTIRE
CILIA
SERRATE
SERRULATE
BISERRATE
DENTATE
LOBED
CLEFT
PARTED LEAF
DIVIDED LEAF

*Apices (the tips):*

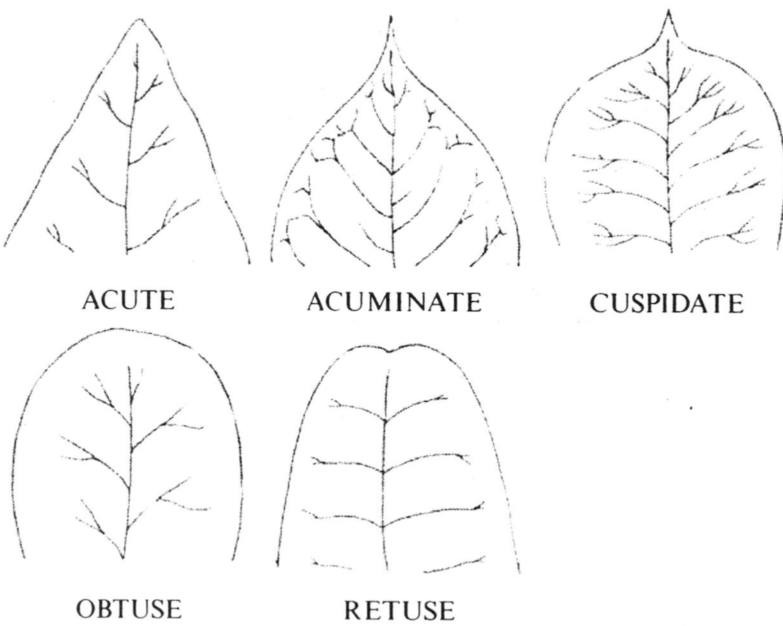


*Bases (the bottoms):*

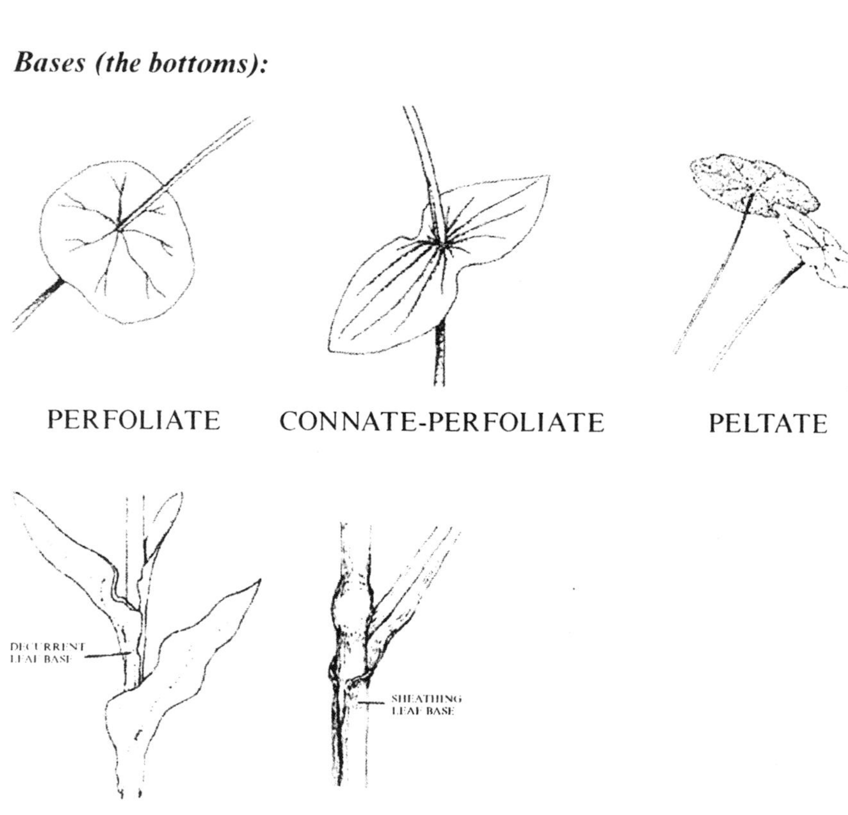

***Bases (the bottoms):***

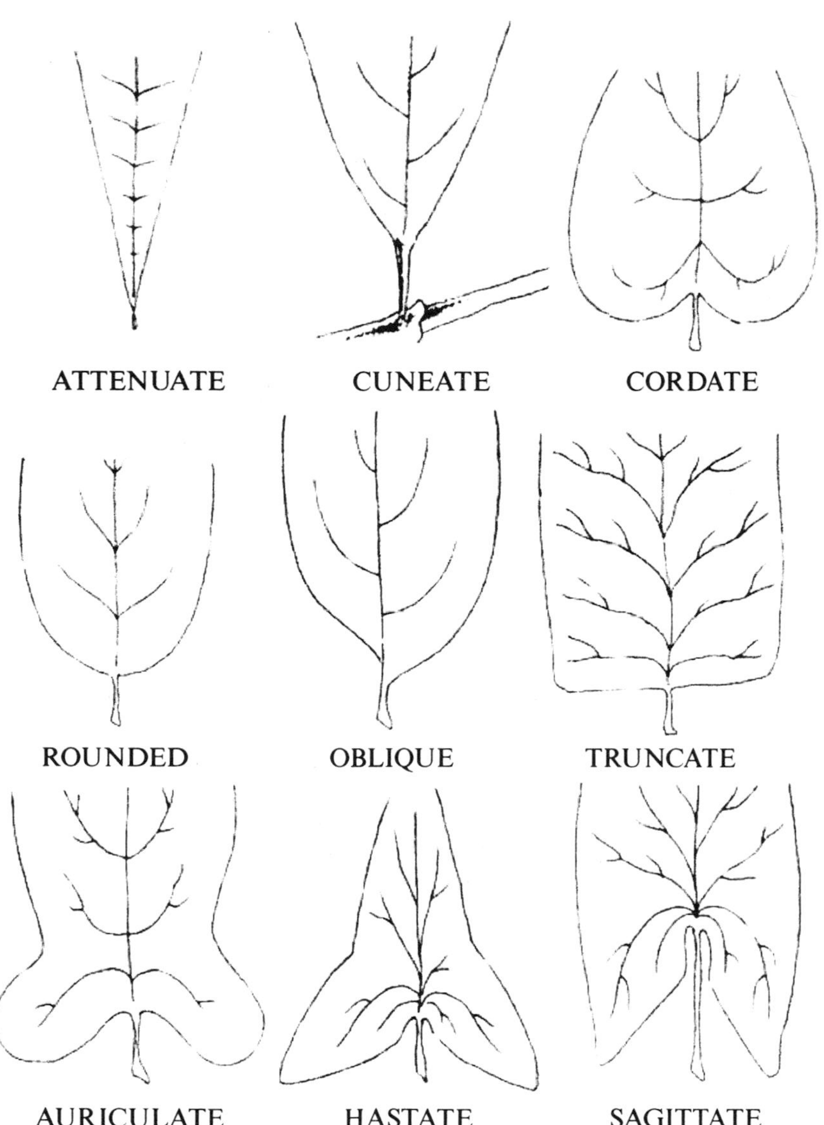

# Flowers:

### *Parts and shapes:*

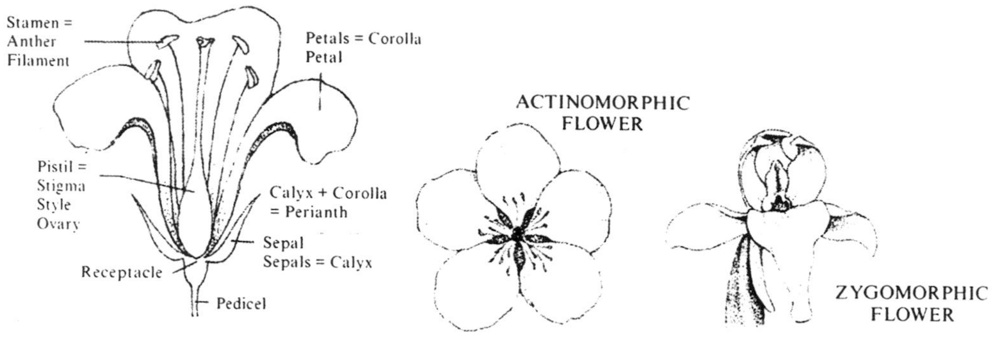


### *Inflorescences:*

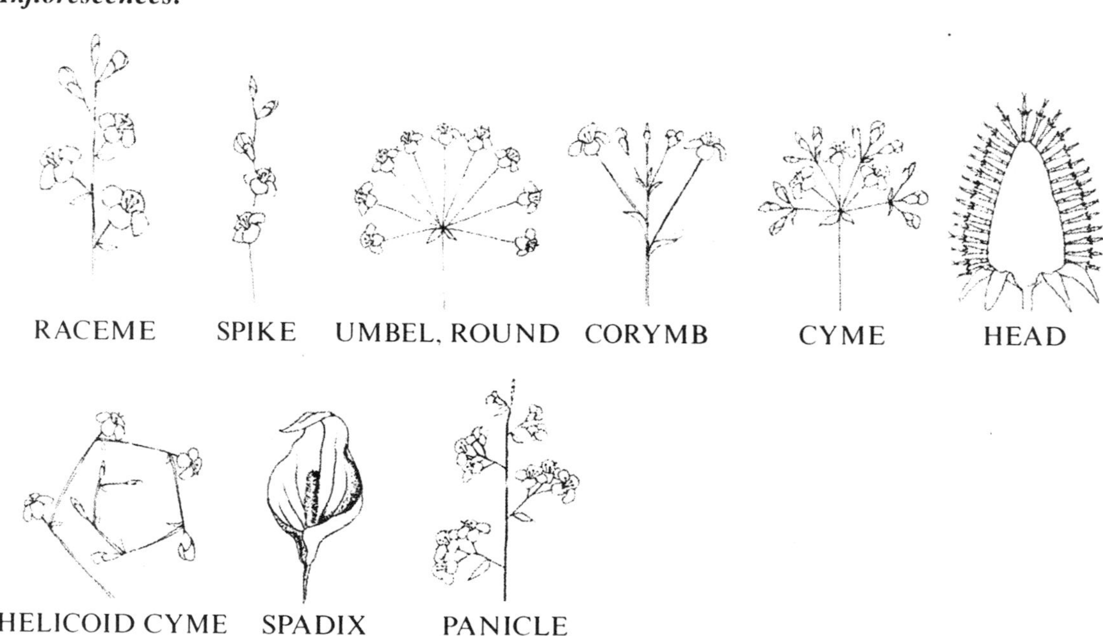

# USDA Plant Hardiness Zone Map

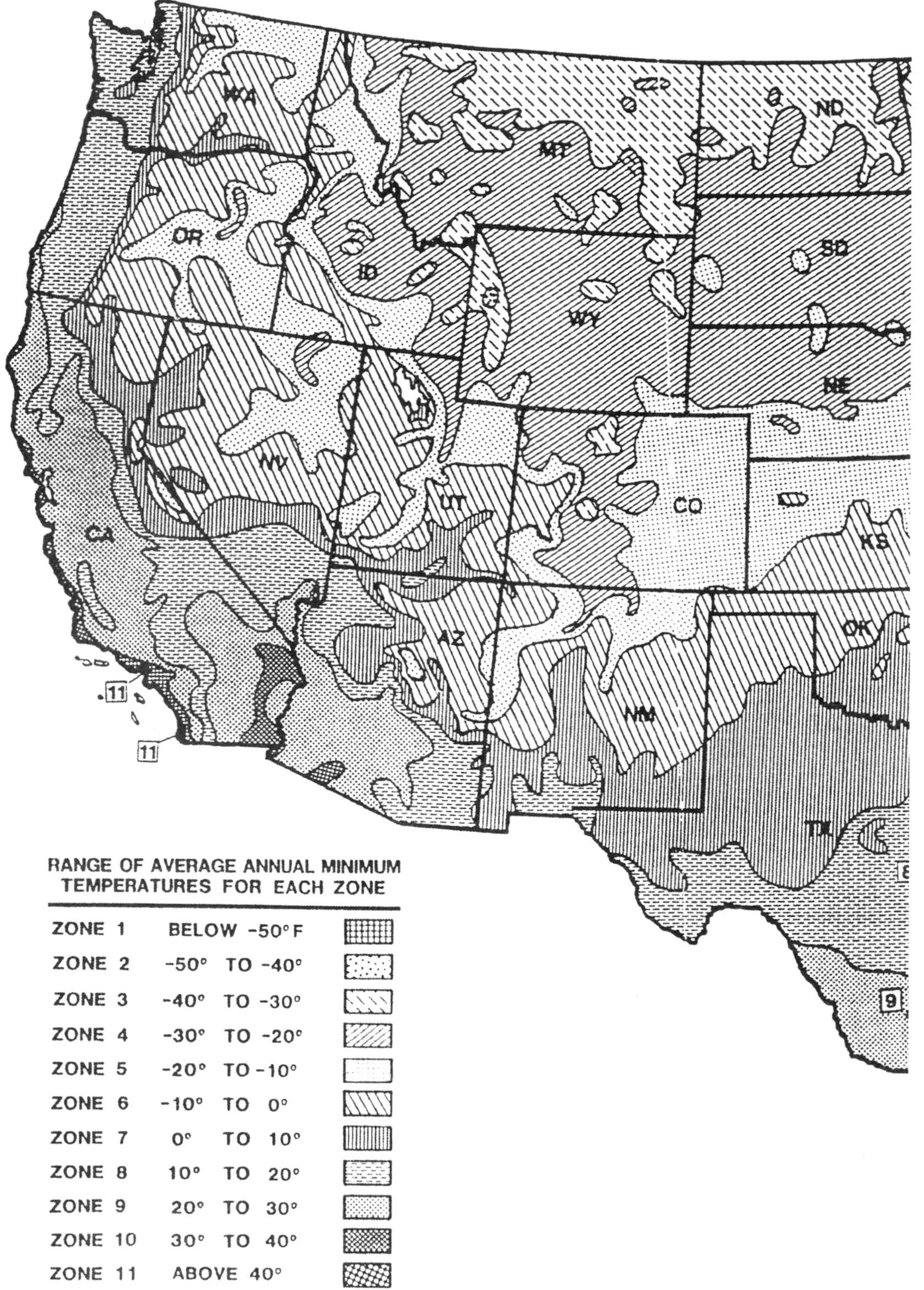

WA
OR
CA
NV
ID
MT
WY
UT
AZ
CO
NM
ND
SD
NE
KS
OK
TX
11
11
9
RANGE OF AVERAGE ANNUAL MINIMUM TEMPERATURES FOR EACH ZONE
ZONE 1 BELOW -50° F
ZONE 2 -50° TO -40°
ZONE 3 -40° TO -30°
ZONE 4 -30° TO -20°
ZONE 5 -20° TO -10°
ZONE 6 -10° TO 0°
ZONE 7 0° TO 10°
ZONE 8 10° TO 20°
ZONE 9 20° TO 30°
ZONE 10 30° TO 40°
ZONE 11 ABOVE 40°

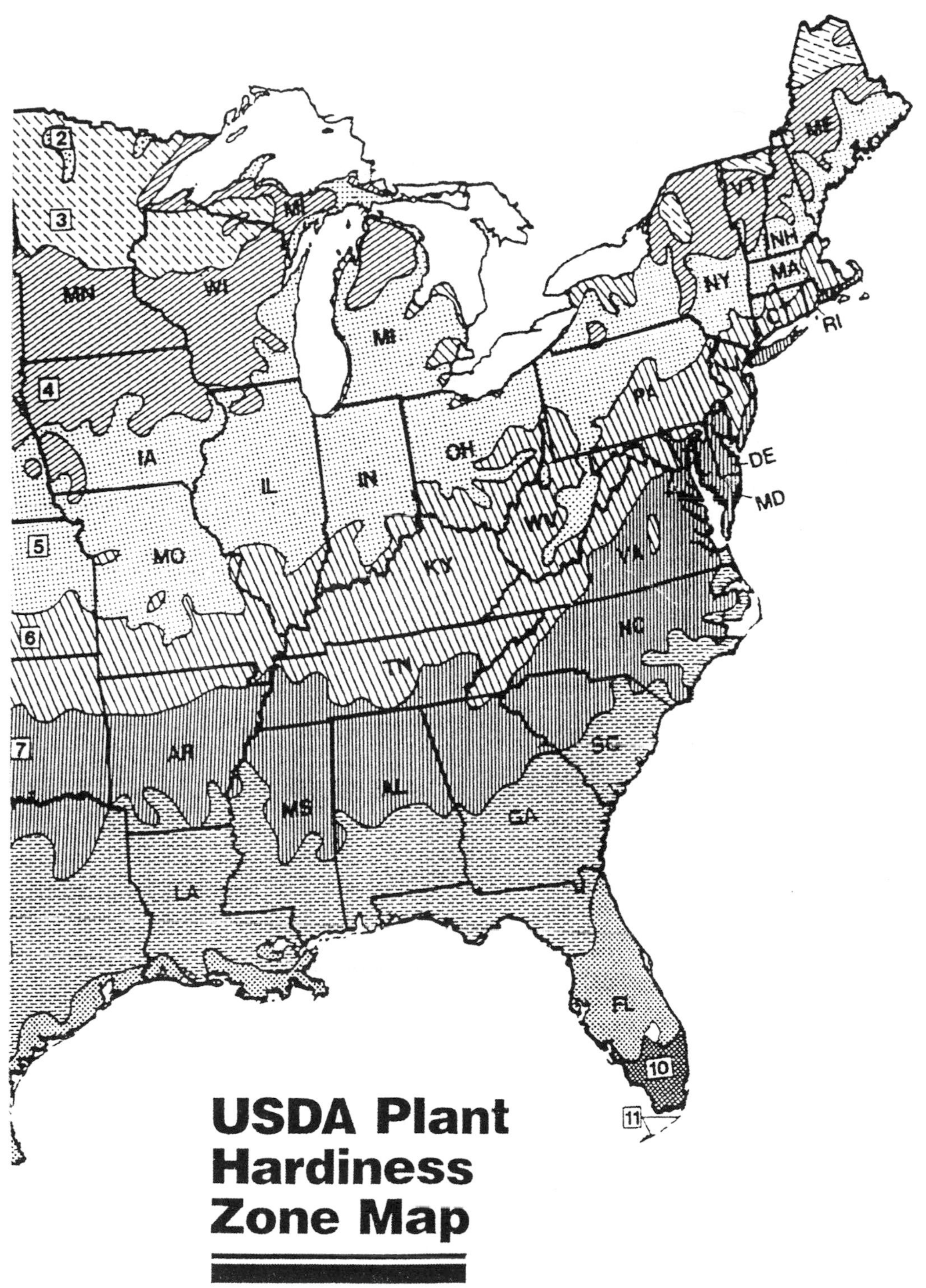


# USDA Plant Hardiness Zone Map

# A

***Acaena*** (a-sane′ a) New Zealand Bur Rosaceae

Of the 100 species in this genus, we are lucky to see a half a dozen in even the better public gardens in North America. As the common name suggests, many species are native to New Zealand, including its namesake, *A. novae-zelandiae*. Other common names for this plant are much more alliterative and any plant with names like pirri-pirri bur, bidgee-widgee and biddy biddy is probably worth the price of purchase alone. The excellent plantings one sees in New Zealand and throughout the British Isles have not made the transition to the North American garden particularly well. Being native to New Zealand generally equates to sure and rapid death for eastern and southern gardeners, but a reasonable chance of success for West Coasters. Nevertheless, where conditions are favorable, the dense, 2-3″ tall mat-forming plants make attractive ground covers and are highly sought after.

Some gardeners find them a little too aggressive (some lucky gardeners call them thugs), as plants can take over significant areas of the rock garden or small border. They root at the nodes and are excellent for placing between stepping stones or trailing over walls. All species prefer full sun, although *A. microphylla*, rosy-spined New Zealand bur, *A. inermis*, spineless acaena, and its cultivar 'Purpurea' and *A. myriophylla*, fern-leaved New Zealand bur, are more shade tolerant than others. All species prefer low humidity and excellent drainage and are cold hardy to about 10°F (zones 7-8), although some sources have them hardy to zone 6.

In general, the flowers are not particularly noticeable, being small, greenish and lacking petals (apetalous). However, the pea-green to steel-blue leaves are pinnately compound and often finely serrated, and colorful bur-like fruit (achenes) keep gardeners wanting more. The burs are carried well above the foliage and are the most interesting part of the plants. Most leaves are about 2″ long but *A. myriophylla* has 6-8″ long green leaves with 15-17 leaflets with burs held at the end of the 6-9″ flower stems. The spherical burs are often spiny and brightly colored relative to the foliage.

The more "burs" I see, the more I would like to see selection work done to enhance their tolerance to "real" weather. Hardiness is always a topic of discussion for those few people who know about these plants. Most books suggest zone 7 for cold hardiness, but Arrowhead Alpines in Fowlerville, Michigan (zone 5) says that *A. inermis*

'Purpurea' is "hardy and nearly indestructible here". 'Blue Haze' seems to be fairly tolerant, but I have managed to kill it in my Athens garden. The vigor of *A. fissistipula* is well known and if crossed with blue foliage forms might provide some potentially tough, handsome offspring. Many other combinations await the bur breeder.

Propagation is usually by division, but cuttings and seed are also used. Seed should be sown in open containers in the fall, and placed in cold frames over winter.

-***anserinifolia*** (an-sir-in-i-foe′ lee-a) Bronze Pirri-Pirri Bur 2-4″/10″
Spring Rose New Zealand Zones 7b-9

This species bears dull green hairy leaves which are paler green beneath, and bronze or red fruit. Five to eight pairs of leaflets are tinged with pink and the combination is handsome indeed. The species is seldom offered but 'Bronzette', a cross with *A. novae-zelandiae*, is occasionally found. Plants have bronze fruit and green-bronze foliage and grow about 6″ tall.

-***microphylla*** (mike′ ro-fil-ah) Rosy-spined New Zealand Bur 2-4″/12″
Spring Dull Rose New Zealand Zones 7-9

The short plant has small silver-blue to blue-green compound leaves with a strong hint of copper and makes an exceptionally good ground cover. The flowers are rather forgettable but the handsome pink to rosy red fruit, nearly an inch across, looks like a spiny wicked thing, but is in fact quite soft. Plants are a little more cold hardy and more tolerant of poorly-drained soils than other species. If conditions are right, it can be quite aggressive.

**Cultivars:**

'Copper Carpet' is about 2″ tall with copper-bronze foliage and showy red burs.

'Pewter Carpet' is similar to the above but with a dull glaze to the foliage.

'Pulchella' is about 4″ tall, with coppery foliage bearing hints of silver. The fruit is reddish-brown.

**Related Species:**

*A. buchananii* is sometimes offered by specialist nurseries and bears pea-green, 3″ long leaves and amber burs. The leaflets, which occur in 3-6 pairs, are about an inch long and have soft silky margins on the underside.

*A. inermis* produces mats of low-growing foliage but has a smooth, rather than a spiny bur. Less fun, but more huggable.

*A. saccaticupula* 'Blue Haze' is still one of the most popular cultivars for the bur gardener. The leaves are a beautiful glaucous blue and the brownish red flowers and red fruit are handsome as well. Plants are 2-4″ tall, spread well, and make attractive ground covers.

**Confusion:**

I often confuse plants of *Acaena* with *Leptinella* (which see), known as brass buttons, particularly when flowers or fruit are not present. They are both low, fernlike ground covers, both can have dark green foliage and both are made for rock gardens and even for walking upon. The flowers and fruit however are obviously different: *Acaena* is grown for the large ornamental fruit and not the rather inconspicuous flower, while *Leptinella* is grown for the opposite reasons, the fruit is unexciting. They are in very different families and are not really confusing if they are seen together in flower, but let's get real here, do you really think anyone actually plants burs and buttons together?

***Acantholimon*** (a-kanth-o-lee′ mon) Prickly Thrift Plumbaginaceae

This large group of plants (about 120 species) occurs predominantly in rocky, high altitude habitats and thus you would not expect to see grand swaths in St. Louis or Atlanta. The genus, however, has a loyal, if small, following among gardeners. Plants are becoming better known in the North where rock gardens and alpine gardens are reasonably common. They are evergreen and grow in dense clumps of short, prickly 3-angled narrow leaves. They look like they belong more to the cactus family than the plumbago family, that is, until they flower, at which time the resemblance to the latter is obvious. To be brutally honest, when not in flower, plants resemble green hedgehogs stuck in the middle of a garden. They are slow growing, but when they produce those long-lasting sprays of small pink flowers, they can be quite irresistible.

Plants are well known by alpine enthusiasts but alpine people are by definition somewhat strange, so this should not be surprising. While these plants will always be thought of as weird, they should be looked upon by other gardeners as exceptionally good subjects for the xeric garden. They need to be used far more often in areas of low rainfall and poor soils.

It is still difficult to find *Acantholimon* in the trade and gardeners are often forced to raise plants from seeds or softwood cuttings. However, hope is on the way, as species such as *A. glumaceum*, with bright rosy pink flowers, *A. olivieri*, with whitish pink flowers held well above the mat, and *A. ulicinum*, with hot pink flowers, are becoming better known. One nursery provides 6 distinct taxa while another lists 20 taxa of *Acantholimon*, once again verifying that there is simply no accounting for taste in American gardening.

Cuttings can be gingerly obtained from other enthusiasts. They can be painful, so root with care. Rooting near the base of the plant is encouraged by spreading sand around the base.

All species need gritty soils but may be grown on dry stone wall, gravel beds or sunny slopes with stony soils. Areas of high rainfall may not be a problem as long as drainage is impeccable. Full sun and cool nights are necessary. An excellent collection is in the alpine garden at the Denver Botanic Garden, but private collections are also well worth searching out.

***Acanthus*** (a-kanth′ us) Bear's Breeches Acanthaceae

The genus contains approximately 30 species of which three or four are particularly ornamental, providing foliage of great beauty and statuesque flowers. The basal leaves are simple, opposite, and often have soft, thorny margins. The flowers are held in long, erect spikes and each flower is subtended by a showy, spiny, leaflike bract. The spikes are lovely, albeit somewhat unnerving, but the true ornamental value of the genus resides in the handsome foliage. Once established, *Acanthus* is almost indestructible and will colonize an area with its invasive roots. If one tires of bear's breeches and wishes to remove same, it is next to impossible not to leave some root pieces behind, which, like amoebae, will regenerate and recolonize their old homesite.

I have always wondered where the name bear's breeches came from, for the combination of the two words makes no sense at all, and it is difficult to even imagine a pair of bear's breeches. Nowhere could I find an explanation, therefore I felt much better when I learned that the eminent British horticulturist Graham Stuart Thomas was equally stumped. He contacted Professor William Stearn who shed some possible light on the subject. Professor Stearn believed that the term resulted from a confusion of the medieval Latin description "*branca ursina*", meaning bear's claw. The upper part of the hooded flower, upon proper squinting, could be said to resemble a bear's claw. But the breeches, where did they come from? Madame Audrey Serreau, a gardener from Pultiers, France, believes that additional confusion between two Latin words resulted in the "breeches". The word "branca" which means claw, was confused with the old Gaul word "braca" which later became "braies" and finally "breeches". Is this clear yet? Such explanations may be confusing in themselves, however, as Madame Serreau stated, "Isn't it fascinating to reflect upon such word changes, bringing, as they do across the centuries, echoes of long-silenced voices?"

*Acanthus* is popular throughout the country although most authors state that it is insufficiently hardy for much of the North. Those authors need to see the wonderful plantings in Gardenview, Henry Ross's fine horticultural park in Strongsville, Ohio (zone 6). And if they need other proof of toughness, they should visit the wonderful garden of Dale and Lila Critz in Savannah, Georgia, where heat, humidity and acanthus are all doing well. Persistent, long-lived and certainly weather hardy.

The leaves are hardier than the flowers, and foliage may survive in particularly cold winters, but plants may not flower. Plants do well in full sun or partial shade and are relatively drought resistant although leaves will wilt often. Poor drainage is synonymous with poor performance and death. The foliage is occasionally evergreen in the South, but in severe winters becomes tattered and torn. In the North, plants are deciduous.

The most effective means of propagation is by 2-3″ long root cuttings taken in the spring. Insert vertically in a well-drained medium and keep moist and warm. Shoots appear in 3-5 weeks. In the garden, I can attest to the wonders of my handy-dandy tiller, with which I inadvertently tilled up a dormant patch of *A. spinosus*. Next spring, every little mangled piece had sprouted. Plants may also be divided in early spring but adequate moisture is necessary to insure establishment. Fresh seed germinates in about 3 weeks if kept moist and warm (70-75°F).

Quick Reference to Acanthus Species

| | Height (in.) | Leaves spiny | Leaf color |
|---|---|---|---|
| *A. caroli-alexandri* | 15-18 | No | Dark green |
| *A. dioscoridis* | 12-24 | Yes | Gray green |
| *A. hungaricus* | 30-48 | No | Dark green |
| *A. mollis* | 30-48 | No | Dark green |
| *A. spinosus* | 36-48 | Yes | Dark green |

***-hungaricus*** (hun-gar′ i-cus) Balkan Bear's Breeches 36-60″/36″
Spring Purple Balkan Countries, Romania Zones 5-9

Sold under the names of *A. balcanicus* and *A. longifolius*, plants are also similar in habit and flower to *A. mollis*. The dull green leaves are lobed with wide gaps between the lobes (the gap is referred to as a sinus). The sinuses are connected to each other with a flange of leaf parallel to the midrib. The sinuses are deep and the lobes are tapered at the base, characteristics which distinguish it from *A. mollis*. The flower stems rise an additional 3-4′ and bear numerous white and purple flowers in mid to late summer. The bracts surrounding the flowers have 5-7 veins and are painfully sharp. Plants are taller than most species, and the leaves more deeply cut. The foliage is more winter hardy than the flowers. After particularly cold winters, the leaves may emerge in the spring but no flowers may occur.

Plants perform well in most gardens and since they are native to the Balkans, Romania and northern Yugoslavia, are probably the most cold hardy. They also perform better in southeastern gardens than *A. mollis*.

***-mollis*** (mol′ lis) Common Bear's Breeches 30-48″/36″
Late Spring Purple Southern Europe Zones 7-9

In the fifth century B.C., one of the species of *Acanthus* was immortalized in the design of the sculptured leaves on Greek Corinthian columns. Some historians believe the design to be based on this species, others believe it is based on the foliage of *A. spinosus*. The lustrous green, 8-12″ wide foliage is lobed but not as deeply as *A. hungaricus*. Although small, soft spines are borne at the end of the lobes, the foliage does not feel at all spiny. The flowers are similar to those of *A. hungaricus*. The plants, having a spread of up to 3′, are best used as specimens or in groups of 3 to 5 plants. I have grown a number of species in the heat of north Georgia (zone 7b) and this one has flowered poorly. The magnificent plantings seen in southern California can not be duplicated in hot, humid weather.

**Cultivars:**

'Albus' has mostly white flowers.

'Hollard's Gold' was originally sold in this country in 1994. The foliage is chartreuse; not bright enough to brag on its beauty but yellow enough to think about a need for fertility. Nevertheless I like this plant, even though it is not as vigorous as the species and tends to disappear in inclement conditions, like my garden. Plants are often sold as 'Fielding Gold', as it originally came from Fielding, New Zealand.

var. *latifolius* is most common although less free flowering than the species. Plants bear 3-5′ tall stalks of mauve-pink flowers and glossy green arching leaves which are sometimes scarcely dissected. Plants appear to be more robust and more cold tolerant than the species. There are a number of similar forms, and plants are often classified as Laterifolius Group.

'Rue Ledan' was found in Matignon, France in the early 1990s. It is an excellent cultivar growing about 3′ tall and producing shiny green leaves. The flowers are white rather than purple, and essentially sterile. It likely belongs to the Laterifolius Group.

'Tasmanian Angel' is the first variegated acanthus and should be a hit. Plants also produce really wonderful pink and cream colored flowers on 4′ tall stems. The foliage is unique in that the leaves have creamy yellow irregular margins. During the summer, the leaves may revert to green.

| | | | |
|---|---|---|---|
| ***-spinosus*** (spine-o′ sus) | | Spiny Bear's Breeches | 36-48″/36″ |
| Late Spring | Mauve | Southern Europe | Zones 6-10 |

The main difference between this species and the previous is the presence of spiny leaf margins which look a good deal more lethal than they really are. The 10″ diameter leaves are lanceolate, and more deeply divided than those of *A. mollis*. The flowers are similar except that three to four veins occur on the purplish bracts rather than five to seven found in common bear's breeches. If late freezes occur, *A. mollis* is killed to the ground while this species is little affected. The flowers are produced consistently each year and the leaves remain fresh all season. Plants also tolerate warm, humid summers better than the previous species, a definite advantage for southern gardeners.

**Cultivars:**

'Lady Moore' is an interesting plant occasionally seen in the British Isles but seldom in the United States. The foliage is creamy white in the spring, greening up as the weather warms up. Named for the wife of Sir Frederick Moore, former keeper of the Botanic Gardens at Glasnevin, Dublin.

var. *spinosissimus* can be a man-eater but taxonomists have placed other plants in this group, diluting the pain. Originally plants bore leaves which were more sharply cut than those of the species, and enjoyed only by masochists or those who could command someone else to handle such vicious plants. I have enough trouble with belligerent people, why tolerate belligerent plants? Today, sufficient variation is thought to exist among plants and they are now referred to as the Spinosissimus Group.

**Related Species and Hybrids:**

*A. caroli-alexandri* has borne other names (*A. syriacus*), but if you want a shorter classy plant, look for this species. Plants grow only about 18″ tall and bear typical white and purple flowers. However, the leaves are deeply cut and the tips can be spiny. The bracts beneath the flowers are also painful. Nevertheless, this is an excellent selection for a smaller garden.

*A. dioscoridis* is 1-2′ tall and has rosy pink bracts. The lanceolate leaves are petioled, gray green, and in var. *dioscoridis* are usually entire, perhaps with a few shallow lobes. Good drainage is essential. Native to mountainous areas of Asia Minor, it is likely hardy in zones 6-9, although not enough plants have been evaluated to provide confident hardiness ratings. var. *perringii* is more common, bearing deeply cut, almost spiny leaves and with more pink in the bracts.

'Summer Beauty' is likely a hybrid between *A. mollis* and *A. spinosus*. The leaves are more deeply cut than *A. mollis* but are still shiny and handsome. The plants are vigorous, 4-5′ tall and bear white flowers with purple bracts. This is far superior than either of the parents, and I rate it highly.

## *Achillea* (a-kill′ ee-a) Yarrow Asteraceae

Although there are approximately 100 species, fewer than a dozen are truly ornamental. They range in height from four inches (*A. nana*) to four feet (*A. filipendulina*) and provide flowers of almost every hue. Leaves of all species are alternate and, with the exception of *A. ageratum*, sweet yarrow, and *A. ptarmica*, sneezewort, the foliage is deeply divided into a fine fernlike appearance. In several species, the foliage has a heavy spicy odor and a gray-green tint. A member of the aster family, its heads are made up of two distinct types of flowers. The outer ray flowers are pistillate (female only), and may be yellow, white, or pink while the inner disc flowers are bisexual (male and female together), and usually yellow. The flower heads (inflorescences) look like small table tops called corymbs. Another advantage of growing yarrow is the gardener's ability to cut the flowers and enjoy them indoors. The flowers of most species make excellent fresh or dried specimens but the pollen must be visible before the flowers are cut or vase life will essentially be nil.

Some yarrows are at times considered weeds, particularly those which multiply rapidly from invasive rhizomes. This characteristic, however, is true for only one or two species; most others behave themselves and stay at home. Unless otherwise noted, all species should be grown in full sun and well-drained soils. They tolerate poor, slightly acid soils (if well-drained), although *A. clavennae* performs well in limey soils. Do not fertilize yarrows heavily; many of the upright species will grow too tall and lanky if fertilized or grown in rich soil.

Quick Reference to Achillea Species

| | Height (ft.) | Flower color | Foliage color |
|---|---|---|---|
| *A.* 'Coronation Gold' | 2-3 | Yellow | Gray-green |
| *A. filipendulina* | 3-5 | Yellow | Green |
| *A. grandifolia* | 2-3 | White | Gray-green |
| *A. millefolium* | 1-2 | Pink, red | Green |
| *A.* 'Moonshine' | 1-2 | Sulphur | Gray-green |
| *A. ptarmica* | 1-2 | White | Green |
| *A. tomentosa* | ½-1 | Yellow | Gray-green |

**-'Coronation Gold'** Coronation Gold Yarrow 2-4'/3'
Late Spring Yellow Hybrid origin Zones 3-9

This hybrid was first offered in 1953 by Miss Pole of Lye End Nursery in southern England to commemorate the coronation of Elizabeth II. An amateur hybridizer, she crossed *A. filipendulina* with *A. clypeolata*, a small yellow-flowered species, to raise the best upright golden yellow yarrow available at that time, and arguably, still the best today. Plants were subsequently sold and distributed by Blooms of Bressingham of Diss, England and rapidly became popular throughout the world. It is sometimes incorrectly listed as a cultivar of fern-leaf yarrow, *A. filipendulina*, but that is unfair to this excellent hybrid.

The plant is shorter than *A. filipendulina*, better branched, and does not require staking. It requires less maintenance and should be the plant of choice for landscapers. The inflorescences are 3-4" across and look like shiny golden plates. Flowering begins in late May in north Georgia, June in the Northeast, late June in the Midwest, and continues for 8-12 weeks. The foliage is gray-green and has a strong aromatic smell. It tolerates a wide range of climates and soils and is grown in gardens from Manitoba to Florida.

'Coronation Gold' is also popular as a cut flower throughout the world. It is interesting to note the differences in stem and flower size between northern and southern climates. In north Georgia, over 50 flowering stems per plant were produced while the same plants growing in Holland yielded fewer than 15 stems but each one was 1½-2 times longer with larger flowers. Propagate by terminal cuttings in spring or early summer, or by spring or fall division every 3-4 years. Stay away from seed labeled 'Coronation Gold'; it will likely be *A. filipendulina* or one of its cultivars.

***-filipendulina*** (fi-li-pen-dew' lye-na) Fern-leaf Yarrow 3-5'/3'
Summer Yellow Caucasus Zones 3-8

The foliage is deeply cut and feathery but bears little of the gray-green tint that is so appealing in 'Coronation Gold'. In general, foliage is greener, flowers are larger and plants are taller than those of 'Coronation Gold'. This is a wonderfully handsome plant but when grown in rich soils, warm temperatures or over-fertilized, it

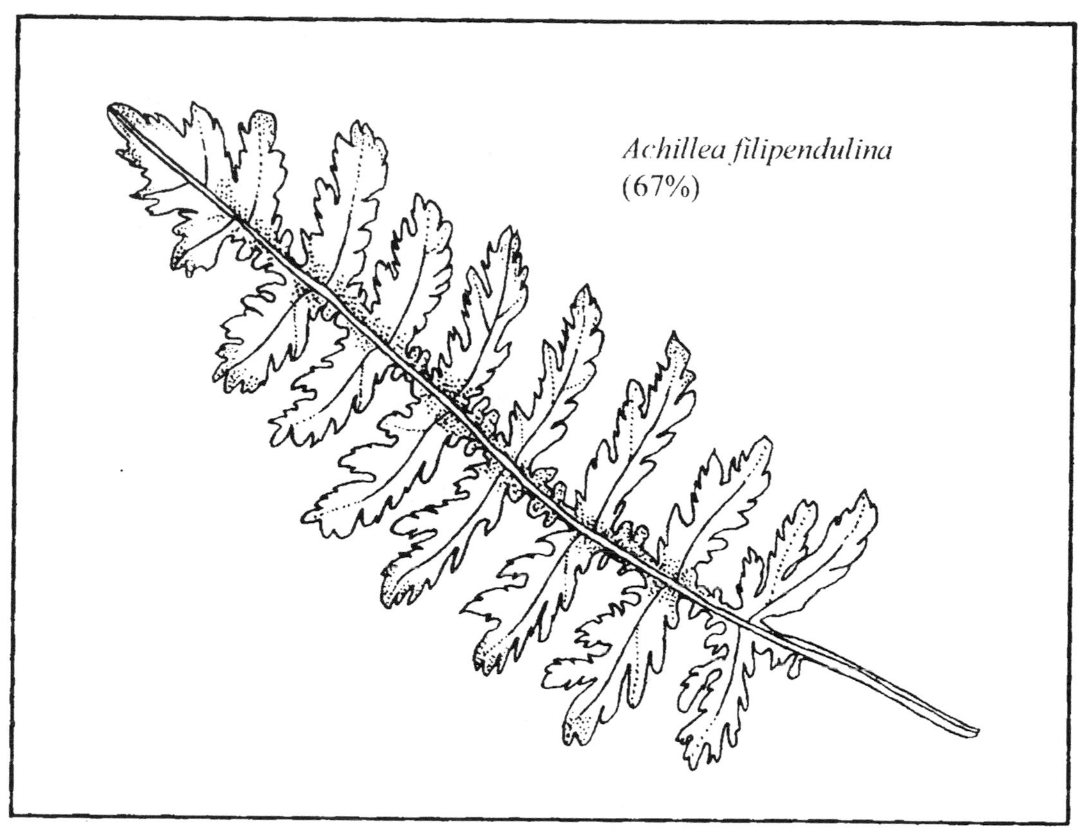
*Achillea filipendulina*
(67%)

generally requires staking, a job most sane people view with disdain. The flat yellow flower heads are 3-4″ across and make excellent cut flowers. Provide full sun. Yellow-flowered yarrows combine well with pink phlox, purple-foliaged plants, blue delphiniums and red hot pokers.

Plants may be propagated by spring division, terminal cuttings in early summer, or by seed. Seed sown in a mixture of 1:1 peat:vermiculite and placed at 70-72°F in a humid area germinates within 21 days. Most cultivars are available from seed.

**Cultivars and Hybrids:**

'Altgold' stands about 3′ tall and bears deep yellow flowers in late spring and again in early fall. An interesting rebloomer.

'Cloth of Gold' bears large pure yellow flowers and grows 3-4′ tall.

'Flowers of Sulphur' is a 2′ tall, slow-spreading hybrid of *A. filipendulina* and *A. ptarmica*. One of the best sulphur-colored flowers in the genus.

'Gold Coin' is a dwarf form of 'Parker's Variety', and grows only about 15″ tall.

'Gold Plate' has deep yellow flowers on stems up to 5′ tall.

'Parker's Variety' bears golden yellow flowers on 3-4′ tall stems. This one and 'Gold Plate' produce large numbers of flowers and have better stem strength than the species but may require support in areas with hot, humid summers.

'Schwellenburg' is likely a hybrid with *A. filipendulina* and a yet to be determined species. The golden flowers sit atop silvery, ferny foliage and stand 1½-2′ tall. Plants do not appear to be particularly vigorous or tolerant of adverse weather, however if old flowers are removed and plants are not over-fertilized, better results can be expected.

***-millefolium*** (mil-lee-fo′ lee-um) Common Yarrow 1-2′/5′
Summer White to Cerise Red Europe Zones 3-9

Common yarrow is "common" because of its ability to spread rapidly and take over any ground available. Often seeded as a wildflower on roadsides, the ferny foliage and off-white flowers fill in median strips and combine well with other roadside plants such as bachelor's buttons and poppies. In Europe, it is often discarded as a troublesome weed not to be included on the grounds of any self-respecting gardener. Yet the same people will find fresh and dried flowers of common yarrow in florist

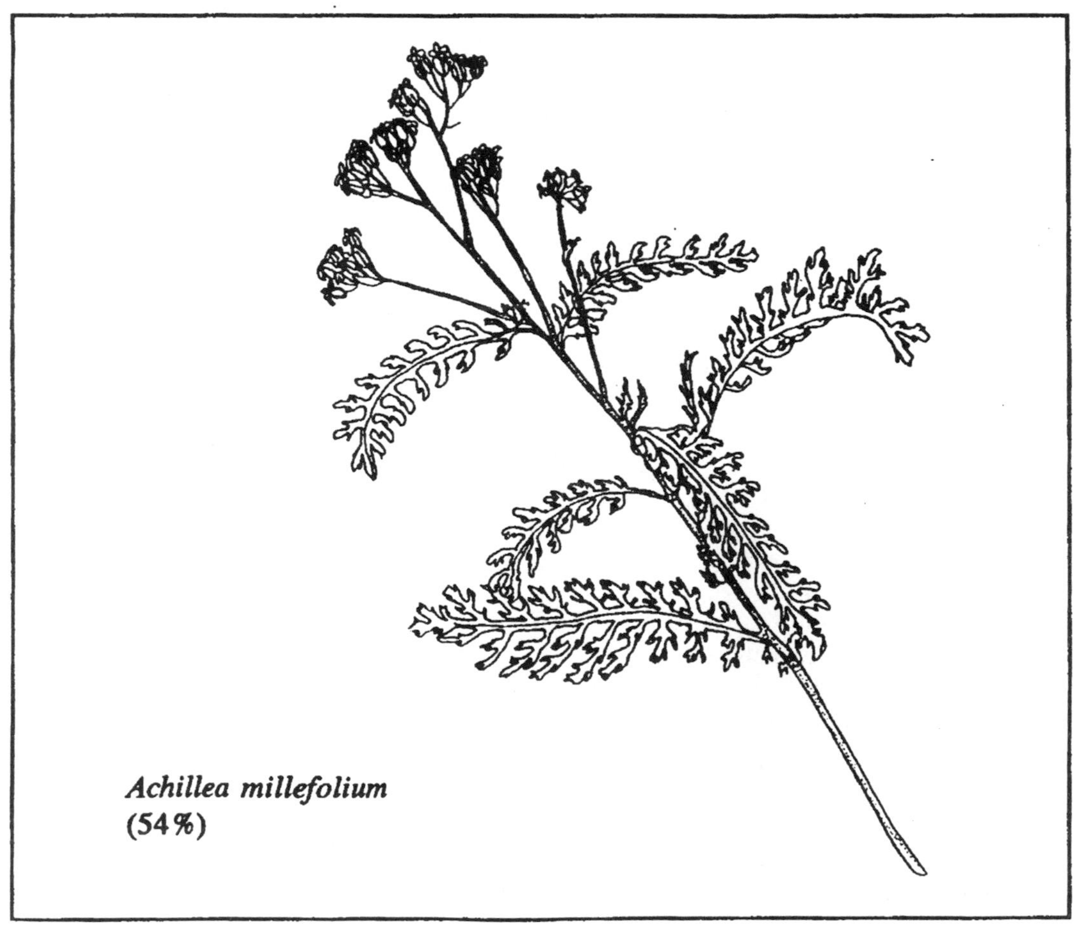

***Achillea millefolium***
**(54%)**

shops where they are widely used in colorful bouquets. The species was cultivated in Europe before 1440, used as a remedy for toothache, and mixed in ale in place of hops to increase the inebriating quality of that drink. It was thought to have a magical quality similar to our "apple a day keeps the doctor away"; and was said to grow in churchyards as a reproach to the dead, "who need never have come there if they had taken their yarrow broth faithfully every day while living". The main use, however, was that of an herb to heal wounds. The genus was named after Achilles, who is said to have used *A. millefolium* to staunch the wounds of his soldiers, thus acquiring the common name of soldier's woundweed and woundwort. And everyone thought this was just a common old flower!

The habit is matlike and the dark green foliage is deeply cut. In early summer, the flower stalks rise about two feet and are quite strong where night temperatures consistently stay below 70°F. Where night temperatures are too warm, the stems do not acquire enough carbohydrates to "fatten up" and topple. Plants fill in rapidly and those placed four feet apart produce an unbroken mat in 2 years. If planted two feet apart, they fill in by the end of the first year.

A number of cultivars are offered from seed but it is just as easy to divide good specimens to retain the desired colors.

**Cultivars:**

Some of the following are selections of *A. millefolium*, many are hybrids. Most of the hybrids are of questionable parentage but all have *A. millefolium* in them. The Galaxy hybrids (*A. aegyptiaca* var. *taygetea* (formerly *A.* 'Taygetea') x *A. millefolium*) have similar foliage to that of *A. millefolium* but the flower heads are larger and the stems much stronger. The only problem I have seen is the tendency of the flowers to fade, particularly when temperatures are above 80°F. In our trials in north Georgia, 'Beacon' and 'Great Expectations' faded less than others. In climates with cool night temperatures, little fading is seen.

'Appleblossom' is a vigorous 3′ tall plant with peach to lilac-pink flowers. A Galaxy hybrid.

'Apricot Beauty' is likely a hybrid. It is difficult to find in this country but with its flat-topped soft yellow to apricot flower heads, it should be more common.

'Apricot Delight', 'Strawberry Seduction', and 'Wonderful Wampee' are part of the Tutti-Frutti series of seed-grown yarrows, designed primarily for rapid greenhouse production. And, no, I have no idea what they were smoking when these names were selected. Flower colors are light apricot, rose and light pink, respectively. All stand 12-20″ tall, the former being the shortest and the seducer being the tallest.

'Belle Epoque' has dusky pink flowers and gray green leaves. Plants earned an Award of Garden Merit (1999) from the Royal Horticultural Society.

'Borealis' (var. *borealis*) bears dense clusters of rose-pink flowers.

'Cassis' is about 2′ tall with flat heads of cherry-red flowers. Plants bloom first year from seed.

'Cerise Queen' is one of the oldest and still popular cultivars. Plants are grown for the cerise-red flowers. It grows about 18″ tall and provides bright drifts of color.

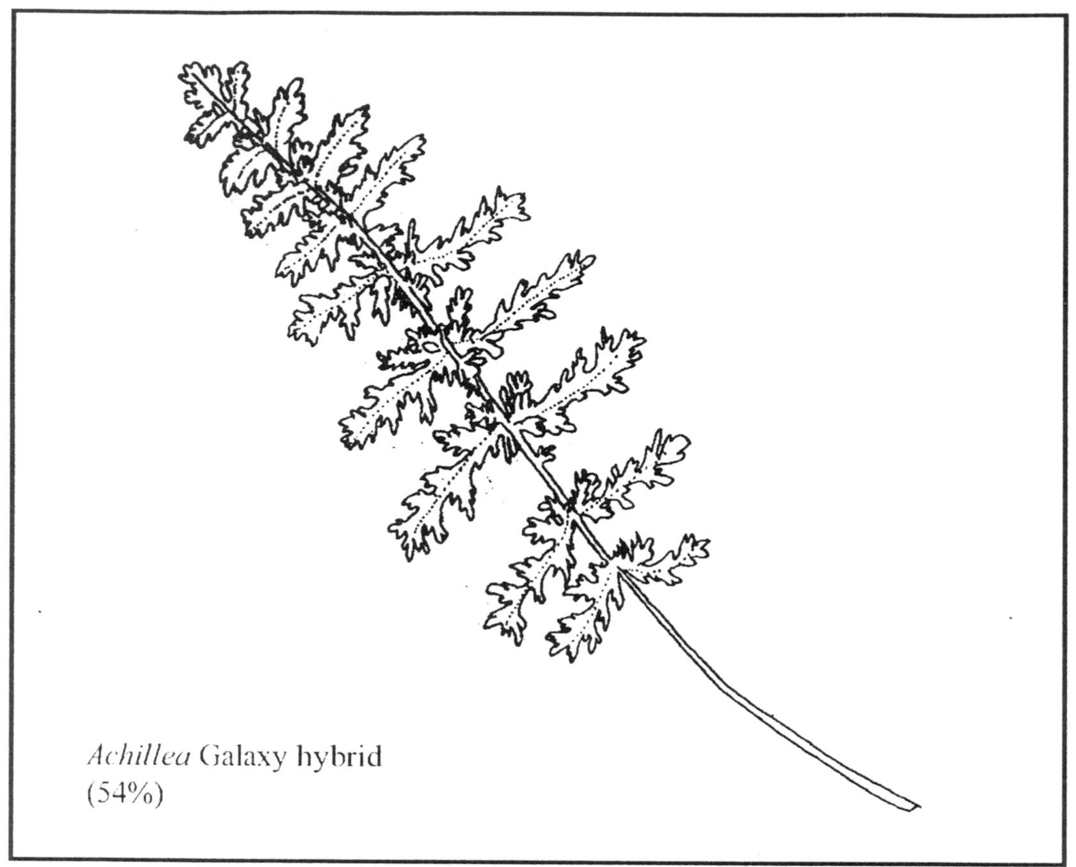

*Achillea* Galaxy hybrid
(54%)

'Chamois' has interesting tan-colored flowers (like a chamois?) which fade somewhat to a creamy yellow. Sounds awful, but not so bad.

'Christel' is a relatively new hybrid, with deeper green foliage than most "millefolium" forms. The flowers are deep rose-pink and if cut back may rebloom.

'Christine' has fernlike foliage, grows about 2′ tall and is topped with light rose flowers.

'Citronella' bears butter yellow flowers on an erect habit.

Colorado mix is grown from seed and provides flowers in a wide range of colors, including apricot, pink, red, russet, yellow, apricot, pink, and cream.

'Creamy' bears large heads of creamy-yellow flowers. Plants fill in quickly.

'Credo' was bred in Germany, resulting from *A. filipendula* x *A. millefolium*. It is a tall (3-4′) cultivar with light yellow flowers that tend to fade to creamy-white. Good for cut flowers.

'Debutante' is a mixture of plants, bearing rose to creamy white flowers. 'Pink Debutante' is also an excellent selection.

'Fire King' and 'Fire Beauty' have dark red flowers; there is little difference between them.

'Fireland' opens red then fades to pink and finally to a tawny gold. The plants grow about 3′ tall but the stems are reasonably stout.

'Great Expectations' ('Hope') produces primrose yellow flowers on 2′ high stems. A Galaxy hybrid.

'Heidi' has pastel pink flowers on 20″ stems in the spring and reblooms a little later in the summer.

'Hidden Pond Pink' is a silly name for a pink-flowered, relatively short (15-24″) yarrow.

'Island Pink' has deep pink flowers and a deep green foliar color.

'Jambo' bears medium yellow flowers on 15-18″ tall stems.

'Jungfrau' has pastel yellow, almost white, flowers on 15″ plants.

'Kelwayi' bears magenta-red flowers on 18″ stems.

'Lansdorferglut' is an ugly name for a pretty 2-3′ tall plant with soft pink flowers in flattened heads. Good for cutting.

'Lilac Beauty' produces lilac flowers on strong upright stems.

'Lilac Queen' has flat heads of pastel lilac flowers and is offered occasionally by mail order nurseries.

'Lusaka' has white flowers and is a vigorous grower.

'Madelein' bears apricot colored flowers on 2′ tall plants.

'Martina' has large, flat yellow flower heads on 2-2½′ tall stems. The foliage is ferny and green.

'Marmalade' has flowers in autumn colors of dark yellow and orange.

'Mary Ann' bears lemon-yellow flowers over silvery-gray foliage and grows only about a foot tall.

'Maskarade' produces interesting pale yellow flower heads with red flecks along the edges as they mature. Quite a different look.

'Moneymaker' has salmon-pink flowers. I'm not sure where the money will be made, as there are many others with similar flower color as well.

'Nakuru' produces purple and white bicolor flowers.

'Natalie' is 2-3′ tall with light pink flowers.

'Orange Queen' has unusual orange-gold flowers. About 30″ tall and 18″ wide.

'Paprika' produces red and yellow flowers on a flattened inflorescence. One of the most handsome cultivars available.

'Petra' resulted from a cross between 'Credo' and 'Fanal'. Plants bear fiery red flowers and stand about 20″ tall. Plants are unique because they are sterile and no wishy-washy seedlings will sneak into the garden.

'Proa' is similar to, if not the same as, the white yarrow that has become naturalized along roadsides in this country. Plants were originally selected for high oil content of the seeds. A pretty enough plant, but quite aggressive.

'Oertel's Rose' was introduced by Goodness Grows Nursery in Lexington, Georgia and blooms heavily with rosy pink and white flowers. A terrific selection for Southern gardeners.

'Red Beauty' bears 2′ tall cerise-red flowers in midsummer.

'Red Velvet' has dark red to rosy red flowers on 18-20″ tall plants. Supposedly the flowers do not fade during the summer, but I have not be able to verify that, at least in zone 7.

'Richard Nelson' was selected at Bluestone Nursery in Madison, Ohio, for its handsome pale pink flowers.

'Rose Beauty' has rather nondescript rose-pink flowers on 2′ tall stems. This name is also used with var. *roseum*, and includes pink seedlings in general.

Rougham series of yarrows were developed at Rougham Hall Nursery, Rougham, Suffolk, England. They are about 2′ in height and separate colors are available. 'Rougham Beauty' is light pink, 'Rougham Bright Star' is cherry-rose with a white eye, 'Rougham Cream' is an off-white, 'Rougham Salmon' is just that, 'Rougham White' is a cleaner white than most white yarrows. Plants do not seem to fade as badly as many others.

'Salmon Beauty' bears large heads of salmon flowers on 3′ tall stems. A Galaxy hybrid.

'Sawa Sawa' bears lavender-purple flowers on 20″ stems.

'Schneetaler' is a hybrid with pure white flowers. Plants are good for cut flowers and may rebloom if cut back hard after the initial bloom.

'Snow Sport' is a vigorous grower with dark green foliage and dozens of clean white flowers on 18″ tall stems.

'Summer Berries' is a seed strain introduced in 2003. Pastel flower colors range from pink to light salmon to cherry.

'Summer Pastels' is a seed-propagated hybrid, which includes numerous pastel colors (pink, rose, lavender, salmon to orange) on 2′ tall plants. Plants flower the first year from seed. The yellow hues are particularly good.

'Summer Wine' is taller than 3′ and is used as a cut flower commercially. The bright wine red flowers are immediately visible, however they fade as they age to a rose pink color. This is not all bad as it provides some color contrast over the season.

'Terracotta' is an exceptional selection, with 2-3′ tall plants of the finest salmon to peach colors I have seen. The foliage has a little silver hue to it as well. Its only drawback is that it may become too tall in rich soils or in areas with warm nights.

'Tickled Pink' is a cute name for a seed-propagated mix of pink to rose colored flowers.

'The Beacon' stands 2-3′ tall and bears rich red flowers with yellow centers. It is the best cultivar I have seen. A Galaxy hybrid.

'Walther Funcke' has gray foliage and deep red flowers on 2′ tall stems. Quite handsome.

'Weser River Sandstone' has deep rose-pink flowers on 2-3′ tall plants.

'White Beauty' produces creamy white flowers.

| **'Moonshine'** | | Moonshine Yarrow | 1-2′/1′ |
|---|---|---|---|
| Summer | Lemon Yellow | Hybrid origin | Zones 3-7 |

This hybrid, between *A. clypeolata* and *A. aegyptiaca* var. *taygetea* (formerly A. 'Taygetea'), was introduced in the 1950s by Alan Bloom of Bressingham Gardens in

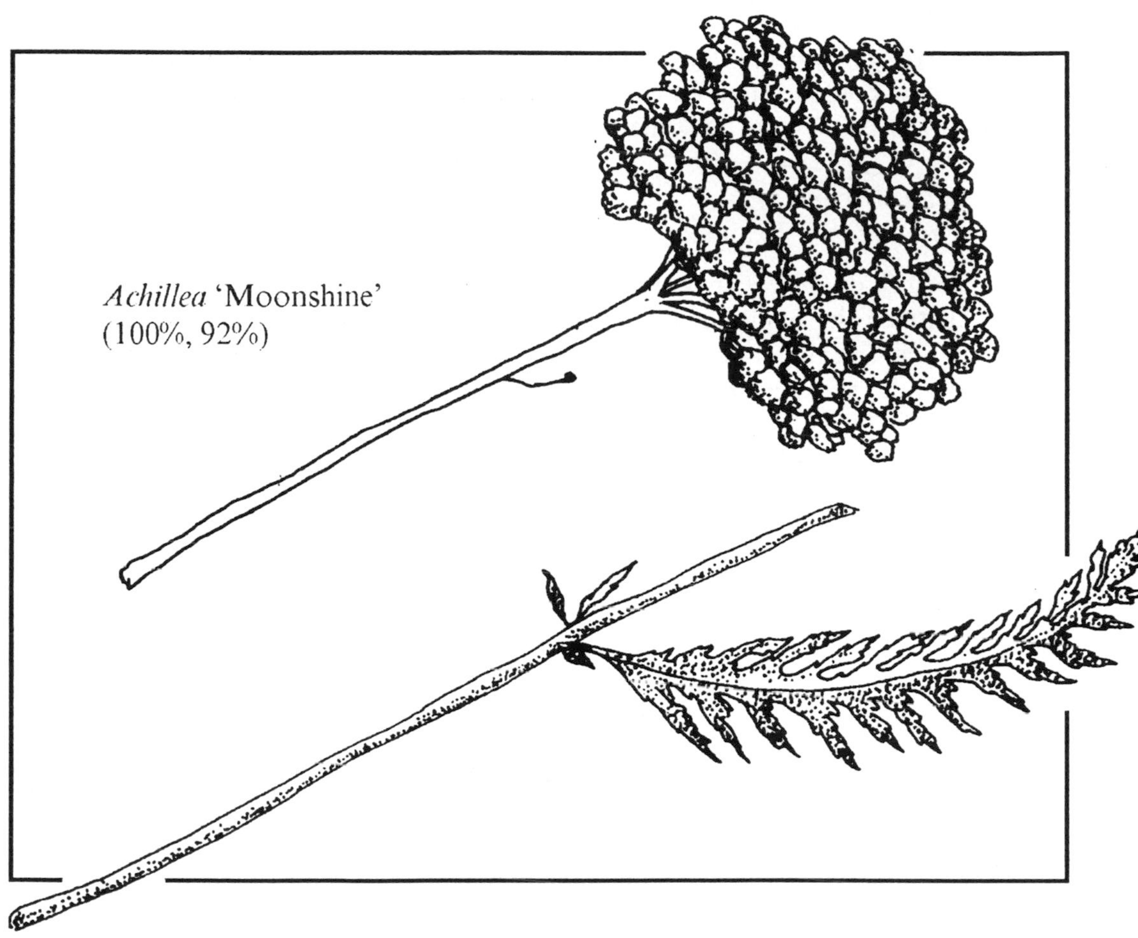

*Achillea* 'Moonshine'
(100%, 92%)

Diss, England. In the garden, 'Moonshine' is similar to 'Coronation Gold' except in size and shade of flower color. The inflorescences are flat-topped, dense, deep lemon-yellow and 2-3″ in diameter while the gray-green foliage is filigreed. It is one of the most popular yarrows in American landscapes and is often recommended because of habit and bright flower color. While a handsome plant, 'Moonshine' tends to become twiggy, lose some of its foliage and die out after 2-3 years in the garden.

The flowers appear in early June (late June in New England) and continue until September. However, it is much more perennial in the North than in the South. In the Southeast where summer days are frequently punctuated by late afternoon rains and high humidity, 'Moonshine' tends to "melt out". This is not surprising considering that one of its parents, *A. aegyptiaca* var. *taygetea*, is also susceptible to many foliar diseases. 'Moonshine' does best during summers with little rainfall, otherwise don't waste your money. The Southeast is particularly taxing on plants susceptible to root fungi, however, regardless of the region of the country in which it is grown, excellent drainage is necessary to ensure more than 2 years garden longevity. Spraying for diseases such as *Botrytis* and root rot organisms such as *Pythium* is helpful and should be practiced in July and August. Regardless of the drawbacks, this was one of the finest hybrid yarrows developed in many years and, if sited properly and grown well, can still be a popular plant for commercial landscapers and gardeners.

Propagate by division any time during the growing season.

***-ptarmica*** (tar′ mah-ca) Sneezewort 1-2′/1′
Early Summer White Europe Zones 2-9

I can think of few other common names in the plant kingdom as ugly as sneezewort. Hearing the name for the first time certainly doesn't endear this species to anyone. The common name is derived from the fact that "the floures make one neese exceedingly". In Victorian England, the leaves and roots were also dried and reduced to powder and used as an inexpensive substitute for snuff.

The species is unusual among yarrows due to the lack of dissected leaves. The sessile foliage is finely toothed and fernlike, and the shape is linear to lanceolate. The species itself is of little ornamental value but a number of good cultivars are avail-

***Achillea ptarmica* (69%)**

able. The cut flowers are occasionally used as a substitute for baby's breath and dry well. It is an aggressive plant and will spread considerably in good soils. Susceptible to powdery mildew in wet soils and shady conditions.

Propagate by division in the spring.

**Cultivars:**

Many of these look the same. Some may differ in height, and perhaps garden performance as well.

'Angels' Breath' bears many half-inch wide clean white flowers on 15-18″ tall plants. Good filler for bouquets.

'Aunt Stientje' has dark green leaves, and bears flowers with large creamy white rays. I don't see this plant in this country at all, however it earned an Award of Garden Merit from the Royal Horticultural Society in 1999.

'Ballerina' is an excellent cultivar with clean white flowers, topping out at about 18″. Good as a dried cut flower. A dwarf form, 'Nana Ballerina', grows only 8″ tall.

'Globe' has small buttonlike blossoms on 12-18″ tall stems.

'Gypsy White' appeared in our trials in 2005, and flowered for months on 9-12″ tall plants. An excellent introduction where a dwarf white is called for.

'The Pearl' is more correctly listed as The Pearl group, consisting of a number of closely related white double-flowered taxa. In general, plants bear a profusion of double white flowers on 2′ high stems but in warm summers, plants sprawl and are weedy looking. All double-flowered cultivars produce some single flowers as well. Up to 30% single flowers may be produced depending on weather and cultivar.

'Snowball' is similar to The Pearl group and may be part of it. The white double-flowered plants are about 2′ tall and are supposed to be a little more compact than plants in The Pearl group. I can see little difference.

'Perry's White' is taller (up to 30″), with flowers similar to the species but opening about a week earlier.

***-tomentosa*** (tow-men-tos′ a) Woolly Yarrow 6-12″/18″
Early Summer Yellow Europe Zones 3-7

The common name provides an excellent description of the deeply cut, light green foliage, which is covered with long hairs, providing a truly woolly appearance. Good drainage is essential and the rock garden is a particularly suitable location, however, plants also make good subjects for the front of the border. It is most handsome in the spring when the hairy new growth begins to clamber over rocks and invades small niches. Many sulphur-yellow flowers, similar to, but smaller than those of 'Moonshine', are produced in June (May in the South) and continue for 3-5 weeks.

Unfortunately, plants are intolerant of hot, humid conditions and cannot be recommended for areas south of zone 6. Although they will survive in zone 7, plants perform well only through early summer and decline by mid to late July, unlikely to be seen again. This is not a species for southern landscapes unless frequent fungicide applications are made. I used to grow it in zone 7 as an annual because I enjoyed the woolly texture enough to replace it in the spring. I am too lazy to do that anymore, but I still enjoy it in other people's gardens.

Most cultivars are usually propagated by division but the species and var. *aurea* may also be seed propagated.

**Cultivars:**

var. *nana* ('Nana') has golden yellow flowers on 3-6″ tall stems. Sometimes sold as 'Little Beauty'.

'Maynard's Gold' produces bright yellow flowers on 10-12″ stems. Some authorities believe var. *aurea* and 'Maynard's Gold' to be one and the same. They are probably correct.

**Related Species and Hybrids:**

*A. ageratum* (formerly *A. decolorans*) 'W.B. Childs' bears single creamy-white flowers similar to sneezewort. If not for the difference in leaf shape, one would be challenged to tell the two apart by looking only at the flowers. The plants, however, have dissected deep green leaves whereas those of sneezewort are almost entire.

'Alabaster', a hybrid from Germany, bears flat heads of pale yellow flowers on stiff 30″ tall gray-green foliage.

'Anthea' was introduced by Alan Bloom by crossing 'Moonshine' with *A. clypeolata*. Plants are more erect and the foliage is soft and silver-gray while the flowers are more sulphur-yellow than those of 'Moonshine'. In our trials at Georgia, the flower heads were about 3″ across but tended to fade to creamy yellow as they mature. At the same time, secondary flowers emerged freely. Flower heads should be deadheaded to extend flowering. A terrific introduction named after Mr. Bloom's daughter, far better than 'Moonshine' in yarrow-challenged environments.

*A. chrysocoma*, yellow yarrow, is similar to *A. tomentosa* but the leaves are more hairy, appear to be coated with white fur and the golden yellow flowers are a little wider. 'Grandiflora' has larger flowers.

*A. clavennae* grows 2-3′ tall and bears up to 25 small white flowers in the inflorescence. Plants form handsome clumps of silky gray foliage. Prefers limey soils. Hardy to about zone 5-8.

*A.* x *jaborneggii* is a hybrid between *A. clavennae* and the alpine species *A. erbo-rotta* subsp. *moschata*. Clean white flowers over deeply cut clumps of gray-green foliage occur in late spring. Plants are only about 4-6″ tall and most suitable for the rock garden.

*A.* x *kellereri* also bears creamy white flowers but with soft yellow centers on 6-8″ tall plants. The plant is a hybrid between *A. clypeolata* and *A. ageratifolia*, which has small white daisies and silver foliage. The resulting hybrid has wonderful fernlike gray foliage that is as pretty as the flowers.

*A.* x *lewisii*, a hybrid between *A. clavennae* and *A. tomentosa*, bears woody stems and soft silver-green foliage. The leaves are not as hairy as *A. tomentosa* and plants are a little taller.

'King Edward' bears primrose yellow flowers on 4-10″ stems. This and the previous hybrid require excellent drainage and are useful only in areas of cool summer nights.

*A. sibirica* is highly variable and still poorly known. Its leathery pinnatifid leaves are sessile, more compact, deeper green and in many ways far more handsome than *A. millefolium* or *A. ptarmica*. The ray flowers are yellow and the discs are brown. 'Stephanie Cohen' was named for our brilliant plant lady in Pennsylvania and bears soft pink flowers all summer. 'Kiku-San' is about 18″ tall with creamy white ray flowers and brown centers. It was an exceptional performer in the Gardens at UGA. The var. *kamtschatica* has pastel pink flowers but its cultivar 'Love Parade' is a wonderful 2′ tall plant with lavender-rosy pink flowers and the same glossy green foliage. Flowers fade to an off-white as they mature.

*A.* x *wilczekii* is a low-growing white-flowered hybrid between *A. ageratifolia* and *A. lingulata*. The plants form mats under conditions of good drainage and sunshine. Particularly useful for the rock garden.

## ***Aconitum*** (ak-ko-ny′ tum) Monkshood Ranunculaceae

*Aconitum* has a number of common names, one of which is monkshood, so called because of the enlarged sepal that resembles a hood, under which the rest of the floral parts are hidden. Roots were used as poison bait for wolves, thus accounting for another popular common name, wolfsbane. All aconitums have poisonous roots, leaves, and stems and warnings concerning their poisonous properties have been sounded since the late 1500s. In *A New Herbal*, William Turner writes, "Let oure Londiners which of late have receyved this blewe wolfes bayne ... take hede that poyson of the rote of this herbe one daye do not more harme than the freshness of the flower hath done pleasure in seven yeres, let them not saye but they are warned." It may even have been used to rid oneself of an unwanted husband or wife, but "it was considered rather a vulgar poison and was not employed by persons of high rank, who probably thought Socrates' hemlock more distinguished." The turnip-shaped tuberous roots, however, are the most toxic and should not be planted near root crops such as potatoes or horseradish in case of accidental harvesting. Roots have even been confused with those of celery while incredibly, some people ate leaves thinking they were parsley! What were they thinking? Use of aconitum alkaloids in modern medicine was largely discontinued by the late 1930s and early 1940s, although they are still available as a local analgesic in liniments and as a heart sedative.

Regardless of the morbid properties, aconitums are excellent garden plants. The ornamental part of the flower consists of 5 sepals, not petals, with the uppermost one enlarged to form a "hood" or "helmet". Petals vary in number from 2 to many, but are found inside the hood. The flowers are arranged in terminal racemes or panicles and flower in summer to early fall. Flowers of the more common species occur in various shades of blue, however, several species have sulphur-yellow flowers, while rose-colored flowers occur in *A. pyramidale*.

All species have been undergoing serious taxonomic reshuffling, and many subspecies have been described. Their identification is difficult at best, impossible without resorting to checking floral parts with a microscope. The leaves are alternate, dark green and usually palmately divided. They superficially resemble those of *Delphinium* but the flowers of the two genera are distinctly different. Among other things, flowers of *Aconitum* usually have two petals whereas those of *Delphinium* have four. If people were to mix up aconitum with delphinium, I can understand, but parsley!

Aconitums should be planted in full sun but will tolerate afternoon shade, particularly when planted near the southern boundary of their range (zone 6). They also tolerate moist soils but abhor swampy conditions. Plants need cool nights to flourish, and languish in southern regions of the country. If summer night temperatures do not regularly fall below 70°F, they should not be planted. A couple of native species, *A. uncinatum* and *A. reclinatum* extend as far south as North Carolina but are always found at higher elevations. One of the few disappointments I have had in gardening in the South is the absence of the stately spires of *Aconitum*. It did well in southern Ontario (zone 4), but try as I may, I cannot grow monkshood well in north Georgia (zone 7).

Most species are at least 3′ tall and look out of place in the front of the garden, however *A.* 'Ivorine', a 2-3′ tall plant with ivory-colored blossoms in early summer, may be planted in the foreground. A few species, such as the Asian *A. volubile* and the eastern United States natives, *A. uncinatum* and *A. reclinatum* are ramblers and can be trained to run through small trees and shrubs.

Flowering time for most of the monkshoods is late summer and fall, however, the 6′ stately dark-purple spires of *A. henryi* open with the summer phlox and late daylilies. *Aconitum* produces good cut flowers but care should be taken not to get any sap from the cut stem on open wounds, or to mistake the leaves for parsley garnish.

Plant the tuberous roots in the fall to establish the root system before the first hard frost. Set the crowns just below the soil surface about 12-18″ apart. Do not disturb established plants as they do not transplant well. Plant in full sun in a well-drained area where you would like them to be for the next ten years for that is where they should stay. If conditions are too wet, various fungi such as *Sclerotinia* will cause root rot and serious decline of the population. The upright forms make excellent cut flowers, persisting in the vase for 4-7 days.

Seed propagation is particularly difficult because the seed develops a deep dormancy upon ripening. Sow seed as soon as collected from the plant. Germination of old seed will occur, but very slowly (12-18 months is not uncommon). Seed-grown plants take 2-3 years to flower. To propagate vegetatively, the brittle tuberous roots can be separated in late fall or very early spring.

Quick Reference to Aconitum Species

| | Height (ft.) | Flower color | Leaves divided all the way to base |
|---|---|---|---|
| *A.* x *cammarum* | 3-4 | Various | Yes |
| *A. carmichaelii* | 3-6 | Dark blue | No |
| *A. lamarckii* | 3-4 | Yellow | Yes |
| *A. napellus* | 3-4 | Dark blue | Yes |
| *A. reclinatum* | 6-8 | Cream | Yes |

**-x *cammarum*** (kam-mar′ um) | Bicolor Monkshood | 3-4′/2′
Summer | Various | Hybrid | Zones 3-7

The plant is often described as a species, but as far as I can tell it is a hybrid between *A. variegatum* and *A. napellus*. The growth habit is quite variable depending on the dominant parent in a particular cultivar. The inflorescences are often branched and the "helmet" may be strongly arched forward. The leaves are 2-4″ long and divided into 5-7 segments. Seldom is the hybrid found, however, a few cultivars call this plant home.

**Cultivars:**

'Bicolor' is 3-4′ tall and has blue and white flowers loosely borne on wide branching panicles derived from *A. variegatum*. This is sometimes sold incorrectly as *A.* x *bicolor*.

***-carmichaelii*** (kar-my-keel′ lee-eye) | Azure Monkshood | 3-6′/3′
Late Summer | Dark Blue | Central China | Zones 3-7

The leaves are thicker and more leathery than those of *A.* x *cammarum* and not as deeply dissected. The leaves are cut about two-thirds of the way to the midrib into 3-5 lobes. It is a sturdy plant that seldom needs staking and has dark blue flowers in late summer and early fall. Afternoon shade and sufficient moisture are necessary for plants to be at their best. When planting, large amounts of organic matter should be incorporated in the planting hole. This species flowers about 2 weeks later than *A.* x *cammarum* and is often referred to as the fall-flowering aconitum. The flowers are deep purple within and lighten to pale mauve on the outside. A planting incorporating Japanese anemones, late monkshoods, and autumn sedums such as 'Autumn Joy' is truly breathtaking. Some taxonomic shenanigans are going on, and some want to separate the species *Aconitum fischeri* from *A. carmichaelii*, others, like myself, see little enough difference, and lump them. For the gardener, either will do well.

**Cultivars:**

'Arendsii' (syn. *A.* x *arendsii*) is a hybrid between *A. carmichaelii* and its var. *wilsonii*. Raised by Georg Arends of Arend's Nursery in Ronsdorf, Germany, this definitely deserves to be used more. Plants bear large helmets of intense blue in September and October and stand 3-4′ tall. The stems are sturdy enough to be self-supporting and, everything considered, is the best late-flowering aconitum in cultivation.

'Barker's Variety' has deep blue flowers and comes true from seed.

'Kelmscott Variety' has lavender blue flowers and is similar in habit to 'Bakers Variety'. Both cultivars were raised by Mr. Barker of Kelmscott, near Ipswich, England. They grow to a height of 6′ under ideal conditions. var. *wilsonii* ('Wilsonii') is up to 6′ tall with 12″ long loose panicles of deep blue flowers.

***-lycoctonum*** (lye-cock′ tone-um) | Yellow Wolfsbane, Badger's Bane | 3-4′/1′
Late Summer | Yellow | Southern Europe | Zones 3-6

It is nice to see some yellow flowers in a genus so seemingly populated with blues and purples. The light green leaves consist of 5-7 deeply divided lobes arranged up the 4′ long stalk. The plants are laden with terminal racemes of small yellow flowers in late summer and early fall and stems may topple on other plants when in flower. This is not altogether bad as a little touch of aconitum can do wonders to some old tired plants in the fall.

Two subspecies are occasionally sold but quite mixed up. subsp. *neapolitanum* (*A. lamacrkii*) has a many-branched inflorescence and flowers quite heavily while subsp. *vulparia* (*A. vulparia*) has a few terminal inflorescences with pale yellow flowers.

'Russian Yellow' has large, deeply cut leaves and pale yellow flowers.

***-napellus*** (na-pel′ lus) | Common Monkshood | 3-4′/1′
Late Summer | Dark Blue | Europe | Zones 3-6

This is the most common of the monkshoods and easiest to locate in catalogs and garden centers. The leaves are divided to the base and divided again into linear or lancelike segments. The flowers are in spikelike terminal racemes. Unfortunately, the species is exceptionally variable, and is divided into numerous subspecies differing in height, flower color and structure of the inflorescence. It is tough enough to determine which aconitum you are growing, without the confusion apparent in a single species.

The popularity of *A. napellus* has declined with the introduction of newer garden cultivars but it is still an outstanding plant. Although plants are toxic, the ground-up leaves have been used as an external treatment for rheumatism and neuralgia, and internally to relieve fevers.

**Cultivars:**

'Album' (*A. napellus* subsp. *vulgare* 'Albidum') bears white flowers on erect 3-4′ tall stems.

'Blue Valley' grows about 3′ tall with deep to medium blue flowers. Plants are upright and strong. The foliage is dull green.

'Snow White' is equally handsome, and may be nothing more than 'Album' with a better name. Regardless, it is worth the effort to try some of these non-blue forms.

***-reclinatum*** (re-clin-a′ tum) | Trailing Wolfsbane | 6-8′/2′
Late spring | Cream | Southeast United States | Zones 4-7

Unlike most others in the genus, this native is a vining, sprawling plant, which needs to be grown through other plants in the garden. The species is native from Virginia to West Virginia and south to north Georgia. Plants look great in the spring as the basal leaves emerge, but they can get a little wild as they loop their way here and there. They provide more of a curious journey than a destination, but they are fun to try. All aconitums are best grown in climates with cool nights—this one is way too weedy-looking in hot, humid climates to even try it.

**Related Species:**

*A. henryi* has leaves divided into 3 segments and indigo blue flowers. 'Spark's Variety' is thought to be a cultivar but may be a hybrid. Regardless, it is dark blue and 4-5′ tall, similar to 'Bicolor' in habit. Both cultivars may require staking, particularly if grown in too much shade.

**Hybrids:**

'Blue Lagoon' grows only 12-15″ tall with medium blue flowers and dark green leaves. Plants flower in mid to late summer.

'Blue Sceptre' has erect 2-3′ stems terminating in dense inflorescences of blue and white flowers. Flowering stems are not as branched as in 'Bicolor'.

'Bressingham Spire' is 2½-3′ tall with violet blue flowers in dense upright panicles suggesting the influence of *A. napellus*. Lateral flowers develop after the terminal flower begins to open. This cultivar is particularly valuable because staking is not required. The latter two cultivars resulted from seedlings from crosses by Alan Bloom between 'Newry Blue' and the bicolored *A. cammarum*.

'Carneum' is a pink to salmon-flowered form that is sometimes offered as 'Roseum' or 'Rubellum'. The pink color adds another dimension to *Aconitum* but plants must be grown where night temperatures are consistently cool or flowers fade to a dingy washed-out white. Spectacular where happy.

'Eleonara' bears terminal racemes of handsome white flowers with blue edges over rigid stems that grow to 3′ tall. The glossy green leaves have 5-7 deeply incised toothed lobes.

'Ivorine' was raised in the early 1950s by Alan Bloom and is an outstanding compact, early-flowering plant. The creamy white flowers are held in short spikes. Becoming more popular as plants become more available. If you can grow *Aconitum*, try this one.

'Newry Blue', raised by Mr. Tom Smith of Daisy Hill Nursery in Newry, Northern Ireland, is 4-5′ tall with navy blue flowers and has the same upright flowering habit as 'Bressingham Spire'.

'Pink Sensation' bears many light pink flowers with a deeper colored margin. Plants are 2-3′ tall and about 2′ wide.

'Stainless Steel' is a relatively new introduction, with many flowering stems of metallic pale lilac flowers with a metallic silver sheen.

***Acorus*** (a-core- us) Sweet Flag Araceae

Looking at the foliage of this fine genus, one would be sure that these are ornamental grasses. The flowers are rather inconspicuous and plants are grown mainly for their handsome grasslike foliage. They are naturalized in shallow water by lakes and slow rivers, therefore excellent for wet areas or bog gardens. While wet conditions are important, they may be grown in well-irrigated garden conditions. These terrific plants have earned a spot in the American garden.

Quick Reference to Acorus Species

| | Height (ft.) | Foliage highly fragrant |
|---|---|---|
| *A. calamus* | 2-4 | Yes |
| *A. gramineus* | ½-1½ | No |

***-calamus*** (kal′ a-mus) Sweet Flag 2-3′/2′
Spring Foliage Asia, Southeast United States Zones 4-8

The foliage, which resembles a large flag iris, releases a pleasing cinnamon scent when crushed or broken. One of the first air fresheners, sweet flag leaves were strewn around rooms to counteract the smells of cooking or garbage. Calamus root was also used at one time in the manufacture of cosmetics. The aromatic chemicals, known as oil of calamus, are extracted from the foliage and roots, and may still be purchased today. Leaves also contain a chemical, asarone, which was once used as a flavoring ingredient.

The leaves may sometimes reach 4′, but around 2½ feet is more common. The flowers are minute and greenish, on a 2-3″ long spadix without the ornamental spathe seen in most members of this family. Full sun and moist soils are preferred but partial shade is also tolerated.

Propagate by division when plants become crowded.

**Cultivars:**

'Argentostriatus' is the proper name of the plant that is often sold as 'Variegatus'. It is by far the most popular cultivated form, bearing long narrow leaves with clean lines of creamy white bands. I grow mine in shallow water in my pond.

***-gramineus*** (gram-in′ ee-us) Dwarf Sweet Flag 6-15″/12″
Spring Foliage Eastern Asia Zones 5-8

The differences between this species and the previous include a smaller stature, shorter, more pendulous sedgelike leaves and a greater choice of cultivars. The foliage is not as sweet as *A. calamus* but the greater choices of leaf color and stature provide worthy plants for the garden. Plants perform well in partial shade to full sun where they form a wide clump, often used as a slow-growing ground cover. I give an ice cream cone to the first student who can find the flowers. They consist of a small narrow spadix enveloped in a 2-3″ long creamy white spathe, well hidden within the leaves. However, after sufficient brushing and combing of the foliage, serious calories are dispensed. The species is not always available but many of the selections are terrific.

**Cultivars:**

'Golden Edge' bears 1′ tall fans of colorful gold and green variegated foliage.

'Golden Pheasant' is similar to but taller than 'Ogon'. Plants bear narrow, straplike leaves, which are chartreuse when young then mature to a handsome gold.

'Licorice' is from the U.S. National Arboretum and must be abused to be enjoyed. Rub your fingers against the foliage or dig a few roots and the anise scent will be quite obvious. From the outside, it is similar to the species.

'Masamune' is a dwarf form (6-8″) with creamy variegation on the narrow leaves.

'Minimus' is only 3″ tall with dark green leaves. 'Minimus Aureus' is a golden form of this dwarf cultivar that is a sock-knocker-offer, particularly when combined with some of the purple heucheras. Because of its small size and brilliant color, it has become a favorite with the garden train enthusiasts. I have also seeen this listed as 'Miniature Gold'.

'Oborozuki' is a robust grower with green leaves and yellow variegation. Plants grow 10-12″ tall. A little more green than 'Ogon', but similar in the winter.

'Ogon' has been and continues to be the most popular cultivar for good reason. The fanlike leaves appear golden yellow because of the chartreuse and cream variegations on the evergreen foliage. Plants are 8-10″ tall. I have grown this one for years in my garden; it keeps trying to grow into the path, but my trusty Lawn-Boy keeps it in bounds.

'Pusillus Nanus' bears fan-shaped fronds of 2-4″ tall dark green foliage. Hard to find much difference between this and 'Minimus'.

'Tanimanoyuki' can't be pronounced but can be enjoyed. The green leaves are brushed with yellow along the blades.

'Variegatus' grows about 12″ tall and bears narrow leaves nicely striped with cream.

'Yodo-no-yuki' has variegated pale green leaves with narrow silver stripes. Growing about 12″ tall, the foliage is slightly more muted than 'Ogon'.

## *Actaea* (ak-tee′-a) Baneberry, Bugbane Ranunculaceae

Since the last edition of this book (1997), the genus has become a Fat Albert, gobbling up *Cimicifuga* while no one was paying attention. As a scientist, I understand the credo of "let's get it right", therefore evaluation and revaluation of scientific issues are normal and important aspects of any field of study. In the field of taxonomy, new techniques have allowed much more in-depth studies, occasionally resulting in lumping and splitting of families and genera, and wholesale changes to species. For the most part, these changes have been of little interest to gardeners, most gardeners did not deal with botanical names anyway. However retailers and producers do, and were caught between what is correct, and what their clients understood. And most changes in the last thirty years were simple enough. However, some blockbusters have recently come our way and we have been forced to come face to face with the science, and accept or ignore the changes. Often, we ignore them. We did not go gently into that good night with the wholesale changes made to *Chrysanthemum*; we hated them and dug our heels in hoping they would go away. Similar changes in the genus *Aster* are upon us, to say nothing of movement between families, an almost daily taxonomic occurrence.

I mention all this now because the genus *Cimicifuga* has all but disappeared. Like every other change, it has been a slow journey from accepted publication in a scientific journal to finding its way into the gardening and industry literature—and even longer before it is accepted by any of us. The official dismissal of *Cimicifuga* occurred in 1998 with a paper from James Compton, and to my amazement, many people have already accepted it, a record for sure. Personally, I dislike it, and have trouble understanding the rationale, however it looks like the changes are here to stay, so let's get with the program. Here we go, welcome to the wide, wide world of *Actaea*.

In the original genus, three common species are grown for their compound leaves and colorful berries. Unfortunately, the berries and roots are poisonous, which accounts for the common name, baneberry. It is reported that eating only 6 berries can produce severe symptoms. For this reason plants should not be grown where children and pets play. The other common name, bugbane, is a translation from *cimex*, a bug, and *fugo*, to drive away. When Linnaeus named this plant in 1750, he knew that *Cimicifuga foetida*, a species from Asia, was dried and ground into powder and used to stuff pillows, mattresses and cushions as a protection against biting insects. For retailers, however, this name does little to attract customers, perhaps we could call it "white spire plant" or something a little less itchy.

All plants are woodland species and do well in moist, shady location and rich, acid soil similar to its native habitat at the edge of woods where leaf mold is plentiful. In early spring, the white flowers appear in terminal racemes, and give way to ¼" long oval berries in late summer and early fall. The fruit is equally ornamental as the flowers, but they are eaten by varmints with tougher constitutions than ours.

With the inclusion of the new species, the genus also includes slender, tall plants with much longer long wands of white flowers. The species of garden value have white flowers with minute petals and the stamens provide much of the beauty. All species have ternately compound leaves, a fancy term meaning that the leaves are divided into three segments, three times. All plants in the genus prefer moist, humus-rich soil.

They often require 3-4 years before decent flowering occurs and patience is necessary. Unfortunately for gardeners dealing with warm summer nights and high humidity, plants are often disappointing. Unless they receive just the right micro-environment in such a setting, they tend to be stunted and do not flower particularly well. Perhaps if plants were never seen growing in their prime in other gardens, people wouldn't be so picky. They continue to flower in the Armitage garden, but I wouldn't put them in a landscape I was designing for someone else.

Seed should be sown when fresh, as old seed is much more difficult to germinate uniformly. In sowing this and other genera of the Ranunculaceae, place the moist seed tray at about 70°F for 3 weeks, then transfer to freezing conditions (28-30°F) for about 5 weeks. After the cold treatment, remove the tray from the freezer and place at 40-50°F until germination occurs. All this is more easily accomplished by sowing in the fall, allowing snow cover or mulch to maintain slightly freezing temperatures followed by cool spring temperatures to satisfy the requirements. A more rapid means of propagation is by root division in the spring.

Quick Reference to Actaea Species

| | Height (ft.) | Fruit ornamental |
|---|---|---|
| *A. matsumurae* | 3-4 | No |
| *A. pachypoda* | 2-4 | Yes, white |
| *A. podocarpa* | 3-6 | No |
| *A. racemosa* | 6-8 | No |
| *A. rubra* | 2-4 | Yes, red |
| *A. spicata* | 2-4 | Yes, black |

**- *matsumurae*** (mat-sue′ mur-aye) Kamchatka Bugbane 3-4′/3′
Late Fall White Russia Zones 3-7
(*Cimicifuga simplex*)

Although Kamchatka bugbane does not have the majesty of some other species, it has gained a significant following. The flower stalks are more arching than those of *A. racemosa* and the secondary stalks are often taller than the terminal raceme. Flowers of this species are generally the last of the bugbanes to open, often taking a minor frost or two, a bonus for gardeners looking for late season color. Plants are more tolerant of basic soils than other species. They are also the best species for the south.

Propagate similar to *A. podocarpa.*

**Cultivars:**

Atropurpurea Group is probably the best way to classify these dark foliage forms. They look alike at first glance and only subtle differences in foliage color can be found. The group includes 'Bernard Mitchell', 'Black Negligee', 'Braunlaub', 'Brunette', 'Hillside Black Beauty', and 'James Compton'. They all have bronze to deep purple foliage, stand 3-4′ tall and can all be spectacular. I am perhaps a little biased towards the latter two selections, but I have never seen them all lined up side by side for a critical comparison.

'White Pearl' has large (over 2′ long), dense white flower spikes. Flowers open in late October in my garden.

'Elstead Variety' has finely cut dark green foliage, over which purplish brown flower buds open to pure white flowers.

'Pritchard's Giant' is an immense cultivar, easily growing 4-5′ tall. All cultivars are vast improvements on the species.

**-*pachypoda*** (pak-ee′ poe-da) White Baneberry, Doll's Eye 2-4′/3′
Late Spring White Eastern North America Zones 3-7a
(syn. *A. alba*)

The species keeps changing from *A. pachypoda* to *A. alba* and back again, but if you ask for doll's eyes, it won't matter at all. The compound leaves, similar to those

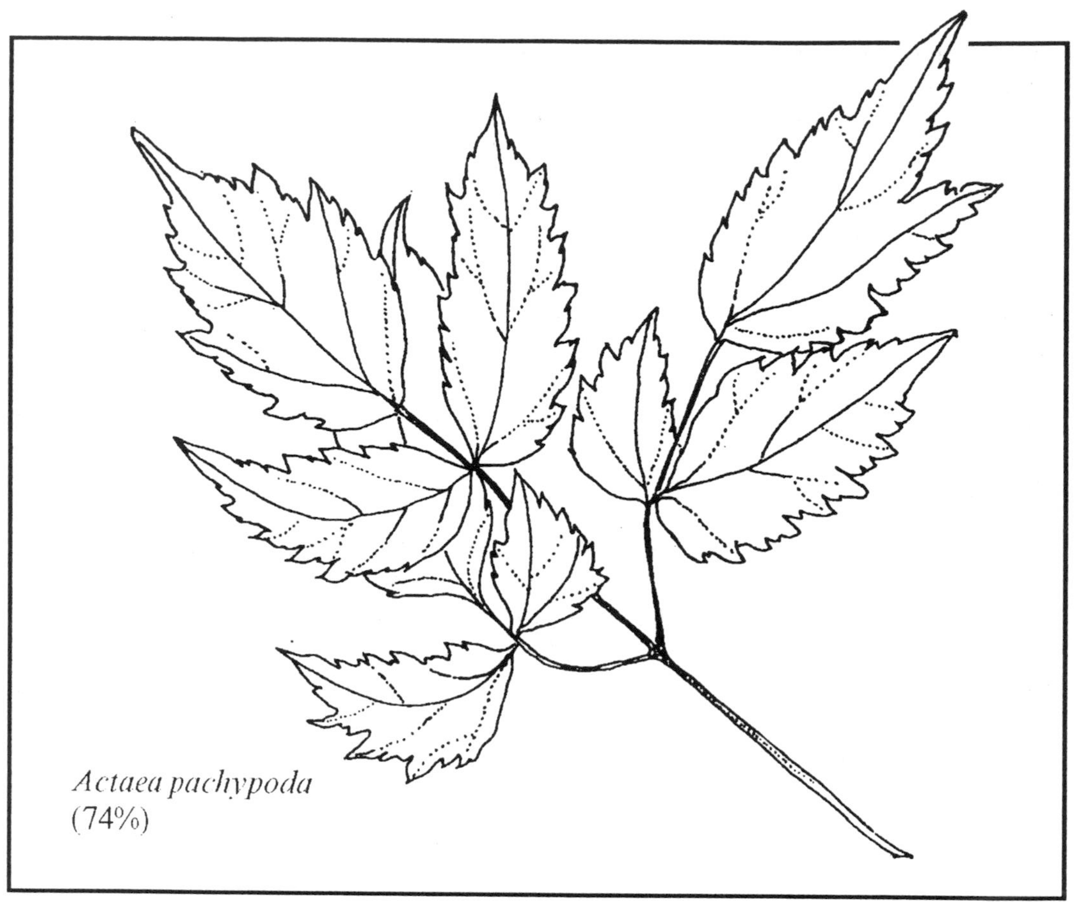

*Actaea pachypoda*
(74%)

of *Astilbe*, are handsome even without the flowers and fruit. The fringed flowers are borne in 2-4″ long terminal racemes on green flower stalks well above the foliage. The flower stalks (pedicels) become thicker (*pachypoda* means "thick foot", referring to the pedicel) and turn a pinkish red as the white berries develop. Although the fruit of *A. pachypoda* and *A. rubra* usually are different colors, there is a red-fruited form of *A. pachypoda* (forma *rubrocarpa*), making the shape of the pedicel the best means of distinguishing the two species. This is a handsome plant for the shady area of a woodland setting or border. The deep green leaves appear fresh well into the late summer and the berries provide interest into late fall. Abundant moisture is required in areas of hot summers; plants perform better in areas of cool nights. I coaxed mine along in my garden in north Georgia for a few years, but it kicked its legs up and finally succumbed.

**Cultivars**:

'Misty Blue' is similar to the species but the showy leaves are blue-green, similar to the color of the foliage of fringed bleeding heart. The plant was named in 1998 by Richard Lighty of Mt. Cuba Center in Greenville, Delaware.

***-podocarpa*** (po-do-car′ pa) American Bugbane 2-6′/3′
Early Fall White Eastern United States Zones 3-7
(*Cimicifuga americana*)

Although not as common in gardens as the other species, it is easier to cultivate. Native from New York to Pennsylvania and as far south as the mountains of Georgia, plants are adaptable to a wide range of conditions. The 1-3″ long, rounded leaflets have 3-5 toothed lobes and heart-shaped bases. The flower stalks are sometimes branched near their base providing additional flowers as the season progresses. If you look closely at the flowers, the bracts at the base of the flower stalks (pedicels) are evident, a distinguishing characteristic of this species.

Propagation by seed is difficult and best results are obtained with fresh seed. Even then, germination is erratic and seedlings emerge over a long time. After collecting the seed, place in sand in the cold (35-40°F) for 6-8 weeks. Sow seed in a 1:1 mix of

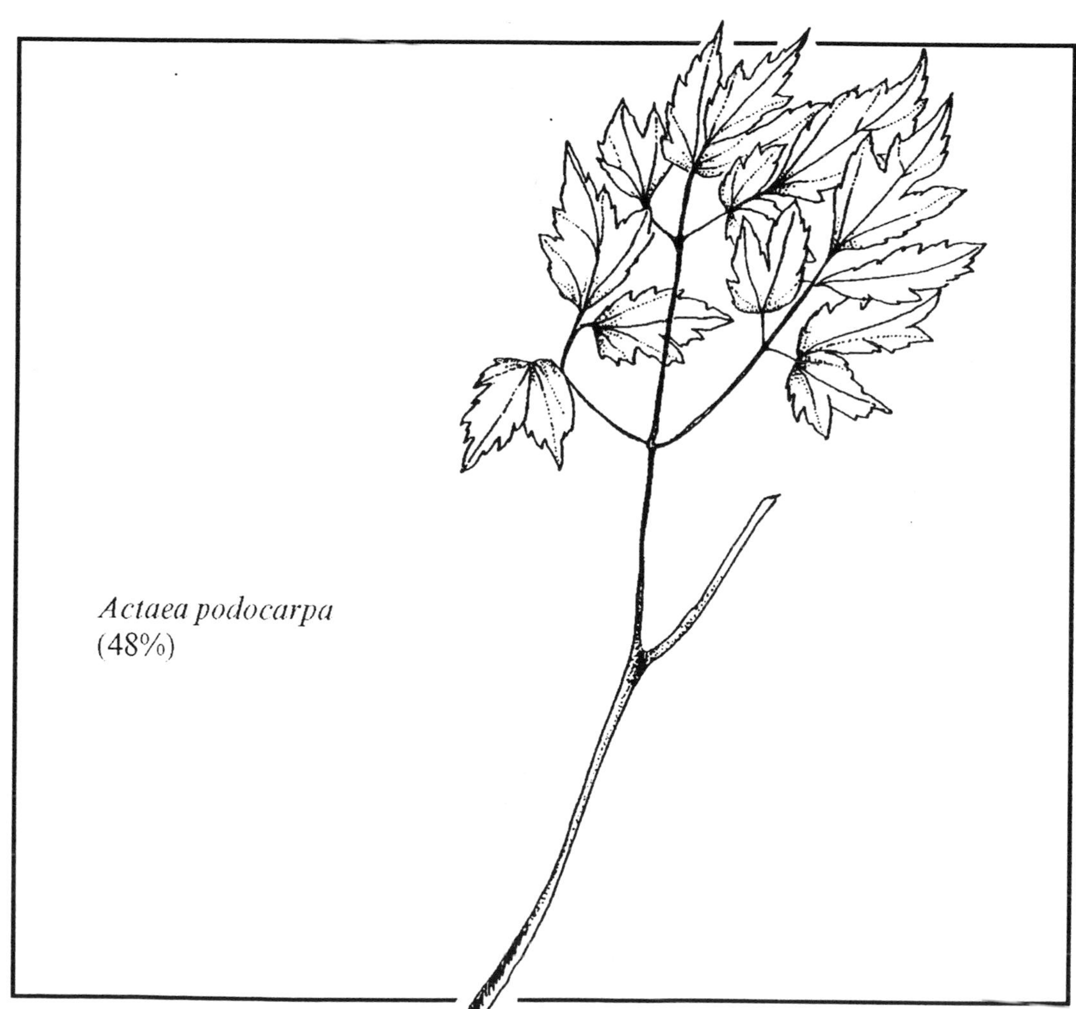

*Actaea podocarpa*
(48%)

peat:vermiculite and place in a warm (70-75°F), humid area. Plants can be divided but this should not be done for at least three years after planting. They have a deep root system and do not divide well.

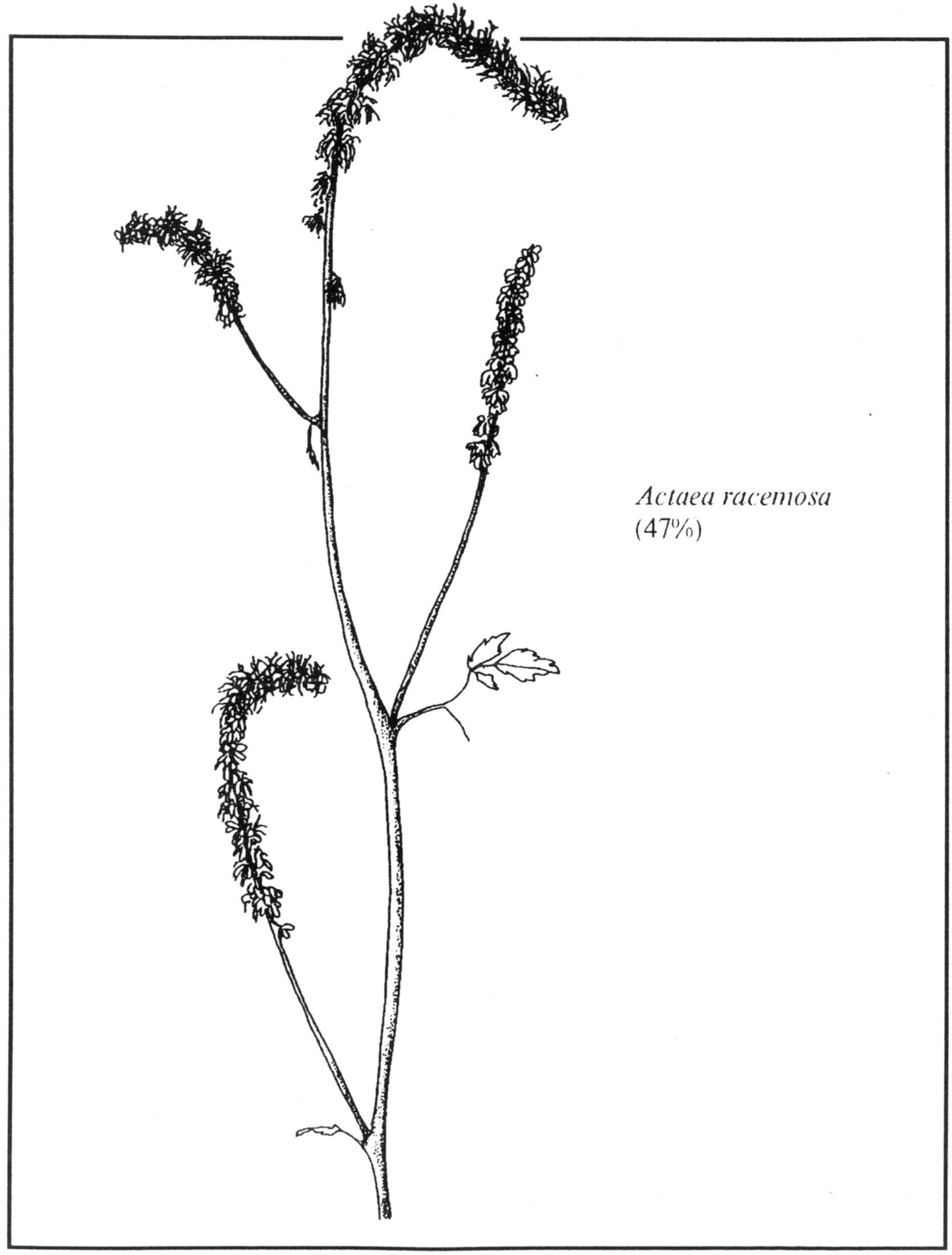

*Actaea racemosa*
(47%)

***-racemosa*** (ray-ce-mo′ sa) | Snakeroot, Cohosh | 6-8′/4′
Late Summer White | Eastern United States | Zones 3-7
(*Cimicifuga racemosa*)

This is the aristocrat of the genus whose tall white spires provide an unforgettable sight in the late summer garden. It is also the easiest to locate at nurseries and from mail order catalogs. The leaves are deeply cut and the 1-3″ long leaflets are ovate and irregularly toothed. The long racemes of creamy white flowers reach 2′ in length, and are often branched near the base of the terminal inflorescence. They may look like rockets on their way to the stars, or bent and twisted in raucous contortions. To the herbalist Patricia Kyritsi Howell, they are reminiscent of a symphony, with gentle music and loud drumrolls. Pat also tells us that these plants are excellent for the treatment of anxiety, or as she calls it "the ax-murderer syndrome." Flowers open in midsummer in zone 7 but not until late summer or early fall in zones 3 and 4. The 1-2 pistils of the flowers are sessile, that is, they have no pistil stem. This lack of stem is not particularly easy to notice, but it is one of the characteristics that make this species unique. The flowers persist for about four weeks and the spent flower spires

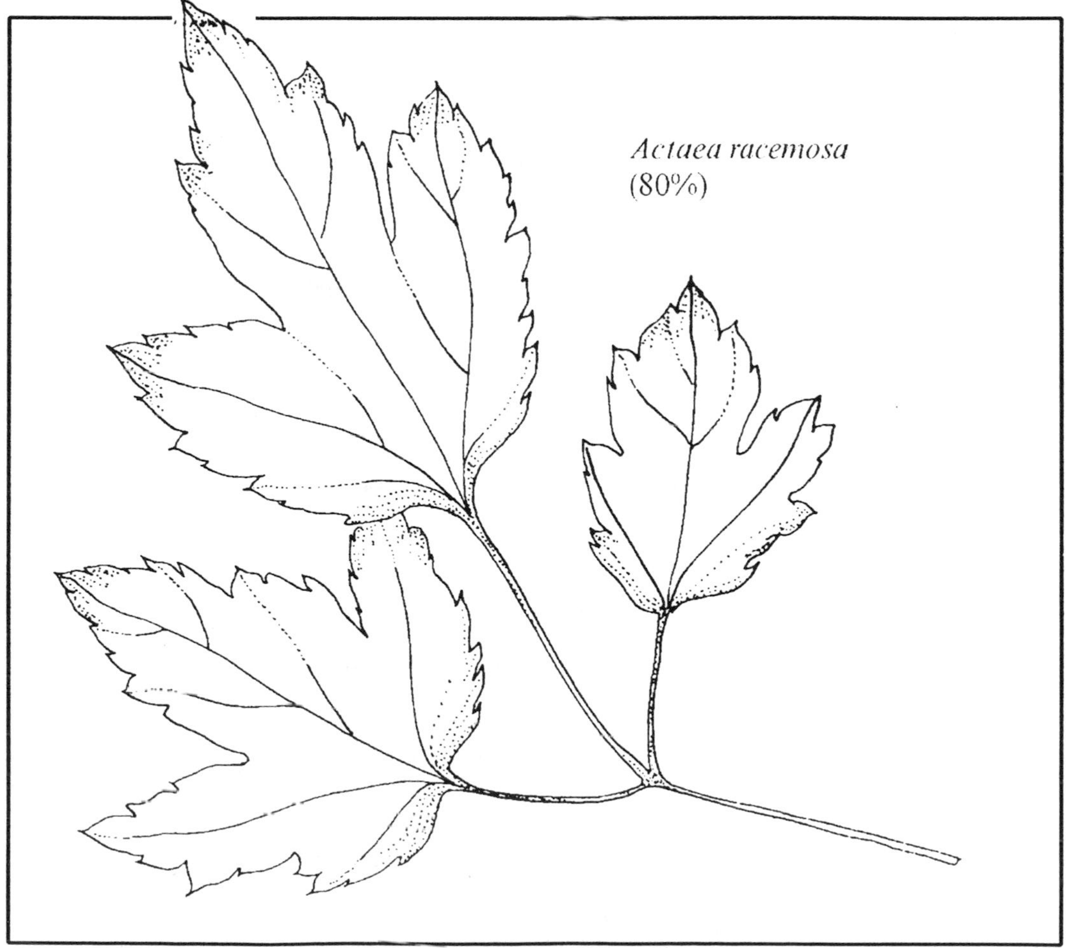
*Actaea racemosa*
(80%)

continue to be decorative for many more weeks. I can't think of a more beautiful planting than at Naumkeag Garden, designed by Fletcher Steele, in the Berkshires of western Massachusetts. Plants have naturalized in the woodland setting and are absolutely stunning in mid July.

Fewer flower stalks are produced on this species than others but its graceful yet wiry form has made it popular in American gardens. They look terrific with many cultivars of *Phlox paniculata*. Plants need a constant supply of moisture or leaf margins turn brown and plants become stunted.

Propagate similar to *A. podocarpa*.

**Cultivars:**

var. *cordifolia*, (*Actaea cordifolia*) grows 4-5′ tall. Leaves consist of 4-10″ long leaflets, the base of the terminal leaflet is heart shaped. Flowers are similar to those of the species.

**-*rubra*** (rew′ bra) Red Baneberry 2-4′/3′
Spring White North America Zones 3-7a

The flowers appear about a week earlier and are larger and not as fringed as those of the previous species. The ¼″ long red berries are borne on slender green pedicels, which turn red as they mature. The berries are particularly poisonous and roots are violent purgatives, irritants, and emetics. The leaves are usually more hairy than those of *A. pachypoda* but except for the color of fruit and shape of pedicels, few differences exist. Plants require the same growing conditions as *A. alba*.

**Cultivars:**

'Filkins' Selection was selected by John Filkins of New York. Plants are similar to the species, but are said to be more vigorous, and bear reliably heavy fruit each year.

'Neglecta' (forma *neglecta*) is a white-berried form with slender stalks. Plants are also a little taller.

**Related Species:**

*Actaea japonica* now includes what was once *Cimicifuga acerina* as well as *C. japonica*. Plants have dark green maple-like leaves with long pointed lobes and purple stems. An outstanding species.

*Actaea dahurica (Cimicifuga dahurica)* is native to China and Japan and is hardy in zone 5 to zone 7. All leaflets are cordate (heart-shaped). Plants grow 5-6′ tall and bear creamy white flowers in simple or compound racemes. Flowers, which occur in midsummer, have a subtle fragrance.

*A. spicata*, also known as *A. nigra*, black baneberry, is similar to *A. rubra* but has jet black berries (also very poisonous) carried on short black slender pedicels.

## ***Adenophora*** (a-den-off′ or-a) Ladybells, Gland Bellflower Campanulaceae

The ladybells are often confused with members of *Campanula* but are unique in having a thick disc-like structure (the gland) at the base of the style of the flower.

If you really don't relish the thought of tearing apart flowers to find such mundane organs, it is helpful to know that *Adenophora* has numerous branched, slender stems and nodding bell-shaped lilac blue flowers. The leaves are alternate, and sessile or have very short petioles. Plants prefer a rich, well-drained soil in full sun or partial shade. In Montreal, I regarded *Adenophora* as an innocuous weedy member of gardens. Although plants are better behaved in Georgia, I still have trouble getting excited about it. More tolerant of heat than many of the campanulas, it may be included in the southern garden where other members of the Campanulaceae must be excluded. There are about 50 species and most gardeners know not a one of them. By far the most available members are *A. confusa* and *A. liliifolia* (often incorrectly listed as *A. lilifolia*), but occasionally species such as *A. pereskiifolia* and *A. bulleyana* are also offered.

Quick Reference to Adenophora Species

| | Height (in.) | Leaf arrangement | Flower color |
|---|---|---|---|
| *A. bulleyana* | 30-36 | Alternate | Blue, lilac |
| *A. confusa* | 24-30 | Alternate | Blue, lilac |
| *A. liliifolia* | 18-24 | Alternate | Blue, lilac |
| *A. pereskiifolia* | 24-30 | Whorled | Blue, purple |

***-confusa*** (con-fuse′ a) Common Ladybells 2-2½′/2′
Late Spring Blue China Zones 3-7

This 2-2½′ tall species bears ¾″ long, nodding bell-shaped, deep blue flowers in late spring. The leaves are ovate, bluntly dentate and are often sessile with leaf bases 2-3″ wide and tapered. The flowers have entire petals and open in late May to early June and continue for about 3-4 weeks. Seed is fine and should be mixed with sand or talcum powder to insure even distribution. Press seed in gently, do not cover. Keep seed tray at 70-75°F soil temperature and moist at all times. Germination takes 2-3 weeks. The roots are deep and fleshy and therefore difficult to divide or move without significant damage.

***-liliifolia*** (lily-foe′ lee-a) Lilyleaf Ladybells 1½-2′/1½′
Late Spring Pale Blue Europe Zones 3-7

This species resembles *A. confusa* but is not as tall and the flowers are paler blue or creamy white. The style of the flowers is obviously exserted (projects from the petals) whereas the style of the former is only slightly so. The petals are finely serrated and the leaves are linear to lanceolate and approximately 1″ wide. This species tolerates heat better than *A. confusa* and is also a good plant for southern gardeners, and even better, it is the most fragrant of the ladybells.

**Related Species and Hybrids:**

'Amethyst Chimes' was introduced by Joy Creek Nursery and grows 3-4′ tall and bears smoky lilac flowers. I believe this is the same as 'Amethyst'.

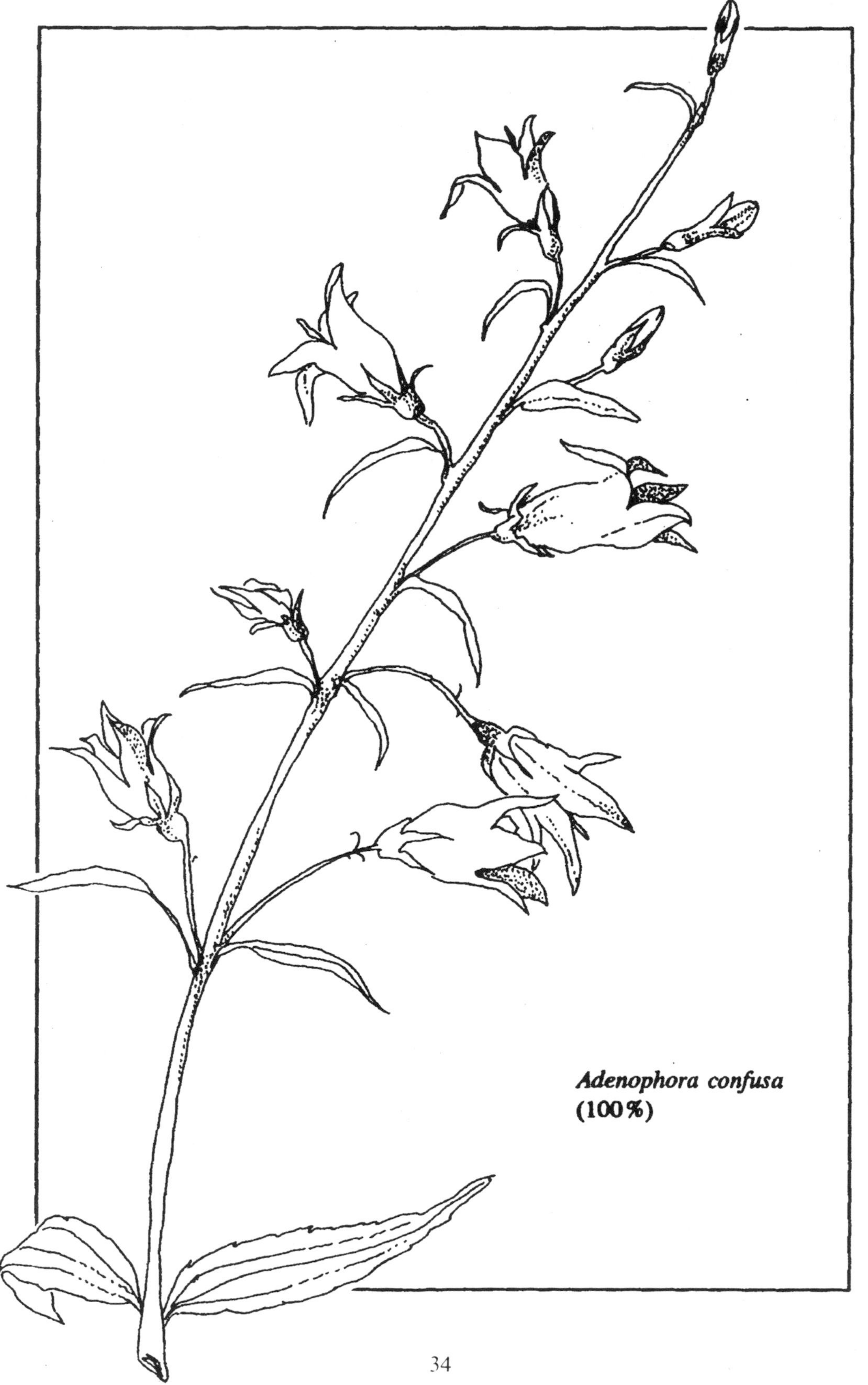

*Adenophora confusa*
(100%)

*A. aurita* has branching stalks of blue bell-shaped flowers with strong basal leaves. Plants grow about 2′ tall.

*A. bulleyana* is native to western China and differs from the above species by having glossy green, ovate leaves with single serrations. The leaves are wider than the above species, all but the uppermost being about an inch wide. The pale blue flowers are often borne in threes. Handsome but uncommon. Hardy to zone 3.

*A. pereskiifolia* bears purple bell flowers on 2-2½′ tall stems. The whorled leaves are pointed and slightly hairy. Excellent plants for heat and humidity.

*A. potaninii* is native to China and hardy to USDA zone 3. The stems are upright but not particularly strong, but the flowers, usually violet to blue, are pendulous. A white form, 'Alba', is occasionally offered.

*A. stricta* is taking a while to find its way to America, but it is a most handsome plant. Seeds of *A. stricta* var. *sessilifolia* were brought to England by Roy Lancaster of Hampshire, England from northwest Sichuan, China. Nodding blue bell-shaped flowers are produced on a branching raceme over kidney-shaped basal leaves. The lower leaves are stalked while the upper ones are sessile. It was originally identified as *A. aurita* and plants may appear in catalogs that way.

*A. tashiroi* is occasionally offered. Native to Japan, plants stand about 15″ tall and bear whorls of nodding blue flowers in summer.

*A. triphylla* is a charming 12-20″ tall plant that flowers in late summer and fall. Long exserted styles protrude from the late summer blue to violet flowers. The leaves are whorled, usually four per whorl. Native to China, hardy in zone 4-7.

***Adiantum*** (add-ee′ an-tum) Maidenhair Fern Pteridaceae

The maidenhairs provide some of the most handsome ferns in the garden. The stems are dark purple to black and the blades are arranged in fanlike segments. Of the 200 or so species, two or three are easily found by gardeners, but others are available with a little searching. Many maidenhairs are not sufficiently cold hardy for much of the country and if seen at all, are seen as houseplants. However, a number of species are quite cold tolerant and may be used as far north as zone 2, if spores or plants are available. The Aleutian maidenhair, *A. aleuticum*, and the northern maidenhair, *A. pedatum*, are the most cold hardy while Argentine maidenhair, *A. lorentzii*, delta maidenhair, *A. raddianum*, and southern maidenhair, *A. capillus-veneris*, are most at home south of zone 7. Trailing or walking maidenhair, *A. caudatum*, is native to the tropics but its long pendulous fronds and attractively lobed segments make a handsome summer fern regardless of winter temperatures.

The maidenhairs do not perform as well in deep shade as many other species. An area with bright filtered light and good air circulation is made for maidenhairs. Well-drained alkaline soils are best and pH may be raised if necessary with the addition of marble chips or dolomitic lime. Sand and peat moss at a pH of about 7 to 8.5 is satisfactory.

Plants are relatively easy to produce from spores.

Quick Reference to Adiantum Species

| | Height (in.) | Foliage arranged in horseshoe shape on stem | Hardy to at least zone 7 |
|---|---|---|---|
| *A. aleuticum* | 6-24 | Yes | Yes |
| *A. capillus-veneris* | 12-18 | No | Yes |
| *A. pedatum* | 12-20 | Yes | Yes |
| *A. raddianum* | 6-12 | No | No |

**-capillus-veneris** (ca-pill′ us ven-er′ is) Southern Maidenhair 12-18″/12″
Spring Light Green Foliage Europe, Tropics Zones 7-10

Southern maidenhair fern is widely distributed from semi-tropical to tropical areas and often grown as a greenhouse plant. My daughter Laura keeps surprising me, she always has flowers in her home, but she also uses 4″ pots of southern maidenhair in decorative containers in her den. Bright girl, that Laura.

Although plants are difficult to perennialize outdoors in cold temperate areas due to lack of cold tolerance and susceptibility to disease, they are showstoppers where they are happy. A great deal of variability occurs, particularly in plant performance. Plants of southern maidenhair exuberantly grow on the rock walls at Birmingham Botanical Gardens; the bright light and sheltered location made these plants glisten. The petioles are dark brown to black and the lacy, delicate foliage is light green, particularly when young. Steve Bender at *Southern Living* recommends southern maidenhair combined with white caladiums and nippon lily (*Rhodea japonica*) as an outstanding combination but they combine nicely with most plants if they are grown well. Bright light is essential for good growth and if overgrown with other plants, they tend to develop dark spots on the fronds and decline. Good air movement and basic pH are essential.

**Cultivars:**

'Fimbriatum' has segments cut into deeply cut finger-like lobes.

'Imbricatum' is smaller with cascading fronds.

'Rock Springs' was found in 2000 in the Edwards Plateau region of Texas near the town of Rock Springs, Texas by Scott Ogden and Tony Avent. Good heat tolerance is a bonus for this 2′ tall cultivar.

**-pedatum** (pe-day′ tum) Northern Maidenhair Fern 12-20″/12″
Spring Mid Green North America, East Asia Zones 3-8

This is one of the most sought-after and popular ferns in temperate gardens. That it is one of our natives to boot provides added pleasure. The northern maidenhair fern provides a graceful and lacy feel in the shaded garden and quickly spreads in moist, bright areas. They thrive in cold areas but are difficult south of zone 7b. The foliage is forked and consists of 8-20 segments held in a horseshoe-like arrangement. The black shiny stems are among the most handsome in the plant kingdom. They are deciduous and slow to emerge in the spring, compared to other more vigorous ferns.

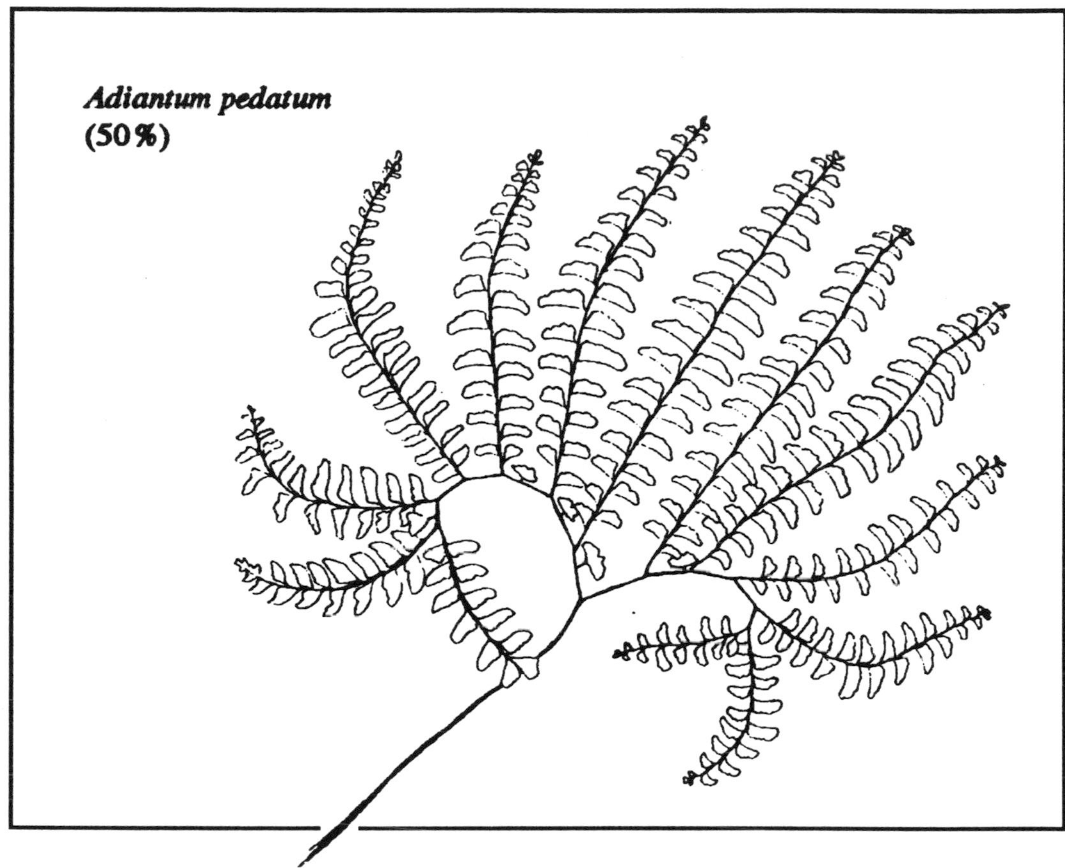


Plants perform well in areas of bright filtered light and good air circulation. A basic pH is also beneficial for best performance.

**Cultivars:**

A number of forms have been selected or developed but few are easy to find, and none is any better than the species.

'Japonicum' has pinkish-bronze new fronds.
'Miss Sharples' produces larger leaflets and has a noticeable chartreuse color.
'Montanum' is much more compact and dense than the species.

**Related Species:**

*Adiantum aleuticum* (*A. pedatum* var. *aleuticum*), Aleutian maidenhair, is native to the western half of the country and as far north as Alaska. USDA zones 2-7. Plants are particularly cold hardy, but not recommended for areas of high heat and humidity. The branches are pendulous and weeping, and the fronds are deeply cut. Two other varieties of northern maidenhair, var. *subpumilum*, a dwarf form, and var. *calderi* have recently been folded into this species.

*Adiantum hispidulum*, rosy maidenhair, has possibilities for gardeners in the southern part of the country and as far north as zone 7. It is variable in form but generally has rough stems and dark glossy green horseshoe-shaped fronds, and is adaptable to a wide range of soil conditions. The new growth is rosy pink, and in the spring well-grown plants are outstanding. Harsh winters will damage the fronds and impede the new growth and some mulching to protect from winter winds may be useful. 'Bronze Venus' bears new foliage that is more bronze than that of the species.

*Adiantum raddianum*, delta maidenhair fern, grows 1-2′ tall and is native to central and South America. Hardy only in zones 8-10. Probably the most common maidenhair in the world, it is little seen in gardens in this country because of its lack of cold tolerance. Even in my garden in Athens (zone 7b), plants overwinter only in mild winters and struggle to multiply. They grow naturally in rocky area and bluffs and generally prefer neutral to alkaline soils. The segments are lobed and narrowly triangular and are borne on handsome black stems. It is renowned for its variability, with over 60 cultivars named by fern growers, but few are commonly available. However, fern organizations may supply spores or plantlets for fern fanciers. 'Bridal Veil' has drooping fronds with small teardrop segments. 'Elegans' bears lobed, wedge-shaped segments and is one of the easiest to raise; 'Fritz Luthi' has overlapping fronds, grows 1-2′ tall and bears similar handsome black stems. Plants appear to be more cold hardy than most cultivars, an RHS Award of Garden Merit plant in 1997; 'Variegatum' produces upright fronds with segments flecked with white. Spores gathered from the strongest variegated fronds tend to produce variegated sporelings.

*Adiantum venustum*, Himalayan maidenhair fern, provides reasonable cold tolerance (to zone 5), but is not particularly heat tolerant. The 1-2½′ tall fern bears large, coarsely divided fronds and each segment is divided. Plants are becoming more available.

**Related Genus**:

*Adiantopsis* appears more similar to *Cheilanthes* than *Adiantum*, however a couple of forms have become available to gardeners. Neither is cold hardy much below 15°F, so think about zone 7b as its limit. So few of these are out there that I, along with all others, am guessing at best. *A. chlorophylla* is about 2′ tall while the more common *A. raddiata* is shorter with fronds arranged in a starfish pattern. Both are native to Costa Rica and northern South America.

## *Adlumia* (add-loom-ee′ a) Allegheny Vine, Climbing Fumitory Fumariaceae

This climbing biennial vine is represented by *A. fungosa*, native to the northeastern United States, thus its common names, mountain fringe and Allegheny vine. The delicate, light green foliage is three times pinnate, resulting in a fernlike appearance. Plants use the petioles of new leaves to clamber and scramble over shrubs and bushes, or gardeners may train the vine along fences or arbors. The pale pink and whitish flowers are similar to those of bleeding heart (*Dicentra*) and are formed in hanging clusters at the axils. Plants are hardy to zone 3 and may be grown as far south as zone 7.

Plants form a low bushy mound the first year and then, after winter, climb as fast as helium balloons released from the football stadium. Growing 10-12′ tall in a few weeks, it is one of those vines that one should plant and then get out of the way. Provide some afternoon shade for best performance. The flowers are not bright or big enough to allow this to ever become a mainstream garden plant, but is fun and easy to grow.

Many European and some American taxonomists put *Adlumia* in the family Papaveraceae. However, the members of the Fumariaceae are quite distinct from those of the Papaveraceae in several respects, including floral symmetry, sap character, and stamen number and fusion. So let's keep it with its friends *Dicentra* and *Corydalis* for a while longer.

Propagate from seed; they will self-sow in areas where plants are happy.

***Adonis*** (a-don′ is) Adonis Ranunculaceae

Greek legend has it that these were favorites of Adonis, who, upon his death, was changed into this flower by the goddess Aphrodite. Adonis was regarded as the God of Plants by the Greeks, and he was believed to disappear every autumn and reappear in the spring.

About 20 species occur but only *A. amurensis* and *A. vernalis* are perennial throughout most of the country. The leaves are alternate, dissected and light green. The plants are erect but normally do not exceed 18″ in height and are most effective as rock garden plants or in the front of a small border. They should be planted in masses as one or two plants do not provide enough "flower power". Although said to perform better at a basic pH, they don't seem particularly fussy about soil as long as it is well drained. An area that receives some afternoon shade should be chosen in the South, although full sun north of zone 5 is satisfactory. Slugs relish them and spring application of slug preventative reduces damage.

Approximately 6 weeks of temperatures below 40°F are necessary for the rhizomes to break dormancy in the spring. Both species go dormant by midsummer. Plant late-emerging perennials such as *Platycodon* or *Gladiolus* or summer annuals to cover the vacant area.

Sow fresh seed in the spring, grow seedlings throughout the summer and transplant to the garden in the fall; plants will likely flower the next spring. Seed is notoriously difficult to germinate if not fresh, and even if collected from garden plants, seeds will need more than one year to germinate. Division is not required, however it the best means of multiplication; divide in late spring after the foliage dies down.

Quick Reference to Adonis Species

| | Height (in.) | Number of leaves | Flower color | Flowering time |
|---|---|---|---|---|
| *A. amurensis* | 9-12 | Few | Yellow | Early Spring |
| *A. vernalis* | 12-15 | Many | Yellow | Late Spring |

***-amurensis*** (am-ew-ren′ sis) Amur Adonis 9-12″/12″
Early Spring Yellow Japan, Manchuria Zones 4-7

This species flowers as early as February in southern gardens and progressively later further north. The stems are branched, each stem branch bearing triangular, 3-6″ long leaves which are cut into 3 sections to the base. Each of those sections is in turn divided into linear segments. At the base of each petiole are leafy stipules. The

2″ wide flowers are usually buttercup-yellow but may occasionally be white, rose, or have red stripes. Each flower has 20-50 petals, slightly longer than the sepals. The flowers generally appear just before the leaves fully emerge.

The leaves unfurl as the flowers begin to open. If the weather remains cool when flowers open, they persist for up to 6 weeks, fewer if hot weather comes along. The golden flowers contrast well with the reticulated iris (*I. reticulata*), crocus, and other spring-flowering bulbs.

Propagation is best accomplished by division in late spring or early summer.

**Cultivars:**

'Flore-plena' is a common double cultivar and is much showier than the species.

'Fukuju Kai' has fully open sulfur-yellow flowers and is the earliest to bloom. Other cultivars with copper, orange, pink, and white flowers have been developed by Japanese nurserymen, but have not been widely distributed.

'Sandanzaki' is certainly interesting, if not calming. Plants grow about 15″ in height and bear flowers consisting of layers of yellow petals often edged in green. Unfortunately, plants are rare at best.

**-*vernalis*** (ver-nah′ lis) Spring Adonis, Pheasant's Eye 12-15″/12″
Spring Yellow Europe Zones 4-7

Plants are more winter hardy (zone 3 with protection) than the former and flowers emerge 3-6 weeks later. It differs from the previous species by having unbranched stems and many more leaves that are sessile (no petioles) and 1-2″ long. The flowers have fewer petals than *A. amurensis* (10-15), which are slightly toothed, and about 2½″ wide. They open as flat as a dinner plate, as if knowing their time in the sun was fleeting, to be enjoyed while they could. Plants do not go completely dormant as do those of *A. amurensis.*

Propagation is more difficult than *A. amurensis* and may take several years to recover from the disturbance of dividing.

**Related Species:**

*A. apennina* is similar to *A. vernalis* but has larger flowers (up to 3″) and the lower leaves are rounded and sheathlike.

## ***Aegopodium*** (aye-go-pow′ dee-um) Goutweed, Bishop's Weed Apiaceae

About 6 species have been described in this genus; all grow by creeping rhizomes and all can be incredibly invasive. The foliage occurs in threes and the flowers are usually white. The only species commonly seen in cultivation is *A. podagraria*, bishop's weed.

**-*podagraria*** (pod-a-grair′ ee-a) Bishop's weed, Goutweed 6-9″/spreading
Late Spring White Europe, Western Asia Zones 2-8

Some people politely call this plant "fast growing and a good filler". Others curse it as they wrench their backs while wrenching out this loathsome invader. No doubt it

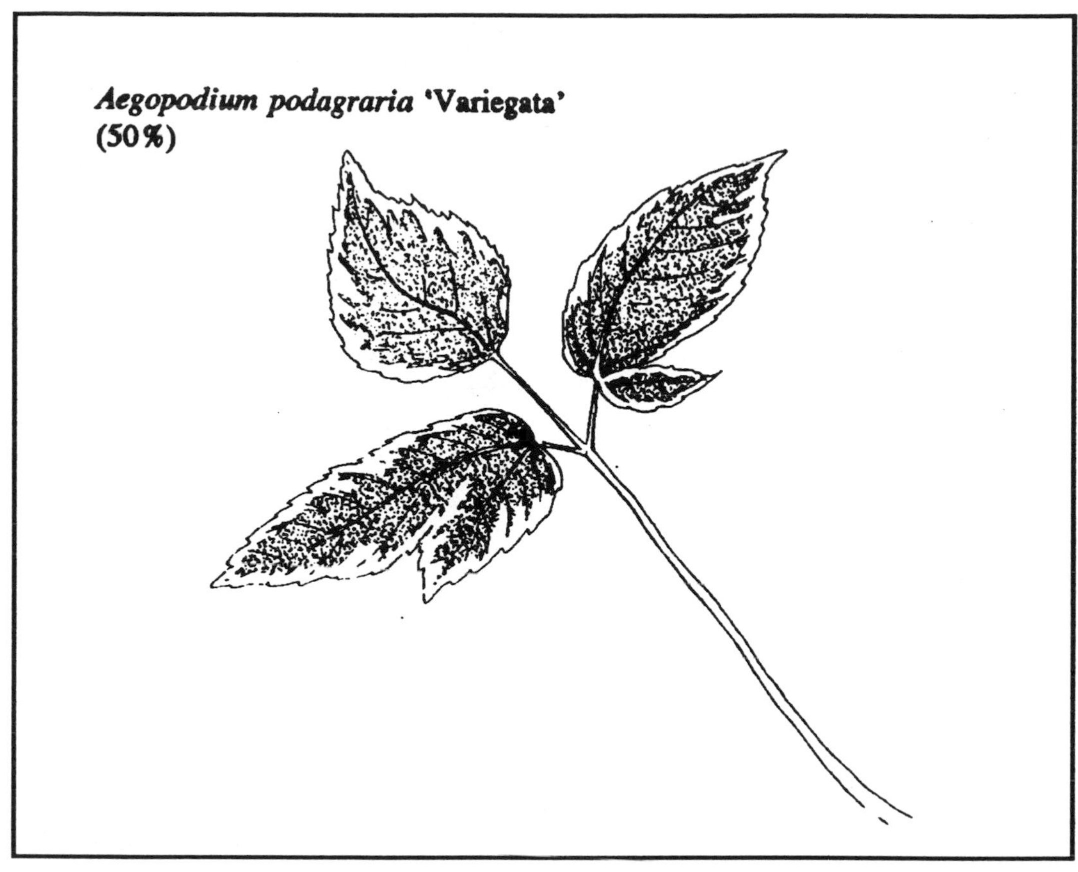


can be invasive, and jump and frolic through the garden. In some cases, this no way diminishes its value, for if areas require some greenery or soil must be conserved, this plant is perfect. The leaves are produced in two groups of three (biternate) and creamy-white flowers are produced in late spring and summer. In Montreal, this plant was everywhere, in Michigan, it was not much different. However, in the southeastern United States, plants are much better behaved. It is still invasive, but takes a few more minutes to take over. Plants are tolerant of nearly all soils, and prefer partially shaded areas. They burn up in full sun, so you end up with an ugly thing all over the place. Plants multiply with creeping rhizomes and spread more quickly in cooler soil temperatures. This plant also looks good in nursery pots, therefore it is a favorite of nursery people who can sell weeds in a pot. Marketing is alive and well in North America. Plants were at one time thought to cure gout, thus one of its common names.

**Cultivars:**

'Bengt' supposedly is a non-running form from Sweden. The margins are somewhat wavy. I have not trialed this, so cannot verify this claim.

'Variegatum' is more common than the species and much more ornamental. The green leaves bear creamy-white margins and plants are only a little less invasive than the species. The leaves, however, are clean and bright and if this genus must be used, the variegated form is far more handsome. I yank it up from my garden and stick it the woods to brighten them up, and it still does well.

***Aethionema*** (ieth-ee-o-nee′ ma) Stonecress Brassicaceae

*Aethionema* has never hit the mainstream of North American gardening, although plants have regional followings where rock gardens and alpine gardening are popular. Plants do poorly in warm climates, but they may be fall planted for spring enjoyment. After flowering, they generally decline. In northern areas, however, *Aethionema* is underused and if small stature and colorful plants are needed, stonecress may fill that need. Numerous handsome species and cultivars are available from seed and given sharp drainage, they are easily grown. All flowers consist of 4 petals and 4 sepals.

Quick Reference to Aethionema Species

| | Height (in.) | Flower color | Foliage color |
|---|---|---|---|
| *A. armenum* | 6-8 | Pink | Light green |
| *A. grandiflorum* | 12-20 | Rose-red | Blue-green |
| *A. iberideum* | 6-9 | White | Blue-green |

***-armenum*** (ar-meen′ um) Turkish Stonecress 6-8″/12″
Spring Pink-white Turkey, Caucasus Zones 5-7

This highly variable species bears narrow, linear light green to gray-green leaves and whitish pink flowers held in tightly clustered racemes. Plants dislike moist clay soils and shade, performing best on sunny, well-drained slopes or raised beds. Plants respond well to slightly alkaline soils. It is difficult to find the species but a number of handsome cultivars can usually be located in the trade.

***-grandiflorum*** (gran-di-flo′ rum) Persian Stonecress 12-20″/15″
Spring Rose-pink Western Asia Zones 5-7

Plants produce dozens of flowers in crowded upright terminal racemes, showy for many weeks. The rose-colored flowers bear petals about 4 times as long as the sepals. The blue-green leaves are needle-like and the base of the plant becomes woody. There is some variability in this species as well, and this variable group is referred to as *A. grandiflorum* Pulchellum group.

***-iberideum*** (i-be-ri′ dee-um) Iberis Stonecress 6-9″/12″
Spring White Eastern Mediterranean Zones 5-7

The white flowers are similar to those of *Iberis*, thus its common name. Gray-green silvery mats of leaves carry many small, fragrant flowers less than 1″ long in a terminal raceme. Plants require excellent drainage and are best used in the rock garden or in raised beds. The diminutive height and free-flowering nature of this plant makes it highly sought after by alpine enthusiasts. In warm humid climates, it melts like an ice cream cone.

**Related Species and Hybrids:**

*A. cordifolium*, heart-leaf stonecress, is similar to *A. grandiflorum* but is smaller in almost every way. The foliage has a blue-green hue. Plants grow to 8″ and the flowers are only about 1/5″ long. Native to Lebanon.

*A. oppositifolium* is only 1-2″ tall but makes handsome mats of pink-lilac flowers. Perfect for the rock garden, this woody-based plant creeps from rock to rock.

*A. schistosum*, Persian stonecress, bears dozens upon dozens of pink flowers in early spring which as a group provide pleasant fragrance to go with the color. The evergreen leaves are tiny with an obvious blue hue.

'Warley Rose' is the most popular stonecress and carries brilliant dark pink flowers densely borne over 6-8″ tall mats of gray-green foliage. The cultivar was awarded an Award of Garden Merit in 1993 by the Royal Horticultural Society. Introduced in the early 1920s by the eccentric Mrs. Wilmott of Warley House, England (see *Eryngium giganteum*).

'Warley Ruber' has dark maroon flowers. Both cultivars have been placed with various species, but now plants are thought to be natural hybrids.

## *Agapanthus* (ag-a-pan′ thus) African Lily Alliaceae

Agapanthus is a rhizomatous plant with fleshy roots and elongated leathery leaves. Most species have strap-shaped, glossy dark green 2-3′ long leaves. The flowers are carried in a rounded umbel on a thick scape and appear in late summer. In favorable climates, plants are extremely tough and durable. In areas of Britain, southern Europe and throughout New Zealand, agapanthus is common and long lasting, used as edgings, roadway dividers and hedging.

The most common species are the evergreen *A. africanus*, lily of the Nile, *A. praecox*, and the deciduous *A. campanulatus*. Few obvious differences occur in foliage and flower, and many selections and hybrids are far more common than the species themselves. Although *A. praecox* and *A. campanulatus* are fully hardy in areas of California and Florida, the hardiest and most available forms of *Agapanthus* are the hybrids; old ones like the 'Headbourne Hybrids' are still popular while newer cultivars are popping up in retail establishments throughout the country.

Even in north Georgia (zone 7b), it is difficult to overwinter agapanthus, yet there are areas as far north as zone 5, where winter temperatures may routinely reach −10°F, where they overwinter. Moderation of temperatures by a lake effect, sandy well-drained soils, and snow cover help create this unusual situation. Without doubt, the majority of gardeners in this country should use agapanthus in a combination container for the deck, porch or around a garden pool, to be brought into a frost-free area during the winter. Many of the newer introductions may be hardy to zone 7.

On a taxonomic note, a good deal of discussion concerns whether the genus should be included in the Liliaceae, where it has resided or in the Alliaceae, a relatively new family. Both are accepted, I have opted to include it with the onions.

Allow the crowns to dry out over the rest period and begin adding water as spring approaches. The crowns should be set approximately 2″ below ground level, watered well and left undisturbed. During the growing season, plants require copious amounts of water and must not be allowed to dry out.

**Cultivars and Hybrids:**

Many beautiful garden forms and hybrids have been developed and a few are gaining popularity. Some cultivars are particularly good for cut flowers.

'Albus' ('Albidus') bears creamy white flowers on 2-3′ tall plants. Evergreen.

'Alice Gloucester' has purple flower buds and stems and bears large warm white flowers in mid to late summer.

'Back in Black' bears dark blue flowers, which in itself is not unusual. The "black" part comes from the flower stem which starts out dark green and ages to black.

'Blue Giant' produces rich blue trumpets on plants that may reach 3½′ tall.

'Blue Globe' is deciduous, growing about 3′ tall with light blue flowers.

'Blue Moon', raised by Eric Smith of Hillier's Nursery, has densely packed pale blue flowers on 2-2½′ tall stems.

'Blue Triumphator' is 2-3′ tall and produces clean blue flowers.

'Bressingham Blue' grows about 3′ tall and produces deep amethyst-blue flowers. 'Bressingham Bounty', with slightly broader leaves and large rich blue flowers was introduced in 1992. 'Bressingham White' is a vigorous plant with clean white flowers. All arose from initial seedlings raised in 1967 at Blooms of Bressingham, Diss, England.

'Cayles Lilac' came from New Zealand and bears soft lilac flowers on 15-18″ tall plants with broad leaves.

'Cobalt Blue', selected by Beth Chatto of Elmstead Market, England, has cobalt blue flowers on 2′ tall plants.

'Elaine' was a wild hybrid found among seedlings at the Los Angeles State and County Arboretum. Plants bear large dense umbels of dark violet-blue flowers. Flower stalks are up to 4′ long.

'Ellamae', also selected by the Los Angeles State and County Arboretum, appears to be a cross from *A. orientalis* 'Praecox' and *A. inapertus*. Very vigorous, plants produce dozens of violet flowers on long stalks.

'Gayle's Lilac' is a good dwarf form, standing about 1½-2′ tall. Plants bear many scapes of pale lilac flowers above the evergreen foliage.

'Getty White' is a hybrid with dense heads of creamy white flowers. Vigorous and handsome.

'Glenavon' is hard to find in the United States, but well worth the effort. Plants bear dozens of blue flowers with deep blue stripes. They are not short, growing up to 3′.

'Headbourne' hybrids arose during the 1950s and 60s from Mr. Lewis Palmer of Headbourne Worthy near Winchester, England. As a mix, they have 2-3″ long deep violet to pale blue flowers. These are among the taller of the available cultivars as well as the most cold hardy. Mr. Palmer was a leader in the breeding of agapanthus and many of his original crosses were used in the continued improvement of this genus.

'Isis' bears large inflorescences (6″ across) of deep blue flowers.

'Kingston Blue' is about 2′ tall and produces blue-black flower buds that open to dark royal blue flowers in early summer.

'Liliput' has 8-12″ long leaves, grows only 12-18″ tall and produces small pendulous dark blue flowers. Terrific for containers but slow to divide.

'Loch Hope' is one of the finest blue agapanthus in cultivation today. It is late flowering and produces flowers of the deepest violet atop 4-5′ tall stems. In many of the older blue selections, the flowers fade to an unsightly reddish purple. This is not the case with this hybrid as the flowers maintain their deep color until they fall from the plant.

'Peter Pan' is a dwarf (about 12″ tall) cultivar with narrow foliage and handsome sky blue flowers. Excellent in containers.

'Profusion' grows to 3′ in height and bears many light to dark blue flowers. The variability in flower color produces a striped effect.

'Silver Baby' has a tinge of blue all over the white flowers. Dwarf (1-2′ tall), handsome and unusual.

'Snow Drops' is a dwarf form with white flowers. Introduced from New Zealand.

'Snowy Owl' is an excellent clone with creamy white flowers on 3′ high stems.

'Snow Pixie' produces many clean white flowers on 9-15″ tall plants.

The Storm series, presently consisting of 'Blue Storm' and 'Snowstorm', has become quite popular due to plants' heavy flowering tendencies. Developed in Australia by the Tesselaar Company.

'Streamline' arose from the Auckland Botanic Gardens and is about 18″ tall and produces blue flowers.

'Tinkerbell' is a short (10-12″ tall) plant with variegated foliage consisting of light green leaves with narrow clean white edges. The foliage is truly beautiful but plants seldom flower. As beautiful as the foliage is, it simply looks like a variegated liriope if the blue flowers don't appear. Beautiful when placed in sunny, moist area.

'White Christmas' is about 2′ tall when not in flower but the white spires of flowers reach nearly 5′ in height.

**Related Species:**

*A. inapertis* bears long narrow blue-green foliage on 2-3′ tall plants. I have always admired the plants in the British Isles but have not seen many in this country. The tubular flowers are dark blue, erect at first, then becoming pendulous. Sometimes the var. *pendulus* can be found where the flowers droop all the time. 'Sky' is one such cultivar with tall stems bearing pendulous, sky blue flowers in summer. A white form, 'Alba', also occurs.

## *Agastache* (a-gah′ sta-kee) Anise Hyssop Lamiaceae

A genus consisting of approximately 20 species, mostly native to southwest United States and Mexico, often smelling of licorice or other childhood fragrances. Plants produce many spikes of flowers in lavender, red, orange and red although yellow flowers are occasionally seen (*A. nepetoides*).

A good many species are not cold hardy north of zone 8, but enough are sufficiently cold tolerant to zone 7 and a few into zone 5 and 6. Many wonderful plants such as *A. foeniculum*, *A. cana* and *A. rupestris* as well as the golden *A. aurantiaca* are native to the United States, and becoming more common as the popularity of native plants increases. However, some species are far more useful as contributing parents for the many hybrids that have recently appeared. As more gardeners discover the xeric properties of these plants, the popularity of the hybrids will continue to increase. All plants do well in full sun and slightly alkaline well-drained soils.

Quick Reference to Agastache Species

| | Height (in.) | Flower Color |
|---|---|---|
| *A. cana* | 12-36 | Rose-pink |
| *A. foeniculum* | 20-30 | Purple |
| *A. rugosa* | 24-30 | Violet-rose |
| *A. rupestris* | 36-48 | Orange-salmon |

***-cana*** (can′ a) Mosquito Plant 1-3′/2′
Late Spring Pink, Rose Southwest United States Zones 7-9

The blue-green foliage and pink-rose tubular flowers on many, branched stems make this an excellent plant to try in the garden. Flower colors are difficult to describe with people calling them deep rose, off-pink, near scarlet and various combinations thereof. The upright racemes consist of 6-12 flowers held in each whorl. The whorls are loosely arranged on 12-18″ flowering stems. The foliage is fragrant but not nearly as much as *A. rupestris*. Full sun and well-drained soils are essential.

Propagate from seed at 72°F and high humidity.

**Cultivars:**

'Sonoran Sunset' grows 12-15″ tall and equally wide and is covered with lavender-rose flowers most of the summer. May be cold hardy to zone 6. A Plant Select® Winner in 2002.

***-foeniculum*** (foe-nick′ ew-lum) Anise Hyssop 20-36″/30″
Summer Purple North America Zones 6-9

Growing tall, bearing many flower stems that are easily dried, anise hyssop is a favorite for cut flower producers and gardeners alike. The flowers are tightly arranged in long dense racemes. The flowers range from lavender to purple and the foliage is distinctly anise-like. They perform well in full sun but get tall and lanky if grown in too much shade. Easily propagated by seed.

**Cultivars:**

'Alba' ('Alabaster') is a common creamy white form of the species.

'Golden Jubilee' has been one of my favorites since we first trialed it in 2002. The anise-scented leaves are a muted yellow, although sufficiently golden to deserve the name, and they maintain their color throughout the summer. Plants produce many upright candles of lavender blue flowers in mid to late summer as well. Probably cold hardy to zone 6.

'Licorice Blue' and 'Licorice White' bear lavender-blue and off-white flowers respectively.
'Snowspire' is offered by only a handful of nurseries, but the 3′ tall plants bear many white flowers atop mid green foliage.

***-rugosa*** (rew-go′ sa) Anise Hyssop 24-30″/2′
Summer Violet-rose China, Japan Zones 5-8

This oriental visitor is offered by a number of nurseries because of enhanced cold tolerance. The branching flower stems carry violet-rose whorled flowers on 2-3′ tall plants over fragrant foliage. The wonderfully mint-scented leaves are 2-3″ long and 2″ wide with serrated margins and are pubescent chiefly along the veins on the underneath. Not as ornamental as some of the hybrids but a good performer.

**Cultivars:**
'Alba' is a white-flowered form of the species.
'Honey Bee Blue' is a uniform long-flowering cultivar. Plants received an Award of Quality from Fleuroselect, an association of flower seed breeders and sales companies in Europe, similar to our All American Selection association.
'Honey Bee White' is similar to 'Alba' and may be the same. The creamy white flowers bloom for a long time on 2-3′ tall plants.

***-rupestris*** (rew-pes′ tris) Rock Anise Hyssop 3-4′/3′
Summer Salmon-orange Southwest United States Zones 5-8

The striking rosy-orange whorled flowers and gray-green foliage provide a lovely wildflower to add color to the garden. One of the hardiest of the native hyssops, it has been used to incorporate cold tolerance to a number of hybrids. The flower color is unusual and flowering persists for at least 8 weeks. The best part of these plants is the fragrance of the foliage. People keep coming back to get their sniff, then bring their friends to get theirs. I call it the licorice plant, and plants transport me to the old-fashioned candy store. A Plant Select® Winner in 1987.

Full sun and well-drained soils are necessary.

***Hybrids***

'Apache Sunset' produces gray, finely cut leaves on 18-22″ plants with salmon-orange flowers in midsummer to late fall.

'Apricot Sprite' and 'Apricot Sunrise' are stunning crosses between *A. aurantiaca*, golden hyssop, and *A. coccinea*, both hybridized by Richard Dufresne of North Carolina. The former is about 2′ tall and filled with apricot flowers in the summer. The latter is taller, up to 3½′ with many golden orange tubular flowers in the summer. Both are eye-catching and attractive to butterflies and hummingbirds. Water and fertilize well. Zones 7-9.

'Black Adder' appears to be a cross between *A. foeniculum* and *A. rugosa*. It is a long bloomer, usually starting in midsummer and flowering until September or October. The flowers are rosy violet and held well above the foliage.

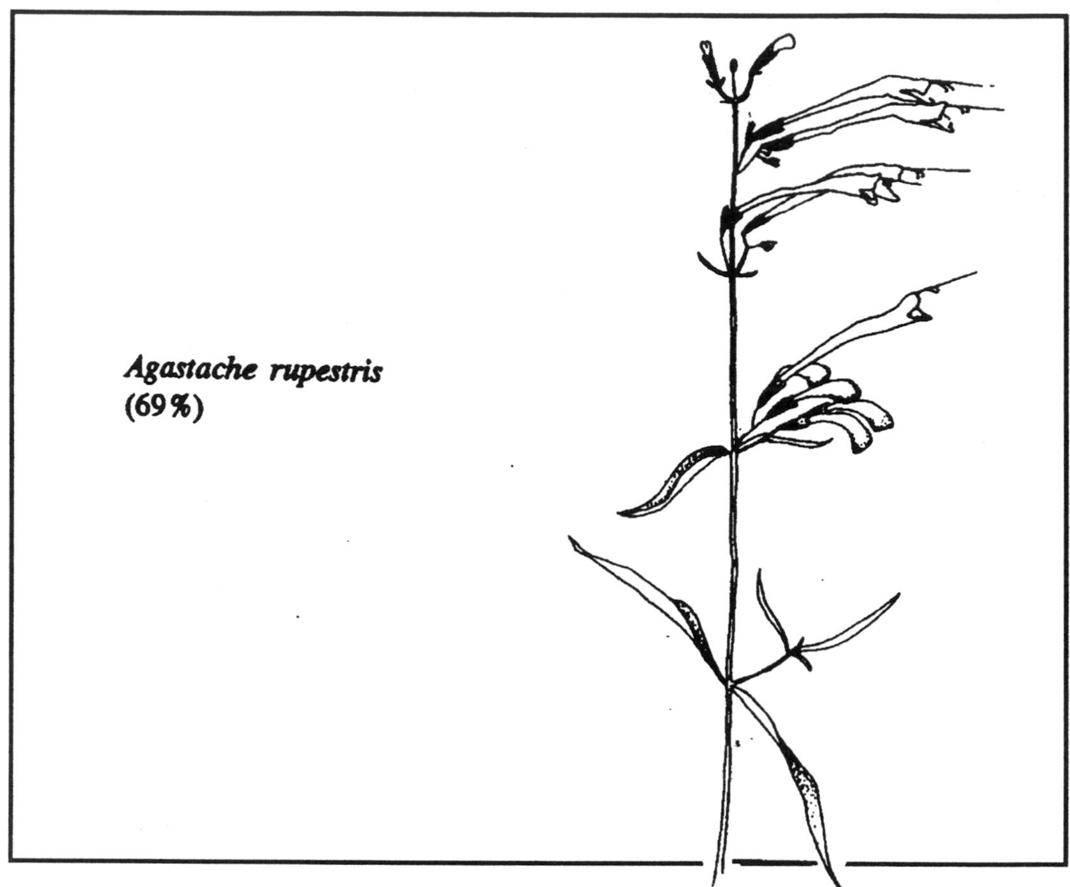
*Agastache rupestris*
(69%)

'Blue Fortune' is also a cross between *A. foeniculum* and *A. rugosa*, and is without doubt one of the best new plants recently introduced to gardens. Plants can grow up to 3′ in height and bear beautiful lavender-blue flowers on upright spires. The foliage has lovely licorice-scented leaves.

'Coronado' is an upright grower with silvery aromatic leaves. The tubular yellow flowers are heavily stained with orange, and open in late summer. Plants grow about 2½′ tall. I have seen this rated to be hardy as far north as zone 4, but more likely to zones 5-6. Selected a winner by Colorado's Plant Select® Program in 2001.

'Firebird', also from Richard Dufresne, is a hybrid of *A. coccinea* and *A. rupestris* and bears many orange-salmon flowers on 3′ tall plants. Plants are fuller than either of the parents and are cold hardy to zone 6. Terrific plant for hummingbirds. Probably hardy to zone 8, perhaps zone 7.

'Fragrant Delight' produces pale blue flowers on 3′ tall stems. The foliage is particularly fragrant.

'Heather Queen' is 2′ tall with many rosy pink flowers.

'Just Peachy', introduced by High Country Gardens of Santa Fe, New Mexico, provides subtle shades of pink- and peach-colored flowers. The 2½′ tall plants are perhaps hardy to zone 6.

'Pink Panther' (*A. coccinea* x *A. mexicana*) grows 3-4′ tall and produces many 1½″ long tubular rose-pink flowers held in long racemes, starting in midsummer.

'Purple Haze' is only about 2′ tall, taller in warmer weather, with lavender flowers in the summer. Not as fragrant as many other hybrids, but plants are consistently hardy to zone 6. Plants were introduced by Dutch plantsman Coen Jansen.

'Red Fortune' did not come as a sport of 'Blue Fortune', thus one should not give the high grades of the latter to this plant. However, having said that, it is still a fine introduction, more like a dwarf form of 'Tutti Frutti'. Probably a hybrid of *A. mexicana.*

'Shades of Orange' was also introduced by High Country Gardens. Plants are about 2½′ tall and produce many tubular blooms from peach to dark orange. Zones 6-10.

'Summer Breeze' is becoming better known as more plants find American gardens. Introduced by Canyon Creek Nursery in northern California, plants are 3-4′ tall and bear dozens of apricot-orange flowers.

'Summer Lustre', also from Canyon Creek, is even more vigorous, easily attaining 4-5′ in height if not trimmed. Flowers are peach colored with a hint of pink.

'Tutti Frutti' (*A. barberi* x *A. mexicana*) has tubular pink flowers from midsummer to frost. The foliage, to some noses, smells like tutti frutti. What does tutti frutti smell like anyway? Many people like this plant, but I was not one of them until I saw plants in Chanticleer Garden in Pennsylvania. They were upright, colorful and an exciting part of the garden; I am a born-again tutti-man. Hardy to zones 7-8.

## *Ageratina* See *Eupatorium rugosum*

## *Ajania* (a-jan-ee′ a) Silver and Gold Asteraceae

*Ajania pacifica* is the accepted name for plants that were classified as *Chrysanthemum pacificum*, and although its name has changed, the beauty and the challenges have not. This native Japanese species grows 1-1½′ tall and bears late yellow pom-pon flowers in late fall. Plants potentially offer a little something for everybody. The foliage is the most ornamental part of the plant, providing mounds of light green leaves edged in well-defined narrow bands of silver throughout the spring and summer. As early as late September and as late as October and November, dozens of flower buds give rise to bright golden yellow buttonlike flowers providing some of the brightest color in the fall garden. They are particularly handsome growing through gray-leafed plants such as *Artemisia* 'Powis Castle' but also are wonderful container plants that can be used as a substitute for fall mums. Because of the outstanding contrast between the bright flowers and the variegated foliage, garden centers offer them for sale as both spring and fall plantings. Plants perform reasonably well in zones 5-8.

However, not all is rosy in silver and gold land. Plants have been plagued with reports of poor winter hardiness, disappearing for no apparent reason. However, such death is as much a problem of poor drainage as cold temperatures. Provide excellent drainage and full sun but regardless, they should not be expected to give more than 3 years of good performance. Enjoy them, then replace with something else. Propagate by terminal cuttings in the spring or summer.

**Cultivars**:

'Pink Ice', introduced in this country in 1994, has light pink petals around a yellow center over 18″ tall plants.

***Ajuga*** (a-jew′ gah) Bugle Weed Lamiaceae

Bugle weed is one of the best-known perennials, even to non-gardeners. Plants popular with "normal" people are those that are easily grown, spread well, and provide good flowers and foliage, all without maintenance. *Ajuga* grows in any reasonably well-drained soil and although tolerant of full sun, growth is more rapid in partial shade. *Ajuga reptans* can become a persistent weed particularly if planted on the edge of a lawn, but other slower-growing species are available.

Approximately 40 species are known, however, only three have become available to American gardeners. Flowers are usually violet-blue although pink- and white-flowered cultivars have also been developed. All have square stems, opposite leaves and whorled flowers. A large drift in full bloom is spectacular but the foliage is the main reason for its popularity. In the South, crown rot (caused by *Sclerotium rossii*) can be a problem, particularly with *A. reptans*. Entire plantings may die or large patches develop infection. Planting in well-ventilated areas, dividing every 2-3 years, and applying fungicides help reduce this problem. Cut away and dispose of affected leaves and often plants recover without long-lasting damage when temperatures cool down.

Seed should be sown in late summer for fall planting or in November for spring planting. Cultivars will not come true to type from seed but cuttings and divisions may be used. Division is the easiest method and may be accomplished any time the ground is workable. Tissue culture techniques have also been developed.

Quick Reference to Ajuga Species

| | Height (in.) | Stoloniferous (Y or N) | Stems (erect or prostrate) |
|---|---|---|---|
| *A. genevensis* | 6-12 | N | Prostrate |
| *A. pyramidalis* | 6-9 | N | Erect |
| *A. reptans* | 4-12 | Y | Prostrate |

***-genevensis*** (gen-e-ven′ sis) Geneva Bugle Weed 6-12″/9″
Summer Various Europe Zones 4-9

This species is becoming more popular because it produces fewer runners, therefore spreads much less vigorously than *A. reptans*. Plants, however, grow faster than *A. pyramidalis*.

If constant moisture is provided, it tolerates more sun than *A. pyramidalis* or *A. reptans*. The dark green basal leaves are coarsely toothed, not hairy, and about 3″ long. The upper leaves are 1-3″ long, sessile and only slightly serrated. The stems are coarsely hairy, which makes it different than common bugle weed. The 4-6″ tall flower spikes are often pink but may be blue or white. Although most *Ajuga* grow in zone 3, this species should receive winter protection in zone 4.

**Cultivars:**

'Alba' bears creamy white flowers.

'Pink Beauty' is 4-5″ tall with light pink flowers in May and June.

'Robusta' is more vigorous and produces larger flowers and bigger foliage. Flowers are lavender-blue.

'Rosea' has rosy-pink flowers but is otherwise identical to the species.

'Tottenham' ('Tottenham Blue') is the best cultivar, bearing dense spikes of lilac-pink flowers.

'Variegata' has dark green leaves, mottled creamy white.

***-pyramidalis*** (pi-ra-mid-ah′ lis) Upright Bugle Weed 6-9″/9″
Late Spring Blue Europe Zones 3-9
(syn. *A. alpina*)

This good-looking plant incorporates the fine flowers and dark foliage of *A. reptans* without the spreading habit. The basal rosette is slightly toothed and hairy. The stems are hairy and the 4-6″ long flower spikes consist of large purple bracts which appear to press against the blue flowers. The leaves subtending the flowers are 2-4 times as long as the violet-blue flowers. Although the plant does not spread as rapidly as *A. reptans*, it does produce short stolons late in the season in response to short days.

**Cultivars:**

'Alba' produces crinkled oval leaves and white flowers.

'Metallica-crispa' ('Crispa') has deep blue flowers and brownish red crinkly foliage with a metallic luster. Ugly as sin, but nevertheless, an outstanding garden plant. Also listed as 'Metallica-crispa Purpurea' and 'Min Crispa Red'.

***-reptans*** (rep′ tanz) Common Bugle Weed 4-12″/24″
Late Spring Violet Europe Zones 3-9

Much of the breeding and selection in this genus has been accomplished with *A. reptans* and remarkable advances in foliage color have resulted. Regardless of cultivar, *A. reptans* is stoloniferous and can spread rapidly. This characteristic makes this species an excellent ground cover and a large clump in flower is a spectacular sight. Plant where its invasive qualities are welcome, such as on a bank or under the dappled shade of trees. Do not plant it as an edging to the lawn or the insidious disease of "buglelawn" will occur. One of the symptoms includes the appearance of small islands of green foliage soon forming a large archipelago in an ocean of lawn. Weapons to destroy these islands include shovels, sprayers, or as one gardener did, simply expanding the flower bed to include all the bugleweed in the lawn. His lawn became smaller every year. (Hmmm, perhaps he is on to something.) The best prevention is proper planning; plan to keep the *Ajuga* away from all grassy areas. If all else fails, remember that the ingestion of leaves of *A. reptans* is a mild narcotic. After trying some of the leaves, buglelawn will not seem as serious.

**Cultivars:**

Some may be hybrids with other species.

*Selections for flower color or size.*

'Alba' has creamy white flowers.

'Linda Applegate' is a reasonably compact form with white flowers.

'Pink Elf' is a dwarf cultivar with clear pink flowers.

'Pink Spire' is a fine green-leaved cultivar bearing 7″ long pink flower spikes.

'Pink Surprise' has bronze-green leaves, narrower than many others species', and purplish pink flowers. Introduced by Terra Nova Nursery, Tigard, Oregon.

'Purple Torch' bears tall torches of 12″ lavender-pink flowers with glossy green foliage.

'Rosea' produces rose flowers.

*Selections for leaf color, all have blue to violet flowers.*

Arboretum Giant came from Tony Avent of Plant Delights Nursery in Raleigh, North Carolina. This is a big robust plant whose large green leaves are outlined in deep purple. Bigger and uglier than 'Catlan's Giant'.

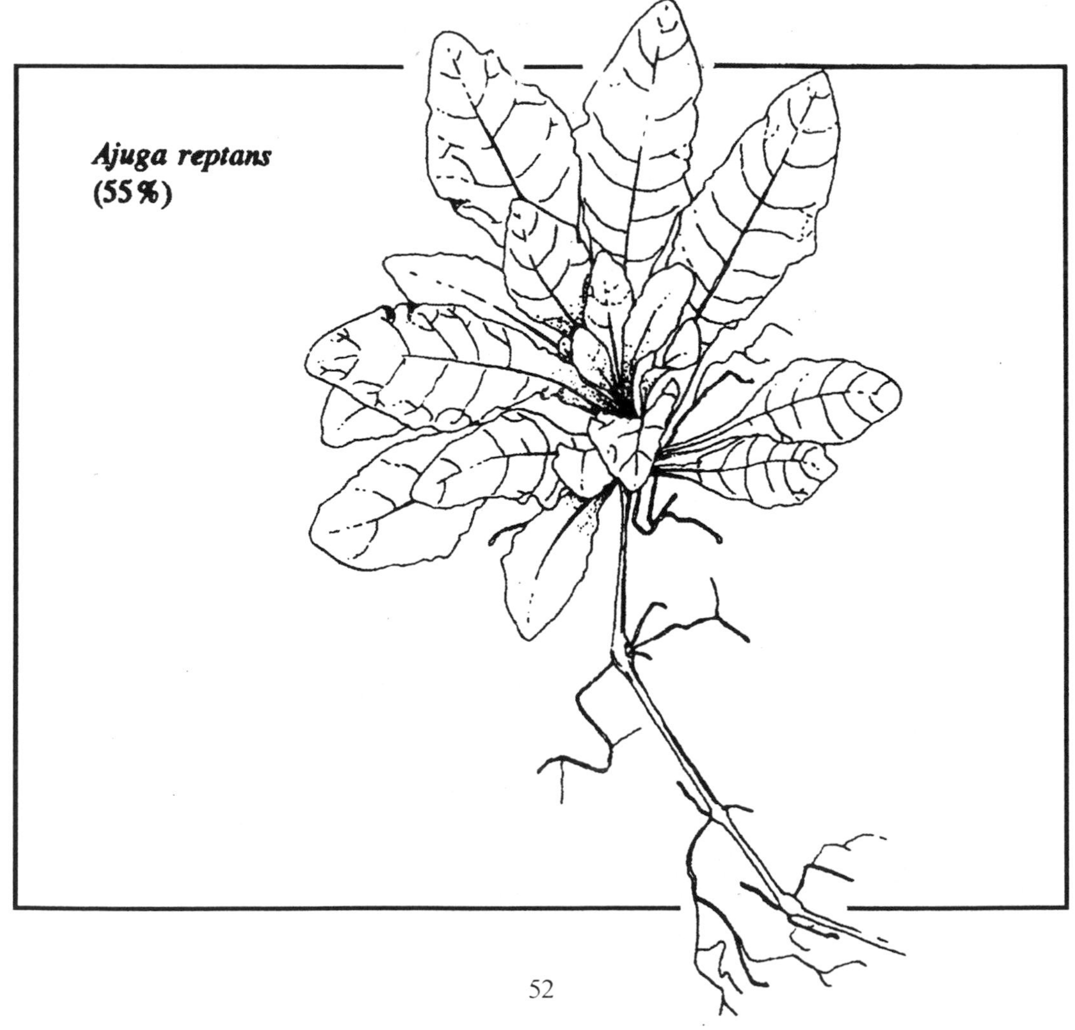

***Ajuga reptans* (55%)**

'Arctic Fox' was introduced by Henry Ross, one of our great horticulturists, whose Gardenview Horticulture Park in Strongsville, Ohio is a must-see venue. 'Arctic Fox' bears small leaves with white centers and green margins, and blue flowers.

'Atropurpurea' ('Purpurea') has dark bronzy-purple leaves that color best in full sun. It is an excellent landscape plant to provide drifts of bronze.

'Black Scallop' produces deep purple, glossy foliage with a wavy or scalloped margin. The flowers are deep blue. Plants were developed by Mike Tristram of the UK.

'Bronze Heart' bears glossy, wine-red leaves and deep blue flowers. Very eye-catching.

'Bronze Beauty' produces metallic bronze foliage with bright bluc flowers. Very popular, very handsome selection.

'Burgundy Glow' has foliage with shades of white, pink, rose and green. In the fall, the older leaves turn a deep bronze and the young leaves have a rosy tint. The combination is interesting if your eyes can stand the clashing hues.

'Catlin's Giant' has tall (up to 8″ long) spikes of blue flowers and bronze-green foliage. Continues to produce fine foliage even after flowering and fills in rapidly.

Chocolate Chip™ ('Valfredda') rapidly became a popular plant soon after its introduction to this country in 2000. Plants are compact, dwarf and bear deep purple foliage. The flowers are also deep blue. Not as rapid a spreader as many other cultivars. They are occasionally sold under the correct name 'Valfredda', from the Italian nursery from which they originated. Arguments abound as to whether the plant is a cultivar of *A. reptans* or *A. tenorii*, from the mountains of Italy and Sicily. Stay tuned.

'Cristata' is probably one of the ugliest little plants available today. The leaves are crinkled and distorted and the whole plant looks like crumpled spinach. To each his own. May go under such names as 'Ripple Leaf'.

'Emerald Chip' supposedly came from Chocolate Chip™, resulting in a green chip. Same properties as Chocolate Chip™ but without the chocolate.

'Gaiety' has bronze purple leaves and lilac flowers.

'Golden Glow' has light golden margins around the green centers of the leaves. A good selection where variegated ground covers are useful. The blue flowers are held on short stems in spring.

'Gray Lady' produces classy gray-green foliage and blue flowers. Growth is relatively slow but clumps are most handsome.

'Jungle Beauty', originally introduced by Allen Bush when he owned Holbrook Farms in North Carolina, bears dark purple leaves outlined with a soft red border. A similar form known as 'Jungle Beauty Improved', selected by Beth Chatto in East Anglia, England, seems to have larger leaves and more persistent purple color. Both are good selections.

'Leprechaun' is a dwarf form with ugly spinach-like leaves. Want spinach? Grow spinach.

'Mahogany' is another dark-leaved short form, similar to Chocolate Chip™, growing about 3″ tall and bearing bright blue flowers in the spring.

'Multicolor' (syn. 'Rainbow', 'Tricolor') is similar to, but more vigorous than 'Burgundy Glow' but the foliage colors are deeper. Sometimes comments concerning leaf colors are best left to the gardener. This is one of those times.

'Pink Silver' produces bronze leaves with a touch of pink.

'Purple Brocade' is 6-8″ tall, with deep purple brocaded leaves. A slow grower, but very handsome.

'Royalty' has some of the darkest purple flowers (almost black) with scalloped edges. Terrific cultivar.

'Ruffled Lace' came from plantsman extraordinaire Dr. Darrell Apps of Woodside Nursery in Bridgeton, New Jersey. It is a clumping form, producing burgundy leaves with ruffled edges. Blue flowers are formed in the spring.

'Silver Beauty' has gray-green leaves irregularly edged with silver-white. Plants are particularly handsome.

'Silver Carpet' produces leaves which are uniformly silver-gray but with green margins. Plants are about 6″ tall.

'Silver Queen' bears white splashes on gray foliage. Blue flowers are produced in the spring.

'Toffee Chip' is as compact as Chocolate Chip™ but bears variegated green and white foliage. Stands out in a crowd in a semi-shaded area.

**Related Species:**

*A. australis* is native to Australia and is a 3-4″ tall mat former. The thick dark green pubescent (hairy) leaves are aromatic when crushed and the light blue flowers rise to about 8″ in height. Probably effective in zones 5-8. Underused and well worth trying.

*A.* 'Brockbankii' (*A. genevensis* x *A. pyramidalis*) is smaller and more vigorous than common bugle weed. Plants have deep blue flowers and shorter stolons.

## *Alcea* (al-see′ a) Hollyhock Malvaceae

Approximately 60 species of biennial and short-lived perennial species are found and some of them are exceptionally popular. Hollyhocks (*A. rosea*) have been gracing gardens for centuries and continue to undergo a renaissance in the United States. All species are found in sunny, well-drained habitats and provide exceptional color for short periods of time. Although hollyhock is the best-known member, one or two other species provide additional interest as well. Flowers are generally large and appear singly or in racemes and the stems are usually hairy. All can be grown from seed and require little more than sun and good air circulation.

The genus is part of the Malvaceae, which contain genera such as *Lavatera*, *Malva* and *Sidalcea*. To me, many of these plants are difficult to distinguish, especially when people ask me "Why is that a hollyhock and not a malva, or lavatera or . . . ?" Since they are closely related and appear so similar, particularly to my leaden brain, I have to find a way to try to answer that question, without resorting to details seen only in a laboratory. If people should be silly enough to ask, I grab a flower, turn it over and say "Look at the bracts." They seldom ask again. Upon close inspection, *Alcea* differs from other genera by having 6-9 bracts (botanically known as the epicalyx) immediately beneath the sepals and they completely envelop the emerging bud. Also, the bracts are joined rather than separate as in the genus *Malva*. This seems a little much for some, but for others it is quite enlightening. For those who like to be lit up, I have provided a basic chart to help discriminate between these genera. Unfortunately, hybrids muddle up this simple scenario, but it is a start.

| | **Bracts below sepals** | **Flower arrangement** |
|---|---|---|
| *Alcea* | 6-11, joined at base | Solitary, raceme |
| *Althaea* | 6-9, united at base | Raceme, panicle |
| *Lavatera* | 3, joined, pointed | Raceme |
| *Malva* | 3, narrow, distinct | Solitary, clusters |
| *Sidalcea* | Usually none | Raceme, spike |

***-rosea*** (rose-ee′ a) Hollyhock 4-8′/2′
Spring, Early Summer Mixed Colors Turkey, Asia Zones 3-7

My mother knew very little about gardening, other than that the lawnmower was a good way to keep her sons out of trouble. But how she loved her hollyhocks. They grew with their backs up the stucco wall of our garage, held up with ugly white strings that extended from rusty nails on either side. Like tape measures across a boxer's chest, these strings were often more visible than the plants. But every year, they would come back from roots or seeds and provide a riot of color along an otherwise drab path. By midsummer, the leaves were eaten up by rust but by that time, hollyhocks gave way to other activities and thus ignored, disappeared once again.

She would be pleased to see hollyhocks today. The old red single flowers are still around, but so are many other colors and forms, including double flowers and saucer-sized singles, up to 5″ across. Plants are generally 3 to 6 feet tall, but 8′ monsters are not uncommon. They are unbranched, thus are rather pole-like, and the stems are hairy to the point of being bristly. The leaves have 3, 5 or 7 lobes and the flowers occur in terminal racemes, made up of 3-10 flowers. The 6-11 bracts beneath the flowers are joined and turn brown as the flowers mature. Cultivars today are also less susceptible to the nemesis of hollyhock, hollyhock rust. Caused by a fungus, *Puccinia malvacearum*, orange-brown pustules occur on the undersides of the leaves and stems. If my mother had known that the spores overwintered on the blistered, ignored leaves by the garage, she would have removed them. Actually, she would have told her sons to do it, and we would have probably taken the trusty Lawn-Boy to them. Fungal sprays are available, removing any affected leaves and rotating cultivars from year to year is much more effective.

Japanese beetles can also crunch, chew, disfigure and destroy hollyhocks within days of their arrival. Japanese beetles love most members of the Malvaceae, and they can be sprayed, picked off, or crushed between two bricks. Regardless, if you have Japanese beetles, think twice about giving them hollyhocks for dessert.

Propagate by planting seeds directly in the prepared soil immediately after the last frost date or in containers about two weeks before that time. If sowing in containers, place the container at 72-75°F and cover the moist soil with a plastic until the seedlings emerge. Do not germinate the seeds too early or plants will be weak and stretched before the transplant date.

**Cultivars:**

*Single flowers*

Barnyard Mix is offered by an enterprising nursery who claim seeds were collected from an old barnyard in Vermont. They are single, in various colors, tall and old-fashioned. I bet they collected them from my mother's house.

'Black Beauty' has deep purple to almost black flowers on 6′ tall plants.

'Indian Spring' is available in white, yellow, rose and pink. Plants are 7-8′ tall. This has been around for quite a while, as noted by its AAS selection in 1949.

'Nigra' has some of the deepest purple flowers of any cultivar. Plants attain about six feet in height.

'Simplex' is a mixture of colors on 4-5′ tall stems.

'The Watchman' has deep purple flowers on 5-6′ tall plants.

*Double, semi-double flowers*

'Appleblossom' bears large light pink to rose fully double flowers.

Chaters Double Hybrids occur in a range of colors. Each double flower resembles a ruffled peony. Plants in single colors may be purchased including 'Chaters Pink', 'Chaters Scarlet', 'Chaters Violet', 'Chaters White' and 'Chaters Yellow'.

'Crème de Cassis' produces mostly semi-double 3-4″ wide flowers of burnished purple with yellow centers. Some flowers may also be single. The petals are also wavy. An interesting look and color.

Fruity Mix is a mixture of pink and rose, bloated, fully double flowers. To each his own.

'Nigrita' has dark, almost purple-red double flowers.

'Peaches 'n' Dreams' bears many fully double, peach and raspberry flowers on 4-6′ tall plants.

'Pinafore' is more branched and compact than other cultivars and bears semi-double flowers in numerous colors. Plants are 3-4′ tall.

'Powder Puffs' grows 6-8′ tall and produces 4″ wide fully double flowers in white, yellow, rose and red.

Queeny series is a seed-propagated mix of semi-double flowers on short (2-3′ tall) plants. 'Queeny Purple' was an All-America winner in 2003.

'Summer Carnival' is name given for a mixture of colors with double blooms on 2½-3′ tall plants.

**Related Species:**

*A. ficifolia* has many common names including figleaf hollyhock, Antwerp hollyhock and Russian hollyhock. The leaves are 7-lobed, irregularly toothed and resemble fig leaves, probably the best means of identification. Flower color is all over the map, many being pale yellow (most common) to deep red, copper or orange. These are robust plants and will easily attain 6′ tall. They are native to Siberia, and their exceptional cold hardiness has made them popular as a parent for the many hybrids of hollyhocks hitting the market today. In the Gardens at UGA, plants are 5′ tall, have nary a smudge of leaf disease, and bear dozens of velvet flowers. Outstanding.

Hybrids of *A. rosea* and *A. ficifolia* with single flowers have been released as 'Summer Memories Mix'.

*A. rugosa*, Russian hollyhock, is becoming more popular due to its classical nature and fewer problems with hollyhock rust. The large 4″ wide single flowers are pale yellow and the leaves are deeply 5-lobed. The 5-6′ tall stems are hairy all over. This can be a terrific plant.

**Related Genus:**

*Althaea*, also known as hollyhock, is often confused with *Alcea*, for obvious reasons. Most of the ornamental hollyhocks belong to *Alcea*. The flowers of *Althaea* are smaller, seldom exceeding 1-1½″ wide and usually rose, rose-pink or occasionally white. While not as flashy as *Alcea*, they are useful for naturalistic plantings. Approximately 12 species are known; the 3-5′ tall *A. officinalis*, which has small rose, pink or white flowers, is best known. The roots of this species were the original source of marshmallows.

## ***Alchemilla*** (al-kem-ill′ a) Lady's Mantle Rosaceae

The genus may have received its name because of its popularity with alchemists and was reputed to have many healing powers. Today we know it as a wonderful low-growing shade tolerant plant with sprays of small yellow flowers in the spring. Some 300 species are known, most of which are palmately lobed and make excellent garden plants. The foliage is light green, pubescent and soft to the touch, particularly on the underside. The apetalous (no petals) flowers are only about ¼″ wide and range from green to yellow. Although many species have been described, only two or three are easily located through catalogs or retail centers in the United States and Canada.

Alchemilla requires partial shade and consistent soil moisture to thrive. Plants will be stunted if planted in full sun or allowed to dry out. Cool climates are preferable but they do quite well as far south as zone 7 providing there is ample shade and moisture. I have grown lady's mantle in Athens, Georgia and it is lovely to those who have never seen large drifts grown under favorable conditions, however, the luxuriant growth taken for granted further north is never attained.

Fresh seed germinates readily but purchased or old seed should be given a cold treatment similar to *Actaea*. *Alchemilla* self-sows readily which helps increase the planting size. Plants should be divided in early spring prior to flowering.

Quick Reference to Alchemilla Species

| | Height (in.) | Lobes cut more than half way | Hairiness on leaves |
|---|---|---|---|
| *A. alpina* | 6-8 | Yes | Lower surface |
| *A. ellenbeckii* | 3-6 | Yes | Both surfaces |
| *A. erythropoda* | 6-9 | No | Both surfaces |
| *A. glaucescens* | 9-12 | No | Both surfaces |
| *A. mollis* | 20-24 | No | Both surfaces |

***-alpina*** (al-pine′ a) Mountain Mantle 6-8″/12″
Spring Green Europe Zones 3-7

Every time I redo this book, I seem to repeat myself: that is, this species is not used enough in the United States. The flowers may not be extraordinary but the silver edges of the deeply cut 2″ wide foliage and the low neat habit make this a wonderful garden plant. The 5-lobed leaves have small, sharp teeth at the end of each lobe and are hairy on the lower surface only, being kind of naked above. Self-seeding is common, and if this becomes a problem, the seed heads may be removed prior to maturity. I have never had that problem in the Armitage garden, being happy just to keep plants alive. Reseeding is more common in the North than in the South. It is native to mountainous areas and as far north as Greenland. Cold hardiness is not a problem in most of the northern states and Canada but they are not as heat tolerant as *A. mollis*.

***-ellenbeckii*** (el-len-beck-ee′ eye) Carpet Lady's Mantle 3-6″/12″
Spring Yellow-green East Africa Zones 5-7

This shade-loving little plant also deserves more use in American gardens. The diminutive height and spreading nature make this a charming ground cover for a shady nook. The 1″ wide leaves are deeply 5-lobed and the plant spreads by rooting at the nodes. The yellow-green flowers are not as freely produced as on the larger species but are handsome nevertheless. Plants are not as cold hardy as others but should be fine to zone 5 with some protection.

Plants are best propagated vegetatively by division.

***-erythropoda*** (e-rith-ro-po′ da) Red-stemmed Lady's Mantle 6-9″/12″
Spring Yellow-green Turkey, Russia Zones 3-7

Similar to other medium-sized species but with small scalloped gray or blue-green leaves and dense hairs on the petioles (leaf stalks). These diminutive plants often develop red stems when grown in a partially sunny location. The lobes of this species look like they were cut across their width with pinking shears whereas the lobes of similar species are rounded. What some people will study!

***-glaucescens*** (glock′ es-sends) Hairy Lady's Mantle 9-12″/18″
Spring, Summer Yellow-green Europe Zones 3-7

This small plant is densely hairy throughout and bears circular leaves with 7-9 shallowly cut lobes. The kidney-shaped foliage may be slightly blue-green (glaucous) but not always. Dense clusters of yellow-green flowers are produced in late spring and into summer. Similar to *A. erythropoda*.

***-mollis*** (mol′ lis) Lady's Mantle 20-24″/24″
Spring Yellowish Asia Minor Zones 4-7

This is grown at least ten times more often than all the other species combined. The common lady's mantle is a splendid ground cover and will grow in almost any

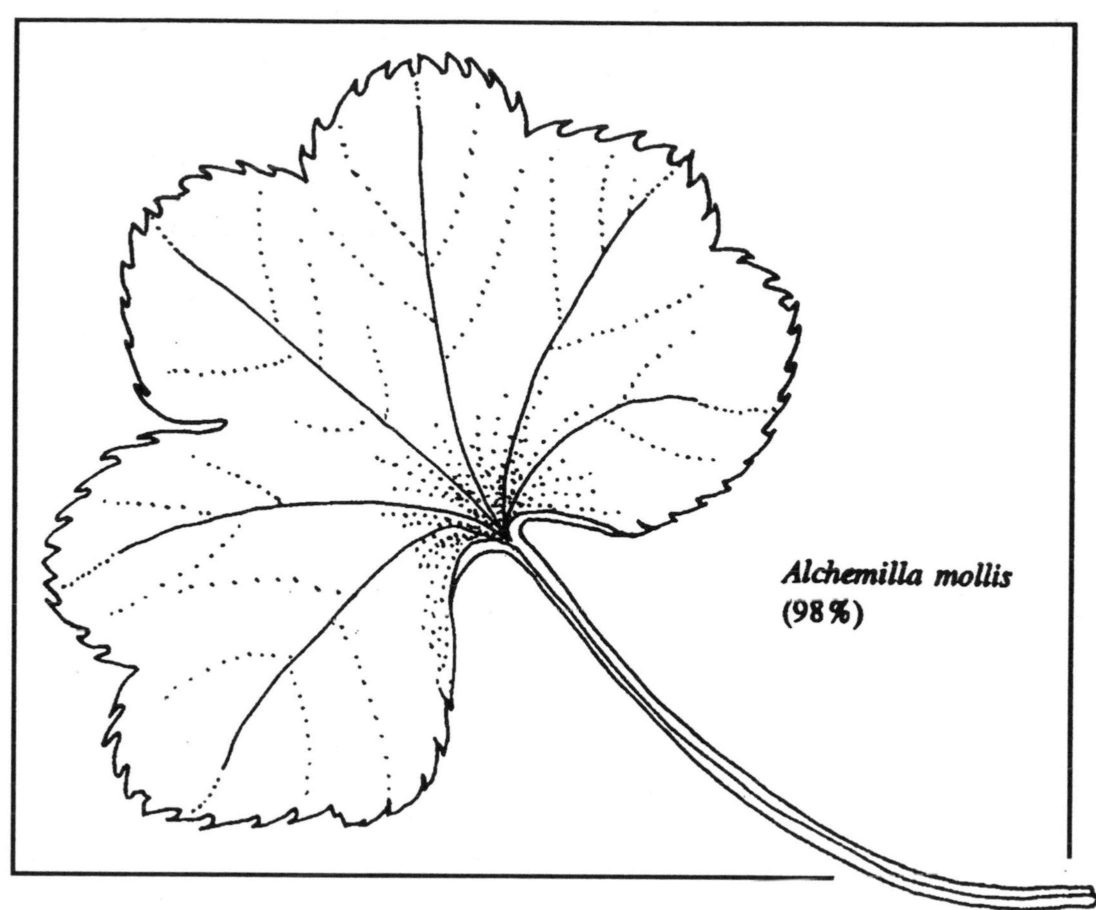

*Alchemilla mollis*
(98%)

moist, shady area except a bog. The dense pubescence gives the foliage a soft velvet feel. Leaves have 9-11 shallow lobes and are particularly pretty after a soft rain when the captured droplets glisten in the sun. The yellow-green starry flowers, which are held above the foliage, make long-lasting cut flowers. When grown side by side, the flowers are obviously the most showy of any of the commonly seen *Alchemilla* species. This species may be too large for the rock garden but can be used successfully to edge a path or border. The densely hairy leaves create a problem in areas such as the Southeast where thundershowers punctuate hot summer afternoons. The water trapped in the leaves and crown does not dry out during the night and provides excellent breeding grounds for a number of foliar diseases. Use of a fungicide during wet, rainy periods partially alleviates the problem.

**Cultivars:**

'Auslese' is offered by a few nurseries and differs little from the species. Perhaps the flowers are more chartreuse and plants are a little more compact.

'Robusta' is more robust and simply larger in every way than the species. However, since most of the *A. mollis* in cultivation is propagated from seed, there may be little difference between a vigorous seedling and this cultivar.

'Senior' is shorter than the species, growing only about 12″ tall.
'Thriller' has large pleated leaves with many chartreuse foamy flowers.

**Related Species:**

Although *A. mollis* dominates, many other species are offered, which are generally less vigorous but equally beautiful. In general, however, lady's mantle, regardless of species, is still more suited to areas where summer night temperatures routinely fall below 70°F.

*A. abysinnica*, Abyssinnian lady's mantle, is similar in spreading habit but differs in having larger (2″ across) 7-lobed leaves. Also native to East African mountains. Little is known about hardiness.

*A. caucasica*, Caucasus lady's mantle, is indistinguishable from *A. erythropoda*, differing mainly in the arrangement of the hairs on the flowering stems.

*A. conjuncta* is closely related to *A. alpina* and is often sold as such. Plants are a little more robust, growing 12-18″ tall. Leaves generally have 7 deep cut lobes but without the sharp teeth found in *A. alpina*.

*A. faeroensis* is another small plant, growing only 3-6″tall. I have grown this in my garden, and one would think that a plant native to the Faeroe Islands would quickly perish in Athens. However, it came back for at least 10 years, and while never overly showy, I always enjoyed it. var. *pumila* is a smaller form yet and terrific for rock gardens, but can easily get lost if crowded with other more vigorous taxa.

*A. pectinata* is the neatest lady's mantle I have seen. Plants produce exceedingly long stems and they are best suited for hanging baskets or tumbling from a stone wall. Dull green leaves and soft yellow flowers are part of the plant's charm.

*A. saxatilis*, rocky lady's mantle, is only about 6-9″ tall, and is normally found in alpine locales, growing among rocks. The foliage has 5 lobes, light green on the top, silvery on the underside. Great for the rock garden, but not the "regular" garden.

*A. sericea* is similar to *A. alpina* but has more conspicuous and irregular teeth in the upper half of the leaves. The upper surface of the leaves have small hairs, whereas those of *A. alpina* are smooth.

*A. vulgaris*, common lady's mantle, is similar to *A. mollis* but is less pubescent and has much smaller, greener flowers. The foliage is also more deeply lobed. Most of the plants of *A. vulgaris* sold in the United States are *A. mollis*.

*A. xanthochlora* is a relatively large plant like *A. mollis*, growing 15-20″ tall. The plant differs in that the leaves are almost hairless on the upper surface and are more kidney shaped compared to the circular leaves of *A. mollis*. Good garden plants with chartreuse, airy flowers.

## ***Allium*** Ornamental Onion Alliaceae

I have always enjoyed growing ornamental onions. They allow me to converse with vegetable gardeners without feelings of guilt. While they don't garnish my hamburgers, they certainly embellish my garden. The genus contains approximately 500 species including onions (*A. cepa*), garlic (*A. sativum*), and chives (*A. schoenoprasum*). Although ornamental forms of chives such as the rosy pink 'Forescate' have been developed, the presence of these tasty but breathy members of the onion family has given the ornamental alliums a particularly difficult time in the marketplace. The species are bulbous or rhizomatous and are all characterized by the presence of a superior ovary, umbels of small flowers and the emission of an onion or garlic smell when crushed. The flowers consist of many petal-like flower parts called tepals. Scientists in several locations have tried to eliminate the odor from alliums, particularly the culinary species, but I, for one, hope they have little success. An allium without odor is like a book without a cover. The odor occurs only when plants are broken or crushed and is not given off spontaneously. In fact, the flowers of some members have a mild fragrance of violets.

The family that *Allium* calls home is in flux. It was a part of the Liliaceae because of the superior ovary but some taxonomists argued that the presence of the umbellate inflorescence should place *Allium* in the Amaryllidaceae. Others then argued for a separate family, Alliaceae, to be created for all genera with a superior ovary and an umbellate inflorescence. After the smoke cleared, it appears *Allium* and 20 other genera, such as *Agapanthus*, *Brodiaea*, and *Ipheion* belong to this onion family. Most gardeners don't really care, but now you know why you don't.

The number of species has also always been in question. When Linnaeus (1707-1778) wrote *Species Plantarum* in 1753, he distinguished 30 species. Many additional species were described since Linnaeus and continue to be discovered today. There is no modern monograph of *Allium*; the last work that embraced all the known species was produced by Eduard von Regel (1815-1892) in 1875 and included 256 species. Other botanists have placed the number at 325 (1925), 400 (1976) and 700 (1987). William Stearn took the major accounts of the genus and subtracted species listed in other accounts and added those not covered in any. Stearn concluded that the genus *Allium* comprises about 750 known species and is the largest genus of petaloid monocotyledons. Two things are self-evident. That the genus is large, and that any self-respecting *Allium* geek will be hard-pressed to run out of onions to plant.

The ornamental alliums range in size from the 2-3″ tall plants of *A. circinatum* to the 4′ tall scapes of *A. giganteum*. Although many onions bear lilac-blue flowers, some species send up umbels of white (*A. neapolitanum*), pink (*A. acuminatum*), mauve (*A. validum*), yellow (*A. moly*), greenish (*A. obliquum*) or interesting multicolors. Most species bear 3-8 linear leaves (except *A. karataviense*) that die back before or soon after flowering. While most species are native elsewhere, a number of fine forms native to America occur, including *A. canadense* and *A. texanum*, both about 1½′ tall and both with white flowers. The seed heads are persistent in many species and extend the ornamental value of plants well into summer.

In general, the planting depth of the bulb should be approximately 3 times the diameter. Bulbs should be fall planted in full sun and in well-drained areas. As lovely as many of these species are, they are poor plants if not combined with other perennials or annuals. Because the foliage dies during or immediately after flowering, many gaps in the garden eventually exist. Planting in ground covers or having other plants growing around them camouflages the empty spaces. That there are so many onions running around out there should be a warning that not all are as wonderful as the photo or catalog says they are. Some can look weedy, others can be aggressive and many will be short lived. Given that as a suitable warning, enjoy as many as you can stand. However, an area devoted strictly to alliums (or any genera of bulbs) is a collection, not a garden, and should be avoided like the plague.

Quick Reference to Allium Species

| | Height (in.) | Flower color | Fragrant flowers | Flowering time |
|---|---|---|---|---|
| *A. acuminatum* | 8-12 | Pink | No | Early summer |
| *A. aflatunense* | 24-36 | Lilac | No | Late spring |
| *A. caeruleum* | 12-24 | Blue | No | Late spring |
| *A. christophii* | 12-24 | Violet | No | Summer |
| *A. giganteum* | 36-60 | Lilac | No | Late spring |
| *A. karataviense* | 6-12 | Lilac | No | Late spring |
| *A. moly* | 12-15 | Yellow | No | Early spring |
| *A. narcissiflorum* | 6-12 | Pink-rose | No | Spring |
| *A. neapolitanum* | 8-12 | White | Yes | Early spring |
| *A. nigrum* | 24-36 | White | No | Early spring |
| *A. oreophilum* | 8-12 | Violet | Yes | Early summer |
| *A. schubertii* | 18-24 | Pink | No | Spring |
| *A. senescens* | 6-12 | Lilac-pink | Yes | Summer |
| *A. sphaerocephalum* | 18-36 | Lilac | No | Late spring |
| *A. thunbergii* | 18-24 | Violet | Yes | Fall |
| *A. triquetrum* | 8-15 | White | No | Summer |

***-acuminatum*** (a-cum-in-aye′ tum) Tapertip Onion 8-12″/12″
Early Summer Rose-pink Western North America Zones 4-7

Two or four narrow, channeled leaves emerge from a round bulb, above which an 8″ scape holds erect, star-shaped flowers with pointed segments. Many ½″ long flowers form a loose umbel approximately 2″ wide. The 10-30 flowers range from deep rose to lilac-pink and bloom for about 2 weeks starting the end of May. Leaves are usually withered by flowering time. Plants do best in dry areas, and in hot, rainy, climates such as the Southeast, do not often persist more than 2 years. Plant in a well-drained sunny location. Flowers dry well when cut from the garden, retaining color when placed in a warm dry room.

It is a pretty plant when used in colonies of at least a dozen bulbs. Bulbils that form at the base of the bulbs result in a slow-spreading colony.

***-aflatunense*** (a-fla-tun-en′ se) Persian Onion 2-3′/2′
Late Spring Lilac China Zones 4-8

This tall allium produces fine 4″ diameter spherical umbels of star-shaped flowers atop 3′ tall scapes. The lilac to violet flowers have yellow anthers and tend to twist and reflex with age. Often thought of as a smaller version of *A. giganteum*, it lacks the majesty and grandeur of the latter. The bulbs, however, are available at one-third the cost and allow the gardener to plant onions with abandon. The 6-8 basal, strap-shaped basal leaves are up to 4″ wide and disappear soon after the flower appears.

This is one of the few species in the genus truly at home among other plants in the border. Plants do well in any sunny well-drained location, however, they are susceptible to root rot organisms prevalent in heavy soils. I have seen wonderful plantings in Philadelphia gardens and as far north as Cleveland. Results in the South have been variable. Some years it is outstanding, others years, disappointing. This may be due to the fact that a number of impostors are sold under the banner of *A. aflatunense*. As cut flowers, they are excellent and last nearly 2 weeks.

Seed should be sown in moist seed trays and placed at about 70°F for 2-4 weeks, then placed at 30-40°F for an additional 4-6 weeks. After the cold treatment, bring the tray to 50-60°F until germination occurs. Keep moist at all times. Plants self-sow on the West Coast and occasionally in the Northeast.

**Cultivars:**

'Purple Sensation' has deeper violet flowers which are more uniform than the species. A little more expensive but more handsome. I have seen this plant all over the country, and while it is not perfect everywhere, it is always colorful, upright and an inexpensive addition to the garden. They were spectacular in combination with colorful annuals in beds and containers at the must-see North Carolina Botanical Garden in Asheville, NC. A number of outstanding hybrids using *A. aflatunense* as a parent have been developed (see hybrids).

***-caeruleum*** (ce-rue′ lee-um) Blue Globe Onion 12-24″/18″
Late Spring Blue Russia Zones 2-7

The deep blue flowers are held very tightly in a 1-2″ diameter umbel. The leaves are 3-sided and 6-12″ long. The cup-shaped flowers, which open in late May in zone 7 and about 2 weeks later in zone 3, persist for about 2 weeks and make excellent fresh or dried flowers. Unfortunately, it is difficult to establish in most American gardens as it comes from the steppes and deserts of Central Asia and requires hot, dry conditions to flourish. Plants may be divided easily to provide good-sized clumps. Occasionally bulbils are formed within the inflorescence (particularly on var. *bulbiliferum*) and may be used for propagation. Seed should be treated as with *A. aflatunense*.

***-christophii*** (kris-tof′ ee-eye) Downy Onion, Star of Persia 15-24″/24″
Summer Violet Turkey, Afghanistan Zones 4-8

Although short in stature, this is one of the largest flowering species in cultivation. Up to 100 metallic blue star-shaped flowers are carried on a spherical umbel often 10-12″ in diameter. The stems and the margins of the 2-7 strap-shaped leaves are covered with white hairs that are responsible for the common name. The leaves die before the flowers have completely opened.

When in flower, there is no more eye-catching member of the genus. It is also one of the best alliums for long-lasting dried flowers, looking good literally for years. A

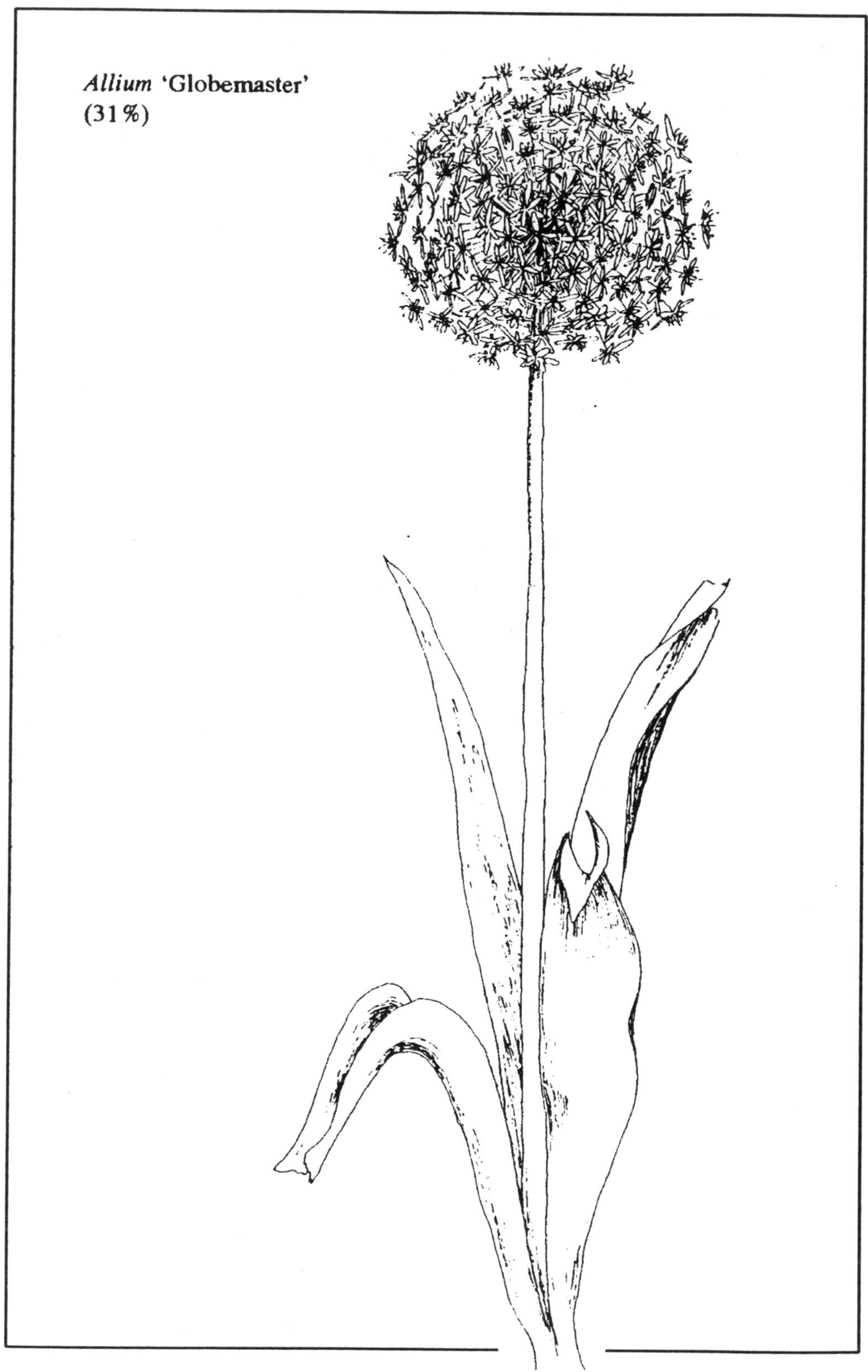

*Allium* 'Globemaster' (31%)

sunny, well-drained area at the front of the border is necessary for best performance. Excellent hybrids, in particular 'Globemaster' (which see), have been developed with this species as a parent.

Propagate by seed similar to *A. aflatunense*.

**-*giganteum*** (gi-gan′ tee-um) Giant Onion 3-5′/2′
Late Spring Lilac Central Asia Zone 4-8

This is, as the name implies, the giant of this genus. The bulb itself is 2-3″ in diameter and resembles a large, round ball. In early spring, 6 to 9 broad (5-8″ wide) gray-green leaves emerge as a rosette followed by a thick, strong scape (flower stem) carrying the many lilac flowers. By the time the scape is 6-12″ long, the leaves lie on the ground. Three to four weeks are required for the scape to grow to a final height of 4′ but the wait is justified. There are over 100 individual flowers, each ½″ long, which are held closely together in a dense, 4″ diameter rounded umbel. The round seed heads are equally beautiful, turning silver-tan color as the flowers age.

Plant in groups of three, more if you can afford more, in full sun and well-drained soils. It is an excellent late spring and early summer flower for the back of the border and because the leaves disappear soon after flowering, there is no "dead time" waiting for the leaves to wither as with tulips and daffodils. Plantings as far south as zone 8 have been excellent and if mulch is applied, the bulbs appear to be cold tolerant to zone 4. In zone 8, flowering occurs in mid May but not until early June in Michigan (zone 4). As a cut flower it is outstanding, and has gained much popularity with florists and designers.

Propagation is accomplished by separating the two portions of the bulb which tend to split after 2 years.

**-*karataviense*** (ka-ra-tah-vee-en′ se) Turkistan Onion 6-12″/15″
Late Spring Silver-gray Turkey, Afghanistan Zones 4-8

This unique species is grown for the foliage as much as for the flowers. The thick, gray-green leaves (usually 2) are up to 4″ wide and mottled purple, particularly underneath and near the base. Many people feel that the leaves are more ornamental than the flower, which is a rather washed-out silver-lilac. I am not one of them. The dense umbels are 6-8″ across and compete with those of *A. christophii* for the largest in the genus. The plant is particularly suited to open, windy locations because of the strong, thick 6″ tall scape that carries the flowers. The leaves and seed capsules persist well after the flowers have abscised and remain handsome until mid June.

Seed-propagated plants (accomplished as with *A. aflatunense*) require about 3 years to flower.

**-*moly*** (mah′ lee) Lily Leek, Golden Onion 12-15″/12″
Late Spring Yellow Southern Europe Zones 3-9

Even before the time of Homer, the lily leek was endowed with magical properties. Reference to the "Moly" can be found in "The Odyssey", in which Ulysses walked unharmed under its protection. It has been looked upon as a good luck charm for many years and this combination of magic and beauty makes the plant difficult not to include in the garden. Having said that, I have little success with these plants in my garden, perhaps because of the warm soil temperatures in the summer. The two flat, lancelike leaves are blue green and up to 2″ wide and 8-12″ long. The small ½″ star-shaped flowers are held in a 2″ wide, open umbel and possess a lovely shade of golden yellow. A dozen bulbs planted in a sunny well-drained area quickly increase to form a golden vista in late spring and early summer.

Propagate by bulb offsets or seed. Seed-propagated plants will flower in one year.

**Cultivars:**

'Jeannine' is a marked improvement on the species. She grows 12-18″ tall but is compact with bright yellow flowers, held on multiple scapes, in late spring.

***-narcissiflorum*** (nar-ciss-i-flo′ rum) Narcissus Onion 6-12″/9″
Summer Pink Northern Italy, Portugal Zones 5-8

A wonderful dwarf species best suited for rock garden or a partially shaded nook in the garden. In bud, the flowers look like those of a small jonquil, but soon open to erect clusters of bright pink bell-shaped flowers. The 3-5 blue-green leaves are persistent through the season. This species and a few others (*A. thunbergii*, *A. tanguticum*) have small bulbs clustered together on a small rhizome.

***-neopolitanum*** (nee-ah-pol-i-tay′ num) Naples Onion 6-12″/12″
Early Spring White Southern Europe Zones 7-9

Two to three linear leaves, about ½ to ¾″ wide and keeled, are held in a basal rosette resembling daffodil foliage. The scape carries a loose, many-flowered umbel (2½″ across) of starry white flowers with rosy stamens. The individual flowers are about ¾″ in diameter and are among the most fragrant in the genus. It is one of the earliest to flower, opening the end of April and persisting for about 4 weeks. Plants are not reliably hardy in zone 6, but if heavily mulched, will overwinter in zone 7a. Mulch should also be applied further south to reduce temperature fluctuations in the soil. Plant about 5″ deep in a sheltered corner of the garden, preferably at the foot of a low, south-facing wall.

The fragrance of the flowers has made this a popular cut flower as well as an excellent species for greenhouse pot plant production. Cover 4-5 bulbs with an inch of soil in a 5″ diameter pot and place at 45°F for 8-10 weeks. Bring to a warm area and enjoy the flowers.

**Cultivars:**

var. *grandiflorum* has 3″ diameter umbels consisting of white flowers with a dark eye. Plants are more vigorous than the species. It is used for forcing in pots and cut flower production and is more ornamental than the species.

***-nigrum*** (nye′ grum) | Black Onion | 2-3′/8″
Spring | White | Southern Europe, North Italy | Zones 5-8

Bulbs produce 3-6 basal leaves in early spring and then send a long straight flower stem up to 3′ in height. The many star-shaped white flowers are borne in a round 4-6″ wide umbel. Sometimes bulbils may form in the inflorescence. The ovary of each flower is dark green to black and appears to give the flowers a black center (thus the name *nigrum*). The flowers occur relatively late in the spring and the seed heads remain highly ornamental for 3-4 additional weeks. These have been excellent additions to the Armitage garden, and persisted for about 3 years.

***-oreophilum*** (o-ray-o′ fi-lum) | Mountain Onion | 4-12″/9″
Early Summer | Rose | Turkey, Afghanistan | Zones 3-8

This is an excellent species for the patio planter or front of the garden. The 2-3 linear leaves are flat, bluish green, and somewhat limp. The dozens of star- to bell-shaped flowers are held in a 2″ diameter umbel. They have a mild pleasant fragrance though the pungent onion smell is particularly noticeable when the leaves and stem are crushed. The flowers persist for many weeks but become thin and papery as they age. The foliage is usually withered by flowering time or may persist for a week or so after flowering. Plant in a sunny, well-drained area.

**Cultivars:**

'Zwanenberg' has carmine-pink flowers that are a little brighter than those of the species.

***-senescens*** (sen-es′ ens) | German Garlic | 6-12″/6″
Summer | Lilac-pink | Europe, Northern Asia | Zones 4-7

The cup-shaped flowers are clustered on a 1-2″ wide umbel in late spring to midsummer. The 4-9 basal green leaves are flat and somewhat grasslike. The plants are best for rock gardens or an area where the small plants will not get lost or overgrown. They tolerate full sun but a little afternoon shade is appreciated. The species itself is nothing to write home about, however, the variety sold as *glaucum* is popular and rather dramatic. The flowers are debatably more pink than in the species but the foliage is blue-green and twisted. Some authorities have named this variant *A. spirale* and it is known as the circle onion. They are not dramatic like 'Globemaster' but garner plenty of comments.

Comments abound in the onion world about two cultivars—'Summer Skies' and 'Blue Skies'. According to Mark McDonough, a well-respected allium breeder in Massachusetts, neither cultivar is particularly outstanding, and he adds that they are not "anything close to being blue flowered, but they do make nice foliage clumps." Personally, I thought they were quite lovely, although not blue. Mature plants stand about 15″ tall. They appear to be happier in the North than the South where they produce many more leaves and far fewer flowers. They probably should be listed as cultivars of *A. lusitanicum* (formerly *A. senescens* var. *montanum*).

**Cultivars:**

'Roseum' has pink flowers and if twisted leaves are not terribly important, then this is the best choice of the species.

***-schubertii*** (shoo-ber′ tea-eye) Schubert Onion, Tumbleweed Onion 18-24″/12″
Spring Pink Mediterranean, Central Asia Zones 5-9

This onion defies description, suffice it to say that the flowers look like the hair on Don King's head (or for my more mature readers, Phyllis Diller's hairdo). I try in vain to teach this species to my students, and while the slides help, seeing the real thing up close and personal makes instant alliophiles. The ½″ wide, pink starry flowers are first produced on short flower stalks (pedicels) like a normal onion but then proceed to form additional infertile flowers on pedicels longer than the first ones. The effect reminds one of the physics experiment with the static machine that makes your hair stand on end.

As gruesome of the above description sounds, it really is a neat garden plant. The 4-8 blue-green leaves are produced early in the spring and deteriorate after flowering has finished. The stems are compact and stout and require no help to support their floral and seed display. The floral fireworks leaves behind the same exploding seed head, ornamental long after the pink of the flowers has faded into memory. The seed heads may be dried for winter decoration, however, if left to their own devices, they eventually fall off and become garden tumbleweeds, rolling around with each gust of wind, resulting in the apt common name. The main reasons so few of these bulbs are found in North American gardens are the cost and relative lack of cold hardiness. But they are worth it, for how else can you bring Don and Phyllis in your garden and not have to listen to them? Plants should be well mulched in zone 5.

***-sphaerocephalon*** (sfay-roe-sef′ a-lon) Drumstick Chives 18-36/15″
Late Spring Purple Europe Zones 4-8

This is one of the finest alliums for both cut flowers and the garden. The 3-5 hollow, semi-cylindrical leaves resemble inflated chive leaves. The oval to round 2″ wide flower heads consist of 50-100 flowers. Each flower bud is green and with maturity, the flowers turn purple, giving the inflorescence a two-tone effect. Flowers open in mid June and persist for two-three weeks. The stamens are longer than the tepals and provide an airy feel to the flower heads. It is excellent in hot climates and performs very well as far south as zone 8. The flowers are persistent on the plant and as a cut flower, last up to 10 days in water. The only reason I can see that this species has been overlooked and underused in North American gardens is that it is rather skinny and at least a dozen bulbs are needed to make a show.

Plant multiple bulbs 6″ apart and 6″ deep in a sunny exposure. One or two plants are not effective and a grouping is essential. By the way, here is another plant whose name neither the taxonomic nor bulb grower communities can agree on. For years, it has been sharing the names *sphaerocephalum* and *sphaerocephalon*. The more recent literature suggests the latter is correct, so end of story. Bulblets may be separated after 2-3 years and seed may be treated similar to *A. aflatunense*.

***-thunbergii*** (thun-berg-ee′ eye) Japanese Onion 18-24″/10″
Fall Violet Japan Zones 5-8

I first saw this onion with my friend Galen Gates of the Chicago Botanic Garden. On that cool fall day, other plants were bedding down but the shiny grasslike green leaves and purple flowers were outstanding. He shared a few bulbs with me and they were equally good in my garden in Athens. The tufts of leaves persist throughout the season and in September to November, the starry violet flowers are fresh and inviting. The stamens and style are elongated and appear to dramatically increase the size of the umbel. Full sun is necessary for best performance.

**Cultivars:**

'Ozawa', introduced by George Schenk, is the best known and most popular, growing about 9-12″ tall.

***-triquetrum*** (tri-kwee′ trum) Three-Cornered Onion 8-15″/12″
Summer White Western Europe Zones 5-9

This is easily recognizable by feeling the three-sided scape which supports a 2½″ diameter inflorescence of six to eight ½″ long pendulous, white flowers, borne primarily on one side of the flower stem. Each bell-shaped flower has a central stripe of green and the stigma is deeply 3-parted, another characteristic useful in separating the three-cornered onion from others. The flowers are fragrant, but not nearly as sweet as those of *A. neapolitanum*. The foliage consists of three to four 1″ wide, keeled leaves. It is common in hedgerows in England and New Zealand. In the Gardens at UGA, this is one of our finest bulbs, spreading over the years through the creeping phlox, making even that colorful plant look better. They are spreading, but not invasive. Yet.

Plant bulbs in well-drained soils in full sun. Seeds germinate readily and can create a weed problem the following spring if growing conditions are conducive. The seeds are dispersed by ants and ants can travel a long way. Some gardeners remove the flowers as soon as flowers have wilted.

Propagate by the many bulblets formed after the first year or by seeds treated similarly to those of *A. aflatunense*.

**Cultivars:**

var. *pendulinum* has larger flowers borne on all sides of the umbel. It is more useful as a cut flower than the species.

**Related Species:**

*A. carinatum*, keeled garlic, has about 30 cup-shaped purple flowers in the pendulous umbels. The inflorescences usually include bulbils. var. *pulchellum* has rosy lilac flowers and lack bulbils.

*A. cernuum*, wild nodding onion, is native to the northeastern United States and bears nodding lilac-pink flowers. The scape never straightens out entirely, thus nodding onion is a particularly appropriate name. Plants are usually about 18″ tall but can be quite variable. Leaves persist into the late summer, and have little onion odor.

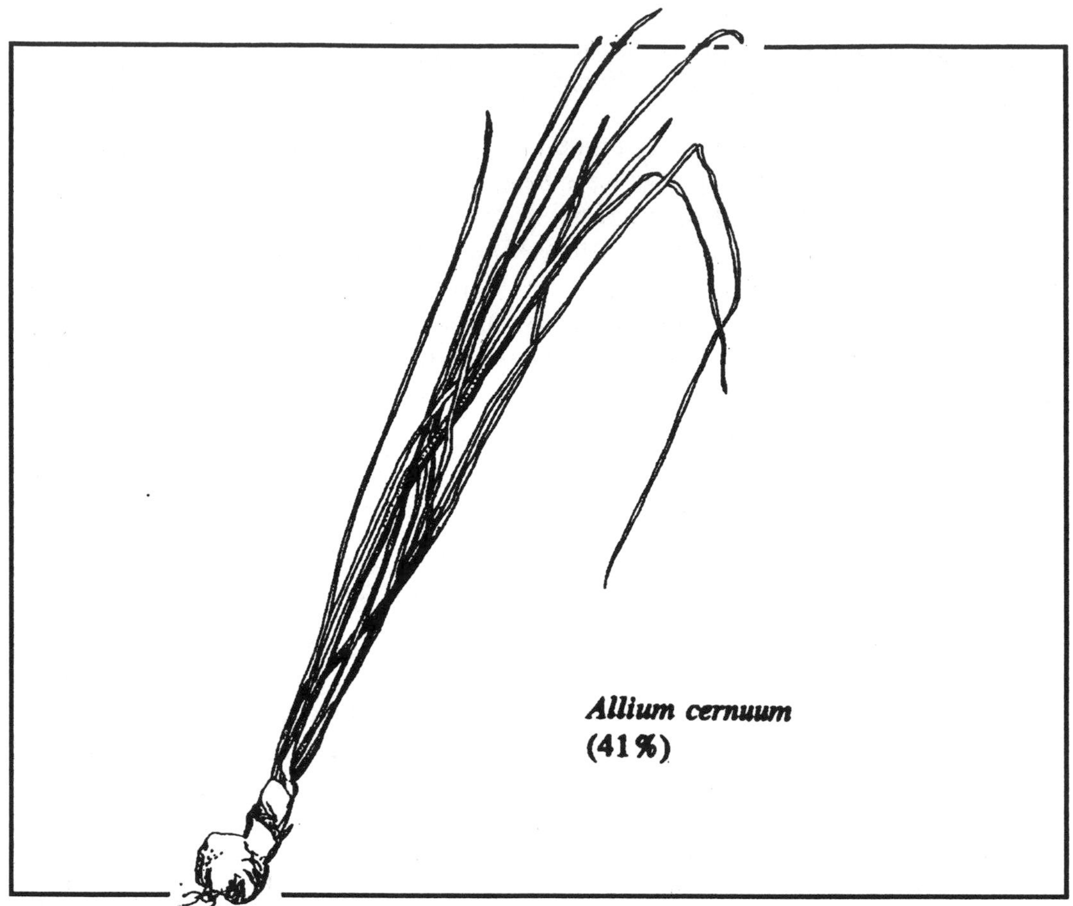

*Allium cernuum*
(41%)

Bulbs are carried on a short rhizome and are easy to grow. They provide a wonderful early summer show when placed in groups of three to six, and will tolerate light shade or full sun. Self-sowing can be a problem, if so, deadhead immediately after flowering.

*A. cyaneum* has dark blue to purple star-shaped nodding flowers on 6-9″ tall scapes borne from small ovoid bulbs, clustered on a small rhizome. Plants are native to western China, and a terrific summer bloomer. The grassy foliage disappears soon after flowering.

*A. insubricum* bears pink bell-shaped flowers and is often confused with *A. narcissiflorum*. Plants differ by having green leaves and flowers that are pendulous both in bud and in flower. *A. insubricum* tolerates wetter conditions than *A. narcissiflorum*.

*A. mairei* var. *amabile* flowers in late summer and fall like *A. thunbergii* and produces slender bulbs clustered on a rhizome and persistent grassy leaves. The funnel-shaped nodding flowers are magenta to deep pink and plants are 5-6″ tall. Plants used to be listed as *A. amabile*. Good garden plants regardless, probably hardy in zones 6-8.

*A. obliquum* is a bright lemon-yellow flowered species, bearing unique cup-shaped flowers. The yellow is a nice break from the more strident yellows of daisies and sundrops often found in the early summer garden.

*A. ramosum*, fragrant flowered garlic, bears many bell-shaped white flowers with a dark red stripe in 2″ wide umbels. The foliage is narrow and persists until the flowers are produced in late summer or fall.

*A. rosenbachianum* easily grows 4′ tall and produces 4″ wide spherical umbels consisting of hundreds of star-shaped deep lavender flowers in the spring. 'Album' is a creamy white form growing about 3½′ tall. The foliage disappears quickly, leaving the long naked flower stem with its cargo of flowers and later seed heads. I grow mine through a large clump of *Baptisia pendula*, so that after the flowers of the *Baptisia* are finished, the globes of the onion continue. They differ from *A. giganteum* in that their tepals become twisted and reflexed but whose umbel remains well formed as it dries and produces large quantities of seed. *A. giganteum* has tepals that remain unreflexed, the umbel falls apart by late summer and seldom produces much seed.

*A. sikkimense* has bell-shaped, pendant, deep blue to purple flowers held on short scapes, each about 8-10″ long. Plants are excellent in rock gardens, blooming in early to midsummer. Likely hardy in zones 6-8.

*A. stipitatum* is another *A. giganteum*/*A. rosenbachianum* lookalike. Plants bear 3-4′ tall scapes topped with globular fragrant lilac flowers. It differs in that the tepals (petals) reflex downward and wither after flowering, while those of *A. giganteum* are persistent. The leaves are narrower, about 1-1½″ wide.

*A. tuberosum*, garlic chives, has creamy white flowers and narrow chivelike leaves. It is similar to *A. ramosum* but differs by having star-shaped flowers with a faint green or brown stripe. Introduced from southeast Asia, it can become an aggressive weed in many parts of the country.

*A. ursinum*, ramsoms, is about 10″ tall and bears 15-20 white flowers in flat 2″ diameter umbels in late spring. The strongly onion-scented plants consist of two to three elliptical leaves with long petioles. Plants are more tolerant of shade than most alliums.

*A. virgunuculae* produces stems with 2-12 pink, star-shaped flowers in October and November. The grassy leaves look good all season. A small grouping makes a lovely setting.

**Hybrids:**

Hybrids of *A. macleanii* and *A. aflatunense* were developed by F. Bijl van Duyvenbode of J. Bijl Nurseries in Holland. Leaves decline quickly and flowers are sterile, therefore they persist on the plant for a long time. More expensive but well worth it.

'Gladiator' is 3-4′ tall with large lilac-purple flowers.

'Lucy Ball' is a sport of 'Gladiator' with dark violet flowers. Stands about 4′ tall.

'Rien Poortvliet' bears great lilac flowers on 3-4′ tall stems.

'Globemaster', a hybrid between *A. christophii* and *A. macleanii*, is without doubt, one of the best ornamental onion I have ever tried. The robust plants stand about 2½′ tall on strong self-supporting stems. The stems must be strong because the lavender flowers are held in 4-6″ wide globular heads. The flowers continue to open over many weeks, the newer ones "replacing" the older ones. While other members of the genus have come and gone, 'Globemaster' still shines. The seed heads remain ornamental well into the summer. It was originally bred as a cut flower in Holland by van Duyvenbode and as more gardeners discovered it, the price decreased significantly.

'Millennium' was bred by Mark McDonough and appears to have a good percentage of *A. nutans* in the parentage. Plants are about 1′ tall and equally wide with rose-purple flowers in late summer. Zones 5-8.

'Sugar Melt' is only about 6″ tall when not in flower, but growing almost to a foot and a half when the flowers open in midsummer. The balls of flowers are light pink. Particularly attractive for rock gardens. Bred by Mark McDonough from *Allium nutans* and *Allium senescens*.

***Alstroemeria*** (ahl-stro-meer-e′ a) Peruvian Lily Alstroemeriaceae

Approximately 50 species, all native to South America, are known. They generally grow from tubers, produce alternate leaves and have wonderfully interesting flowers. Peruvian lilies have become extremely popular as cut flowers, produced in fields and greenhouses in California, Holland, Colombia, Israel and other cut flower-producing regions. Generally cut flower production involves hybrids of *A. ligtu* and *A. aurea* but most of these are poor garden plants in all but a few areas of the country. In areas on the West Coast, the orange-yellow flowers of *A. aurea* brighten gardens and once established can roam about at will. *A. aurantiaca* is another wonderful golden-orange species but seldom survives extremes of heat and cold common to most areas of the United States. 'Lutea' is particularly handsome.

***-psittacina*** (sit-a-seen′ a) Parrot Lily 2-3′/3′
Summer Red/Green South America Zones 7-9

This is a rather common plant in the Southeast, and once established, can become a bit of a nuisance. Having said that, they are a joy when the flowers, which are an odd mix of green and wine red, spotted or streaked with maroon, start to open in early to midsummer. The color combination sounds rather weird, but they are weirdly delightful. Flowers begin in early June and continue for 4-5 weeks. Like all members of the genus, they are excellent cut flowers, albeit a rather difficult color to place with anything else. That's why bud vases are sold. Two to three flowers are produced in each terminal inflorescence. *A. psittacina* performs best in partial shade, but too much shade results in leafy, poor-flowering plants. Easy to divide, these are the ultimate pass-along plants.

**Cultivars:**

'Variegata' has far more handsome foliage than the species and should be used more often. Perhaps not quite as aggressive but you will be giving some away soon enough.

**Hybrids:**

Large-flowered colorful alstroemerias, such as seen in the florist shop, have not been particularly resilient in the much of the country. However, a couple of fine fellows, Mark Bridgen, presently at Cornell University, and George Hare of California, have provided a number of hybrids that combine cold tolerance with excellent flowers. This are wonderful breakthrough plants for gardeners, although I still would not recommend them for my daughters in the Southeast. However, many more people have considerably more choice than ever before.

'Freedom' bears rose-pink flowers in early summer atop 2′ tall stems. All Dr. Bridgen's breeding was done in Connecticut, and plants are cold hardy to at least zone 5b.

'Glory of the Andes' is a variegated leaf form of 'Sweet Laura'. The leaves have a nice creamy yellow margin.

'Sweet Laura' provides golden flowers with red petal tips, speckled with brown, on 1-2′ tall plants. Flowers open in mid to late summer. A Bridgen hybrid.

'The Third Harmonic' sports plants about 3′ tall. The backs of the golden flowers are maroon. Each flower is flecked with black. Bred by George Hare, cold hardy to zone 7.

Other beautiful hybrids are also available, but are more suited for containers, lacking the weather tolerance of the above cultivars. They include the coral peach and yellow flowers of 'Princess Victoria', the yellow and burgundy flowers of 'Yellow Friendship' and the light and dark pink blossoms of 'Dusty Rose'.

## ***Alyssum*** (a-lis′ um) Madwort Brassicaceae

The large genus consists of over 150 species, mostly native to alpine and northerly areas, and most do poorly in hot, wet summers. Plants are usually small in stature and are outstanding for rocky crevices or rock garden areas. The majority bear yellow flowers. Taxonomists removed the most popular old alyssum (*A. saxatile*) to the genus *Aurinia*.

A number of fine species are occasionally offered and seed may also be found through specialty organizations, such as the North American Rock Garden Society. *A. montanum*, mountain madwort, is an 8-10″ tall ground cover, with finely cut foliage and masses of bright yellow spring flowers. 'Mountain Gold' is a more compact, floriferous cultivar and 'Luna', a Fleuroselect winner in 2003, may be even better, at only 5-6″ tall. Hardy in zones 2 to 7.

*A. wulfenianum* is prostrate, about 8″ tall, with gray leaves and light yellow flowers in early spring, while *A. argenteum* produces handsome foliage with gray on the top and green beneath.

All require excellent drainage and do best in full sun. None does particularly well in the South, although if planted in the fall, they are wonderfully bright in the spring, but decline as the heat of summer arrives.

## X ***Amarcrinum*** (a-mare-cry′ num) Amarcrinum Amaryllidaceae

The intergeneric cross between *Amaryllis belladonna* and *Crinum moorei* is way underused, particularly in southern gardens. The hybrid, known as *A. memoria-corsii*, bears 1½′ long straplike dark green leaves in the summer and fragrant pink flowers on 15″ long scapes in late summer to fall. Plant bulbs to a depth of about three times their diameter in late fall or early spring for best performance.

I think these are wonderful bulbs, and can't imagine my garden without them. Their biggest limitation for the rest of the country is the fact that they are cold hardy only to zone 7. However, there is enough beauty here to treat them as annual bulbs in containers or bring them in as you would with dahlias.

**Cultivars:**

'Dorothy Hannibal' has lighter pink flowers than the species.

'Fred Howard' has light pink flowers with a darker pink streaking throughout the flowers. A handsome plant named in 1920 for Mr. Howard, a breeder in Los Angeles. This is occasionally (and incorrectly) labeled as *A. howardii.*

***Amianthium*** (am-ee-an-the′ um) Fly-poison Liliaceae

Who said fly traps have to come in a spray can or sticky strips? All parts of the plant are poisonous, although the folklore about poisoning flies is a bit of a mystery. Perhaps because an excellent fly poison results when the small bulbs are mixed with honey or syrup, although fly paper is a lot cheaper.

Only one species occurs in this genus, *A. muscaetoxicum*, and it is native from Pennsylvania and New York south to Florida and west to Arkansas. Grazing cattle have been known to be poisoned, thus names like fall-poison and stagger grass have also been attached to these plants. Such morbidity makes for good stories but plants are also quite ornamental. They produce long racemes of clean white flowers, and when allowed to grow in large groups, brighten the woodland landscape. The basal leaves are usually more than a foot long but only about an inch wide. They flower in May in the South and in June further north. A wonderful population may be seen at the Atlanta History Center in the terrific native garden tended with great care by Sue Vrooman.

***Amorphophallus*** (a-mor-fo-fal′ us) Snake Palm Araceae

That plants of this genus belong in a garden is a given, that they belong in yours or mine may be debatable. Membership in the Araceae puts them in the same company as caladiums, calla lilies and jack-in-the-pulpits, characterized by the unmistakable spathe and spadix arrangement of flowers. Approximately 100 species of these bulbous plants are known, all are denizens of leafy moldy places in moist, shaded habitats. Some are used for their edible tubers, but if grown in the garden, their compound foliage, marbled stems and dramatic, often evil-smelling inflorescences should be enjoyed.

Flowers of this group of plants have memorable effluvia, often assailing the nostrils with a barrage of odor. Sir Joseph Hooker described the odor of the huge flower of *A. titanum* as a "mixture of rotting fish and burnt sugar, which turns your stomach over and makes your eyes run". Perhaps that is why its common name is corpse flower! Knowing my fondness for such weird plants, Tony Avent of Plants Delight Nursery in Raleigh, North Carolina brought me a tuber of devil's tongue many years ago. I have since planted dozens more, mostly for their fabulous stems and foliage. Not all plants want to flower every year, which is probably just as well as my neighbors, let alone my wife Susan, would not be impressed. The scent of this species was described by a visitor at a flower show when "We detected the scent of pure rot. Following our noses, we came across two huge, liver-colored inflorescences atop five-foot stalks which arose from naked corms the size of pumpkins." I have not been as vigorously assailed, but when they are flower in May, it is tough to walk by without noticing.

They seem to be most at home in heavy shade and a reasonably moist area. When they do not flower, it is easy to forget they are there. However in June, long after most plants have risen and are growing well, *Amorphophallus* gives a big yawn, stretches, and breaks through the soil. Seeing that purple mottled stem rise like a phoenix and watching the foliage unfurl can keep me occupied for days. Generally a single leaf emerges and branches repeatedly, the two branches of each division basically equal. The name for this kind of leaf shape is "dichotomous", in case one cares. Regardless of my ineptness at describing them, let's just say the leaves and stem are by far the best parts of the plant.

There has been an awakening in American gardening to plants in this genus, and one can now find a handful of species through specialty nurseries, or through the Internet.

Other similar genera occasionally presented to the gardener such as *Dracontium* and *Sauromatum* offer weirdness of habit, foul odor and curious, often disparaging comments. Who could ask for more?

If you are confused by all the voodoo lilies, here are a few of the more obvious differences.

| | *Amorphophallus konjac* | *Dracontium vulgaris* | *Sauromatum venosum* |
|---|---|---|---|
| Spathe color | Dark purple | Dark purple | Dull violet with yellow |
| Spathe shape | 3-4′ wide | 1′ long, 6″ wide, arching | 2′ long, pointed, flattened back |
| Spadix | Purple | Purple | Deep purple |
| Leaf number | Usually one | Several | One |
| Leaf shape | Dichotomous | Sickle-shaped | Sickle-shaped |

***-konjac*** Devil's tongue 3-5′/3′
Summer/fall Purple India, Sumatra Zones 6-10

This was the beast that Tony shared with me, putting me on the slippery slope of aroids. At one time, it was called *A. riveri* subsp. *konjac*, but it has recently been reclassified. It is the most common simply because it is the most cold hardy and most easily available. While its garden attributes may be debated, its importance as a food crop is well known in Indonesia, Southeast Asia, India and the Pacific Rim. In many regions, the corms are important standbys when the rice crop fails. In Japan, a traditional food made from the corm is known as konnyaku, and industrial uses for the carbohydrates (mannose, starches) in the dark-skinned corm have also been discovered. Gelling properties for convenience foods and dietary supplements for weight loss are being investigated.

Plant tubers in partial shade, approximately 3 times deep as the tubers are wide. This may be a large hole. Do not be concerned if they do not flower, it may take 3-5 years before the tubers are significantly mature. Plants do not normally emerge until late spring or even early summer. Hang in there, the stems and leaves are well worth the wait.

**Cultivars:**

'Leo Song' is similar to the species but has quite lovely creamy white stems, still mottled in purple.

**Additional Species:**

Gardeners have always lusted for additional species, and today there are more than ever before. The aforementioned Mr. Avent lists nine different taxa in his 2007 catalog, unheard of 5 years ago. The International Aroid Society is a wonderful source of photos and growing information. However, be prepared to pay top dollar, and once paid, say thank you to the people who are making them available. If you are fortunate to find a good species, you have ornamental value, dietary value and nasal exercise all in one. Have fun.

*A. bulbifer*, the voodoo lily, has 30-36″ tall mottled stems and palmately lobed foliage. The leaves form small tubers in late summer that may be removed for new plants. The spadix is green with a tinge of pink and appears in the spring before the foliage. Hardy in zones 8, perhaps to 7 to 10.

*A. dunnii* bears a white bulbous spadix half surrounded by a green and white mottled spathe. Plants are about 2′ tall and still produce the wonderful speckled stalk and voodoo leaves. Plants have not been tested sufficiently but are likely hardy in zones 8 (7)-10.

*A. muelleri* was introduced to gardeners by Tony Avent of Plant Delights Nursery in 2005. Plants have a large white spadix enclosed with a pink-purple spadix. The flower stem is mottled purple but the petioles are often mottled white. Like *A. bulbifer*, this also produces small tubers on the stems.

*A. thaiensis* holds flowers on a foot-long stalk, the inflorescence consists of a green spathe suffused with pink and a spadix that is white at the base, progressing to pink at the top. The plants are characterized by a single petiole marked with brown to purple spots.

*A. titanum*, titan lily, giant voodoo lily, is certainly the most famous, and in its native Indonesian environment has flowers up to 15′ tall. The mottled stems and foliage are equally impressive. Many botanical gardens now grow the tuber and often announce when the titan lily will be flowering. Do people actually stand in line to see something that smells, even if it's huge? In 1999, when the titan lily flowered at Huntington Botanical Gardens in California, more than a few people showed up. According to the garden staff, "During the 19 days it was on public view, before and after blooming, the *Amorphophallus titanum* drew an unprecedented total of over 76,000 enthusiastic flower fans. Television coverage alone lasted for 18 consecutive days. Numerous front-page newspaper stories appeared, and countless radio interviews and news stories were broadcast, ranging from National Public Radio and the

BBC to alternative rock station KROQ." This does not even mention the refrigerator magnets, coffee cups and t-shirts that were sold by the hundreds. So, yes, people really do line up for the weird and wonderful. You have reached la-la land when you find yourself in such a line. Plants are seldom for sale, and if they are, they cost as much as a Beamer. Like the Beamer, they need to be brought in for the winter.

*A. yuloensis* is probably hardy to at least zone 7b; produces wonderfully deeply cut foliage and cream-colored spathe and spadix.

***Ampleaster*** (am-plee-as′ ter) See *Aster*

***Amsonia*** (am-sown′ ee-ah) Blue Star Flower Apocynaceae

This North American genus contains some fine low-maintenance, resilient species for the garden. Light blue to almost white star-shaped flowers are held in terminal panicles above the alternate leaves. There are approximately twenty species in the genus although only 3 or 4 are available to the gardener. Amsonias provide early blue flowers, disease and insect resistance, and fall color. The fruits (follicles) are long and narrow; in some species they are erect while others bear spreading or pendant fruit. Certainly one of my favorite plants is the common blue star flower, *A. tabernaemontana*, however, the Arkansas amsonia, *A. hubrichtii* and the downy amsonia, *A. ciliata*, are also excellent garden plants.

Quick Reference to Amsonia Species

| | Young leaves obviously hairy | Approx width of leaves | Flower color |
|---|---|---|---|
| *A. ciliata* | Y | 1.5″ | Light blue |
| *A. hubrichtii* | N | ¾″ | Light blue |
| *A. tabernaemontana* | N | 2″ | Blue |

***-ciliata*** (sill-e′ a-ta) Downy Amsonia 1-3′/3′
Spring Sky Blue Southeastern United States Zones 6-10

An excellent plant for many gardens, plants provide handsome ½″ wide unblemished foliage and good flowering in the same package. The linear to lanceolate dark-green leaves have a fringe of silky hairs that are particularly handsome in the early season, but with maturity, they lose much of their silkiness. However, if the plant is cut back after flowering, the new growth returns as feathery as before. The leaves are crowded toward the upper end of the stems and the margins slightly curled back toward the underside of the leaves (revolute). The foliage is seldom touched by insects or disease. The light blue starry flowers open in spring and persist for 3-4 weeks. Some species of amsonia provide marvelous fall color in the garden. The foliage of downy amsonia is one of them, providing a golden yellow hue until frost.

Plant in full sun or light, dappled shade and provide sufficient moisture to survive dry periods. Although no serious pests occur, stems may need cutting back at least once during the season to keep them from falling over, particularly if planted in a shady area. If plants remain evergreen, cut back hard in very early spring.

Seed, division, and terminal cuttings taken during the spring are all viable means of propagation. Store the seed at about 40°F for 4-6 weeks because untreated seed germinates irregularly. Chipping or cutting away a small piece of one end of the seed and soaking overnight in water results in better germination. Division is not necessary for 8-10 years but is a quick way to increase a planting. Cut through the crown in late spring or fall so that each division consists of at least one growing point. Terminal cuttings from lateral branches collected in May and treated with a rooting hormone (one labeled for herbaceous plants) root faster and more uniformly.

**Cultivars:**

var. *filifolia* is really a neat-looking amsonia. I first saw this plant in the garden of plantsman Allen Bush in Louisville, Kentucky and was most impressed. Plants are prostrate, much like a ground cover, and have wonderfully feathery leaves. The light blue flowers occur in the spring. It is being sold as the variety and as 'Georgia Pancake', a particularly unattractive name for such an attractive plant.

**-*hubrichtii*** (ew-brickt-ee′ eye) Threadleaf, Arkansas Amsonia 2-3′/3′
Spring Pale Blue South-central United States Zones 6-9

Many writers (this one included) have written the name incorrectly as *hubrectii*, which is as wrong as E before I except after C. If there was one reason to update this book, it was to apologize, belatedly, to Leslie Hubricht, an extraordinary man who found the plant in 1942. Leslie (and others), apologies from me and my less than bright colleagues.

When I wrote my original book in 1989, hardly anyone knew this plant; today it is probably as popular as any species in the genus. The foliage is feathery, like *A. ciliata*, but leaves are threadlike and longer (3″). The flowers are lighter blue than blue star flower and, in fact, are almost white as temperatures warm up in spring. The early flowers are easily visible but the foliage tends to cover the flowers that open later. The narrow foliage makes a marvelous display throughout the season, and some people claim that the golden-yellow spectacle in the fall is quite spectacular. While it is true that they turn golden in the fall, let's not get too carried away with this spectacular thing. Without doubt, they provide excellent color compared to other herbaceous plants, but they certainly don't compete with a maple. Plants are more colorful in the North than the South.

In the Armitage garden, it tends to get a little too tall and floppy, and while I prefer common blue star, I enjoy the look of the foliage of this plant as well. Fall color in warm climates is highly overrated, and although a little better than blue star flower, plants are not as exciting in my garden as in the Midwest or North. Plants grow about 3′ tall and equally wide. Full sun is best; plants do not tolerate shade well.

Cut back in early spring. Division or cuttings are effective methods to increase numbers.

**Hybrid**:

'Seaford Skies' was discovered by Pamela Harper, from Seaford, Virginia, one of the great grand-dames of American gardening. Plants appear to be hybrids between *A. hubrichtii* x *A. tabernaemontana*, providing the fernlike foliage and good fall color of the former with the vigor of the latter.

***-tabernaemontana*** (tay-ber-nay-mon-tan′ a) Common Blue Star Flower 1-3′/3′
Spring Sky Blue Eastern United States Zones 3-9

Leaves are wider, flowers are darker and plants are among the best for full sun to partial shade in most gardens in America. Plants are native from Pennsylvania to South Carolina and west to Kansas, and are found along roadsides or in sunny fields. This species is more cold hardy than the previous and much more common. The flowers are a good dark blue, but they may fade a little over time. The foliage also turns golden yellow in the fall, but does not compete with threadleaf amsonia. For me, blue star flower is always on my list of "no-brainers". Plant and get out of the way.

Plants have alternate willowlike leaves and many ½-¾″ pale blue star flowers clustered in loose terminal inflorescences in spring to early summer. They are particularly

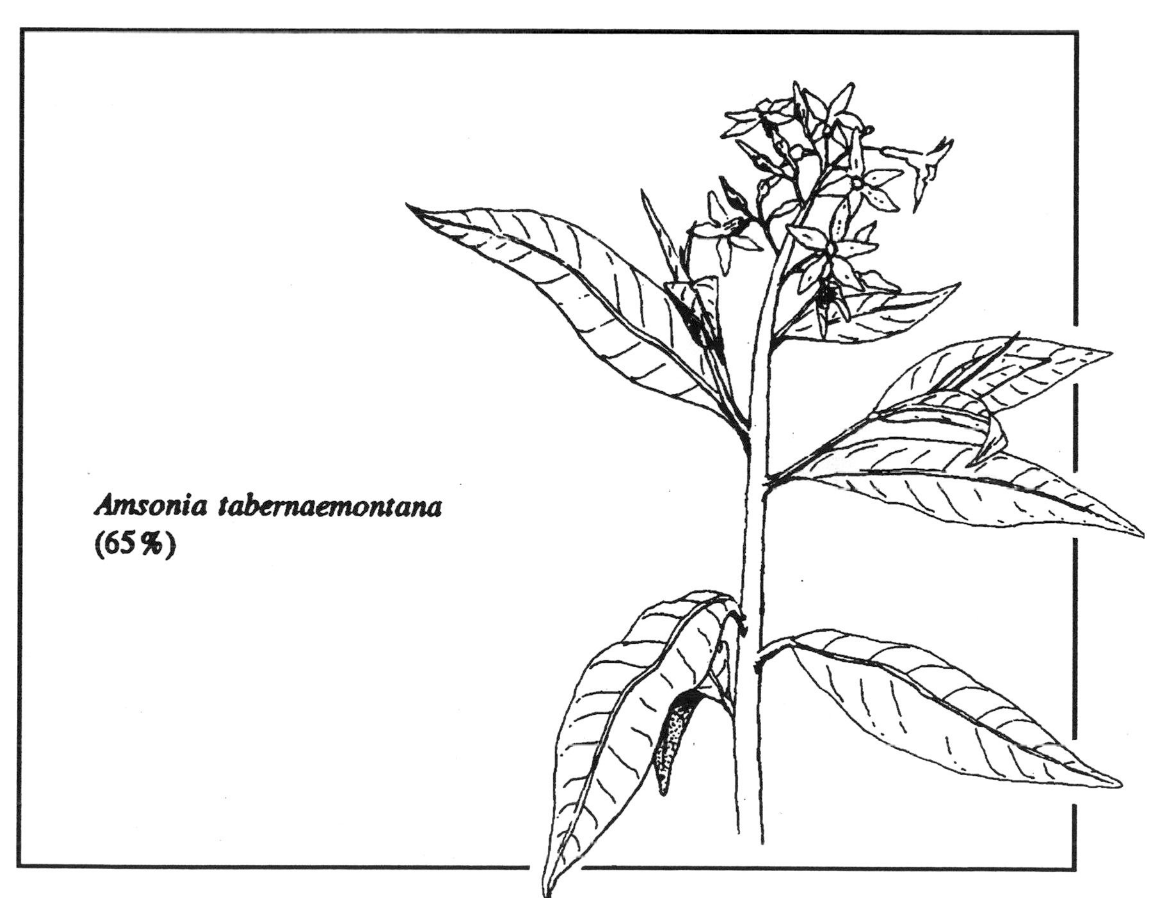

***Amsonia tabernaemontana* (65%)**

lovely in the early spring as they break through the ground and rapidly extend to their mature stature. If grown in full sun, pruning is not necessary, however, if grown in shade, plants must be supported or cut back after flowering to maintain shape. Plants perform best in full sun, but they tolerate some shade as well. In my shaded garden, I grow plants through a circular support frame to keep plants from falling over. Deep, moist soils and partial shade are ideal.

**Cultivars:**

'Blue Ice' is the best-known cultivar, and is grown because of its compact habit (12-18″ tall). However, it does not appear to be as vigorous or as persistent as the species. It may be a hybrid, which may help to explain its relative wimpiness.

var. *montana* (zones 5-9) is a dwarfer version of the species. Some taxonomists have split it into *A. montana*. An exceptionally good plant, small enough to even find a place in the rock garden. 'Short Stack' was selected by Plant Delights Nursery as a more consistent, vigorous form. Plants are 10-12″ tall.

var. *salicifolia* (sometimes listed as *A. salicifolia*) has leaves 5-10 times longer than they are wide and is less erect than the species. The flowers have a white throat and a small beard within. Native to the southeastern United States. Propagation is similar to *A. ciliata*.

**Related Species:**

*A. illustris* is native to the central United States and resembles *A. tabernaemontana*, bearing similar foliage and flowers. Plants differ by having thicker leathery leaves and pendant fruit. Cold hardiness to about zone 5.

*A. ludoviciana*, Louisiana blue star, is native to southern Louisiana only and is distinguished by the white wool on the undersides of the leaves. Handsome even without flowers.

*A. orientalis* superficially resembles *A. tabernaemontana* but is native to southern Europe. On close inspection, one can see short hairs along the margin and midribs of the leaves, whereas the leaves of *A. tabernaemontana* are smooth (glabrous). Plants do not appear to be as cold hardy as common blue star flower.

*A. rigida* is occasionally offered, bearing 2′ tall stems and light blue flowers. Native to the Southeast, likely cold hardy to zone 6.

**Related Genera:**

*Rhazya orientalis* is so similar to *A. orientalis* that it is considered a synonym. The late spring and summer flowers range from bright blue to violet. Plants are native to Greece and Turkey.

## ***Anacyclus*** (an-a-psyc′ lus) Mount Atlas Daisy Asteraceae

Of the approximately 9 species of annual and perennial species, only the Mount Atlas daisy, *A. pyrethrum* var. *depressus* (*A. depressus*) is easily available to North American gardeners. Plants produce fine basal foliage, forming ferny mats with a lovely gray-green cast. Plants grow 4-6″ tall and bear 1-1½″ wide single white daisies with yellow centers and purple to red backs. Being native to the Mediterranean, excellent drainage is a necessity, at least in the East, and plants are more persistent in sunny, dry rock gardens, gravel pathways or embedded in rock walls than in the border. Plants are more productive in areas of low rainfall and low humidity. Our plants at Georgia were wonderful the first year but succumbed to the winter wetness. Hardy from zone 5 to 7.

Propagate by division or easy from seed.

**Cultivars:**

'Garden Gnome' is occasionally listed but I see no difference from the species. It is likely a common name that someone put some single quotation marks around.

'Silberkissen' is even more compact than the species and bears gray foliage with silver hairs and pink-tinged white daisies.

***Anaphalis*** (an-naff′ al-iss) Pearly Everlasting Asteraceae

Anaphalis produces masses of small white flowers in August and September, usually with a brownish yellow center, but it is the foliage that is special throughout the growing season. The gray-white leaves create a cooling effect in the border and tone down the bright reds and oranges of flowers beside them. They are reasonably tolerant of moisture and are particularly useful in areas that are too wet for other gray-green plants such as *Artemisia* and *Perovskia*. This is not to say they will jump with glee when placed in a swamp, but they are especially tough and can withstand significant abuse. Rich soil is not a prerequisite, but evenly moist soils are recommended because the foliage looks shabby under dry conditions. They are also at home in the naturalized or wildflower garden in full sun to partial shade.

The leaves are alternate, entire, and sessile. The flower heads are small and crowded like small pearls at the ends of the branches. They can be cut and dried to make excellent "everlastings".

Seed sown in late summer will produce flowering plants the next year but division is the most rapid means of propagation. Plants should be divided every 3-4 years.

Quick Reference to Anaphalis Species

| | Height (in.) | Underside of leaves woolly | Flower color |
|---|---|---|---|
| *A. margaritacea* | 24-36 | Yes | White |
| *A. triplinervis* | 12-24 | Yes | White |

***-margaritacea*** (mar-ga-ri-tay′ see-a) Western Pearly Everlasting 24-36″/24″
Late Summer White North America, Northeast Asia Zones 4-7

The 2-4″ long gray-green lanceolate leaves have a white, woolly pubescence on their undersides and the margins are rolled in. The rounded flower heads consist of dozens of ¼ to ½″ diameter flowers that cover the plants like a carpet of snow in late summer. The common name refers to the long-lasting dried flowers. Under evenly moist conditions, plants grow up to 3′ tall and equally wide. These are outstanding plants when a touch of gray is needed, and although they may take a couple of years to look their best, once established, gardeners cherish it for its usefulness in the garden design. One of my favorite garden designers, Bobby Schwartz, of Shaker Heights, Ohio recommends it "be placed in the front of a deep border with tall asters, Joe Pye Weed or *Helianthus* 'Lemon Queen' behind it. Alternatively, it could be placed in the middle of a border with any of the above perennials behind it and *Coreopsis verticillata* 'Moonbeam' in front of it." I love designers who understand that good garden design is based on knowing good plants from bad.

Plants are native to the western United States but also extend across the entire northern half of the country and into Canada. They are not found in the Southeast of the Rocky Mountains.

**Cultivars:**

var. *cinnamomea* is probably the most common form available. The 1″ long leaves are 3-nerved and bear a lovely cinnamon hue on the undersides. Hardy in zones 4-7. It is interesting to note that much of the taller anaphalis offered by American nurserymen is var. *cinnamomea*, native to India, while the majority of everlastings in English gardens is our native *A. margaritacea*.

var. *yedoensis* produces about 2″ long, 1-nerved hairy leaves. Native to Japan and likely a little more cold hardy.

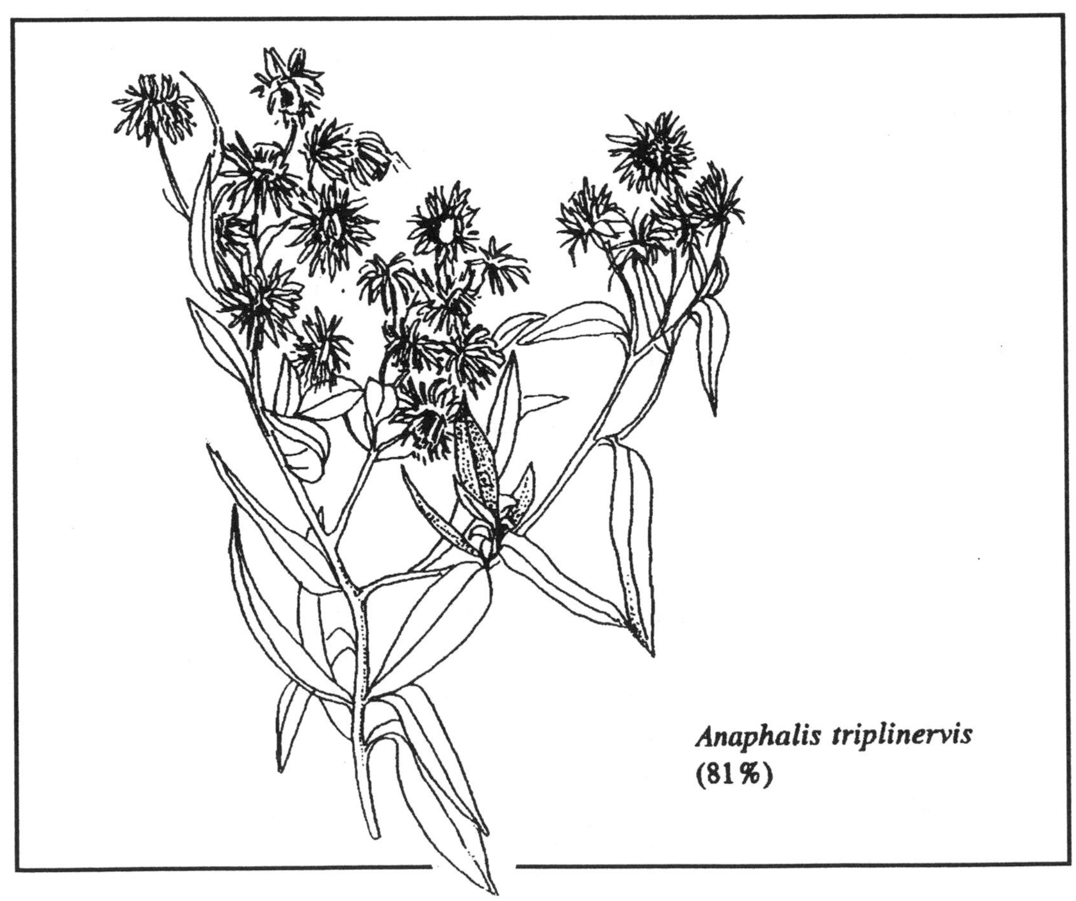

***Anaphalis triplinervis* (81%)**

***-triplinervis*** (tri-plee-ner′ vis) Three-veined Everlasting 12-24″/12″
Late Summer White Himalayas Zones 3-8

I think I like this plant even more than the former because I can satisfy my "what is it?" curiosity. Trying to guess what these gray-leaved plants are is a challenge, but the obvious three veins (three nerves) on the undersides of the leaves makes my guess a little more accurate. The dense, white, woolly pubescent leaves, like other species, contrast and soften other green leaves and bright flowers in the garden. The stems have a more or less zigzag or wavy form (flexuous) which is especially evident if a few leaves are removed. The flowers, which open in July, are long lasting and continue until frost. This makes an excellent low-growing plant for the front of the garden and should be used more often.

**Cultivars:**

'Summer Snow' has clear white flowers over tufts of silvery gray foliage. The flowers are a "cleaner" white than those of the species.

**Related Species:**

*A. nepalensis* var. *monocephala* (*A. nubigena*) is similar to *A. triplinervis* but is only 6-9″ tall.

## ***Anchusa*** (an-koo′ sa) Alkanet Boraginaceae

Of the 30 or so species, gardeners are lucky to see more than two or three. This is a good thing as most of the others are best left to nature; we have enough weeds without raising others. All are biennials or short-lived perennials (living for 2-3 years) and provide flowers in the blue range, a color often difficult to find in the spring and summer garden.

Most members of the Boraginaceae are characterized by the presence of alternate leaves, hairy stems, and flower buds arranged in the shape of a scorpion's tail (scorpioid cyme). Members of *Anchusa* also bear these characteristics. *A. capensis* may be one of the prettiest species for the front of the garden, but the 1-2′ tall plant is best treated as a biennial or an annual. *A. caespitosa* grows about 3-5″ tall and bears extraordinary blue flowers, and is worth a try in the rock garden if plants or seeds can be obtained. The most popular and most tolerant species is *A. azurea*, available in a number of stately cultivars. All species require excellent drainage for best performance.

***-azurea*** (a-zewr-ree′ a) Italian Alkanet 3-5′/2′
Late Spring Blue Caucasus Zones 3-8

This tall-growing, coarsely hairy species can be a beautiful background specimen for full sun in the late spring garden. The 4-8″ long entire leaves are sessile or attached to the stem by the clasping base. The bright blue flowers are ½-¾″ across and persist for about four weeks, depending on temperature. The important words in this discussion are "can be", as they also can be a mess, with leaves turning black and plants askew. In the South, plants may reach 4′ in height and require support. Do not fertilize as they may become too lanky. I have seen some reseeding in rich soils but this is not a widespread problem.

Propagation is mainly by root cuttings. Take ½-¾″ diameter cuttings, 2-3″ long, in early spring, place horizontally in moist, loose, well-drained soil at 65-75°F (also see *Anemone*). Seed is commonly used: sow 1-2″ deep, place at 70-75°F and cover to maintain high humidity.

**Cultivars:**

'Dropmore' was selected in 1905 and the deep blue flowers are still in demand. It reaches a height of 4′ and is one of the more commonly offered cultivars.

'Feltham Pride' has deep blue flowers and grows about 3′ tall.

'Little John' is a compact version of the species (1½′ tall) with dark blue flowers and a compact habit.

'Loddon Royalist' is still the most popular and most available cultivar today. Plants grow about 3′ in height and have lovely gentian-blue flowers.

'Morning Glory' bears gentian-blue flowers on 4′ tall plants.

'Opal' was raised in 1906 and has azure blue flowers. This and 'Dropmore' are untidy in habit and occupy a great deal of garden space.

'Royal Blue' is similar to 'Loddon Royalist' but has a deeper blue color.

## *Andropogon* Bluestem Poaceae

Grasses never go away, they only go to seed. The movement to ornamental grasses has continued unabated for years, and the inclusion of our prairie grasses into mainstream gardens simply accentuates the trend. There are number of bluestems, most are tall and rangy, but with the introduction of a few cultivars, gardeners and landscapers are more ready to try them out. Once established, they are all extremely drought tolerant and are favorites for reclamation purposes. Grow in full sun, mow or cut back hard in early spring.

The common name bluestem is often confused with little bluestem, *Schizachyrium scoparium* (which see).

**- *gerardii*** Big Bluestem, Turkey Foot Grass 5-7′/4′
Summer Tan America Zones 3-8

Its height lends the plants more towards windbreaks, or along highways for erosion control, than in the garden. However, its reliable cold hardiness and drought tolerance have also made it a favorite for large landscapes and naturalizing areas such as meadows. Plants are essentially clump formers, although in warmer areas of the country like parts of Texas, they tend to be more rhizomatous. They are gaining popularity as landscape plants because of quick growth and the blue-green foliage that turns a handsome red in late fall. The summer flowers are formed on branched inflorescences, which some say resemble turkey feet, then are followed by drooping seed heads. Both the seed heads and the flowers make useful cut stems for drying.

**Cultivars:**

'Niagara' has been selected for vigorous growth and tolerance to moist soils. Used mainly in conservation sites, but handsome in their own right. They grow up to 7′ tall and sport red coloration in the fall.

'Pawnee' was introduced to gardeners because it is only 4-5′ tall, somewhat shorter than the species. Plants have a little darker green foliage and often take on a handsome red tinge in the fall.

**Related Species:**

*A. capillipes*, sometimes called chalky bluestem, bears narrow bluish foliage that turns a bronzy red in the fall. Plants grow 2-4′ tall in clumps and do not spread aggressively. The silvery flowers occur in late summer and persist into the fall. Plants are native to warm areas in the southeastern U.S. and cold hardy only to zone 7. 'Valdosta Blue' was found by Bob McCartney near Valdosta, Georgia, and has deeper blue foliage than the species.

*A. glomeratus*, bushy bluestem, broom grass, is tolerant of moist soils, rather unusual in this genus, and is a clump-forming grass. I think the broomlike inflorescences (hence the common name) and the habit make this a far more attractive and user-friendly species than big bluestem. The bronze to red foliage color and the soft flowers make it a winner even in the winter. Plants are not without problems: they are still big (4-6′ tall), and can reseed, so some caution is needed. Clumps should be cut to the ground in early spring. Zones 3-8.

***Androsace*** (an-dros′ a-kee) Rock Jasmine Primulaceae

This relatively unknown group of plants consists of more or less xerophytic, low-growing alpines, all of which require excellent drainage. They are grown for their open, flat-faced flowers with a marked eye, borne over tight rosettes of leaves. In general, they prefer light sandy soils, low nutrient status, and good air movement. Most of the 100 or so species perform well in full sun, although *A. geraniifolia* is best in partial shade. While no species in this genus relishes the hot humid summers so common to the eastern United States, *A. sarmentosa*, *A. carnea*, *A. lactea* and *A. lanuginosa* are a little more forgiving. *Androsace* is most popular with gardeners on the West Coast and in Plains states where temperatures are cool and/or rainfall is limited.

**Related Species and Hybrids:**

A few species and cultivars are offered by mail order nurseries as well as a few retail garden centers.

*A. brigantiaca* is larger, more robust and bears white flowers. *A. carnea* is a 4″ tall tufted ground cover with white or pink flowers. The species, along with the subspecies *laggeri* and *rosea* have all earned Medal of Honor awards from the RHS Garden Wisley in England. *A. pyrenaica* has gorgeous white flowers with a yellow eye.

Hybrids between *A. carnea* and *A. pyrenaica* have become more popular in recent years. 'Callisto' bears white flowers with a red eye, 'Jupiter' produces white flowers with a dark red eye, 'Millstream' bears light pink flowers, 'Rhapsody' has clean pink flowers with a red eye, and 'Venus' bears many white flowers, each with a small yellow eye.

*A. sarmentosa* is offered by most nurseries that sell plants of this genus. Plants produce hairy, silver rosettes in early spring, later becoming less hairy. Plants spread by stolons to make a small patch and bear pink flowers with tiny yellow eyes. Most grow about 6″ tall. The variety *chumbyi* is more dwarf (about 3″) and bears deeper pink flowers. *A. villosa* is densely tufted with rosettes that look like little cushions, and usually bears lots of shaggy hairs on the leaves. Flowers are pink to white; var. *jacquemontii* bears pink flowers.

## ***Anemone*** (a-nem′ o-nee) Windflower Ranunculaceae

Talk about a diverse genus! *Anemone* consists of approximately 100 species, from fibrous to tuberous rooted forms, from spring- to fall-flowering species. They are enjoyed around the world as greenhouse potted plants, florist cut flowers and garden plants. In 1629, John Parkinson wrote in *Paradisi* that "the sight of them doth enforce an earnest longing desire in the minde of anyone to be a possessour of some of them at the least, for ... is of it selfe alone almost sufficient to furnish a garden with their flowers for almost halfe the yeare ...". Most species have compound leaves and apetalous (no petals) flowers, most of the color the result of the showy sepals. Three main groups of *Anemone* occur, based on their rootstalks and growth habit.

| Rootstalk | Flowering time | Examples |
|---|---|---|
| Fibrous | Late summer, fall | *A. hupehensis*, *A.* x *hybrida*, *A. tomentosa*, *A. vitifolia* |
| Tuber, rhizomes | spring | *A. blanda*, *A. canadensis*, *A.* x *lesseri*, *A. nemorosa*, *A. sylvestris* |
| Tuberous rooted | spring, early summer | *A. coronaria*, *A.* x *fulgens*, *A. pavonia* |

The tuberous types (*A. blanda*, *A. coronaria*) are best planted in mid to late October, approximately 3″ deep. All species appreciate shelter from the afternoon sun and do poorly if allowed to dry out. The early spring-flowering tuberous species usually become dormant by the time the hot sun of the summer arrives.

Confusion reigns about those ubiquitous Japanese anemones, which include a complex of closely related plants, none of which originated in Japan. It makes more sense to call them fall-flowering anemones. They include *A. vitifolia*, *A. tomentosa*, *A. hupehensis* and *A.* x *hybrida* and are all vigorous growers.

Propagation by seed is possible but for most, division is the quickest and surest method of multiplication. For tuberous/rhizomatous species, the tubers may be lifted in early June and divided. Ripe seed should be rubbed in dry sand to remove the cottony down adhering to the seed. The autumn-flowering forms are easily increased by division in the fall. Root cuttings of the fibrous forms are commonly employed to propagate those species.

Quick Reference to Anemone Species

| | Height (in.) | Root | Number of sepals | Flower color | Flowering time |
|---|---|---|---|---|---|
| *A. blanda* | 6-8 | Tuber | 9-14 | Blue | Early spring |
| *A. canadensis* | 12-24 | Rhizome | 4-5 | White | Spring |
| *A. coronaria* | 7-15 | Tuber | 6-20 | Various | Early spring |
| *A.* x *hybrida* | 30-48 | Rhizome | 6-11 | White, pink | Fall |
| *A. multifida* | 6-8 | Rhizome | 5-10 | White | Early spring |
| *A. nemorosa* | 6-8 | Rhizome | 5-9 | White | Spring |
| *A. sylvestris* | 10-18 | Rhizome | 5-8 | White | Spring |

***-blanda*** (blan′ da) Grecian Windflower 6-8″/8″
Early Spring Sky Blue Greece Zones 4-7

The Grecian windflower is one of the earliest harbingers of spring. The plants' small stature makes them suitable for naturalizing or for filling in small areas of the garden. Fernlike foliage arises from an oval tuber, followed by the flower. The narrow sepals are about ½″ long and the flowers nearly 2″ across. The flowers last but 2 weeks and then give rise to hairy seed heads known as achenes. These fruiting bodies persist for 3-4 weeks but are not particularly attractive and should be removed unless seeds are being collected. Although the flowers of the species are dark blue, cultivars are available in sky blue, white, pink or purplish red. Plant the tubers 1-3″ apart in dappled shade and in soil amended with organic matter. In the South (south of zone 6), plants do not spread as rapidly as in the North nor are they as long-lived. Regardless, plants will flower the first spring after planting, but one to two years is necessary to fully establish the tubers in the garden, especially if dried out when purchased. Once established, plants will self-sow and the seedlings will flower the next year. However, after all is said and done, given marauding critters like squirrels, chipmunks and voles combined with heat, drought and cold, an expectation of more than 3 years may be a tad unrealistic. They are inexpensive, buy some each year. Provide winter protection in zone 4 with leaves or pine boughs.

**Cultivars:**

'Charmer' produces deep rose flowers.

'Blue Star' has dark-blue flowers about 2-2½″ in diameter.

'Bridesmaid' and 'White Splendor' both bear flowers of pure white. There is little difference between them.

'Pink Star' and 'Rosea' have differing shades of purple. The former has larger flowers than the latter.

'Radar' is one of the finest cultivars and has large mauve flowers with white centers.

'Violet Star' bears violet flowers with white centers.

'White Splendour' has lovely single creamy white flowers.

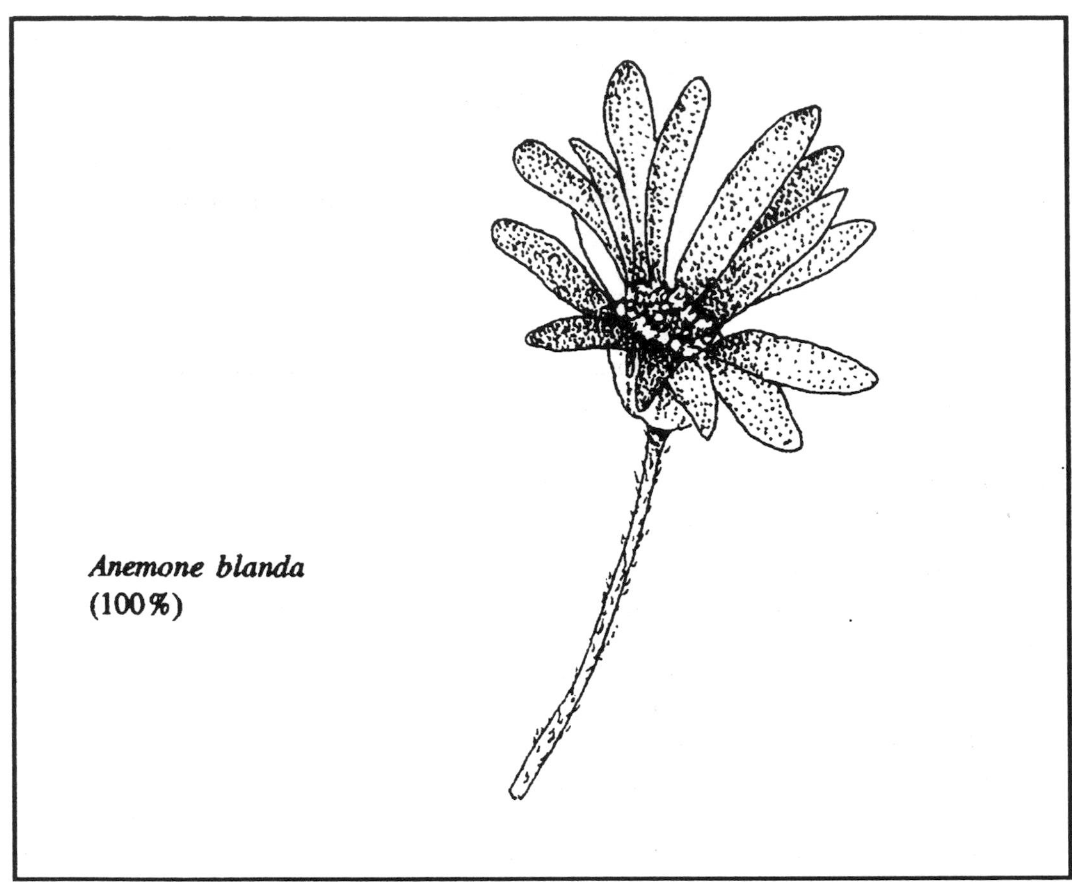

***Anemone blanda***
**(100%)**

-***canadensis*** (kan-a-den′ sis) Meadow Anemone 12-24″/spreader
Spring White Northern United States, Canada Zones 3-7

The common name is particularly appropriate because the species will spread and fill an entire meadow. That it is somewhat invasive is probably its only flaw, and if placed in a difficult corner or other area where it can run, it will reign supreme in the spring and into early summer. The light green leaves are 5-7 parted and broader than long. They are hairy beneath and the leaf segments are toothed. Each clear white flower is almost 2″ across and consists of 4-5 sepals.

Plants do best in partial shade but tolerate full sun. It is native to low-lying areas and thus requires moist conditions to become established. As long as its exuberant habit can be enjoyed, this is an excellent plant for those who think they can't grow anything.

Propagate by division any time from May to September.

-***coronaria*** (ko-ro-nah′ ree-a) Poppy Anemone 7-10″/8″
Early Spring Various Mediterranean Zones 6-9

Poppy anemone is similar to Grecian anemone in that it is planted as a tuber and generally available from bulb catalogs or in colorful containers at garden centers.

Gardeners seldom see the actual species anymore, for it has been replaced with more colorful hybrids. All strains have finely divided foliage and rounded sepals in various colors. Regardless of the pedigree, they make lovely spring garden plants as well as excellent cut flowers. They may be planted in the North (zone 6) as late as October and in the South in November for early spring flowering. Further north than zone 6, pot the tuber at the beginning of March and plant outside after threat of frost, and flowers will emerge in late May and early June.

Research in Georgia (zone 7b) has shown that planting as late as December does not affect the number of flowers (4-5 flowers/plant). The flowering season was also extended a few weeks with late planting. However, plantings in January, February, and March resulted in very few flowers, all of questionable quality. This was probably because insufficient cold was accumulated by the tubers.

This research also indicates that tubers are best treated as annuals, dug up and discarded after flowering. Flower production declines and tubers decline after two years in the ground. Like *A. blanda*, tubers are inexpensive and can be replaced at nominal cost.

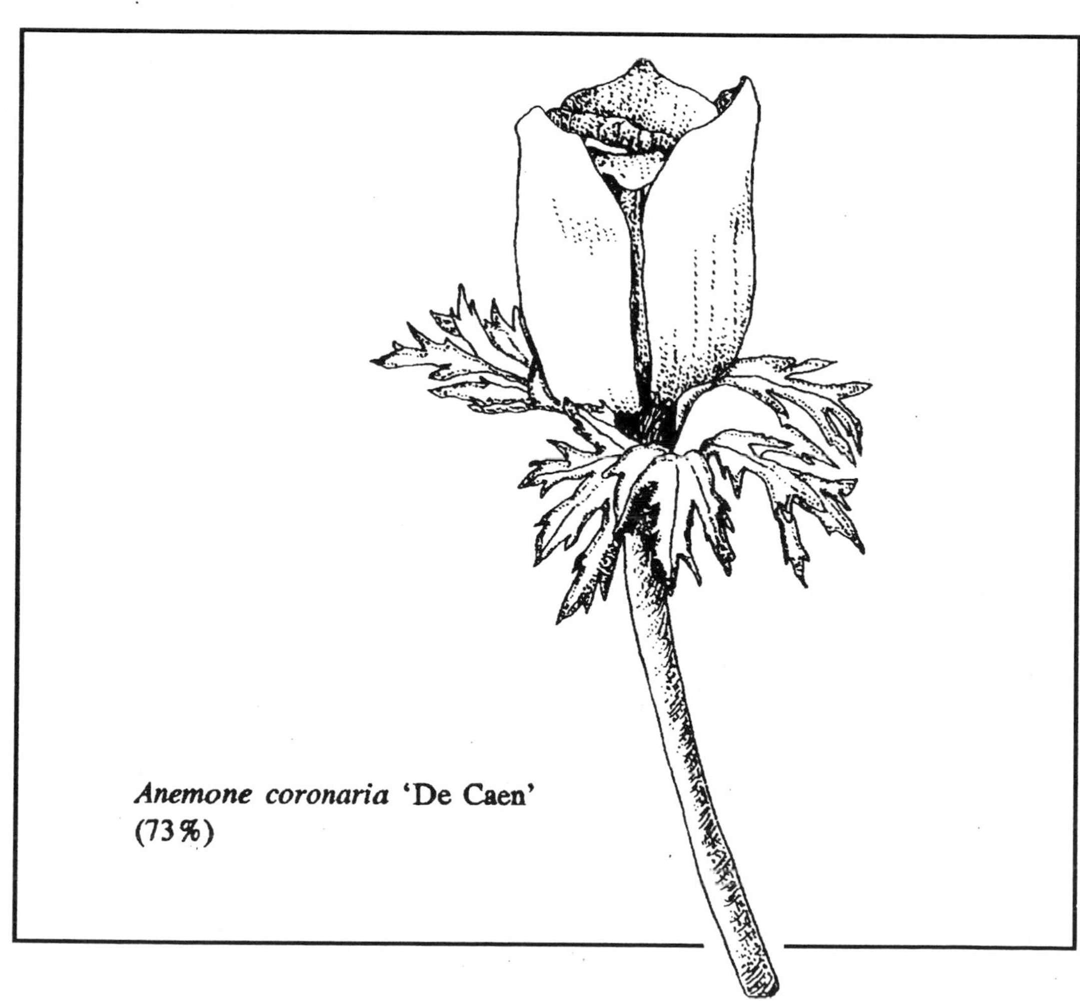

***Anemone coronaria* 'De Caen'**
**(73%)**

**Cultivars:**

'De Caen' hybrids were developed early in the 18th century around the Caen and Bayeux districts of northern France and became known as the De Caen anemones. The flowers are single, saucer shaped and available as 'Florist Mix' or as separate colors. 'The Bride', white; 'Mr. Fokker', violet-blue; and 'Sylphide', violet rose are only a few of the cultivars that were developed within the De Caen series. 'Hollandia' (syn. 'His Excellency') has scarlet sepals with white bases surrounding a black center and appears to be a cultivar of *A. coronaria*.

'Mona Lisa' series is a strain of poppy anemone that is much preferable to the 'De Caen' series. Separate colors as well as a mixture have been developed. The flowers are larger, the stems are 1½ to 2 times longer and the vase life of the cut flowers is longer.

'St. Brigid' series has semi-double flowers and is available as a mixture or in separate colors. 'Lord Lieutenant', purple blue, 'Mt. Everest', white, 'The Admiral', pink-red, and 'The Governor', crimson scarlet are available in this series.

***-hupehensis*** (hew-puh-hen′ sis) Japanese Anemone 2-4′/3′
Fall Pink Japan Zones 4-7

Plants are similar and often confused with *A.* x *hybrida*. This species has 5-7 rosy-mauve sepals, grows 2-2½′ tall and flowers a week or so earlier than the hybrid. It is generally shorter and may produce flowers that lack fertile pollen. Plants with 10-20 narrow sepals were found in 1695 in Japan, and finally sent to England in 1844 by Robert Fortune where they were called *A. japonica*. Its proper name has finally been established as *A. hupehensis* var. *japonica*, and has never been found in the wild except where it has been introduced. However, many fine cultivars belong to this variant.

**Cultivars:**

'Bodnant Burgundy' has handsome dark flowers and stands 2-3′ tall.

'Bowles' Pink' is hard to find in this country but has shown excellent performance in Europe. Single pink to rose-colored flowers occur in the fall.

'Bressingham Glow' produces deep rose-pink semi-double flowers.

'Hadspen Abundance' has pink-rose single flowers with dark and light pink petals, and prominent golden-yellow stamens on 3′ tall plants. Plants arose from Hadspen House, England.

'Pamina' has proven to be an excellent addition to the Gardens at UGA, showing tolerance to heat and student abuse. The semi-double rose-pink flowers consist of overlapping sepals, and persist for weeks.

'Prince Henry' has deep rose, semi-double flowers stands nearly 3′ tall.

'Splendens' has purple to pink flowers and is quite early to flower, up to 2 weeks earlier than other cultivars in some climates.

**-x *hybrida*** (hi-bred′ a) Hybrid Anemone, Japanese Anemone 2½-3′/2′
Fall White, Pink Hybrid Origin Zones 3-7

The nomenclature of *Anemone* is rather confused but nowhere is it as befuddled as with Japanese anemone and the various hybrids, however, things are becoming a little more clear. A few plants are still sold as *A. japonica*, but those are actually hybrids. It now seems clear that almost all fall-flowering anemones have been lumped in this hybrid category, including favorites once classified as *A. tomentosa* and *A. vitifolia*. So far, only the closely related *A. hupehensis* remains split from the hybrids. I research these names long and hard, but like a sack full of puppies, the name game moves all over the place. There is no universal acceptance of this latest lumping, and in the next edition, everything may be changed again. So don't get too concerned, especially with this group, because regardless of the name, the late flowerers are wonderful garden plants.

They are often slow to establish, but after the second or third year become free flowering and can often be overly aggressive. In the South, plant early in the fall to allow root establishment or early in the spring. Planting in midsummer is possible but often plants don't establish well. They perform best in well-drained soils and partial shade.

Propagation by division in the spring can be accomplished and is the easiest means of moving plants around the garden and avoiding overcrowding. However, root cuttings are also effective. Take thick sections of root approximately 3-4″ long from lifted plants and place vertically in a moist well-drained medium. Cover the tops of the root sections with a thin layer of sand or vermiculite and place in a cold frame or unheated greenhouse. This method of propagation should be accomplished when the plants are dormant in the winter.

**Cultivars:**

Some absolutely wonderful hybrids are available and although my preferences in anemones reside with the single forms, many cultivars are available with semi-double or double flowers. The only defect with many of the cultivars is that they are 4-5′ tall and may need some support to look their best.

'Alba' bears single, clear white 2-3″ diameter flowers and stands 3′ tall. This is often listed in catalogs but is probably the same as 'Honorine Jobert'.

'Alice' has semi-double light pink flowers and is 2-2½′ tall.

'Andrea Atkinson' is 3-4′ tall with semi-double white flowers with chartreuse eyes. Plants bear handsome dark green foliage that makes the white flowers stand out even more.

'Coupe D'Argent' literally translates to "cut silver".

'Elegans' is early to flower and bears light pink single flowers that can be extraordinary in bloom. Plants may stand up to 4′ tall and carry dozens of single, 3-4″ wide, clean pink flowers. The cultivars 'Albert Schweitzer' and 'Max Vogel' have been lumped into 'Elegans'.

'Elegantissima' grows 3-4′ tall and bears double rosy sepals. A tetraploid plant, it is very vigorous.

'Honorine Jobert' was a sport of the pink-flowered *A.* x *hybrida* discovered in the garden of M. Jobert in Verdun, France in 1858. It has graced European gardens since the beginning of the American Civil War and is still the most popular and highly sought-after white anemone today. It is 3-4′ tall and the clean white sepals contrast beautifully with the yellow stamens in the center. The flowers are only

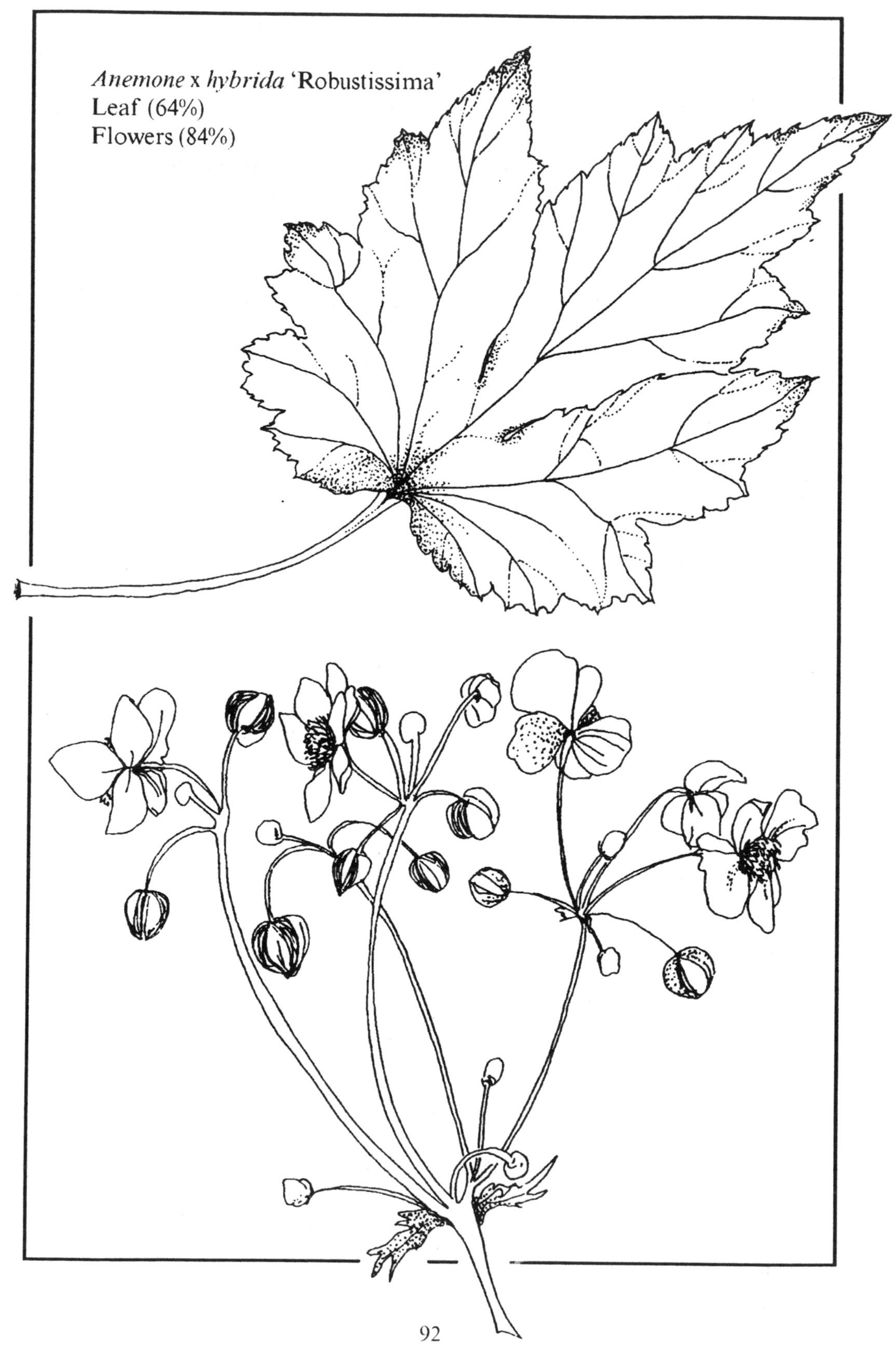
*Anemone* x *hybrida* 'Robustissima'
Leaf (64%)
Flowers (84%)

2-3″ across, not as large as some of the newer clones, but the plant is floriferous and worthy of a place in the garden. It is difficult to know if you are purchasing this cultivar or 'Alba'.

'Kriemhilde' is still one of the finest semi-double pink flowering cultivars available today with 10-15 broad overlapping sepals. Introduced in 1909.

'Loreley' is seen more often in Europe but sometimes finds its way over here. Flowers are 3-4′ tall with silvery pink semi-double flowers.

'Luise Uhink' was bred by the German nurseryman Wilhelm Pfitzer, but is little known in this country. This is unfortunate as it has 3-4″ diameter semi-double white flowers on 4′ tall stems and is a prolific flowerer.

'Margarete' has semi-double to double deep pink flowers and is about 2-3′ tall. Sterile flowers.

'Montrose', introduced in 1899, bears semi-double to double deep rose sterile flowers on 3′ tall stems. Flowers consist of about 40 slightly twisted narrow sepals. The cultivar 'Lady Gilmour' has been determined to be the same thing.

'Queen Charlotte' bears lovely pink semi-double flowers which measure 3″ across. The tips of the sepals have a ragged appearance. It grows about 3′ tall and was also bred by Pfitzer in Germany.

'Richard Ahrens' produces pink-lilac single to semi-double flowers that fade to almost white.

'Robustissima' produces mauve-pink flowers held well above the foliage. The leaves are gray-green underneath. It is more winter-hardy than the species and can be grown in zone 4. Plants are robust, to the point of thuggery, in the shade, better behaved and quite tolerant of full sun. Plants are still offered as *A. tomentosa* (*A. vitifolia*) 'Robustissima'.

'September Charm' is quite popular and with good reason. Plants produce an abundance of single rose-pink flowers that are darker on the outside than inside. Plants used to be classified as *A. hupehensis*.

'Victor Jones' has single rose-pink flowers held up by 3-3½′ tall purple stems.

'Whirlwind' is 4-5′ tall and produces 4″ wide semi-double pure white flowers consisting of 20-30 narrow flattened sepals.

'White Giant' grows to 4′ tall and produces large semi-double flowers.

***-multifida*** (mul-tee′ fi-da) Magellan Anemone 6-8″/6″
Early Spring White Chile Zones 2-6

The main claim to fame of this low-growing garden species is that it is one of the most cold-tolerant species of this genus, allowing gardeners from Alaska to North Carolina to enjoy it. The hairy leaves are much divided and plants are covered with numerous 1″ creamy-white flowers on 12″ long scapes. The seed heads (achenes) are densely hairy. Culture is not difficult in sun or light shade.

**Cultivars:**

'Annabelle White' grows about 12″ tall and is covered with creamy white flowers in early summer.

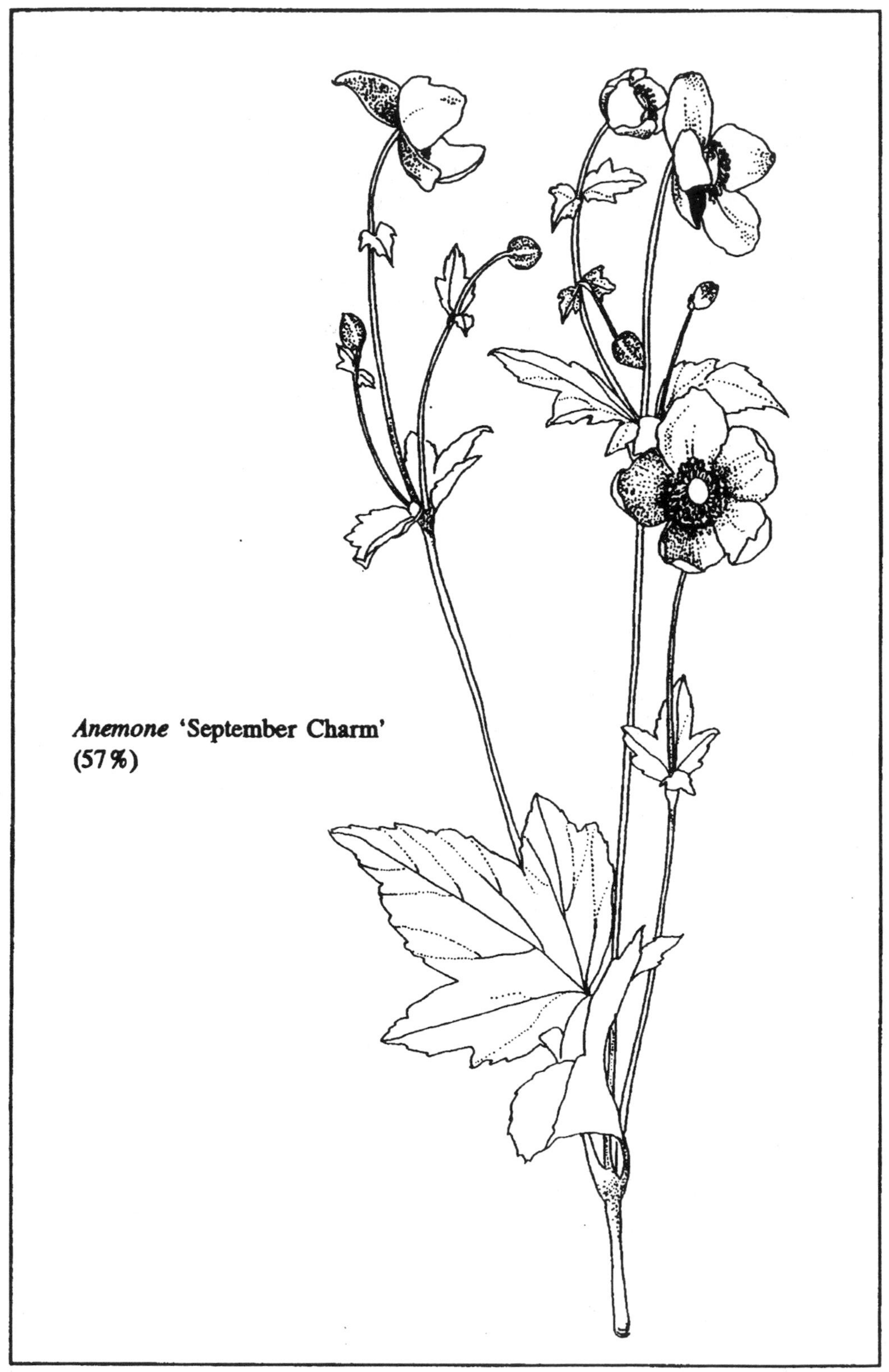

*Anemone* 'September Charm'
(57%)

***-nemorosa*** (nem-o-ro′ sa) | Wood Anemone | 6-8″/8″
Early Spring | White | Europe | Zones 4-8

Wood anemones are widely distributed in Europe, absent only in the more southerly Mediterranean areas, so it should not be surprising that plants are extremely variable in size, color, and even structure of the flowers. There are usually 5-8 sepals, but forms lacking sepals, and those with 50 or more are known. The flowers are about 1½-2″ wide and often tinged rose on the margins. The solitary stems bear leaves halfway up, and terminate in a solitary flower. The common flower color is white, but a number of clones have blue or pink flowers and a yellow-flowered variant has also been described.

The foliage is three times divided into deeply toothed linear segments. Plants arise from a wormlike rhizome that branches extensively beneath the ground. *A. nemorosa* performs best in slightly acid soil (pH 5.5-6.5) containing liberal amounts of peat or leaf mold and in dappled to deep shade. Plant in fall only.

**Cultivars:**

Many cultivars and varieties have been described but not all are easily found.

*Blue flowers:*

var. *allenii* is about 1′ tall and has large (2″ diameter), deep lavender-blue flowers. The reverse is streaked with purplish red dots of varying intensity.

'Blue Beauty' is the tallest of the blue forms growing 15-18″ in height and bears perfect sky blue cup-shaped blooms. It is the best blue form of the species.

'Bowles' Mauve' has lavender-blue flowers.

var. *caerulea* is about 6″ tall with sky blue ¾″ wide flowers. The flower reverse is paler blue. Perhaps all the blue forms should be lumped under this category, as there is little difference between them.

'Robinsoniana' has 1½″ diameter bright lavender-blue flowers. It grows 12-14″ tall and is one of the oldest varieties still offered by perennial growers. Probably discovered by William Robinson in Oxford Botanical Garden, having "been sent there by a lady in Ireland".

*Pink flowers:*

var. *rosea* is 10-14″ tall and carries nodding 1″ wide light rose flowers with a paler reverse. It is slow to increase vegetatively and seed production is poor.

*White flowers:*

'Flore Pleno' ('Alba Plena') stands 10″ tall and has semi-double to double flowers. It is an excellent garden plant.

var. *grandiflora* has the largest flowers, sometimes attaining 3″ in diameter. Plants are vigorous and grow 20″ tall in rich soil.

'Lady Doneraile' is similar to 'Lychette' but only 10″ tall.

'Lychette' is one of the best white-flowered cultivars, bearing large 2″ diameter flowers that are pure white above and beneath. There are green blushes around the bases of the 6-8 sepals. I have seen plants grow up to 20″ tall, but they are normally 10-12″ in height.

'Vestal' has pure white sepals surrounding a center filled with broad stamen filaments (petaloid stamens). Closely resembles 'Flore Pleno' but the flowers are larger and petaloid segments are more regular. They are different but in commerce, I am not sure what is being sold out there.

'Viridifolia' is for those gardeners who can't get enough green. Flowers consist of dozen of green bracts making it look like the Jolly Green Giant on a bad hair day. However, since it flowers in early spring, there is not a lot of green competition at the time, so it is certainly interesting.

***-sylvestris*** (sil-ves′ tris) Snowdrop Anemone 10-18″/12″
Spring White Europe Zones 4-8

I have been in a Denver snowstorm in March and the next day seen these plants push through the white stuff as if it were no more than a minor nuisance. One of the prettiest spring anemones, it combines light green, 3-5 parted leaves with fragrant 1½-2″ diameter, dainty, white flowers. The 5-sepaled flowers are slightly nodding when fully open and are solitary on the flower stalk. The lovely flowers give way to interesting white, woolly fruit.

*A. sylvestris* requires light soil and a partially shaded area for best performance. The major drawback is that it runs freely, particularly in loose soils, and can overrun less aggressive plants. Plantlets, however, are not difficult to remove and gardening friends will be more than happy to accept a few. It visits me every now and then in Athens, but without doubt is more comfortable in Denver and Montreal. Cold weather is to its liking and it is more aggressive in northern climates than in the South.

**Cultivars:**

'Compacta' is offered by a few nurseries and is a more dwarf, more compact form of the species. I have never found the species to be particularly large or in need of compaction, but such is the benefit of diversity.

var. *macrantha* has larger and more abundant flowers.

'Elise Feldman' is a relatively new introduction with almost fully double white flowers in the spring. The flowers are quite heavy and may fall over in inclement weather. Similar to 'Flore pleno', perhaps more consistent.

'Flore pleno' is a double-flowered white cultivar but is not nearly as pretty as the species.

**Related Species:**

Dozens of species and hybrids are sold and can be dramatic additions to the garden. Most are more difficult to locate, and some may disappoint a little, but for the anemone enthusiast, there is no such thing as a bad anemone.

*A. altaica* is a tuberous form native to northern areas of Russia and the Arctic and therefore particularly cold hardy. Plants are about 8″ tall and bear single white flowers with blue or purple veins in the spring. Great for the rock garden.

*A. apennina*, Apennine windflower, is also tuberous and has a similar form to *A. altaica*, but is not as cold hardy. Plants have larger leaves and bright blue spring flowers with yellow stamens.

*A. leveillei* has kidney-shaped leaves basal leaves divided into three sessile lobes, each divided deeply. Plants grow 15-18″ tall. The 1-2″ wide white flowers are stained blue to pink on the outside. Hardy to about zone 6.

*A. multifida* is native from Alaska to Quebec and Saskatchewan and south to California and Colorado. This fine native species forms 8-12″ high mounds of light green delicately cut foliage with two to three long stalked yellowish flowers in early spring. Flowers may be clear red or tinged with blue or purple. The styles are red or pink, and silky seed heads add additional interest after flowering. Some handsome colonies occur in the alpine area of the Denver Botanic Garden. 'Major' is better than the species due to the larger creamy yellow flowers. 'Magellanica' is taller, growing 18-24″ in height. Plants perform well in zones 3 to 6 as well as in the Northwest. Poor choices for the South.

*A. narcissiflora*, native to the mountains of Europe and Japan, grows about 12-18″ tall over deeply divided foliage. Plants bear 2-6 white to cream-colored flowers in an umbel in the spring. Each flower is about an inch wide. Plants do well in zones 4 to 7a.

*A. pavonina* is native to southern Europe, mainly around the Mediterranean, and also arises from a tuber. Plants grow about 9-12″ tall and bear solitary 2-3″ wide flowers in the spring. The flowers, consisting of 7-9 segments, are often scarlet, however pink, purple and violet colors occur.

*A. quinquefolia*, American wood anemone, was initially considered to be a variety of *A. nemorosa* (*A. n.* var. *quinquefolia*). It is native from Quebec to Georgia and common in moist rich woodlands. The white flowers are ¾-1″ across and appear in spring.

*A. rivularis* is native to India and China and grows up to 3′ tall in zones 5-7. The white flowers are stained blue throughout and are borne in 3-5 flowered umbels in late spring and summer. It is a terrific plant, particularly suited around semi-shaded ponds and water features.

*A. rupicola* is another white-flowered species with blue or pink staining on the sepals but is only about 6-9″ tall. The basal leaves are three parted and strongly lobed while the solitary flowers are up to 2-3″ across. Hardy in zones 4-7.

*A. virginiana*, thimbleweed, is a native woodland species with greenish white to white 1″ wide flowers. The early spring flowers usually occur in 3's and consist of 5 sepals. Plants grow about 2′ tall and are particularly suited to the woodland garden. Thimbleweed is hardy from zones 3 to 7.

***Anemonella*** (a-nem-o-nell′ a) Rue-anemone Ranunculaceae

The rue-anemones have to be one of the prettiest diminutive woodland plants for the garden. They are native to a large slice of North America, from southwest Maine to northern Florida, west to Minnesota and Oklahoma. The genus is represented by *A. thalictroides* only. Many taxonomists have transferred the species to *Thalictrum* (*T. thalictroides*) but the jury is still out, so I'll leave it here for now. Plants with an eastern nativity tend to be white but as the plants extend west, flowers appear to have more pink in them.

In woodland gardens throughout the eastern United States, rue-anemone is a welcome and familiar sight in early spring. And in the Armitage garden, plants compete with the roots of a large white oak without complaint, and make the base of that noble tree even better. Plants grow about 8-10″ tall and bear foliage similar to anemone, except much daintier and finer. They are blue-green, basal and 1-2 ternate,

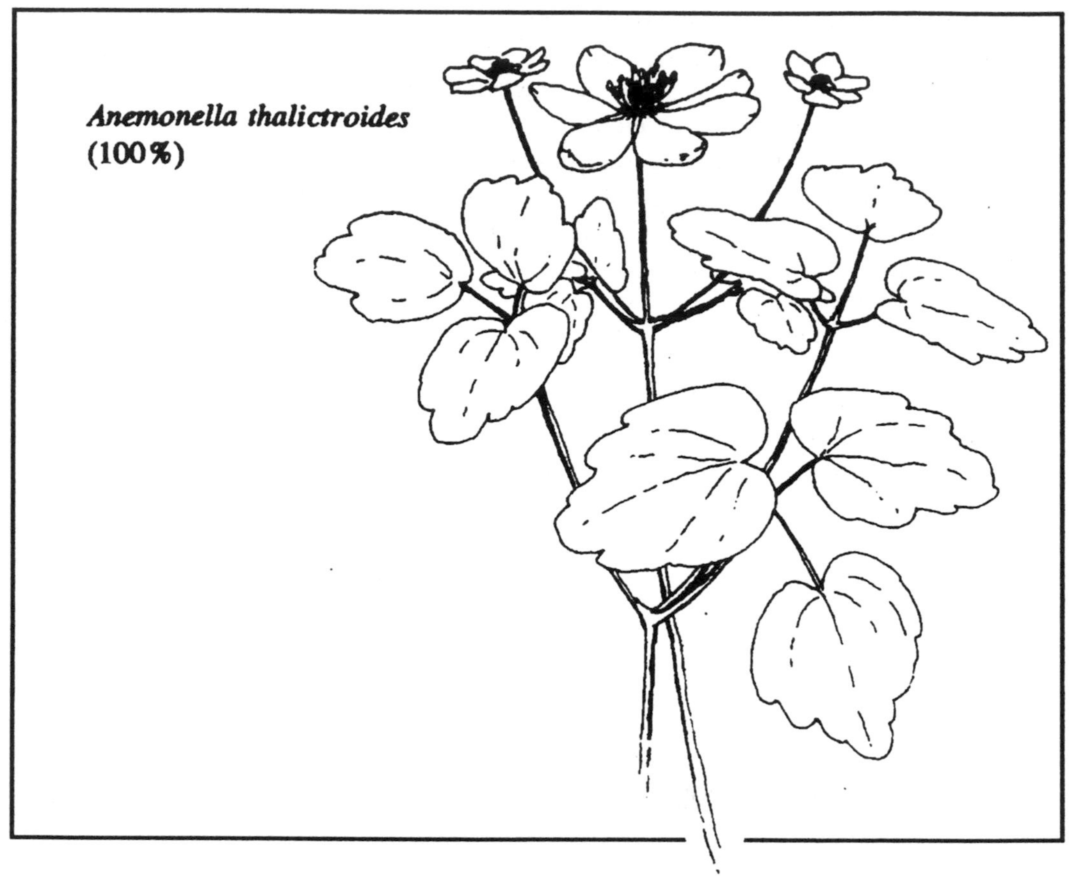


each terminal leaflet being 3-toothed at the apex. The ½″ wide flowers are arranged in 2-5 flowered umbels and consist of 5-10 petal-like sepals and numerous stamens. There are no petals.

They love to be grouped in partially shaded areas with moisture-retentive soils. If they dry out, they look ratty early. With the exception of slugs, few diseases or insects bother them. Plants are hardy in zones 4-9. By the way, the suffixes "opsis", "ella" and "oides" means "looks like"; this plant resembles both an anemone and a thalictrum.

Propagate by seed or division of well-developed clumps.

**Cultivars:**

There has been an explosion of cultivars in the last few years. None of them is inexpensive but I see an "Anemonella Stage of Life" coming to a few gardeners.

'Betty Blake' produces light green to yellow green double flowers and flower for a long period of time.

'Cameo' is a light pink-flowered double form. They are similar in form to 'Schoaf's Double Pink' but differ by having much lighter-colored flowers.

'Double White' is similar to 'Cameo' but with cleaner white flowers.

'Eco Pink' from Don Jacobs of Eco-Gardens in Decatur, Georgia, has single pink flowers.

'Eco Starry Night' has unique pointed sepals and bronzy foliage. Quite different.
'Eco Atlas Double' bears white pompon double flowers.
var. *favilliana* is a handsome double white form. Flowers persist much longer than the species but plants are slow to increase. Difficult to locate.
'Jade Feather' is also known as 'Green Dragon' or 'Green Hurricane'. Regardless of the name, they are scary. The plants produce strange double flowers with twisted green sepals.
'Rosea' bears single light pink flowers.
'Schoaf's Double Pink' bears double rose-pink flowers. It was the result of a chance sighting by a Mr. Oscar Schoaf in a graveyard in Owatonna, Minnesota. While Mr. Schoaf brought the plants into cultivation in his garden, it was Mrs. Louise Koehler of Bixby, Minnesota who sent plants to friends and nurseries and so brought the plant out of obscurity. Propagated only by division, plants are slow to increase but now are relatively easy to locate. Like other anemonellas, they are expensive, but they are worth the hunt. They are stunning in Garden in the Woods, Framingham, Massachusetts.
'Tairin' has deep pink to rose single flowers and performs well for a long period of time in the spring.

## ***Anemonopsis*** (a-nem-o-nop′ sis) False Anemone Ranunculaceae

As I stared at this plant in a shady Cleveland garden, I knew the glossy foliage looked like an anemone but I couldn't for the life of me place the flowers. All I could say to my inquisitor about this most handsome plant was that it looked like an anemone. It turned out to be a pretty good guess when one considers that the name *Anemonopsis* is translated "resembles anemone". Only one species, *A. macrophylla*, native to Japan, has been described and it is occasionally offered by specialty nurseries. The 1″ wide waxy lavender-pink flowers are held in loose racemes well above the glossy green basal leaves. The pendulous flowers occur in late summer and are particularly lovely if plants are planted on a bank where the flowers can be viewed from beneath. Partially shaded, moist conditions serve plants well. A terrific garden plant, they likely perform well in zones 4-7. Propagate from seed or division.

## ***Angelica*** (an-gel′ i-ca) Angelica Apiaceae

Plants are better known for their medicinal properties than as an ornamental garden plant. The 50 or so species are found in the northern United States and Canada to Japan and Europe. In general, they are tall and stout, and at home in semi-shaded moist areas. The leaves are in 3's (ternate) to pinnate and the petioles are usually sheathed around the stem. The garden forms available are impressive but often short lived.

Quick reference to Angelica Species

| | Height (ft.) | Flower color |
|---|---|---|
| *A. archangelica* | 5-6 | Creamy-white |
| *A. gigas* | 3-5 | Purple |

***-archangelica*** (ark-an-gel′ i-ka) Wild Parsnip 5-6′/4′
Early summer Creamy-white Europe, Asia Zones 5-7

Say the name *Angelica archangelica* a few times and it begins to take on poetic qualities of its own. The specific name came from the Archangel Raphael. As you know archangels are high-ranking angels, and Raphael was charged to heal the earth. St. Raphael has a special charge of protecting the young, the innocent, and travelers. The Feast of St. Raphael is October 24.

The plant has been cultivated for generations in Asia and Europe for its confectionery properties and as a vegetable. The stems and petioles may be crystallized for candying and the young shoots are prepared similar to asparagus or cooked with rhubarb, to reduce the tartness. However, let not your taste or lack of it for rhubarb limit the use of this plant! As a cultivated plant, it lends a stateliness of its own to the garden. The large, flat, creamy-white to greenish compound umbels are handsome enough but the resulting seed heads can be absolutely majestic. These large plants can take over an area and will reseed if allowed to do so. Plants are monocarpic, meaning they die after seeding. Some gardeners have found that removing the flowers before they go to seed increases the chance of perennialization. Seedlings require two years to flower.

***-gigas*** (gee′ gas) Purple Parsnip 3-5′/4′
Late summer, Fall Purple Japan, Korea, China Zones 5-7

Introduced to this country from Korea by Barry Yinger of Asiatica Nursery, this large coarse plant never fails to draw attention when in flower. The light green leaves are attached to the thick stems with inflated purple sheaths. The flowers are deep purple, in umbels 3-4″ across. Similar to the above species, the drying seed heads are also magical. Although tolerant of shade, if placed in too heavy shade, the dark flowers get lost. Plants love moisture and will be stunted in dry summers. Only recently finding its way into American nurseries, this is an exciting biennial plant for the late summer and fall garden. Plants will self-sow in favorable conditions and may be considered a "perennial biennial". Seed-grown plants generally require two years before flowering. In the shaded Armitage garden, plants were magnificent in June into July although the seed heads never developed as well as I would have liked. The quality of the seed heads increases with sunny areas, cool night temperatures and low humidity.

**Related Species**:

*A. keiskei*, otherwise known as ashitaba, is a medicinal herb from Japan. I grew this in the Gardens at UGA and was most impressed with the ornamental value. The plants were robust, but compact, never growing taller than 2½′. However, the foliage was glossy, shiny green and always caught the eye. Plants shone even more as temperatures became cooler and in our zone 7 climate were at their best in the fall, winter and spring. The flowers were white. Most of the time plants behave like a biennial and once flowered, it will disappear. However, I have seen this in John Elsley's garden in Greenwood, South Carolina and he claims it was there for at least three years.

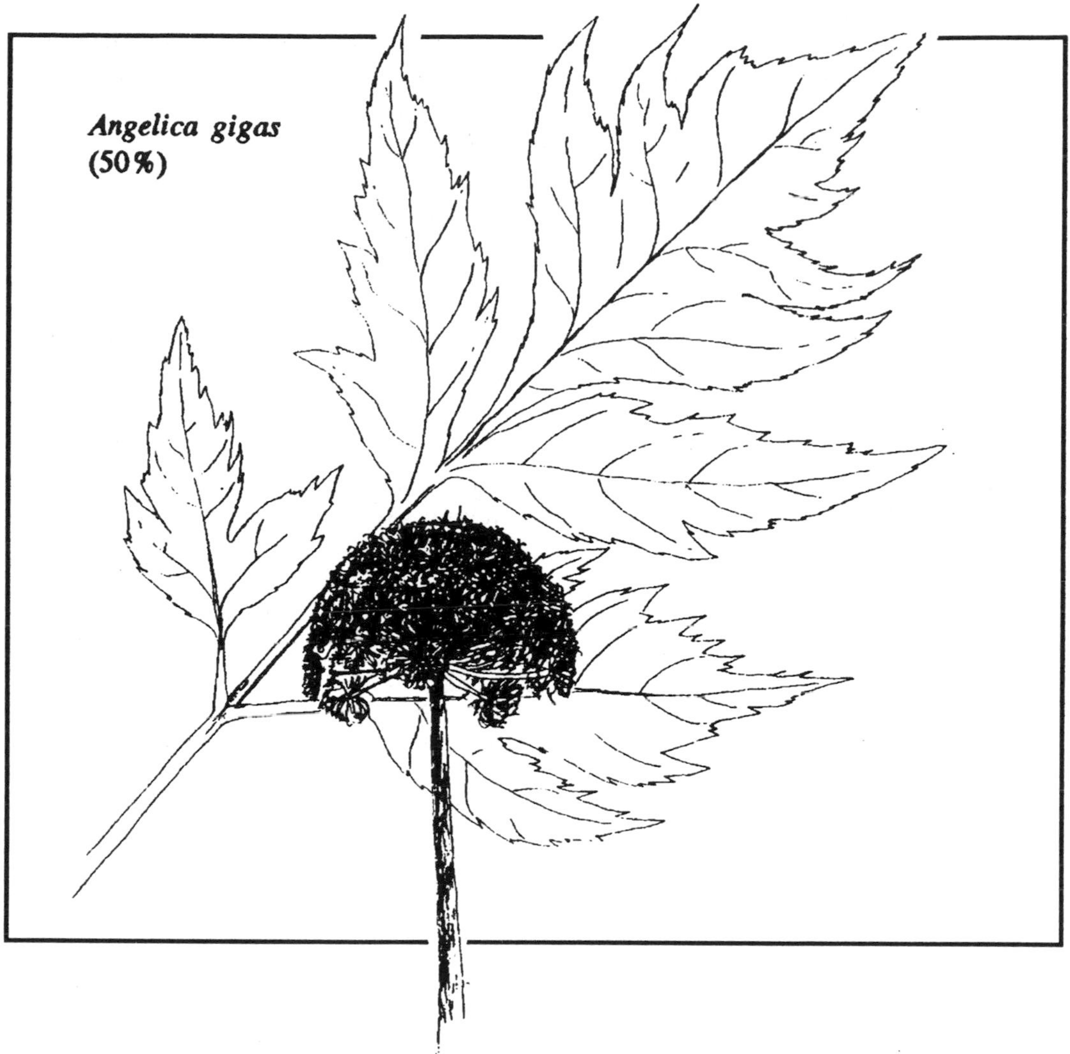


*A. pachycarpa* also has glossy green leaves and is also a biennial. Leaves are smaller and plants are more branched. Plants grow 4-6′ tall, and are wonderfully ornamental.

## ***Antennaria*** (an-ten-ar′ i-a) Pussytoes Asteraceae

About 15 species are used in gardens, primarily because of the gray foliage that carpets the ground. The flowers are dioecious, meaning that male and female occur on separate plants. The actual flowers are nondescript but are surrounded by dry, chaffy scales which provide the color. However, the gray foliage is the most valuable garden asset.

Plants tolerate poor infertile soils and hot, dry locations. They are best suited for the front of the garden or rock garden. Pussytoes are gaining a steady following due to their toughness, their well-behaved habit and the gray-silver foliage. Some of the more common forms are native to Europe, however, a number of good species call

North America home. *A. neglecta* var. *gaspensia* is one of the neatest, bearing small silvery leaves on 2-3″ tall ground-hugging mats over which rise silvery-white flowers. *A. parvifolia*, Contock pussytoes, native to southwest Canada and the western United States is also an excellent rock garden plant.

***-dioica*** (die-o-i′ ka) Common Pussytoes 4-10″/18″
Early Summer White Europe Zones 4-7

Plants send up crowded corymbs of light green flowers with pinkish tips that resemble the toes of your favorite pussycat. The spatulate basal leaves are about 1″ long and gray-green (some call them silver). The foliage becomes less gray-green as the season progresses and may be almost green by midsummer. The stoloniferous plants fill in rapidly and are occasionally used as an herbaceous lawn by more creative gardeners. If not used as a ground cover, they should be divided every 2 years. Plants are tolerant of poor soil but good drainage is necessary to reduce root rot.

Propagate by division in the spring or by seed. The seeds are small and should be mixed with fine sand to insure even distribution in the seed tray. Provide temperatures of about 72-75°F and maintain consistent soil moisture. Transfer seedlings to 60°F conditions for subsequent growth.

**Cultivars:**

'Devil's Tower' is about 4″ tall with silver leaves and pink flowers. Available from seed.

var. *hyperborea* (var. *tomentosa*) produces wide, densely hairy leaves.

var. *minima* ('Minima') is only about 1″ tall and forms a dense carpet. Best for containers or sunny rock gardens.

var. *minima rubra* is similar to the above but bears rosy red flowers.

'Nyewood' is a more compact and slower-growing form than the species. The cherry-red flowers cover the tight silver-gray leaves in late spring to early summer. About 3″ tall.

var. *rosea* ('Rosea') and var. *rubra* ('Rubra') have pink and rosy red flowers respectively and are 8-10″ tall.

**Related Species:**

*A. plantaginifolia*, ladies' tobacco, is an interesting if not dramatic native species. The basal rather smooth leaves have three to seven conspicuous veins, resembling those of plantain. From this basal rosette arise the light tan tight flower heads on 8-12″ tall stems, which slowly form a colony of gray-green foliage. Useful in zones 3 to 7.

*A. rosea* (*A. dioica* 'Rosea'), rose pussytoes, is the most common offering and produces rose-pink flowers on 8″ tall plants. The leaves are a little thinner than those of *A. dioica*. The fluffy rose-pink flowers rise well above the permanently gray-green foliage in late spring and early summer. Native to the mountains of western North America.

*A. rupicola* is native to the northeastern United States and forms 2-3″ tall loose mats of gray-green foliage which turn beet red in the fall.

***Anthemis*** (an' them-is) Golden Marguerite Asteraceae

Of the 80 species in the genus, only a few are worth growing and fewer yet are easily available in the United States. All have strongly scented, alternately arranged foliage that is divided 2-3 times. Flowers of some species such as *A. punctata* are white, and many hybrids also sport white ray flowers. However most of the species of anthemis have yellow or orange flowers borne singly on long stems. All need full sun and well-drained soils for best results. Most tolerate relatively poor soils and, in fact, become too leggy if fertilized heavily. The genus is most suitable for northern climates and while *A. tinctoria* prospers during spring and early summer in southern gardens, it usually collapses into a messy heap making it rather useless south of zone 7.

Propagation is easy by division and is necessary within 2-3 years for all species listed. Seeds germinate readily and are available for some cultivars of *A. tinctoria.*

Quick Reference to Anthemis Species

| | Height (in.) | Foliage color | Flower color |
|---|---|---|---|
| *A. punctata subsp. cupaniana* | 6-9 | Gray-green | White |
| *A. marschalliana* | 12-18 | Silver-green | Yellow |
| *A. tinctoria* | 24-36 | Green | Yellow |

***-punctata*** (punk-tah' ta) Sicilian Chamomile 8-12"/36"
Early Summer White Italy Zones 5-7

The species is handsome enough but the only plant offered is subspecies *cupaniana*. Scientists have been battling over this plant for a good while but for now, this is its taxonomic slot. Plants form sprawling gray-green mats that remind me of lacy artemisia and provide wonderful contrasts to other plants in the garden. They are most useful as edging or placed strategically at the front of the border or as an integral part of the rock garden.

The 1-2" diameter white daisies consist of 20-25 rays around yellow centers and are borne on 10-12" stems. The flowers are nothing to write home about but the contrast with the ferny, aromatic leaves is terrific. This subspecies remains relatively compact compared to others in the genus. Good drainage helps prevent plants dying during cool, rainy winters. If plants are not in flower and you are not sure if you are looking at *Anthemis* or *Artemisia*, simply smell the foliage. The characteristic artemisia scent is totally lacking.

***-marschalliana*** (mar-shal-ee-ah' na) Marschall's Chamomile 12-15"/24"
Early Summer Yellow Caucasus Zones 5-7

Plants are dressed in finely divided silvery foliage atop which are borne 1-2" diameter golden yellow daisy flowers. The pinnately segmented foliage has long hairs and is silky to the touch. If spent flowers are removed immediately, flowering will continue throughout the summer. This is a better species for the South than *A. tinctoria*. Excellent drainage is necessary and full sun is best but some afternoon shade is tolerated. subsp. *biebersteiniana*, named for Baron Friedrich August Marschall von Bieberstein, is even more silvery and more compact.

***-tinctoria*** (tink-to′ ree-a) Golden Marguerite 2-3′/2′
Summer Yellow Europe Zones 3-7

This is the most common *Anthemis* available and, with proper culture, is a magnificent plant in the northern United States and Canada. The 3″ long toothed leaves look a little like parsley and are somewhat downy beneath. The stem is not round but angled and the 1½″ diameter flowers are single, yellow and plentiful, even if rather short-lived.

If grown in rich soil, plants often grow 3′ tall and require staking. Do not fertilize heavily or the plants will be a mess. Cut back severely after flowering to encourage basal growth, and divide every 2 years. Sharon Illingworth, of Thunder Bay, Ontario, Canada takes cuttings from overwintered young shoots in early spring and roots them in vermiculite covered with plastic bags. Roots are formed within 14 days and good-sized plants for transplanting result by early June.

**Cultivars and Hybrids:**

*A. tinctoria* and *A. sancti-johannis* (a similar species with deep orange-yellow flowers) have hybridized freely and some of the listed cultivars may be hybrids between them.

'Alba' is very un-alba-ish, bearing pale cream-colored flowers over dark green finely divided leaves.

'E. C. Buxton' ('Buxton's Variety') is a superb 2-2½′ tall cultivar which bears off-white daisies with lemon yellow centers. Probably still the best of the *Anthemis* cultivars.

'Beauty of Grallagh' includes plants sometimes sold as 'Grallagh Gold' and 'Grallagh Glory'. Plants may bear bright gold to pale yellow to yellow-orange flowers atop 3′ tall stems.

'Kelwayi' ('Kelway's Variety') has been popular for many years. Plants bear a profusion of bright yellow flowers.

'Moonlight' bears handsome light yellow blossoms with a deeper yellow center.

'Sauce Hollandaise' bears pure white ray flowers surrounding yellow centers. Grows about 2′ tall. Cheryl Greenwood Kelly of Washington State University compares the flowers to "softly poached eggs; a feast for the eyes". I have seen a plant listed as 'Sauce Béarnaise' but can not find it sold anywhere. I will let the chefs sort this one out.

'Suzanna Mitchell' bears silver-green mounds of feathered foliage and light cream yellow ray flowers surrounding gold centers. Plants are about 2′ tall, cold hardy to zone 6.

'St. Johannes' has bright orange flowers. The three previous cultivars are more compact than the species but even more dwarf cultivars would still be most welcome.

'Tetworth' is a welcome addition to this plant group. A hybrid between *A. tinctoria* and *A. punctata* subsp. *cupaniana*, plants bear the gray foliage and small stature of the latter but the profusion of flowers of the former. The semi-double white daisies are produced in early summer on 10-18″ tall plants.
'Wargrave' bears masses of pale yellow daisy flowers and deep green ferny foliage.

**Related Species:**

*A. carpatica* (*A. cretica* subsp. *carpatica*) forms 6″ tall cushions of gray-green hairy foliage and white daisy flowers. 'Snow Carpet' occasionally appears in catalogs. It seems to be the same as the above but is a much better name. Hardy from zones 3-7.

*A. triumfetti* is similar to *A. tinctoria* but carries many handsome white flowers with yellow centers. Plants grow 18-24″ tall. Likely hardy only to zone 6 or 7.

## ***Anthericum*** (an-ther′ i-cum) St. Bernard's Lily Asphodelaceae

About 50 species of this little-used genus are known but two are cultivated with some success in North America. Plants emerge from rhizomes, and flowering occurs in late spring and summer. All species are native to southern Europe, Turkey or Africa. Not easy to locate but well worth a spot in the garden.

Quick Reference to Anthericum Species

| | Flower color | Flower stem branched | Height (in.) |
|---|---|---|---|
| *A. liliago* | White | No | 24-30 |
| *A. ramosum* | White | Yes | 15-24 |

**-*liliago*** (lil-ee′ a-go) St. Bernard's Lily 24-30″/12″
Summer White Southern Europe Zones 4-7

Native to alpine meadows, where it bears racemes of small, starry white flowers in the late spring or summer garden. The flowers are even more handsome up close where the upwardly curled styles and yellow stamens can be admired. Plants will grow 2-2½′ tall, but for best results, plant in groups of at least three. Full sun and well-drained soils are necessary. Plants do not perform well in the South.

**Cultivars:**

'Major' is taller (3′) than the species and bears flattened pure white flowers.

**-*ramosum*** (ray mo′ sum) 15-24″/12″
White Summer Southern Europe Zones 4-8

Native to lower valleys than *A. liliago*, this species is a little more heat tolerant and a better choice for hot summers. The gray-green upright foliage combines with many white flowers on a branched inflorescence. The flowers have yellow stamens and straight styles. Full sun and well-drained soils help make this plant successful in the garden.

***Aquilegia*** (ack-wi-lee′ gee-a) Columbine Ranunculaceae

A garden without columbine is simply unacceptable. The genus consists of approximately 65 species, and if all were available, they would probably all be outstanding garden plants. The flowers, which may be nodding or upright, consist of 5 petals with a short broad tube in front (petal tube) and backward-projecting spurs. The spurs were thought to resemble the claws of an eagle, the Latin translation being *aquila*, thus the genus name. They are useful determiners of a species, in that some are reasonably straight, in others, the ends are hooked like a fish hook, yet others are curved. The 5 sepals are often the same color as the petals but may be different in some species and hybrids. After flowering, the seed is held in erect long, narrow follicles that are ornamental for many weeks.

The leaves are held in groups of 3 leaflets (ternate), and in some species they are arranged in two groups of three (biternate). The leaves are always attached to the stem by long petioles. All columbines are spring or early summer flowering and perform best in a rich soil, light to moderate shade and with plenty of moisture. Many columbines are short lived, particularly if drainage is poor, and considered a bonus if they return after two or three years (although many reseed).

Species vary considerably, ranging from 3′ tall species to miniatures, and vary in color from white to blue and purple to pink. In fact, for those gardeners who can't control their columbine habit, there is even a green-flowered species, *A. viridiflora*, which no one will like but you. The white-flowered *A. fragrans* is even sweetly fragrant. Several columbines reseed freely, particularly *A. canadensis* and *A. vulgaris*. Natural hybridization occurs among species, so they should be planted in separate areas of the garden if one does not want illegitimate seedlings among the parents. In general, the hybrids do not come true from seed, however, many of the chance offspring that do result are handsome in their own right and often quite vigorous. Many gardeners, myself included, feel that the hybrids are not nearly as stately as many of the species; however, they do satisfy the needs of the "bigger is better" crowd.

A huge amount of confusion still exists as to what cultivar and hybrid belong under what species. A trial of 96 columbines in 2003 by the Royal Horticultural Society found that nearly one-third were incorrectly labeled. Many of the cultivars and series are raised by one company and then introduced, often under different names, by one or several other companies over a short period. In our studies at the Gardens at UGA, we have seen the same problems, where one series is essentially the same as another, but with a quite different name. As a gardener, I really do not fret about it; as a researcher, it rots my socks. However, I have listed cultivars and hybrids to the best of my ability; someday DNA profiling will sort it out.

Nearly all the hybrids, cultivars and species are grown from seed. Propagation from seed is not difficult, however most respond to a cold treatment. Sow the seed in a well-drained medium, place in the cold (a refrigerator will do) for about 6 weeks. Many of the named cultivars of the hybrids as well as species may be purchased from seed.

Quick Reference to Aquilegia Species

| | Flower Color (sepals/petals) | Spurs straight (S) hooked (H) curved (C) | Spur length (in.) | Flower nodding (N) upright (U) |
|---|---|---|---|---|
| *A. alpina* | Blue/blue (white) | C | ¾-1 | N |
| *A. caerulea* | Blue/white | S | 1-2 | U |
| *A. canadensis* | Yellow/red | C | ½-1 | N |
| *A. chrysantha* | Yellow/pale yellow | H | 2-2½ | U |
| *A. flabellata* | White/white | C,H | ¾-1 | N |
| *A.* x *hybrida* | Various | S | 2-6 | U |
| *A. longissima* | Yellow/pale yellow | S | 4-6 | U |
| *A. vulgaris* | Blue/blue | H | ½-¾ | N |

***-alpina*** (al-pine′ a) Alpine Columbine 1-3′/2′
Spring Blue Switzerland Zones 3-8

This species belies its name as some of the most vigorous and stately plants in the Armitage garden have been *A. alpina*. Most columbines will be a little taller in the South compared with the same plants in the North and this one is usually only 1-1½′ in northern areas but is 2½-3′ in the South. The gray green foliage is deeply divided into linear lobes. The basal leaves are biternate and the stem is hairy, particularly near the top. The abundant nodding flowers have short curved or slightly hooked spurs, flared 2″ wide sepals, and are usually blue throughout, although the petal tube is occasionally white. This is, without question, one of the finest classic columbines available for the garden. Plants often reseed, providing years of enjoyment.

Propagation from seed is easy and although a cold treatment is beneficial, it is not necessary.

**Cultivars:**

var. *alba* is a white form whose flowers contrast well with the dark green foliage. It grows a little shorter than the species.

'Atroviolacea' bears purple flowers.

'Blue Spurs' is taller and has longer spurs than the species.

var. *superba* is larger than the species but otherwise similar.

***-caerulea*** (ce-ru′ lee-a) Rocky Mountain Columbine 1-2′/2′
Spring Blue/White Rocky Mountains Zones 3-8

This long-spurred blue and white-flowered species really isn't much different than many of the hybrids of the same color but to encounter a stand of these flowers in the spring mountain meadows is close to a religious experience. The state flower of Colorado bears large (2-3″ across) upright facing flowers and has been an important

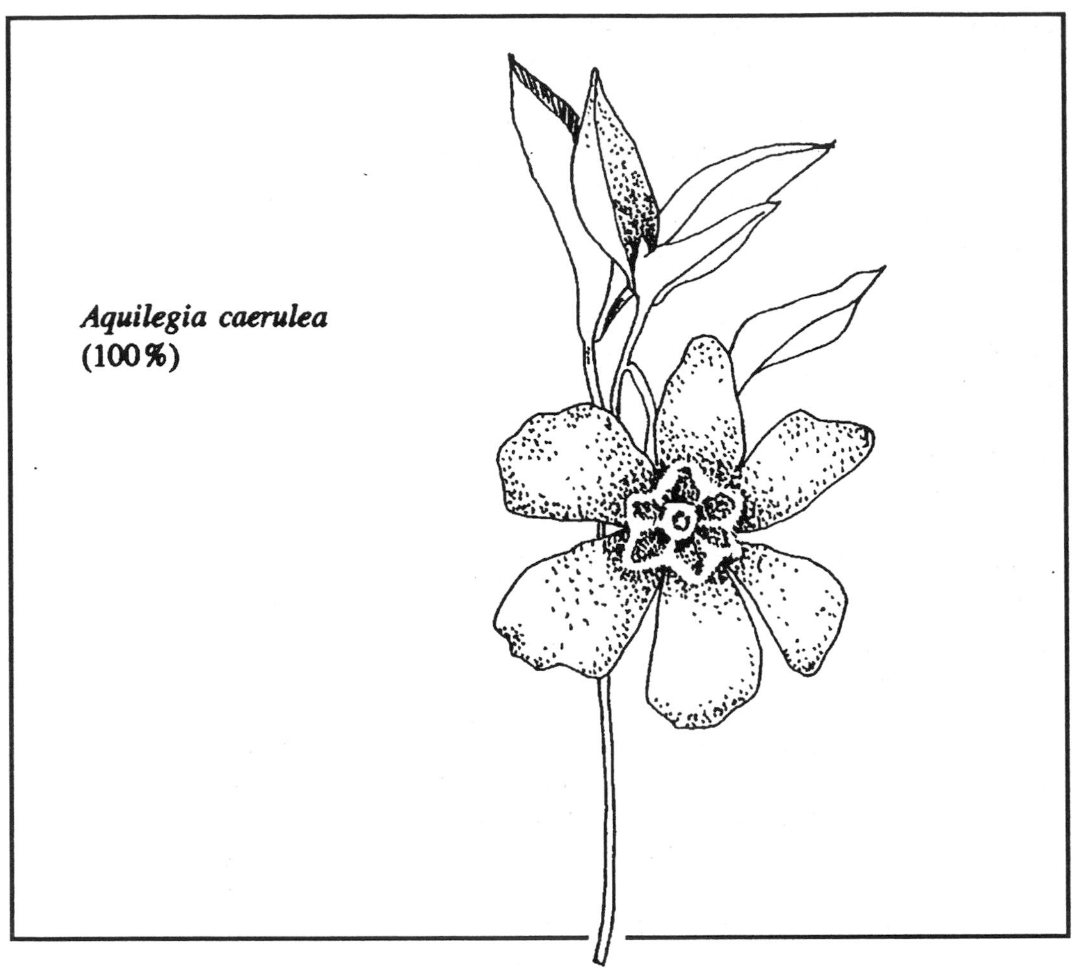

*Aquilegia caerulea*
(100%)

parent in the development of long-spurred hybrids. The spurs are straight or outward curving and are often tipped with green. Although not as vigorous as many of the other species or hybrids, it is longer lasting, 4-5 years in the garden not being uncommon. Propagation is similar to *A. alpina*.

**Cultivars:**

Some catalogs provide an impressive list of cultivars but most belong with the hybrids, of which *A. caerulea* is only one of the parents.

'Mrs. Nicholls' has 3″ wide Cambridge blue outer petals and whitish blue inner petals. It is an old cultivar and, unfortunately, difficult to find.

var. *ochroleuca* (syn. 'Albiflora') has creamy white flowers but is otherwise similar to the species.

'Red Hobbit' is an *A. caerulea* hybrid having been selected from 'Crimson Star'. Rose-red flowers are produced on a compact 12-15″ tall plant.

'Rose Queen' produces large long-spurred rose and white flowers.

***-canadensis*** (kan-a-den′ sis) Canadian Columbine 2-3′/1′
Early Spring Yellow/Red Eastern United States, Canada Zones 3-8

This is one of my all-time favorite spring-flowering plants. To be sure, they are not as spectacular as many of the hybrids but have a certain grace and elegance that puts them in a class of their own. People in North Carolina certainly appreciated it when they named it the North Carolina Wildflower of the Year in 1987. Native to much of eastern North America, they are found in moist, shady areas. Plants look best in clumps of three or more and reseed to double the area within 2-3 years. The 1½″ long nodding flowers appear in early spring and remain in bloom for approximately 6 weeks. The short spurs are slightly curved but do not have the obvious hook seen in *A. vulgaris* or *A. flabellata.* In my garden, plants range from light pink/yellow to blood red/yellow. In climates with cooler nights the sepals are decidedly redder. Plants have somewhat evergreen foliage in southern climes and new growth begins as soon as temperatures rise above 40°F. Due to its vigor, this is one of the few columbines that can be placed at the back of the bed or used to hide a distracting object

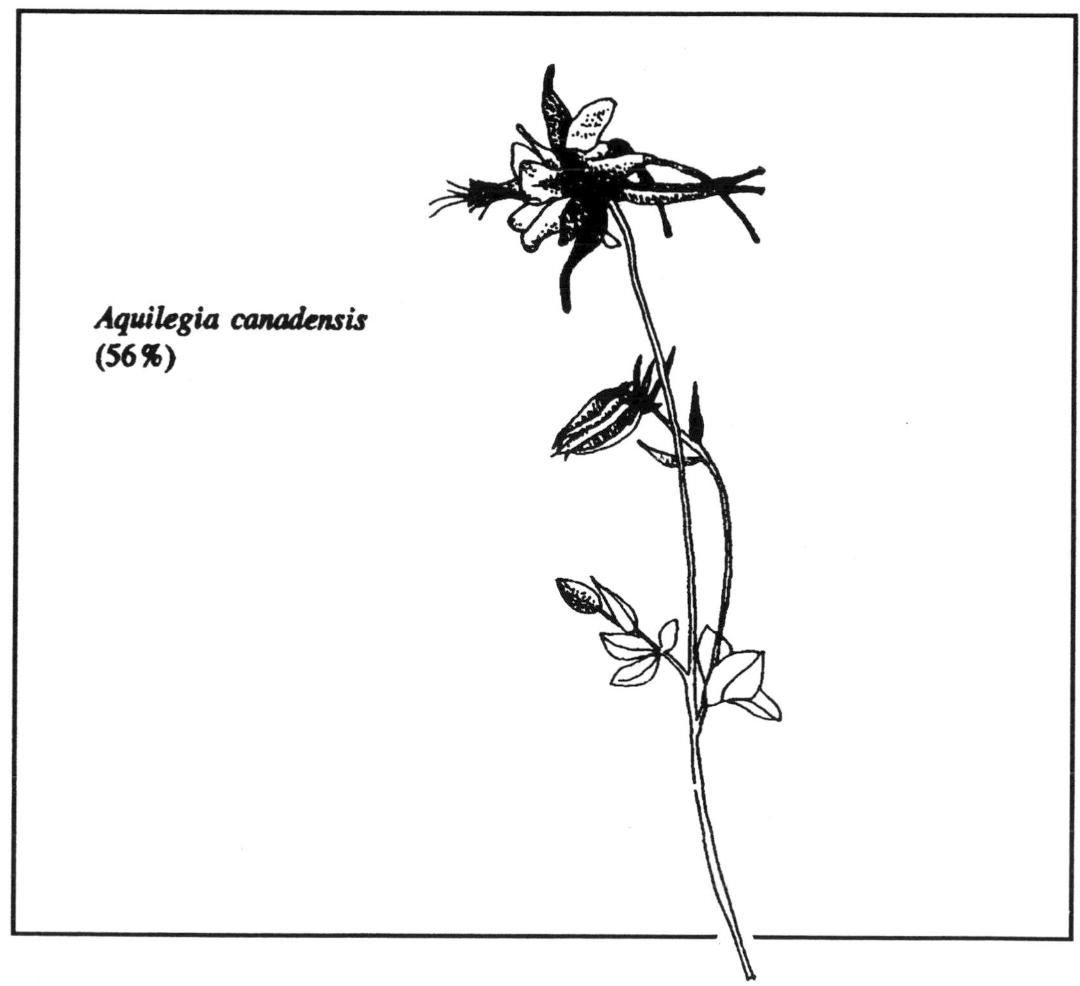

***Aquilegia canadensis***
**(56%)**

such as an electrical box or fire hydrant (although my dog Hannah was not fooled and learned the meaning of respect).

This species also shows a relative disdain for that voracious enemy of columbine—the leaf miner! Based on observations over the years, there is little doubt that when grown side by side, *A. canadensis* is less susceptible to leaf miner damage than many other species and certainly much more so than the hybrids. Leaf miners will mine this species also and eventually cause significant disfiguration, but not as rapidly as with others.

Propagation by seed is easy. Do not be surprised to find plants emerging quite a distance from the initial planting. If fresh seeds are needed, wait until the seeds loosen and turn jet black. One of the favorite projects in my perennials class at Georgia is to place each student beside a plant in my garden just after the seeds have ripened in their cozy follicles. The assignment is to gather the seeds and fling them around the garden, leaving a legacy for the student and increasing my harvest for next spring. Everyone gets a grade of A; no worries about grade inflation here. Plants flower the second year from seed. Thinning the seedlings by transplanting young plants rejuvenates the clump as well as increases numbers.

**Cultivars:**

'Corbett' was selected by Richard Simon of Bluemont Nursery in Monkton, Maryland. This happens to be near another quaint town called Corbett, Maryland, a town in which the Clemens family lived. In the late 1960s, two young brothers, Andrew and Larry Clemens, went walking in the woods near their house, found some short yellow columbine plants, and brought them home. Their mother Shirley eventually shared some seed with their neighbor, Richard Simon, who introduced it under the town name approximately 25 years later. It is one of the great stories of American gardening, reaffirming the axiom "If you want to save a plant, share it with others." Plants grow 8-10″ tall and bear pale yellow flowers. It is not as vigorous as the species and does better in areas of cooler nights. I still love it.

'Little Lanterns' is a dwarf form of the species, mirroring flower color, foliage and vigor, except that plants are no more than a foot tall. This is very similar to, or the same as, 'Canyon Vistas'. I cannot tell the difference.

**-*chrysantha*** (kris-anth′ a) Golden Columbine, Texas Columbine 2-4′/1′
Spring Yellow New Mexico, Arizona Zones 4-8

The flower size of Texas columbine is the antithesis of those of Canadian columbine, figures, eh? Although not possessing flashy colors, it is probably one of the most spectacular columbines when in flower, particularly when planted against a blue-flowered background. My students pointed out that my plants would probably be a little easier to see if they were not planted in the middle of late yellow daffodils. I have to find that darn color wheel. The flowers are 2-3″ across and the petals are a deeper yellow than the sepals. The 3″ long spurs spread away from the flower. This is a tall, loose grower that has been used as one of the parents of the long-spurred hybrids. If provided with sufficient moisture, no staking should be necessary.

**Cultivars:**

'Alba-plena' has very pale yellow (almost white) flowers that are occasionally tinged with pink and about 1¾″ across.

'Denver Gold' is likely the same as var. *hinckleyana,* but has a better name. A 2001 Plant Select® winner.

var. *hinckleyana*, Hinckley's columbine, is native to Texas and is more compact than the species. Seems to be more persistent.

var. *jaeschkanii* and *nana* are dwarf varieties (1½′ tall), the former bearing yellow flowers and red spurs while the latter is the same color as the species.

'Silver Queen' has 3″ diameter white flowers.

'Yellow Queen' bears 2-3″ wide lemon-yellow flowers. This is a great plant, and looks even better when combined with blue or gray-foliaged plants. In the 2003 trials of the Royal Horticultural Society, this cultivar was presented the Award of Garden Merit.

***-flabellata*** (flay-bel-lah′ ta) — Fan Columbine — 8-18″/1′
Spring — Blue — Japan — Zones 3-9

The leaves are unique in that they are thicker and bluer than most species and the fan-shaped, round leaf segments often overlap. The overlapping leaf segments and the bluish tinge to the leaves make this one of the easiest species for my students to identify and separate from the other dozen columbines I throw at them. Plants have been described as "squat or short and fat", however, the term compact is kinder and more accurate. It is an excellent plant for the front of the garden or the rockery. The species bears lilac to blue flowers and the spurs are curved to hooked. The terminal flower opens first followed by those in the lower axils.

Propagate from seed.

**Cultivars:**

'Alba' is the most common form offered by nurseries. The creamy white nodding flowers are often tinged pink.

var. *pumila* is the dwarf form of the species. var. *pumila* forma *alba*, ('Nana Alba', 'White Angel') has white flowers. Expect to see these sold as 'Dwarf' or 'Dwarf White', or whatever creative terms are most marketable to garden centers.

Cameo series consists of short compact forms, all of which do well in the shaded garden. The best are blue-white and pink-white. 'Cameo White' does not appear to be as vigorous.

Fantasy series is among the most dwarf of the columbines offered. Similar to Cameo but even shorter, the series consists of numerous colors. Plants are excellent for protected areas, but not as good where other plants may overrun them.

'Kurilensis' (var. *pumila* 'Kurilensis') is only 4″ tall with blue, or blue and white flowers.

'Mini-Star' is a dwarf 6-8″ tall cultivar with blue sepals and white petals. One of the best selections for the rock garden.

var. *nana* is similar in habit and flower to the above cultivar. They appear to be different names for the same thing.

Spring Magic series is useful for the front of the garden bed and for containers. They are only a foot tall and are available in many colors.

- x ***hybrida*** (hy-brid′ a) Hybrid Columbine 18″-3′/1′
Spring Various Hybrids Zones 3-9

The hybrids are particularly popular and with good reason. The flowers are large, upright, and in a wide range of colors. There are two generally accepted divisions in this group, long-spurred and short-spurred hybrids. Crosses involving *A. canadensis*, *A. chrysantha*, *A. caerulea*, and *A. formosa* became known as the long-spurred hybrids and are most popular.

The recent upsurge in passion for hybrid columbines began with the McKana hybrids, an All-America bronze medal winner in 1955, which brought large flowers and pastel shades to the gardener. McKana hybrids superseded 'Mrs. Scott Elliott', another excellent strain. The breeding of hybrids continues at a furious pace and many excellent cultivars are available today.

**Cultivars:**

'Biedermeier' is a 9-12″ compact blue and white cultivar, but other colors are also available in the mix. Often referred to as nosegay columbine. These contain a good deal of *A. vulgaris* parentage.

'Dragonfly' consists of a mix of colors on 18-24″ tall plants.

'Fairyland Mix' is a group of dwarf plants with short-spurred upright-facing flowers in various colors.

'Firecracker' is an exuberant 3′ tall plant with dozens of flowers in explosive colors, mostly in rose and canary yellow with long yellow stamens. An outstanding plant in the Gardens at UGA in 2005.

Fairytale series is a series of 2′ tall plants, available in various colors such as 'Fairytale Violet', 'Fairytale Yellow', etc.

'Kristall' ('White Star', 'Kristal Star') grows 2½-3′ tall with large white flowers and long straight spurs. A good deal of *A. caerulea* in the parentage.

McKana hybrids are a series of columbines that have stayed the test of time. Large long-spurred flowers, which occur in many colors, are borne over 18-24″ tall plants.

Musik series is almost as good as the Song Birds. They are available in many colors although yellow is the best. They are free flowering and relatively compact.

Origami series consists of numerous colors (blue/white, rose/white, etc.) on 2½′ tall plants. These are the same as plants sold under the Butterfly series. 'Origami Rose and White' and 'Origami Yellow' earned the RHS Award of Garden Merit in 2003. These contain a good deal of *A. caerulea* in their parentage.

Song Bird series is the work of the late Charles Weddle, one of this country's finest plant breeders. The plants are 2-3′ tall and come in vibrant colors which are truly impressive. Some of those available include 'Blue Bird', light blue and white; 'Blue Jay', deep blue and white; 'Cardinal', rich violet and white; 'Chaffinch' (rose pink and white), 'Dove', nodding small blue and white flowers; 'Nightingale', lavender

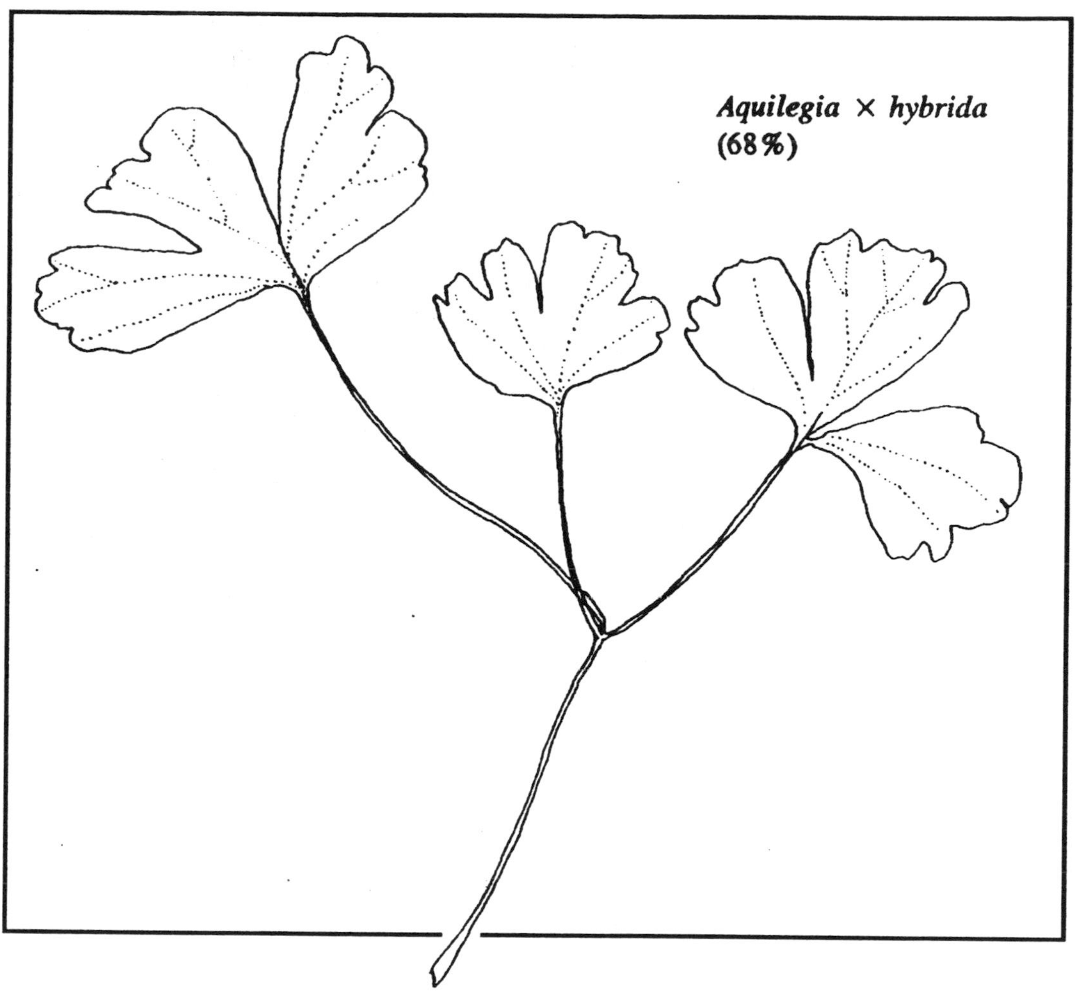
*Aquilegia* × *hybrida* (68%)

and white; 'Robin', pale pink and white. 'Chaffinch' and 'Dove' were also Award of Garden Merit winners in 2003. The Songbird series is still popular but is being replaced by others such as the Spring Magic and Origami series.

'Spring Song' consists of 3′ tall plants with spurs up to 3″ long. The flowers are available in mixed colors and some are nearly double.

Star series consists of 2-2½′ tall plants in various colors. 'Blue Star' and 'Crimson Star' (crimson sepals and white petals) are the most common. 'Maxistar' is yellow and at least 3′ tall, and may be a cultivar of *A. longissima*. All others have a good deal of *A. caerulea* in the parentage.

State series is also sold as Swan series but at least in America, state names will sell more plants than swans any day. Some are listed as cultivars of *A. flabellata*, others as *A.* x *hybrida*. Many state swans are out there, including (but not inclusive) 'Alaska' ('Swan White'), 'Colorado' ('Swan Violet and White'), 'Florida' ('Swan Yellow'), 'Georgia' ('Swan Red and White'), 'Kansas' ('Swan Red and Yellow'),

'Louisiana' ('Swan Burgundy and White'), 'Montana' ('Swan Rose and White') 'Vermont' and 'Virginia' ('Swan Blue and White'). In a large columbine trial by the Royal Horticultural Society in 2003, 'Alaska', 'Florida' and 'Georgia' earned the Award of Garden Merit.

'Windswept' has short-spurred deep blue flowers on a 12-15″ tall plant.

Winky series consists of tall plants (2-3′) in various colors. Red/white, purple/white and even 'Tiddlywinks' (mix) are part of this group.

Many of the older long-spurred hybrids were crossed with *A. vulgaris* to yield the short-spurred hybrids. These are more popular in Europe than in the United States and are smaller in stature and bear smaller flowers.

Some hybrids are available from seed but self-sown seed will not necessarily resemble the parent. Leaf miner can be a serious pest and is more disruptive to the hybrids than to many of the species. If leaf miner damage makes you nauseous, the easiest control is to simply cut the plants down to the ground after flowering and destroy the leaves. New growth will soon appear at which time the life cycle of the miners will have been completed. An all-purpose insecticide may be applied in early spring as a preventative measure but is seldom effective once the damage is evident.

***-longissima*** (long-gis′ si-ma) — Longspur Columbine — 2-3′/2′
Early Summer — Yellow — Southern United States — Zones 4-8

The obvious attributes of this species are the very long (4″) slender spurs on pale yellow flowers. A grouping of 5-6 plants makes an impressive display. Unfortunately, though vigorous, it is a short-lived perennial seldom persisting for more than 2 years.

**Cultivars:**

'Longissima Hybrids' resulted from crosses among some of the long-spurred hybrids and *A. longissima* and contains different colors.

***-vulgaris*** (vul-gah′ ris) — Granny's Bonnet — 1-2′/1′
Spring, Early Summer — Blue — Europe — Zones 3-8

So much natural interbreeding among *A. vulgaris* and other species has occurred that it is becoming more and more difficult to find the true *A. vulgaris*. There is a great deal of variability but in general the flowers are blue or violet, with short incurved spurs which end in small knobs. It does not possess the classic statuesque form of *A. alpina*, the sparkle of *A. canadensis*, or the airiness of *A. chrysantha*. However, it is a durable performer and has persisted well in gardens throughout the country, and has good heat tolerance, as shown by its performance in the State Botanical Garden of Georgia. Although I may be in the minority, I believe that some of the ugliest flowers in the plant kingdom are the doubles and near triple cultivars of *A. vulgaris*.

**Cultivars:**

'Adelaide Addison' bears double purple and white flowers. For some reason, this is sometimes listed as 'Nora's Sister'.

'Altrosa' produces rose-pink nodding flowers on 2-2½′ tall stems.

var. *alba* is a good single white-flowered form.

Barlow series started out with 'Nora Barlow', a most interesting and unusual cultivar. Flowers are fully double and look more like small dahlias than columbines. The sepals are reddish pink with white margins and plants grow 2-2½′ tall. Nora was the granddaughter of Charles Darwin, and I can't help but thinking of tortoises when I look at Nora. Association comes in strange forms. Nora has been around for decades but recent additions of 'Blue Barlow', 'Rose Barlow' and 'Black Barlow now fill out the series.

'Cap de Rossiter' has wonderful small pink and white dahlia-like flowers and even though I am not keen on double columbines, this one quickly became a favorite in the Armitage gardens. Plants grow 2-3′ tall and flowers are persistent.

'Clematiflora', stormy columbine, bear lovely light pink to burgundy spurless flowers. The flat, nodding flowers are carried on 2′ tall branching stems. These are often sold under the Clementine series, and may appear under names like 'Clemantine Blue', 'Clementine Purple' and 'Clementine Red'.

'Dorothy Rose' has pendulous "hose in hose" dark pink flowers (looks like one flower is in another). Plants are about 2′ tall.

'Double Rubies' ('Burgundy Double') produces deep maroon double flowers on 3′ tall plants. Flowers are very persistent. I have seen a very similar plant listed as 'Ruby Port'.

'Grandmother's Garden' is simply a mix of *A. vulgaris* seedlings, each plant a different color, all plants 18-24″ tall.

'Heidi' bears handsome light pink nodding flowers on 18-24″ tall stems.

'Lime Frost' is a yellow and green variegated form with few flowers. Similar plants may be found under 'Variegata' or 'Woodside Gold'.

'Lime Sorbet' produces interesting, if you like them, double, spurless, off-white flowers. How many ways can we mess up this beautiful plant?

'Mellow Yellow' has golden yellow foliage with white or pale blue flowers in the spring. Plants are about 20″ tall.

'Miss Jekyll' produces nodding white flowers on 2′ tall plants.

'Nivea' has single white flowers and pale gray foliage. It is vigorous, often attaining 3′ in height. Plants may be seen as var. *nivea* and are also referred to as Munstead white columbine, in reference to Gertrude Jekyll's fondness for the plant.

'Raspberry Tart' is yet another gruesome deformed columbine offering, with raspberry red double flowers.

'Ruby Port' is a tall double-flowered form with ruby flowers. Great name, great plant, similar to 'Double Rubies'.

var. *stellata* is the correct name for most of the spurless forms of columbine. Once classified as 'Clematiflora' or *A. vulgaris* var. *clematiflora*, all stand about 2½′ tall and have double flowers with minute or no spurs. 'Pink Spurless', 'Firewheel', 'Green Apples' and 'Iceberg' are color variants in this variety. All are interesting, but none is beautiful.

'Trevor Bath', introduced by Canyon Creek Nursery in Oroville, California, carries rosy, short-spurred semi-double flowers with white petals and rose-red sepals.

'Variegata' (*A. vervaeneana* 'Variegata') or 'Woodside Variegated' has foliage marbled with yellow or gold. The foliage is reasonably handsome in the spring but tends to fade as temperatures rise. Flowers are usually blue but may be white or purple.

'Woodside Gold' produces less marbled and more golden foliage than 'Woodside Variegated'.

'William Guinness' ('Magpie'), as would be expected, bears flowers the color of that fine stout. Double flowers are produced over the 2-3′ tall plants in late spring.

**Related Species:**

Hybrids are reasonably easy to find in today's gardening market but there are dozens of lesser-known species that are fun to try. The only thing stopping gardeners is their availability. Here are few related species that, with a little hunting, may end up in your garden one of these days.

*A. atrata* is a handsome 18-30″ tall columbine with 1-2″ wide, nodding purple-violet flowers. This is similar to another dark-flowered form, *A. nigrescens*. Hardy to about zone 4.

*A. bertolonii*, alpine rock columbine, is only 4-9″ tall and bears rich blue-violet flowers. This is a wonderful dwarf columbine for the front of the border or rock garden.

*A. buergeriana* produces nodding flowers of dull yellow petals and purple sepals on one- to two-foot tall plants. The straight short spurs are dull purple. 'Calimero' is a compact form with pendulous purple and cream yellow flowers.

*A. einseleana* is another alpine species with nodding blue-violet flowers and short (½″) straight spurs. Plants are smaller than *A. alpina* and usually grow 9-12″ tall.

*A. formosa*, formosa columbine, is native to the western United States and similar to *A. canadensis*. Plants are taller and have sepals longer than the spurs. Even grown side by side, this species and *A. canadensis* are difficult to separate. The var. *truncata* is sometimes offered as *A. eximia* and differs from the species in having much reduced petals. The formosa group does not perform as well as *A. canadensis* in Eastern gardens.

*A. glandulosa*, Siberian columbine, is almost identical to *A. flabellata*, having fan-like bluish foliage and nodding blue flowers. If one looks closely, the pistils of this species are pubescent while the pistils are smooth in the fan columbine. The spur is strongly hooked in this species while it is curved in *A. flabellata*. Var. *jucunda* has white petals and is similar to *A. flabellata* 'Alba'.

*A.* x *helenae* ('Helenae') is a hybrid between *A. caerulea* and *A. flabellata*. It has the blue and white flowers of *A. caerulea* and the short half-inch long spurs of *A. flabellata*.

*A.* 'Hensol Harebell' was always believed to be a hybrid between *A. alpina* and *A. vulgaris*; however, recent evidence suggests it may be a cultivar of *A. alpina*. Plants bear deep blue flowers that continue well into summer. The branched flower stems produce an open, airy effect. Plants persisted about 2 years in the Armitage garden, and then various unrecognizable offspring took over.

*A. laramiensis* is also native to the Rocky Mountains and bears small white flowers that barely surpass the foliage. Plants grow 6-9″ tall and are best for well-drained rock garden sites

*A. olympica* is native to southern Europe and sports blue and white flowers with incurved spurs. Plants stand about 2½′ tall. Hardy in zones 4-8.

*A. oxysepala* is closely related to *A. buergeriana*, and grows 2-3′ tall with interesting claret sepals and yellow petals. The spurs are strongly hooked. Native to Siberia, the plants have not enjoyed great success in the Armitage garden, but I have seen excellent plants in the Northeast and Midwest.

*A. pyrenaica*, native to the Pyrenees in northern Spain, bears nodding violet blue flowers with straight or slightly curved spurs. They are suitable for small areas or rock gardens due to their 8-12″ height.

*A. viridiflora*, green columbine, has nodding bicolored flowers with chocolate petals and yellow green sepals over blue-green foliage. Growing less than one foot tall, it is excellent for the rock garden.

## ***Arabis*** (ar′ a-bis) Rock-cress Brassicaceae

Most of the approximately 120 species distributed over the northern hemisphere are alpine in habit. All produce basal rosettes then send up stems that produce racemes of rose, purple or white flowers. Species are difficult to separate unless one looks closely at the stem leaves and flowers. The cultivated species are effective for the front of the garden or rock walls and are all less than 12″ tall. For the most part, the leaves persist in the winter, and if snow cover is not heavy, the foliage looks good at that time.

*Arabis* is also well known to butterflies such as Mustard white, Sara orange-tip, Boisduval's Marble, Edward's Marble and California white butterfly, which all feed on rock cress.

Since the last edition was written, somebody snuck in a few taxonomic changes to the genus, but nothing too confusing. The most popular plant in gardens used to be known as *A. caucasica*, wall rock-cress, but it is now properly classified as *A. alpina* var. *caucasica*. Certainly, other species also have garden value. *A. blepharophylla* (native to California) has rose-purple flowers but is quite tender and needs winter protection in much of the country. A compact, white-flowering species with a large following in the United States is *A. ferdinandi-coburgii*. The species has gray-green foliage but only the variegated forms are easily available to the gardener. *A. procurrens* grows to 9″ tall, has entire evergreen leaves, and larger white flowers. *A. soyeri* is about 10″ high with white flowers. One of my favorites is *A.* x *sturii*, which is only 2-3″ tall with glossy leaves and relatively large white flowers.

The majority of species are cool climate plants and perform far better in the North than in the South. In hot weather, the centers tend to "melt out" and the stems become long and spindly. I have been successful with *A. procurrens*, *A. alpina* var. *caucasica* and *A.* x *sturii* in north Georgia, but none spread vigorously during the summer, and none persisted more than 2 years. All species should be planted in full sun in the North or afternoon shade (in the South), preferably in areas where drainage is excellent. Cut back after flowering if plants start to look a little dog-eared.

All are easily propagated by division, cuttings, or seed.

Quick Reference to Arabis Species

| | Height (in.) | Flower color | Stem leaves sessile |
|---|---|---|---|
| *A. alpina* var. *caucasica* | 8-15 | White | Yes |
| *A. blepherophylla* | 4-8 | Rose, pink | Yes |
| *A. ferdinandi-coburgii* | 4-6 | White | No |

**-*alpina*** (al-pine′ a) Mountain Rock-cress 8-15″/18″
Early Spring White Mediterranean Zones 4-7

The plant forms a loose mat and the hairy, succulent foliage is particularly effective climbing over rocks or cascading down walls. The numerous white flowers are held in a loose raceme in early spring. Plants should be cut back severely after flowering, or by midsummer branches will be nude except for the terminal leaves. The subsequent year's performance is also enhanced by late spring pruning. In the North, plants make a wonderful spring show and form large clumps that may need division every 2-3 years. In north Georgia, flowers are present by the end of February and persist until the end of April. Plant in the fall in the South for enjoyment the following spring (similar to a pansy) as plants tend to decline in the summer heat south of Zone 6.

**Cultivars:**

All plants listed are cultivars of var. *caucasica*, whose gray-green leaves and more compact habit help distinguish it from the species itself.

'Bakkely' is a compact (4-6″) plant with single white flowers.

'Corfe Castle', discovered at Corfe Castle in England, is a handsome 6-8″ tall plant with deep magenta flowers.

'Douler Angevine' has green leaves with a thick golden edge. The bright pink flowers contrast well with the leaves.

'Flore-pleno' is an excellent plant because the double white flowers are mostly sterile and little seed is produced. The lack of seed production results in more persistent flowers.

'Gillian Sharman' bears gold-edged leaves and white flowers. Handsome, but difficult to locate.

'Pink Pearl' has deep pink flowers on mat-forming plants.

'Red Sensation' produces rose-red flowers over silvery-green leaves.

'Snow Cap' is a large white-flowered cultivar more ornamental than the species.

'Snow Drop', 'Snow Flake' and 'Snow White' are all white, about 4-5 inches tall, and compact. I am not sure even the breeders could tell them apart, so don't fret if you cannot.

'Variegata' has yellow-white stripes on the leaves. It is an interesting cultivar but the leaf color detracts from the flowers and the plant is altogether too busy.

***-blepharophylla*** (ble-fa-ro-fil′ a) Fringed Rock-Cress 4-8″/12″
Early Spring Rose-purple California Zones 4-7

This tufted rock garden plant generally consists of rosettes of 1-3″ long entire to toothed leaves. The flower stems bear sessile, oblong leaves and terminate in short, dense racemes of carmine-red flowers. The petals are about ½″ long and the flowers are slightly fragrant.

**Cultivars:**
'Alba' bears white flowers.
'Spring Charm' is the best cultivar of this species, bearing fragrant rose-pink flowers on compact plants.

***-ferdinandi-coburgii*** (fer-di-nahn′ dye ko-burg′ eye) Alpine Rock-Cress 4-6″/10″
Early Spring White Bulgaria Zones 4-7

Named after King Ferdinand of Bulgaria, these plants provide carpets of white flowers over narrow-oblong leaves with long petioles. Like other members of the genus, plants require excellent drainage and cutting back in the summer. The species itself is seldom offered by nurseries, however, variegated forms are quite common. All bear white flowers.

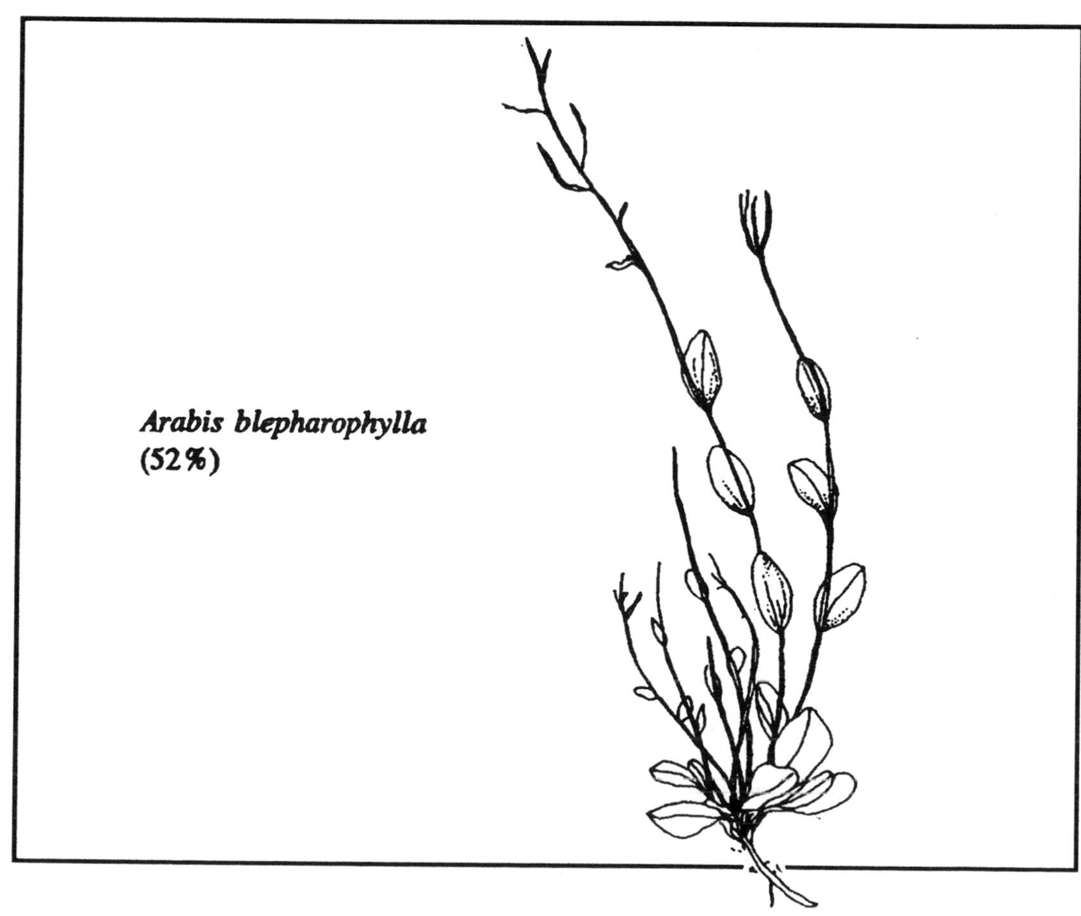

***Arabis blepharophylla***
**(52%)**

**Cultivars:**

'Limedrop' bears deep green leaves with a lime-green center. Plants grow 4″ tall.

'Old Gold' produces shiny green leaves variegated with gold. This is probably the most common cultivar offered, however, there is little difference between this and 'Aureo-Variegata'.

'Reversed' has mostly white leaves with green margins.

'Variegata' is the most available of the cultivars and bears handsome leaves splashed and edged with clean white. Debate continues as to whether this is a cultivar *of A. ferdinandi-coburgii* or *A. procurrens*.

**Related Species:**

*A.* x *arendsii* resulted from the natural hybridization of *A. aubrietoides* and *A. alpina* var. *caucasica* and includes a few excellent selections. 'Compinkie' has handsome pink flowers; 'La Fraicheur' bears deep rose-red flowers; 'Rosabella' produces rose-colored flowers that become paler as temperatures rise in the spring; 'Rubin' bears wine-colored flowers.

*A. procurrens* is a stoloniferous species similar to *A. ferdinandi-coburgii* but has shiny ovate leaves rather than narrow leaves. Plants appear to be more heat tolerant than other species. 'Glacier' has dark green leaves and white flowers. 'Variegata' is similar to plants of *A. ferdinandi-coburgii* 'Variegata' and may in fact be the same. Who cares, if rock-cress grows well in your garden, the variegated forms will look terrific and won't die because they aren't named correctly.

*A.* x *sturii* is one of my favorite rock garden plants. It has small (<2″ long) dark green lustrous leaves arranged in compact mounds. Plants produce many small (½″) clean white flowers in early spring. The clean leaves, the white flowers and the compact growth habit make this a wonderful species. 'Glacier' is similar and is a good choice if *A.* x *sturii* cannot be located.

## *Arachnoides* (a-rack-noi′ deez) Shield Fern Dryopteridaceae

The shield ferns are some of the most outstanding plants for the shaded garden, and have become more popular but are still not the easiest to find, and terribly underused. Those useful for American gardeners are native to China, Japan and Korea and are probably not hardy much north of zone 6. I have seen outstanding plantings of *A. standishii*, the upside-down fern, in the wonderful garden of Mr. Charles Cresson in Swarthmore, Pennsylvania. This fern forms thin, bright green, narrow fronds whose black sori are visible from above, hence the common name. A far more coarse relative is spiny leatherfern, *A. aristata*, whose glossy, dark green fronds are almost prickly to the touch.

The pearl of the genus, however, has to be *A. simplicior* 'Variegata', East India holly fern or variegated shield fern, which has finally found its way out of obscurity and is no longer the unknown gem it once was. In fact, it is probably the most easily obtained of the shield ferns. The leathery fronds are notable for the prominent yellowish bands on each side of the glossy-green midribs; the color does not fade in hot summers and the plant is evergreen to about 10°F. In the Armitage garden, plants ducked underground when temperatures fell to about 5°F, but emerged unscathed in early spring. Everyone stops to admire the clump and this handsome variegated species should be much more widely planted. Certainly, it is a winner for gardeners in zones 7-10, who have been desperate for some decent ferns for a long time. It may be marginally hardy in zone 6, with protection.

Plant in partial shade and provide lots of water, particularly in early spring. Variegated shield fern is more tolerant of drying out than the upside-down fern.

***Arisaema*** (a-ris-aye′ ma) Jack-in-the-Pulpit Araceae

Some of the wildest, weirdest, most handsome and therefore most highly sought-after plants are found in the genus. With over 150 species of mostly tuberous plants, there is something for everyone. *Arisaema* is widely distributed, occurring from Tanzania (7°S) to Mexico through eastern North America and all the way north to about 51°N latitude. Leaves are almost always palmately compound and generally only one or two mottled stems are produced from the tuber. The flowers consist of a bewildering array of spathes and spadices, which provide some of the most unusual architectural arrangement of flowers in the plant kingdom. *Arisaema* is also unique in its ability of individual plants to change gender. Plants of some species start out bearing male flowers only on the spadix and spontaneously change to female (and vice versa) the next year.

Plants are woodland in nature and perform best in cool, moist areas with plenty of organic matter. Nearly all species go dormant in the summer after flowering and fruiting is complete. Some of the most interesting are native to Korea and Japan, growing to 3′ in height (*A. angustatum*) and bearing distinctive large flowers.

A few years ago, it was difficult to find nurseries that offered more than one or two species, but today availability is not a problem. Jacks, along with other genera in this family, have become collectors' favorites as well as those who simply like plants from the untrodden path. If you search the Internet, not only will you find impressive lists of species and cultivars, but also entire websites devoted to the Araceae. Scary, but most of the people swapping Jack stories don't bite.

The downside is that as the demand continues, the difficulties of propagation still keep prices high for most species. Without doubt, this problem is being quickly resolved as modern propagation techniques make the tubers more available for the clamoring public.

Plant tubers approximately 3-4″ deep and allow to remain undisturbed unless propagation is necessary. Commercial propagation of *Arisaema* is nearly always by seed. If collecting seed, the seed coat contains germination inhibitors and must be removed (use gloves, as some people are quite allergic to the pulp). Plant the clean seed; expect a couple of years before plants are mature. In the garden, tubers can be lifted and separated. However, try to control yourself and don't disturb unless necessary.

Since the provenance of *Arisaema* is so diverse, it is not surprising that the tolerance to cold and heat would also be diverse. The International Aroid Society updates records annually concerning hardiness, based on locations and temperatures without snow cover.

Quick Guide to Arisaema Species

| | Spathe | Spadix | Height |
|---|---|---|---|
| *A. candidissimum* | Pale pink and white | Yellow-green | 15-18″ |
| *A. consanguineum* | Green, purple, white stripes | Green | 24-60″ |
| *A. dracontium* | Green | Green | 18-30″ |
| *A. ringens* | Striped green and white | Yellow-white | 10-20″ |
| *A. sikokianum* | Striped purple | White | 18-25″ |
| *A. taiwanense* | Purple | Purple | 15-30″ |
| *A. triphyllum* | Greenish, mottled purple | Green, brownish | 12-30″ |

**-*candidissimum*** (kan-di-dis′ si-mum) White Jack 15-18″/15″
Late Spring Pink and White Spathe Western China Zones 5-7

I first saw a group of these plants in the garden of Mrs. Helen Dillon in Dublin, Ireland and quickly became a convert to the white jack. The solitary leaf consists of 3 leaflets and generally emerges with or just after the flower. It is late to emerge (mid May in most areas) and is therefore less susceptible to late frosts. The loveliest part of the plant is the white spathe that is suffused with delicate pink. The spathe is only slightly hooded therefore the pink can be seen inside as well. The spadix is yellow-green and slightly fragrant. A pure white-flowered form is also occasionally offered.

This is one of the easiest species to find, but its popularity also results in sold-out stocks at the nursery. I have since planted this in the Armitage garden and seen it used as a summer plant in the garden of Wayne Winterrowd and Joe Eck in southern Vermont. In the North, plants are overwintered in a cold greenhouse and brought out again for summer bloom. A pure white-flowered form (without the pink) may occasionally be offered.

Plant in groups of a half dozen in a slightly shaded area rich in organic matter.

**-*consanguineum*** (con-san-gwin-ee′ um) Himalayan Cobra Lily, Palm Tree Jack 2-5′/2′
Spring Red China Zones 5-8

One of the most diverse species, plants under this name can be native to lowland areas all the way to elevations above 10,000′. Well-grown plants can easily attain 5′ in height, and with its impressive palm tree-like leaf, consisting of 10-12 leaflets, each with an extended tip, it is an impressive sight. Heck, who even needs a flower? The green to purple inflorescences are often striped white and the tip of the pulpit has been teased out into a long, thin piece of spaghetti.

I have often read how easy this plant is to grow, but not so in the Armitage garden. Perhaps the warm summer temperatures or lack of a long Himalayan winter are to blame, or perhaps I am buying the ones from the 10,000′ mountain range rather than those that originated in the lowlands. I have lost my fair share, and those that do survive grow about 2-3′ rather than the 5-6′ I see in Oregon gardens. Regardless, I keep trying.

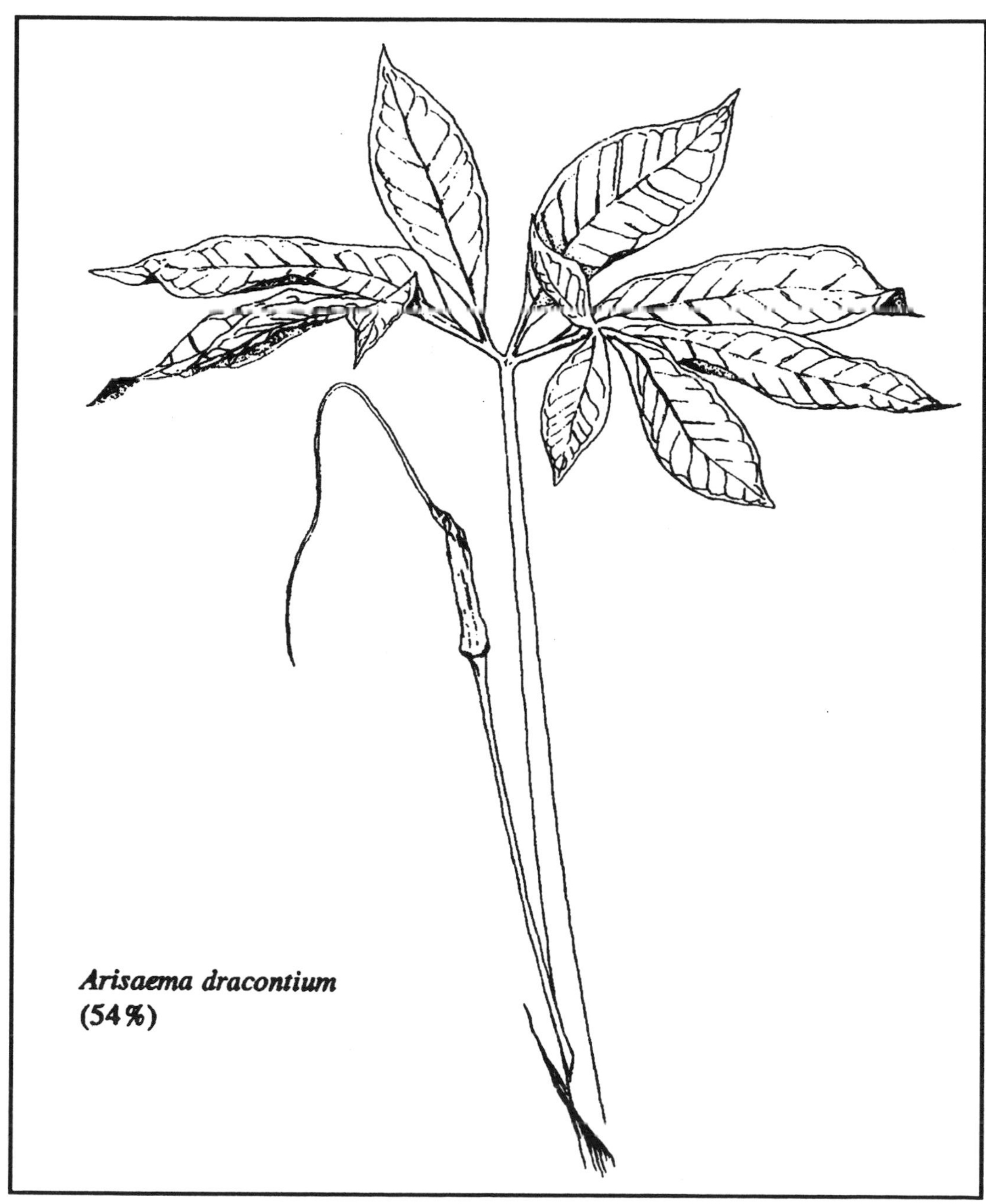

***Arisaema dracontium***
**(54%)**

***-dracontium*** (dra-kon′ tee-um) Green Dragon 18-30″/20″
Spring Green Eastern North America Zones 4-8

Extending as far north as Maine and south to northern Florida, green dragon is a frequent, if not common, woodland inhabitant. Although plants are distinctive, their complete green color also makes them easy to walk by without being noticed. However, those who stop a moment quickly enjoy this most interesting species. The single leaf consists of 7-15 oblong leaflets arranged in a horseshoe shape, underneath which the green spathe may be found. The narrow spathe is only about 2-3″ long but the spadix looks like cotton candy that has been pulled out to form a 10-12″ long string-like tail.

Plants arise from strong thick green stems and quickly rise to 3′ in height; flowers appear by late spring to early summer. They are best placed in a shady area where they can be viewed along a path or walkway. To be honest, plants are as interesting than they are handsome, and the oblong tubers are inexpensive and easy to locate, and what's the matter with interesting, anyway?

***-ringens*** (rin′ gens) Cobra Jack 10-20″/20″
Early Spring Striped Green and White Japan Zones 5-7

A most wonderful species, the tubers produce two leaves each composed of three leaflets and an incurved contorted spathe that looks like a striped helmet. The hood of the spathe is a deep chocolate color while the white to yellow spadix is almost entirely enclosed. Plants are robust and produce some of the largest spathes, relative to the overall size of the plant, in this genus. It is easy to find and grow the cobra jack, and if cold hardiness is not a problem, this is probably the jack I would start with.

Plants are best suited to groups of three or more and tolerate wetter conditions than other species. Partial shade and soils with sufficient organic matter are essential for best performance.

***-sikokianum*** (si-koke-ee′ aye-num) Gaudy Jack 18-25″/20″
Early Spring Striped Purple and White Japan Zones 5-7

I have grown nearly a dozen different jacks in the Armitage garden, but if I had to pick but one jack for my garden, it would come to a vote between this species and *A. ringens*, and this one would probably win. The two leaves consist of five leaflets in the lower, three in the upper and emerge about the same time as the flower. The beauty of this plant lies in the contrast of the purple spathe and the elegant white spadix. The spathe forms a funnel-shaped tube ending in a long narrow projection. Inside the spathe nests the lovely pestle-shaped spadix, easily visible in early spring. The only drawback to this plant, other than cost and availability, is that it emerges very early in the spring and has been clubbed to death by late frosts on more than one occasion. I use peat moss and baskets to cover the plants in the spring if a frost is forecast, but I have lost my share. The later emergence of other jacks strains one's patience but helps the wallet.

Plants with silver markings on the leaves are also being selected, for foliar interest even when plants are not in flower. I hesitate to give cultivar status ('Variegata'), however, if a variegated form is offered, this is what it is.

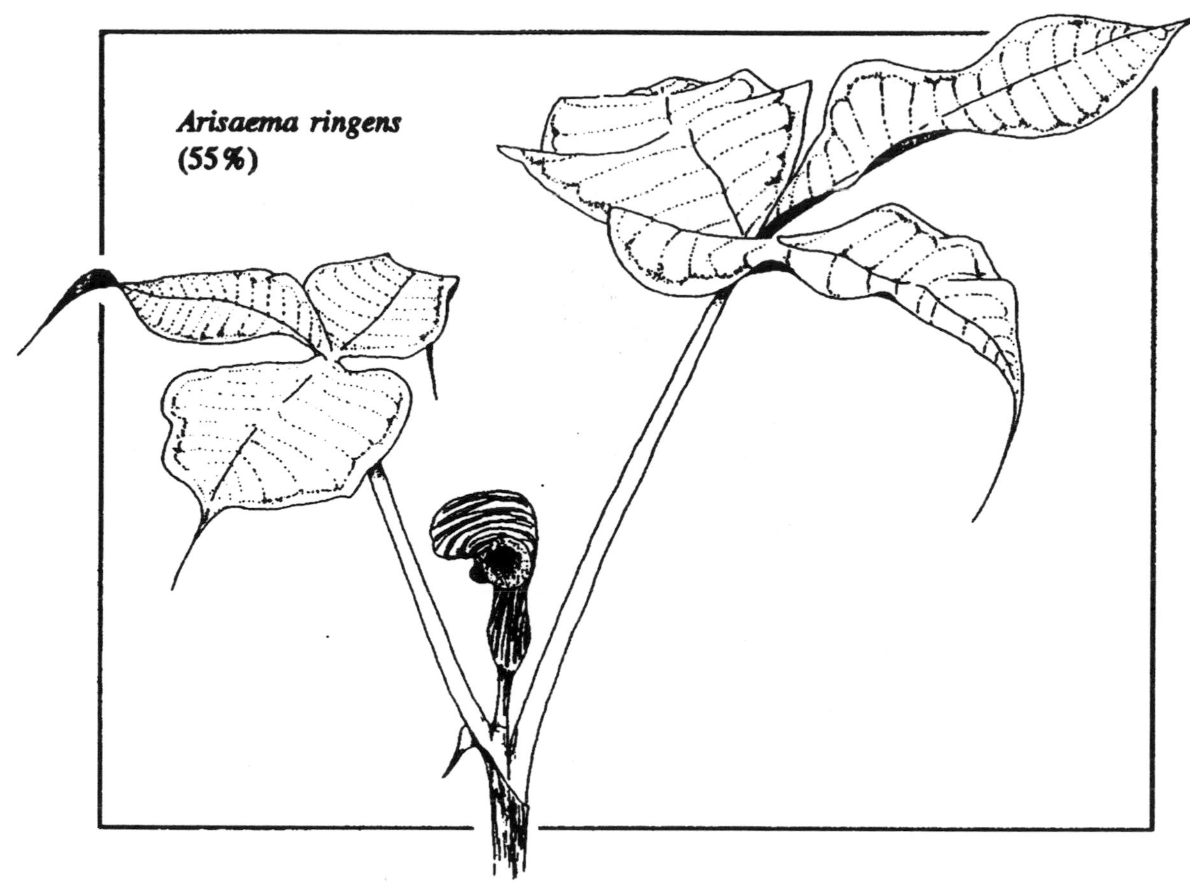


***-taiwanense*** (tie-wan-en′ se) Taiwan Jack 1½-2½′/2′
Spring Purple/Black Taiwan Zones 6-9

I love this plant because it is a doer in the garden. Plants emerge with a strong cinnamon-colored tip, giving way to a wonderfully light green stem mottled with purple. The leaf consists of a dozen or so thin leaflets, each with a short thread at the end. The large purple to almost black inflorescence is also bizarre, forming at the base of the stem, tossing out a long thread from its mouth, and persisting for weeks and weeks. Plants grow 2-2½′ tall but are worth the bending down to admire.

**Cultivars**:

'Silver Heron' is a silver-leafed form that I am lusting for. I have not tried it so don't know how really silver the leaves are, particularly in the heat of summer.

***-triphyllum*** (tri-fil′ lum) Jack-in-the-Pulpit 12-30″/25″
Spring Green, Mottled Purple Eastern North America Zones 4-8

By far the most common species in the genus, it is nevertheless a most satisfying plant for the woodland garden. Plants are found from southern Canada to Louisiana and Texas, therefore variability should not be surprising. And variable it is! I have

*Arisaema sikokianum* (46%)

seen plants a mere 12″ tall with 3-leaflet leaves, and giants that easily attain three feet in height and bear large 5-leaflet leaves. The color of the spathe also varies from deep purple to green with a few purple stripes. I am sure there is a taxonomist who could split out at least three botanical varieties from the populations commonly found in eastern North America.

The entire plant, including the tuber, contains numerous microscopic bundles of needle-like crystals of calcium oxalate. If one is crazy enough to bite into it, one bite will be enough. The crystals pierce the tender tissues of the mouth, tongue and throat.

These are not at all like the potato chip ads that bet you can't eat just one! The best soothers are cool liquids and antihistamines. Despite these irritants, the dormant tubers were cooked by native Indians to produce a fine flour, similar to arrowroot. They were peeled, mashed and washed through sieves to obtain a fine starch solution that was dried, boiled or roasted, then ground to flour. The tubers were known as Indian turnip and that common name still is used today.

Plants bear two leaves and emerge from early spring to early summer. The spathe may be striped with green or purple or possess a handsome deep purple hue. The green to brown spadix is generally exserted (sticks out) from the spathe. New tubers are formed in abundance and a source of small dormant tubers is not difficult to locate. Plant in groups of a dozen or more.

**Related Species:**

From a few plants a few years ago, today's specialty catalogs offer dozens of species for the jackite. Here a few others I have tried, but many more are out there.

*A. costatum*, Chinese cobra lily, produces one of the dark purple flowers in the group. The single 3-parted leaf is atop a 3-4′ tall stem. The long-tailed spathe has handsome white striations.

*A. flavum*, yellow jack, has relatively small flowers that are purple on the inside and somewhat yellow on the outside. Some catalogs go overboard with the golden yellow nonsense; they are not golden and not particularly vigorous. Zone 4-7.

*A. fargesii* has been a terrific plant, coming back for many years. It is one of the trifoliate jacks, each large leaf consisting of three leaflets. The inflorescence is held above the foliage and with its white-striped purple spathe, it is really quite handsome, a word not often associated with the genus (weird perhaps, but not often handsome). For me, it grows about 1½′ tall. Although some think this and the next plant are the same, this species has done well in my garden. Zones 5-8.

*A. franchetianum* is so similar to *A. fargesii* that many aroid enthusiasts simply treat them as the same. All parts of the plants, but especially the foliage, are similar. It also produces its flowers near the base of the stalk. The large trifoliate leaves (up to a foot across) are part of its mystique, and the striped purple and white spathe with its long narrow beak is particularly handsome. I have not had a great deal of luck with this species, but it may simply be too warm and too heavy a soil structure in my garden. 'Hugo' claims to big a more vigorous clone with larger flowers. Zones 6-8.

*A. griffithii*, Griffith cobra jack, is another fine dark-flowered jack that flowers at the base of the 18-22′ tall stem. The spathe is curled back on itself and a long tongue also protrudes. Generally 3 leaves are produced at the top of the plant. Heat tolerant only to zone 7a, cold to zone 5.

*A. heterophyllum*, dancing jack, is one of the easiest species to be successful with. The green stems with the folded leaflets emerge in early spring, topped by a green inflorescence with a little purple on the spathe. Sounds kind of boring, but the spadix inside bears a 12″ long tongue that lolls outside the spathe then stands straight up. Great fun. Plants grow 2-3′ tall, zones 5-8.

*A. speciosum*, big-leaf jack, is native to southwestern China and has only recently been introduced. The 2′ tall plants have three, one-foot long leaflets and bear a blackish purple spathe and a long white spadix. Plants are hardy to zone 7, but may make it to zone 6. 'Himalayan Giant' is a taller (3′) and more robust form and has more pink in the spathe than the species.

*A. tortuosum*, whipcord jack, is also of great interest in that the long S-shaped spadix sticks out from the enveloping spathe like the tongue of a tired bulldog. These shade-tolerant plants grow 24-36″ tall and are useful in zones 7-10.

*A. takedae*, fancy-stalk jack, grows about 3′ tall with a purple-splotched stem and a purple spathe. A beautiful plant in its own right, it has also become a parent. Hybrids between this species and *A. sikokianum* have been developed and they are absolutely lovely. The 2′ tall plants with a purple spathe and whitish spadix is intermediate between the parents. Outstanding in the Armitage garden.

## ***Arisarum*** (a-ris-ar′ um) — Mouse Plant — Araceae

An interesting group of 3 species from the Mediterranean and southwestern Europe that are grown for the fun of growing rather than their beauty. The most common species is *A. proboscideum*, mouse plant. The tip of the long spadix dangles like a mouse's tail in the air in early spring, eventually becoming covered by the dark green rounded foliage. The leaves make a pleasant mound but then poof, they want to go dormant in early summer. They are slow growers but if you like tails of mice, then it is indeed fascinating. Partial shade, moisture and humus-rich soil are necessary for success. Likely hardy to about zone 7 (zone 6 with protection).

## ***Armeria*** (ar-meer′ ee-a) — Sea Thrift — Plumbaginaceae

*Armeria* consists of approximately 80 species, several suitable for edging, the rockery or front of the garden. Flowers appear in solitary, dense, globe-shaped heads high above the foliage on leafless stems. They are great garden plants and useful for cut flowers. Plants perform best in sunny locations but benefit from afternoon shade particularly in the South. Plants are tough as nails, and can be found in rock-hard clay upon which pedestrians trample, as well as poor sandy soils near any coast. The foliage is tufted, similar to tufts of grass, and flowers occur in dense heads. The most common species is *A. maritima*, sea thrift, because of its availability, cultivars and toughness. However, a few other species are sold as well, although few obvious differences exist and horticultural classifications are principally based on stature and size of leaves.

Propagation is by division and seed. Seeds placed under warm (70-75°F), moist conditions germinate in 14-21 days.

Quick Reference to Armeria Species

| | Height (in.) | Leaves less than one inch wide | Flower color |
|---|---|---|---|
| *A. alliacea* | 12-18 | Yes | White-Pink |
| *A. juniperifolia* | 2-4 | No | Lilac |
| *A. maritima* | 6-12 | No | Various |

***-alliacea*** (al-lee-ah′ say-a) Plantain Thrift 12-18″/12″
Summer Whitish-pink Central and Southern Europe Zones 4-9
(*A. plantaginea*)

The white to pink flower head is approximately 3/4″ across and more oblong than the rounded flower shape of *A. maritima*. The flowers are more white than pink but are particularly handsome. The leaves are much wider (1-2″ across) than the previous species, resembling those of plantain. They are mostly erect and have 3-7 veins running lengthwise.

**Cultivars:**
Formosa hybrids (*A. alliacea* x *A. leucocephala* 'Corsica') form cushions of green and bear deep pink to white flowers.
var. *leucantha* is a white-flowered form.

***-juniperifolia*** (jew-ni-pe-ri-fo′ lee-a) Pyrenees Thrift 2-4″/6″
Summer Lilac Spain Zones 4-8

This low-growing plant is occasionally offered by rock garden plant specialists but deserves greater use. It is densely tufted with peculiar linear, 3-angled leaves seldom longer than 3/4″. The small pale lilac flower heads are only about 3/8″ across and held on 1″ scapes. Place in a sunny location and well-drained soil.

**Cultivars:**
'Alba' produces a dense canopy of creamy white flowers.
'Beechwood' is a compact growing plant with short, compact, deep pink flowers.
'Beven's Variety' is a real gem. The tiny, green compact hummocks bear short, almost stemless, pink flowers. A 1993 Award of Garden Merit winner from trials at RHS Gardens Wisley.
'Rubra' bears rosy red flowers.

***-maritima*** (ma-ri′ ti-ma) Common Thrift 6-12″/10″
Summer Pink Europe Zones 4-8

This diverse species contains over 20 unique botanical varieties. Common thrift has pink, mauve-red, lilac, or white flowers depending on the variety or cultivar. The specific epithet is derived from the species' salt tolerance and plants may be found growing on coastlines where few others can survive the saline conditions. As the name implies, it is the most common species of the genus and has undergone extensive selection. The 1-1 1/2″ diameter flower head consists of many tiny flowers attached to the central flower dome, and persists for about 3 weeks in the North, a week less in the South. The plant forms a tuft of narrow, 4-8″ long linear leaves, each of which has one vein running lengthwise. It is relatively easy to grow, however in the South, it should be shaded from the afternoon sun.

*Armeria maritima* is also grown as a flowering potted plant. Approximately 12 weeks are required from seed to produce a flowering plant under greenhouse conditions. No cold treatment is necessary to induce flowering.

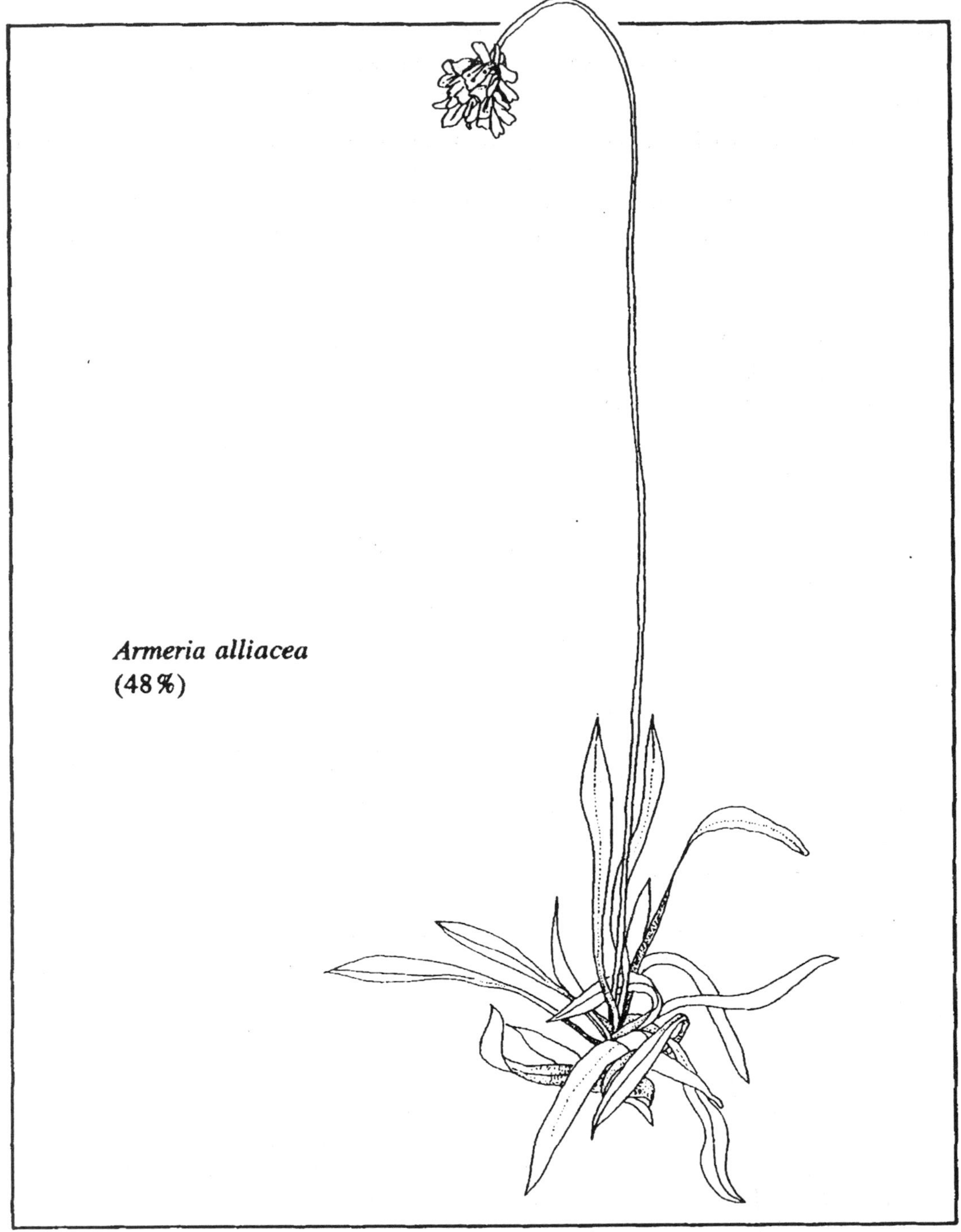


Seeds sown under high humidity and warm conditions produce seedlings ready to transplant in 3-4 weeks. They can be overwintered in a cool greenhouse or outside, and flower in the spring. Division is risky; more plants are damaged than reproduced.

**Cultivars:**

'Alba' is about 5″ tall with a creamy white flower, unusual in this species. It is handsome in the garden but, unfortunately, the white flowers discolor faster than colored flowers and decline more rapidly in heavy rains or winds.

'Bees' Ruby' is one of the most spectacular of the plantain thrifts. The intense bright cerise flowers are carried on smooth 18″ stems. This is probably a hybrid of *A. alliacea* x *A. maritima.*

'Bloodstone' produces a 9″ tall stem of intense blood-red flowers, some of the largest in the group. This also may be an *A. alliacea* x *A. maritima* hybrid.

'Cotton Tail' is quite a handsome plant, for an armeria, producing white flowers on 8″ tall plants.

'Dusseldorf Pride' grows 6-8″ tall and carries large wine-red flower heads. It is gaining a following in this country.

Joystick series includes large flower globes in white ('Joystick White') and rose ('Joystick Lilac') on 12″ tall plants.

'La Pampa' bears deep pink flowers over 6-9″ tall plants.

'Laucheana' produces 20-40 leaves resulting in a highly tufted rosette. It is about 6″ tall and has outstanding deep rose-pink flowers.

'Little Penny' is tiny, only about 2″ tall, and is most at home in a container or small niche in the rock garden. Plants produce many rose-pink flowers.

'Merlin' is only 6-9″ tall with pastel-pink flowers.

'Nifty Thrifty' has a great name along with pink ball-shaped flower heads on 6-8″ stems. The leaves are variegated white and green.

'Ornament' is an excellent hybrid with evergreen foliage and large white and rose flowers.

'Robusta' is the most vigorous form I have seen. It grows 12-15″ tall and produces 3″ wide pink flower heads.

'Rubrifolia' is 8-10″ tall with many rose-red flowers over the grassy leaves.

'Ruby Glow' grows 8-10″ tall with ruby-colored flowers similar to 'Dusseldorf Pride'. It can get rather washed out in the South.

'Splendens' is 8-10″ tall and bears intense red flowers. This is one of the most ornamental cultivars.

'Victor Reiter' is a clump former, only about 6″ tall, with narrow leaves (less than a quarter inch wide) and many pink flowers.

'Vindictive' is a compact, free-flowering cultivar growing 6″ tall and bearing bright rosy-red flowers.

**Related Species and Genera:**

*A. girardii* (*A. setacea*) bears many pink flowers on 3-4″ tall stems over tufts of grasslike foliage. This is an excellent plant for the front of the garden.

*A. pseudoarmeria*, pinkball thrift, is similar and has large, 1-2″ diameter, white to rose flower heads. When well grown, the flowers look like those of chives. The foliage can appear limp and flaccid and in constant need of water when conditions are unfavorable.

*Arenaria montana*, mountain sandwort, is a similarly tough plant, but with white flowers and growing no more than 6″ tall. Plants are exceptional rock garden additions but do poorly in poorly-drained soils and hot climates. Zones 4-6.

***Arnica*** (ar′ ni-ca) Arnica Asteraceae

The genus consists of about 30 species, all similar in appearance to each other and confused with the leopard's banes and inulas. *Arnica* differs from similar genera such as *Doronicum* and *Inula* by having opposite stem leaves rather than alternate. A good number of species are native to the Northwest and the Rocky Mountains and a couple are useful for the rock garden in areas with cool summer nights. They are relatively difficult to locate but two species, *A. montana*, mountain arnica, and *A. chamissonis*, are sometimes available. Both have deep yellow flowers on upright stems and flower in late spring and early summer. *A. montana* bears light green basal leaves and is easily the most popular in European gardens while *A. chamissonis* bears lustrous deep green foliage and a lighter yellow flower. The former is native throughout Europe while the latter is native from Alaska to the mountains of New Mexico.

***Artemisia*** (are-ti-meez′ ee-a) Wormwood Asteraceae

This large genus (about 200 species) has an ancient and curious history, the aromatic properties having attracted herbalists for many hundreds of years. The common name resulted from the fact that many species were recommended to expel worms from the intestinal tract by herbalists such as Dioscorides and Pliny the Roman. The chemical santonin, derived from some of the Asiatic species, is still used for treatment of intestinal worms. Mugwort, *A. vulgaris*, was widely used to flavor beer prior to the introduction of hops while hypochondriasis, gout, scurvy, kidney stones, and liver problems all received the medical attention of *Artemisia* prior to the 19th century.

The large genus contains 4-6′ tall plants that become woody with age, as well as mat-formers that never grow over 18″ tall. Some of the famous members of this noble genus are French tarragon, *A. dracunculus*; the symbol of the Old West—the tumbling sagebrush, *A. tridentata*; and the cause of much heartache and headache, absinthe, *A. absinthium*. All species except *A. lactiflora* are characterized by having small, alternate leaves and inconspicuous, often dioecious flowers (male and female flowers on separate plants). The leaves on many species are finely divided, and are highly aromatic when crushed. Smelling crushed leaves is one of the best ways to determine the difference between plants of this genus and gray-leaved plants of closely-related genera such as *Anthemis* and *Senecio*. Fragrance of the foliage is now being analyzed in laboratories as a means to separate cultivars within a species. For example, in the *A. arborescens* group of plants, 'Powis Castle' and other similar selections, 'Faith Raven' and 'Brass Band' had similar fragrance "fingerprints". The major component was identified as thujone. Other plants in the same species had different fingerprints, often exhibiting little thujone. Fragrance fingerprinting may be the only way to tell some of these cultivars apart, or find out that they are all the same but with 3 or 4 different names. Some species like to hide behind the fragrance of other herbs. *A. chamaemelifolia*, chamomile wormwood, is a terrific little mat former that has a distinctive chamomile smell when leaves are bruised.

Many species are from arid regions and are particularly suitable for dry, sunny areas and make few soil demands. In the South, however, where summers are humid and hot, many of the mat-forming species tend to open their centers and fall apart. Some species such as the lovely *A. splendens* are sensitive to wet soils and must be grown in loose rocky areas. The shrubby forms are more useful as they can be rejuvenated in the spring with hard pruning. This gives the pruner a wonderful sense of power and teaches the prunee to behave. Prune woody forms, such as 'Powis Castle', in the spring, not the fall. I killed a good number of artemisias by cutting the plants back hard in the fall. Woody perennials like salvia, perovskia and artemisia can all be given a "haircut" to clean them up but wait until active growth starts in the spring before severely cutting back. Most of the ornamental species have silvery-green foliage and are used as a foil for harsh colors in the garden, providing a cool note in hot, sunny weather. Applying fertilizer, particularly nitrogen, causes more harm than good to most species and tall, spindly growth results. Except for *A. lactiflora*, plants are best grown lean and dry.

The method of propagation differs for herbaceous and shrubby species. In general, herbaceous species are divided in the fall or early spring. Cuttings with a small piece of stem attached may be taken in late summer and placed in a clean bed consisting of a 3:1 ratio of perlite and peat. With the shrubby species, take 3-4" long semi-hardwood cuttings in late summer or fall and place in a cold frame in a similar medium. A rooting hormone is beneficial. Roots should be present in 3-4 weeks. Artemisia may be propagated under intermittent mist but cuttings rot quickly so plantlets must be removed as soon as roots form.

A number of silver foliage plants are similar to *Artemisia*, including *Achillea*, *Senecio* and *Seriphidium*. The foliage of *Artemisia* is usually palmately divided or finely dissected and aromatic whereas the foliage of *Seriphidium* is generally simple and non-aromatic. One of the finest foliage plants for warm, dry areas is *S. palmeri*, native to southern California.

Quick Reference to Artemisia Species

| | Height (in.) | Woody | Silver Foliage |
|---|---|---|---|
| *A. abrotanum* | 36-48 | Yes | No |
| *A. absinthium* | 24-36 | Yes | Yes |
| *A. lactiflora* | 48-72 | No | No |
| *A. ludoviciana* | 24-48 | No | Yes |
| *A. schmidtiana* 'Nana' | 6-12 | Yes | Yes |
| *A. stelleriana* | 15-24 | Yes | Yes |

***-abrotanum*** (a-broe′ tan-um) Southernwood 3-4′/18″
Summer Gray Foliage Southern Europe Zones 5-8

All sorts of common names are also associated with this species. Romance overflowed everywhere with names like boy's love, lad's love, maiden's ruin, maid's love and maid's passion but others like medicinal wormwood, Sabbath day posy, slovenwood and sweet Benjamin were also tagged on to the plant.

This species has light green (sometimes with some silver-green), finely divided, intensely fragrant foliage. Under good cultural conditions, plants grow 4′ tall. The pinnately divided foliage is softly hairy at first and becomes less so later in the season. Some people like to plant it near a garden bench or a path so that the foliage can be brushed against to take advantage of the fragrance. Prune back hard in spring and early summer if necessary, otherwise plants will look weedy by midsummer. Flowers are yellowish-white but rather inconspicuous.

**Cultivars:**

'Tangerine' has finely divided, feathery light green foliage on upright stems. Leaves have a citrus scent. Plants, like most artemisia, are deer-resistant.

***-absinthium*** (ab-sin′ thee-um) Wormwood, Absinthe 2-3′/2′
Late Summer Gray Foliage Europe Zones 3-9

Many of the artemisias have been used as herbal remedies and as local curatives for various ailments. *A. absinthium* was used to cure stomach aches and intestinal worms. Perhaps it is best known, however, as an important ingredient in the preparation of absinthe, a dry, bitter popular spirit containing 68% alcohol. Scientists then discovered that *A. absinthium* contains thujone, which, if ingested repeatedly, caused a disorder known as absinthism. Effects of absinthism included delirium, hallucinations, and permanent mental illness. First made by Pernod in 1797, production was banned in Switzerland, then France, but continued to be manufactured in Spain until 1939. The effects of absinthe were graphically displayed by the French painter, Degas, in his famous painting, "Absinthe". Absinthe may still be purchased today, but is an imitation and contains no parts of the absinthe plant. Tea was also made from this plant and as L.H. Bailey stated in 1944, "Wormwood tea is an odorous memory with every person who was reared in the country".

This woody artemisia has deciduous, finely divided silvery-gray foliage. The 2-5″ long leaves are more silvery than the previous species but not as fragrant. The flowers are tiny, gray and carried on long branched panicles. Plant in a dry, well-drained location in full sun.

**Cultivars:**

The Lambrook name, from East Lambrook Manor, the garden of Margery Fish, is associated with a number of artemisias. 'Lambrook Mist' has gray-green aromatic foliage. For the most persistent foliage, remove the flowering shoots.

'Lambrook Silver' is about 2½′ tall and more gray-green than the type. If necessary, cut back heavily in the summer to discourage floppiness. This is the best artemisia for the North and the gray, finely divided foliage provides an effective break for green-leaved plants in the garden. Both 'Lambrook Mist' and 'Lambrook Silver' were given Garden of Merit awards from the Royal Horticultural Society in 1993. 'Lambrook Giant' is a taller form and occasionally offered.

'Silver Frost' bears finely cut silver-green foliage and grows 15-18″ tall.

***-lactiflora*** (lak-ti-flo′ ra) White Mugwort 4-6′/4′
Late Summer Cream China, India Zones 3-8

This is the oddball of the group, having green foliage, conspicuous flowers, and growing best in moist areas. The 8-9″ long leaves are pinnately compound, each leaflet is about 3″ long, coarsely lobed and toothed, and the green rosette is evergreen in milder zones. Under suitable growing conditions, it easily attains 6′ and requires staking. The magnificent cream-white flowers are borne in large 1-2′ long plumelike panicles and persist well into the fall. This is an ideal background plant whose late-season flowers provide a nice change from the daisies that are so abundant at that time. It is also useful to cut for dried flowers. Plants do best in sunny locations in soils that do not dry out (unlike other species).

Propagate by division every 3-4 years.

**Cultivars:**

'Guizhou' has a good deal of variability, and is now referred to as the Guizhou Group. Plants were selected by Blooms of Bressingham and bear dark green (close to black) foliage and stems. Sprays of creamy white flowers are formed above the foliage in early summer. A handsome plant.

'Jim Russell' is 3-4′ tall with white flowers and dark green foliage, not as dark as 'Guizhou'. Plants grow as a clump, they do not run.

'Variegata' has green and gray leaves with white flowers. Propagation is exacting and plants are particularly difficult to locate.

***-ludoviciana*** (loo-do-vik-ee′ aye-na) White Sage 2-4′/2′
Late Summer Gray Foliage North America Zones 4-9

This deciduous, non-woody species provides compact growth and good silver foliage color. It differs from most of the other gray-leaved species in having entire, rather than dissected leaves. The 2-4″ long leaves are white-woolly beneath and almost hairless above. The stems are white, and branched towards the top. The gray flowers are produced in late summer on narrow, branched, compound panicles. The roots can run rampant underground and quickly result in large clumps. This is the best species for southern gardens as it tolerates warm temperatures, is less prone to disease, and grows back quickly after pruning.

Propagate by division in late summer or fall and cuttings in late spring and summer.

**Cultivars:**

'Latiloba' has wide (3″ across) gray-green leaves with 3-5 lobes near the ends. It stands 12-24″ high and makes an effective ground cover. It is not as heat tolerant as the species.

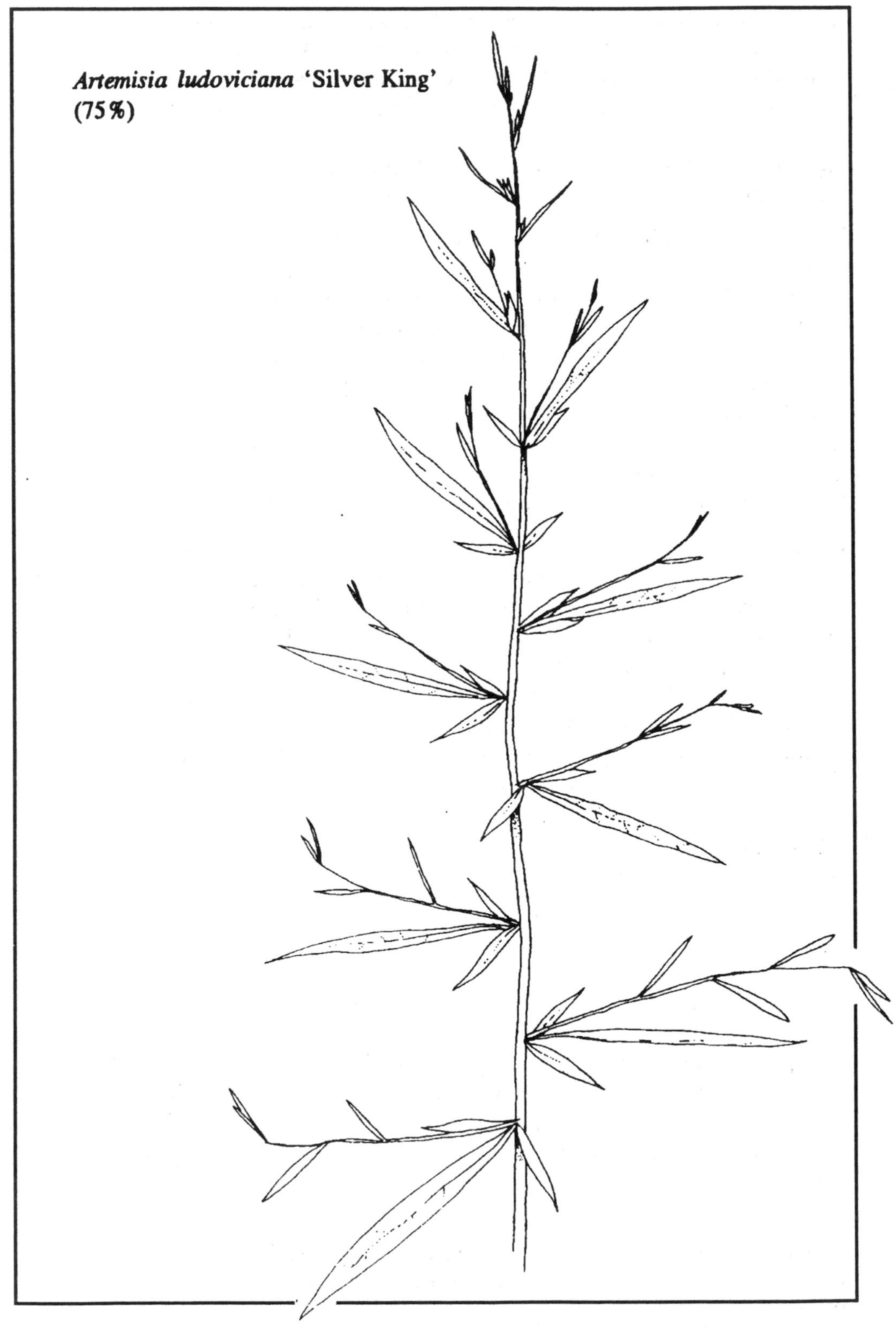
*Artemisia ludoviciana* 'Silver King'
(75%)

'Silver King' may not really exist, but may simply be a variant of 'Silver Queen'. Hardy to zone 3 and offers excellent deep silver foliage. The flower plumes sport red fall color not found in the species. Very invasive where comfortable.

'Silver Queen' produces sparse female flowers and wide silvery leaves with deeply cut jagged margins. 'Silver Queen' is a little shorter, but with slightly larger leaves, than 'Silver King'.

'Valerie Finnis' stands only 15-18″ tall and produces handsome silver entire leaves. Unlike the previous two cultivars, she is non-invasive. I have not yet been impressed with her performance in the heat as plants tend to lose lower leaves in warm weather. Years of heavy summer rains are also destructive. However, if placed in well-drained soils, plants can be handsome.

***-schmidtiana*** (shmit-ee′ aye-na) Silvermound Artemisia 15-24″/18″
Summer Silver Foliage Japan Zones 3-8

The species is about 2′ tall but seldom seen in gardens. It is represented by the dwarf form 'Nana' and usually sold as 'Silver Mound'. The finely cut silver foliage grows in a silky cushion that completely covers the small, drooping yellow flowers. The handsome mounding habit has resulted in this plant being immensely popular in the North. The mounded shape is retained most of the season in the Northeast and Canada but, unfortunately, it "melts out" in hot summers and is disappointing south of zone 6. Melt out also occurs in the Midwest, only later. The center of the plant opens and any semblance of a mound is lost, making it a particularly poor choice for southern gardens. It is rather woody at the base and cuttings consisting of the leaf, petiole and a piece of the stem should be taken in the summer.

***-stelleriana*** (stel-la-ree-ah′ na) Beach Wormwood 15-24″/30″
Summer Silver Foliage Northeast Asia, United States Zones 4-8

Plants are known as old lad and perennial dusty miller as well as beach wormwood and are cold hardy to zone 4. They are highly tolerant of salt air and saline water but intolerant of poorly drained soils. The white silky leaves are densely hairy, lobed and divided. Many ¼″ wide yellow flowers are borne in a narrow panicle.

**Cultivars**:

'Broughton Silver' is also known as 'Mori's Form', a compact, low-growing silvery plant recently introduced from Japan. A handsome selection for rock gardens or raised beds. It is probably the same as 'Silver Brocade'.

'Silver Bouquet', recently released from the University of British Columbia, is a low-growing mat former with excellent silver foliage.

'Silver Brocade' is another low-growing (6-12″) gray-leafed form that is becoming a standard for low-lying artemisias. Its prostrate and compact habit sets it apart from other cultivars. Excellent drainage is necessary. Plants have a tough time in the Southeast, but if planted in containers, it is terrific. Also introduced by the University of British Columbia Botanical Garden.

'Silverado' is offered by a few nursery people as a non-melting substitute for 'Silver Mound'. Similar foliage but not quite as "moundy".

**Related Species and Hybrids:**

*A. frigida*, mountain fringe, native to the Plains States, bears deeply cut silver foliage with woody stems and tufts of yellow flowers. Plants grow 8-12″ tall and are useful for the front of the garden. 'Laramie' is a compact selection (8-10″ tall) from Rice Creek Gardens in Blaine, Minnesota. An Award of Garden Merit winner in 1993 from the Royal Horticultural Society.

*A.* x 'Huntington' ('Huntington Gardens') is likely a hybrid with *A. absinthium* in its bloodlines. Plants become woody at the base and grow about 18″ tall, but can reach 4 feet. The handsome silver foliage is deeply cut and soft to the touch. As with other taxa of wormwood, wet soils are sure death. However, plants appear to be relatively heat tolerant. Hardy in zones 5 to 7.

*A. pontica*, Roman wormwood, is also very fragrant and bears finely divided light green foliage, somewhat resembling the leaves of common yarrow. Plants grow up to 2′ tall but can be pruned to stay low to the ground. Handsome plants, however, they can reseed where comfortable and have been cursed as thug-esque as often as lauded as garden-esque. 'Old Warrior' is shorter (18″) and more silver than the species.

'Powis Castle' took the gardening world by storm when it was introduced and is still one of the finest plants in cultivation. Two stories of its origin may be found. Graham Stuart Thomas suggested that it was a hybrid of *A. arborescens* and *A. absinthium* raised by Mr. J. Hancock at Powis Castle in Wales. However, according to Dr. J.D. Twibell, Mr. Hancock obtained the material as a cutting from a gardener in Yorkshire, England and was already propagating and distributing the plant when he moved to Powis in 1972. Regardless of its origins, is an outstanding filigreed silver artemisia. It blends relative hardiness with beauty and combines with many plants to perfection. Plants are sterile, or occasionally throw out a small flower, and are uniform. They are reliably cold hardy to zone 6 and heat tolerant to zone 8. Although not as popular as it once was, this is still an excellent plant. Prune in spring or summer, not fall.

*A. purshiana*, pursh sagebrush, is similar to 'Silver King' but only 2-3′ tall with narrower, less divided, almost entire, leaves. It also flowers about a week earlier and more profusely. This is listed as a synonym of *A. ludoviciana* by some authorities or a selection of *A. ludoviciana* by others.

*A. pycnocephala* is native to California and has handsome gray-green cut foliage. However, 'David's Choice' is better, forming 1′ tall mounds of finely textured silver foliage, much like 'Powis Castle'. Selected near Point Reyes, California, plants do best in coastal climates. Zones 6-9.

*A. rupestris* is a finely cut sub-shrub growing to about 18″ tall. Cold hardy to zone 4, plants are tough and easy to grow in well-drained soils.

'Tiny Green' is a low-growing (3-5″ tall) spreading wormwood with gray-green foliage small yellow flowers in midsummer. An excellent choice for the sunny rock garden. Zones 5-9.

*A. vulgaris* is simply an aggressive ground cover for some but an invasive weed for most others. Plants grow only 6″ tall and produce green foliage, rooting at every node.

For thuggishness, 'Limelight' is the worst of all, promising a beautiful green and yellow variegated foliaged ground cover. What most people get after a few years is an impossible-to-remove invader, whose variegated leaves do nothing for you when hurting your back trying to get rid of it.

***Arum*** (ar′ um) Arum Araceae

Approximately twenty species belong to this genus and all are characterized by a spadix consisting of unisexual flowers, the females at the base, the males above them with sterile flowers between (similar to the genus *Arisaema*). The large spathe is the showy part and envelops the spadix in the spring. Plants emanate from tubers; the shoots generally arising from the top of the tuber and the roots produced from the base of the shoots. More and more woodland species are being offered to gardeners for use in shady, moist areas. Some of the most handsome foliage to be found on any garden plant belongs to *A. italicum* 'Pictum'.

***-italicum*** (ee-ta′ li-kum) Italian Arum 12-20″/18″
Spring Creamy White Southern Europe Zones 5-9

*Arum italicum* is a woodland species native to Italy, the Mediterranean and south to the Canary Islands. The habit is unusual to most gardeners in that new foliage appears late in the fall (November in my garden) and remains green over winter. The leaves are followed by creamy-yellow spathes in spring similar in structure to jack-in-the-pulpit (*Arisaema triphyllum*) flowers. They are easy to distinguish from jack-in-the-pulpits because arum has simple leaves while "jacks" have compound leaves. The flowers disappear in summer and are replaced with strong columns of bright orange-red berries as ornamental as any part of the plant. The berries are equally common in northern and southern gardens, but may persist longer in the North. Although most at home in the woodland garden, plants are particularly handsome at the front of any shade area. The 12″ long, hastate (like an arrowhead) leaves are at their best in late fall and winter. For this reason, it is an exceptional plant for the winter garden. Combined with the winter foliage of *Bergenia* or *Heuchera*, and the architectural forms of ornamental grasses such as *Miscanthus*, the garden may be enjoyed 12 months of the year. Of course, these handsome scenes are not quite as handsome if 3 feet of snow is on the ground. Similar to *Arisaema*, plants contain calcium oxalate; try to refrain from eating them.

Propagate the species and cultivars by division after leaves appear in fall. Seed of the species must be stratified (provided with cool, moist conditions) in the fall and left until spring at which time some germination may occur. Seed often requires a year to germinate.

**Cultivars:**

A number of nurseries, mostly in Europe, have introduced slight variants ('Bill Baker', 'Cyclops') to well-known cultivars, but few are available in North America.

'Dick and Dot', from Heronswood Nursery is certainly interesting if not beautiful. The white spathe has purple dots throughout and surrounds a white spadix. You

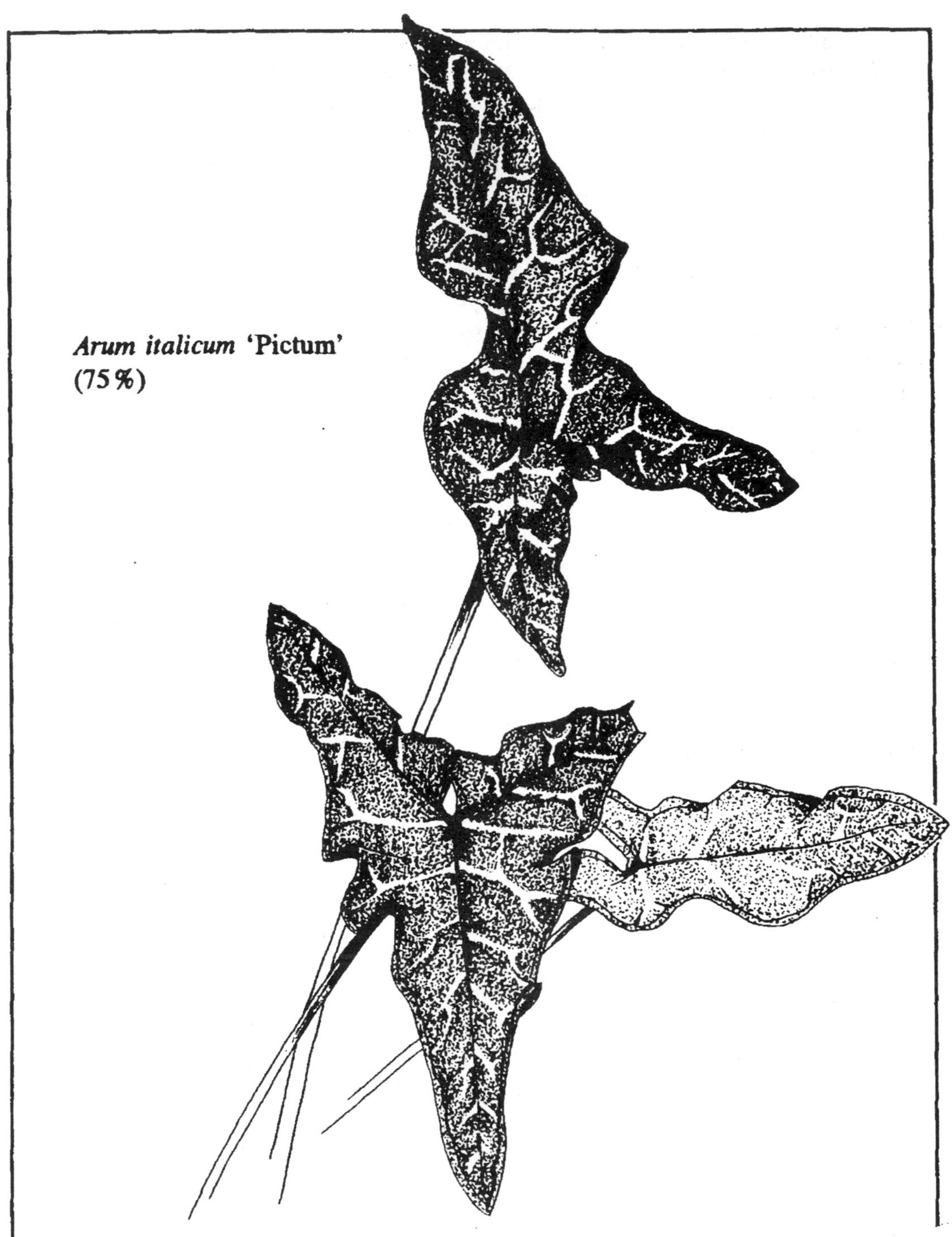

*Arum italicum* 'Pictum' (75%)

have to get down on your hands and knees to enjoy the sight, but it is worth the creaky joints.

'Eco Italian' is similar but the foliage is much lighter in color, with more white than the species.

'Jet Black Wonder' (not to be confused with the *Alocasia* of the same name) was introduced by Plant Delights Nursery. The dark green leaves have some black spotting, but the purple petioles are its saving grace. They bear greenish spathes and a white spadix.

'Marmoratum' has broad gray-green leaves marbled with splotches of yellow-green. The leaves are larger than those of the more common 'Pictum' and the yellow-green spathe is purple at the base. Unfortunately, it is difficult to find in the trade. This may be because the name is used interchangeably with 'Pictum' and the distinction between the two has almost disappeared.

'Pictum' is still the best form of this species and has dark green leaves that are narrowly spear shaped and conspicuously blotched with gray and cream. It grows approximately 18″ tall, spreads by tuberous roots, and is an excellent ground cover. In the fall, shiny clustered spikes of bright orange berries brighten the landscape.

'White Winter' is probably the most ornamental form I have seen but difficult to find. The green leaves are heavily mottled with silvery lines.

**Related Species:**

*A. creticum*, from Crete and Turkey, has green leaves similar to more common species, but bears golden yellow spathe and a dull yellow spadix. Zone 7b.

*A. dioscoridis* is extremely variable but generally has large triangular leaves and purple-spotted spathes with a dark spadix within. Flowers are rather malodorous, smelling of dung and carrion. Bet you can't wait to find this one. Plants are winter hardy only to zone 7 or 8.

*A. maculatum*, lords and ladies, or cuckoo-plant, bears glossy green leaves, often with black spots and creamy-yellow spathes. They differ from *A. italicum* by having a violet-yellow or violet flushed spadix compared to the yellow spadix of *A. italicum*. Orange-red berries are produced in late summer and fall.

*A. pictum* is interesting in that its flowering time is quite different than that of the above species. Dark green leaves in the fall are accompanied by dark purple spathes and spadices are quite beautiful, and smelly enough for crazy gardeners as well. Native to the Mediterranean area, plants are likely hardy only to zone 7.

## ***Aruncus*** (ah-run′ kus) Goat's Beard Rosaceae

Only two species occur and each possesses excellent qualities for the garden. Male and female flowers occur on different plants (dioecious) and are carried in tall showy panicles (compound inflorescences). The light green foliage is bipinnately compound. A little afternoon shade is useful and moisture is necessary for best growth and flowering in southern areas of the country (zone 5 to 7), although plants perform best in full sun further north. Consistent moisture is important regardless of locale; the leaf margins of plants grown in dry areas will turn brown and crispy. In general, species of *Aruncus* do terribly south of zone 7a.

Propagate by division in the spring or by seed collected fresh and placed in a warm (70-75°F), humid area. Germination will occur in two to three weeks. If seed is old, place at 40°F for about 4 weeks prior to putting them in the warmth.

***-dioicus*** (die-o-eye' kus) Goat's Beard 4-6'/6'
Late Spring Creamy White Europe, Asia, North America Zone 3-7

This is a spectacular plant when given sufficient moisture, dappled shade, and plenty of room. The flowers of *Aruncus* are either male or female but the two sexes are rather unisexual in appearance and difficult to tell apart from a distance. The 2-3' long light green leaves are bi- to tripinnately compound and each lanceolate leaflet is sharply doubly serrated. Plants are similar to some of the tall white forms of *Astilbe* and can be confused. Three ways may be used to separate *Aruncus* from taller astilbes such as *Astilbe biternata* and 'Prof. van der Wielen'. In general, leaves of *Astilbe* are usually singly serrated , those of *Aruncus* are doubly serrated, there are always 10 stamens in *Astilbe* flowers, there are either 20 (male) or 0 (female) stamens in *Aruncus*. They are small and difficult to count but nobody will laugh. Finally, in each fruit *Astilbe* has many seeds, *Aruncus* has two to four seeds.

In the northern states, plants are far more tolerant of afternoon sun than in the South. I have tried to grow goat's beard in Athens, Georgia (zone 7b) for many years and have not succeeded. It is either too hot or I can't provide sufficient moisture or both. However, I have seen fine specimens in Raleigh, North Carolina (zone 7a). Because of these experiences, I don't recommend its use south of zone 7a (although it will survive even further south, it will not perform well).

Where well grown, large plumelike panicles of small (1/8") creamy flowers appear in late spring and provide a magnificent sight. I read that males are more sought-after than females because the plumes are supposedly fuller. I have stared at clumps of goat's beard for hours trying to determine the garden differences between male and female plants. As I stuck my head through foliage, flowers and fruit, the conclusion was painfully obvious—gender makes little difference. One can argue that the male plumes are more feathery and upright than the drooping seed-laden females, but unless you are a chauvinist of some kind, it does not matter. Plants form large clumps in rich soils but unfortunately many of today's smaller gardens can not afford the space.

In an earlier edition of this book, I casually mentioned that one could divide plants if additional plants were desired. A letter arrived a few months later showing me the error of my ways. *"I would like to know what kind of mischievous smile you had when you wrote ... that Aruncus is propagated ... by division ... Let me briefly tell you my experience with a 6-7 year old clump. It took: 1 pick (which broke), three shovels (one of which broke), an ax and two people (in your next book, you might suggest that a husband/wife team not attempt this project together). Then it went through pruners (dumb on my part) to loppers (still quite dumb), to a pruning saw (we're getting smarter), to a big hand saw, with serious consideration on getting out the chain saw.*

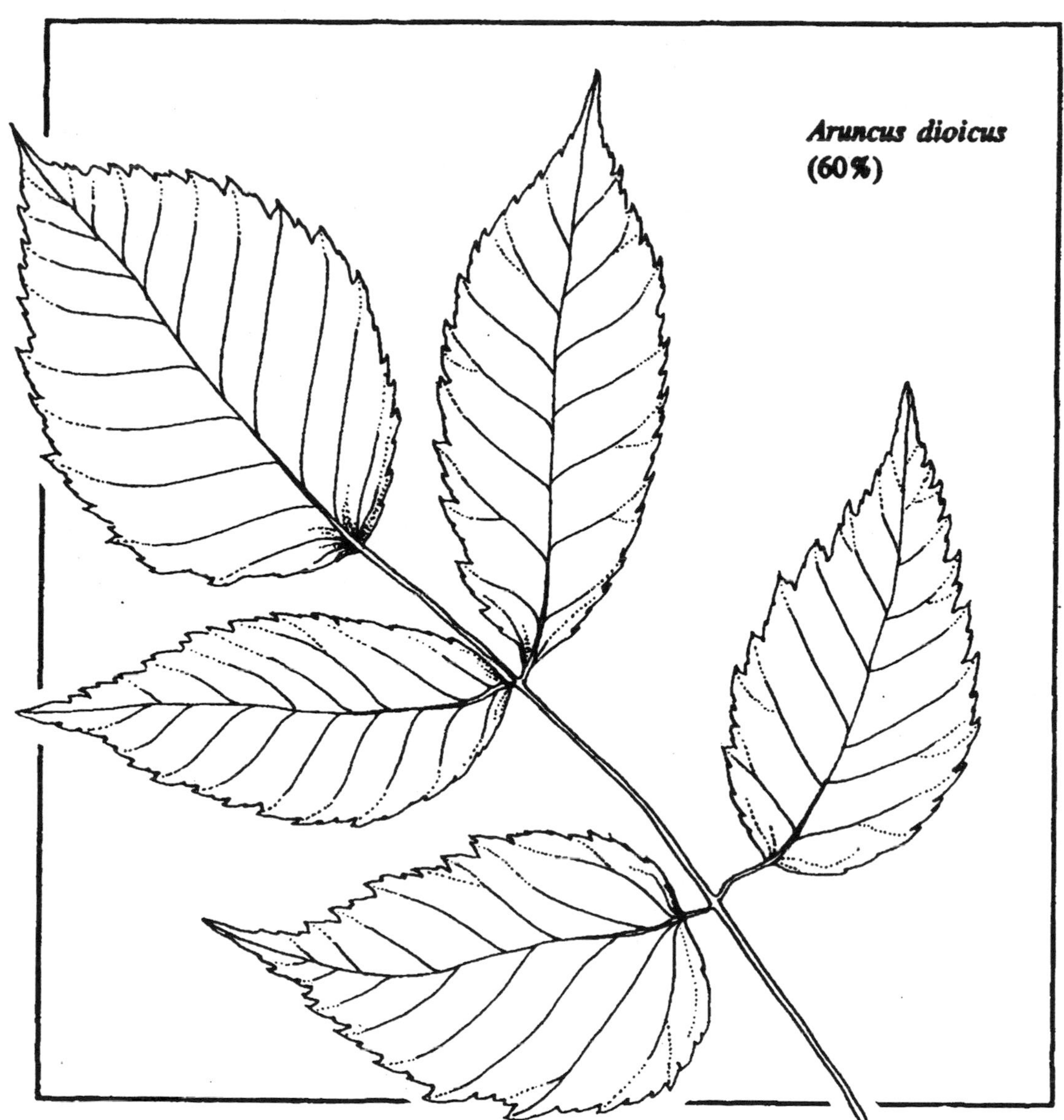


*At one point there was discussion of laying it on its side, varnishing it, and making end tables out of it. Anyway, it was an experience to remember."* Robyn Duback, Robyn's Nest Nursery, Vancouver, Washington.

**Cultivars and Hybrids:**

var. *astilboides* is a smaller version (18-24") of the species, and although difficult to find in the American trade, is worth the hunt. The leaves are more deeply serrated and the inflorescence less compound.

'Glasnevin', from the wonderful Botanic Gardens at Glasnevin, Dublin, bears deeper green fuller leaves and is dwarfer than the species. Apparently, it is also more tolerant of dry soils.

'Kneiffii' is only 3′ tall with foliage deeply cut into threadlike segments. This foliage is wonderfully handsome but the flowers are not as dramatic.

'Misty Lace' is a terrific hybrid that is intermediate between *A. dioicus* and *A. aethusifolius*. It had its beginnings at Bluemont Nursery in Maryland, the excellent establishment of Richard Simon. Three plants were brought back to the University of Georgia, two immediately died, but one grew vigorously. With the help of Dr. Hazel Wetzstein, plants were successfully propagated in tissue culture and were released in 2005. Its attributes are the compact habit (2-3′ tall), tolerance to heat and cold (zones 3-7b) and excellent foliage even after flowering. This is a great addition to the genus.

'Child of Two Worlds' is a shorter, more airy form with pendulous white flowers. This cultivar is thought to be a form of *A. sinensis*.

**Related Species:**

*A. aethusifolius,* native to Korea, is an nice addition to the perennial trade and is a true miniature. It attains a mature height of 8-12″, has deeply cut dark green leaves and a panicle of creamy white flowers. Plants tolerate partial shade, and are most at home in the rock garden or the front of the border. A little more heat tolerant than *A. dioicus*.

## *Asarum* (a-sar′ um) Wild Ginger Aristolochiaceae

*Asarum* contains about 70 species, most of which are native to north temperate areas. The common name comes from the ginger-like smell that arises from the roots when bruised or cut. The plant that provides true ginger, however, is *Zingiber officinale*. Wild ginger spreads by rhizomes, produces only a few leaves and is generally less than 6″ tall. Many excellent species are native to North America, but recent explorations to China and Japan have resulted in a cornucopia of ginger delights. Whereas I was hard-pressed to come up with 6-7 selections for the second edition of this book, it is easy to find a couple of dozen today. One of our great plantsmen, Barry Yinger, offered over 120 selections in his Asiatica catalog in 2007! These include species with outstanding foliage textures, variegations, small flowers and immense ones. *A. splendens* is an outstanding Chinese species with large dark green leaves mottled with silver throughout. It has remained evergreen in the Armitage garden to 10°F. *A. kumageanum* (my favorite) and *A. magnificum,* one of the biggest species (12-15″ tall), were introduced from Japan by the Arnold Arboretum. A good deal of study and collection have occurred in this genus and Japanese species continue to be described. Recently, two additional Japanese species, *A. fudsinoi* and *A. minamitanianum* were described from plants at Kew Gardens. Many of these species will never be common garden plants but with the possible aid of tissue culture, they may be available on a limited scale in the future.

All species prefer woodland conditions of slightly acid soils, heavy shade, constant moisture and good drainage. In the wild, plants generally occur in the dappled shade of deciduous forests. In the garden, they are used mainly as shade-tolerant ground covers whose glossy green leaves, often mottled with white or yellow, are amazingly eye-catching for such diminutive plants. The urn-shaped flowers consist of sepals only and are borne underneath the foliage. The "little brown jugs" are wonderfully handsome but are seldom seen by the uninitiated. The sepals usually end in turned-back lobes, referred to as the calyx lobes, and may be handsome in their own right. Hidden from flying insects, the flowers are pollinated by ground-hugging insects.

Some taxonomists have split this genus into 2 main sections, placing evergreen species in the genus *Hexastylis* and the deciduous species in *Asarum*. I have retained all species under *Asarum*.

Species may be propagated by seed although the most foolproof method is division in spring or early fall.

***-arifolium*** (ar-i-foe-lee′ um) Arrow-leaf Ginger 6-8″/12″
Spring Dull Brown Southeastern United States Zones 4-8

In this large native ginger, the evergreen leaves are up to 8″ long, 10″ across and usually visibly mottled. They are triangular to arrow-shaped (deltoid to sagittate) and smooth throughout. A great deal of variability occurs, resulting in some plants having different degrees of leaf mottling, which shows up more in the spring than in the summer. The leaves and roots also have a pleasant smell when crushed. In early spring, the tan-colored buds are easily visible, especially if the old leaves are removed. In later spring, flask-shaped brown flowers with prominent spreading lobes occur, although significant variability also occurs with the flowers. For most gardeners, this is a reliable, excellent ginger.

**Cultivars:**

'Beaver Creek' was selected by Jean Frett at the Mt. Cuba Center in Delaware. Plants are similar to the species but appear to be more vigorous.

***-canadense*** (can-a den′ see) Canadian Ginger 4-8″/10″
Spring Dull Brown Canada, United States Zones 3-7

Most of the popular gingers today are evergreen but for the toughest and most cold tolerant, this aggressive deciduous species fits the bill. Down and out in the winter, two soft-green kidney-shaped downy leaves emerge early in the spring about the same time as the flowers. Plants tend to ramble (some say rocket) a good bit, and given cool, moist areas, large colonies may occur within a few years. The 1″ wide flowers are obviously hairy, greenish on the outside and brown within. The three flared, pointed flower lobes look they have been peeled back to allow ground-hugging bugs to do their pollinating. They are certainly not as exciting as the flowers on the Asian species, but fun to look at regardless.

Canadian ginger is probably the most cold hardy of the gingers and one of the most popular, even as far south as Zone 7.

**Cultivars:**

'Eco Choice' and 'Eco Red Giant' are more dense and larger than the species, respectively.

***-europaeum*** (eur-o′ pay-um) European Wild Ginger 6-8″/8″
Spring Dull Brown Europe Zones 4-7

This excellent ground cover is at home in the woodland garden. The 2-3″ wide kidney-shaped leaves are leathery, glossy dark green, and evergreen. The leaves are hairy, particularly on the veins on the upper surface. The small dull brown flowers are also hairy and bear three pointed lobes about half as long as the flower.

I believe the foliage is some of the most handsome in the genus, but the flowers are among the most forgettable. This is one of the hardiest and easiest species to establish in the North. I have seen this stuff taking over pathways and shade gardens of my gardening friends in Long Island and like Santa Claus, I always return with a sack of ginger on my back. Unfortunately, plants don't tolerate high temperatures associated with southern summers as well, and although they still work in the South, they are better in the Northeast and Midwest. Moist, shady conditions are needed for best performance.

***-maximum*** (max′-i-mum) Panda Face Ginger 6-12″/12″
Spring Brown China Zones 7-9

This plant has made significant headway in the American market for good reasons. The 6″ long, evergreen leaves provide a handsome clump of glossy green foliage and plants are well worth giving a try. The 2″ wide flowers are larger than others, and they are also among the most eye-catching, being purple on the outside and white with dark purple margins on the inside. The plants are useful in the shade garden or in containers where the flowers can be enjoyed without having to get on one's knees. Plants are cold hardy only to about zone 7.

**Cultivars:**

'Green Panda' is offered, however it does not seem to be different than the species.

'Ling Ling' is one of the more sought-after forms, bearing handsome mottled foliage with the same beautiful flowers.

***-shuttleworthii*** (shut-tle-worth-ee′ eye) Shuttleworth Ginger 4-9″/8″
Spring Brown Southeastern United States Zones 5-8

Plants bear beautiful mottled evergreen heart-shaped to rounded foliage. The 1-2″ long urn-shaped flowers are pale brown to red with broad calyx lobes. Plants are not as winter hardy, but are more heat tolerant than the Canadian or European gingers. They are native from Virginia to Alabama and Georgia.

**Cultivars:**

'Callaway', selected from Callaway Gardens in Pine Mountain, Georgia, is probably a selection of *A. shuttleworthii* var. *harperi*. Plants were introduced by one of America's great plantsmen, Fred Galle. Plants are more compact than the species, growing only about 6″ tall with handsome mottled foliage. This is one of the finest mat formers but unfortunately, one of the slowest growers. In the Armitage garden, it has taken about 8 years to form a clump 18″ square, but oh what a clump it is!

'Cahaba River' also has silver mottling and relatively large purple flowers beneath the foliage. Plants were found by Barry Yinger near the Cahaba River in central Alabama.

'Velvet Queen' is similar to, but produces larger leaves than 'Callaway'. The same beautiful silver mottling may be found on this selection but the larger leaves and flowers provide a larger clump in less time.

| ***-speciosum*** | | Alabama Ginger | 9-12"/12" |
|---|---|---|---|
| Spring | Purple | Southeastern United States | Zones 5-9 |

I include this species not only because it is a beautiful native ginger but also because it is making a comeback, at least in American gardens. Plants are native to small areas of the Southeast, mainly Alabama, and lack of availability has made plants difficult to include in gardens. The large triangular leaves are lightly mottled and evergreen, and can be mistaken for arrow-leaf ginger. However, the flowers are much larger, and deep purple around the edges, with purple lines radiating from the center. I only wish it were more cold hardy so growers in the North could enjoy it as much as I do.

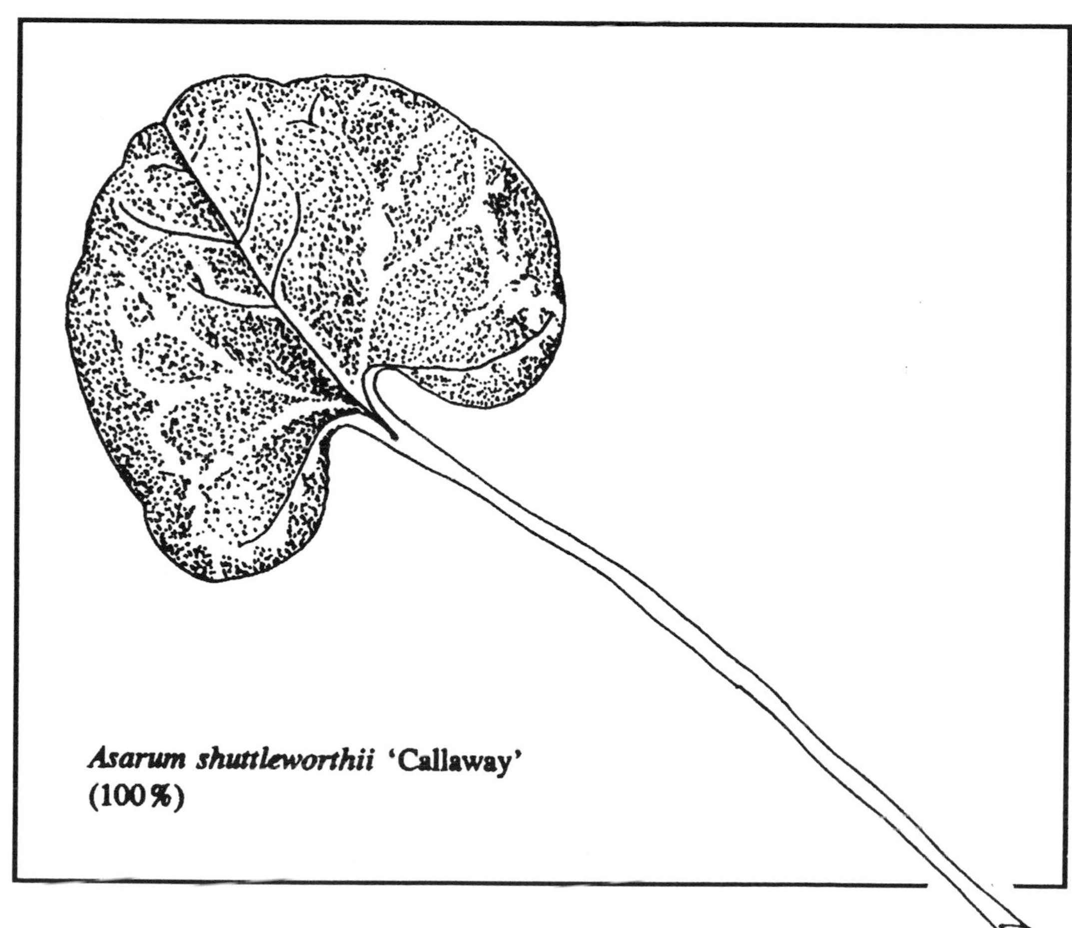

***Asarum shuttleworthii* 'Callaway'**
**(100%)**

**Related Species:**

There has been such an incredible influx of gingers since the last edition, thanks mainly to people like Barry Yinger, Ozzie Johnson, Tony Avent, Dick Lighty and other forward-looking plantspeople, that it is impossible to list them all. In fact, it is impossible to list even those I am enamored with, and I know but a small fraction. Here is a decent effort.

*A. caudatum* has slightly hairy rounded evergreen leaves and densely hairy petioles when young. The reddish brown flowers are most fascinating due to the long twisted tails ("cauda") on the lobes. Native to Washington eastward to western Montana, and south to northeastern Oregon. A white-flowered form, forma *alba*, is an interesting plant, although the flowers are mostly hidden by the foliage. Zones 4-8.

*A. hartwegii*, Sierra wild ginger, is a western representative, native to Oregon and California. The green leaves have conspicuous silver veining and the outstanding mottling has earned the common name of cyclamen-leafed wild ginger. 'Silver Heart' has a silver streak through the midsection of the green leaf. Terrific plants but excellent drainage is a must.

*A. heterophyllum* generally bears round green leaves and urn-shaped flowers. While walking around the woodland at Mt. Cuba in Delaware, Dr. Richard Lighty, the former director of the garden, pointed out a clump of marvelously variegated *A. heterophyllum*. Seeing that beautiful form simply reinforced the fact that all species of this genus are highly variable and that green and mottled forms will occur in most of them. Plants are native to the eastern United States.

*A. virginiacum* is native to Virginia and the Carolinas and has evergreen, heart-shaped, 2-3" long dark green leaves often with white spots on the upper side. Similar to *A. minor* and *A. shuttleworthii*, however the flowers are smaller. 'Silver Splash' has a more distinctive silver mottling pattern on the foliage. Zones 5-9.

*A. splendens*, Chinese ginger, is a fine spreading form with large silver-mottled glossy leaves and 2" purple flowers with white centers. Plants are evergreen and quite at home in zones 6-9.

## *Asclepias* (as-klee' pe-as) Silkweed, Milkweed Asclepidaceae

Although many plants in this genus are highly ornamental, some argue that few, if any, milkweeds are worthy of inclusion in the formal garden. *A. curassavica*, blood flower, is as ornamental as any species but is considered an annual in most of the country. However, if people loosen up a little, and get out of the formal garden frame of mind, then milkweeds become exceptional plants. Meadow gardens, native plantings, and informal wildlife sanctuaries are the domain of many of these plants. And to be sure, planting milkweeds is part of good stewardship, as they attract butterflies from all over the neighborhood. I have a love/hate relationship with these things, so I am quite impressed when I find an entire nursery like the Milkweed Farm, Bluemont, Virginia devoted to distributing milkweed

A couple of species are crossover plants, popular in both formal and informal settings. The most brilliant is probably butterfly weed, *A. tuberosa*, but swamp milkweed, *A. incarnata* has also turned a few gardeners' heads. Once established, milkweeds usually prosper. Anyone who has farmed and tried to rid fields of one of the great agronomic pests, common milkweed, *A. syriaca*, knows how tenacious members of this genus can be. Oh, how I remember, as a lowly "weeder" on a farm in southern Quebec, cursing this plant. However, to be fair, some highly creative people have found that other creative people will actually pay a pretty good dollar for the inflated pods of the common milkweed to be used as dried ornaments. And if you stick your nose in the flowers, you will be rewarded with a wonderful honey scent.

All members of this genus have milky sap (although butterfly weed is much less obvious than others), inflated seed pods (follicles), and silky seeds. All species are highly coveted by aphids and if you grow milkweed, you will also be farming aphids. A horde of ladybugs or a strong stream of water will help keep them under control.

<u>Quick Reference to Asclepias Species</u>

| | Flower Color | Leaf Arrangement |
|---|---|---|
| *A. incarnata* | Rose-pink | Opposite |
| *A. tuberosa* | Orange | Alternate (spiral) |

**-*incarnata*** (in-kar-nay′ ta) Swamp Milkweed 3-4′/2′
Spring Rose-pink North America Zones 3-7

Swamp milkweed has opposite 3-6″ long leaves and clusters of rosy pink flowers atop 3-4′ tall plants in late spring and summer. The flowers have a faint vanilla scent and are real come-ons for many butterflies. In particular, the foliage is a primary source of food for monarch butterflies. The sap of this species is milkier than in butterfly weed, thus complicating cutting for flowers. Plants can be found in ditches, swamps and any moisture-retaining soil. In the garden, find a low area, although well-drained sites are tolerated. All taxa have red-brown seeds with a silky tail within the seed pods.

**Cultivars**:

'Cinderella' has been selected for the larger rosy pink flowers and more compact flower heads. Flowers have an interesting fragrance of vanilla.

'Ice Ballet' produces persistent white flowers on 3-5′ stems. When butterflies hover, which they will, the contrast is fabulous.

'Soulmate' bears rose-purple clusters of flowers.

**-*tuberosa*** (tew-be-ro′ sa) Butterfly Weed 2-3′/2′
Spring Orange Eastern North America Zones 4-9

The orange flowers of butterfly weed are so vibrant that they seem to jump out at you. There is a good deal of variation in flower color and I've seen plants ranging from pure yellow to dark red at the edge of woods in north Georgia. Plants were and may still be used in the treatment of pleurisy, a common ailment in early colonial times in which inflammation of the pleura around the lungs resulted in coughing, wheezing and great pain. It was so effective in treating this ailment that it became known as pleurisy weed.

Mature plants do not transplant well, thus removing plants from the wild should not be attempted. The 4-4½″ long leaves are more or less alternate but may spiral up the stiff stems. The stems are topped by umbels of many small flowers in spring and continue to bloom at least six weeks in the garden. Cut flowers have a good vase life if immediately placed in warm water, then transferred to the refrigerator for 12 hours. Some gardeners flame the base of the stem to reduce the flow of sap, but flowers will not decline if flaming is not attempted, and you will not burn your house down either. Cutting the flowers also results in additional flowering three to four weeks later.

Flowers allowed to remain on the plant give way to narrow 3-6″ long ornamental follicles that provide an additional dimension to the plant. They should be removed before they open because the seeds spill out at that point, and ornamental soon gives way to messy. Butterfly weed is slow to emerge in the spring and patience is a must.

Some research on forcing the flowers in the greenhouse has shown that *A. tuberosa* requires short nights (i.e. long days) in order to flower. Growers use a 60W incandescent light bulb from 11:00 p.m. to 2:00 a.m. each night to "trick" the plants into thinking the nights are short. Under the normal long nights of winter, plants just sit there and decline.

Seed germination is highly variable and results as low as 5% to as high as 90% have been reported. If fresh seed is collected, cleaned, and sown immediately, 50-80% ger-

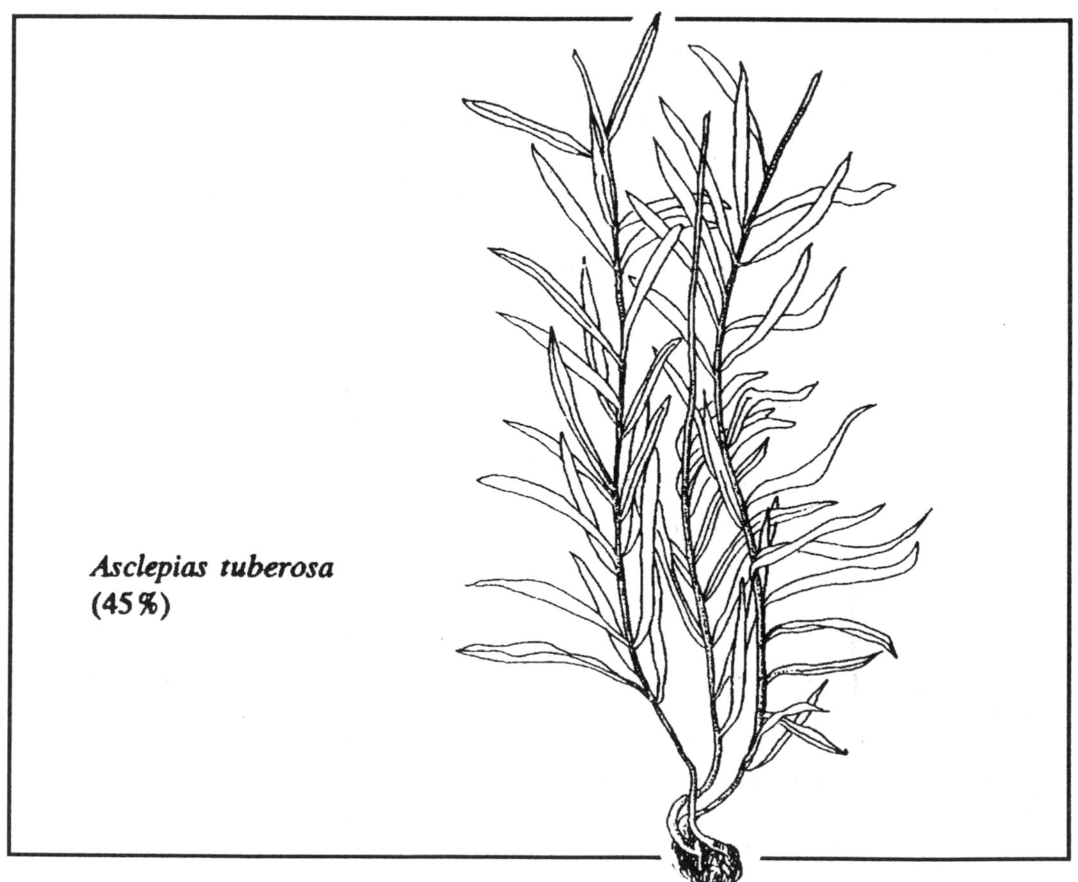

***Asclepias tuberosa***
**(45%)**

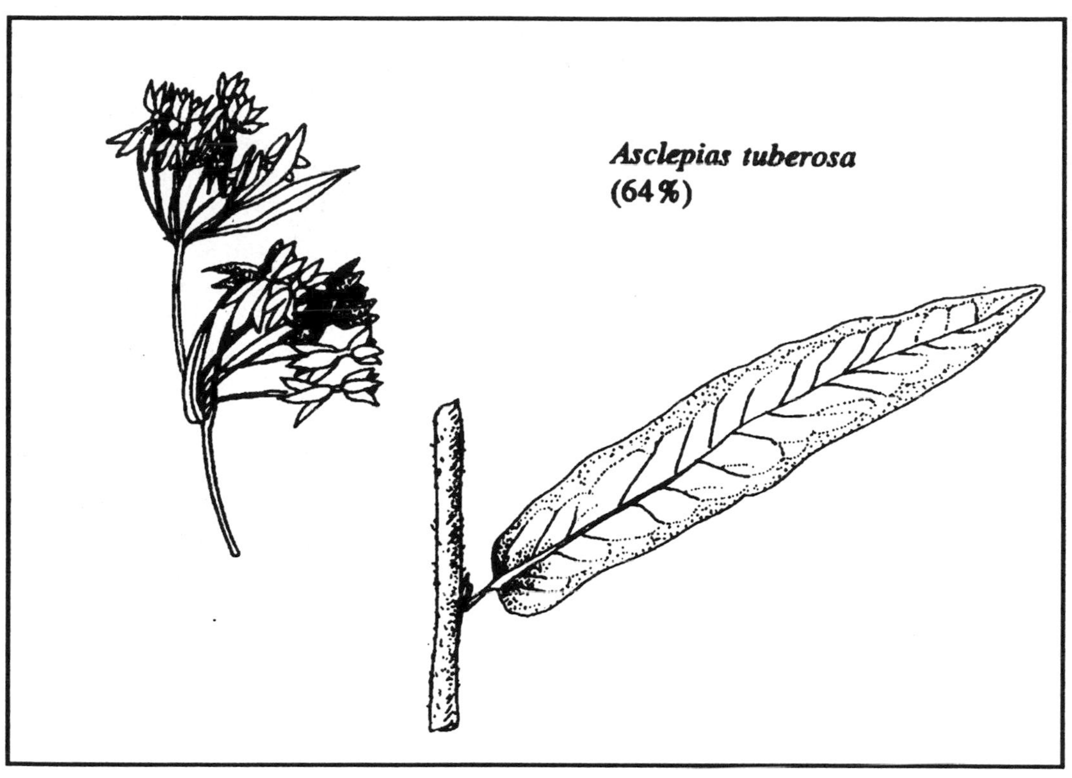


mination will result. Old seed or seed that is purchased germinates more uniformly if seeds are sown in a well-aerated soil mix, watered in well, covered with plastic, and placed in the refrigerator or other cool place for about six weeks. A good deal of variation in flower color results from seed-sown material. Root cuttings can be used to increase forms that have merit (see *Anemone*).

**Cultivars:**

'Gay Butterflies' is a mix of yellow-, orange- and red-flowered forms. Plants are generally 2-3′ tall.

'Hello Yellow' bears vibrant yellow flowers atop 24-30″ plants. A showstopper.

**Related Species:**

*A. purpurascens*, purple milkweed, caught me totally by surprise. As a real skeptic of anything milkweed-ish, you can imagine my own surprise at embracing this beautiful deep purple-flowered plant. It is a milkweed, but the flowers catch your eye immediately on turning the corner. Plants are about a foot tall, and flower in late May to early June. Not as fragrant as *A. syriaca*, but not bad either.

*A. verticillata*, horsetail milkweed, has narrow, sessile, whorled leaves and small creamy white flowers along the length of the unbranched stems. Flowers occur from June to September. Native to open areas of Massachusetts, southern Ontario west to the Canadian prairies and south through Texas, Mexico and Florida. Handsome and tough.

***Asphodeline*** (as-fo-de′ line) Jacob's Rod Asphodelaceae

Eighteen to twenty species occur in the Mediterranean area and north to Austria. The leafy unbranched stems arise from rhizomes and produce many-flowered conical inflorescences. All species were at one time part of the genus *Asphodelus*, but in 1830 this genus was created. They are most easily distinguished from *Asphodelus* by having erect and leafy stems. Taxonomists are also arguing about the family, and recently the Asphodelaceae was formed, to which the genus belongs.

Stems of plants of *Asphodelus* are generally leafless and branched. Plants perform best in full sun and can be spectacular in late spring and early summer. Of the numerous species found in the wild, only king's spear, *Asphodeline lutea*, is readily available.

***-lutea*** (loo-tee′ a) King's Spear 3-4½′
Late Spring–Early Summer Yellow Mediterranean Zones 5-8

This is the true asphodel of the ancients, connected in Greek mythology with the dead and the underground. It was planted on graves and associated with Persephone, goddess of agriculture and fertility, who was kidnapped by Hades, god of the dead. In this gruesome story, Persephone appears crowned with a garland of asphodels. It was suggested that the grayish foliage and the yellow flowers intimated the gloom of the underworld and the pallor of death. Sounds pretty awful, doesn't it?

It really is a fine plant, regardless of what the mythologists did to it. The deep green leaves are grasslike with paler veins and are found all the way to the inflorescence. Each of the many starlike fragrant flowers is about an inch long and open from bottom to top on a 6-18″ long raceme. I have seen outstanding plants in cool summer climates but seldom have they reached their potential in the harsher summers of the South and central plains. In the heat, the open flowers decline rapidly while the top flowers are still waiting to open. The stems are rather ugly; this should be interplanted among other plants so the flowers can be the focal point.

**Cultivars:**

A double form, var. *flore-pleno*, has been described but is difficult to locate.

**Related Species:**

*A. liburnica* has soft yellow flowers but the racemes are more lax and plants grow only 1-2′ tall. The primrose color makes this a fine plant for the garden. The foliage extends only about halfway up the stem and flowers open a little later than those of *A. lutea*. Native to southern Europe, plants perform well in zones 4 to 7, as well as on the West Coast.

*A. taurica* is 1-2′ tall and bears handsome white flowers. Sometimes confused with *Asphodelus albus*, however, the leafy stem and more diminutive stature of *A. taurica* should help to keep them separate.

***Aster*** (as′ tur) Aster Asteraceae

This large genus consists of species native to North and South America, Europe, Africa and Asia. While many remain weedlike, horticultural improvements have greatly enhanced their garden value in recent years. Many species are native to the

United States and have common names such as New York aster and New England aster. Perhaps it is this familiarity with our roadside asters that have held back the popularity of the named cultivars in this country. Although many useful species are native to North America, credit for much of the improvement must be given to English and German nurserymen. Many selections were raised in the late 1890s and new ones continue to be introduced every year. Asters are also raised in greenhouses and fields as commercial cut flowers and are becoming an important item in the flower designer's palette. The most important species for cut flowers are *A. ericoides* and *A. novi-belgii.*

The leaves are alternate and the daisy flowers are borne either singly on the flower stem or in multiple-flowered panicles or corymbs. Some species of the genus *Aster* are similar to some *Erigeron* species, particularly our native forms. In general, *Erigeron* mostly flowers in the spring and summer and has bracts beneath the flower in a single circle all about the same length. *Aster* generally flower in summer and fall and the bracts underneath the flowers occur in two rings of different sizes.

Species and their cultivars range in height from 6″ (*A. alpinus*) to the giant 8′ *A. simplex*, however, so much hybridization has occurred in cultivation that proper identification is highly questionable. If you don't know what species you are looking at, don't worry about it, it is probably a hybrid of some kind. A great deal of breeding work has been accomplished with *A. novi-belgii*, and cultivars and hybrids of that species alone are now available in heights from 6″ to 6′. Flower color of most species is white or in the blue-purple range (although many pink cultivars have been selected). Yellow does or does not occur in aster depending on whether you follow the taxonomic lumpers or splitters. Goldilocks is the common name of the 18″ tall fall-flowering *A. linosyris*, however, the taxonomic splitters have renamed this plant as *Linosyris vulgaris.*

Speaking of taxonomists, the *Aster* genus has taken a major hit, similar to the genus *Chrysanthemum*. Based on characteristics such as chromosome number, inflorescence shape, the presence of rhizomes, and characteristic basal leaves, the genus has been split into new and gruesomely unspellable genera. The main genus to which the asters have been transferred is *Symphyotrichum* (sim-fee-o' trick-um), but other equally tongue-twisting genera have also been constructed. This is mainly the case of the American asters (New England, Carolina aster, etc.) but Old World asters are also undergoing change. They have all been coolly embraced by botanists and totally ignored by gardeners (perhaps because we can't pronounce them). For the latest in names of native species, check the Integrated Taxonomic Information System (*www.itis.usda.gov.*). However, as far as the all-knowing Royal Horticultural Society goes, nothing has changed anywhere in the genus. As for me, I am at a crossroads: I want to give the new names some love, but I also realize that no one will have a clue what I am talking about if I toss out the old ones. So in keeping with other taxonomists, I too will sit on the fence, and provide both names as the various species are discussed.

Division is the easiest means of propagation. The outside portions of the clumps should be split and replanted in early spring or fall. The centers of stronger-growing species become bare within 1-2 years and if not divided every few years, plants will degenerate and lose their ornamental usefulness (an exception to this *A. amellus*, which should be left undisturbed for 2-3 years). Terminal cuttings of most species can also be rooted. Collect 1-2″ long cuttings with two to three leaves in the spring or early summer and insert in a clean mixture of sand and perlite and rooting will occur within 2-3 weeks. This is the best and sometimes the only method to clean up prized plants that suffer from aster wilt caused by *Verticillium vilmorinii.* Since the fungus resides in the rootstock, terminal cuttings of new growth may result in clean plants. *A. novi-belgii* types are most susceptible while *A. novae-angliae* is least affected. The other major problem of New England and New York asters is powdery mildew (*Erysiphe cichoracearum*). Some cultivars are more susceptible than others, but fungicides should be applied to all cultivars starting around July 1 to reduce infection. Rust can also be troublesome with many species of asters. Maintain good air circulation, cut out stems if the plants are too dense, and stay away from highly susceptible cultivars.

Asters are useful for fall flowering but some flower in the summer and may reflower in the fall if spent blossoms are removed immediately. Tall varieties need staking and should be avoided if one is an anti-staker. This is still a major drawback to asters, particularly the New England and New York types. Regardless of where they are grown, most cultivars must have support or they look shabby. Staking can be reduced and even eliminated in many medium-sized cultivars if plants are grown in full sun, and pinched back once or twice in spring and early summer. This is also a good practice for all tall flowering plants and results in more compact, dense plants. Pinch back 4-6″ of growth from each growing point but do not do it later than June 15 in the North and July 1 in the South, or you may remove the developing flowers. A sharp pair of hedge trimmers does the job in the Armitage garden.

Plants that are sold under the name of China aster are *Callistephus chinensis.* These are beautiful plants but are annuals and not to be confused with the perennial asters.

Quick Reference to Aster Species

| | Height (ft.) | Flowers single or in clusters | Flowering time |
|---|---|---|---|
| *A. alpinus* | ½-¾ | Single | Early Summer |
| *A. amellus* | 2-2½ | Single, Cluster | Summer |
| *A. carolinianus* | 7-12 | Single | Late Fall |
| *A. cordifolius* | 4-6 | Cluster | Early Fall |
| *A. divaricatus* | 1-2 | Cluster | Summer |
| *A. ericoides* | 3-4 | Cluster | Late Summer |
| *A.* x *frikartii* | 2-3 | Cluster | Summer |
| *A. lateriflorus* | 2-3 | Cluster | Fall |
| *A. novae-angliae* | 4-6 | Cluster | Fall |
| *A. novi-belgii* | 1-6 | Cluster | Fall |
| *A. oblongifolius* | 3-4 | Cluster | Late fall |
| *A. sedifolius* | 2-3 | Cluster | Fall |
| *A. tataricus* | 3-6 | Cluster | Late Fall |
| *A. thomsonii* | 1-3 | Cluster | Early Fall |
| *A. tongolensis* | 1-2 | Single | Early Summer |

***-alpinus*** (al-pine′ us) | Alpine Aster | 6-9″/1′
Early Summer | Purple | Europe | Zones 4-7

Plants are variable, but usually bear solitary, 1-2″ diameter purple flowers with 20-40 ray flowers and yellow centers. The foliage is entire and is gray-green in the spring but loses the gray color in the heat of the summer, particularly in the South. This is an excellent front-of-the-garden plant for cooler areas of the country. "Cooler" is the most important word in that sentence. It is absolutely not tolerant of hot, humid climates, and at the best of times is not a particularly long-lasting species in much of the country, 3-4 years being an average life span. Terrific plant for the West and upper plains states. Plants perform better with excellent drainage and gritty soils.

Seed germinates readily when placed in moist, warm (70-75°F) conditions.

**Cultivars:**

var. *albus* has white flowers but is a rather spindly grower.

'Beechwood' is seldom offered but has flowers of clear blue with yellow centers.

'Dark Beauty' has dark blue, almost purple flowers in early summer. This is also sold as 'Trimix'.

'Goliath' is so called because of the 2½-3″ diameter light blue flowers. It is taller than the species and grows to 15″.

'Happy End' offers soft pink flowers, gray foliage in the spring, and a compact habit.

'Pinkie' has bright pink 2″ wide on 10-12′ tall plants.

'Wargrave Variety' ('Wargrave Park') has pale pink flowers tinged with purple, which, unfortunately, tend to fade in bright sun.

***-amellus*** (a-mel′ lus) | Italian Aster | 2-2½′/2′
Summer | Purple | Italy | Zones 5-7

Plants have pubescent stems and leaves giving a rough appearance and feel. The leaves are entire, sessile and about 5″ long. The large, 2-2½″ diameter purple flowers consist of 20-30 narrow petals with orange-yellow centers. They are borne singly or in dense corymbs in early fall and bloom continuously to frost. The species itself, however, is seldom seen and improvements have been made to reduce height, increase color range, and reduce floppiness. Most of the new cultivars are 1-2′ tall and do not need staking unless overfertilized or if temperatures become exceptionally high. It is a particularly fine species for zones 5 and 6 and is good, but not as spectacular, in the heat and humidity of zones 7 and 8. *A. amellus* is one of the parents of the hybrid *A.* x *frikartii*.

**Cultivars:**

'Blue King' bears large violet-blue flowers on 2′ tall stems.

'Brilliant' has bright purple-pink flowers with yellow centers on 2½′ tall plants.

'Butzemann' produces sprays of small, violet-blue flowers. Only about 2′ tall.

'Joseph Lakin' has flat heads of blue flowers, 18″ to 2′ tall.

'King George' is an exceptionally fine selection offering deep purple flowers on 2-3′ tall stems. It is floriferous and requires no support.

'Nocturne' is often cited as a pink-flowered form but appears to be more bluish purple than pink. Although not as floriferous as 'King George', it is nevertheless a good selection.

'Peach Blossom' has violet-pink flowers.

'Pink Zenith' and 'Lady Hindlip' bear pink flowers with yellow centers on 2-3′ tall stems. The former is darker pink and shorter (2′) than the latter.

'Rudolph Goethe' was selected in 1914 and is still popular today. It bears violet flowers on 2-3′ tall stems.

'Sonia' is probably the best pink-flowered form, producing many 2″ diameter rich pink flowers with yellow centers on 1-2′ tall plants.

'Violet Queen' produces many deep violet-blue flowers with yellow eyes. This plant is probably as close to the species in color as any cultivar.

***-carolinianus*** (car-o-lyn-ee-aye′ nus) Climbing Aster 7-12′/4′
Fall Pink Southeastern United States Zones 6-9
(*Ampleaster carolinianus*)

If you are fortunate enough to live in mild areas of the country, you might want to give this aster a try. Its common name is a bit deceptive because plants don't climb by themselves but consist of long, lanky, arching stems. The plant is actually a big, messy shrub and but if you train it on a fence or run it through a trellis or even chicken wire, it is really rather impressive. Not a clematis, but then how many clematis flower in October?

This is a terrific rollicking plant, but takes up a good deal of space. Growing up to 12′ in length, each stem produces dozens of 1-2″ wide pink to purple flowers with yellow centers along their lengths. Easy to grow in full sun but partial shade is tolerated.

Propagate from divisions or terminal cuttings. Plants may be grown further north if a few cuttings are taken indoors before frost.

***-cordifolius*** (kord-i-foe-lee′ us) Heart-leaf Aster 4-6′/2′
Summer Pale Blue Eastern North America Zones 3-8
(*Symphyotrichum cordifolium*)

Plants are usually highly branched with many small flowers, each generally less than 1″ wide. Ten to twenty narrow ray flowers ranging from dark blue to off-white surround a yellow center. Although a good deal of variability occurs, smooth stems and scabrous (with short stiff hairs) pointed leaves are common. The thin, sharply toothed leaves have provided the plant with common names such as bee weed and bee tongue. Although plants often look bedraggled in the wild, cultivation tends to make them stand up straight and put their shoulders back. The lower leaves are heart shaped (cordate) and the upper leaves are ovate to lanceolate. The small blossoms lend themselves to cut flowers, particularly as fillers with larger flowers in arrangements. The species itself is offered but numerous cultivars have also been selected. Plants grow well in both the North and the South but leaf spotting becomes a bigger problem in the humidity of the South.

**Cultivars:**

'Avondale' has light blue flowers on 18-24″ stems.

'Elegans' bears many white flowers and is one of the best selections.

'Ideal' is 4-6′ tall with many violet-blue flowers. In the cut flower trials at the University of Georgia, plants were vigorous and yielded dozens of flower heads. Unfortunately, without fungicide applications, leaves tend to develop black spots in the summer.

'Photograph' produces lilac flowers in arching sprays rather than upright inflorescences.

'Silver Spray' has small white flowers with yellow centers. Plants are 3-4′ tall.

***-divaricatus*** (di-var-i-cah′ tus) White Wood Aster 1-2′/3′
Summer White North America Zones 4-8
(*Eurybia divaricata*)

This spreading aster is native from Maine to Georgia but for some reason is seen far more often in European gardens than in this country. It bears many thin, nearly black, cascading branches, at the end of which are corymbs of small (¾″ diameter), starlike white flowers with yellow centers, that are quite attractive to butterflies.

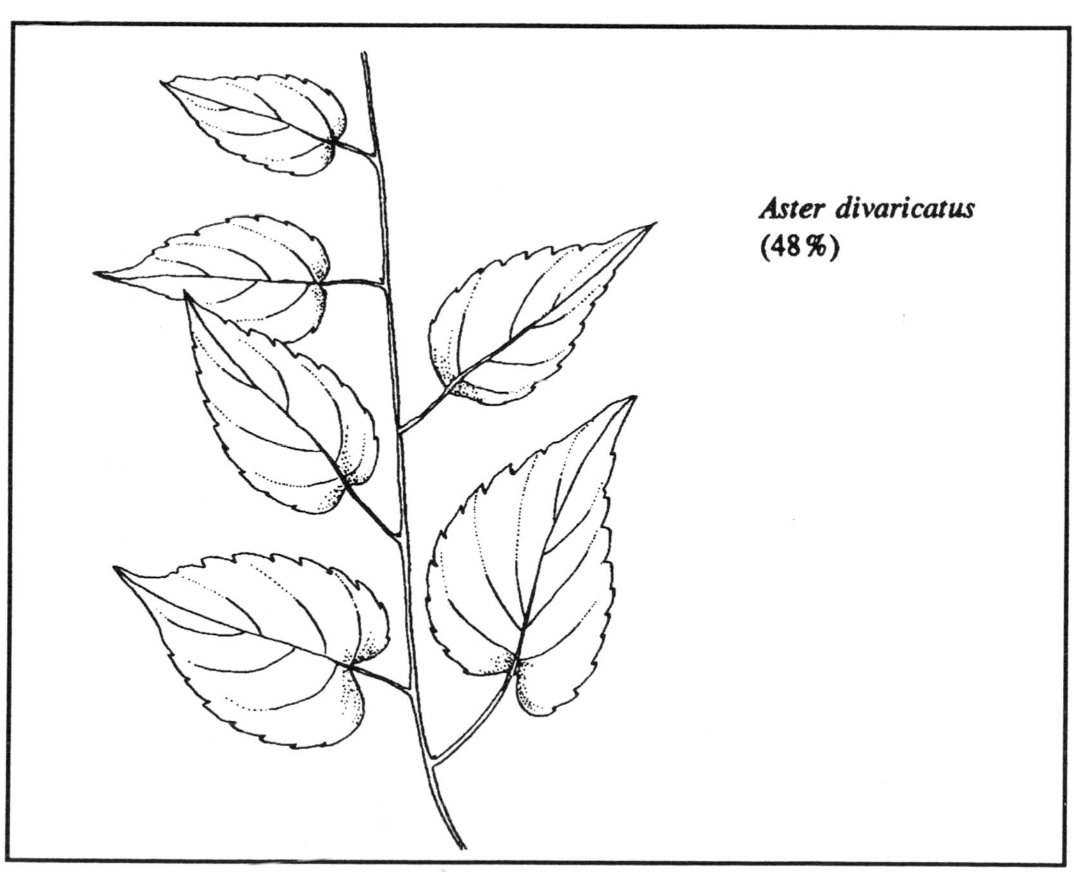

***Aster divaricatus* (48%)**

The blossoms may be small, but they are so plentiful that the plant is covered with clouds of flowers from mid August through September in the South and as late as October in the North. The leaves are about 3″ long, heart shaped, and coarsely toothed.

This is one of the few asters that tolerates shade. Plants may be used at the edge of woodlands or placed at the front of the border to grow through other plants. However, while shade is tolerated, more flowers and fewer foliar diseases occur in areas of morning sun and good air movement. Flowers are particularly pretty running in and among bergenias, a combination made popular by Gertrude Jekyll, the grand dame of English gardening. If, like me, you are not a big bergenia fan, allow the plants to ramble over hostas. In hot summers, in the Midwest and further south, it tends to be leggy. I cut my plants back to about 12″ in early June.

Division, terminal cuttings taken in the spring, or seed sown in the spring or fall are appropriate methods of propagation.

**Cultivars:**

'Eastern Star' is only about 12-18″ tall, a endearing characteristic to be sure. The same dark stems and white flowers with yellow centers occur. Plants have done well in the Gardens at UGA and have become quite popular. Plants bloom from late summer to early fall.

***-ericoides*** (e-ri-koi- deez) Heath Aster 3-4′/2′
Summer, Fall White United States, Mexico Zones 5-8
(*Symphyotrichum ericoides* var. *ericoides*)

Another roadside weed, but one that can become a fine garden plant and an economically important one to boot. The many needlelike, sessile leaves are pubescent, stiff, and very narrow, seldom more than an inch long (like *Erica*, heath). One of its old names was *A. multiflorus* (many-flowered), an equally descriptive name for this plant. The leaves are generally paler green than many other aster species. The daisies consist of 15-25 ray flowers, each only about ¾″ wide, giving each head a starry appearance. The bracts beneath the flowers end in broad, conspicuous green tips and a minute spine. Useless information, unless one wants to try to identify various species in this frustrating genus.

The small but numerous flowers (literally hundreds of flowers are produced) have resulted in cultivars used as commercial cut flowers from South America, Holland and the United States. They are used as fillers (like baby's breath) and are harvested by the acre in fields and greenhouses. Most available cultivars were selected mainly for cut flower production but these are useful for garden plants as well.

Plants multiply efficiently by rhizomes, and division is the quickest and easiest means of propagation.

**Cultivars:**

'Blue Star' bears hundreds of star-shaped dark blue flowers on 3′ tall stems.

'Blue Wonder' has blue flowers with a tinge of pink.

'Esther' has white flowers with a tinge of pink and is similar in growth habit to 'Monte Cassino', but is only about 18-24″ tall.

'Golden Spray' has wiry stems and grows 3-4′ tall. The small white flowers have a large golden center that lends a somewhat golden appearance to plants in full bloom.

'Monte Cassino' is not particularly well known to gardeners but it is a most popular cultivar for cut flower producers. It bears many stems with clusters of small white flowers on 24-30″ stems.

'Pink Cloud' produces clouds of starry light pink flowers on 3′ tall plants.

'Ringdove' was selected for its multitude of half-inch wide lilac-rose flowers.

'Snow Flurry' is more of a ground cover than an upright grower. The arching stems are only 6-9″ tall and covered in small white daisies. Good for falling over banks and walls. This is a neat plant.

'White Wonder' is similar in growth habit to 'Blue Wonder' but has creamy white flowers.

**-x *frikartii*** (fri-kart′ ee-eye) Frikart's Aster 2-3′/3′
Summer Lavender Hybrid Zones 5-8

*A.* x *frikartii* was raised in Switzerland around 1920 and was the result of crossing *A. amellus* x *A. thomsonii*. The large flowers of *A. amellus* combined with the long flowering season of *A. thomsonii* provided one of the best and most popular asters when it was introduced. Interestingly, it is a little taller than either parent. The dark green, pubescent foliage is mildew resistant and remains reasonably disease free throughout the season. The 2-3″ diameter, lavender-blue flowers start in late June in the South, late July further north and continue for about eight weeks. Plants should be placed in full sun and fertilized sparingly. The cultivars that resulted from this cross became instantly popular because of their mounding habit and summer flowers. However, their popularity has diminished considerably in this country in the last 10 years, as the mounding habit became sprawling and the persistence in the garden was questionable.

**Cultivars:**

Four selections were named from the original Swiss hybrid: 'Wonder of Staffa', 'Monch', 'Eiger' and 'Jungfrau' but the latter two are seldom seen in North America. 'Flora's Delight' was bred by the late Alan Bloom of Blooms of Bressingham using *A. thomsonii* 'Nana' and *A. amellus* 'Sonia' in the hope of widening the color range offered by Frikart. Named after his wife, 'Flora's Delight' is a little shorter than the Frikart hybrids and produces daisies of lilac-blue. Plants require well-drained soils and full sun.

'Monch' is reputed by many garden authorities to be the best *A.* x *frikartii* clone. It bears lavender blue flowers and stands 2½-3′ tall with a 3′ spread. Plants differ from 'Wonder of Staffa' by being less prone to falling, and having darker blue flowers.

'Wonder of Staffa' supposedly has lighter blue flowers than 'Monch' but the differences between these cultivars have been overstated. It is a challenge, to say the least, to distinguish between the flowers of each cultivar even when placed side by side. 'Wonder of Staffa' may be slightly taller (although I have seen little difference) than

'Monch' and in warm climates might require more support. Perhaps differences in cultivars have been obscured over the years as the demand continued to grow. It is possible that some material has been seed propagated to keep up with demand or that stock blocks have been mixed up on occasion.

Seeds of Frikart's aster are available but are phonies. The resulting flowers occur in many different shades of lavender and blue.

***-lateriflorus*** (lat-er-i-flor' us) Calico Aster 2-3'/3'
Late Summer, Fall White North America Zones 5-7
(*Symphyotrichum lateriflorum* var. *lateriflorum*)

One description of this species reads "many branched stems with narrow lanceolate dark green leaves and small bristly white flowers". Hardly makes you want to run out and buy a dozen. The species itself stands about 3' and flowers are often borne along one side (*lateri-*) of the stem in late summer and early fall. The tiny toothed leaves turn a nice coppery hue in the fall. If no improvements had occurred, it is doubtful that plants would have made their way into many gardens. However, a number of cultivars have gained this plant many fans. Native to the Plains states, plants need well-drained soils and full sun. Plants will tolerate hot days and warm nights, but are far better in areas where the night temperatures cool off.

**Cultivars:**

'Coombe Fishacre' is likely a hybrid with *A. lateriflorus* in its blood. Plants have dark green leaves with small pink ray flowers and dark centers. Not as horizontal as the favorite, var. *horizontalis*.

var. *horizontalis* ('Horizontalis') is one of the oldest and still a marvelous plant when grown in full sun and well-drained soils. Dark green leaves on horizontal branched stems make this bushlike aster unique. Add the white flowers with reddish centers, also borne on one side of those stems, and one has a wonderful garden plant. It may be used as a shrublike mass or even as a low-growing hedge. Flowers in mid fall.

'Lady in Black' has superceded most of the other offerings. Plants possess dark purple foliage that usually remains attractive throughout the season if temperatures are not consistently in the 90s. Tiny white asters with rosy centers appear in dense, branching sprays in early fall on rigid, purplish stems.

'Prince' is as good as if not better than 'Horizontalis'. Plants are about 3' tall, have the same small white flowers but also have handsome deep purple foliage. The foliage and flowers make an excellent contrast. In hot summers and in shady areas, the purple color turns green. Much better in climates with relatively cool nights and lower humidity.

***-novae-angliae*** (no'vay-ang' glee-aye) New England Aster 4-6'/4'
Late Summer Violet-purple Eastern United States Zones 4-8
(*Symphyotrichum novae-angliae*)

This common wild flower is one of the largest and prettiest in the genus but is seldom seen, having been superceded by newer but not always better cultivars. The

*Aster* × *frikartii* 'Monch'
(92%)

entire, 4-5″ long leaves are numerous and very hairy. This species and a few others similar to it may be separated from many others by looking at the base of the leaves. The two basal lobes of the leaves clasp the stem, poking out on either side. The flowers are 1½-2″ across and consist of 40-50 ray flowers surrounding a yellow center. The flowers are excellent for cutting and last longer in water than those of *A. novi-belgii*, New York aster. My friend Chris Hussey found out the hard way that harvesting the hairy stems of New England asters can cause a serious skin rash on hands and arms. Chris strongly recommends gloves and a long-sleeved shirt when tackling these fellows.

**Cultivars:**

'Alma Potschke' is an excellent 3-4′ tall bright rose selection. The flowers are 1-2″ across and have slightly curled petals. It is more compact (but still requires support) than other selections and less prone to topple.

'Barr's Pink' has 1½″ wide bright rose-pink, semi-double flowers on 4′ tall stems. 'Barr's Blue' and 'Barr's Violet' are similar in habit with blue and violet flowers respectively.

'Harrington's Pink' was developed by Mr. Millard Harrington of Williamsburg, Iowa, and is still a popular aster today. This 3-5′ tall plant bears large (1½″ diameter) salmon-pink flowers in September through October.

'Hella Lacy', named for the wife of garden writer Allen Lacy, is 3-4′ tall and covered with 2″ wide violet-blue daisies in the fall. Quite big and lanky in the heat.

'Honeysong Pink' bears pink flowers with bright yellow centers. Plants are strong growers on 3′ tall stems. A favorite of Mr. Bud Heist of Heistaway Gardens in Conyers, Georgia. In the South, people know that if Bud endorses a plant, it is a winner.

'Lye End Beauty' has lovely cerise flowers but grows 4-5′ tall and must be supported.

'Lyon's White' produces dozens of clean white flowers on 4-5′ tall plants in late September (October in the South).

'Martha' has silvery pink flowers growing 3-4′ tall and may be a cross between 'Hella Lacy' and 'Alma Potschke'. Selected by Allen Lacy.

'Mt. Everest' is 3′ tall with good, clear white flowers.

'Purple Dome' is a terrific introduction from Mt. Cuba Center in Delaware. Late-flowering on compact 18-24″ stature, the plants maintain a mounded habit even while supporting hundreds of deep blue flowers. Under high humidity environments, leaf and stem diseases can become problems in mid July and August. In Atlanta, plants do well most years but the heat and humidity take their toll in a cumulative manner. Its popularity has waned significantly but it can still be a great aster for the front of the sunny garden.

'Rosa Sieger' has large salmon-rose flowers on 4′ tall plants. Very eye-catching.

'Rose Serenade' is about 30″ tall and bears soft pink flowers in early fall.

'September Ruby' has 1″ diameter, deep ruby red flowers on 3-5′ high stems. If planted in rich soils or overfertilized, heights up to 5′ are not uncommon for this cultivar. Although classified as a late bloomer, flowering begins in late May in north Georgia and continues through late June. If the flowers are removed, it blooms again in September. Flowering is 3-4 weeks later in the Northeast but seldom do flowers peak in the fall. This is true with many so-called fall-flowering asters.

'Treasure' is 4-6′ tall with light purple to violet flowers.

'Wedding Lace' is 3-4′ tall with clean white flowers in early fall.

***-novi-belgii*** (no′ vee-bel-gee′ eye) New York Aster, Michaelmas Daisy 1-6′/3′
Late Summer Violet Eastern United States Zones 4-8
*Symphyotrichum novi-belgii* var. *novi-belgii*

There are literally hundreds of cultivars of this roadside weed. The specific epithet, *novi-belgii*, arose when the state of New York was once known as New Belgium. The history of breeding of Michaelmas daisies is a who's who of horticulture including the Honorary Vickary Gibbs, Ernest Ballard, A.H. Harrison, Barrs of Taplow and Alan Bloom, all of whom threw their talents into the aster fray. The smooth or nearly glabrous leaves differentiate them from New England asters. The leaves clasp the

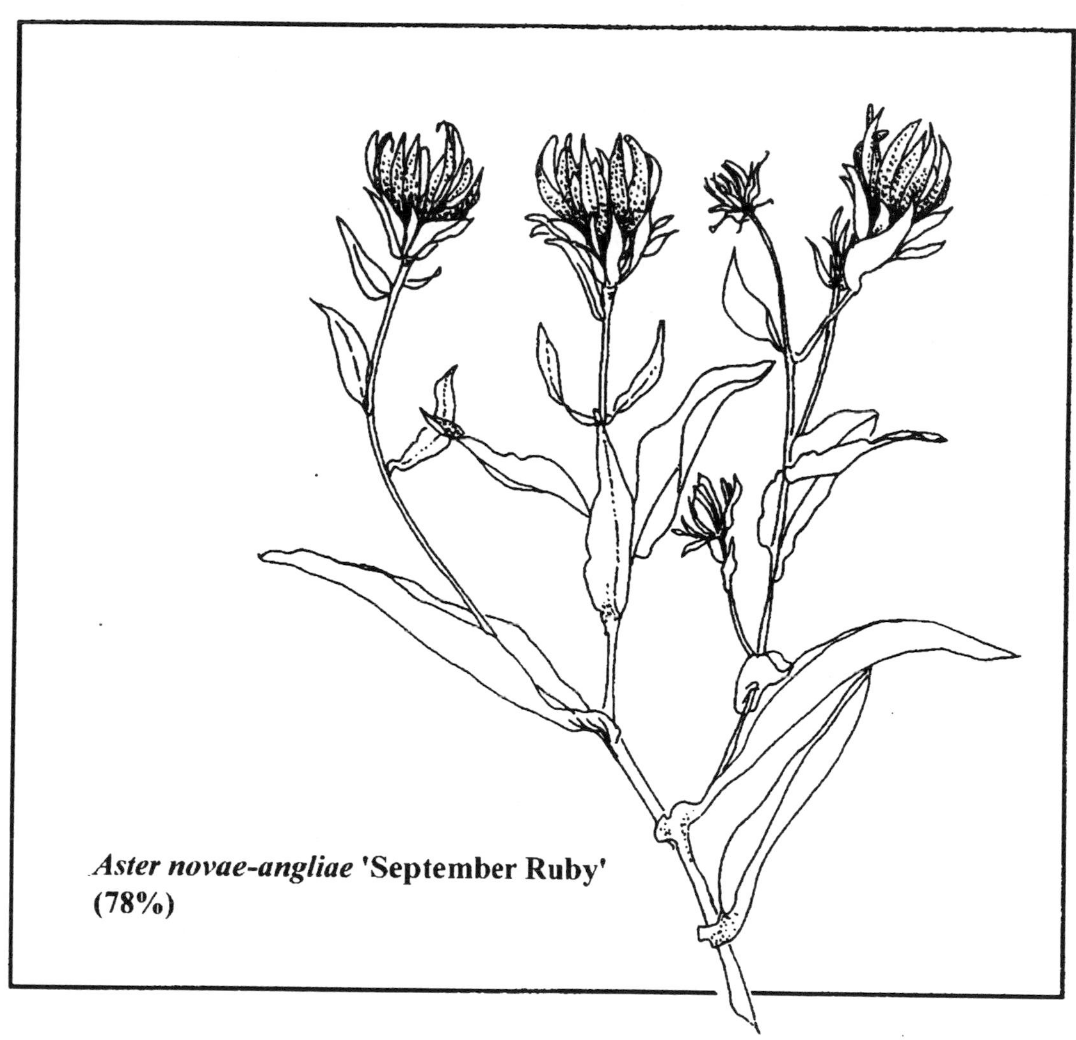

*Aster novae-angliae* **'September Ruby' (78%)**

stem similar to New England asters, but flowers normally have only 15-25 ray flowers. The flowers are not as good for cutting as the New England asters but provide excellent color in the late summer and fall garden. They are called Michaelmas daisies because they bloom around September 29, St. Michael's Day in the British Isles.

Somewhere along the way, many cultivars were placed under the name *A.* x *dumosus*. This was likely the result of European growers listing plants under this name and American growers following suit. The species, *A. dumosus* (*Symphyotrichum dumosus* var. *dumosus*) is a bushy, rather short plant (1-3′) native to fields and meadows from Florida to Texas, and north to Maine, Ontario and Illinois. It seems that any cultivar under 15″ tall has summarily been pushed into *A.* x *dumosus*. I can find no taxonomic evidence for the name change so I will maintain the listing of short cultivars under *A. novi-belgii*. It is likely that all the cultivars I list under "dwarf cultivars" are listed in most catalogs under *A.* x *dumosus*.

Propagate all cultivars by division or by terminal cuttings.

**Cultivars:**

*Dwarf cultivars* (less than 15″ tall). (*A.* x *dumosus*). Many of the dwarf cultivars are excellent for the front of the garden and, best of all, require no staking. Dozens more are available than these listed, but how many can we use?

'Alert' produces double crimson-red flowers on 12-15″ plants.

'Alice Haslem' was raised in the 1950s by Mr. A. H. Harrison of Gayborder Nurseries, in Derbyshire England. She has wonderful double rosy pink flowers.

'Audrey' bears 1″ wide lilac flowers on 12″ tall plants.

'Buxton's Blue' is only 4-6″ tall but produces many small dark blue flowers.

'Daniela' produces sculptured mounds of lavender-violet flowers, about 1-1½′ tall.

'Heinz Richard' forms compact 12″ mounds of foliage covered with semi-double salmon-pink flowers in late summer and early fall.

'Jenny' ('Jenny Margaret Rose'), also from the Gayborder Nursery, bears lovely red flowers on 12-15″ tall stems. Many Michaelmas daisies bear the Gayborder name and all are in this height range.

'Kassel' has semi-double carmine-rose flowers in early fall.

'Kristina' bears white daisy flowers on 15″ tall plants.

'Lady-in-Blue' is about 12″ tall with blue flowers in the fall.

'Little Pink Beauty' is one of my favorites, becoming covered in semi-double pink flowers in the fall. There is a complementary 'Little Blue Beauty' lurking about in catalogs as well.

'Nesthakchen' sounds like a sneeze but bears rather striking compact pinkish red flowers on 12″ tall plants. More mildew resistant than most others.

'Newton Pink' is another good pink, bearing semi-double flowers, on 12-15″ tall plants.

'Niobe' produces single white flowers with yellow eyes on 6-10″ tall plants.

'Peter Harrison' is a handsome Gayborder gentleman offering pink flowers in September and October on his trim 15-18″ frame.

'Pink Bouquet' is about 12″ tall with soft pink, daisylike flowers in late summer and fall.

'Prof. Anton Kippenburg' is 9-12″ tall and carries lavender-blue semi-double flowers. This excellent cultivar has withstood the test of time.

'Rosemarie Sallman' is about 2′ tall with pink-purple semi-double flowers.

'Sapphire' was introduced to North American gardeners in 2005. Plants are covered with lavender ray flowers surrounding yellow centers on a 12-16″ tall mounding plant.

'Snow Cushion' is a late bloomer (late September-October) with white flowers on 6-8″ tall plants.

'Snowsprite' has semi-double white flowers with yellow centers. It grows to 15″ tall.

'Violet Carpet' bears rich violet daisy flowers forming 8″ tall carpets.

'Wood's Dwarfs' are wonderful 8-12″ tall plants with purple-blue ('Wood's Purple') and pink ('Wood's Pink') and light blue ('Wood's Light Blue') flowers. In the Armitage garden, they begin flowering around mid September and persist for 4-6 weeks.

'Zwergenhimmel' is included because nobody can pronounce it, find it or grow it. However, it does exist, once more pointing out that breeders really don't care if anybody in the English-speaking world ever buys the plant. In case you are wondering, plants have light blue flowers.

*Medium cultivars* (less than 4′). Many require staking, especially those with large flowers.

'Ada Ballard' has double lavender-blue flowers atop 3′ tall stems. Most of the asters bearing the Ballard name will be medium to tall.

'Arctic' bears double white flowers.

'Beechwood' Rival' produces wine-red flowers on 3′ tall stems. At least five cultivars carry the Beechwood name, a popular series of cultivars all with rather large flowers and about 3′ tall.

'Bonningdale Blue' and 'Bonningdale White' grow nearly 3′ tall and produce 1-2″ wide blue and white semi-double to double flowers in September and October.

'Carnival' has rosy red flowers on 3′ tall plants.

'Christine Soanes' produces carmine-rose flowers on 2 ½′ plants.

'Crimson Brocade' is about 3′ tall and produces crimson-red flowers in late fall.

'Eventide' produces 2″ wide semi-double violet-blue flowers on 3-4′ high plants.

'Ernest Ballard' has reddish pink semi-double flowers up to 3″ wide. Many of the medium-sized cultivars are the result of the work of Mr. Ernest Ballard of Colwall, Malvern, England, who stands as a leader in the breeding of Michaelmas daisies. One of his traits was breeding large (1-3″ diameter) flowers on 2½ -3′ tall plants. Most Ballard family members have at least one cultivar as their namesake.

'Patricia Ballard' has semi-double rose pink flowers.

'Priory Blush' is at least 4′ tall with double white flowers tinged with a little pink. Very handsome but needs some judicious early summer pruning.

'Royal Ruby' and 'Royal Velvet' are 20-30″ tall and produce semi-double red and violet-purple flowers, respectively. Both raised by Alan Bloom of Bressinghams.

'Sailor Boy' is about 3½′ tall with semi-double violet-blue flowers.

'The Bishop' ('The Archbishop') bears deep red flowers on 2-3′ tall plants.

'Winston Churchill' would be proud of the handsome red daisy flowers on 2-3′ tall stems. They were fantastic in our cut flower trials at Georgia.

*Tall cultivars* (over 4′). I recommend none for the South and hesitate to recommend them at all. They are too tall for most gardens, require extensive support, and can become highly aggressive. All could use some pruning in the summer; however, if grown well, they are showstoppers. They are exceptional in flower and can be grown as long as they are pinched at least once in the spring or early summer and then supported.

'Cardinal' has deep rosy-red flowers surrounding a yellow center.

'Climax' is a 5′ tall giant with outstanding large (3-4″ across), light blue flowers in early fall. This was raised over 80 years ago and is one of the few old-time Michaelmas daisies still in cultivation.

'Fellowship' bears large clear semi-double pink flowers on 4-5′ tall stems.

'Mount Everest' has large (2-3″) semi-double white flowers in September and October.
'White Ladies' is 5-6′ tall with clear white flowers and an orange-yellow center.

***-oblongifolius*** (ob-long-i-foe′ lee-us) Aromatic Aster 2-4′/3′
Fall Blue-purple United States Zones 3-8
(*Symphyotrichum oblongifolium*)

The aromatic aster is loaded with blue-purple daisylike flowers that persist into late October, and is one of the last wild flowers to bloom. Plants are native to dry prairies and rocky bluffs from Pennsylvania to Wisconsin and south to North Carolina and Texas. The base of the flowers contains glandular hairs, which when brushed lightly, release a fresh, hard to describe but pleasant fragrance. This aster grows from rhizomes (as do most asters) and will attain height of about 2-4′ in the wild. Up to a dozen well-branched stems occur on a mature plant, and each holds narrow 1″ long leaves. The flowers are violet to pink to blue, each about an inch wide. The plants are spectacular at the San Antonio Botanical Garden, and they earned a Plant of Merit designation from the Missouri Botanical Garden in 2003. Enough said.

**Cultivars:**

'English Countryside' is still being sorted out. She appears to be mostly *A. oblongifolius*, but also seems to have a hefty chunk of New England aster in her as well. Plants bear beautiful lavender-blue flowers that absolutely smoother the plant in late fall. However, it may too late for Northern gardeners or as Judy Laushman of Oberlin, Ohio so aptly states "It flowers so late in northeast Ohio it's in danger of being snowed on." Plants definitely need a hard prune by early June in the South, late June in the North, or they will be far too vigorous. Found in Athens, Georgia. by the great garden designer Anne English.

'Fanny's Aster' is covered with blue flowers in late fall and grows up to four feet tall. An absolutely terrific aster, particularly in the South. Introduced by Nancy Goodwin, nursery lady and plantsperson extraordinaire, who acquired it from Ruth Knopf of Boone Hall Plantation in South Carolina. Turns out her maid, Fanny, passed it on to Ruth.

'October Skies' is a low-growing version of 'Raydon's Favorite', introduced by the Primrose Path Nursery. They have excellent lavender flower power but grow only about 2′ tall, even without pruning.

'Raydon's Favorite' may be even better, with purple flowers with yellow centers in the fall on stiff, hairy 2-3′ tall plants. The foliage also has a nice hint of mint. Plants originally came from south Texas, and are especially beautiful at the San Antonio Botanical Garden, a treasure of a place that should be on every plantsperson's map. Plants need full sun and well-drained soils.

***-sedifolius*** (say-di-fo′ lee-us) Rhone Aster 2-3′/3′
Fall Lilac Southern Europe Zones 4-7

This relatively unknown aster has rough hairy, linear, entire leaves and many stems resulting in a bushy habit. Each stem terminates in a corymb of 30-40 small

(1-1¼″across) starry blossoms. The individual flowers are not particularly ornamental but the plants are literally covered in a sea of lavender blue. The ray flowers are widely spaced around the yellow center. Plants should be grown in full sun and tolerate most soils assuming drainage is adequate.

Division is the surest and easiest means of propagation but seed sown and placed at 70-75°F under constant moisture germinates readily.

**Cultivars:**

'Nanus' is the most common form, the species seldom seen anymore. It is 18″-2′ tall and the flowers are only slightly smaller (1″) than those of the species.

***-tataricus*** (ta-tar′ ri-cus) Tatarian Daisy 3-6′/3′
Late Fall Blue Siberia Zones 4-8

One of the reasons for the popularity of this tall aster is that plants rarely require staking. Although it will reach heights of 6′ or more, seldom does growth exceed 3-4′ the first year. Plants resemble Swiss chard in the spring and summer but in early fall, flower stalks begin to emerge from the leafy mass. The erect stems are covered with straight bristly hairs (hispid) and the entire, lanceolate leaves are large (the basal leaves are up to 6″ wide and 2′ long), and sessile. The flower stems branch near the top resulting in dozens of blue to purple ray flowers with yellow centers. One of the best features of this aster is its late flowering. Although many asters flower until frost, they often look tired and worn out. This species does not start flowering until late September or early October so it still looks fresh in November. Tough to beat as a late-flowering garden plant. Plants will make large colonies within a few years, and division not only allows for more plants but keeps the garden from becoming one big chard patch.

**Cultivars:**

'Blue Lake' absolutely puzzles me. Looking at the plant in bloom, it has all the characteristics of *A. tataricus*, however, it blooms in the summer, unlike the very late flowering of the species. Stunning and a showstopper, give it a go.

'Jindai' was found by Rick Darke and Skip March, two excellent American plantsmen, in the Jindai Botanical Garden near Tokyo. It is a better selection for most gardens in that it is only 3-4′ tall. I have grown plants side by side with the species, the difference in height is dramatic, and 'Jindai' may flower a little later than the species.

***-thomsonii*** (tom-son′ ee-eye) Thomson's Aster 1-3′/2′
Late Summer Lilac Western Himalayas Zones 4-8

The leaves are coarsely toothed and the 1-2″ diameter lilac flowers are borne on long slender flower stems. One of the outstanding characteristics is its long blooming period and, as one of the parents of *A.* x *frikartii*, this trait was passed on to that hybrid.

**Cultivars:**

'Nanus' is only 12-18″ tall and is essentially the only form of *A. thomsonii* represented in gardens. It resembles a dwarf *A.* x *frikartii*. The 1-3″ long, pointed foliage is gray-

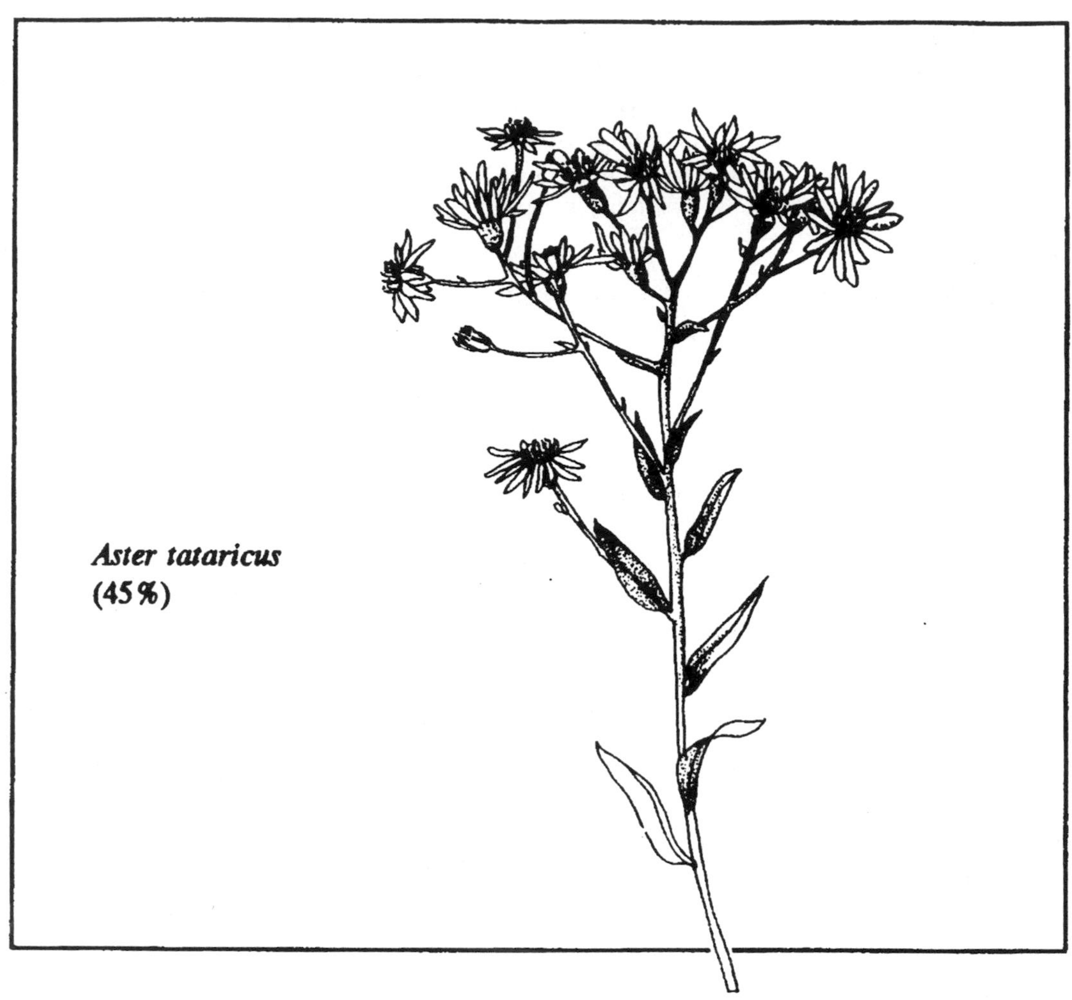

*Aster tataricus*
(45%)

green and the starry, blue flowers are about 1-1½″ in diameter. This is an excellent plant for the front of the garden where late color is desired. One of the favorite species of aster lovers.

***-tongolensis*** (ton-go-len′ sis) East Indies Aster 1-2′/1′
Early Summer Violet Western China Zones 5-8

Rosettes of dark green hairy leaves and solitary, 2″ diameter violet-blue flowers with bright orange centers are characteristics of this aster. The strong stems carry the flowers well and no support is necessary. Plants are stoloniferous and significant clumps can form under suitable conditions. Unfortunately, this summer-flowering aster is not long lived and survives only 2-3 years in the South, perhaps a little longer in zone 5.

Divide after flowering to keep plants vigorous.

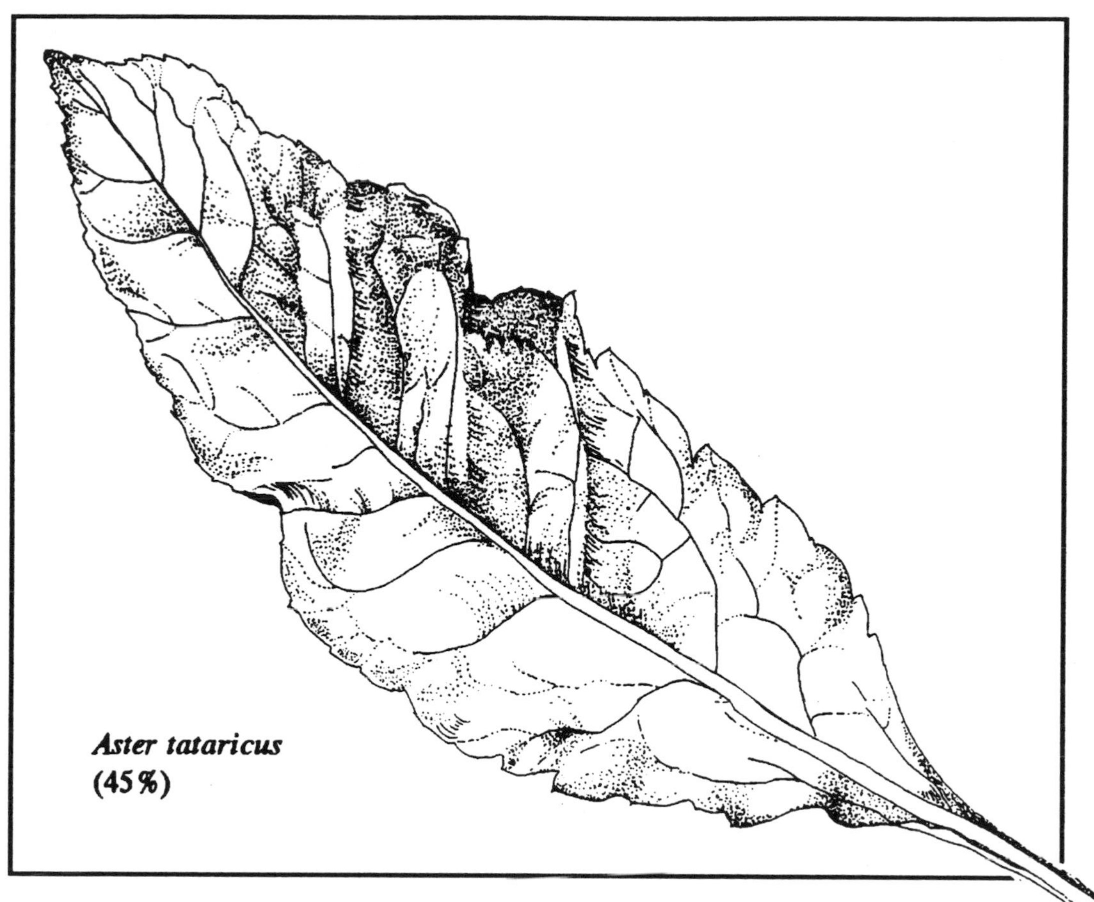
*Aster tataricus*
(45%)

**Cultivars:**

'Berggarten' has 2-3″ diameter violet-blue flowers with orange-yellow eyes.

'Napsbury' has violet blue daisies consisting of narrow ray flowers around a bright orange center.

'Wartburg Star' bears 1½″ diameter lavender-blue flowers with orange centers. Flowers are 2″ across and can bloom for weeks on end. The foliage is dark green and usually looks good. Flowers appear in June. The best of the cultivars offered.

**Related Species and Hybrids:**

Good grief, only hard core asterites can still be reading this stuff. Yet, believe it or not, there are still many little-known species are out there, just waiting to be discovered. Our native asters are becoming much more appreciated as the movement to more natural landscapes becomes commonplace, while the European breeders have added dozens of cultivars and hybrids to the palette. Here are a few I have fallen over, there are many more I have yet to trip on.

*A.* x *alpellus* is a cross between *A. alpinus* and *A. amellus*. 'Summer Greeting' has light blue ray flowers around orange centers; 'Triumph' has darker blue ray flowers. Plants are 12-15″ tall.

*A. azureus*, (*Symphyotrichum oolentangiense* var. *oolentangiense*) is also one of our native asters from the Plains states. Plants grow 2-3′ tall and bear deep blue to violet flowers and heart-shaped leaves. Sometimes called the sky blue aster. Zones 4-9.

*A. diplostephioides*, native to southeastern Tibet and western China, bears narrow reflexed lavender ray flowers with dusty lavender to reddish orange disc flowers. Plants are about 2′ tall and flower in late spring and early summer.

*A. grandiflorus* (*Symphyotrichum grandiflorum*), great aster, is one of the latest asters to flower and bears some of the largest flowers (up to 1½″ wide). They are violet-blue and held on 2-3′ tall plants. Native from Virginia to Florida and hardy in zones 5-9.

*A. laevis* (*Symphyotrichum laeve* var. *laeve*), smooth aster, combines dozens of blue ray flowers with yellow centers, dark stems and slightly blue-green smooth foliage on 3′ tall plants. Although a fairly common roadside plant, a little tending can make an eye-catching garden plant. 'Bluebird' bears 1″ wide violet-blue flowers and arching stems with handsome blue-green foliage. Plants are best if pinched by June 15th, otherwise they look leggy and un-catalog like. This selection was introduced by Richard Lighty of the Mt. Cuba Center.

*A. linariifolius* (*Ionactis linariifolius*), savory-leafed aster, is 1-2′ tall with 1″ entire, linear, stiff, sessile leaves. The many 1″ wide flowers are porcelain-blue to violet. Zones 4-8.

'Little Carlow' is a hybrid between cultivars of *Aster cordifolius* and *Aster novi-belgii*. It typically grows to 2′ tall with a similar spread and features clusters of 1-1½″ diameter sky blue asters (blue rays and yellow discs) which bloom in fall. The blue flower color (as opposed to the more common purple) sets this plant apart from most other asters.

*A. macrophyllus* (*Eurybia macrophylla*), bigleaf aster, native to the eastern United States, is about 4′ tall and flowers in August and September. It produces 8-10″ long serrated, heart-shaped (cordate) basal leaves with long petioles. The uppermost leaves become less cordate and are sessile (no petiole) at the top. Plants produce dense mats of foliage in the spring, and with sufficient light and moisture, produce leafy stems carrying 1″ diameter pale blue to violet flowers in a rounded, many-flowered corymb in the fall. They are late to flower but not as late as *A. tataricus*. A white-flowered form ('Alba') is also known.

*A. pilosus*, (*Symphyotrichum pilosum* var. *pilosum*) is one of the first perennials to invade abandoned agricultural fields and is considered a weed by most people who drive by it on the side of the road. However, with a little love and care, plants will become much less sprawling and will be covered with white flowers in late fall. The leaves are almost needlelike and similar to those of *A. ericoides*. I have seen wonderful garden specimens at the Mercer Arboretum and Botanic Gardens in Houston.

*A. ptarmicoides* (*Oligoneuron album*), upland aster, bears many white flowers in the summer on low-growing plants. The foliage is still erect, up to 6″ long and less than ½″ wide. Likely hardy from zones 3 to 8.

*A. puniceus* (*Symphyotrichum puniceum* var. *puniceum*), swamp aster, can produce thick treelike stems up to 6′ tall although a great deal of variability occurs in the wild. Plants are most at home in damp swampy conditions and look particularly ragged in dry soils. The stems and leaves are generally quite hairy and the leaves clasp the stem in the same manner as New England aster. Flowers are usually light blue, not the Phoenician purple that the Latin name suggests.

*A. sibiricus*, Siberian aster, are well-branched plants producing violet flowers with yellow discs in the early fall. A handsome plant.

*A. spectabilis*, (*Eurybia spectabilis*), looks similar to Frikart's aster but grows only 1-2′ tall and flowers much later. Plants are covered with showy violet-blue flowers on many-branched stems. Native from Massachusetts to North Carolina, plants are way underused.

*A. umbellatus* (*Doellingeria umbellata* var. *umbellata*), is found from Newfoundland to Georgia and bears umbel-like heads of small white flowers with yellow centers on 4-5′ tall stoloniferous plants. Plants spread aggressively by rhizomes. This is another example of a species that perks up significantly given a little garden care.

*A.* x *versicolor*, bicolor aster, resulted from a cross between *A. laevis* and *A. novi-belgii*. Plants grow 3′ tall with ray flowers that open blue or white and change to purple.

*A. vimineus* (*Symphyotrichum lateriflorum* var. *lateriflorum*), native to Kansas and Oklahoma, also bears very stiff narrow leaves but has a twiggy dense appearance. The leaves are slightly gray-green and many off-white flowers are held on slightly arching branches. 'Lovely' bears lovely lilac-pink flowers in late summer and early fall. Not well known and deserving of far more use. The new nomenclature system lumps this species in with *A. lateriflorus*.

*A. zzzzzz* I give up, haven't you?

### ***Asteromoea*** see *Kalimeris*

### ***Astilbe*** (as-til′ bee) False Spirea Saxifragaceae

Astilbes have enjoyed immense popularity for many years and can be excellent plants for shady, moist conditions. The individual flowers are small and without much merit, but the plumelike inflorescences range from 6″ to 2′ tall and can be extraordinarily striking. About 25 species of *Astilbe* have been described, and hundreds of cultivars are offered. Some are less than 1′ tall and useful for the front of the garden or rockeries while others are over 4′ in height and better suited for the back of the garden. No cultivar requires staking, and all last for years under good garden conditions. The mid to deep green foliage is 2 or 3 times divided into groups of three (biternate to triternate) and is often copper colored when young (particularly red-flowered hybrids). The biggest enemy of *Astilbe* is dryness; if the soil dries out, the foliage develops brown margins and whole leaves may wither and die prematurely. Ample moisture and rich soils result in a rewarding planting. This is more of a problem in areas of hot days and warm nights, but that can be said for the performance of many perennials. In my garden, I revel in the many astilbes that look good, but I don't try to compare them to those in Banff, Alberta.

Plants are particularly effective grouped around the edge of ponds or other water features in the garden. If grown in areas to their liking, they provide incomparable beauty during flowering and then will fade nicely as the season progresses.

Astilbes can also be used as potted plants forced into flower in the greenhouse. Plant the crowns in 6" pots in late summer and allow them to establish good root and foliage systems during the fall. Place them in a cold frame or bury under straw mulch so they receive approximately 3 months of sub 40°F temperatures. At that time, bring the pots inside and water and fertilize as foliage and flowers appear. Astilbes also make excellent cut flowers if harvested when the inflorescence is half open. Propagate from divisions in spring or fall. Some of the species may be raised from seed but the hybrids must be propagated vegetatively. Seed should be sown in moist sand-peat mixture and placed at 70-75°F for 2 weeks followed by 40°F for 4 weeks.

Quick Reference to Astilbe Species

| | Height (in.) | Flowering season | Flower color |
|---|---|---|---|
| *A.* x *arendsii* | 24-48 | Late Spring | Various |
| *A. biternata* | 36-60 | Late Spring | White |
| *A. chinensis* | 8-15 | Summer | Red-pink |
| *A. chinensis* var. *taquetii* | 24-48 | Late Summer | Lilac |
| *A.* x *rosea* | 24-36 | Summer | Salmon, pink |
| *A. simplicifolia* | 12-18 | Summer | Pink, white |

**-x *arendsii*** (ah-rendz' ee-ie) Hybrid Astilbe 2-4'/2'
Late Spring Various Hybrid Origin Zone 4-8

Over 95% of the astilbes sold in this country probably belong to this group of hybrids. Not enough can be said about the accomplishments of Georg Arends (1862-1952), of Ronsdorf, West Germany, who studied and hybridized such genera as *Bergenia, Sedum, Phlox* and *Campanula.* His passion, however, was *Astilbe.* One of his first introductions (1903) using *A. chinensis* and *A. japonica* was a light pink cultivar called 'Peach Blossom', still enjoyed by gardeners today (this has since been reclassified as *A.* x *rosea* to designate hybrids of *A. chinensis* and *A. japonica* parentage only).

Additional clones arose from crosses among other species including *A. grandis, A. thunbergii, A. davidii,* and *A. astilboides.* In 1933, a major breakthrough came with the appearance of a bronze leafed, red-flowered cultivar later named 'Fanal'. Arends continued crossing combination after combination and between 1902 and 1952 introduced over 74 cultivars, many of which are available in North American nurseries. Astilbes also caught the attention of other nurseries such as the Lemoine Nursery in Nancy, France and Blooms of Bressingham in Diss, England. Well over fifty cultivars are available, ranging from those with copper to dark green foliage; flower colors from clear white to blood red; and flowering times of early June to mid August.

**Cultivars:**

It is impossible to name all cultivars within the confines of this book but the following list includes some personal favorites as well as other popular selections.

Many cultivars have been reclassified under *A.* x *hybrida*, *A.* x *japonica*, *A* x *rosea* and *A.* x *thunbergii*, but differences from the garden point of view are absolutely inconsequential.

*White flowers:*

'Avalanche' is about 2′ tall with wide, arching inflorescences.

'Bridal Veil' is about 2½′ tall with white-pink flowers.

'Bumalda' produces rosy white plumes and grows about 2′ tall.

'Deutschland' bears dense flower spikes on 2′ tall plants.

'Diamond' has fairly clean white flowers on 2-3′ tall plants.

'Ellie' bears large white flowers on thick mid to dark green foliage. Showier than most whites.

'Gladstone' ('W.E. Gladstone') produces 18-24″ tall plants with creamy white inflorescences.

'Irrlicht' has rosy white flowers over dark green foliage. It grows 2-2½′ tall.

'Professor van der Wielen' has loose flower spikes on 3′ high plants. A terrific plant which can also substitute for goat's beard. A hybrid of *A. thunbergii.*

'Queen of Holland' bears white flowers tinged with pink and bronze foliage.

'Snowdrift' is a sport of 'Irrlicht' and produces clear white flowers over 2½′ tall stems.

'White Gloria' is an early-flowering cultivar about 2′ tall. The tight flowers are not as graceful as some of the more airy-flowered forms, but they flower well and without complaint.

*Pink to salmon flowers:*

'Anita Pfeifer', bred in 1930 by the Arends nursery, produces bright salmon-rose flowers on 24-30″ plants.

'Astary Pink' is a seed-propagated form that grows only 10-15″ tall.

'Betsy Cuperus' is one of the oldest cultivars, bred in 1917, and is occasionally offered today. Long sprays of blush pink flowers are held on 3′ tall plants. A hybrid of *A.* x *thunbergii.*

'Bremen' grows about 3′ tall and bears deep pink flowers.

'Bressingham Beauty' has arching plumes of clear pink flowers on 3½′ tall plants.

'Catherine Deneuve' is almost as beautiful as her namesake. Fluffy rose-pink flowers top 24-30″ tall plants.

'Cattleya' bears orchid-pink, long blooming flowers on 3′ high plants. A cultivar that performs well all over the country.

'Country and Western' grows about 20″ tall and sports light pink flowers.

'Düsseldorf' grows 2-2½′ tall and produces salmon-pink flowers.

'Elizabeth Bloom' has dark green foliage with handsome pink flowers.

'Erica' is about 3′ tall and has large open panicles of clear pink flowers.

'Europa' is an early-flowering cultivar bearing pale pink flowers over 2′ tall plants.

'Flamingo' has bright pink flowers produced on many branched stems. The dark green foliage is a nice contrast. 18-20″ tall.

'Gloria' flowers in midsummer with rosy lavender flowers on 30″ tall plants.

'Grete Pungel' is at least 3′ tall, has pink flowers and blooms in early to midsummer. An Arends introduction dating back to 1924.

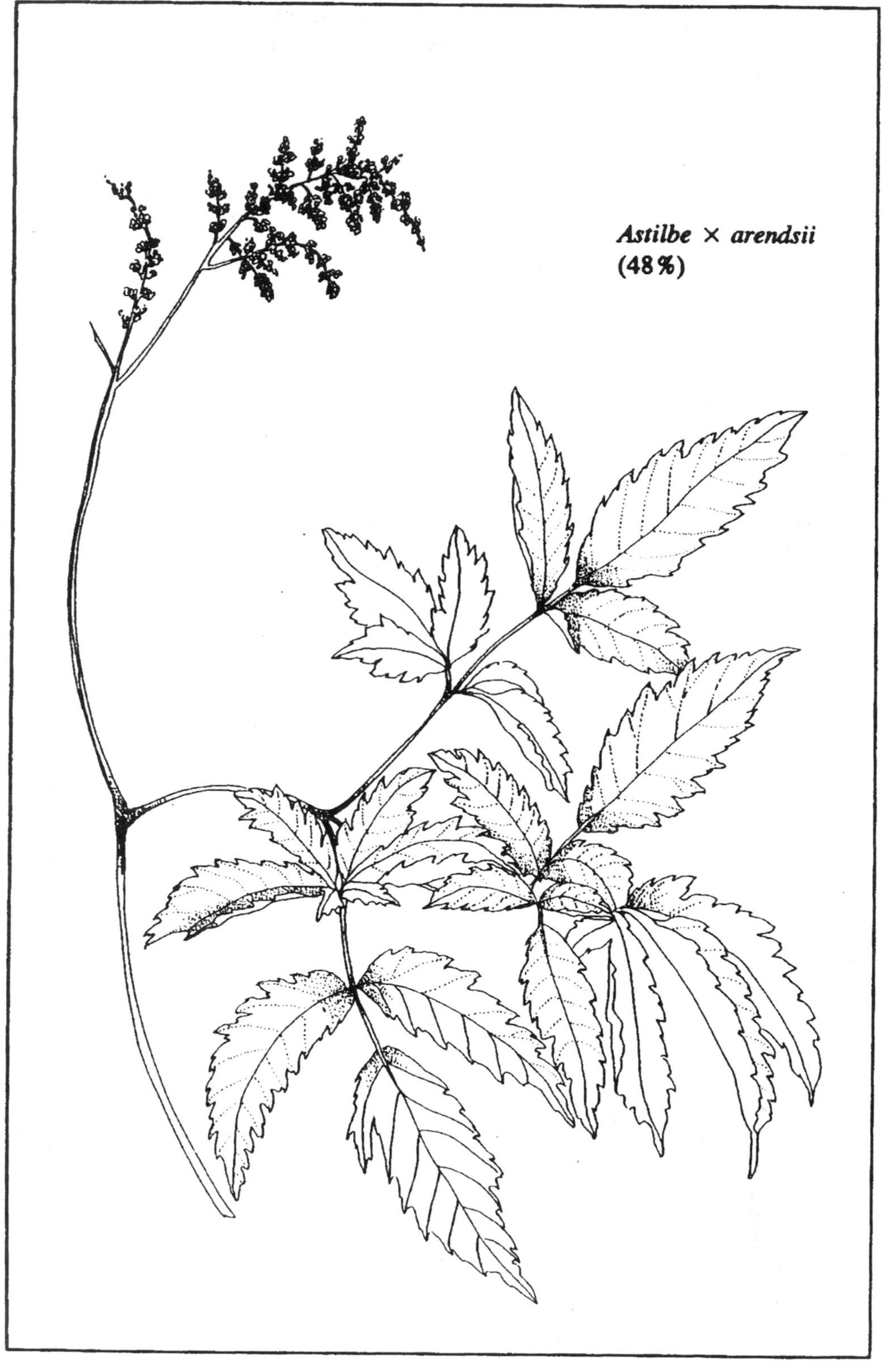
*Astilbe × arendsii*
(48%)

'Irene' has lovely light pink flowers on 2′ tall plants.

'Lollypop' is a reasonably new deep pink-flowered form with dark green foliage, which looks good even when not in flower.

'Love and Pride' (who names these things?) has purple-pink flowers on 2½′ tall plants. The foliage is bronze in the spring, but greens up later.

'Mainz' produces handsome lavender-pink flowers with dark green foliage.

'Ostrich Plume' bears many bright pink arching spikes over 3′ tall plants. An *A.* x *thunbergii* hybrid.

'Peaches and Cream' is more pink than white, but the two colors on the same plume account for the name. Plants are about 2′ tall.

'Pink Lightning' grows about 2′ tall with handsome, deep pink flowers over dark green foliage.

'Rheinland' is popular and has early clear pink flowers on 2′ tall plants.

'Sheila Haxton', a new introduction from Blooms of Bressingham, has *A. chinensis* 'Pumila' in its parentage. The flowers are deep pink and a little over 2′ tall. Plants have performed very well in the Gardens at UGA.

'Touch of Pink' is 2-2½′ tall with glossy green leaves. The flowers are sort of white with pink or pink with white, depending on climate.

*Red to magenta flowers:*

'America' bears lilac rosy flowers on open plumes. Old-fashioned but tough.

'August Light' produces intense red flowers on 2-2½′ tall plants. Red stems in the spring add to its appeal.

'Burgundy Red' has dark red flowers over glossy green foliage.

'Etna' has dark red plumes with dark green foliage on 2′ tall plants.

'Elisabeth van Veen' bears raspberry red flowers on stiff upright 2′ tall plants. This is sometimes sold as 'Elizabeth'.

'Fanal', first offered in 1933, is one of the most popular astilbes offered. It is small (2′ in height), early to flower, and produces blood red blooms above dark bronze leaves.

'Federsee' adapts well to dry conditions. Plants produce 2′ long panicles of carmine-rose flowers.

'Fire' ('Feuer') produces eye-catching fiery-red flowers on 30″ plants.

'Gertrud Brix' is also carmine-red and plants are only 2′ tall.

'Glow' is only 1-1½′ tall with intense red flowers.

'Granet' is about 2′ tall and bears carmine red blooms.

'Jo Ophorst' has late-flowering, stiff magenta spikes on 3′ tall plants.

'Lilli Goos', raised in 1930, is still a handsome red to pink late-flowering cultivar. About 30″ tall with dark green foliage.

'Mars' is an early violet-flowering cultivar growing about 2′ tall.

'Montgomery' is a terrific scarlet-red flowering plant 2-3′ tall.

'Radius' is an exceptionally good red-flowered cultivar. Plants grow 2-3′ tall and the flowers persist for weeks.

'Red Charm' has a good deal of *A. thunbergii* in its pedigree, accounting for its robust size (3-4′ tall) and arching red flower plumes. Close to true red as any cultivar I've seen.

'Red Light' has intense red flowers and exceptionally handsome shiny green foliage.
'Red Sentinel', an early-flowering cultivar, produces red flowers on 3′ tall plants.
'Spartan' bears dark red flowers on 2-3′ tall deep green plants.
'Spinell' bears salmon-red flowers atop 3′ tall stems.
'Vesuvius' has early bright salmon flowers on 2′ tall plants.

***-biternata*** (bye-ter-nay′ ta) Native Astilbe 3-5′/3′
Spring White Southeastern United States Zones 4-8

Must be me. I have written about this plant for years and years, in fact, in the last edition I said that it was "an uncut diamond . . . just waiting to be discovered." Still waiting, I am afraid. I may be the only person in North America who enjoys this plant. I still keep hoping others will give it a try.

Plants grow at least 3′ tall and 5′ plants are not uncommon in moist organic soils. The serrated foliage is biternate (blade divided into 3 segments, which are again divided into 3 segments) and slightly hairy. The yellowish white flowers are held in large drooping panicles which, while they can't compete with the shocking reds and carmines of some of the cultivars, lend a wonderful classical feel to the garden. Compared to the hybrids, it is most similar to 'Professor van der Wielen', which can be substituted if *A. biternata* cannot be located. Partial shade, rich soil and ample moisture are necessary for best performance.

Plants can be propagated from seed, division or root cuttings. One of the most successful propagations occurred inadvertently when we tilled our University garden in the fall. The next spring a half dozen plants emerged, the result of our tiller cutting the roots of dormant plants. Not recommended but effective.

***-chinensis*** (chin-en′ sis) Chinese Astilbe 1½-2′/2′
Summer Rosy White China Zones 4-8

The species is seldom seen in gardens, and was once almost totally represented by the dwarf variety *pumila*. Recently, renewed interest in this tough species has resulted in a number of new cultivars for North American gardeners. The dark green ternate (in 3 segments) foliage is rounded at the base of the hairy segments and is doubly serrated. A group of plants makes an excellent ground cover for a moist, shaded area. The flowers are held in branched, rather narrow panicles and while the species itself is rosy white, most of the cultivars are rose to purple. Plants are doubly handsome due to the deeply incised bronze-green foliage. Although garden performance is far better in moist soils, it is one of the more drought-tolerant astilbes.

**Cultivars:**

'Finale' grows about 18″ tall and bears handsome spikes of light pink flowers.
'Intermezzo' has salmon-pink flowers on 24-30″ tall plants.
'Maggie Daley' bears fuzzy lavender-purple flowers over glossy green foliage. Plants stand about 2½′ tall.
'Pumila' (var. *pumila*) is the most common form offered. Plants bear dense branched inflorescences of lavender-purple. It is obvious that not all material labeled as var.

*pumila* has been propagated vegetatively or originated from the same parent stock. I have seen this variety as an 8″ ground cover and as a 2-2½′ border subject. Some of the variations can be attributed to climate and presence of soil moisture (plants will be taller and more vigorous in consistently moist soils than in those that dry out), however, even in the same climatic zones and in relatively similar moisture regimes, variation in height is considerable (or plants are mixed up).

'Purple Glory' stands about 2′ tall with tight purple inflorescences.

'Serenade' bears rosy pink flowers a little later than other cultivars on 15-18″ plants.

'Sister Theresa' is a stiff upright grower, with light pink flowers. Plants grow about 2′ tall.

'Spatsommer' is very late and produces bright rose flowers on 2′ plants.

'Veronica Klose' grows 18-24″ tall with many purple-rose flowers.

Visions series has more upright flowers than others in the species and deep bronze green foliage. The flowers are pink-purple. In the Armitage garden it is outstanding. Recently, two selections of 'Visions' were introduced with similar habits and good flowering characteristics. 'Visions in Pink' and 'Visions in Red' appear to be as good as the original cultivar and should become popular.

var. *taquetii* has always been known as *A. taquetii* (ta-get′ ee-eye) but has recently been reclassified as a variant of *A. chinensis*. This variety is most commonly represented in gardens by the very vigorous and late-flowering 'Superba' but other cultivars have been offered. Compact columnar panicles up to 5 inches tall extend the flowering season of *Astilbe* into late summer and occasionally early fall. In north Georgia, flowering ceases in early to mid June whereas those of *A.* x *arendsii* hybrids finish 2-4 weeks earlier. Further north, flowering may continue into late August. The flower stems are far more hairy and the flowers are more dense than those of the *A.* x *arendsii* hybrids and make excellent cut flowers, persisting over a week in water. The seed heads retain the majesty of the flower spires and persist throughout the winter. Many cultivars (and hybrids) of this variety have recently appeared. They will still often be found under *A. taquetii* in most catalogs.

'Pink' produces flowers that are more pink than they are purple, the common color of this variety. The pink is still not a true pink, but is a little less harsh than the common forms.

'Purple Candles' bears purple-red flowers on 3′ tall plants.

'Purple Lance' is large (4-4½′ tall) with big purple-red blooms appearing in late summer. The flower plumes are longer and considerably narrower than others. In cool summers, even the flower stems will be red.

'Superba' is the most common form, bearing tall narrow stalks of lavender-purple flowers.

| **-x *rosea*** (ros′ ee-a) | | Rose Astilbe | 2-4′/2′ |
|---|---|---|---|
| Summer | Pink | Hybrid | Zones 4-8 |

The result of crossing *A. chinensis* and *A. japonica*, a 3′ tall white-flowered species, this hybrid has the habit of *A. japonica* and the flower color of *A. chinensis*. The original hybrid is seldom seen in gardens, having been superseded by various selections.

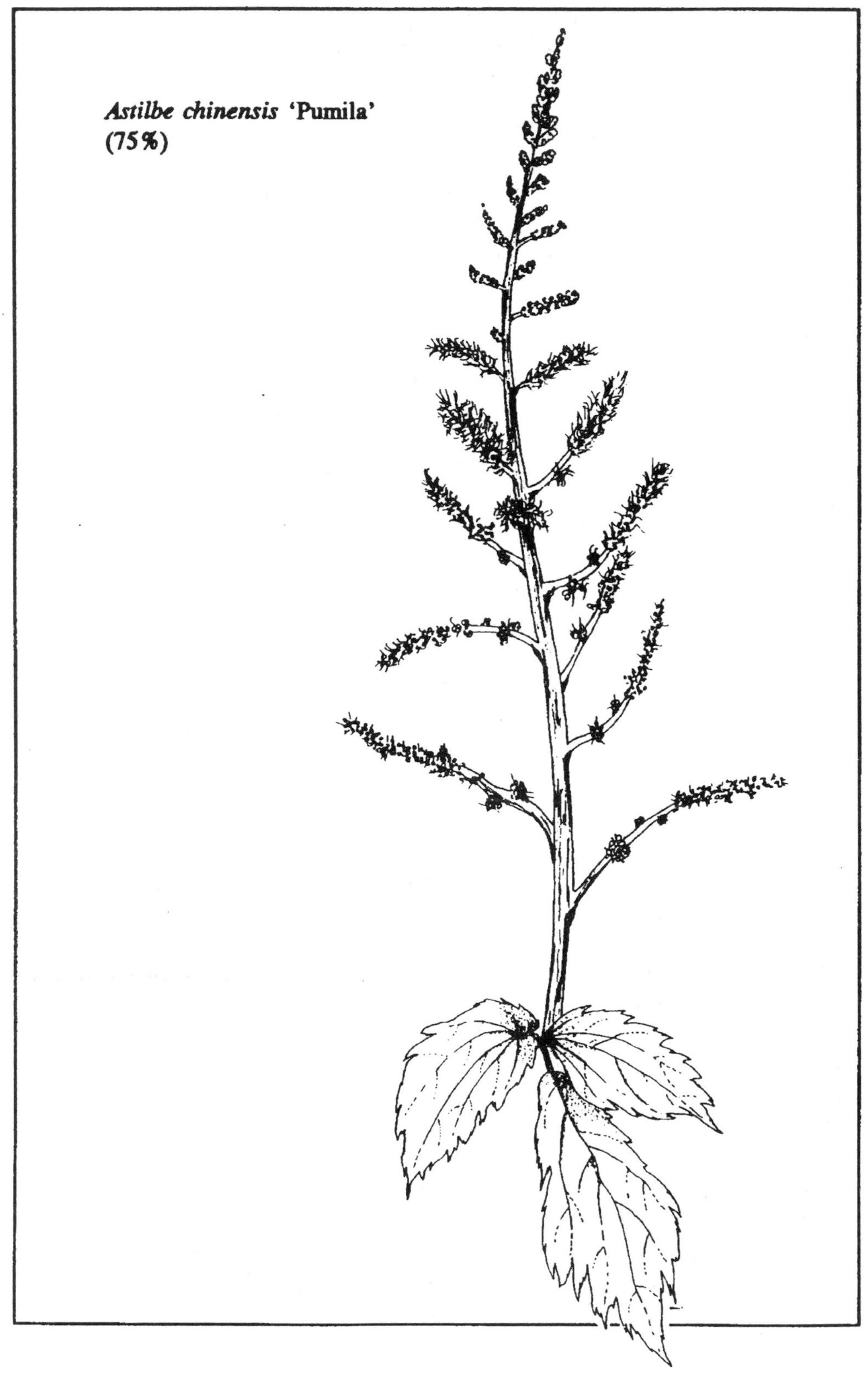

*Astilbe chinensis* 'Pumila'
(75%)

**Cultivars:**

'Peach Blossom' is 3-4′ tall and produces salmon-pink blooms clustered in large racemose panicles.

'Queen Alexandra' is a deeper pink but otherwise similar to 'Peach Blossom'. These cultivars are both excellent for damp places, and intolerant of drought conditions. They were some of the first hybrids (1903) raised by Georg Arends.

**-*simplicifolia*** (sim-pli-si-fo′ lee-a) Star Astilbe 1-1½′/2′
Summer White Japan Zones 4-8

This dwarf species has undergone considerable selection and hybridization, having caught the attention of Arends in 1911. The 3″ leaves are either simple (not compound) or a single group of three (ternate leaves). Hybridization has resulted in more compound leaves than simple leaves and has made identification more difficult. The leaves are nearly always glossier than other hybrids or species and are good looking even without flowers or fruit. It forms compact mounds of medium green, glossy, deeply cut foliage that gives rise to white starlike flowers in airy, open panicles in June and July in the South and July and August in the North. The seed heads are nearly as ornamental as the flowers and provide an additional 1-2 months of useful garden effect.

**Cultivars:**

Most cultivars are likely hybrids between *A. simplicifolia* and other species, but resemble *A. simplicifolia*. They are slower to establish than the *A.* x *arendsii* hybrids and require 2-3 years to reach mature size.

var. *alba* has white flowers which are "cleaner" than those of the species.

'Aphrodite' is one of the larger cultivars in this species, growing 15-20″ tall, and bears salmon-red flowers over dark green leaves. The upright, rather than arching, plumes set this plant apart from the others.

'Atrorosea' has 18-20″ tall bright rose-salmon plumes.

'Bronze Elegance' produces rose pink blooms in August over bronze foliage. Very handsome.

'Carnea' grows about 15″ tall and bears deep salmon flowers in late summer.

'Dunkellachs', raised in 1940, has recently appeared in the United States. A little taller than other cultivars, plants grow about 2′ tall and produce large trusses of salmon flowers over deep bronze foliage.

'Hennie Graafland' grows about 16″ tall and produces rosy flowers over shiny dark green leaves. Flowers in July and remains handsome for 4-6 weeks.

'Inshriach Pink' produces 10″ tall pink spikes over bronze-green crinkled foliage. Raised by the nurseryman Jack Drake of Inshriach Nursery in Aviemore, Scotland.

'Sprite', raised by Alan Bloom, is the most popular cultivar and was named the 1994 Perennial Plant of the Year by the Perennial Plant Association. It has airy, shell-pink blooms over bronze foliage and grows 12-18″ tall. The rust colored seed heads are particularly outstanding.

'White Sensation' is a relatively new offering characterized by many white-flowering stems and glossy green foliage. Plants stand about 18″ tall.

'White Wings' appears to have *A. simplicifolia* in its veins. Plants are about 18-24″ tall, with bright dark green leaves and white flowers.

'William Buchanan' is one of the most dwarf cultivars. Growing only about 6-8″ tall, pale pink flowers are formed over dense curly foliage.

**Related Species:**

*A.* x *crispa* has been in horticultural literature since 1924, however, compared to other hybrids, it is relatively unknown. The 12-15″ tall hybrid, also raised by the Arends nursery, forms a mat of dark green fernlike foliage that turns bronze in the fall. The flowers of the species are creamy white but flowers of 'Liliput' are salmon-pink. 'Perkeo' is the most available cultivar in North America and bears dark pink flower spikes and grows 8-10″ tall.

*A. glaberrima* reaches only about 3-5″. The leaves are bronze and the flowers are purple. It is generally offered as 'Saxatilis'.

## *Astilboides* (a-stil-boy′ deez) Saxifragaceae

This genus is the result of a taxonomic split from the genus *Rodgersia*, and in this case, the split seems to make sense. Only one species is recognized, *A. tabularis* (syn. *Rodgersia tabularis*). Leaves are not compound as in *Rodgersia* but are immense, circular and slightly lobed. They are peltate, meaning that the petiole attaches to the middle of the leaf, and may be 3′ across. The leaves resemble those of *Darmera peltata* while the flowers resemble those of a large astilbe. The inflorescence is made up of long plumes of creamy white flowers that extend well above the foliage. Both sepals and petals are found on the flowers, whereas those of *Rodgersia* are apetalous.

Plants grow at least three feet tall and equally wide. These are not plants for the small garden. Although hardy in zones 5-7, plants are not easy to establish unless assured of moist, cool conditions. A wonderful plant where well-grown, sure to elicit all sorts of comments.

## *Astrantia* (a-stran′ tee-a) Masterwort Apiaceae

This interesting genus encompasses about 10 species although none is particularly common in American gardens. Plants are useful for moist, shady areas and benefit from copious amounts of organic matter. The white to pink flowers are surrounded by a "collar" of bracts which produce a starlike effect. The flower head is a compound umbel and consists of both sterile and fertile flowers. The sterile flowers have long flower stalks (pedicels) and the fertile flowers are short stalked. Night temperatures are too warm to grow *Astrantia* much further south than zone 7a unless at higher altitudes. Cool night temperatures, partial shade, and consistent soil moisture are necessary for best performance. *Astrantia major*, the most common garden species, is well known in flower gardens in Europe, particularly the British Isles, and is now finding its way over here. It is about time! They persist for 10-14 days as a cut flower and are produced commercially as such in the Netherlands and California.

*Astrantia* is easily increased by division of the black roots in autumn or early spring. It also spreads by runners just below the surface and reseeds itself where it is comfortable.

Quick Reference to Astrantia Species

| | Height (ft.) | Flower color |
|---|---|---|
| *A. major* | 2-3 | Greenish white to white with tinge of pink |
| *A. maxima* | 2-3 | Rose-pink |

***-major*** (may′ jor) Great Masterwort 2-3′/1½′
Late Spring Greenish White Europe Zones 5-7

The 2-3″ diameter flowers are greenish white with a collar of green bracts and borne in a many-flowered umbel. The basal leaves have a petiole, 3-7 deeply cut lobes and are toothed while the leaves on the flower stem have widely expanded petioles which clasp directly to the stem, and are seldom toothed. The bracts are often tinged purple which give the effect of pink flowers. Plants spread rapidly under good growing conditions and form a formidable clump. A tremendous amount of variation occurs within the species, due to the large amount of seed and the propensity to shift colors. White, rose, and pink flowers can all occur in the same planting over a few years. I've noticed that some enterprising nurserypeople have taken advantage of this natural occurrence and offer a range of colors under the name Rainbow. The rainbow will only get more colorful if planted where they can multiply.

Plant in semi-shaded moist areas. They are at their best in cool, moist, shaded areas.

**Cultivars:**

'Abbey Road' is a recent introduction with dusky purple flowers on 18-22″ stems. This may be a hybrid with *A. maxima*.

'Alba' bears white flowers. In shaded areas, flowers light up the area more than the species.

'Claret' has become quite popular, being another dark red-flowering form on 20-24″ stems. Plants have dark stems and appear to be quite floriferous. It is difficult to tell the many dark red forms apart so try what is available in your local garden center.

'Hadspen Blood' is about 2′ tall with deep crimson bracts. Plants originated in the gardens of Nori and Sandra Pope in Hadspen, England.

*involucrata* is a subspecies and includes a number of cultivars with an extra long collar of pink bracts. One of the most impressive cultivars is 'Margery Fish', better known as 'Shaggy', a most apt description of the flowers. The true cultivar should be vegetatively reproduced from cuttings, although some seedlings with long bracts will occur.

'Lars' has shown excellent vigor and produces dark red flowers.

'Magnum Blush' has creamy white flowers with a tinge of pink.

'Moira Reid' is a most interesting plant with large pink flowers and salmon-peach collars.

'Moulin Rouge' is one of the newer cultivars and bears dark red flowers. Plants grow 18-24″ tall.

'Roma' is about 2½′ tall and produces deep pink flowers.

'Rosea' bears rose-colored flowers with deeply incised leaves.

'Rose Symphony' is a wonderfully handsome plant with rosy pink flowers with a silver collar of bracts. Plants are about 2′ tall.

'Ruby Wedding' has ruby red centers surrounded by ruby red bracts beneath. One of the darkest red of the bunch.

'Silver Glow' bears pale green, almost to the point of being silvery white. About 3′ tall.

'Snow Star' ('Star of Snow') has white flowers with tinges of green throughout. Plants grow 2½ to 3′ tall.

'Sunningdale Variegated' is most handsome in the spring when the margins of the light green leaves are splashed with yellow and cream. The variegation fades in summer. This is an elegant plant.

***-maxima*** (mahk′ si-ma) Large Masterwort 2-3′/2′
Late Spring Rose-pink Southern Europe Zones 5-7

I really like this species and it is good to see its availability increasing in this country. The flowers are larger and much more rose-pink than white, as in *A. major*. The foliage is usually 3-parted, although some 5-parted leaves may occur. The basal leaves are petioled, however, the upper leaves are usually sessile and appear wrapped around the stems.

The plants are not as vigorous or self-sowing as *A. major* but the flowers are subtly eye-catching.

**Cultivars:**

'Alba' is a white-flowered form, but quite difficult to locate.

'Buckland' appears to be a hybrid of *A. major* x *A. maxima*, bearing flowers similar in color to the former and intermediate in size. Perhaps one of the best characteristics is that flowers are sterile, and persist considerably longer than on either parent.

**Related Species:**

*A. carniolica*, lesser masterwort, is similar but smaller (6-12″ tall) than *A. major*. The purple flowers of 'Rubra' contrast well with the greenish bracts surrounding them. Some taxonomic authorities lump this species with *A. major*.

## ***Athyrium*** (a-thi′ ree-um) Lady Fern Dryopteridaceae

Approximately 68 species of *Athyrium* have been listed by one fern expert or another but only half a dozen are found in North American gardens. Some of the most common and handsome hardy ferns are to be found in the genus. *Athyrium* is a large genus widespread in temperate and tropical regions in which the sori (spore cases) are generally curved and the indusium, a thin layer of cells surrounding the sorus, is attached only on one side. Most have a delicate texture and thrive in moist, humid conditions. All species are deciduous and die down over the winter. Ferns in this genus are some of the most reliable, colorful and easiest ones to grow. Some taxonomists have placed the genus in the Woodsiaceae, but that change has not been universally accepted.

Quick Reference to Athyrium Species

| | Amount of color on fronds | Habit |
|---|---|---|
| *A. filix-femina* | None | Upright, 2-3′ |
| *A. niponicum* | Highly | Spreading, 1-2′ |

***-filix-femina*** (fi′ liks fem′ mi-na) Lady Fern 2-3′/2′
Northern Hemisphere Zones 4-8

Valued for ease of cultivation, this graceful fern is one of the most satisfying for new fern gardeners. Although the frond shape can be highly variable, they are often up to 3′ tall and 1′ wide and generally stand up on their own. The vigorous flush of new growth in the spring is wonderful. If placed in dense shade, they will grow well enough, however they may not be sufficiently strong to withstand winds, rabbits or dogs. Morning sun and loamy humus-rich soils are highly recommended.

**Cultivars:**

Dozens of cultivars have been selected. The RHS Plant Finder lists well over 30 variants, subspecies and cultivars of the lady fern. They range from dwarf forms ('Congestum'), bunched fronds ('Corymbiferum'), crested like a celosia ('Cristatum', 'Glomeratum'), slender pinnae ('Setigerum'), balled-up pinnae ('Frizelliae'), and long terminal narrow crest ('Victoriae'). I can handle the Victoria lady fern reasonably well and even the dwarf 'Cruciato-cristatum' (otherwise known as 'Dre's Dagger'), but many of these ulcerated forms are ugly enough to induce nausea and few can compete with the classic beauty of the species itself.

var. *asplenoides*, southern lady fern, grows 2-3′ tall and spreads more aggressively than its northern cousin. Native to southern and eastern United States. Plants tolerate more sun than most other green ferns. Zones 4-8.

'Aurea' is a light green (not really golden) selection of *A. filix-femina* 'Plumosum'. The fronds consist of lacy pinnae. Introduced by Carol and Angelo Randaci of The Fernery, Covington, Kentucky.

'Axminster' is also of 'Plumosum' parentage, having highly divided fronds, providing a lacy appearance.

'Encourage' is a selection of *Athyrium filix-femina* 'Vernoniae Cristatum', crested lady fern. It is distinctly crested and tasseled but is faster growing than other crested forms and is also notable for producing light green fronds. Another Randaci introduction.

'Lady in Red' is a selection of *A. filix-femina* var. *angustum*, northern lady fern, and is slow grower. However, her red stems, particularly in the spring, are quite pleasant.

**-*niponicum*** (nip-on-i′ cum) Japanese Painted Fern 1-2′/2′
East Asia Zones 3-8

The Japanese painted fern is native to China, Korea and Japan and has handsome green fronds. Although a reliable and useful plant, it is usually offered as its colorful variant, var. *pictum* ('Pictum'). This is a great plant, and has been a great plant for many years. It took a while, but finally the Perennial Plant Association chose it as the Perennial Plant of the Year for 2004.

The fronds, a soft metallic gray suffused with reddish or bluish hues, are among the most colorful on any fern. The color is maintained in the old fronds and the emerging shades of the new ones paint a pleasant contrast. Plants tolerate deep shade but display their best color when they receive some direct sunlight, preferably in the morning. Even though a great deal of variability occurs, they will be of bragging quality in 2-3 years. Provide a humusy soil and sufficient water for best performance.

**Cultivars:**

All of these are cultivars of var. *pictum* or have it in the parentage. Many have appeared only in the last three to five years.

'Apple Court' has its moments, bearing the purple, silver and green markings of a typical Japanese painted fern, but is also crested at the end of the fronds. Originating from Apple Court Nursery in the UK, introduced by Plant Delights Nursery.

'Branford Beauty' is an upright, clump-forming selection with subtle shades of green, purple, silver, and gray on the fronds. Plants are hybrids between lady fern and Japanese painted fern.

'Burgundy Lace' has eye-popping purple fronds with streaks of silver. The purple coloring is more intense in the spring, but the silvery sheen remains all season. Upright grower to about 2′.

'Ghost' is probably the best known, producing upright ferns with silvery markings (ghost-like?) on the fronds. Plants are hybrids between lady fern and Japanese painted fern. These are some of the best hybrids in the Armitage garden.

'Ocean's Fury' produces light silver fronds with crested pinna and red midribs. Personally, I can't see the fury or the ocean, but it could be an excellent hardy fern.

'Pewter Lace' bears handsome metallic foliage. A little less silver than 'Silver Falls' and no red to speak of on the fronds.

'Red Beauty' has red veins and stems in the silvery green foliage. Seems very similar to 'Branford Red'.

'Silver Falls' has long arching fronds clothed and bedecked in silver patterns, which is highlighted by the red-purple veins.

'Wildwood Twist' has smoky gray and green fronds that twist a little as they grow. Probably a hybrid between *A. niponicum* x *A. otophorum*.

'Ursula's Red' has more red in the fronds than the normal species. Selected by Ursula Herz in South Carolina.

**Related Species:**

*A. distentifolium*, alpine lady fern, has light green finely textured fronds. Native to the alpine areas of North America and Eurasia, plants are extremely cold hardy.

*A. japonicum* (*Lunathyrium japonicum*) black lady fern, Japanese lady fern, grows about 18″ tall and produces blackish-green, upright arching, triangular fronds. Fiddleheads begin to unfurl in late spring after most other ferns are already leafed out. Spreads slowly by creeping rhizomes. According to Missouri Botanical Garden and USDA plant databases, this fern is synonymous with and sometimes sold as *Deparia petersenii*, (*Athyrium petersenii*).

*A. otophorum*, Asian lady fern, is native to China and Japan. This is a taller, more subtle, colored fern with large pewter green fronds with a reddish to purplish stem (stipe) and midrib (rachis). Not quite as hardy (Zone 6) as Japanese painted fern but almost as handsome. Provide some direct sun and humus-rich soil.

*A. thelypteroides*, silver spleenwort, silver glade fern, is a southeast American native. Plants have silvery sori (spore cases) on the undersides of the fronds, which together with small yellowish hairs, give a pale sheen to the plants as they wave in the breeze. Plants grow vigorously upright (to 4′ in height), but are not invasive.

## *Aubrieta* (o-bree′ sha) Rock Cress Brassicaceae

The genus consists of about a dozen species and a large number of cultivars. Some of the available garden forms are cultivars of *A. deltoidea*, although most are hybrids, listed as *A.* x *cultorum*, probably with *A. deltoidea* and *A. gracilis* in the parentage. *Aubrieta* is closely related to *Arabis*, also commonly known as rock cress. The differences are not obvious and with the introduction of many cultivars, it is more difficult for the uninitiated to tell them apart. In general, *Aubrieta* is more compact with smaller foliage having 1-2 teeth on each side of the leaf blade. The flowers are larger and have a cylindrical calyx (sepals) below the petals about half as long as the petals. Flowers of *Aubrieta* are lilac to red with a few blue forms, while flowers of *Arabis* are usually white or pink. A summary follows.

| | **Habit** | **Petal length** | **Flower color** | **Foliage toothed** | **Sepals tubular** |
|---|---|---|---|---|---|
| *Aubrieta* | More compact | ¾″ | Lilac, red | Yes | Yes |
| *Arabis* | Less compact | ½″ | White, pink | No | No |

Plants in both genera have alternate, silver-green, pubescent, evergreen foliage. Neither genus is tolerant of warm nights, often declining in warm climates, and should be treated the same in the garden. Many cultivars can be propagated by seed and those not available from seed may be propagated by terminal cuttings or division.

### *-deltoidea* (del-toi′ dee-a) Rock Cress 6-8″/2′

Spring Lilac Sicily to Asia Minor Zones 4-7

The species and hybrids (*A.* x *cultorum*) perform best where sunny conditions and well-drained soils are present. So much interbreeding occurs within varieties that a great deal of variability occurs. The foliage is somewhat wedge shaped with large teeth. The ¾″ long, red to lilac flowers are clustered in racemes that emerge from the leaf axils. They are best grown cascading over rocks or walls where water will not collect. After the plants flower in the spring, the stems continue to grow and become leggy by midsummer. Some of the hybrids are more compact, but in general, they are best cut back to 6-8″ to allow new growth to emerge, otherwise stems will be naked in the middle with a few leaves on the end. This is especially true in the South where plants will not survive if allowed to deteriorate. Plants tend to lose vitality and may deteriorate badly after a few years unless new plants are purchased.

Seed is available for many cultivars and germinates in about 2 weeks under moist, warm (70-75°F) conditions. Division, however, is the easiest means of propagation. Stem cuttings may also be taken from new growth in the spring or after cutting back in late spring or early summer.

**Cultivars:**

'Aurea' has golden green foliage and blue to violet flowers.

'Aurea Variegata' ('Golden King') has green leaves with yellow variegation. It is otherwise similar to 'Aurea'.

'Barker's Double' has double purple-blue flowers.

'Bengal Hybrids' are seed-propagated forms with a mixture of lavender, purple and rose flowers on 6-8″ tall plants.

'Bressingham Red' produces double red flowers.

'Campbellii' has double rose-purple flowers.

'Carnival' is very free flowering and produces hummocks of purple-violet flowers.

'Cascade Hybrids' provide flowers in shades of purple, red and lavender.

'Dr. Mules' is similar to 'Carnival' but a little less floriferous.

'Greencourt Purple' has semi-double to double lavender-purple flowers.

'Gurgedyke' also has maroon-purple flowers. Free-flowering and compact.

'J.S. Baker' bears bluish flowers with a white eye.

'Leichtlinii' has handsome bright red flowers on 4″ tall plants.

'Purple Gem' bears deep purple flowers over 6″ tall plants.

'Red Carpet' produces 6″ tall plants that form a mat of red-rose flowers.

'Royal Blue' has dark blue flowers.

'Royal Red' bears flowers in shades of red and magenta.

'Whitewell Gem' produces 6″ mats of deep blue flowers.

'Vindictive' has large (up to 1″ wide) rosy-red flowers.

'Variegata' has yellow-edged foliage in a tight clump. Lavender-blue flowers are a bonus.

## *Aurinia* (ow-rin′ ee-a) Basket-of-Gold Brassicaceae

There is general agreement among taxonomists that this plant should be called *Aurinia*, so we can finally dispense with the old name of *Alyssum*, although from the gardener's point of view, it matters not at all. Of the approximately seven species, *A. saxatilis* is the most popular because of the intense yellow early spring flowers. I grew

*Acanthus hungaricus*

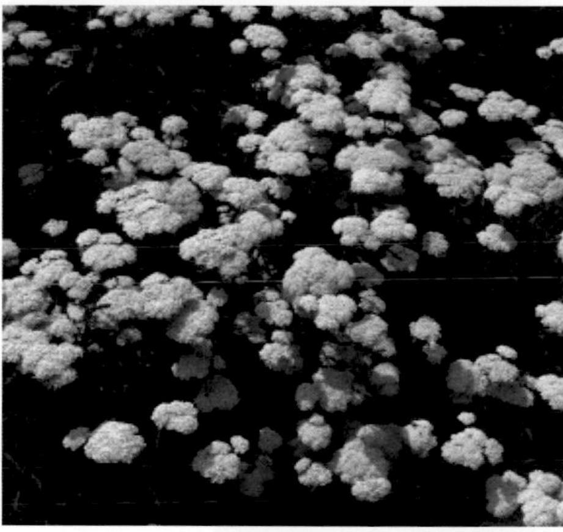

*Achillea*
'Flowers of Sulphur'

*Aconitum napellus*

*Actaea*
'Black Negligee'

*Adiantum pedatum* with *Osmunda cinnamomea*

*Aegopodium podagrarium* 'Variegatum'

*Agapanthus* Headbourne hybrids

*Agastache* 'Blue Fortune'

*Ajuga reptans*
'Black Scallop'

*Allium giganteum* with
canna lily

*Allium giganteum* fruit

*Allium*
'Globemaster'
(with *Delphinium*)

*Amsonia hubrichtii* with *Iris pallida* 'Variegata'

*Amsonia hubrichtii* (fall color)

*Aquilegia canadensis* with *Adiantum pedatum*

*Aquilegia canadensis* 'Little Lanterns'

*Aquilegia* × *hybrida* 'Blue Bird'

*Arisaema dracontium*

*Arisaema taiwanense*

*Arisaema triphyllum*

*Artemisia lactiflora*
'Guizhou'

*Arum italicum*
'Pictum'
(fruit)

*Aruncus*
'Misty Lace'

*Asarum canadense*

*Aster*
'English Countryside'

*Astilbe chinensis*
'Visions'

*Astilbe simplicifolia*
'Sprite'

*Astilbe × arendsii*
'Radius'

*Astilboides tabularis*

*Astrantia maxima*

*Baptisia australis*

*Baptisia*
'Purple Smoke'

*Baptisia bracteata* var. *leucophaea*

*Begonia grandis*

*Bergenia emeiensis*

*Beschorneria yuccoides*

*Bletilla striata*

*Boltonia asteroides*
'Jim Crockett'

*Brunnera macrophylla*
'Jack Frost'

*Brunnera macrophylla*
'Looking Glass'

this species with ease in East Lansing, Michigan and Guelph, Ontario, but had little success in north Georgia. In the South, if planted in early fall, performance is beautiful the first spring but plants gradually melt out during the summer. Planting under the shade of summer-flowering perennials may help it return in subsequent years but it should be replanted each fall for best form and color.

***-saxatilis*** (saks-ah′ ti-lis) Basket-of-Gold 12″/18″
Spring Yellow Eastern Europe Zones 3-7

When *Aurinia* is in flower, the canary-yellow flowers can be seen shimmering across the length of a football field. It requires full sun and excellent drainage and should be cut back after flowering. The foliage is gray green and spreads into clumps very rapidly. The yellow flowers combine beautifully with purple flowers of *Verbena* 'Homestead Purple' or *Phlox divaricata* 'Louisiana'. It is a classic rock garden and wall plant.

Seed germinates in 2-3 weeks in moist, warm (70-75°F) conditions. Seeds are available for the species and a few cultivars but division in the fall is the easiest method of propagation. Cuttings may also be taken in the spring or fall.

**Cultivars:**

'Citrina' ('Sulphurea') has lemon gold flowers and grows 12-15″ tall.

'Compacta' is similar to 'Gold Ball' but more compact.

'Dudley Nevill Variegated' has apricot-salmon flowers over leaves with cream-colored margins. Interesting if you like the color combination.

'Flore' ('Flore-plena') has double flowers but is generally less vigorous than the singles.

'Gold Ball' starts to flower in early to mid April in the South and about 2 weeks later further north. Plants have a globose habit and grow about 8″ tall.

'Golden Queen' is certainly not much different than 'Gold Ball'. The plants grow into a 9-12″ mound with light yellow flowers.

'Sunny Border Apricot', raised by the fine nursery, Sunny Border of Kensington, Connecticut, has apricot flowers. Very handsome.

'Tom Thumb' is only 3-6″ tall but vigorous.

# B

***Baptisia*** (bap-tis′ ee-a) · False Indigo Papilionaceae

Plants in this genus have been "hanging around" for years, favorites of hardcore gardeners, but totally ignored by those just getting started. It is as if one can call himself a gardener only after he has had a baptisia in his garden for a couple of years. This is probably because plants look so scruffy in containers in the garden center that only those who know the future virtues of the plant will spend the money on sticks in a pot. I am a proponent of the genus, I can wax poetic on the virtues, the beauty and the longevity of baptisias, but there is no way my daughters would ever buy one of those containers if I did not personally talk them into it.

The name comes from the Greek *bapto* meaning "to dip", referring to the flower extract once used as a substitute for indigo. *B. australis* was often used for blue dyes while *B. tinctoria* was a source of yellow dye in the southern United States. *Baptisia* is one of the most rewarding and historically fascinating genera among our garden plants. Native to large areas of the United States, plants afford exceptional garden performance and a mini-lesson in early American history. The common name refers to its use as a substitute, albeit not a great substitute, for the true indigo, *Indigofera*, of the West Indies. When *Indigofera* was in short supply, the English government contracted with farmers in Georgia and South Carolina in the mid 1700s to "farm" the plant to augment the supply of the dye. The farming of *B. australis* was one of the first recorded examples of agricultural subsidies. The process used to extract the dye was very cumbersome and time consuming. A report in The Georgia State *Gazette* on May 10, 1788 provided directions "For the Cultivation and Manufacture of Indigo" by "an Indigo Planter". What with planting, cutting, beating, draining and pressing, the process was doomed to a short life. Today, *Baptisia* provides gardeners with a living example of Americana and, more importantly, with reliable and beautiful garden plants.

*Baptisia* produces racemes of pea-like flowers over alternate, gray-green, usually 3-parted compound leaves. They are sometimes confused with, or even marketed as, lupines. They are not even close. Baptisias have all the garden features we don't find in lupines. That is, they are heat tolerant, drought tolerant, relatively disease resistant and persistent in the landscape. Some people confuse the yellow-flowered species with false lupine, *Thermopsis*, but the habit of baptisia is larger, and the flowers are far less densely arranged, and all in all, baptisia is a far better choice. *Baptisia* offers numerous colors and with minor effort, you can find plants with white, blue, deep yellow, light yellow, and hybrids in between. The flowers are wonderful, as are the stems, green in some and black as night in others. Even the fruits are interesting, and may be round, elliptical, or pointing up or hanging down. Get out and baptize!

The baptisias themselves are confusing to tell apart, as is obvious with the knotted taxonomy. One of the ways to separate similar species is the presence or absence of the small leaflike stipules at the base of each leaf. They are not always obvious but for those who enjoy such sleuthing, they can be found. Several studies have shown that significant natural breeding takes place and interspecific hybrids are common in nature. The taxonomic reshuffling of the genus is settling down a little, but taxonomists continue to disagree. There is an ongoing movement to split the very large bean family (Fabaceae) into three smaller families (Caesalpiniaceae, Mimosaceae, and Papilionaceae), *Baptisia* now belonging to the latter. I don't like it, but that's the way it is. What I say here will not change the world of indigo nomenclature, but I will no longer be wishy-washy. Wrong perhaps, but with conviction.

In recent years, a good deal of interest in collecting wild species and more importantly, in breeding new hybrids, has arisen. Already some excellent hybrids have become well established, ('Carolina Moonlight', 'Purple Smoke'), but they are but the tip of the iceberg. Look for chocolate, red, pink and bicolors very soon. The race is on, and the gardeners and landscapers are the winners.

Plants tolerate warm temperatures and require full sun for best performance, although the white forms tolerate partial shade. All grow best in deep, rich soils but are tolerant of poor soils. I think these plants are some of the most trouble-free and marvelous plants for American gardeners, however, I also hear those who have had problems. It appears that voles love the roots of *Baptisia* and can cause no end of frustration.

Quick Reference to Baptisia Species

| | Height (ft.) | Flower color | Flowering time |
|---|---|---|---|
| *B. alba* | 2-3 | White | Late Spring |
| *B. bracteata var. leucophaea* | 2-3 | Creamy yellow | Spring |
| *B. australis* | 3-4 | Blue | Spring |
| *B. sphaerocarpa* | 3-5 | Bright yellow | Spring |
| *B. tinctoria* | 2-4 | Yellow | Early Summer |

***-alba*** (al′ ba) White Wild Indigo 2-3′/3′
Late Spring White Southeastern United States Zones 5-8

This is one of my favorite plants for the garden. I like the blue baptisias, but I enjoy the white-flowered forms even more. I find they are earlier and more consistent performers. The plants' popularity began in southern gardens but the species can be found around the country.

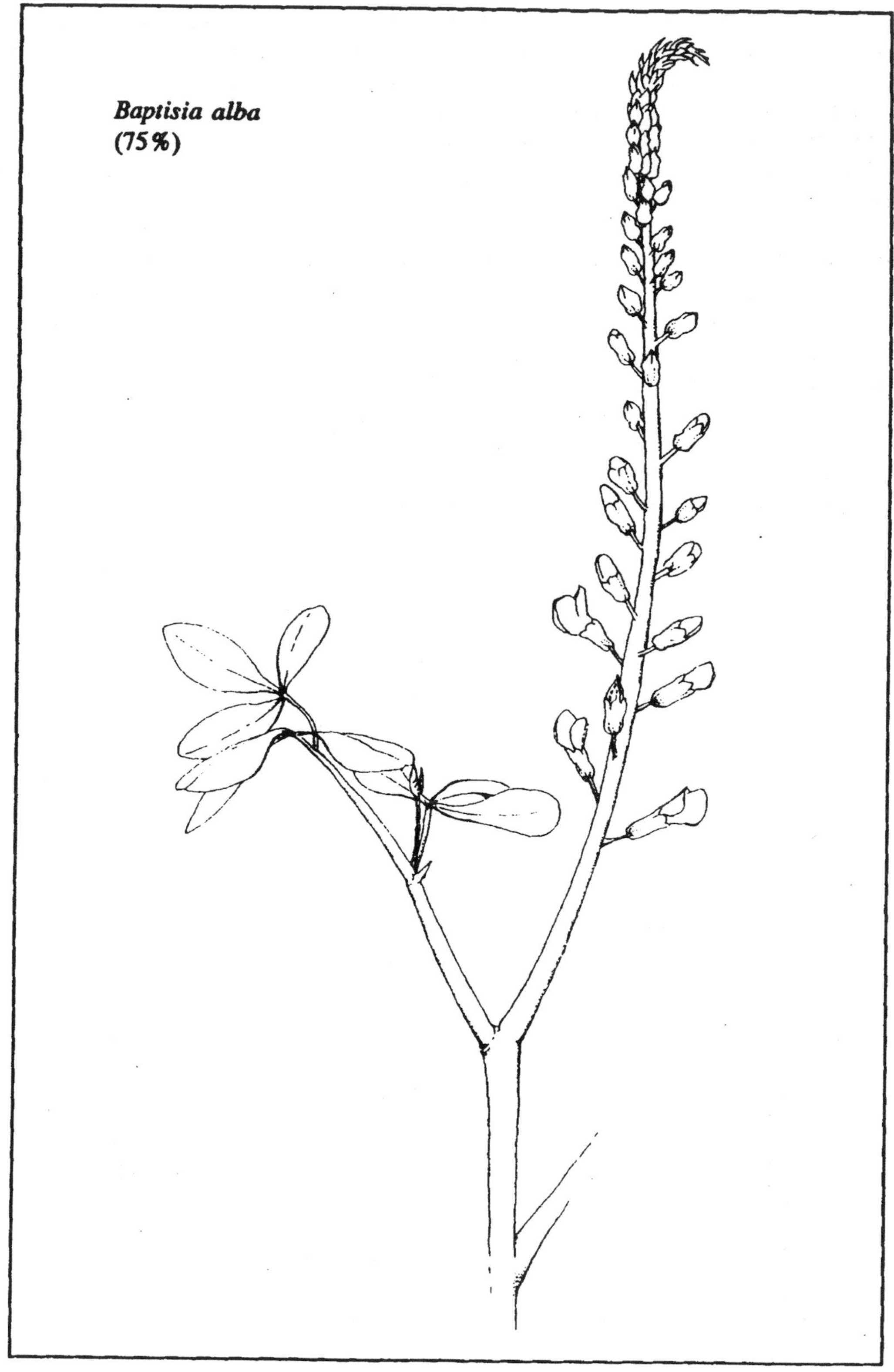
*Baptisia alba*
(75%)

When plants first emerge in the spring, they resemble dark shoots of asparagus. The new shoots often maintain this handsome black-purple tint throughout the season. It grows best in full sun but tolerates partial shade better than the blue form, *B. australis*. The 12-20″ long racemes of ½″ long white flowers persist at least 3 weeks on the plant. The flowers often are blotched purple and are not as dense as those of *B. australis*. The stems are smooth but often covered with a thin whitish or bluish fuzzy pubescence. The leaves are divided into 3 segments, each widest near the rounded end. Stipules are minute and most are soon lost. The foliage of most species of *Baptisia* can look ragged and diseased during the fall, particularly in the South. The foliage of *B. alba* tends to remain attractive even into the fall. The seedpods are cylindrical, yellow-brown, and persistent. This is a stunning specimen for the smaller garden where an easy-to-grow, long-lived plant is desired. It looks good with almost everything.

Propagation by seed is slower and more difficult than *B. australis* and a scarification (cold, moist) treatment is beneficial. Division of the roots may be accomplished in early spring or fall. Care must be taken to make a clean cut of the roots with a sharp knife and provide abundant water upon transplanting.

**Cultivars:**

var. *macrophylla*, prairie false indigo, was forever sold and still is sold as *B. leucantha* and/or *B. lactea*. Unfortunately, intermediates of all the white forms are also out there with variations of white, and fruit size and shape. Like *B. alba*, the flowers are white (but not quite as clean a white), stems are gray black, and plants are upright. Unlike *B. alba*, plants are native to the Midwest, and differ by having thinner, more leathery fruits than those of *B. alba* and var. *alba*. When all is said and done, a gardener should not think twice about these names. The white-flowered forms are all terrific garden plants.

'Pendula' is an equally stunning plant, whose only difference I can see is that the upright racemes give way to pendulous seed pods in late spring. Plants may not be as tall as *B. alba* but I may be making this up. Plants are classified as *B. alba* var. *alba*, *B. pendula*, *B. alba* var. *pendula* and *B. alba* 'Pendula'. It matters not.

'Wayne's World' was propagated from a wild form in Wayne County, North Carolina by Tony Avent of Plant Delights Nursery. Plants appear to be bigger (up to 4′ tall), with white flower spikes. More robust than the species.

***-australis*** (ow-strah′ lis) False Blue Indigo 3-4′/4′
Spring Indigo Blue Eastern United States Zones 3-8

Compared to the white-flowered forms, the blue baptisias are reasonably well known. This is the most cold-hardy species and performs well over a wider range of environments than others. In the early spring, it may still be emerging (later than the white-flowered forms) but the gray-green leaves quickly fill out into a substantial sized bush. The 10-12″ long flowering stalks arise in the spring, carrying 1″ long, indigo-blue pea-like flowers that persist for 3-4 weeks. Although the flowers are violet blue, there is considerable variation when plants are raised from seed. Flowers will

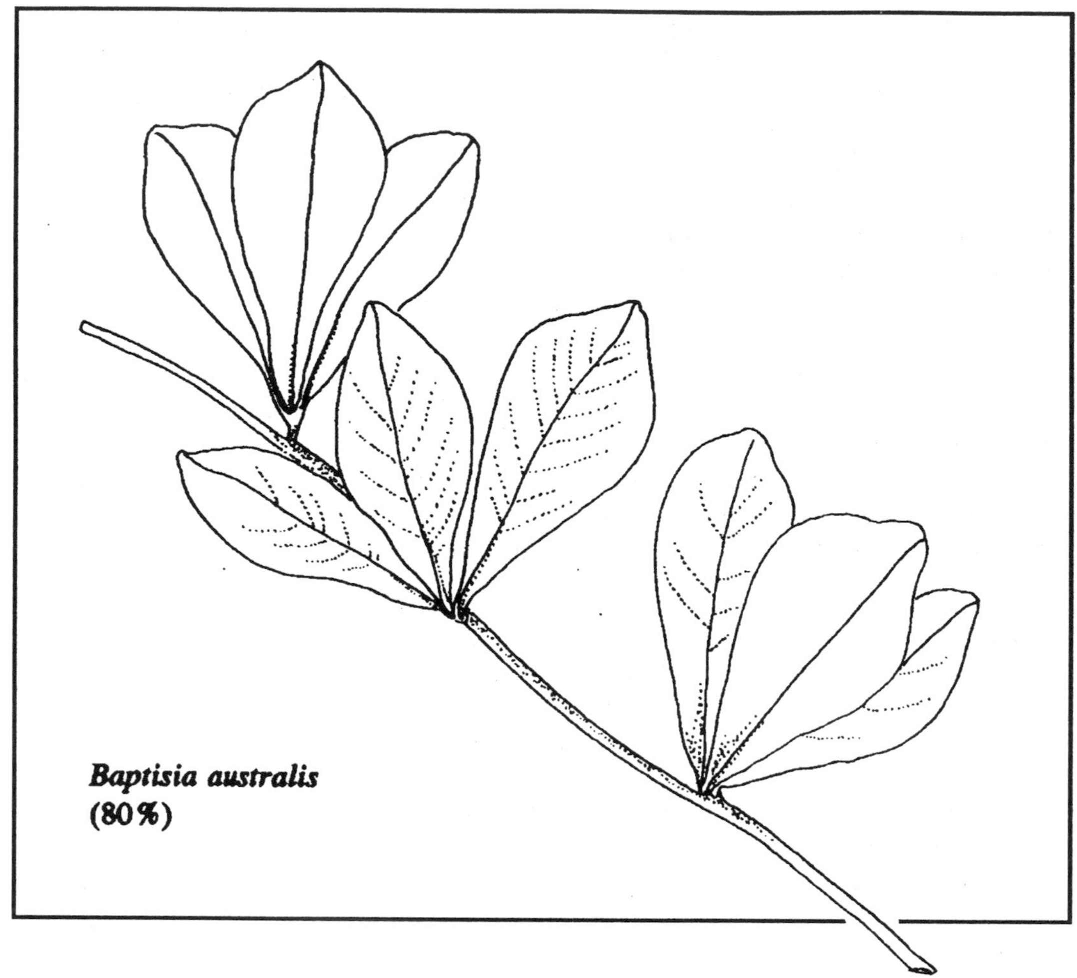

**Baptisia australis**
**(80%)**

vary from light to deep indigo blue, the latter much preferable to the former. The flowers were once used for indigo (see introduction to *Baptisia*) but are now simply viewed as good garden plants.

The flower looks a little like lupine flowers but the leaves and habit are distinct. Some people also confuse it with *Thermopsis* which has dark green rather than blue-green leaves and yellow flowers. Although *B. australis* is cold hardy to zone 3, the leaves turn black with the first hard frost.

Two to 2½″ long brown to black pods appear in early summer and remain until the plant dies back in the fall. The pods become dry by midsummer and the seeds inside rattle around and should be collected at this time. Arrangers find these pods attractive and use them as dried ornaments in the house. In my partially shaded gardens, I must support my plants; if grown in full sun, however, no staking is required. The plant spreads by rhizomes and well-grown plants can consume considerable garden space.

The key to successful seed propagation is to harvest the seed as they turn black and sow when fresh. Seed propagation is less erratic when seeds are given a scarification treatment. Piercing or scraping the seeds with sandpaper or other abrasive substance is helpful, but not essential. This allows moisture and oxygen to penetrate the seed coat. Acid scarification is used commercially but should be performed only by trained individuals. Once the seeds have been treated, place them in a peat-vermiculite mix in a moist, warm environment. Germination of over 90% occurred regardless of acid and mechanical scarification, cold and hot water soaking or cold stratification. A cold treatment (40°F) is also useful and can be accomplished in a cold frame or in a refrigerator or incubator. From the plant's point of view, no division is required, but doing so every 5 years or so may ease overcrowding. Divide in very early spring or not at all.

**Cultivars:**

'Big Ben', selected by Minnesota plantsman Ben Gowen, has many tall, rich blue flower stems. Bigger in every way compared to the species.

***-sphaerocarpa*** — Yellow Wild Indigo — 2-4'/3'
Spring — Yellow — Midwest United States — Zones 5-9

The more I grow baptisias, the more I realize how mixed up they are, and how mixed up I am. I have seen this plant bear bright butter-yellow flowers, creamy yellow flowers and then watched it undergo name changes as well.

Plants which bear this name should have brilliant yellow spikes of flowers, the cream-flowered forms are probably *B. bracteata* var. *leucophaea* (see related species). They are early to emerge and bloom with the white-flowering baptisias. Probably the most eye-catching baptisia, but they may scream at you a little much. The upper leaves may have two leaflets, rather than three. A marvelous plant, and easily available.

**Cultivars:**

'Screamin' Yellow' is just that, as well as being up to 5' tall and about 3' wide. Nothing subtle here.

***-tinctoria*** (tink-tor-ee' a) — Yellow Wild Indigo — 2-4'/1'
Early Summer — Yellow — Eastern United States — Zones 5-8

This species has not been widely embraced as a formal garden plant but is excellent in a meadow garden or sunny informal area. The lower leaves have petioles but the upper leaves are nearly sessile (with very short petiole). The 4-20 terminal flowers are less than an inch long and held in arching 4-5" racemes. There is also considerable variation within the species and flowers range from clear yellow to cream colored. Full sun is necessary.

**Related Species and Hybrids:**

*B. bracteata* var. *leucophaea*, otherwise known as *B. leucophaea*, is a more spreading plant with soft pubescence throughout. A distinctive feature is the large stipules (4/5" to 1-3/5") which persist longer than on other baptisias. Flowers are not as densely clustered and generally are a soft yellow. The 8-10" long racemes slope downward and the fruit are somewhat pendulous. Full sun is necessary. 'Little Texas' is only 9-12″ tall and is at home in a rock garden or container.

'Carolina Moonlight' comes from the great plant breeder, Rob Gardner, of North Carolina Botanical Garden in Chapel Hill. Plants are a cross between *B. sphaerocarpa* and *B. alba*. The flowers are a light yellow as would be expected and rise 2-3′ above the blue-green foliage.

'Chocolate Chip' has a neat name, and is a wonderful addition to the baptisia bonanza. However, it is really good only if you enjoy dull-looking brownish flowers. Other than that, they are terrific. Plants are about 3′ tall.

*B. minor*, lesser wild indigo, is essentially the same as *B. australis* except half the size. Equally beautiful for sure, but my experiences with plants sold under that name have been gruesome; perhaps zone 7b is too hot for them. I have not seen 'Blue Pearls' but plants were apparently selected to have more flower stems and with luck, will do for me what the catalogs say. Fat chance. Zones 4-7.

'Purple Smoke', also from the plant easel of Rob Gardner, has been a hit in the trial gardens at the University of Georgia, as it has been elsewhere. The 4′ tall plants are covered with smoky purple flowers in spring, and persist for up to 4 weeks.

'Twilight Prairie Blues' was bred by Dr. Jim Ault at the Chicago Botanic Garden from *B. australis* and *B. sphaerocarpa*, the result being a strong grower with yellow and purple bicolored flowers. Plants are 3½-4′ tall.

*B. perfoliata*, Georgia wild indigo, and *B. arachnifera*, hairy wild indigo, an endangered species in Georgia, have yellow flowers and simple, perfoliate leaves (the stem passes through the leaf) rather than compound leaves. Interesting but hardly garden worthy.

## ***Barbarea*** (bar-bar-ee′ a) St. Barbara's Herb, Bittercress Brassicaceae

Of the 12 species of this mustard relative, most are grown as leafy salad greens. One of our introduced weeds from Europe is bittercress or wintercress, *B. vulgaris*, which has become naturalized all over North America. However, it is this weed that also possesses some ornamental value in its double-flowered and variegated forms. Plants are biennial, occasionally perennial, but reseed themselves with abandon. Generally the yellow flowers are formed early in the spring and plants soon decline in most areas of the country. They may be discarded after seed has formed.

No sane gardener would introduce the species to her garden, however the double-flowered form 'Flore-pleno' is a little more handsome. The best form is 'Variegata' with yellow splashes on the green foliage. The variegation is most obvious in the winter or early spring. and flowering and seeding are less prolific than on the green-leafed species. This was one of the many ornamental "weeds" in Janette Waltmath's fabulous Portland garden that she allowed me to abscond with. They were in the Horticulture gardens for a few years and were not nearly as aggressive in Georgia as in Oregon. However, if you grow this plant, in any form, you take your chances.

All forms prefer full sun or partial shade and well drained soils. Plants perform well in zones 5-8.

**Begonia** (beg-on′ ee-a) Begonia Begoniaceae

When residents of the province of Quebec are not trying to separate from the rest of the country, they can take some pride in knowing that the name of this great genus commemorates Michael Begon, a governor of that province-to-be in the mid 1670s, and a great supporter of botany. Although *Begonia* is an unusually large genus, with approximately 900 species at last count, only one or two species can be embraced as perennials in North America. The American Begonia Society is an excellent source of information on this wonderfully diverse genus. Hardy begonias tolerate shade and prefer moist but not wet conditions.

***-grandis*** (gran′ dis) Hardy Begonia 15-24″/12″
Summer Pink Southeast Asia Zones 6-9

This is a true perennial species, reported hardy to –15°F if mulched, and to 5°F when unprotected. I have seen vigorous plantings from Rochester, New York to Atlanta, Georgia. Plants are handsome for the large heart-shaped leaves, green above and red beneath. The red veins on the underside of the leaves are particularly appealing and the foliage contrasts beautifully with ferns and annual caladiums. Sprays of slightly fragrant pale pink flowers are produced in early summer and continue until frost. Plants can get out of control where comfortable.

Plants are tuberous and are propagated by bulblets, although they often reseed themselves with abandon.

**Cultivars:**

'Alba' bears white flowers and green foliage, lacking the red pigment found in the species. Brightens up the shade.

'Heron's Pirouette' originated at Heronswood Nursery and bears much larger clusters of deep pink flowers compared to the species.

'Wildwood Purity' has deep red undersides to the leaves and white flowers on red stems. Bred by Thurman Maness of North Carolina (see *Lobelia*).

***-pedatifida*** (pe-dat-if′ I-da) Finger-leaf Begonia 12-15″/12″
Late summer Pink Zones 7b-9

I originally obtained this plant from ItSaul Plants in Atlanta and have been growing it for a number of years. The more I see it, the more I feel it should be much more popular. The best part of the plant by far is the foliage: each dark green leaf is many times divided and the venation has a nice pink hue. For me, I get few if any flowers, but that does not stop me from bragging on it.

Plants grow in partial shade, although morning sun is beneficial. Well-drained soils seem to be important, particularly in aiding winter survival. Cold tolerance has not been determined, but perhaps to zone 7a.

Propagate by division.

**Related Species and Hybrids:**

'Barbara Rogers' looks and grows like a tall, vigorous wax begonia with wonderful white flowers over leathery green foliage. In 1999, I spoke at Clemson University and met the begonia guru, Rehka Morris of Clemson, South Carolina, who wanted me to see a "hardy white begonia". She had obtained it from her friend Barbara Rogers and that was the name we christened it with when we placed it in our trials many years ago. Plants perform best in full sun, but if placed in too much shade will stretch up to 4′ in height, a little too unruly for me. Plants have come back in zone 7b, and I suspect they may be a little cold hardier than that. They are now available from a number of nurseries.

*B. emeinsis* was collected by Dan Hinkley on China's Mt. Emei. The large, serrated, deep green leaves cover the ground, and light pink flowers emerge in late summer or fall. Probably not much hardier than zone 7.

*B. sinensis*, introduced by We-Du Nursery in North Carolina, is similar, but smaller (10-12″) than *B. grandis*. Flowers are light pink and leaves are consistently green throughout.

'Shaanxi White' has white flowers over 10″ tall plants. Hardy to at least zone 7, perhaps zone 6.

***Belamcanda*** (bel-am-kan′ da) Blackberry Lily Iridaceae

Of the two species, the most common is *B. chinensis*. Both are tolerant of almost all environments and bear handsome flowers and even better seedpods.

***-chinensis*** (chin′ en-sis) Blackberry Lily, Leopard Flower 3-4′/2′
Summer Orange, Red Spotted China Zones 5-10

In early to midsummer, stems bear loosely arranged clusters of 3 to 12 orange flowers, each peppered with gaudy red spots from which one of the common names—leopard flower—is derived. The flowers are about 2″ across and the petals and sepals barely distinguishable from each other. The 6 segments are narrow at the base and are, unfortunately, very fleeting. The pear-shaped seed pods are persistent and contain the shining, black, round seeds for which the blackberry lily is named. In the fall the black seeds line up like kernels of corn inside the open pod and are an attractive part of the autumn garden. The stoloniferous roots give rise to about six swordlike clustered leaves that resemble those of gladiolus. Plant in full sun in a well-drained soil and mulch heavily above zone 5. Iris borer can be a problem but removal of dying or decaying leaves will greatly reduce the damage.

I have seen dwarf forms at Longwood Gardens but plants raised from that seed grew almost as tall as the species in my Georgia garden. Seeds germinate within 3 weeks if provided with moist warm conditions. Rootstocks may be divided in early spring.

**Cultivars:**

'Freckle Face' is a welcome addition to the species due to its shorter (12-15″) stems. The flowers are similar but slightly paler.

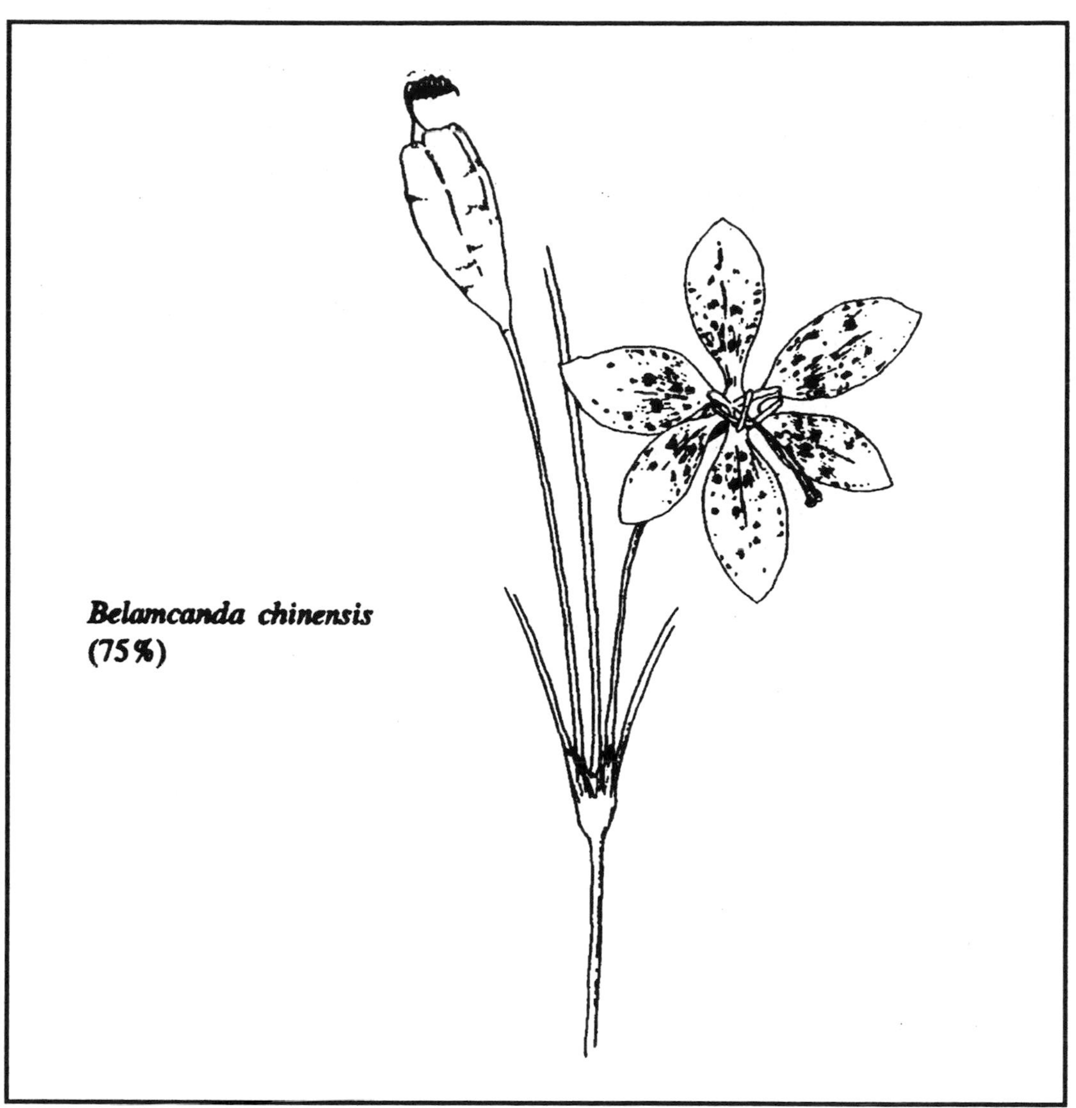

*Belamcanda chinensis* (75%)

**Related Species:**

*B. flabellata* has handsome gray-green leaves and unspotted yellow flowers on 2′ tall plants. Plants are often sold as 'Hello Yellow'. Stunning, terrific plants.

***Bergenia*** (ber-gen′ i-a) Bergenia, Pigsqueak Saxifragaceae

The genus contains about eight species, most of which have leathery evergreen leaves and flower in early spring. Plants tolerate full sun in the North but prefer afternoon shade in the South. Most of what is sold out there consists of evergreen forms, but ever-brown is a more apt description, the foliage often being badly damaged in the winter. To be fair, where bergenias are happy, they can be quite spectacular. When planted in groupings of 10 or 20, the cabbage-like leaves make an impressive sight. The flowers of most species are rose to red colored but hybrids exist with pink and white flowers. The flower buds, however, are less cold hardy than the foliage and may abort during particularly cold winters. When well grown, the foliage of bergenia softens the hard lines of paving and brickwork and accentuates the curves of beds and borders. The large, shiny leaves are often used to provide greenery for florist bouquets since they persist for a long time after cutting.

However, before we get too carried away in praise of pigsqueak, let us be honest. At times, plants look like a cold homeless drunk, whose leafy blanket is torn and nose is red. With all the cultivars available and so much hype about the plants, I have tried to become a bergenia lover, but except for the overlooked fringed bergenia, I have been blatantly unsuccessful with the leather-leaf evergreen forms. The only good thing about these plants is their entertainment value. If you rub the leaf between thumb and forefinger just right, it sounds just like a pig squeaking. Talent comes in many forms; learning pig squeaking is not to be taken lightly.

Plants are at their best in the northwest and southern California but I have not seen a great many "English" plantings in the East. To obtain best performance, place plants in moist shade and morning sun. They perform poorly in heavy soils and standing water. Most of the cultivars offered today are hybrids and are superior to many of the cultivars offered ten years ago. Bergenia can be propagated easily from seed or by division in early spring.

Quick Reference to Bergenia Species

| | Height (in.) | Flower color | Leaf shape | Flower season |
|---|---|---|---|---|
| *B. ciliata* | 12-18 | Pale Pink | Heart | Early Spring |
| *B. cordifolia* | 12-18 | Rose-pink | Heart | Early Spring |
| *B. crassifolia* | 12-18 | Rose-pink | Oval | Early Spring |

***-ciliata*** (sil-ee-ah′ ta) Fringed Bergenia 12-15″/12″
Early Spring Pale Pink Nepal, Kashmir Zones 5-7

Now I can write about a bergenia with a hop in my step and a smile on my face. This is by far the most handsome in leaf of all the bergenias, and fortunately, plants are becoming easier to locate.

The large (up to 12″ across) undulating round leaves are pubescent on both sides and look like a well-behaved African violet in weight training. This differs from the other species in that the leaves are deciduous, which is good for most of us in that we don't have to look at those ugly leaves in winter. I seldom see flowers on our plants, but in their native habitat, the pale pink flowers are pale pink, almost white, and appear before the new leaves unfurl. Even without flowers, this is still the best species if you can grow it.

The "if you can grow it" may be a problem because plants are cold hardy only to about zone 5 at best. In their native habitat, the mountains of west Pakistan, south

Kashmir and Nepal, plants are covered with a winter-long canopy of snow, therefore a light mulching in the fall may be useful. Early frosts and late frosts will decimate the flowers and foliage but the growth buds are reasonably hardy, and plants will come back. Good drainage is also beneficial to winter survival.

Propagate the rhizomes in late spring or fall by cutting them into one-inch long pieces, each with a growth bud and bit of root attached. Place the cut piece in a container and allow to grow before placing in the garden.

**Cultivars:**

'Patricia Furness' was selected for the deep rose flowers. Outstanding, although the flower buds are no more cold hardy than those of the species.

***-cordifolia*** (kor-di-fo′ lee-a) Heart-leaf Bergenia, Megasea 12-18″/12″
Early Spring Rose-pink Siberia Zones 4-8

This is the most common species available and it is a vigorous grower. The 10″ long, glossy evergreen leaves are leathery, waxy and thick. They turn a deep burgundy with the advent of cold weather, and if not buried by snow, make an effective show in the winter. However, even in my north Georgia garden, the purple foliage becomes damaged and is not particularly attractive in the winter. The panicles consist of a dozen or so flowers but do not rise much higher than the foliage. To provide the best show, plant in groups of at least half a dozen in partial shade. Most of the cultivars of bergenias are hybrids and can be found there.

***-crassifolia*** (kra-si-fo′ lee-a) Leather Bergenia 12-18″/12″
Spring Purple Siberia Zones 4-8

Few differences occur between this species and *B. cordifolia* and they serve the same garden function. The toothed undulating leaves are obovate (like a hen's egg with the broad part above the middle) rather than heart shaped. The flowers are held higher above the foliage than those of *B. cordifolia* and the inflorescence is more branched. The leaf blade of *B. crassifolia* runs down along the petiole (decurrent) rather than being two obviously distinct parts of the leaf (i.e. petiole and blade) as with heart-leaf bergenia. Performance is better in the North than the South.

**Hybrid Cultivars:**

If ever a genus had too many cultivars with too few differences, this is it. My descriptions are based on well-grown plants, certainly not those in my garden.

'Abendglut' (Evening Glow), raised by Arends Nursery in Germany, is one of the more popular selections in this country. It is shorter and more prostrate than most other clones and richly colored in the winter.

'Admiral' has cherry-pink flowers over bronze-green leaves in the spring. Good bronze and crimson foliage during the winter.

'Autumn Red' is so named because of the vivid red foliage in the winter. Flowers are soft pink.

'Baby Doll' is about 12″ tall with soft pink flowers and small leaves.

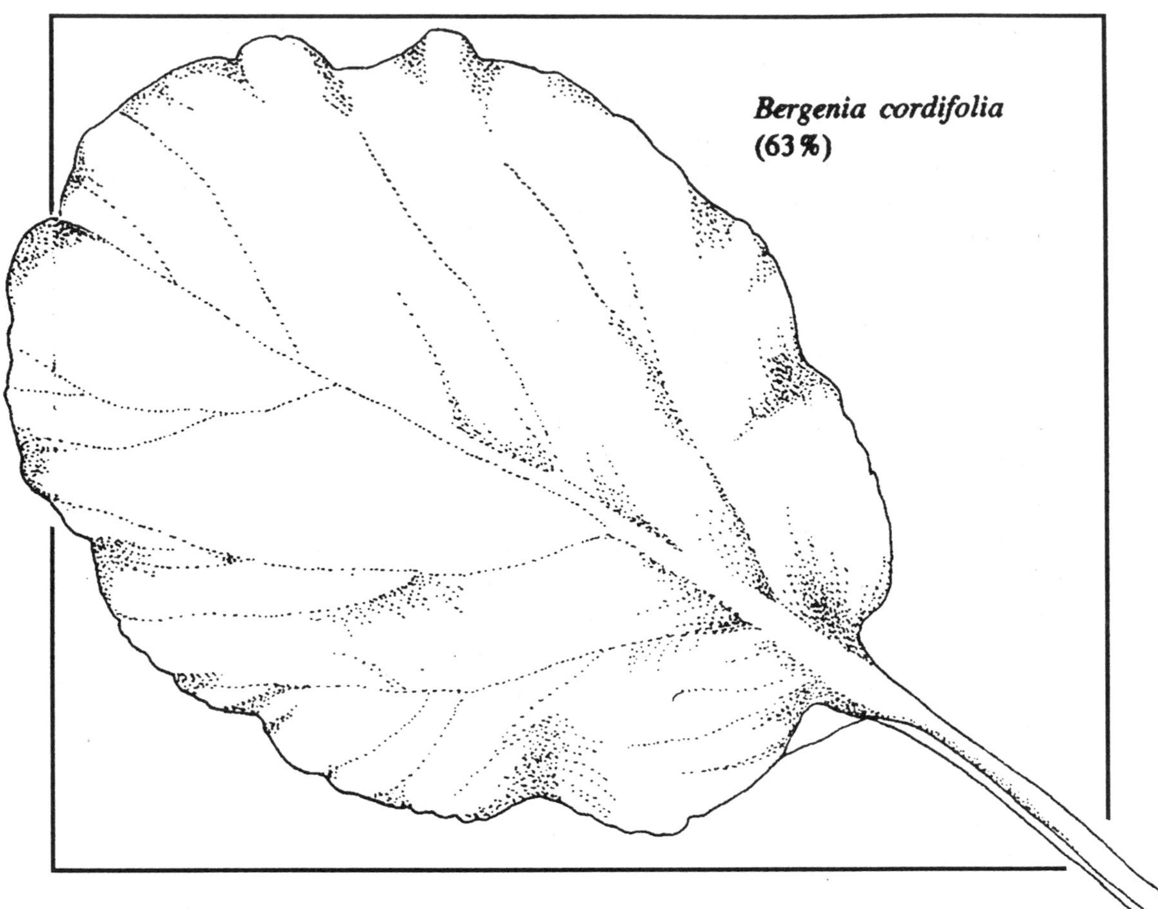


'Bach' is one of a series of cultivars raised by Eric Smith of England and named after composers. This selection has light pink to cream flowers and dark green leaves.

'Ballawley' is a massive plant with 8-12″ wide leaves. It makes a wonderful ground cover in areas where moisture is available. Plants are grown more for the foliage than the sprays of 2′ tall magenta flowers, which are not freely produced.

'Beethoven' bears large clusters of white flowers surrounded by coral red sepals. About 1′ tall.

'Bell Tower' bears pinkish red flowers on 15″ tall plants.

'Brahms' bears creamy white flowers over long light green foliage.

'Bressingham Bountiful' is vigorous with much-branched inflorescences of pink flowers.

'Bressingham Ruby' bears glossy reddish purple leaves in cool weather, fading to dark green as the weather warms up. Flowers are bright pink.

'Bressingham Salmon' resulted from crossing 'Silberlicht' ('Silver Light') with some pink cultivars. It bears salmon-pink flowers.

'Bressingham White' also resulted from the same batch of seedlings that produced 'Bressingham Salmon'. Plants produce clean white blooms that are smaller than those of 'Silberlicht'.

'Distinction' has pink flowers on 1′ long brownish red pedicels.

'Eco Pink Cherub' has pink flowers and compact 3″ long leaves.

'Eden's Dark Margin' has rosy red flowers in the spring over maroon foliage. Leaves have a somewhat darker red margin but the claim to fame is that the foliage remains maroon all season.

'Eric Smith', named after the excellent plant breeder of the United Kingdom, has some of the finest winter foliage, with polished bronze-tints on the upperside and carmine-red on the lower side.

'Morning Red' is 8-12″ tall with carmine red flowers.

'Perfecta' has rosy red flowers held well above the foliage and has performed well in many regions of the country.

'Pink Butterfly' is a recent introduction from Terra Nova Nurseries in Oregon. Its claim to fame are the narrow leaves (like dragonfly wings), coral pink flowers, and shiny plum-red winter color.

'Profusion' is another pink hybrid. Both this cultivar and 'Perfecta' were some of the original plants raised near the turn of the century by Mr. Thomas Smith at Daisy Hill Nursery in County Down, Northern Ireland. The rounded foliage is characteristic of their *B. cordifolia* parent.

'Pugsley's Purple' and 'Pugsley's Pink' grow 2′ tall and are purple and pink-flowering hybrids respectively.

'Purple King' bears rose-red flowers with a touch of salmon.

'Red Start' has good winter color and roe-purple inflorescences.

'Rotblum' has, as the name suggests, red flowers. The flowers are produced over deep green foliage.

'Silver Light' ('Silberlicht'), also raised by Arends, has pink-tinged white flowers with red centers and shiny dark green foliage. Both this and 'Abendglut' have *B. ciliata* in their pedigree.

'Snow Queen', also from Germany, bears large pale pink flowers, almost to the point of being white.

'Sunningdale', one of the better hybrids for winter color, is approximately 12″ tall with excellent foliage color all year. The coral red flower stalks support rich carmine flower heads.

'Sunshade' has lilac-rose flowers and maroon foliage in the fall and spring.

'Sunshine' bears rose-red flowers that have a slightly darker center. Quite handsome.

'Tubby Andrews' differs by having variegated green foliage splashed with yellow, and large pink to purple flowers. Rather gruesome combination, and not for the faint of heart.

'Winter Glow' produces bright red flowers in the spring. The leathery leaves turn purple in the fall and winter. About 12-15″ tall.

'Winter's Tale' has small narrow pointed leaves and grows only about one foot tall. Some leaves turn brilliant red in the winter and deep rose flowers are formed in the spring.

**Related Species:**

*B. emeiensis* was recently found on Mt. Emei in Japan. Handsome brown calyces carry the nodding white flowers with soft pink centers. They are some of the largest flowers I have seen. This is a heat-tolerant bergenia, and although not hardy in most areas, plants may make a good container item in the summer, and also can be an excellent breeding parent. 'Appleblossom' is the result of a *B. emeiensis* cross by Robin White of the UK. The flowers have more pink in the centers. The cross has allowed more cold tolerance, and plants may be hardy to zone 7, perhaps 6.

*B. stracheyi* is useful for the rock garden or small garden and is perfect for those who enjoy more diminutive garden plants. A small plant from Afghanistan and the western Himalayas with rounded leaves and clusters of rose-pink flowers. 'Alba' is a white-flowered form.

*B. purpurascens*, purple bergenia, is about 15″ tall and has larger (petals ¾-1″ wide) deep magenta flowers. The foliage is green with a red blush. One of the best features of this species is the new growth in the spring. The leaves are deep purple, shiny and much less messy from winter damage than any of the other species or selections.

*B.* x *schmidtii*, a cross between *B. ciliata* and *B. crassifolia*, is a hardy evergreen cross, first described in 1868. The toothed leaves are bright green and the clear pink flowers appear as the foliage appears. It performs more similar to *B. crassifolia* than *B. ciliata*. To avoid confusion with other bergenias, it is sometimes offered under the name 'Ernst Schmidt'.

*B.* x *smithii* (syn. *B.* x *newryensis*) encompasses some of the more common garden cultivars. Plants arose from crosses between *B. cordifolia* and *B. purpurascens*.

## ***Beschorneria*** (besh-or′ neer-ee-a) False Red Agave Agavaceae

Plants in this genus are amazing. When I first saw them many years ago, I swore they were yuccas, then the name agave came to mind, then ... well, to be honest, I had no idea. The soft yucca-like leaves emerge as a rosette in the spring, and from the middle arises a great fat elongating-as-we-speak reddish flower stem. They keep growing until red bell-shaped flowers open in spring along the 5-6′ long stem. I was not going to include them until I saw that my friend and excellent plantsman, Scott McMahan of McMahan's Nursery in Clermont, Georgia was selling them. I figured I should include one in the Armitage garden, and there it sits, obnoxiously tall and dramatically theatrical. I also almost omitted it because of its limited cold hardiness. The cold hardiness recommendations are somewhere between zone 7 and 8, depending on whom you believe. I have read they will tolerate temperatures as low as –4°F while others say more like 15°F. However, why should that stop us trying one of these crazy plants, even in containers to be wheeled in the garage for the winter.

Plants found their way into this country as a result of a plant hunting expedition to northeastern Mexico in 1991 by John Fairly of Peckerwood Nursery, Martin Grantham from the University of California Botanical Garden at Berkeley, Eduardo Estrata Castillon, a student at the College of Forestry Science at the State University of Nuevo Leon, Linares, Mexico and Carl Schoenfeld of Yucca Do Nursery.

The most common species is *B. yuccoides*, but others such as *B. septentrionalis* may also be offered. In the mid 1990s, the aforementioned Mr. Grantham made crosses between *B. septentrionalis* and *B. yuccoides*, and many of these hybrids are being tested at Peckerwood Garden. 'Ding Dong' is a hybrid between *B. septentrionalis* and *B. decosteriana* selected at Plant Delights Nursery in Raleigh, North Carolina. Plants are 7′ tall with red and white bell-shaped flowers, and they appear to have a little more cold hardiness.

Plants should be grown in a shaded part of the garden, with excellent drainage. They are xeric plants and too much water may prove lethal. Propagate by division if the clump gets sufficiently large.

***Blechnum*** (bleck′ num) Deer Fern Blechnaceae

The deer ferns have been appearing on and off in catalogs and nurseries for years, but none is sufficiently easy to garden to have made this a "must have" plant. The best known is the western deer fern, *B. spicant*, with its leathery lustrous green fronds and outstanding compact habit. Plants are native to the northwestern United States and do reasonably well in the heat and humidity common across the mountains. Others are appearing that may be good for eastern gardeners, the most common being the Japanese *B. nipponicum*, and its dwarf relative var. *minimum*. Plants are symmetrically shaped with dark green fronds. The former grows 9-12″ tall, the miniature form may attain only 3-4″. Zones 6(7)-9.

***Bletilla*** (ble-til′ la) Bletilla Orchidaceae

There are a few orchids suitable for the outdoor garden, and *Bletilla* is one of the better choices. These terrestrial orchids produce pseudobulbs useful for propagation while the flowers, consisting of similar sepals and petals, are produced on terminal racemes. The bulbous roots should be planted no deeper than 2″ below the surface.

***-ochracea*** (oh-cray′ see-a) Yellow Bletilla 18-24″/15″
Spring Light Yellow China Zones 7-9

I received this plant about five years ago and did not know it from Adam's house cat. I have been so impressed that I believe this is the best of the group, although I have not yet tried all the hybrids that have recently appeared. I have read that plants are slower growing than *B. striata*, but our experience has been exactly the opposite. Plants are robust, growing to 1½ to 2′ in height, and produce rather ordinary leaves, but dozens of flowering stems, compared to the handful that normally occur on *B. striata*. The flowers are light yellow with a hint of pink on the lips. Plants are later to flower than *B. striata* and are not as susceptible to late freezes.

Unfortunately, plants are not as cold hardy, although I doubt there have been too many northern data collected, and they are more difficult to find, but finding any bletilla is in itself a bit of a challenge. Propagate by division or collect seeds and sow in a warm greenhouse.

**-*striata*** (streye-ah′ ta) Hyacinth Bletilla 8-12″/10″
Spring Purple China Zones 5-9

Three to six pleated papery leaves emerge early in the spring and look rather nondescript, but later give rise to rosy-purple sprays of orchidlike flowers. Racemes consist of about 6-10 flowers, each measuring 1-1½″ across and persisting for 2-3 weeks.

Partial shade and well-enriched soil are ideal, allowing a single plant to enlarge into a fine garden clump in a few years. They are suited to growing in large containers on the patio or deck. This method is most useful for gardeners north of zone 5 who can bring the container in for the winter to be returned outside in the spring. It is too fine a species to ignore simply because winters are cold. I like the idea of having orchids in my garden and *Bletilla* adds a touch of class to any deck or border planting.

The only problems I have seen result from late frosts. Leaves emerge so early that the ends often get nipped, resulting in tattered tips. Summer drought causes poor initiation of flowers resulting in little or no flowering the following spring. Late frosts occasionally result in death of the flowers although I have seen plants in Houston knocked down hard by a late frost only to quickly rise again. Propagate by division of the pseudobulbs. They are tuber-like structures about ¾″ in diameter. Separate them from the mother plant in the fall or simply divide the clump with a sharp shovel.

A number of bletillas have been bred in Asia and are available to those willing to look for them and pay a little money.

**Cultivars:**

'Alba' has creamy white flowers, occasionally with pink tips, that contrast better with the dark green leaves than the purple flowers of the type. This is likely var. *japonica* 'Alba'.

'Albostriata' ('Variegata', 'Albo Marginata') is the most ornamental form and has white stripes along the length of each leaf. Purple flowers similar to the species are produced and the foliage remains ornamental all season. Best growth occurs in a rich, cool, moist soils.

'Eco White Edge' has larger white margins around the leaves. From Eco-Gardens in Decatur, Georgia.

'First Kiss' has clean white flowers and white-margined leaves. Quite beautiful. Perhaps a selection from var. *japonica alba variegata*.

**Hybrids**:

Penway series is a group of hybrids incorporating parentage from (*B. formosana*, *B. striata*, *B. szetschuanica* and *B. yunnanensis*. 'Penway Dragon' typically has purple-pink petals and sepals, white lip with purple pink margin and spot. 'Penway Paris' produces rose purple petals, sepals and lip with white keels on lip; 'Penway Princess' bears light rose pink sepals and petals, darker on the reverse. Lip spotted red and yellow with purple red margin.

'Sunset' is a cross between *B. szetschuanica* x *B. ochracea* and has light yellow petals and sepals, sometimes with pink on reverse. Lip yellow with light purple front margin.

'Yokohama' bears pale lilac petals and sepals, with a yellow throat. The result of a cross between *B. striata* x *B. formosana*.

*Bletilla striata* 'Alba'
(68%)

***Boltonia*** (bowl-tone′ ee-a) Boltonia Asteraceae

Most species of *Boltonia* are native to the United States and are easy to grow, producing vast numbers of daisylike white or purple flowers in late summer. The leaves are alternate, lance shaped, and sessile. Many species are too large and lanky to be considered for anything but the wild flower garden, however, a number of excellent cultivars are quite garden friendly.

***-asteroides*** (as-tur-oide′ ees) White Boltonia 5-6′/4′
Late Summer White, Purple Eastern North America Zones 4-8

The 3-5″ long, blue-green leaves are entire, broadly lanceolate and narrowed at both ends. The numerous ¾-1″ wide flowers are held in large billowy terminal panicles. Although the species produces showy flowers, it is too large, floppy, and weedy for my liking and should not be grown in the "formal" garden. However, 'Snowbank' is a selection of this "weed" and is a fine garden plant. Propagation is by division in the spring; a small shovel of basal rosettes yields dozens of offspring. Divide every 3-4 years. Seed of the species may be collected and will germinate readily. Seed of 'Snowbank' will not come true.

**Cultivars:**

Nearly all cultivars offered are selections of var. *latisquama*.

var. *latisquama*, violet boltonia, native from Missouri to Oklahoma, is similar to the species in habit but is about 4′ tall and has larger, purple flowers. A dwarf form of this variety, 'Nana', is only 18-30″ tall and requires no staking.

'Pink Beauty', found by the plantsperson Edith Eddleman in a North Carolina garden, has been offered under various names, including *Boltonia rosea*. Plants are more open and lanky than 'Snowbank' and bear dozens of pale pink flowers in late summer and fall. Provided with sun and decent soil, they grow 5′ tall and will likely require some support.

'Jim Crockett' was developed by Dr. Thomas Boyle of the University of Massachusetts in 2003. Plants are dwarf, well branched and flower all season. Excellent new introduction from an excellent plant breeder. The plant was named for James Underwood Crockett, an author and the host of PBS's "The Victory Garden", first televised in 1975. Crockett's personality and presence made the show instantly popular with a loyal audience of gardeners. Jim Crockett passed away July 11, 1979, and I speak for many gardeners in thanking Dr. Boyle for the memories.

'Snowbank' is a cultivar of which I am also most fond. It is about 3-4′ tall but benefits from a hard prune (remove about one-third of the growth) by midsummer. If this is done, staking is not required when grown in full sun. In partial shade, however, plants will not be as compact and will require support. The simple foliage is blue green, and the top half of the plant is blanketed by clear white daisies with yellow centers. In my garden, flowering begins in early August and continues well into September. Although plants perform best in deep, moist, organic soils, plants have tolerated two severe Georgia droughts with only occasional watering.

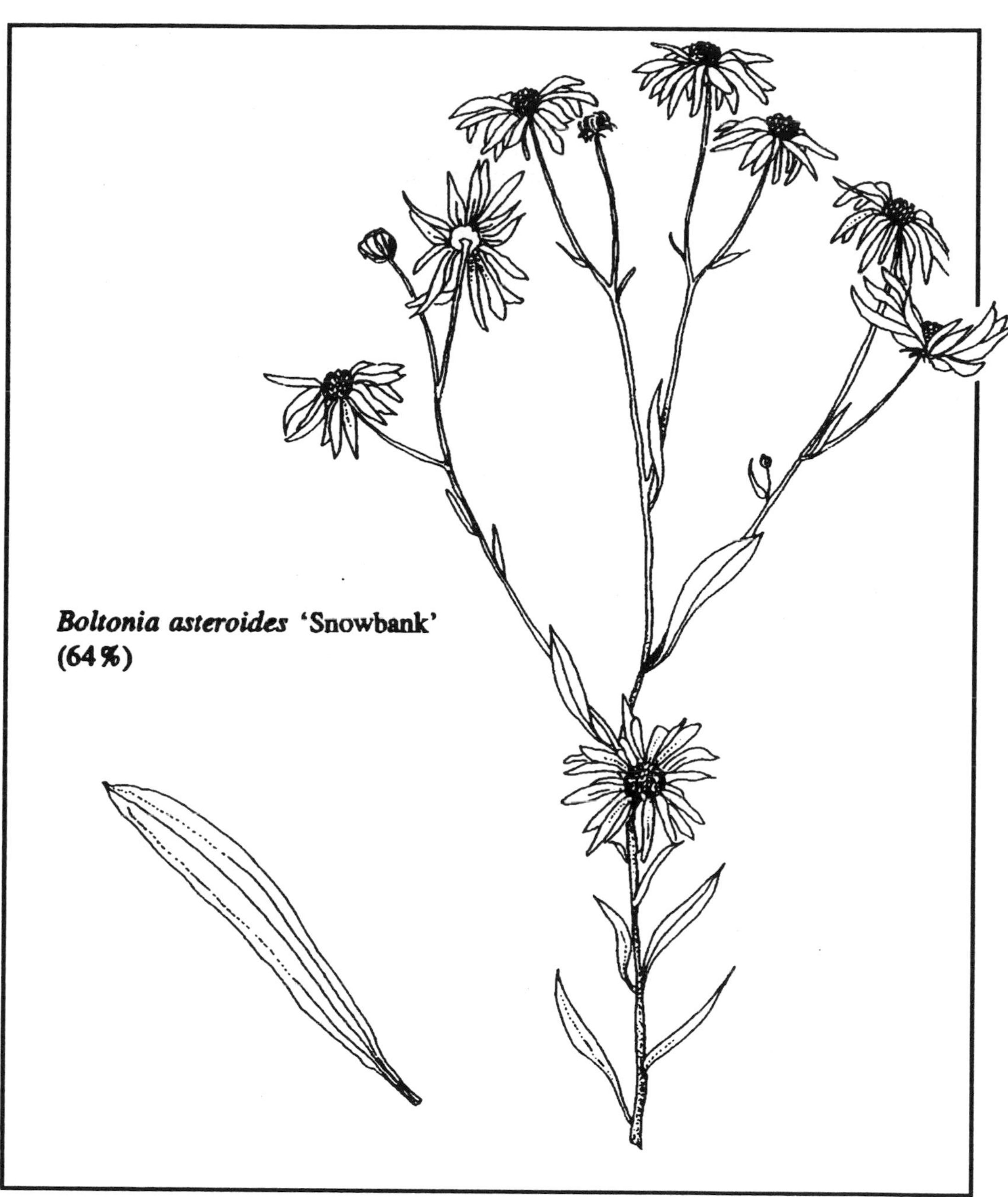

***Boltonia asteroides* 'Snowbank' (64%)**

***Borago*** (bor-rah′ go) Borage Boraginaceae

Most species of borage are annuals but the flowers are such a lovely shade of blue, it is worth the effort to include at least one species. Borage has long been used as a pot-herb and young leaves were often (and still are) included in salads. Medicinal properties attributed to borage (mainly *B. officinalis*) include relief for stomach distress and a curative for local inflammation.

**-*laxiflora*** (laks-i-flo'ra) Corsican Borage 1-2'/1'
Early Summer Blue Corsica Zones 5-9

Most appropriate for wall or rock gardens, this borage bears light blue, drooping flowers about ¾" across similar in shape to flowers of tomatoes (rotate). The loose racemes are produced in late spring and persist for approximately 4 weeks. The many stems are covered with short backward-pointing bristles and the 4-6" long leaves are rough and coarsely hairy. Plants need deep mulching in the fall in most parts of the country, but are drought tolerant. Plants resemble a kind of scrambling forget-me-not that can self-seed everywhere.

Propagate by division in the spring, by seeds sown in the fall, or by 2-3" long terminal cuttings in summer.

## ***Boykinia*** (boy-kin-ee' a) Brook Saxifrage Saxifragaceae

About 9 species of this moisture-loving genus occur, and plants are best suited to moist woodlands or shady rock gardens. Named after Dr. Samuel Boykin of Savannah, Georgia, most are native to the United States. The alternate, kidney-shaped leaves are held on long petioles and flowers are held in lax panicles with the foliage.

Only two species are used to any degree in Canada and the United States, but with the continued discovery of our native flora, more of these interesting plants are being offered. *B. aconitifolia* is an eastern native, hardy in zones 6 to 8, and has rounded lobed basal leaves and white flowers in late spring. Plants are 10-15" tall. *B. rotundifolia,* native to southern California, also has white flowers but the lobed foliage is rounded with hairy stems. Plants are about 12" tall and likely hardy only to zone 7.

## ***Brunnera*** (brunn' er-a) Brunnera Boraginaceae

The genus contains three species but only one is of ornamental interest. *Brunnera* is most at home in moist, shady areas and does particularly well along shaded stream banks or around shaded water features in the garden. Flowers occur as leaves are forming or sometimes even before they have emerged. Large, basal heart-shaped leaves are produced, somewhat reminiscent of Virginia bluebells (*Mertensia virginica*) or even hostas. The flowers and inflorescence remind people of forget-me-nots (*Myosotis*) resulting in the common name, false forget-me-not.

**-*macrophylla*** (mak-ro-fil' a) Heartleaf Brunnera 12-18"/20"
Spring Light Blue Caucasus Zones 3-7

The azure blue flowers arise early from the hairy, light green foliage and may continue into late spring. Plants branch from the base, spread quickly and produce mounds of green foliage. The basal leaves are much larger (up to 6" across) and held on longer petioles than those near the top, resulting in a light, airy effect in the landscape. The ¼" diameter flowers have a yellow center and are carried in a loose 1-2" wide panicled raceme.

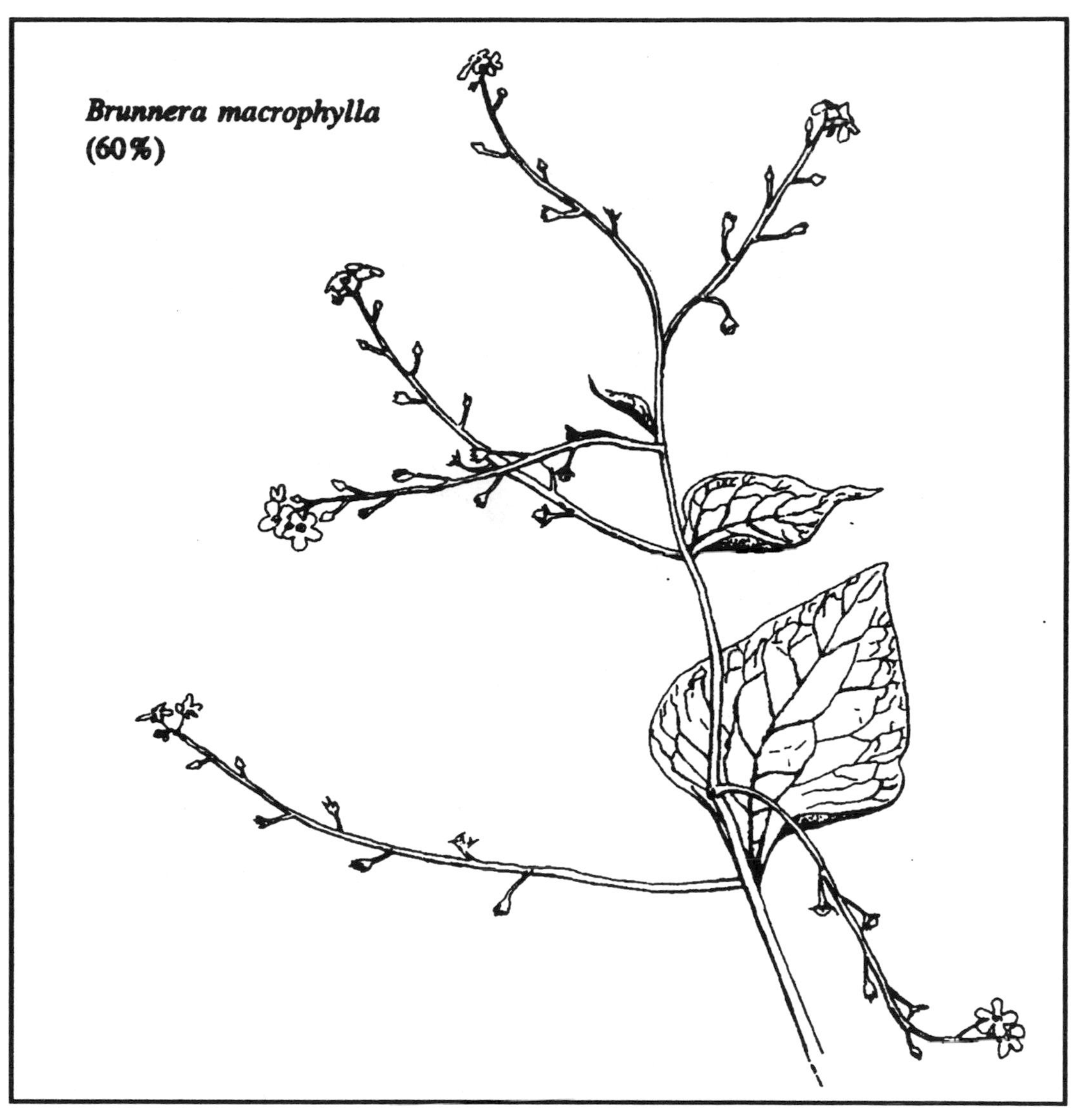
*Brunnera macrophylla* (60%)

In the past, if you gardened in hot, humid weather, you might as well have thrown your money in the trash as plant brunnera. However, tougher plants have been introduced (see cultivars), and while they are still suspect, they give one more than a fighting chance. Regardless of North or South, morning sun is welcome, but afternoon shade and consistent moisture are necessary for vigorous growth. I have seen moist woodlands (not mine) covered with these plants and their quiet understated beauty is soothing to the soul. Some of the finest plantings in this country are in Gardenview Horticultural Park, the fine garden of Henry Ross in Strongsville, Ohio, and at Old Westbury Gardens on Long Island, where they romp about in the company of forget-me-nots and poppies. However, it is the variegated forms that most people want to grow, and none of them are rompers.

Propagate the species by seed sown in moist, warm (70-75°F) medium in late summer and transplant in the fall. Root cuttings (similar to *Anemone*) may also be used. Variegated forms are slow to increase but may be propagated by division. However, it is difficult to propagate them commercially to obtain large numbers. They do not come true from seeds and root cuttings seldom survive as variegated forms. They will continue to be difficult to locate and continue to be relatively expensive. Tissue culture is the most efficient way to obtain sufficient numbers for commercial production and as plants increase in numbers, they will become more available and less expensive.

**Cultivars:**

'Betty Bowring' has large heart-shaped green leaves and clean white flowers. Sometimes sold under 'Alba'.

'Hadspen Cream' produces light green leaves with irregular creamy-white borders. Somewhat more tolerant of sun and dryness than 'Variegata' but if subjected to full afternoon sun, the leaf margins will turn brown. Strikingly beautiful where well grown, miserable looking where abused.

'Jack Frost', a sport of 'Langtrees', is one of the newer cultivars that is not only handsome, but seems to be sufficiently vigorous to tolerate hot summers. The leaves are silvery white with green venation and a thin green margin. The tiny, forget-me-not-like flowers are held on thin stems in spring.

'Langtrees' has dark green leaves with silver-white spots on the border. Sometimes called 'Aluminum Spot', it is more tolerant of dry conditions than other cultivars. A bust south of zone 6.

'Looking Glass', a sport of 'Jack Frost', has heart-shaped silver leaves without the obvious green veining of its parent. For me, this is the most heat tolerant of any of the cultivars I have trialed, and although it is certainly not bulletproof, it is worth garden space even in my zone 7b garden.

'Smith's Gold' has handsome yellow margins around light green leaves.

'Variegata', also known as 'Dawson's White', is characterized by large clear white borders which may take up most of the leaf, and lavender-blue flowers. It is intolerant of drought and prefers cool, moist, shady areas. It is a most handsome plant if grown well. I have seen good specimens in the wonderful Yew Dell Gardens in Lexington, Kentucky, a sure sign of heat tolerance.

## ***Bulbinella*** (bul-bi-nel′ a) Bulbinella Asphodelaceae

This is not a genus one can find without a bit of searching, and the species is perennial only on the West Coast and in areas of moderate zone 8 winters. Of the 15 or so species, *B. nutans*, nodding bulbinella, and *B. hookeri*, Maori onion, are reasonably easy to find and grow. The former is native to the Cape area of South Africa, the latter to New Zealand. In both species, the flowers at the base of the inflorescence open and finish first, the upper third is still in bud, while the middle one third is open. Plants require copious amounts of organic matter and grow well in full sun. Mulch well in late frosts, plants can't handle much more than 25°F. Plants may be raised in pots in cold areas of the country and brought in like caladiums and dahlias.

Differences between the two are not particularly striking, however, the biggest difference may be that *B. nutans* grows during the winter (February-March) and is summer dormant. Plants are 2-2 ½′ tall with grassy foliage. The many starlike yellow flowers open along a tight cylindrical racemc.

The individual flowers of *B. hookeri* are less than 1″ across, however there may be more than 100 yellow/orange flowers on each raceme. The flowers remind me of a not quite ripe cob of corn eaten at one end only. The foliage is narrow and in a basal tuft.

Propagate by separating the bulblets.

***Buphthalmum*** (buf-thahl′ mum) Oxeye Asteraceae

Although the genus features rather common yellow, dark-centered daisies, they have their moments in the sun. The name is derived from *bous*, ox, and *opthalmos*, eye, in reference to the appearance of the disc of the flower head. I suppose I have not seen the eyes of enough oxen but the flowers don't look a great deal different than most other daisies. They are best in moist areas and tolerate poor soil. The large blossoms make reasonably good cut flowers. The foliage is alternate, dark green, and toothed. All species may be easily propagated by division in early spring or immediately after flowering. Seeds germinate in 14-21 days if placed in warm (70-75°F) moist conditions. Only one genus, *B. salicifolium*, is offered; the former *B. speciosum* has been reclassified as *Telekia speciosa*.

***-salicifolium*** (sa-li-si-foe′ lee-um) Willowleaf Oxeye 1-2′/2′
Late Summer Yellow Southeastern Europe Zones 5-8

The alternate leaves are long and narrow like those of a weeping willow, and usually are toothed and have white pubescence on the undersides. The terminal, solitary flower heads are about 2″ wide. The stems are slender and without support tend to topple, particularly in rich soils. Fertilization should be discouraged or foliage will be produced at the expense of flowers. Like most daisies, flowering continues for many weeks if spent flowers are removed.

**Cultivars:**

'Dora' grows 24-30″ tall and bears 2″ wide daisies. She has handsome dark purple stems that contrast well with the willowy leaves and yellow flowers.

'Sunwheel' is about 2′ tall with golden yellow flowers from July to September.

# C

**_Calamagrostis_** (kal-a-ma-grost′ is) Feather Reed Grass Poaceae

Approximately 250 species of this genus occur, however, only a couple of forms have been extensively used in gardens for the last ten years. The plants are stoloniferous and thrive on permanently damp, fertile, even heavy soils. This is an understated genus, which, as Kim Hawks, the former owner of Niche Gardens in North Carolina states, "Go quietly unnoticed until they bloom".

**-*x acutiflora*** (acute-i-floor′ a) Feather Reed Grass 3-4′/3′
Summer Tan Hybrid Zones 6-8

These tight, tufted, erect grasses are the result of hybridization between *C. arundinacea*, reed grass, and *C. epigejos*, rush grass, both natives of Europe and Asia. The foliage is lax and the loose inflorescence is branched with flowers ranging from silvery bronze to purple-brown. Full sun is best. Some terrific cultivars with strong erect flower stems are offered, and are far better than the species.

**Cultivars:**

'Avalanche' is about 4′ tall and produces a wide white band down the center of each leaf blade, essentially the reverse of 'Overdam'. The tan flowers appear in the late summer and fall. Plants resulted as a sport of 'Karl Foerster' and were introduced by Steve Schmidt of American Ornamental Perennials. The variegation pattern is far more noticeable than in 'Overdam'.

'Karl Foerster' produces feathery golden inflorescences on 4′ tall plants in early summer. Plants grow tightly together and should be grouped for best effect. They make a marvelous vertical element in the garden, marvelous enough to have been named the Perennial Plant of the Year in 2001. The best display I've seen is the hundreds of plants at the Chicago Botanic Garden. A terrific botanical garden; their use of grasses is instructive at all times but spectacular in the fall.

'Overdam', striped feather reed grass, starts out striped yellow and changes to more noticeable white stripes on the green foliage and 2-3′ tall mounding plants. Golden plumes of flowers occur in mid to late summer. Plants are not as vigorous as 'Karl Foerster'.

'Stricta' was the original garden offering of this grass and may still be found in gardens today. People often use 'Stricta' as a synonym for 'Karl Foerster' but it is a foot taller, earlier to bloom and the flowers are not as full.

**Related Species:**

*C. arundinacea*, reed grass, is quietly spectacular in its own right. The tall clumps of green to blue-green grass bear handsome airy plumes in late summer. The foliage looks like silvery wheat as late fall and winter occurs. I have seen striking plants in containers around pools and ponds; a beautiful setting is Cornell Plantations in Ithaca.

*C. brachytricha*, feather grass, is also known as *C. arundinacea* 'Brachytricha'. Handsome, blond inflorescences give rise to purple spikelets in the fall on 2-3′ tall plants. Plant *en masse*. They have shown excellent heat tolerance in the Gardens at UGA.

## *Calamintha* (kal-a-min′ tha) Calamint Lamiaceae

Some 7 species of these aromatic mints may be found and a few of them make handsome low-growing garden plants if provided with full sun to partial shade and well-drained soils. They are often woody at the base, and may be cut back heavily when overgrown to provide good ground covers for the rock garden or border. A number of species have been reclassified to other genera. *Calamintha acinos* is now *Acinos arvensis* and *C. clinopodium* is *Clinopodium vulgare*, both of which are fine garden plants. The most popular species is *C. nepeta*. None of the calamints performs particularly well in warm, wet climates.

***-nepeta*** (nep-e′ ta) Savory Calamint 9-12″/12″
Early Summer Lavender Southern Europe Zones 4-7

The small (less than 1″ long), hairy leaves are strongly mint scented and the whorled light blue to pale lavender flowers are produced slightly above the 12″ tall mats. Plants make good fillers and are terrific if one wants to attract bees to the garden. Cut back if plants become overgrown. They do well in the Northwest, look fine in the Northeast and upper Midwest, but struggle in the deep South. Good drainage or raised beds are necessary for areas of hot, wet summers. Cut back hard after flowering in all but areas of the coolest summers.

**Cultivars:**

'Alba' bears dozens of small white flowers on plants about 1′ tall.

'Blue Cloud' has many small lavender-blue flowers on 12″ tall plants. The foliage is fragrant and plants appear to be vigorous growers in a well-drained garden site.

subsp. *nepeta* has more flowers per inflorescence and leaves about 1½″ long.

'Gottlieb Friedkund' sounds like a crazed serial killer but plants have been great performers in the Gardens at UGA. They are less than a foot tall and bear many lavender flowers.

'White Cloud', an introduction from Canyon Creek Nursery in Oroville, California, bears many small white flowers with oregano-scented foliage. Similar to 'Alba' but appears to be a little more floriferous. However, it is difficult to see a great deal of difference between them.

**Related Species:**

*C. grandiflora*, large-flowered calamint, is also aromatic but bears ½″ long rosy pink flowers in midsummer. Plants grow to about 18″ tall. 'Variegata' ('Forncett Form') has creamy flecks on the leaves, bears pink flowers and is usually a little shorter than the species.

*C. sylvatica*, common calamint, is similar to *C. nepeta* but may be distinguished by the paler green leaves and pale pink flowers with white spots.

## *Calanthe* (kal-an′ thee) Hardy Orchid · Orchidaceae

I remember first being introduced to these plants by the great plantsman Barry Yinger, who was speaking in Athens about some of his introductions. As a fund-raiser, we had an auction, and sure enough, after a strenuous bidding session, I was the proud owner of three plants I'd never heard of, each looking to be half dead. Did I mention I was also now broke?

I don't totally blame my living under the bridge on these plants, and I have been able to visit them at my old house every now and then. Now, when you visit my garden, I hope the new owner will take great pains to show you those original calanthes.

Numerous species and hybrids are available through specialty catalogs and if I could afford them, I would have them all. They are also expensive, which is one of the reasons to be quite selective. The hardiest is probably *C. tricarinata* (zone 6), with frilly flowers in tones of yellow, green and red; most others will be reliably hardy in zone 7, although with consistent snow cover, hardiness will extend further north.

The foliage is pleated and evergreen during the winter; not much to get excited about. As weather warms, the growing apex can be seen beneath the leaves (or snow). The flowers emerge in early spring and are in potential danger from late frosts. Be sure to cover if buds are up and temperatures are down. I enjoy this group of plants, and although they are relatively slow and certainly not for everybody, they are reasonably easy to grow and once established will persist for years.

### -*discolor* (dis′ color) Hardy Orchid 9-12″/12″

Spring Purple with White Tips Japan Zones 6b-9

This is not the most colorful orchid but certainly among the most interesting. In spring, the flower stems arise bearing purple and white orchids in April to May. The pleated leaves are about 6″ long and 2″ wide. After flowering, they remain part of the shaded garden, blending in with the ferns and wildflowers. Plants tolerate morning sun but should be shielded from the hot afternoon rays.

Propagation is slow from seed, as plants require 5-7 years to produce flowers. They arise from pseudobulbs and if grown well, division is easily possible.

***-sieboldii*** (cye-bold′ ee-eye) Hardy Orchid 9-12″/12″
Spring Yellow Japan Zones 7-9

Of the calanthes I have tried, I enjoy this one the most. It is similar in habit to *C. discolor*, but the flowers are brilliantly yellow, showing up easily even though it struggles to reach a foot in height. Foliage is similarly pleated, and about 8″ long and 2″ across. Fortunately, prices have come down, and I am back home. However, if you are anywhere near Greenwood, South Carolina, call on my friend John Elsley, whose calanthes have nearly taken over his garden. I am sure he will be pleased to share some with you, so you do not share the same fate as I in my unbridled lust for calanthe. Tell him I sent you.

Grow and propagate similar to *C. discolor*.

**Related Species and Hybrids:**

Hizen hybrids arose from *C. discolor* x *C. aristulifera* and bear flowers in a wide range of pastel colors, from cream to light pink and an occasional darker purple. Zones 7b-9.

Kozu hybrids (*C. discolor* x *C. izu-insularis*) provide colors in white, pink red or brown. The flowers stand about a foot tall, and are mildly fragrant. A number of colors have been stabilized and are available, including pink/purple and red, as well as a mixture of light pastels and yellows ('Kozu Spice').

Takane hybrids combine *C. discolor* and *C. sieboldii*, resulting in a range of flower colors from yellow to orange, even red and brown. Plants are about a foot tall and a bit more vigorous than either parent.

*C. tricarinata* comes from Japan, and may be a little hardier (zone 6) than other selections. Plants bear yellow flowers with amber margins. Plants are about 15″ tall.

## ***Callirhoe*** (ka-lee-ro′ ee) Poppy Mallow Malvaceae

In his outstanding three-volume work, *The Standard Cyclopedia of Horticulture*, L.H. Bailey wrote that "callirhoes are of easiest culture and deserving of a much greater popularity". That was written in 1944. In my second edition (1997), I wrote "... and fifty years later callirhoes are still no more difficult to grow and have earned no greater respect. Why is this genus so difficult to find?" Today, I can happily report that we have finally caught up to Dr. Bailey, and poppy mallows are everywhere.

About 8 species, all native to the United States, have been described. All bear alternate leaves that are lobed or palmately cut, and showy cup-shaped white to purple flowers. Most are cold hardy to about 5°F and tolerate heat, but prefer cool summers. They require full sun and well-drained soils. Plants are particularly effective growing over walls and raised beds. The main species seen in gardens is the purple poppy mallow, *C. involucrata*, but bush's mallow, *C. bushii* is also going through a happy renaissance.

*Callirhoe* can be easily distinguished from other members of the Malvaceae by the five sticky threadlike style branches in the flower. The styles of other genera in the Malvaceae are either more numerous or are tipped with round sticky stigmas. Feel free to take my word for it.

***-bushii*** (bush-ee′ eye) Bush's Wine Cups 2-2½′/3′
Late Spring Purple Central United States Zones 4-8

I remember seeing this plant in gardens in the UK and then in the Midwest and wondering how it differed from common wine cups, *C. involucrata*. The flowers seemed to be the same shape, size and color, and I wondered if the label was simply incorrect. However, when I finally planted the two side by side, I noted the larger, thicker and less divided leaves of this species compared to common wine cups. Bush's form was a little less aggressive, at least in the Southeast. Still not a great deal of difference, but this is an excellent plant to try, especially if you cannot find the common one. It is a highly drought-tolerant species, flowering throughout the summer regardless of abuse. Another consideration for gardeners is that plants tolerate more shade than common poppy mallow. This is not to say it romps with ferns, but some afternoon shade is useful.

Plants were first described in 1909; the plant was named in honor of Benjamin Franklin Bush (1858-1937), a prominent botanist of the time. Perhaps I was not the only one confused about the differences; after considerable debate over the true taxonomic status of the species, *C. bushii* has been accepted as correct. In the past the plants were referred to as *C. involucrata* var. *bushii*.

***-involucrata*** (in-vol-yew-krah′ ta) Purple Poppy Mallow 1-2′/2′
Early Summer Purple Central United States Zones 4-7

The rough hairy stems and palmately divided leaves tend to grow horizontally, which results in a good deal of ground being covered. The leaves are covered with short, stiff hairs and are dark green with pale veins. The handsome 2″ wide wine-colored cup-shaped flowers are found throughout the plant but mainly on the terminals. Generally, flowers are entirely wine to magenta in color but occasionally the bases of the flowers may be white. This is a terrific plant that starts flowering after the main flush of spring plants, beginning in June and often continuing for months. Beneath the flower are three bracts that are similar to the sepals. Most other species of *Callirhoe* do not possess these bracts.

Plants are easy to grow from seed and if placed in well-drained soils in full sun, they provide a long show of eye-catching flowers. They are particularly popular in the Plains states, and it is almost impossible to visit gardens in Kansas, Missouri or Iowa and not run into a poppy mallow or two. In some gardens, they self-sow prodigiously. They do poorly in wet conditions and can get leggy under conditions of high heat and humidity. However, if plants get too leggy, simply whack them back, if you have the heart for it.

**Cultivars:**

var. *tenuissima* has deeply divided leaves and is only about 9″ tall. A terrific ground cover for full sun gardens.

**Related Species:**

*C. alcaeoides*, pale poppy mallow, has triangular basal leaves and often produces white to rose flowers with at least a tinge of pink, and no bracts are found beneath the flowers. 'Logan Calhoun' differs from the species by having pure white-cupped flowers on 8-12″ plants, with a spread of 4′. In 2000, plants were introduced in the GreatPlants® program, a joint effort of the Nebraska Nursery and Landscape Association and the Nebraska Statewide Arboretum.

*C. digitata* grows 3-4′ tall, has palmately divided leaves and beautiful long-stalked rose-red deeply cleft petals.

*C. triangulata*, clustered poppy mallow, bears triangular basal leaves and a cluster of red-purple flowers.

## *Caltha* (kal′ tha) Marsh Marigold Ranunculaceae

About 10 species of these moisture-loving plants occur and their garden value is finally being recognized. They flourish in wet areas near running water, but can succeed in rich, well-irrigated garden sites. The early spring flowers are white or yellow and made up entirely of sepals with numerous stamens. The leaves are alternate, usually basal and have an entire to slightly lobed margin.

***-palustris*** (pal-lus′ tris) Marsh Marigold 1-2′/1′
Spring Yellow North America Zones 5-7

Growing in shallow water or boggy ground, plants are less adaptable to common garden conditions than some of the other species. One- to two-inch-wide bright yellow flowers open over succulent kidney-shaped leaves which tend to get smaller as they progress up the stem. Plants simply make larger clumps but var. *palustris* is more spreading and forms large colonies. Plants may grow to two feet but 12-15″ is more common. Full sun is necessary for best performance.

Occasionally, plants can be confused with buttercups, *Ranunculus*. Both groups of plants love it wet, are low growers and have yellow flowers. *Caltha* has simple (not compound) leaves and the flowers usually have 5 sepals and no petals. *Ranunculus* often has compound leaves (or at least divided) and its flowers have 5 petals and 5 sepals.

**Cultivars:**

'Alba' produces white flowers but is much more difficult to obtain than the species. The white flowers make a striking contrast to the green foliage. Expensive but striking.

'Flore plena' ('Multiplex') is an outstanding plant with double yellow flowers.

'Tyermannii' is a more dwarf plant with dark stems and clear yellow flowers.

**Related Species:**

*C. leptosepala* (*C. biflora*), Western white marsh marigold, has basal leaves and no stem. The scape (flower stem) is slender and bears 2 marvelous white flowers with gold stamens. Native from California to Alaska.

## *Camassia* (ka-ma′ see-a) Quamash Liliaceae

*Camassia* is a true bulb and was used extensively by the Indians of the Northwest as a food staple. Bitter battles were fought over possession of the quamash grounds.

All are native to North America, extending from the West Coast to Georgia, yet are still undervalued in gardens in this country. The foliage is long, lancelike and grassy, and flower stems are erect and may be up to 4′ tall. The star-shaped flowers consist of six petal-like segments (called tepals), blue, purple, white, or cream colored, and appear at about the same time as the late tulips. The genus is closely related to *Scilla* and *Ornithogalum* but the veins on the tepals provide a handy clue to their identification. In *Camassia*, the tepals are distinctly veined, in *Scilla*, there is only one vein on the tepals and in *Ornithogalum*, the veins are quite indistinct. They are inhabitants of rich meadows, wet in spring and dry in summer. Plants tolerate some shade but perform better in full sun. Plant in the fall approximately 3 times deeper than the diameter of the bulb and in groups of at least a dozen. Nothing looks worse than one lonely quamash.

The foliage is not as persistent as that of daffodils, and bulbs may be planted in the formal garden. However, they still look rather scruffy after flowering and some gardeners prefer to plant them in a slightly more out of the way area such as the naturalized garden, where enough can be planted to insure a good supply of cut flowers for indoors. As for me, my garden is suitably scruffy to plant a few bulbs without guilt.

Bulb offsets are produced after several years, but natural production is very slow. Wounding the bulbs greatly enhances offset production and is practiced commercially. Seed propagation is not difficult if seed is fresh. Seeds germinate readily but 3-4 years are required before plants flower.

Quick Reference to Camassia Species

| | Height (ft.) | Number flowers open at once | Total flowers on stem |
|---|---|---|---|
| *C. cusickii* | 3-4 | Many | 30-100 |
| *C. leichtlinii* | 3-4 | 1-4 | 20-50 |
| *C. quamash* | 2-3 | Many | 10-40 |

**-*cusickii*** (kew-sik′ ee-eye) Cusick Quamash 3-4′/1′
Early Summer Blue Oregon Zones 3-8

These large bulbs can weigh up to half a pound! Numerous, slightly wavy leaves about 15″ long and 1½″ wide appear in a basal cluster. The lovely pale blue star-shaped flowers are approximately 1½″ across and up to 100 flowers are held in long racemes on 3-4′ long scapes. Each narrow flower segment has 3-5 faint veins running its length. The flowers do not twist together as they wither.

This is the cold-hardiest species and grows as far north as zone 3 with suitable winter protection.

**Cultivars:**
'Zwanenburg' has large deep blue flowers.

***-leichtlinii*** (liekt-lin′ ee-eye) California Quamash 3-4′/1′
Early Summer Various California to British Columbia Zones 5-9

This is probably the best species of *Camassia* for the garden. The foliage is broader than in *C. quamash* but not as wide as in *C. cusickii.* Plants are strong and stout and seldom need support except in windy areas. Up to 50 large (up to one inch across) flowers occur and may be white, cream, blue or purple. Each segment has 5-7 nerves. When the flowers wither, they twist around the capsule before falling away. This is one of the few characteristics that distinguishes this species from others, clearly pointing out how few differences exist among members of the genus.

There is tremendous variability in the species and a number of subspecies have been defined to try to bring some order to the chaos. Subspecies *typica* includes those with whitish flowers and sold under 'Alba' while subsp. *suksdorfii* embraces the blue to violet-flowered forms to which many of the cultivars below belong. When you purchase bulbs, you seldom will have to deal with subspecies, because, as luck would have it, nobody but camassia taxonomists gives a flip.

**Cultivars:**

'Alba' is a handsome white form of the species.
'Atroviolacea' has single flowers of deep violet.
'Blue Danube' produces dark blue flowers.
'Caerulea' produces light blue flowers. The soft coloration is wonderfully handsome.
'Electra' bears large flower heads of deep blue.
'Eve Price' is the finest cultivar I have seen and produces a magnificent clump of light blue flowers.
'Plena' bears creamy yellow double flowers.
'Semi-plena' produces semi-double creamy white flowers.

***-quamash*** (kwah′ mash) Common Quamash 2-3′/1′
Early Summer Various Western North America Zones 4-8

The 12″ long leaves are linear and grasslike (about ½″ wide). The flowers are usually white or in various shades of violet with 3-5 nerves per segment. This is also a highly variable species and the segments taking up the flowers may be closely or loosely spaced, often on the same raceme. It is distinguished by the irregular flowers that have 5 segments, more or less on one side, and the last one on the other. Each of the 10-30 flowers in the inflorescence is persistent but don't twist around as in the former species. The colors are not as deep as in *C. leichtlinii.*

The same lecture on variability and subspecies found in the former species could be provided for this one as well.

**Cultivars:**

'Blue Melody' has become popular for the violet blue flowers which rise above variegated foliage of creamy white and green.

'Flore-alba' is a handsome semi-double, white-flowering cultivar.
'Orion' bears dense inflorescences with purple buds and dark blue flowers.
'San Juan' has even darker blue flowers than 'Orion'.

**Related Species:**

*Camassia scilloides*, wild hyacinth, eastern camas, is not as bold or handsome as the western forms. The leaves are grasslike and rather floppy, although the pale blue to lavender flowers, borne on a 1-2′ tall stalk, are attractive. For eastern gardeners, their sites may mirror more closely the native range of this species and quamash success may be a little easier, if not as brilliant. Native to southern Ontario to Michigan and west to Wisconsin, and Kansas, and south to Texas and Georgia.

## ***Campanula*** (kam-pahn′ ew-la) Bellflower Campanulaceae

This fascinating genus consists of approximately 250 species, many of which are terrific garden plants. Campanulas can get into one's blood and bring out the collecting urges in many people. The great horticulturist, Liberty Hyde Bailey, took immense pleasure in his garden which "was fully inhabited by bellflowers, representing genera and species of *Campanula*, and related plants ...". The British authority Alan Bloom stated that he had "furtively accumulated 109 species and varieties of campanula before the nurseryman in me took control." Shades of blue tend to dominate but flowers are often tinted with lilac, lavender, violet and other hues. Species with white and pink flowers can also be found. They range in height from the low-growing rock garden species to five foot tall monsters.

The leaves are simple, usually alternate, and toothed. The basal leaves of the upright forms are usually different in size and shape than the stem leaves. The genus includes annuals (*C. americana*, *C. ramosissima*), biennials (*C. medium*), and even food crops (*C. rapunculoides*), but most are long-lived perennials. Although many wonderful species for the American garden occur, unfortunately most of the upright bellflowers do not perform particularly well in hot, humid climes (*C. persicifolia* is one exception). This is certainly a generalization and at higher altitudes or in cooler microclimates in the South, experiences with other upright forms are more positive. Bellflowers do not appreciate night temperatures above 70°F, although the dwarf forms are more forgiving than most of the erect species.

Propagation for all but double-flowered cultivars is easy by seed. Even most named cultivars come true from seed. Terminal stem cuttings, root cuttings, and divisions can be used when necessary. Most are sun loving but a few species may benefit from partial shade.

To quote L. H. Bailey once more is to understand the finer qualities of *Campanula*. "They are eminently plants for the garden-lover, for those persons who graciously accept cool nights and soft rains and dews, who respond to the milder sensations and derive sustaining satisfactions from gentle experiences. They are for those who love to grow plants for the joy of growing them."

Quick Reference to Campanula Species

| | Height (in.) | Habit (erect/low) | Flower color | Flower shape | Flower (pendulous or upright) |
|---|---|---|---|---|---|
| *C. carpatica* | 9-12 | L | Blue | Cup | U |
| *C. cochlearifolia* | 4-6 | L | Blue | Bell | P |
| *C. garganica* | 5-6 | L | Blue | Star | U |
| *C. glomerata* | 12-18 | E | Purple | Bell | U |
| *C. lactiflora* | 36-60 | E | Lilac | Bell | U |
| *C. latifolia* | 48-60 | E | Purple | Tubular | U |
| *C. latiloba* | 12-36 | E | Lilac | Saucer | U |
| *C. persicifolia* | 12-36 | E | Blue | Saucer | U |
| *C. portenschlagiana* | 4-6 | L | Blue | Bell | U |
| *C. poscharskyana* | 8-12 | L | Lilac | Bell | U |
| *C. pyramidalis* | 36-48 | E | Blue | Bell | U |
| *C. rotundifolia* | 6-12 | L | Purple | Bell | P |
| *C. takesimana* | 24-36 | E | Off-white | Tubular | P |

***-carpatica*** (kar-pa′ ti-ca) Carpathian Harebell 9-12″/12″
Summer Bright Blue Eastern Europe Zones 3-7

Perhaps because Carpathian harebell tolerates a wide range of conditions (although not heat), it has become one of the most popular bellflowers in the country. The numerous bell-shaped flowers are solitary and up to 2″ across. The leaves are triangular, toothed and dark green. Plants are excellent for containers, the rock garden or the front of the border and may spread readily as long as adequate drainage is provided. It is a floriferous species and will be covered with blooms in summer under good conditions.

I have not found this species particularly good in my north Georgia garden but I haven't tried all available cultivars. I have been more successful with some of the other smaller-flowered, low-growing species. All cultivars of *C. carpatica* prefer to have roots in cool soil, therefore, a summer mulch is useful, particularly in hot summers. If slugs are a problem, be prepared to have them feed on your plants.

Plants are relatively easy to force in the greenhouse. They may be cooled at temperatures around 40°F or can even be frozen, by leaving outdoors in large containers. Once temperatures are above 55°F, bring in and provide plants with artificial long days (turn on incandescent lights from dusk to midnight, or from 11:00 p.m. to 2:00 a.m.). Plants will flower 30 to 45 days later. Long days are a condition necessary to the flowering of *Campanula* and a few other genera as well.

Propagation of most cultivars is easiest by seed. Place the seed on top of medium and lightly cover with a thin layer of vermiculite. Keep the seed moist by covering with plastic and keep out of direct sun. Germination should occur within 3 weeks and seedlings can be transplanted 2 weeks later. Plants should be divided every other year to maintain habit and vigor.

**Cultivars:**

'Alba' has white flowers. Numerous white-flowered forms are available under names ranging from 'White Cloud', 'Snowdrift' and 'Albescens'. They are essentially all the same.

'Avalon' is a hybrid between var. *turbinata* x *C. raineri*. Plants are less than a foot tall, with a mounding habit and violet bell-shaped flowers.

'Blue Clips' is an excellent compact, 6-9″ tall plant bearing blue flowers up to 3″ wide. In the Clip series, one may find 'Deep Blue Clips', 'Light Blue Clips' and 'White Clips'.

'Blue Moonlight' bears china blue cups on 6-9″ tall mounds.

'Bressingham White' has 2-3″ wide clean white flowers.

'Chewton Joy' produces interesting two-toned flowers over 10″ tall plants. The petals are pale blue with much deeper blue margins.

'China Cup' and 'China Doll' are about 9″ tall and have azure blue flowers. Habits are similar.

'Jingle Bells' produces a mixture of white and blue flowers and grows 8-12″ tall.

'Kobalt Bell' has intense cobalt-blue flowers on 6-8″ tall plants. Stunning color.

'Pearl Deep Blue' has violet-blue upward-facing flowers with pale blue centers. Grows 6-9″ tall.

'Samantha' is relatively new, forming slow-spreading mounds of violet-blue upward-facing flowers. Like all members of this species, they are far better in cool climates.

var. *turbinata* has a more compact habit, growing 6-9″ tall and producing purplish blue flowers. A number of cultivars belong to this variety but, unfortunately, few are offered in the United States. The most popular is 'Karl Foerster', mainly used as a forced greenhouse plant or hanging basket which bear saucer-shaped flowers of deep blue. Other cultivars include 'Hannah' with white bell flowers, 'Isabel' with wide spreading deep violet flowers, 'Pallida' which bears blue flowers up to 1″ in diameter and 'Snowsprite' with white flowers on a 4″ tall frame.

Uniform series is designed for rock gardens or hanging baskets. Large flowers of blue ('Blue Uniform') or white ('White Uniform') are available. Not long lived.

'Wedgewood Blue' bears 2½″ diameter violet-blue flowers over 6″ tall plants. 'Wedgewood White' is one of the most compact white-flowered cultivars.

'White Star' is similar to 'Alba'. The flowers are a little cleaner white but plants are not as compact as 'Wedgewood White'. To be honest, it is almost impossible to tell the whites apart, and it is not much easier to separate the blues. If plants grow well in your area, you will likely enjoy them all.

***-cochlearifolia*** (kok-lee-ah-ree-i-fo' lee-a) Spiral Bellflower 4-6″/12″
Summer Blue-violet European Mountains Zones 4-7

A campanula that is easily grown in spite of the fact that nobody can pronounce the name. Another common name is fairies' thimbles, which attests to its diminutive habit and the creativity of taxonomists to create tongue-twisting names. The mat-forming plants, suitable for the front of the garden or along pathways, produce ¾″ diameter pendulous sky-blue flowers on wiry stems. The lower leaves are heart shaped and deeply serrate while the upper leaves are more narrow, almost elliptical. Nothing more than good drainage and mid-afternoon shade are required for success.

Propagate by seed similar to *C. carpatica* or by division in spring or fall.

**Cultivars:**

'Alba' bears clear white flowers and is particularly vigorous.

'Bavaria Blue' and 'Bavaria White' are about 4″ tall, more compact than the species and bear dark blue and white flowers respectively.

'Cambridge Blue' bears light blue flowers on 2-3″ tall plants. The latter two cultivars were bred by Alan Bloom in the 1930s.

'Elizabeth Oliver' is interesting not because of the pale blue flower color but because they are fully double. She is now available in this country and should be a hit.

'Miranda' is a vigorous grower which produces pale icy blue flowers.

'Patience Bell' bears large diameter deep blue flowers on 6-9″ mounds of foliage.

'Temple Bells' is 12-15″ tall with white flowers.

***-garganica*** (gar-gah' ni-ca) Gargano Bellflower 5-6″/12″
Spring Blue Italy Zones 5-7

This species was discovered in 1827 at the base of Mt. Garganica in Italy. Although treated by some authorities as a variant of *C. elatines* or *C. portenschlagiana*, it is usually offered as *C. garganica*. The basal leaves are kidney shaped while the stem leaves are heart shaped. Both are grayish green with rounded teeth. Starlike blue flowers with white eyes are produced in clusters in the leaf axils and persist for 2-3 weeks.

This is an aggressive species and needs to be divided often. Full sun is preferable but partial shade is tolerated, particularly in the southern range of cultivation. It is a hardy rock garden plant which should be grown for the unique non-campanulate flowers, prostrate habit and gray-green leaves.

Propagate by seed (similar to *C. carpatica*), terminal cuttings or division in early spring or fall.

**Cultivars:**

'Alba' bears white flowers.

'Blue Diamond' produces icy blue flowers with a dark blue center.

'Constellation' is a clumper that grows 3-6″ tall and 9-12″ wide. The lavender-purple starry flowers formed in late spring to early summer are held above the serrated dark green leaves. Best as a container or rock garden plant.

'Dickson's Gold' ('Aurea') is unique for its golden foliage. The contrast between the foliage and the blue flowers is striking, although not particularly easy on the eyes. Plants need some protection to maintain the golden hue. Some afternoon shade in the South is essential.

'E.K. Toogood' is quite common in Europe but difficult to find in the United States. Plants form 6-9″ tall mounds of heart-shaped smooth leaves that are covered with

blue star-shaped flowers with paler centers in spring and early summer. Probably hardy in zones 4-7. Some taxonomists believe this may be a hybrid between *C. garganica* x *C. poscharskyana*.
'Glandore' bears dark blue flowers with a lighter blue center.
var. *hirsuta* is a gray downy-leafed form with lighter blue flowers and longer stems than the species.
var. *hirsuta alba* has the same form as var. *hirsuta* but with white flowers.
'W.H. Paine' produces star-shaped flowers with a clean white center.

**-*glomerata*** (glo-me-rah' ta) Clustered Bellflower 12-18"/12"
Summer Blue, Purple Eurasia Zones 3-8

The common name of this showy bellflower comes from the clustered arrangement of flowers atop the flowering stem. There may be as many as 15 flowers in the inflorescence which persists for 2-3 weeks. Cut flower stems also last up to 2 weeks when placed in water. The ovate, toothed foliage is hairy above and below and varies in size. The stem leaves are 3-4" long, sessile or short petioled, and usually narrower and more pointed than the 5" long basal leaves. Plants may be single stemmed or branched.

Full sun in the North or partial shade in the South is recommended. None of the cultivars is particularly persistent, regardless of where one gardens. Plantings in the State Botanical Garden of Georgia held up for approximately 3 years, and trials in the Gardens at UGA and elsewhere have shown that plants may be recommended for the warm humid climes as long as partial shade and water are present. For most aesthetic results, place in groups of at least three plants.

Propagate using 2-3" long terminal cuttings in summer after flowering. Seed is available for many of the cultivars as well as the species and should be treated similar to *C. carpatica*.

**Cultivars:**
var. *acaulis* is a dwarf early-flowering violet-blue form which is almost stemless and only 3-5" tall. Plants taller than 8" with bluish flowers are not likely this variety. A white form (var. *acaulis alba*) is 8-12" tall. These have been quite useful for rock gardens where small stature may be important.
'Caroline' has lilac to light pink flowers with a little darker edge. Plants are about 18-24" tall.
'Crown of Snow' is nearly 18-24" tall and bears large white flower clusters.
var. *dahurica* (syn. *C. dahurica*, *C. speciosa*) has large (clusters 3" across) deep-violet flowers and stands about 2-3' tall.
'Joan Elliott' sends up many flowering stems of deep violet-blue flowers and is 1½' tall. Probably the most floriferous of the group and an excellent choice for cut flowers.
'Odessa' bears upright facing clusters of deep purple flowers. Plants are 2-3' tall.
'Purple Pixie' is about 1½' high with lavender-blue flowers. Plants remain in a tight clump, displaying no spreading tendencies common in many other cultivars.
'Snow Cushion' is a clean white form and grows 2' tall.

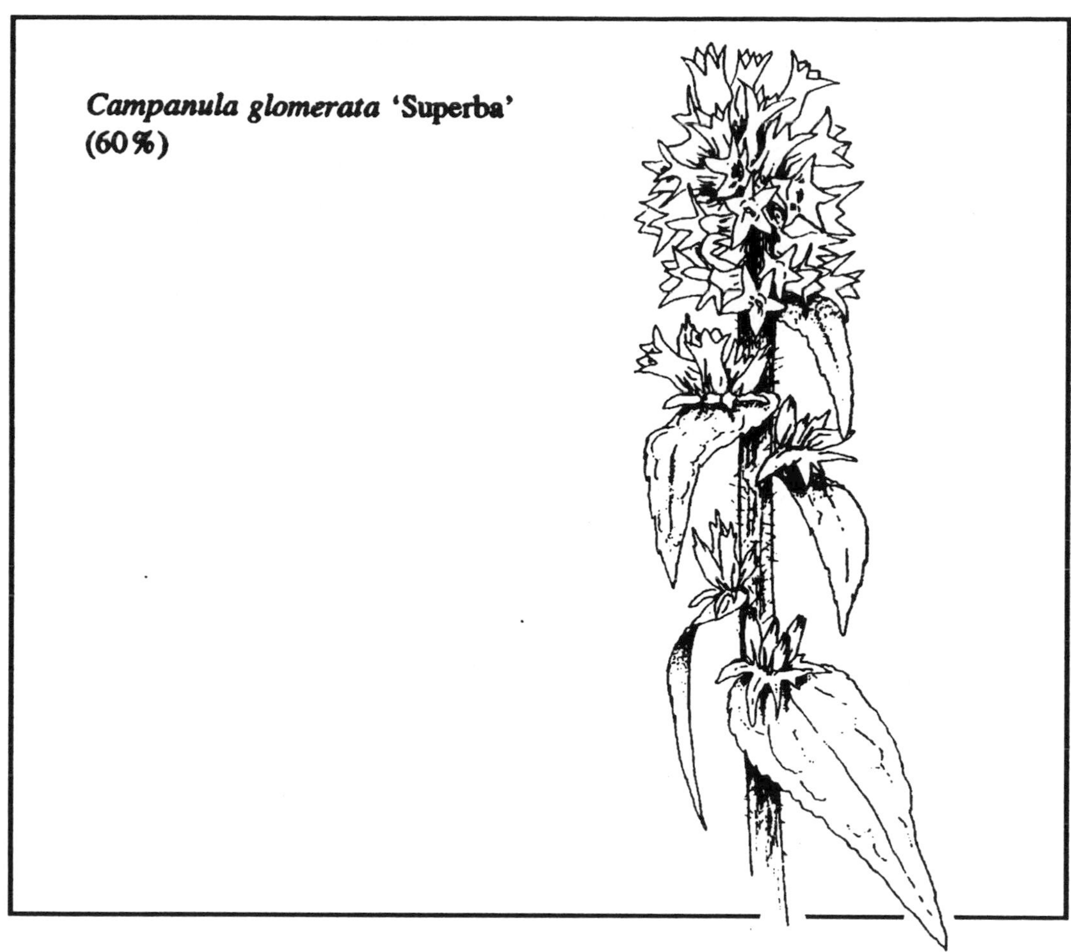
*Campanula glomerata* **'Superba'** **(60%)**

'Superba' has violet flowers and grows 2½′ tall. It is vigorous and tolerates heat better than many other selections.

'Superba Alba' is a white form of the above cultivar.

'White Barn', introduced by Beth Chatto, has dense heads of violet-purple flowers on short 12-15″ tall spikes. An excellent habit.

***-lactiflora*** (lak-ti-flor′ a) Milky Bellflower 3-5′/3′
Summer Lavender-blue Caucasus Zones 5-7

This tall bellflower has a bushy habit and can reach up to 5′ under optimum conditions. The 3-5″ long basal leaves are serrated and have short petioles. They become smaller, more pointed and sessile as they ascend the stem. The 1-2″ long bell-shaped flowers point upwards and are often milk white (thus its common name) to pale blue. They are borne on 12-15″ long leafy terminal panicles on each axillary shoot. Hundreds of flowers can occur on well-grown plants, distinguishing it from other tall campanulas such as *C. latifolia* and *C. latiloba*. People often have trouble distinguishing some of the tall species apart, and I am one of them. This table helps me, it may help you also.

| | Flowers | Flower attachment | Comments |
|---|---|---|---|
| *C. lactiflora* | Many | Pedicel | With many flowers, think "flora" |
| *C. latifolia* | Few | Pedicel | Few flowers compared to *lactiflora* |
| *C. latiloba* | Few | Sessile | Spikes remind me of a delphinium |
| *C. persicifolia* | Many | Pedicel | Leaves narrow, not serrated |

The many flowers and the tall bushy upright habit help to separate this one from other similar bellflowers. I still get confused, but if you want flower power, this is the one to try first.

Although milky bellflower is tolerant of full sun in northern climes, plants are more at home with a few hours of afternoon shade and do not look out of place in a semi-shaded wild flower garden. A consistent moisture level is helpful for vigorous growth, but well-drained soils are necessary, especially in the heat. Plants do not transplant particularly well and direct sowing (i.e. sowing seeds directly in the garden) helps them establish. In fact, once established, plants multiply rapidly due to the prolific self-sowing tendency. This is particularly true in the Northwest where much to the chagrin of Easterners, they can get a little weedy. If a problem, flowers should be removed immediately after flowering. If plants are cut back immediately after flowering, a second flush of flowers may occur in the fall.

Propagate the species and varieties by seed or division, the cultivars by division. Treat the seeds similar to *C. carpatica*. All varieties exhibit a great deal of variation when raised from seed.

**Cultivars:**

var. *alba* is a 4-5′ tall white-flowering variety.

'Avalanche' was discovered by Adrian Bloom as a chance seedling in his garden, Foggy Bottom in Bressingham, UK and released in 2005. Plants bear large white flowers and are particularly floriferous. There is also a cultivar with blue flowers that goes under the name of 'Blue Avalanche' but I am not sure if it is simply a sport of the above, or a "made up" name.

var. *coerulea* ('Caerulea') bears violet blue flowers.

'Favourite' is about 4′ tall with dark violet-blue flowers.

'Loddon Anna' is a strong 4′ tall plant with soft pale pink flowers. This is old fashioned yet still a lovely cultivar.

'Pouffe' is a dwarf cultivar that stands only 10-18″ high and is covered with pale blue flowers for 4-5 weeks. Many of the taller cultivars are floppy; this is not.

'Prichard's Variety' can bear hundreds of purple-blue flowers on its 3-4′ tall stems. It is the most common cultivar available, and for good reason.

var. *rosea* has pink flowers.

'Superba' has large (1½-2″) dark violet-blue flowers and is more vigorous than the type.

'White Pouffe' is similar to 'Pouffe' but with white flowers.

***-latifolia*** (lah-ti-fo′ lee-a) Great Bellflower 4-5′/3′
Early Summer Purple-blue Europe Zones 3-7

This erect plant has a running rootstock that results in rapidly spreading clumps. The 5-6″ long basal leaves are held on a long, slightly winged petiole but become smaller and virtually sessile as they ascend the stem. All are slender-pointed, double toothed and hairy. The erect, bell-shaped flowers are about 2-3″ long and held in a short leafy terminal raceme as well as in the leaf axils. The old basal flowers turn down while the new ones are still opening.

Plants are not as showy as *C. lactiflora* but do make reasonably good garden specimens. Support is required to remain upright and plants are best placed in the rear of informal settings. I have had no success establishing plants in my garden and I have seen few good stands south of zone 6. Where plants are successful, seed capsules should be removed prior to maturity if new colonies are not wanted.

Propagate the species by seed or division in early spring. Seed normally germinates quickly but may first require 2-4 weeks of 40-50°F to assure a high germination percentage. Cultivars should be divided in early spring.

**Cultivars:**

'Alba' has white flowers but is otherwise similar to the species.

'Brantwood' is violet colored and the best-known cultivar of the species.

'Gloaming' has pale blue flowers and is particularly attractive. Plants are 2-3′ tall and seem to spread less aggressively than others. Plants must be propagated vegetatively for best results.

'Macrantha' has larger flowers but otherwise is similar to the species.

'Macrantha Alba' is a good white form although not remarkably different from 'Alba'.

'White Ladies' bears clear white flowers.

***-latiloba*** (lat-ee-lobe′ a) Delphinium Bellflower 3-4′/3′
Summer Blue, White Europe Zones 5-7

One of the many taxonomic suggestions made in recent years was to officially change the name of *C. latiloba* to *C. persicifolia* subsp. *sessiliflora*. Although it is much more of a mouthful, it better describes the sessile flowers and the peachleaf bellflower-leaves found in this plant. It is the sessile flowers, arranged in a spike, that makes identification of this species so easy.

However, *C. latiloba* is still used in the trade and the name slips off your tongue so much better. I also made up the common name, delphinium bellflower, because the plants remind me of a delphinium when I first look at the flower stalks. The flowers are large (2-3″ long) with wide lobes, thus *latiloba* (wide-lobed) is also appropriate. The species itself is seldom seen, however, some good cultivars occur.

**Cultivars:**

'Alba' is one of the best white-flowered plants I have seen. Clean, clear and handsome.

'Hidcote Amethyst' bears pale amethyst flowers with a faint median stripe of deeper blue.

'Highcliffe Variety' produces deep violet-blue flowers.
'Percy Piper' is similar to 'Highcliffe' but is significantly shorter.
'Splash' has blue flowers "splashed" with pale lavender. Plants are 3-4′ tall.

***-persicifolia*** (per-sis-i-fo′ lee-a) Peachleaf Bellflower 1-3½′
Summer Blue-violet Europe, North Africa, Asia Zones 3-7

This popular European cut flower is becoming more familiar to American consumers and gardeners. The erect flowers are 1-1½″ long and broadly bell shaped, almost resembling a saucer. Flowers occur in various shades of blue in open terminal racemes. The evergreen, basal leaves are 4-8″ long while the sessile stem leaves are 2-4″ long. All are narrow, leathery, and have rounded teeth or are wavy and certainly don't resemble peach leaves. Clumps increase in size by shoots arising from the base of the plant and new colonies are formed everywhere through self-sowing. Flower color, plant habit and size are variable.

In zones 3-6, this is an excellent garden plant. Garden performance in the South has been mixed. In zone 7, plants perform fairly well and persist for 3-4 years but in zone 8, flower color is faded and plants decline after one summer.

Peachleaf bellflowers are among the best cut flowers in the genus, providing strong sturdy stems and persistent flowers in the vase. Propagate by seed (similar to *C. carpatica*), division, or terminal cuttings.

**Cultivars:**

'Alba' has white flowers.
'Alba Coronata' bears semi-double white flowers.
'Alba Flore-pleno' has fully double white flowers.
'Beechwood' bears pale, soft blue flowers.
'Bluebell' has single blue flowers and grows 2-3′ tall.
'Blue Gardenia' produces double blue flowers. This may be the same (they look the same) as 'Coerulea Flore-plena' but certainly sounds better.
'Boule de Neige' bears large, double white flowers.
'Chettle Charm' is a marvelous plant producing creamy white flowers with light lavender margins.
'Coerulea Coronata' produces semi-double purple-blue flowers.
'Coerulea Flore-plena' has double flowers of the same color.
'Grandiflora Blue' and 'Grandiflora White' have larger (2″ diameter) blue and white cup-shaped flowers respectively.
'Hampstead White' is a particularly handsome white form, bearing semi-double hose-in-hose flowers. Also occasionally listed as 'Hetty'.
'Kelly's Gold' arose in the garden of Ann Holt on Bainbridge Island, Washington. It is unique in having golden foliage and white flowers with a touch of blue on the margins. The foliage is brighter in spring, but is still noticeable in summer. Like others upright forms of the genus, better in zone 4 than zone 7. However, well worth a try in the garden.
'Powder Puff' has fully double white flowers that are a little larger and certainly as double as any other whites out there. Plants grow 2-3′ tall.

'Snowdrift' also has large 2″ diameter white flowers.

'Telham Beauty' is 3-4′ tall with bell-shaped pale china-blue flowers. Still one of the most popular and handsome cultivars.

***-portenschlagiana*** (por-ten-schlag-ee-ah′ na) Dalmatian Bellflower 4-6″/12″
Spring Blue-purple Southern Europe Zones 4-8

This is a particularly effective plant for rock gardens, rock walls or as potted plants. In the British Isles and the Northwest, it scampers over walls and transforms rockeries and walls into glorious seas of blue. I use it in my garden, and although the performance does not compare to English standards, it makes an effective ground cover at the front of the bed. The 1-2″ long foliage is triangular and forms low-growing dark green mats. The 1″ diameter bell to cup-shaped flowers virtually cover the plant in late spring and early summer. Plants are easily confused with another species whose name also catches in the throat, *C. poscharskyana.* Tricks for telling them apart are found in that species.

Although the flowers are smaller than those of *C. carpatica*, it is a better plant for the heat. Plants persist for three to four years. They are not particularly fussy about growing conditions except for good drainage.

Propagation of the species is easy from seeds or divisions; cultivars are easily divided. The seeds are extremely small and should not be covered. Water from the bottom so seeds will not be washed away. A four-week treatment at 35-40°F promotes germination.

**Cultivars:**

'Alba' is a lovely white-flowered cultivar, otherwise similar to the species.

'Bavarica' is a named cultivar but it looks so similar to the species that I cannot see any difference.

'E.H. Frost' is similar to 'Alba' but the flowers may be more of a milky white. Nice to have a choice in whites.

'Major' has larger flowers than the type.

'Resholdt's Variety' bears the most vivid blue of the bunch. The best by far.

***-poscharskyana*** (po-shar-skee-ah′ na) Serbian Bellflower 8-12″/12″
Spring Blue-lilac Yugoslavia Zones 3-7

The 18″ long stems are prostrate resulting in excellent plants for dry walls, rockeries, or edgings of paths. The ½-1″ wide star-shaped flowers have deeply cut petals about 4 times as long as the flower tube. The easiest way to remember the difference between this unpronounceable species and the former unpronounceable one is the following. When you see a prostrate blue campanula with small flowers growing in cracks or on walls, look at the flower shape. If the flowers are star shaped, star rhymes with *shar* in *poscharskyana*. If they are bell or cup-shaped, then it is likely the other one. I never claimed to be a rocket scientist!

The 1½″ long leaves are rounded with wavy margins. This is a good species where a rapidly spreading, low-growing plant is needed for a sunny area. Propagate by seed (similar to *C. carpatica*) or division in early spring or fall.

**Cultivars:**

'Blue Gown' has larger, blue flowers than the species.

'Blue Waterfall' produces mounds of bell-shaped lavender-blue flowers in early to mid summer late June and July.

'E.H. Frost' bears milky white flowers.

'Lilacina' produces lilac-pink flowers.

'Stella' has wide star-shaped flowers of vivid violet-blue. An Award of Garden Merit winner from the Royal Horticultural Society in 1994.

***-punctata*** (punk-tah′ ta) Spotted Bellflower 2-3′/3′
Summer White to Pink Korea Zones 5-7

Plants bear pendulous tubular flowers spotted or flecked with tiny purple spots. They are somewhat lanky in warm climates but better than their close cousin, *C. takesimana*. I find that they can be thuggish and look weedy even when in flower, however, there is no doubt they are eye-catching. The species itself is seldom seen, but breeders are working hard to develop more garden-worthy cultivars.

**Cultivars**:

'Alba', 'Rosea' and the handsome 'Rubrifolia' have white rose and deep rose flowers spotted with bright red respectively.

'Bowl of Cherries' is a recent introduction and should become quite popular. It is nice to see dozens of dark, purple-red bells falling off the plant, but the best part may be that it is less than 18″ tall. If old stems are removed, additional flowering may occur.

'Hot Lips' may be a hybrid with *C. punctata*. Regardless, plants are only 10-12″ tall and bear tubular pale pink flowers with purple spots within. Good for a container or small space in the garden.

'Kent Bells' is probably the best known of the Bells series, bearing cobalt blue flowers on 2-3′ tall plants. However, 'Cherry Bells', and 'Wedding Bells' provider gardeners with red, and white bell-shaped flowers respectively. 'Wedding Bells' consist of hose-in-hose flowers (i.e. look like double flowers) on strong upright stems.

'Little Punky' had to have been named by a man, on a bad day. Regardless, plants are short (8-10″ tall) and have light lavender flowers with many red spots within.

'Milkshake' combines chartreuse foliage spotted with green freckling and lavender-pink flowers on 2′ tall plants. An interesting, if somewhat scary combination.

'Pantaloons' produces pendulous pink "hose-in-hose" flowers over mounded 2′ tall plants.

'Pink Chimes' produces dozens of pendulous pink bells on short 14-18″ plants.

'Sarastro' is probably a hybrid between this species and *C. trachelium*, throatwort bellflower, originating from Austria. Plants are slower to grow than *C. punctata*, but do not take as much room. Purple bell flowers hang down from the plants in early summer. Better behaved than other cultivars and a better choice where space is at a premium.

*Campanula poscharskyana*
(110%)

'Summertime Blues' is likely a hybrid but has pendulous bell-shaped flowers similar to those of *C. punctata*. The silver-blue flowers are formed on 2′ tall stems and appear to be much more persistent than other similar cultivars. According to the breeder, they seldom reseed or spread.

***-pyramidalis*** (pi-ra-mi-dah′ lis) Chimney Bellflower 3-4′/3′
Summer Blue, White Southern Europe Zones 3-7

This plant is grown as a biennial as it deteriorates badly after the second year. The 2″ long heart-shaped basal leaves have 6-8″ long petioles and dentate (teeth point straight out, not up, as in serrate) margins. Twelve- to fifteen-inch-long pyramidal panicles of bell-shaped blue flowers arise from the axil of each stem leaf. More flowers open at the base of the flower stem than at the top, resulting in the pyramidal shape of the inflorescence.

Similar to most other upright species, chimney bellflower does not tolerate heat and humidity and struggles even in zone 6. Regardless of locale, stems are brittle and the plant should be supported. This is a good species for growing in patio containers (perhaps the only good place) where the size will be restricted by root compaction in the container.

Propagation is similar to other species.

**Cultivars:**

'Alba' is similar to the type but with clear white flowers.

'Aureovariegata' has yellow variegated foliage.

'Compacta' is a dwarf 2-3′ tall form. It is easier to manage in the garden and requires less room than the type but lacks the characteristic pyramidal shape.

***-rotundifolia*** (ro-tund-i-fo′ lee-a) Harebell 6-12″/12″
Summer Blue-violet Northern Hemisphere Zones 2-6

This species is circumboreal in distribution and is found in many regions of North America. Known as the bluebells of Scotland, it is well entrenched in song and verse in that country. Probably the most cold tolerant of the available bellflowers; there is even a var. *alaskana*. As cold hardy as it is, it is one of the least heat tolerant. The 1″ wide basal leaves are rounded, thus "rotundifolia", but often disappear by the time flowering occurs. The 2-3″ long stem leaves are linear and grasslike. Many flowering stems are formed and several ½-1″ wide, bell shaped, nodding flowers are borne in each terminal raceme.

Performance is far better in mountain or northern climates, and plants are ideally suited to the northern United States and Canada. In the South, they are much more sprawling and weedlike, and not worth the nickel to buy them (see 'Olympica' below).

Propagate by seeds (similar to *C. carpatica*) or division.

**Cultivars:**

'Alba' has creamy white flowers but is otherwise similar to the species.

'Flore-plena' has double blue flowers that are more persistent than the species.

'Olympica' is a good bright blue-flowered cultivar with 12″ tall stems. In the Gardens at UGA, this was pretty the first year, weedy the second, and dead the third.
'Purple Gem' bears rich purple bell flowers in early summer and the rosette turns a handsome maroon in winter.
'Soldanelliflora' is a unique semi-double variety whose blue flowers are split to the base into about 25 divisions.
'White Gem' has clean white bell-shaped flowers on 1-1½′ long stems.

***-takesimana*** (tak-ease-ee-mane′ a) Korean Bellflower 2-3′/3′
Summer Creamy White Korea Zones 5-7

Relatively new to gardeners, the plants are beginning to enjoy some popularity. From a rosette of heart-shaped leaves, each measuring about 3-4″ long, tubular lilac pink to off-white flowers are suspended from the stems in mid to late summer. The flowers are usually spotted inside which may be visible from the outside through the thin tissue. Plants can get large and gangly and require a lot of space. Actually, they can take over the world. Well-drained soils and full sun are necessary. It is similar in habit to *C. punctata* but larger and even more poorly behaved.

**Cultivars:**
'Elizabeth' has light green foliage and arching stems carrying dozens of purplish-pink bells. She has been lauded wherever she has been planted.
'Pink Octopus', from Terra Nova Nursery, has long, narrow petals that kind of look like octopus tentacles. Sounds gruesome, doesn't it? However, the pink flowers are produced in abundance, so octopi lovers can take heart.

**Related Species and Hybrids:**

The genus *Campanula* is not only one of my favorite genera in the entire plant kingdom, it is also one of the most complex to describe. This is because so many species are ornamental and so much breeding and hybridization has occurred. The following taxa are some of my best friends but not all have reached mainstream American gardens.

*C. alliariifolia*, spurred bellflower, grows large and lush, starting out as a rosette of large heart-shaped leaves, followed by 2-3′ tall stems bearing many white 1-2″ long bell-shaped flowers on one side of the inflorescence only. Interesting, but can get weedy due to their lankiness. 'Ivory Bells' is sometimes listed as a cultivar or sometimes used as a common name for the species. There is so little difference between the two, I believe it is more accurately used as a common name. 'Flore-pleno' bears double flowers but is quite difficult to locate.

*C. americana*, tall bellflower, is native to moist shady areas in eastern North America. Although not as showy as other upright forms, the spikes of 1″ wide, pale blue flowers associate well with other shade-tolerant perennials. Unfortunately, plants are short lived and should be treated as biennials.

*C. barbata*, bearded bellflower, bears 1″ long lilac-blue pendulous, bell-shaped flowers which have woolly hairs (bearded) within. In the summer, the rosettes of dark green leaves send up the strong 12-18″ tall flower stems. So many flowers are produced that it has been said to "flower itself to death." A white form, 'Alba', is occasionally listed. Likely hardy in zones 5-7.

*C.* 'Birch Hybrid' resulted from a cross between *C. portenschlagiana* and *C. poscharskyana*, Serbian bellflower. Nodding cup-shaped purple blue flowers smother the 6″ tall plants. Effective for walls and crevices.

*C.* 'Burghaltii' is a cross between *C. latifolia* and *C. punctata*. Plants bear pale mauve flowers which arise from amethyst-colored flower buds. I find the long pendulous flowers on the lanky stems messy at best but if room allows, it is worth a try.

*C. collina*, Armenian bellflower, produces 8″ tall mounds of good-looking heart-shaped leaves, and bears handsome purple bell flowers in early summer. Plants can spread.

*C. divaricata*, southern harebell, is native to the southern Appalachians from Maryland to Georgia. It is one of few useful native campanulas. The many, small, pale blue flowers are pendulous and are borne in terminal panicles. Little known, but should be more used, particularly by southern gardeners.

*C. elatines*, Adriatic bellflower, is similar, but has heart-shaped leaves compared to the ovate leaves of *C. garganica*. The blue or white flowers are borne in a spike. A number of variants occur, including var. *fenestrellata* with a more upright habit and larger leaves, which is also listed as *C. fenestrellata*. None is useful for warm, humid conditions, much preferring cool night conditions.

*C.* x *fergusonii* (*C. pyramidalis* x *C. carpatica*) has erect 2′ tall stems with carpatica-like blue flowers. It is seldom seen in North American gardens.

*C.* x *haylodgensis* is a hybrid between *C. carpatica* and *C. cochlearifolia*, both low-growing forms best suited for walls or rock gardens. The best known cultivar is 'Warley White', with white double flowers on 5-6′ tall plants.

*C.* x *hendersonii* is a cross between *C. alliariifolia* and *C. carpatica*. Plants are about 18″ tall with pale lilac flower spikes.

*C. medium* (*C. media*), Canterbury bells or cup and saucer, are some of Grandmother's favorites, however, perhaps because they are biennials, plants are less available than "in the old days". The species, bearing single flowers up the 3′ tall stem, is known as Canterbury bells, while the double forms ('Calycanthema') with white, rose or purple flowers are known as cup and saucer plant. Plant one-year-old plants in the fall, flowers will occur next spring or early summer. Some spectacular cultivars are available but the best of the Canterbury bells by far is the Champion series. Each plant bears dozens of large flowers and are excellent not only in the garden but also make the best cut flowers for the house. 'Champion Blue' and 'Champion Pink' are the most common, although other colors may soon be available.

*C. ochroleuca* resembles *C. alliariifolia* but the lower leaves are deltoid rather than heart shaped. The flowers, which range from white to very pale yellow, may be distinguished by the style which extends beyond the petals. A handsome, although similarly lanky plant. Plants are likely hardy to zone 5.

*C. pulla* is among the smallest species in the genus. This tufted 3-4″ tall plant bears small dark blue nodding flowers. Often seen in rock gardens. I saw this at the wonderful Northwest Nursery near Eugene, Oregon. Fabulous.

*C. rhomboidalis* is an upright plant, growing about 2′ tall with racemes of bell-shaped lilac to blue flowers. The flowers are nearly an inch long and held almost horizontally. Seldom seen in North America but worth trying in zones 3 to 6.

*C.* 'Royal Wave' is sometimes listed under *C. punctata* but is obviously a hybrid. The upward-facing cup-shaped flowers are deep blue with white centers and are nicely fragrant.

*C. thyrsoides* is the most un-bellflower bellflower I have seen. It forms a 2-3′ tall plant with pale yellow flowers in a compressed narrow, almost cylindrical, spike. It is a lot more interesting than ornamental but because it is so different, it has appeal to the crazy gardeners of the world. The variety *carniolica* has yellow-white flowers in an even narrower inflorescence. The main drawback, other than weirdness, is its tendency to be monocarpic, meaning that it will die after setting fruit. Plants may self-sow where they are happy.

*C. trachelium*, throatwort bellflower, has an angular stem and somewhat bristly stems and leaves. The blue or white bell-shaped flowers are initially erect then later droop in a loose raceme. Very hardy and dependable. 'Bernice' is the best, growing about 2′ tall and producing double blue flowers. 'Snowball' produces double white flowers.

## ***Canna*** (kan′ na) Canna Lily, Indian Shot Cannaceae

Approximately 50 species occur in the genus but finding a true species in American gardens is well nigh impossible. The plants that adorn gardens today are known as *C.* x *generalis*, *C.* x *hybrida*, or just plain garden hybrids. They resulted from crosses among *C. glauca*, gray canna; *C. speciosa*; *C. iridifolia*, Peruvian canna; *C. warscewiczii*, and the native *C. flaccida*, southern marsh canna. Suffice it to say the nomenclature is rather confusing and I prefer "garden hybrids". Nomenclature aside, many beautiful hybrids are available which outperform their parents 100 times over.

Cannas placed in rich, well-drained soil in full sun begin to flower in midsummer and continue well into the fall, depending on cultivar. In most of the country, the rootstocks must be lifted after frost has knocked down the leaves. Allow the roots to dry in a warm area for a few days and then store them in moist (not wet!) peat moss where temperatures will remain above 40°F. In zones 7b-10, the plants may be over-wintered in the ground but no damage will be done if rootstocks are lifted. In the spring, start the rhizomes indoors in pots about 4 weeks before the date of the last frost. Do not plant them too early as they are tender and may be killed by late frosts. Plant single colors *en masse* 3′ apart for maximum effect. Plants are excellent choices for wet areas, along the sides of streams or even as additions to the garden pond. They tolerate dry conditions but are right at home in the neighborhood swamp.

However, other than minimal frost tolerance, two other major problems can occur. Leaf rollers (*Calpodes ethlius* and *Geshna cannalis*) lay their eggs in the folds of emerging foliage and damage is seen as rolled-up leaves with holes throughout. The larvae of these small moths roll up the edge of a young or fully expanded leaf and use silk to hold the edges closed, preventing further expansion. Depending on the type of leaf roller, the entire leaf surface will be eaten or just the upper surface will be disfigured. Cutting plants to the ground in the late winter and disposing of the cut material will reduce populations of leaf rollers. Once infested, it is difficult to spray chemicals to reach the larvae, but if attempted, add a spreader-sticker like soap to the insecticide because the waxy leaf surfaces repel water. Products that contain *Bacillus thuringiensis* (Bt) are least toxic to beneficial organisms and work well but slowly on leaf rollers. Japanese beetles can also seriously disfigure cannas. Both have resulted in gardeners getting rid of cannas rather than fight the little buggers.

**Cultivars:**

Hundreds of cultivars are available but be careful how you buy them. Purchasing dried-out rhizomes in a bar-coded plastic bag from a shelf in a nondescript store is just plain stupid. Buy prestarted plants or freshly dug rhizomes.

The number of cultivars is astounding, ranging from single to multiple colored flowers and green, dark bronze or purple foliage. We have trialed dozens at the Gardens at UGA and have barely touched the tip. Heights range from 1½′ to 7′.

A List of Some Reliable Hybrid Cultivars:

| | Height (ft.) | Leaf color | Flower color |
|---|---|---|---|
| 'Apricot Dream' | 3½ | Gray-green | Salmon |
| 'Australia' | 5 | Purple | Red |
| 'Bengal Tiger' ('Pretoria') | 4 | Yellow, Green | Orange |
| 'Black Knight' | 3 | Bronze | Dark Red |
| 'Brandywine' | 5 | Green | Dark Red |
| 'Cleopatra' | 4 | Green with Purple | Red, Yellow |
| 'Conestoga' | 5 | Green | Lemon-yellow |
| 'Constitution' | 5 | Gray-green | Light Pink |
| 'Ermine' | 3 | Green | White |
| 'Grande' | 3 | Green | Orange-scarlet |
| 'Intrigue' | 7 | Purple-gray | Orange-red |
| 'Musifolia' | 12 | Green | Red |
| 'Lucifer' | 3 | Green | Red and Yellow |
| 'Minerva' | 5 | Striped White, Green | Yellow |
| 'Orange Beauty' | 4 | Green | Orange |
| 'Nuance' | 7 | Gray-green | Gold, Red |
| 'Orange Punch' | 4 | Green | Orange |
| 'Pacific Beauty' | 6 | Gray | Orange |
| 'Panache' | 6 | Gray-green | Apricot |
| 'Pink Sunburst' | 3 | Multi colored | Pink |
| 'Pink President' | 3 | Green | Pink |
| 'Red Stripe' | 6 | Green with Red Midrib | Red |
| 'Richard Wallace' | 4 | Green | Yellow |

A List of Some Reliable Hybrid Cultivars *(continued)*:

| | Height (ft.) | Leaf color | Flower color |
|---|---|---|---|
| 'Rosamunde Cole' | 3½ | Green | Red |
| 'Stuttgart' | 7 | Green and White Blocks | Peach |
| 'The President' | 3 | Green | Red |
| 'Tropicanna Gold' | 4 | Stripped Yellow, Green | Orange |
| 'Tropicanna (Phaison') | 5 | Multi-colored | Orange |
| 'Valentine' | 3 | Green | Red |
| 'Wyoming' | 5 | Bronze | Orange |

The variegated forms such as 'Minerva' and 'Tropicanna Gold' tolerate afternoon shade, 'Stuttgart' absolutely requires it. Those with pendulous flowers such as 'Panache' and 'Nuance' are generally more upright and are better suited to the rear of the garden. All require heavy feeding, consistent moisture and except where noted, full sun.

Propagation of cultivars is accomplished by division of the rootstock. On the roots are many dormant buds, and at least one bud must be present to reproduce the plant. The strongest buds yield the strongest plants. Large clumps can be produced by using root pieces with multiple buds.

Seed is available for a number of cultivars and germination is easy if the seed is first soaked in water for 24 hours to soften the hard coat. The spherical black seeds of Indian shot (*Canna indica*) are so hard and perfectly round that they resemble oversized BB's or buckshot from a shotgun shell. In fact, they are so dense that they readily sink in water. The seeds are called "Indian shot" because of their superficial resemblance to lead shot ammunition of the 18th and 19th centuries. Seeds germinate in 14 days and plants may flower the first year.

**Related Species:**

*Canna indica*, Indian shot, is native to South and Central America (not India) and has thin green leaves and small red flowers. I include it for its place in history and breeding, and although it cannot compete in ornamental value with the hybrids, it is a pleasant enough plant in its own right. We have grown it for years in the Gardens at UGA. 'Red Stripe' may well be a cultivar of this species.

*Canna musifolia*, banana canna, has been slid from cultivar to species to cultivar again. It is usually listed as *C.* 'Musifolia', which is probably correct. Regardless of its name, this is one impressive plant. Plants grow at least 10′ tall, 12′ is not all that uncommon, and to realize this is in a single growing season makes it even more remarkable. The large banana leaves provide that architectural element landscape architects are always going on about, and that is its value. I first saw the plant at Cornell Plantations and then on the campus at University of Georgia, and in both locales, they were the centerpiece of the planting. The small, red flowers are produced sparingly, but who needs them anyway?

***Cardamine*** (kar-dah′ mi-nee) Bittercress, Cardamine Brassicaceae

The majority of the 100 species in this genus inhabit cool temperate climates, usually in areas of shade and moisture. Some are terrible obnoxious weeds, such as our native hairy bittercress, *C. hirsuta*, but a few are excellent plants for the woodland garden. Recently, the genus *Dentaria*, to which the native toothwort, *D. diphylla* belonged, has been reassigned to the genus *Cardamine*. With the lumping of species, the genus is even more difficult to characterize. Many species have pinnately divided foliage (*C. diphylla*) while others have round undivided leaves (*C. bulbosa*). The flowers are usually white, occasionally pink, and are borne on racemes in early spring.

***-diphylla*** (die-fill′ a) Toothwort 9-12″/12″
Spring White Eastern North America Zones 3-7

This popular woodland plant is easily distinguished from others by having two leaves (*diphylla*) per stem, both of which are palmately (like a hand) divided into three toothed segments. The yellowish veins contrast nicely with the light green leaves, over which white 4-petaled flowers arise in April or May. I have grown plants in my southeastern garden and they do well, but perform more vigorously further north. They need shaded, moist conditions to be at their best. Plants grow from a pockmarked rhizome, accounting for another common name, crinkle root. In mild winters, plants arise in fall to early spring and may go dormant again in late summer. This native species is easy to grow, easy to maintain and essentially asks nothing but gives much. The suffix *wort* refers to a supposed medicinal use for, and the teethlike marks on the roots suggested the plant might relive toothache, thus its common name.

**Cultivars**:

'American Sweetheart' is characterized by the silver veining on the dark green leaves. The back of the foliage is purple. A vigorous clone, an improvement over the species.

'Eco Cut-leaf', from Don Jacobs of Eco-Gardens in Decatur, Georgia, is a smaller form of toothwort with deeply cut leaves.

'Eco Moonlight' bears unusually large creamy white flowers. This is an outstanding addition to this little-cultivated plant.

**Related Species:**

*C. bulbosa*, spring cress, is about 10″ tall and bears smooth rounded leaves and small (½″ long) white spring flowers in the spring. Native in wet places north to Quebec, south to Florida and west to South Dakota and Texas.

*C. concatenata* (*C. laciniata*), pepper root, has a similar native range to *C. diphylla* and is characterized by having three whorled leaves, each with three segments. The toothed segments are often so deeply lobed that each leaf appears to have five parts. Flowers are also similar to *C. diphylla*. They are also a little more heat tolerant than common toothwort and may be a more useful choice for deep south gardeners. Pepper root comes from the fact that the roots have a peppery taste that was supposedly used in cooking by Native Americans. Roots were pickled, fermented (to make them sweet), boiled and eaten raw with salt. 'Eco Flamingo' has pink flowers.

*C. pratensis,* meadow cress or cuckoo flower, has rosettes of finely dissected gray-green to glossy green foliage. The small white to pale pink flowers are blushed with lilac and held on racemes approximately 15″ tall. 'Edith' is unique in that she bears lovely double rose-like white flowers, which are pink in bud. This may be a renaming of 'Flore-pleno', which is occasionally offered through specialist nurseries. Native to Europe and hardy in zones 5-7.

*C. trifolia,* also native to Europe, has three-parted dark green leaves with long petioles. The plants tend to creep along the ground and send up dozens of white flowers with yellow anthers in the spring. Good looking in moist woodland gardens and shaded rock gardens. The European species may often be found in the western part of the country but does poorly in the East.

***Cardiocrinum*** (kar-dee-o-kry′ num) Giant Himalayan Lily Liliaceae

A genus of about 3 species, but only *C. giganteum* is ever seen or offered. The flowers resemble true lilies but the foliage is heart shaped in *Cardiocrinum* rather than linear in *Lilium.* And other than the fact that these plants dwarf most lilies, another major difference is that the main shoots die after flowering, although offshoots continue.

Non-flowering shoots may take five to seven years to flower. Flowering shoots can grow 8-10′ tall and require considerable room. The huge basal leaves give rise to the leafy stem at the top of which are formed large (6-12″ long) white fragrant trumpets, that persist for about 2 weeks. No written description can do justice to these remarkable plants. Unfortunately, one generally must travel considerable miles to find such treasures. I have seen them in various gardens in the United Kingdom, and they are equally beautiful but far less abundant in North America. However, things are changing for the better in America. West Coast gardeners in Canada and the U.S. have enjoyed Himalayan lilies for many years and a few southeast gardens have been experimenting successfully as well. That the bulbs are difficult to find, require ages to flower, are susceptible to voles, moles and mice, cost a small fortune, die immediately after flowering and are cold hardy only to about 15°F may explain their relative lack of abundance. However, such minor details never stopped real gardeners. Three- to four-year-old bulbs are offered by good nurseries and seed is not difficult to locate. Go find, go spend and go enjoy.

Bulbs should be planted with the growing tips at the surface of the organic soil in semi-shaded conditions. After flowering, remove the offsets and redistribute about 3′ apart. The offsets will reflower in about 5 years, which is faster than the 7 years required from seed.

**Related Species:**

*C. cathayanum* and *C. cordatum* are offered by the wonderful Asiatica Nursery in Lewisburg, Pennsylvania. The former grows 3′ tall and has wonderful large white flowers with wine red interiors, hardy in zones 6-8. The latter is also about 3′ tall with pure white flowers. Both die back after flowering but offshoots may reflower in as little as 2 years.

***Carex*** (kah′ reks) Sedge Cyperaceae

It must be only me, but I have such a gardener's and writer's block when it comes to this genus for the garden. The explosion in cultivars, the majority of which look the same, reminds me of the explosion of bergenia cultivars. Ninety percent could be incinerated and they would not be missed. I feel guilty because not only do many gardeners treasure their sedges, but it is probably blasphemy not to embrace them because many are native to this country, therefore they must be good. So many nurseries offer them that I continue to include them, but except for one or two, I have not been able to love them as I should.

In my last edition, I stated that they "are laboring as unknown little grasses ..." and "... perhaps they are ignored because there are about 1000 species, many of which are absolutely indistinguishable without keys, magnifiers and a touch of insanity." Today, they are no longer unknown nor ignored, but the rest is still true. Plants are native to many areas of the world, including the United States, Japan and New Zealand, often occurring in moist areas and swales, helping to form large areas of marshland. Many nurseries are offering a wide range of species for wetland reclamation, prairie establishment and other worthy projects.

Plants are often grown for the foliage, but to say flowers of some species are not ornamental would be an injustice. The unisexual flowers (male and female flowers separate, but on the same plant) are one of the ways to separate the genus from the closely related genera *Cyperus* and *Scirpus*, both of which bear bisexual flowers. To be honest, many sedges are easy to grow, relatively available and provide some marvelous foliage colors for the garden.

They are frequently described in catalogs and texts under grasses or sold as "grass look-alikes". The foliage is the most difficult means of telling them apart, but sedges differ from true grasses in a number of ways. The first four points are relatively easy to determine, the last one requires a little patience. In general:

1. The flowering stems of sedges are triangular, easily distinguished by rubbing them between your fingers. When looking at sedges and grasses, I think "if stems are a wedge, it must be a sedge".
2. The flowering stems are solid and without nodes; in grasses they are usually hollow with nodes.
3. The flowers of sedges are either male or female; in grasses they are perfect.
4. Ligules (appendage at junction of sheath and blade) of sedges are obsolete or absent; those of grasses are usually conspicuous.
5. Lastly, the presence of a sac-like structure enclosing the pistil, known as a perigynium, is unique to the genus. This is the structure that eventually forms the fruit, called a nutlet.

Many species do well in normal garden conditions and their diversity has led many a nurseries to go on a sedge binge. Today we have plants in which the foliage is thin and grassy (*C. albula*) while others have wider, coarser leaves (*C. siderosticha*). Plants have been selected for colored or variegated evergreen foliage that often make a handsome contrast to other low-growing garden species. Every year more species and selections pop up and differences between them are tough to discern, unless one is a nursery person trying to sell them to you. No particular problems occur in growing them in lightly shaded and moist conditions. I cut back last year's foliage in the spring to allow the new leaves to take over as quickly as possible.

Quick Reference to the Carex Species

| | Leaf color | Leaf width | Height (in.) |
|---|---|---|---|
| *C. buchananii* | Red-brown | Less than ½″ | 15-18 |
| *C. conica* | Green | Approximately 1″ | 4-15 |
| *C. flacca* | Green | Approximately 1″ | 24-30 |
| *C. glauca* | Blue-green | Less than 1″ | 6-10 |
| *C. morrowii* | Deep Green | Approximately 1″ | 12-18 |
| *C. muskingumensis* | Light Green | Less than 1″ | 18-30 |
| *C. siderostricha* | Green | 1-2″ | 6-9 |

***-buchananii*** (bew-kan-an-ee′ eye) Leatherleaf Sedge 15-18″/18″
New Zealand Zones 7-9

A interesting sedge for architectural features; the dense tufts of evergreen, very narrow leaves (about 1/16″ wide) are coppery-red, bronze to light brown and look good with many golden and variegated plants. Flowers are inconspicuous. This is one of the bronze sedges that people, not in the know, will simply call dead sedge. To each his own. Plants perform well in the Northwest but are finicky in most other areas. Beautiful where happy, unfortunately, not often happy. They are best planted in full sun to partial shade in moist soils. Propagate by seed or division.

***-conica*** (kon-i′ ca) Birdfoot Sedge 6-15″/10″
Japan, South Korea Zones 5-8

The tufted plants bear 3-angled stems and flat evergreen leaves, around 1″ wide but up to 1½″ wide. The purplish flowers consist of a terminal male spike, below which are the small erect lateral female flowers. Plants are quite variable in height, shortest in areas of cool summer nights and tallest in the heat. A popular sedge for rock gardens and effective even between stepping stones. Plants are evergreen in mild climates, but cutting off old leaves in the spring provides for a much more handsome plant.

**Cultivars:**

'Gold Fountains' is a hybrid form with narrow leaves bordered in gold stripes. Plants grow 12-18″ tall.

'Marginata' bears leaves with silver margins.

'Snowline' has a thin green line down the middle of the creamy-colored leaves. Makes an attractive plant that can help light up a shady area.

'Variegata' has variegated white foliage. One of the most handsome and popular cultivars within the species.

**-*elata*** (ee-lay′ ta) | Tufted Sedge | 2-3′/3′
Northern Europe | Zones 5-8

This tufted sedge forms dense hummocks of light green-yellow ½ to 1″ wide leaves. Plants can grow well at the edge of ponds or streams but also perform well in consistently moist soils. They look terrible if allowed to dry out. Not as good for warm climates as for cool areas. The flowers are brownish and arch up and out of the foliage, but are not particularly showy. The species is seldom found but a couple of cultivars are well known.

**Cultivars:**

'Aurea' has deeper yellow margins, sometimes sold as 'Bowles Golden' and in fact may be the same thing.

'Bowles Golden' is terrifically handsome and most available. The leaves are golden-yellow with thin green margins. The yellow color fades as temperatures rise in the summer.

'Knightshayes' is similar, not quite as big, but the foliage has no green margins.

**-*flacca*** (flah′ ca) | Blue Sedge | 6-10″/10″
Europe | Zones 5-8

Some sedges have bluish foliage, and this slow grower is one, with narrow leaves and a creeping growth habit that makes it quite effective as a ground cover. They are tolerant of a wide range of soils, and being stoloniferous, make decent colonies after 2-3 years. The foliage is bluer (it used to be known as *C. glauca*) on the underside than on top but makes a good contrast with dark green leaves of neighboring plants. Prefers moisture but quite tolerant of drying out.

**Cultivars:**

'Burton's Blue' has bright blue-green leaves about 3/8″ wide. Plants grow 9-15″ tall.

**-*morrowii*** (mo-row-ee′ eye) | Japanese Sedge | 12-18″/12″
Japan | Zones 5-9

Compact clumps of plants occur under partial shade or sun. In my densely shaded garden, the dense growth keeps getting denser, until the shade became too heavy. Plants of the species grow about 15″ tall, the stiff evergreen leaves have margins rough to the touch and tapered at the tip. Species are seldom seen but some of the more handsome cultivars occur here.

**Cultivars:**

'Goldband' ('Aureovariegata') has a clean golden variegation around the margins of the green leaves. Plants produce rigid semi-upright growth about 12″ tall. Similar to 'Variegata' but the gold margins provide a distinctive golden cast.

'Hime-kansuge' is relatively new to the United States, with dark green stiff leaves with a clean white edge.

'Ice Dance' was brought into cultivation by Barry Yinger and is similar to the more common 'Variegata' except that it spreads rather than forming a clump.
'Silk Tassel', also sold as 'Temnolepis', has looked terrific in the Armitage shade, producing long lax narrow leaves resulting in a 6″ tall mophead. Narrow white bands run the length of the long leaves.
'Silver Sceptre' is yet another choice in variegated sedges. Plants produce thin green leaves with white margins. Plants are clumpers, and stay well behaved. Excellent for brightening up the shade.
'Variegata' is the most popular of the cultivars of the genus, has silvery white margins on 12″ tall plants. Similar in habit to 'Goldband'.

***-muskingumensis*** (mus-king-u-men′ sis) Palm Sedge 18-30″/18″
Eastern North America Zones 5-8

One of the most distinct sedges, the crowded willowy green foliage forms atop the 1-2′ tall stems, resembling miniature palm trees. The "palmlike" form can be more easily seen in mid-season than at the beginning of the year. The plants tend to flop, spill and then slowly creep. They prefer a little shade, but full sun is tolerated, as long as moisture is present. Too much shade results in toppled plants.

**Cultivars:**
'Ice Fountains' provides narrow green and white variegated leaves on 10-15″ tall plants. Flowers occur in early to midsummer.
'Little Midge' gives a hint of what characteristic this plant brings to the table. It is a far more compact and dense form of the species.
'Oehme', selected from the garden of the wonderful designer Wolfgang Oehme, has a clear yellow border around the leaves. Similar in habit to the species, but brighter in the summer.
'Sentry' is similar but with handsome weeping foliage. More architecturally pleasing than the species.

***-siderostricha*** (sid-er-o-stric′ ha) Broad-leaved Sedge 6-10″/9″
Japan, Korea Zones 5-8

Plants form a slow-growing colony and produce some of the widest leaves (1-2″) in the genus. Plants are deciduous in all but the mildest climates. They grow well in semi-shaded moist conditions. In some areas, the new growth is tinged pink as it emerges.

**Cultivars:**
'Banana Boat' has wonderful golden leaf centers inside dark green margins. About 6-8″ tall.
'Island Brocade' has yellow margins on the broad green leaves. Almost as handsome as 'Variegata'.
'Variegata' is the most popular cultivar due to the white stripes along the margins of the leaves.

**Related Species:**

Far too many species, cultivars and hybrids of sedge have been introduced, several from Japan and Asia, while other nurseries have concentrated on providing visibility for some of our native species.

*C. appalachia*, Appalachian sedge, mophead sedge, best fits the second common name. Long thin leaves which resemble unkempt hair contrast well with coarse-leaved plants. Hardy to zone 4.

*C. ciliatomarginata*, hairy sedge, is a Japanese native, and grows only 3-6″ tall. The cultivar of real value is 'Treasure Island', with handsome white to yellow margins. Zones 5-8.

*C. comans*, New Zealand hair sedge, native to New Zealand and forms long, very thin (less than 1/16″ wide), lax, evergreen leaves. Foliage color ranges from light green to pale whitish green. Inconspicuous flowers are tucked into the foliage in the summer. Some cultivars offered include 'Bronze' whose fine brownish foliage gives the appearance of dry dead plants throughout the season and looks like it belongs in a 1963 horror movie. I can kill plants myself without having to buy them looking that way. 'Frosted Curls' is similar to the species but has weeping iridescent frosty white leaves. Plants grow about 1′ tall. One of the more attractive cultivars; probably winter hardy to zone 6.

*C. dolichostachya* 'Kaga Nishiki' was brought back by Barry Yinger from a Japanese collection trip. Plants bear narrow green leaves with a pleasant golden variegation and grow less than a foot tall. Zones 5-9.

*C. flaccosperma*, wide blue sedge, is an excellent native plant, and provides compact (about 18″) plants with wide (1″) blue-gray evergreen foliage. Moisture is needed for best performance. A good choice for the beginning sedger. Zones 5-8.

*C. oshimensis* 'Evergold' forms dense clumps with a pale yellowish or white center on the narrow weeping leaves. The lush arching foliage is used to advantage spilling over rocky slopes or into pools. Quite similar to 'Silk Tassel'. Zones 5-9.

*C. pendula*, drooping sedge, is tall (2-3′) and bears pendulous 3′ leaves and drooping inflorescences. It is noted for its long arching flower spikes and vertically hanging flowers. Needs moisture and semi-shaded conditions.

*C. phyllocephala* 'Sparkler' is a Japanese evergreen sedge with white margins on the thin leaves, resulting in an eye-catching display. Plants are upright and grow 12-18″ tall. Zones 7b-10.

*C. plantaginea*, plantain sedge, also has wide (over 1″ wide), flattened green leaves. The showy flowers are brownish black and emerge before the foliage matures in early spring. Plants are native to the eastern United States and are among the most cold hardy, growing in zones 3-8.

## ***Caryopteris*** (ka-ree-op′ te-ris) Bluebeard Verbenaceae

Although this genus consists of woody species, plants lose leaves and may die back to ground in the winter, thus are often treated as herbaceous perennials. Violet-blue to lavender-blue flowers that almost encircle the stem appear in late summer and fall on the current season's growth. Excellent plants for the garden with few insect or disease problems. There are about 10 species from eastern Asia, of which two are valuable and overlooked garden plants.

Quick Reference to Caryopteris Species

| | Height (ft.) | Flowers whorled all the way around stem |
|---|---|---|
| *C. x clandonensis* | 3-4 | No |
| *C. divaricata* | 3-5 | No |
| *C. incana* | 3-5 | Yes |

**-x clandonensis** (klan-don-en′ sis) Blue Mist 3-4′/4′
Summer Blue Hybrid Origin Zones 5-9

This hybrid, between *C. indica* and *C. mongholica*, was raised in West Clandon, England (thus its specific epithet), in 1930. The opposite leaves are narrow, up to 3½″ long and the undersides are gray-white. They are usually entire but occasionally may be coarsely toothed. Up to 20 flowers are held in a tight 1-2″ diameter cyme and two cymes are borne in each of the upper 3-4 leaf axils. The inflorescences lean toward the outside of the plant giving the appearance of the flowers being one-sided. The flowers, which are magnets to butterflies, are a welcome late summer relief from the many yellow daisies that flower at that time. They contrast well with those same yellows.

Full sun and well-drained soils result in maximum performance. Wet winters can cause significant dieback when plants releaf in the spring. On a maintenance note, it is important not to cut back plants to the ground in the late fall or winter. You can give them a haircut to clean them up, but wait until new buds break in the spring before cutting back hard. This is true for other woody-stemmed perennials, such as *Artemisia*, *Perovskia* and *Salvia*. I have killed many a plant with impatience.

Propagate by terminal cuttings in spring or early summer.

**Cultivars:**

'Arthur Simmonds' was selected in the 1930s in the garden of the late Arthur Simmonds of West Clandon, Surrey, England. Plants are 2′ tall and consist of dull green 1-2″ long leaves and dark blue flowers.

'Blue Mist' has gray-green foliage and light blue flowers.

'Dark Knight' bears the darkest blue flowers of any other cultivars.

'Ferndown' has dark green foliage and dark blue flowers. Raised in Ferndown Nurseries, Dorset, England. As dark-flowered as 'Dark Knight', and looks very similar.

'First Choice' is an excellent smaller, more compact form and has garnered excellent reviews from gardeners across the country.

'Grand Bleu' is a selection from 'Heavenly Blue'. Plants have glossier leaves and grow only about 2′ tall.

'Heavenly Blue' is of American origin and has darker green leaves, deeper blue flowers, and is altogether a superior plant to *C.* x *clandonensis*. Seed propagation of

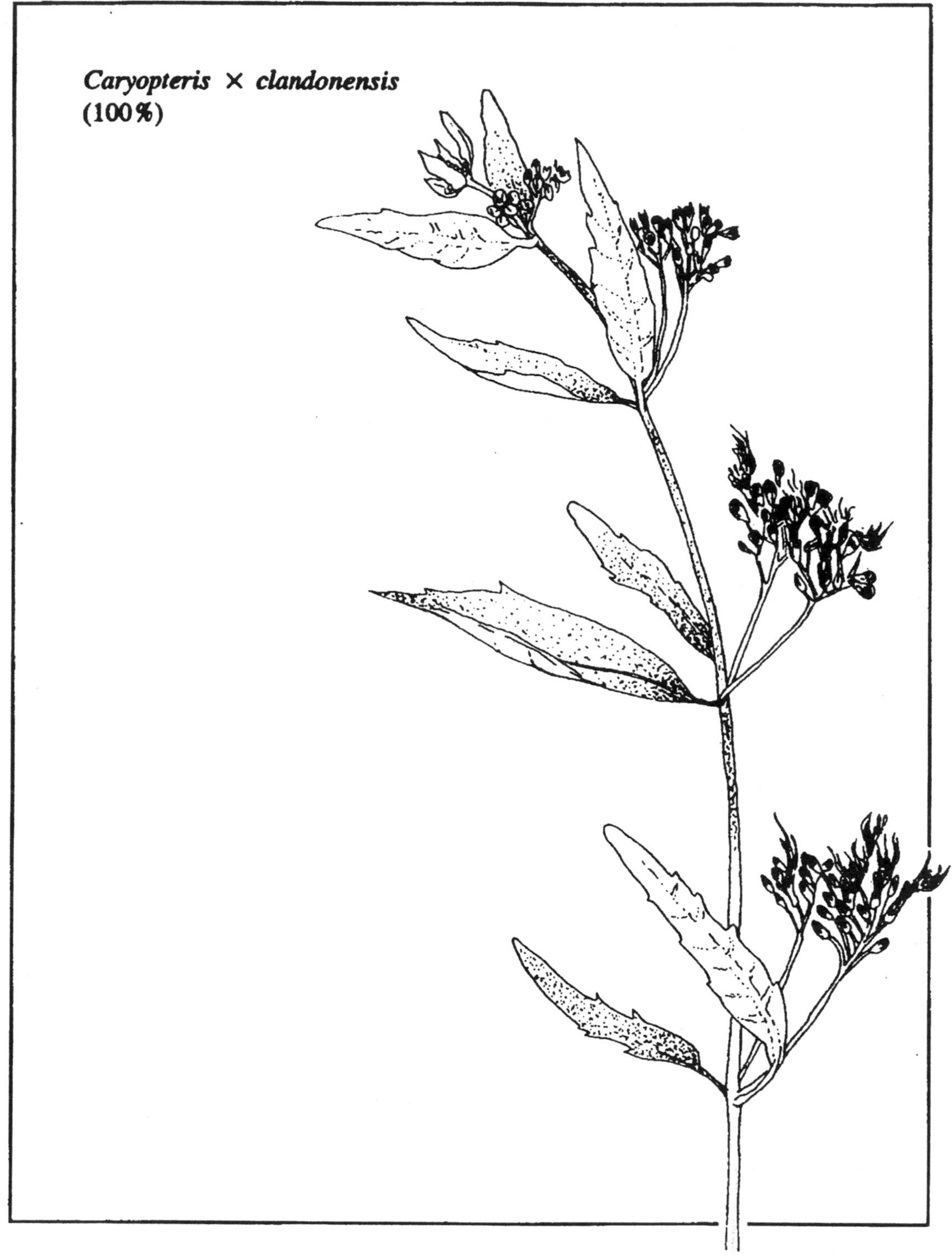

*Caryopteris × clandonensis*
(100%)

this cultivar has resulted in much variation, making it more difficult to distinguish. 'Blue Mist' and 'Dark Knight' may have resulted as sports of 'Heavenly Blue'.

'Kew Blue' resulted from a seedling of 'Arthur Simmonds' and was raised in Kew Gardens. Flowers are a darker blue than 'Arthur Simmonds'.

'Longwood Blue' was selected at Longwood Gardens, Kennett Square, Pennsylvania. Plants have silvery foliage, bear sky blue flowers in late summer and grow 1½-2′ tall.

'Petite Bleu' has a compact habit with deep blue flowers and glossy green foliage. The Bleu series is useful where smaller plants are desired. Raised by Minier Nurseries, Angier, France.

'Pink Chablis' has dull green leaves but handsome pink flowers. Plants arose from the breeding efforts of Mr. Dalton Durio of Louisiana Nursery.in Opelousas, Louisiana.

'Summer Sorbet' was new in 2005 and was likely a sport from 'Kew Blue', although some authorities contend there is a good deal of *C. incana* in the parentage. Regardless, the foliage is quite extraordinary, having yellow margins around the green leaf blades. Flowers are blue but plants are grown mainly for the foliage. Hardiness appears to be zones 6-8, perhaps suggesting that *C. incana* is indeed part of this hybrid.

'Sunshine Blue' has golden leaves and blue flowers. We have trialed it against 'Worcester Gold', and leaves appear equally bright and plants are far more compact.

'Worcester Gold' is the easiest form to distinguish due to the yellow-gold foliage and strong habit. Flowers are fine but unimportant. The foliage fades in climates with hot summers, but looks wonderful in the spring and early summer. Cut back hard in the spring every 2-3 years to maintain habit and color. Raised by St. Johns Nursery, Worcester, England.

| | | | |
|---|---|---|---|
| ***-divaricata*** (dye-var′ i- cah-ta) | | Bluebeard | 3-5′/3′ |
| Late Summer | Blue | Asia | Zones 6-9 |

The species has existed on the periphery of garden plants for many years. It hardly looks like a caryopteris, the leaves smell bad and the flowers are closer to those of *Clerodendron* than to *Caryopteris*. However, the cultivar 'Snow Fairy' has pulled the species into the bright lights and it has performed on center stage well.

'Snow Fairy' grows in an upright habit up to 4′ tall. The best and only redeeming characteristic is the handsome white and green variegated foliage. We have trialed the plant for years and heat and humidity do not lessen the variegation, a wonderful contrast to other plants which are colored only in the spring. The blue flowers are handsome enough but they are small and are obscured by the leaves anyway.

The biggest drawbacks are the variable cold hardiness, and the late spring emergence. Zone 6 is pushing the envelope although I have seen this listed as far north as zone 5. The late emergence is similar to balloon flower, *Platycodon*, and waiting an extra 3-4 weeks is simply something to get used to.

***-incana*** (in-cah′ na) Common Bluebeard 3-5′/2′
Late Summer Blue China, Japan Zones 8-9

We grew many, many plants of common bluebeard while researching their potential as cut flowers. My colleague, Judy Laushman, cut and evaluated them and, like me, believed them to be among the best cuts we trialed. They grew 3-4′ tall, producing flowers from late summer until frost. However, a couple of drawbacks occur. The first is that hardly anyone knows this species exists, it having been tsunamied by the more popular hybrids. The second is the relative lack of cold hardiness. Plants are not suitable north of zone 7b and even there, mulch should be applied around the base of the plant. The first hard frost kills back the top growth and plants may be cut back to 18-24″ any time. I have seen references to this being hardy to as far north as zone 5, but it certainly was not for us. It is also interesting to note all the new selections of this plant in recent years. For an upscale annual, it is doing just fine.

The leaves of this species are not quite as gray green or as long (only 1-3″) and linear as the hybrids, and are always coarsely toothed. The flowers are violet-blue and held in cymes in the upper leaf axils. The main difference is in the habit (more upright) and the flower arrangement. Each cyme has many more flowers than *C.* x *clandonensis* and they totally envelop the stem, unlike the more one-sided arrangement found in the hybrids. Plants require full sun and well-drained soils.

Propagate by seed in warm, humid conditions. Two- to three-inch terminal cuttings of new growth also root readily.

**Cultivars:**

'Alba' and 'Rosea' are white and pink forms of the species.

Cultivars with names like 'Blue Billows' and 'Blue Cascade' are occasionally seen in the literature but are likely fancy names for the species.

## *Catananche* (kat-a-nan′ ke) Cupid's Dart Asteraceae

The common name comes from the fact that the plants were once used by the ancient Greeks as an important ingredient in love potions and its presence in bouquets is still used to symbolize love. Flowers are useful for fresh or dried cut flowers. Plants should be placed in full sun in well-drained soils. There are five species in the genus but only one, *C. caerulea*, is grown to any extent.

***-caerulea*** (se-ru′ lee-a) Blue Cupid's Dart 18-30″/12″
Summer Blue Southwest Europe Zones 4-7

The foliage is mostly basal and narrow, and usually entire or with a few small teeth. Each leaf is woolly pubescent on both sides with three veins running its length. The 8-12″ long leaves are silver-green, particularly when young, as are the flower buds. The blue dandelion-like flowers are about 2″ in diameter and borne singly on long naked flower stems. The bracts beneath the flowers are arranged in many series, like shingles on a roof. Each ray flower is strap shaped while the disc flowers (the center) are darker blue. The yellow stamens provide a pleasing contrast. Warm temperatures and high humidity in the summer result in floppy plants.

Propagation of the species is not difficult from seed. If sown in March or April, plants will flower the first year. Barely cover the seed in the seed tray. Cultivars can be raised by root cuttings (see *Anemone* x *hybrida*) in the spring.

**Cultivars:**

'Alba' is a white-flowering form that I have come to admire more and more. Although it is not as handsome as the type, I enjoy it among the blues and yellows of my garden.

'Amor Blue' and 'Amor White' are some excellent seed-propagated cultivars, each growing about 2′ tall. The former has blue flowers while the latter has white flowers with a distinct red eye.

'Bi-color' may be the solution for those who can't decide between white- or blue-flowered cultivars. It has white petals with a dark center, and is often used for dried floral bouquets.

'Blue Giant' has dark blue flowers decorating a 2′ tall stout plant.

'Major' produces lavender-blue flowers and is nearly 3′ tall.

'Perry's White' is similar to 'Alba' but is reputed to be a better performer.

**Related Species:**

*C. caespitosa* is a yellow-flowered form of the genus, growing about 12″ tall with handsome blue-green foliage. I saw this growing in the Edinburgh Botanical Garden but seldom see it in North American gardens. Interesting possibilities.

## *Caulophyllum* (kaw-lo-fill' um) Blue Cohosh Berberidaceae

This little-known genus contains 2 species, one Asian and one North American. Only the latter is occasionally offered by nurserymen. They are plants for the lightly shaded garden and thrive in moist conditions, doing poorly if allowed to dry out. They may be propagated by seed or division in the fall or spring.

***-thalictroides*** (tha-lik′ troi-deez) Blue Cohosh 12-18″/12″
Spring Yellow-green Eastern North America Zones 4-7

Go to any website for *Caulophyllum* and nine times out of ten, the site will have nothing to do with gardening. Plants have soared in popularity as a holistic treatment of any number of ailments, including labor problems and menstrual cramps. That blue cohosh is available in a vial is a good thing, but whole hillsides are being harvested to obtain it. Hopefully, the balance between supply and demand will not result in disaster for the species.

This woodland plant is native from southeastern Canada to Alabama and Mississippi. The thickened rootstock sends up fleshy grayish green stems with one many-divided (triternate) leaf. The leaf is 3-lobed at the base with each lobe deeply cut into three 1-4″ long narrow segments. The small, ½″ long yellow-green flowers occur before leaves mature. They are rather nondescript and are held in a loose panicle. The main reason for including this species in the shade garden, however, is the appearance of the blue grape-like berries in late summer which stand erect above the foliage. The berries remain even after the foliage has withered and provide a rich, deep blue for the late fall landscape. These are outstanding in Garden in the Woods in Framingham, Massachusetts, but have not stood the test of time in the Armitage garden.

***Centaurea*** (sen-tor′ ree-a) Cornflower, Knapweed Asteraceae

*Centaurea* contains approximately 500 species of which a dozen are useful garden plants. A number of excellent annuals such as *C. cyanus* (bachelor's button), *C. americana* (purple basket flower), and *C. moschata* (sweet sultan) provide easy-to-grow color in the garden. The latter two also produce excellent cut flowers. *C. cineraria* (dusty miller) is a popular gray-leaf bedding and edging plant. The cornflowers are a diverse group of plants but all have overlapping bracts immediately beneath the petals as one of the identifying characteristics of the genus. The leaves are alternate and may be once or twice divided.

Plants prefer full sun and good drainage. If placed in too much shade, they become lanky and weedy. They are easily propagated from seed and no particular problems with germination should be encountered if the seed is fresh. Many of the hardy species can also be propagated from divisions and should be divided every 2-3 years.

*Centaurea* is a genus awash in ancient Greek folklore. It is said to have healed Chiron the centaur. This in itself may not seem reason enough to name a genus after such an event because as we all know, most centaurs were wild and lawless. Chiron, however, unlike most of his kind, was wise and just. He was a magnificent teacher and having been healed by that innocuous cornflower, went on to teach many Greek heroes, including Achilles. Next time you see a bachelor's button, think of Chiron.

Quick Reference to Centaurea Species

| | Height (in.) | Flower color | Flower diameter (in.) | Foliage color (top) |
|---|---|---|---|---|
| *C. dealbata* | 20-30 | Lavender | 2½-3 | Green |
| *C. hypoleuca* | 8-24 | Rose, Pink | ½-2 | Gray-green |
| *C. macrocephala* | 36-48 | Yellow | 3-3½ | Green |
| *C. montana* | 18-24 | Blue | 1-2 | Green |
| *C. nigra* | 12-18 | Violet | 1-1½ | Green |
| *C. pulchra* | 24-36 | Pink | 3-3½ | Gray-green |

***-dealbata*** (deel-bah′ ta) Persian Cornflower 20-30″/18″
Late Spring Lavender Asia Minor, Persia Zones 3-7

The basal foliage is up to 2′ long, coarsely cut into pinnate lobes with long whitish hairs on the underside. The deeply fringed flower heads are solitary and carried atop a slender stem bearing small, sessile, entire leaves. The bracts at the base of the petals (involucre bracts) are deeply fringed like the flowers. The 2-3″ diameter flowers appear in late spring in the South (early summer in the North) and continue for approximately 4 weeks. Warm days and nights tend to make them stretch and require staking. South of zone 7a, plants melt out in the summer and decline within 3 years. They are better plants for the North where their stems are thicker and less likely to fall over.

**Cultivars:**

'Steenbergii' is more compact in plant habit and flowers longer than the species. The flowers have clear white centers surrounded by deep rosy petals.

**-*hypoleuca*** (high-po-loo′ ka) Knapweed 18-24″/18″
Summer Rose-purple, Pink Armenia Zones 4-7

There is little difference between this and the previous species except that *hypoleuca* is more compact and the leaves are grayer. The flowers are smaller (1½-2″ diameter) although named cultivars may have flowers up to 4″ across.

**Cultivars:**

'John Coutts' is an excellent lavender-colored plant and has been a good performer in North American gardens.

**-*macrocephala*** (mak-ro-ceph′ a-la) Armenian Basket Flower 3-4′/2′
Summer Yellow Armenia Zones 3-7

This is one of my favorite plants when grown in a favorable environment. The large bright yellow flowers are 3-4″ in diameter and are excellent cut flowers. Stems last up to 10 days in water and are well established in upscale florists' shops. The coarse 5-6″ long leaves are entire with wavy margins. The involucre bracts (see *C. dealbata*) are brown and papery and add to the coarse appearance of the flower. In Michigan (zone 5), it reaches 4′ tall with full yellow flowers and deep green leaves. On the other hand, in our trials in North Georgia (zone 7b), it struggles to reach 2½′ and the flowers are small and persist but a short time.

**-*montana*** (mon-tan′ nah) Mountain Bluet 18-24″/12″
Early Summer Blue Europe Zones 3-8

In the North, this plant is a weed—a very pretty weed, but a weed nevertheless. I remember this plant taking over almost the entire garden in Montreal and the difficulty in removing it. Where we could keep it confined, it was lovely, but little did we suspect its traveling ways when so innocently planted. Even aware of its dark side, I still enjoy the bluets for their rich blue flower color and unique flower shape. It is a cool-season species, and does not have the same vigor in the South as in the North. Regardless of locale, it is stoloniferous and will be something of a rover. Plants perform best in high pH soils. The 2-2½″ diameter flowers consist of long ray petal flowers around the margin and short disc flowers in the center. The outer ray flowers are tubular and the ends are divided into 3-5 short segments. The normal color of the flowers is deep blue with a reddish center. Another lovely characteristic of this species is the black margin around each involucre bract (see *C. dealbata*). The bracts overlap like shingles and add to the value of the flower. The foliage is entire and silvery-white when young.

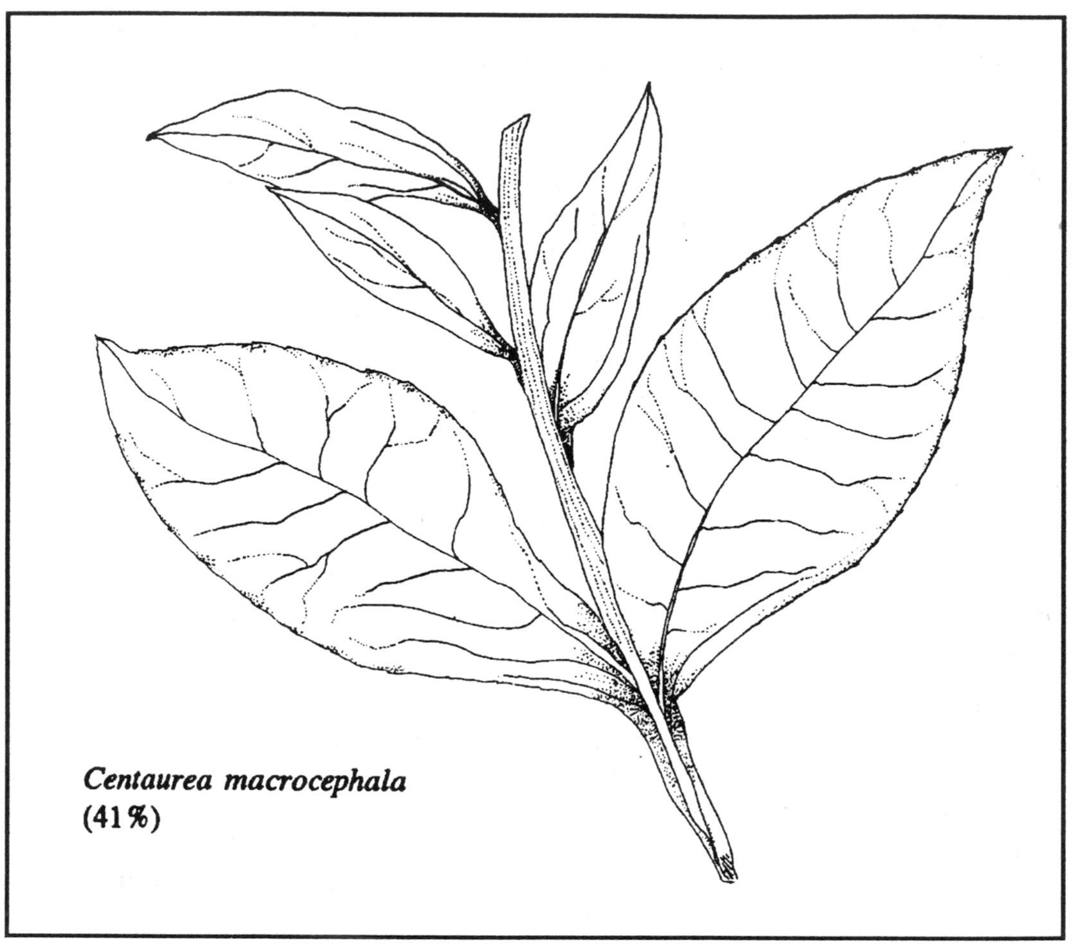

*Centaurea macrocephala*
(41%)

**Cultivars:**

'Alba' has white flowers and is truly beautiful.

'Gold Bullion' is exciting, bearing the same blue flowers as the species but over golden foliage.

'Grandiflora' has larger violet-blue flowers than the species.

'Purple Heart' is similar to 'Alba' but has more pronounced purple stamens, a handsome contrast.

'Rosea' ('Carnea') bears pink flowers.

'Violetta' produces amethyst flowers.

***-nigra*** (ni′ gra) Hardhats 1-1½′/1′
Summer Violet Europe Zones 3-7

Having escaped from cultivation, plants can be found in fields throughout the eastern United States. The flowers and petioles are dark violet and the solitary, ball-like flowers are responsible for the common name. This is a coarse, somewhat weedy species but the violet color contrasts well with the whites and pale yellows of summer.

**Cultivars:**
'Rivularis' is similar to the species but more compact.
'Variegata' has leaves edged with creamy white and is most striking.

***-pulchra*** (pul' kra) Pink Knapweed 2-3'/2'
Summer Rose-pink Kashmir Zones 5-7

This species is seldom seen in North America, a fact I cannot figure out. There is no reason this handsome species should not be as common as *C. macrocephala.* In Holland, I have seen fields of this plant grown for cut flower production and in many countries of northern Europe it is an outstanding garden plant. In *Hardy Plants of Distinction,* Alan Bloom states "the real aristocrat amongst centaureas is surely *C. pulchra* 'Major'." Still extraordinarily difficult to locate. What are we waiting for?

It is similar in habit to *C. macrocephala* and without the flower, the two may be confused. The pinnately compound leaves are smooth and more gray-green than the former species. The flowers are large (3" in diameter), borne singly on stout stems, but differ from *C. macrocephala* in being pink and having almost white flower buds, compared to the tawny brown flower buds of the Armenian basket flower. It may be slightly less hardy than *C. macrocephala* but limits of hardiness have not been established with certainty in North America.

**Cultivars:**
'Major' is larger and more vigorous than the type and is a better garden plant.

**Related Species:**

*C. kotschyana,* Kotschy's cornflower, grows 3' tall and bears deep purple to blood red flowers. Plant in full sun in well-drained soil.

*C. pulcherrima,* pink bachelor button, bears large heads of rosy pink flowers in late spring and early summer. Persistent flowerer and attractive to butterflies and goldfinches. Hardy in zones 3 to 7.

*C. simplicicaulis* is shorter, growing only 9-15" tall. The deeply segmented foliage has handsome whitish venation on the top and gray coloration on the underside of the leaves. The pink flowers occur in June and July. Full sun and good drainage are necessary. Hardy in zones 4-7.

## *Centranthus* (ken-tran' thus) Red Valerian, Jupiter's Beard Valerianaceae

The genus consists of about a dozen species but only one is used in North American gardens. They are all good border plants and grow in alkaline soils in full sun. The name comes from *kentron,* spur and *anthos,* flower, as the corolla (the petals) is spurred at the base.

***-ruber*** (rew' ber) Red Valerian 18-36"/24"
Spring Pink-red Europe Zones 5-8

This old-fashioned garden plant is still one of the great "cottage plants" still used today. Red valerian thrives on infertile, limey soils and there are few stone walls this plant does not like. The white cliffs of Dover, England take on a red hue in spring as the precariously perched plants flower profusely up and down the limestone faces. In fact, there are few nooks and crannies in northern Europe that this plant does not inhabit. In the United States, southern California is the Dover of America, where *Centranthus* beautifies side streets and sidewalks to the point that some native Californians consider it a pesky weed. Wander through much of coastal California and you will find this plant right at home. Plants are almost as aggressive in the North and in the West; gardeners yank it out of the ground, stomp all over it and toss it nonchalantly into the compost pile. In the South, plants are not nearly as tough.

The sessile, opposite blue-green leaves are about 4" long, often entire but sometimes toothed at the base. The individual flowers are only ½" long but so many occur on the terminal inflorescences in late spring and summers that the individual flowers are hardly noticed. Insects and pests are non-existent and little more than irrigation and sunshine are required. Cut flowers last about one week in water.

Propagation is easy by seed and in most seed batches, reds, whites, and sometimes rose-flowered plants will occur. Plants flower the first year from seed. Division in the spring or fall is necessary to maintain true colors.

**Cultivars:**

var. *albus* has clean white flowers, var. *coccineus*, deep red flowers and var. *roseus*, rose-colored flowers. However, other seed-raised cultivars in the trade may be the same as the varieties.

'Snowcloud' has clean white flowers and grows about 18" tall.

'Star Mixed' is a seed mixture containing all colors of the species.

## ***Cephalaria*** (seff-al-ay′ ri-a) Cephalaria Dipsacaceae

Although the genus consists of over 60 large, coarse species, few are encountered in the United States and Canada. They are closely related to *Scabiosa* and bear opposite, toothed or pinnate-like leaves and terminal white or yellow flowers. Of the many species identified, one is commonly available and three or 4 others are occasionally found in catalogs. *C. scabra* is about only 3′ tall and bears white flowers and *C. radiata* is a little over 3′ tall with creamy white flowers. Double-flowered forms may also be found in selections of *C. uralensis*. All these little-known species are marvelous and if you can find them, I would recommend a try. However, the most impressive and the most available is the giant cephalaria, *C. gigantea*.

***-gigantea*** (gi-gan′ tee-a) Tatarian Cephalaria 5-7′/4′
Summer Yellow Caucasus Zones 3-7

*C. gigantea* is a big coarse plant whose height can dominate the summer garden. Grown in full sun, plants may not need staking, however, if soils are too fertile, too much nitrogen fertilizer is applied or plants reside in too much shade, they will topple over at the first thunderstorm. Plants can be pinched early, and if so, they may mature at 5-6′ and be 4′ wide. The striped stem produces dark green pinnatifid leaves (leaves are deeply divided in broad divisions almost to the midrib, but without separating into distinct leaflets) with each division having toothed margins and hairy undersides. The primose-yellow flowers produced at the end of the 2′ wiry flower stems are flattened and look like the flowers of *Scabiosa* (at one time this species was in that genus). The 2″ diameter flower heads are made up of many individual 4-parted florets and the marginal florets are enlarged and radiate outwards. Flowering persists on and off throughout the summer.

Plants look best at the back of the garden where their coarseness may be reduced but where their attributes may still be enjoyed. The flowers provide a lovely soft yellow not often found in gardens. Place in full sun and provide adequate moisture. If allowed to dry out, the leaf margins turn black and the foliage quickly deteriorates. Plants decline in the fall and should be cut back after flowering.

Occasionally I get confused between this species and the very similar-flowered *Scabiosa ochroleuca*, cream scabious. Both bear primrose yellow flowers, similar pinnatifid leaves and flower at the same time. The most obvious difference is the much larger stature of *Cephalaria gigantea*, being triple or quadruple the height, and the larger flowers. However, height and vigor can be affected by light, temperature and soils, so height differences are not particularly precise. Some additional distinctions may be of interest. The flower heads of *S. ochroleuca* are seldom wider than a half inch. The leaves are coarser; each division of *C. gigantea* leaves is roughly toothed while those of *S. ochroleuca* are finer and almost entire. Last, the most fundamental, though least obvious, difference occurs under the flower heads. In all species of *Cephalaria*, the bracts immediately under the flower heads occur in many series (more than two) while in all *Scabiosa* species, the bracts always occur in one or two series only.

Propagation by seed is easiest if seed is placed in sand at 40°F for approximately 6 weeks. After 6 weeks, sow seed and sand in peat:vermiculite mix under warm (70-75°F), humid conditions. Divisions may also be used and plants need dividing every 2-3 years to maintain vigor. Plants will reseed where comfortable.

**Related Species:**

*C. alpina*, yellow cephalaria, is shorter and differs mainly in the marginal flowers which are not as enlarged and are about half the size. The plants are 3-4′ tall and the stems are covered with fine soft hairs, giving an appearance and feel of velvet. Sometimes plants offered as *C. alpina* are simply variants of *C. gigantea*.

## ***Cerastium*** (ser-ass′ ti-um) Snow-in-Summer Caryophyllaceae

The genus is so confusing that taxonomists can not decide if there are 60 or 100 species; the number is probably somewhere between. The main species found in gardens, however, evoke emotions of love or hate from gardeners. When in flower, the plants literally look like shiny mounds of snow in summer. Perhaps because I often see *Cerastium* "melt out" in summer in the East, I appreciate it more than most when I see it shining. In England, it is rampageous, and has been described as a "a thug and a strangler", and an "unpromising race of weeds" by Alan Titchmarsh in *The Rock*

*Gardener's Handbook*, 1983. Few areas, other than the Pacific Northwest, enjoy such luxurious cussing. In any event, *Cerastium* provides several excellent species for the wall, rock garden, or borders along path, and if plants gets out of hand, simply "tear them up by the roots ... or burn by the barrow-load" (Titchmarsh).

Ideally full sun is required in the North and partial shade in the South. Shear off the flowers after they fade to maintain plant vigor. The fact that it will grow in pure sand is a telling reminder that drainage should be excellent and feeding minimal. In the Gardens at UGA, the plants are wonderful until about the first of July, then rapidly decline.

Propagate by seed collected in summer, by divisions in spring or fall or by softwood cuttings.

| ***-tomentosum*** (toe-men-toe' sum) | | Snow-in-Summer | 6-8″/12″ |
|---|---|---|---|
| Late Spring | White | Italy, Sicily | Zones 2-7 |

This is the most common species and the silvery leaves and bright white flowers are a welcome sight in late spring and early summer. Plants do not tolerate heat well and the centers decline where summers are hot and humid. The leaves are ½-¾″ long and the tips resemble the end of a spatula (spatulate). The petals are deeply divided so there appear to be ten petals instead of the actual five. Plants spread by underground runners and quickly fill in an area or cover a wall. They look terrific around dwarf conifers but contrast handsomely with almost any dark-colored upright feature.

This is a fine, tough plant for northern areas and is often cursed by its own performance. Where it does well, people take it for granted and belittle its contributions to the spring garden. In the South, gardeners hold their breath in the summer hoping that it will establish itself well enough to provide another show next spring. Unfortunately, they are usually disappointed.

Sow seeds on the top of a peat:vermiculite mix but do not cover. Place the tray in warm (70-75°F) humid conditions. Germination occurs in 14-21 days, after which the seedlings should be placed at 55-65°F. Division may be accomplished any time during the growing season.

**Cultivars:**

'Columnae' and 'Silver Carpet', which may be the same, are more matted and more compact than the type. 'Columnae' may be less aggressive.

'Yo-Yo', has a compact growth habit (about 6″ tall), silvery gray leaves and does not spread as rapidly as the species.

**Related Species:**

*C. alpinum*, alpine chickweed, forms silver-gray 2-3″ tall mats more or less densely covered with wavy, gray-white hairs. Hardy as far north as the Arctic.

*C. biebersteinii*, taurus chickweed, is similar except that leaves are larger (1-1½″ long, 1/5″ wide), and are not spatulate. The petals are deeply notched at the ends and about twice as long as the calyx. The foliage is silvery gray because of the long white hairs covering the plant. The minor differences between these two species and others have resulted in some authorities lumping them all together in a collective sense, and the two species are often placed in the "*C. tomentosum* group".

***Ceratostigma*** (ser-at-o- stig′ ma) Leadwort Plumbaginaceae

This genus of 7-8 species has alternate, rather bristly leaves. There are two excellent garden species, one commonly available, and one which deserves greater use in the American landscape, particularly in the South.

Quick Reference to Ceratostigma Species

| | Height (in.) | Fall color |
|---|---|---|
| *C. plumbaginoides* | 8-12 | Yes |
| *C. willmottianum* | 24-36 | No |

***-plumbaginoides*** (plum-bah-gi-noi′ deez) Leadwort 8-12″/18″
Late Summer Blue China Zones 5-8

The 1-2″ long alternate leaves have short petioles, and are borne on many, branched angular stems which die back to the ground in the fall. The deep gentian blue, ¾″ diameter flowers are arranged in terminal heads, and flower from late summer well into fall.

This is a terrific species, looking equally good in Athens, Georgia and Niagara, Ontario. They tolerate full sun but afternoon shade results in more open plants which spread more freely. As a ground cover in sunny areas or as a plant to ramble over small rocks, it is difficult to beat. In the fall, the foliage turns bronzy-red and although plants don't quite compete with red maple or kochia for fall color, they are quite striking. Leaves emerge late in the spring so patience is important. Plants in zone 5 should be mulched.

Plants are also good subjects for forcing into flower in the greenhouse. The use of artificial long days in the winter or spring causes flower initiation and development. Plants which are forced to flower in the spring will also flower in late summer if placed in the garden.

Propagate by cuttings, spring division or seed. Seed germinates more uniformly if placed in sand in a plastic bag, and stratified for 4-6 weeks at 40°F. Root cuttings may also be used (see *Anemone*).

***-willmottianum*** (wil-mot-ee-a′ num) Chinese Leadwort 24-36″/2′
Late Summer Blue Western China Zones 7-9

This shrubby member may grow 4′ tall, although 2-3′ is more realistic. I have seen glorious shrubs in Capetown, South Africa and while not as impressive, I have also enjoyed my 2-2½′ tall plants in Athens. The 2″ long pointed leaves have coarse hairs on both sides and taper at the base and are much prettier than common leadwort. The 5-lobed flowers are violet blue with a rosy red tube and persist for 6-8 weeks. The leaf buds are covered with short scales in this species but are naked in *C. plumbaginoides*.

This is a most interesting plant, being a subshrub similar to *Caryopteris* and *Perovskia*. The leaves are smaller than those of the previous species yet the plant is twice as tall. The greatest drawback is the relative lack of cold hardiness, but it is a

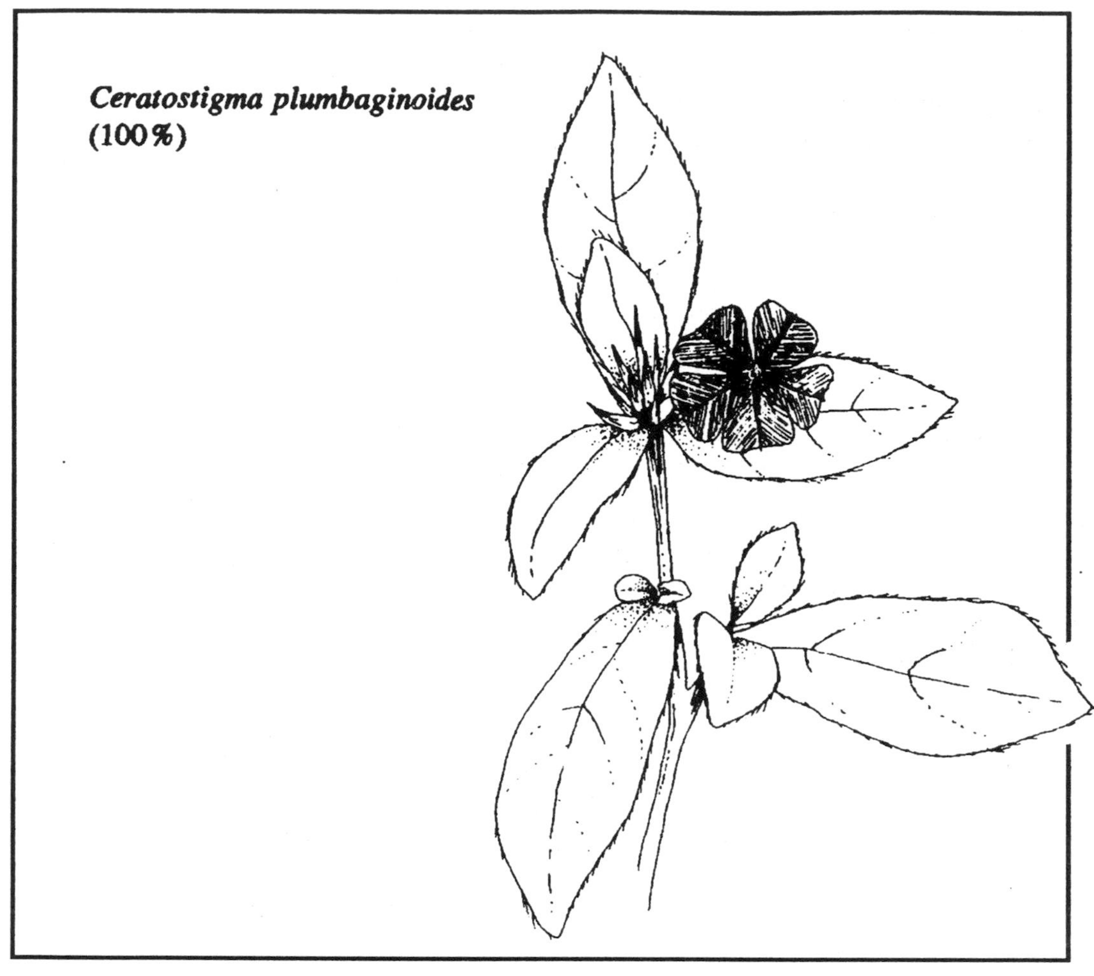
***Ceratostigma plumbaginoides* (100%)**

fine plant in areas where it is hardy and can also be used in summer containers where hardiness is an issue. I would like to see this genus and its cultivars used a great deal more, or perhaps encounter some breeding that would pair these two parents.

Propagation is similar to *C. plumbaginoides*.

**Cultivars**:

'Forest Blue' arose from the UK, and has been growing for about 10 years in the Gardens at UGA, and every year the new foliage is handsome and the blue flowers impress. An excellent addition to the genus.

'My Love' is quite spectacular, bearing bright chartreuse leaves all season, and true blue flowers in the fall. Plants may grow to about 18″ in height.

'Palmgold' provides golden foliage, better in spring, and the same wonderful blue flowers as the species. This cultivar and 'My Love' are similar and will only be sorted out by garden performance and availability.

**Related Species:**

*C. griffithii*, Griffith's leadwort, differs from *C. plumbaginoides* in that the leaves have a red margin and are evergreen. A handsome plant with deep blue flowers. Probably hardy in zones 6 to 8.

***Chamaelirium*** (cam-aye-leer-e′ um) Fairy Wand Liliaceae

Only one species occurs, *C. luteum*, which extends from eastern Massachusetts to Ontario and Michigan south to Florida, Mississippi and Arkansas. All sorts of common names exist for this plant, but most make no sense at all. Names such as blazing star (neither starlike nor blazing), and devil's-bit or devil's-bite (nothing devilish here) are also bandied about. The name *Chamaelirium* means "dwarf lily", but it is not lily-like and the specific epithet *luteum* means yellow and the flowers are white. Plants do, however, resemble a wand, fairy's or otherwise.

The plants are about 2-3′ tall, although they can reach four feet. The basal leaves are blunt and broadest at the tips and the stem leaves are narrow and generally point upward. Plants arise from rhizomes and the plants bear cylindrical racemes of either male or female flowers (similar to *Aruncus*). Male flower stems are longer and more pendant than the shorter upright female flower stems. This is not well known except to native plant enthusiasts but it is a terrific plant for shady woodland conditions. Do not dig from the wild or I will hunt you down!

***Chasmanthium*** (chas-man-the′ um) Northern Sea Oats Poaceae

Although about 6 species occur, only *C. latifolium*, northern sea oats, is grown for the garden. Plants produce many linear to narrow lancelike leaves followed by panicles of small silvery flowers. The flowers, however, give way to groups of flattened spikelets, the most ornamental part of the plant. The pendulous spikelets occur in groups of 5 to 10 at the end of the flowering stems. They start green and turn a handsome bronze as fall approaches. They may be picked when mature and are terrific in fresh or dried arrangements. They are at their best in late summer and fall. Hardy in zones 3-8.

Plants are North American natives and I use this as an example that not all natives are perfect. Their main drawback is their tendency to reseed everywhere and travel underground with fervor. They can fill in large areas in a few years, but they look much better in large drifts than as single specimens anyway. It is so aggressive that many gardeners have eradicated it from their gardens. At the University, my students, fellow workers and I took a poll when we planted *Chasmanthium* in a bed that was being taken over by *Oenothera speciosa*. Since both species are very invasive, a bloody brawl was anticipated. The betting was wild while the plants went at it root to root and node to node. The outcome: come see the *Chasmanthium* bed when you visit, it isn't going anywhere.

Propagate by seed or dig a shovelful of plantlets from the base of the plants.

***Cheilanthes*** (chee-lan′ thees) Lip Fern Adiantiaceae

The lip ferns fight for respect among their more colorful and robust fern colleagues, but they are not without their admirers. It is not the type of fern to use in a glade or a ground cover. but rather for small areas, such as a nook in the rock garden or where a small fern is needed to fill in a gap in the landscape. Most of the 150 or so recognized species are native to North America but a few reside in South Africa, Europe and Asia.

***-spicant*** (spi- cant′) Hairy Lip Fern 8-12″/12″
Green Eastern United States Zones 5-8

Plants are endangered in some parts of the East, such as Connecticut, but are relatively easy to produce, so there is no excuse or need to dig them from the wild. The wiry and brittle stipe (leaf stalk) is dark brown or purple, and quite hairy. The spores are borne in purple cases on the undersides, and are partially hidden by the in-rolled margins of the fronds.

Plants are deciduous and hide during the winter, and can generally be counted on to return if provided with a moist, shady environment. Plants will multiply by self-sporing.

**Related Species:**

*C. argentea*, silver lip fern, is native to Japan and easily recognizable by the silvery undersides of the finely cut fronds. Plants are about a foot tall and hardy in zones 7-9.

*C. quadripinnata*, four-angled lip fern, is found in South Africa and bears black stems and closely spaced pinna on the fronds. Zones 7b-9.

***Chelidonium*** (chel-i-do′ nee-um) Greater Celandine Papaveraceae

A pretty, although rather weedy member of the poppy family. Only one species is known, *C. majus*, native to Europe and western Asia but naturalized all over the eastern United States. When bruised, stems and leaves exude an orange sap, which was once used as a cure for warts (wartweed or wortflower), but is really no more than a skin irritant. The leaves are alternate, usually deeply divided, the terminal leaflet 3-lobed. The 1″ wide yellow terminal flowers have 2 sepals, 4 petals and about 20 stamens. Plants self-seed everywhere but are useful for shady woodland areas. Best propagated from seeds; plants do not transplant well.

Some people confuse this plant with the native wood poppy, *Stylophorum diphyllum*, sometimes known as celandine poppy. The flowers of the wood poppy are about 2″ wide and generally bear two paired pinnately divided leaves on the stem while the true greater celandine has smaller flowers (about half the size of those of wood poppy) and generally the leaves are more deeply cut.

**Cultivars:**

'Flore Pleno' has double flowers and is more ornamental than the species.

'Grandiflora', sometimes known as 'Asiatica' has bigger flowers and is much more ornamental than the species.

***Cheiranthus*** see ***Erysimum***

***Chelone*** (chel-o′ nee) Turtle-head Scrophulariaceae

The flowers in this genus were once described as being rather reptilian and if you squint your eyes and count to 10, you may see the resemblance to a turtle head. The sessile flowers are inflated and held in a terminal spike. Plants are native to North America and prefer partial shade and rich, moist soil. They are particularly useful for shady areas and are excellent plants for bog gardens and stream bank areas with acid soil. Pinching the shoot tips in the spring results in better performance in all species. Flowers occur in late summer and fall.

Quick Reference to Chelone Species

| | Height (ft.) | Flower color |
|---|---|---|
| *C. glabra* | 2-3 | White |
| *C. lyonii* | 2-3 | Rose-pink |
| *C. obliqua* | 2-3 | Deep Rose |

***-glabra*** (gla' bra) White Turtle-head 2-3′/2′
Summer, Fall White Tinged with Red United States Zones 3-7
(syn. *C. obliqua* var. *alba*)

Native from Newfoundland to north Georgia, and west to Minnesota, these natives have become more popular as the movement to native plants continues. Part of their appeal is the dark green color of the opposite, lanceolate leaves. The veins on each leaf, which is borne on a short petiole, are barely visible. The flowers are white with a red to rose tinge and are borne in a dense, terminal spike for three to four weeks in late summer.

Plants do well in full sun and constantly moist areas, but do not perform in areas of high heat and humidity. However if moist conditions are provided, they tolerate heat better. This species is handsome because of the contrast of flowers and foliage not seen in the other species.

Sow seed in moist peat:vermiculite and cover with ¼″ of fine peat. Place the tray at 40°F for six weeks for best germination. Bring out to 60°F and maintain moisture. Seed germinates in 10-14 days and may be transplanted to larger containers in 4-6 weeks. Vegetative cuttings (4-6″ long) may also be used in the spring and summer. Divisions are possible in early spring and fall.

**Cultivars**:

'Black Ace' has white flowers in late summer and fall but earns its name from the deep green, almost black (well, not quite) pigment of the leaves. Actually, in the heat of summer, the leaves return to plain old green. A vigorous grower (4′ is not uncommon), and quite pretty in the spring.

**-*lyonii*** (lie-on′ e e-eye) Pink Turtle-head 2-3′/1 ½′
Early Fall Rose-pink Southeastern United States Zones 3-7

The 3-7″ long leaves are smooth, pointed, and evenly toothed. They differ from other species by being broadly ovate and long petioled. The 1″ long rose-pink flowers have a yellow beard on the lip of the outermost petals and are held in a dense terminal spike. Flowers persist for about 4 weeks in the summer.

This is the most common turtle-head in North America but, similar to the previous species, is most suitable for cool climates. It can be planted in full sun, although afternoon shade is useful, and prefers moist, rich soils. Plants tolerate basic (i.e. non acidic) soils better than the other species of *Chelone*. With sufficient moisture, large clumps develop within 3-4 years.

Propagate similar to *C. glabra*.

**Cultivars**:

'Hot Lips' has wonderful deep green foliage and rosy pink flowers in fall. In general, the red stems that characterize this selection persist most of the season.

**-*obliqua*** (o-blee′ kwa) Rose Turtle-head 2-3′/2′
Late Summer, Fall Deep Rose Southeastern United States Zones 5-8

Plants have smooth, large (up to 8″ long) and prominently veined leaves which are sharply toothed and broadly lanceolate. Some references claim that this is much shorter than C. *lyonii*, but I have seen little difference between them. The flowers are also similar to those of *C. lyonii* but are deeper rose.

While *C. lyonii* is native to the mountains of the Southeast, *C. obliqua* is native to wetlands, and is less cold hardy. Late flowering makes it a desirable addition to an area where moisture is plentiful. Plants make fine companions to *Anaphalis*, *Aster*, *Anthemis* and *Sedum* in the fall garden. Its upright habit, rosy-red flowers and handsome foliage make it a perfect companion for many plants. It is in its glory at the Royal Botanical Gardens in Hamilton, Ontario, in September.

Propagate similar to *C. glabra*.

**Cultivars:**

'Alba' is a white-flowered form of the species.

'Bethelii' has many more flowers on each spike and the deep rose color is more vibrant than the species.

**Related Species:**

*Chelonopsis* is a genus that is little known but starting to appear here and there in catalogs and webpages. The "opsis" means "looks like" or "resembles", and this is similar to *Anemonopsis*, *Codonopsis*, even *Coreopsis*, in looking like something else. *Chelonopsis* is native to Asia, and the flowers more resemble penstemon than turtles. *C. yagiharana*, which was introduced by Barry Yinger of Asiatica Nursery, bears deep red flowers and stands 18-24″ tall. Plants tolerate afternoon shade and should be tried much more often than they are now. Hardy to about zone 5.

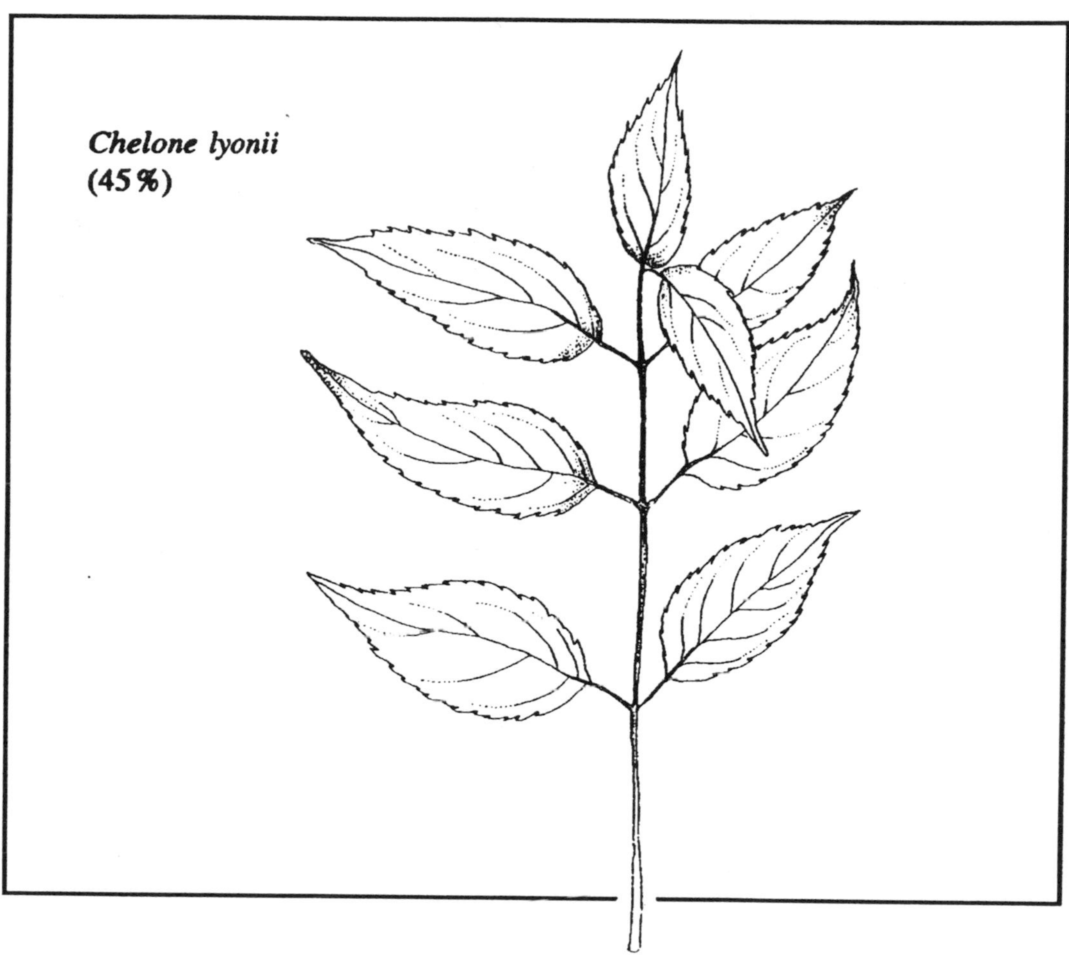
*Chelone lyonii* (45%)

***Chiastophyllum*** (ky-as′ to-fy-lum) Cotyledon Crassulaceae

This is a monotypic genus, having only one species, *C. oppositifolium* (syn. *Cotyledon simplicifolia*). I first discovered this little gem in England many years ago and was intrigued with this unique plant. From the 3 to 4 pairs of rounded, opposite, fleshy basal leaves emerge upright inflorescences of dangling chains of pea-like yellow flowers in spring and early summer.

The plant is most suited for draping over walls or in a rock garden and requires excellent drainage and afternoon shade. The species occurs in limestone outcroppings in its native habitat, therefore garden soils should be well limed. A grouping of three or four will definitely draw attention if well grown. Plants failed their test in the Gardens at UGA (zone 7b) but are doing well further north. Milli Piccione gardens in Rochester, New York (zone 5) and she told me her clumps have been returning for at least 10 years. I still have not seen many plants around the United States or Canada, but Evermay Nursery in Old Town, Maine is making plants available. Plants should be hardy in zones 4 to 6 (maybe 7a).

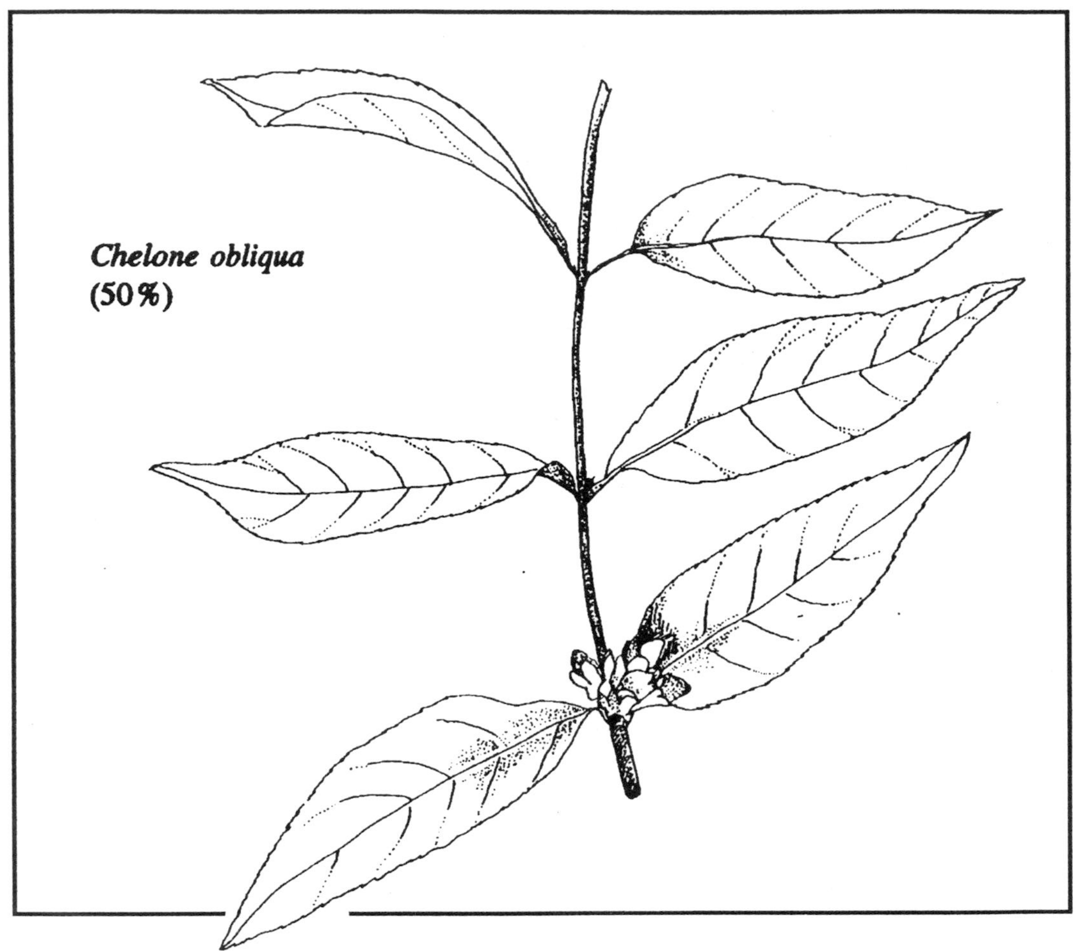


Propagate by division in the spring or late summer. Seed propagation requires that the tiny seeds be mixed with sand and then spread out on the seed flat uncovered. Place the seed flat at 60-70°F for 2-3 weeks, then transfer to 40°F for 4-6 weeks. After cooling, remove and germinate at 65-75°F. This is more easily accomplished by sowing in flats in the fall, placing outside in a cold frame, and waiting until spring after Mother Nature has done her job.

**Cultivars**:

'Goldtrop' is, as far as I can tell, almost identical to the species. Plants may be a little more compact, but I wouldn't pay extra for it.

'Jim's Pride' is a creamy white variegated form with scalloped margins. An interesting cultivar, not sure of the vigor.

## *Chimaphila* (chim-a-fil′ a) Pipsissewa Pyrolaceae

This group of native woodland species arises from rhizomes and bears pink to white flowers in the spring, and unusually handsome leaves. Of the 6 species, two are common to eastern North America, one to the Northwest (*C. menziesii*) and one to eastern Asia (*C. japonica*). Probably the best known is *C. maculata*, spotted pipsissewa, with widely-toothed, pointed green leaves with a pale white stripe along the midrib of each leaf. The white, waxy, 1″ wide nodding flowers are fragrant and occur in early to midsummer. The plants spread well but are not aggressive. They are wonderful in the woodland garden but don't expect to be overwhelmed with their vigor and panache; they are subtle, not in your face. Native to woods from southern New Hampshire to Georgia, west to Alabama and Michigan.

Another fine species is *C. umbellata*, prince's pine, native further north and west than the previous species. The leaves are sharply toothed and are broader and wider than common pipsissewa. The flowers are pale pink to white, also hanging from a leafless flower stem. The leaves of both species are refreshing when chewed and those of *C. umbellata* have been used in making root beer. *Chimaphila* belongs to the rather nondescript shinleaf family (Pyrolaceae), a family derived from the early use of the leaves of the native shinleaf (*Pyrola rotundifolia*) in making plasters for injured shins. No part of the human anatomy seems to have escaped the attention of the plant world, but shins?

## ***Chionodoxa*** (ky-on-o-dox′ a) Glory-of-the-Snow Liliaceae

*Chionodoxa* contains a wonderful group of spring-flowering bulbs which, in their native habitats, bloom even through the snow. Plant bulbs approximately 3″ deep in the fall in full sun or partial shade; flowering will occur the following March-April. *Chionodoxa* is often confused with *Scilla* (squills) however the flower segments are obviously united at the base whereas those of *Scilla* are not. Also, there are usually only 2 leaves in *Chionodoxa* and they are thicker, stiffer and darker green than those of *Scilla*.

***-forbesii*** (for-bes-ee-eye) Glory-of-the-Snow 4-6″/4″
Early Spring Blue with White Eye Asia Minor Zones 4-8

Plants were formerly classified as *C. luciliae* (named after Lucille Bossier, the wife of a Swiss botanist) and are still listed and sold as such. This is the best species of the genus. The two linear leaves arise in the spring followed by three to six flowers on each flower stem. Each intense blue flower is about 1″ wide with a large white center. They flower early, thus the common name, and if the weather remains cool, will persist for 3-4 weeks. Warm weather accelerates flowering (as in all spring bulbs) and results in reduced flowering time.

Bulbs require good drainage and if planted on sides of hills or banks, they soon spread to make a spectacular display. They are also at home in the garden but at least 50, preferably one hundred or more, should be planted together. People have naturalized glory-of-the-snow in turf areas for years. They are low, usually early enough that the lawn is not in need of cutting, and if blades are raised a little, the turf can still be cut before the plants go dormant.

Propagation is by offsets, small bulbs that form around the older bulbs, just after flowering. Fresh seed should be sown in seed flats at 65-70°F. If seed dries out, cold moist stratification (35-40°F) for 4-6 weeks provides more uniform germination.

**Cultivars:**

'Alba' has white flowers on 6″ tall stems and 'Rosea' has pink flowers on 8″ stems. Other than flower color, they are similar to, although not as pretty as the species.

var. *gigantea* has large (2″ diameter) blue flowers. Because of plant variability, the specific variety has been lumped into a "Gigantea" group. 'Blue Giant' and 'Pink Giant' are offered in this giant group. They are quite marvelous. A white form, 'White Giant', is also available in the group, although I seldom have seen it.

'Pink Giant' is taller than the species and produces bright pink flowers. It is surprisingly attractive.

**Related Species:**

*C. albescens* bears pale blue to whitish flowers which are only about ½″ in diameter, the smallest of the genus. Plants are often confused with *C. forbesii* 'Alba' and differ mainly in size.

*C. sardensis*, lesser glory-of-the-snow, has 6-8 sky blue flowers which have no white disc (or very diminutive) at the throat of the flower. Some gardeners find that the lack of white center intensifies the flower color, however, I feel the white of *C. forbesii* provides interest as well as beauty. It flowers about a week earlier than *C. forbesii*.

X *Chionoscilla allenii* is a natural intergeneric hybrid between *C. forbesii* and *Scilla bifolia* but is hard to find. It is similar in habit to *Chionodoxa* but is subject to the same fungal diseases that attack *Scilla*.

## ***Chrysanthemum*** also see *Ajania*, *Dendranthema*, *Leucanthemum*, *Tanacetum*

The chrysanthemum is one of the oldest cultivated plants in existence. Chrysanthemums provide a common bond with the people of China who lived 500 years before the birth of Christ. As happens with plants in cultivation that long, name changes inevitably occur. The genus has undergone extensive taxonomic dismantling. Scientific study of the plant structure and the date in which the plants were originally named has resulted in the overflowing *Chrysanthemum* genus being a shadow of itself. The only species remaining are *C. carinatum*, tricolor daisy, *C. coronarium*, crown daisy and *C. segetum*, corn daisy. Wonderful plants all, but annuals in most North American gardens. All others have been placed in "new" genera.

I have waited to see if the new names would "stick" in taxonomic circles, and if producers, breeders, and retailers would adopt the new genera. The fact is, debate continues. According to the Integrated Taxonomic Information System (ITIS) and others, some of the chrysanthemum names, such as *C. coccineum*, painted daisy, *C. frutescens*, marguerite daisy, and *C. morifolium*, florist mum, have retained dual citizenship. However, in this, the third edition of this tome, I have reluctantly put away the chrysanthemum and have adopted the taxonomically accepted counterparts. While there has been a good deal of teeth gnashing and spirited academic debate over which names are correct, they mean little from the gardeners' point of view. It is important to remember that all this rearrangement changes nothing about the plants themselves. And to be honest, gardeners will never fully give up the chrysanthemum name, regardless of what taxonomists decide. All plants in the various genera are best planted in full sun and need little more than adequate drainage to thrive.

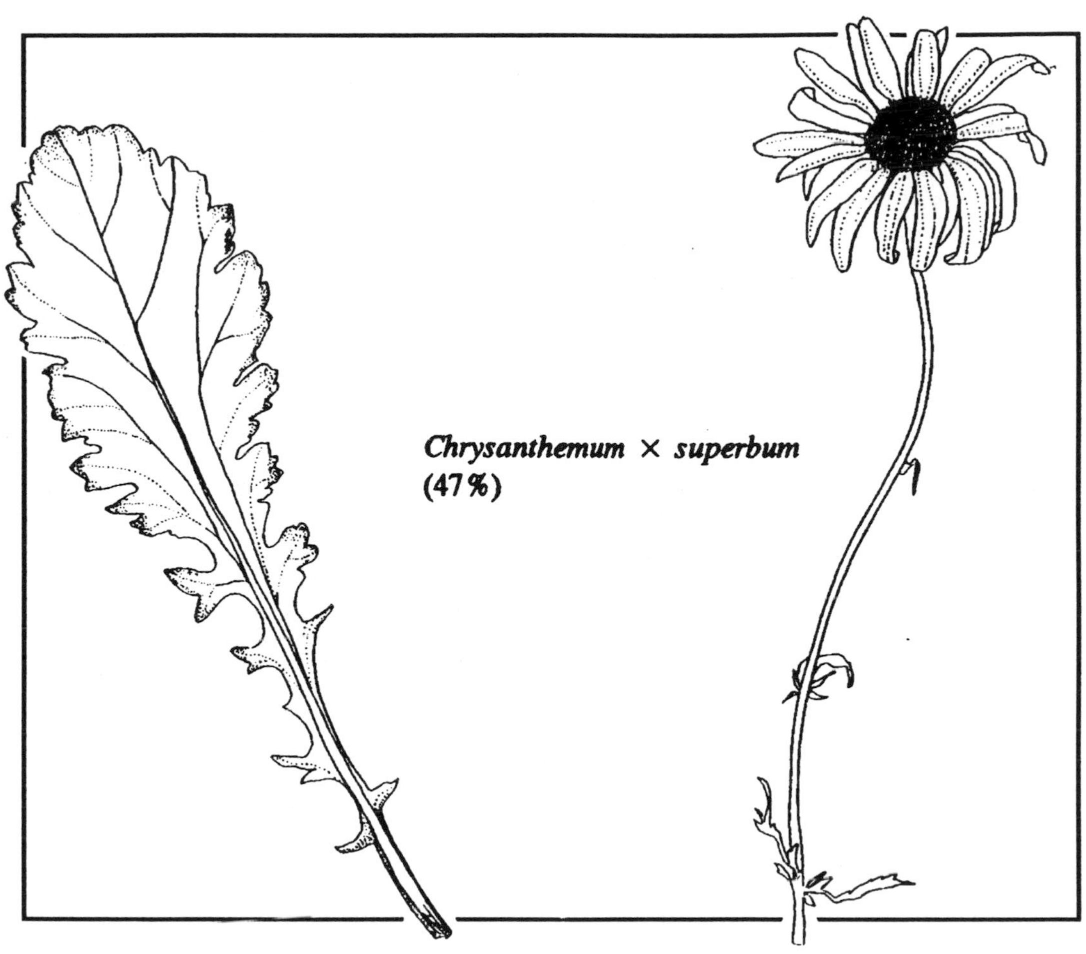

Chrysanthemum × superbum (47%)

Here are the new names, see you there.

| Old/Previous | New/Current | Common |
|---|---|---|
| *C. coccineum* | *Tanacetum coccineum* | Painted daisy, Pyrethrum |
| *C. x morifolium* | *Dendranthema x grandiflorum* | Garden Mum |
| *C. nipponicum* | *Leucanthemum nipponicum* | Nippon Daisy |
| *C. pacificum* | *Ajania pacifica* | Silver and Gold |
| *C. parthenium* | *Tanacetum parthenium* | Feverfew, Matricaria |
| *C. leucanthemum* | *Leucanthemum vulgare* | Oxeye Daisy |
| *C. x superbum* | *Leucanthemum x superbum* | Shasta Daisy |

***Chrysogonum*** (kris-og′ o-num) Goldenstar, Green and Gold Asteraceae

This genus is represented by one species, *C. virginianum*, a wonderfully useful, shade-tolerant ground cover. Plants are "doers" although they are not terribly imaginative. They tolerate heavy shade but also do fine in sunny moist areas as well.

**-virginianum** (vir-jin-ee-aye′ num) Green and Gold 6-8″/12″
Spring Yellow Eastern United States Zones 5-8

This is such a popular plant in many parts of the country that nurseries cannot keep up with demand. The 1-2″ long toothed leaves are triangular and dark green. The ends of the petals are slightly notched and the stamens are brown, nicely contrasting with the 1″ diameter bright yellow daisy flowers.

Many catalogs state that plants bloom constantly all summer, however they peak in spring, flower on and off in May and June, and come to a standstill in the heat of the summer. This is particularly so in zones 6 through 8, although flowers are more persistent in northern gardens. Plants should be placed in moist, well-drained soil and medium shade, particularly at the southern end of their range. *Chrysogonum* may be grown in full sun only if soils are constantly moist. Although cold hardy to zone 5, an application of mulch in that zone may be prudent. The much respected *RHS Dictionary of Gardening* states that *Chrysogonum* is "of no striking beauty", but I strongly disagree. While it is surely not endowed with eye-catching attributes, it most certainly deserves a place in the wild flower or moist shade garden. W.H. Pierce stated it best in his book *North American Rock Plants* (1937) when he wrote "I must admit I do not know why I am so fond of this little plant: it has neither splendor nor prodigality of blossom; it gives forth no intriguing perfume; it has neither airy grace nor stately form ... its habit is humble and lowly; just the same, to grow it is to love it."

Division is the surest means of propagation, and should be accomplished in late spring every two to three years. Seed germinates within 3 weeks when sown in warm (70-75°F), moist conditions. Seedlings may also be found at the base of mature plantings and transferred to other areas of the garden.

**Cultivars:**

A couple of variations to the species and a few named cultivars have appeared, however, except for one, the difference between any of them is debatable. All bear five-rayed bright yellow flowers and make excellent ground covers.

var. *australe* is similar to the species but has above-ground stolons and shorter stems. Plants spread more rapidly than *C. virginianum* but the flowers appear to decline more rapidly. 'Mark Viette' is an example of this variation.

'Eco Laquered Spider', an introduction from Don Jacobs at Eco-Gardens, has lacquered gray-green foliage and long stolons. Plants grow at an amazingly rapid speed, growing on top of itself in its zeal to cover all available space. It is truly different from the others.

'Springbrook' is the most compact, growing only 4-8″ tall.

var. *virginianum* has light green leaves, grows 4-8″ tall and the flowers occur well above the foliage. It also appears to remain in flower for a longer period of time than var. *australe*. 'Allen Bush', named for the great plantsman living in Louisville, Kentucky, is an example of this variety. 'Pierre', for Pierre Bennerup of Sunny Border Nursery, is also a long-blooming form.

***Chrysopsis*** (kris-op′ sis) Goldaster Asteraceae

Approximately 10 species may be found in this native genus, two or three are occasionally found in the flower garden. As gardeners experiment with more native genera, this one will find an ever greater following. All species have entire, alternate foliage and dozens of golden yellow flowers. There is so little difference between this genus and *Heterotheca* that plants are undoubtedly mixed up. See the latter genus for generic differences. The only species of importance in American gardens is the southeastern native, *C. mariana*, Maryland goldaster, that grows 1-3′ tall and bears many 1-1½″ wide yellow flowers. Plants perform best in full sun, sandy soils and good drainage, and are exceedingly drought tolerant.

**Related Species:**

*C. falcata*, (syn. *Pityopsis falcata*), sickleleaf goldaster, is only 5-12″ tall with linear leaves and small (less than 1″ across) flower heads. For those looking for small wild flowers, the plant has merit.

***Cimicifuga*** see ***Actaea***

***Cirsium*** (sir-see′ um) Plume Thistle Asteraceae

Thistles can be found in most cool-season habitats, and this genus includes some of the more prominent species. Our neighbors to the north boast the Canada thistle, *C. arvense*, while others bear names like melancholy thistle, marsh thistle and bull thistle. No doubt, most cirsiums are noxious weeds, found only in gardens of masochists or hermits. That they are usually thorny and not at all user-friendly however, just gets certain gardeners all excited, and soon enough a cirsium cult develops. Over 200 species exist and one or two have found their way into garden gentrification and are handsome in a contradictory way. *C. japonicum* is usually used as an annual and the red flowers are harvested (carefully) and dried for bouquets. Occasionally fresh flowers are seen in roadside markets or florist shops but they do not have enough flower power to be in great demand.

The most common perennial species is the purple-flowered *C. rivulare*, which does relatively well in gardens on the West Coast and in the Midwest. Plants grow 3′ tall and bear 2-5 flowered clusters of 1-2″ wide rounded globes. The spiny leaves are entire to slightly pinnate and are not fun to handle. Plants, however, are striking in the middle or as a backdrop to other flowers in the garden and provide some height in late spring and summer. Where content, they will self-sow with abandon. Removal of the flowers immediately upon their decline may be good housekeeping. The cultivar 'Atropurpureum' is sometimes offered with deeper purple flowers than the type.

***Claytonia*** (klay-ton-ee′ a) Spring Beauty Portulacaceae

One of the earliest American botanists, John Clayton, was honored with the name of these woodland native species, which provide small handsome flowers on unobtrusive plants. Plants occur from Newfoundland to Minnesota, and south from Georgia to Texas. The genus is characterized by 2-leafed stems, persistent sepals and a raceme of white to pink 5-petaled flowers, usually with deeper veins.

Quick Reference to Claytonia Species

| | Height (in.) | Stem leaves | Flower color |
|---|---|---|---|
| *C. caroliniana* | 4-9 | Oblong | Pink |
| *C. virginica* | 4-6 | Linear | White |

***-caroliniana*** (car-o-lin-ee′ ane-a) Wide-leaved Spring Beauty 4-9″/6″
Spring Pink North America Zones 4-7

Plants are less well known than *C. virginica* and are characterized by weak upright stems with oblong leaves and distinct petioles. About 2-10 pink flowers (sometimes white flowers with pink stripes) with deeper veins occur in late spring. Plants are less tolerant of humidity and heat than *C. virginica.*

Propagate by terminal cutting or division immediately after flowering.

***-virginica*** (vir-gin-i′ ca) Narrow-leaved Spring Beauty 4-6″/8″
Spring White to Pale Pink North America Zones 4-7

These ground-hugging plants (decumbent) consist of many long stems that arise from small corms. The two opposite stem leaves are 1-2″ long, less than ½″ wide and without well-defined petioles. The 10-15 white flowers are generally tinged with pink and are held in long racemes.

Propagate similar to *C. caroliniana.*

**Related Species:**

*C. lanceolata* is a western representative in the genus, and is similar to *C. virginica* but flowers a little earlier. Plants have 1-2 stalked basal leaves but the stem leaves are sessile. The petals are whitish pink, although some variants may be yellow. Native from the Cascade Mountains to Wyoming and Colorado.

## ***Clematis*** (klem′ at-is) Clematis Ranunculaceae

Over 230 species of woody and herbaceous species have been described in this diverse genus. Certainly, the best known are the large-flowered vines and there is no lack of exceptional hybrids and species for the garden. One of the most vigorous climbers, *C. vitalba*, Dutchman's beard, traveller's joy, is quickly strangling many of the forests of New Zealand. It has been designated a noxious weed and eradication programs are being carried out. I grow clematis vines over every shrub in my garden from 'Nellie Stevens' holly to *Fothergilla* 'Mt. Airy'. It is difficult to beat the hybrid vines for color and vigor but numerous species and their cultivars are becoming more available to American gardeners. In the North, most hybrids are winter hardy to zone 5; a number of species such as *C. macropetela*, *C. orientalis* and *C. ternata* grow well to zone 4. In the South, most hybrids and species do well, however, I have had difficult times with *C. orientalis* and *C. tangutica*. In the spring, they seem to grow a few feet a day, but in midsummer, they succumb to the infamous "clematis wilt". They die back to the ground, only to go through this frustrating cycle the next year. On the other hand, *C. montana* takes over the place. *C. cirrhosa*, the winter clematis, has some of the best glossy green foliage and flowers in late winter, although in the South, the foliage looks poor in the summer. An excellent viner is the Texas clematis, *C. texensis*, with chalice-shaped flowers and long flowering time, however the cultivars of the species are much superior. One of them, 'Duchess of Albany', scrambles through my sweetshrub and flowers from May to July, while 'Princess Diana' provides even rosier flowers.

The genus also includes some fine herbaceous non-climbing species and they shall be discussed in some detail in this book. These are essentially clumpers, although recently the breeders have turned their attention to hybridizing the climbers and non-climbers, resulting in scrambling, weaving forms. Most people feel that the clumping forms are not as showy as the climbers but I would not be without the solitary clematis, *C. integrifolia*. The non-climbers can be handsome garden plants ranging from 1-3′. The leaves are opposite and may be lobed, entire, or divided. All plants bloom on new wood, therefore can be cut back hard in winter or early spring.

Quick Reference to Non-climbing Clematis Species

| | Height (ft.) | Flower color | Number of leaflets |
|---|---|---|---|
| *C. heracleifolia* | 2-3 | Blue | 3-5 |
| *C. integrifolia* | 1½-2 | Blue | Entire |
| *C. recta* | 3-4 | White | 5-7 |

**-*heracleifolia*** (hare-a-klee-i-fo′ lee-a) Tube Clematis 2-3′/3′
Late Summer Blue China Zones 3-7

This subshrub has compound foliage, each leaf divided into three, 3-6″ long leaflets with sharply pointed teeth. About 6-12 tubular, hyacinth-like blue flowers are produced in short axillary clusters. They have four reflexed sepals (there are no petals) and some flowers are male while others are perfect (male and female parts present). The 1″ long fragrant flowers are produced in late summer and fall and followed by fluffy seedheads.

These are interesting plants but sprawl everywhere by late summer and fall. They are vigorous growers and should not be fertilized unless necessary. Interplant closely with plants of equal size or provide support to keep them from falling over. They are a bit of a pain in the behind when they fall everywhere. Plants prefer full sun and plenty of moisture.

Propagate by 2″ long terminal cuttings in the spring and summer. Seeds may be cooled for 2-4 weeks at 40°F and then sown in a warm, humid area.

**Cultivars:**

'China Blue' is 18-24" tall with deep blue to purple flowers. May be the same as 'China Purple', which claims the same colors.

'Cote D'Azur' has lighter blue flowers but otherwise is similar to the type.

var. *davidiana* (*Clematis tubulosa*) has wider flowers and less reflexed sepals than the species. The flowers are violet-blue and plants are 6-12" taller than the type. The foliage is heavily scented when dried and may be used in potpourri. var. *davidiana* is one of the parents of *C.* x *jouiniana*, a vigorous lavender-white flowered sprawler.

'Mrs. Robert Brydon' was bred in 1935 but has taken its time showing up in North American gardens. It is likely a hybrid of *C. heracleifolia* var. *davidiana* and *C. virginiana*. The small, pale violet flowers have white stamens and appear in mid to late summer. She is a romper and sprawler, and not easy to keep in bounds. Effective as ground cover, suitable for covering tree stumps and stones.

'Wyevale' (*C. tubulosa* 'Wyevale') has darker blue flowers than the type and the small flowers are lightly scented.

***-integrifolia*** (in-teg-ri-fo' lee-a) Solitary Clematis 1½-3'/3'
Summer Blue Southern Europe Zones 3-7

The common name comes from the single, urn-shaped, nodding flowers borne at the ends of the stems. They are indigo-violet, 1-2" long with the sepals turned up at the ends. The 2-4" long leaves are sessile and entire (not trifoliate as in most species). The whole plant is slightly hairy. This species contains some of the most handsome plants for the herbaceous garden. This has to be one of the finest, most overlooked plants in American gardening. In the Armitage garden, it starts flowering in mid May and continues on and off for 6 to 8 weeks. Further north, flowering occurs in late summer, about one to two weeks earlier than *C. heracleifolia*, followed by the appearance of ornamental, plumose seed heads. I used to think the Armitage planting was my favorite, but I have since viewed wonderful specimens in late May in Asheville, North Carolina, beautiful specimens at the great Quailcrest Farm in Wooster, Ohio, and admired a wonderful planting, covered with spiral translucent seed heads, on an early August trip to the superb Montreal Botanic Garden.

Plants do not sprawl as much as the previous species but should still be supported. I place twigs and old stems around the emerging plant (pea staking) and let the plant grow through and over this homemade support. Place in full sun although partial shade is tolerated (shade causes fewer flowers and thinner stems). The best of the non-vining clematis.

Propagate similar to *C. heracleifolia*.

**Cultivars:**

'Alba' has creamy white flowers.

'Olgae' produces lightly scented light blue flowers with long, recurved sepals.

'Pastel Blue' and 'Pastel Pink' have powder blue and light pink flowers respectively.

'Rooguchi' has deep blue flowers with light lavender margins.

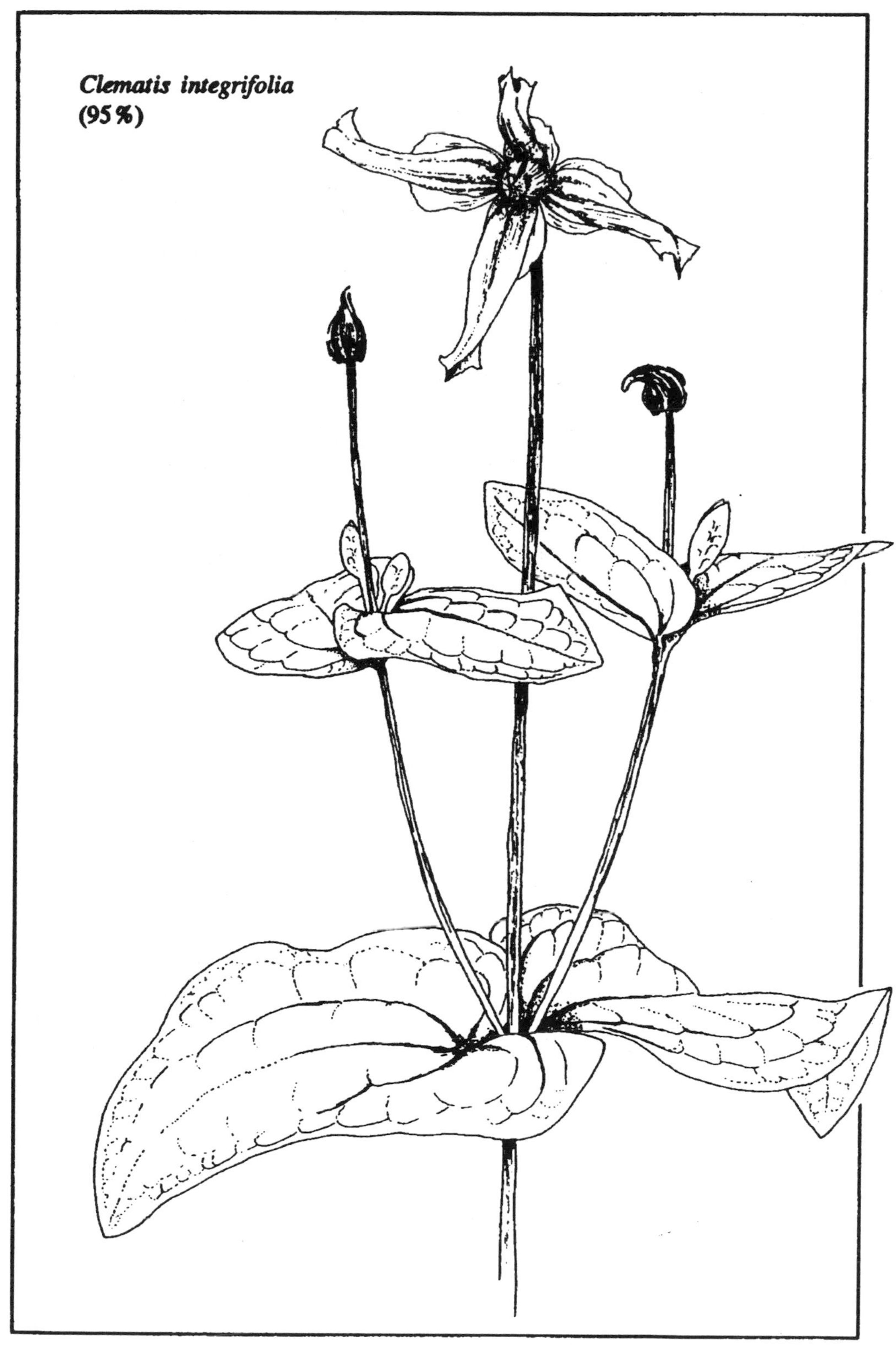
Clematis integrifolia
(95%)

'Rose Colored Glasses' (really, I don't make these up), is a large-flowered sport of 'Rosea'.
'Rosea' bears rose-colored flowers.
'Tapestry' provides large mauve to red flowers.

**Hybrids:**

Some old hybrids such as *C.* x *durandii* are still outstanding, however newer forms that incorporate the large flowered climbers have garnered a good deal of attention.

'Alionushka' (*C. integrifolia* x *C.* 'Nezhdanny') has long, narrow, pink- to rose-colored flowers on 4-6′ long stems.
'Blue Pirouette' (*C.* 'Warszawska Nike' x *C. integrifolia* 'Rosea') bears light blue flowers with obvious white stamens on 4-6′ long stems.
*C.* x *durandii* (*C. integrifolia* x *C. lanuginosa*) incorporates the non-climbing tendencies of the former but the large beautiful deep blue-purple flowers of the latter. It is almost unfailingly on every list of great clematis for the garden.
*C.* x *eriostemon* (*C. integrifolia* x *C. viticella*) is a sprawling semi-woody shrub that is more vigorous than tube clematis. Flowers are often borne in sets of three and leaves generally consist of seven leaflets.
'Fascination', a hybrid between *C. integrifolia* and *C. fusca*, is quickly becoming popular. Plants are dark blue to violet with white edges.
'Hendersonii' (*C. integrifolia* x *C.viticella*) has single violet-blue flowers and is a popular selection.
'Inspiration' has handsome rosy star-shaped flowers on 10′ tall stems. Same parentage as 'Blue Pirouette'.

***-recta*** (rek′ ta) | Ground Clematis | 3-4′/3′
Summer | White | Southern Europe | Zones 3-7

This is different than either of the previous species as it bears hundreds of fragrant white, fringed flowers. They are borne in terminal and axillary panicles in summer and followed by silky fruits. The pinnately compound leaves are divided into 5-9 entire pointed leaflets, each about 1-3″ long. Plants can be allowed to crawl along the ground or supported similar to other non-vining climbers. This species does not know whether to climb or crawl but I have seen plants climbing through hollies and supported around pea staking at the back of the garden bed. At Longwood, it was supported and in full flower in late May and early June. Looks good no matter what it does.

Propagate similar to *C. heracleifolia.*

**Cultivars:**

'Flore-plena' has double flowers that persist longer than the type.
'Peveril' is more upright to about 3′ tall and is quite floriferous.
'Purpurea' bears purple leaves that make a wonderful contrast to the creamy white flowers. Absolutely wonderful.

**Related Species:**

*C. stans*, japtube clematis, is similar but has ¾″ long light blue flowers borne in terminal as well as axillary clusters. It is less woody and must be supported. It is not as good a garden plant as *C. heracleifolia* or *C. integrifolia*.

***Clerodendrum*** (kle-ro-den′ drum) Glory Bower Verbenaceae

Over 400 species of woody trees, shrubs and vines occur with opposite or whorled leaves. However, nearly all are tropical plants, better suited for the greenhouse than the garden. The species may be divided into shrubby or vining forms, however, the only species to enjoy some popularity in gardens is *C. trichotomum*, a large vigorous plant cold hardy to about zone 7b.

***-trichotomum*** (tri-ko′ to-mum) Harlequin Glory Bower 8-10′/10′
Summer White Eastern China, Japan Zones 6-9

Here is a crazy big tree that sets records for the amount of growth per day, growing up to 10′ in one year, and almost as wide. Plants often die back to the ground in severe winters but have survived as far north as New York City. The white 5-petaled flowers are tubular at the base starting in July and are crowded together in stalked cymes, 6-9″ across. The reddish, leathery sepals are at the base of the flowers, and the ¼″ diameter bright blue pealike fruits (drupes) occur in late summer through the fall. The fruit are amazing but are not particularly showy until they are right in front of your nose. The dark green leaves are opposite, simple, usually entire and smell awful when bruised. Spreads by root suckers that can be divided and replanted.

Certainly not a plant for everyone, but a plant to look forward to if it is happy. One of the best specimens I will show you when you visit me in Athens is at Goodness Grows Nursery, just down the road in Lexington, Georgia. There, the 12′ tall plants with dark red calyces, clean white flowers and bright blue fruits make one want to sing the national anthem. Place plants in an area of full sun and well-drained soils. Propagate by terminal cuttings in late spring.

**Related Species:**

*C. bungei* is a spreading 3-4′ tall shrub with opposite pubescent malodorous foliage and spiny stems. The handsome ¾″ wide rosy-red flowers 3-4 times longer than the calyx, lull you into believing this is a lovely plant for the garden. Beware, they will be everywhere if given half a chance. Plants are hardy only to about zone 8, but may survive as far north as Philadelphia if the crown is protected.

*C. indicum*, Turk's turban, is native to Asia and bears glossy green leaves and long (4″) tubular fragrant white flowers very late in the season. In zone 7, it is hardy but flowers seldom occur before a hard frost. It is far more common in the deep South. Plants are invasive, appearing like magic late in the season. I pinch mine to obtain more branched stems but in general they are totally unsuitable for zones north of zone 8.

*C. ugandense* grows to a substantial subshrub and bears handsome light blue flowers and dark green foliage. Terrific for indoor displays but seldom winter hardy north of zone 8.

***Clintonia*** (klin-tone-ee′ a) Wood Lily Convallariaceae

The governor of New York State in the early nineteenth century had tremendous foresight and aggressively promoted the building of the Erie Canal. The canal, built between 1817 and 1825, connects the Hudson River to Lake Erie and made New York a major shipping port. The governor, whose name was DeWitt Clinton, was also a plant enthusiast and was honored with this marvelous genus. Five species are known, two native to the American West (*C. andrewsiana*, *C. uniflora*), one native to the Himalayas and Japan (*C. udensis*), and the two most common forms native to eastern North America (*C. borealis* and *C. umbellulata*). Wholesale changes to the lily family have occurred and many genera including this one have been placed in the Convallariaceae.

Quick Reference to Clintonia Species

| | Flower color | Flower number | Fruit color |
|---|---|---|---|
| *C. borealis* | Greenish-yellow | 2-8 | Blue |
| *C. umbellulata* | White | 10-30 | Black |

***-borealis*** (bore-ee′ al-is) Bluebeard, Dogberry 9-15″/12″
Spring Greenish-yellow Eastern North America Zones 4-7

The flower stems generally arise from 2-5 (usually 3) obovate, thin, glossy green basal leaves. The slightly drooping green-yellow flowers occur in umbels and consist of 6 spreading petals. The flowers are handsome but sparsely produced. The shining blue fruit are more familiar and account for the common names of bluebeard and dogberry.

Propagate by removing the seed from the fruit and germinating in cool conditions.

***-umbellulata*** (um-bel-ewe-lah′ ta) Speckled Wood Lily 9-12″/12″
Spring White Eastern North America Zones 4-8

Although not as widely distributed as the previous species, it may still be found in mountains from New York to Ohio and south to Georgia and Tennessee. The white flowers are held in a 5- to 30-flowered umbel in early spring above light green shiny basal leaves. The flowers are often spotted with green and purple and are only about 1/3″ long. After flowering, black berries are formed which provide food for birds and other small critters.

A most handsome woodland plant. Provide rich soils and partial shade. Propagate similar to *C. borealis*.

**Related species:**

*C. andrewsiana*, native from middle California to southwestern Oregon, is far more colorful and striking than the previous species, bearing deep rose-purple flowers on 2-3′ tall stems. Five to six shiny basal leaves are produced in the spring, and blue fruits occur after flowering. Worth trying, although cold hardy only to about zone 7.

## *Codonopsis* (ko-don-op'sis) Asia Bell Campanulaceae

This little-used genus consists of about 40 species of herbaceous plants, often with twining stems, native to Central Asia, the Himalayas, and southeast to Java. I never understood why plants are so ignored by gardeners and growers, as they are handsome, easy to grow and fit well with other garden selections. Might it be because the foliage has a distinctly unpleasant odor? Heck, no, that's simply us on a hot summer's day. Perhaps it is because the bell-shaped flowers are nodding and require a little more bending to appreciate. Regardless, I hope to see more of them offered in the future.

The genus is from the Greek *kodon*, bell, and *opsis*, appearance, alluding to the shape of the corolla. The genus differs from the genus *Campanula* in subtle ways, mostly having to do with the ovary and fruit capsule. The ovary is inferior and the fruit splits open from the side in *Campanula*, superior and splits open on the top in *Codonopsis*.

***-clematidea*** (klem-a-tid′ ee-a) Asian Bell Flower 2-3′/2′
Summer Light Blue Asia Zones 5-7

The stems are erect when young but eventually begin to sprawl and twine. The ¾″ long lanceolate to ovate leaves are entire, lightly pubescent and alternate or sub-opposite. The 1″ wide, nodding, light blue, bell-shaped flowers have lovely orange centers that remain hidden from view unless you take the trouble to pick them up and look inside. The flowers are usually solitary at the ends of the many branches. The lobes of the calyx (sepals) are about half the length of the corolla (petals) and reflexed. Plants require a good deal of room because of their sprawling habit and are best planted on banks or other areas where the inside of the flowers can be admired. Otherwise they are not particularly interesting. Place them in full sun to moderate shade and provide plenty of moisture.

Propagate by terminal cuttings or seed. Take 2″ terminal cuttings of basal shoots emerging in spring and root in a peat:vermiculite mix. Seeds should be covered lightly and placed in a warm (70-75°F), humid atmosphere. Germination occurs within 2-3 weeks.

**Related Species:**

*C. cardiophylla* is similar to *C. clematidea* but differs by having smaller flowers and more cordate leaves. The leaves also have narrow, white, slightly thickened margins.

*C. ovata* is also often confused with *C. clematidea*. Plants are shorter (9-12″) and less sprawling. The calyx, which is less than half the length as the corolla, consists of spreading sepals, rather than the reflexed sepals of *C. clematidea*.

*C. lanceolata* is a twining species with 2-3″ long pointed leaves with a very short petiole and flowers which are light blue and lilac outside and violet inside. Often confused with *C. ussuriensis*, which differs by having obtuse smaller leaves (1-1½″ long). They are lumped together by some authorities.

***Colchicum*** (kol-chi′ kum) Autumn Crocus Liliaceae

Approximately 45 species of plants occur, all of which arise from corms. The name comes from Colchis, a former country on the Black Sea, now part of the Republic of Georgia, where these plants are plentiful. The common name comes from the flowering time and the resemblance of the blossoms to crocus. Flowers in nearly all species occur in late summer or fall. The basal leaves usually arise in early spring and die down by early summer. The tubular flowers are often solitary or in short stalked clusters, each one sporting six stamens. In general, flower color is rose, pink or white but can occasionally be purple (one species, *C. luteum* is yellow and blooms in the spring).

*Colchicum* and *Crocus*, particularly the fall-flowering species, may be confused. Four major differences occur between the two: (1) *Crocus* has three stamens, *Colchicum* has six; (2) there are 3 distinct styles in *Colchicum*, in *Crocus*, there is just one, which is divided into three just below the tip; (3) the leaves of *Crocus* are narrow and always have a whitish line down the center, in *Colchicum* they are broad and never have a line down the center; (4) the corm of *Crocus* is symmetrical with the shoot on top, in *Colchicum* the corm is irregular and the shoot is produced on the side.

In general, cultivation is easy, however, their reputation for beauty is way overdone. Without foliage, the flowers often fall over and look like tired pink- to rose-colored dogs. They are much more effective when planted through some low-growing ground covers such as dwarf artemisias, mossy saxifrage, sedums or phlox, where they stand up much more effectively and are protected from splashing rain. I have had reasonable success when I planted some corms through low-growing blue-leaved hostas, such as 'Blue Cadet' or 'Blue Wedgewood'. Blooms are short lived, but some species produce numerous flowers in quick succession. Although flowers are beautiful, the corms are relatively expensive, particularly for the length of bloom time. On the other hand, they open at a time when many other flowers are declining in the garden.

Corms must be ordered to arrive and be planted in late summer or early fall or they may bloom in the box. Plant in partial shade to full sun so that one to two inches of soil covers the corm. Add organic matter and provide good drainage. Do not disturb unless they are in need of division or if the flowering has declined in recent years. Slugs are a major nuisance as they love to attack the emerging flowers. Heavy summer rainfall can also result in significant loss of corms, particularly where drainage is suspect. And oh yes, they are also on the poisonous plant lists of many states, containing the chemical colchicine. Try not to eat them. Other than that, they are fine.

Quick Reference to Colchicum Species

| | Height | Flower color | Number of flowers |
|---|---|---|---|
| *C. autumnale* | 3-4″ | Purple-pink | 1-4 |
| *C. byzantinum* | 2-3″ | Lilac-purple | 12-20 |
| *C. speciosum* | 4-5″ | Violet | 1-4 |

***-autumnale*** (ow-tum-nah′ lee) Autumn Crocus, Naked Boys 4-6″/6″
Fall Purple-pink Europe Zones 4-7

This is the best known and most widely distributed species. The flowers occur before the leaves and vary from purple to rose to lilac. The flower tube is 4-8″ long and about 1-2″ wide and flowers are among the earliest to appear, often as early as late August or early September. The five to eight narrow leaves may be up to 12″ long where they are happy. My experiences have been similar to the comments above; I look forward to their arrival but am often disappointed by their rapid demise.

Plant in partial shade to full sun, by the time the hot summer sun arrives, little remains of the plant. Well-drained soils are important as boggy soils contribute to corm rot. Probably the most cold hardy of the available species, tolerant to at least –5°F soil temperature.

**Cultivars**:
'Album' is a white-flowered form
'Alboplenum' produces double white flowers.
'Pleniflorum' bears large double flowers.

***-byzantinum*** (bi-zan-tee′ num) Byzantine Colchicum 4-6″/6″
Fall Lilac-purple Turkey Zones 6-8

Introduced to gardens in the 16th century and still unexcelled in its generosity of flowers, each corm bears up to 20 lilac flowers per corm, although 10-12 is more common in most North American gardens. The starry flowers are generally lilac-pink with a white center and appear in September and October. The pleated leaves are dark green, wide (up to 4″ across) and appear in late winter or early spring. One of the best species, but not as well known as the more common ones.

**Cultivars**:
'Album' is white with a touch of purple at the tips of the flowers.

**Related Species:**

*C. cilicicum* is similar to *C. byzantinum*. Plants differ by having deeper lilac flowers with leaves appearing just after the flowers disappear.

| ***-speciosum*** (spe-cee-o′ sum) | | Showy Colchicum | 4-6″/6″ |
|---|---|---|---|
| Fall | Violet | Southern Turkey | Zones 5-7 |

Plants differ from others by having stronger colors, although a good deal of variability occurs. The species bears one to four blooms per corm and some of the largest in the genus. Flowers in September and October, with 4-5 leaves, each 3-4″ wide and up to 15″ long. The leaves are produced in the late winter and spring.

**Cultivars:**

'Album' is a fine white-flowered form, which some gardeners feel is the best white autumn "bulb".

'Maximum' has even larger flowers.

'Ordu' is named for the area in Turkey from which this selection arose. Flowers are amethyst-violet with white centers and appear in early September. Among the most cold hardy of the available selections.

**Related Species:**

*C. giganteum* flowers a little later than *C. speciosum* and may be somewhat more robust. The flowers are more broadly funnel shaped than campanulate, as in *C. speciosum*.

**Hybrids**:

A number of hybrids have been developed which incorporate *C. speciosum*. *C. giganteum* and others in their parentage.

'Autumn Queen' ('Princess Astrid') has purple flowers with a white center. Flowers have a crisscrossed pattern (tessellated) on the petals.

'Lilac Wonder' has large rosy-purple flowers with a long narrow tube. The flowers soon flop over.

'The Giant' bears large lilac-pink flowers, white in center with faint tessellation.

'Violet Queen' produces flowers that are dark purple throughout.

'Waterlily' is the best-known double form. The deep rose-pink flowers resemble a waterlily and can be quite handsome. After a heavy rain, they can also look like a forlorn dog.

## *Conradina* (kon-rah-deen′ a) Cumberland Rosemary Lamiaceae

Seven species of low-growing shrubby plants occur, all native to the southern United States. Plants are characterized by two-lipped flowers, and narrow leaves that are usually rolled under at the edges. Most are native to Florida, however, the best garden plant, *C. verticillata*, extends north to the Cumberland Mountains of Tennessee and Kentucky. The needlelike foliage resembles rosemary and has a strong herbal fragrance. The pink-lavender flowers are produced at or near the end of the procumbent stems. Plants are found growing in sandy soils indicating the need for excellent drainage. These are not the easiest plants to grow—I have managed to kill my fair share—but in well-drained soils and full sun to partial shade, they can be excellent. While I have been a mass murderer of *Conradina*, Willis Hardin, of Commerce, Georgia has been quite successful by planting them in a sandy, very well-drained area. He has a nice collection that benefits from the chance to get out of the normally wet Georgia clay. Hardy in zones 5 to 8. This species, and any varieties or cultivars, is a federally protected species and plants can be purchased only by nurseries with the appropriate propagation permit. A beautiful white-flowered form, 'Cumberland Snow', was found by Leo Collins of North Carolina and is available at selected nurseries.

*C. canescens* is native to the pinelands of the gulf coast of Florida and Alabama. Plants can grow to 3′ tall and have gray foliage and rosy pink flowers. Native to sandy soils, excellent drainage is necessary. A compact form can also occasionally be found.

## *Convallaria* (kon-val-air′ ee-a) Lily-of-the-valley Convallariaceae

The creeping rootstock of *C. majalis* allows rapid spread under optimum conditions, a condition northern gardeners are well aware of. There, it is often looked upon as a benevolent, aggressive weed but welcomed nevertheless. However, as one travels further south, the creeping tendency is severely retarded and plants do not fill in nearly as rapidly or as well. Growing up in Montreal, I loved and hated it with equal passion. Plants filled in everywhere and dynamite was needed to dislodge them. However, nothing compared to the thick fragrance of the flowers in the spring. Living in Georgia, where it struggles to send up a few flowers in the spring, I have decided that I know of no finer weed.

The 2-3 basal leaves are lanceolate-ovate and about 8″ long. The arching one-sided racemes carry 5-8 drooping, white, wonderfully fragrant flowers which should be brought inside the house to be fully enjoyed. The plants are 8-12″ tall in flower and thrive in zones 2-5, do well in zones 6 and 7a, and struggle in zone 7b and further south. Grow in semi-shade and consistently moist conditions.

Plants should not be overlooked by those in the commercial cut flower arena. Cut flowers are always sought after and during the wedding season, they are sold at an exorbitant price. Fathers with daughters should think about planting a large patch today and talking the bride and groom into a spring wedding. Also, plants may be forced relatively easily in the greenhouse for flower and pot plant use.

Propagate by division immediately after flowering.

**Cultivars:**

'Bordeaux' appears to be unique in that the flowers are held well above the foliage, compared to older forms in which the flowers are found within the leaves. Flowers are larger than those of the species.

'Fortin's Giant' is 12-15″ tall and has larger flowers (¾″ long) than the species.

'Hardwick Hall', named for the wonderful English garden with the same name, has thin yellow margins around the leaves and the same fragrant white flowers as the species.

'Plena' has cream-colored double flowers, larger and more persistent than the type.

'Prolificans' is a most unusual form of this handsome species. Plants bear tiny flowers congested in a tightly branched inflorescence. They appear to be double but

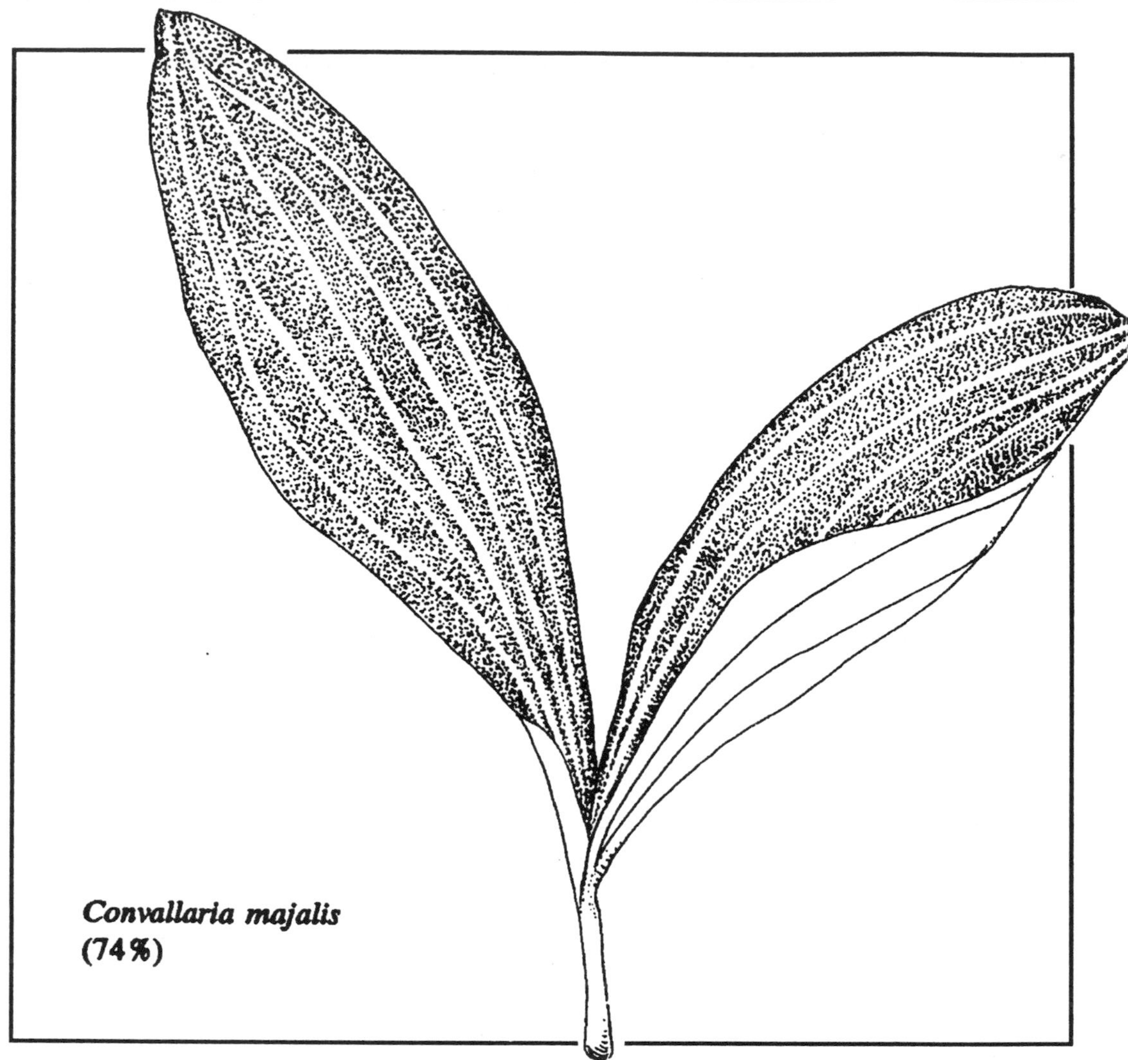

***Convallaria majalis* (74%)**

are occasionally malformed in appearance. Difficult to find but an interesting addition.

'Rosea' has light pink flowers but is otherwise similar to the species.

'Striata' ('Aureo-variegata', 'Lineata', 'Variegata') has green leaves with pale yellow stripes and white flowers. Very handsome.

***Convolvulus*** (kon-vol′ vew-lus) Bindweed, Morning Glory Convolvulaceae

Few of the 250 species are ever voluntarily planted in gardens, but the appearance of the strangling common bindweed, *C. arvense* is certainly not uncommon. This can be an incredibly voracious weed, eating garden beds for breakfast then looking for more. Deep digging or dynamite are the only remedies I know of. The fear of bindweed and the lack of cold hardiness in most ornamental species has limited their availability to American gardeners. Few species do well in eastern gardens but their tolerance of hot, dry conditions allow them to perform well in the Southwest and on the West Coast.

A number of species are offered but only a few can seriously be considered. Mallow bindweed, *C. althaeoides*, can be handsome, producing pink flowers with dark venation over trailing silver-leaved stems. Cold hardy to zones 7 or 8; plants can also be weedy and quite invasive. The compact *C. boissieri* is occasionally offered and grows only 3″ tall and 8″ wide. White flowers are produced over cushions of silver rosettes. Best for the very well-drained rock garden in zones 7-8.

One of the brightest forms available is silver bush morning glory, *C. cneorum*. This is a 2-4′ tall shrubby plant whose white, pink-tinged flowers contrast beautifully with the silvery-gray foliage. Sun and absolutely well-drained soils are essential. If plants begin to look ratty, renew them by hard pruning when necessary. Plants are a landscape mainstays in places like Scottsdale, Arizona, where rain is sparse and day temperatures routinely rise above 95°F. Although I would not recommend them for areas of high heat or humidity, I have seen stunning specimens in the State Botanical of Georgia in a scree-like area. 'Snow Angel' is a wonderfully compact cultivar with a pink blush to the white flowers. Hardy to zone 7.

Perhaps the most handsome of all is *C. sabatius*, a non-weedy, trailing evergreen rambler with violet-blue flowers, often with a yellow center. Plants are well suited to climb over and around other plants or trail over walls. Good drainage and full sun, zones 7-10. A number of fine cultivars are available, differing in the intensity of blue in the flowers.

For those of you who can grow only bindweed and have been frustrated trying to untangle it from other plants without success, this tip may be helpful. Put posts (bamboo, tomato stakes) in the plantings in the spring and allow the bindweed to scramble up the posts. Once they are above the good plants, paint some Round-Up or other systemic herbicide on the leaves. The bad guys will be knocked back if not out, and the good guys will be forever thankful.

Propagate the good species by root cuttings or seed.

## *Coptis* (kop' tis) Goldthread Ranunculaceae

The goldthreads, so named for the golden slender underground stolons, are terrific small plants for shady, moist places. Native to northern areas, they are seldom seen in the South because they do poorly in hot, humid conditions. The small white flowers consist of 5-7 showy sepals and occur in early spring. The flowers, much like small buttercups, are held over shiny, dark green, fernlike leaves. In the Northwest, or if buried under some mulch, plants may remain evergreen throughout the winter.

Three or four species are sometimes offered, usually by rock garden specialists. *C. asplenifolia*, native to the Northwest, has fine lacy foliage and greenish white flowers on 8-10″ tall plants. Grows well in zones 3 to 7. *C. laciniata*, native from Washington to California, is more robust with larger leaves and flowers but is not as cold tolerant, hardy in zones 5-8. *C. trifolia*, native to the Northeast, has handsome, shining trifoliate leaves and similar white flowers. Hardy in zones 3-7.

Propagate by dividing the mats at any time.

***Coreopsis*** (ko-ree-op′ sis) Tickseed Asteraceae

Coreopsis has been a mainline group of plants for decades, and little has changed to dislodge that popularity. There are well over 100 species, and most are ornamental. Two major changes have occurred in the genus. First, the movement to hybridization has been strong, as seen by such newcomers as 'Autumn Blush', 'Creme Brulee' and many others (see Hybrids). But an even bigger change has been the acceptance of more marginal native species into mainstream garden space, species such as the whorled-leaf tickseed, *C. major*, Atlantic coreopsis, *C. tripteris*, stiff coreopsis, *C. palmata* and Chipola River coreopsis, *C. integrifolia*, to name just a few. Such species were always on the favored list of hardcore native-ites, but have become more respectable as the native plant movement has gained mainstream status. Many of these "wild" species simply need a little love and care (i.e. sunshine and water) and they will do just fine.

*Coreopsis* is characterized by opposite leaves (a few have whorled leaves), which may be entire or lobed, and yellow daisylike flowers. Another telling characteristic of *Coreopsis* is the presence of two distinct circles of bracts around each flower head. The outer bracts are generally green, like small leaves, the inner broader and thinner and often yellowish. A number of fine annuals exists, particularly plains coreopsis, *C. tinctoria*. The name *Coreopsis* translates "like a bug", and refers to the shape and color of the seeds. This is likely how the common name, tickseed, evolved.

*Coreopsis* should be planted in well-drained soil in full sun. All perennial members can be propagated by division and several are easily raised from seed or terminal cuttings. Seeds germinate in 2-3 weeks if sown in a well-drained medium such as peat: perlite (1:1) in warm (70-75°F ), moist conditions.

Quick Reference to Coreopsis Species

| | Height (in.) | Flower time | Leaf shape |
|---|---|---|---|
| *C. auriculata* 'Nana' | 12-24 | Spring | Entire |
| *C. grandiflora* | 12-24 | Summer | Deeply Cut |
| *C. lanceolata* | 12-24 | Summer | Moderately Cut |
| *C. rosea* | 3-6 | Summer | Entire |
| *C. verticillata* | 18-36 | Summer | Threadlike Segments |

***-auriculata*** (ow-rik-ew-lah′ ta) Mouse Ear Coreopsis 1-2′/1′
Spring Yellow Southern United States Zones 4-9

The 1-2″ diameter solitary flowers, made up of about eight yellow petals surrounding yellow disc flowers, are held well above the dark green, evergreen foliage. The rounded, pubescent leaves are 2-5″ long and often have 1 or 2 small lobes at the base of the blade. Plants are usually close to 2′ tall. They are stoloniferous, but do not spread rampantly.

The species is easily propagated from divisions and can be divided every two to three years to maintain vigor. Plants may also be propagated from seed. Cover seeds lightly and place seed tray in warm, humid area.

**Cultivars:**

'Elfin' is a dwarf form, similar to 'Nana', but with a longer flowering time. Propagated from seed by Jelitto Seed Company in Germany. This is a terrific substitute for 'Nana' if that plant is not what you thought it should be. Probably zones 5-8.

'Jethro Tull' originated from ItSaul Plants in Georgia, and is somewhat similar to 'Zamphir', but with more consistently fluted ray flowers. Plants grow 12-15″ tall.

'Nana' has been an excellent cultivar and one of the best of the whole genus. There is nothing flashy but flocks of bright yellow flowers are produced in April and May over foliage that remains in good condition all season if moisture is provided. If plants dry out, however, the foliage can self-destruct. Like the species, it is stoloniferous, but not invasive. This is a terrific plant for the front of the border or along a path. Flowers of the true 'Nana' are sterile and the leaves are less than 1″ long. Over time, some natural hybridization has occurred with cultivars of *C. grandiflora*. The resultant hybrid is taller than 'Nana', shorter-lived, not as stoloniferous and the flowers are not sterile. Therefore, if plants are grown from seed, it is probably not 'Nana'. I am not sure what it is, and there may be nothing wrong with that hybrid, but it is not the true 'Nana'. 'Nana' may be propagated by division or cutting the stolons and inserting them vertically in a tray, and putting them under long days.

'Superba' has large (2-3″ diameter) orange flowers with a maroon center and is good for cutting.

'Zamphir' has proven to be a winner, although not as good a performer as 'Nana'. Plants are also dwarf, although 10-15″ is normal. The flowers are a golden yellow, but what is most unusual is that the ray flowers are "open" at the ends, and look like wine flutes, quite different from cultivars other than 'Jethro Tull'.

| | | | |
|---|---|---|---|
| ***-grandiflora*** (gran-di-flo′ ra) | | Tickseed | 1-2′/1′ |
| Summer | Yellow | Southern United States | Zones 4-9 |

This is the mainstay of many a summer garden. The lowermost leaves are simple while the upper ones are often deeply 3-5 lobed. The flower heads are 1-2½″ across and orange to yellow. It has a particularly long flowering season when handled properly, but unfortunately, plants are short lived, usually lasting 2 years in the South and 3-4 years in the North. In California, it never winter kills in milder climates and often self-sows.

Flowers must be deadheaded if plants are to flower to their potential. Flowering occurs late May to early August if spent flowers are removed, a tiring task but one well worth the fatigue. Don't get lazy and simply flick off the flower heads with your thumb or all that will appear above the foliage is naked sticks. Not only will the potential of the plants be unfulfilled by the lack of deadheading but the worn-out flowers are excellent candidates for disease. Plants in areas of hot summers and high humidity are short lived but even in the best of climes, you will need to rejuvenate or replace plants after 3-4 years. Cultivars, which come true from seed, have been produced and singles, semi-doubles, and doubles are now available.

Propagate by divisions in the spring or fall, or from seeds.

**Cultivars:**

'Badengold' bears bright yellow flowers. An old fashioned cultivar, but still popular.

'Domino' produces single golden yellow flowers with dark centers. Plants are only about 1½' tall.

'Early Sunrise' was an All-America winner in 1989. Plants are easily raised from seed and bear bright yellow semi-double 2″ wide flowers. Not persistent but excellent for a couple of years. It was a breakthrough plant because it could be raised from seed and flower the first year, an obvious advantage to producers. Others such as 'Heliot' and 'Rising Sun' followed with similar first-year qualities.

'Flying Saucers' is a compact form of the species, with good flower productivity and habit. Flowers are yellow to gold.

'Heliot' has 2″ wide single daisylike blooms. A Fleuroselect winner in 2004.

'Mayfield Giant' is an old cultivar with 2-3″ diameter gold-yellow flowers, grows 2-3′ tall and useful for cut flowers.

'Rising Sun' is another of these seemingly endless yellow coreopsis. This one produces 2″ wide double yellow flowers with mahogany bases. Flowers first year from seed. A Fleuroselect winner in 2005.

'Ruby Throat' bears yellow flowers with a deep claret throat.

'Schnittgold' produces golden yellow flowers.

'Sunburst' is about 2′ tall with large semi-double golden-yellow flowers.

'Sundancer' is an exceptionally good plant from Dupont Nursery in Plaquemine, Louisiana. Plants, which were selected from 'Sunray' in 1992, exhibit a dwarf habit, semi double flowers and a long period of bloom. They have looked very good in the Gardens at UGA.

'Sunfire' has fringed yellow ray flowers and obvious wine-red markings in the center.

'Sunray' is an exceptional selection that bears 2″ diameter double flowers for 8-12 weeks on 2′ plants.

'Tequila Sunrise' is a variegated form with golden single flowers. I have always enjoyed the plant, but I seem to be in a minority. The variegation pattern with its hint of pink is not bold but is still obvious and flowers are plentiful. It does not have the vigor of other tickseeds, and probably will not be persistent for more than three good years. However, an interesting color combination.

***-lanceolata*** (lan-cee-o′ lah-ta) Lanceleaf Coreopsis 1-2′/2′
Late Spring Yellow Eastern United States Zones 3-8

There is little difference between this and the previous species and some cultivars are hybrids between the two. Plants are rather variable but the flowers are always borne singly and are up to 2½″ across. The stems are leafy mainly toward the base of the plant compared to *C. grandiflora*, which is leafy throughout. The leaves are not as deeply cut as *C. grandiflora* and sometimes may be entire. It is a good garden performer, perhaps a little longer lived than *C. grandiflora* but not as floriferous. Comments concerning deadheading of *C. grandiflora* also pertain to this species.

Propagate similar to *C. auriculata*.

**Cultivars:**

'Baby Sun' provides excellent compact 12-18″ tall plants with yellow-orange flowers.

'Brown Eyes' is an excellent long-lived cultivar with single yellow flowers that have a maroon ring near the center. We grew plants for about five years in the Gardens at UGA before we removed them.

'Goldfink' produces many 2″ wide single yellow flowers with an orange center yet grows only about nine inches tall. Plants are excellent for the front of the garden. Should be raised from cuttings or divisions.

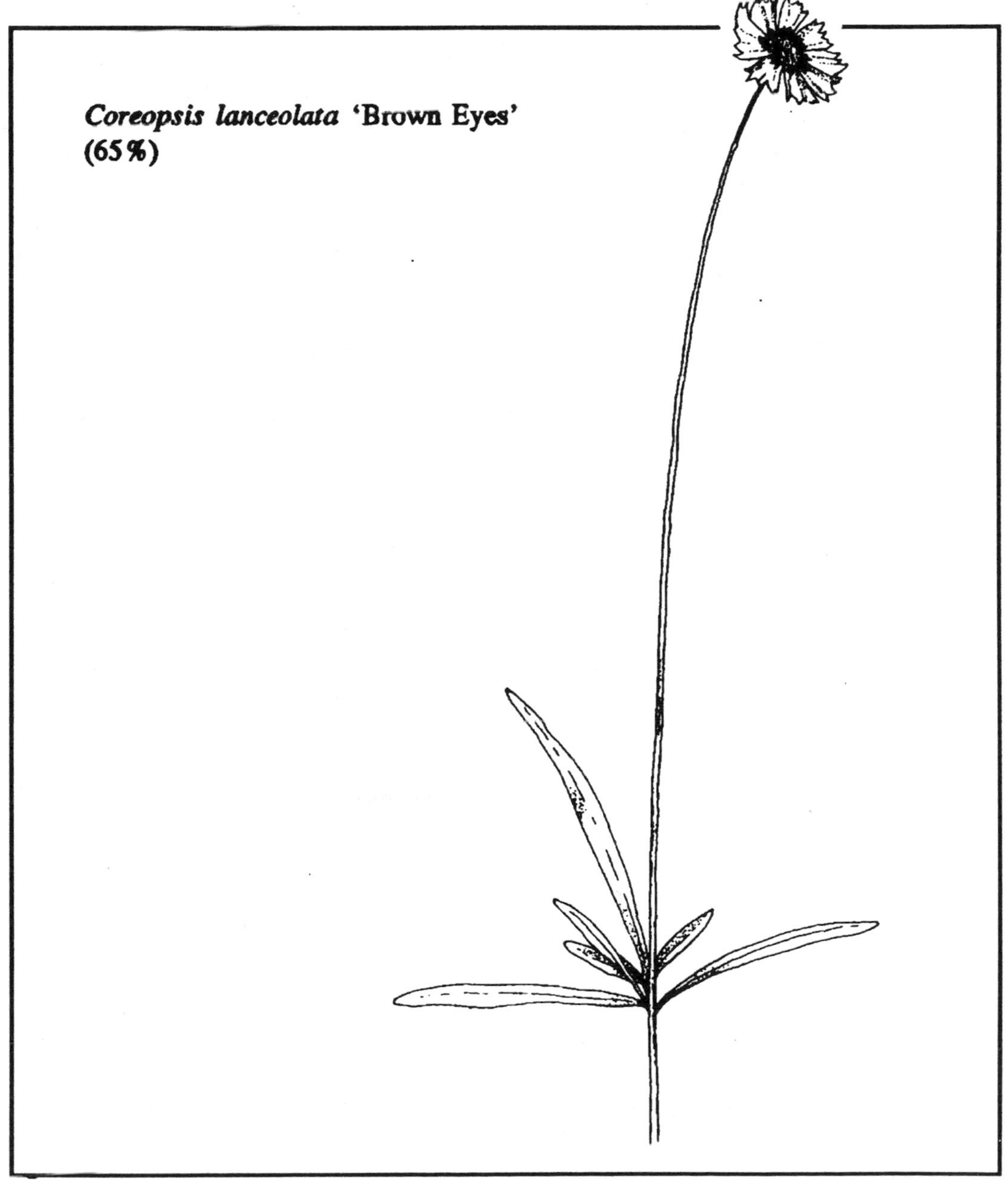

***Coreopsis lanceolata*** **'Brown Eyes' (65%)**

'Sterntaler' is similar to 'Brown Eyes' and has gold flowers with a brown ring over 12-18″ tall plants.

'Summer Sprite' was introduced by Carroll Gardens of Westminster, Maryland. Plants produce single yellow flowers with a mahogany-red ring around the center on 10-12″ tall plants.

'Sundancer' is also bright yellow and has been an excellent performer.

| **-*rosea*** (rose-ee′ a) | | Pink Coreopsis | 8-10″/spreader |
|---|---|---|---|
| Summer | Rose-pink | Eastern United States | Zones 4-7 |

I have seen wonderful rosy pink spreading mounds in northern Ohio and lousy spotty plants in many areas of the country. At their best, the threadlike leaves are covered with ¾″ flowers, each with a yellow center. Plants are rhizomatous and rapidly form handsome 8-10″ tall colonies that combine well with many taller plants. At their worst, they survive by sending up a few spindly stems and flowers, whose only need is to be ripped up and put out of their misery. Those who enjoy the plant find that it comports well with *Echinacea* and *Rudbeckia* where the rose and yellow of the *Coreopsis* are repeated in the flowers of the other two species. Best in cooler climates, but still useful as far south as zone 7. Plants offered in the trade are probably var. *nana*, since the species itself is almost 2′ tall. Plants are native from southwest Nova Scotia to Maryland.

Place in full sun and provide excellent drainage. Planting on a sloping bank helps with the drainage and enhances the view of the flowers. Propagate by division any time.

| **-*verticillata*** (ver-ti-si-lah′ ta) | | Threadleaf Coreopsis | 18″-3′/3′ |
|---|---|---|---|
| Summer | Yellow | Eastern United States | Zones 5-9 |

The combination of brighter, better colors with drought tolerance, persistent flowering, and long life put this species at the top of the coreopsis list. The sessile, 2-3″ long leaves are palmately divided into threadlike segments and therefore little leaf area remains from which to lose water under times of drought. The 2″ diameter, single flowers are borne in a few-flowered inflorescence (corymb) and held on slender stalks. Two or three plants grouped in a well-drained, sunny location grow into a sizable clump by the end of the summer. After the burst of summer flowering, cut off the flower heads and an additional autumn flush follows. I have not been as successful with the species in north Georgia as expected. Hordes of flower buds are produced which proceeded to blacken and rot. This has not been the case, however, with several cultivars.

Propagate similar to *C. auriculata*.

**Cultivars:**

'Golden Gain' is one of my favorites, forming 2′ tall mounds covered with golden flowers most of the season. Nothing fancy, just good performance.

'Golden Showers' ('Grandiflora') is 18-24″ tall, produces 2½″ diameter bright yellow flowers, and is larger in every way than the type.

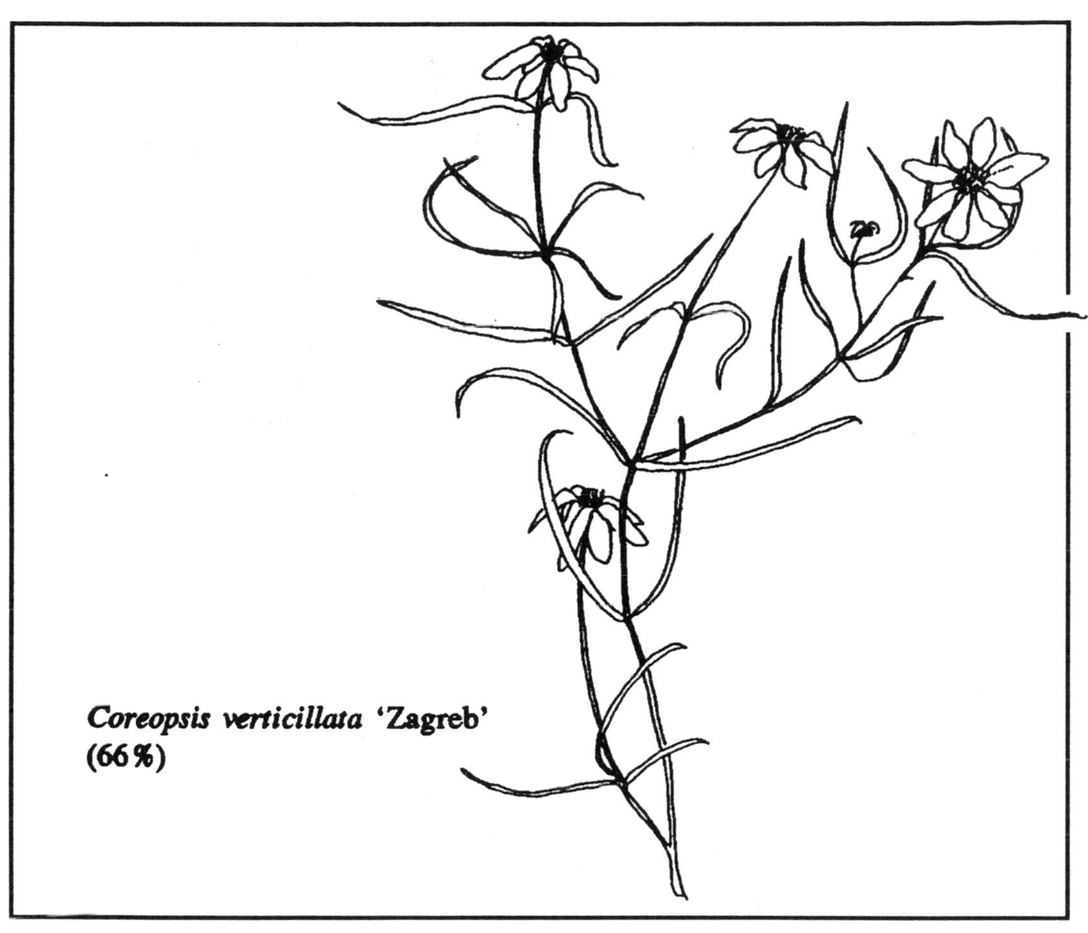

*Coreopsis verticillata* **'Zagreb' (66%)**

'Moonbeam' was the most popular cultivar for years and still may be in certain areas. Plants are 18-24″ tall and bear many soft muted yellow flowers which never fail to catch the eye. Flowers open continuously from late June to October and combine well with purple foliage of everything from *Setcreasea* to *Pennisetum setaceum* 'Rubrum'. Plants have performed well throughout the country.

'Zagreb' has deeper yellow flowers than 'Moonbeam'. Compact upright plants are bushy, upright and only 8-12″ tall in the North. In the South, 18″ tall plants are not uncommon. This is the toughest and best performing cultivar of this species.

**Related Species:**

*C. integrifolia*, Chipola River coreopsis, has entire leaves and grows 2-3′ tall. Plants are native to northwest Florida and produce beautiful dark-eyed daisies in August and September. They spread by rhizomes, but are not rapid colonizers. This is not a dry soil species, being indigenous to moist areas, but plants do fine under normal garden situations. Zones 6b-9.

*C. palmata*, stiff coreopsis, is native to the American prairie and bears seven to eight-rayed yellow flowers on 2-3′ tall plants. The distinctively pale yellow ray flowers combine with the flat yellow centers to form 1-2″ wide blossoms atop stiff, upright stems from late spring to midsummer. The stem leaves are sessile and the upper half of each leaf is divided into three narrow sections, sort of resembling a palm leaf. Zones 3-8.

*C. pulchra*, beautiful coreopsis, has similar foliage as *C. verticillata* and produces handsome yellow flowers, each with a red eye. Flowers in summer, hardy in zones 6-9. Requires excellent drainage for best performance. Native to Alabama.

*C. tripteris*, tall coreopsis, grows 4-10′ and bears dozens of dark-centered single yellow flowers. Very showy, but can get very big. Foliage has 3-5 narrow leaf segments. Native from southern Ontario to Wisconsin, south to Florida, Louisiana and west to Kansas. Both the leaves and the flower heads have a faint smell of anise when crushed. Plants flower in mid to late summer and are excellent for areas with poor, dry soils. Regardless of the area planted, tall tickseed will reseed. We don't see this plant too often in gardens because of its height and reseeding tendencies. Zones 3-8.

**Hybrids**:

No one is really sure of the parentage of some of the more extraordinary cultivars, but without doubt, hybridization has occurred.

'Autumn Blush', from Terra Nova Nursery, appears to have *C. auriculata* and *C. rosea* (at least) in the bloodline. Plants are about a foot tall and at least as wide, and at their best are covered with light yellow daisy flowers with a copper-colored center. Excellent for containers. Zones 5-7b.

'Creme Brulee' probably includes 'Moonbeam' and *C. grandiflora* in its parentage, combining the color of the former with the vigor of the latter. The latter species can be short lived, however 'Creme Brulee' has proven to be tougher than I thought it would be. Plants are about 18″ tall in our garden. Introduced from The Plantage on Long Island. Hardiness is zones 5-7b, but we have had some trouble overwintering plants, although it cannot be said our beds are particularly well drained.

'Heaven's Gate' is another one of the many dwarf colorful cultivars that have arisen lately. This one has thin stems topped with rose-pink flowers, each with a darker center. Plants grow about a foot tall and equally wide. Zones 5 or 6-8.

Lemonade series from Terra Nova Nursery provides low-growing compact plants most suitable for containers and garden edges. 'Cherry', 'Pink' and 'Strawberry Lemonade' bear rose-red, pink and red flowers respectively. The foliage has a golden tint that provides interest before the summer flowers get going. Hardiness is being evaluated, but it's likely they are not consistently winter hardy north of zone 8. Excellent drainage and some protection may allow some additional hardiness.

'Lightning Flash' was new in 2007 and is characterized by bright chartreuse foliage, follwed by light yellow flowers with a dark center in spring and early summer. It is quite outstanding in the spring, however, I have not yet trialed it long enough to know how long into the summer the foliage will remain golden. Height is about 3', hardiness is said to be zones 3-8.

'Limerock Ruby' and 'Limerock Passion' are also not sufficiently hardy to be in a book on perennials, but' Limerock Ruby', when introduced, was touted as a hardy coreopsis. Beautiful it is with ruby flowers and short, compact habit, but if you treat it as an annual, you will enjoy it far more. Plants were discovered as a natural cross by Mary Ann Faria of Limerock Plant Farm in Rhode Island. Excellent drainage enhances the weather tolerance. 'Limerock Passion' has pinkish lavender flowers.

'Pinwheel' came from the breeding program at Terra Nova in Oregon and produces creamy yellow fluted ray flowers and darker centers. Plants are about 2′ tall. Zones 6-8.

'Snowberry' may have some *C. auriculata* in its parentage. Plants produce creamy white flowers with wine-red eyes during late spring and summer. The foliage is a good dark green.

'Sweet Dreams' may be a hybrid of *C. rosea* but appears to have better vigor. Plants were in our trial gardens at Georgia for many years and never ceased to stop people in their tracks. They are short (12-15″) but need to be cut back hard in late spring or early summer, especially in warm climates. Doing so allows for many thin stems that carry a white daisy flower with a wonderfully contrasting red center all season. Cut back again if plants become unruly. Zones 5-7b.

## *Cornus* (kor′ nus) Bunchberry Cornaceae

To include a species of this woody genus testifies to the incredible diversity of structure and form within a single group. Bunchberry (*C. canadensis*) is anything but woody, seldom attaining more than 6″ in height and disappearing in the fall. However, the dark green foliage and the handsome 2″ wide white flowers that blanket the leaves make a spectacular show as a ground cover in the spring. The white of the flowers consists of 4-6 bracts subtending a very small greenish flower. The 4-6 oval to obovate leaves are whorled on top of the stem and multiply thanks to an aggressive creeping rootstalk. After flowering, red fruit, about ¼″ across, are formed and persist until eaten by wildlife. Plants are native in North America from Greenland to Alaska and south to Indiana, West Virginia and Colorado. Unfortunately for many gardeners, plants abhor sustained warm weather but in semi-shaded moist, cool areas, they are beautiful where allowed to naturalize. Growing up in Quebec, I took this plant for granted but now that I live in north Georgia, never more. Acid soil, semi-shaded and moist areas are necessary for best performance. Propagate by division in the early spring.

## *Cortaderia* (kor-ta-dare-ee′ a) Pampas Grass Poaceae

Pampas grass consists of about 24 species of robust, tussock-forming perennials from South America, New Zealand and New Guinea. Plants are highly ornamental and favored for the showy, feathery flowers and tough, thin foliage. Most species bear either male or female flowers and while the panicles of female flowers are more fluffy and often more showy, all flower plumes are eye-catching. The only species grown to any extent in this country is *C. selloana*, although occasionally a few others are offered by specialty growers.

***-selloana*** (sel-oh-ah′ na) Pampas Grass 4-7′/4′
Whitish Summer South America Zones 7-9

This evergreen grass is the royalty of ornamental grasses. The ugliest trash-strewn treeless yard (remind anyone of anywhere you know?) can be made almost inviting when the magnificent plumes proudly rise above the light green foliage. Plants are tough as nails; even the aforementioned yard cannot dull its vigor.

The leaves are ½-1″ wide and sharply edged, with the ability to snag clothing and shred hands. The flowers individual flowers are very small but the panicles may be three feet long and 6-12 inches wide. Flower color varies from silver to creamy-white and cultivars also include pink forms. Flowers generally emerge in July and are handsome throughout the winter.

After a few years, plants make a dense, wide clump that must be maintained from one year to the next. People often ask me if the old foliage must be removed in the spring before new growth gets under way. Plants growing on the pampas of Argentina don't have any caballeros out there hacking away the old growth to make prettier plants. Yours will do just fine without this intervention. Occasionally, fire does the same thing in wild plantings. However, most people do housework on their pampas grass simply because they look better when cleaned up in the spring. Do not attack these plants without being fully armed! Leaves are lethal, even in the spring, and plants do not accept attacks to their person mildly. Use long-handled secateurs or a sharp chain saw. Some people burn the old foliage in the spring, however, along with attendant air pollution, throwing a match into the plant results in an inferno, potentially dangerous to home, people and other plants. Burning, however, seldom harms the plants if done before the new growth gets underway.

I have seen pampas grass escaped from gardens in the South and West of the United States and become weedlike along fields and roadways. It is causing trouble to native plantings and may not be welcome in your state. Check with your local nursery or extension office to be sure that plants are not on your state's invasive plant list.

Propagate by division; a small pie-shaped wedge is sufficient to start a new clump.

**Cultivars:**

'Andes Silver' is 5-7′ tall and bears full silver plumes. Plants appear to be a bit more cold hardy than others.

'Bertini' is more dwarf than the common dwarf form, 'Pumila'. Plants grow only 2-3′ tall with handsome female panicles.

'Carminea Rendatleri' is one of the most handsome forms when it looks good, disastrous at other times. The flowers are pinkish but unfortunately all too weak, frequently pushed down by the wind. Difficult to locate today.

'Carnea' is a better plant than the former, bearing tougher soft pink flowers.

'Gold Band' ('Aureo-lineata') has green foliage with bright yellow bands on each side. Slow growing but grows 4-6′ tall.

'Marabout' is one of the most handsome cultivars, producing huge plumes of pure white flowers.

'Patagonia' is 5-6′ tall with blue-green foliage.

'Pumila' is a dwarf form of pampas grass. Creamy white flowers grow 3-4′ above the foliage in August and remain handsome in the winter. A terrific choice for gardens of limited space. Probably the most floriferous of available cultivars.

'Rosea' is the pink pampas grass that looks good in clumps of two or three. Rather washed-out color.

'Silver Stripe' ('Albo-lineata') has thin white margins on the leaves. A slow-growing but effective variegated foliage plant. Plants bear female flowers.

'Sun Stripe' bears leaves reverse of those of 'Gold Band', that is, yellow centers with green margins. Flowers tend to flop over more than those of other variegated forms.

'Sunningdale Silver' bears robust, tall (6-9′) female plumes of silvery white. Very vigorous and strong rigid flower stems that withstand all but the fiercest storms.

'Violacea' produces violet panicles. Distinct coloring but almost impossible to locate.

**Related Species:**

*C. jubata*, purple pampas grass, generally bears thin dark green foliage and loose, pinkish flowers. Plants grow 9-12′ tall and flowers may be pink, reddish, and even creamy yellow. Plants can be weedy, are even less cold hardy then common pampas grass and the flower stems are weak.

*C. richardii*, black pampas grass, is native to New Zealand and grows 6-10′ tall with showy, cream white, outward-arching flower plumes. More tolerant of wet soil conditions, less tolerant of cold weather.

## ***Corydalis*** (ko-ri′ dal-is) Corydalis Fumariaceae

All 300 species produce 4-petaled irregular flowers and many have finely divided fernlike foliage. The genus has long been well represented throughout northern Europe, and emergence of the genus in North American gardens is welcome indeed. Many species are ornamental and while *C. lutea*, yellow corydalis, has always been easily available, others such as the blue corydalis, *C. flexuosa*, and a number of hybrids are gaining popularity. Species range in size from the 4-6″ yellow-flowered *C. thyrsifolia*, native to the high mountains of the Himalayas, to the 3′ tall robust *C. nobilis*, native to central Asia. Most are yellow flowered but a good number also bear pink to purplish flowers such as *C. anthriscifolia*, *C. popovii*, a low-grower from central Asia, and *C. solida*, (*C. bulbosa*), fumewort. *C. solida* includes a particularly handsome cultivar, 'George Baker', with rich terra cotta flowers. The foliage of all species is an important ornamental characteristic and for some, like *C. ophiocarpus*, the lacy gray-green leaves are probably the best part. A tremendous potential exists in this genus and it should not be long before a dozen good species can be found in gardens. However, to be fair to gardeners, many have learned the hard way that warm summer temperatures are not to the liking of corydalis in general. Once burned, twice shy. Good drainage, basic soils (pH lower than 6.5) and partial shade are useful for best performance.

Quick Reference to Corydalis Species

| | Height (in.) | Rootstock | Flower color |
|---|---|---|---|
| *C. cheilanthifolia* | 9-12 | Stolons | Yellow |
| *C. flexuosa* | 12-15 | Stolons | Blue, Purplish |
| *C. lutea* | 6-12 | Rhizome | Yellow |

***-cheilanthifolia*** (chee-lanth-i-fo′ lee-a) Ferny Corydalis 9-12″/10″
Spring Yellow Central China Zones 3-6

Growing in rock walls and well-drained crevices, this gray-leaved plant produces dozens of bright yellow flowers over a dense rosette. The 2-3 pinnate leaves are 4-6″ long and look more like the fern (*Cheilanthus*) than a corydalis. Plants are winter hardy to zone 4 or 5 but do not take well to warm humid climates. They can distribute themselves with abandon by throwing out seed everywhere. In the quarry garden at Longwood, these plants are cropping up like dandelions. At Branklyn Garden outside Perth, Scotland, I was also astonished to see these spreading like weeds everywhere in early spring. The head gardener looked at them disdainfully as only one who must remove such obnoxious things can. As for me, I have tried three times in my southern garden, but without success. This is such a favorite of mine that I am thinking of building a stone wall if for no other reason than to grow these crazy plants.

Propagate by divisions after flowering or from seed.

***-flexuosa*** (flex-ewe-o′ sa) Blue Corydalis 12-15″/12″
Spring Blue China Zones 5-8

Few plants have caused the excitement or the frustration that plants of blue corydalis have. The finely divided glaucous foliage is similar to *C. lutea* but the deep blue to lavender-blue flowers seldom fail to catch the eye. In late spring or early summer, up to 10 thin, tubular-spurred flowers are held on 12″ pedicels (flower stems). They were first collected by the French missionary naturalist Pere Armand David (of *Davidia* and *Buddleia davidii* fame) in 1865 in western China. They were "rediscovered" and brought back in 1989 from steep shady slopes around 5000 ft. elevation in western Sichuan province. Their native habitat helps to explain why they perform best in cooler climates and in areas of sharp drainage. Try them in containers if you are unable to find the right site. Where they do well, they are outstanding and persistent in flower.

As marvelous as these plants can be, the jury is no longer out on their worthiness in parts of this country. They perform well in the Northwest (as do most other *Corydalis* species) and that is the best area to see vigorous stands. However, they appear to grow reasonably well at Longwood Gardens, and I have seen good colonies at Old Westbury Gardens in Long Island, New York. In the Midwest, they are but fair, and cannot be recommended in the Southeast. Performance is questionable in the Northeast and lower Midwest, although reports of winter hardiness to 5°F have been reported. Plants appear to self-destruct after flowering, but this is because they are summer dormant, dismaying many a gardener who first tries them. Unfortunately, they may not reappear after a difficult winter. Barry Glick of Sunshine Farm, West Virginia, has also been fed up paying perennial prices for an "annual" but was so enamored with the plants, he provided these suggestions. "Right before it goes dormant, break a chunk off and bring it inside. Pot it up in a 6″ pot and let it go dormant in a bright shady window. Keep it moist, but not wet during its summer dormancy. In late Autumn, about Thanksgiving, it will awake and start growing again. Start feeding it a liquid fertilizer at ¼ strength weekly. In about a month or so, it will run you out of house and home. Repeat this process yearly and you'll always be in good supply and probably end up starting your own nursery to get rid of them."

If drainage is reasonably good, plants may return early the following spring. Most species of *Corydalis* perform better in more basic soils, so add some lime to the soil.

A number of other species and hybrids of blue corydalis are occasionally available (*C. elata*, *C. curvifolia*) and similar comments hold true for them.

Propagate by division or seed immediately after flowering.

**Cultivars:**

Good grief, but it is difficult to tell the difference between any these cultivars, as intensity of color is so tied to soil and temperature.

'Blue Panda' was discovered in the 1986 and bears sky blue flowers, particularly in cooler climates, on 9-12″ tall plants. Like most of the other cultivars, the blue color is more intense in areas with cool nights and mornings. A chance seedling with more purple-blue flowers arose in the original Heronswood Nursery and was offered as 'Purple Panda'.

'Blue Dragon' has smoky blue flowers on 10″ tall plants.

'China Blue' has more smoky blue flowers than the species. The foliage is brownish green in winter and flowers fade to purple after blooming. This is the tallest cultivar.

'Pere David' has lavender to light blue flowers. Leaves distinctly blue-green.

'Purple Leaf' is the earliest to bloom and has purplish blue flowers and leaves with a central purple blotch in the center. The leaves are purple, especially in winter, with blood-red markings at the base of the leaflets. The smallest and neatest clone.

***-lutea*** (loo′ tee-a) Yellow Corydalis 6-12″/18″
Spring Yellow Europe Zones 5-7

The 1-4″ long leaves are blue-green on the top sides and two to three times pinnately compound, resulting in divided fernlike foliage. Many wiry stems push through the soil terminating in small, golden yellow, spurred flowers. The flowers superficially resemble those of the fringed bleeding heart, *Dicentra eximia*.

Plants bask in shady, moist areas and are tolerant of soils with basic pH. This is a most ubiquitous plant in the Northwest and in the British Isles where it grows in cracks of walkways and fissures in walls and revels in areas scorned by more "uptown" plants. When you visit Portland and Seattle gardeners, and up to Vancouver and Victoria, you will also find similar yellow pools everywhere. The rest of our

North American climate is not as much to their liking but yellow corydalis is still a useful addition in the shaded rock garden.

The species is well known for its self-sowing tendencies, however purchased seeds are notoriously difficult to germinate because they are not fresh. The best means of seed propagation is to collect fresh seed and sow immediately. All seed should be sown in a seed tray in 1:1 mixture of peat:vermiculite and placed in a warm (70-75°F) area for 6-8 weeks. After the warm treatment, place at near-freezing conditions for an additional 6-8 weeks. Warm the trays slowly and germination will occur, although erratically. Fortunately, nature takes care of these conditions. If seed flats are placed outdoors in late summer and allowed to overwinter under snow or other protection, germination will begin as the weather warms in the spring. Plants may also be divided in spring or fall.

**Related Species:**

*C. cashmeriana* is native to the Himalayas and bears dark blue flowers on short (less than 9″ tall) plants. They are best used as an alpine plant in well-drained rock gardens. Perfectly hardy but require outstanding drainage and partial shade, and cannot be allowed to dry out.

*C. chaerophylla* has a taproot and is reasonably drought tolerant. Plants produce many stems of bright yellow flowers and distinctly triangular biternate basal leaves. The stem leaves are sessile and 3-parted. Plants differ mainly from *C. cheilanthifolia* by having stems and growing up to 3′ tall. A little easier to grow than ferny corydalis.

*C. incisa* has pink to purple-lavender flowers on 8-12″ tall plants. These vigorous plants are biennial but their reseeding tendencies will keep them forever in the garden if conditions are to their liking. Native to Japan, plants are well suited to areas of cool nights and warm days. Best guess on zones is likely 5-7.

*C. nobilis* is native to central Asia and mountainous areas in China. This early-flowering plant (late April in Denver) bears 18-24″ tall upright stems terminating in a cluster of 20-30 yellow flowers with a dark spot in the inner petals. The weight of the flowers causes the stems to bend over slightly. Plants can be robust and grow three feet tall and equally wide under optimum conditions. Summer dormancy occurs in dry soils. Good drainage and sunny areas are necessary for best performance. Likely performs well in zones 3 to 6.

*C. ochroleuca*, white corydalis, resembles *C. lutea*, but bears pale yellow flowers, often with green lips. The foliage is glaucous blue on both sides rather than on the top sides only. Plants are native to southern and eastern Europe. Terrific in the Northwest, needs to be proven elsewhere. Tolerates sun but prefers moisture and shade. Grow similarly to *C. lutea*.

*C. sempervirens*, rock harlequin, is a 2-4′ tall biennial which naturalizes by reseeding. Flowers are pale pink to purple with yellow tips and the fernlike foliage is gray green. Plants are native from Newfoundland to Georgia and west to British Columbia. Plants can become a nuisance due to their reseeding tendencies.

**Hybrids:**

'Berry Exciting' has very exciting chartreuse foliage, and does not go summer dormant, except in hot, humid gardens. Purple, somewhat fragrant flowers top the foliage in the spring. Plants arose from a sport of 'Blackberry Wine'.

'Blackberry Wine' produces lilac flowers in the spring over 1-2′ tall plants. The main claim to fame of this selection is its apparent increased tolerance to heat and humidity, not exactly traits associated with corydalis. In the Armitage garden, it has performed handsomely.

'Blue Heron', from Heronswood, is similar to other blue-flowering corydalis but is a totally different species (*C. curvifolia* var. *rosthornii*). I have read accounts that this is more robust than other blues, so you might want to give it a go. However, as disappointing as other blue ones have been, don't spend too much money quite yet. Plants are summer dormant.

'Canary Feathers' has large bright yellow flowers over 1½′ tall plants bearing narrow soft green foliage. Heat tolerance has not been adequately tested but cold hardy to about zone 6.

'Rainier Blue' looks terrific, but I believe the same can be said as for 'Blue Heron', at least in the East.

## ***Cosmos*** (kos′ mos) Cosmos Asteraceae

Most gardeners think of *Cosmos* only as an annual but there are a couple of marginal perennials lurking among the 26 species that make up this genus. To be accurate, the perennials are cold hardy only in the mildest areas in the South and the moderate climes of the coastal Northwest (zone 8-11). The best perennial species, arguably, is the elusive chocolate cosmos, *C. atrosanguineus*. Native to Mexico, it tolerates no less than 10°F (zone 8, zone 7 with lots of protection) but perhaps because it is so difficult to establish, it is highly sought after. Plants grow from tuberous roots (like a dahlia) that may be dug in colder climates and overwintered in loose peat in moderate temperatures. The compound leaves are often lobed at the bases and are attached to the stems by winged petioles. The velvety deep-crimson flowers are formed on 2-3′ tall stems. The flowers smell like chocolate to some noses; mine seems uncooperative and I often smell vanilla. But then, I am a boring Canadian.

Propagate by seed. Sow seed at 70°F in moist medium and humid conditions. Germination occurs in 14-21 days.

## ***Crambe*** (kram′ bay) Kale Brassicaceae

The genus contains several exceptional cultivars, some with highly ornamental foliage, others with monstrous proportions and yet others quite forgettable. All plants produce many small 4-petaled flowers in large branching inflorescences (racemes). Two species are reasonably well known and if space allows, are well worth including.

Quick Reference to Crambe Species

| | Flower Color | Height (ft.) | Basal Foliage |
|---|---|---|---|
| *C. cordifolia* | White | 4-7 | Thin, Heart shaped |
| *C. maritima* | White | 2-3 | Thick, Fleshy |

**-*cordifolia*** (kord-i-foe-lee′ a) Giant Kale 4-7′/4′
Summer White North Caucasus Zones 5-8

When in flower, this is a 55-mph plant, which can be seen from cars, trains and mopeds. A perfect plant to hide the Dempsey Dumpster or the entire trailer park. The basal leaves are heart shaped and more or less hairy but as the leaves ascend the stem, they become larger (2′ across), thicker and more variable in shape. They are great big cabbages when not in flower but are stately, even graceful, in bloom. Hundreds of small white flowers are produced above the foliage, giving the appearance of huge plants of baby's breath.

These are not specimens for the small garden and are best used as accent plants in open areas. They require full sun and well-drained soils for best performance. While they are quite happy in the zone 8 of the West Coast and Northwest, they are useless in the eastern zone 8, and not much better in zone 7.

Propagate by root cuttings of 3-4 year plants in early spring. Seed takes 2-3 years to flower.

**-*maritima*** (ma-ri-ti′ ma) Sea Kale 2-3′/3′
Summer White Western Europe Zones 5-8

Plants historically were grown for shoots that were blanched in the spring by covering the plant with a pot or box and eaten as a salad, far more common in European cuisine than in America. This plant brings a few additional uses to the garden other than its questionable ornamental value. They were particularly useful in coastal areas where salt spray and saline soils were common. The wavy, thick, bluish foliage is handsome in its own right and in the early summer, stiff sprays of creamy white flowers are carried above the leaves. The basal stems become woody at the end of the first year. In areas of cool nights, many of the flowers have a decided yellowish tint as well. I have seen a dusky form known as purple bush form, but it does not appear to be particularly dusky in the Eastern and Midwestern heat. Plants need full sun and are tolerant of moist soils, but not waterlogged conditions. Similar problems of heat tolerance occur with this species as with the former one. I have tried plants in my north Georgia garden and while they are decent the first couple of years, they seldom persist much longer. However, they can be most ornamental in the Midwest and lower Northeast. Propagate by root cuttings or seed.

**Related Species:**

*C. koktebelica* is seldom seen in this country and I have seen it in only one or two gardens in the British Isles. It is similar to *C. cordifolia* but is a little shorter (3-4′) and bears white flowers with yellow sepals. The flowers are more stiffly held than those of giant kale.

***Crocosmia*** (kro-caws′ me-a) Crocosmia, Montbretia Iridaceae

Crocosmia has become exceeding popular as new cultivars and hybrids emerge. The swordlike leaves arise from a corm and myriads of one-sided nodding flowers resembling small funnels are produced along the length of the arching flower stems. As well as being excellent in the garden, they are widely sought after as cut flowers and are used commercially by florists in arrangements and bouquets. They can be grown by gardeners in almost all areas of the country, ranging from those who pray for their survival to those cussing them while pulling them out from wherever they have invaded.

About seven species occur but many of the cultivars available today are interspecific hybrids, mainly with *C. paniculata* (formerly known as *Curtonus paniculatus* and *Antholyza paniculata*) and most are listed under *C.* x *crocosmiiflora*. Their additional vigor and colors continue to win converts.

Plant in full sun, in soil that isn't waterlogged. In the North, corms should be lifted in the fall and treated similar to gladiolus. Plants are generally hardy from zones 5 to 6 to 8. Alan Bloom, who bred many fine cultivars, stated that the degree of cold hardiness depended on the corm size. The larger the corm, the more tolerant of cold. Plant the smaller corms about 3″ deep, the larger about 4″ deep. Plants can be propagated by division or by lifting and removing offsets from the corms. They become crowded after a few years and flowering and in areas where they do well, will be reduced if not divided after 2 or 3 years.

**-*x crocosmiiflora*** (kro-kos-mee-i-flo′ ra) Crocosmia, Montbretia 2-3′/1′
Summer Various Hybrid Zones 6-8

This hybrid occurred in the early 1880s when the French hybridizer Lemoine introduced a hybrid between *C. aurea*, a golden, large-flowered but tender species, and *C. pottsii*, a vivid red, hardy species. This was once listed as *Montbretia* x *crocosmiaeflora* by Lemoine and became known as *Montbretia*, a name which no longer has any botanical stature. Additional selections and hybridization in England resulted in free-flowering, brilliantly colored plants. The nodding to erect flowers are borne on a zigzag rachis (the central axis of the inflorescence which bears the flowers) and persist for up to 4 weeks. They were included in our research on commercial cut flower production and produced 8-10 stems per plant for 2-3 years before requiring division.

Plant in full sun and in well-drained soils. The corms should be planted in spring about 3″ deep and 6″ apart. Spider mites can cause a great deal of damage to the foliage and discourage flowering. A number of chemicals are available and although I do not enjoy the idea of spraying, these plants are worth the trouble.

**Hybrids**:

The parentage of many of these cultivars is not known, and all are thought to be hybrids. Most cultivars have been bred in England and have filtered our way. With luck, more will make it across the pond. Most flower in early to midsummer. To be on the conservative side, I would say that most are reliably hardy to zone 7, many to zone 6, and a few to zone 5.

'A. E. Amos' is a brilliant orange-red.

'African Gold' is about 1½′ tall and bears golden yellow flowers.

'Babylon' is 2-3′ tall with red-orange flowers. Plants are vigorous and bright.

'Bressingham Beacon' produces many orange and yellow bicolored flower sprays on dark stems. Stunning.

'Bressingham Blaze' has intense orange-red flowers on 2-3′ tall plants.

Bright Eyes™ are 18-24″ tall with orange flowers with red centers.

'Citronella' (syn. 'Citrinum') has small, pretty, orange-yellow flowers above the light green foliage.

'Coleton Fishacre' has apricot flowers and bronzed foliage. Plants are similar to, but more vigorous than 'Solfatare'.

'Eastern Promise' claims to have "mango-yellow blooms with tangerine centers." I don't know whether to grow it in the garden or the orchard.

'Emberglow' produces burnt orange-red flowers atop 2-3′ tall plants.

'Emily McKenzie' is truly impressive. It was introduced in the mid-1950s and I have yet to see a more vibrant cultivar. The large orange flowers contrast beautifully with the crimson throat.

'George Davidson' is one of the granddaddies of the group, bred prior to 1902. Small soft yellow flowers are produced on 2′ tall plants. The flowers are small by modern standards but plentiful.

'Irish Sunset', from Blooms of Bressingham, provides red-tipped yellow buds that give rise to sprays of yellow and orange red flowers in the summer.

'Jackanapes' is best known for its wonderful name. An older cultivar, plants bear small flowers of yellow and red.

'James Coey' has deep red flowers with yellow centers. Not as vigorous as some of the new cultivars.

'Jenny Bloom', named after Mr. Bloom's youngest daughter, is a vigorous selection with butter-yellow flowers on 2-3′ plants. Really lovely, one of my favorites.

'John Boots' has golden yellow flowers and stands 2-3′ tall.

Little Redhead™ is only about 2′ tall and bears bright red flowers with yellow throats.

'Lucifer' is exceptional and is covered with scarlet-red flowers in the summer. It has been grown in the United States for a number of years and has proven its garden value over and over. Plants are probably among the most vigorous and can become a problem in rich soils. Divide every three years or plants will stop flowering.

'Meteore' bears red and yellow bicolored flowers in midsummer. About 2′ tall.

'Mistral' produces orange-red flowers on 2-2½′ tall plants.

'Norwich Canary' is a late-flowered form with bright yellow flowers on 2′ plants.

'Red King' reminds people of 'Lucifer' but is not as vigorous, a good thing in many areas of the country.

'Solfatare', one of the oldest hybrids, was bred in the late 1800s by the French nurseryman, Lemoine. It is 2′ tall with apricot-yellow flowers and dark green leaves.

'Spitfire' is a cross between *C. masonorum* and *C. x crocosmiiflora* 'Jackanapes'. It is a large plant with stunning orange-red flowers with a yellow throat.

'Star of the East' bears orange flowers with maroon coloration in the center. Plants are about 3′ tall and gorgeous in flower.

Walburton Yellow™ has golden yellow upward-facing flowers. This is a relatively old cultivar but we have trialed it for only about 3 years. It is the best yellow I have ever tried, not too vigorous but tough, and with flowers to leave your spouse for.

'Walburton Red' has flaming red flowers, quite beautiful, but not as vigorous as its yellow cousin. Probably hardy to zone 6.

'Venus' is only 18-24″ tall and produces peach-yellow flowers on darkened stems.

'Vulcan' is also relatively short, compared to 'Lucifer', and bears scarlet-orange flowers.

**Related Species:**

*C. masonorum* has 3′ long flower stems, narrowly lanceolate leaves and bright orange-red upright flowers, each measuring about 1½″ long. 'Firebird' has fiery orange-red flowers with a bright yellow throat and is jaw-dropping in its brilliance. 'Rowallane Yellow' has apricot-yellow flowers and commemorates Rowallane Garden, in County Down, Northern Ireland. May require additional mulching.

***Crocus*** (kro′ kus) Crocus Iridaceae

"All the world loves a crocus. There can be no two opinions about this," states Louise Beebe Wilder in her delightful book *Adventures with Hardy Bulbs* (1936). Most gardens boast a few plants in March and April, and while these plants are surely exquisite gems for the gardener, they show but a fraction of the potential of the 75 species in the genus. Crocus may flower in September, October, November, February, March, and April. In some places, they can be coaxed into bloom even in December and January. Of course, not all are available to the gardener nor are all of them as easy to grow as the common Dutch hybrids, but at least a third of them may be successfully grown in the United States and Canada. The common crocuses of gardens are the large-flowered hybrids of *C. aureus* and *C. vernus*, comprised of innumerable spring-flowering cultivars, but fall-flowering species and cultivars of *C. chrysanthus* have their adamant admirers.

The genus also includes a plant of great historical interest, the saffron crocus, *C. sativus*. The bright yellow stigmas of this plant were dried and made into "karcom" of the ancient Hebrews, and corms were widely cultivated by the ancient Greeks and Romans. Saffron took on medicinal and culinary uses as well as being an important dye and perfume. It is still cultivated today in Spain, India and a handful of other areas but is difficult to grow well in this country because of the need for a long dry period. It is estimated that it requires about 75,000 flowers to produce one pound of saffron, making it arguably the most expensive spice in the world. Interestingly, a fair amount of saffron is grown today in east Texas. There are, however, many species more ornamental, and except for the engaging stories you can tell your garden visitors, it probably is not worth the space.

The crocus corm is covered by scaly leaves from which arise leaf and flower buds, as well as buds that form the new corm. The leaves are usually channeled white-veined and appear before the flowers with their bright yellow or red stigmas. Crocuses may be divided into two groups, the first consisting of late winter and early spring-flowering species, the second being the autumn flowerers (these are different from *Colchicum*, often referred to as the autumn crocus, which has 6 stamens instead of the 3 found in *Crocus*). The first group should be planted from September to November while the second must be planted no later than early September. Plant in full sun about 4″ deep and close together, in groups of 25 or more. The spring-flowerers perform reasonably well in shady areas, particularly the early-flowering species, but are at their best in the sun. Fall-flowerers must soak up the sunshine. Corms require well-drained areas and all are suitable for the rock garden.

Flowers of all crocus are short lived, persisting for only 1-2 weeks, but what glorious weeks they are. Naturalized in grassy meadows, they are a beautiful sight when in bloom. I have seen large drifts in March on sides of highways or along grassy verges, and nearly always cause an accident as I slam on the brakes of the car. However, they should not be planted in lawns if the lawn is to be kept cut. Seldom is mowing finished for the year that the emerging buds of autumn-flowering species will not be injured, and mowing starts in the spring before the leaves of the spring-flowering types have yellowed.

Propagation can be accomplished by lifting the corms, dividing them into various sizes, and replanting in a larger area. Most species can also be raised from seed. Unfortunately, many animals love the corms as much as gardeners love the flowers. Squirrels, chipmunks, rabbits, mice and voles can be an awful nuisance and desperate measures must sometimes be taken. As Ms. Wilder also concludes, "It is easy to see what a rabid state of mind the gentlest and most humane of persons may be brought by the destruction of his beloved Crocuses. The gun in a sure hand is the most unfailing weapon."

Many of the differences between species are found in the covering of the corm, the color of the anthers and branching pattern of the styles. Many species are not commonly found in catalogs for the home gardener, and botanical gardens are often worth a visit to appreciate the diversity of the genus, particularly those that flower in the fall.

Quick Reference to Crocus Species

| | Flower color | Flowering season |
|---|---|---|
| *C. ancyrensis* | Yellow | Spring |
| *C. biflorus* | White, light blue | Spring |
| *C. chrysanthus* | Various | Spring |
| *C. kotschyanus* | Rose | Fall |
| *C. speciosus* | Blue | Fall |
| *C. tommasinianus* | Mauve | Spring |
| *C. vernus* | Various | Spring |

***-ancyrensis*** (an-see-ren′ sis) Golden Bunch Crocus 4-6″/6″
Early Spring Various Turkey Zones 3-8

One of the earliest of the spring-flowering crocus to bloom, plants bear 1″ long, ½″ broad flowers that are bright yellow inside and out. Occasionally the outer segments may be feathered with bronze. Normally, each corm produces 2-3 flowers and 3-4 narrow leaves which appear with the flowers.

**Cultivars:**

'Golden Bunch' was said to be selected for its prolific flowering and may have up to 10 golden-yellow flowers per corm, 5 being average. However, in many cases 'Golden Bunch' is nothing more than a fancy name for the species itself.

***-biflorus*** (bi-flo′ rus) Scotch Crocus 4-6″/6″
Early Spring White, Blue Italy to Iran Zones 5-9

This reliable plant flowers as early as February and often bears two flowers at once, thus accounting for the specific name. Although not native to Scotland, it has become naturalized there as an escapee from gardens. Typically the flowers are white with a yellow throat and purple stippling on the outer petals. This combination gives the flowers a slight metallic sheen resulting in its other common name, cloth-of-silver. Performance is better in dry summers than wet ones and, like all crocus, full sun is preferable to shade.

**Cultivars:**

'Adamii' bears flowers that are lilac inside and light brown outside with darker veining.

var. *alexandri* produces flowers of pure white with glossy purple outside but no yellow throat.

'Miss Vain' proved to be a good performer in the Armitage garden. I was taken by the small white flowers, each with a blue base and yellow styles.

'Pusillus' has small flowers of white with an orange throat.

var. *waldenii* has small white flowers with a bluish base and is one of the best forms of the species.

***-chrysanthus*** (kris-anth′ us) Golden Crocus 4-6″/6″
Spring Various Greece, Asia Minor Zones 4-7

One of the best known of the spring-flowering crocus species, plants are available in a wide range of colors. It flowers earlier than the hybrids and helps provide a longer flowering season when combined with them. The wild species is yellowish orange throughout and has a honeylike scent. A couple of features of the flowers distinguish the species from others, but neither is obvious without some squinting. The anthers are tipped in black (although some are more brown than black), and the styles are tri-lobed, as opposed to many-branched in other species. Plants bear more than one flower per corm and produce 3-6 narrow leaves.

I have tried many cultivars in my garden and I can get excited about most of them. However, as wonderful as they are, most are not as long lived as the Dutch hybrids, returning for 2-3 years before needing replanting.

**Cultivars:**

The following are but a few of the dozens of cultivars available. Refer to a reliable bulb catalog for additional selections.

'Ard Schenk' produces clean white flowers with yellow centers.
'Advance' has blue-violet outer petals and lemon-yellow inner petals.
'Bluebird' is lavender blue throughout with white tinges on the inside of all petals.
'Blue Pearl' has been one of my favorites, bearing flowers of a delicate blue that darken at the base.
'Cream Beauty' is light yellow with contrasting orange stamens. The base of each flower is bronze-green. A lovely plant and a reliable performer.
'Dorothy' is eye-catching, bearing bright yellow flowers with a hint of bronze on the outside.
'E.A. Bowles' was named after one of the authorities on this genus and has canary yellow flowers with bronze veining towards the base.
'E.P. Bowles' is a little shorter than the former but the petal markings are more pronounced. Flowers have a hint of purple.
'Elegance' bears handsome flowers of brown and gold.
'Gypsy Girl' has yellow flowers with brown stripes on the petals.
'Herald' is unique in having bright yellow inner and purple outer sepals and petals.
'Lady Killer' is lilac-white outside and violet-white inside.
'Moonlight' is one of the earliest to flower, unfolding deep yellow flowers as soon as the soil warms up in the least. I have had flowers as early as January 15 in mild winters, February 1 not uncommon.
'Prins Claus', Santa's brother, is another bicolored cultivar, bearing white flowers heavily blotched with purple on the outside.
'Snow Bunting' is white with a small purple spot at the base, and yellow inside.
'Snow White' bears white to yellow outer petals with a bluish purple veining at the base and white inner petals with a blotch of yellow.
'Zwanenberg Bronze' is yellow on the inside with an interesting bronze exterior.

| **-*kotschyanus*** (kot-shee-ah′ nus) | | Kotschy's Crocus | 4-6″/6″ |
|---|---|---|---|
| Fall | Rose-lilac | Europe to Syria | Zones 5-8 |

The flowers open a little earlier than *C. speciosus* and the rose-lilac goblet-shaped flowers appear before the leaves. The flowers have a white or deep yellow throat and usually have two deep orange-yellow spots at the base of the flower segments. The anthers are creamy white compared with the orange anthers of Dutch crocus (*C. vernus*). Plants are often recommended for naturalization due to their vigor and ability to quickly multiply.

**Cultivars:**

'Albus', a white-flowered form, is sometimes available.

***-speciosus*** (spe-see-o′ sus) Showy Crocus 4-6″/6″
Fall Light Blue Southern Russia, Western Turkey Zones 5-7

This is one of the easiest fall crocus to grow. The lavender-blue petals and the large, much divided orange-scarlet stigma make the flowers particularly attractive. The outside of the segments is painted with three main purple veins. It is one of the earliest fall crocus and emerges while the foliage is very short. The 3-4 leaves are broad, dark green, and grow 15″ long after flowering.

As beautiful as these plants are, I have had little success relative to the tales of the bulb catalogs. The first year, they flower "picture perfect" but perhaps because temperatures are still warm in north Georgia in late September and early October, they persist for less than a week. The other problem is that the flowers tend to stretch if placed in any shade resulting in a long-eared floppy puppy look. Obviously, full sun (rock garden is terrific) and well-drained soils are recommended. In cooler climates, plants are better behaved.

It seeds freely and increases by offsets. When first planted, locate them in a permanent place as corms do not like to be disturbed.

**Cultivars:**
var. *aitchisonii* has 1½″ broad, pale lavender flowers.
var. *albus* has flowers of white.
'Cassiope' flowers about one week after the species and has rich blue petals.
'Conqueror' has clear, deep blue flowers.
'Oxonian' has large dark blue flowers.
'Pollux' has large, violet-blue outer segments and is silvery blue on the inside.

***-tommasinianus*** (tom-a-see-nee-ah′ nus) Tommasini's Crocus 4-6″/6″
Early Spring Lavender-blue Western Yugoslavia Zones 5-9

Plants increase rapidly by self-sowing and this is one of the better species to naturalize for large drifts and masses. Three to five leaves are present when the flowers appear, each leaf growing about 5-8″ long. The flowers are lavender to silvery blue outside and when warmed by the sun, they unfurl to boast a soft amethyst center. It flowers very early and is excellent to naturalize with hellebores or snowdrops (*Galanthus*). Winterthur House and Gardens in Delaware bears spectacular drifts of these crocus in early spring. This is the best species of crocus for the new crocus gardener to try.

**Cultivars:**
'Albus' produces milky white flowers but is otherwise similar to the species.
'Barr's Purple' has flowers of soft lilac mauve.
'Lilac Beauty' is one of my favorites with lilac flowers that contrast with the orange stigmas.
'Ruby Giant' produces large blooms of deep ruby purple. Outstanding.
'Whitewell Purple' bears flowers of deep reddish mauve that contrast beautifully with the yellow stigmas.

***-vernus*** (ver′ nus) Dutch Crocus 4-6″/6″
Spring Various Europe Zones 3-8
(syn. *C. albiflorus*)

Plants are widely distributed in alpine regions from the Pyrenees to the Carpathian Mountains. The 3-4 narrow leaves usually have a white line running their length and eventually grow 12-14″ long. *C. vernus* has given rise to the many Dutch hybrids available today, all of which are more vigorous and generally larger-flowered than those of the species. Occasionally, varieties of the true species are offered and are well worth trying if space is unlimited.

**Cultivars:**

var. *albiflorus* bears small white flowers.

var. *leucostigma* has blue flowers with cream-colored stigmas.

'Obovatus' has feathered purple veins on the outer segments, giving it an interesting appearance.

**Dutch hybrids**:

The Dutch hybrids have been selected for size and color and include other parentage such as *C. aureus* and/or *C. tommasinianus* as well as *C. vernus*. Flowers are 2-4″ long, 1-3″ wide, and the color range is extensive. All are equally useful in containers as they are in the garden.

**Related Species:**

*C. gargaricus* has some of the brightest orange flowers in the genus. With orange-yellow sepals, yellow anthers and orange styles, it is a March to April stoplight in the garden.

*C. goulimyi*, native to southern Greece, produces star-shaped pale to deep lavender flowers with a white throat and pale yellow anthers. Flowers emerge with or slightly before the leaves in October and November. Corms increase rapidly by offsets. An excellent fall-flowering crocus.

*C. laevigatus* is quite late to flower, opening in late fall to early winter, depending on climate. The leaves appear first, followed by flowers that vary from white to deep purple. The most common form available is 'Fontenayi' which has pale violet flowers strongly striped deeper purple on the outside and yellow in the center. An excellent, relatively unknown crocus.

*C. sieberi* has broad, dark green leaves and flowers with a tapering rounded perianth tube. Flower color of the species itself is are lavender-purple with a deep yellow throat. Cultivars sometimes offered are 'Bowle's White', with clean white petals and yellow anthers, 'Firefly', light blue outside, white inside, 'Herbert Edelsten' with pale flowers banded with purple and white, and 'Violet Queen' with stunning iridescent violet flowers in the spring. Short-lived but memorable.

**Cultivars:**

There are numerous hybrids offered in bulb catalogs, too many to mention here. Some I am familiar with include:

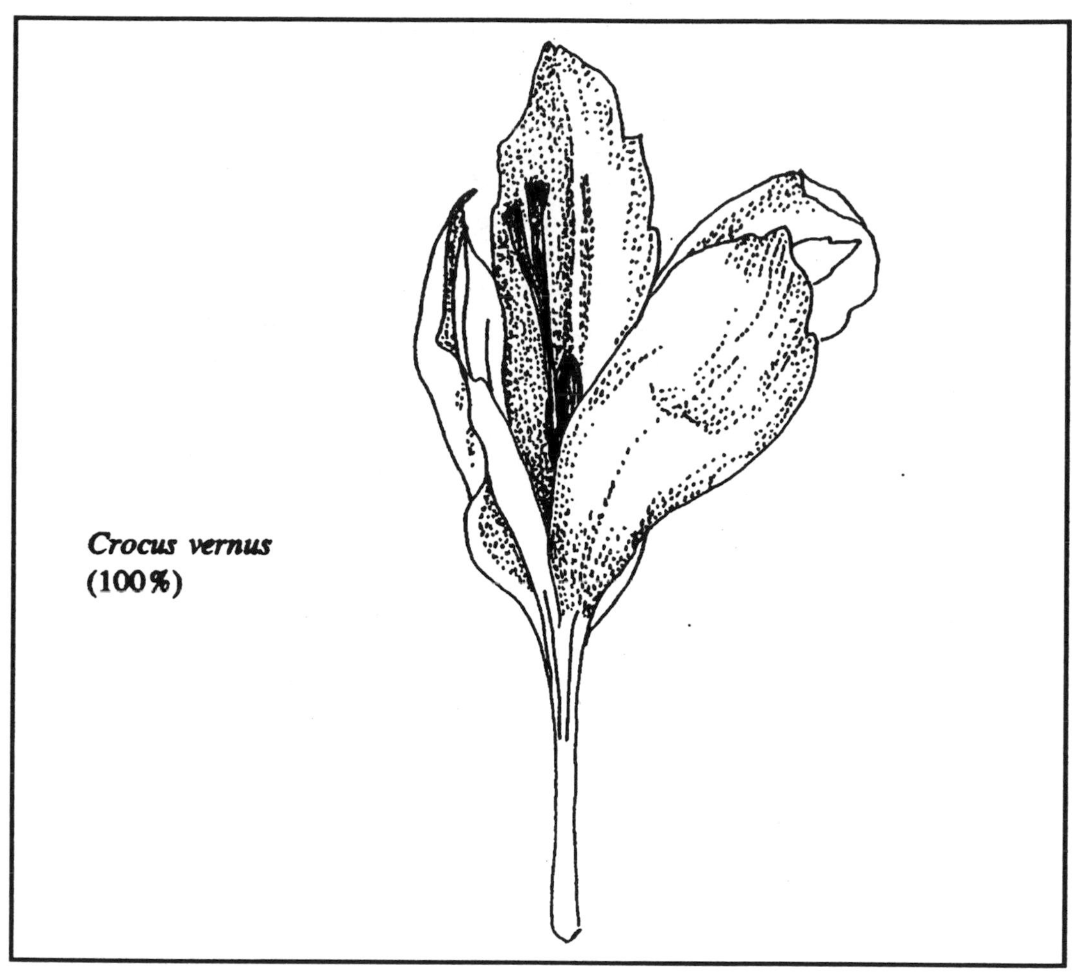

*Crocus vernus*
(100%)

'Enchantress' has lovely pale blue flowers.

'Flower Record' bears many dark purple flowers. Probably a little more long-lived than 'Queen of the Blues'.

'Jeanne d'Arc' is a clean white-flowered form that has performed well in many gardens.

'King of the Striped' must be a jealous rejoinder to 'Queen of the Blues'. Regardless, corms provide large creamy white flowers with many ugly purple stripes on the outside.

'Peter Pan' has large white flowers.

'Pickwick' ('Mr. Pickwick') has lilac flowers with dark blue stripes on the outside. It is the most popular of the striped cultivars.

'Queen of the Blues' has large deep violet flowers with yellow stamens.

'Remembrance' has purple flowers with a dark blue flower tube. This cultivar is often forced in dish or bowl gardens for Valentine's Day.

'Vanguard' has light mauve to purple flowers.

'Yellow Mammoth' is an apt name for this very popular large-flowered bright yellow selection. Although commonly offered as a typical Dutch hybrid, it is likely a hybrid of the yellow crocus, *C. flavus*.

***Cyclamen*** (cyke′ la-men) Hardy Cyclamen Primulaceae

Most people are familiar with the greenhouse cyclamen (*C. persicum*), a wonderful houseplant to cheer people up during the doldrums of winter. If given a plant in early spring, rise from your sick bed and place it in the garden after flowering. Although not meant for outdoor use, their mottled foliage makes them reasonably handsome garden plants, at least for the spring season. Chances are pretty good they will die over the winter if left in the ground.

However, there is a wealth of other useful species in this genus. Approximately 19 species are known and a half dozen are used in semi-shaded gardens for winter and early spring color. All arise from large, flattened corms and often have heart-shaped leaves and handsome mottled foliage. The distinctive fragrant flowers have reflexed petals borne on slender stalks.

The genus is centered in the Mediterranean basin with species in all countries except Spain, Morocco, Syria and Egypt. Most are native to rocky terrain in semi-arid locations, and excellent drainage is necessary for best performance and longevity. Without serious attention to drainage, success in the garden is unlikely. Some authors claim that five species are hardy in zones 5 (possibly 4) although I would not want to bet my house on their cold tolerance. Certainly many can be grown south of zone 6. One of our best growers of this genus is Nancy Goodwin, whose former nursery, Montrose Gardens, in Hillsboro, North Carolina, was an excellent source of information and hardy plant material. She separated the many species into fall, winter, spring and summer bloomers according to the following table.

| **Fall** | **Winter** | **Spring** | **Summer** |
|---|---|---|---|
| *C. africanum* | *C. coum* | *C. balearicum* | *C. purpurascens* |
| *C. cilicium* | *C. libanoticum* | *C. creticum* | |
| *C. graecum* | *C. parviflorum* | *C. pseudibericum* | |
| *C. hederifolium* | *C. trochopteranthum* | *C. repandum* | |
| *C. intaminatum* | | | |
| *C. mirabile* | | | |

The most cold hardy include *C. coum*, *C. hederifolium* and *C. trochopteranthum* followed by *C. cilicium*, *C. intaminatum* and *C. purpurascens*. *C. hederifolium* tolerates cold temperatures to about 0°F (zone 7) as do *C. coum* and *C. purpurascens* if soil is particularly well drained. If snow cover occurs regularly, then these species can tolerate temperatures as low as –20°F (zone 5) for short periods of time.

All cyclamen, except *C. purpurascens*, are summer dormant and can rot if drainage is poor and summer rains are excessive. I generally add some organic matter and small gravel to the soil when I first place the tubers. I place, not plant, the tubers almost on top of the soil, having barely scraped out a small crater. Once the plants become established, they will find their own comfort depth. In the heavy clay of north Georgia, about the only things covering the tubers are the oak leaves that fall each year. Even then, I lose my fair share. Some people are fortunate enough to have critters carry seed about the garden, but I have not yet found such friendly fellows. Most of the critters at my place scratch, dig, eat or smother; precious few have caught on to the "carry" bit. Although many species can be found with sufficient persistence, the easiest to locate and most hardy species is *C. hederifolium*.

One of the best reasons to plant hardy cyclamen is the least known, as it is a plant that can give the "no such thing as evolution" gang a run for their money. The environment under which they evolved was difficult and it was to the species' advantage to distribute seed near the parent plant. As the flowers fall off, the flower stem bearing the seeds begins to twist and coil until the stem capsule is brought close to the ground. The coiling was to insure that seeds fell in an area suitable for the plant, that is, right around it. Get down on your hands and knees and pull the fruit stem; it is like the small intestine, lots of length in a small space. I love demonstrating this unique characteristic, another great reason to be a gardener. The spiraling of the peduncle is responsible for the genus name, after the Greek *kyklos*, meaning circular.

Propagation is usually by seed. Soak newly collected seed for 24 hours prior to sowing in moist medium at temperatures of 60-65°F. Keep seeds in the dark until germination occurs. Germination occurs within 4 weeks; if not placed in darkness, seeds can take up to a year to germinate. After germination, place in the light and wait until small corms form at the base before transplanting. As a side note, there was, and still is to some degree, a huge trade in tubers dug from the wild. You are doing the world a favor by buying only nursery-produced tubers. Please check before you buy or better yet, buy the seed and produce your own. Two to three years is needed to reach flowering size.

***-hederifolium*** (he-de-ri-fo′ lee-um) Hardy Cyclamen 4-6″/12″
Fall Pink, White Southern Europe Zones 5-7

Few garden scenes are as delightful as a bed of pink and white hardy cyclamen gracing the base of a mature tree in a fall garden. One of the finest examples I have seen is at Snowshill Manor in the Cotswolds of England, although the scenes at Montrose Gardens, Chapel Hill, North Carolina are a close second. The pointed flower buds arise in the fall before the foliage and open into glorious stands of warm pink and white. The ivy-shaped leaves are up to 4-6″ long but more beautiful than any ivy. They are gray-green and have attractive patterns of purple marbling. The foliage persists all winter before going dormant in late spring. The leaves vary from deep green to a silver sheen. In the Armitage garden, the leaves begin to emerge in October, and fill in to a wonderful clump by mid-November. Flowering occurs from October to December, but the foliage continues into April, then plants are totally dormant by the first of June. Reseeding results in all sorts of wonderful foliage patterns.

Cyclamen should be planted in partial shade and out of afternoon sun in a soil amended with lime. They do not tolerate deep planting, particularly in areas of hot summers. Plant them so the top of the corms are only about ½″ below the surface.

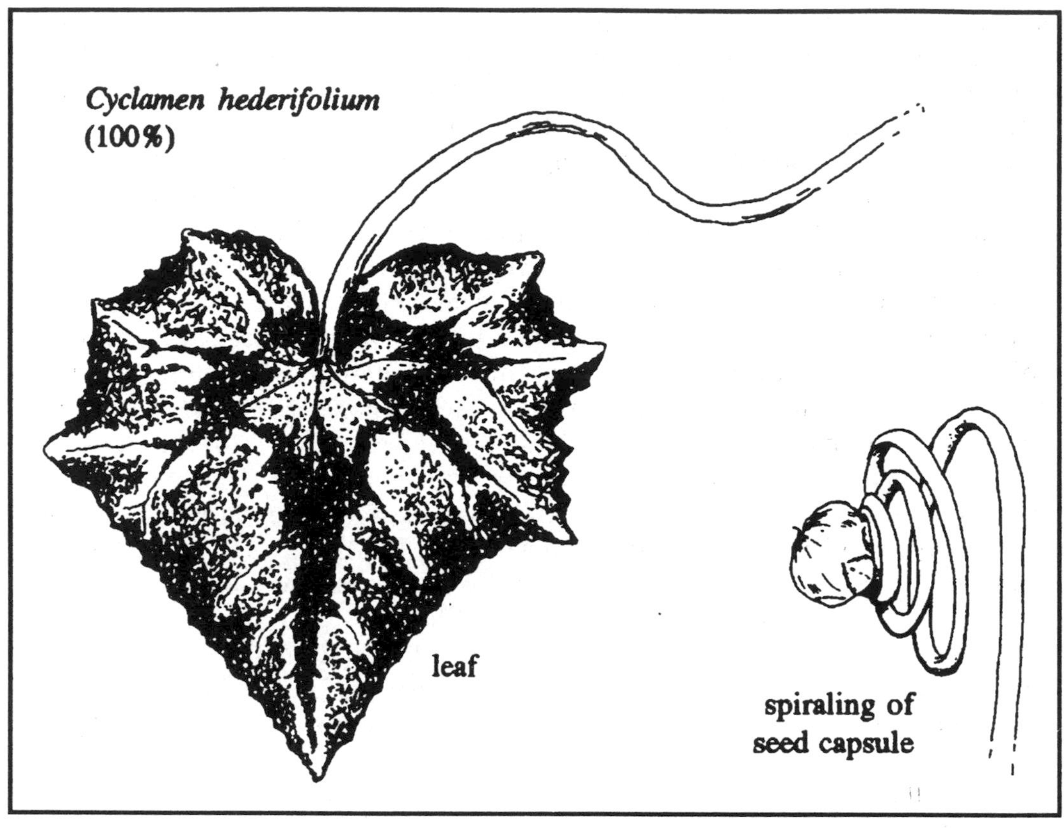


Since they are dormant in summer, supplemental water should not be applied where cyclamen are resting or corm rot may occur. Annuals such as begonias, which do not wilt readily, are excellent for overplanting. Once established, they persist for many, many years and need not be moved.

In the garden, plants multiply by seed or cormels. Dense plantings are the result of liberal formation of cormels, which may be removed in the fall after flowering has occurred

**Cultivars**:

A number of cultivars are available from bulb and specialty dealers. Because most are seed propagated, there are few absolutely stable clones, and leaf groupings are more sensible. That is, look for marbled leaf, or silver leaf or pewter leaf groupings, rather than a single cultivar name. The plants in that group may not be identical but they will have similar characteristics. The lack of similarity makes for some wonderful surprises. This is true for this species and maybe even more so for *C. coum*.

'Album' has white flowers. This variety is often interplanted with the pink species, making a beautiful combination.

'Silver Cloud' is the name given to silver-leafed forms of the plant. While the markings of some of the species forms are more definitive, this group is more subtle but equally beautiful.

**Related Species:**

*C. africanum* is quite beautiful but lacks the cold hardiness necessary to be an in-ground perennial. I love them in containers that can be brought in over winter. Flowers are pink and foliage is large and mottled.

*C. coum* are gaining in popularity as their availability increases. They may be a little more difficult to establish but are as cold tolerant as *C. hederifolium*. The flowers, which occur after *C. hederifolium*, are a vivid magenta to white, the leaves glossy green and plants are perhaps a little more dwarf than other hardy species. Flowering occurs in late fall and winter. This species and the selections are less well known than *C. hederifolium* but are at least as good, if not better, garden plants.

*C. pseudibericum* is cold hardy to zone 8 but more difficult to find. It is considered by many the most beautiful of all cyclamen. The flowers open with *Anenome blanda*. The rosy-red flowers that have a faint fragrance of violets.

***Cymbalaria*** (sim ba-lah′ ree-a) Kenilworth Ivy Scrophulariaceae

Approximately 10 species of short-lived creeping and vining plants are known but they are not seen nearly as much in the United State as they are in Europe. A few species are occasionally offered, growable in zones 6/7-10, but none does well in hot, humid areas. All can be rampant, aggressive growers in cool summers and moderate winters but can also provide a cool delight to the summer morning. *C. aequitriloba* hugs rocks, thrives in cracks and crevices of old walls and bears hundreds of tiny lavender-pink snapdragon-like flowers in late spring through the summer.
*C. hepaticifolia*, cold hardy to zone 7, uses its stoloniferous habit to creep and climb on walls and over rocks. Growing to about 2″ tall, the species bears small violet-blue flowers. A white-flowered form, 'Alba' is even more handsome.

The most common species is *C. muralis,* Kenilworth ivy, also known as coliseum ivy, pennywort and ivy-leaved toad flax. The shallowly lobed leaves are kidney shaped (reniform) to semi-circular and roots form at each node. Like English ivy (*Hedera*), the tenacious roots can find any moisture in walls or bark of trees to secure the plant. Covering walls or any cool, shady crevices with small scalloped foliage and lilac-blue flowers, they make pleasant backgrounds to old gardens. Provide areas of ample moisture for best performance.

'Alba' is a white-flowered form whose flowers make a terrific contrast to the light green foliage. A more compact form, var. *compacta* or var. *nana*, may also be used. 'Apple Court' is listed every now and then, but it is exceedingly difficult to find. Leaves are mottled and flowers are pink. 'Maxima' has larger flowers, but plants should not be selected for the flowers, but rather for the foliage.

Propagate by rooting the stems at any node.

***Cynara*** (si-nah′ ra) Cardoon Asteraceae

The genus is probably best represented by the globe artichoke, *C. scolymus*, a vegetable best known for the stares of disbelief from people expected to eat the thing. However, every now and then gardeners want a plant for its architectural value, and cardoon, *C. cardunculus*, is such a plant. Why else would anyone put a 6′ tall seriously prickly plant with lavender-purple flowers in his garden? The architectural part comes from the robust stature and deeply cut, handsome foliage, gray-green above and white, hairy below. They are at their architectural best from spring to midsummer, then depending on the severity of the summer, can look like an old, tired field thistle. People love them for their size and the contrast with other green-leaved plants growing with them. The flowers can be rather drab, but on the other hand, I have seen some spectacularly bright heads in my travels. More good luck and good locale than good management. Plants are native to the Mediterranean area and can be used as a short-lived perennial in zones 7-10, and as an annual elsewhere. They are worth the planting each year for the machismo. Provide full sun and well-drained soils.

## *Cynoglossum* (sy-no-gloss′ um) Hound's Tongue Boraginaceae

The fifty-five species have hairy stems and alternate, long stalked basal leaves that were said to resemble the tongue of a dog; hence the common name. Plants are valued for the intense blue of the flowers, but also may exhibit a range of colors from flower bud to flower death. The flowers are less than 1″ across and held in coiled inflorescences called scorpioid cymes. This genus differs from others in the Boraginaceae by having tubular flowers that evolve into small nutlets covered with prickles.

None of the perennial species is easy to locate but *C. nervosum*, with dark blue flowers and *C. virginianum*, with lighter blue flowers, are useful garden plants. The Chinese forget-me-not, *C. amabile*, is a 1-2′ tall biennial and has lovely funnel-shaped flowers of blue, pink, or white. 'Firmament' is more compact and bears particularly ornamental intense blue flowers.

It is difficult to tell the difference between some genera in the Boraginaceae and people ask me how to distinguish the genus *Cynoglossum* from *Lithodora*, particularly *L. diffusa*. Separation of the genera in the Boraginaceae is based on the flowers being rounded (*Borago*) or tubular (all others). The fruit is the easiest way to tell the difference between the two; the fruit of *Cynoglossum* is covered with prickles, the fruit of *Lithodora* is smooth. Another distinction is that the flowers on the inflorescence have small bracts (such as *Brunnera*, *Myosotis* and *Lithodora*). *Cynoglossum* does not have bracts at the base of the flowers. It takes a good bit of staring the first few times but then is a little easier. The people who asked were sorry they did.

**-*nervosum*** (ner-vo′ sum) Hairy Hound's Tongue 2-2½′/2′
Spring Blue Himalayas Zones 4-7

The leaves and stems are quite rough due to the presence of short stiff hairs. The 6-8″ long basal leaves are narrowly lanceolate, entire and petioled while the upper leaves are more oblong and sessile. Branching sprays of intensely blue forget-me-not-like flowers are produced in the upper axils as well as on the terminal shoot. The ½″ long flowers first appear in a rounded head which uncoils to a 6-9″ long erect inflorescence. Flowers persist for about four weeks.

Plants require abundant water and do not tolerate dryness. They may be planted in full sun in the northern part of their range but afternoon shade should be provided in zones 7 and 8. Rich soils are beneficial but heavy doses of fertilizer cause plants to grow tall and weak. Growing plants well in the South is difficult because the hairy leaves trap water and the high temperatures and humidity result in foliar disease.

Propagate from seed or divisions in fall or spring. Seed requires no special treatment other than sowing in a warm (70-75°F ), humid environment.

**Related Species:**

*C. grande*, Pacific hound's tongue, native to western North America, is occasionally seen in gardens in the West but seldom in the East. Plants are 1-2′ tall with bright blue flowers and oval, hairy leaves.

*C. virginianum*, wild comfrey, is native to open woodlands from Connecticut to Missouri and south to Texas and Florida. This little-known plant, with a basal rosette of soft-hairy leaves and ½″ wide pale blue spring flowers, is terrific for shade gardens. Plants return year after year and are innocently unaware of drought or flood. Much easier to grow, if not quite as colorful, for gardeners in the South or those with warm summers.

## *Cypripedium* Lady's Slipper Orchidaceae

People, including myself, love the pleated leaves, the slow-growing colonies and the slipper-like perfection of the pink and yellow flowers. They are a great deal tougher than they appear, but that is not to say I haven't lost my fair share. My orchid thumb seems to have atrophied years ago, but I am happy to report that due to better availability and more accessible information, other people are finding slippery success.

Sitting down beside a lady slipper and probing around the leaves and flowers is an exercise in plant diversity and adaptability. And who needs to apologize for being curious? Botanically, plants have two pollen-bearing stamens near the opening of the "slipper" but the third rudimentary stem bears no pollen and has a shield-like object visible in the center of the flower. A single green bract, similar to but smaller than the foliage, stands behind each flower. The leaves are always pleated by conspicuous veins that run from the base to the apex without branching.

Interest, however, is high among slipper aficionados and entire web sites and chat rooms help the addicted find and succeed with these marvelous orchids. I visit every now and then to enjoy the cacophony of sound and spirit as diehard orchidites provide spiritual guidance. Isn't gardening great?

I can think of two genera of native plants that everybody wants in their gardens, two genera that have been removed from the wild way too much, and two genera that usually die by the transplant shovel: *Trillium* and *Cypripedium*. And compared to travails of lady's slippers, trilliums have enjoyed a walk in the park.

Half a dozen species and selections are offered, and all have a high price tag (but so does a good steak, and these are far better for you). All are native to this country, but that does not mean they will love your soils. One of the easiest to purchase species is the 12-18″ tall pink lady slipper, *C. acaule*, which differs from others in that the stem is essentially underground. Plants generally bear two dark green leaves and a flower pouch that is usually pink, although the color can be almost white to deep rose. Plants are widespread in Canada (it is the provincial flower of Prince Edward Island) and extend as far south as the Smoky Mountains.

Two other marvelous species are the large yellow lady's slipper, *C. pubescens*, and *C. reginae*, showy lady's slipper. The flowers of the former consist of green to slightly brown petals and sepals and a yellow pouch with brown dots. They are big, bold and may have a dozen stems in a showy clump. The showy lady's slipper may be the most spectacular and beautiful of the lady's slippers, not lost on the fine citizens of Minnesota, who adopted it as their state flower. A century ago, the plant was a favorite summer adornment of rural church altars, however since 1925, it has been protected by Minnesota state law. In general, plants produce 5-7 pleated leaves and are one of the taller forms, growing 2-3′ in height. They are often found in moist, almost boggy conditions. The entire plant is hairy, and has been known to cause dermatitis on those trying to dig it from the wild. Well deserved, may they itch for ages.

Propagation is not easy but can be accomplished by seeds and division. Orchid seeds are extraordinarily small, and lack sufficient food sources necessary for germination. In nature, orchid seeds have developed a symbiotic relationship with beneficial fungi known as mycorrhiza, that provide nutrition to the developing seed. It is an interesting relationship, one that is difficult to reproduce in the garden. The fungi are beneficial throughout the life of the plant, but are essential in the early stages of development. Clumps can be divided by digging in early spring. The separated plantlets should have 1-3 fat, pointed buds on the division. Purchasing mature plants allows for more chance of success because the conditions for growth are less stringent as they mature.

Lady's slippers are routinely propagated today through tissue culture, allowing more and more growers to produce them. Therefore being a smart shopper is not difficult and highlights your intelligence; digging them from the wild shows you are dumber than a rock. That is not to say that the plants will thrive in your garden, but now instead of breaking the law to bring home plants that die, you can pay good money to do the same thing. At least your friends will still talk to you.

**Related Species:**

*C. parviflorum*, small yellow lady's slipper, is similar to *C. pubescens*, having smaller and brighter yellow flowers. The petals of *C. parviflorum* are brownish with little green color, and its range extends a little further south. Equally beautiful. Numerous hybrids have been developed in Germany using this and European species, under such names as 'Aki' (pink), "Emil' (yellow) and 'Sabine' (light pink).

## ***Cyrtomium*** (cer-tom-ee′ um) Holly Fern Dryopteridaceae

Holly ferns are often seen in floral decorations and dish gardens, but of the 20 or so species, two or three are candidates for the shaded, moist garden. They are prized for the evergreen, shiny, once-pinnate fronds that contrast well with other plants. I think some of the finest plantings occur at Sea Island Resort on Sea Island, Georgia.

*Calamagrostis × acutiflora* 'Karl Foerster'

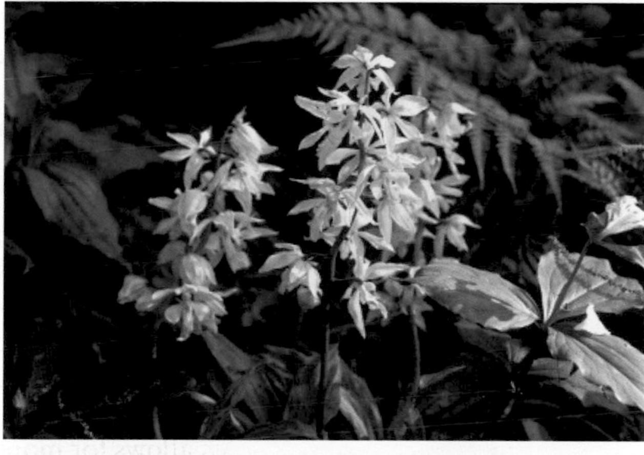

*Calanthe sieboldii*

*Callirhoe bushii*

*Camassia leichtlinii* 'Lady Eva Price'

*Campanula carpatica*
*'White Clips'*

*Carex ciliatomarginata*
'Treasure Island'

*Carex elata*
'Bowle's Golden'

*Caryopteris divaricata*
'Snow Fairy'

*Caryopteris* × *clandonensis*
'Longwood Blue'

*Ceratostigma plumbaginoides*

*Chionodoxa forbsii*
'Pink Giant'

*Clematis integrifolia*

*Colchicum autumnale*
'Waterlily'

*Coreopsis grandiflora*
'Sunfire'

*Coreopsis*
'Autumn Blush'

*Coreopsis*
'Pinwheels'

*Coreopsis*
'Sweet Dreams'

*Coreopsis rosea*
'Heaven's Gate'

*Crocosmia*
'Lucifer'

*Crocosmia*
'Star of the East'

*Dahlia*
'Moonfire'

*Dahlia*
'Murdock'

*Dianthus barbatus*
'Sooty'

*Dicentra*
'King of Hearts'

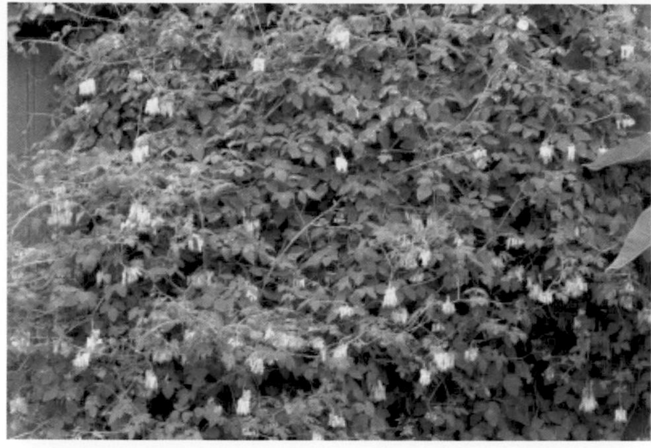

*Dicentra scandens*
'Athens Yellow'

*Dicentra spectabilis*
'Gold Heart'

*Digitalis parviflora*

*Diphylleia cymosa*

*Dodecatheon meadia*

*Doronicum carpetanum*

*Dryas octopetala*

*Dryopteris celsa*

Shining in the landscape, they act as lustrous green fillers in the landscape as well as bringing out the colors in the annuals nearby.

The Japanese holly fern, *C. falcatum*, with its glossy, leathery fronds that are curved sideways, resembling a scythe or sickle (falcate) is the most common. The margins are entire or slightly wavy (undulate). They are hardy in zone 7 to 10 but can be devastated by winter winds and abnormally cold temperatures. They have survived winter temperatures of about 0°F with no snow cover in the Armitage garden but the fronds were badly desiccated and brown on the margins. The next summer was a slow one indeed. 'Butterfieldii' has sharply serrated foliage, 'Rochfordianum' is a popular cultivar that differs by having coarsely toothed or lobed margins.

The most cold hardy of the group is *C. fortunei*, native to Japan and cold hardy to zone 6 (5 with adequate protection). It differs from *C. falcatum* by having more pairs of pinnae or segments (12-26 pairs in *C. fortunei*, 3-11 pairs in *C. falcatum)*, and narrower and longer, more drawn-out segments. I have this throughout my garden and it is less prone to winter damage and has a wonderful upright habit. This is, without doubt, the best choice of the holly ferns for most outdoor situations north of zone 8.

Another handsome fern in this little-used group is large-leaved holly fern, *C. macrophyllum*, hardy in zones 7-10. The plants are not as full as the others mentioned, having only 2-8 pairs of entire or slightly toothed pinna on each frond. Each pair, however, is larger and the terminal segment is usually 3-lobed.

Site all species in light to heavy shade and water well in the spring and early summer. If fronds are badly damaged over the winter, trim back in the spring and fertilize with a slow-release fertilizer.

# D

***Dactylorhiza*** (dak-til-o-rise′ a) Marsh Orchid Orchidaceae

There is no overwhelming or even sensible reason to include this genus in a book for most North American gardeners; however, like the alluring *Meconopsis*, its beauty combined with its degree of difficulty brings out the obstinance in many gardeners. If these stately, terrestrial orchids can be established, they are quite trouble-free. The main problem is that they nearly always die, but other than that, they are terrific. If the masochist in you still wants to give them a try, you will then find that most species are almost unavailable to gardeners in this country anyway. However, if you have persevered, and once you have them in your hand, be sure that you place them in moist, but not wet, conditions and temperate temperatures.

*Dactylorhiza* is one of the most eye-catching garden orchids, and while they may be successfully grown in the Northwest and a few areas of the Northeast, seldom will they look as good as they do in the British Isles or wherever else you fell in love with them. After saying all that, I know that some readers will be growing these plants everywhere. My friend, Don Jacobs of Eco-Gardens in Decatur, Georgia contends that a number of them are reasonably easy given proper conditions for growing. If you are successful, ignore the previous remarks and spread the word.

Approximately 30 species are known, all of which arise from finger-like tubers. Most are native to Europe, Asia, and North Africa, although *D. aristata* is also found in North America. The pink to deep purple flowers consist of lipped flowers (like snapdragons) and are spurred (like columbine). The most common species, *D. elata*, robust marsh orchid, is 1-2″ tall and bears pink to maroon flowers. *D. foliosa* also produces unspotted, light green foliage with stately, purple flowers. *D. maculata*, spotted marsh orchid, is similar to the above but has spotted foliage, and is perhaps the most handsome.

The tubers persist for one year, and new tubers are produced on the fingers of the old ones. Do not disturb unless necessary. Provide areas rich in compost with high water-holding capacity. Afternoon shade is helpful. Beautiful plants, but don't buy a dozen until you first try one or two.

***Dahlia*** (dah′ lee-a) Dahlia Asteraceae

Although approximately twenty species occur, it is mainly the hybrids that grace gardens today. Dahlias originate from Central and South America and have a long history of cultivation. Dahlias were probably an important crop to the Aztecs, used as animal feed and in the treatment of urinary disorders. The Aztec word for dahlia was *cocoxochitl*, meaning water pipes, and their use as a urinary treatment was based on the Doctrine of Signatures (see *Pulmonaria*). The long stems of the tree dahlia (*D. imperialis*) were also used to transport water from mountain springs to villages. The modern garden dahlia is thought to be derived from three Mexican species: *D. pinnata*, Aztec dahlia, with double, purple flowers; *D. coccinea*, fire dahlia, with single, red flowers; and *D. rosea*, old garden dahlia, with single, pink flowers. Dahlias have a natural tendency to hybridize, and breeders in the 19th century took full advantage, deriving new hybrids from chance seedlings. Throughout Europe and the United States, the passion for dahlias in the 1840s matched the tulip mania of the 17th century in intensity and exorbitant prices realized.

Since its introduction to Europe in the early 1800s, thousands of cultivars have been raised, particularly in France, England, Germany, Holland, and United States, resulting in approximately 20,000 cultivars listed in the *International Register of Dahlia Names*, first started in 1966. These efforts have resulted in plants ranging from 1-8′ tall, with flowers up to 12″ across. Plants may bear huge, spider-like flowers or tiny, pompon-like balls. One of the more recent trends in dahlias is the use of seed-propagated dwarfs for bedding plants. They can be raised true from seed, allowing greenhouse operators to offer them far more inexpensively than before. The demand for shorter plants combined with the desire for ornamental foliage has resulted in cultivars with dark mahogany to rich purple foliage. One such recent development (2007) is the Mystic series; plants which grow 3-3½′ tall and bear rich purple filigreed leaves. Four colors of single flowers have been introduced.

There are so many shapes, colors, and sizes of flowers that they have been arranged into different groups by the International Registration Authority and used by the American Dahlia Society. The groups are based on the morphology of the head and flowers and are listed below. To obtain a more in-depth listing and definition of various classifications, and appropriate cultivars for each, consult the American Dahlia Society.

Regardless of the seemingly infinite hybrids, occasionally one can find a few species offered. Perhaps these have been saved for those who love a combination of beauty and history. While in Auckland, New Zealand, I had the pleasure of seeing the 12′ tall tree dahlias, *D. imperialis* upon which dozens of pink flowers occurred in the fall. Quite unbelievable to people used to seeing manicured hybrids. In this country, they are likely frost-tolerant to zone 7b; however, they are not particularly happy with high humidity and heat. In the Northwest, they are marginal in that an early frost may cut down the flowers before they open, but well worth trying. Another tree species that flowers over a much longer period of time is *D. tenuicaulis*, with single,

| Group Name | Description |
|---|---|
| Single | Open-centered blooms with one or two outer rows of ray flowers surrounding a disc. Common in bedding plant forms. |
| Anemone | One or more rows of ray flowers surrounding a dense group of upward-pointing, tubular florets. |
| Collarette | Open-centered, surrounded by an inner ring of short florets (the collar) and one or two outer rows of usually flattened ray flowers. |
| Waterlily | Fully double blooms, with broad ray flowers which are flat or slightly incurved. The overall effect is a flat or shallow bloom, as in a waterlily. |
| Decorative | Blooms fully doubled, with no central disc, with broad, flat or slightly inwardly rolled ray flowers. The tips of the ray flowers may also be cut (fimbricated). |
| Ball | Ball-shaped or globose, often slightly flattened at the top. The ray flowers are blunt or rounded at the tips. |
| Pompon | Similar to Ball types, but more globose in shape. Flower heads are not flattened but almost circular. |
| Cactus | Fully double blooms showing no central disc. The ray flowers are long and narrow and tightly rolled (revolute) for over half the length. Subdivided into those with long, straight rays and those in which the ray flowers curve upward. |
| Semi-cactus | Fully double blooms, with slightly pointed ray flowers which are broader at the base than at the tips. Revolute for less than half their length and either straight or curving. |
| Miscellaneous | A group of relatively small, variable classes. Examples include Orchid-flowered, Peony-flowered, Star-flowered, etc. |

lavender flowers on 6′ tall plants. Both are woody when mature. However, my favorite has to be *D. merckii,* Merk's dahlia, with its hundreds of lavender flowers on a shrub-like 3′ structure. Find it, buy it. Zone 7.

Dahlias have tender, tuberous roots, normally lifted at first frost. Although they can be left in the ground in zones 7(7b)-10 (assuming good winter drainage), some gardeners report that lifting the roots even in those zones results in better performance the following year. After lifting, soak the roots in a fungicide, and store in a cool area in moist, but not wet, peat moss or sand. Inspect them occasionally over the winter for rot and moisture.

Propagation is accomplished by separating the tubers at planting time. At least one bud or eye must be present on the separated piece of tuber; otherwise no growth will occur. Use a sharp knife for separation of the tubers. Dipping the knife in rubbing alcohol or peroxide before each cut reduces the spread of disease organisms. Cuttings from the base of the plant can also be used as propagation material. Take 1-1½″ long terminal growth from the basal shoots, apply rooting hormone, and root in a warm, humid area. If cuttings are taken early in the season, plants should flower the first year.

Dahlias are certainly not low-maintenance plants in most areas of the country. Many require support to prevent flopping and are prone to mosaic, stunt, and ring spot viruses, as well as fungal and bacterial problems. Insects feast on them, the worst are aphids and spider mites. However, some people would not have a garden without dahlias and are willing to spend the time necessary to show off their brilliance, because brilliant they are when properly grown.

I have been fortunate to see three of the loveliest plantings anywhere in the Western world. One of these was in Vancouver, British Columbia when my colleagues and I visited Queen Elizabeth Park. Brilliant beds of decorative-, spider-, and anemone-flowered dahlias shimmered in the late afternoon light, and we marveled at their uniformity and color range. On my return to Georgia, I looked at the gaps in my garden where I had yanked out my 4′ tall, lanky, spider mite-infested plants and again pondered the fact that certain species of plants are simply more content in some climates than others. The beauty of the Vancouver planting was challenged by the dahlia garden at Anglesey Abbey near Cambridge, England, where a great semicircular swath of 3-5′ tall plants boasted magnificent flowers of every shape and color. Each photograph I took was to be the last, but each new plant found me exclaiming and firing away with my Nikon. I finally pulled myself from that glorious Garden of Eden, very proud of the self-discipline I demonstrated. Running out of film and the onset of darkness also helped. And not to be outdone, any trip to Swan Island Dahlias in Oregon will leave you breathless and broke. There should be a law against selling plants in gardens that beautiful.

In the South, dahlias need to be sprayed every other week for spider mites, something I am not willing to do. I must admit that for me, dahlias are not worth the problems involved trying to raise them well. I no longer grow dahlias in my southern garden, but now I have a great excuse to travel to Oregon, Vancouver and England again.

***Darmera*** (dar-mer′ a) Umbrella Plant Saxifragaceae

A single, water-loving species, *D. peltata*, is grown, which used to be known as *Peltiphyllum peltatum*. The species is large and aggressive and definitely not a plant for the small backyard garden. Sometimes known as the "poor man's gunnera."

***-peltata*** (pel-tay′ ta) Umbrella Plant, Indian Rhubarb 3-5′/6′
Spring Pink California, Oregon Zones 5-7

The peltate leaves (the petiole is attached to the leaf inside the margin, usually near the middle) are 6-18″ across, have 6-10 lobes, and are much paler beneath than above. The leaf petioles arise directly from the rhizome and are cylindrical and hairy. Plants are best suited for shaded stream banks, beside ponds, or any watery environment where the roots may be constantly cool and moist. The flowers are small, about ½″ across, pink to white and are borne in tall (3′) terminal cymes, providing a bergenialike appearance. They appear on bristly stems before the leaves appear but remain attractive long after the plant has leafed out. Plants do well as far south as zone 7 (occasionally zone 8) but only if constant moisture is provided. The thick, matted roots make plants most effective as stabilizers for muddy or marshy banks. However, be warned, not even your trusty John Deere will get these out of the ground once established.

This species is often confused with *Peltoboykinia tellimoides* (syn. *Boykinia tellimoides*, *Saxifraga tellimoides*), also a relatively large, coarse, water plant. *D. peltata* is taller and has larger leaves with more lobes. However, the flowers of *P. tellimoides* occur with the leaves in early summer and are white, much larger, and somewhat campanulate. To be sure, the number of stamens may be counted. They both have 10; however, those of *P. tellimoides* are arranged in two groups of five, while those of *D. peltata* are separate. See the section on *Peltoboykinia* for differences between some of the large-leaved water plants.

Propagate by division with a pickaxe or backhoe in the summer or fall.

**Cultivars:**

'Nana' is a dwarf (12-18″ tall) plant that allows some smaller water gardens the luxury of including this species. Much better behaved as well.

***Delosperma*** (del-o-sperm' a) Ice Plant Aizoaceeae

The hardy ice plants are mostly native to the hot-dry climates of South and East Africa and form mats of succulent foliage and bright, daisy-like flowers. They are terrific plants for hot sunny locations where soils are well drained. There are approximately 150 species in this variable genus, and more and more are being offered each year. It was not so long ago that I was hard pressed to come up with two or three, today I can find ten selections in the Bluebird Nursery catalog (Clarkson, Nebraska) alone.

The two main species are *D. cooperi*, purple hardy ice plant, and the more popular *D. nubigenum*, orange-yellow hardy ice plant. The main difference between them is pretty obvious from the common names. Both are native to South Africa, need full sun, and do best on banks or in dry rock gardens. Flowering starts in mid-spring and persists for 4-6 weeks, after which light green, succulent foliage remains as a handsome reminder of the bright flowers. The fluorescent, purple-red flowers of *D. cooperi* are almost 2″ wide and plants are about 6″ tall, while the orange-yellow flowers of *D. nubigenum* are a little less than 1″ wide on 2-3″ tall matted plants. The other main difference is that *D. nubigenum* is more cold tolerant, performing as far north as zone 5, while planting *D.* cooperi north of zone 7 is risky. I have seen only one cultivar offered, that of *D. n.* 'Basutoland', perhaps being more yellow than the species.

**Additional Species:**

*D. aberdeenense* is hardy to zone 6 and produces red-purple flowers on 3″tall plants.

*D. congestum* 'Gold Nugget' has dozens of golden flowers on 2-3″ tall plants. Tolerates afternoon shade, hardy to zone 4.

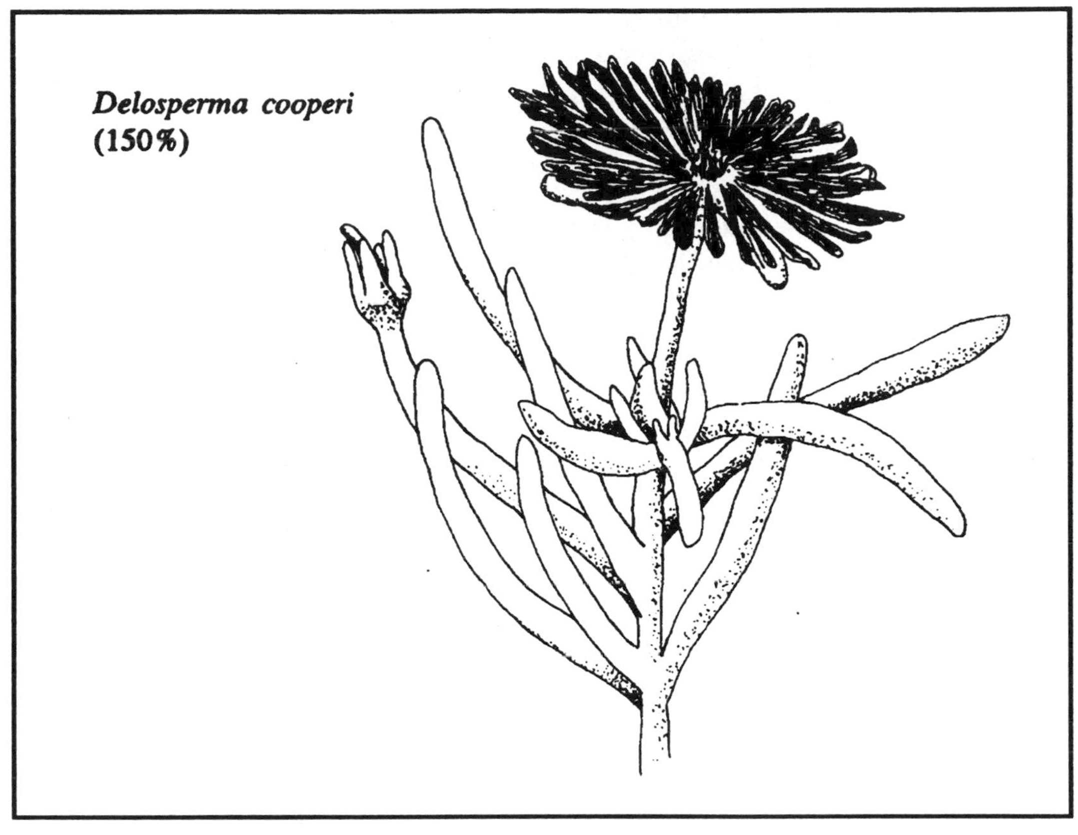
*Delosperma cooperi*
(150%)

*D. sphalmanthoides,* tufted ice plant, is known by few and offered by fewer. It only grows 1″ or so tall but spreads well if provided dry sunny conditions. Plants bear fuchsia flowers in the spring. Zone 4.

**Hybrids:**

Additional ice plants have recently become available through the interest of nurserymen and plant hunters, including Panayoti Kelaidis and the people at the Denver Botanic Garden. In all cases, plants do best in hot dry conditions; wet feet result in a sure, quick death. All perform in zones 5-8 unless otherwise indicated. They should become more available as gardeners discover their versatility. Excellent drainage is a must for all ice plants.

'Beaufort West' is only about 1″ tall, but bears small succulent leaves and pink flowers in the spring. Discovered at high elevations in South Africa, plants do far better in the summer in Denver than in areas with more heat and humidity. Cold hardy to perhaps zone 6.

'Grahamstown Ghost' has clean white daisies with long narrow petals. Plants grow about 3″ tall. Zones 7-8.

'John Proffitt', named for the former director of the Denver Botanic Garden, has deep purple to magenta flowers on 3″ tall plants.

'Kelaidis' is about 2″ tall with salmon-pink flowers. Plants flower for a long time, compared to many others. Perhaps more cold hardy than others, zone 5.

'Starburst' is thought to be a cultivar of *D. floribunda*, has 2″ wide lilac flowers with white centers. The leaves are narrow, almost needlelike. Plant Select® is a cooperative program administered by Denver Botanic Gardens and Colorado State University, and this plant was highlighted there in 1998.

***Delphinium*** (del-fin′ ee-um) Delphinium Ranunculaceae

There is nothing more "English" in an English garden than spikes of delphiniums soaring to the heavens. Although over 300 species of annuals, biennials, and perennials occur, most delphiniums seen in today's gardens are usually complex hybrids whose development began in the late 1800s. However, with the rediscovery and increased availability of native species and dwarf forms, that is changing slowly.

The leaves are palmately lobed, or divided, and plants grow from 9″ (*D. tatsienense*) to 6′ tall (*D. elatum*). Although blue is the dominant color in the genus, red (*D. nudicaule*) and yellow (*D. zalil*) flowers also occur. *Delphinium* is closely related to *Aconitum*, differing in having a spurred, rather than a hooded, sepal and four, rather than two, petals. The flowers consist of five sepals, one of which is spurred into a distinctive spur and small petals. However, the two genera are similar in that they both prefer northern latitudes and are poor perennials in the South (further south than zone 6).

Larkspur is the common name for annuals of this genus, but taxonomic changes placed two popular annual species in the genus *Consolida*. The common larkspur, *C. ambigua*, and the candle larkspur, *C. regalis*, are still occasionally listed as *D. ajacis* and *D. consolida*, respectively. Is it any wonder why so many people prefer common names?

In most areas of the country, delphiniums are short-lived perennials and often lose vigor after 2-3 years. Many excellent cultivars can be raised from seed, and new plants should be grown for replacement each year. In the South, plants are placed outside in fall or early winter to flower in early spring. After flowering, they should be pulled and replaced with warm-season plants. A well-drained soil with a basic pH (adding lime to the soil helps provide this condition) and full sun are preferable. They are heavy feeders, and the use of well-rotted compost or manure, in combination with granular fertilizer such as 5-10-5 or 8-8-8, results in stronger, more vigorous plants. The two common hybrids of delphinium are the *elatum* and *belladonna* types; both have hollow and brittle stems, which if not staked, can be ravaged by rain and wind. Removing spent flower stems as soon as possible allows formation of secondary blooms in the fall.

Numerous native species may be seen in the higher elevations of several central and southern states and in the Rocky Mountain area. On each and every visit to the Smoky Mountains of North Carolina, I screech to a halt whenever *D. elatum* is spotted. As my family peels themselves off the backs of seats and the windshield, I jump out to admire the 6′ tall spires of blue or occasionally white flowers. The segments of the leaves are wide and shallowly cut. Plants are native from Pennsylvania to Ohio and south to North Carolina and Alabama. Smaller species include the greenish white *D. virescens* and the 4′ tall, deep blue or purple flowers of the Carolina delphinium, *D. carolinianum*. The Carolina delphinium is the most heat-tolerant species, extending to the sand hills of Florida. In the central and western states, there are dozens of species from the creamy yellow *D. xantholeucum* of the Wenatchee Mountains to the variable blue flowers of *D. geyeri* of the western plains. It is unfortunate that so few nurseries raise these wonderful native plants, but perhaps it is best that they are admired from a distance.

Propagation can be accomplished, albeit with difficulty, by seed. Germination is most successful if seed is collected fresh and sown as soon as possible. If this is not possible, store the seeds in the refrigerator (35-40°F) for 4-6 weeks. Germination should occur in 14-21 days. A more reliable method of propagation is basal cuttings in the spring. Take 3-4″ long terminals of new shoots arising from the base of the plants. The base of the cutting should be solid (i.e., not hollow) and white. They can be rooted in partial shade in sand or sand/peat mix in 3-4 weeks.

The major pest is slugs, which find delphinium shoots particularly delectable, while crown rot is a severe disease in poorly drained soils or where plants have been planted too deeply. Powdery mildew and various leaf blights can also be serious problems in all delphiniums.

Quick Reference to Delphinium Hybrids and Species

| | Height (ft.) | Single/double flowers | Branched or single flower spike |
|---|---|---|---|
| *D. belladonna* hybrids | 3-4 | Single | Branched |
| *D. elatum* hybrids | 4-8 | Single, double | Single |
| *D. exaltatum* | 4-6 | Single | Branched |
| *D. tricorne* | 1-2 | Single | Single |

***-belladonna*** (bell-ah′ don-a) Belladonna Delphinium 3-4′/3′
Summer Blue Shades Hybrid Zones 3-7

The belladonna hybrids resulted from crosses between forms of *D. elatum* and *D. grandiflorum*, a 2′ tall, blue-flowered species. Most cultivars are shorter and more branched than *D. elatum* cultivars. Instead of a central flower stem followed by smaller branches, as in *D. elatum*, many flower stems of belladonnas occur at the same time, although the central stem still dominates. Flowering occurs from midsummer to fall. Most cultivars have single, cup-shaped flowers which are often sterile.

**Cultivars:**

'Bonita' has gentian-blue flowers.

'Bellamosum' produces deep blue flowers on 4′ tall plants.

'Casa Blanca' has pure white blossoms.

'Cliveden Beauty' bears sky blue flowers and grows 3′ tall.

'Lamartine' has deep violet flowers on 4′ high stems.

'Moerheimii' has white flowers but is not as vigorous as 'Casa Blanca'.

'Pennant Mix' is a seed-propagated strain with blue, lavender, creamy white, and rose flowers. Flowers tend to be single.

'Volkerfrieden' ('World Peace') is a fabulous selection with deep blue flowers. This is an unusually good cut flower form.

'Wendy' bears gentian-blue flowers on 12-15″ tall plants.

***-elatum*** (ee-lay′ tum) Hybrid Bee Delphinium 4-8′/3′
Summer Various Hybrid Zones 2-7

These hybrids likely resulted from crosses between *D. elatum*, *D. exaltatum*, and *D. formosum*, and although early records were lost, *D. elatum* was surely one of the parents. Hybridization and selection by nurseries in England, Germany, and America resulted in groups of plants referred to as strains or series. Within these groups are plants with different flower colors, but similar in habit and culture. They include the Blackmore and Langdon strains, Pacific Hybrid series (also known as the Round Table series), Wrexham strain, New Century hybrids, and others with equally imaginative names. All are characterized by having large, flat flowers on a central flower raceme. This group of plants has long been the favorite of gardeners everywhere, and in areas with cool summer nights and days, they still are. Seeing them in their glory, as we did to a trip to the Gaspe area of eastern Canada, is a near religious experience. However, enough people in other parts of the continent have spent so much time and money and come away with little else but frustration that the use of hybrid delphiniums, except for the most northern states and Canada, is on the wane.

Additional flowering spikes arise from the base, especially if the first inflorescence is removed immediately after flowering. These are the aristocrats of the garden, and in cool climates, such as in the Pacific Northwest and the Northeast, and much of Canada, plants will last up to 5 years, performing better each year. In the Midwest and Central Plain states, 2-3 years of enjoyment is not uncommon.

**Cultivars:**

For simplicity's sake, cultivars are arranged by height. The following are but a small fraction of those available.

Tall (greater than 4′):

*Giant Imperial Series:*

'Blue Spires', 'Blue Bell', and 'Rosalind' belong to this series. They are often listed as perennials but are mainly derived from annual larkspur, *C. regalis*. Due to the short-lived nature of delphiniums in most parts of the country, there is often little difference in longevity between these and the previous hybrid types.

*Mid-Century Hybrids:*

This relatively new strain bears flowers of pink ('Rose Future'), white ('Ivory Towers'), light blue ('Moody Blues'), and dark blue ('Ultra Violet'). They are 4-5′ tall, have stronger stems than other tall delphiniums, and are more resistant to mildew.

*New Millenium series:*

Bred by Dowdeswell's Delphiniums in New Zealand, at least ten selections have been made available. More are surely on the way. Most are 3-4′ tall.

'Blue Lace' has lavender blue flowers with a tinge of pink.
'Blushing Brides' has large pink to rosy-colored flowers.
'Green Twist' bears white flowers with a tinge of green. Areas of full sun should be avoided, a little afternoon shade results in better performance.
'Innocence' produces pure white flowers, occasionally double.
'Misty Mauves' bears frilly light blue flowers with a darker eye.
'Morning Lights' has lavender-pink flowers with white eyes. More lavender than pink.
'Pagan Purples' usually has double blue to purple flowers.
'Purple Passion' bears deep purple flowers with a white center.
'Royal Aspirations' produces a mix of blue to purple flowers with white centers.
'Sunny Skies' bears single and double light sky blue flowers, quite beautiful.

*Pacific Giant Hybrids:*

It has been stated by several experts that the original strains of Pacific Hybrids have been lost, and a great deal of variability is now commonplace. However, seeds and plants are still commonly available. All the Pacific Hybrids are usually raised from seed; therefore, variation in color is common.

'Alice Artindale' has bright blue double flowers on dense racemes.
'Astolat' has lavender-pink flowers with a black center.
'Black Knight' is the darkest of the series, bearing dark purple, almost black, flowers.
'Blue Bird' has clear blue flowers with a white center.
'Cameliard' is 6′ tall, with lavender-blue flowers.
'Galahad' has magnificent white flowers and is one of the latest of the series to flower.
'Guinevere' bears lavender flowers with a tinge of pink and a white bee. The contrast in color sometimes gives the impression of a bicolor.
'Lancelot' has lavender flowers with a white eye.
'King Arthur' is a most impressive 3-5′ tall, dark blue-flowering selection.
'Summer Skies' is light blue with a white center.

*Independents:*

Many delphiniums have been bred as independent cultivars, not closely allied to a particular strain or series, and because of this, they may be more difficult to locate.

'Betty Hayes' has pale blue flowers with a white eye.
'Canada' is sky-blue with a black eye.
'Coral Sunset' has handsome coral flowers in 4′ tall plants. Zone 5.
'Cressida' bears pale blue flowers with a white eye but is taller and more vigorous than 'Betty Hayes'.
'Jack Tar' is very late flowering and has large, rich, dark blue flowers.
'Xenia Field' produces beautiful pale lavender flowers with a creamy white center.

Small (2½-3½′ tall):

These require less staking and are most impressive in groups of 3-5 plants.

*Centurion Series*

Bred by the Sahin Company in the Netherlands, they feature upright stems with semi-double flowers. They offer plants with blue, rose and white. About 3′ tall.

*Connecticut Yankee Series:*

Similar to the belladonna types, cultivars are more heavily branched than many of the previous selections. 'Blue Fountains' is one of my favorites because of its reliability as far south as zone 7. Flowers are produced in various shades of blue, white, and mauve. 'Baby Doll' has pale mauve flowers with a yellow-white eye.

*Magic Fountains Strain:*

Plants occur in lilac, white, white with a dark center, dark blue, sky blue, and pink. Generally they grow about 2½-3′ tall.

***-exaltatum*** Tall Larkspur 4-6′/2′
Spring Blue North America Zones 5-7

Mainstream gardeners have finally discovered native delphiniums, and nurseries who have forever been shouting their merits into gale force winds for years are now trying to keep up with demand. This species is probably the most commonly offered native delphinium, although others are hot on its tracks. The vigorous plants typically grow 4-6′ tall, bearing loose terminal racemes of gentian blue flowers, each only about an inch long. Although the flowers don't bloom until late summer or early fall, the palmately divided 3-5 lobed, deep green foliage is handsome nearly all season. Not only that, the flowers are persistent for weeks. People are actually suggesting that their delphinium money should be spent on these, and not on those English hybrids. What a refreshing thought. Plants perform better in afternoon shade than in full sun, particularly in the South. Plants are native to woods and rocky slopes in higher elevations from Pennsylvania to Ohio, south to Alabama and North Carolina.

Plants are grown from seed. Deadhead spent flowers if you wish the foliage to remain healthy. Otherwise allow seeds to fall and additional plants may occur.

***-tricorne*** Dwarf Larkspur 12-18″/12″
Spring Blue North America Zones 4-7

Wonderful plantings occur at the must-see Mt. Cuba Center in Delaware as well as many other gardens featuring native plants. It is also more readily available through mail order nurseries, so it might get into a few gardens yet. The antithesis of tall larkspur, plants attain only about 16″ in height and bear but a few blue to dark purple flowers in the spring. Regardless of its diminutive height and less than All-American flowering, they are handsome in their own right. Flowers fade quickly once they have been pollinated. Plants prefer a good deal of moisture, so keep them moist if possible. Plants are native to woods and rocky slopes from Pennsylvania to Minnesota and Nebraska, south to Oklahoma, Arkansas, Alabama and Georgia.

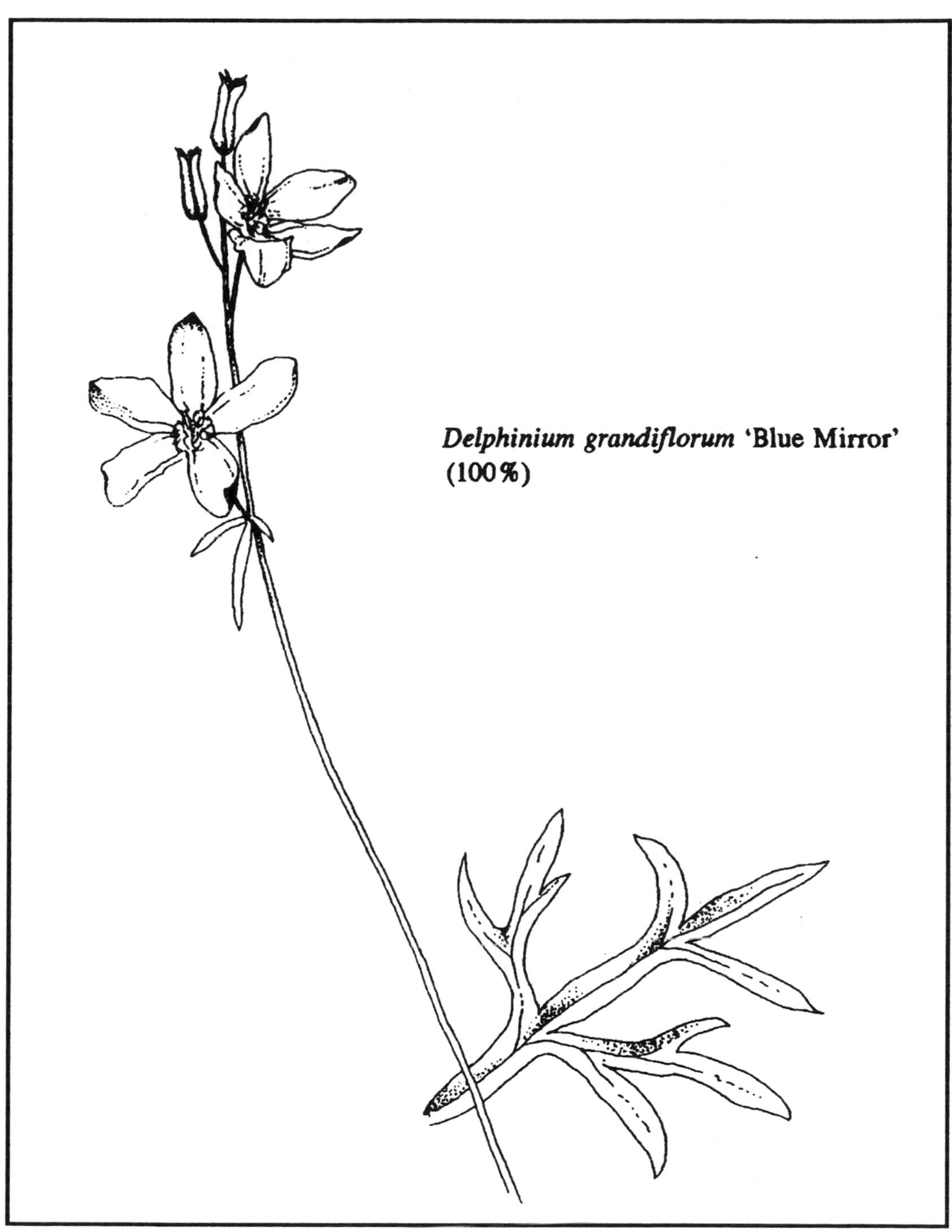

*Delphinium grandiflorum* 'Blue Mirror'
(100%)

**Additional Species:**

*D. caroliniana* produces loose racemes of blue flowers from a basal rosette in the spring. A number of subspecies of the plants are offered, differing by shape of the foliage, color of the flowers (subsp. *virescens* has white flowers) and height. That they were found in sandy areas of Texas tells gardeners that plants can tolerate more heat and that good drainage is essential.

*D. cardinale*, scarlet larkspur, is one of the many species native to the western coastal states. Plants bear vibrant scarlet flowers held in tall loose racemes in late summer. Because of the late flowering, the foliage is quite handsome for most of the season. Plants can reach up to 5′ tall and are commonly used as a parent in making orange, red and scarlet hybrids for the cut flower industry. Plants grow best in full sun and moist soils. Native from central to Baja California. An annual in most of the country.

*D. grandiflorum* is gaining a following in this country, even though it is a short-lived plant. The few flowers in the lax inflorescence may be violet, blue, or white. 'Azureum' is a light blue dwarf form, 'Blue Butterfly' is only about 16″ tall and bears deep blue flowers, and 'Blue Mirror' has dark blue flowers on 3′ tall stems. 'Summer Blues', 'Summer Morning' and 'Summer Nights' have sky blue, dark pink and deep blue flowers on 18′ tall plants, respectively.

***Dendranthema*** (den-dran-the′ ma) Chrysanthemum Asteraceae

Fall-flowering mums (*Dendranthema* x *grandiflorum*) are hardy from USDA zones 5-9, however, in recent years, the mass production of fall mums has made them less useful as garden perennials. The fall-flowering mums (once known as *Chrysanthemum* x *morifolium*) are complex hybrids which have been derived over hundreds of years using wild species in China and Japan. I remember seeing my first fall chrysanthemum show many years ago in rundown display greenhouses in Hamilton, Canada and the colors, habits, and flower shapes were absolutely phenomenal. I have seen many such shows since but perhaps because it was my first visit to the "land of the mum", I remember it to this day. There are many shapes and sizes of flowers for outdoor culture as well, although not the diversity of forms being grown under protection.

All fall mums flower in response to the length of the night. As fall approaches the night length increases and when it reaches a certain number of hours (critical night length), the flowering response is triggered. The difference between late-flowering and early-flowering mums is simply the number of weeks of critical night length required to flower. Obviously it is important to purchase early-flowering cultivars in areas where frost comes early. In the North, florists' mums received as gifts may be planted outdoors but these decorative forms usually require too many weeks of long nights before frost and often freeze before flowering. In the South, early and late flowering mums can be used. There is no relationship between quality of flower or plant and flowering time.

The importance of night length was made very obvious to me when I moved south and noticed chrysanthemums flowering in April. It took me a while to realize that in southern latitudes, long early spring nights occur when temperatures are warm enough for plant growth. In the North, plants do not respond to the long nights of early spring because they are still shivering in the ground. Although plants flower in the South in the spring, they make a poor display and should not be allowed to do so. Flowering stems should be pinched to encourage vegetative growth.

Plant mums in full sun and well-drained soil. They are heavy feeders but should be fertilized no more than 2 times a year. If fed too heavily, it is impossible to keep the height down. Except for dwarf cultivars, cut the plants back heavily once or twice (up to 3 times in the South) to keep plants compact and encourage flowers. Don't cut back later than August 1 in the North or August 15 in the South or all the developing flowers will be removed. Aphids and spider mites are serious pests and pesticides should be used when necessary.

All mums can be propagated by division in spring and fall. In fact, division once every three years is advisable. New plants may also be propagated by 2-4″ long terminal cuttings taken from vegetative stems in spring and summer.

**Cultivars:**

The hundreds of cultivars of hardy mums are bred by a handful of flower breeders. They are bred for ease of production and self-branching. So many new cultivars are introduced and grown for the mass-market outlets that it is difficult to find much difference between them. Plants are classified by flower shape.

*Cushions*: Double-flowered forms with compact growth, usually less than 20″ tall.
*Daisies*: Single daisy-like flowers with yellow centers.
*Decoratives*: Taller forms with larger double or semi-double flowers than cushion mums.
*Pompons*: Very free-flowering plants with small ball-shaped blooms, usually less than 18″ tall.
*Buttons*: Plants with small double flowers (less than 1″ across), usually less than 18″ tall.

**Related Hybrids and Species:**

Some of the early garden hybrids referred to as Korean mums were developed by an American breeder, Mr. A. Cumming, and were the result of crossing an early-flowering cultivar with forms native to Korea. They are variously colored, well branched and go under names such as 'Venus' and 'Apollo', with pale pink and dark red flowers, respectively. Plants are distinguished by being extremely floriferous in late fall, so much so that the foliage seems to disappear when flowering. The following appear to have Korean hybrid parentage, but I do not know how much. There may be some Nippon daisy (*Leucanthemum nipponicum*) in these as well.

'Apricot Single' is covered with flowers in late fall. I saw plants absolutely smothered in soft apricot flowers at Bluemont Nursery in Maryland in late October and had to have one. Richard Simon, the owner of Bluemont, took pity on me and I now have it in Georgia. It has been flowering without fail now for over 10 years. A cultivar known as 'Sheffield's Pink' is essentially the same.

'Clara Curtis' may still be a chrysanthemum or perhaps a dendranthema—who cares? However, it is a wonderful cultivar, growing 18-24″ tall and covered with 2-3″ diameter deep pink daisy flowers with raised yellow centers.

'Mei-Kyo' produces many small (2″ diameter), double rose-colored flowers with yellow centers. They do not open until late October in my garden and continue until frost. Plants are hardy in zones 4-9.

'Ryan's Daisy' is a marvelous fall-flowering plant that bears dozens of single rosy pink daisy in September through November. The plant is likely winter hardy to about zone 6, but flowers appear so late that early frosts in the North may knock off developing flowers. Plants were found in the garden of Mr. Ryan Gainey, a fine garden designer in Atlanta.

***Dentaria*** see *Cardamine*

***Deschampsia*** (des-camp-see′ a) Hairgrass Poaceae

Hairgrass consists of approximately 50 species of grasses, including annuals and perennials. Plants are generally native to woods, meadows, and plains, but are best grown in moist fertile soils. Some people love this grass, others find it tolerable at best. Describing the merits of *D. caespitosa*, the folks at Los Pilitas Nursery in Santa Margarita, California stated the following: "Tufted hairgrass is a perennial bunchgrass from mountain meadows. It grows very poorly at lower elevations and looks like hell here at all times. If you live in a mountain meadow at 6000 ft. or in an awful climate like Vermont, this is a decent plant, if you live in L.A. I can sell you a plant that looks dead 12 months of the year." Ah, honesty in advertising is so refreshing!

Plants do tolerate some shade, and are quite drought tolerant. All species are tufted, and leaves are generally narrow and inrolled, looking like strands of long, thin hair. There are probably no other grasses that look quite so delicate in flower and they may be the most ethereal of our available grasses, if you can keep them alive.

The most common species are *D. caespitosa*, tufted hairgrass, and *D. flexuosa*, crinkled hairgrass, both native to North America. Flowers are handsome on the plant and also popular as dried flowers for arrangements. One or two unusual forms may occasionally be found, such as *D. caespitosa* 'Vivipara' ('Fairy's Joke'), that produces small plantlets on the flowers at the ends of the stems.

***-caespitosa*** (ces-pi-tose′ a) Tufted Hairgrass 2-3′/3′
Spring Bronze to Cream North America, Eurasia Zones 4-8

Tufted hairgrass produces handsomely pleated leaves which are less than ½″ wide, often flattened or occasionally inrolled. Plants may be used in zones 4 to 8, but they do not perform well under hot, humid conditions. In most of the country, plants will be winter dormant, but where winters are mild, leaves turn bronzy yellow and remain evergreen. Hundreds of flowers arch upward and outward in loose, airy panicles in such numbers as to almost obscure the foliage. It is one of the earliest grasses to flower, and its tolerance of minimal shade makes it a handsome addition to ferns and hostas. Moisture is more important for good performance than the amount of shade or sun. If consistent moisture is provided, plants will tolerate significant shade. Deep shade, however, results in poor flowering and death.

**Cultivars:**

'Bronze Veil' is more heat tolerant than other forms. Plants grow 2-3′ tall and bear bronze-yellow arching panicles of flowers.

'Holciformis', Pacific hairgrass, is only 1-2′ tall and suitable as a ground cover in northern and western gardens. Plants produce bright green foliage and dense, narrow panicles, very much unlike previous forms.

'Gold Dew' blooms a week later than most of the hair grasses and has golden inflorescences that start out dark green. Plants are only 1-2′ tall.

'Gold Veil' bears large plumes of silvery to yellow slightly arching flowers in late summer and early fall on 1-3′ tall plants.

'Northern Lights' was introduced in 1998 by Bluebird Nursery, Clarkson, Nebraska and has enjoyed popularity in America and Europe. Plants have creamy white and gold variegated foliage with the same soft flowers. Flowers are not as abundant as on other cultivars, but foliage is more handsome.

'Schottland' is wonderfully tall, but seldom falls over even in brisk winds. Flowers are tan to silver and tower to nearly 4′ in height.

'Tardiflora' is a late-flowering selection, bearing flowers in early fall on 2-3′ tall plants.

***-flexuosa*** (flex-ewe-o′ sa) | Crinkled Hairgrass | 1-2′/2′
Summer | Purple-Tinged | North America, Eurasia | Zones 4-7

Crinkled hairgrass, with its narrow, wiry leaves and nodding, purple-tinged flowers in June and July, makes an excellent small, cool-season grass. The panicles are slightly twisted, thus accounting for the botanical name. These fine-textured plants are useful as small accents in moist, partially shaded gardens and best planted in groups of at least three. Plants grow well in zones 8 and 9 of the West Coast, but do poorly in similar zone numbers in the South. They do not tolerate high heat and humidity.

**Cultivars:**

'Aurea' is only about 18″ tall with particularly golden foliage in early spring. The color fades as summer approaches.

## ***Dianthus*** (dye-an′ thus) | Pinks, Carnations | Caryophyllaceae

To recreate Grandmother's garden, one need only start with this genus as pinks have been in gardens as long as there have been gardens. That they are called pinks has nothing to do with the flower color, rather that the petals look like they have been cut with pinking shears. By the way, try teaching that to a group of twenty year olds: seems the old pinking shears aren't quite as common as they used to be.

Most species are low growing and suitable for rock gardens and border edging. Natural and planned hybridization of the 300 species have occurred for at least two centuries, so today the parentage of many of the pinks is somewhat cloudy, even muddy. However, garden interest in these plants has always been steady, and some of the oldest hybrids are still available to gardeners today. Considerable selection of annual pinks (*D. chinensis*) has occurred for the greenhouse trade, but wonderful breakthroughs in the breeding of this and sweet William, *D. barbatus*, have produced exceptional landscape hybrids. In many parts of the country, these hybrid pinks are hardy enough to overwinter and are seen in combination with pansies and violas in fall and winter landscapes. Examples include the Amazon series, Telstar series, Ideal series and many others. The modern-day carnations used for corsages and cut flowers are selections of *D. caryophyllus* and require greenhouse conditions to grow properly.

Perennial species may be hardy from zone 2 to zone 10, so there is no excuse for not having some *Dianthus* in the garden. Unfortunately, many are short lived, and propagation every 2-3 years is required to keep plants vigorous and attractive. All should be provided full sun, excellent drainage, and slightly alkaline soils.

Propagation of many species is relatively easy from seed, but taking terminal cuttings is the most foolproof method for all of the garden species.

Quick Reference to Dianthus Species

| | Foliage color, gray or green | Height (in.) | Flowers solitary, in 2s or clusters | Flower color |
|---|---|---|---|---|
| *D. allwoodii* | Gray | 12-20 | 2s | Various |
| *D. alpinus* | Green | 3-6 | Solitary | Pink |
| *D. barbatus* | Green | 10-18 | Clusters | Various |
| *D. deltoides* | Green | 6-12 | 2s | Red |
| *D. gratianopolitanus* | Gray | 9-12 | Solitary | Pink |
| *D. knappii* | Green | 15-24 | Clusters | Yellow |
| *D. plumarius* | Gray | 18-24 | 2s | Various |

***-allwoodii*** (awl-wud′ ee-eye) Allwood Pinks, Modern Pinks 12-20″/12″
Summer Various Hybrid Zones 4-8

This hybrid was raised in the 1920s by the English nurseryman Montague Allwood, who crossed a hybrid of garden pink (*D. plumarius*) with a carnation type, *D. caryophyllus*. Plants are highly variable, but in general, the foliage is gray-green and usually bears two flowers per stem. Plants flower for up to eight weeks, have a more compact habit than the "plumarius" types (which see), and are more vigorous, requiring division every 2-3 years. Many fine cultivars have been raised, and although it is difficult to be sure of their parentage, a large number have been assembled under this hybrid group. All have some fragrance, some strong and spicy, others less so. The degree of fragrance is dependent on the amount of *D. plumarius* parentage remaining. A few single-flowered forms are available, but most are double. Plants can be cut back if they become lanky. Some have been raised specifically for exhibition and are known as show or imperial pinks.

Propagate by division in spring or fall or take 1-2″ long, terminal cuttings immediately after flowering. Root in a warm, humid area. All need excellent drainage to be successful.

**Cultivars and Hybrids:**

*Border Selections (10-18″ tall):*

'Alba' has clear white flowers on 10-15″ tall stems.

'Annabelle' bears handsome pink, double flowers.

'Aqua' grows 10-12″ tall with clear white, double, fragrant flowers.

'Baby Treasure' is a free-flowering plant and produces fragrant, shell pink flowers with a scarlet eye.

'Becky Robinson' bears double, pink, rosy flowers over tufts of blue-green foliage.

'Constance' is a silver-pink form with red flecks on the petals.

'Candy Dish' has double flowers of pink, each one streaked in red.

'Danielle' (sometimes 'Danielle-Marie'), a recent sport of 'Helen', is a vigorous 10-12″ high plant bearing deep salmon flowers most of the summer.

'Doris' is one of the most popular cultivars and has wonderfully fragrant salmon-pink flowers with a deep pink eye. 'Doris' underwent a number of mutations resulting in two sports, 'Laura' and 'Doreen', both with orange-pink flowers.

'Frosty Fire' is about 6″ tall with double red flowers and blue-green foliage.

'Helen' has fragrant, deep pink with salmon flowers. The color is a little deeper than 'Doris' and free blooming.

'Horatio' has double pink flowers with a handsome red eye. Grows to approximately 6″ tall.

'Ian' is a long-blooming plant bearing rich scarlet flowers, but it is not quite as cold hardy as many other cultivars (zone 5).

'Laced Romeo' has deep red flowers fringed with creamy white.

'Little Blue Boy' has single white blooms over bluish foliage. Plants are 8-12″ tall.

'Loveliness' was bred by Montague Allwood prior to 1926, and consists of flowers whose frilly lacy-cut petals are in shades of pink and rose. Highly fragrant. They are appearing in this country as 'Rainbow Loveliness Mix'.

'Mrs. Sinkins' is still one of my favorites whenever I happen to see it. Bred in 1868, she is one of the oldest, and seen less and less as new cultivars arise. Plants are about 15″ tall and bear wonderfully fragrant double white flowers (with a tinge of pink) and gray-green foliage.

'Rachel' has spicy, fragrant, double, pink flowers over dense blue-green foliage. Grows 10-15″ tall.

'Robin' is one of the brightest of the garden pinks, having bright coral-red flowers.

'Susan' is pink with a crimson center.

'Thomas' has deep red flowers over blue-green foliage.

'War Bonnet' bears double red flowers in early summer.

*Miniatures (3-6″ tall):*

The miniatures can be used to advantage in rock crevices and as fillers in the rockery, and are finally becoming easier to locate in the trade.

'Alpinus' is the result of crossing *D. allwoodii* with other dwarf species. Plants bear single, fragrant flowers and are exceptionally free blooming. Flowers are produced in a mixture of colors ranging from light pink to red and an occasional bicolor. Plants are also more cold hardy (zone 3) than most others.

'Dainty Maid' has single, bright purple flowers with a red eye.
'Elizabeth' bears pink flowers with a small crimson eye.
'Essex Witch' is one of the most popular cultivars with flowers in a range of pink hues, as well as whites and salmons.
'Evangeline' has double, rose pink flowers.
'Fay' has bright purple flowers on 6″ tall stems.
'Frosty Fire', an excellent selection from Canada, is only about 6″ tall with double, brilliant red flowers and blue-green foliage.
'Little Bobby' ('Bobby'), named by John Donofrio of Carroll Gardens over 50 years ago, has cerise-colored, single flowers. The foliage is blue, and the height is about 6 inches.

***-alpinus*** (al-pine′ us) Alpine Pink 3-6″/1′
Late Spring Pink Austrian Alps Zones 3-7

The grass-green leaves are about 1′ long and 1″ wide with a prominent midrib. The leaves are entire and plants form a loose, matted clump that can multiply to cover large areas. The 1½″ diameter flowers are large relative to the plant, and can literally hide the foliage for 4-6 weeks. The 5 petals are fringed, and the scentless flowers usually have a white central disc.

This is a garden gem if soils are well drained, somewhat alkaline, and temperatures are not consistently above 85°F. It is an excellent rock garden or edging plant in moderate summers. Plant in moderate shade and minimize full afternoon sun. In the Armitage garden (zone 7b) it was spectacular until the end of July, whereupon it gave up, pooped out, and was not seen again. This is not uncommon in the southeastern states, and cuttings and/or divisions need to be taken each year.

Propagate vegetatively similar to *D. allwoodii*. Seed germinates within 3 weeks if placed in warm (70-75°F), humid conditions.

**Cultivars:**
'Albus' has white petals with small purplish spots.

***-barbatus*** (bar-bay′ tus) Sweet William 10-18″/1′
Late Spring Various Eastern Europe Zones 3-8

A little English history helps to undercover the origin of the intriguing common name. Sweet William is so named for that most likable fellow, William, Duke of Cumberland, who brutally crushed a number of rebellions, the most famous being the Jacobite Rebellion led by Bonnie Prince Charlie, which came to a bitter end at the battle of Culloden in 1745. Sweet is hardly an appropriate description for William's activities. English history aside, sweet William is as well known in Edmonton, Alberta as it is in Athens, Georgia. Since many of the cultivars are seed propagated, there is a great deal of variation even within cultivars. Although classified as a biennial, it self-sows so prolifically that it is always a guest in the garden. The 2-3″ long lanceolate leaves are short petioled and have a prominent midrib. The unscented flowers have toothed or fringed petals, often with a distinct eye of either a darker or different color than the petals. Although many species of *Dianthus* have only 1-2 flowers per stem, sweet Williams have a characteristic flat-topped cluster of flowers (cymes).

In the southern states, plants act as true perennials, particularly if flowers are removed before seed is produced. However, regardless of locale, plants are not long-lived and decline if not divided every 2-3 years.

Lime should be added to the garden yearly to provide a slightly basic soil. Like the rest of the genus, they are sun lovers, although in the South, partial shade is tolerated. It makes a desirable cut flower, having an excellent shelf life in water. More and more sweet Williams are appearing in bouquets and on dining room tables as florists take advantage of their excellent properties.

Division is the surest means to maintain true colors, but terminal cuttings or starting plants from seed is not uncommon and in fact, often easier. Germination takes 7-14 days when seeds are placed in warm (70-75°F), humid conditions.

**Cultivars:**

Many cultivars have come and gone, and it is quite difficult to find some of the "old fashioned" forms any more. What with the hype for compact, no-maintenance plants, the taller forms have all but disappeared.

'Blood Red' has one of the darkest red flower colors in the species and grows to 15″ tall.

Double Tall Mix is a descriptive name for this group of 15-18″ tall plants suitable for cut flowers.

'Harlequin' bears semi-double to double, pink and white flowers.

'Heart Attack' surely brings warm and cozy feelings when you give this cultivar to an elderly gentleman. Nevertheless, red leaves emerge in the spring, which later change to green. The carnation-like flowers are crimson red atop 12-15″ tall plants. Plants appear to be longer lived than many other selections of sweet William.

'Homeland' and 'Nigricans' are both deep red-flowered cultivars.

'Indian Carpet' is about 10″ tall and comes in various colors. A dwarf form ('Dwarf Indian Carpet') is a selection of shorter (6-8″ tall) plants. There is little difference between the two.

Messenger Mix is similar to 'Indian Carpet' but is about 15-24″ tall and one of the earliest cultivars to flower. Useful for cut flowers because of the strong stems.

Midget Mix and Double Midget Mix are mixes of semi-double and double flowering 4-6″ tall plants.

'Newport Pink' bears deep pink flowers and is 10-12″ tall. One of the prettiest plants ever, and unfortunately getting more and more difficult to find.

'Pink Beauty' has soft salmon-pink flowers on 15″ tall plants.

Pinocchio is a 6-12″ tall mixture. What's with the "Pinocchio" name?

Roundabout Mix is another seed-propagated mix of low growers with bicolor flowers of white and pink or rose.

'Scarlet Beauty' bears flowers of rich scarlet.

'Sooty' is one of my favorites. Plants stand only 12-18″ tall and produce some of the most eye-catching flowers of all the sweet Williams. They are not exactly violet, nor deep lavender, but rather kind of sooty purple.

***-deltoides*** (del-toi′ deez) Maiden Pinks 6-12″/24″
Summer Red, Rose Europe Zones 3-8

This species forms loose mats and is an excellent ground cover when planted in full sun or partial shade. Two types of stems are found: the 8-12″ long flowering stems which are usually branched at the base as well as near the top, and non-bearing stems which are prostrate and 4-6″ long. The grasslike green leaves are narrow (less than ½″ wide), and 3-6″ long. They often have a rosy purple flush, especially at cooler times of the year. The ¾″ wide, solitary flowers usually bear a V-shaped pattern in the throat. They are purple to rose colored and borne at the end of the branched stems. Flowers persist for 8-10 weeks and can totally cover the foliage. Shearing the plants after flowering promotes more vigorous growth and additional flowers later in the summer.

Plants spread rapidly under conditions of good drainage and moderately rich, alkaline soil. The species is as good as many of the named cultivars, particularly in the South, where some of the larger-flowered cultivars melt out in the summer. Sifting a layer of sand: soil mix on the centers of the planting helps alleviate that problem.

Propagation is not difficult from seed or cuttings. Remove 2″ long side shoots after flowering with a bit of the main stem attached and place in warm, humid conditions. Seed should be treated as with *D. alpinus*.

**Cultivars:**

'Albus' has clear white flowers.

'Arctic Fire' is a relatively recent discovery, bearing small white flowers with a pink center, around which is a fuchsia ring. Plants grow about 8″ tall.

'Bright Eyes' bears white flowers with handsome red centers, about 3-6″ tall.

'Brilliant', 'Coccineus' and 'Fanal' have scarlet-red flowers.

'Confetti Carmine' and 'Confetti Cherry Red' are about 6″ tall with deep crimson and cherry red flowers, respectively.

'Flashing Light' bears deep ruby-red flowers.

'Garland' produces pure pink flowers on 4-6″ tall plants.

'Inshriach Dazzler' is 4-6″ tall with chrome-red flowers. Some *allwoodii* parentage can be seen in this cultivar.

'Nelli' grows flat along the ground and bears many flowers, each one dark red with a deeper red circle.

'Red Maiden' has reddish purple flowers that totally cover the 6″ tall plants. Terrific performer in the heat.

'Vampire' and 'Wisley Variety' have carmine-red flowers with dark green foliage.

'Zing Rose' has large deep red flowers. While it is magnificent in flower, it is not as well adapted to hot, humid summers as the type.

***-gratianopolitanus*** (grah-tee-ah-no-po-li-tay′ nus) Cheddar Pinks 9-12″/12″
Spring Rose, Pink Europe Zones 3-8

This is a fragrant but highly variable species. The common name refers to the Cheddar Gorge in Southwest England, one of the native habitats of this plant. This is

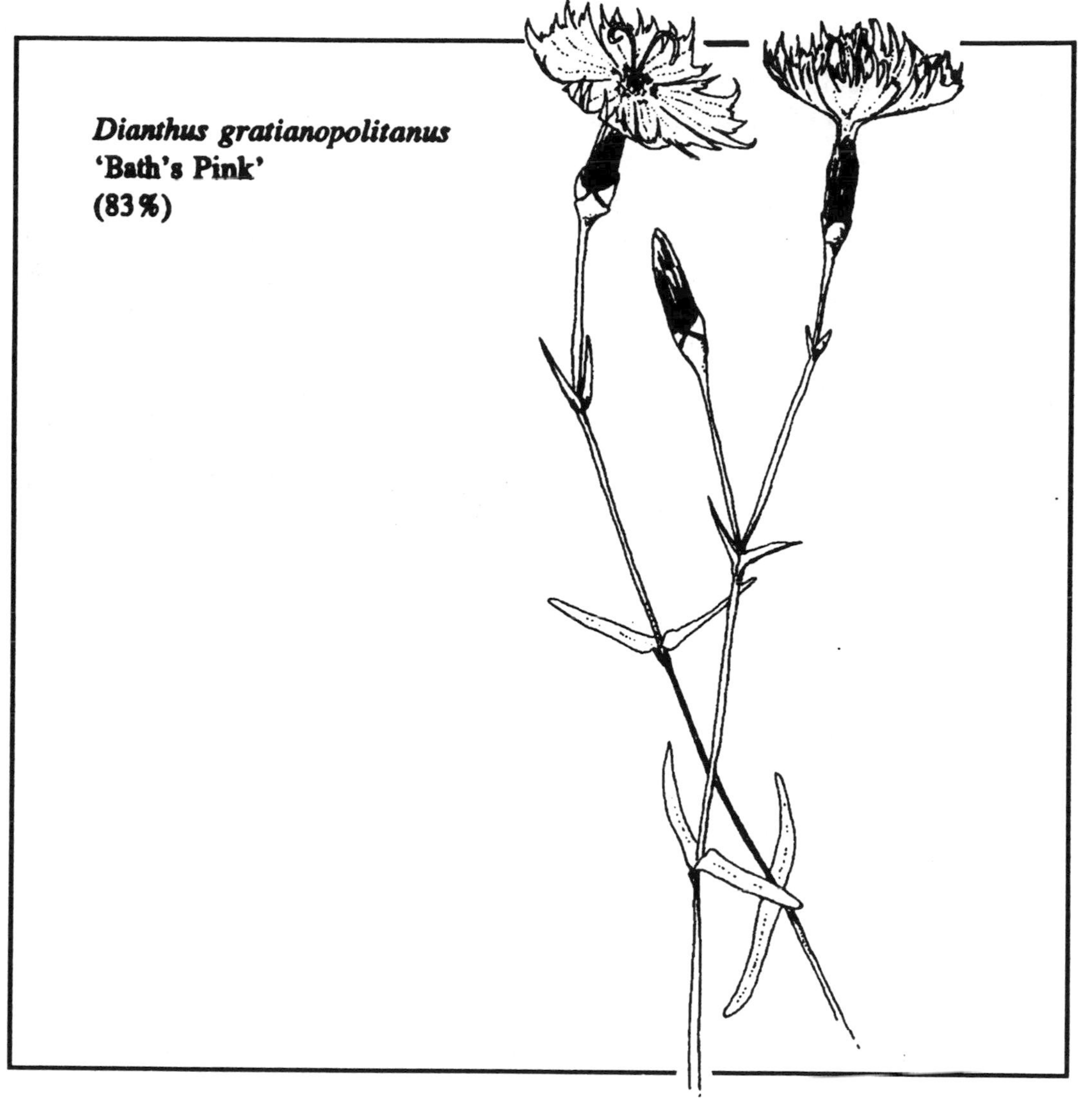

***Dianthus gratianopolitanus***
**'Bath's Pink'**
**(83%)**

also the location of the Cheddar Caves, well known for their delightful cheese. When my colleague, Dr. Michael Dirr, and I visited there, it seems we ate far more cheese than we saw native pinks. Man cannot live by pinks alone!

The gray-green entire foliage is narrowly lanceolate (less than ½" wide) and forms compact tussocks. The 1" diameter flowers are carried singly or in twos and are usually rose, pink, or any shade between. If the flowers are not allowed to produce seed, flowering will continue from spring to late summer. In the Gardens at UGA, plants are in full flower from late March to mid May. There is a great deal of variation within seed-propagated plants, but their fragrance and ease of culture make this species one of the best in the genus. In the South, this is an almost indestructible species.

Propagate terminal cuttings. Treat similar to *D. alpinus*.

**Cultivars:**

So much natural interbreeding occurs that one can never be sure of absolute pedigree. However, most of the following have a reasonable percentage of Cheddar pinks within.

'Bath's Pink' was introduced in the late 1990s and is still one of the finest soft pink cultivars available. The flowers are fringed, 1″ across, and plants are particularly floriferous. They are tough, easy to grow, and handsome. The gray-green foliage is also attractive when not in flower. Plants were originally found by Jane Bath, one of America's grand dames of the garden world, of Stone Mountain, Georgia.

'Bewitched' is a sport from 'Firewitch'. The pink flowers have a dark inner ring and are pleasingly fragrant. Similar foliage and habit to 'Bath's Pink', introduced by ItSaul Plants.

'Dottie' ('Pretty Dottie'), raised by Mr. Jim Fleming of Nebraska, is a hybrid between 'Spotty' and 'Snow Flurries'. The flowers are white with a maroon eye, and borne on a 6-9″ tall plant.

'Feuerhexe' (Firewitch) has handsome deep blue foliage and single magenta flowers. Plants flower in the spring and again during the summer. The Perennial Plant Association's Plant of The Year for 2006.

'Ginger's Kiss' is only 5″ tall but provides persistent light pink with white flowers over blue-green foliage.

'Greystone' has grayish blue leaves and white flowers remarkably close to those of 'Bath's Pink'.

'Karlik' is covered with wonderfully fragrant, deep pink, fringed flowers.

'La Bourbrille' has clear, single, pink flowers over mounds of silver-green foliage.

'Petite' produces an interesting, tiny 4″ tall tussock of gray-green leaves over which appear small pink flowers. For those looking for a truly dwarf dianthus, this is a good choice.

'Pink Feather' has pink flowers with feathery petals.

'Pixie' has pink fringed flowers with a red center that bloom for a considerable time. Plants bear blue-green foliage and grow about 12″ tall.

'Red Devil' is similar to 'Feuerhexe' but with cherry red flowers.

'Splendens' has deep red flowers.

'Spotty' ('Spotti') is an interesting red and white bicolor. This lovely cultivar from Jim Fleming (see 'Dottie') is well worth trying.

'Tiny Rubies' is a double-flowered, deep pink form, which has rapidly become popular in American gardens. Its carpetlike stature lends itself to rock gardens and ground covers.

***-knappii*** (nap-pee′ eye) Hairy Garden Pink 15-24″/15″
Summer Pale Yellow Central Europe Zones 3-7

I remember first reading about this species in a catalog which stated that it was "very rare and uncommon, the only yellow-flowered species of pinks." The way this advertisement ran on, the plant was so rare that if I didn't purchase it, I would seriously add to its chances for extinction.

The truth is that although *D. knappii* is the only yellow-flowered dianthus in cultivation, it is anything but rare. Plants are easy to grow from seeds (which are plentiful), and are short lived, but reseed themselves everywhere. They have no fragrance, and their washed-out yellow flowers are dismally unexciting. Other than that, they are fine.

The 2-3″ long, hairy, gray-green leaves are less than ¼″ wide and carried on 4-sided upright stems. Eight to ten flowers are clustered in an inflorescence that persists for 4-6 weeks. It grows better and has brighter flower colors in the North than in the South, but it dies after one or two years, regardless.

Propagate similarly to other species.

**Cultivars:**

'Yellow Beauty' is occasionally offered but I have not seen too much difference between it and the species. May just be my love for this plant.

***-plumarius*** (ploo-mah′ ree- us) Cottage Pinks, Grass Pinks 18-24″/12″
Early Summer Various Eastern Europe Zones 3-8

The wild *D. plumarius* species is seldom seen but closely resembles *D. gratianopolitanus*, differing by having petals which are more deeply cut, and generally bears flowers in groups of two; seldom solitary as in the latter species. The foliage is gray-green and grasslike, and plants can be vigorous. Beautiful in its own right, the species is also valuable because it is the dominant parent of the garden pinks, so popular in today's gardens.

The garden pinks are also known as old fashioned pinks. They are usually listed separately from the Allwood types, known as modern pinks, previously discussed under *D. allwoodii*. The garden pinks grow more slowly than the allwoods and need to be divided every 2-3 years. Since the nomenclature is so mixed up and so many terms have come into use, some people put the allwoods and plumarius types in the same grab bag. However, in trying to maintain some semblance of scientific decorum, I believe the following cultivars have a good deal of *D. plumarius* in their bloodlines.

**Cultivars (Garden and Cottage Pinks):**

'C.T. Musgrave' ('Musgrave's White') bears marvelously fragrant, white flowers with a green eye, and is one of the few singles.

'Dad's Favorite' is a double bicolor of white with red fringes on the petals. Very old fashioned, selected in the early 18th century.

'Excelsior' has carmine-colored flowers with a darker eye.

'Inchmery' has pale pink flowers on an 8-10″ tall compact plant. Nicely fragrant.

'White Ladies' produces clean white, strongly scented flowers.

'Spring Beauty' produces wonderfully fragrant flowers in shades of pink over gray foliage.

**Hybrids:**

*Series hybrids*:

This is where today's action is on dianthus. New introductions to the greenhouse trade have resulted in large numbers of plants being made available to retail and mail order outlets. Some are excellent. I list but a few. All are generally cold hardy to zone 5, sometimes 4, and heat tolerant to zone 7b.

Dessert series include 9-15′ tall plants, all with single flowers in a "clock" pattern of colors (white petals surrounded with dark edges and a dark center. The series includes 'Cranberry Ice', 'Raspberry Swirl' ('Siskin Clock'), and 'Strawberry Sorbet'. You can probably imagine the colors but if not, the dark colors are mauve-purple, magenta-red and red respectively.

Devon Cottage series sounds like a classy name, until you discover that someone must have been in the sauce when naming the individual plants. They include 'Blushing Maiden' (white with light pink), 'Miss Pinky' (salmon-pink), 'Fancy Knickers' (white), 'Rosy Cheeks' (rose-pink), and 'Ruby's Tuesday' (red). All flowers are double (carnationlike), plants are about 15″ tall and nicely fragrant. We trialed all of them at the Gardens at UGA, and found 'Miss Pinky' and 'Fancy Knickers' to be the most reliable.

Garden Spice series has provided an outstanding group of carnationlike flowers for the landscaper and gardener. All are short, less than 1′ tall and flower in very early spring and continue for weeks. They include baby pink (pink with white), pink, coral, fuchsia, marble (pink and white), pearl white (white with pink), red, and white. They are particularly heat tolerant and we have gushed over the performance of coral and fuchsia in particular. 'Garden Spice Coral' was awarded the Classic City Award from the Gardens at UGA in 2003.

Star series consists of half a dozen low-growing (6-9″ tall), single to semi-double forms. They have become quite popular for their ease of production and reasonable garden performance. Plants include 'Brilliant Star' (white with red center), 'Eastern Star' (red with darker center), 'Pixie Star' (large pink), 'Neon Star' (neon pink), 'Spangled Star' (red and white bicolor), 'Shooting Star' (pink with dark ring in near center), and 'Fire Star' (bright red), for now. All require excellent drainage in the landscape. 'Neon Star' has been the best performer in our evaluations.

*Other hybrids*:

So many hybrids are out there, some of which have lost sight of their parentage altogether. However, here are a few I am impressed with, there are many more. All are generally cold hardy to zone 5, sometimes 4, and heat tolerant to zone 7b-8.

'Bouquet Purple' is an excellent plant for cut flowers, but are more lavender than purple. Plants generally attain 2′ in height but have wonderfully stout stems, and need no staking.

'Duchess of Westminster' is an old cultivar with a strong clove fragrance.

'First Love' seems to have been around forever. We first trialed this a dozen years ago as an entry from Takii Seed in Japan and it has become one of the few seed pinks offered by perennial growers. The plants are about 18″-2′ tall, with abundant flowers of white, pink and rose on the same plant. Catalogs suggest cold hardiness to zone 3, I am a bit of a skeptic on that one.

'ItSaul White' produces white, double flowers. Also marketed as 'Vanilla', one of the most fragrant flowers on the market.

'Lady Granville' bears white flowers with raspberry markings and a red center. An old cultivar, but wonderfully fragrant.

'Little Boy Blue' also has lovely blue foliage. The single white flowers have pink centers.

Miss series are tall plants designed for cut flowers. The seed-propagated series includes 'Miss Biwako' (rosy red), 'Miss Kobe' (magenta), and 'Miss Kyoto' (pink flowers).

'Mountain Mist' is another blue-green foliaged plant, but with many single pink flowers on 10″ stems. I think this is the next great dianthus, with foliage which looks good in the winter (in the South) and summer and covered with pink flowers in the spring. Does not flower well south of zone 7b.

'Oakington' grows about 4″ tall, spreads well, and bears semi-double to double warm pink flowers. Raised by Alan Bloom in the 1930s and named for the site of the original Bloom nursery.

'Painted Lady' is a mat former (8-10″ tall) with single, light pink flowers splotched with red.

'Peppermint Patty' came from Rice Creek Nursery in Minneapolis, and has fragrant, double, pink flowers over blue-green foliage. Grows about 12″ tall.

'Prairie Pink' is a 2006 introduction from Dale Lindgren at the University of Nebraska. Plants bear double fuchsia to pink blooms over glaucous blue foliage. Plants grow 15-20″ tall.

'Pheasant's Eye' bears white semi-double flowers with reddish centers. Noteworthy not only because of the pleasant 12″ tall plants, but because it is one of the oldest cultivars still available, selected in 1671.

'Pike's Pink' has double pink flowers only about 4″ tall. Spreads to 1′ across.

'Raspberry Surprise' will constantly be confused with 'Raspberry Swirl', however this has a fragrant double white flower with pink and raspberry red flavoring in the center.

'Rosish One' from the Fleming Brothers of Lincoln, Nebraska, grows 8-12″ tall, has handsome foliage and bears semi-double rose flowers edged in white margins.

'Wink' has lovely light pink to almost white flowers on 4″ high mounding plants. Selected by Dr. Roger Uhinger at the University of Northern Iowa.

## ***Dicentra*** (dy-sen′ tra) Bleeding Heart Fumariaceae

Year after year, one of the most popular plants for the shaded garden is the bleeding heart. The common name comes from the heart-shaped flowers whose inner petals protrude from the outer petals giving the appearance of a bleeding heart (rather a morbid name for such a lovely flower). The genus includes other wonderful names such as Dutchman's breeches (*D. cucullaria*), golden eardrops (*D. chrysantha*), and squirrel corn (*D. canadensis*). In the garden, common bleeding heart, *D. spectabilis* is the most popular, but the virtues of fringed bleeding heart, *D. eximia*, and Pacific bleeding heart, *D. formosa*, have elevated them to the top tier of mainstream garden plants.

Plants of common bleeding heart were first introduced to England from Japan in the 1840s by one of the great plant explorers, Robert Fortune. About 15 species of *Dicentra* occur, characterized by deeply cut, compound leaves and flowers in racemes. All prefer rich moist soil in a shaded location. Propagation is accomplished by taking 3-4″ long root cuttings (see *Anemone*) in the summer or fall, division in the fall, or by sowing seed in late summer. Seed should be placed at 60-65°F for 2-4 weeks, 40°F for 4-6 weeks, and finally warmed slowly to 65°F until seed germinates. If placed in a seed flat in the fall and put outside under mulch or snow, nature will take care of these requirements. Sometimes fresh seed may germinate well without any special treatment but if stored for more than a few weeks, the above program should be followed.

Quick Reference to Dicentra Species

| | Height (in.) | Flower color | Dormant in summer | Inflorescence branched |
|---|---|---|---|---|
| *D. cucullaria* | 6-9 | Creamy white | No | No |
| *D. eximia* | 9-18 | Rose-pink | No | Yes |
| *D. scandens* | 36-60 | Yellow | No | No |
| *D. spectabilis* | 18-24 | Rose-pink | Yes | No |

***-cucullaria*** (kuk-ew-lah′ ree-a) Dutchman's Breeches 6-9″/9″
Spring Creamy White Eastern United States Zones 3-7

A well-known native plant, found in sunny forest floors from Nova Scotia to Georgia, and west to Missouri. Plants arise from a loose cluster of whitish tubers, each eye giving rise to gray-green finely dissected leaves. The short tapering spurs stick upward, looking like a pair of upside-down breeches.

I love "discovering" these plants in gardens, they do not jump out at you but they add a quiet charm all their own. Place in a shaded moist area. If plants dry out, they may go dormant in the summer.

Propagate by breaking apart the tuber after flowering. Do not allow to dry out.

***-eximia*** (eks-ee′ mee-a) Fringed Bleeding Heart 9-18″/18″
Spring Rose-Pink Eastern United States Zones 3-9

The fringed bleeding heart is native to forest floors from Georgia all the way up to northern New York. It is stemless, that is, the foliage and flowers arise directly from the scaly rootstock. The leaves are deeply cut, fernlike, and usually gray-green in cultivation. The inner petals of the 1″ long rosy pink, heart-shaped flowers protrude from the outer petals and are easily visible. Flowers are carried on long branched racemes (an elongated inflorescence with stalked flowers) resulting in a more floriferous species than common bleeding heart when optimal growing conditions are provided. 'Alba' has lovely milky-white flowers over light green foliage.

**Cultivars and hybrids:**

Considerable confusion exists as to the parentage of most of the garden cultivars. The debate is centered on whether the cultivars are selections of *D. eximia*, *D. formosa*, Pacific bleeding heart (the western form of fringed bleeding heart), or hybrids. All may be divided after about 3 years.

'Alba' has handsome white flowers and good blue-green foliage.

'Adrian Bloom' was a chance seedling from 'Bountiful' and produces ruby-red flowers on blue-green foliage. Can tolerate a bit more sun than many others.

'Aurora' is an improved form of 'Alba', appearing to bloom for a longer time and possess additional heat tolerance. May be a selection of *D. formosa*.

'Bacchanal' has some of the deepest wine-colored flowers of these hybrids. The persistent flowers arch over the darkly pigmented foliage.

'Boothman's Variety' is a magnificent soft pink-flowered form with blue-green foliage.

'Bountiful' has soft rosy-red flowers and finely cut foliage.

'Candy Hearts' has bright rosy pink flowers.

'Dolly Sods' was introduced by Plant Delights Nursery in 2003, and has turned out to be a superior performer in many gardens, particularly those in the South. Plants have good blue-green foliage, emerge early in the spring and produce abundant, if not overwhelming, numbers of pink flowers. I recommend it for my daughter Heather, the highest accolade I can give a plant.

'King of Hearts' is a vigorous selection with rosy pink flowers.

'Langtrees' bears dozens of white flowers over blue-green deeply cut foliage. One of the best whites.

'Luxuriant' is almost certainly a hybrid between the two species and bears cherry-red flowers over 15″ tall blue-green foliage. An exceptional cultivar.

'Margery Fish' is a relatively new introduction from England. She has white flowers and some of the bluest foliage I have seen.

'Pearl Drops', selected in 1977, is similar to the other white-flowering forms with blue-green foliage. Flowers are slightly tinged pink. Similar to, if not the same, as 'Langtrees'.

'Silversmith' has white flowers flushed with pink, and is quite different from other cultivars.

'Snowdrift' has pure white flowers without the pink tinge of 'Silversmith'. Lovely, deeply divided foliage.

'Snowflakes' is really handsome. A low-growing clump former, discovered by Joyce Fussey in Goathland, Yorkshire, plants have beautiful finely cut light green foliage and creamy white flowers.

'Stuart Boothman' is similar to 'Boothman's Variety', but the specimens I have seen have redder flowers and more glaucous foliage.

'Sweetheart' appears to be a cultivar of *D. formosa*. Plants bear snow white flowers on 12″ stems.
'Zestful' grows about 18″ tall and has large deep rose flowers over blue-green foliage.

***-scandens*** (scan′dens) Climbing Bleeding Heart 7-8′/3′
Summer Yellow Himalayas Zones 7-9

This quite unusual bleeding heart may be for those looking for a vigorous vine but wanting something other than a clematis. When it's in flower, most gardeners become excited and must have it. I generally check pockets for cuttings after people have seen this one. The light green vines have thin tendrils at the end of the divided foliage which allows them to climb over and around by themselves. While the foliage is handsome, it is the beautiful butter-yellow lockets which seize the attention of visitors. They are held in loose racemes of 5-14 flowers and occur in late spring and throughout early summer.

Although they should be planted in partial shade, they require less shade than common bleeding hearts. Too much shade results in few flowers. Provide consistent moisture and some support to allow the plants to climb. This is a vine which one needs to be close to in order to appreciate. It is not eye-catching from a distance like the clematis. The only drawback I have seen is that the tips of the individual flowers turn brown as they age, distracting from the new flowers just emerging.

Propagate from terminal cuttings; little seed is produced.

**Cultivars:**
'Athens Yellow' is similar to the species but the flowers are brighter yellow and more vigorous. In the wonderful Atlanta garden of my colleague Linda Copeland, I have seen this selection grow 18-20′ in a single season. Selected by the author and named after Athens, Georgia.

***-spectabilis*** (spek-tah′ bi-lis) Common Bleeding Heart 18-36″/18″
Spring Rose-Pink Japan Zones 2-7

Common bleeding heart is difficult to beat when grown in partial shade and provided with adequate water. The leaflets are the largest of *Dicentra* species and the flowers, made up of white inner petals extending from rosy outer petals, look like they have been hung out to dry on the arching flower stems. It is a great joy to watch the foliage, and the flowers that follow soon after, emerge in the spring. If well watered, the foliage is attractive until early summer in the South and into the fall in the North. However, if rainfall is light or plants dry out, the foliage yellows and disappears by mid June. This is one of the differences between this species and *D. eximia*, which does not go summer dormant.

This is a much more robust plant in the North than the South. The plants that line the drive at the Arnold Arboretum in Boston grow 4′ tall and can smother a young child, whereas those in the South might get to 2′ and hardly be noticed.

Bleeding hearts can easily be forced in greenhouses or cool conservatories. Plants should be dug early in the spring when dormant, potted and brought into a cool

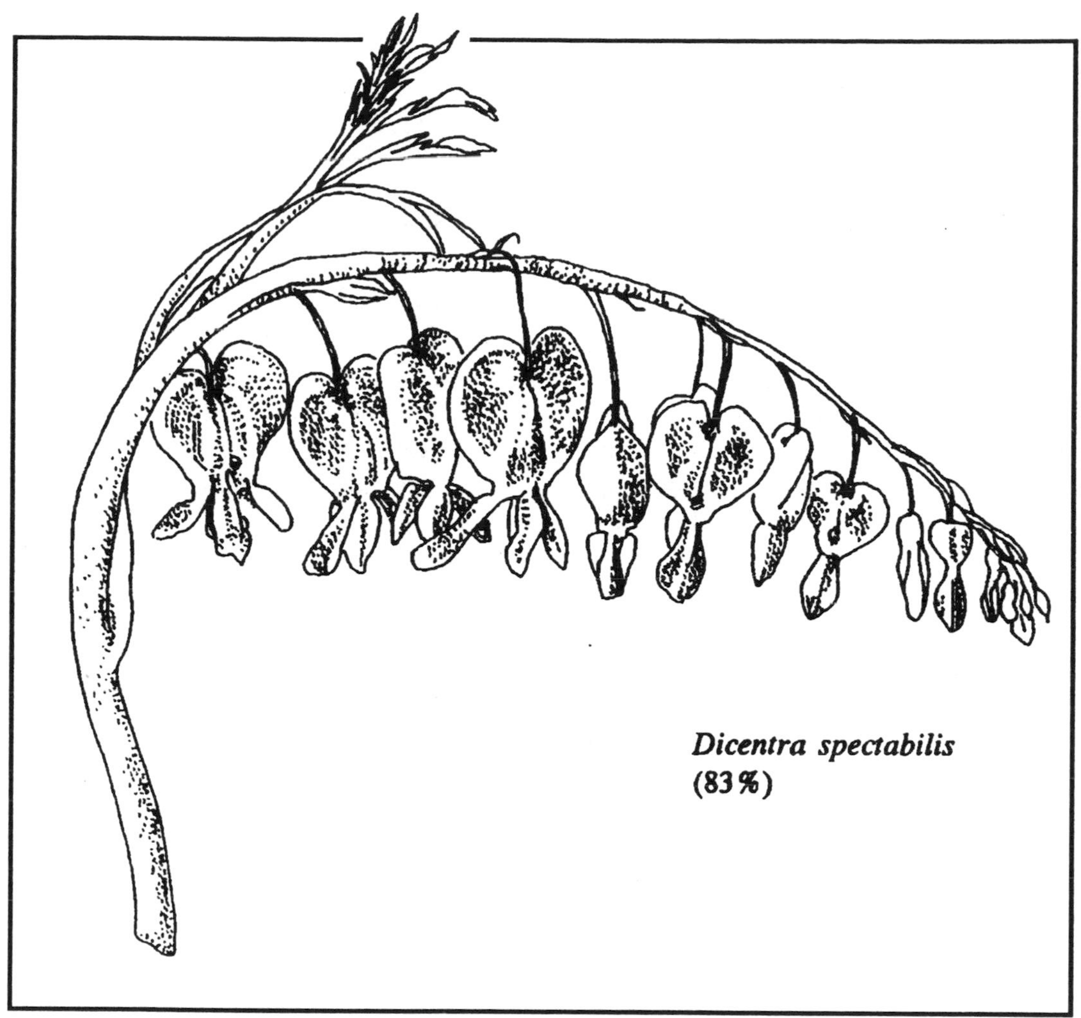

*Dicentra spectabilis*
(83%)

greenhouse (55°F) for forcing. With the addition of heat and water, leaves appear in 10-14 days followed by open flowers four weeks later. It is one of the fastest species to force and is particularly appreciated on St. Valentine's Day.

The dormant rhizome is divided after flowering or 3-4″ long root cuttings are taken in March and inserted in a cold frame in clean soil. Pot up or line out when young leave are well developed and plant in the garden in the fall.

**Cultivars:**

'Alba' is the ever-present white form, which although quite impressive, is not as vigorous as the type.

'Gold Heart' is truly spectacular, especially when it emerges in early spring. The foliage is golden yellow and is eye-catching from across the parking lot. The foliage hardly loses its color as summer progresses. This is proving to be a great new introduction. The same rose-pink flowers occur.

'Pantaloons' is pure white and is a more vigorous selection of 'Alba'.

**Related Species:**

*D. formosa*, Formosa bleeding heart, is similar to *D. eximia*. The main difference is that the inner petals barely protrude from the outer petals. Native from British Columbia to central California, it is more drought tolerant but less resistant to hot, wet summer weather than *D. eximia*. 'Alba' has white flowers over blue-green foliage, 'Ruby Mar' bears reddish flowers over glaucous bluish foliage.

***Dichelostemma*** (dy-kel-o′ stem-uh) Firecracker Plant Liliaceae

This group of plants, which arise from corms, are native to the Northwest, mainly from northern California into Washington. The flower stems, about 18″ tall, are not going to knock anyone out with their beauty, but in late spring to early summer, the red to pink tubular flowers are simply great fun to have in the garden. That they are so poorly known will have everyone asking you what they are, so practice pronouncing the name. I had no idea what they were until Brent Heath from Brent and Becky's Bulbs in Gloucester, Virginia sent me a few to try, and I have been trying them ever since. Three of four selections are offered; all produce thin gray-green leaves and are absolutely nondescript until they flower. The most common species is probably *D. ida-maia* whose pendulous dark red flowers are tipped in green. I have also been impressed with *D. congestum*, which differs in having shorter, upright-facing flowers and are usually purplish in color. A cultivar 'Pink Diamond' is offered with pink flowers.

Corms persist for only a couple of years in most eastern and midwestern gardens, but they are inexpensive and easy to replace. Zones 5-8.

***Dicliptera*** (die-klip′ ter-a) Hummingbird Plant Acanthaceae

I never believed any plants in the genus should be included in a book on perennials, however, my experience with this old houseplant, *D. suberecta*, has changed my mind. Certainly, it is not going to be a favorite of gardeners in Minneapolis or even Columbus, Ohio, but it is probably consistently winter hardy to zone 7. The gray-green fuzzy foliage itself is enough to grow the plant, and nary a bug or spore seems to bother it. The orange upright tubular flowers occur from early summer on and off through fall. A hummingbird attractor and a gardener magnet. Plants require well-drained soils, I have the most success growing the plant on a slope, where the water runs off easily. Truly wonderful!

Propagate by division or terminal cuttings.

***Dictamnus*** (dick-tam′ nus) Gas Plant Rutaceae

The genus contains few species however, the main one can be so outstanding that it makes up for lack of members. Gas plants are rich in volatile oils, which supposedly can be lit on a still, warm evening. I have gone through many a match, but have yet to see even a tiny spark. I have recently been told that it is the roots that emit this flammable stuff, but I have no intention of yanking up any of my meager plants to test them. If pyrotechnics are not your thing, you may want to rub the leaves and smell the lemon fragrance present in the foliage.

Regardless of what is rubbed or ignited, this is an exquisite plant when established. The alternate leaves are glossy green and the plants are long lived. Two-year-old plants are usually purchased and require at least two more years to look their best.

***-albus*** (al′ bus) Gas Plant 3-4′/3′
Early Summer White Europe, Asia Zones 3-7

The alternate pinnate leaves are divided into 9-11 finely toothed leaflets about 2″ long, each covered with translucent dots. The 1″ white or purple flowers have long exerted stamens and are held in an extended terminal raceme. Although plants can grow 4′ tall, the bases of the stems are woody and support is unnecessary.

Plants should be placed in a well-drained, sunny location and left undisturbed. Where comfortable, large clumps bearing magnificent displays of flowers can develop over a number of years. Unfortunately this plant is not comfortable in all parts of the country, and cool nights are a must for best performance. I tried a number of plants in the Gardens at UGA, and although they hung on for a number of years, they never came close to reaching the proportions of which they are capable. While the plant is one of my favorites, I cannot recommend it for southern gardens. However, fine specimens can be found in the gardens of the Biltmore Estate in Asheville, North Carolina, illustrating the value of cool nights, regardless of latitude, to the performance of this plant.

Propagation is time-consuming with *Dictamnus*. They are difficult to divide and the resulting injury may considerably damage the parent plant. Root cuttings have been used successfully (see *Anemone*), but the donor plant must be disturbed to harvest the roots. Although feasible commercially, it is not a good idea for the home gardener. The most common method is to gather the seeds in late summer (do this before they are ejected all over the garden) and plant them in a container and place outdoors. Keep the seed container moist. Do not expect germination until the following spring, at which time some seedlings should emerge. Do not throw away the seed flat as seedlings will continue to emerge for an additional 12 months. This is one of the species that has been the subject of a good deal of seed research, and as yet no results have suggested there is any way to hurry Mother Nature.

**Cultivars:**

'Purpureus' has flowers of soft mauve-purple with darker veins on the petals. It is most attractive and quite common.

## ***Dierama*** (die-e-rah′ ma) Wandflower Iridaceae

A genus of about 45 species, native to South Africa, 3 or 4 of which are beginning to find their way into American gardens. The cold hardiness has yet to be firmly established, but it is doubtful that plants would be perennial north of zone 7b, and the heat and humidity tolerance is also poorly understood.

Plants are quite spectacular when in flower, producing long arching flower stems that carry dozens of pendulous funnel-shaped flowers above the basal grasslike foliage. The shape of the long inflorescences with its suspended small flowers results in the other common name, angel's fishing rod. Plants arise from corms that are renewed each year. I have seen many marvelous plantings during my travels to the British Isles, where they are particularly common in the Republic of Ireland, but not too many in this country, other than the Northwest, where they are quite at home.

*D. pulcherrimum* is one of the prettiest species, bearing 3-4′ long narrow (½″ wide) arching leaves and many pink to red bell-shaped flowers on the terminal and lateral flower stems. 'Album' is a beautiful white-flowered selection. The development of named cultivars occurred in two general phases. The first was the selection of color variants of *D. pulcherrimum* and *D. pendulum* and marketed mostly under names of birds. They included 'Falcon' (wine-purple), 'Blackbird' (violet), 'Kingfisher' (pale pink), and 'Windhover' (lilac rose). The second phase involved crosses with dwarf forms (probably *D. dracomontanum*) and *D. pulcherrimum*, and resulted in intermediate hybrids often bearing Shakespearian names such as 'Puck' (rose-pink), 'Oberon' (peony-purple), and 'Iris' (violet).

Other wand flowers are occasionally offered, such as the soft pink-flowered *D. cooperi*, the hybrid 'Titania' with light pink blooms, the brick red flowers of *D. dracomontanum*, and its more diminutive cousin, var. *pumilum*. Unfortunately, if conditions are not quite right, plants produce foliage but may not flower. Many an experimental gardener has thrown plants away out of frustration and impatience. Don't spend the entire savings account on these plants quite yet, but trying one or two may provide a pleasant surprise.

## ***Digitalis*** (dij-i-tah′ lis) Foxglove Scrophulariaceae

If one surveyed private flower gardens for foxglove, one would probably assume that only a single species, *D. purpurea*, existed in the genus. There are, however, over 20 species, and at least a half dozen deserve a place in the shaded garden. The common foxglove is a biennial but many others are true perennials, and although not as spectacular, are nevertheless fine garden plants. The flowers are borne in tall racemes whose spikelike colorful spires can dominate a garden in late spring. The leaves of all foxgloves occur in basal rosettes as well as alternately up the stem. Soil requirements are minimal but plants perform well in soils rich in organic matter. They should be planted in partial shade and not allowed to dry out.

The name "digitalis" means finger-like. They were called finger flowers because "they are like unto the fingers of a glove, the ends cut off" (Parkinson, Paradisi, 1629).

Quick Reference to Digitalis Species

| | Height (ft.) | Flower color |
|---|---|---|
| *D. ferruginea* | 4-5 | Rusty red |
| *D. grandiflora* | 2-3 | Yellow |

| | | |
|---|---|---|
| *D. lutea* | 2-3 | Yellow |
| *D. mertonensis* | 3-4 | Rose |
| *D. purpurea* | 4-5 | Purple, white |

***-ferruginea*** (fe-roo-gin′ ee-a) Rusty Foxglove 4-5′/1½′
Early Summer Brown-Red Southern Europe Zones 4-7

This biennial has leafy spikes that arise from a rosette of lance-shaped mid-green leaves. The brownish red pendant flowers are borne on 2-3′ long racemes. The lower lip of the flower is considerably longer than the other lobe.

Place in areas of partial shade where plants will not dry out. I have had little success with this species in the Southeast, but I have seen it in flower well further north. They were outstanding in the beautiful gardens on the campus of Smith College in Massachusetts.

Propagate the species by seed similar to *D. grandiflora* in the spring or fall. A minimum of 2 years is necessary for flowering.

**Cultivars:**
'Gigantea' has large yellowish brown flowers and grows 4-5′ tall.
'Krik-Island' bears pure yellow flowers on 3-5′ tall plants.

***-grandiflora*** (gran-di-flor′ a) Yellow Foxglove 2-3′/1½′
Summer Yellow Europe Zones 3-8

This is one of the toughest and best performing foxgloves in the genus. Plants are made up of hairy, toothed, dark green, sessile leaves. The 2″ long pendant flowers are yellowish on the outside and netted with brown on the inside, and fit comfortably into almost any setting. The common name refers to the large flowers whose size helps separate this species from the small yellow flowers of *D. lutea*. The more I see this plant, the more I am taken with its understated charm and its tough disposition.

Seed germinates rapidly under warm conditions (70-75°F) and high humidity.

**Cultivars:**
'Carillon' grows 12″ tall and produces yellow flowers.
'Temple Bells' is shorter and bears smaller (1″ long) flowers than the species. Plants will bloom first year from seed.

***-lutea*** (loo-tee′ a) Straw Foxglove 2-3′/1′
Summer Yellow Europe Zones 3-7

The 4-6″ long serrated glossy leaves are oblong to lanceolate. The ¾″ creamy yellow, nodding flowers are borne on one-sided branched racemes. The flowers are tiny relative to those of *D. grandiflora*, and the upper surface of the leaves and flower stems are smooth.

Plants tolerate some shade but prefer moist, sunny areas. They are not as heat tolerant as *D. grandiflora*, and are not as common in areas of high heat and humidity.

**Cultivars:**

var. *australis*, the smaller-flowered Italian form, is often used in place of the species. There is little difference in garden appearance or performance between the variety and the type. Propagate similar to *D. grandiflora.*

**-x *mertonensis*** (mer-ton-en′ sis) Strawberry Foxglove 3-4′/2′
Summer Rose Hybrid Zones 3-8

This hybrid was raised at the John Innes Horticultural Institute in 1925, in Merton, England, by crossing *D. purpurea* and *D. grandiflora.* The offspring is tetraploid (twice the number of chromosomes of either parent) and the 6-8″ long leaves and 2½″ long flowers are bigger than those of either parent. It inherited the perenniality from *D. grandiflora*; however, the bienniality of *D. purpurea* results in plants that generally persist for only 2-3 years.

This is an excellent plant for a number of reasons. It is one of the few spike-like flowers in a rose-colored shade, and unlike many other species in the genus, the foliage always looks fresh. Even when not in flower, the large, mid green, velvety leaves catch the eyes of the passers-by. In flower, the tall spires of coppery-rose flowers are interesting as well as ornamental. This species received a Gold Medal Award for excellence from the University of Georgia Horticultural Gardens in 1987.

Seed propagation is not difficult (see *D. grandiflora*). Dividing plants is difficult but can be attempted every two years to maintain vigor.

***-purpurea*** (pur-pewr′ ree-a) Common Foxglove 3-5′/2′
Spring Purple, White Europe Zones 4-8

This old fashioned plant is still the stateliest of the foxgloves, and when in flower, is difficult to be rivaled. They are native to the British Isles and seldom does a summer day go by when visitors to England or Ireland fail to comment on the beauty of "that old English weed" in fence rows and the wood's edge. They make the lofty views on the Irish Ring of Kerry even more beautiful, but are equally handsome in gardens in Ohio and Kentucky, or planted in decorative urns. One of the finest displays I have seen was some potted foxgloves at Longwood Gardens in Kennett Square, Pennsylvania. Plants had been raised in greenhouses and moved to the containers when the flowers were at their peak. The 5′ tall displays beckoned to the crowds passing by and those who stopped to admire them knew they were privileged to have visited that day.

The wrinkled, somewhat downy, oblong leaves form a large rosette the first year followed by 1-3 flowering stems the next spring. The basal leaves have long petioles and the smaller stem leaves become sessile as they ascend the stem. The 2-3″ long pendulous flowers are usually lavender with large purple and white spots inside and are held on a long one-sided flower stem.

Plants require a good deal of water to "strut their stuff" and should be placed in a moist, semi-shaded area. Flowering begins in early spring and persists for about 4 weeks, after which the spent flower stalks should be removed. Unless sprayed with

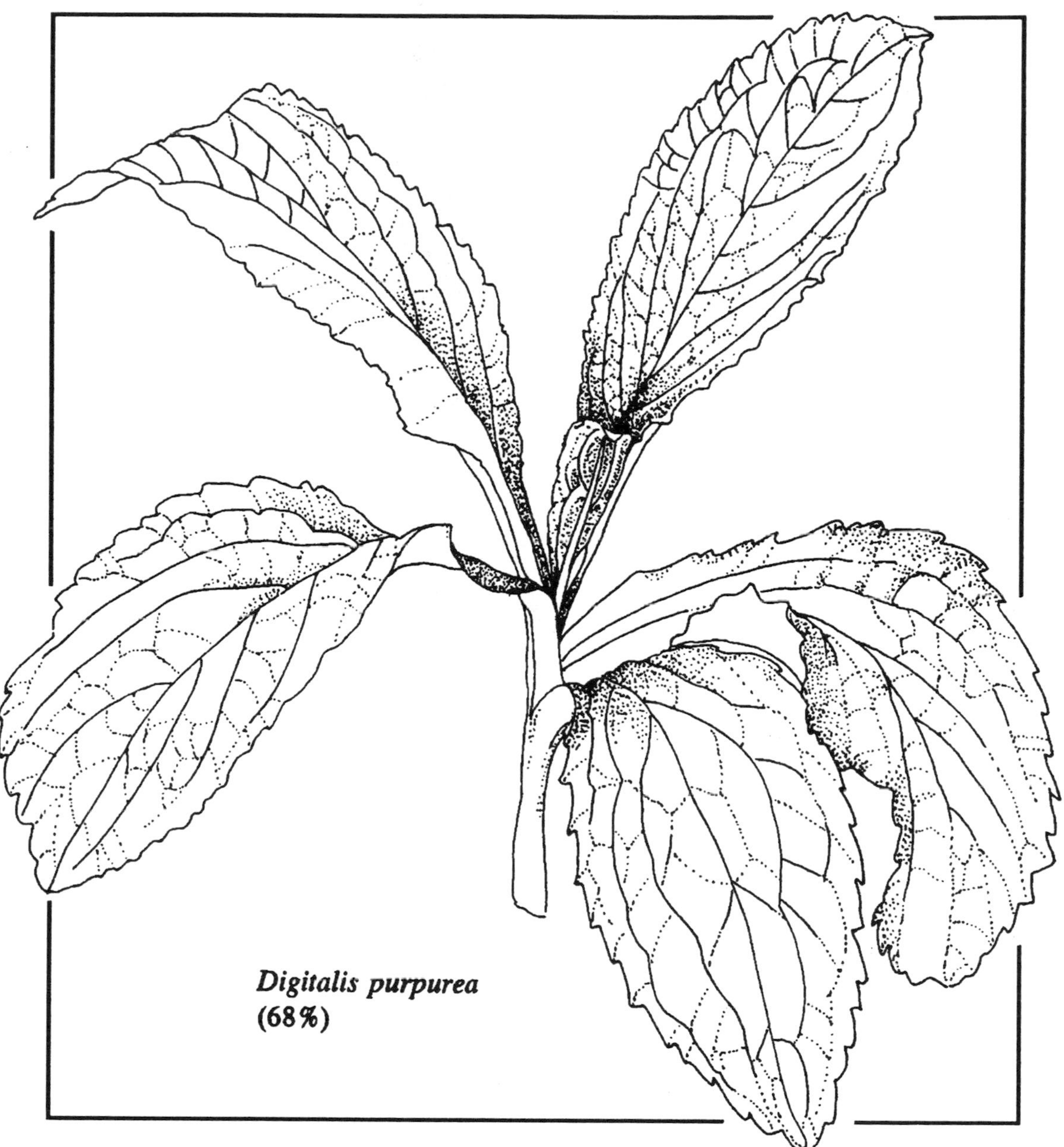

*Digitalis purpurea*
(68%)

fungicides, the foliage often becomes ragged by late summer. Since plants are biennials and will likely not survive the winter, they can be removed and replaced after flowering without guilt. I leave mine in the garden long enough to release seed for next year's plantlets.

The species is the source of the powerful drug digitalin, used for heart diseases, but there is no way to know exactly when the value of the plant as a cardiac medicine was first understood. The first mention occurred in 1640 in Parkinson's *Herbal*

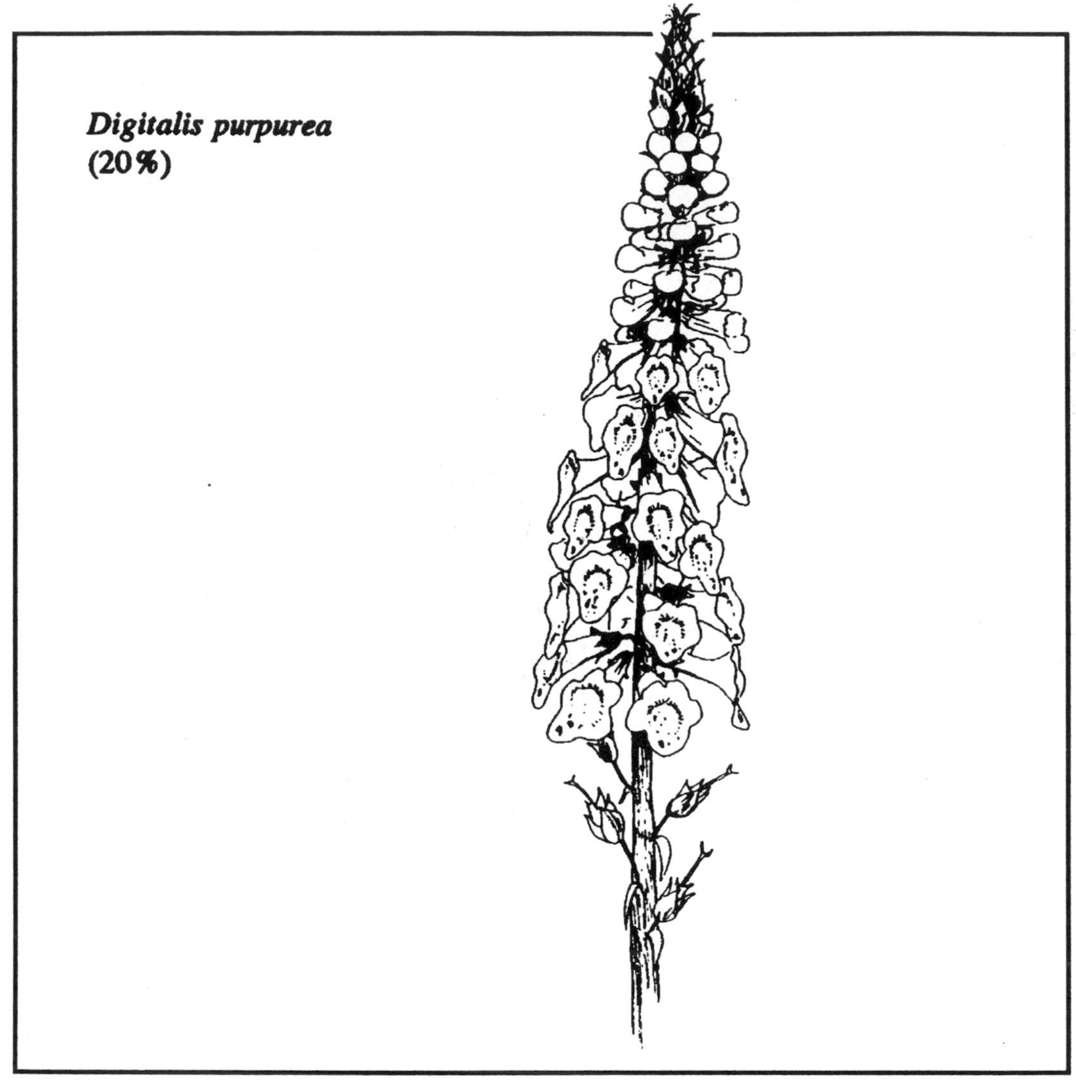


and was introduced into *London Pharmacopoeia* in 1650, but its use by native people probably went back many hundreds of years. It received its earliest scientific attention in 1776 when Dr. Withering, a British physician, tested *Digitalis* on his patients and kept careful records. In 1785 he published *An Account of the Foxglove, and Some of Its Medical Uses, with Practical Remarks on Dropsy and Other Diseases.* Withering was the first to understand the correlation between heart activity and dropsy (today often described as edema) by observing the action digitalis had on his patients' hearts. Prior to that, all sorts of fabulous medicinal properties were attributed to these plants. In the 13th century, leaves were used to treat "scrofulous complaints" and this is thought to be the origin of the family name to which it belongs.

Propagate from seed in the spring or fall. Older cultivars required 2 years between seeding and flowering, many new cultivars however, flower the first year from seed.

**Cultivars:**

'Alba' is a white form of the species and is particularly pretty when naturalized at the edge of woods.

'Apricot' has marvelous apricot-colored flowers on 4′ tall stems.

'Campanulata' has large bell-shaped flowers near the top of the raceme.

'Camelot Lavender, 'Camelot Rose' and 'Camelot White' appear to be crosses between *D. purpurea* and *D. grandiflora*. Lavender, rose-pink and white flowers respectively arise on stout stems on the 3-4′ tall plant. Plants flower first year from seed.

'Emerson' is a particularly good strain of white foxglove selected by Marc Richardson of Goodness Grows Nursery in Lexington, Georgia. Plants stand about 4′ tall and bear strong stems.

'Excelsior Hybrids' produce their flowers around the entire flower stalk and are held more upright than those of the species. The 2-3″ flowers are held almost horizontally, allowing an easier view of the handsome markings. Plants grow 5-7′ tall.

'Foxy' is similar but is only about 2½′ tall and has more side shoots. A breakthrough in foxgloves, 'Foxy' flowers the first year from seed. An All-America silver winner in 1966.

'Giant Shirley Hybrids' (bred by the Reverend Wilkes, see Shirley poppies) are similar to the type but are 4-5′ tall, with the potential of reaching 8 to 9′ in height. The large bell-shaped flowers are densely packed and usually mottled in shades of pink.

'Heywoodii' ('Silver Fox') bears pastel colored flowers in lavender and soft pinks. The foliage is hairier than others, resulting in a more silver color.

'Pam's Choice' is 3-4′ tall with white flowers on the outside, each having a dark velvet spotted throat within.

'Primrose Carousel' is only about 12″ tall and produces primrose yellow flowers with brown spots within.

'Spice Island' was introduced at the Chelsea Flower Show in 2004, but is now available in this country. It is definitely a hybrid, perhaps with the closely related genus *Isoplexis*, or with other cultivars of foxglove. Plants are upright, with evergreen glossy green foliage and bear peach to light yellow flowers. This is an interesting plant for gardeners wanting to try something a little different.

'Snow Thimble' has 2-3″ long clean white flowers on 3-4′ tall stems. The flowers are somewhat pendulous.

'Sutton's Apricot' bears large flowers in shades of apricot and salmon. Very handsome.

**Related Species:**

*D. lanata*, Grecian foxglove, has 1″ long pale flowers held in an erect dense raceme. The flowers are almost white with purplish netting within. It differs from *D. grandiflora* by being somewhat shorter (1-2′ tall) and by having the lower lip of the flower longer than the other flower segments. It is more or less perennial, and while not as showy as many others, is worth a try in the garden. Reseeds happily in Oberlin, Ohio.

*D. obscura*, sunset foxglove, is native to Spain and northwest Africa. Plants are 12-20″ tall with entire, linear leaves and nodding, beige-yellow flowers with red veins within. They tend to have a shrubby appearance, and the narrow smooth leaves have resulted in the other name, willow foxglove. Plants perform best in sunny conditions.

Plants were suitably impressive to industry leaders in the plains states, receiving a Plant Select designation for 2004. Likely hardy in zones 5-7.

*D. parviflora*, native to northern Spain, bears 2½ to 3′ tall unbranched stems with cylindrical racemes of densely-packed, small, reddish brown flowers. Flowers appear in late spring and early summer. A true perennial.

## *Diphylleia* (die-fell-ee′ a) Umbrella-Leaf Berberidaceae

*D. cymosa* is one of a number of eastern wildflowers that can so easily enhance the woodland or shade garden, but still remains in relative garden obscurity. Native to woods by mountain streams from Virginia to Georgia, plants require cool nights and consistent moisture to do well in a "civilized" garden. A large peltate leaf, roundish in outline but with jagged margins, arises from a thick, knotty, jointed rhizome. The flowering stem also arises from the rhizome bearing two similar but smaller alternate leaves and a small inflorescence of about 10 white flowers. They are not particularly showy in flower but the indigo blue berries formed after flowering are absolutely eye-catching. The rhizome spreads reasonably rapidly and many leaf/flower stem pairs may occur on the same plant. Plants are strikingly handsome where comfortable. Plants are closely related to the may apple, *Podophyllum peltatum*, but leaves differ and flowers are held above the foliage.

They do not transplant well from the wild, they are slow to establish, and do not grow well in areas where night temperatures do not consistently fall below 70°F, nor where soils dry out. This is an understated plant for subtle gardens. Hardiness is probably from zones 4-7.

*D. grayi* is native to Japan, with smaller leaves that are not as deeply divided and bearing fewer flowers. Almost never available in this country.

## *Dipsacus* (dip-sa′ cus) Teasel Dipsacaceae

Some people claimed I was getting desperate for plant material when I included this 5-6′ tall prickly biennial weed in the last edition. Desperate though I may appear, gardeners looking for a rugged coarse architectural feature have found that teasels provide terrific interest in summer and winter, perhaps behind the shed, but useful nevertheless. Plants form a nondescript rosette of coarse dark green leaves the first year and throw up the flower stem the next. Plants reseed so soon you will have both juvenile and mature plants behind the shed.

The main species, *D. sativus* (*D. fullonum*), is native from Asia to Europe, but has escaped to become a common roadside inhabitant in eastern Canada, the Northeast and central states. The elongated flower heads carry dozens of small lilac flowers in circular arrangement around the egg-shaped inflorescence, each flower guarded by sharp bracts. This plant is not, in every respect, for the faint of heart, nor for those without heavy gloves. The stem, the leaves, and the flowers can puncture all but the most calloused hands.

Their main garden usefulness comes from their longevity as a dried flower, which can create attention in the house for many years. The ripe flower heads, or teasels, were also used extensively for raising the nap (teasing) of woolen cloth and earned the plant the common name of fuller's teasel. Plants were raised in the 1930s and 40s in central New York for this purpose. Their use in wool mills in the eastern and middle states accounted for their escaping throughout the country. Apart from its industrial uses, teasel is also known as a "fracture healer" to denote its ability to help heal broken bones and sinews and as a tonic, provides nutrients to maintain strong bones, sinews and cartilage. In Chinese medicine, this herb is also used for promoting energy and blood circulation. Moreover, an ointment produced from the roots of this plant was traditionally used to cure warts.

*Dipsacus* derives from Greek and means 'to thirst'. This name was given because of the way rainwater collects at the base of leaves, where the leaf and the stem together to form a little bowl. This is also the reason why Romans called it Venus' basin and why early Christians in Ireland called it Mary's basin. Its other highly descriptive common name is Johnny-prick-the-finger. Good grief, what a shed planting this has become.

*D. laciniatus* is occasionally offered by specialists and worth a try. Flower shape is similar to *D. sativus*, but the bases of the stem leaves form "cups" to hold water and are of considerable interest after a rain. The flowers are whitish pink and not as prickly as *D. sativus*.

## ***Disporopsis*** (die′spore-op-sis) Evergreen Solomon's Seal Convallariaceae

The term *opsis* means "looks like" and in some ways these plants do look like the much better known fairy bells, *Disporum*. However, they look a lot more like Solomon's seal, *Polygonatum*, in that they have the ladder-like foliage and 1-3 small white pendulous flowers hanging from the nodes. Seems like they should be called Polygonatopsis. They belong to what is known as the Disporum/Polygonatum complex, confirming the similarities that exist between these genera.

*Disporopsis*, native to China and Taiwan, are excellent plants for the shaded area, and their mature height of 1-2′ makes them easy to use and enjoy. They form reasonably large colonies in 4 or 5 years and can easily be divided. Plants are evergreen in as far north as zone 7, and can be so further north in mild winters.

There are a number of species and 2-3 are offered to shade gardeners. Plants are somewhat taxonomically confused, so it is a bit of a crapshoot when you order plants. Do so from a nursery that at least sounds like they know a little about the genus. Regardless of catalog-speak, they look very much the same, although dwarf forms such as *D. jinfushanensis* are available. The most common species is the glossy-leaf *D. pernyi*. The new growth in the spring is slow to emerge through the evergreen foliage but when it does, the small white flowers are clearly visible beneath the 1′ long arching stems. 'Low Man' is a dwarf form, about 6″ tall and 'Bill Baker' is about 12″ tall with arching stems, but looks quite similar to the species.

Other species include *D. fuscopicta*, whose stems are not as long and has creamy white flowers with dark markings within (*fuscopicta* means dark painted). It is not a fast grower, and a clump large enough for division has taken about 5 years in the Armitage garden. A species I have not grown is *D. arisanensis*, from Taiwan, which has 2″wide leaves (wider than *D. pernyi*) and similar small flowers from the axils.

In the case of the evergreen foliage, removing the winter foliage in the spring allows for even more enjoyment of the new foliage and flowers. Propagate by division.

***Disporum*** (die′ spor-um) Fairy Bells, Mandarin Convallariaceae

Some of the more handsome shade-loving woodland species reside in this genus and nursery-grown plants have become much more available. Approximately 15 species are known, native to eastern Asia, the Himalayas, and North America. *Disporum* differs from similar woodland genera such as *Uvularia* (bellwort) and *Polygonatum* (Solomon's seal) by having white, whitish green, or yellow flowers borne singly, or in a few-flowered umbel at the end of the stems. The flowers of *Uvularia* (yellow) and *Polygonatum* (white) usually appear at the axils of the leaves. The fruit of *Disporum* is a red berry, in *Uvularia* it is a three-lobed pod, and in *Polygonatum*, a dark blue to black berry.

The family in which it resides has historically been the lily family (Liliaceae) however, most taxonomists have now placed *Disporum* in the lily-of-the-valley family (Convallariaceae) and recently to family Ruscaceae.

***-flavens*** (flay′ vens) Yellow Fairy Bells 1½ -2′/2′
Early Spring Yellow Korea Zones 4-8

Although politically incorrect, this is my favorite disporum, bar none, perhaps because it grows so well in the Armitage garden. The green leaves are sessile, and essentially clasp the stem. The bright yellow flowers unroll with the leaves and pop open within days of the plant emerging. Plants are robust and grow 18-24″ tall. I have them near a small water feature and they add a perfect touch of class in early spring. In summer, plants may produce some black fruit, however, I have seen few berries in my plantings. They perform better under high shade but can tolerate 3-5 hours of direct sunlight as well. Shade during the afternoon is beneficial.

Propagate by division.

***-lanuguinosum*** (la-noog′ i-nos′um) Yellow Mandarin 2-4′/2′
Spring Yellow North America Zones 5-7

The flowers are yellow-green, 1″ long and the tepals (petals and sepals together) flare outward. They are far showier than those of spotted fairy bells, that is not to say that they will turn too many heads, but they show up well in early spring. Flowering occurs in late spring and early summer. One of the best parts of all disporums are the fruit, and the brilliant yellow to orange berries on this species are no exception.

Propagation is by seed or division after a few years' growth.

***-maculatum*** (mack-ew-lay′ tum) Spotted Fairy Bells 1-2′/1′
Spring White North America Zones 4-7

The whitish flowers on this eastern North American native have many purple spots, providing the common name. The flowers are small, however, fall off readily and are enjoyed only if you make the effort to look closely. Stems are branched at the

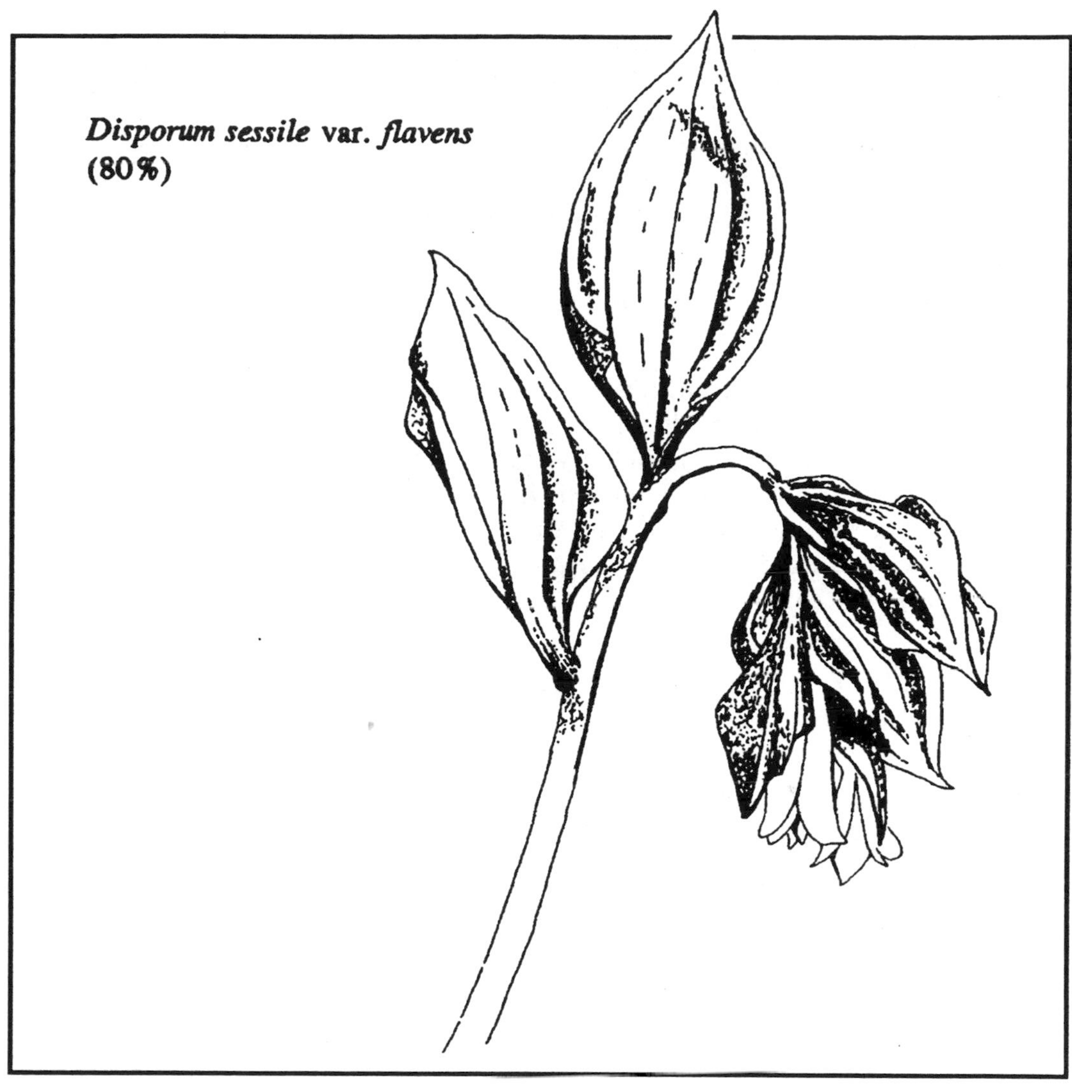
*Disporum sessile* var. *flavens* (80%)

base and the foliage is heavily veined. The leaves are more handsome than the flowers by far, however, the yellow fruit in late summer is quite beautiful. They perform well in the Northeast but struggle somewhat in areas of high heat and humidity. Much better in Boston than Atlanta.

Propagate similar to *D. lanuguinosum*.

-***sessile*** (sess′ isle) Fairy Bells 6-12″/6″
Spring Green China Zones 4-8

I have never had, or been interested in having, the green-leaved species in my garden. However, I love the green and white variegated form ('Variegata') for lots of reasons. Plants are tolerant of heavy shade and cavort freely with ferns and voodoo lilies. The foliage is white enough that it brightens up a rather dark area of the garden. In areas of such heavy shade, I am always on the lookout look for colorful ground covers rather than more spurge or vinca. Even the flowers have a tinge of variegation and closely mimic the leaves, and later in the season, black fruit is produced. They spread rapidly, but I do not consider them invasive; at least not after 5 years or so in the ground.

Propagate by division, you will have lots to share.

**Cultivars:**

Numerous cultivars from China and Japan have hit these shores, all are still rather rare.

'Chigger' and 'Cricket' were introduced by Barry Yinger of Asiatica Nursery, along with a half dozen others. Both are low growing (3-6″ tall), the former has a central yellow stripe on the leaves, the latter white central leaf markings.

'Sunray' has similar green leaves but with yellow streaks. Plants are quite handsome but much less vigorous than those of 'Variegata'. This may be a good thing.

'Tightwad' is a name only the folks at Plant Delights could dream up, but the dense tight growth has earned its name.

**Additional Species:**

*D. cantoniense*, Canton fairy bells, is native to China, and can be quite wonderful. The bamboo-like shoots emerge in early spring and can soar to 3′ in length. Stems branch about 2/3 of the way up and creamy, bell-shaped flowers appear. I have them in the Armitage garden, they are handsome but do not stand out as I hoped they would. The heavy shade is likely impeding their progress. Provide at least morning light for best performance. Hardy in zones 6b-9. 'Aureovariegata' produces green foliage with yellow streaking. The variegation is not distinct, but the yellow brightens up the leaves considerably. 'Night Heron' has dark musky foliage as it emerges, but turns green later on.

*D. hookeri* has creamy white flowers and scarlet berries. Native to the western part of the country, they enjoy some following there, but are seldom seen in the East.

*D. smilacinum*, from Japan and Korea, has tall unbranched stalks with creamy white flowers. A number of cultivars have recently been introduced. A dwarf golden-margined form ('Aureovarigata') is only about 8″ tall. It looks like *D. cantoniense* 'Aureomarginata' except for the height.

*D. smithii* is native to cool, moist areas of evergreen and redwood forests in the northwest United States and Canada. Shrublike in habit, the many branched stems form a 2 to 2½′ tall clump in 2-3 years. The nodding, narrow, creamy white bells usually occur in groups of 3-6 in early spring, then yield to orange berries in late spring and early summer. Probably hardy in zones 5 to 7 in the East, to zone 8 in the West.

## ***Dodecatheon*** (do-de-kath-ee′ on) Shooting Star Primulaceae

Grown for its elegantly reflexed flowers and "shooting" stamens, the approximately 14 species may be found from damp grasslands to prairie flatlands and mountain meadows. Species differ in the amount of reflexing of the petals, but all have shuttlecock-like flowers and basal rosettes of leaves. All species flower in early to late spring and are summer dormant. Most are native to the central and western states of America, and a couple are native to the eastern United States. Plants prefer excellent drainage, protection from the afternoon sun, and moist but not wet soil.

Not commonly offered but well worth the effort are *D. jeffreyi*, Sierra shooting star, and *D. pulchellum*, both native to the Cascade and Rocky Mountain states. The former is one of the larger species (up to 2′ tall), bearing large leaves and many reddish purple flowers with purple stamens. The flowering stems are slightly sticky to the touch. *D. pulchellum* is more difficult to establish and extremely variable. The range encompasses northern California to Alaska. The flared flowers are pink to rosy-purple. Plants have escaped to the east and may be found in woodland and moist areas. Selections have resulted in a white-flowered form, 'Album', and a carmine-red form, 'Redwings'. Another extremely handsome but more difficult species of the western states is the white-flowered *D. dentatum*, with toothed or wavy margins on the leaves, and 10-14″ tall flower stems.

Certainly the best known and easiest to grow for most gardeners, east and west, is the common shooting star, *D. meadia*. The tuft of smooth, narrow leaves, often reddish at the base, gives rise to a 6-12″ leafless flower stem. The flower head is an umbel of 3-7 lilac to pink blossoms whose petals are sharply bent back. Stamens are usually yellow. Flower color ranges from light to dark pink, but white flowers ('Alba') are also handsome. The species is found in open woods and meadows from Pennsylvania to Wisconsin, and south to Georgia and Texas. 'Aphrodite' appears to be a hybrid, bearing purple to pink flowers on vigorous 18-24″ tall plants.

For all species, provide some protection from the afternoon sun and plant in consistently moist, but not wet, conditions. Allow to grow through other plants in order to cover the area after summer dormancy occurs.

## ***Doellingeria*** See *Aster*

## ***Doronicum*** (dor-on′ i- kum) Leopard's Bane Asteraceae

Leopard's bane consists of approximately 35 species with bright yellow daisy flowers and alternate leaves. They range in height from the 12″ hybrids of *D. orientale* to 3′ tall *D. carpetanum*, and flower in the spring. A number of species, such as *D. pardalianches* and *D. plantagineum*, are useful for meadow planting and naturalize in dappled shade and moist woodland conditions. I have seen large meadows of *D. plantagineum* interspersed with forget-me-nots and coltsfoot in Europe, a particular outstanding planting being at Leith Hall in Scotland. In this country, they are not used as often because of the warm summers compared to northern Europe. In fact, under warm conditions, a number of species go dormant in the summer and must be overplanted. They are not fussy as to soil type, thrive in full sun or partial shade, and may be propagated by seed or division. Few leopard's banes do well under warm conditions, where night temperatures do not consistently fall below 70°F. High humidity is also a curse. All species, however, make excellent cut flowers.

Quick Reference to Doronicum Species

| | Height (ft.) | Flower color |
|---|---|---|
| *D. carpetanum* | 2-3 | Yellow |
| *D. orientale* | 1-2 | Yellow |

***-carpetanum*** (kar-pe-tane′ um) Spanish Leopard's Bane 2-3′/2′
Spring Yellow Spain Zones 4-7

This tall, coarse species may only be suitable for larger gardens where the bright yellow flowers can be used to wake up the spring garden. The 6-8″ long, heart-shaped leaves have smooth margins and are carried on long petioles. Plants are stoloniferous, and the tuber-like roots spread rapidly into large clumps. The 2-3 flowers per stem are 1-2″ across and open a little later than other *Doronicum* species. The numerous ray flowers are thin and the buttonlike discs are dark yellow. Cut flowers are excellent fresh or dried. Excellent plants for moist soils and full sun to partially shady conditions

Plants can be divided in spring. Seed germinates within 3 weeks if placed in warm (70-75°F), humid conditions.

***-orientale*** (ore-ee-en-tal′ ee) Caucasian Leopard's Bane 1-2′/1′
Spring Yellow Europe, Asia Zones 4-7

This is the most common species in American gardens. Plants send up bright yellow daisy flowers over bright green clumped foliage. The leaves are kidney to heart-shaped and deeply toothed but in warm climates, plants go dormant resulting in gaps in the garden. Plants spread slowly by fleshy underground rhizomes and can form wide patches with many flowering stems. The flowers are solitary and the bright splash of color can be a spectacular addition to the spring garden. This is a poor subject in the South as it tends to look limp unless given a good deal of water. Plants are not long lived even in the Midwest due to warm summer temperatures and humidity. Its summer dormancy is of great survival value but other plants must be used to cover the bare ground.

Propagate similar to *D. carpetanum.*

**Cultivars and Hybrids:**

Hybrids of *D. orientale* are usually more vigorous and better garden performers, and have less tendency toward summer dormancy.

'Finesse' has semi-double, yellow-orange flowers on 15-18″ tall stems. A good plant for the front of the garden.

'Little Leo' is 9-12″ tall with semi-double yellow flowers. A fine plant.

'Magnificum' is the most common form, growing 2-2½′ tall with 1-2″ diameter flowers in early spring. The foliage is dark green and heart shaped. An excellent hybrid.

'Miss Mason' is a hybrid of *D. orientale* and *D. austriacum*, a dwarf species with canary-yellow spring flowers. Plants are 1-2′ tall and bear single daisies in May and June.

'Spring Beauty' has large double flowers on 12″ tall stems. Although a fine hybrid, the double flowers can look particularly bad in warm wet summers, causing a friend to describe it as "botrytis on a stem." Another double-flowered hybrid ('Spring Bouquet') is also offered, but I have not noticed any significant difference between the two.

**Related Species:**

*D. macrophyllum* is a handsome large-leaved species from Iran. Growing about 3′ tall, plants bear terminal clusters of 1″ wide daisy yellow flowers. Less hardy than other species, probably useful in zones 6-8.

*D. plantagineum*, native to southern Europe, is a tall (2-4′) plant with spreading rhizomes that form extensive colonies. The basal leaves are ovate to elliptical with a clasping stem. The 1-2″ wide daisy yellow flowers are similar to other species, but these large colonizing plants can be quite impressive. Plants tend to fall apart after flowering. 'Excelsum' (also known as 'Harpur Crewe') has branched stems with many large flowers with yellow centers.

***Dracocephalum*** (dra-ko-cef′ a-lum) Dragonhead Lamiaceae

The common name refers to the shape of the hooded sage-blue flowers. This little-known genus consists of over 40 species, most of which are native to Asia. The foliage is opposite and entire, or sometimes dentate (sharp indentations), and many species are pleasantly aromatic. The flowers are held in loose whorls and may be axillary or terminal. The four stamens distinguish it from salvias, and the lack of a crest or fold on the sepals distinguish the genus from *Scuttelaria*.

Planted in full sun and well-drained soils, plants are often most useful in sunny rock gardens. A number of lovely plants have been moved out of this genus, including *D. virginicum*, (now *Physostegia virginiana*), and *D. sibericum*, (presently *Nepeta sibirica*), leaving a few rather unexciting salvia-like plants.

*D. argunense* has thin, almost needlelike foliage. Two cultivars are commonly available, 'Fuji Blue' and 'Fuji White'. The flowers of the former are dark blue, with a light blue lip while those of the latter are white, but the lower petals carry a bit of light blue. Hardy to zone 5.

*D. grandiflorum* has larger flowers in more compact whorls that look like short spikes. Plants are about 15′ tall. Flowers are an intense violet-blue with a conspicuous hood over each flower. Native to Siberia, hardy in zones 3-7. 'Altai Blue' can be equally intense.

*D. nutans* is only about 12″ tall with 1-2″ long serrated foliage and bright blue flowers in open whorls. Useful for rock gardens in full sun.

*D. ruyschianum* has many blue to violet 1″ long flowers on 8-12″ tall plants. A much more handsome form is the white-flowered 'Alba'. Tolerates partial shade and drought conditions. Hardy in zones 3-7.

Plants may be propagated from seed or terminal cuttings.

***Dracunculus*** (dra-kun′ kew-lus) Dragon Arum, Voodoo Lily Araceae

Another plant that once again demonstrates that gardeners' great passion for the bizarre can even overcome the senses, at least the sense of smell. Most who approach

*D. vulgaris* in flower end up holding their nose and gasping for breath. About 3 species occur, and each vie for the most obnoxious smell. Related to other malodorous genera (see *Amorphophallus* and *Sauromatum*), this tuberous plant produces a spotted stem and sickle-shaped leaves, divided into about 10 finger-like, white-streaked leaflets, resembling a dragon's claw. The foliage is similar to *Arisaema dracontium*, dragon-root, but differs in having purple flowers instead of green. The wavy spathe is up to a foot wide and purple throughout. The long narrow spadix is also deep purple and erect, extending well beyond the spathe. After flowering, green berries may be formed which become orange-red as they mature.

Some of the neat things about gardening are the stories that occur in your garden. This plant will always remind me of my daughter Heather. We were thrilled that Heather was engaged to be married, and so we invited our prospective in-laws, a wonderful family from Augusta, Georgia, for an initial meeting in Athens. Heather is the kind of young woman who does not suffer fools well, and who always has an opinion (remind anybody of any other daughters?). On the fateful day, she went on the deck, and said "Dad, something stinks!" Sure enough, my voodoo lily was in full stinking glory and was attracting every fly in the county. Heather and I met each other in the foyer, she looking for scissors and me looking for my camera. I kept Heather at bay long enough for the guests to arrive and the voodoo lily was a great conversation piece for the meeting. Heather and David continue to be in love and the in-laws still enjoy each other's company.

Place tubers in well-drained soils in partial to heavy shade. They are slow to emerge in areas where they overwinter, often not arising until late spring. Two to three years are needed for flowering. In most of the country, treat tubers like a dahlia, digging each fall and replanting in the spring. Cold hardiness can surprise gardeners, however, as plants sometimes return as far north as Philadelphia, but are usually marginally hardy north of zone 7. Remove the offsets from the tubers every 2-3 years to keep the plants vigorous. Seeds collected from the ripened fruit may also be propagated.

## ***Dryas*** (dry′ as) Mountain Avens Rosaceae

A group of plants native to arctic areas of North America, found on rocky ledges, sea cliffs, and sand dunes. Such a nativity points out the need for cool nights and good drainage when transferring them to a garden. The 3 species bear evergreen leaves which superficially resemble oak leaves. The genus name comes from the Greek *dryas,* referring to the wood nymphs to whom the oak was sacred. Plants are 6″ to 2′ tall and are actually small shrubs (shrublets) bearing white to yellow flowers. The most ornamental aspects of the genus, however, are the feathery seed heads, similar to those of *Pulsatilla*. They are terrific for planters, containers, and rock gardens.

The showiest species is *D. octopetala*, which consists of leaves that are dull green above and white-hairy below. Plants grow 9-12″ tall in open gardens, but are shorter in containers where roots are restricted. If sited well, plants can form dense mats and have been recommended as an alternative to grassy areas. The white 8- to 10-petaled flowers are erect, and flower over a long period of time in late spring and early summer. The flowers also have many golden stamens while the cottony seed heads are formed by persistent styles (part of the female pistil) that elongate to about 1″ long, after flowering. As the seeds ripen, they begin to turn brown.

A number of forms, such as the diminutive var. *minor* and var. *lanata*, have grayish hairs on the top surface of the leaves. *D. drummondii* is smaller than *D. octopetala* and has nodding yellow flowers, and longer feathery styles. The upper surface of the leaves are slightly tanned and covered with long silky hairs, pressed close to the leaf surface. It seems more difficult to establish than *D. octopetala*. A hybrid between the two species is greatly sought after because of the increased vigor. *D. suendermannii* bears nodding white flowers and grows about 12″ tall. Everything is a little larger than either of the species.

None of the species is particularly easy to propagate or establish. Seeds may be collected as soon as the seed heads turn brown and may germinate in 2 weeks, or may germinate in 2 years. Seedlings tend to produce only one root and are notoriously difficult to transplant. If you are patient, additional side roots will form and transplanting will be easier. Cuttings, with some new growth and a heel of old growth, may be taken in summer and rooted in shady, moist but well-drained medium. Divisions from a naturally layered plantlet may be cut off the mother plant, but allow it to root in a rooting area before planting to the garden. All are recommended from zones 2-6. Don't waste your money in the South.

***Dryopteris*** (dry-op′ ter-is) Wood Fern Dryopteraceae

The wood ferns include evergreen and deciduous forms, and are adaptable over a wide range of growing areas. The name comes from *drys* (oak) and *pteris* (fern), an early indication of the abundance of this genus in oak forests. There are believed to be over 1200 species, one of the largest genera in the plant kingdom. Such a community of ferns naturally produces many hybrids resulting in all sorts of shapes and sizes. Given such incredible diversity, we ought to be able to find one or two that do well in our gardens. Even though other ferns like the Japanese painted fern (*Athyrium*) or East India holly fern (*Arachnoides*) may be more colorful, gardeners attest to the toughness and adaptability of this group of ferns.

Plants of *Dryopteris* are usually medium-sized woodland ferns, often evergreen, with their sterile and fertile fronds the same shape and size. The leaflets or subleaflets are generally deeply cut or toothed. The indusia (structures which cover the spores) are usually kidney-shaped, whereas those of other genera are rounded, star-shaped, or elongated. All sorts of species are finally coming to the market, and we, as gardeners, are the winners.

*D.* x *australis*, Dixie wood fern, is unusual in that it is essentially sterile and produces no spores. For gardeners, that is not an issue, for plants are easily divided when needed. However, it slows the commercial availability significantly. Plants are hybrids between *D. celsa* and *D. ludoviciana* and make a 3-4′ tall clump. Upright and slow to multiple, but an excellent fern for shady areas. Zones 6-9.

Plants of marginal woodfern, *D. marginalis*, are marvelous, leathery evergreen ferns, which along with Christmas fern, *Polystichum acrostichoides*, make islands of green through the snowy landscape in the winter. The fiddleheads are covered with a golden-brown "fur" and the numerous leaf stalks are similarly shaggy. The top of the fronds have a subtle blue-green cast, while beneath they are light green. The sori are found around the margins (*marginalis*) on the bottom of the fertile fronds. Native to Nova Scotia to the mountains of Georgia, plants are best in northern zones.

A fern similar to the marginal woodfern is the male fern, *D. filix-mas*, native to Europe and northern North America. The main differences are the lack of the blue cast, they are shorter and stouter, and the sori are nearer to the midveins than to the margin. This has been one of the best performers in the Armitage garden, always looking fresh and green. Should probably be used more in this country. Numerous forms of male fern are offered to gardeners, from the handsome narrow-leaved 'Barnseii' to the easy to grow and robust 'Undulata Robustá' to the mutilated 'Linearis Polydactylon', which is about as grotesque as the name and the new 'Parsley', with ruffled fronds. Both the marginal woodfern and the male fern are tolerant of relatively dry conditions, although consistent moisture is helpful. Another fine native fern is the narrow buckler fern, *D. carthusiana* (*D. spinulosa*), a northern fern from Alaska to Virginia with opposite leaflets and light green fronds. Needs moisture and cool nights to succeed.

If large size is a requirement in the shaded woodland, then Goldie's fern (*D. goldiana)* should surely be considered. Plants grow up to 4′ tall and 12-15″ wide, probably the largest of our native ferns. The large backward-tilting fronds are abruptly pointed at the tips, wider in the middle than at either end, and are a golden green. The leaflets are cut almost to the midrib and the rootstalks are long and scaly. Native from New Brunswick to North Carolina and Tennessee, hardy in zones 3-8. This is a marvelous plant and vies for attention with some of the large ferns of *Matteuccia* and *Osmunda*.

Southern gardeners may have trouble establishing some of the more northern species; however, *D. ludoviciana*, southern shield fern, has glossy, bold, evergreen foliage and is one of the best choices for hot summers. Native west from Texas to Florida and north to North Carolina. plants perform well in zones 6-10. Another southern fern that is occasionally offered is the log fern, *D. celsa*, with 2-3′ long fronds which gradually taper at the tip. Plants perform well in semi-shady areas and soils rich in organic matter. Moist but not wet areas are best. Native along the Gulf Coast from Louisiana and up the eastern coast to New York, hardy in zones 5-9.

One of the finest and widely available evergreen is the autumn fern, *D. erythrosora*. Plants are found in China, Korea, and Japan and do well in zones 5-9. The best characteristic is the coppery-red color of the new fronds which contrast pleasantly with the older green fronds. The back of the fronds are densely speckled with red sori. One of the easiest ferns to establish, this goes with Japanese painted fern and Christmas fern as some of the "no-brainer" ferns out there. Autumn fern provides a picturesque fern for shade and partially sunny areas. The cultivar 'Brilliance' has excellent young frond color and color reappears in the fall.

Another fine species is Wallich's fern, *D. wallichiana*, notable for its strong flush of new growth in the spring and leathery green foliage. It is a widespread and diverse species and does well in shady areas and organic soils. Neither autumn fern nor Wallich's fern likes wet feet.

For wet areas, the best species is probably the crested shield fern, *D. cristata*. The fronds are leathery and have the same bluish tinge found with *D. marginalis*. The leaflets are curiously arranged like a ladder, widely spaced and almost horizontal to the stem. They don't do well in warm areas, and do poorly regardless of location if roots are not kept consistently wet.

There are many other species in the genus that make good subjects for the woodland garden. Differences between them are found in their adaptability, heat and cold tolerance, and shape and hue of the fronds. Many can be propagated from division, and spores may be purchased from specialist societies.

# E

***Echinacea*** (ek-in-ay′ see-a) Purple Coneflower Asteraceae

The rise in popularity of this common native plant has been nothing short of spectacular. As if by magic, the early 2000s have brought the gardener and landscaper a potpourri of colors and flower forms that did not exist before. Of course, magic had nothing to do with it; the breeding and selection of coneflowers has been going on for many years. Many hands have been involved but those of Dr. Jim Ault, Richard and Bobby Saul, Dan Heims, Kim Hawks, and others have been instrumental in raising cone consciousness. Creativity is alive and well in America.

*Echinacea* has always been a popular genus, consisting of 8-9 species of tough, coarse plants native to the eastern and central United States. Because the base of the flower is rather prickly, Konrad Moench of Germany named the genus in the late 1700s after the Greek word for hedgehog, "echinos". *Echinacea* is closely related to *Rudbeckia*, a genus of yellow and orange coneflowers and was originally included there. General differences between them can be found under *Rudbeckia*. The dark green leaves are alternate, simple, and tend to clasp the stem. Roots are thick and black and the purple flower petals are usually slightly reflexed. All species are drought and heat tolerant, require full sun and attract hordes of butterflies.

Many people have accepted *Echinacea*, particularly *E. angustifolia*, as a bona fide health supplement. From a vitamin C supplement to combating colds and flu, the coneflower has become the rock star of herbal medicine. The chemistry, pharmacology and clinical applications of *Echinacea* have been the subject of over 350 scientific studies. Tests have proven that tissue regeneration, anti-inflammatory and stimulation of the immune system are possible. Interest in the plant's ability to help in the treatment of cancer, AIDS and other debilitating diseases continues. The cultivation of these plants for their medicinal rather than their ornamental use is becoming much more widespread.

Propagate by division and seed. The seed of the various species is easy to germinate. Sow fresh seed at 70°F under humid conditions.

Quick Guide to Echinacea Species

| | Height (ft.) | Flower color |
|---|---|---|
| *E. pallida* | 3-4 | Creamy white |
| *E. paradoxa* | 2-3 | Purple, Yellow |
| *E. purpurea* | 2-3 | Purple, White |

***-pallida*** (pal′ li-da) Pale Coneflower 3-4′/2′
Summer Pale Purple South-Central United States Zones 4-8

This most interesting wildflower is well worth trying in the herbaceous border, providing plants with dark green, hairy, 3-5″ long leaves that have 3-5 parallel veins. The lower leaves are held on long petioles while the upper are sessile. The leaves may not be terribly exciting but the 3-4″ diameter flowers, consisting of dark central cones surrounded by 8-10 narrow straplike, drooping petals (ray flowers), tend to catch the eye. The drooping, thin rays make the flowers more interesting than beautiful, and they do not compete with those of purple coneflower and its many selections. Plants have all sorts of supposed pharmacological uses and were commonly used by native Americans of the central plains to treat the pain of burns, snake bites and stings.

Placed in full sun, plants attain 3-4′, however if grown in partial shade, 5′ tall, weak-stemmed plants result. Pinching in late spring may induce additional branching and may make support unnecessary. The species tolerates poor soils and additional fertilization need not be applied. Plants are not long lived and 2-3 years is all that should be expected without division, especially in warmer zones. Plants are generally found in dry open places from Illinois to Minnesota and Montana south to Texas and Georgia.

Propagate by seed or by division every two to three years. Seed germinates in 2-4 weeks if placed in warm (70-75°F), humid conditions. Cover the seed lightly as darkness inhibits germination.

***-paradoxa*** (par-a-dox′ a) Yellow Coneflower 2-3′/2′
Summer Pale Yellow Ozark Mountains Zones 4-7

I wrote in the last edition that the species is "an interesting if not a terribly vigorous plant." The vigor may not be a great deal better, but the interest certainly is. I see it a good deal in Kansas and Missouri and I marvel at yellow ray flowers on a purple coneflower. However, while it may not be a remarkably outstanding plant (after all, there are a lot of yellow daisies out there), it has some of the most wonderful perfume. It has been an important parent in the breeding of yellow, gold and orange forms of coneflowers, and many of the new hybrids take the fragrance with them. I still do not see many plants sold in nurseries or online, but that is likely because the new hybrids have swamped sales of everything else.

***-purpurea*** (pur-pewr′ ree-a) Purple Coneflower 2-3′/2′
Summer Purple Central United States Zones 3-8

In order to truly appreciate the glory and grandeur of this common species, you need only visit the Great Plains garden at the Holden Arboretum outside Cleveland, the Chicago Botanic Garden, Powell Gardens near Kansas City, or any native prairie gardens in the eastern and central United States. To have seen them growing alongside natural natives such as *Liatris*, *Filipendula* and *Silphium*, the incredible beauty of the prairies as our ancestors saw them must have been awe-inspiring to the pioneers.

Although purple coneflower has been a common garden plant for many years and untold cultivars are now available, the species itself is still a must-have for American gardeners almost anywhere. The 4-8″ long, dark green leaves are coarse, serrated, and have short stiff hairs. The 3-4″ diameter flowers consist of a brown central cone with a bronze tint, surrounded by broad, rose to purple petals. These droop slightly although not as much as those of the previous species. Plants are tough and handle summer heat well, performing as well in zone 8 as in zone 4. They do best in full sun and do not benefit from additional fertility, particularly if in partial shade. Plants begin to flower in midsummer, make a grand display about two weeks later, and continue sporadically until frost. The flower is also useful as a cut flower. Many flower arrangers remove the ray flowers and use the naked cone in bouquets and arrangements. It makes a fascinating and long-lasting specimen.

**Cultivars:**

A number of beautiful new introductions are available, some are hybrids to be sure and some are just downright weird. Will *Echinacea* become another heuchera, whose hundreds of cultivars simply confuse the gardener and landscaper?

When I recommend coneflowers to my children or friends I always suggest they buy those that have a good deal of purple. The more *E. purpurea* germplasm in the parentage, the more vigorous a hybrid is likely to be.

'Abendsonne' has lighter, more cerise-pink flowers than the species.

'Alba' has cream-white petals surrounding a greenish disc.

Big Sky™ Series is the work of Richard and Bobby Saul, who spent many years hybridizing coneflowers and have introduced at least five colors, with more likely on the way. All are about 2½-4′ tall, most are fragrant, and all are outstanding. After Midnight™ ('Emily Saul') is the latest introduction to the series and claims a short stature (12-18″) with black stems and overlapping magenta ray flowers. Harvest Moon ('Matthew Saul') has wide, overlapping golden ray flowers and an amber golden cone. 'Summer Sky' ('Katie Saul') has reddish flowers, 'Sundown ('Evan Saul') has eye-catching orange-red and wide ray flowers. This has essentially taken the place of 'Sunset', an early burnt orange introduction. Grows 3-4′ tall. 'Sunrise' is lemony yellow with narrow ray flowers and a golden disc, 'Twilight' produces both ray flowers and the disc in shades of red.

'Bressingham Hybrids' are a seed strain arising from seed of 'Robert Bloom'. Plants vary slightly from light rose to red and are excellent garden performers.

'Bravado' has 4-5″ wide rosy-red flowers with excellent horizontal ray flowers.

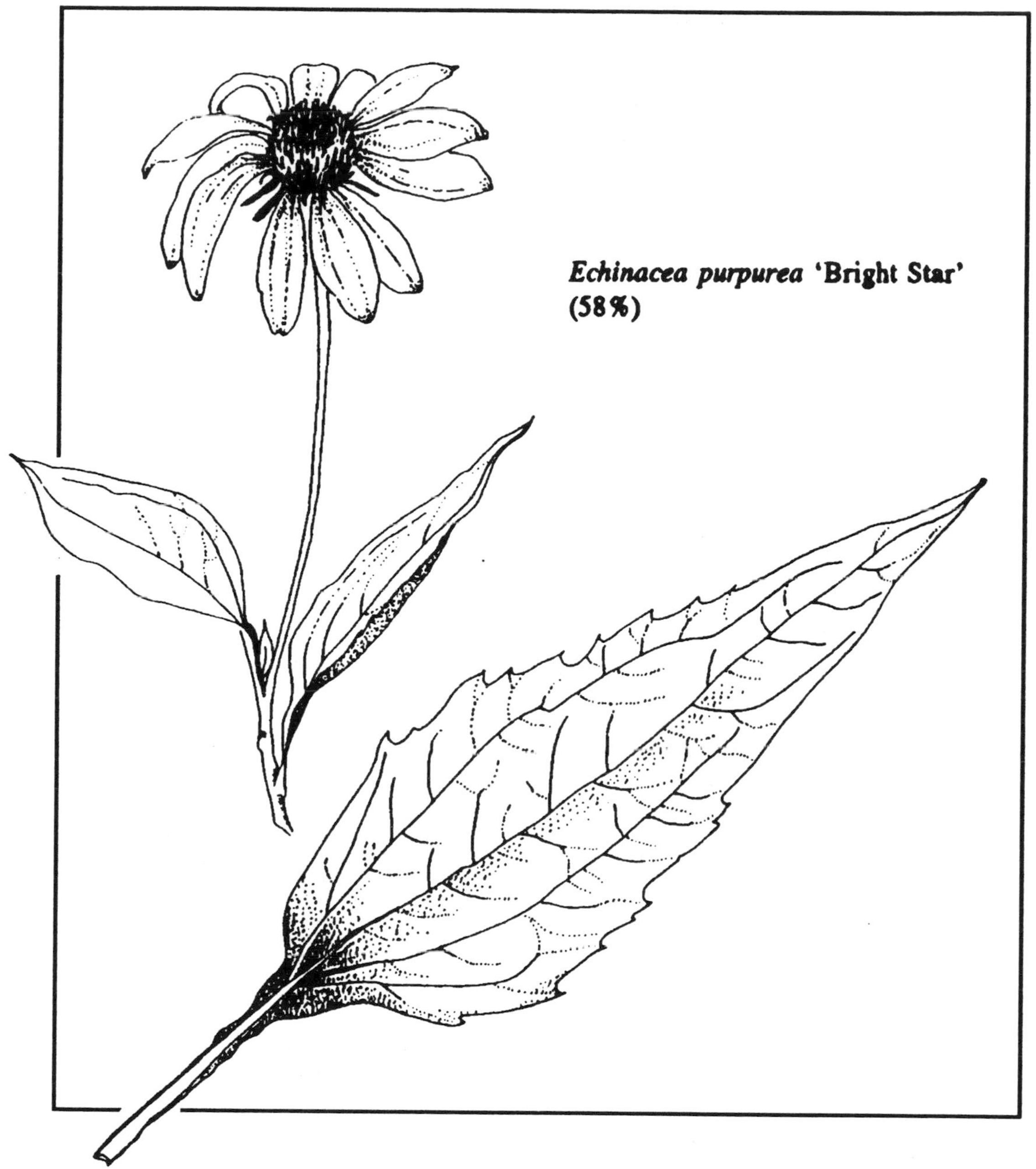

***Echinacea purpurea* 'Bright Star' (58%)**

'Bright Star' is a rose-colored, free-flowering cultivar that has performed well throughout the country. Plants are seed propagated and significant variability occurs. An old cultivar, but still popular.

'Coconut Lime' is similar to 'Pink Double Delight' but has creamy white flowers instead. Bred by dutch breeder Arie Bloom, this is the first double white coneflower introduced to the American market. It has yet to be trialed in many sites, but here's hoping its performance is as good as its promotion.

'Cygnet White' is a compact (18-20″ tall) form which is most suitable for the front of the garden or in containers.

'Doubledecker' reminds me of plants gone berserk. Believe it or not, the flowers are in two tiers (like a salvia), the short ray flowers of the uppermost flowers cling to the cone, perhaps hoping that somebody will put the entire thing out of its misery. But I can't argue with the uniqueness. Bluebird Nursery in Clarkson, Nebraska, one of America's premier growers, calls it "a exciting new novelty." Who am I to argue with the Bluebird folks?

'Fancy Frills' has pink petals that look like they were attacked by an insect. They are often described as frilly or shaggy, much better than "moth-eaten."

'Fatal Attraction' bears rosy-pink flowers on 2-3′ long black stems.

'Fragrant Angel' bears white upright ray flowers held horizontally around a golden disc. Plants are vigorous and flowers are nicely fragrant.

'Green Envy' is one of those offerings that you are either enamored with or wonder what the breeder was smoking. It is interesting, to be sure, with green ray flowers and a darker green center. Unfortunately, I have seen too many green-flowered plants dissolve in warm summers, so my amour is definitely lacking. So, I must ask—what was that smoke anyway?

'Hope' has fragrant pink flowers on 3′ tall plants The proceeds from the sale of this plant benefit the Susan Komen Foundation for Breast Cancer Research. A worthy joint venture between Terra Nova Nurseries of Tigard, Oregon and Walters Gardens of Zeeland, Michigan.

'Jade' produces dirty white ray flowers around a green center. Flowers are lightly fragrant and plants stand about 4′ tall.

'Kim's Knee-High' is my favorite coneflower because plants are vigorous, flowers are numerous and plants stand only about 2′ tall. The ray flowers overlap and are pendulant. Developed by Kim Hawks, who started Niche Gardens in Chapel Hill, North Carolina. And who says the Europeans don't show glimpses of brilliance? This plant was named the best new perennial in Holland in 2000, dispelling all doubt in the minds of non-believers.

'Kim's Mophead' is small in stature like 'Kim's Knee-High' but with white flowers. Persistent bloomer.

'Lilliput' is on of the many coneflowers developed by Dan Heims of Terra Nova Nurseries. The claim to fame of this light rosy-colored plant is that it stands only about 16″ tall.

'Little Giant' is only about 1½-2′ tall but bears large purple flowers.

'Magnus' is also rosy colored with petals that don't droop as much as those of the species. This is an old-fashioned selection but its popularity soared when it was designated the 1998 Perennial Plant of the Year by the Perennial Plant Association. An excellent selection!

'Mars' has outward facing intense purple ray flowers on 2-3′ tall stems.

Meadowbrite series was developed by Dr. Jim Ault at the Chicago Botanic Garden and put the perennial world on its ear when first seen. 'Orange Meadowbrite' ('Art's Pride') was a major breakthrough and the first orange coneflower in cultivation.

This was followed by 'Mango Meadowbrite' with mango-colored flowers. Both are fragrant and were exceptional breakthroughs in color. 'Pixie Meadowbright' is about 18″ tall and bears pink flowers for a long time during the summer.

'Merlot' has large purple flowers, with a orangey hue to the cone. Plants stand about 2½′ and sport black stems in the spring.

'Overton' is a seed-propagated form with rosy pink drooping ray flowers.

'Paranoia' first reminds me of the yellow-flowered *E. paradoxa*; the name is even similar. However, the ray flowers are more upright and the stems are stronger.

'Picca Bella' almost pushed me over to the dark side of *Echinacea* hell, but I suppose every plant deserves a try. This thing has a large dark cone surrounded by narrow wiry ray flowers that look like the thrips got at them. At least they are still sort of purple. Who knows, it may be a huge hit.

'Pink Double Delight' has bright pink double flowers on strong stems, growing 2′ tall. It is a more recent introduction than 'Razzmatazz' and is shorter and sturdier.

'Prairie Frost' has white margins around the green leaves, and pink flowers. It has been a mediocre performer in our gardens. Variegated coneflowers have a ways to go before they take their place in American gardens.

'Prairie Giant' has very large (up to 4½″ wide) rose-pink flowers on 3′ tall stems. Plants appear to be strong enough to be self-supporting, even with the size of the flowers and the length of the stems.

'Primadonna' boasts large white inflorescences with overlapping ray flowers. The disc is amber. Well branched and good garden plants where a whiter bloom is needed.

'Raspberry Tart' is only about 2′ tall and sports deep magenta flowers. Reasonably fragrant as well.

'Razzmatazz' is a cultivar you will either love or abhor. I think it is great. The double flowers are like little pompons, and are deliciously fragrant. While many agree with me, others look at this and say "Look what they have done to my plant!" To each his own. This is not the most vigorous coneflower in the cupboard, so give it plenty of sun and lots of air movement. Other additions to the double-flowered coneflowers, such as 'Pink Double Delight', 'Coconut Lime' and 'Doubledecker' are keeping the ice cream cone mentality alive and well.

'Robert Bloom' bears 3-4″ diameter purple-rose flowers, upright petals, on 3′ tall stems.

'Ruby Giant' is an excellent large-flowered form with purple flowers. Flowers are obviously bigger than other cultivars we've trialed. The plants were sufficiently impressive to receive a Classic City Award from the Gardens at UGA in 2005.

'Ruby Star' ('Rubinstern') is simply a "doer", an excellent coneflower with normal coneflower looks, except for the deeper purple color and the more horizontal ray flowers. A seed-propagated cultivar, it is terrific for mass plantings, like the one seen at the Chicago Botanic Garden. It was named "Fresh Cut Flower of the Year" for 2006 by the Association of Specialty Cut Flower Growers.

'Sparkler' looks like the leaves have either been splashed with white paint or spider mites have had a field day. Its vigor leaves something to be desired but if you are looking for something different (as if there is not enough), this is worth a try. Flowers are light pink.

'The King' is 4-5′ tall with 4-5″ diameter rose-red flowers. Its height is a disadvantage in today's smaller gardens and it has been superseded by more compact cultivars such as 'Bright Star' and 'Robert Bloom.'

'Tiki Torch' has large (4″ across) orange flowers, bigger and more robust than 'Orange Meadowbrite'. Plants stand about 3′ tall.

'Vintage Wine' from Piet Oudolf in Holland has deep purple flowers on 2-2½′ tall plants. One of the deepest colored coneflowers available.

'White Lustre' differs from 'White Swan' by having a little more bronze-orange center and more horizontal ray flowers. Plants are more uniform because they are often vegetatively propagated.

'White Swan' is a seed-propagated white form with drooping ray flowers.

**Related Species:**

*E. angustifolia*, narrow-leaf purple coneflower, is the western representative of this species. Plants are 1-3′ tall and have narrow, entire 4-6″ long leaves. They are as tough as any species but do not perform quite as well in the East as *E. purpurea*, although I have seen some wonderful stands in Georgia and North Carolina. The flowers are pink to creamy white with drooping ray flowers.

*E. laevigata*, smooth coneflower, has leaves up to 3″ long but differs from common purple coneflower by having smooth, rather than hairy, leaves on upper sides.

*E. simulata* is similar in form and flower habit to *E. pallida* but flowers are far more colorful. I don't know what the problem is but I never see this for sale outside the Great Plains.

*E. tennesseensis*, Tennessee coneflower, is a southeastern native and on the Federal Endangered Species List. A small number of nurseries now offer nursery-propagated plants to the gardener. The foliage is linear and plants grow 1½-2′ tall. Dark mauve flowers with upturned ray flowers and greenish-pink centers open from early June until August. In the garden, its lack of vigor compared with other plants often results in being overrun after a year or two. 'Rocky Top' is a selection with more vigor and bright pink flowers that will allow this endangered plant back into our gardens.

## ***Echinops*** (ek′ in-ops) Globe Thistle Asteraceae

I don't see as many globe thistles in gardens as I used to. Either they are less popular than they were 20 years ago, or I am visiting the wrong gardens. About 120 species are known, but only a few are common to gardens in North America. There is good reason for this; consider species such as *E. nivens* and *E. spinosissimus*. They both have handsome leaves that are white on the undersides but the foliage is almost lethal to the touch. The main species in cultivation is *E. ritro*, and its foliage only looks scary, appearing far more prickly than it really is. The flowers, however, are surrounded by bristly bracts and are not at all bare-hand friendly. The leaves are alternate and often have white hairs beneath while the small individual flowers are bunched in a steely blue, globelike inflorescence. Plants should be placed in full sun in well-drained soil.

***-ritro*** (rit′ ro) | Globe Thistle | 2-4′/3′
Summer | Blue | Europe, Western Asia | Zones 3-7

This is probably the best of the globe thistles, although considerable confusion exists as to the true identity of many of the plants sold as *E. ritro*. According to some sources, no changes are needed, but others have essentially replaced it with *E. bannaticus*. That taxonomists are still arguing about which is which tells me that we should not worry at all about what to buy, plants bearing either name will perform in the same way.

The 6-8″ long leaves have deep wavy margins. The upper surface is smooth while the underside is gray green and hairy (originally, in *E, bannaticus*, the upper surface of the leaves were hairy). The stems branch near the top and numerous 1-2″ diameter globose dark blue flowers are formed in early summer (mid-June to mid-August in zone 7, about 1 week later in zone 6). The flowers are a beekeeper's delight as they are particularly attractive to bumblebees and nocturnal moths.

I have grown *Echinops* in southern Ontario, Michigan, and north Georgia and found it to be a reliable plant. The cooler nights in the North, however, result in much deeper blue flowers compared with plants in the South, and it can be recommended as far north as Alaska. Dry, poor soil is quite suitable for all species.

Globe thistle produces 4-10 flowers per branched stem which can be used fresh or as long-lasting dried flowers. If placed in a dry, warm environment, flowers dry without loss of color, and have become popular with florists and floral designers.

Propagate by seed, divisions, or root cuttings. Seeds germinate within 3 weeks if planted in peat-vermiculite and placed at 70-75°F and under high humidity. Division should not be attempted until plants are at least 3 years old. At that time, basal plantlets are visible. Approximately 2-3″ long pieces of roots may be cut in the spring. Treat root cuttings similarly to those of *Anemone*.

**Cultivars:**

These may be listed under *E. ritro* or *E. bannaticus*. Buying by cultivar rather than by species should keep you out of trouble. Most of these cultivars look almost the same anyway.

'Blue Globe' ('Blue Ball') is about 3′ tall with dark blue flowers.

'Blue Glow' has flowers of deeper blue than the species, grows 3-4′ tall.

'Blue Pearl' has mid-blue flowers on 3′ tall plants.

subsp. *ruthenicus* differs by having deeply divided basal leaves whose segments are quite narrow, giving the plant the appearance of a cutleaf form of globe thistle. It is usually listed as a distinct species or as a subspecies of *E. ritro*. The undersides of the leaves are generally whiter and plants are shorter than those of *E. ritro*. A handsome garden form, but not as cold hardy.

'Taplow Blue' is the most popular cultivar and bears 2″ wide steel-blue flowers. It is now generally listed under *E. bannaticus*.

'Taplow Purple' is bluish purple and not as attractive as 'Taplow Blue'.

'Veitch's Blue' has steelier blue flowers than 'Taplow Blue' and is very popular in European gardens. The darker flower color also makes it the best choice for Southern gardens.

**Related Species:**

*E. exaltatus*, Russian globe thistle, is the tallest of the globe thistles and can grow to 8 feet in height. The stems are unbranched and the leaves are more spiny than the previous species. The flowers are silvery white and flower later than those of *E. ritro*. Native from eastern Europe to western Russia.

*E. sphaerocephalus*, great globe thistle, grows up to 3′ in height and has narrow foliage with sharp spines on the margins. The round flowers are silvery blue. This is quite striking and while the species is seldom sold, the cultivar 'Arctic Glow' is commonly offered. Flowers are a little more silvery than the species.

***Echium*** (e′ kee-um) Viper's Bugloss Boraginaceae

Most of the 40 species are native to Europe and the Canary Islands and one or two of the short forms such as *E. plantagineum* and *E. vulgare* are becoming popular as annual or biennial garden fillers. *E. vulgare* has been around for centuries and has acquired more than a few colorful names. Some of them include viper's bugloss, adderwort, blue devil, blue thistle, blueweed, bugloss, cat's tail, North American blueweed, snake flower, viper's grass and viper's herb. The best cultivar is 'Blue Bedder', which provides a better habit and more colorful flowers.

A few very impressive species appear like large rockets whose missiles of blue flower spikes look ready to launch. Between 6′ and 10′ tall, plants bear hundreds of terminal blue or white flowers. Many are biennials, producing large basal rosettes of smooth leaves the first year, then after the winter, sending up their tall spikes of flowers. Once they flower, they make seeds and die. The 6-8′ tall hybrids of *E. pininana*, giant viper's bugloss, also known as the tower of jewels, can be seen happily growing in southern California, and other areas where temperature fluctuation is minimal. I was indeed fortunate to be in the garden of Evelyn Alemanni in Escondido, in southern California, where these blue rockets had reseeded and were spectacular. There was nothing short-lived about them! Cultivars in pink and white are available, but why mess with a good thing? Each time I see them, I marvel at the diversity of plant life on this great planet. *E. pininiana* and *E. wildpretii*, also known as tower of jewels, are said to be cold hardy to around 15°F, although no hybrids or species enjoy hot or humid summer conditions. Others that may be fun for the explorative gardener are the tall and unbranched *E. simplex*, pride of Tenerife, and *E. candicans*, pride of Madeira, which often behaves as a biennial.

Just for the heck of it, I tried *E. russicum*, red bugloss, in the Gardens at UGA, and have been quite impressed. The red spikelike flowers rose about 18″ to 2′ but the foliage was healthy all season and plants have come back for 3 years. I certainly recommend this to gardeners; it is not a rocket, but it is a fun plant to try.

All plants of viper's bugloss are easy to propagate from seed. Sow seeds in a warm, humid area and overwinter seedlings in a cool greenhouse. If planted out in the spring, after the last frost, flowering often occurs in the summer. Place in full sun in relatively poor soil, fertile soils result in leafy plants. Most attractive to bees and butterflies.

***Endymion*** See ***Hyacinthoides***

**Enemion** See **Isopyrum**

**Eomecon** (ee-om e′ con) Snow Poppy, Chinese Bloodroot Papaveraceae

A genus of just one species, *E. chionantha*, the snow poppy has understated beauty when young, but can become a major nuisance as the years pass. The leathery leaves, emerging from the rootstalk, have wavy margins and three to four main whitish veins. The sap is orange. The 1-2″ wide white flowers arise in early to mid-spring with centers of yellow stamens, somewhat similar to bloodroot, thus its other common name. Flowering is usually sparse.

The nuisance part of this plant results from the traveling tendencies of the vigorous creeping rhizomes, creating large mats of snow poppies where there were few before. This is obviously a major benefit if a ground cover is preferred.

Plants are native to eastern China and cold tolerant to about –5°F; I do not know their heat tolerance limit, but at least to zone 7b. They require cool, moist conditions but can tolerate more sun providing the roots are constantly moist. They look miserable under drought conditions, but once water is applied, they move on, and on and on ...

**Epilobium** (e-pi-lo′ bee-um) Willowherb Onagraceae

Over 200 species of *Epilobium* occur, and now that the genus *Zauschneria* has been folded in, this group of plants just keeps expanding. They are native mainly to western North America but also may be found in many temperate areas of the world. *E. glabellum*, for example, has attractive rose-violet flowers with yellow stamens and is native to New Zealand. Although the genus is large and plants are found over large areas, plants are seldom found or used east of the Rocky Mountains. Many of the garden-worthy species bear handsome flowers in late summer to fall but all can be very invasive. The most prolific and spreading species is *E. angustifolium*, rosebay willowherb, also called fireweed, so named because of its ability to colonize waste ground after a fire. Willowherb spreads by long white stolons and airborne seeds, which can carry a tremendous distance. Both *E. angustifolium* and *E. hirsutum*, affectionately known as codlins and cream, make massive stands where conditions are to their liking.

Nearly all the species have pink to rose flowers, with occasional white varieties or cultivars available. The easiest species to distinguish is *E. luteum* with its yellow flowers while the most common by far is *E. angustifolium*. The flowers of all species consist of 4 sepals and 4 petals as well as 4 short and 4 long stamens and are typically held in racemes above the foliage. The seed pods are long slender rods and look like flower stalks of the spent flowers.

***-angustifolium*** (an-gust-i-fo′ lee-um) Rosebay Willowherb, Fireweed 4-9′/4′
Summer Rose, Purple Western North America Zones 3-7

Its common name was particularly appropriate in England during and after the London blitzes, when fireweed quickly colonized burnt-out areas, not only in London but throughout devastated areas in Europe. That it is capable of such behavior should also make gardeners cautious about its use in any formal setting. Gardeners who enjoy the beauty of a mass of these plants (and they are beautiful) allow them to "do their thing" for a year or two, then religiously remove the flowers before seed is produced. On the West Coast, plants are every bit as rambunctious as in Europe but they are a little better behaved in the northern plain states and in Canada. They do poorly in the South and are not worth the effort.

The reflexed, irregularly shaped (zygomorphic) 4-petaled flowers, which may be rosy, purple or lavender, are held in many-flowered racemes. The stigma is 4-lobed and protrudes from the flowers on the long style. The alternate leaves are 4-8″ long and less than ½″ wide (much like a weeping willow leaf). The attractive seed heads are silky and translucent but if you see them, you will likely be seeing a lot more plants next spring.

They spread by stolons to make handsome colonies. Full sun is preferred but a little shade may be tolerated. Soil is not particularly important. It will grow almost anywhere where climate is reasonably cool.

Propagate by division or seed.

**Cultivars:**

'Album' is a beautiful white-flowered form with green sepals. Seeds produce mainly white plants, with some rose.

'Isobel' has pale pink flowers and crimson sepals.

| -***canum*** (cay′ num) | | California Fuchsia | 1-2′/18″ |
|---|---|---|---|
| Late Summer | Scarlet | California | Zones 6-9 |

(syn. *Zauschneria cana*)

Recent discussion in taxonomic circles had placed all species of *Zauschneria* into *Zauschneria cana*, and now all of those have been blended into various subspecies of *Epilobium canum*. While such wholesale movements are not the least conducive to gardeners, we might as well be aware and bite the bullet. However, such changes take years to filter down to producers and retailers and thus plants known as California fuchsia are still sold under *Zauschneria*.

The linear to linear-lanceolate leaves are white-woolly and velvety to the touch. The lower leaves are opposite while those toward the top are alternate. The 1-1½″ long bright scarlet flowers are held in racemes and look like fuchsias. The bright red-orange flowers are great hummingbird attractors, explaining the other common name, hummingbird trumpet. The showy flowers and low-growing habit make plants suitable for the front of the border or the rock garden. Plants tolerate full sun or partial shade but good drainage is essential, particularly in the Southeast, where winter rains are common. One of the drawbacks is the hairy, messy seeds which detract from the plants in the fall. Removal of the spent flowers reduces the problem. Hardiness range is difficult to make sense of, although most hardiness ratings are purely speculative anyway. Since humidity and afternoon rain are not preferred, they do better in zone 6 of Denver than zone 7b of Athens and do much better in zone 8 of Portland, Oregon than zone 8 of southern Alabama. The soils also make a huge difference. Sandy or gritty soils are much better than heavy clay soils.

Propagate by seed in a moist, warm (70-75°F) environment. Seed emerges within 3 weeks. Terminal cuttings may also be used in early summer. Cut 2-3″ long terminals and place in sand or a peat-vermiculite mix. Maintain moisture and warmth until roots appear (usually within 2-3 weeks).

**Cultivars:**
'Albiflora' is unusual in that the flowers are white.
'Dublin' is smaller than the species, growing only 12-18″ tall. This is still the most popular form of *Zauschneria* (oops, *Epilobium*). From the fine Glasnevin Botanical Garden outside Dublin, Ireland.
'Sir Cedric Morris' has rosy red flowers on more compact plants.
'Solidarity Pink' bears pale pink flowers.

**Related Species:**

*E. dodonaei* is only 1-2′ tall and is a multi-stemmed plant with reddish stolons. The linear leaves are only about 1″ long, and the deep rose-purple flowers, with a slightly protruding style, are held in loose inflorescences. Native to central and western Europe and Asia. Probably hardy in zones 6-7 (8 on the West Coast).

*E. garrettii* is less than 8″ tall with handsome reddish flowers. However, 'Orange Carpet', about 6″ tall, has wonderful orange-scarlet flowers. This received a Plant Select® award from the Denver Botanic Garden and Colorado State University in 2001.

*E. fleischeri* resembles *E. dodonaei* but has a much longer style and less deeply colored flowers. Plants grow about 18″ tall and bear gray-green foliage on red stems. Native to the European Alps, cold hardy to zone 5. A Plant Select® winner in 2002.

## *Epimedium* (ep-ee-mee′ dee-um) Barrenwort Berberidaceae

In the last edition I wrote that this was "a genus whose time has come, with plenty of attributes and very few faults." Today, barrenwort is well established and earns great marks in nearly all parts of the country. Whenever I speak to audiences about perennials, enthusiasm about this genus is always high, and good garden centers stock up on plants for the spring season. The travels and breeding work of people like Barry Yinger, Dan Hinkley, Robin White and especially Darrell Probst have opened up the epimedium world; the development and availability of plants has never been greater.

How times have changed. In his classic work (1938) on the genus "Epimedium and Vancouveria", Dr. W.T. Stern recognized 21 species. However, in the last 15 years, with expanded access to China, the number has more than doubled, with new species and cultivars regularly being introduced. In 2005, I counted 155 taxa from one catalog, 15 from another, and 45 from yet another. And this was just scratching the surface. For gardeners, half a dozen will do, for collectors, it appears that more space is needed.

Once established, most species make magnificent ground covers, and many are evergreen. They do best in soils which have been amended with copious amounts of organic matter such as peat moss. They compete well with roots of trees and tolerate heavy shade, growing in barren areas where many other species perish.

Somewhere along the garden lecture circuit, some speaker must have shouted that the genus enjoyed dry shade conditions, and if one had those conditions (which everyone does) one should run out and plunk in barrenwort. He or she must have been good, because everyone believed him (or her). The speaker was correct, and such conditions scream for epimediums. However, the fact is that these plants *tolerate* such conditions better than many others, but they grow a great deal better in light shade with even moisture. It is unfair to judge the performance of a genus based on the worst conditions found in the garden. Have a heart—plant an epimedium where you plant a hosta.

They can be slow to establish, but they also will form wonderful colonies in a few years. They consist of compound foliage (leaves in 2 groups of three), and each leaf has an oblique leaf base (one side of the base is bigger than the other) which makes the genus easy to identify. The flowers consist of four petals and eight sepals. The sepals are arranged in two groups. The outer sepals are usually small, early deciduous and hardly noticeable while the colored inner four look more like petals. These petals may be spurred (like columbine) or hooded, giving rise to common names like bishop's hat or bishop's mitre.

In the spring, the leaves are often tinged pink or red and in the fall they usually turn yellow, red, or bronze. If the foliage of evergreen forms is clipped low to the ground very early in spring, the flowers are far easier seen and better appreciated, otherwise they are lost in the leaves. Another reason for cutting off old leaves is to appreciate the beauty of the new foliage. A little effort in cleaning goes a long way in admiring. All plants are excellent ground covers and persist for many years if provided the proper environment, although the hardiness of new species has yet to be well established.

A useful public collection of epimediums may be found in the trial gardens at the University of Georgia. At least 15 taxa are grown side by side so that differences and similarities can be compared.

Propagate by division in late spring, after flowering has been completed, or summer. They are easy to divide and move at any time.

Quick Guide to Epimedium Species

| | Plant height (in.) | Flower color (Y/N) | Flowers with conspicuous spurs | Evergreen or deciduous |
|---|---|---|---|---|
| *E. acuminatum* | 12-15 | Pinkish | Y | E |
| *E. alpinum* | 6-9 | Dull red | Y | D |
| *E. grandiflorum* | 8-15 | Pale pink | Y | D |
| *E. perralderianum* | 10-12 | Yellow | N | E |
| *E. pinnatum* | 8-12 | Yellow | N | D |
| *E x rubrum* | 8-12 | Bright red | N | D |
| *E. x youngianum* | 6-8 | White | N | E |

***-acuminatum*** (a-kew-mi-nah′ ta) Pointed Barrenwort 12-15″/15″
Spring Pinkish China Zones 5-8

Plants were originally discovered in 1858 by the French missionary Perny, and a number of forms have come into cultivation since the early 1980s. It is relatively easy to distinguish this species from others because of the long tapered apex (acuminate) on each leaf. The large dark green leaves are also hairy along the margins. The flowers are magnificent, with creamy or pale pink outer sepals and larger pink, rose or purple-spurred inner parts, making a wonderful contrast. Protect from strong winds and provide a shaded, cool spot.

**Cultivars:**

'Hot Lips', from Collector's Nursery in Battle Ground, Washington, bears deep red long spurred petals and red tinged flower stems. The long narrow foliage emerges reddish pink.

'Pink Constellation' has wonderfully large pink flowers, but the dark green, sharp-tipped foliage is equally handsome.

***-alpinum*** (al-pine′ um) Alpine Barrenwort 6-9″/12″
Spring Dull Red South and Central Europe Zones 4-7

The leaves are arranged in two groups of three and the 2-3″ long leaflets are pointed at the end, although not as obvious as *E. acuminatum*. Up to 20 small flowers occur in a loose raceme above the foliage in April and May. The outer sepals are grayish with specks of red; the inner sepals are dark crimson while the petals are yellowish and slipper shaped. This is an excellent ground cover, particularly in the northern end of the range. The species has served well as a parent of numerous hybrids such as *E.* x *warleyense*, *E.* x *rubrum* and *E.* x *cantabrigiense*.

**Cultivars:**

'Rubrum' has brighter red inner sepals and petals that are more yellow than the type. Plants are vigorous and multiply rapidly.

**- *brachyrrhizum*** (brack-ee-rise′ um) Short-root Barrenwort 8-12″/12″
Spring Pale Pink China Zones 5-8

I include this relatively unknown species because it is an excellent performer and reliable every year. The plants are short and produce almost round, leathery leaves that emerge with a fine rose to purple tinge in the spring. The flowers are spread out on the rhizome; each rose-pink bloom bears wonderful long spurs.

Plants come back reliably but are not fast growing.

***-grandiflorum*** (grand-i-flo′ rum) Longspur Barrenwort 8-15″/15″
Spring Pale Pink Japan Zones 5-8

Plants produce some of the larger flowers in the genus and are some of the best performers in the eclectic Armitage garden. The large flowers combined with some of the smaller leaves helps to identify these plants. The bright green leaflets are spiny-toothed and are only about 1″ long. The young spring foliage is beige-brown, greening up in early summer. Outer sepals are white, inner ones pale yellow, and the petals are rose or violet with a conspicuous ½ " long spur. About a dozen ¾-1½″ diameter flowers are arranged in a tight raceme. Plants are intolerant of alkaline soils.

**Cultivars:**

'Album' has creamy white flowers.

'Benedict's Violet' grows 9-12″ tall and bears large flowers with purple backsides and even darker purple spurs. From the late Herb Benedict, renowned hosta and epimedium breeder.

'Dark Beauty' has purple and white flowers with long spurs, over 6″ tall plants.

var. *higonse* makes orderly compact mounds of more deeply cut leaves and clean white flowers. The cultivar 'Bandit' has creamy white flowers over 6″ tall plants with handsome foliage, particularly in the spring.

'Pierre's Purple', brought to you by Darrell Probst and named after Pierre Bennerup of Sunny Border Nursery, bears dark purple flowers in the spring. Plants are quite tall, up to 15″.

'Lilafee' bears lavender-violet flowers and has become a popular cultivar in many areas.

'Nanum' is only about 4-6″ tall with chocolate brown margins on the leaves. Creamy flowers occur in spring.

'Purple Prince' bears many entirely purple flowers, interesting if not spectacular.

'Red Queen' has red backs with white spurs. One of the most colorful forms out there, and that is saying a great deal.

'Rose Queen' is one of the prettiest cultivars and has crimson leaves. The flowers are among the more visible in the genus and are rose-pink with long white-tipped spurs. They are larger but borne in smaller numbers than the species. There is a bit of controversy concerning this cultivar. According to epimedium expert Robin White of Blackthorn Nursery in England, the real 'Rose Queen' has deep rose to crimson flowers without white or just a little white on the tips of the spurs, while a lighter-colored form bearing the same name may be something else. They are all terrific, but the darker form without white spurs is probably the true 'Rose Queen'. A subsp. *koreanum* produces handsome long-spurred creamy yellow flowers, but they are often scarcely produced and hidden by the foliage. Plants bear large leaves; the young ones are bronze in the spring.

'Sirius' is old (1990) in epimedium years but still one of the best white-flowered forms being offered. From Dick Weaver of We-Du Nursery.

'White Queen' is similar to 'Rose Queen' but with silvery-white flowers.

'Violaceum' has large murky violet flowers. The new foliage has bronze veins.

***-perralderianum*** (pe-ral-der-ee-ah′ num) 10-12″/12″

Spring | Yellow | Algeria | Zones 5-8

Each evergreen leaf consists of 3 spiny-edged shiny leaflets, each about 3″ long, usually light green when young and later tinted red-brown. The unbranched inflorescence consists of 20-25 yellow flowers. This species is similar to *E. pinnatum* but not as good a garden plant. The small brownish spur is hardly noticeable.

***-pinnatum*** (pin-nay′ tum) 8-12″/12″
Late Spring Yellow Northern Iran Zones 5-8

Plants were collected by Roy Lancaster in 1979 and the species, particularly subsp. *colchicum*, has been quickly embraced in cultivation. The leaves are composed of 5 or more leaflets and the whole plant is hairy, particularly when young. The bright citrus yellow flowers have very small petals and short brownish spurs and are arranged in a loose inflorescence of 12-30 flowers. Plants have no stem leaves; all the leaves arise directly from the root.

**Cultivars:**

subsp. *colchicum* is the most common form of the species. Leaves are sparsely toothed and smooth on the margins. Plants have larger flowers and are more free flowering than the type. This is one of the more vigorous and floriferous epimediums in the Armitage garden, second only to 'Sulphureum'.

***-pubigerum*** (poo-big′ er-um) Barrenwort 18-24″/15″
Spring Yellow with Tan Southeast Europe Zones 5-8

With all the similar-looking epimediums around, I really enjoy finally seeing one that I can identify with confidence. It is one of the tallest species and makes wonderful mounds, rather than the spreading ground cover common to many others. The foliage is evergreen in mild climates but deciduous further north. The new leaves are tinged red in the spring. The flowers are held well above the foliage, so there is no losing them in the leaves. I like this plant because of its unique habit, many, if not showy, flowers and reliability.

**-x *rubrum*** (rew′ brum) Red Barrenwort 8-12″/12″
Spring Red Hybrid Zones 5-8

A hybrid between *E. alpinum* and *E. grandiflorum*, with the robustness of the latter and the height of the former. Each of the 15-20 flowers is up to 1″ across and clustered in a loose inflorescence held slightly above the many leaflets. The heart-shaped leaflets are particularly pretty in the spring and fall when tinged red. The foliage remains red in cool summers but changes to green in warm summers. The long thin rhizomes are adaptable to many soils and result in one of the fastest growing ground covers. The inner sepals are crimson red and the petals are pale yellow or tinted red. Absolutely one of the best species to chose for a ground cover.

**Cultivars:**

'Sweetheart' from Darrell Probst, was originally introduced as 'Cobblewood Form' and may occasionally still be seen under that name. Plants are more vigorous, the leaves are richer in red, and the flowers stand up against the foliage. When grown well, an outstanding introduction.

**-x *versicolor*** (verse' i-color) | Bicolor Barrenwort | 7-12"/12"
Spring | Yellow | Hybrid | Zones 5-8

Plants are the result of a cross between *E. grandiflorum* and *E. pinnatum* subsp. *colchicum*. They usually have 9 leaflets that are conspicuously red mottled when young, turning to green in early summer. The sepals are light rose, the petals yellow, and the spur has a red tinge. The most popular selection from this cross is 'Sulphureum', an excellent clone and one of the no-brainers for beginning gardeners. Plants are evergreen in all but the hardest winters. The 5-11 leaflets give rise to a leafy flowering stem bearing pale yellow sepals and bright yellow petals. This has been one of the toughest epimediums in the shady, dry conditions under the oak trees in my garden. 'Cherry Tart' has two tone pink and bright red flowers. 'Neosulphureum' is similar but has 3-9 leaflets, brownish when young, and slightly shorter spurs. All cultivars flower earlier than most other barrenworts.

**-x *youngianum*** (yun-gee-aye' num) | Young's Barrenwort | 6-8"/8"
Spring | White | Japan | Zones 5-8

This hybrid resulted from crossing *E. diphyllum* and *E. grandiflorum* and is one of the easiest to establish. The leaves, which are deciduous, arise from the base of the plant and are usually divided into nine ovate pointed leaflets. The leaflets are sharply serrated, marked with red upon emergence in the spring, and turn a deep crimson in the fall. Plants form small clumps of leaves with 2-6 small leaflets. The 3-8 pendulous flowers are about ¾" across and light pinkish white. Flowers are essentially spurless. Plants require more humus-rich soils than many others and are relatively slow growing. The species itself is seldom offered, being superseded by the cultivars.

**Cultivars:**

'Merlin' arose from a chance seedling in a garden in Dorset County, England. Plants are similar and flowers are a dusky purple.

'Niveum' is the most common cultivar and bears lovely small white flowers. Similar to a form called 'Milky Way' and may be the same thing.

'Pink Star' should supersede 'Roseum' as the plants are more vigorous and the flowers held well above the foliage. An excellent cultivar just recently available.

'Roseum' has rose to pinkish lilac flowers.

'Tambabotan' is the latest of the many stars of the epimedium world to emerge from Japan. The flowers are slightly two toned, light lavender changing to darker lavender near the tips. The foliage is beautifully dusky purple in the spring, changing to green as summer progresses.

**Related Species:**

With the incredible explosion in species, cultivars and hybrids, there is no way to make this listing complete. Going online or reading some of the better catalogs will provide many more names than I can bring. But here are a few more of my favorites.

'After Midnight', from Collector's Nursery in Battle Ground, Washington, produces many white starry flowers that contrast with the chocolate brown leaves in spring.

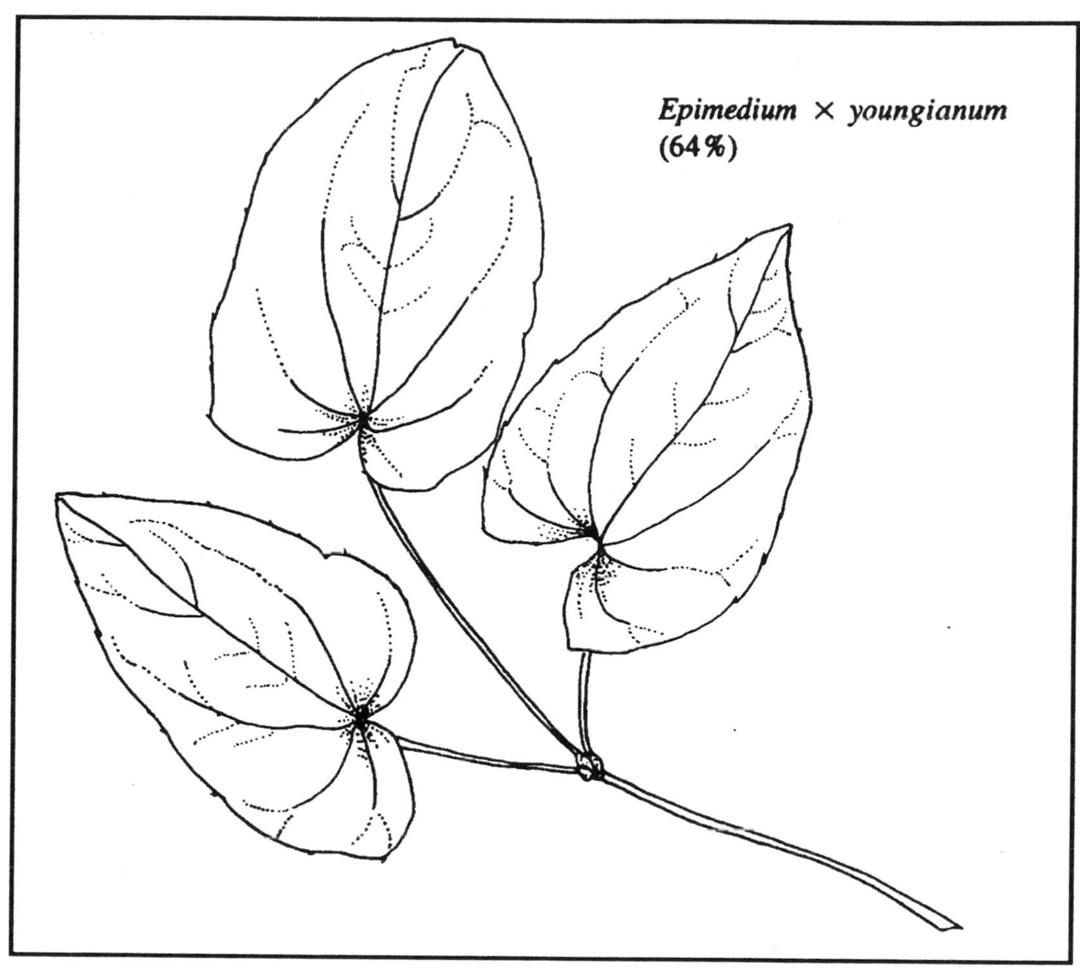


'Amber Queen' has wonderful yellow to orange flowers over green leaves marked with reddish borders.

*E.* x *cantabrigense*, a hybrid with *E. alpinum* and *E. pubigerum*, a species with glossy leaves and creamy white yellowish flowers, has become popular. Plants arose in St. John's College in Cambridge, England and consist of 1-2′ tall mounds of evergreen nine-leaflet leaves. Hardy to zone 4.

'Cherry Heart' has the habit of 'Sweetheart' but produces much larger red margins on the foliage and white flowers in the spring.

*E. davidii* is a small, low-growing species, but bears small bright yellow flowers with a conspicuous spur. Slow to grow but bright and beautiful.

*E. diphyllum* has been mentioned as a parent in a number of crosses. Plants produce small gray-green leaves and small white flowers, and is a wonderful small-bodied plant. It's just plain small. The cultivar 'Variegatum' has white speckles on the leaves and makes the term "gruesome" an understatement. However, how many variegated epimediums do you know?

'Enchantress' (*E. dolichostemon* x *E. leptorrhizum*) has been in my garden for many years. Plants produce rough leathery evergreen foliage with long narrow apices, more resembling *E. acuminatum* than anything else. The spidery flowers bear long spurs and are purple in color. Plants are 4-6″ tall.

'Fire Dragon' bears yellow and purple flowers on 1½′ tall plants.

*E. leptorrhizum*, native to Sichuan, is a low-growing species with leathery evergreen leaves and large rose-red flowers. Plants spread rapidly.

'Lilac Cascade' appears to have a good deal of *E. grandiflorum* and produces equally large flowers as found in that species. The lilac flowers are beautiful and the leaves are tinged with pink to lilac throughout.

*E.* x *perralchicum* 'Frohnleiten', selected in Germany, grows 4-8″ tall and is one of the most robust forms available. Plants are natural hybrids between *E. perralderianum* and *E. pinnatum* subsp. *colchicum*. The evergreen, spiny leaves have a reddish tint both when young and in the winter. They have exceptional yellow flowers (sometimes with red centers) held on leafless stems. A fabulous plant, on the Armitage top five list of epimediums for the garden. The cultivar 'Wisley' also resulted from the same parentage and is somewhat similar to 'Frohnleiten'.

'Pink Elf' has many flowers of pink and red above dark green leaves.

*E.* x *setosum* is a low-growing hybrid, supposedly between *E. diphyllum* and *E. sempervirens*, two species from Japan. The leaves are lime green in the spring and green up in the summer. Small, starry white flowers occur in early spring. Dainty and truly wonderful.

*E.* x *warleyense* arose in the early 1900s in Warley Place, Essex, England, the garden of Miss Willmott (see *Eryngium giganteum*). The hybrid, a result of natural pollination of *E. alpinum* x *E. pinnatum* subsp. *colchicum* has dull green leaves and eyecatching flowers of coppery red inner sepals and yellow petals. I do not find it to be particularly vigorous, but it certainly is beautiful when in flower.

## ***Eranthis*** (er-anth′ is) Winter Aconite Ranunculaceae

The seven species comprising the genus bear solitary bright yellow flowers in late winter and early spring. The petals are modified into small nectaries and the showy part of the flower consists of sepals only. The winter aconites have short stems and are best massed under deciduous trees or along river banks where they can be naturalized. Flowers do not show up well when planted in grass. Where they are happy, pastures of aconites produce a riot of yellow in early to mid-March followed by fine fernlike foliage. Unfortunately for gardeners in the South, happiness seldom occurs. Plants are far better in the North where hard winters and cold soil temperatures are the norm.

Tubers do better in alkaline soils but will increase if left undisturbed in almost any soil, as plants seed prolifically. Plant tubers about 2″ deep in late summer or early autumn. Propagation is most successful by lifting the tubers after they have been undisturbed for two to three years and breaking them into smaller pieces. The pieces may not flower the first winter but will the next. Plants raised from seed require three to four years to flower.

***-hyemalis*** (hye-e-mah′ lis) Winter Aconite 4-6″/4″
Winter, Early Spring Yellow Western Europe Zones 3-7

The solitary 1-2″ diameter flowers are made up of 6 sepals and appear before the attractive 3-5 lobed palmately cut leaves. Beneath each flower is a large collar-shaped bract which appears to support each blossom. These are so early that many gardeners cannot be without them because they bring the hope of spring. The late great gardener H. Lincoln Foster certainly could not be without his aconites. They "thrust their shining yellow cups through .... the snow that overlay them, and they were spread in a profligate scattering of doubloons, as though flung across a white damask table cloth, each golden coin surrounded by a ruff of deep green leaves." (*Rock Gardening*, 1968).

The tubers are ridiculously inexpensive so there is little excuse not to plant in masses of 50 or more. Plant immediately upon purchase as I have had great disappointments with dried-out tubers never emerging. Judy Laushman, in northeast Ohio, suggests tubers be soaked in water overnight for best garden emergence. Within a few years those 50 bulbs will form a golden carpet to welcome the onset of spring. They are particularly beautiful meandering down a slope or naturalized in a wildflower setting. They do not spread as rapidly in zone 7 as in zone 4 but are still effective. If less than successful in the garden, use them in containers where drainage is better. Another alternative is to purchase green started seedlings in early spring to insure establishment. Finding such seedlings, unfortunately, is a major challenge.

**Cultivars:**
'Glory' has large lemon-yellow flowers.

**Related Species:**

*E. cilicica* is similar to *E. hyemalis* but flowers earlier and is more robust. The leaves are tinged bronze on emergence, turning green with age. The flowers are the same bright yellow.

*E.* x *tubergenii* is a hybrid of *E. hyemalis* and *E. cilicica*. It has 2-2½″ wide flowers that, because they are sterile, persist longer than those of *E. hyemalis*. 'Guinea Gold' has leaves tinged with bronze and deep yellow, fragrant flowers. It is the most handsome form of all but not particularly easy to locate in the trade.

***Eremurus*** (air-uh-mure′ us) Foxtail Lily Asphodelaceae

Few plants are as impressive as a foxtail lily in flower. The most stately species may be *E. robustus*, which bears 8 to 10′ tall spikelike inflorescences of peach-colored flowers. *E. stenophyllus*, narrow-leaf foxtail lily, on the other hand, is only 2 to 3 feet tall with bright yellow flowers but is equally handsome. Of the thirty species, many of which have been hybridized, only a few are widely available in North America.

The genus belongs to the same group of plants as the red hot poker (*Kniphofia*) and lesser-known bulbs like bulbine and asphodeline. All the leaves arise from the thick fibrous root and disappear shortly after flowering. In their natural habitat, many species grow in steppe vegetation, often on mountain slopes. They need a thoroughly drained, rich soil and will not do well in heavy clays. To grow them successfully, it is necessary to mulch the plants as soon as the leaves emerge in the spring because spring frosts are deadly. Plant the crowns about 6″ deep as soon they are received, for they must not be allowed to dry out. In the Gardens at UGA, I must have planted foxtails a dozen different times. We simply don't get along, not once have I seen a decent plant emerge and flower. However, if they work for you, choose a site in full sun out of prevailing winds. Although they are not the easiest plants to grow, they are well worth the effort.

- x ***isabellinus*** (is-a-bell-eye′ nus) Shelford Foxtail Lily 4-8′/3′
Summer Various Hybrid Zones 5-7

These hybrids were originally raised in Great Shelford, Cambridge, England and are often listed as Shelford hybrids. Plants are variable and 3-4′ long racemes in shades of yellow, pink, white, and copper are produced in summer. These free-flowering hybrids are the result of crossing *E. stenophyllus*, a short species with bright yellow flowers, and *E. olgae*, a medium to tall, white-flowered species. The spider-like roots should be spread out carefully in early spring or fall in planting holes 6-8″ deep and 18″ apart. Do not bury the crown more than 1-2″ below the surface as it may rot if rains occur before plants are well established. Plants do well in full sun and well-drained soils and generally look best against a green background, such as a hedge of Leyland cypress. Protection from high winds is essential if plants are to look their best. The flowers open from bottom to top and remain in flower for 2-3 weeks. The leaves decline after flowering and foliage and flowers self-destruct by late summer. Plant annuals or perennials which flop over such as *Boltonia asteroides* or *Clematis heracleifolia* to hide the foliage and fill in the gap when the leaves go dormant. I have had only moderate success in zone 7b.

Propagate by division after 3-4 years. When the leaves have died back, carefully lift the crowns and gently separate into individual plants. Plants grown from seed will take four to six years to flower.

**Cultivars:**

'Cleopatra' has burnt orange flowers, growing 4-5′ tall.
'Isobel' has pink-orange flowers on 5-6′ plants.
'Moonlight' bears pale yellow flowers.
'Pinocchio' is 4-5′ tall with bright yellow flowers.
'Lemon Meringue' has soft yellow flowers on 3-5′ tall stems.
'Romance' is stunning, with light salmon flowers combined with yellow/orange stamens. Plants are only 3-4′ tall.
'Rosalind' displays bright pink flowers and is 5-6′ tall.
'White Beauty' has clear white blossoms.

**Related Species and Hybrids:**

*E. aitchisonii*, (*E. elwesii*), Elwes foxtail lily, is similar to *E. robustus*. It is 6-8′ tall with soft pink fragrant flowers. 'Albus' is a white-flowered form.

*E. himalaicus* is 6-7′ tall with pure white flowers. Outstanding when planted in front of a dark background.

Spring Valley hybrids are a mix of species and cultivars bred by Ken Romrel of Idaho. They were bred for strong stems and have proven to be a good mix for windy areas. Plants are 4-6′ tall in a mix of colors.

*E. stenophyllus* is a dwarf member of the genus, growing 2-3′ in height. The yellow flowers turn burnt orange as they mature, providing a two-toned effect. Plants require less maintenance because little support is required. 'Magnificus' bears large, bright yellow flowers on a 3-foot flower stalk.

## ***Erianthus*** see ***Saccharum***

## ***Erigeron*** (e -rij′ er-on) Fleabane Asteraceae

Many of the 200 species are native to North America. Several are big-time weeds, including horseweed, *E. canadensis*. Although only 2-3 species are useful for the garden, many cultivars have been named and a good deal of hybridization and selection has taken place. They are attractive for many weeks in the summer, make good cut flowers, and are not fussy as to soil. Unfortunately this genus, like other roadside flowers, is often ignored by gardeners because it is considered so common. While many of the species are of little value, some selections are indeed garden worthy. All require full sun and the taller forms should be deadheaded to provide a second flush of flowers. The taller, showier cultivars (generally forms and hybrids of *E. speciosus*) are not particularly good plants for areas of high heat and humidity.

Flowers of fleabane suggest native asters and are easily confused. If interested in telling them apart, it helps to get eyeball to eyeball with them and count a few of the flower parts. In general, flowers of *Erigeron* open earlier, have two or more series of ray flowers and the bracts under the flowers are in 1-2 series (usually one). In *Aster*, flowers usually open later (often late summer and fall), the ray flowers occur in only 1-2 series and the bracts occur in more than two series. Not much to go on, but the best we can do without a microscope. The common name suggests its usefulness in repelling fleas, however, I have seen no modern mention of this. If it worked, every neighbor's dog, not to mention a few neighbors, would be dipped in a fleabane stew.

Propagation is not difficult by seed, division, or cuttings. Sow the seed when collected or sow purchased seed in late fall. Seed should be covered very thinly, and placed at 70-75°F in a humid atmosphere. Seeds germinate in 10-14 days. Divide the plants in the fall every 2-3 years. Two-inch terminal shoot cuttings may be taken any time, but preferably before flower buds have formed.

Quick Reference to Erigeron Species

| | Height (in.) | Flower color |
|---|---|---|
| *E. aurantiacus* | 9-12 | Orange |
| *E. philadelphicus* | 18-30 | Pale lavender |
| *E. pulchellus* | 18-24 | Rose-purple |
| *E. speciosus* | 20-30 | Purple |

***-aurantiacus*** (ow-ran-tee' ah-cus) Orange Fleabane 9-12"/1'
Summer Orange Turkestan Zones 4-8

While most of the fleabanes are rose, white, or purple, this one has bright scarlet-orange 1-2" diameter flowers atop 9-12" high plants. The foliage is somewhat velvety and the leaves appear twisted at first glance. The basal leaves are 3-4" long and shaped like a spatula (spatulate) while the upper leaves are ovate and sessile. The solitary flowers have a small green center and open for six to eight weeks in early summer. Plants tolerate partial shade, particularly in the South. A unique color but a short-lived plant.

Propagates readily from seed.

**Cultivars:**

var. *sulphureus* bears lovely pale yellow flowers and looks particularly nice in the rockery or the front of the border.

***-philadelphicus*** (fil-a-del-fi' cus) Common Fleabane 18-30"/18"
Early Summer Whitish Pink North America Zones 3-8

Actually, this is a weed but a handsome weed it is. No one striving for the tidy garden look would include it, but it certainly grows and flowers well. The species extends from New Brunswick to British Columbia and south from Texas to Florida. The narrow basal leaves are toothed or scalloped and the stem leaves have lobes at their bases which extend to either side of the stem.

The flowers are among the smallest in the genus but many of them open over a long period of time. They consist of numerous rays which can vary from white to pinkish on the same plant. This is truly an easy plant to grow and if you are looking for the "wild" flower look, this should be on your list.

Propagate by division or seed.

***-pulchellus*** (pul-chel' lus) Poor Robin's Plantain 18-24"/2'
Early Summer Rosy-Purple Eastern and Central U.S. Zones 3-7

This is one of the few stoloniferous fleabanes in cultivation, eventually resulting in larger and larger clumps. The 2-6" long, hairy, toothed basal leaves are tufted and attached to the slender stem with a short petiole while the stem leaves are usually sessile and entire. The solitary 1" diameter flowers consist of about 60 ray florets and are lavender with yellow centers. Although this can be one of the showiest fleabanes, they lose all semblance of tidiness when given too much fertilizer or rich soils. The poorer the soil, the better. This is a fair garden species, at best.

***-speciosus*** (spiece-ee-o' sus) Daisy Fleabane 20-30/24"
Summer Purple Western United States Zones 2-7

Although the species itself is seldom seen in gardens, selections are the most common of the garden fleabanes. The lanceolate stem leaves clasp the stem but the 3-6" long basal leaves have winged petioles. The numerous flowers usually consist of over 100 ray florets. Flowers are 1-2″ across and occur in clustered corymbs held well above the foliage. Plants are upright and well branched.

Plants should be grown in full sun and moist soil. Native to the western United States, they do poorly further south than zone 7, although occasionally worthy specimens are found in zones 7 and 8. Plants may be cut back after flowering to reduce weediness and rejuvenate the foliage.

**Cultivars and hybrids:**

Many cultivars are available and while they are usually listed under *E. speciosus*, they are more likely hybrids that may include genetic infusion from *E. speciosus*, *E. s.* var. *macranthus*, *E. alpinus*, *E. aurantiacus*, and/or *E. glaucus*. In most of the hybrids listed, the first two appear to be the dominant parents. The following cultivars are showy, but those taller than 24″ need support.

'Adria' has many narrow lavender-blue ray flowers with pale yellow centers, growing about 2′ tall. Flowers early in May.

'Azure Beauty' is one of a series that includes 'Azure Blue' and 'Azure Fairy'. These are usually propagated from seed resulting in a great deal of variation. 'Azure Fairy' and 'Azure Beauty' appear to be the same cultivar but sold under different names by different companies. They have semi-double lavender-blue flowers on 30″ tall stems. 'Azure Blue' is similar to the above but has lighter blue flowers.

'Black Sea' is about 2′ tall with deep violet ray flowers around a prominent yellow center.

'Darkest of All' is a much-planted cultivar with violet-blue flowers on 2′ tall stems. It is one of the best.

'Dimity' is only 10-12″ tall and produces orange-tinted flower buds which open to light pink flowers with orange centers. Dwarfness is an asset as no support is necessary. Many of the "ity" cultivars ('Dimity', 'Dignity', 'Festivity') were raised by Alan Bloom in the 1950s but only about a half dozen of the thirteen cultivars are still in cultivation.

'Foerster's Darling' ('Foerster's Liebling') is a wonderful double pink form, only 18″ tall, and needs little staking.

'Gaiety' is about 2′ tall with bright pink flowers comprised of narrow ray segments.

'Loveliness' is one of the most handsome cultivars because of the very narrow foliage and semi-double pink flowers.

var. *macranthus* is similar to the type but has ovate rather than lanceolate leaves and slightly larger flowers.

'Pink Jewel' was selected from 'Rose Jewel' and has a variety of pink shades.

'Prosperity' has large, almost double, lavender-blue flowers with yellow centers on 18″ tall plants. This has been a winner in the trials in the Gardens at UGA. Plants have come back for many years and are still going strong.

'Quakeress' and 'White Quakeress' ('Alba') appear to be hybrids between *E. speciosus* and *E. s.* var. *macranthus*. The former has light mauve-pink flowers while the latter has off-white blooms. Both grow 18-24″ tall.

'Rose Jewel' has lilac-rose flowers and can grow 30″ tall. 'Rose Triumph' bears semi-double rose-pink blossoms on 24″ tall plants.

'Rose Ballet' has lavender-rose flowers on about 2′ tall plants.

'Shining Sea' has pink flowers with fine narrow ray segments. About 2′ tall.

'Unity' is about 20″ tall with bright pink narrow ray flowers.

**Related Species:**

*E. aureus*, gold fleabane, is native to mountainous areas of western North America. It has solitary ½ to ¾″ diameter yellow-orange flowers and is only 3-6″ tall.

*E. caespitosa*, tufted fleabane, is native to the central United States and bears blue to pink daisy flowers and silver-gray foliage.

*E. glaucus*, beach aster, native to western North America, is about 6-12″ tall but with a somewhat sprawling habit. Hardiness range is zone 5 or 6 to 8. Numerous lilac to violet ray flowers occur in summer. A white form ('Albus') and a rosy form ('Roseus') are both handsome. 'Arthur Menzies' sports handsome pink flowers with yellow centers on compact plants. 'Cape Sebastian' has lavender daisies on 8-10″ tall plants, hardy to zone 5. However, the best cultivar is 'Elstead Pink', with good bright pink flowers. This fine cultivar was raised by Ernest Ladham's nursery at Elstead, Surrey, England. Best in areas with cool summer nights.

*E. grandiflorus* is native to the Rocky Mountains and bears large flowers with numerous lavender ray flowers. One of the better fleabanes for cut flowers.

*E. karvinskianus* is another easy, and perhaps not quite as wild a plant as *E. philadelphicus*. The flowers are small (less than an inch across) and can be incredibly plentiful. They range from pink to whitish pink, on the same plant. Native to Mexico, plants are not cold hardy much below 10°F (zone 7, possibly 6b), however, plants reseed well. Where they overwinter, they will get larger over time. 'Profusion' is a 6-8″ tall selection with flowers that open white and fade through pink and lilac; plants spread like crazy.

*E. scopulinum* is also tiny, growing only about 4″ tall. The white flowers are equally small, but in a rock garden, it stands out well. Cold hardy to zone 5, heat tolerant to zone 7, with excellent drainage.

## ***Eriophyllum*** (e-ree-o-fill′ um) Woolly Sunflower — Asteraceae

About 12 species of this little-known genus occur, but only one, *E. lanatum*, is reasonably available through American nurseries. The beautiful silver, hairy leaves are borne on tumbling woody stems which form large silvery gray mats. In general, they are useful only when pouring over retaining walls or in gritty, well-drained areas. However, when they smile upon you, you are aglow in hundreds of small yellow daisies that match the sunshine ray for ray. Native to the West Coast, some Oregonians have taken to calling it "Oregon Sunshine". Perhaps a little overdone, but plants can be lovely.

They are best grown in areas of cool nights and low humidity, which excludes two-thirds of the country. Probably cold hardy only to about zone 6, leaving about 100 gardeners who get all that Oregon sunshine.

***Erodium*** (e-ro-dee′ um) Heron's Bill Geraniaceae

Heron's bill is often recognized as a weed in many areas, most likely the escaped Old World species *E. cicutarium*, known as filaree. Of the 50-60 species, only two or three have gained much popularity in gardens. To the naked eye, the flowers are similar to those of hardy geraniums and plants are often initially confused. If one feels highly curious, one can see that the flowers differ because those of *Erodium* have 5 stamens instead of the 10 in *Geranium*. The leaves, however, are the easiest way to discriminate between the two genera. The leaves in *Erodium* are usually in a rosette and they are pinnately lobed or compound and wavy around the margins. Those of hardy geraniums are usually palmate and not in a rosette. The fruit is similar in both genera, having the long beak of a crane or heron.

Quick Reference to Erodium Species

| | Height (in.) | Flower color | Garden use |
|---|---|---|---|
| *E. manescavii* | 15-24 | Purple | Border |
| *E. reichardii* | 4-6 | Rose-pink | Rock garden |

***-manescavii*** (man-es-kav′ ee-eye) Manescau Erodium 15-24″/18″
Spring Purple France Zones 3-7

Plants are mostly native to the French Pyrenees, and are some of the bigger species in the genus. They are about 18″ tall and the basal 6-8″ long leaves are pinnatisect (deeply lobed) to pinnately compound. The rosy purple flowers are about 2″ across and occur in 5-20 flower umbels in early June through September. Useful for any well-drained flower garden or containers. Plants perform better in cooler climates than warm but are most useful in zones 3-6. Plants are also listed as *E. manescaui*.

***-reichardii*** (ree-chard-ee′ eye) Rock Geranium 4-6″/12″
Spring Whitish Balearic Islands Zones 5-7

Plants used to be listed as *E. chamaedryoides*, and make handsome (dare I say cute) additions to the rock garden or other well-drained areas. The flowers, which are borne singly, are white with rosy veins. Excellent drainage is absolutely necessary, particularly in warmer, more humid areas. The filigree leaves make for eye-catching plants where they are comfortable.

**Cultivars:**

'Album' has white flowers.

'Charm' is only about 3″ tall and is perfect for rock garden situations. Small pink flowers are formed in late spring and early summer.

'Plenum' produces double pink blossoms.

**Related Species:**

*E. castellanum* is a similarly large plant with compound leaves and pinkish red flowers. Most impressive, for an erodium.

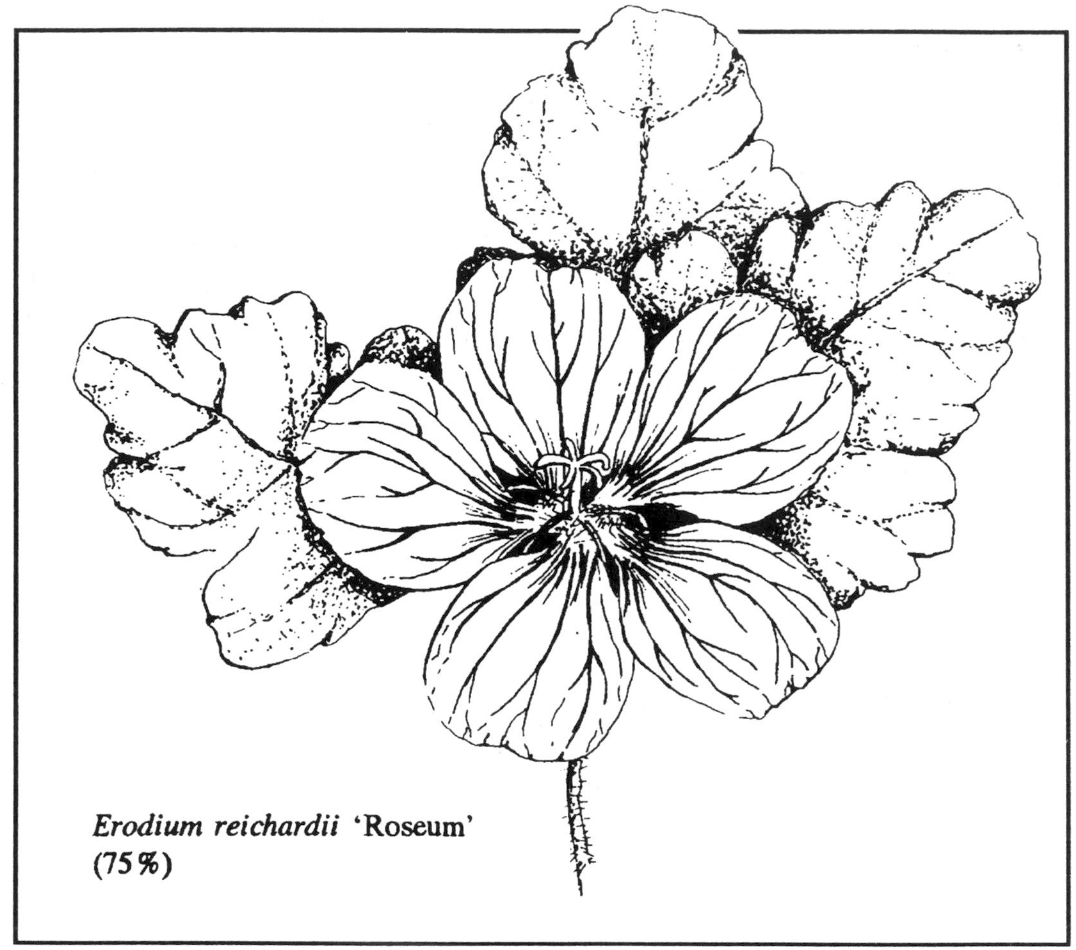

***Erodium reichardii* 'Roseum'**
**(75%)**

*E. chrysanthum* is a diminutive (6″) tufted plant with finely dissected silvery hairy leaves and yellow flowers. Plants are wonderfully handsome in the spring, and look good in summer months as well. Plants are also of interest because they are dioecious, meaning that male and female flowers occur on different plants. A pink-flowered form has become recently available. Native to Greece, plants don't do well unless very well-drained and dry sites are provided. Hardy in zone 5-9.

*E. guttatum* grows about 6″ tall on short woody stems and produces pale pink to white flowers. Two of the petals have deep purple blotches.

*E. leucanthemum* is a small rock garden candidate of the genus. Growing only 6-9″ tall, it nevertheless bears handsome 1″ clean white flowers.

*E.* x *variabile* is a hybrid between *E. reichardii* and *E. corsicum*. Many of the erodiums sold today likely belong to this cross. 'Bishop's Form' bears rose-pink flowers and 'Flore-Pleno' has double flowers. 'Roseum' is the most common form and bears pink-rose flowers with deeper rose veins. An RHS Award of Merit Plant in 1993.

***Eryngium*** ( e-rinj-ee′ um) Sea Holly Apiaceae

Of the 100 or so species, only a half dozen are seen in gardens. This is changing as some leaders in the nursery business are expanding the palette with South American species such as the giant 4-6′ tall *E. pandanifolium*. The roots of the European sea holly, *E. maritimum*, were reported to have been given to "old and aged people that are consumed and withered with age, and which want natural moisture" and also "amended the defects of nature in the yonger" (Gerard). This species, from which the common name arose, is still available from specialist nurseries and thrives in coastal gardens where sandy soils are common. It may sometimes be found naturalized on the East Coast.

Sea hollies tolerate a wide range of environments. Some thrive in poor, dry, even salty soils; some prosper in typical garden soils; and one, *E. aquaticum*, is a favorite among garden pond enthusiasts. They are native to coastal areas, particularly the Mediterranean, although *E. yuccifolium*, rattlesnake master, is native to the eastern United States. The rigid, spiny leaves are often long and narrow in American species, superficially resembling bromeliads. In European species, leaves are frequently rounded or lobed, and often have attractive contrasting white veins. The leaves are more or less sheathed at the base and are usually lobed or deeply cut with spiny margins.

This genus differs from other members of the Apiaceae (formally Umbelliferae) by not having flowers in umbels. In general, the individual flowers are small but are held in dense oblong or roundish heads, which turn gray-green to bright blue under cool temperatures, as do the supporting bracts and upper stems. The bracts (known as an involucre) range in shades of silver-blue to almost purple and look like the flared collar of an English Beefeater. They are often the most ornamental part of the inflorescence. The terminal flower colors first and persists sufficiently long that the lateral flowers start to color while the terminals still look fresh. Of course, exceptions to the above description occur. Try planting some *E. ebracteatum* and see how many of your gardening friends will look at the long, skinny, burnet-like flowers and not have a clue what it is. The sea hollies are usually thought of as large plants and while *E. agavifolium* and *E. pandanifolium* can be up to 6′ and 10′ tall respectively, *E. varifolium* is only about 18″ tall. Most of the common species are 2-3′ tall.

Lethality of spines varies greatly among species, but flat sea holly, *E. planum*, is probably the least offensive while the dense barbs on the flowers and foliage of *E. spinalba* and *E. tricuspidatum* do not beckon friendship. Full sun is preferable because plants will be more dense and more intensely colored than in partial shade. In areas of warm nights, the catalog-blue color never occurs, as the intensity of color is dependent on the persistence of cool temperature.

Separating the plantlets produced at the base of the mother plant is the easiest method of propagation. Buying seed is usually a waste of money because the seed goes into dormancy rather quickly and 1-2 years may be required for germination. A 55% germination rate was obtained with seeds of *E. planum* collected fresh and sown within two weeks but germination plummeted to 5% or less after 3 months. I do not know if this is true of all species but suspect it is a problem with many.

Quick Reference to Eryngium Species

| | Height (ft.) | Shape of basal leave |
|---|---|---|
| *E. alpinum* | 1-2 | Heart-shaped |
| *E. amethystinum* | 1-1½ | Pinnately divided |
| *E. bourgatii* | 1-2 | Palmate, 3-5 parted |
| *E. giganteum* | 4-6 | Heart-shaped |
| *E. planum* | 2-3 | Heart-shaped |
| *E. varifolium* | 1-2 | Rounded |
| *E. yuccifolium* | 2-4 | Straplike |

***-alpinum*** (al-pine′ um) Alpine Sea Holly 1-2′/2′
Summer Blue Europe Zones 4-7

The slightly toothed basal leaves are heart shaped while the upper leaves are 3-lobed or palmately divided. The flower head is oblong like a pineapple, and one of the bluest of the sea hollies. The upper part of the stem also turns a dark blue. Twelve to 18 finely divided, rather soft, involucre bracts extend prominently from the flower head and give the species its marvelous ornamental value. The flower and associated involucre look like exploding fireworks. The involucre of immature flowers is almost white, then becomes bluer with age. For flower power, this is the best species.

Plant in full sun and well-drained soil. It is a popular cut flower and lasts for at least 2 weeks in water. If the terminal flowers are cut, the side branches reach flowering maturity earlier.

**Cultivars:**

'Amethyst' is 2½-3′ tall with metallic light blue bracts and serrated foliage.

'Blue Star' has been popular because it has been one of the few cultivars available from seed, even though half the seed may never come up. Plants grow 2-3′ tall and bear large lavender-blue involucres.

'Opal' is 2′ tall and bears more silvery blue flowers than 'Amethyst'.

'Slieve Donard', named for the fine Irish nursery, has handsome light blue bracts around dark blue flowers.

'Superbum' has large dark blue flowers on 2-3′ tall stems.

***-amethystinum*** (a-me-thist-eye′ num) Amethyst Sea Holly 1-1½′/2′
Summer Blue Europe Zones 2-8

This is one of the most cold-hardy species and one of the most common in North America. The basal leaves are pinnately parted, differing from those of most other common species. The stems branch near the top, and bear many small (½-¾″ long) flowers. The 7-8 involucre bracts are much longer than the flower heads and sharply pointed. The color is a steely blue and the flower stem is also deeply colored, adding a good deal of interest to the garden. Its cold hardiness allows plants to be used where others can not be grown successfully.

***-bourgatii*** (bour-gat′ ee-aye) | Mediterranean Sea Holly | 1-2′/2′
Summer | Blue-Green | Pyrenees | Zones 5-8

An excellent compact plant, this underused species has palmately cut foliage resembling a hand with 3-5 fingers. The dense, coarse foliage has conspicuous silver-white veins and is grayer than most species. Leaves are entire or with 1-2 pairs of spiny teeth. The flowers are ovoid and subtended by 12-18 silver, lancelike, spiny involucre bracts which are much longer than the flower head. The ¾″ long flowers are silver-blue to blue-green and borne on wiry stems which associate well with the silvery venation of the foliage. This is a good garden plant, although a little too spiny for my liking.

***-giganteum*** (gi-gan′ tee-um) | Miss Willmott's Ghost | 3-6′/4′
Summer | Blue | Caucasus | Zones 4-7

For those gardeners who want a large-flowered, rather large plant, get out your shovels. The oval 3-4″ long flowers are subtended by 8 or 9 rigid, long toothed, silvery white involucre bracts. The spineless basal leaves are deeply heart shaped and entire. The leaves are pale green in and consort well with other plants. The silvery flowers and pale green color give the plants a rather ghostlike appearance. They are biennial and flower in the spring to early summer of the second year. This can be a most lovely plant but looks rather menacing. Provide sufficient room and protect from winds. I have been unsuccessful in establishing Miss Willmott's plant in the Armitage garden but it seems to do just fine further north.

Ellen Willmott was beautiful, enormously wealthy and not one to trouble much about the sensibilities of others. At her peak in the early 1900s, she would walk around the gardens of friends, neighbors or nurseries, and surreptitiously scatter the seed of plants which she felt were unjustifiably missing. One her favorite additives was *E. giganteum*, and the conclusion of her forays was a great deal of head-scratching by those she visited, wondering where all those ghostly plants came from. The charming result was that plants became known as Miss Willmott's ghost. In my garden, all I ever have visit is the Chickweed Ghost, who is not nearly as much fun.

Seeds germinate easily where plants are happy and may pop up here and there. To reduce the size of this plant, use it in containers where root restriction will restrict overall growth.

***-planum*** (plane′ um) | Flat Eryngium | 2-3′/3′
Summer | Blue | Eastern Europe | Zones 5-8

The silver-blue flower heads are small (½-¾″), oval, and numerous. The 6-8 involucre bracts are about the same size or slightly longer than the flower head. The scalloped basal leaves are heart shaped and not spiny. Plants are not as ornamental as those of *E. alpinum* and in fact may be less ornamental than most of the species listed. However, they do well under conditions of heat and humidity and are excellent long-lasting cut or dried flowers. Its popularity has resulted in a number of cultivars more showy than the species.

*Eryngium planum*
(81%)

Interestingly, it is a more popular export flower in some countries than *E. alpinum*. The small flower heads ship well and more stems may be placed in each shipping box.

**Cultivars:**

'Blue Cap' bears deep blue flowers on 2′ tall plants.

'Blue Diamond' is a dwarf form selected for the deep blue flowers. Not a great deal different than the next form.

'Blue Dwarf' is similar to the species but grows 15-18″ high.

'Blue Ribbon' has larger flowers, appearing to be double blue. Plants grow about 2′ tall.

'Paradise Jackpot' is about 2′ tall with long blue bracts around lighter blue flowers.

'Silver Stone' has creamy-white flowers and stands 3-4′ tall.

***-varifolium*** (var-ee′ fol-ee-um) Moroccan Sea Holly 1-2′/2′
Summer Silver-Blue Morocco Zones 5-8

Another unused, rather unknown species, this is a delightful garden plant. It is one of the few evergreen members of the genus and is also unusual in that the leaves are as striking as the flowers. The small, rounded, spiny leaves have conspicuous white veins and appear variegated. The round flower heads are small but showy with narrow involucres of white-blue bracts. The small size allows it to be used in smaller areas where some of the other species may be too large.

***-yuccifolium*** (yuk-i-fo-lee′ um) Rattlesnake Master 3-4′/3′
Summer Creamy-Chartreuse United States Zones 5-9

Many sea hollies are native to this country and none bear the bright blue flowers of the European species. Native from New Jersey to Minnesota and south to Texas and Florida, these plants enjoy a wide range of habitats. Plants can grow up to six feet tall but 3-4′ is more common. The stiff, narrow leaves with their unbranched parallel veins led to the yucca-like species name. Widely spaced bristles line the leaf margins. The creamy white flower heads are buttonlike and the bracts are insignificant. All in all, they don't provide a great deal of color but are fun to grow for the habit and yucca-like foliage. The common name comes from the belief that plants could cure rattlesnake bites or even drive them away. Fat chance.

As native plants become more popular, more of them are finding a place in American gardens. Without doubt, rattlesnake master is the most popular, but *E. agavifolium*, agave sea holly, whose foliage resembles the common agave, is similar to but much spinier than *E. yuccifolium*. Although the flowers are a little bluer, they won't keep the rattlesnakes away from the posy patch either. A few other similar species that can be confusing are *E. bromeliifolium*, which is taller than *E. agavifolium* and, of course, resembles a bromeliad, and *E. serra*, whose bright green vases of swordlike foliage also resembles an agave. These plants have a definite identity crisis.

Propagate from seed.

**Related Species and Hybrids:**

Some interesting hybrids have been produced but may be difficult to locate.

*E. aquaticum*, sea holly, rattlesnake master, is similar to *E. yuccifolium*, but is larger (up to 4′) and does best in poorly-drained soils, tolerating continuously wet feet. Zones 6-8.

*E.* x *oliverianum* is a 3′ tall hybrid whose parentage is confused but is likely the result of crosses between *E. giganteum*, *E. alpinum*, and *E. planum*. It bears pale blue, 1½-2″ long flower heads and stiff involucre bracts. The foliage is deeply cut, often with white veins, adding to the ornamental value of the hybrid.

*E. proteiflorum* appears to be deeply envious of other forms of plant life. The flowers really do look like proteas, mainly because the flower head is brownish while the 15-30 stiff bracts are white to light blue. The spiny foliage is deeply cut. Native to Mexico; performs in zones 7-9.

*E. serbicum* looks more dangerous than it is, bearing soft spines on the palmately cut dark basal green leaves. The spines get tougher as the leaves move up the stem. The flowers are blue but there are only 5-7 very narrow silvery white bracts beneath.

*E.* x *tripartitum* is a 3½-4′ tall hybrid of unknown origin. Plants bear massive numbers of metallic blue flowers. The basal leaves are 3 lobed and coarsely toothed and nearly all the leaves have a gray venation. The 6-9 involucre bracts are twice as long as the base of the flowers. Probably zones 5-8.

*E.* x *zabelii* is a magnificent hybrid and is likely a cross between *E. alpinum* x *E. bourgatii*. It grows 1½-2′ tall and has 1-2″ long flower heads with 10-12 long rigid lavender-blue bracts. Some of the resulting offspring from this cross are: 'Donard Blue' produces extra large flowers on 2′ tall plants. 'Sapphire Blue' may be the best of all. Plants bear small flowers but long, deep blue bracts. 'Spring Hills' has long lavender bracts and is quite special. 'Violetta' and 'Jewel' bear light and dark blue and light blue involucres respectively.

## ***Erysimum*** (e-ri′ si-mum) Wallflower Brassicaceae

All the plants commonly grown as wallflowers, which used to be encountered under the name *Cheiranthus*, have now been lumped under this one genus. This is a good thing because I never could tell the difference between the two. I have a tough time telling the differences between various species of the old *Erysimum*, let alone the new expanded one. All flowers have four petals and are arranged in a raceme. There are six stamens, but four are longer than the other two. The fruit is a silique (long, narrow splitting open longitudinally).

In the old taxonomic classification, differences were found in insignificant parts of the flower and within the seed. *Erysimum* has no nectary glands at the base of the stamens, the fruit (silique) is not as flat, and seeds within the fruit are in a single row compared with two rows in the compressed fruit of *Cheiranthus*. In general, plants of *Cheiranthus* bore orange-yellow flowers but as more of the *Erysimum* species were introduced, it soon became obvious that flower color could not be used to discriminate between the two genera. In this case, the lumpers had a good argument, unlike the ones in *Actaea* (which see).

Wallflowers are common in the British Isles. Europe, and New Zealand, however, with the exception of a few annuals and one or two short-lived perennials, they have not enjoyed the same popularity in North American gardens. This may be because of the rather short-lived nature of most species and their need for well-drained soils and neutral to slightly basic soil. They should be placed in full sun in the North and afternoon shade in the South. All should be cut back hard after flowering and not be expected to persist longer than two years. Good drainage is a must and many species do much better in alkaline soils than acidic ones. In the South, fall plantings result in the best spring performance.

Propagate by seed, division, or cuttings.

Quick Reference to Erysimum Species

| | Height (in.) | Flower color |
|---|---|---|
| *E. helveticum* | 2-4 | Yellow |
| *E. kotschyanum* | 3-6 | Yellow |
| *E. linifolium* | 12-15 | Purple |
| *E x marshalii* | 12-24 | Orange-yellow |

***-cheiri*** (cheer-ee′ eye) Common Wallflower 6-12″/12″
Spring Orange, Yellow Europe Zones 5-8

Plants are native to southern Europe but have undergone many developments in breeding to develop the "English" wallflowers. Flower color ranges from white to pale yellow through browns and purples. They are generally low growers but some tall forms have been developed for cut flower use. They are less cold tolerant (zone 6 or 7) and are best used as an annual or biennial. Many cultivars have been developed, which are likely hybrids with Siberian wallflower, *E.* x *marshallii*, *E. bicolor* and *E. sempervirens*. Treat as biennials although some may also perform as annuals or occasionally as perennials.

**Cultivars and hybrids:**

'Aunt May' is only about 6″ tall, bearing rose-lavender flowers.

'Aurora' has apricot, bronze, orange and mauve flowers.

'Bredon' is a well-known hybrid with reddish buds and golden-yellow flowers. About 8″ tall.

'Butterscotch' has orange flowers.

'Constant Cheer' grows about 15″ tall and bears dull rose to amber flowers in late spring. Flowers start brownish orange before turning amber. Long flowering.

'Covent Garden' bears fragrant deep magenta flowers.

'Golden Bedder' produces dozens on golden flower heads on 9-12″ tall plants. This has been an excellent perennial in the Gardens at UGA.

'Golden Gem' produces deep yellow flowers on 9-12″ tall plants.

'Harpur Crewe' is a double-flowered form of *E. cheiri*. This is one of the oldest wallflowers still in commerce, selected in the 17th century. Very fragrant, often listed as *E x kewensis*.

'Jubilee Gold' has gold flowers over 6″ bushy plants. Similar to 'Bredon' but with toothed leaves. One of the shortest forms.
'Scarlet Bedder' has rich red flowers.
'Turkish Bazaar' bear very fragrant yellow to gold flowers on 6″ stems in the spring.
'Wenlock Beauty' produces yellow flowers with a bronze tint.
'Yellow Bird' is about 12″ tall with yellow-gold flowers.
'Variegatus' has leaves variegated with cream.

***-helveticum*** (hel-vet-i′ kum) Tufted Wallflower 2-4″/6″
Spring Yellow Alps Zones 4-7

This little-known species bears many pale yellow, fragrant flowers on tufted compact plants. The basal leaves are narrow, gray-green and somewhat toothed. This is more perennial than most of the other species and should be planted in limey soil in full sun.

Propagate similar to *E. kotschyanum*, however, non-flowering stems may be used for cuttings any time from emergence to midsummer.

***-kotschyanum*** (kot-shy-aye′ num) Kotschy Erysimum 3-6″/12″
Spring Yellow Asia Minor Zones 6-8

This excellent rock garden plant grows in compact tufts and is covered with bright yellow flowers in the spring. The half-inch long basal leaves are narrow, and finely toothed. The half-inch long flowers are carried in crowded racemes and are not only pretty but also pleasantly fragrant. They grow well in full sun in cracks and crevices in walls and rock gardens. Plants perform well as far south as zone 8 if planted in the fall, however, summer heat and humidity result in decline and plants seldom recover.

Seed sown in a warm (70-75°F) environment begins to germinate within two weeks. Germination is erratic, however, and seedlings may continue to appear over a 4-6 week period.

Two-inch terminal cuttings may be taken immediately after flowering or in the fall.

**Cultivars**:
'Orange Flame' is about 6 inches tall and produces orange-yellow flowers in the spring. Not much different from the species other than its name.

***-linifolium*** (line-i-fo′ lee-um) Alpine Erysimum 12-15″/12″
Spring Purple Spain Zones 5-8

One of the most common perennial wallflowers, this large species can be used as an edging specimen but is equally at home cascading from rock walls. The narrow leaves are gray-green, entire, and evergreen if winters are not too severe. The ¾″ long flowers are held in a dense raceme well above the foliage and the purple color is particularly brilliant early in the early spring. The stems are woody and as plants age, they become like little shrubs.

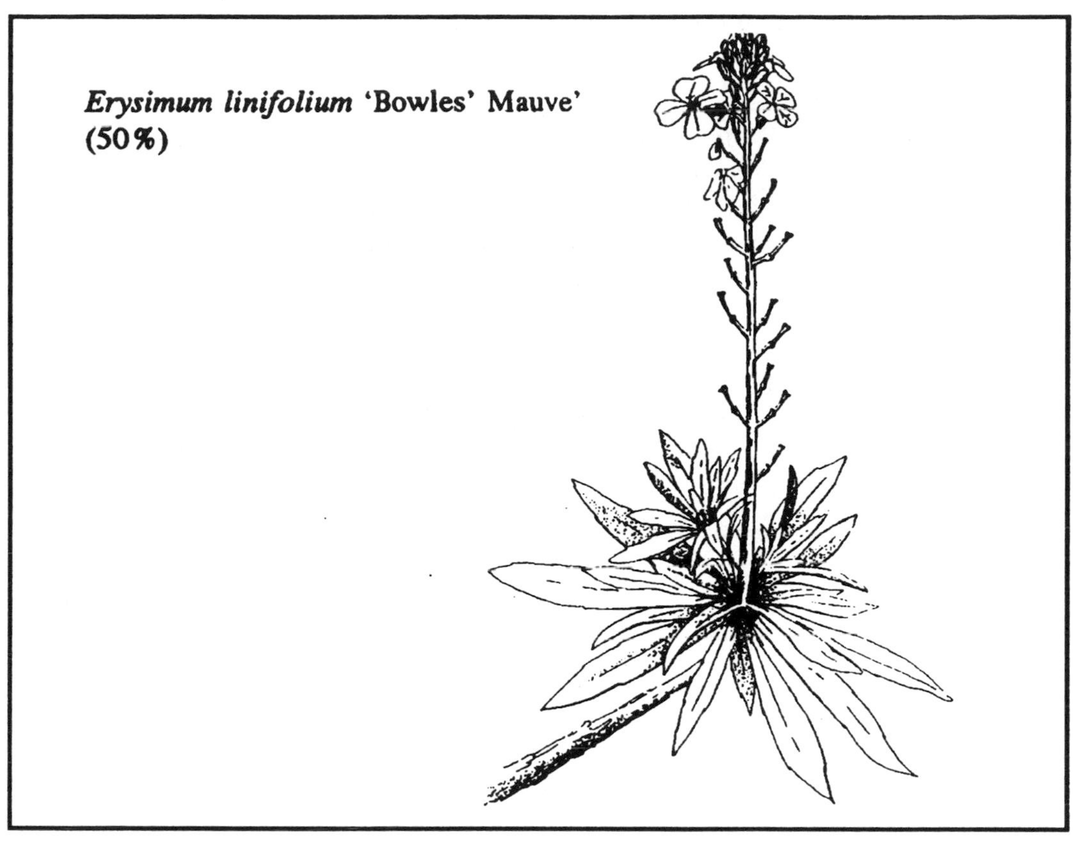

***Erysimum linifolium*** **'Bowles' Mauve' (50%)**

Although plants are not long-lived (2-3 years), I consider them "no-brainers" for southern gardens and excellent early-planted species for all gardeners.

Propagate similar to *E. kotschyanum*.

**Cultivars:**

'Bowles' Mauve' is named for one of the greatest English amateur gardeners, Edward Augustus Bowles, and is probably the best known of the many plants that bear his name. Plants have longer flower heads and are clearer purple than the type. In the Armitage garden (zone 7b), the leaves are evergreen and the flower buds appear in the winter, culminating in brilliant purple flowers in late winter and early spring.

'Variegatum' has variegated foliage and lilac flowers. A particularly handsome form.

| -x ***marshalii*** (al-lee-own-ee′ eye) | | Siberian Wallflower | 12-24″/12″ |
|---|---|---|---|
| Spring | Orange-Yellow | Garden Origin | Zones 4-7 |

This hybrid of unknown parentage (once known as *E.* x *allionii*) forms tufts of foliage and dozens of bright orange flowers with a strong spicy fragrance. The 2-3″ long leaves are narrow and coarsely toothed. Plants are best grown as biennials, although they may prove more reliable in cooler climates. They are similar to the more popular

*E. cheiri*, the common wallflower, but are longer lived, more cold tolerant and flower a little later.

**Related Species:**

*E. hieraciifolium* (*E. alpinum*), alpine wallflower, has woody stems and bright yellow flowers on 9-12″ tall plants.

*E. pulchellum* forms tufts of green foliage, the stems branching at the base. The stem leaves are sessile and the bright golden yellow flowers are most handsome. More perennial than many others. 'Auranticum' bears flowers which are mauve and yellow.

*E. purpureum*, purple wallflower, is difficult to tell from *E. linifolium*. Generally, it is shorter (about 12″ tall) with smaller leaves. It does have he same handsome gray-green foliage and purple to violet flowers held in long racemes. Not as cold hardy as 'Bowles' Mauve'.

## ***Erythronium*** (e-rith-roan′ ee-um) Trout Lily Liliaceae

Trout lilies consist of approximately 25 species, and all are handsome in flower and foliage. Plants arise from small pointed fleshy corms and are tolerant of extreme weather conditions. They fit wonderfully well in woodland areas, and are particularly suitable for naturalizing in shade or near streams where moisture is constantly available. Some of the species are particularly cold hardy and can be grown in northern Canada.

The name *Erythronium* came from the Greek *erythros*, red, a reference to the leaf mottling found on most, but not all, species. In general, the plant bears two leaves, one narrower than the other, although up to four leaves may sometimes be formed. The nodding flowers are borne singly or in twos or threes and the anthers protrude well away from the reflexed petals. The fruit, which is formed in early summer, is a green capsule. The American species usually have yellow or white flowers while European species are red or purple.

Many common names have been applied to species in the genus. The first species to be named had long, white, shiny tuberous roots resembling canine teeth and was called "denscaninus", and later dog-tooth violet. The term violet was used at the time for many small, purple-flowered plants. That particular species is now known as *E. dens-canis*, a native of central Europe. The mottled leaves have given rise to the common names of trout lily, fawn lily and adder's tongue.

Quick Guide to Erythronium Species

| | Height (in.) | Flower color | Mottled leaves |
|---|---|---|---|
| *E. albidum* | 6-12 | White | Yes |
| *E. americanum* | 6-9 | Yellow | Yes |
| *E. dens-canis* | 4-6 | Purple | Yes |
| *E. grandiflorum* | 12-24 | Yellow | No |
| *E. revolutum* | 10-16 | Varied | Yes |

***-albidum*** (al′ bi-dum) | White Trout Lily | 6-12″/9″
Late Spring | White | Eastern North America | Zones 4-8

One of the latest species to flower, the 1½″ long drooping blossoms are a lovely clear white, with a tinge of yellow at the base. The elliptical 4-6″ long leaves are occasionally mottled with silver-green but under heavy shade, little mottling is apparent. This species recently came into commercial propagation and is slowly becoming more available. Plant in light shade and provide adequate soil moisture. One of the few species to have stoloniferous roots, significant colonies are formed, albeit slowly, within 3-5 years.

Propagation by seed is slow and frustrating, particularly if not fresh. Keep seed warm (70-75°F) and moist for 2-4 weeks, cool seed to 30-35°F for 4-6 weeks and then raise temperatures again to 75°F. This sequence may be done naturally through the cycles of fall, winter, and spring. Place the seed flats outside in the fall in an area which will not fall below 25°F, such as a cold frame. A covering of snow will do the same thing. Seedlings appear in the spring as temperatures rise. Three to four years are required to obtain flowering plants from seed. Offsets may also be taken from mature plants. Offsets require two years to produce flowering plants.

***-americanum*** (a-me-ri-kay′ num) | American Trout Lily | 6-9″/9″
Late Spring | Yellow | Eastern North America | Zones 3-8

This common trout lily is found in damp woodlands and pastures from Nova Scotia to Florida. Two dark glossy green, 3-8″ long leaves mottled with brown and purple markings appear in late winter in mild climates to early spring. The 1-2″ wide, nodding, pale yellow flowers are occasionally tinged with purple and are borne singly, opening a little earlier than *E. albidum*. The anthers, sometimes a means of distinguishing species from each other, are usually yellow to brownish. Additional studies found that plants are tetraploids, with 48 chromosomes rather than the 24 found in most other species.

The drawbacks of growing trout lilies are that they are expensive, and difficult to procure from nurseries. Unfortunately, one trout lily or even three is inadequate and buying at least a dozen is necessary for most of us, resulting in richer gardens and poorer wallets. The flowers are not numerous, and persist for less than a couple of weeks. Lastly, the foliage is summer dormant and may in fact be gone before summer actually arrives. Regardless, I would not be without them, but not all readers may be quite so smitten.

Plants are known as common trout lily, fawn lily and yellow adder's tongue because of the leaf markings. Partial shade and adequate soil moisture must be provided. More nursery-propagated plants are becoming available, hopefully reducing the number of plants being wrenched from the wild. Each bulb produces abundant stolons and plants multiply readily

Propagate similar to *E. albidum*.

***-dens-canis*** (dens-kay′ nus) | Dog Tooth Violet | 4-6″/6″
Spring | Purple | Central Europe | Zones 2-7

This is the most common species in Europe and has been cultivated since the late 1500s. Plants have a more limited southern range than the American trout lily but are more cold hardy. The 4-6″ long lanceolate leaves are variable but often heavily splotched with dull crimson, through which rise the solitary 2″ long flowers. The tepals (petals and sepals look alike) of the nodding rose-purple flowers are narrow with sharply reflexed tips and purple stamens. Flower color ranges from pink to deep purple, but all flowers have a ring of red-purple markings around the base. Many cultivars have been selected over the years, although they are seldom seen outside botanical gardens. Plants do not go summer dormant as early as *E. americanum*.

Propagate similar to *E. albidum*. Cultivars must be vegetatively propagated.

**Cultivars:**

'Charmer' has white flowers mottled with crimson on 8-12″ tall plants.

'Lilac Wonder' has large muted lilac flowers with a small brown spot at the base of each segment.

'Pink Perfection' is early flowering and has clear pink flowers larger than the species.

'Purple King' is a particularly eye-catching cultivar. Mauve flowers are edged with white and centers are marked with dark brown spots.

'Snowflake' has pure white flowers.

'White Splendour' has white flowers larger than the species.

***-grandiflorum*** (grand-i-flo′ rum) Lambstongue Trout Lily 12-24″/18″
Spring Yellow Western United States Zones 5-8

Plants are native to the Cascade Range of northwestern California and Oregon and north into Washington, and can be difficult to establish, particularly in the East. This early-flowering species has large, golden yellow star-shaped flowers with dark red or maroon anthers. The flowers may be up to 2″ long and are held in 2-6 flowered racemes. The 4-8″ long elliptical leaves are dark green and unmottled. The size of the flowers is arresting and the lack of leaf mottling seems to make the flowers even brighter. Plants are less tolerant of warm, humid climates than many others.

**Cultivars**:

'Albiflorum' has white flowers tinged with green.

var. *candidum* has greenish to creamy white flowers with white anthers and a yellow interior.

'Parviflorum' has cream-colored anthers instead of the normal crimson color.

***-revolutum*** (re-ve-loo′ tum) Mahogany Trout Lily 10-16″/10″
Spring Rose-Pink Western North America Zones 5-8

A favorite, particularly among West Coast gardeners, the mahogany trout lily or coast fawn lily is well adapted to western gardens and reseeds itself vigorously to quickly establish large colonies. The 6-8″ long, deep green leaves are mottled with brown and white, and sport crinkled margins. The one or two rose-pink flowers, 3″ across and up to 1¾″ long, have yellow bands inside the flower and yellow anthers. Although the species is worthy of a place in the garden, several cultivars are much more common than the species.

**Cultivars:**

'Branklyn Form' is a sterile form found in Branklyn Garden in Perth, Scotland.

'Kondo' (*E. revolutum* and *E. tuolumnense* ), has 3-5 large sulphur-yellow flowers shaded brown at the center. Anthers are also yellow.

'Pagoda' has leaves slightly marbled with bronze and pale yellow flowers. This has been growing successfully in the Armitage garden for many years. Each year, the clump gets better but unfortunately, plants have not spread very far. This is also a hybrid between *E. revolutum* and *E. tuolumnense*.

'Pink Beauty' has reflexed petals of clear pink.

'Rose Beauty' bears rose-pink flowers.

'White Beauty' has creamy white flowers with crimson-brown centers but the petals are less reflexed.

**Related Species:**

*E. tuolumnense* is also native to California and produces 4-8 golden-yellow flowers above unmottled yellow-green foliage. Flowers are up to 3″ wide and persist for about 2 weeks. Similar to *E. grandiflorum* but has yellow rather than red anthers. Plants are far easier to establish.

*E. umbilicatum* is similar to *E. americanum*, bearing yellow flowers and mottled leaves. It differs morphologically with the absence of a toothlike structure at the base of the petals found in *E. americanum*. Bulbs do not produce as many stolons and are less likely to fill in as rapidly.

***Eucomis*** (ewe comb′ us) Pineapple Lily Liliaceae

One of the many oversights in the earlier editions of this book was the omission of this great genus. Unfortunately, plants are not cold hardy much further north than zone 6b, but dozens of plants in the book are equally limited. The more I play with the various members of the group, the more I appreciate its diversity and its usefulness. Plants are deciduous, grow about 1-4′ tall and are characterized by the straplike leaves and gorgeous stalks of lily flowers ending in pineapple-like leaves at the top. If you live too far north to overwinter them, plant them in containers and bring them inside in the fall. Propagation is not difficult and with limited facilities, plants can also be multiplied.

***-comosa*** (coe-moe′ sa) Common Pineapple Lily 2-3′/2′
White Early Summer South Africa Zones 6b-9

We have grown half a dozen hybrids and cultivars and the common pineapple lily is part of all of them. The 2-3′ tall species is a wonderful plant, especially in flower. Although the leaves are simply green and flowers are "normal" pineapple lily flowers, they make wonderful additions to the garden. If you have never tried a pineapple lily, you will love it.

**Cultivars:**

'Innocence' and 'Toffee' were dropped off on my doorstep by Eddie Welsh, a marvelous horticulturist in Palmerston North, New Zealand. Both are about 1½-2′ tall with sturdy flowers useful for cutting. I have seen them offered for sale, but I am not sure of the availability. They were selected for cut flower use.

'Sparkling Burgundy', without doubt, provides the greatest wow factor, particularly as the burgundy leaves emerge in the spring. Plants grow 2-3′ tall and produce purple-tinged flowers in early summer. The leaves lose some of their color in hot weather, but the further north, the longer the burgundy effect. Outstanding!

'Tegula Ruby' is another excellent burgundy-tinged plant, particularly the center of the flowers. Like all eucomis, it simply gets better with age. Not as intense as 'Sparkling Beauty', but still brings great panache to the garden. Both this and the previous cultivar may well be hybrids.

***-pole-evansii*** (pole-ev-an′ see) Giant Pineapple Lily 3-4′/3′
White Early Summer South Africa Zones 7-9

This is simply for the gardener who says "if it must be green, let it be seen." Once established, these plants can definitely be seen! Plants are said to attain 6′ in height, but methinks that is overly generous or growing on a manure field. Four feet is not uncommon, and the green pleated leaves—along with the always wonderful pineapple flowers—make it worth a try in the garden.

Hardiness is still an issue, but even as an annual, it is stunning.

**Related Species:**

*E. vandermerwei* is only 6-8″ tall and is best planted in a well-drained rock garden. The leaves are spotted with purple, the flowers are dark purple.

*E. zambesiaca*, dwarf pineapple lily, has been fun to try out. It is similar to other green pineapple lilies, but plants are only about 9-12″ tall. They can get overrun easily, so put them where they can be seen; a good container plant for sure.

## ***Eupatorium*** (yew-pa-tor′ ium) Boneset Asteraceae

A half dozen of the 600 species are common wildflowers in the eastern half of the country and make excellent garden plants as well. Easily grown in moist well-drained soils and full sun or partial shade, the larger species reach seven feet in height and dominate the fall garden. One of our roadside plants, *E. capillifolium*, dog fennel, starts to flower in late September and covers itself in small white flowers throughout the fall. This is a wonderful plant in the wildflower garden but I respect its toughness even more as I see it smothering cars in junkyards. There should be a law that for every car junked, half a dozen dog fennels should be planted around them.

*E. hyssopifolium*, also a native with white flowers, is excellent for dry, sandy sites. This native has narrow leaves that occur in whorls up the 4′ tall stems. A more compact selection has been named 'Bubba' by Tony Avent of Plant Delights Nursery. Ol' Bubba grows only about 3′ tall. Both *E. capillifolium* and *E. hyssopifolium* are terribly underused, and should be found at least in the wildflower garden. All Joe Pye weeds are effective because of their late summer and fall flowering and architectural beauty.

Quick Reference to Eupatorium Species

| | Height (ft.) | Flower color |
|---|---|---|
| *E. cannabinum* | 4-5 | Mauve |
| *E. coelestinum* | 2-3 | Blue |
| *E. purpureum* | 4-7 | Purple |
| *E. rugosum* | 3-5 | White |

**-cannabinum** (kan-a-been′ um) Hemp Agrimony 4-5′/4′
Late Summer Mauve Europe Zones 5-8

The 5″ long leaves are palmately 3- to 5-lobed and resemble those of *Cannabis*, or so I am told. They are soft, opposite and more or less sessile. Not seen much in this country, perhaps because of the plethora of useful native species, it nevertheless is a handsome addition to the late-flowering garden. Plants make large clumps, but grow more slowly than many of the native forms. The flat-topped inflorescence consists of many small mauve-pink flowers and like all of the eupatoriums, they are much visited by butterflies and moths.

**Cultivars**:
'Album' is a white-flowered form.
'Flore-Pleno' is the best selection in the species with sterile, fully double flowers which persist for weeks on end.

**-coelestinum** (sow-les-teen′ um) Hardy Ageratum 2-3′/36″
Late Summer Blue Eastern United States Zones 6-10
(syn. *Conoclinium coelestinum*)

The 2-3″ long leaves of hardy ageratum are opposite, triangular, and coarsely toothed. The flower heads consist of up to 70, one-half inch wide flowers clustered in dense racemes or corymbs, very similar to the annual *Ageratum*, for which they are named. In fact, at first glance they are almost identical. The rhizomatous nature is the best clue to their difference, and plants of *Ageratum* smell awful when crushed. Because plants steal around by rhizomes, they may become a menace, competing fiercely even with other thugs like *Lysimachia*. Cut them back once or twice during the summer to force additional lateral shoots. With ample water and a sunny location, an outstanding fall show develops. Supporting the plants is helpful to avoid the weedy look but they may flop in warm summers. Numerous azure blue flowers celebrate the fall season in the garden and they should be welcomed, just not too warmly. Often, they have been relegated to the edge of woods or in waste ground, however, they can be quite handsome especially if combined with asters, *Sedum* 'Autumn Joy' and other fall bloomers.

Plants seem to travel from *Eupatorium* to *Conoclinum* and back again. They will likely officially fall under *Conoclinum* eventually, but for now, take your choice.

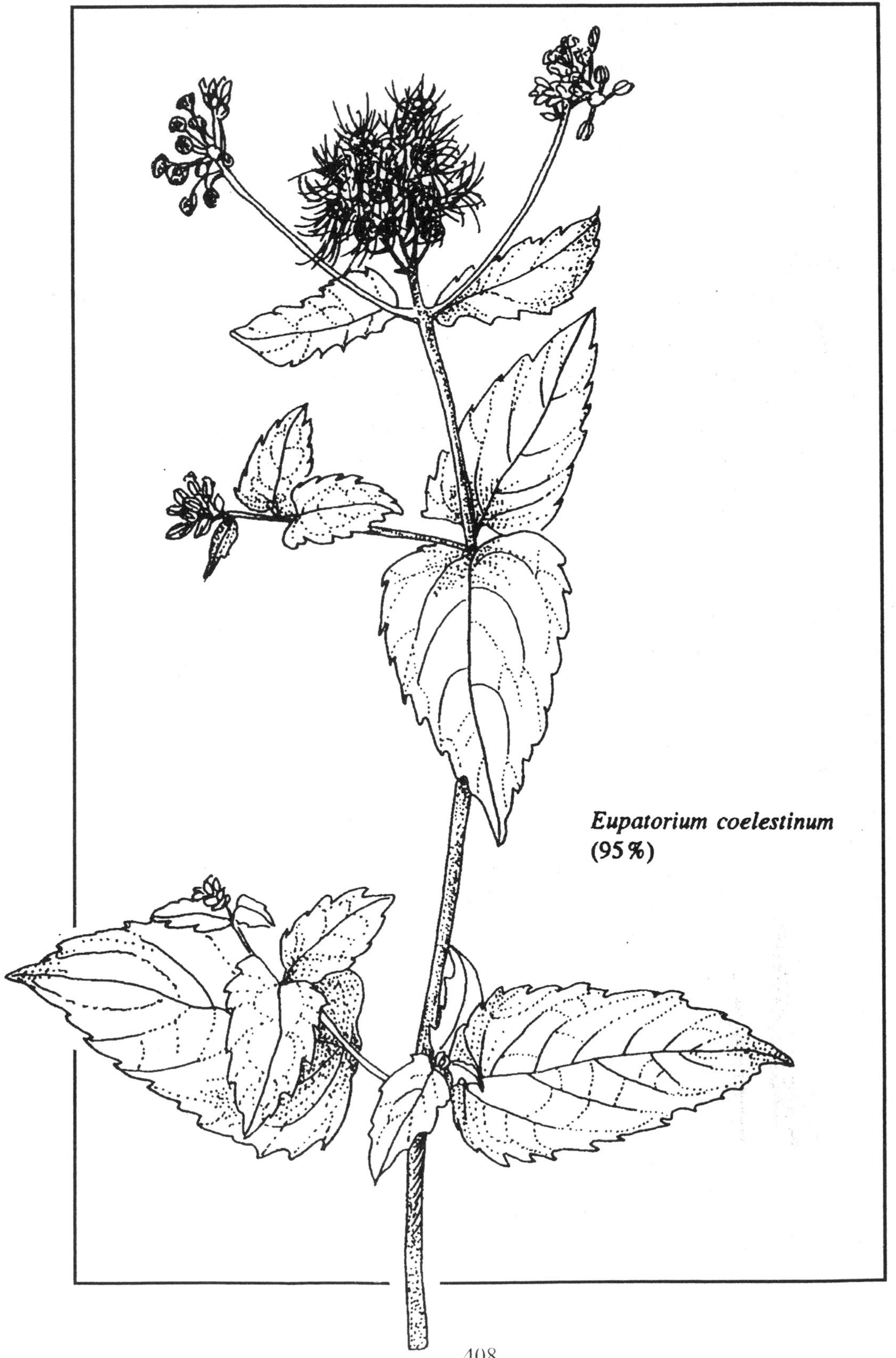

*Eupatorium coelestinum*
(95%)

Divide plants in the spring every 2-4 years. Seed may require 4-6 weeks of cold moist treatment (35-40°F) if germination does not occur within 3 weeks. Cuttings may also be rooted or as Judy Laushman of Oberlin, Ohio so eloquently states "or just wait until they crawl under the sidewalk, around the dogwood and past the mailbox."

**Cultivars:**

'Album' has white flowers but is otherwise similar to the species. I saw some wonderful stands at Huntsville Botanical Garden, resembling dusky shadows at the edge of the woods.

'Cori' is a selection with clearer blue flowers than the species.

'Wayside Variety' is a little shorter than the species and flowers heavily. I have trialed it in the Horticulture Gardens and am impressed with its shorter, less weedy stature.

***-maculatum*** (mack-ew' lay-tum) Spotted Joe Pye Weed 5-7'/4'
Late Summer, Fall Purple Eastern North America Zones 4-8

*Maculatum* means "spotted" and the stems have purple speckling and mottling rather than the plain green in *E. purpureum*. Plants are similar in height and form to *E.purpureum*, however, the flower heads consist of 9-15 flowers compared with 5-7 in *E. purpureum*. It is more cold hardy than *E. purpureum*, extending as far north as zone 4.

**Cultivars:**

'Atropupureum' is a magnificent plant, eye-catching from a distance and impressive close up. It bears purple flowers, leaves, petioles and upper stems. This is the architectural and color highlight of the fall garden.

'Carin' bears light lavender flowers over 5-7' tall plants. Introduced by North Creek Nursery, the plant recognizes its plant propagator, Carin Bonafacio.

'Gateway' is similar but more compact and shorter. 'Gateway' was hailed as a dwarf cultivar but plants routinely grow 6' in height.

'Purple Blush' is only 4-5' tall with purple flowers in the fall.

***-purpureum*** (pur-pewr' ree-um) Joe Pye Weed 4-7'/3'
Fall Purple Eastern North America Zones 4-8

Although this wildflower occurs from Quebec to southern Maine, to the mountains of north Georgia and as far west as Texas, one must often search high and low for its presence in American gardens. On the other hand, it is one of the architectural building blocks of British gardens. People with whom I have traveled overseas in the fall always wonder why our native plant is so well used and cherished there and so scorned and ignored here. Perhaps knowing we can find it on meadows and hills everywhere provides some skewed justification not to use it in our cultivated areas. Plants are tolerant of cold winters, common throughout the Laurentian Mountains and Eastern Townships which encompass Montreal, Quebec on the north and southeast respectively. The more I see this in the wild, the more I understand why one common name is queen of the meadow.

Another common name is gravel root, because the roots were used to help reduce the size of kidney stones, and to prevent their formation. The leaves are also used to treat fevers and infections. Joe Pye is said to have been a North Carolina Indian who used these plants to cure many ailments, including typhoid fever, and plants became known as Joe Pye's weed. Perhaps changing the name to Joe Pye plant would enamor it to gardeners a little more.

The foliage is whorled, generally 3 to 5 leaves to a whorl, each 8-12″ leaf coarsely serrated and pointed. The leaves have a distinctive vanilla scent when crushed. The stems are hollow, green with purple nodes and usually not mottled with purple. About 5-7 small purple flowers make up one of the flower heads but 5-9 flower heads are packed together to make an impressive 12-18″ diameter compound inflorescence.

Plants require abundant water and full sun to be at their best. In shady locations, they become excessively tall. This is a large plant and is not for everyone's garden, nor should it be relegated to the back pasture. Unfortunately, Joe Pye weed does not tolerate the constant high summer temperatures in my Georgia garden. It is a cool-season species and is a better plant for areas where night temperatures remain below 75°F.

Propagate similar to *E. coelestinum*. The divisions have long fibrous roots and a sharp spade is useful when separating the plantlets.

**Cultivars:**

var. *album* is an uncommon white-flowered form which I have yet to see.

'Big Umbrella' grows 7′ tall and 2-3′ wide. Selected in Germany, it has dark stems and broad flowering heads.

'Joe White' has cleaner flowers than those of other white-flowered eupatoriums. Introduced by ItSaul Nursery in Atlanta, Georgia.

'Little Red' is a purple-flowering dwarf form, about 4′ in height.

***-rugosum*** (roo-go' sum) White Snakeroot 3-5′/4′
Late Summer White Eastern North America Zones 3-7
(syn. *Ageratina altissima*)

This is seldom seen in cultivated gardens but makes an attractive and unusual display if conditions are favorable. The 5-7″ long pointed leaves are opposite, ovate, and sharply toothed. The veins on the underside are often slightly hairy. Mature plants are covered with 3-4″ diameter white inflorescences, consisting of 12-24 one-quarter inch wide flowers arranged in dense corymbs. The flowers are long lasting, persisting well into the fall.

Plants look particularly good at the end of a flower bed where the whole plant may be appreciated, rather than just one side if viewed only from the front. Full sun and well-drained soils are prerequisites for success as well as cool night temperatures. Plants are more shade tolerant than most species of *Eupatorium* and can be used in areas of a few hours of afternoon shade. This is not a good plant south of zone 7 because warm nights result in loss of vigor. Plants should be cut to the ground after flowering.

Plants have been reclassified by some taxonomists into the genus *Ageratina*. It may be listed as *A. altissima*, or it may not.

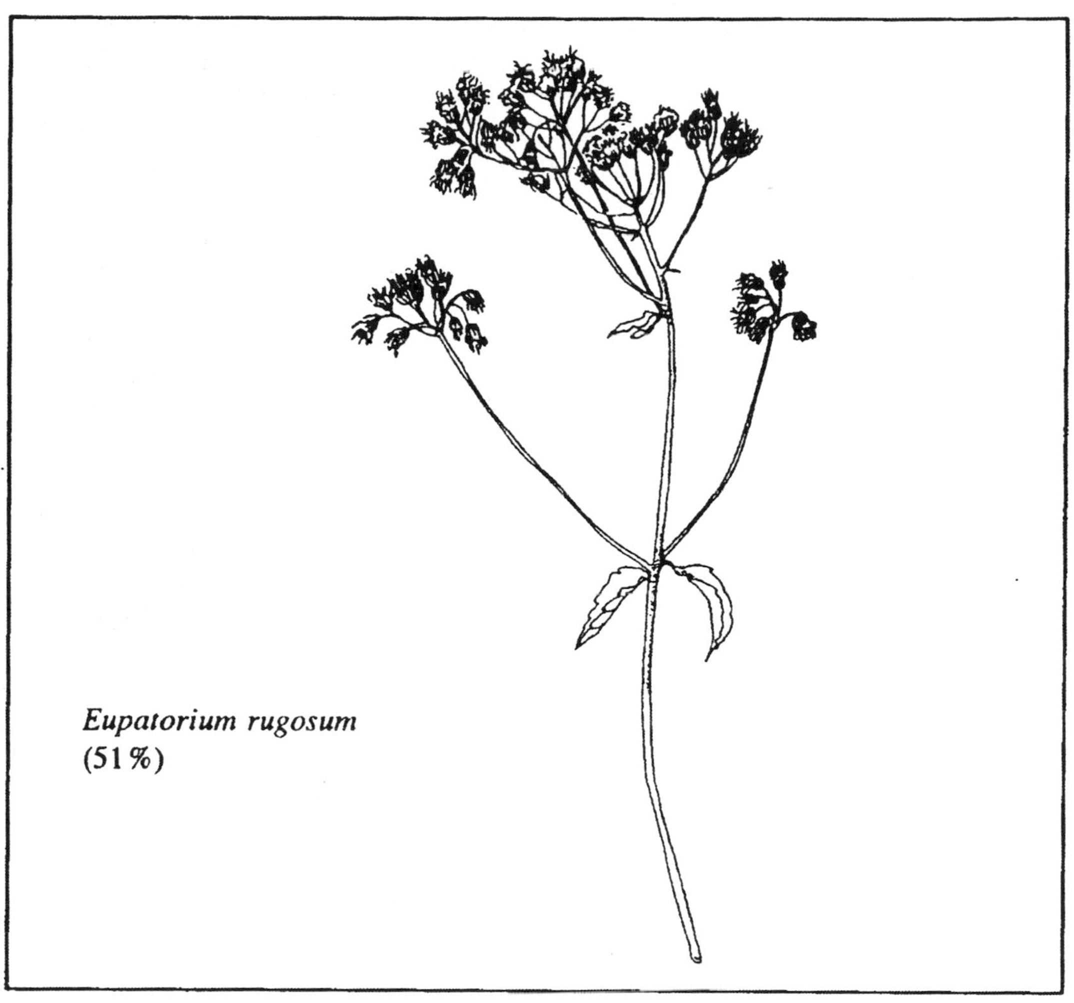
*Eupatorium rugosum*
(51%)

Propagate similar to *E. coelestinum*.

**Cultivars:**

'Braunlaub' has handsome bronze to purple foliage that contrasts well with the white flowers.

'Chocolate' was introduced by the Mt. Cuba Center in Delaware and hit the nurseries with a bang, showing off dark foliage topped with many white flowers. Chosen as the 1998 Native Plant of the Year at the Millersville Native Plant Conference in Millersville, Pennsylvania. Plants can grow up to 4′ tall, but a good shearing in late spring or early summer provides a far more handsome plant. Zones 4-7a.

**Related Species and Hybrids:**

Many of these big purple-flowered species are difficult to tell apart, and hybridization also seems to have occurred, making the job even harder.

*E. dubium* is a shorter form (3-5′) of Joe Pye and may be more useful in smaller gardens. Plants flower a little earlier than *E. purpureum* and are a bit more shade tolerant. The cultivar 'Little Joe' is shorter yet, but still about 4′ high.

*E. fistulosum*, hollow Joe Pye weed, differs by having four to seven leaves per whorl and hollow stems. The flower heads consist of five to eight flowers. Plants grow to seven feet. A white-flowered form, 'Album' is occasionally offered under a couple of names. The white form is sold as 'Bartered Bride', but I agree with Allen Bush, backing the common name 'Joe Pye's Bride'. Family values, please. The cultivar 'Gateway' is sometimes included here.

*E. fortunei*, Chinese boneset, does not have a lot of devoted gardening fans, but as an ingredient used in Chinese medicine, the plant has attracted legions of people. Plants stand 4-6′ tall with pink flowers. A white-flowered form is available that is a nice contrast with the green foliage, and a variegated form, 'Pink Frost' that provides pink flowers and leaves with white edges is also sold.

*E. lindleyanum*, native to China, is 2-3′ tall and smothered with small creamy white flowers in late summer. The lancelike foliage is whorled and irregularly toothed.

*E. perfoliatum*, common boneset, bears stems which appear to grow through the middle of the narrow, leathery leaves. The flowers are creamy white and open on 4-6′ stems in late summer. An excellent and overlooked native plant. This was probably one of the most common medicines used in the 1800s and routinely used by Civil War doctors. It was used to break up coughs and treat fevers, and was found in the medicine cupboard of most every settler in the East. In fact, it is said to be the best cough medicine in the last 100 years (Patricia Kyritsi Howell, *Medicinal Plants of the Southern Appalachians*). Typhoid fever was far more common a hundred years ago, and those suffering often described the brutal pain as if "their bones were going to crack." The term boneset had nothing to do with setting bones, but rather described its soothing affect on the symptoms of this painful and often fatal disease. Plant extracts were also said to have tonic, cathartic and emetic effects. Quite a plant, I'd say.

'Phantom' is a hybrid with *E. maculatum* 'Purpureum' and *E. rugosum* and grows only 3′ tall. Plants bear lavender flowers. This appears to be the best form for persistent dwarf habit.

*E. triplinerve*, also smothered in white flowers, has cordate, scalloped leaves and grows 5-6′ tall.

## ***Euphorbia*** (yew-for′ bee-a) Spurge Euphorbiaceae

I bet Euphorbius, the Greek physician to King Juba II of Mauritania in the 1st century A.D. did not realize his immortality would be found in some milky plants. Euphorbius was a pioneer, he used the latex from his namesakes for medicinal purposes. This large genus contains approximately 2000 species, yet the best known is still the greenhouse poinsettia, *E. pulcherrima*, a deciduous shrub reaching heights of 15′ in its native habitat. A number of attractive annual species such as *E. heterophylla*, painted spurge, and the white-flowered *E. marginata*, snow-on-the-mountain, make wonderful conversation pieces, and six to nine perennial species are reasonably easy to find. However, the number of cultivars has risen dramatically in the last 5 years as "euphorbs" have been rediscovered.

None of the species has petals or sepals and the "flowers" are actually highly colored bracts. The true flowers are reduced in the male to a single stamen and in the female to a long-stalked ovary. Fused, they are called a cyathium. Most bracts are yellow but *E. corollata*, flowering spurge, are white and petal-like while *E. griffithii* has orange to red bracts. Another characteristic common to all species is the presence of milky sap, which in some species is acrid and poisonous, especially if it comes into contact with open cuts. Always keep it away from your eyes.

The flowering stems of the upright forms, especially *E. characias*, *E.* x *martinii*, *E. amygdaloides* and their hybrids occur in early spring, then decline in summer, looking woozy by mid to late summer. The new stems are at the base and if the old stems are removed, these will grow rapidly, providing the framework for next year's flowers. This is not necessary for the creeping forms like *E. cyparissias*.

Propagate the herbaceous species by terminal cuttings in midsummer, by division, or by seed.

<u>Quick Reference to Euphorbia Species</u>

| | Height (in.) | Bract color | Flowering time |
|---|---|---|---|
| *E. amygdaloides* | 12-20 | Yellow | Late Spring |
| *E. characias* | 30-60 | Green-Yellow | Spring |
| *E. cornigera* | 24-30 | Yellow | Early Summer |
| *E. corollata* | 12-24 | White | Spring |
| *E. cyparissias* | 12-15 | Yellow | Spring |
| *E. dulcis* | 12-15 | Yellow | Spring |
| *E. epithymoides* | 18-24 | Yellow | Early Spring |
| *E. griffithii* | 24-36 | Red | Summer |
| *E. myrsinites* | 6-9 | Yellow | Spring |

***-amygdaloides*** (a-mig-dal-oi′ deez) Wood Spurge 12-20″/15″
Late Spring Yellow Europe Zones 5-7

Plants are native from Ireland to Portugal and Algeria and to woodlands and grassy banks of Turkey and the Caucasus. They prefer moist soils and cool climates. The stems have tufted spoon-shaped (oblanceolate) leaves and the habit is more or less upright. The plant is distinguished from many others by having purple stems with greenish yellow bracts.

Plants do well in full sun or partial shade but are best at higher elevations and where humidity is relatively low. They are susceptible to mildew in warm, wet areas.

**Cultivars:**

'Golden Glory' has done well in the Gardens at UGA, providing good chartreuse flowers on 4′ tall plants.

'Purpurea' is the most handsome form, bearing deep red stems and bronze foliage, especially when young. Plants come true from seed.

var. *robbiae*, Mrs. Robb's bonnet, has green-yellow bracts and green foliage. It differs by being rhizomatous, thus making a useful evergreen ground cover by filling in rapidly. The wide spoon-shaped foliage is evergreen and plants are about 2′ tall. Plants tolerate dry shade and blend well with a wide assortment of plant material. 'Redbud' has red stems and deep red apical growth.

***-characias*** (ka-ra′ kee-as) Mediterranean Spurge 3-5′/3′
Early Spring Yellow Mediterranean Zones 6-8

Probably one of the most common spurges in European gardens; and many North American gardeners have also discovered its charm, along with its persistent nature. The green thick stems are woody at the base and somewhat purplish, and the 4-6″ long linear leaves are arranged spirally along its length. Plants can look bare at the base but leaves become more closely spaced near the top. Dozens of green-yellow flowers with purple glands are held in a large inflorescence above the foliage.

Plants look terrific in foliage in the winter, and in early spring flower, and except for their size, tend to retreat in the background in the summer. In the South, these are exceptionally handsome plants in the border, but persist no more than three years. After flowering, they mysteriously decline, going soft and mushy for no apparent reason. This is also the case a little further north, but happens faster in the South. Fortunately, seedlings appear with regularity and may be moved around the garden. For some gardeners, they have taken on a weedlike status, particularly if all the seedlings are allowed to remain.

They are full sun plants and will be a little weaker if given too much shade.

**Cultivars:**

'Black Pearl' is 3-4′ tall in the Gardens at UGA, with outstanding performance and eye-catching flowers. Best tall euphorb we have trialed.

'Blue Hills' has somewhat blue-green leaves and larger yellow flowers than the species.

'Ember Queen' is a recent introduction with clean green and white variegation on the leaves. It is also sold as 'Variegata'.

subsp. *wulfenii* is shorter (2-3′ tall) and bears similar flowers, although the glands are a little more purple than the species. This is the most common form in gardens and includes a number of interesting cultivars. 'Burrow Silver' is a fine, although slow-growing plant with yellow and green variegated foliage and creamy yellow flowers and golden centers. 'Humpty Dumpty' is shorter (about 2′ tall) and more compact with large flower heads and dark red glands. 'Lambrook Yellow', arising from Lambrook Garden in England, bears impressive large green-yellow flowers. 'Lambrook Gold' has golden yellow flowers with blue-green foliage. Both are exceptional.

***-cornigera*** (kor′ nig-er-a) Wallich Spurge 24-30″/18″
Early Summer Yellow Himalayas Zones 6-9

The 4-6″ diameter yellow-green bracts occur in groups of three and encircle the small flowers. Combined with the large eye-catching bracts are lanceolate, dark green leaves with clear white midribs. Although tolerant of full sun, plants do best with some afternoon shade and abundant water. Given these conditions, plants will remain attractive all season. Like many others in the genus, some name rattling is going on. This may appear as *E. cornigera* or by its older names *E. wallichii* or *E. longiflora.*

Seed may require a cold treatment (35-40°F) for 4-6 weeks prior to placing in a warm area for germination. Propagate by cuttings similar to *E. epithymoides.*

***-corollata*** (kor-o′ lat-a) Wild Spurge 1-3′/2′
Summer White Central United States Zones 5-8

One of the few garden-useful native euphorbs, wild spurge is a long-flowering species with white bracts at the tip of the radiating branches. Plants are native to the prairies and dry open woodlands from southeastern South Dakota to southeastern Nebraska, Kansas and Oklahoma. The star-shaped "flowers" are excellent for cutting and are sometimes known as false baby's breath. Plants bloom from summer to early fall and the foliage turns glossy wine-red at that time.

Full sun and relatively rich soil are needed for best performance.

***-cyparissias*** (sigh-pa-ris′ ee-as) Cypress Spurge 9-15″/8″
Spring Yellow Europe Zones 6-8

Looking like a dwarf cypress or tiny spruce tree, plants are easily distinguished from most other garden euphorbias. Plants are stoloniferous and will run like crazy if provided with full sun and rich soil. The willowy leaves are blue-green and compact throughout the stem. This old-fashioned plant is most handsome where happy. Be forewarned, however, plants can become a nuisance, even a cuss-worthy plant, because of their running roots. They can be terrible re-seeders as well and have become naturalized in some western and southern states. You will soon be sharing it or tossing it over the fence.

Good drainage is essential; plants grow well in sandy soils or rocky areas.

**Cultivars:**

'Baby' is a dwarf form, only about 8″ tall.

'Bush Boy' bears featherlike branches, almost soft to the touch.

'Fen's Ruby' is my favorite, having ruby growth tips in the spring, changing to green in late spring and throughout the rest of the season. It is equally aggressive as the species.

'Orange Man' has bright yellow flowers that turn orange in the spring. Quite outstanding.

***-dulcis*** (dull′ chiss) 12-18″/15″
Spring Yellow Europe Zones 5-7

The species itself has 1-2″ long succulent oblong leaves that occasionally have a tinge of purple. The flowers are yellowish green; the plants are handsome enough but would not have seen the light of popularity if not for the purple-leaved cultivar 'Chameleon'. This popular form grows in a tight mound, quite a different shape compared to most of the other species. In full sun, the small leaves are deep purple on the outside, but quite green if you look in the interior. In shade, the plants open up and are far less purple. Plants do well in cool climates but do not perform according to the catalogs in warm, humid summers. In fact, they have been a disappointment in many parts of the country, being floppy, short-lived and less than colorful.

***-epithymoides*** (e-pi-thi-moi′ deez) Cushion Spurge 12-18″/18″
Early Spring Yellow Europe Zones 4-7
(syn. *E. polychroma*)

A dazzling plant in early spring, the pale green leaves give way to shiny yellow bracts which light up the early spring garden. When in flower, the clump-forming plants look like yellow cushions. The 2″ long, oblong, alternate leaves remain attractive throughout the year if planted in the right conditions, and produce some red fall color.

Cushion spurge tolerates full sun in zones 4 and 5 but even there, protection from afternoon sun is beneficial. Shade is essential in the South. I have grown it in north Georgia in full sun and partial shade: those in full sun performed poorly while plants in afternoon shade prospered, spread, and lived up to expectations. The habit, however, becomes a little leggy and the clump opens up as the heat of a southern summer progresses. This is especially true after 2-3 years in the garden, at which time it should be re-propagated.

Seed germinates irregularly but no special problems are encountered if seed is placed in a warm, humid area. Plants may be carefully divided after 2-3 years. Care must be taken to provide adequate roots on each of the divisions. Two- to four-inch long terminal cuttings may be rooted after flowering is completed. Remove all vestiges of bracts and flowers, insert cutting in equal parts sand:vermiculite, and place in a warm (70-75°F ), humid area.

The proper botanical name of this species is constantly in doubt. *E. polychroma*, named by an Austrian, Anton Josef Kerner in 1875, was superseded by *E. epithymoides*, given by Linnaeus, in 1770. Normally the first name takes precedence and thus *E. epithymoides* should be the correct name. However, that name had been given to another species. Because of this confusion, cushion spurge will be listed by both names for many years to come: choose the one you like and stay with it.

**Cultivars:**

'Bonfire' has bright yellow flowers over burgundy foliage, which holds the color reasonably well into the summer. Plants are about a foot tall.

'Emerald Jade' is smaller than the species and boasts brighter fall color.

'First Blush' bears leaves with creamy margins and rosy pink coloring on the blades. Plants are about 1′ tall.

'Midas' bears brighter yellow flowers.

'Major' is more compact than the species, resulting in tighter mounds of growth. Flowers are also bright yellow.

'Pilosa Major' was selected for its larger flower heads.

'Purpurea' has purple-suffused foliage which makes a handsome contrast with the yellow foliage.

'Sonnegold' is vigorous with bright yellow flowers.

***-griffithii*** (gri-fith′ ee-eye) Griffith's Spurge 24-36″/24″
Summer Orange-Red Himalayas Zones 5-7

I have been excited about the future of this species ever since it become available in North America. The mounding habit of the plants is similar to but larger than *E. epithymoides*. The unique characteristic is the many brick-red bracts held above the lancelike mid-green leaves with pale pink midribs. After flowering and when the bracts fade, an attractive herbaceous shrub remains. I have seen wonderfully good-looking colonies in the Northeast and West, and reasonable plantings in the Midwest. However, they are shy of heat and humidity and southern summers result in plants that languish, begging to be put out of their misery. Don't waste your money!

Partial shade is best although full sun can be tolerated in the North. As with other species of this genus, it must not be allowed to dry out.

**Cultivars:**

'Dixter' arose from the garden of Christopher Lloyd at Great Dixter, Northiam, England, and has red flushed foliage and orange bracts. Flowers are more orange and stems are redder than 'Fireglow'.

'Fern Cottage' bears red stems and red margins on the leaves. Plants are more compact than 'Fireglow'.

'Fireglow' is most common and is similar to the species but has flame-orange bracts, red midveins, and orange-brown stems. It is particularly attractive in combination with yellow-flowering plants such as tall *Coreopsis*.

***-myrsinites*** (mur-sin-ee′ teez) Myrtle Euphorbia 6-9″/12″
Spring Yellow Southern Europe Zones 5-9

This evergreen trailing plant produces many gray-green, almost blue, sessile leaves in tight spirals along the prostrate stems. The 2-3″ wide inflorescences are made up of sulphur-yellow bracts at the end of each 8-10″ long stem. The foliage color is an excellent contrast to the bracts. Plants tolerate heat well and have proven excellent for the Southeast. These can get away from even the most patient gardener, filling pathways and byways with little euphorbettes. Be tough.

Propagate by seed and cuttings similar to *E. epithymoides*.

**Related Species:**

*E. lathyris*, caper or gopher spurge, is an unusual-looking spurge, with pointed white-midribbed leaves and small greenish bracts. Each solitary flower gives rise to a capsule which superficially looks like a caper (the unopened bud of a caper bush, used in cooking), thus its common name. It has reseeded in the Armitage garden and pokes its way through baptisias and my garden bench. Not a bad combination. In my curiosity about capers, I read Susan's cookbook which specifically told me not to confuse them with fruit of the caper spurge, which are poisonous. Good thing! Plants are biennial but can grow 2-3′ tall. They reseed everywhere and are thought to repel moles, voles and gophers from the garden. Whether they do is debatable but gardeners looking for any remedy to these burrowing rodents tend to leave nothing to chance. Rodents aside, this is a great plant.

*E. palustris* grows 2½-3′ tall and bears bright yellow green bracts from late spring through July. They are vigorous growers which form large clumps from woody rootstocks. The foliage is long and narrow and numerous side branches occur. Plants are tolerant of wet soils and can grow in shallow water. Native throughout Europe, sometimes escaping in the southeast United States, they perform well in zones 5-7, zone 8 if placed in moist conditions in afternoon shade. Cut back after flowering.

*E. schillingii*, Schilling's spurge, also has large bright yellow bracts but is taller and later to flower than the previous species. Native to the Himalayas, plants are likely hardy in zones 5-7.

*E. seguieriana* bears bracts which are fire engine red, certainly redder than 'Fireglow'. The plant is woody at the base and has light green linear to oblong stem leaves. Plants grow at least three feet tall. The species is native to central and western Europe, east to Siberia and may possibly be cold hardy to zone 5.

*E. sikkimensis*, native to Nepal, is one of the most handsome species in the garden. Plants grow to 3′ in height and form significant colonies. The young shoots are bright red and as the plants mature, turn a more dull purple-red. The leaves have white midribs which provide a notable brightening in the garden. The bright yellow flower heads are large and showy and easily seen from a distance. Flowers are formed in late spring and summer.

**Additional Hybrids:**

Many new hybrid euphorbias have been released in the last 5 years, with confusing parentage to be sure. Here are a few of them.

'Autumn Sunset', a hybrid between *E. epithymoides* and *E. griffithii*, grows up to four feet in height, and produces interesting red, orange and yellow mottling on the upright foliage. The yellow-orange flowers occur in the spring. Cold hardy to zone 6, perhaps 5.

'Blackbird' is outstanding everywhere I have seen it. The dark purple foliage holds all season on 2′ tall plants. Flowers are chartreuse but the foliage is the best part. Plants are a sport of 'Red Wing'. The cold hardiness is suspect, however they may be cold hardy to zone 7, perhaps 6.

'Blue Lagoon' is similar to var. *robbiae* but taller. Plants have blue-green foliage and chartreuse flowers. This can be an aggressive grower, spectacular in flower.

'Despina' is only about 15-18″ tall with blue-green leaves and yellow flowers.

'Efanthia' is popular, growing 2-4′ tall, with chartreuse flowers and good weather tolerance.

'Glacier Blue' was introduced by Gina Falcetti-Arnold of Skagit Gardens and is a sport of 'Tasmanian Tiger.' Plants provide good looking silvery blue foliage edged with white. It appears to be much more vigorous than 'Tasmanian Tiger'

'Helena's Blush' is a variegated form of 'Efanthia'. Handsome pink and green foliage and extraordinary winter color. In the winter, leaves and stems are a spectacular dark purple.

'Helen Robinson' (*E. robbiae* x *E. characias*) seems to be very vigorous, making large clumps in a very short time. Plants produce deep yellow flowers.

'Jade Dragon' is a cross between *E. characias* subsp. *wulfenii* and *E. amygdaloides* 'Rubra'. The foliage is purple as it emerges and turns green as it matures. The yellow flowers are held in wide inflorescences over compact plants.

'Jessie' was popularized by Barry Glick of Sunshine Farm and Nursery in Renick, West Virginia. Plants are hybrids of *E. griffithii* and *E. epithymoides* and provide yellow bracts edged in orange. Interesting to be sure, little information is available on garden performance.

'Kalipso' is cute, growing only about 12″ tall, with dark green leaves and chartreuse flowers.

x *martinii* is a natural hybrid between *E. amygdaloides* and *E. characias*. They are very similar to, but significantly more dwarf than *E. characias*. The flower heads are not as elongated but the glands are redder than in *E. characias*. A good garden plant, more easily grown, but similar in longevity to *E. characias*. A couple of reasonably good garden selections have been offered. 'Cherokee' is similar to 'Chameleon' but is said to be much more vigorous and a better plant. I have not trialed it, but if that is so, it will be well worth trying. 'Rudolph' is a selection with red terminals, à la Rudolph's nose, particularly noticeable in the fall. It has looked outstanding in trials. 'Tiny Tim' is a mounding dwarf form with similar red centered flowers as the species.

'Orange Grove' is a cross between *E. amygdaloides* 'Rubra' and *E. amygdaloides* var. *robbiae*. The flowers are yellow, which later turn to a good-looking orange. From Terra Nova Nursery, Canby, Oregon.

'Redwing' is a *martinii* x *amygdaloides* cross, resulting in a mounding habit about 18″ tall. The flower buds are red prior to opening, the bracts are chartreuse and flowering stems are so numerous as to almost hide the foliage.

'Royal Velvet' appears to be a cultivar of *E.* x *martini*. The foliage is hairy, sort of velvety, the stems have a pink to purple caste and the flowers are chartreuse.

'Tasmanian Tiger' is truly spectacular with its white and green variegated leaves. However, it lacks vigor in areas with heat, humidity or excessive rainfall. Stunning where happy, probably best in a container where soils and irrigation are more controlled.

'Shorty' has chartreuse flowers in the spring, bluish green summer foliage and red tips in the winter. Plants have proven themselves to be tough and handsome. Plants are only about 12″ tall. Bred by ItsSaul Plants.

## *Eurybia* See *Aster*

## *Euryops* (ew-ree′ ops) Euryops Asteraceae

The genus consists of about 100 species of mostly tender woody shrubs or herbaceous plants, but only one or two are occasionally seen in gardens. Much of the recent interest in the most popular species, *E. pectinatus*, has come from the many gardeners who travel to the British Isles or the West Coast. They discover plants at Sissinghurst, Powis Castle, Kew, Wisley, or Minter Gardens and see how wonderful this subshrub can be when provided with good growing conditions. The deep green deeply divided foliage makes an outstanding contrast with the bright yellow daisy flowers. Plants grow 3-4′ tall and are about 3′ across. They are best displayed in containers where drainage is well controlled.

Unfortunately, few places in this country show off euryops as well as such gardens in the British Isles. Except for gardeners on the West Coast, and in zones 7b to 10, plants are not consistently cold tolerant to be considered a perennial. While they certainly have no trouble surviving hot summers, flowering is poor in the hot summer months. Plants flower nearly all season in the North, and look good in the spring and fall in the South. The foliage is probably the best feature of the plant, so if flowering is sparse, one need not despair. However, do as the Brits do and plant them in large containers in full sun or in an area with afternoon shade.

Another possible choice for containers or well-drained areas of the garden is a low-growing species, *E. acraeus*, likely hardy to zone 7. It is about half the height of the previous species and tends to be more spreading. Flowers are bright yellow, and plants may be trimmed back after flowering.

**Cultivars**:

'Athens Sun' has bright yellow flowers and has proven to be perennial in the Gardens at UGA.

# F

## ***Fallopia*** (fal′op-ee-a) Fleece Flower Polygonaceae

The genus *Fallopia* is closely related to and associated with the genus *Polygonum*, and in fact, numerous species of these genera have been dumped, lumped and split, so the taxonomy is still confusing. *Fallopia* can be big, bodacious and invasive and is not generally associated with small gardens, but if placed in the correct setting, plants can be quite beautiful and always impressive.

The most impressive of all, and the only one I would have in my garden is *F. japonica* 'Variegata', a large (4-6′ tall and equally wide) plant with wonderful white and green spotted leaves and a tinge of pink on the leaves. The petioles are often pink to red as well. Hundreds of small white flowers occur on elongated inflorescences in midsummer, attracting butterflies and at least a bazillion bees.

Plants will spread, faster in the North than the South, but can be contained if the new stems are removed in the spring. We have grown it for years in the Gardens at UGA and it maintained its impressive stature without too much effort. However, for small gardens and weak backs, this plant cannot be recommended. Propagate by division.

Another species that got caught in the taxonomic crossfire is now known as *F. baldschuanica*, the plant we used to know as *Polygonum aubertii*, Chinese fleece vine. Growing to heights of 15′ or more, and covered with silky white flowers, this plant is a treat to see. Of course, it is better to see it in other peoples' gardens as it will reseed from here back to China. However, if that is not a concern, use it to cover a few posts and cell phone towers.

## ***Farfugium*** (far-fuug′ ee-um) Leopard Plant Asteraceae

After considerable taxonomic shuffling and debate, leopard plant, once known by the totally unpronounceable *Ligularia tussilaginea*, is now *Farfugium japonicum*. I have had little use for the green form in the past but I have come to see the light—well, at least some light. The rounded glossy green leaves are handsome and usually left alone by insects and diseases. The plants are less needy of moisture than their old partners, the ligularias, and can make handsome tussocks in a shaded, reasonably moist area. Heat is still a bit of a nemesis and the yellow daisy flowers that occur in mid to late fall are still quite ugly. Other than that, it is a pretty green thing.

Propagate by division; hardy in zones 7-9.

**Cultivars:**

Many new and quite weird forms, all from Japan, are being ballyhooed to the garden public. Most are winter hardy to zone 7 (7b) although with some care, perhaps a little colder.

'Aureomaculatum', leopard plant, is the most popular form with leaves splashed with yellow dots. One author, to remain nameless, stated that it looked like a "pretty green thing with ugly yellow spots". However, it too can look stunning given mild summers, consistent moisture and a little shade. May be a little cold hardier than the species.

'Crispatum' is one of my favorite "fargs". The leaves are gray-green and the margins are wavy, truly quite wonderful in the moist shaded garden. I have lost it in my garden more than once, but I have come to believe my garden simply eats things when I am not looking. Zones 7-9.

'Jitsuko's Star' has handsome mounds of light green foliage and is topped with double, yellow flowers, easier on the eye than the singles of the species. Introduced by famed plantsman Ozzie Johnson for his late wife Jitsuko.

'Kagami-Jitsi' has yellow spots similar to 'Aureomaculatum' but also has the crested leaf margins of 'Crispata'.

'Kaimon Drake' is interesting, to be sure. Introduced by Barry Yinger of Asiatica Nursery, Lewisberry, Pennsylvania, the new leaves emerge pure white to white-speckled while leaves that emerge later in the season are green. By midsummer, most of the variegation is gone.

'Tsuwabaki' is truly ugly. Shiny green leaves repulsively crested and recrested make it look like large green droppings. No doubt, this will be a hit in gardens everywhere.

## *Festuca* (fes-too' ca) Fescue Poaceae

Almost all turf mixtures have at least some fescue grass in their composition, but many gardeners are unaware of the potential beauty of some members in this large (over 300 species) genus. In general, the leaves are flattened and the flowers are held in narrow panicles. They prefer full sun and well-drained soils although, as can be expected in a genus this large, exceptions occur. Fescues are cool-season grasses and are at their best in spring and fall and are poor grasses for southern gardens. Heat is anathema to all the blue-leafed grasses, resulting in summer dormancy or even death, particularly if rainfall is plentiful. From the garden perspective, find a well-drained sunny location, plant a grouping of about four to six plants and plan on replanting every two to three years.

A great deal of confusion exists as to the proper names of some of the garden species and the same plants are likely sold under two or three different names. But what else is new? Certainly the most popular group of fescues are the blue-foliage forms, sold as cultivars of *F. glauca*, *F. ovina* and *F. cinerea*. Botanically, there are few enough differences between them and horticulturally even fewer.

While some of the most ornamental garden forms are characterized by their blue foliage, *F. tenuifolia*, fine-leaved fescue, has beautiful green, narrow foliage. The diminutive size and need for good drainage of many of the cultivars suggest that they are best suited for containers or rock gardens. Most of the fescues are short (6-18″ tall) clump-formers that prefer well-drained soils, although *F. californica*, California fescue, and *F. gigantea*, giant fescue, can easily reach 3′ feet, while *F. viviparia* prefers moist conditions and does well at the edge of lakes or streams.

The oldest selection is probably *F. ovina* 'Glauca', which is now properly known as *F. glauca*, and has been propagated from seed for many years. Thus, foliage ranges from deep blue to a washed-out gray-blue. Recently, numerous cultivars have been selected and propagated vegetatively to maintain the subtle differences between them.

Propagate the species by seed, cultivars by division.

**Blue-leaved Cultivars and Hybrids:**

Many of these look the same, and choosing *F. glauca*, which is the easiest to procure, will be more than satisfactory. However, richer blues and often more compact habits may result from choosing a selection.

'April Green' grows about 8-12″ tall with olive-green foliage and handsome flowers. Likely a cultivar of *F. amythestina*.

'Azurit' has blue-gray foliage and is taller than most, growing to about 18″ in height.

'Blue Finch' bears fine-textured dull blue leaves.

'Blue Fox' was an Award of Merit winner from the Royal Horticultural Society in 1993. Handsome striking blue foliage.

'Blue Silver' is a particularly handsome fine-textured form with silvery blue leaves. A planting at Longwood Gardens was outstanding.

'Boulder Blue' is a bit like a boulder, I guess. The clumping habit is certainly boulderlike.

'Tom Thumb' grows only 4-6″ tall. The blue foliage may fade to green as the season progresses.

'Elijah Blue' is my favorite, at least this year. Plants bear soft blue leaves and grow 12″ tall. Even in flower, this is a handsome form. I saw this at the home of Dennis Mareb of Windy Hill Farm, Great Barrington, Massachusetts in late July, and it was as outstanding as Dennis and the business he runs there.

'Spring Blue' is likely a cultivar of *F. cinerea*. Plants have intense blue, fine foliage and grow 8-10″ tall.

'Harz' bears medium-textured olive green foliage, sometimes tinted plum at the tips in the summer.

'Sea Blue' is more blue-green than many others. Medium textured, strong grower.

'Platinum' has blue leaves with a tint of green . Grows 8-12″ tall.

'Sea Urchin' produces fine silvery blue leaves.

'Silver Heron' bears silvery blue foliage on 6-12″ tall plants.

'Solling' is blue-gray, grows about 10″ tall, and was selected for its lack of flowering.

'Superba' is a fine-textured form of *F. amethystina* with weeping blue-green foliage and ornamental pink flowers in the spring.

***Filipendula*** (fil-i-pen′ dew-la) Meadowsweet Rosaceae

This genus of nine or ten species was once part of the genus *Spiraea* and is still frequently referred to as false spirea. Plants have alternate, pinnately or palmately lobed foliage and panicles of many small white or pink flowers. The genus name comes from *filum*, thread; and *pendulus*, hanging; and alludes to the root tubers hanging on the fibrous roots of *F. hexapetala*, the species after which the genus is named. Most species are found in moist areas in nature and should be grown where high moisture levels can be maintained. The exception to this is *F. vulgaris* which is more drought tolerant than the others.

Plant in alkaline soil (pH, 7.0-7.5) in full sun to partial shade. Flowers appear in early summer. Propagate by division in fall, or by seed.

Quick Guide to Filipendula Species

| | Height (ft.) | Flower color |
|---|---|---|
| *F. palmata* | 3-4 | Pink |
| *F. rubra* | 6-8 | Pink |
| *F. ulmaria* | 3-6 | White |
| *F. vulgaris* | 2-3 | White |

**-*palmata*** (pahl-may′ ta) Siberian Meadowsweet 3-4′/3′
Summer Pink Siberia Zones 3-7

The 4-8″ wide coarse leaves are palmately divided into 3-5 sections. The leaves are white and hairy beneath. A multitude of 6″ wide flattened heads (corymbose panicles) of pale pink flowers rise above the foliage in June, and turn white as they mature. Although the flowers persist for only 2-4 weeks, they make a wonderful show. In north Georgia, flowering begins the end of May, about two weeks later in zone 6, four weeks later in zone 4.

This excellent garden plant lends a bold texture to the garden, remaining attractive all season if moisture is constant. However, if allowed to dry out, the margins of the leaves turn brown, and if continued, the leaves shrivel up and fall off. Copious amounts of compost or other moisture-retaining material incorporated in the garden are beneficial. I have grown this for years and have always been rewarded with its graceful habit and excellent performance. Plants are highly persistent, returning for at least 10 years.

The two drawbacks for this plant are that it must be grown in full sun for best performance and that it is highly attractive to Japanese beetles (what a mess!).

Propagate by fall division or by seed. Seed germinates within 3 weeks when lightly covered with soil and placed in warm temperature (70-75°F) and high humidity, although germination is erratic.

**Cultivars**:
'Alba' has cleaner whiter flowers.

'Digitata Nana' ('Nana') is similar to the species but only 8-10″ tall.
'Rosea' bears pink flowers.
'Rubra' produces darker redder flowers than the species.

***-rubra*** (rew′ bra) Queen-of-the-Prairie 6-8′/4′
Summer Pink Eastern United States Zones 3-8

This native, found from Pennsylvania to Iowa to Georgia, is large and impressive and perhaps the common name is the result of its ability to support itself even in high winds. A most imposing species, although its size somewhat limits it to larger gardens. The foliage consists of pinnately divided leaflets: the large 5-8″ long terminal leaflet has 7-9 small lobes and the laterals have 3-5. The lateral leaflets, however, are absent on the upper stem leaves. The pink to peach flowers are arranged in a 6-9″ wide, dense panicle with conspicuous stamens that stick out from the flowers. This is a classic accent plant, and one which can be as impressive in your garden as it must have been to Lewis and Clark.

Propagation is similar to *F. palmata*.

**Cultivars:**

'Albicans' has white cotton candy flowers and is a little shorter than the type. Flowers open earlier than the species.
'Venusta' is the most available cultivar and has deep pink to carmine flowers. This is a most visual plant, easily seen from a speeding vehicle.

***-ulmaria*** (ul-mah′ ree-a) Meadow Sweet, Queen-of-the-Meadow 2-4′/2′
Summer White Asia, Europe Zones 3-7

This large, stout species is closer in size to *F. vulgaris* than *F. rubra*. The leaves consist of 7-11 large, toothed leaflets. The leaflets are whitish and hairy beneath. The creamy white flowers are carried above the foliage in a flat 4-6″ wide inflorescence, similar to *F. vulgaris*.

Divide similar to *F. palmata*. Seed, however, should be placed in a seed flat at room temperature for about 2 weeks, then cooled for 4-6 weeks at 40°F. After the cool treatment, place at 70-75°F under high humidity.

**Cultivars:**

'Aurea' is the best cultivar and is grown for the foliage rather than the flowers. The flowers are rather insignificant but the foliage is a lovely golden yellow. The flowers should be removed as they start to develop to encourage foliage vigor. Discourage the growth of seedlings as they will be green leaved. The foliage holds up better in cooler climates than in the South.
'Flore Pleno' is also superior to the species. The flowers are double, more showy, and more persistent.
'Variegata' ('Aureo-Variegata') has a central yellow stripe in the foliage, providing contrasting variegated foliage.

***-vulgaris*** (vul-gah′ ris) Dropwort 2-3½′
Summer White Europe Zones 3-7

The 4-10″ long shiny mid-green leaves are pinnately divided into many 1″ long leaflets resulting in a somewhat fernlike appearance. The creamy white flowers are borne in many 4-6″ diameter, branched, flattened inflorescences and are often tinged with pink. I have seen an effective use of the small double form as a handsome edging to stone paths. The rootstock is tuberous, allowing an almost ground cover habit. Plants prefer constant moisture but tolerate dry soils. Plant in full sun to partial shade.

Propagate similar to *F. palmata*.

**Cultivars**:

'Grandiflora' bears larger flowers.

'Multiplex' ('Flore Pleno') is a commonly available double-flowered form, usually 1-2′ tall and more ornamental than the species.

'Rosea' has light pink flowers and is particularly handsome.

**Related Species**

*F. camtschatica*, giant meadowsweet, is even more vigorous and taller than our native "Queen". The large 12″ wide leaves are dark green and sharply toothed. The white to pale pink flowers occur in large inflorescences at the top of the plants in late summer and early fall. Native to Japan, Manchuria and the Kamchatka peninsula and likely hardy to at least zone 4.

*F. purpurea*, Japanese meadowsweet, has much deeper pink flowers and crimson stems and is truly spectacular in flower, probably the most beautiful species in the genus. Each leaf consists of 5-7 serrated, long, pointed segments. A little-known white form, 'Alba', is also occasionally offered. 'Elegans' is an excellent performer and is more compact than the type. It has whitish flowers with red stamens, giving the appearance of rose-colored blooms.

## ***Foeniculum*** (fee-nik′ ew-lum) Fennel Apiaceae

Here is a plant for everyone's garden; one which satisfies the environmentalist, the ornamentalist and the herbalist within us. Two forms of fennel are grown for seasoning and salads. *F. vulgare* var. *azoricum*, is known as Florence fennel or finocchio, and the swollen base of this annual is harvested and served fresh in salads or cooked as a vegetable. Common fennel, *F. vulgare*, native to southern Europe, is offered everywhere and provides light airy, finely cut foliage and the fragrance of anise. The leaves may be harvested throughout the summer and, freshly chopped, impart a unique flavor to the evening salad. Young shoots may also be peeled and chopped and tossed in. The seeds may also be used, further infusing a taste of anise to bread or salads.

As an ornament in the garden, the cultivar 'Purpureum', also sold as 'Bronze' or 'Rubrum', is particularly handsome, providing purple-flushed foliage that earns the plant a garden place regardless of its culinary value. The leaves make a great foil for the light green or variegated foliage of neighboring plants. Another half-dozen fennels have been selected, but it is tough to beat this old-fashioned favorite for straight ornamental value.

The other reason some people like to have this plant around is that it is the preferred host for the swallowtail butterfly. While I like watching these beautiful creatures flit about my fennel as much as the next person, I really have not reached the stage of environmental altruism where I enjoy watching the resulting caterpillars voraciously devouring the plant. I suppose the caterpillars are pretty enough, but I am happy to knock them off and give them to my friends with a wildflower meadow. Since that time, I have given them the plants as well. Now I enjoy the butterflies while they admire the caterpillars.

The yellow-green flowers occur in summer in a compound umbel and are quite useful as cut flowers. Fennel has something for everyone and has made the transition from the herb garden to the main garden relatively painlessly. Performs as a perennial in zones 6-9.

Propagate from seed or by dividing established plants.

***Fragaria*** (fra-gah′ ree-a) Strawberry Rosaceae

Small fruits and vegetables have become common denizens of the ornamental garden. Purple fennel, ornamental peppers, asparagus fern, sweet potato vine, and ornamental kale are but a few. The strawberry has also been hanging around the fringes of ornamental horticulture for some time. The compact habits of the sweet-tasting alpine strawberry, *F. vesca* 'Semperflorens' and its variegated form, 'Variegata' lend themselves well to edging. 'Alexandria' has no runners and is grown for the mounding habit while 'Alpine Yellow' is grown for the ornamental yellow fruit. The common cultivated strawberry, *F.* x *ananassa*, has many cultivars for agronomic selection, however 'Shades of Pink', with light and deep pink flowers and the creamy variegated form, 'Variegata', can also add excitement to the potager.

About ten years ago, 'Pink Panda' ('Lipstick') become a much sought-after container plant and ground cover. Bred by Blooms of Bressingham, this hybrid resulted from the marriage of *Potentilla palustris* and an unnamed culinary strawberry. Plants are excellent ground covers, filling large areas in a single growing season, while producing handsome rosy pink flowers in early spring. Unfortunately, flowering was sparse, perhaps people expected more fruit, and demand fell off. Plants are still occasionally available and are still fine plants for window boxes or hanging baskets. Occasionally, but not in great numbers, small strawberry fruit are produced, but they will never take the place of the real thing on anyone's granola.

***Francoa*** (frang-ko′ a) Francoa Saxifragaceae

A beautiful member of the saxifrage family (*Astilbe*, *Heuchera*) but seldom seen but in northwest coast gardens. Perhaps this is because none of the 5 species are easy garden plants nor do they tolerate a wide range of climates. The most dependable of the species is *F. sonchifolia* which may be hardy to about 15°F (zone 8). Due to its lack of heat and humidity tolerance, it is suitable only to western zone 8 rather than southern zone 8. However, since plants can't read and because plants are so beautiful, it may be worth a try for gardeners willing to take a chance. Be warned, it may not be a great return on investment.

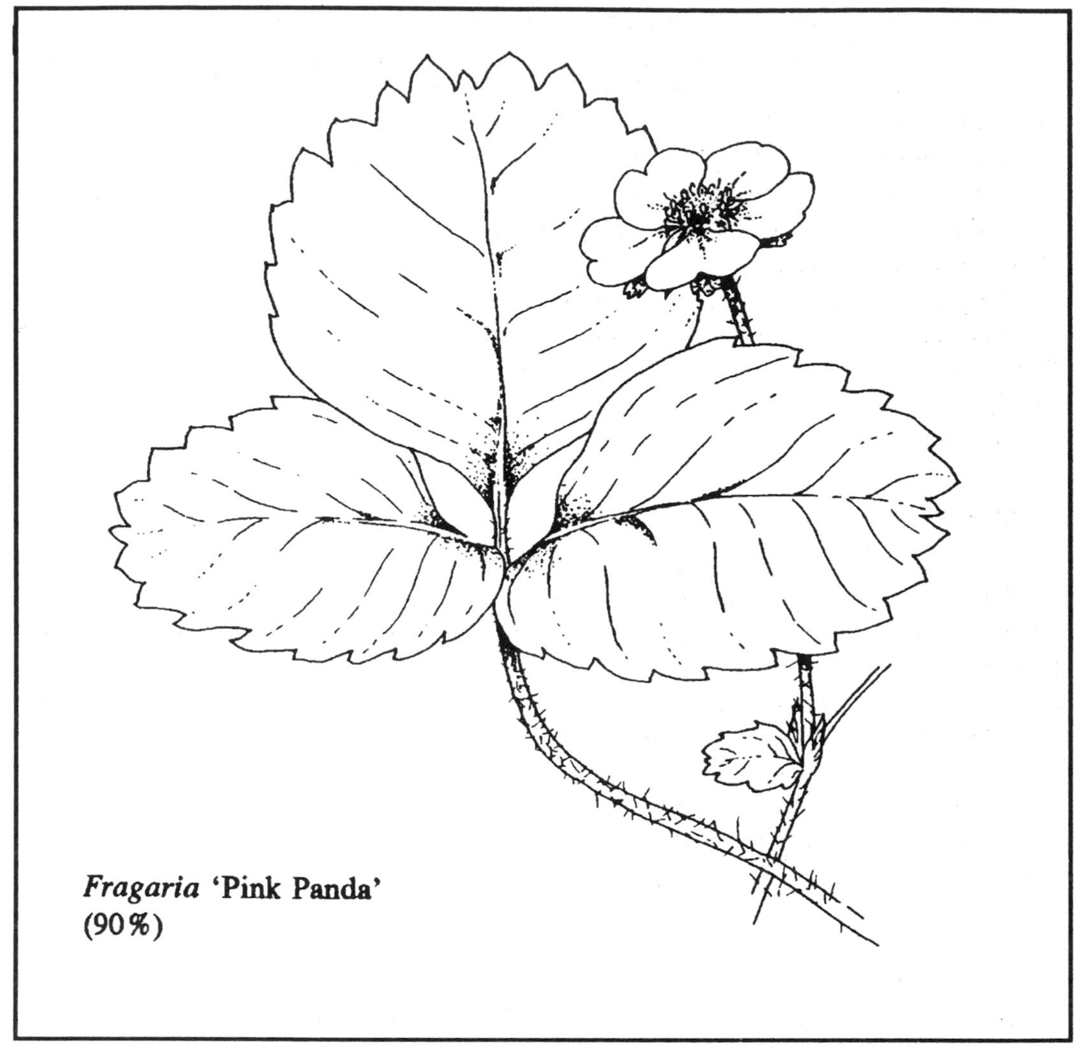

*Fragaria* **'Pink Panda'**
**(90%)**

The basal hairy evergreen foliage is shallowly divided and dense. Above the leaves arises a raceme of closely spaced pink flowers with darker splotches on each of the four petals. Below the terminal inflorescence are smaller branches of flowers which open after the terminal. Altogether a handsome and interesting plant, particularly in gardens in Vancouver and Victoria Canada.

The other species which may be found once in a while are the white-flowered *F. ramosa* and the shell pink *F. appendiculata*. While they are fine garden plants where sited well, neither is as densely flowered nor even as weather tolerant as *F. sonchifolia*.

They may be treated as biennials by starting seed in the spring or early summer, growing on and then placing in cold frames or other protected winter area. Plant out in early spring and enjoy.

***Fritillaria*** (fri-ti-lah′ ree-a) Fritillary Liliaceae

The genus takes the name from *fritillas*, a chessboard or dice-box because the flowers of many species are checkered on the outside. Over 80 species are known but only a small number are available or useful. All species have unbranched leafy stems, with leaves arranged in whorls or in pairs. The flowers on all but the crown imperial are arranged up the stem. When I gardened in Montreal, the guinea hen flower, *F. meleagris*, was everywhere in the spring and people constantly commented on its unusual appearance. I thought it was kind of ugly, but then again, I thought all girls were ugly then too. The crown jewel of the species, however, is the crown imperial, *F. imperialis*, which when grown well, is truly impressive. I have visited the tulip fields of Holland in spring and it is always an enlightening and spectacular time. However, a field of crown imperials is a sight never to be forgotten and easily trumps another tulip patch.

Numerous little-known species are also offered to collectors and a few are finally seeing the light of the garden world. *F. pallidflora*, a handsome pale yellow form, is one example, and I have noticed plantspeople like Brent and Becky Heath offering some of the more exotic forms like *F. michailovskyi* with its beautiful yellow and purple flowers, and *F. pudica* with handsome flowers, small but beautifully scented. These lesser-known species really need to be used more. They may not persist for more than a few years, but what a wonderful few years they provide.

All require full sun and well-drained soil. The fleshy bulbs must be handled carefully and planted 4-6″ deep as soon as received in early fall. If you are to receive bulbs in the mail, be sure that the shipper protects them from drying out. If allowed to dry out, it is unlikely that many bulbs will emerge in the spring. This is true with all the species, although *F. imperialis* is a little more tolerant of shipping and handling.

Propagation from offsets is not difficult. Bulbs should be lifted and offsets potted and grown until ready to replace in the garden. The offsets will bloom in about 12-18 months. Scales may also be used (see *Lilium*), however, the number of scales taken from each bulb must be limited so as not to reduce the vigor of the parent bulb. Fresh seeds require about four years to reach flowering size (Just buy the bulbs!).

Quick Reference to Fritillaria Species

| | Height (in.) | Flower mottled |
|---|---|---|
| *F. imperialis* | 30-36 | No |
| *F. meleagris* | 12-15 | Yes |
| *F. persica* | 24-36 | No |

***-imperialis*** (im-pe-ree-ah′ lis) Crown Imperial 2½-3′/1′
Spring Orange, Yellow Turkey, Iran Zones 5-7

When the crown imperial is planted in groups of a dozen or more, there are few species that compare. The alternate, lanceolate leaves are 4-6″ long, dark green and have a skunklike odor when crushed (as do the flowers). On a calm spring evening, one does not linger by the fritillaries. The foliage persists into midsummer and is difficult to hide when senescence begins. The numerous 2-3″ long flowers hang down beneath a crown or whorl of leaves which protect the flowers from nature's elements. The stigma (part of the pistil) protrudes from the flowers like the clapper in a church bell. Large nectar drops reside inside the flowers and defy all laws of gravity by refusing to fall. Gerard compared each drop to a "pearl of the Orient".

Plant in full sun or afternoon shade. The bulbs may not perform well the first year, patience is often rewarded the second. Bulbs may be divided after 3-4 years.

**Cultivars:**

'Aurora' has orange-scarlet flowers.
'Lutea bears lemon-yellow flowers.
'Lutea Maxima' has yellow flowers which are even larger than the previous selection.
'Orange Brilliant' produces clear orange flowers.
'Rubra has red flowers; 'Rubra Maxima' has larger flowers.

***-meleagris*** (mel-ee-ah′ gris) Guinea Hen Flower 12-15″/12″
Spring Pale Mauve Western Europe Zones 3-7

Although significantly more winter hardy, plants are not nearly as magnificent as the previous species. The 1-2″ long solitary, drooping, checkered flowers are borne on 12-15″ stems and are mauve, marked with squares of dark purple "like the board at which men do play at chesse" (Gerard). It is also known as the snake's head daffodil, for before it opens, the broad budded flower resembles the head of a snake. The 3-6″ long foliage is narrow, alternate, and dark green but not as persistent as *F. imperialis*. Bulbs may be divided in 2-3 years. Plants are highly tolerant of alkaline soil and may be naturalized in grass or in banks.

**Cultivars:**

Bulbs are usually offered in an awful assortment of mixed colors but occasionally single colors are available.

'Alba' has creamy white flowers and is much more visible than the dark camouflage colors of the species. It has no markings but is an excellent cultivar.
'Aphrodite' is also white, but with larger flowers than 'Alba'.
'Artemis' bears purple checkered flowers with hints of green.
'Charon' probably has the darkest flowers of the species.
'Saturnus' bears bright violet with a reddish cast.

***-persica*** (per′ si-ka) Persian Fritillary 24-36″/12″
Spring Purple Asia Zones 5-8

Native to Cypress, southern Turkey and Iran, plants are hardy in about zones 5 to 8. They are tall (up to 3′) and have gray-green alternate, sometimes twisted, stem leaves. Approximately 15-20 musky purple pendant flowers open up along the long

*Echinacea purpurea* with *Perovskia atriplicifolia*

*Echinacea purpurea* 'Fragrant Angel'

*Echinacea purpurea* 'Mars'

*Echinacea purpurea* 'Pink Double Delight'

*Echinops ritro*
'Taplow Blue'

*Epimedium grandiflorum*
'Rose Queen'

*Epimedium* × *versicolor*
'Sulphureum'

*Epimedium* × *warleyense*

*Erigeron* 'Prosperity'

*Eriophyllum lanatum*

*Eryngium alpinum* 'Amethyst'

*Eucomis comosa* 'Sparkling Burgundy'

*Eucomis comosa*
'Tegula Ruby'

*Eupatorium dubium*
'Little Joe'

*Eupatorium purpureum*
'Bartered Bride'

*Euphorbia cyparissias*
'Fen's Ruby'

*Euphorbia*
'Glacier Blue'

*Euphorbia*
'Tasmanian Tiger'

*Euphorbia*
'Blackbird'

*Fallopia baldschuanica*
(aka *Polygonum aubertii*)

*Filipendula kamtschatica*

*Francoa sonchifolia* with
*Gladiolus*

*Gaillardia* × *grandiflora*
'Fanfare' with
*Salvia* 'Rugen'

*Gaillardia* × *grandiflora*
'Oranges & Lemons'

*Galega officinalis*
'Bicolor'

*Gaura lindheimeri*
'Stratosphere Pink Picotee'

*Geranium*
'Orion'

*Geranium*
'Rozanne'

*Geranium maculatum* with *Zizia aptera*

*Geranium phaeum* 'Margaret Wilson' with *Tiarella cordifolia*

*Geranium pratense* 'Plenum Violaceum'

*Gunnera manicata*

raceme with a leafy bract at the base of each flower. They open wide to reveal a hint of green within.

They may be grown in light shade and moist, but not wet soils.

**Cultivars:**
'Ivory Bells' bears green and white flowers.

**Related Species:**

*F. assyriaca*, native to Turkey, is about 12-15″ tall with many greenish white flowers. Flower color may be variable and occasionally have some maroon tinge.

*F. biflora*, mission bells, is native to the southwest United States. Plants have basal glossy green leaves with 1-6 (usually 2) nodding purple flowers tinged with green on each flower stem. 'Martha Roderick' is about 8″ tall, bearing green hanging bells with brownish burgundy blotches at the base and green and burgundy striped interiors. Hardy in zones 4-8.

*F. glauca* is a dwarf species, best used in containers or rock gardens. The foliage has a decided blue tint. 'Goldilocks' has bright yellow flowers.

*F. pallidiflora* has four to eight, 1-2″ wide pale yellow flowers on 2′ tall stems with bluish green leaves. Not as eye-catching as crown imperials but much more pleasant than *F. meleagris*. I first saw them in Rob Proctor's splendid garden in Denver and have since seen their popularity rise. They open at the same time as other fritillarias. Hardy to zone 4.

# G

***Gaillardia*** (gay-lard′ ee-a) Blanket Flower Asteraceae

Blanket flower is one of the best-known herbaceous plants, valued for its midsummer flowers in a range of hot colors, from deep yellows to rich burgundy. The reasons for its popularity are ease of culture, tolerance to drought and heat, and extremely long blooming season. Of the approximately 30 species, only two, *G. aristata* and *G. pinnatifida*, the western blanket flower, are available as perennials. A good deal of work has been done with the hybrids, expanding the range of colors and habits. Plants perform best in full sun, well-drained soil and occasional removal of spent flowers. They do poorly in wet winters, particularly if temperatures fluctuate a great deal.

***-aestivalis*** (aye-stee′ vah-lis) Firewheel 2′/2′
Summer Purple with White Southern United States Zones 7-9

I first saw this plant in Mercer Arboretum and Botanical Gardens in Humble, Texas and was taken by its many colors and its total disdain of the heat and humidity that was draining all my energy. I gathered some seed and went to work to determine if plants would tolerate a Southeastern summer and subsequent winter. They loved it, and after about four generations of seed gathering, four distinct color groups emerged.

Heat and humidity tolerance is not an issue, winter tolerance is. Plants have been trialed as far north as Wisconsin with positive results, however, they will consistently tolerate zone 7, perhaps zone 6. They will be far more tolerant if in well-drained areas; we lost ours that were in a low spot in the garden, but those in a higher area just keep getting bigger.

As excited as I am about these plants, they are difficult to propagate by cuttings, thus keeping the colors separate will be almost impossible. The use of tissue culture could overcome that dilemma, however, prices would rise dramatically if this became the main method of commercial multiplication. Presently they are difficult to find, but I am confident they will be in the market by 2010.

Propagate by division.

*Gaillardia* × *grandiflora* (61%)

**-x *grandiflora*** (grand-i-flo′ ra) Blanket Flower 2-3′/2′
Summer Red, Yellow Hybrid Zones 5-9

This hybrid is a cross between *G. aristata*, a 2-3′ tall perennial, and *G. pulchella*, a 2′ tall annual species. Although blanket flowers are often listed under *G. aristata*, that species is seldom seen in gardens today. The resulting tetraploid hybrid is vigorous and easy to grow. The 4-6″ long leaves are alternate, coarsely toothed and usually gray-green. The 3-4″ diameter solitary flower heads are yellow with various amounts of maroon at the base of the petals. The center is often burgundy and the many colors result in a somewhat garish flower of many colors.

One of the decided disadvantages of the above-mentioned cross is that with the addition of genes from the annual species, the hybrid is more short-lived than *G. aristata*. In the Gardens at UGA, plants of *G. aristata* and *G.* x *grandiflora* 'Goblin' were planted side by side. Although 'Goblin' is a better garden plant from the point of view of habit and flowering time, it disappeared after 2 years while *G. aristata* was still prospering. Longevity may not be an important selection criterion but this example points out the fact that desirable characteristics can be lost in breeding in order to gain other qualities. The lack of consistent snow cover and increasingly wide fluctuations of winter temperatures may explain the relative lack of winter hardiness seen in recent years (see 'Fanfare'). On the other hand, the genes of *G. pulchella* and other annual species have given the hybrid the distinction of having one of the longest flowering periods and most extensive environmental ranges of any perennial.

Many of the resulting cultivars may be propagated from seed, and germination is rapid under warm, humid conditions. Seedlings should be ready to place in the garden within eight to ten weeks after sowing. Flowering occurs the first year from seed. 'Baby Cole', 'Mandarin' and 'Goblin' especially result in a good deal of variation. However, cultivars like 'Goblin', 'Fanfare' and 'Oranges and Lemons' are vegetatively produced. In general, cuttings of gaillardia are poor rooters compared to, for example, asters and coreopsis. Take more than you think you would need; rooting percentage for some is less than 20%.

**Cultivars:**

'Amber Wheels' has large, fringed, yellow flowers with a red eye on 18-24″ plants. Quite outstanding.

'Arizona Sun' is similar in flower to, but a better breaking plant than 'Goblin'. Plants were All-America winners in 2005, but winter hardiness is suspect.

'Baby Cole' is an excellent dwarf (6-8″) selection with 2-3″ diameter yellow, red-banded ray flowers.

'Bijou' has red flowers with yellow tips and a red center. Plants are about 15″ tall. Zone 4-7.

'Bremen' has coppery-scarlet flowers on 2-3′ tall stems.

'Burgundy' bears rich wine-red flowers and grows 2-3′ tall.

'Chloe' has yellow flowers on 2′ tall plants.

Commotion™ series was introduced in 2007 by a terrific plantsman and breeder, John Dixon, of Skagit Gardens in Washington. They resemble 'Fanfare' in that the petals are flared and fluted and have a somewhat similar habit. Two cultivars are presently included. 'Frenzy' is a deeper burgundy and tipped with brighter yellow than the other cultivar 'Tizzy'. Both have more burgundy and less yellow that 'Fanfare'. I have not trialed them sufficiently to know if winter problems will occur; the breeders suggest zone 5.

'Dazzler' produces blooms with blunt rosy flowers and yellow centers. Similar to 'Goblin'.

'Fanfare' was greeted with just that when introduced in the early 2000s. The petals (ray flowers) bore similar colors to 'Goblin' but they were flared at the end, somewhat like a trumpet, thus the fanfare name. They flower for a long time, however their Achilles heel appears to be intolerance to winter stress. Although we go gaga over them in the summer, they seldom return for us the next spring. It likely has to do more with wetness than cold, but the problem is not uncommon wherever I go. Perhaps we can call it a great temperennial.

'Goblin' was for many years the best cultivar of gaillardia. Plants are short (9-12″) with flowers up to 4″ in diameter, each sporting red petals with yellow edges.

'Golden Goblin' bears pale yellow flowers on sturdy frames.

Lollipop series is a double-flowered, multicolored group whose extra petals and many colors result in particularly loathsome plants.

'Mandarin' comes from Blooms of Bressingham and is taller than 'Goblin' but more compact than the species.

Monarch Strain (Portula hybrids) is a seed-propagated color mix.

'Oranges and Lemons' reached the market in 2005 with a good deal of acclaim. Orange- and lemon-colored daisy flowers are borne on 18-24″ tall plants. Plants stretch a little and flowers tend to fade a little in the heat, however I have been impressed with their performance and recommend it to others. Winter tolerance has not yet been determined, but likely zone 5 or 6.

'Summer Fire' is a dwarf form with yellow flowers and red zonations.

'Tokajer' was introduced in the early 2000s and bears 3″ wide orange-red flowers on 2′ tall plants. Plants struggle a bit in the heat of summer.

**Related Species:**

*G. aristata* is a fine flowering plant but is much more variable than the hybrid. It grows to 3′, often requiring support. Unlike the hybrids, plants raised from seed will not flower the first year.

## *Galactites* (gal-ac-tee′ tees) — Asteraceae

Winter hardy only south of zone 7, the garden plant *G. tomentosa* is not a common denizen of North American gardens. However, these are eye-catching specimens and when grown well, always have people wondering where they can be obtained. The 2′ tall plants stand out in the landscape due to the gray-green spiny pinnately cut foliage with milky white veins while the underside of the spiny leaves are hairy (tomentose).

The genus name comes from the Greek *gala*, milk, alluding to the leaf veins. While the main garden value is the foliage, the small, pink daisylike flowers that occur in the summer contrast well with the rest of the plant. Plants can look like centaureas to the casual observer, but the flowers of *Centaurea* are seldom pink, and the leaves are not spiny.

Place in a sunny well-drained location, perhaps in containers that can be moved to a protected area during the winter.

## *Galanthus* (ga-lanth′ us) — Snowdrop — Amaryllidaceae

How I enjoy drifts of snowdrops. In Montreal, they were as taken for granted in the spring as dandelions in the summer. Unfortunately, where I live in north Georgia, the drifts I planted must have drifted somewhere else. Warm soil temperatures are the bane of many temperate bulbs, and this one is obviously affected. However, where they grow well, snowdrops never fail to provide pleasure in late winter and early spring, sometimes even before the snow has disappeared. These cool climate plants are known as *pierce neige* ("snow piercing") in France, and are totally intolerant of heat. They persist longer in the northern parts of the country than in the South but still can be enjoyed as far south as zone 6, where they flower in February.

A mix of various kinds of snowdrops provides flowers from January to April, gladdening hearts at the dreariest time of year. I was fortunate enough to visit Scotland in March with my good friend and well-known woody expert, Michael Dirr. Looking over drifts of snowdrops naturalized around clear streams and through woodlands rendered both of us speechless. That the impact was immense was proven by the continuous clicking of the great tree-man's camera. It makes one want to go out and purchase bulbs in the thousands or move to Scotland. Similar scenes have unfolded in the northern states, the Midwest, and in Canada. I sure wish I hadn't taken them so lightly in Montreal.

In all species, the buds are solitary and erect but the flowers nod on short wiry stems. They have 3 outer and 3 shorter inner petals held above straplike leaves. Bulbs should be planted in groups of 25 or more, bulb to bulb, otherwise they make no impact. The spring landscape comes alive when snowdrops are combined with hellebores and winter aconites.

Plants need to be established early in the fall, and should be ordered earlier than other spring-flowering bulbs. Plant about 3″ deep in well-drained soil in full sun. The combination of heavy soils and cold winter rains results in the loss of many bulbs, regardless of where you garden. Where conditions are favorable, however, multiplication is rapid. Clumps may be lifted immediately after flowering, separated carefully into sections of 3-4 bulbs and replanted as soon as possible.

Snowdrops are sometimes confused with snowflakes, *Leucojum*, another spring-flowering relative, mainly because of the names. The flower segments of snowflakes are all equal in size, plants are significantly taller, and they bear 2-3 flowers on each stem.

Quick Reference to Galanthus Species

| | Height | Leaf width |
|---|---|---|
| *G. elwesii* | 8-10 | >1″ |
| *G. nivalis* | 4-8 | ½″ |

***-elwesii*** (el-wez′ ee-eye) Giant Snowdrop 9-12″/6″
Spring White Asia Minor Zones 4-7

The outer segments of the flowers are usually about an inch long, but can be up to 2″ long, and 1¼″ wide. The inner segments have green blotches at the base (point of attachment) and the tip. The two gray-green straplike leaves are about 1¼″ wide, 4″ long and deeply channeled. Everything about this plant is larger than the more common *G. nivalis*. Plants flower about one week later than *G. nivalis*.

**Cultivars:**

'Giant Form' is just that, although "giant" is perhaps being a little opportune.
var. *globosus* has broad outer segments resulting in flowers up to 1″ wide.

***-nivalis*** (ni-vaal′ is) Common Snowdrops 6-9″/12″
Early Spring White Northern Europe Zones 3-7

One of the earliest species to flower, plants may open as early as January in its southern range and push through the snow by March at the northern end. The foliage consists of 2 narrow (usually no wider than a half inch) straplike leaves above which the 1″ long and half-inch wide flowers are borne. They are pure white except for a green crescent at the apex of the inner segments. Bulbs multiply rapidly but must be planted in large numbers to fulfill their potential. This species naturalizes better than others and can create large drifts in moist, cool climates.

**Cultivars:**

'Angustifolius' is a dwarf form with single white flowers and narrow leaves.

'Atkinsii' is a vigorous form, growing 9″ tall and bearing many 1″ wide flowers.

'Cilicicus', Cilician snowdrop, is likely a sub-species (subsp. *cilicicus*). Flowers earlier than *G. nivalis* and the leaves are narrower, particularly at the base.

'Flore Pleno' has 1″ wide double flowers, although the "doubleness" is noticeable only when the flowers are turned up. They are interesting and quite ornamental.

'Ophelia' bears large double flowers filled with green-tipped segments.

'Lutescens' has inner segments marked with yellow rather than green.

'Sam Arnott' is vigorous, nicely scented and has large flowers.

'Viridi-apice' differs by having a green patch on both the inner and outer petals.

'White Dream' has a white stripe on the leaves and good clean white flowers.

**Related Species:**

*G. ikariae*, Nicarian snowdrop, is similar but has flared outer segments and broad, recurved, shiny green, rather than gray-green, leaves. The green leaves contrast beautifully with the white flowers. The inner segments are green only at the apices. I think this is the most handsome of all the species. What is Nicaria, you ask? Nicaria is a derivation of Ikaria, one of the wonderful Greek islands of the Eastern Aegean Sea and the home of the mythical Ikaros. Who is Ikaros, you ask? Ikaros is a variation of Icarus, who flew to close to the sun and ... enough, read about him and have fun with his snowdrops.

*G. reginae-olgae*, native to Greece, differs from *G. nivalis* by having dark green leaves with a gray stripe along the center. It differs from all other species by flowering in the fall, before the leaves appear, rather than in the winter or early spring.

## ***Galax*** (gay′ lax) Wandflower, Beetleweed Diapensiaceae

Only one species of this American plant occurs, *G. urceolata* (formerly *G. aphylla*), native to the eastern mountains of Virginia through North Carolina and extending into Georgia. The circular leathery leaves persist for weeks after being cut from the plant and are highly sought after for flower arrangements. Tremendous numbers of leaves are harvested from native populations and exported to Europe and Asia. The evergreen foliage is tufted at the base and dull green throughout the summer. In the early spring and late fall and winter, the leaves turn bronze, even red, especially in the sun. The tiny white flowers are held in a spikelike raceme on a long leafless scape in spring.

A wonderful place to visit is the Southern Highland Reserve in Sapphire, North Carolina, the far-sighted venture of Robert Balantine of Atlanta. There are treasures everywhere, but the galax in spring envelops the eyes with its beauty and the nose with its delicious perfume. The Reserve is a fabulous place to see North American

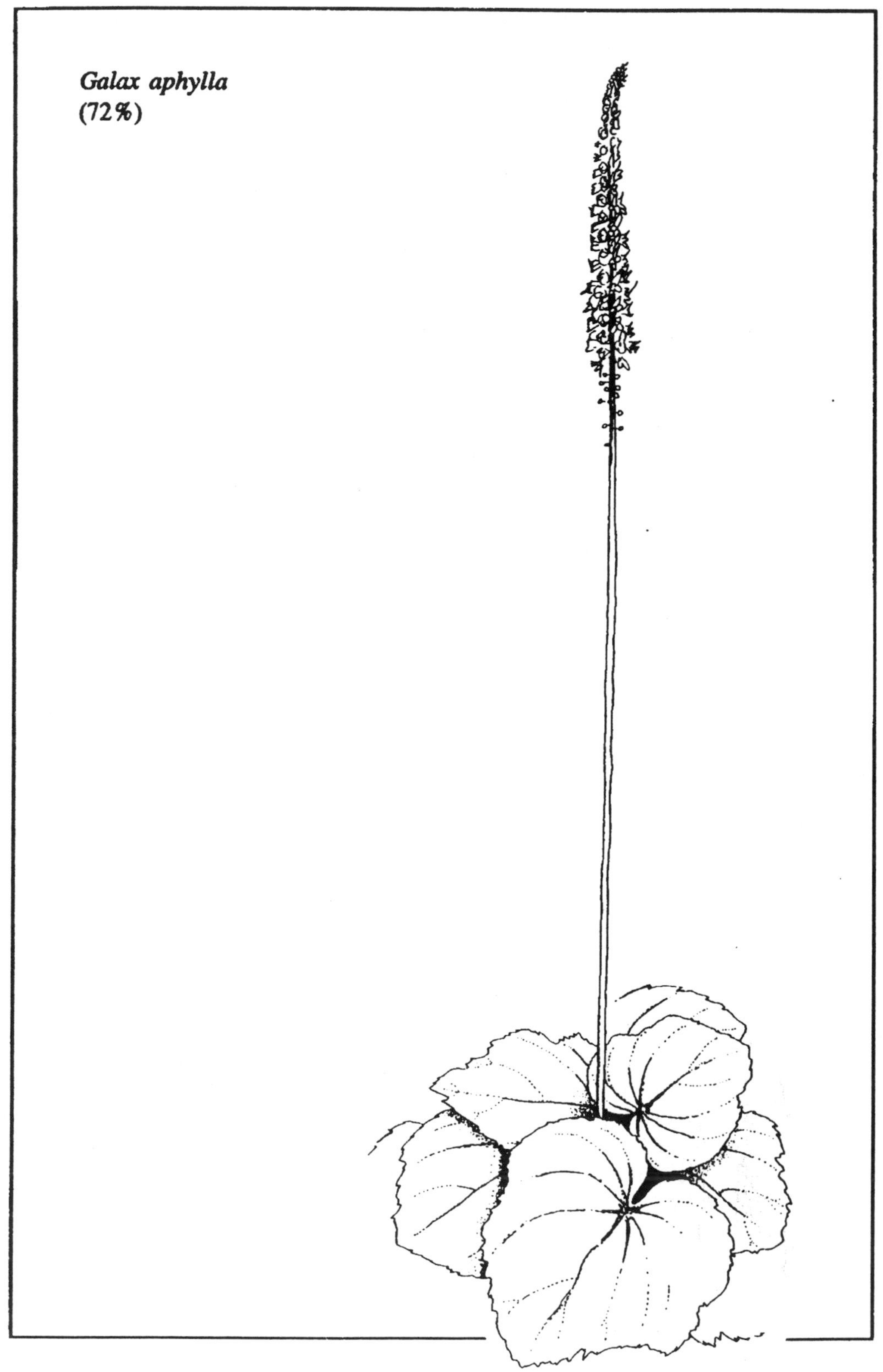
*Galax aphylla*
(72%)

native species in their natural habitat, and the vision of people like Balantine bodes well for the future of American horticulture.

Plants are wonderful in woodland and shady gardens, mainly for their foliage, however, the flowers are also handsome. When not in flower, plants are 6-9″ tall but extend to 18″ in bloom. Hardy from zones 5-8. They may be propagated by careful division or from seed.

## ***Galega*** (gal-ee′ ga) Goat's Rue Fabaceae

Of the 6-8 species, only *G. officinalis* and *G. orientalis* are of particular garden value. Plants were once grown for forage and were prized for feeding to goats to increase milk flow. This was so common that the genus was named after the Greek word *gala*, meaning milk. The pea-like flowers are sometimes confused with those of *Baptisia*. Plants are useful for the back of the garden and bear odd-pinnate foliage and purplish blue or white flowers.

Common goat's rue (*G. officinalis*) is a federally listed noxious weed but has a limited distribution nationwide. However, the species also appears on the noxious weed list of 12 states and it is illegal to sell, propagate or transport the species in these states. One site in Utah reports 38,000 acres (60 square miles) of infested cropland, irrigation waterways, pastures, fence lines, roadways and wet, marshy areas. Eradication efforts in Utah have been costly and time-consuming. Goat's rue is capable of forming a monoculture in wetland communities, displacing native or beneficial plants. Wetland wildlife vacate these areas once their food source or nesting material is gone. So those of you in the other 38 states, think wisely.

Regardless, plants are still grown for their ornamental value, and many cultivars are thought to be hybrids (see *G. officinalis*), thus reducing the risk to native populations.

Quick Reference to Galega Species

| | Height (in.) | Number of leaflets | Flower color |
|---|---|---|---|
| *G. officinalis* | 3-4 | 4-8 pairs | White, lavender |
| *G. orientalis* | 3-4 | 6-12 pairs | Blue-violet |

**-*officinalis*** (o-fi-chi-nah′ lis) Common Goat's Rue 3-4′/3′
Late Spring Blue, White Southern Europe, Asia Minor Zones 3-7

The 1-2′ long pinnately compound leaves consist of 9 to 16 entire leaflets held on short petiolules (stalk of leaflet). At each leaf node is a lancelike stipule, less than 1″ long. The 1-1½″ long flowers can be pale blue, lilac, blue-pink to white, and are held in long, many-flowered racemes pointing upward like colored candles. There is much confusion as to whether *G. officinalis* and the hybrid *G.* x *hartlandii* (considered by some to be a hybrid between *G. officinalis* and *G. bicolor*) are the same. The discussion is important because of noxious weed debate, mentioned above. They certainly look the same to me. Therefore, you may see *G. officinalis* 'Hartlandii' or the hybrid listed separately. Similarly, cultivars may be listed either way as well.

*Galega officinalis*
(56%)

The species is tolerant of poor soils and if over-fertilized, grows tall and lanky and requires support. Plant in full sun in any well-drained soil. Cut back after the flowers are finished. Not only are the flowers not particularly attractive after flowering, a problem common to many members of the pea family, but reseeding will also be minimized.

*Galega* is tolerant of cool conditions but does not adapt well to the heat and humidity in much of the country, and is seldom used in the eastern half of the country. A number of cultivars are sterile and should be chosen whenever possible.

Propagate by division every 3-5 years. If seed forms, you have a non-sterile cultivar or species. Look about, if seedlings are a problem, you may want to compost the plants to be on the safe side.

**Cultivars:**

'Alba' is an excellent form which bears showy white flowers.

'His Majesty' is synonymous with 'Her Majesty'. Plants have clear white and mauve-pink to lavender flowers. Plants are sterile and the flowers are nicely scented.

'Lady Wilson' bears lilac-blue flowers.

***-orientalis*** (o-ree-en-tah′ lis) Oriental Goat's Rue 3-4′/3′
Late Spring Violet-blue Caucasus Zones 3-7

Similar to the previous species except having larger, more numerous leaflets which are slightly more tapered at the ends and with wider stipules. The violet-blue to lavender flowers are held well above the foliage, resulting in handsome, if somewhat aggressive plants for the garden. This species does not appear on any noxious weed lists.

Propagate as with *G. officinalis*.

***Galium*** (gay-lee′ um) Sweet Woodruff, Bedstraw Rubiaceae

The genus name comes from *gala*, meaning milk, because of the former use of *G. verum*, yellow bedstraw, in curdling milk for cheese manufacture. Most of the 400 species are weeds and have little place in the garden. Smooth bedstraw (*G. mollugo*) is a common weed in many parts of the country. The only garden plant that is easily available is *Galium odoratum*, sweet woodruff, a useful and popular ground cover.

***-odoratum*** (o-dor-ah′ tum) Sweet Woodruff 4-9″/12″
Spring White Europe Zones 4-7
(syn. *Asperula odorata*)

The half-inch long, half-inch wide, sessile leaves are borne in whorls of 6-8 at each node along the length of the square stems. The roots are slender and creeping, making the plants particularly effective ground covers. The fragrant white flowers are only 1/8-1/4″ long and held in loosely branched cymes. When in flower in the spring, plants look like newly fallen snow.

The entire plant smells like new-mown hay when crushed or dried, thus one of its common names, bedstraw. It is also known as ladies' bedstraw, because it was thought to be part of the plants in the hay on which the mother of Christ rested. The leaves are an ingredient for potpourri and sachets and are used traditionally as a moth deterrent. Plants have also been used to flavor everything from wine and brandy to sorbets and fruit salads.

In the garden, plants tolerate partial shade in the North and require it in the South. To grow rapidly and cover large areas, a consistent water supply is necessary. It is particularly pretty in the dappled shade of trees like locust (*Gleditsia*) or beneath high canopy trees.

However, for some gardeners, bedstraw is a little too rambunctious, covering significant acreage far too quickly, and is much more useful in the compost pile than in the garden. Propagate by division in the spring or fall.

***Galtonia*** (gawl-tone′ ee-a) Summer Hyacinth Liliaceae

A group of three species of bulbous plants, native to South Africa, closely related to the garden hyacinth. They are all ornamental, however, *G. candicans* is the only one sufficiently winter hardy to be used in large areas of the country.

***-candicans*** (kan′ di-kanz) Summer Hyacinth 2-4′/3′
Summer White South Africa Zones 6-9

The strap-shaped leaves are 2-3′ long, 2″ wide and have conspicuous midribs. A leafless scape arises from the basal leaves carrying a loose raceme of 20-30 dangling, bell-shaped flowers on 1-2½″ long pedicels. The 1½″ long flowers are slightly scented and clear white.

Plants should be grown in full sun and watered and fertilized copiously. If planted in a proper site, staking is not necessary. However, if grown in excessive shade or in lean soil, scapes will not be strong enough to support the heavy flowers. Plant bulbs in early spring about 6″ deep in groups of a dozen or more for the best show. Cut back foliage after flowering as plants tend to look weedy as leaves decline. Bulbs need to be lifted, similar to gladiolus, north of zone 6, although bulbs in zone 5 may overwinter if well protected.

Propagate by lifting bulbs in spring and removing small offsets, which flower after two years. If seed is purchased, sow the small seeds in well-drained soil under warm (70-75°F), humid conditions. Approximately 3 years is necessary for flowering plants from seed.

**Related Species:**

*G. princeps* has broad gray-green foliage and bears greenish white flowers 1-2 weeks earlier than *G. candicans*. Hardy only in zones 8 to 10.

*G. viridiflora* bears many (15-20) pale green flowers on 2′ tall plants. They were handsome in the trials at Georgia but did not overwinter.

***Gaura*** (gaw′ ra) Gaura Onagraceae

In the last edition, I commented that the genus was a relative newcomer to the American garden scene. No more; *Gaura* has become a garden staple and the number of cultivars has exploded. In our trial gardens, we have evaluated at least two dozen, many quite similar to the one before. Although there are about 20 species of annuals, perennials and biennials only one, *G. lindheimeri*, is used as breeding stock. Plants have proven well-suited to many areas and highly useful for the warmer regions of the country.

***-lindheimeri*** (lind-hay′ mer-eye) White Gaura, Whirling Butterflies 3-4′/3′
Summer White Louisiana, Texas Zones 5-8

The species itself is seldom seen but many cultivars have been developed and are used extensively throughout the country. Plants have been a boon to Southern gardens as they tolerate heat and humidity well, although some problems with legginess and lack of flowering are still obvious.

In areas of consistently cool summer nights, flowering occurs throughout the season on reddish stems. The 1-3″ long, lanceolate leaves are alternate and sessile. The flowers are carried on a loose, open panicle well above the foliage. The 1″ long white flowers are rose tinged and open up the spike much like a gladiolus, although they don't open all at once. As they age, the white gives way to pale rose. Although not the most showy plant in the landscape, gaura is one of the most tolerant of poor soils and difficult conditions. They perform best in full sun, but well-drained soils are necessary. Plants are adaptable to many conditions as stated by Texas gardener Elizabeth Crenota Clark who wrote that gaura "is tough as a boot, delicate as a butterfly". Yet it was also highly valued by Mr. Jack Hobbs of the Auckland Botanic Gardens in New Zealand. Two more diverse climates you will not see.

Plants will flower like fireworks, and dazzle the eyes, however, once flowered, the blooms can look ragged and ugly after a few weeks. Be tough, cut back the flower stems, one and all, when they detract instead of awe. If you do so, additional flowers will form and plants may bloom from late spring to fall.

Plants grow three feet tall and this has become a problem. Breeders have concentrated on providing pink and red flowers, but the most important breakthroughs have been better compactness in newer cultivars. They still flop but it may take a couple of years before they do so.

Seed germinates within 14-21 days when sown in a warm, humid area. Cuttings may be used and plants may be carefully divided when sufficiently large.

**Cultivars:**

So many cultivars, so similar in appearance. Boy, it is tough to tell them all apart without a label. Hardiness is zone 5 or 6 to zone 8.

Ballerina series was bred to be compact and even in the heat of the Georgia gardens did not flop. The best performer was 'Ballerina Blush' but 'Ballerina Rose,' with her darker flowers, was also excellent.

Butterfly series was also bred to be shorter and more compact than others. I was impressed with 'Crimson Butterfly', although the red color in the leaves and stems faded rapidly in the heat. 'Bijou Butterfly' has red and green variegated foliage and rosy red flowers but can get terribly long and lanky. 'Sunny Butterfly' bears white flowers and is certainly more compact than the species but still gets a little lanky. White-flowered gauras all are genetically large, compared to the darker forms.

'Cherry Brandy' has some of the most handsome light pink flowers in the spring.

'Corrie's Gold' is a variegated form with creamy and gold markings on the foliage. The flowers are similar to the species. The plant arose as a chance seedling in the garden of Beth Chatto near Colchester, England and was named for the daughter of one of her employees.

'Dauphin' is the most vigorous, upright cultivar, bar none. I have seen 4′ tall plants at the Royal Botanical Gardens in Ontario, and 5′ tall plants in Annapolis, Maryland. It is an extraordinary flowerer as well but can reseed and become quite a pest. It is a parent of some of the more upright forms like 'Pink Cloud' however, most of the new ones are far more compact. This is better for producers but not necessarily for gardeners.

Fountain series is excellent, the best being 'Pink Fountain', which earned a 5 out of 5 in our trials. 'Snow Fountain' is significantly taller, but blooms well.

Geyser series is all over the place. For excellent vigor and good flowering, 'Geyser White' is tough to beat, but it is tall and gets leggy. 'Geyser Pink' is better behaved but not an outstanding color.

Karalee series is quite variable. All members make an unforgettable display. 'Karalee White' was short the first year but big and bodacious the next. 'Karalee Petite Pink' was also compact the first year and remained so in subsequent years. The best of the bunch with good color and great habit.

'Passionate Rainbow' has deep pink flowers which fade to light pink. Foliage is bronze edged in white.

'Perky Pink' is an exceptionally good pink cultivar only about 20″ tall. This is an excellent plant for containers.

'Pink Cloud' has one of the longest flowering times of any gaura we looked at. Plants grow 2-3′ tall but can be cut back without trouble.

'Siskiyou Pink' was the first breakthrough in gauras. Gauras were relatively unknown until 'Siskiyou Pink' was introduced by Baldassare Mineo of Siskiyou Rare Plant Nursery in Medford, Oregon in 1995. Mr. Mineo and his cultivar can claim responsibility for mainstreaming the genus to perennial growers around the world. The flowers are a deep pink and when first introduced, were a welcome departure from the normal white flowers. Now it seems all new cultivars are pink or rose, thanks to this cultivar.

Stratosphere series was introduced by Proven Winners in 2005, and plants can get big. At River Farm, headquarters of the American Horticulture Society in Alexandria, Virginia, 'Stratosphere White' and 'Stratosphere Pink' were 3′ tall and absolutely full of flowers in late May.

## ***Gentiana*** (gen-tee′ ah-na) Gentian Gentianaceae

Gentians are some of the most handsome, highly sought-after plants for the cool season garden. Every gardener I have ever met lusts after gentians, however, only a few of the more than 300 species are successfully employed in gardens east of the Rocky Mountains and south of zone 4. They are widespread across cool temperate and alpine zones of the world and most thrive in regions with cool summers. Gentians are found in a wide range of habitats and soil types and display a corresponding diversity of habit, size and cultural requirements. Because of the diversity, it is difficult to generalize about gentian culture. Some gardeners find them as easy as dandelions, others build monuments when one plant lives. However, the great majority of gentians are alpines, needing full light, lots of water, excellent drainage and cool nights. Colors range from common deep blues, to which the genus has given its name, to yellows (*G. lutea*), whites (*G. alba*) and scarlet and gold (*G. scarlatina*). While numerous species are native to North America (including the wonderful fringed gentian, *G. crinita* or more properly, *Gentianopsis crinita*), they are not the easiest plants to propagate and therefore not always easily available.

Some mail order nurseries offer an extensive collection of gentians, and since plants can't read, it may be worth planting a few types in the fall or early spring. For Midwestern and Eastern gardeners with marginal "gentian conditions", probably *G. acaulis*, *G. andrewsii* and *G. puberulenta* are good places to start. Southern gardeners should not spend too much of their childrens' inheritance on gentians, however, *G. saponaria*, *G. septemfida* and *G. asclepiadea* may be somewhat useful. Tall gentians are suitable for borders and landscape planting and include *G. lutea*, *G. andrewsii*, *G. asclepiadea*, *G. saponaria* and *G. septemfida*. Low-growing forms generally have sessile flowers and are suitable for rock gardens and include *G. acaulis* and *G. dahurica*. Most gentians flower in late summer and fall. There are also numerous cultivars, however not many are available from North American nurseries compared to those in the United Kingdom or Europe.

| | Flower color | Height (in.) | Flowering time |
|---|---|---|---|
| *G. acaulis* | Azure blue | 4-6 | Spring |
| *G. andrewsii* | Dark blue | 16-30 | Early fall |
| *G. asclepiadea* | Blue-purple | 20-30 | Late summer |
| *G. cruciata* | Blue | 8-12 | Summer |
| *G. dahurica* | Deep blue | 6-12 | Summer |
| *G. lutea* | Yellow | 48-72 | Summer |
| *G. makinoi* | Pale blue | 18-24 | Late summer |

**-*acaulis*** (a-kaw′ lis) Stemless Gentian 4-6″/8″
Spring Azure Blue South, Central Europe Zones 3-7

The stemless gentian is one of the more common gentians in European gardens; plants produce a dark green rosette of many 1″ long lancelike leaves. The term *acaulis* means "without stem" and the flowers appear to emerge from the rosette itself. The lack of a stem results in short plants with relatively large (2″) solitary, terminal flowers. The azure to dark blue flowers consist of a long tube ending with five lobes, sometimes flared back (recurved). The flower tube is usually spotted green within. This handsome species requires exceptional drainage, cool nights and lime-free soils. Avoid constant sun; four to five hours a day is sufficient.

Propagate by placing seed on light porous sandy mix and place under 55-65°F and high moisture. Seeds should not be covered as they require light to germinate. Best success occurs with newly ripened seed; if they are old, they descend into a deep dormancy which results in slow and erratic germination. Many seeds are set but they lose vitality quickly. If seed must be stored, store in an airtight container, with a desiccant, in the refrigerator.

**Cultivars:**

'Alba' is a white-flowered form.

'Belvedere' is more vigorous, forming larger clumps in less time. Flowers are deep blue.

'Rannock' is even shorter than the species, growing only about 2″ tall. The deep blue flowers are striped green and white within.
'Trotter's Variety' flowers in the spring and fall.

***-andrewsii*** (an-drooz-ee′ eye) Bottle Gentian 16-30″/2′
Fall Deep Blue North America Zones 3-7

One of our prettiest but lesser-known natives, bottle gentian occurs as far north as Quebec, west to Saskatchewan, into Nebraska, south to Arkansas and the mountains of Georgia. The opposite leaves occur all the way up the one-and-a-half-foot-tall plant. The deep blue terminal flowers are sessile and occur in groups of two to five. This is one of the last plants in the garden to bloom. This species is one of the easiest to recognize, at least in flower, because the flowers never really open. Their frustrating habit of expanding but never opening have lent them the common names of bottle gentian and closed gentian. *G. clausa*, closed gentian, native to the Appalachian Mountains, is similarly mute.

Not quite as finicky as some of the alpine forms, nevertheless, good drainage and cool nights are necessary for success.

Propagate by seed similar to *G. acaulis* or by 1-2″ long cuttings.

**Cultivars:**
'Albiflora' has white flowers.
'Creamy' has creamy white flowers.

***-asclepiadea*** (a-sklay-pee-ah′ dee-a) Willow Gentian 20-30″/18″
Late Summer Blue-Purple Europe Zones 3-7

The plants bear arching stems with 2-3″ long bright green, willow-like 3-5 veined leaves. The blue-purple, narrow, sessile flowers occur in axillary clusters of two to three flowers. The flowers are variable but most are purple-spotted within the tube and are often striped white at the throat.

**Cultivars:**
'Alba' has white flowers.
'Knightshayes' is smaller and bears bluer flowers (less purple) with white throats.
'Phyllis' is a vigorous selection with pale blue flowers.

***-cruciata*** (cruc-ee-ah′ ta) 8-12″/12″
Summer Blue Eastern Europe Zones 3-7

One catalog states, "If you kill every gentian you touch, this one is safe even with you." This may help in raising confidence in growing gentians, but it is not one of the showier forms. In late summer, the small (less than a half inch) dark blue flowers are formed in terminal and axillary clusters in the nodes of the 3-4″ long and 1-2″ wide stem leaves. Those with anti-gentian tendencies should give it a go.

Plants are tolerant of some shade and are more tolerant of drought than many other species. A good gentian to start with.

***-dahurica*** (da-her-i′ ca) 6-12″/12″
Summer Deep Blue China Zones 4-7

Flowering in mid to late summer, the intense blue flowers are showy but not exceptional. They are held at the end of the 12″ stems as well as in the leaf nodes. The long narrow leaves are both basal and held on the stem. The flowers are only about 1″ long and are often slightly spotted with white.

This has also proved to be one of the easier gentians to grow, although cool nights and well-drained soils are still recommended.

***-lutea*** (loo′ tee-a) Yellow Gentian 4-6′/2′
Summer Yellow Europe Zones 3-6

At first glance, this robust perennial looks nothing like a gentian, especially when not in flower. The broad basal leaves are 10-12″ long and strongly ribbed. The vigorous stems rise 4-6′ in height and carry paired, narrow sessile leaves. The nodes of the upper five to seven stem leaves carry 3-10 bright yellow flowers that can be seen from miles away. A most unusual plant, but the one for which the genus was named.

·Yellow gentian is native to the Alps and Pyrenees at elevations of 3000 to 6000 feet and is most at home in areas where nights and days are cool. Plants must be at least two years old before they will flower. This is a problem in most American gardens because plants are not as vigorous in our diverse climates as they are in their native habitats or in mild gardens found in the British Isles, and may not persist long enough to reach their flowering potential. However, some handsome specimens may be seen on the West Coast as well as in the Denver Botanic Garden.

The bitter yellow-brown root of this plant has been used as a medicine and may still be purchased as gentian bitters, an extraordinary effective tonic for soothing stomach ailments as the bitter taste stimulates digestive enzymes and secretions.

Propagate by seed in the fall and plant out in spring.

***-makinoi*** (mack-in′ oy) 18-24″/18″
Late summer Light Blue Japan Zones 3-7

Plants are erect, tall and useful for cut flowers. The pale blue spotted flowers are clustered at the top of the plant and in the last few nodes and never completely open. The 2-3″ long, lanceolate leaves are paired and have 3-5 veins.

Propagate by seed.

**Cultivars:**

'Marsha' is about a foot tall, bearing purple-blue flowers in late summer to fall.
'Royal Blue' has deeper blue flowers than the species.

**Related Species:**

*G. flavida*, cream gentian, is a Midwest native, bears handsome creamy white flowers and is similar to bottle gentian, *G. andrewsii*, in its refusal to fully open. Requiring little moisture and tolerant of limey soils, this little-known plant is much more available now than in the past. Quite handsome.

*G.* x *macaulayi*, Macaulay's gentian, is a hybrid between *G. sino-ornata* and *G. farreri*. The hybrid is best known for the cultivar 'Kingfisher', which bears large, upright-facing blue flowers over narrow foliage in the fall. Hardy to zone 5.

*G. saponaria*, soapwort gentian, is also similar to bottle gentian in that the flowers never open. The leaves are arranged in pairs or fours. Native from New York to Florida, Minnesota to Texas. Flowers occur in the fall, bringing the rather nondescript plants into the limelight. Hardy in zones 5-8, one of the easiest with which to succeed.

*G. septemfida* is somewhat prostrate and grows 6-12″ tall, and has been called "everyman's gentian", for its relative ease of growing. The leafy stems bear clustered, light blue, bell-shaped flowers in summer. There are many color variants within the species; the best and the brightest may be var. *lagodechiana* with deeper blue flowers on more or less prostrate stems.

*G. sino-ornata* is also a prostrate gentian, only about 4″ tall, with basal leaves forming loose rosettes. The stems root at the nodes. Plants bear large (2″ long) tubular, azure blue tubular flowers with bands of deep purple-blue in the fall. Numerous handsome cultivars have been developed.

*G. triflora* has deep blue to purple-blue flowers banded white on the outside. The flowers occur near the top of the upright 1-2′ tall stems in late summer and fall. They never open very wide, even in full sun.

## ***Geranium*** (jer-aye′ knee-um) Cranesbill Geraniaceae

This wonderfully diverse genus, consisting of well over 250 species, is known as cranesbill because of the beak-like fruit. Plants are often referred to as hardy geraniums to separate them from the annual geraniums, *Pelargonium*. Hardy geraniums were woefully underused in American gardens but in the last 20 years, they have been discovered and are thriving in this country. As additional species become available in North America, the good, the bad, and the ugly are being separated. Alas, we cannot expect equal performance from all species on this continent as in Europe, but many are well worth including in the garden. In this renaissance, the garden attributes of our native spotted geranium, *G. maculatum*, have been discovered and plants have outperformed many of their more sophisticated relatives. A niche may be found in every garden for at least one species of geranium as their diversity is extraordinary. A few species such as *G. renardii* appear to have narrow growing ranges, but most are far more adaptable.

Plants typically grow from basal rosettes of palmately lobed or dissected leaves. The flowering stems bear alternate or opposite stem leaves. The flowers have 5 equal and usually overlapping petals and 10 stamens. When teaching my students how to distinguish *Geranium* from other genera, I suggest looking for palmate leaves, five-petalled flowers and cranesbill fruit. If all three characteristics are present, it is a geranium. The seeds are often explosively expelled from the fruit and the method of seed expulsion helps distinguish between similar species. However, to be honest, the more species and cultivars I learn, the fewer I seem to know. If you have a problem telling geraniums apart, you are not alone.

In general, most geraniums prefer moist soils and full sun to partial shade although one or two may be tolerant of shade. In the southern limits of their range, late afternoon shade should be provided. Propagation is by division in spring or fall, terminal cuttings in the spring or after flowering, or by seed.

Hardiness (cold and heat tolerance) is always an issue with all genera grown in North America, and as expected from so diverse a genus, great variation in adaptability occurs. Those native to Europe (e.g. *G. pratense*) often withstand cold better than heat, those native to Madeira such as the giant and incredibly beautiful *G. palmatum* and *G. maderense* are best grown in areas with a Mediterranean climate or in the greenhouse. Species native to New Zealand such as *G. traversii* are difficult to establish almost anywhere. While the last few statements are somewhat depressing, that still leaves another 240 or so species to experiment with.

Many geraniums can be divided every 2-4 years, however, some species have deep taproots making division difficult. Most of these may be raised by root cuttings (see *Anemone* for details), cuttings or seed. Seed generally requires a ripening period before germination. If seed is collected from garden plants, store it for 2-4 weeks at room temperature prior to sowing in a warm (70-75°F), humid area. Some seed may require a cold treatment of 3-5 weeks, but this is not usually necessary.

Quick Reference to Geranium Species

| | Height (in.) | Flower color |
|---|---|---|
| *G.* x *cantabrigiense* | 6-8 | Rose, pink |
| *G. cinereum* | 6-12 | Red, pink |
| *G. clarkei* | 15-20 | Purplish violet |
| *G. dalmaticum* | 4-8 | Pink |
| *G. endressii* | 15-18 | Pink |
| *G. himalayense* | 10-15 | Lilac, purple veins |
| *G. macrorrhizum* | 15-18 | Magenta |
| *G. maculatum* | 12-24 | Pink |
| *G.* x *magnificum* | 18-24 | Blue |
| *G. phaeum* | 18-24 | Dark purple |
| *G. platypetalum* | 18-24 | Purple |
| *G. pratense* | 30-36 | Purple |
| *G. procurrens* | 6-9 | Magenta, black center |
| *G. psilostemon* | 24-48 | Magenta, black center |
| *G. sanguineum* | 9-12 | Magenta |
| *G. sylvaticum* | 30-36 | Violet blue |

**-*x cantabrigiense*** (can-tab-rig-ee′ en-se) Cambridge Geranium 6-8″/8″
Spring, Summer Rose, Pink Hybrid Zones 5-7

In 1974, Dr. Helen Kiefer of Cambridge University made a number of reciprocal crosses between *G. macrorrhizum* and *G. dalmaticum*. With *G. macrorrhizum* as the female parent, she successfully raised a seedling that was planted in the University gardens. The color of the petals was purple-violet and the light green leaves grew into a weed-proof carpet. The flowers persist for a long time because little seed is produced. Plants have the inflated calyx associated with *G. macrorrhizum*, but not nearly as obvious. The species name was coined by geranium expert Dr. Peter Yeo in 1985 and commemorates the city of Cambridge, England. A number of excellent cultivars have arisen from this cross.

**Cultivars:**

'Biokovo' is best known, bearing white flowers tinged with pink on 6-8″ tall plants. The somewhat inflated calyces (sepals) are redder than the petals making a handsome contrast, and flowers are much easier on the eyes than the above hybrid. Plants were found in the Biokovo Mountains of the Dalmatica region of present-day Croatia.

'Biokovo Karmina' ('Karmina') has deeper, almost raspberry, red flowers. The more I see this, the more I like it.

'Cambridge' is offered by a number of nurseries and bears purple-violet flowers. It is likely the original Cambridge clone from the initial cross.

'Westray' has deeply lobed leaves and lavender pink flowers on 12″ tall plants. It was created by the British breeder, Alan Bremner, who named it after the Orkney Island of Westray.

***-cinereum*** (si-ner′ ee-um) Grayleaf Cranebill 6-12″/12″
Spring Red, Pink Pyrenees Zones 5-7

The cultivars of this species are some of the most colorful in the genus. The leaves consist of 5-7 wedge-shaped lobes divided almost to the base. Each division is 3-lobed for about one-third the length. The pale purplish pink flowers have dark veins and are 1″ wide. The plant is essentially stemless and its small stature dictates its placement at the front of the garden or in a well-drained rock garden. One of the most demanding as to siting, plants do poorly north of zone 5 or south of zone 7, although I have seen plants thriving in zone 8 Portland gardens. This is unfortunate as there are some stunning forms available. The cultivar 'Ballerina' did wonderfully well in the Gardens at UGA (zone 7b) in the spring, but struggled for life during the summer. When placed in partial shade and well-drained soil, it can be a knockout.

Much variation within the species occurs and confusion exists in the classification. Two major varieties have been named, although differences require a taxonomist's eye. var. *cinereum* differs from var. *subcaulescens* in that the latter has darker leaves, magenta petals, and blackish stamens and stigmas. Natural hybridization occurs readily, thus making separation even more difficult. From the garden and gardener standpoint, the parentage or history of the garden forms is unimportant if the plants perform well.

Propagate by divisions, stem cuttings or by seed.

**Cultivars:**

An impressive number of cultivars has been produced in the last few years. They are all quite beautiful, but none does well south of zone 6 in the East. This does not mean they are not worth a try elsewhere, especially in well-drained sunny areas.

'Album' (of var. *cinereum*) has completely white flowers.

'Alice' has silver-green foliage and 1½″ wide lilac-pink flowers on 4-6″ tall plants.

'Ballerina' (*G. cinereum* var. *cinereum* x var. *subcaulescens*), raised by Blooms of Bressingham in England, has received numerous awards. Plants stand only 4-6″ tall and bear 2″ diameter lilac-pink flowers with a dark center and purple veining on the petals. Flowers are largely sterile which accounts for the long blooming time.

'Giuseppii' belongs to var. *subcaulescens*. It has deep magenta flowers with a dark spot in the center.

'Laurence Flatman' is similar to 'Ballerina' but more vigorous and with a deeper venation on the flowers. This was also raised by Alan Bloom and named for a valued employee of the firm.

'Memories' has burgundy flowers with a purple eye.

Purple Pillow™ bears deeply lobed gray-green foliage and plum-colored round flowers, each with darker veins on the petals.

'Sateene' is similar to many other forms of the species, bearing pink-purple flowers with a dark eye on 6″ tall plants.

'Splendens' (of var. *subcaulescens*) is 5-6″ tall and covered with vibrant deep red flowers with dark centers. It appears to be one of the least vigorous of the species.

| | | | |
|---|---|---|---|
| ***-clarkei*** (clar-key′ eye) | | Clarke's Geranium | 15-20″/18″ |
| Spring | Violet, White | Nepal | Zones 5-7 |

The 4-6″ wide basal leaves are deeply divided into seven divisions, each division deeply pinnately lobed. The ½-¾″ diameter flowers are upward facing (as are the seed capsules) and purplish violet or white with dark veins. Plants are completely covered with flowers in late spring and summer and are among the prettiest geraniums I have seen.

The species was separated in 1985 from *G. pratense* (which see) by Dr. Peter Yeo of Cambridge University. Plants are lower growing, leaves are much more deeply cut, more basal leaves are formed, and a more open inflorescence is produced than plants of *G. pratense*.

Propagate by division in spring or fall.

**Cultivars:**

'Kashmir Blue' bears deep blue flowers and comes relatively true from seed.

'Kashmir White' (syn. *G. rectum* 'Album') has clear white, 2″ wide flowers with pale lilac-pink veins. Can be totally covered in white when happily sited. When raised from seed, some plants will be purple flowered.

| | | | |
|---|---|---|---|
| ***-dalmaticum*** (dal-mat′ i-cum) | | Dalmatian Cranesbill | 4-8″/6″ |
| Late Spring | Pink | Balkan Peninsula | Zones 4-7 |

This low grower has trailing stems and spreads rapidly by rhizomes without being invasive. The smooth foliage is up to 2″ wide and deeply divided. Each of the 5-7 divisions is 3-lobed for about ¼ its length. The light pink, 1″ diameter flowers have entire petals (i.e. not notched) and are usually borne 3 to a flower stem. The foliage has red to orange fall color and persists well into the winter. I do not see this plant in many

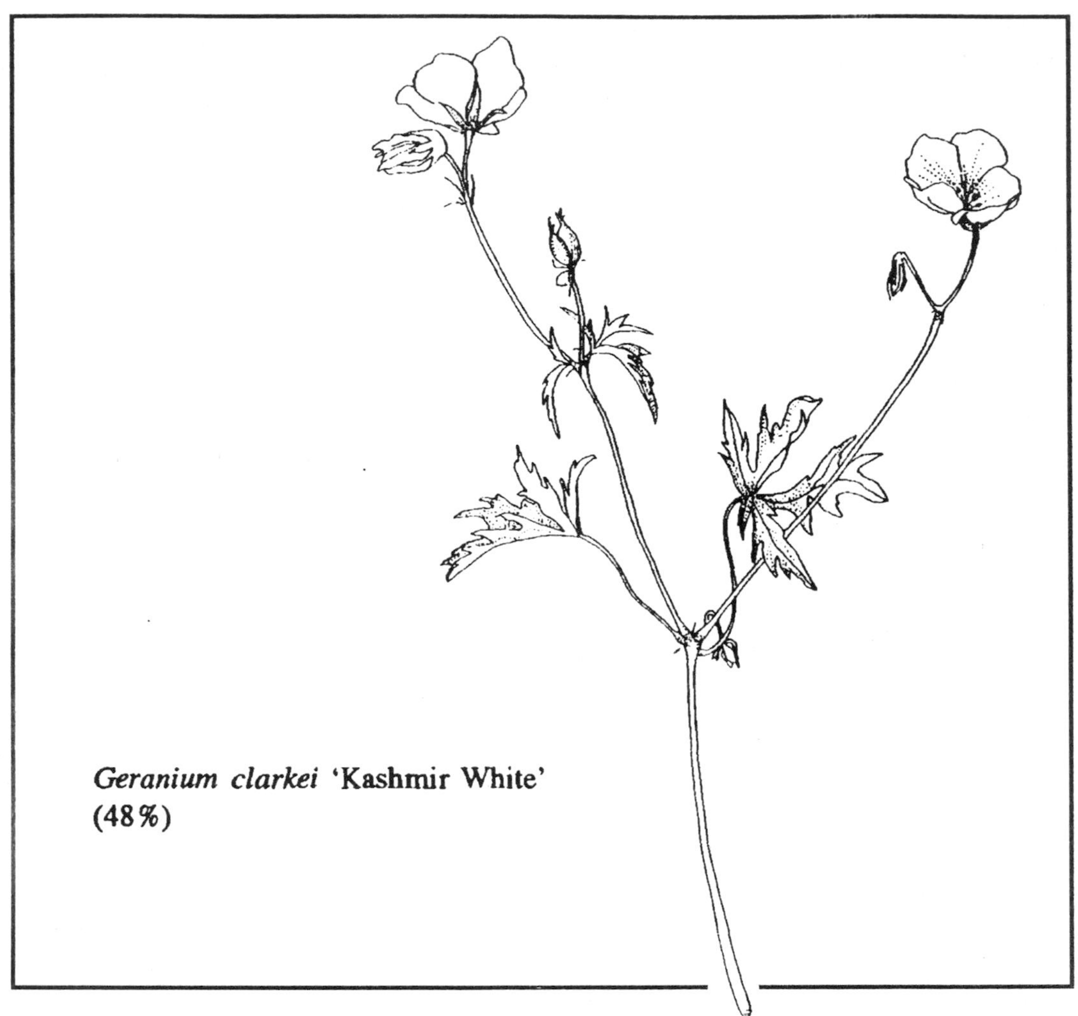

*Geranium clarkei* **'Kashmir White'**
**(48%)**

gardens in North America, perhaps because it is not as colorful or robust as some of the newer material. Place in full sun in well-drained soil. Plants tolerate partial shade but will be taller and not as floriferous.

Propagate by division of the rhizome or from seed.

**Cultivars:**
'Album' is a lovely white-flowered form but not quite as vigorous as the type.

| ***-endressii*** (en-dres′ ee-eye) | | Endress' Geranium | 15-18″/18″ |
|---|---|---|---|
| Summer | Pink | Pyrenees | Zones 4-7 |

This vigorous species bears light pink 1″ diameter flowers above 3-5″ wide shiny green leaves. Leaves are deeply 5 times divided, each division having 3 lobes cut about halfway down. Plants flower from early summer through the fall in northern gardens but stop flowering in mid June in the South. Plant in full sun in the North but provide afternoon shade in the South. Good drainage is essential to plant survival. This species is a terrific plant in itself, but is also an important parent in a number of very useful hybrids.

Propagate by division every 2-3 years. Seeds of the species germinate within 3 weeks if placed in warm (70-75°F), humid atmosphere.

**Cultivars:**

'Wargrave Pink' superseded the species years ago and is still the most popular cultivar. It is a vigorous clone with salmon-pink flowers held well above the foliage. The petals are more distinctly notched than those of the species. Excellent plant for North or South.

***-himalayense*** (hi-mah-lay-en′ se) | Lilac Geranium | 10-15″/15″
Summer | Lilac | Northern Asia | Zones 4-7
(syn. *G. grandiflorum*)

Plants are large enough for most gardens but since they tend to sprawl, are better placed near pathways where their unruly growth can be used to advantage. The 3-6″ diameter leaves are deeply cut into seven divisions, each division 3-lobed at the apex. The petioles are up to 6″ long, resulting in a sprawling habit. In the fall, the foliage turns bright orange and red before disappearing. The 1½-2″ diameter, violet-blue flowers have a warm reddish center and are among the largest of any geranium species. They are saucer shaped with prominent red-purple veins and flower continuously for 4-6 weeks. Plant in full sun in well-drained soil and do not allow to dry out.

Propagate by division every 2-3 years or from seed.

**Cultivars:**

'Birch Double' (syn. 'Plenum') has half-inch diameter washed-out double lavender flowers. It is less vigorous and less attractive than the species. The flowers, however, are sterile and persist much longer than the singles.

'Gravetye' bears 2″ wide bright blue flowers with reddish centers and dark veins. It is shorter (about 12″ tall) and less unruly than the species. This cultivar is a knockout.

'Irish Blue', found in Ireland in 1947 by the noted horticulturist Graham Thomas, bears large pale blue flowers with a large purplish center area. The petals are slightly notched at the ends.

***-macrorrhizum*** (mak-ro-rise′ um) | Bigroot Geranium | 15-18″/15″
Spring | Magenta | Southern Europe | Zones 4-8

One of the earliest geranium species in cultivation, plants were likely cultivated for their fragrant oil (oil of geranium) as early as 1576. When surrounded by dozens of geranium species, it is nice to know that at least one is easily distinguished from the rest. Crushing a leaf provides the unmistakable medicinal smell of *G. macrorrhizum* that some people enjoy, others do not, but all remember. The 6-8″ wide leaves have seven divisions, cut two-thirds the way down, each division shallowly lobed. The 1″ diameter purplish magenta flowers, held on a slightly hairy flower stem, have entire petals and dark red calyces (the sepals) inflated like tiny balloons. The plant has thick, fleshy rhizomatous roots and spreads well in areas of full sun to partial shade. The vigorous root system allows it to compete during drought when others falter and thus plants make excellent ground covers. Plants are heat tolerant, performing well in zone 7 in partial shade. This is one of the easiest geraniums to grow and certainly one of the easiest to identify.

Propagate by dividing the thick rootstock using the rosette bearing stems as cuttings, or by seed. Seed should not be covered before placing it in a warm, humid area.

**Cultivars:**

See hybrids for additional plants with this parentage.

'Album' bears white petals with pink calyces and is a lovely garden plant.
'Beven's Variety' is 8-10″ tall with 1″ wide flowers consisting of deep red sepals and magenta petals.
'Czakor' has a low habit, growing at most 15″ tall. The rosy sepals contrast with the magenta petals.
'Pindus' appears to be a dwarf form of 'Czakor'.
'Ingwersen's Variety', named after the noted English horticulturist, Walter Ingwersen, has pale pink flowers with slightly glossier leaves than the type. It may be the finest cultivar for the garden.
'Spessart' originated in Germany and is already mixed up in the trade. Although white- and pale pink-flowering forms are sold under this name, the original name refers to plants with dark pink to rose-colored petals.
'Variegatum' has leaves irregularly variegated with cream, with typical flowers of the species. Fair at best.

***-maculatum*** Spotted Cranesbill 1-2′/1′
Spring Pink Eastern North America Zones 3-8

Our native geranium has for too long taken a back seat to its European brothers, but no more. It is not that the plant all of a sudden transformed into garden gold or others transmuted to garden garbage, it is simply that we have finally come to appreciate the understated merits of this shade-tolerant geranium. The foliage is subtly spotted, sometimes hard to see, particularly in the summer, and it is the spotting that is responsible for its botanical name (*maculatum* means spotted). The flowers are pink, but I have seen creamy white to purple in populations as well. They were and still are used for their astringent properties and are effective in treating skin conditions, like rashes and minor burns.

Plants are tough as nails and are one of the few geraniums that tolerate some shade and come back with vigor every year. Propagate by seed.

**Cultivars:**

A number of selections may be offered with different flower colors but most will be highly variable.

'Espresso' is a vegetatively-propagated selection from North Creek Nursery in Landenburg, Pennsylvania, with chocolate-colored foliage and pink flowers. It is one of our favorites at the Gardens at UGA and been well received throughout the country. The foliar color is strongest in the spring, and in areas of hot days and warm nights, the color fades to dark green.

**-x *magnificum*** (mag-nif′ i-cum) Showy Geranium 18-24″/24″
Summer Dark Blue Hybrid Zones 3-8

This sterile hybrid resulted from *G. ibericum* x *G. platypetalum* and bears hairy foliage with 5-7 deeply cut divisions. Plants are more vigorous than either of the parents. The peduncles are 4-5″ long and the 1½″ diameter, deep violet-blue flowers are held erect and upright. Plants are similar to *G. ibericum* and are distinguished by their more vigorous growth and sterility. They are large and tend to flop over in rain and wind, but if cut back after flowering, new sets of leaves will appear, although additional flowers may not. Grow in full sun to partial shade in well-drained soil. There apparently are a number of clones here and there in botanic gardens, but I am not aware of any accepted cultivar names.

Propagate by division every 2-3 years.

**-x *oxonianum*** (ox-own′ ee-aye-num) Hybrid Geranium 1-2′/2′
Spring Pink Hybrid Zones 4-7

This hybrid arose as a natural hybrid between *G. endressii* and *G. versicolor* and bears funnel-shaped pink flowers with darker veins. Such hybrids seem to occur with impunity when these two species are planted close to each other and a number of fine cultivars have been named. Plants are generally taller than either parent and have larger flowers. Full sun and well-drained soils are best for good performance. This species name, adopted by Yeo in 1985, commemorates the city of Oxford, England. Many cultivars have been named, all of which should be propagated by division.

**Cultivars:**

'A.T. Johnson' was named for the Welsh horticulturist, Arthur Johnson, and is supposed to be dwarfer than *G. endressii* and have silver-pink flowers. However, plants I have seen are similar to the cultivar 'Rose Clair', also from A.T. Johnson, which has salmon-pink flowers. The true 'A.T. Johnson' may be lost.

'Claridge Druce', named after its discoverer, is vigorous with hairy grayish green foliage and lovely purple-pink flowers with dark veins. The foliage is vigorous, but can look terrible after the plant flowers. Foliar diseases such as rust can disfigure the plants. Cut back hard after flowering and the fresh growth will help to renew your interest in this hybrid. Unfortunately, significant variation occurs and 'Claridge Druce' includes any plants having approximately the characteristics given above.

'Lady Moore' has lighter pink flowers than 'Wargrave Pink' and may be a cultivar of *G. endressii.*

'Phoebe Noble' was raised in the garden of Phoebe Noble, a noted horticulturist and geranium expert in Victoria, British Columbia. Plants bear dark pink flowers.

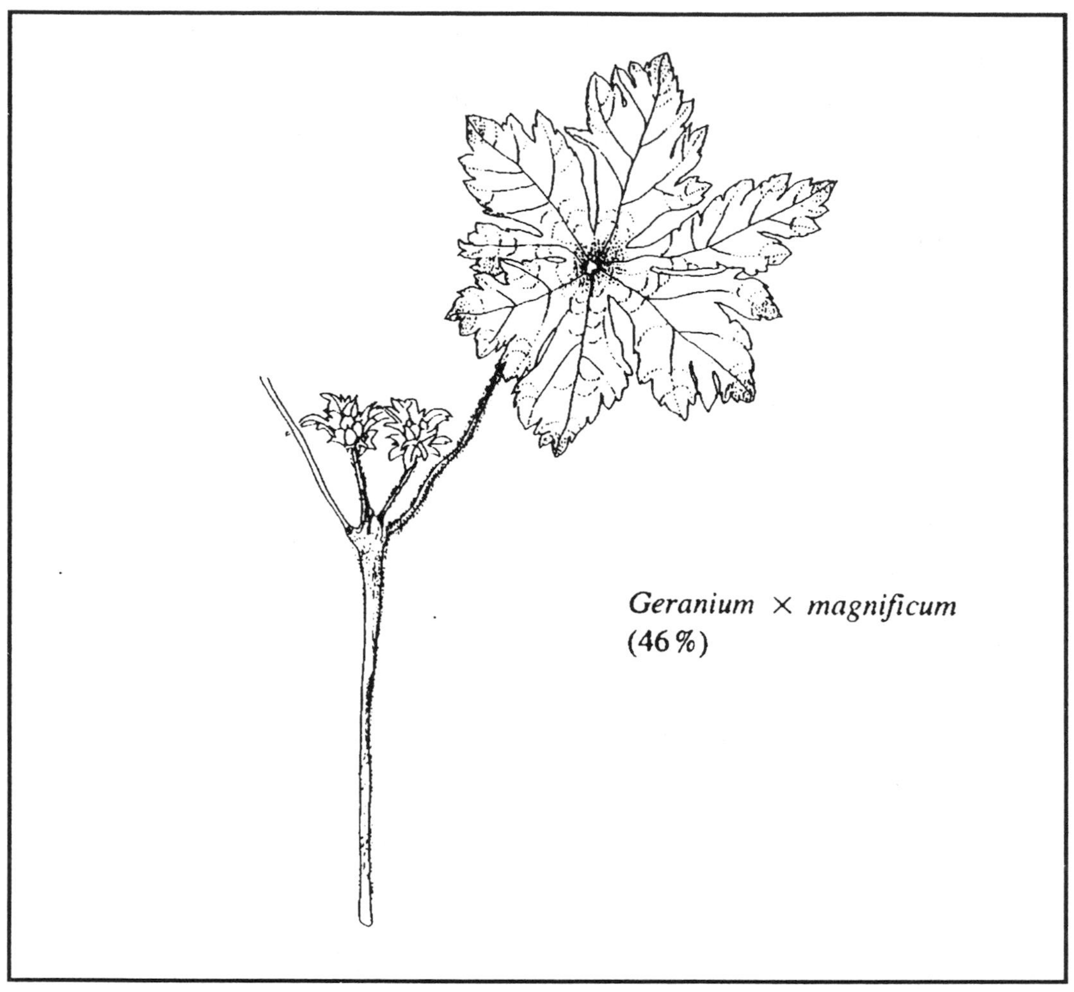

*Geranium* × *magnificum* (46%)

'Rebecca Moss', introduced by the original Heronswood Nursery, has light silver pink flowers and is unique in having little or no conspicuous veining.

'Rose Clair' bears rose-salmon flowers with a hint of veining. Almost indistinguishable from 'A.T. Johnson' in habit and foliage.

'Sherwood' has light pink flowers consisting of narrow petals.

'Southcombe Star' bears flowers with many narrow bluish pink petals, often providing the appearance of double flowers. The habit is more spreading than many other selections.

'Thurstonianum' has purple flowers, occasionally semi-double, consisting of narrow, strap-shaped petals. It is more interesting than pretty. Quite variable, differing in the intensity of flower color and the amount of leaf blotching.

'Wageningen', named for the Dutch research station of the same name, has coral petals and compact growth.

'Walters Gift', another Heronswood selection, differs by having strongly bronze-zoned foliage. Flowers are similar to 'Claridge Druce'.

'Winscombe' is a little smaller than 'Wargrave Pink' and is distinguished by a greater change of petal color during the flowering time, from white to a moderately deep pink. The petals are slightly notched and veined. Found in the village of Winscombe, Somerset, England by the great gardener and writer Margery Fish.

***-phaeum*** (fie' um) Mourning Widow 18-24"/18"
Early Summer Dark Maroon Europe Zones 5-7

This distinct species produces dark, almost black, nodding flowers that suggest "a widow in mourning". The petals, which are about as long as broad, are slightly reflexed resulting in the pistil and stamens being totally exserted (sticking out from the flower). Flowers look like can-can girls raising their purple skirts. The erect stems bear 5-7 deeply divided leaves, each division having small purple spots at their bases. The thick rhizomes allow plants to tolerate some drought although they perform best under moist conditions. Plants are native to damp meadows and shady roadsides and can be grown in shady, moist areas of the garden. This is not a plant that will knock you over with color, however after noting it a few times in my travels, I tend to agree with Walter Ingwersen's comments from 1946. He stated that plants "will appeal to those who have an eye for unusual and quiet charm". Little success has occurred in establishing plants in zone 8, and likely zone 7 is the southern limit.

**Cultivars:**

'Album' has white or faintly blushed petals.

'Lily Lovell' bears flowers of a deep mauve but not as dark as the species. The leaves are lighter green and produce a handsome contrast with the mauve flowers. Plants flower a little earlier and are larger than the species.

var. *lividum* has paler flowers occasionally streaked with lilac spots. They are more colorful and easier on the eyes. Within this variety is a large-flowered and tall form called 'Majus'.

'Margaret Wilson' is quite beautiful, producing green and white foliage along with purple flowers, each with a white center. A wonderful addition to this species.

var. *phaeum* probably bears the darkest flowers of the group, producing purple-black nodding blooms with white, star-shaped centers.

'Samobor' is characterized by the large purple markings on the leaves and small, reflexed burgundy flowers. The markings vary among plants, sometimes almost making a deep ring in the leaf, other times rather blotchy. Plants can self-seed.

'Springtime' produces dark maroon flowers with foliage that starts out with white marbling then develops red spots. Sounds awful, but not bad. Plants grow 18-24" tall.

'Variegatum' has leaves with irregular yellow margins, and often with purple blotches. Unusual and most difficult to locate.

***-platypetalum*** (pla-ti-pet-ah' lum) Broad-petaled Geranium 18-24"/18"
Late Spring Deep Violet Caucasus Zones 3-7

The sticky flower stalks carry deep violet 1" diameter flowers with reddish veins. The 4-6" wide rounded leaves have 7-9 divisions, each cut about halfway into the leaf.

Partial shade, particularly in the South, is preferable to full sun. All parts of the plant are noticeably hairy. Although not as showy as one of its children, *G.* x *magnificum*, it is reasonably heat tolerant and makes a good show in the garden. The foliage persists all season and does not require cutting back as do most other species.

Propagate by divisions or seed.

***-pratense*** (prah′ ten′ see) Meadow Cranesbill 24-36″/24″
Late Spring Purple Northern Europe Zones 5-7

Meadow cranesbill is widely distributed in Europe and quite variable. The 3-6″ wide leaves are deeply cut into 7-9 divisions, each of which is deeply serrated. The ½″ diameter flowers have reddish, sometimes translucent veins on the dark blue petals. This is one of the tallest and most vigorous of the cranesbills and plants often need support to remain upright. One of the problems with the species is its enthusiasm for seed production, often resulting in rapid and messy shedding of flowers. When grown in warm climates, they can quickly look weedy, and foliage must be cut back after flowering. Plants tolerate limey soils better than many others, naturally occurring on calcareous soils in Europe. Place in full sun and provide plenty of moisture.

Propagate by division or seed.

**Cultivars:**

'Dark Reiter' has dark plum-colored foliage with lilac-blue flowers, and grows only about 10″ tall. This is a seed-propagated form that originated from the vegetatively-produced 'Midnight Reiter' (which see).

'Galactic' is over 2′ tall, with flat-topped inflorescences of white flowers with translucent veins. The petals overlap and are sometimes slightly notched. A number of white forms have been sold as 'Album' and 'Albiflorum'. They are all about the same.

'Hocus Pocus', introduced in 2003 from the Netherlands, is a deep bronze-leaf geranium that grows only about 12″ tall. Plants bear handsome lavender-blue flowers. Plants are similar to 'Cheryl's Shadow' and seem to have some heat tolerance as well.

'Midnight Reiter' is truly an eye-catching plant. I first saw this dwarf plant in the wonderful Northwest Garden Nursery of Ernie and Marietta O'Byrne near Eugene, Oregon. A couple of great plantspeople, a great garden and a great nursery, where the cool nights allowed the plants to darken up and maintain their tight habit. The blue flowers were handsome but the foliage was the best part. Plants grow slowly, so they can be overrun with more vigorous plants if sited incorrectly. In hot climates, the foliage will fade a little and the plant will not be as dense, but may be worth a try to determine if you can grow it. Best for containers and rock gardens. Plants were sports from another dark-leaved geranium,'Victor Reiter Jr', named for the noted gardener in San Francisco.

'Mrs. Kendall Clarke' has pale blue flowers with rosy-white venation. Really a handsome clone. The cultivar was first described in 1946 and there appears to be more than one form in commerce. It is definitely a pale blue suffused with rose veins, but the same name has mistakenly been given to darker forms as well.

'Plenum Album', 'Plenum Caeruleum', and 'Plenum Violaceum' have 1″ diameter, double flowers of white, pale blue, and purple, respectively. The flowers persist longer than the single flower types.

'Silver Queen' is 3′ tall and bears 1-2″ diameter silvery-blue flowers.

'Striatum' ('Bicolor') has white petals spotted with varying amounts and intensities of violet-blue.

'Summer Skies' is a double-flowered form of the species with lavender flowers, not blue. Plants are vigorous and can open up in the middle by the second year. We enjoyed the plant in the Gardens at UGA, unfortunately, it did not persist more than a couple of years.

***-psilostemon*** (sye-lo′ ste-mon) Armenian Geranium 24-48″/36″
Summer Magenta with Black Center Armenia Zones 5-7

I first saw this plant at Sissinghurst Castle and Garden, Kent, England in the late 1980s. I observed and studied well over a thousand plant species that trip, but the stateliness and beauty of this one was unforgettable. The 6-8″ wide, heart-shaped, basal evergreen foliage is cut nearly 4/5 of the length into 5-7 sections while the stem leaves are triangular. The 1½-2″ diameter bright magenta flowers have a conspicuous black spot in the middle. It is a color one either hates or loves.

This is not a small plant; heights of 3 to 4′ are not uncommon and the stems often need support, certainly in areas of warm summer nights. Plants should be placed in broken shade and in rich moist soil to perform their best. They look better planted against a dark background where their luminous flowers will stand out even more. At the time of the writing of the first edition, plants were almost non-existent in the United States. I grew some plants in the Armitage garden (zone 7b), and they stood only 2′ tall after 4 years. As the shade of the oaks grew, I finally replaced them with other plants more adaptable to the changing conditions. Today, plants are much more available than ever before, and have been hybridized to provide some of the beauty without all of the problems. In general, plants in the East will disappoint if compared to those in the British Isles, but so what? They are handsome plants if sited well and have found their way into North American gardens.

Propagate by division of the root stalk or by seed.

**Cultivars:**

'Bressingham Flair' is about 2′ tall and does not require as much support as the species. The flowers are a little less intense and with a hint of pink in the magenta.

***-procurrens*** (pro-cure′ ens) Trailing Geranium 6-9″/3′
Summer Magenta Himalayas Zone 5-7

Plants bear 1″ diameter flowers of blinding rich magenta with black centers in the summer. The petals do not overlap and the flowers are not as full as those of

*G. psilostemon*. Essentially, plants are ground covers that can ramble and scramble through and about other plants. The red stems trail for long distances like strawberry runners and they will root at the nodes, making them effective ground cover plants for a sunny area. They are effective but both flowers and foliage are harsh to the eyes.

***-sanguineum*** (sang-guin′ ee-um) Bloody Cranesbill 9-12″/12″
Spring Magenta Europe, Asia Zones 3-8

Of the cultivated geraniums, this may be the most common one in the United States and Canada. Plants are adaptable, able to tolerate heat and cold better than other species, and are free flowering. They generally grow in mounds, consisting of small, shallowly divided basal leaves and thinner, deeply divided stem leaves. The foliage also provides a touch of fall color, turning crimson red. The 1-1½″ diameter flowers are a rich magenta, often too fierce for the tastes of many gardeners. The *Geranium* genus has more than its share of that often intolerable magenta color, however, one man's ceiling is another man's floor. The flowers are solitary and the petals are not notched.

Plants should be placed in full sun or partial shade in the front of the garden. If grown in too much shade, they are less compact, less floriferous and taller than in the sun. This is the most trouble-free species for southern gardeners as the deep root stalk ferrets out moisture in times of drought and the thick basal leaves tolerate hot weather. Many cultivars have been introduced but differences between some are minimal, at best.

Propagate carefully by division every 3-4 years or from seed.

**Cultivars:**

Many cultivars of this tough old bird have been developed since the second edition, and while all are good, many are quite similar to each other.

'Alan Bloom' is a short plant with relatively large magenta flowers.
'Album' has clear white flowers and grows 10-18″ tall. It is an excellent cultivar; far easier on the eyes than the species.
'Alpenglow' grows about 8″ tall with vivid rose-red flowers.
'Ankum's Pride' was developed by the Dutch breeder Coen Jansen and bears good-looking pink flowers with darker striations. Competes in beauty with var. *striatum*.
'Cedric Morris' has large rosy magenta flowers over vigorous one-and-a-half-foot tall plants. Plants flower earlier in the spring and occasionally throughout the season.
'Elsbeth', a fine English name, has some of the largest flowers of the species. She is bright purple and grows only about 9″ tall.
'Glenluce' has 1½-2″ diameter clear pink flowers on compact plants.
'Holden' is a spreading plant, with small leaves and rosy pink flowers. Named for Holden Clough Nursery in Lancashire, England in the early 1970s.
'John Elsley', named in honor for one this country's premiere horticulturists, was selected by Blooms of Bressingham at the same time they selected the cultivar

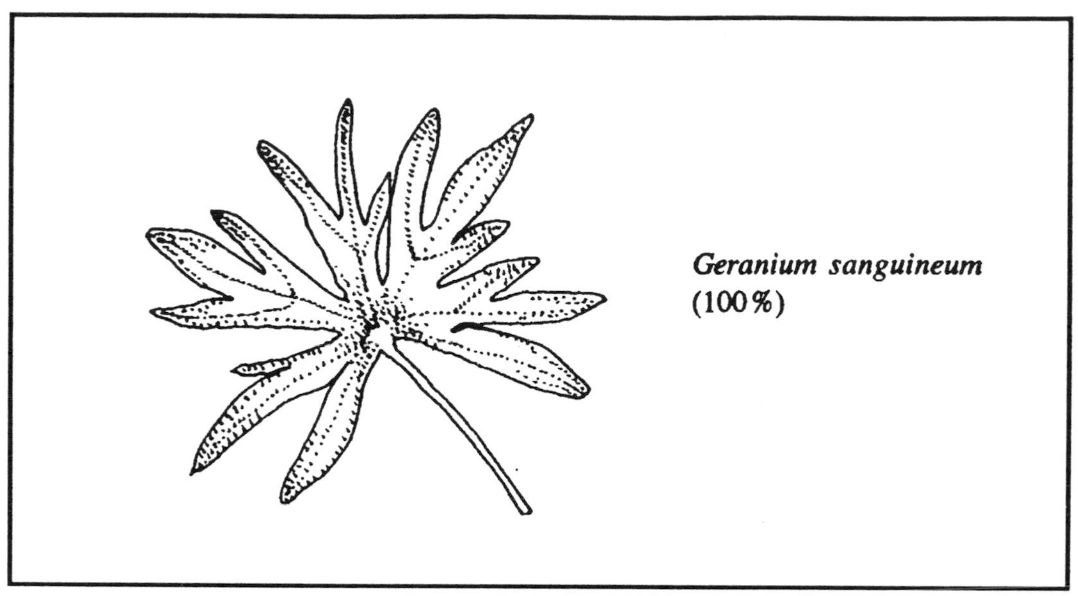

*Geranium sanguineum*
(100%)

'Alan Bloom' (above). Little differences can be seen between them, however, 'John Elsley' is a little taller.

'Jubilee Pink' has magenta-pink flowers over compact foliage.

'Max Frei' bears purple-pink saucer-shaped flowers over compact plants.

'New Hampshire Purple' is 15-18″ tall and maintains a good compact habit, at least for the first two years. Flowers are more purple than magenta.

'Minutum' grows only a few inches tall and bears deep rose flowers less than one inch wide.

'Shepherd's Warning' is an outstanding compact form with deep rose-pink flowers. Raised by nurseryman Jack Drake, in Aviemore, Scotland, along with 'Jubilee Pink'. Plants are excellent as rock garden or wall plants.

var. *striatum* is still one of the best of the lot and is often sold under the name 'Lancastriense' or 'Prostratum'. It is only 6-8″ tall and although flower color is somewhat variable, light pink flowers with crimson veins are usually produced.

| **-*sylvaticum*** (sil-va′ ti-kum) | | Wood Cranesbill | 30-36″/30″ |
|---|---|---|---|
| Spring | Purple-Violet | Europe | Zones 5-8 |

One of the earliest-flowering geraniums, flowers appear as early as late April in the South and May further north. The 6-7″ wide roundish leaves are deeply cut into 7-9 divisions. The 1″ wide purplish violet flowers have a white base and are like tiny chalices open to the sky, borne neither horizontal or nodding. They are usually violet-blue with a white center but may be pink or white. The seed capsules are thrust in the air like athletes showing the crowd they are number one. This species is not as garden worthy as some of the cultivars. Plants are best placed in partial shade and in a moisture-retentive soil.

Propagate by division every 2-3 years or by seed.

**Cultivars:**

'Album' is a white-flowered cultivar with light green leaves. It comes true from seed. Quite tolerant of shade.

'Mayflower', introduced around 1972, is the best of the group, bearing rich violet-blue flowers with a white base.

**Related Species and Hybrids:**

You would think with all the species and cultivars described above that I would be exhausted and tired of this glut of geraniums. I am tired of writing about them, but never tire of looking at them. And certainly, nobody has told the retailers and breeders that perhaps we have enough, so here we go into the geranium stage of life. May you exit unscathed.

'Ann Folkard' is a natural hybrid which occurred in 1973 between *G. procurrens*, a trailing ground cover species, and *G. psilostemon*. This can be a stunning plant when scrambling over shrubs and bushes. It is not a climber, nor a ground cover, but best described as a scrambler. The leaves are always light green, sometimes appearing chlorotic, and require a second look to appreciate. The rich magenta flowers have black centers that contrast brightly with the leaves. Plants struggle in the East and the South, and the light green look becomes tiring if not at its best. The picture in the catalogs certainly was not taken in my garden. Best on the West Coast and does reasonably well in zones 5 to 7 east of the Rockies. We owe this plant to an amateur gardener, Rev. O.G. Folkard, from Lincolnshire, England who set out to collect and hybridize geraniums that appealed to him, one of which he named for his daughter Ann. Such plants are powerful testimonials to the ability of amateur gardeners to have a significant impact on horticulture.

'Ann Thompson' came from the same parents but claims of better performance and more heat tolerance are being batted around by reputable nurserypeople. However, I have only started to test it so I cannot yet recommend it any higher than 'Ann Folkard'. If you do well with the first Ann, you will probably do even better with the second.

*G. argenteum*, silverleaf geranium, has leaves that are densely covered with a silvery-gray pubescence. The notched flowers appear singly and are light pink with netted veins. Good drainage is essential; plants are at their best in rock gardens or raised containers.

*G. aristatum* is similar to *G. phaeum* but not as upright. The flowers are white to lilac-pink and the reflexed petals have lovely lilac veins. The leaves are also more pubescent. Zones 5-7.

'Brookside' has beautiful large blue flowers. The lanky plants remind me of meadow geranium, *G. pratense*, which is no doubt part of the parentage. They are heat tolerant and a good choice for hot summer gardens.

'Cheryl's Shadow' is another dwarf dark-leaved geranium, this one sporting pink flowers. As with all these dark-leaved forms, they are exceptionally beautiful in the first year, but their heat tolerance is somewhat suspect and are best in containers or rock gardens.

'Dilys' is a cross between *G. sanguineum* and *G. procurrens* with late purple flowers on prostrate stems. The leaves are close to those of *G. sanguineum*. Highly recommended for zones 4-7. Named for the well-known English gardener, Dilys Davis.

*G. donianum* is a low-growing species which lends itself to well-drained sunny spots in the garden. The flowers are reddish purple or magenta and the plant grows about 12″ tall. Native to the Himalayas, plants are quite wonderful but also difficult to find and difficult to establish. The deeply divided leaves are carried on a compact plant, and flowers occur in late spring.

*G. ibericum*, Caucasus geranium, is best known as a parent of *G.* x *magnificum*. Plants differ by having the divisions cut about three-quarters of the way down the leaf and flowers are fertile. Caucasus geranium is also more drought tolerant but a little less vigorous than the hybrid.

'Johnson's Blue' is a wonderful hybrid between *G. himalayense* and *G. pratense* that arose around 1950 from seed of *G. pratense*, and named for famed British horticulturist, A.T. Johnson. Seed set is minimal so flowering continues for a long time. At 15-18″ tall, it is taller than *G. himalayense* but not as big as a well-grown *G. pratense*. The 1½-2″ diameter clear blue, unnotched flowers are similar in color to those of *G. himalayense* but without the reddish center. This hybrid is the epitome of an "English garden", and every gardener who comes back from the British Isles must have the plant in his garden, often to be disappointed. In the North and West, plants do fine in the summer but don't always return, particularly after a cold winter. In the South, the heat results in blue bacon, scorched, crispy and totally inedible. Fabulous if you can grow it!

'Jolly Bee' has handsome violet-blue flowers that are continuously formed for at least two months. Plants are essentially the same as 'Rozanne'; I have them planted side by side and cannot see any obvious differences.

'Katherine Adele' is more of a sprawler that is at her best growing in and around plants, rather than on her own. She is not large, growing only about 18″ in height, but her dark leaves combined with light pink flowers and darker veins make her a reasonable addition.

*G. malvaeflorum* is a tuberous plant and acts as a ground cover. Native to Northwest Africa, plants are cold tolerant only to zone 7 but are likely heat tolerant to at least zone 7b. They tolerate summer heat by going summer dormant. Don't be upset if your plants disappear in midsummer; that is what they are supposed to do. The mauve to violet flowers are about 1″ wide and produced in early to mid spring. In mild winters, the foliage arises in winter; in harsher winters, foliage may not arise until early spring. A good plant for everyone, but particularly good for Southern gardeners to try.

*G.* x *monacense* is a hybrid between *G. phaeum* and *G. reflexum*, with characteristics intermediate between the two. The hybrid was first described in Germany and commemorates the city of Munich. Leaves may be blotched or not. I see it offered occasionally, particularly the cultivar 'Muldoon', named after Spotty Muldoon, a British radio show character played by the late Peter Cook.

'Nimbus' can be a robust plant, growing at least 2′ in height and equally wide. However, it is a bit more refined than 'Orion' or 'Brookside' and also bears smaller leaves and more lavender flowers.

*G. nodosum* has the habit of *G. endressii* but with glossy green leaves and saw-toothed edges on the leaf divisions. The lilac flowers have an obvious purple venation pattern. Does well in relatively deep shade. Works well in zones 5 to 7.

'Orion' is a large vigorous grower like 'Brookside' and claims the latter as one of its parents. The lavender flowers are large and many, and plants have performed particularly well in the Gardens at UGA in Athens, Georgia. Highly recommended by this author.

*G. orientalitibeticum* is not closely related botanically to *G. sanguineum*, however, the flowers are similar in color and form. The foliage of the former is deeply divided, almost to the base, and marbled with yellow throughout. Plants are aggressive ground covers but require cool nights and excellent drainage to do well.

'Orkney Cherry' may belong closer to the *G. cinereum* group as plants are less than 6″ tall. Bright pink flowers with white centers are produced over bronze foliage.

'Patricia' has been one of my favorite geraniums since I planted it in 2000. The dark flowers remind me of those of *G. psilostemon*, one of the parents. Plants are large and vigorous but a little more civilized due to the presence of the other parent, *G. endressii*. Plants are cold hardy to zone 4, heat tolerant to zone 7 and show exceptional persistence.

'Pink Penny' is said to be a pink form of 'Rozanne'. I like the idea of a pink-flowered geranium with similar garden performance of 'Rozanne', but the jury is still out.

*G. reflexum* is also similar but the flowers are smaller and not as dark purple. The petals, which are twice as long as broad, are the most reflexed of any species. The immature fruits are downwardly inclined in this species but upwardly inclined in *G. phaeum*.

*G. renardii* is a beautiful but temperamental species not often seen in American gardens. The 5-7 divisions of the dull gray-green foliage are shallowly lobed and the flowers are unmistakable. Each 1″ diameter white flower is vividly marked with violet feathered veins. Excellent drainage and a sheltered location are required. I have seen excellent plants in Asheville, North Carolina and expect that reasonably good garden performance can be expected in zones 5 and 6.

'Rozanne' was found in Somerset, England, in the garden of Rozanne Waterer, and was introduced to this country in 2002. It quickly became the "must-have" geranium almost everywhere. The violet blue flowers continue to open for months on end and have had no disease or insect problems. The foliage is also handsome, showing slight yellow striations. The plant was given additional recognition when it was named 2008 Perennial Plant of the Year by the Perennial Plant Association. Similar to 'Jolly Bee', which see.

*G.* x *riversleaianum* is a little-known hybrid between *G. endressii* and *G traversii*, native to New Zealand. Flowers are pink to magenta and plants grow approximately 12″ tall. Two good cultivars have become available in the United States and Canada from the many progeny that have undoubtedly occurred. It is likely that these hybrids are less cold tolerant than *G. endressii* due to the New Zealand presence of one of the parents. 'Mavis Simpson' has deeply indented leaves with broad lobes. The 1″ wide, light pink flowers have dark purple veins and tend to fade with age. The centers of the flowers are creamy white. Plants grow about 18″ tall. Named for a staff member at Kew Gardens. 'Russell Pritchard' is a well-known cultivar with 1½″ diameter magenta flowers and dull gray-green, lobed foliage. The flower color is much more intense than either parent, leading to speculation that this may be a hybrid between *G. sanguineum* and *G. endressii.*

'Tiny Monster' is another example of a name that makes one pause. However, I enjoy oxymorons as well as the next person, so into the Gardens at UGA it went. It is more similar in leaf and flower color to bloody cranesbill (*G. sanguineum*) than to its other parent, Armenian cranesbill (*G. psilostemon*). Plants are vigorous, get to be monstrous in spread but stay less than a foot tall. They are beautiful in the spring but open in the middle with the onset of summer. Even in the Northeast, it can outgrow its place. Not a bad thing, just something to be aware of.

*G. thunbergii* makes an effective ground cover, particularly for southern gardens. It is a weedy species, consisting of light green hairy leaves on sprawling stems and dozens of half-inch white to pink flowers that appear in late summer. Not at all recommended for the formal garden.

*G. wallichianum*, Wallich geranium, is a prostrate species with 2′ long trailing stems making this an excellent geranium for growing over stone walls or in patio pots. The late summer flowers are purple and not outstanding. However, the cultivar 'Buxton's Variety' has small white marbled foliage, and saucer-shaped, campanula-blue flowers with a distinct white center. A planting laden with flowers romping over rocks and walls is a magnificent sight. Plants commemorate E.C. Buxton in whose garden it appeared around 1920. It may be raised from root cuttings and comes true from seed. 'Crystal Lake' has the same marbled foliage but with larger flowers on 16-20″ plants. 'Rosetta' was new in 2007 and is characterized by rose pink flowers with a small white eye.

## *Geum* (jee′ um) Avens Rosaceae

Over 50 species are included in this genus known for its bright, showy 5-petaled flowers and dark green leaves. The compound foliage is cut in various ways, depending on the species, but the terminal lobe is always the largest. In some species, their charm is extended by the production of fluffy seed heads, similar those of *Pulsatilla.* Species such as *G. reptans* are small enough to be included in the rock garden while taller ones such as *G. montanum* are large enough for inclusion in the border. All require good drainage, ample moisture and some protection from full afternoon sun. Geums are easily grown in the northern part of the country but many struggle in areas of high heat and humidity.

Taxonomic confusion has rippled through the genus. *G. chiloense* and *G. coccineum* are used interchangeably, sometimes separated, other times united. Cultivars may be listed as one or the other or as hybrids. Perhaps this is a moot point, for except for our native species, *G. triflorum*, which has benefitted from the movement to native plants in this country, few nurseries offer more than two or three cultivars of avens.

Propagate by division in spring or fall or from fresh seed. Multiplication of cultivars should be accomplished vegetatively. Unfortunately, natural hybridization takes place readily between species and the resulting seedlings are often inferior.

**-*chiloense*** (chill-o' en-se) Chilean Avens 20-24"/18"
Spring Scarlet Chile Zones 4-7

This species is the most common of garden avens and, in my opinion, highly overrated. The 6-12" long hairy leaves are pinnately divided into 5-7 lobes: the terminal being about twice as large as the other leaflets. The 1-1½" wide scarlet flowers may be single or double. The species does not tolerate the excesses of the North American climate, struggling a great deal in the summer and often dying out in the winter. Plants are short-lived even under the best of conditions. To be fair, some cultivars can look stunning when grown in a well-drained area out of the hot afternoon sun and kept consistently moist.

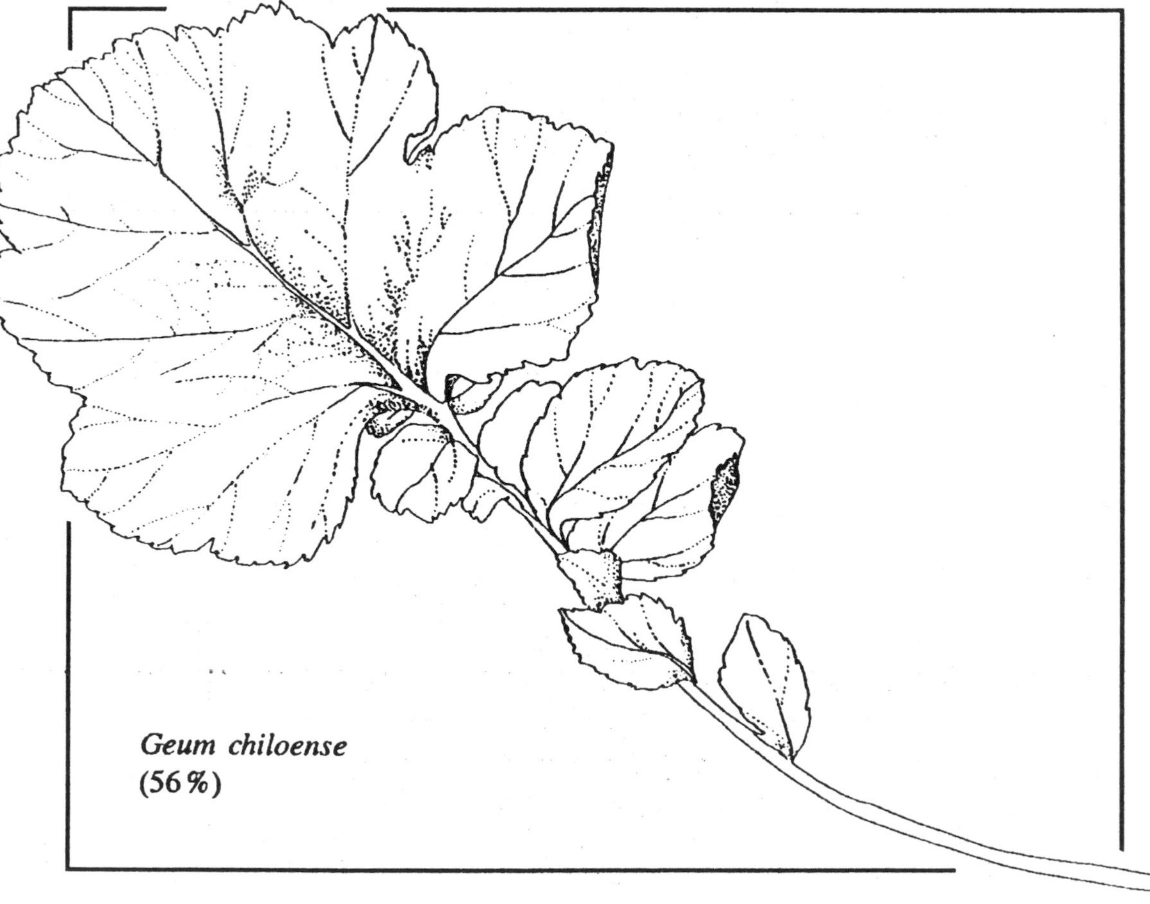

*Geum chiloense*
(56%)

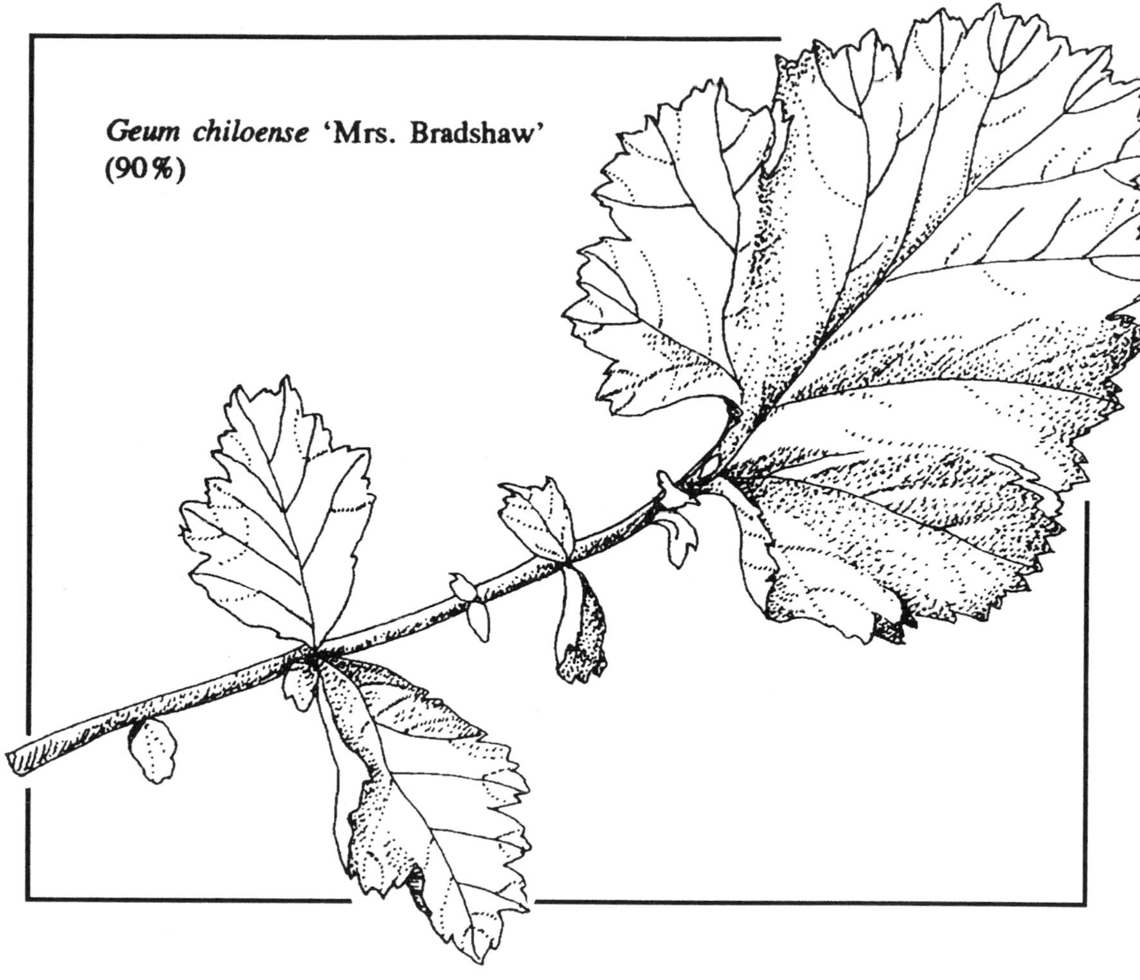
Geum chiloense 'Mrs. Bradshaw' (90%)

***-montanum*** (mon-tah′ num) Mountain Avens 6-9″/12″
Spring Golden Yellow Southern Europe Zones 3-7

The foliage of the species is among the prettiest and long-lasting of the genus. The leaves are about 4″ long and densely pubescent; the terminal leaflet about 2′ long. Leaves remain fresh well into the summer, unlike many species whose leaves deteriorate soon after flowering. The 1″ wide flowers are held in 1-3-flowered inflorescences well above the foliage and are a lovely golden yellow. The seed heads are feathery and as pretty as the flowers.

Plants are native to sub-alpine areas around 6000′ elevation and do best in areas of cool summers or at least cool summer nights.

***-x heldreichii*** (hel-dritch-ee′ eye) 1-2′/2′
Summer Orange-Red Hybrid Zones 4-7

A hybrid of confused lineage but thought to be a hybrid between *G. montanum* and *G. coccineum*. Plants are taller than *G. montanum* and the 1-2″ diameter reddish

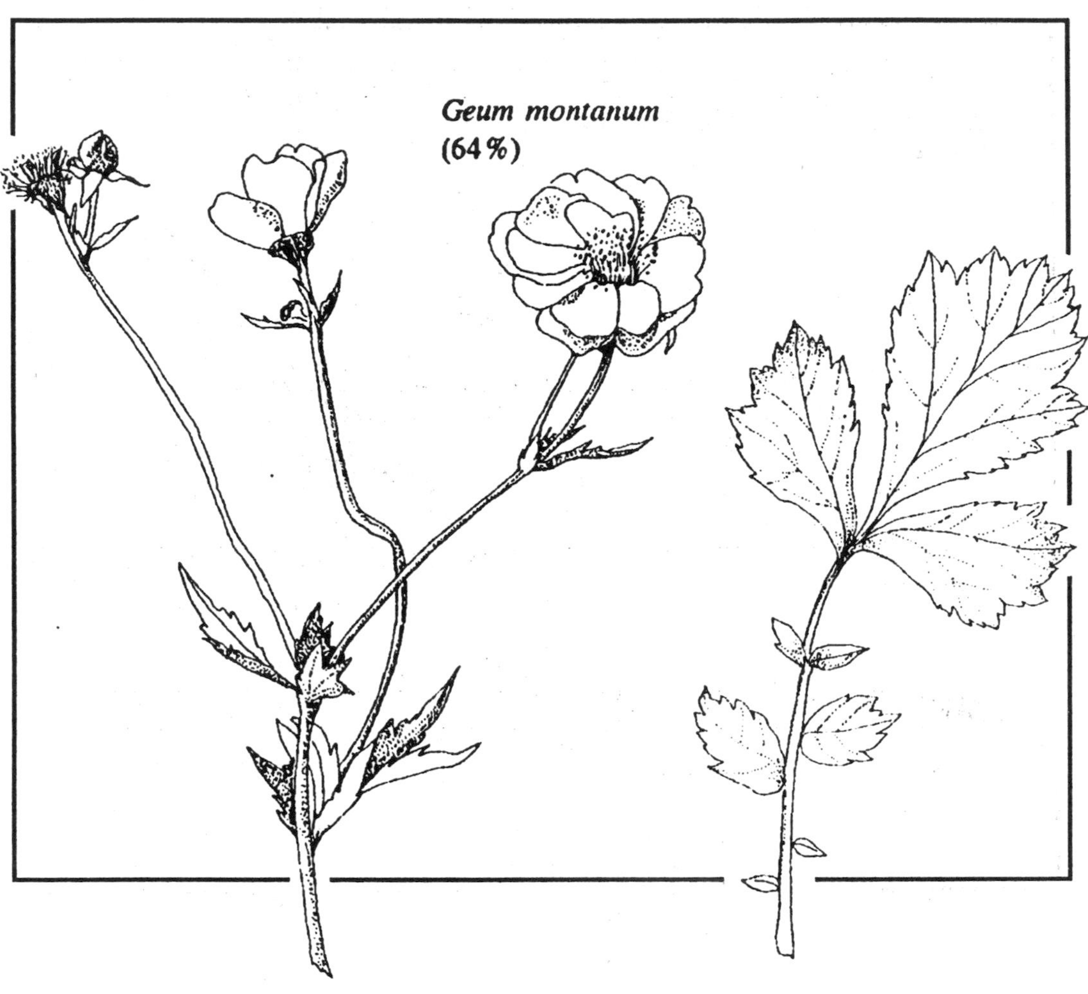


orange flowers are borne in twos and threes. It is not terribly well adapted to heat and persisted for about two years in north Georgia gardens.

Propagate by division in the spring.

***-reptans*** (rep′ tanz) Creeping Avens 6-8″/8″
Spring Yellow European Alps Zones 3-7

If full morning sun, excellent drainage, and somewhat basic soils are provided, this little plant can be a definite asset to the garden. However, if not given these conditions, it will throw its runners in the air, give up and die. The leaflets are deeply toothed and unlike many others, the terminal leaflet is about the same size as the laterals. As a ground cover, plants multiply by rooting along the nodes of non-flowering runners. Many solitary 1-1½″ diameter pale yellow flowers are borne in early summer.

Propagate by cutting the rooted runners and replanting in the final location. Seed germinates within 2-3 weeks under warm (70-75°F), humid conditions.

***-rivale*** (ree-vah′ lee) Water Avens, Indian Chocolate 8-12″/10″
Spring Red-Orange Eurasia, North America Zones 3-7

While most species bear upright flowers and require consistent moisture and sharp drainage, this species has nodding, bell-shaped, flowers and is, for all intents and purposes, a bog plant. The foliage consists of 7-13 leaflets, the terminal twice as large as the lateral ones. The leaflets are hairy and noticeably serrated. This is a good ground cover plant for cool, wet areas where little else does well. However, it is also useable in non-boggy areas but constant moisture must be available. It performs poorly in the heat.

The rootstock is thick and brown and if boiled in water, the resultant liquid tastes faintly like chocolate, a tale I have fortunately not had the pleasure of verifying.

Propagate by seed or division.

**Cultivars:**

'Album' bears nodding white flowers with calyces (sepals) in early summer.

'Leonard's Variety' has drooping, mahogany-red, bell-shaped flowers and deeply cut green foliage. Very floriferous. Plants show hybrid vigor and may be a hybrid, possibly with *G. coccineum*.

'Leonard's Double' is similar to the above but carries double flowers.

'Lionel Cox' is about 12″ tall and has nodding primrose flowers with light green leaves.

***-triflorum*** (try-flor′ um) Prairie Smoke 9-12″/12″
Summer Mauve Central United States Zones 3-7

These distinctive plants are native from the High Plains to the Cascade Mountains to the Sierra Nevadas, Colorado and Nebraska. The drooping purplish red nodding flowers are generally cup shaped. Flowers occur in one or more-flowered inflorescences, but often in threes. The flowers give rise to feathery silver and pink cottony fruit, which persist for many weeks after flowering, leading to regional descriptive common names like torch flower, long-plumed purple avens, prairie smoke, lion's beard and old man's whiskers. Plants were used by Native Americans to treat wounds and sore throats. The leaves are quite different from other species in that there are about 30 leaflets on each 6″ long leaf. The entire plant is softly hairy. Unusually cold hardy, handles Midwest heat reasonably well. Place in moist but well-drained areas in full sun.

Plants multiply by runners, propagate by division.

**Related Species and Hybrids:**

Many of these may be cultivars of *G. chiloense, G. coccineum* or hybrids between them. Most are short-lived, perhaps performing well for a couple of years, then declining.

'Bernstein' carries light golden flowers on 18″ plants.

'Blazing Sunset' produces fully double scarlet flowers in early spring. A knockout color.

'Cooky' has been one of the few new success stories in geum for years. Probably a selection of *G. coccineum*, plants bear vibrant orange flowers early in the spring and the foliage persists throughout the summer. In the Gardens at UGA, plants have been carrying on like this for at least three years, unheard of for geums in the South.

'Coppertone' is less than 1′ tall, bearing early wide open apricot flowers.

'Dolly North' has golden orange, semi-double flowers.

'Fireball' bears orange to yellow semi-double flowers on 2-2½′ tall plants.

'Fire Opal' produces many intense orange-scarlet, semi-double flowers.

'Flames of Passion' is 12-15″ tall, compact and free flowering. Flowers are red to scarlet and appear in late April to early May on red stems.

'Georgenberg' has soft, pale yellow flowers arising from nodding buds. Often listed as a cultivar of *G. chiloense*.

*G.* x *intermedium* is a hybrid between *G. rivale* x *G. urbanum* and forms aggressive ground-covering clumps about 18″ tall. Plants bear pale yellow flowers enhanced by reddish brown sepals. Happy in wet areas.

'Lady Stratheden' ('Goldball') has deep buttercup-yellow semi-double flowers.

'Magnificum' bears semi-double orange flowers.

'Mrs. Bradshaw' bears scarlet, semi-double flowers. 'Mrs. Bradshaw' and 'Lady Stratheden' are still widely available, mostly because they can easily be raised from seed. While both have their admirers, they produce too few flowers for the amount of leaf area.

'Prince of Orange' has many deep orange flowers.

'Princess Juliana', raised in 1923, bears soft yellow semi-double flowers that open about one week later than the others.

'Red Wings' is similar to 'Fire Opal' but has more orange in the flower.

*G.* x *rhaeticum*, a hybrid between *G. montanum* and *G. reptans*, has foliar characteristics intermediate between the two. One-inch diameter golden-yellow flowers cover 6-8″ tall plants.

*G. rossii* grows 9-12″ tall and produces relatively large (1-1½″ wide) yellow flowers. The plants form a coarse mat made up of deeply divided leaves. They are stoloniferous and spread rapidly.

'Rubin' bears semi-double crimson flowers, about 12-15″ tall.

'Sea of Fire' grows about 12″ tall and produces fire engine red flowers.

'Tim's Tangerine' is really quite wonderful. These vigorous plants have a mounding rounded habit and dozens of orange-yellow (tangerine?) flowers in the spring. Plants have performed well in hot, humid conditions, particularly when placed in an area of afternoon shade.

*G.* x *tirolense* is a hybrid between *G. rivale* and *G. montanum*. 'Lemon Drops' has nodding wide open yellow flowers with purplish centers.

'Werner Arends' carries many semi-double orange flowers tinted red.

## ***Gillenia*** (gil-ee′ nee-a) Bowman's Root, Physic, Ipecac Rosaceae

Still an overlooked genus, *Gillenia* contains 2 species native to the United States that are wonderfully ornamental. Moist areas and partial shade are requirements for best performance. Propagate by division in the spring or by seed. Many common names occur, but syrup of ipecac, used to induce vomiting for food poisoning comes from a Brazilian shrub *(Psychotria ipecacuanha)*. However, American history (non-fiction and historical fiction, such as Diana Gabaldon) American ipecac is also mentioned as an early emetic. Native plants have similar although less effective properties.

***-trifoliata*** (tri-fo-lee-ah' ta) Bowman's Root, Indian Physic 2-4'/3'
Summer White Central, Southern United States Zones 4-7

I was first "turned on" to this species in the 1980s in Aas, Norway, where it shimmered in the late afternoon sun. I was embarrassed to learn that it was native from New York to Georgia and that it was seldom commercially available to gardeners in America, which is certainly no longer the case. The 3-foliate leaves are borne on short leaf stalks and each 2-3" long ovate leaflet is serrated and pointed. Small insignificant stipules (leaflike structures) are found at the base of the petiole on the upper nodes.

In summer, plants bear such masses of 1" wide white star-shaped flowers that they look like clouds of butterflies. The five white petals emerge from small tubular wine-colored sepals that persist long after the petals have fallen. The flowers are held above the foliage on wiry stems terminating in paniculate corymbs. Place in partial shade and moist areas or plants will languish. Unfortunately, support is usually required, particularly in areas of high temperatures. A half dozen plants are well worth trying if you have the space.

**Related Species:**

*G. stipulata*, American ipecac, is similar but does not have the persistent red sepals. The leaflets are narrower and the stipules are larger and more leaflike than those of the previous species. Plants are native from New York to Georgia and Louisiana and are easier to establish in the South than the previous species.

## ***Gladiolus*** (glad-ee' o-lus) Gladiolus Iridaceae

The many species and their hybridization can be discussed only superficially in this book. Although there are over 250 species, it is difficult for the home gardener to find anything but the large-flowered and miniature-flowered hybrids, one must search to find any of the actual species. Arguably, in point of beauty, the natural species do not compare with today's garden hybrids, many of which evolved from *G.* x *gandavensis*, x *childsi*, x *nanceianus*, and x *lemoinei*, all of which are of little garden interest today. So much hybridization has occurred that it is almost impossible to know what parents produced what cultivars. All modern hybrids have been lumped together under *G.* x *hortulanus*.

Named varieties abound and are usually classified as large-flowered, with flowers 4-7" across; butterfly flowers, which are half the size of the large-flowered types with striking throat markings or blotches; miniatures, evolved from *G. primulinus* with 2-3" wide flowers borne on shorter stems; and open face types whose flowers are wide open and point more upright than those in the other classes. For those interested in the history of gladiolus and the cultivars available, a number of good books on bulb species and excellent bulb catalogs are your best sources.

Although hybrids abound, a few species are still available. These cannot compete with the colors and flower size of the hybrids, but they add a touch of class and dignity to the garden.

***-byzantinus*** (bi-zan-teen′ us) Byzantine Gladiolus 2-3′/2′
Summer Maroon Mediterranean Zones 7-10

The leaves are narrower than the hybrid gladiolus and the 1-3″ long flowers are loosely arranged on the 6-12 flowered raceme. They are mostly maroon but are sometimes red or copper and are borne on one side of the spike only. Corms are hardy in southern areas of the country but must be dug in the North. They are lovely plants, provide long-lasting cut flowers and give the serious gardener a glimpse into the genus before the hybridizers "improved" it.

Plants grew with enthusiasm in the garden of the late Laura Ann Segrest, my gardening mentor in Athens, but she hated the color. Other gardeners love the color and vigor of the plants. Plants were grown by Southern gardeners for years and are often found today around old homesteads and cemetery plots, particularly in Texas and the Southeast. In the North, corms should be treated like those of hybrid gladiolus and dug in the fall after flowering but before the first severe frost, and dried in a warm room.

Plant in a sunny area in moist soils. Similar to all gladiolus, thrips can be a terrible nuisance.

***-callianthus*** (cal′lee-an′ thus) Abyssinian Gladiolus 2-3′/1′
Late Summer-Fall White with Purple Throat Ethiopia Zones 8-10
(syn. *Acidanthera bicolor*)

The proper name for this plant keeps flip-flopping from the old name, *Acidanthera*, to its new home, *Gladiolus*. It looks like, behaves like, and even smells like a gladiolus. This is one of the loveliest of the summer-flowering bulbs (actually a corm) and it is unfortunate that the species has such a limited range and color. The swordlike, mid green leaves are topped with long tubed, star-shaped, fragrant 2″ diameter white flowers with purple throats. Each flowering stem consists of 4-6 flowers arranged in a loose spike. The species is often grown for cut flowers and, when placed in a commercially available floral preservative, displays excellent vase life.

Remove cormels, dead roots, stems, and store corms and cormels in a dry warm place (60-70°F) until spring. One of my gardening friends, Sharon Illingsworth, who lives near Thunder Bay, Ontario (USDA zone 3), starts them inside in early May and sets them out at the end of the month. This way she is able to enjoy the late flowers before frost cuts them down in early fall. Those who live in areas where it is perennial must be patient in the spring as it is slow to emerge. It is a good species to combine with some of the spring-flowering plants that go dormant in the summer, such as *Mertensia* and *Doronicum*. Abyssinian gladiolus has barely emerged when these species are at their peak. As they decline, it fills in those areas vacated due to summer dormancy. Unfortunately, flowering declines if corms are not lifted and divided every year. Even in Athens, I consider them annuals because flowering the second year is reduced and the third year is non-existent.

**Cultivars:**
'Muralis' is similar to the species but more vigorous, growing to 3½′ tall.

## *Glandularia* see ***Verbena***

## *Glaucidium* (glow-sid-ee′ um) Glaucidiaceae

In my classes and at home, we have this game called GKQ, which stands for General Knowledge Question. I ask a silly GKQ, like "What is the capital of Canada?", and my students pray I don't call on them to answer. Here's one for all your gardening friends: What genus can be found in both the plant and animal kingdom? There are probably many, but *Glaucidium* is also the proper name for many species of pygmy owls, such as the northern pygmy owl of California. Useless, eh, but interesting.

Only a single species of *Glaucidium, G. palmatum*, exists in the plant kingdom, and is native to mountainous woods of Japan. Plants are highly sought after because of the large-lobed leaves (much like those of May-apple) and handsome peony-like flowers in the spring. The leaves are palmately lobed and the solitary terminal mauve to lilac flowers are about 2″ across. Sounds boring, I know, but they are quite beautiful when well grown.

They are difficult to establish in many areas because of their inability to perform well in warm climates and their need for protection from desiccating winds in the winter. If planted in a protected area, away from such drying winds, and planted in moist but not wet soils, they can be outstanding. They are quite marvelous in the Northeast and can do well in zones 4-6, and on the West Coast. A white form, var. *leucanthum*, (often listed as 'Album') occurs and is well worth looking for.

Propagate from seed or careful division in the spring.

## *Glaucium* (glow-kee′ um) Horned Poppy Papaveraceae

Approximately 25 species occur, many of them annual or biennial with a few true perennials. The genus comes from the Greek *glaukos*, meaning gray-green, referring to the foliage color. In fact, for most gardeners, the color of the foliage is the most handsome part of many of the species. The sap is yellow and the roots are poisonous. The striking hornlike seed pods have given rise to the common name.

The yellow horned poppy, *G. flavum*, is most common and bears 2″ wide golden yellow flowers over pinnately divided gray-green foliage. They are native to coasts of the British Isles, the Mediterranean and North Africa. The plants grow 2-3′ tall and become very lanky in areas of warm temperatures, although the foliage remains subtly colorful in the summer if soils are well drained. Drainage is important and plants are generally terrific on the West Coast, in the Northeast and in low rainfall climates such as Denver and parts of the Midwest.

Occasionally the biennial *G. corniculatum*, red horned poppy, is grown. Plants bear red, orange or yellow flowers, often with orange or red spots at the base. The gray-green leaves are similar to the previous species. Beautiful foliage, handsome flowers yet marginal performance unless cool and dry.

Easily propagated from seed at 65-70°F in humid conditions. No cold treatment is necessary.

***Globularia*** (glob-ew-lah′ ree-a) Globe Daisy Globulariaceae

About 20 species of this little-known group of plants occur, many of them on the line between herbaceous perennial and small shrub. Those which are useful are generally found in rock gardens where their evergreen foliage and low-growing habit are best taken advantage of. *G. cordifolia*, heart-leaved globe daisy, bears many 1″ diameter lavender-blue flower heads over flat mats of shiny leathery foliage on creeping woody stems. A white-flowered 'Alba', and a rose-pink 'Rosea' also occur. *G. repens* is similar but shorter and smaller. A more vigorous form occasionally seen is *G. tricosantha,* with long creeping stolons and stems which rise 5-7″ above the mats of evergreen foliage. The flower heads are larger but otherwise similar.

All species require full sun and excellent, well-drained soil. Success is more likely in a gritty area such as a rock garden than in the regular garden. Performance range is about zone 5-7 and zone 8 in the West. Propagate from seed, division or softwood cutting.

***Goniolimon*** (gone-ee′ o-lim-on) Tatarian Statice Plumbaginaceae

Only one species, *G. tataricum*, tatarian statice, has any bearing on gardeners in North America, although flower stems are common in florist shops everywhere. The plant had for years been part of *Limonium* (*L. tataricum*) but was changed sufficiently long enough that I am reluctantly changing as well.

Plants are similar to statice (*Limonium latifolium*, but are shorter (15-18″ tall) and have smaller flowers. The flowers appear in the summer and are whitish to light blue, but upon close inspection, ruby-red inner petals are evident. The rosette leaves are smooth and about 4-6″ long. Plants are not terribly ornamental but the flower stalks make excellent dried cut flowers. Plants are successfully grown in zones 4-8.

*Goniolimon* differs from *Limonium* by having hairy styles and capitate stigmas (compact cluster of stigmas). Propagate by seed, root cuttings or division.

**Cultivars**:

'Woodcreek' has off-white flowers in rounded inflorescences.

***Goodyera*** (gud-yer′ a) Rattlesnake-Plantain Orchidaceae

Resembling neither a rattlesnake nor a plantain, this group of terrestrial orchids is nevertheless a favorite for native plant enthusiasts. Of the approximately 30 species known, three or four are offered for sale through mail order sources. The common name is related to the network of white leaf veins common to many species, thought to resemble the skin of rattlesnakes and to be useful remedies for snake bites. The botanical name comes from the seventeenth-century English botanist, John Goodyer. The flowers are held in a slender spike and are relatively small, compared to other members of the orchid family.

*G. pubescens*, downy rattlesnake-plantain, is the most common species, extending from Newfoundland and Quebec, west to Minnesota and south to Arkansas and Georgia. The 3″ long leaves are produced in circles at the base of the stems and have an obvious white midrib with a network of white veins throughout the leaf blades. Dozens of small white flowers (about one-fifth of an inch long) form a dense cylindrical spike from late spring to late summer, depending on locale. The hairy plants grow about 12-18″ tall.

**Related Species:**

*G. oblongifolia* is native to Oregon and bears smaller, but equally handsome mottled leaves, and spikes with greenish white flowers.

*G. repens*, creeping rattlesnake-plantain, produces slender runners, thus its name, and small (about 2″ long) leaves often marked with dark rather than white veins, although white-netted forms are common in North America (var. *ophiodes*). The greenish white flowers are about one-eighth of an inch long and grow on one side of the flower stem only. Plants prefer cool damp woods and are more successful further north than the previous species.

## *Grindelia* (grin-del′ ee-a) Gum Plant Asteraceae

A group of plants largely ignored by North American gardeners, even though most of the 20 or so species are native to the western United States. If you're looking for garden information, an Internet search will lead to far more notes on the medicinal uses rather than the landscape uses of the genus. In fact, it is believed that grindelia acts to relax smooth muscles and thus is used in the treatment of asthma and bronchitis.

The fact that they are native does not mean that they are wonderful garden specimens and try as I may, I can find few listings of these plants anywhere in this country. Of course, it may be that nursery people have decided that a plant with flowers that look like dandelions may not enjoy a particularly robust market. The plants of all species are rather lax and unkempt and the daisies are always in various tones of yellow.

While at first glance the flowers look like dandelions, simply touching the buds or beneath the flower will quickly reveal the origin of the common name. They secrete a glutinous substance which is unmistakably sticky. They are native to open ground, along roadsides and dry, rocky places. Therefore, decent drainage and full sun are required for some success. In their native habitats, plants grow on very poor soils. If heavily fertilized, they explode.

All species are similar but *G. robusta* is a good vigorous native to start with while some of the brightest flowers may be found in the non-native *G. chiloense*. Probably hardy in zones 5-8. Worth a try, if for nothing more than a conversation piece.

Propagate from seed or cuttings after flowering.

**Gunnera** (gun-e′ ra) Gunnera Gunneraceae

The inclusion of *Gunnera* in a book meant for North American gardeners is pushing credibility a little; next thing you know I'll be telling you how wonderful *Meconopsis* is in American gardens. Although plants are grown successfully only in the most forgiving climates, adventurous gardeners are always pushing back the climatic envelope. Plants are offered for sale by West Coast growers in Oregon, Washington, and British Columbia. L.H. Bailey in his *Standard Cyclopedia of Horticulture* states that "with protection... may be grown in some of our northern states. He was likely referring to parts of northern California, coastal Oregon or Washington. Accounts of winter survival to around 15°F have been penned, therefore there may be some hope yet. Mind you, once you see some of these monsters, you might change your mind. The big species are huge, the smaller ones are relatively normal but spread without conscience.

While all this talk of winter survival is interesting, the necessity for cool summer climates, particularly in the evening, and moist roots, are even more important and often more difficult to provide. All species grow on stream banks, bogs and even in shallow water. If they are allowed to dry out, the leaves decline into crispy candy. The smaller species, such as *G. magellanica*, require even more consistent moisture than the larger ones such as *G. manicata* and *G. tinctoria*.

*G. manicata* is the most common and most highly prized member of the genus. The stems are thick and short and the colossal orbicular leaves arise from the basal crown. The prickly petioles are as tall as your father and the leaves may be 8-10′ across with great striking channelled veins. The small flowers are packed together in a large corn-on-the-cob-like spike at the crown in early summer. Altogether impressive, but perhaps not tucked into the back yard. Protect in winter with the fallen foliage and any other mulch available. Some crazy people actually grow them in a deep pit, allowing the leaves to surface in the summer, then bury the crown in said pit in the winter. Geez, get a life!

Plants of *Gunnera* may be raised from seed or divided with a newly sharpened chainsaw.

**Related Species:**

*G. hamiltonii* is a slow-growing, compact, mat-forming species. The slate green triangular leaves are evergreen. Native to Stewart Island off the coast of New Zealand where it is an endangered species.

*G. magellanica* has small (2″ across) dark green, kidney-shaped leaves and is my favorite swampy ground cover. Plants are stoloniferous, taking over moist areas in no time. However, they are likely a little less hardy than *G. manicata*, not that thousands of gardeners in the United States or Canada are in deep debate as to which species of *Gunnera* they should use in their Midwest garden.

*G. tinctoria* is similar but a little smaller and more compact than *G. manicata* with reddish flowers.

***Gymnocarpium*** (gim-no-kar′ pee-um) Oak Fern Polypodiaceae

A small group of North American ferns which includes the popular oak fern, *G. dryopteris* and the lesser-known Robert's fern, *G. robertianum*. Both are relatively small, less than 2′ tall, and bear similar sterile and fertile fronds. The fronds are in the shape of a triangle, the base of the frond of the oak fern being much wider than that of Robert's fern. They are both useful for shady moist conditions, although Robert's fern is more at home in limestone areas. They add a layered carpet effect to the shady garden and are a handsome deep green. Oak ferns are terrific deciduous plants with small fist-like fiddleheads emerging all summer.

Oak fern is native as far north as Greenland and winter hardiness is not a concern to most gardeners. However, heat tolerance is marginal south of zone 5, perhaps to zone 6 when conditions are shady and moist.

***Gypsophila*** (gyp-soff′ ill-a) Baby's Breath Caryophyllaceae

This genus contains plants that are almost indispensable to the florist as fillers for arrangements. If one thinks of the many bouquets sold each day across the world, the economic importance is quickly realized. Although the commercial production of baby's breath, *G. paniculata*, is big business in many countries, it is also a lovely garden plant. The name gypsophila comes from the Greek word *gypos*, meaning gypsum and *philos*, meaning friendship. This refers to its love of soils with a high pH, a soil condition that must be present if plants are to thrive. *G. elegans* is an excellent, easy-to-grow annual species for those wishing white or pink baby's breath-type flowers on much smaller plants.

Propagation of the perennial species may be accomplished by seed or terminal cuttings taken immediately after flowering, or by divisions.

Quick Reference to Gypsophila Species

| | Height (in.) | Flower color |
|---|---|---|
| *G. paniculata* | 24-36 | White, pink |
| *G. repens* | 4-8 | White, pink |

***-paniculata*** (pa nik-ew-lay′ ta) Baby's Breath 2-3′/3′
Summer White Europe, Northern Asia Zones 3-7

Common baby's breath is a graceful plant covered with wispy blooms in midsummer. The narrow, 4″ long gray-green leaves are opposite and provide a lovely contrast for the myriad branches of tiny white flowers. Over 1000 flowers may be produced in a single panicle. The more flowers that are picked, the more that will be produced. If the first flowers are cut back immediately upon fading, a second bloom occurs in the fall. Although they are most valued for cutting, the plants make excellent fillers to cover barren areas left by oriental poppies, common bleeding hearts or other plants which go dormant early. They should be grown in basic soil, full sun, and in areas of good drainage. In areas of south Florida (zone 9, 10), it is treated as an annual and replanted from November to January every year.

Gypsophila is a long-day plant and flowers faster when daylength is greater than 14 hours long, information only useful in year-round forcing of baby's breath for cut flowers. It is also interesting to note that when the leaves of *G. paniculata* are analyzed for various nutrients, the level of calcium is about five times higher than most other garden genera. Magnesium is also very high. This means that soils high in calcium and magnesium or additional applications of these elements are helpful to optimize growth. This is true for most species of *Gypsophila*, the exception being the pink-flowered *G. pacifica*, which appears to be the most tolerant of acid soils.

Many of the double-flowered cultivars have been grafted to single-flowered forms. Plants should be planted below the graft union to encourage rooting from the stem of the cultivar. Another means of propagation is by terminal cuttings. In the garden, plants develop large fleshy roots and should be left undisturbed. Tissue culture is becoming the most common means of commercial propagation of large numbers of clonal material.

**Cultivars:**

'Bristol Fairy' is the traditional double white-flowered baby's breath and grows about 2-2½′ tall. It was one of the standards for cut flowers, but has been replaced with newer cultivars.

'Compacta Plena' is a smaller (18″) form of 'Bristol Fairy' but not as floriferous or as double.

'Festival' is a seed-propagated series consisting of 'Festival Pink' and 'Festival White'. Both are relatively short (12-18″ tall) and bear both single and double flowers.

'Flamingo' has double pink flowers and is vigorous, attaining heights of 3-4 feet.

'Perfecta' has larger white double flowers and is more robust than 'Bristol Fairy', growing at least 3′ tall.

'Pink Fairy' is a pink version of 'Bristol Fairy', about 18″ tall.

'Pink Star' has bright pink flowers on 18″ tall, compact plants.

'Red Sea' bears double rose-pink flowers on 3-4′ tall stems.

'Rosy Veil', a hybrid between *G. paniculata* and *G. repens*, grows 12-18″ tall and bears handsome pale pink flowers.

'Single White' is as the name implies. About three feet tall.

'Snowflake' consists of pure white double flowers. Also sold as 'Double Snowflake'.

'Viette's Dwarf', from the excellent Andre Viette's Farm and Nursery in Virginia, is a dwarf form (about 12-18″ tall) with pinkish double flowers. Terrific for the small garden.

'Virgo' stands three to four feet tall and carries mostly double white flowers.

***-repens*** (ree' penz) Creeping Baby's Breath 4-8"/12"
Summer White Europe Zones 3-7

This wonderful little plant is most useful for edging or the front of the border. It tolerates heat but not wet feet. The ½-1" long leaves are grayer than those of *G. paniculata* and form a large mat in less than 2 years. The white to lilac flowers are not as delicate as those of its larger cousin but still cover the foliage with hundreds of blooms during the summer.

This species is not as fussy about pH as *G. paniculata* and plants do reasonably well in acid soils. Provided with good drainage and sunshine, they perform well as far south as zone 7b. Plants are excellent rock wall plants and cascade with abandon. This overlooked species should be used much more in American gardens.

Propagate by division in the summer or by seed. Seed is very small and should not be covered. Germination occurs in 3-4 weeks under warm (70-75°F ), humid conditions.

**Cultivars:**

'Alba' has clear white flowers.

'Bodgeri' produces sprays of double light pink flowers.

'Dorothy Teacher' bears blue-green leaves and soft pink flowers.

'Dubia' is compact with dark green leaves and red stems. The white flowers are flushed pink.

'Fratensis' has rich pink flowers.

'Jolien' has a pink hue to the white flowers, stands 18-22" tall, and bears yellow markings on the green leaves.

'Rosea' has pale pink flowers but is not as compact as 'Fratensis'.

'Silver Carpet' is about 1½' tall with white margins around the dark green narrow leaves. White flowers appear in late spring or early summer. A sport of 'Jolien'.

**Related Species:**

*G. aretoides* forms dense cushions consisting of small, smooth, fleshy leaves over which are produced single or few-flowered inflorescences of small white flowers. 'Caucasica' is even more dense, with handsome blue-green foliage.

*G. cerastoides* has the general appearance of *Cerastium*, snow-in-summer, with blue-green hairy foliage. The flowers have 2 styles rather than the five in *Cerastium* and are white to lilac with pink veins.

# H

***Hakonechloa*** (ho-kon-ee-klo′ a) Hakone Grass Poaceae

When I see a well-grown clump of Hakone grass, it stops me in my tracks. This terrific lime green grass adds beauty wherever it is planted, in a rock garden or the front of the border. Native to Japan, plants have been grown there for years but only in the last 15 years have they made inroads in American gardening. They are only about a foot tall with layers of 4-6″ long leaves, each about ½″ wide. The cascading foliage makes them wonderful candidates for hillsides or overflowing from containers. The only species, *H. macra*, spreads by stolons but is not invasive. The flowers occur in late summer but plants are essentially grown for the foliage and not the flowers.

Other than the obvious ornamental value, particularly of the cultivars, I find two attributes most appealing. The first is its tolerance for shade. In areas of partial shade, growing alongside hostas, plants are at their best. Full sun burns them up, however too much shade also causes the variegated forms to fade. The other characteristic is the handsome fall and winter color of the foliage, turning pinkish-red in the fall and bronze in the winter.

Unfortunately, plants are winter hardy only to about zone 7, perhaps zone 6 with protection, which limits their northern use. They also do poorly where summers are consistently warmer than 80°F, also somewhat limiting their southern use. They may be propagated by division, but are slow growers and need not be divided for many years.

**Cultivars:**

'Albo-aurea' has longitudinal stripes of cream and yellow along with narrow bands of green. It is less vibrant than 'Aureola' but still rather elegant.

'Albo-striata' is similar to the above but has white stripes on the leaves.

'Aureola' is the most available and the brightest of the listed cultivars. Known as golden variegated hakone, the leaves are golden yellow with thin stripes of green running the length of the leaf. They glow from a distance and draw viewers like a magnet. If variegated or golden plants are to your liking, this is a no-brainer. However, if variegated plants cause slight nausea, best to enjoy this in someone else's garden. They are less vigorous and slower growing than the species.

'Beni-kaze' may be someone's idea of a great plant but I don't see it. The leaves turn pink to magenta in the fall, but look like they are simply about to die. Otherwise the plant is green. Have at it, it might be the greatest thing since sliced bread.

'Stripe It Rich' has golden leaves with a white stripe, similar to 'Albo-striata'. The stripes may be a little wider and for sure, the plants are easier to find.

## *Hedychium* (he-dee′ chee-um) Ginger Lily Zingiberaceae

The ginger lilies consist of about 40 species, mostly native to the tropics. Those suitable for the garden are generally perennial south of zone 6, but all may be enjoyed as annuals and dug like dahlias in areas of cold winters. In the southern states, the two common perennial species are the orange or red-flowered *H. coccineum,* scarlet ginger, and the white-flowered *H. coronarium*, butterfly ginger. Both are strong, coarse plants with numerous reedlike stems that can grow 4-6′ tall. The leaves of *H. coccineum* are long and narrow, sessile and often with a well defined white midrib. The many orange or scarlet (occasionally red) flowers with their long projecting red stamens are held at the top of the stem in dense spikes. 'Tara' is a spectacular orange-flowered cultivar, growing about 4′ tall.

Plants of *H. coronarium* have broader leaves with wonderful white butterfly-like flowers with yellow centers. Not only are the flowers exquisite, they are sweetly fragrant. Less winter hardy, slightly more difficult to locate but very special.

Plants do best in full sun with plenty of water. In the Armitage garden, my plants are in far too much shade, and I must support them because of their tendency to stretch. In more sun, they are self-supporting. Propagate by division

**Additional Species:**

A number of other species and hybrids are also making their appearance in the era of the "tropical look" in gardens.

*H. gardnerianum*, Kahili ginger, bears clear yellow flowers with projecting red stamens. When I visited the extraordinary glasshouses at the Irish National Botanic Garden in Glasnevin, Dublin, this plant absolutely stopped the crowd. Plants are winter hardy only in the deep South but can be planted in areas where summers are warm and enjoyed all season, to be brought in during the winter.

*H. greenii*, salmon ginger, has unusually large flowers but a rather short flowering stem, so that the orange-red flowers appear to be almost on top of the leaves. The dark green foliage is also particularly handsome. The only drawbacks are that flowers have no fragrance and the plants are likely hardy only to zone 8.

*H. kewense* produces myriads of small salmon-peach flowers with orange throats. Plants grow up to 8′ tall. All species perform better in moist soils with partial shade to full sun.

*H. thrysiforme* is unusual in that it hails from Nepal and that it is a very late flowering species, perhaps not until late November. The flowers are white and the foliage is significantly wider than other species. Zone 7.

**Hybrids**:

Most are cold hardy to at least zone 7b, perhaps further north with a little mulching or snow cover.

'Daniel Weeks' has long-blooming fragrant flowers of yellow, each with a darker yellow center. Plants grow rapidly, and can fill in a large area within a couple of years. Zone 7b at least.

'Elisabeth' can grow 8-10′ tall in a single season! In late summer, she is topped with handsome, fragrant, peachy rose flowers. If nothing else, she is impressive.

'Gold Flame' bears white flowers with golden yellow centers on 5′ tall plants. The flowers are late, not appearing until the fall.

'Kanogie' comes from Ogie's nursery in southern Louisiana, and arose when one of Ogie's friends asked him to play. "Can Ogie come out and play?" became the basis of its name. Plants are 5-6′ tall and have orange-yellow flowers in late summer. Ogie's mother would be proud.

'Light Yellow' has pale yellow flowers on 6′ tall plants.

'Short White' is not exactly short, attaining heights of 5-6′. The fragrant flowers are white with a yellow throat.

'Tahitian Flame' produces beautifully fragrant apricot flowers on 5′ tall stems.

Tai series of gingers comes from intensive breeding work by my colleague Doyle Smittle of Tifton, Georgia. He has crossed various species and cultivars and come up with plants such as 'Tai Alpha' (4′, light yellow), 'Tai Conch Pink' (5′, salmon-peach), 'Tai Empress' (5′, salmon with a darker eye), 'Tai Golden Goddess' (4′, deep orange, eye-catching), 'Tai Mammoth' (6′, light yellow with darker yellow stripe), 'Tai Monarch' (4′, creamy yellow), 'Tai Pink Princess' (5′, pink), 'Tai Savannah' (5′, cream white), and 'Tai Sunlight' (5′, light yellow), with likely more yet to come.

## ***Hedysarum*** (he-dis′ a-rum) French Honeysuckle Papilionaceae

Perhaps because of the similarity in name to *Hedychium*, plants are often mixed up. In fact, this group of plants is not even remotely related to the gingers, being much more closely affiliated with the common bean and pea. Although plants are difficult to locate (I traced only one nursery who sold it online), the brilliantly red-flowered *H. coronarium*, French honeysuckle, may still be worth trying. The bluish green leaves are pinnately compound and the flowers are held above them. Plants grow 3-4′ tall and while they are self-supporting in full sun and cool areas, they are flip-floppy in climates with hot summers. They can be cut back after flowering to keep in bounds and in general, will be ugly if not trimmed up. The blood-red flowers are fragrant and when in bloom, are impossible to walk by. A white-flowered form, 'Alba', is also quite handsome, if not as brilliant. Plants are probably cold hardy to zone 5.

*H. multijugum* is larger in every aspect, and is essentially a shrub. The flowers occur on new wood and plants can be cut back hard in the spring, like butterfly bush, *Buddleia*. The purple flowers occur in the axils of the leaves as they develop.

Plants are best suited to the West Coast or the northern part of the country. Winter hardiness is not a problem; however, where summers are warm, they are untidy and require significant maintenance. Full sun and good drainage are necessary for best performance.

***Helenium*** (hel-ee′ ne-um) Sneezeweed Asteraceae

Of the 35-40 species, most are native to the United States, which is why it is difficult to understand why the genus is said to be named for Helen of Troy. That fine lady notwithstanding, the ornamental value of the genus is enjoyed worldwide. Plants were first introduced into Europe from North America in 1729 but around 1910, new cultivars started appearing ('Riverton Gem', 1909) in this country. However, the 1930s and 1940s saw a plethora of new cultivars from German and English breeders, many of which are still grown today.

The inflorescences are characterized by orange to yellow broad, fan-shaped ray flowers, each with three or more lobes at the end and a rather conspicuous dome of disc flowers. They are particularly useful for their extended blooming time. Most appear in mid to late summer and combine well with summer-flowering species lilies. They also flower naturally at about the same time as ragweed, thus being falsely accused of making one sneeze.

They are adaptable to many climates and tolerate cold temperatures and moist conditions, dry soils resulting in unsightly plants. Most gardeners, especially those in the South, should be ruthless with these plants, cutting them back hard in early to mid June to encourage branched plants, healthy foliage and many flowers. In general, sneezeweeds are large plants and require support to look their best. The leaves are alternate, often sessile, and have few or no serrations. They resemble *Helianthus*, sunflower, but differ by having a naked receptacle (the base of the flower) instead of pale bracts, long fruit rather than 4-angled fruit, and alternate basal leaves rather than opposite in *Helianthus*.

Propagation is by division or seed.

Quick Reference to Helenium Species

| | Height (ft.) | Flower color |
|---|---|---|
| *H. autumnale* | 3-5 | Yellow, orange, mahogany |
| *H. hoopesii* | 2-4 | Yellow |

***-autumnale*** (ow-tum-nah′ lee) Common Sneezeweed 2½-5′/3′
Late Summer Yellow, Mahogany Eastern North America Zones 3-8

These large plants are best used at the back of the garden or in the center of island beds. The 4-6″ long serrated leaves are lance shaped and the base of each leaf runs down the stem, thus being winged (decurrent). The 2-3″ wide yellow flowers usually have brown to black centers. Flowering starts in early to mid summer and continues for 8-10 weeks. Plants should be fertilized sparingly or tall spindly growth results.

Heleniums do well in gardens from zone 3 to zone 8, but as night temperatures rise, plants require additional support and flowers become smaller. Cut plants back hard in early to mid June to encourage better flowering in late summer and fall. Regardless of location, the dense foliage should be partially cut back after flowering to keep disease and insect pressure minimized. Plant in full sun and keep well watered.

Propagate by division every 2-3 years or by seed. The seed may be cooled for 3-4 weeks but this is not always necessary. Germination is not particularly uniform but should occur within 4 weeks after cooling.

**Cultivars:**

The many cultivars, each claiming to be bigger and better than the others, are probably hybrids between *H. autumnale*, *H. bigelovii*, and *H. hoopesii*. However, as I look at all the similar heleniums out there, perhaps it is time to say enough is enough. In the last edition I stated "What today's gardeners need, however, are smaller, not larger, cultivars. Only 'Crimson Beauty', 'Mardi Gras' and 'Wyndley' are sufficiently short and sturdy for today's smaller gardens." Help has come in the last 10 years and a few more cultivars are now available to fit smaller garden spaces.

'Adios' bears drooping red ray flowers with yellow edges. The cone is handsome and obvious.

'Butterpat' is still one of the best of the yellow heleniums. It stands 4-5′ tall and the horizontal petals are attached about two-thirds the way down the central disc.

'Bruno' bears bronze-red flowers on 3-4′ tall stems in late summer.

'Brilliant' is covered with hundreds of bronze flowers in late summer.

'Can Can' bears flowers with an even tawny yellow coloring. Otherwise quite similar to 'Zimbelstern'.

'Chelsey' grows 2-3′ tall and bears red flowers with bright yellow flecking in the summer. This plant has received a good deal of attention in the British Isles and may be introduced here soon. Plants were named for Chelsey Shippers, the granddaughter of the breeder, Nic Geerlings. In a related story, Terry Lloyd, a British news reporter, was killed March 22, 2003 in Basra when the car he was traveling in was attacked. In appreciation of the work carried out by the Red Cross to bring his body home for burial, his daughter, Chelsey Lloyd, began campaigning to raise funds for the charity. With the Geerlings family's blessing, and the support of Darwin PlantSpotters and retailers of the plant, *Helenium* 'Chelsey' has been adopted by Chelsey Lloyd as a part of her fundraising activities.

'Chipperfield Orange' has large reddish orange flowers with yellow bases. Big and bold.

'Coppelia' flowers earlier than many of the fall forms and bears large coppery orange flowers on sturdy three foot tall stems.

'Crimson Beauty' grows only 2-3′ tall and bears mahogany brown ray flowers with a dull brownish center.

'Double Trouble' has more petals (ray flowers) than most other selections. The sterile yellow flowers still have a center cone, but not as obvious. Perhaps "Semi Double Trouble' may be a better description. Originally bred as a cut flower therefore strong stems and a height of almost 3′ can be expected.

'Dunkle Pracht' defies pronunciation but is a brilliant red cultivar growing up to six feet tall. The centers are delineated by a whitish circle formed by white markings at the base of each ray flower.

'El Dorado' is 3-4′ tall with large golden flowers. Plants flower in midsummer.

'Fiesta' is a hybrid between 'Koningstiger' and 'Rubinkuppel' and produces copper flowers with a wide yellow band on the base of each ray flower. Plants are about 3′ tall.

'Gartensonne' is one of the tallest forms, up to 6′ tall. Plants bear primrose yellow flowers with reddish brown centers.

'Helena Red' and 'Helena Gold' have been colorful additions to gardens, growing only about 3′ tall.

'Kanaria' is 2-3′ tall with bright yellow single flowers. Cutting them back in late spring may provide more flowers later on.

'Lambada' is only 2-3′ tall and produces bright red flowers with a golden disc.

'Mardi Gras' is only about 2½-3′ tall and has performed well in the heat of the UGA gardens and has been outstanding around the country. Plants are self-supporting. The flowers are orange with a hint of red. Highly recommended.

'Moerheim Beauty' bears brownish red petals around a black disc on 3-4′ high stems.

'Potter's Wheel' has flowers with dark brown cones and crimson rays, each with a touch of gold at the tip.

'Pumilum Magnificum' is similar to 'Butterpat' but has softer yellow flowers. The name 'Pumilum' means dwarf but this cultivar reaches heights of 5 feet.

'Ring of Fire' has tawny red flowers, with a band of yellow close to the disc and one at the tips. Plants are easily 4′ tall.

'Riverton Beauty' has golden yellow ray flowers around bronze centers. Plants are 3½-4′ tall.

'Rotgold' (Red-Gold) has been around for some time. Plants grow 4′ tall and bear red and gold flowers. Usually raised from seed.

'Rubinzwerg' is translated as 'Dwarf Red' and is only 2-3′ tall with dark red flowers.

'Rubrum' produces beautiful 2-3″ wide mahogany flowers on 6′ tall plants.

'Sahin's Early Flowerer' is a red-flowering form with streaks of yellow and a brown cone. This was an Award of Merit plant (RHS) in 2001 and flowers look similar to those of 'Mardi Gras'. Plants developed by K. Sahin Seed of the Netherlands.

'Sunshine' is interesting in that the golden petals (ray flowers) are flecked with crimson. Unique.

'Sun Sphere' is 3-4′ tall and bears many butter yellow flowers.

'Waltraut' has golden brown flowers on 3′ tall plants.

'Wyndley' produces 2-3″ diameter handsome coppery brown flowers and is only 2-3′ tall.

'Zimbelstern' has yellow ray flowers surrounding a red and yellow bicolor disc.

***-hoopesii*** (hoop-ess′ ee-eye) | Western Sneezeweed | 2-4′/2′
Early Summer | Yellow | Rocky Mountains | Zones 3-7

The 2″ diameter yellow-orange flowers are held in a 5-20 flowered inflorescence and are similar to those of the previous species. The basal gray-green leaves are up to one foot long and entire (no teeth). The stem leaves are smaller and sessile and are not decurrent like those of *H. autumnale*. The wingless stems are fuzzy (tomentose) when young but become smooth later. The ray flowers are more straplike and occur earlier than *H. autumnale*. Although this is a shorter species, support may still be required. Plant in full sun and provide sufficient water to keep roots consistently moist. It is not as tolerant of hot summers as the previous species and does not do as well in the South. However, both this and *H. autumnale* make excellent cut flowers. Plants grow on meadows and moist slopes and along streams throughout the southern half of the Sierra Nevada and east to New Mexico and Wyoming. Plants have been known to cause poisoning in grazing sheep.

Propagate similar to *H. autumnale*.

**Related Species:**

*H. bigelovii*, bigelow sneezeweed, is native to the Pacific Northwest and bears solitary 2″ wide yellow daisies, composed mainly of the wide yellow-brown centers. Plants are 2-4′ tall. 'The Bishop' should be classified here, but may also be seen as a cultivar of *H. autumnale*. Plants produce clean yellow flowers on 2-2½′ tall stems. It is one of the more dwarf forms available.

## ***Helianthemum*** (hee-lee-an′ the-mum) Sun-Rose Cistaceae

Of the approximately 120 species, one of them, *H. nummularium*, is recognized as a useful garden plant in the United States and Canada. The sun-roses are actually evergreen shrubs, much like *Artemisia* and *Caryopteris*, with woody stems and persistent foliage. Five-petaled, 1-2″ diameter, single rose-like flowers are produced in numerous colors over green to gray-green foliage. Plants are particularly useful as edgings in gardens or along walkways. They are not winter hardy north of zone 5 or warm hardy south of zone 7. The most important factor in successful culture is to provide rocky, sandy, or any well-drained soil. Otherwise they will rot before you can say *Helianthemum nummularium*.

***-nummularium*** (num-ew-lah′ ree-um) | Common Sun-Rose | 1-2′/2′
Summer | Various | Mediterranean | Zones 5-7

When I travel in the Northeast or overseas and see these plants tumbling over rocks and walls and alight in pastel pinks or yellows, I want to go home and build a three-acre rock garden to accommodate them. However, as rock gardens are not particularly popular in Georgia and my garden is in the shade, I accept the fact that they look better in someone else's garden. This low-growing subshrub with opposite 1-2″ long evergreen gray-green leaves is the finest of the genus. The mature plant is usually wider than tall and bears many 1-2″ wide flowers in loose 4-12 flowered,

1-sided terminal inflorescences. Where well-sited, the flowers cover the plants and totally obscure the foliage.

I grew several in my heavy red clay soil, amended with compost. They were spectacular in the spring and early summer but rain and humidity during the summer killed the plants. However, on moving to sharper ground, I enjoyed moderate success with the cultivar 'Mutabile' for about three years. While areas of high humidity may not be sun-rose country, there are no excuses for not trying these further north and west. In the Northwest, they should be as common as grass. There is little doubt that most cultivars do better in cool summers and mild winters.

Plant in full sun in the North and partial shade in the South. They have few soil requirements other than excellent drainage. After flowering, shear plants back to encourage new growth. Propagate by division every 4-5 years or from 1-2″ long softwood cuttings taken in the spring.

**Cultivars:**

Most of the plants available are hybrids of *H. nummularium*, *H. appenninum* and others. Well over 100 hybrids have been named, but usually fewer than a dozen are available through North American nurseries.

'Annabel' bears double pink flowers with deep green foliage.

'Ben Heckla', one of approximately seventeen cultivars which start with "Ben", bears orange flowers with a red eye.

'Ben More' provides deep orange flowers with dark centers on 8″tall plants.

'Ben Nevis' has terrific tawny-gold flowers borne over green foliage.

'Ben Ledi' has deep rose-red flowers.

'Broughton' ('Broughton Double Primrose') produces dozens of primrose yellow double flowers. Outstanding.

'Buttercup' is 6-10″ tall and bears clear, clean yellow flowers.

'Cerise Queen' produces double red blooms. Although the double flowers detract from the charm of the singles, the flowers are more persistent.

'Cheviot' has silver leaves, salmon- to peach-colored flowers, each with a yellow center.

'Dazzler' has dark red flowers over green foliage.

'Fireball' has deep red double flowers.

'Fire Dragon' bears coppery-red flowers over gray-green foliage in early summer.

'Georgeham' has handsome rose-pink flowers with a white base and yellow stamens.

'Henfield Brilliant' has green foliage covered with terra cotta flowers.

'Jubilee' has double yellow flowers.

'Mutabile' is an interesting cultivar whose flowers open light pink then change to lilac, and finally to white. This variety is difficult to place in a specific color scheme but has proven somewhat heat tolerant.

'Orange Sunrise' has golden orange flowers with a dark orange central ring.

'Raspberry Ripple' has gray-green foliage and raspberry red and white flowers. Plants are less than 10-12″ tall.

'Red Orient' ('Supreme') produces single deep red flowers.

'Rice Creek Rose', named by Betty Ann Addison of Rice Creek Nursery in southeast Minnesota, is about 10″ tall with pink flowers. A good rebloomer.
'Rose Queen' bears double rose-pink flowers. This and 'Cerise Queen' seem to retain their color in the heat.
'Snowball' bears double white flowers on 3-6″ tall plants.
'Spotlight' bears gray foliage and bright cherry-coral flowers. Well-named.
'St. Mary's' has large white flowers over green leaves.
'Sudbury Gem' produces handsome rose-pink flowers over green foliage.
'Wisley Pink', a lovely muted pink-flowering plant with gray-green leaves, is one of my favorites. Anyone who has visited Edinburgh's Royal Botanic Garden in June will remember this plant draped over rocks at the top of the rock garden like pink icing on a resplendent cake.
'Wisley Primrose' is a light yellow-flowered form similar in habit to 'Wisley Pink'.
'Wisley White' is the white-flowered sister.

**Related Species:**

*H. apenninum*, apennine sun-rose, is closely related but not as winter hardy (to zone 6 with protection). It is taller (18″) than *H. nummularium* and has long, arching branches bearing clusters of 1-2″ diameter white flowers with a yellow blotch at the base of the petals. Cultural requirements are similar to the previous species. var. *roseum* has clear pink flowers.

*H. croceum* is a compact shrub growing about 15″ tall with many yellow to apricot flowers borne in early summer. Native to southern Europe and North Africa, plants are only cold hardy to about zone 7.

*H. scoparium* are less than a foot tall with bright yellow flowers. Plants tolerate a great deal more heat than other species. The foliage is more green than gray-green. Probably useful in zones 7-9.

## ***Helianthus*** (hee-lee-an′ thus) Sunflower Asteraceae

The 150 species include ornamental plants as well as commercially important food and oil crops. The annual sunflower (*H. annuus*) yields seeds with high oil content, and the tuberous roots of *H. tuberosum* (Jerusalem artichoke) are a valuable food crop in many areas of the world and an obnoxious weed in many areas of this country. In the 1990s, the commercial world went mad over the ornamental value of sunflowers. Sunflowers became the Michael Jordan of the flower world with t-shirts, aprons, hats, cookware, place settings and anything else that can be sold sporting brightly adorned portraits of the sunflower. Perhaps that was its fifteen minutes of fame, however as Kansans have long known, it may simply be a wonderful flower.

The perennial species are much less well known than the annuals, but are easy to grow in full sun and tolerate a wide range of soil types. All species are relatively tall and require considerable room. The flowers are always yellow and the leaves are usually rough and coarse. Most flower in late summer and fall and all provide excellent sources of food for birds.

Propagate by division after flowering or by seed.

Quick Reference to Helianthus Species

| | Height (ft.) | Color of disc flowers | Flower time |
|---|---|---|---|
| *H. angustifolius* | 5-7 | Brown, purple | Fall |
| *H. giganteus* | 7-10 | Yellow | Fall |
| *H. mollis* | 4-5 | Yellow | Late Summer |
| *H.* x *multiflorus* | 3-5 | Yellowish | Late Summer |

***-angustifolius*** (an-gus-ti-fo′ lee-us) Swamp Sunflower 5-7′/4′
Fall Yellow Eastern United States Zones 5-9

This fall-flowering plant is as beautiful as ever, particularly in the South, but it has lost some of its luster because plants were overused in the 1990s, and its aggressive tendencies became tiring. The 5-7″ long narrow, entire leaves are mostly alternate, although opposite at the base of the unbranched stem. Leaves are stiffly hairy but not as coarse as those of other species. In the fall, the plants are smothered with 2-3″ wide bright yellow flowers which light up the garden at a time when other plants are going downhill. Each flower has 10-18 narrow petals surrounding a dark brownish to purplish center. When placed in full sun, the plants are strong and self-supporting, however, in partial shade, they are more open, less floriferous and taller. In my partially shaded garden, they grew over 10′ tall and stems broke in high winds. The same plants, in the sunny Horticulture Gardens, grew no more than 6′ tall and required no support. If they must be planted in partial shade, pinch plants once or twice in early summer to encourage branching, but understand that they will not be as good. They are heavy feeders, require abundant moisture, and should be well fertilized if grown in full sun. The main problem is that they can be aggressive, to the point of being thugs. Dozens of plantlets are produced around the base. If not removed, the garden will consist of little else within 2-3 years.

Propagate by divisions, cuttings, or seeds.

**Cultivars:**

'First Light' is quite wonderful. Plants are certainly shorter than the species, topping out at 3-4′ in height. It is more compact in every way, and still bears delightful sunflowers in late fall. Bred by the excellent plantsman Keith Hammett of Auckland, New Zealand.

'Gold Lace' is about 5′ tall with golden yellow flowers.

'Low Down' is the shortest form, attaining a full-bodied one foot in height. Flowers and foliage are similar, but smaller. It is as if someone sprayed the species with pixie dust. In the Gardens at UGA, we enjoyed it for a year or so, but it did not have the staying power of the species. That is certainly not a bad thing, but the vigor was somewhat suspect.

'Table Mountain' is similar to Low Down', but the breeders claim it is even shorter. I have not trialed it yet so I cannot comment on the vigor. Give any of these short ones a go, they are certainly cute and bouncy.

***-giganteus*** (gi-gan-tee' us) | Giant Sunflower | 7-10'/4'
Fall | Yellow | North America | Zones 5-9

Many years ago, I received a plant of unknown identity from Kim Hawks, formerly of Niche Gardens in Chapel Hill, North Carolina, and was chased down for its proper name by anyone who saw it in flower. The species was big, grew at least 6' tall in full sun, and had alternate, shallowly toothed slightly hairy leaves. The many yellow flowers are 1-2" across, borne in a panicle-like inflorescence, and appear in late summer to fall. It was a monster, a wonderful monster to be sure. It has since gone to sunflower heaven.

This is a good plant to hide or soften obstacles or corners. Our plant in the Horticulture Gardens effectively softens the end of our 5' tall fence. Only one is needed.

**Cultivars:**

'Marc's Apollo' was bred by the fine plantsman Marc Richardson at Goodness Grows Nursery in Lexington, Georgia. Plants, which are crosses between 'Lemon Queen' (see related species) and *H. giganteus*, easily grow 7' tall. They put on a spectacular display in late fall. Place a 2-3' tall plant at the base as the bottom leaves often fall off by the fall.

'Sheila's Sunshine' became the name of the aforementioned plant sent to us by Kim Hawks. The flowers are a soft pastel yellow and is much easier on the eyes than the species itself. Named after Sheila Goff, an herb grower and gardening friend of Ms. Hawks.

***-mollis*** (mall' is) | Downy Sunflower | 3-5'/3'
Summer | Yellow | Midwestern States | Zones 4-8

I have fallen in love with this American native plant in the last few years even though it can be somewhat thuggish. The reason I enjoy it is not for the large handsome sunflowers; I can see those on many other such plants, but because of the wonderful gray felty foliage. It makes me think of a lamb's ear plant that simply happens to be 4' tall.

In the spring and early summer, the plants make handsome clumps of felt, with many strong stems. Once the flower buds form, however, the additional weight may cause the stems to bend. This may be a bigger problem in the South than the Midwest, but regardless, this is no shrinking violet. The flowers are sunflower-like, and fine enough, but I am thinking that I would just as soon stop all growth by late July, and suspend the plants as they are then. Plants will spread, not like swamp sunflower, but there will be more the third year than the first, to be sure.

Plant in full sun, support if necessary. Propagate by division in the spring.

**-x *multiflorus*** (mul-tee-flo' rus) | Many-flowered Sunflower | 3-5'/3'
Late Summer | Yellow | Hybrid | Zones 4-8

This hybrid, *H. annuus* x *H. decapetalus*, has become far more popular in European gardens than in North American gardens. Many cultivars have been bred but for some reason, few seem to have caught on in this country. Plants have hairy, coarse leaves, up to 10″ long, 4-6″ wide and oval to heart shaped. They are usually 4-5′ tall but may reach heights of 7′ or more. The 3-5″ diameter flowers may be single or double and are usually yellow or yellow-orange. Flowers persist for 4-6 weeks and continue well into the fall. One of the problems I have noticed is that leaves degenerate after flowering and plants can look bedraggled. If you notice the same thing, cut back soon thereafter. In warm climates, fungi are more of a problem on the hybrid than on other species. Place in full sun and provide copious water and fertilizer.

Propagate by division or cuttings similar to *H. angustifolius*.

**Cultivars:**

'Capenoch Star' has single lemon-yellow flowers that are a little cooler to the eye than the others.

'Flore-pleno' is a 5′ plant with fully double (little or no center) bright yellow flowers. This is by far the most commonly available cultivar sold by nurseries.

'Loddon Gold' bears fully double, 5-6″ diameter bright yellow flowers and grows 4½-6′ tall.

'Maximus' has large golden flowers, 'Maximus Flore Pleno' is similar but with double flowers.

'Meteor' grows about 5′ tall with deep gold semi-double flowers.

'Morning Sun' has lovely single yellow flowers with large yellowish brown centers and grows 5′ tall.

'Soleil d'Or' (Golden Sun') was selected in 1889 and has semi-double flowers with thin quill-like ray flowers.

**Related Species and Hybrids:**

*H. atrorubens*, darkeye sunflower, grows 2-5′ tall with thin, opposite leaves and branched stems. Two inch wide flowers consist of deep yellow rays surrounding a dark red disc. A good southern wildflower for well-drained areas.

*H. decapetalus*, thinleaf sunflower, has rough sharply serrated thin leaves above which are borne 3″ diameter single light yellow flowers. The 4-6′ tall plants are covered with flowers in late summer and always make a handsome display. They are an important parent of *H.* x *multiflorus* but not as showy.

*H. maximilianii*, Maximilian sunflower, differs by having spikelike inflorescences rather than the paniculate inflorescence of *H. giganteus*. The leaves are usually folded lengthwise and usually entire. Also big and tall. All sunflowers make useful cut flowers and this species was heralded by Dr. John Dole at North Carolina State University.

*H. resinosus*, hairy sunflower, native throughout the southeastern United States, grows 6-8′ tall with densely hairy stems. The leaves are dotted, as if with resin, and sessile. Flowers with yellow central discs and golden yellow ray flowers are produced in August and September.

*H. salicifolius*, willowleaf sunflower, is much more prevalent in the Midwest and Plains states than in the East. Plants have much narrower leaves and smoother stems than *H. angustifolius*. The very narrow leaves that are constantly being produced at

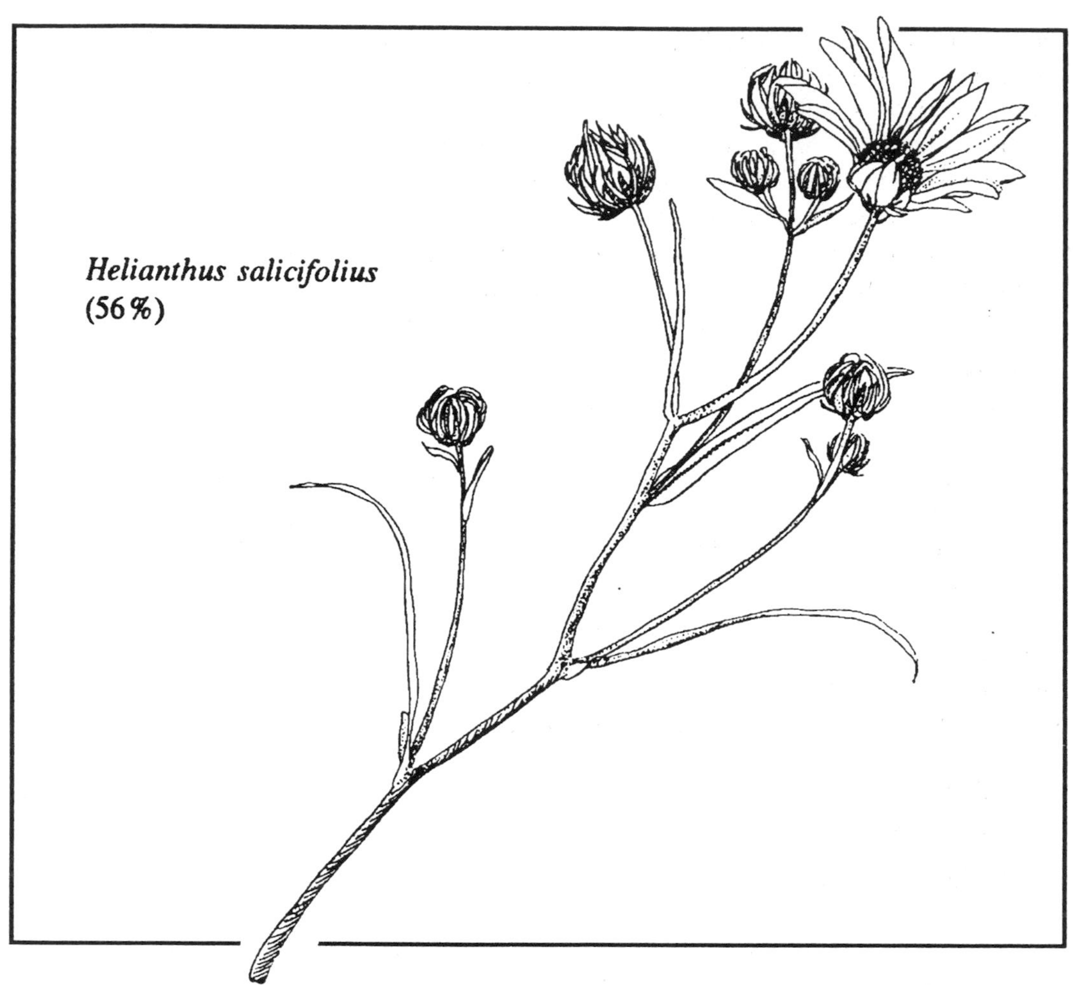

*Helianthus salicifolius*
(56%)

the tops of the plants look like bands of green silk, a much different look than the swamp sunflower. Otherwise the habit and flower color are similar. Not only are they more handsome, they are more drought tolerant, and more winter hardy (zone 5) than swamp sunflower.

'Lemon Queen' is a spectacular cultivar whose parentage is still being debated. It is believed that they arose as natural hybrids between *H. pauciflorus* var. *subrhomboideus* (prairie sunflower) and *H. tuberosus* (Jerusalem artichoke). Regardless, plants bear hundreds of 2½″ wide pale yellow flowers on 5-7′ tall plants. The parents should tell you that they will move around. They may not be invasive, but they definitely will be aggressive.

*H. schweinitzii* is a terrific plant but unfortunately available only in local areas. The narrow lanceolate leaves grow on 5′ tall stems and 1-2″ wide yellow flowers are borne in late summer. The best part of this species is its non-aggressive nature, and plants simply get better, not weedy. Native from Georgia to Alabama and North Carolina. Plant in full sun.

*Helianthus* × *multiflorus* 'Morning Sun' (72%)

***Helictotrichon*** (he-lik-toe-tri′ kon) Blue Oat Grass Poaceae

Grown primarily for the blueness of the foliage, *H. sempervirens* is one of about 100 species in this genus of handsome grasses. Plants are tufted with distinctly ribbed leaves and are overtopped with showy, arching one-sided flower heads. Plants are about 18″ tall without flowers, then top out at 2-3′ when in flower. The flower heads are brownish and dry to a golden wheat color in the fall.

Plants look good in a group, but occasionally a single plant may make a handsome specimen. They perform best in full sun with good air circulation and fertile, well-drained soil, in zones 4-7, and in zone 8 on the West Coast. Plants are cool-season grasses and due to their dislike of hot, humid summers, are not good choices for Southern gardens.

**Cultivars:**

'Sapphire' ('Sapphire Fountains') grows 2-3′ tall and differs from the species by having slightly wider leaf blades, better blue color and, according to the Missouri Botanical Garden, "better disease resistance (especially to rust) and better tolerance for heat and humidity."

***Heliopsis*** (hee-lee-op′ sis) Heliopsis Asteraceae

This genus closely resembles the true sunflower (*Helianthus*) and the literal translation of the name is "sun-like". About 12 species are known, many of which are rather weedy but those used in cultivation have a much smaller habit than *Helianthus* cultivars and flower in midsummer. In fact, this is a far better genus for gardens than most of the sunflowers. The leaves are simple, rough and opposite. Plants should be grown in full sun and fertilized sparingly.

***-helianthoides*** (hee-lee-anth-oi′ deez) Sunflower Heliopsis 3-6′/4′
Summer Yellow, Orange North America Zones 3-9

This short-lived perennial has smooth, occasionally hairy above, 4-5″ long serrated leaves and can grow up to 4′ tall. The 2-3″ diameter daisylike flowers consist of pale yellow ray flowers surrounding brownish yellow central discs. The species itself is weedy, too tall, and is not floriferous enough to be a good garden plant. However, many cultivars that have subsp. *scabra*, often referred to as *H. scabra*, in the parentage, are much better and more popular in today's gardens. They all flower in shades of yellow and in fact, there is not much difference among them. Plants flower in late summer to early fall.

Plant in full sun in well-drained soil. Support is necessary, particularly if plants are shaded. All cultivars should be divided every 2-3 years. The species and some cultivars come true from seed and are easily germinated in a warm (70-75°F ), humid area.

**Cultivars:**

'Ballerina' ('Ballet Dancer') is about 2′ tall with 2-3″ wide bright yellow ray flowers surrounding a brown center. An excellent cut flower choice.

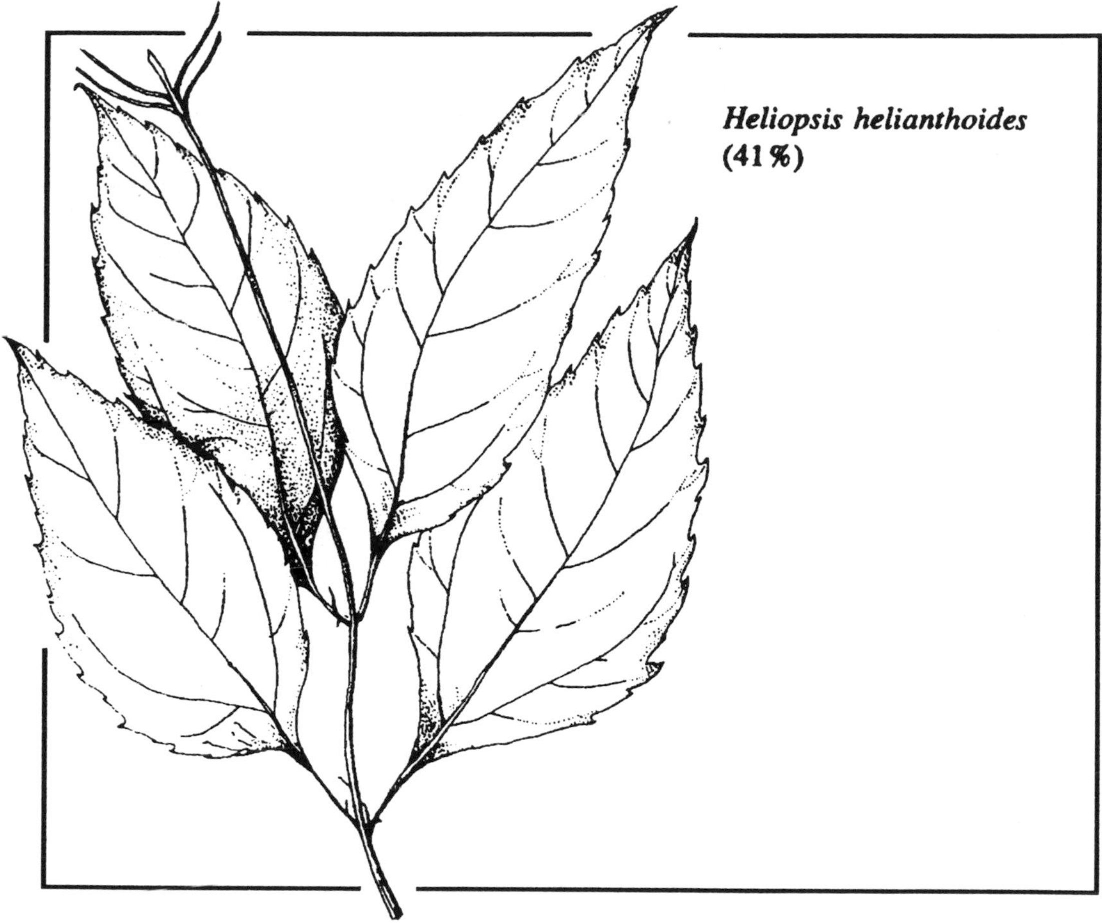

***Heliopsis helianthoides* (41%)**

'Golden Plume' is a floriferous, double-flowered 3-3½' tall cultivar. This is the best of the double-flowered heliopsis.

'Goldgreenheart' has interesting if somewhat gaudy chrome-yellow double flowers surrounding a slightly green center.

'Goldspitze' produces 2-3" diameter gold-yellow flowers on 3' tall plants.

'Concave Mirror' has dark orange concave semi-double flower heads.

'Incomparabilis' bears 3" wide semi-double flowers with warm orange overlapping petals.

'Karat' is about 3' tall with bright yellow flowers.

'Loraine Sunshine' has turned many heads because of its beautiful green and white foliage. Leaves are more striped with green rather than variegated. The flowers are orange. I have seen some beautiful plants here and there but in many cases the variegation was unstable and the plant vigor was poor, resulting in disappointment after a couple of years. As with many variegated plants, the leaf patterns are more stable in the northern states. Plants were discovered by Loraine Mark in Rhinelander, Wisconsin.

'Light of Loddon' is similar to 'Karat' but grows 4' tall. Both may need support, particularly in the South.

'Patula' is 2½-3′ tall with golden orange semi-double flowers.

'Prairie Sunset', introduced by Neil Diboll of Prairie Nursery, Westfield, Wisconsin, bears good-looking yellow flowers with wine-red discs in the summer and fall. This is a fine plant.

'Summer Sun' is a delightful 2-3′ tall plant with 3″ diameter bright yellow flowers. This is also an excellent cultivar for warm climates as it tolerates heat well and does not get too leggy. Plants flower for 10-12 weeks and come fairly true from seed.

'Summer Nights' is the best cultivar since 'Summer Sun' to come our way. Introduced by Dale Hendricks of North Creek Nurseries in Landenberg, Pennsylvania, this plant looks good everywhere I travel. The yellow flowers have a slightly darker disc. *Heliopsis* is not known for the showy stems, but this one bears black stems from the time it emerges from the ground. An excellent plant for the South as well as the North.

'Toe Dancer' bears semi-double golden yellow flowers on 4′ tall stems.

'Tuscan Sun' is the shortest of the group, blooming when only about 18" tall. Similarly beautiful single yellow flowers are produced in summer.

**Related Species:**

subsp. *scabra* (*H. scabra*) is characterized by sandpapery (scabrous) stems and leaves. Plants grow 2-4′ tall and 2-3′ wide. The upper leaves are often entire while the basal leaves may be toothed. The ray flowers are orange-yellow and the center varies from greenish yellow to brown. Leaves should be cut back in the South after flowering. This is more important as a parent of a number of cultivars, rather than a plant sought after by gardeners.

## *Helleborus* (hell-e-bor′ us) Hellebore Ranunculaceae

Unless hardiness is an issue, no garden should be without hellebores. Period! The budding and blooming of hellebores herald the dawn of a new season. Strolling by a clump of hellebores on the edge of a path or on a hillside where flowers nod their greetings, the stroller knows that spring has sprung and all is right with the world. The genus consists of about 15 species, all with some ornamental value and in addition, dozens of selections have been raised that combine the better characteristics of their parents. We have come a long way and we are using more hellebores than ever before. Many of the better garden centers and mail order nurseries now offer a choice of species, although only two are grown to any extent. All prefer moist soils and shaded conditions. I am certainly not the only one who thinks the world should know more about this great plant; *Helleborus* x *hybridus* was selected as the Perennial Plant of the Year in 2005 by the Perennial Plant Association.

Most species have evergreen, divided leathery leaves. The margins are coarsely serrated or even spiny, depending on species. The nodding flowers are white, rose, green, or purple. The sepals are the showy part of the flower, the petals reduced to inconspicuous nectaries. Part of their charm is the early flowering time, resulting in such neat names as Christmas rose and Lenten rose. Because they flower when the weather is cool, they have an exceptionally long bloom time, often flowering from

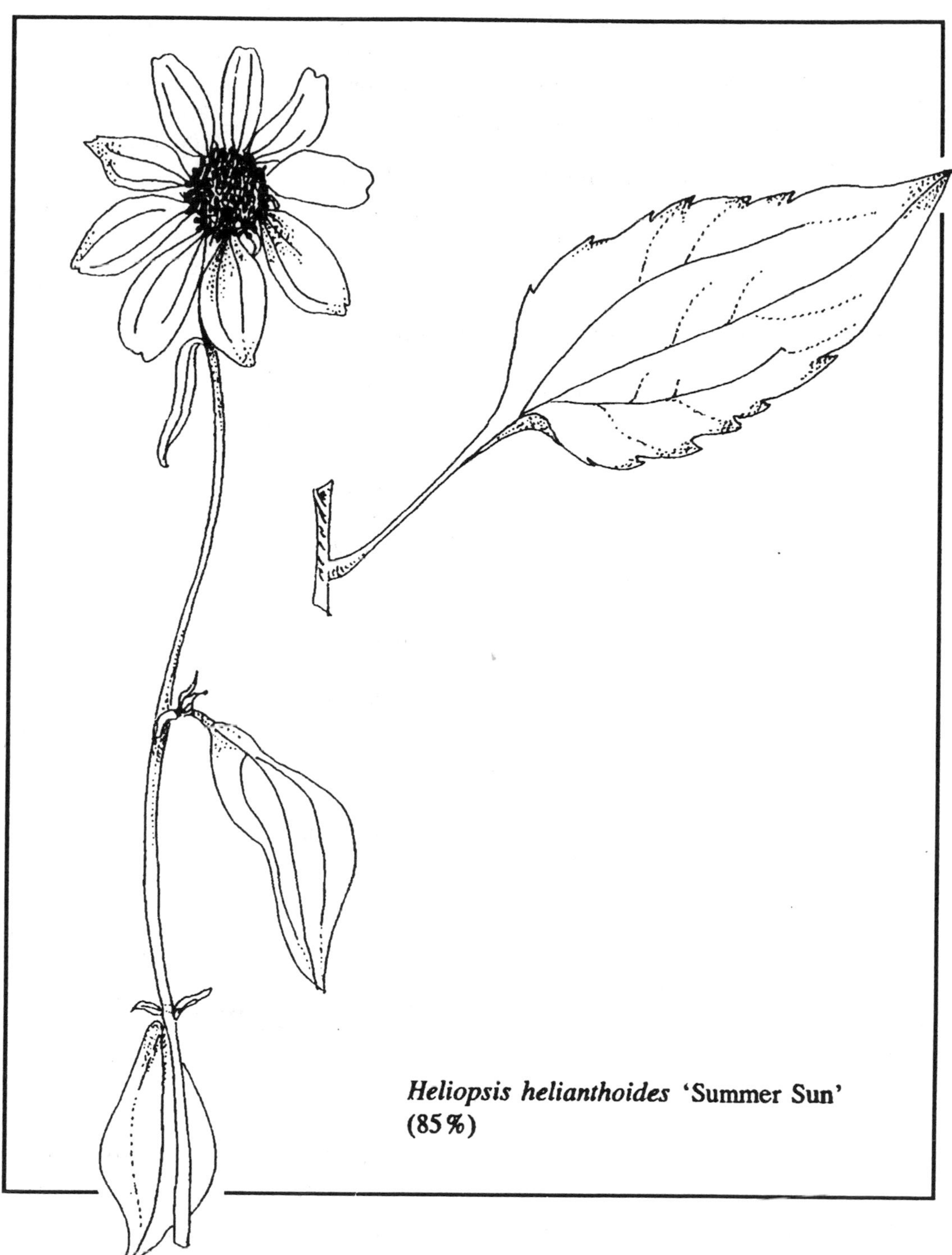

*Heliopsis helianthoides* 'Summer Sun' (85%)

February to May. Fruit consists of 3-10 sessile follicles containing numerous seeds. Seed may be collected when follicles are papery and dry.

Teaching my students plant identification is not always easy. However, telling hellebore species apart is simple enough that even my most dim-witted rookies can get it. The garden species may be divided into two categories. The first group includes those with a leafy stem (caulescent) and flowers carried at the ends of the stems, such as *H. argutifolius*, Corsican hellebore, *H.lividus*, and *H. foetidus*, bearsfoot hellebore. In the second group are those whose leaves and flowers rise directly from the rootstock, i.e. stemless (acaulescent). These includes *H. niger*, Christmas rose, and *H. orientalis*, Lenten rose.

The desire to introduce new hellebores continues more fervently than ever. Strains with double flowers or upright flowers are available: hybrids incorporating silver leaves, marbled leaves and variegated foliage are well established through mail order outlets but we are also now seeing them on retail shelves. The future of this great genus will only get better.

Propagation from seed is difficult and exacting. Sow seeds in well-drained medium and place at 75-80°F for 7 weeks. Move tray to approximately 32°F for 8 weeks and then raise temperatures slowly to 40°F. Germination should commence at that temperature after which soil temperature may be elevated to 50-55°F until germination is complete. This technique is used for many members of the Ranunculaceae such as *Actaea* and *Clematis*. Mother Nature, however, has no such difficulties and is much more efficient than gardeners. Seedlings of most species may be found under the plant litter at the base of 2-3 year-old plants. Gentle removal and subsequent transplanting provide abundant plants for the spring garden. If necessary, roots of mature plants may also be divided in the spring but large showy clumps will result only if plants remain undisturbed.

<u>Quick Reference to Helleborus Species</u>

| | Height (in.) | Flower color | Number of leaflets | Stem (Yes/ No) |
|---|---|---|---|---|
| *H. argutifolius* | 18-24 | Light green | 3 | Yes |
| *H. foetidus* | 18-24 | Light green | 7-10 | Yes |
| *H. niger* | 12-18 | White | 7-9 | No |
| *H. orientalis* | 15-18 | White, plum | 7-9 | No |

***-argutifolius*** (ar-gew-ti-fo' lee-us) Corsican Hellebore 18-24"/18"
Early Spring Greenish Corsica, Sardinia Zones 6-8

Plants have become more available and thus more popular in the last 5 years. They bear green flowers but should be grown as much for the foliage as for the flowers. The rough foliage is unique in that there are only 3 leaflets, and they are gray-green. The individual leaflets are thick and bear rather sharp teeth. The many green, cupped flowers have a tinge of white and are held well enough above the foliage so as not to be lost, but are not as decorative as those of *H. niger* or *H. orientalis*. It is a stout, bushy plant with thick stems, which after a few years may become large and almost like a short hedge. In the Northwest I have seen clumps easily 4′ tall, in southern Ontario, 2–3′ is not uncommon. In warm climates, they may need some support. I use some stout sticks I find in the garden to prop the stem up if needed. Plants tolerate more sun than others. Without doubt, the coarsest of the species, but this in no way diminishes its appeal. *H. foetidus* and *H. orientalis* are easier to establish, but this one is certainly fun to grow.

Many seeds are produced and if mulch is placed at the base of the plant, seedlings will arise. Division may be accomplished in spring or fall.

**Cultivars:**

'Janet Starnes' is almost 2′ tall and produces speckled leaves. If that is your thing, you may fall in love with this selection. The speckling gives the foliage a silvery appearance.

'Pacific Frost' has white-spotted foliage with a little pink and cream as well. Plants grow about 20″ tall and bear green flowers.

'Silver Lace' produces silvery-gray foliage and is quite handsome. The plants are 18-22″ tall and bear large greenish flowers.

***-foetidus*** (fe-ti′ dus) Bearsfoot Hellebore 18-24″/18″
Early Spring Light Green Western, Southern Europe Zones 5-9

The evergreen foliage is deeply divided into 5-9 narrow dark green leaflets. The first year, stems and leaves are produced. In the second year, several branched stems bear many cup-shaped, light green nodding flowers often rimmed with purple. The specific name, *foetidus*, means fetid or bad smelling and refers to the flowers, although one must stick his nose in the flowers to get a good whiff. However, it is not a flower one brings in the kitchen to brighten the day. The plant does best in zones 6-7, and struggles with the heat in areas further south. Partial shade and well-drained soils are the only requirements for establishment. It develops quickly and can be as ornamental as *H. orientalis*. I visited the lovely garden of Mrs. Weezie Smith in Birmingham, Alabama (zone 7b), in late February. Dozens of plants of *H. foetidus* shone beneath her shade trees, *H. niger* was flourishing, and *H. orientalis* welcomed me at every corner. Who says February has no charm? Plants are not as persistent as the easier *H. orientalis*, usually succumbing to fungal problems (leaf spot, *Coniothyrium hellebori*) after about three years, especially in humid climates.

Plants self-seed readily and may be left in place or moved carefully. If plants are many years old, they may be separated, but that is a tricky operation at best. Plants resent being disturbed and if lifted for division, the parent plants may take considerable time to re-establish. New cultivars have recently become reasonably available.

**Cultivars:**

'Chedglow' has golden foliage in the spring, fading during the summer. Flowers are similar to other other forms of bearsfoot hellebore. Plants arose from Chedglow Nursery, UK.

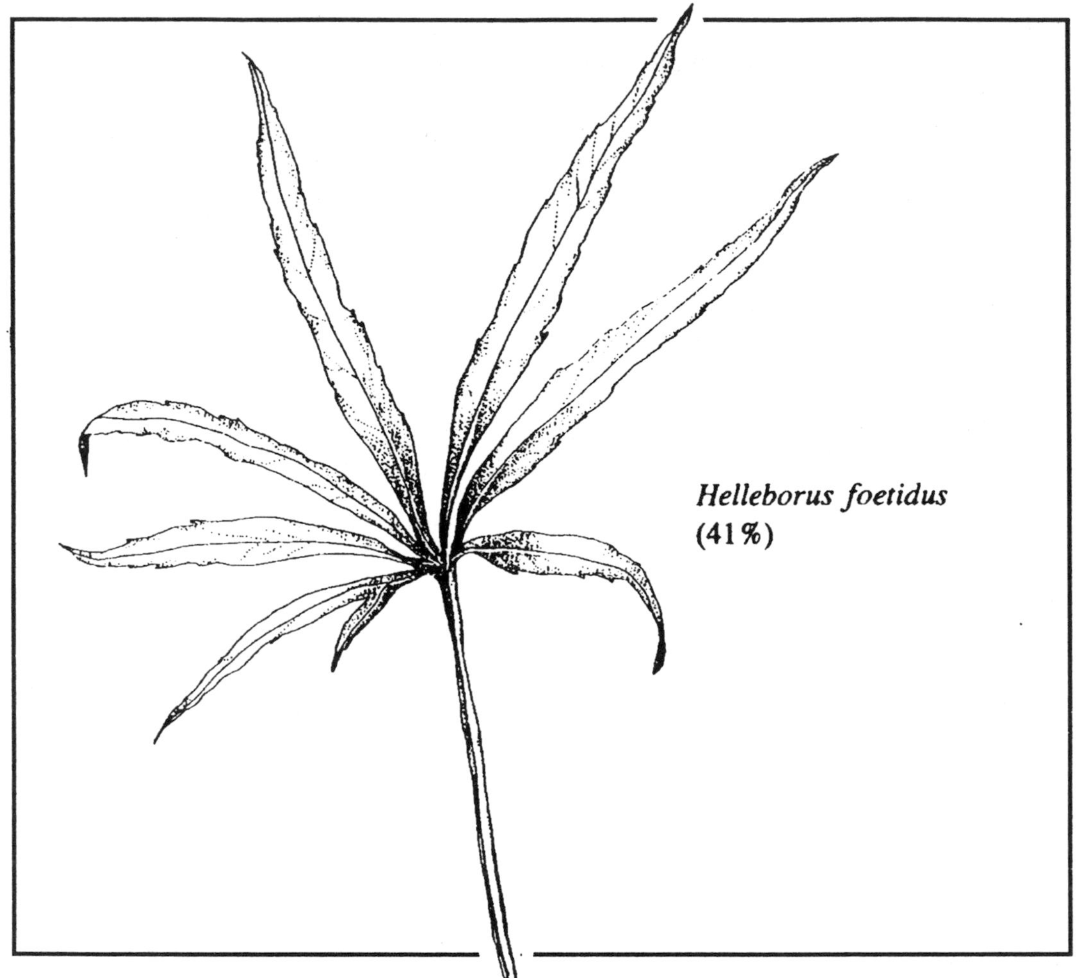

*Helleborus foetidus*
**(41%)**

'Frenchie' was introduced by Barry Glick of Sunshine Farms in Renick, West Virginia. Plants have narrower leaflets and a red tinge to the tips as they unfold.

'Golden Showers' has green leaves with lots of random gold streaking throughout. Eye-catching, particularly in spring when the variegation is most obvious. Introduced by Plants Delight Nursery, Raleigh, North Carolina.

'Krenitsky' comes from Tom Krenitsky of Chapel Hill, North Carolina, also via Plant Delights Nursery. Plants produce deep green serrated foliage and are topped with lime-green flowers in early spring.

'Piccadilly' arose from a chance seedling at the wonderful Piccadilly Farm in Bishop, Georgia. Plants are very dark green with a bit of silver, and may have a touch of pink in the leaf axils. The flowers are whitish green.

'Sopron' is a large plant, selected from a population near Sopron, Hungary. The foliage has more gray in it and the flowers are a little larger most other selections.

'Wesker Flisk' was one of the first cultivars introduced. Plants have long narrow leaflets with stems, petioles and inflorescence branches tinted red. The yellow-green flowers have a slight maroon tinge.

***-niger*** (nigh′ ger) | Christmas Rose | 12-18″/12″
Winter, Early Spring | White | Europe, West Asia | Zones 3-8

The saucer-shaped, 2½″ wide flowers bear yellow stamens which contrast well with the clear white petal-like sepals. Flowers are held on red-spotted peduncles. The flowers are usually solitary, but I have seen many plants with 2-3 flowers per flower stem. Tremendous variation in flower color, size, and earliness to flower occurs, particularly because most of the commercially available plants are seed propagated. Although flowering may occur at Christmas in sheltered locations, this seldom happens and plants are usually at their best in early spring. The dark green leaves are divided into 7-9 leaf segments, the margins toothed only towards the apex of each segment. Plants are more difficult to establish than *H. foetidus* or *H. orientalis*, being less tolerant of extremes of climate, including heat, cold, drought and wet feet. In one garden, plants may die at every corner, yet down the road, the microclimate may be to the plants' liking. It is not the species one should choose if success is important, but, my, they can be beautiful. Consistent moisture, shade and slightly basic soils are necessary.

**Cultivars:**

'Altiflorus' has long-stalked, larger and more distinctly toothed leaves than the species. The petioles, peduncles (flower stalks) and the 2-3″ wide flowers are tinged with red spots.

'Blackthorn Strain' arose from the efforts of a single individual, Mr. Robbie White, at Blackthorn Nursery in Hampshire, England. When I escorted 25 keen gardeners to his nursery in March, no one could refrain from marveling at the beauty of the hybrid. Each plant results from a controlled cross (that is, the pollen of one parent is introduced by hand to the flowers of the maternal parent). This F1 hybrid has large white flowers suffused with pink, each flower on stout stems close to the foliage. Absolutely breathtaking. The best part is knowing that each plant results from a controlled cross, and is not going to be a hit and miss seedling. Unfortunately, obtaining such plants is next to impossible, but that does not mean they do not exist.

subsp. *guttatus* is similar in habit and has white to cream flowers with red-purple spots inside.

'Louis Cobbett' has strong pink suffusion on the flowers.

subsp. *macranthus* has small spiny leaves and white flowers tinged with rose held well above the foliage. The peduncle is not purple spotted as in *H. niger*.

'Maximus' is someone's selection of plants with especially large flowers. The definition of 'large" is a slippery slope in the plant world, since flower size is also greatly affected by the environment in which the plants are grown. Anyway, size isn't everything.

'Potter's Wheel' is vegetatively propagated and has been selected for its large rounded white flowers with a distinct green eye. This is still probably the best-known clone in the hellebore world, but others are rapidly surpassing it.

'White Magic' has clean white flowers and a compact habit.

**Related Hybrids of *H. niger*:**

*H.* x *ericsmithii*, once known as *H.* x *nigristern*, is a cross between *H. niger* and *H.* x *sternii*. (This stuff is crazy, isn't it? I am exhausted simply trying to describe the hybrids, let alone actually uncover the crosses). The offspring are variable but bear large white flowers, tinged pink-brown or green on the outside. The foliage is often marbled and stems are purplish. 'Pink Beauty' has silvery gray leaves and flower buds with pink backs, which open to a dusky cream color. Quite beautiful. 'Sunmarble' comes from Barry Glick of Sunshine Farm and Gardens in Renick, West Virginia. Plants show handsome marbling on large leathery evergreen leaves and produce long lasting, sterile 3-4′ wide white flowers.

Ivory Prince™, whose true name is 'Walheliver', a name that the world will totally ignore, is outstanding. Probably involving *H. niger* and *H.* x *ericsmithii*, the compact silver- to gray-leaved plants produce dozens of off-white upright flowers that stand well above the foliage. It is nice to be able to admire the flowers without getting on hands and knees. I have been most impressed with this plant, one of the very few clonal offerings that can support the demand.

*H.* x *nigercors* is a cross between *H. argutifolius* and *H. niger*. The flowers of the latter have been combined with the profusion of the former to produce large white flowers with a hint of green. Plants are sterile and persist for months. They bear coarse, jagged-edge foliage and "Christmas rose" type flowers at the end of short stems. 'Alabaster' is a cultivar similar to the above description that resulted from a cross between *H. argutifolius* and *H. niger* 'Potter's Wheel' by Elizabeth Strangman of Washfield Nursery in England. I cannot find this offered in the United States. 'Green Heron' from Heronswood Nursery, produces dark green obviously veined leaves and outward facing creamy white flowers. A winner for sure. 'White Beauty' has silvery gray leaves and off-white flowers that stand above the foliage. Quite similar to newer offerings like Ivory Prince™ (which see).

***-orientalis*** (o-ree-en-tah′ lis) Lenten Rose 15-18″/15″
Early Spring White, Purple Greece, Asia Minor Zones 4-9
(syn. *H.* x *hybridus*)

Even the plants are getting dizzy with all the head-spinning taxonomic arguments. Some experts claim that most cultivars and strains of this species should be called *H.* x *hybridus*. They may be correct, for surely there are additional parents in some of those cultivars. You can call them whatever you like but, until all the experts agree, I am not muddying the water further, and have elected to maintain the "orientalis" moniker.

Regardless, this group of plants provides some of the finest low-growing, early-flowering flora in cultivation, so easy that no garden should be without several clumps. The 8-12″ wide, leathery dark green leaves are divided into 7-9 serrated segments and remain attractive all year, particularly in areas of mild winters. The nodding 3-4″ wide flowers last for 8-10 weeks and vary from white to plum-colored and are often spotted inside. Similar to *H. niger*, there is a great deal of variation in color and size of flowers.

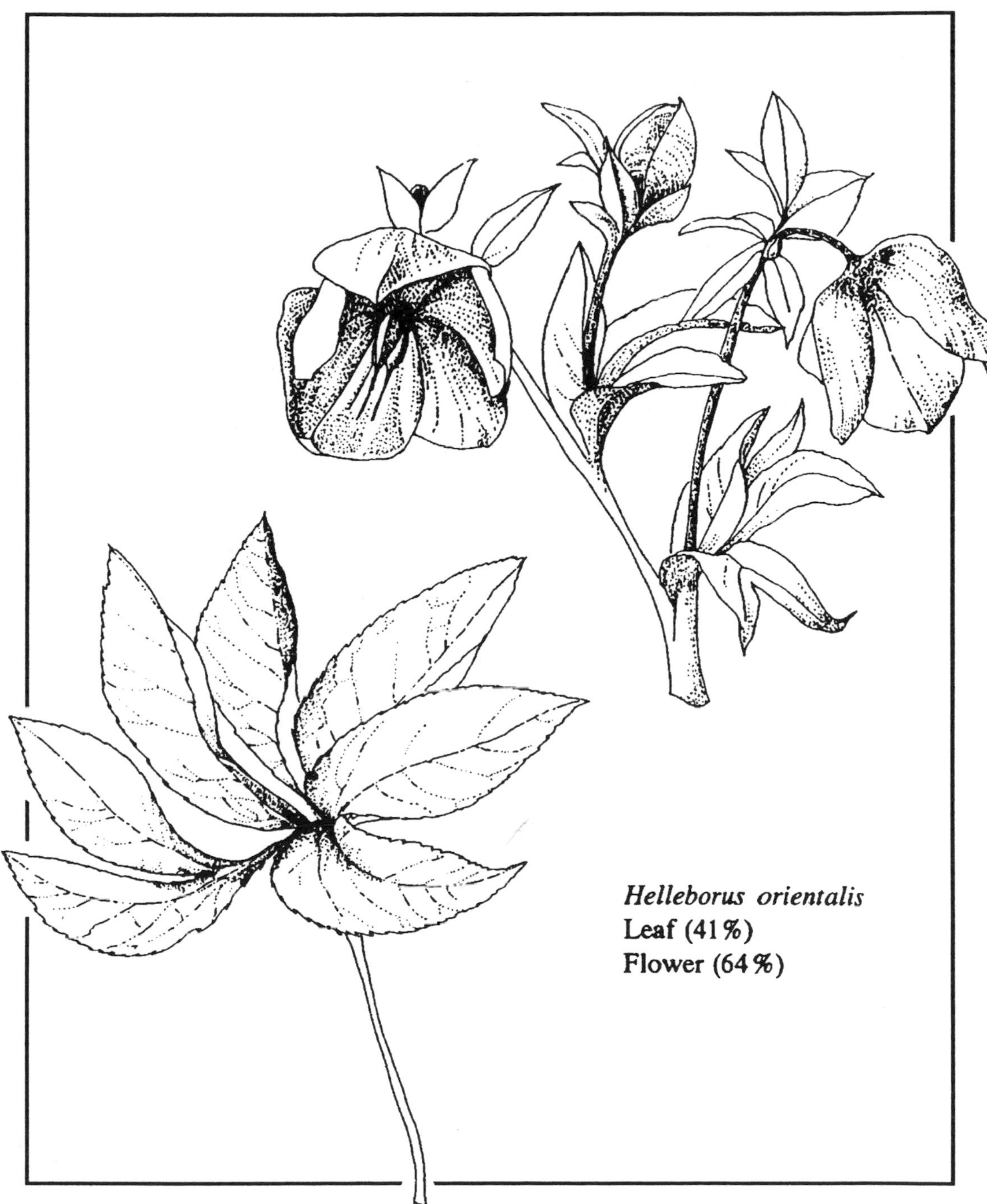

*Helleborus orientalis*
**Leaf (41%)**
**Flower (64%)**

Without doubt, like a chick struggling to break out of the egg, the patience of breeders and growers will soon be paying dividends to gardeners. New cultivars of hellebores have teased gardeners for years; we have seen marvelous pictures in books and occasionally seen some new colors in gardens, but we have never had the opportunity to purchase many new clones of hellebores. Ballard, Chatto, White,

Smith and Strangman are English breeders who have raised handsome cultivars, and have been joined by breeders from North America like Elsley, Tyler, Hinkley, Heims, Culp, Glick, O'Byrne and many others, as well as plantsmen from New Zealand and Europe. The pictures of yellow, black, red and double-flowered forms have caused instant Pavlovian salivation in avid helleborists. It is easy enough to find a better hellebore, either with improved habit or different flower color or size, but the difficulty has always been the ability to propagate enough plants of the clone to offer to the public.

Full-scale vegetative propagation is difficult so most of the plants offered are seedlings. However, if the parents are isolated, sufficient uniformity of the offspring results in new varieties. Clonal propagation is a reality and the hellebore world is exploding as we speak. However, if patience is a virtue, gardeners looking for new hellebore cultivars must indeed be righteous.

In almost all parts of the country, the Lenten rose is the easiest species to grow, requiring only shade and occasional water. Fertilizing in early spring as the new leaves emerge results in rapid growth of the clump. Clumps establish quickly and plants can be increased rapidly from the numerous seedlings produced in any rich soil. For best flower viewing, cut back the old leaves in early spring. The new leaves, which are also quite handsome as the emerge, will quickly fill in.

**Cultivars:**

As stated above, numerous crosses and selections have been made, and may appear as this strain or that, but many more F1 hybrids and clones are being tissue-cultured and becoming available as single colors. However, Hellebore Fever is upon us, and we are quickly getting too many with too few differences, resulting in a dilution of their uniqueness. Look for many of these new offerings listed under *H.* x *hybridus*.

Ballerina Mix is one of Marietta O'Bryne's introductions, producing double flowers in many colors, including single colors and flowers painted with other hues as well. Marietta has bred many hellebores and gardeners are the richer for her. Other mixes from Marietta include Brushstrokes Mix, with single flowers, and Mellow Yellow Mix with colors ranging from light yellow to deep gold and a few apricot flavors for good measure.

Brandywine strain came from the talented work of Robert Culp, who has been working with hellebores in the Brandywine region of Pennsylvania for many years. The vigorous plants provide a mix of colors and shapes, all single.

'Cosmos' was selected by Beth Chatto of the UK, and has white flowers with heavy spotting of pink on the sepals. Plants are almost impossible to find in the United States or Canada.

Double Queen series from Elizabeth Strangman in England has mostly double flowers in an array of colors. Lots of double-flowered strains are available today, a marked departure from just a few years ago. None is 100% double, so purchase as many as you can to ensure a good percentage of doubles.

Double Vision is a mix of double flowers edged in coral, white or pink. Plants stand about 16″ tall.

'Filigree Pink' was developed by Chris Hansen, one of America's excellent plantsmen, and has light pink flowers with darker pink venation.

'Gold Finch' comes from Dan Hinkley of Washington State, and produces single, gold-colored flowers with pink markings in the center.

'Grand Burgundy', from Chris Hansen, has large outward-facing flowers and dark green foliage.

'Hansen's Shamrock' provides bright green, rounded flowers.

Heronswood strain consists of double-flowered forms mostly in shades of pink, however, hues of cream, purple, rose and lilac are also produced.

'Kingston Cardinal', also from Mr. Hinkley, consistently produces large, rosy red double flowers.

'Party Dress' hybrids resulted from the breeding work of Mr. White at Blackthorn Nursery and flowers are consistently double. The nectaries of the normal flower have been transformed into a pinwheel appearance so the resulting flowers look more like a semi-double than the convoluted appearance of a double mum or daffodil. Seed set is poor, therefore numbers are difficult to build up. The flowers are generally pink to purple, occasionally a few creams and primroses result. Numerous other double strains have resulted.

Pine Knot strain, from Pine Knot Farms in Virginia, has produced a vigorous group of hybrids, many with pink, purple or white flowers.

'Pink Picotee' produces large, off-white flowers with pink venation. An introduction from Ernie and Marietta O'Byrne of Northwest Garden Nursery in Eugene, Oregon.

'Regal Ruffles Double Mix' includes light and dark flowers that are semi-double to fully double. An O'Byrne introduction.

Royal Heritage strain is the result of work of John Elsley of South Carolina. The plants vary in flower color, but are vigorous and among the best growers I have tried.

Slate strain produces a combination of dusky to deep purple single flowers.

'Snow Bunting' bears clean white flowers that face out and up for easier viewing. They remind me of the flowers of Christmas rose.

Southern Belles strain, from Pine Knot Farms, consists mainly of double-flowered forms.

Sunshine strain is the result of intense selection by Barry Glick of Sunshine Farm and Garden in Renick, West Virginia. Plants are vigorous and flowers may be found in many colors. Barry has focused on hellebores for some time and is always adding new ones to the mix.

**Related Species:**

*H. atrorubens* (sometimes listed as var. *atrorubens*) is much darker than the type and usually bears 9 leaf segments. The rich plum-purple flowers are some of the first to open (early January in my garden). It is winter hardy only to zone 5 or 6.

*H. lividus* has similar flowers but is only 12-18″ tall, and has smooth-edged dark green leaves with obvious netted white veins and often, entire margins. It is less winter hardy than *H. argutifolius* and difficult to grow in most areas of the country. All leaves arise from the flowering stem and plants often die after fruiting. 'Pink Marble' is a hybrid with a good deal of *H. lividius* in its system. Its vigor makes it a more choice plant, hardy to about zone 7.

*H. odorus* is only about 1′ tall with 3-5 lobed basal leaves with coarsely serrated margins. Three to five saucer-shaped greenish flowers are produced in early spring.

*H. olympicus* (sometimes listed as var. *olympicus*) has 5-7 leaflets and many spreading white flowers with a green tinge.

*H.* x *sternii* is a handsome hybrid between *H. argutifolius* and *H. lividus*. The foliage is more gray-green than other species, with obscure silver-white veins. The margins are usually rather spiny, however, leaves are occasionally entire. The flowers are lime-green to green with purplish flush. A fair number of cultivars have arisen, a few in just the last 5 years. Blackthorn hybrids, from Blackthorn Nursery in Hampshire, England, have gray-green foliage and are more compact than the original hybrid. 'Broughton Beauty' was one of the first selections of this cross and was more compact than the hybrid but still a large specimen plant. Plants combine the greater size of *H. argutifolius* with the color of *H. lividus* and are truly handsome where well grown. 'Broughton Beauty' has a compact habit, with flowers suffused rose and the foliage tainted a rosy purple. 'Eagle Crest' arose from Eagle Crest Nursery in Oregon and bears silvery foliage and many greenish flowers. 'Fire and Ice' is "interesting" if you like speckled leaves. Not my cup of tea, but may be quite popular for those into the spider mite look. Plants are hardy from zones 6 to 8.

*H. torquatus* produces dark flowers on the ends of leafy stems. The plants are deciduous, disappearing totally over the winter. Seldom used in America, it is a useful parent in the breeding of dark-flowered hybrids. 'Dido' is a double lime-green form. 'Wolverton Strain' is a seed-propagated strain raised by Blackthorn Nursery and consists of many pastel colors.

*H. viridis*, green hellebore, is an overlooked species of delicate beauty. It is only 15-18″ tall, has 7-11 very narrow, light green leaflets and about 1″ wide drooping green flowers. Much more subtle than most other hellebores, and well worth trying. subsp. *occidentalis* has wider, coarser margins with more obvious serrations. Not as good as the species.

## ***Helonias*** (hel-own-ee′ as) Swamp-pink Liliaceae

An evergreen plant growing in swamps and bogs (*helos* translates to swamp). *H. bullata* is the only species in the monotypic genus. The basal leaves are about a foot long and grow in a leathery tuft. Dense racemes consisting of many pink flowers with blue stamens occur in the spring. The flower stem is hollow but strong and 2-3′ tall. In the garden, plants require copious moisture to succeed, otherwise they languish and never rise to their full potential. I have seen plants flourishing in gardens in North Carolina and as far north as the Montreal Botanic Gardens.

This is a wonderful plant for the same boggy areas needed for many *Primula*, *Ligularia* and *Petasites*. If you have a wet area, find some seed of *Helonias* or plants from a native plant center and beautify the area.

***Hemerocallis*** (hem-er-o-kal′ lis) Daylily Liliaceae

The modern daylily is a mainstay of gardens and landscapes all over the world, and in North America, it is as ubiquitous as grass. This is particularly true of commercial installations designed for public buildings, parks, entrances to malls and condominiums where toughness and longevity are so important. In few other genera has hybridization proceeded at such a rapid pace. Daylily breeders have done a magnificent job in bringing outstanding cultivars to the gardener so that today almost any size, color and shape is available for the daylilyer.

The clamor for larger flowers, more colors, more flowers, and greater vigor results in the introduction of dozens of cultivars every year. In the first edition (1989), I mentioned that the American Hemerocallis Society had registered approximately 20,000 cultivars and that I figured it would increase by about 500 a year. As I sit here in August, 2007, I see there are 58,469 cultivars starting with 'A Babbling Baboon's Bouncing Babies' (really!) registered in 2003, which just beat out 'A Bauble for Bilbo' (2001) for alphabetical honors, and finishing 11,694 pages later with 'Zyzanie' (1990). I wasn't even close. Don't ever go to a daylily lecture, especially if the speaker begins with the letter A. Although, if you're suffering from insomnia, this may not be such a bad idea.

To try to bring some organization of the chaos of cultivars, a number of categories of daylilies have been artificially constructed by the American Hemerocallis Society. Plants are classified into evergreen, semi-evergreen and dormant. They are also arranged according to height of flower into dwarf, below 6″, ('Buffy's Doll', 'Eenie Weenie'); low, 1-2′, ('Catherine Woodbury', 'Joan Senior', 'Stella d'Oro'); medium, 2-3′; tall, over 3′ tall, ('Marion Vaughan', 'Whichford'). Flower diameter, flower color and pattern and flowering season are also convenient categories for the hybrids. The wave of new cultivars is certainly not all bad and the new cultivars' popularity speaks for itself. The greater use of *H. minor* and *H. nana* to instill genetic dwarfness in hybrids has also opened up a new era of daylily use that has become the norm for landscape plantings. There is little doubt that the breeders have done a tremendous service to horticulture by transforming some of the rather bland species into the wonderful flower colors and excellent garden performers found in today's hybrids.

Unfortunately, in our pursuit of hybrid hipness, the old folks got left behind. The parents of the hybrids, i.e. the species, have been forgotten. In looking through garden catalogs, there are pages and pages of descriptions and lovely pictures of daylily hybrids, each seemingly better than the last. It is, in fact, uncommon to see anything but hybrids being offered. The dark brown buds of *H. dumortieri*, the fragrant, dense cluster of *H. middendorffii* flowers and the fragrant old-fashioned lemon-lily, *H. lilio-asphodelus* are becoming more difficult to locate. Some species like *H. citrina* with their lemon-colored fragrant flowers arising from long pointed buds, provide nocturnal flowers that open in late afternoon and remain abloom all night.

It is still nice to see the common tawny daylily, *H. fulva*, having escaped from old gardens, with orange flowers shining alongside roadways and in wild meadows. They are everywhere! Recently visiting family outside Montreal in July, I could not believe the number of orange daylilies in gardens throughout Quebec, which alongside white hydrangeas, pink mallow and monarda were the backbones of small gardens. Perhaps hybrids aren't the cat's pajamas after all.

Daylilies have well-known culinary and medical properties. As treatment for abscesses of the breast, dropsy, bowel disorders and as an anti-arsenic agent, daylilies have been recognized in Chinese literature since 1000 BC. In Japan, the buds and flowers were eaten in salads and many people find the tight buds "crunchy to the teeth and nutty to the taste".

Perhaps the relative disdain for the species is a small price to pay for today's garden plants which are tough, reliable, and in colors and sizes enough to suit every taste. However, a few of the better species are included here for those still interested in old-fashioned charm for the garden.

Diseases are few and far between, however, in 2000, a rust disease caused by *Puccinia hemerocallidis* was first observed in the Southeast. Daylily rust has now spread to nearly all states. According to the Cornell Plant Diagnostic Clinic Fact Sheet, August, 2002, the most obvious symptoms are yellow to brown streaks on the leaves. You may see very bright, small, yellow spots on the surface of the leaves while the undersurface of the leaves will have numerous small, orange to yellow pustules that poke out of the undersurface of the leaf. The pustules grow and release numerous

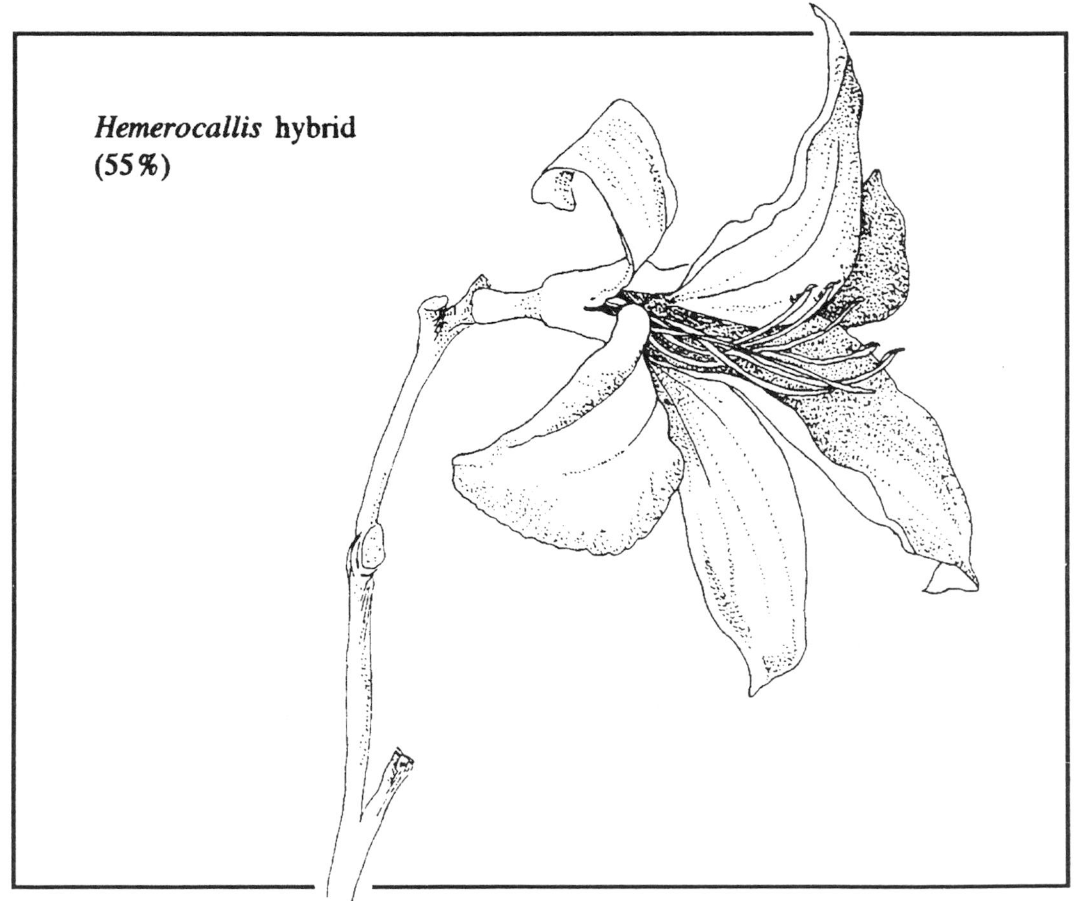

***Hemerocallis* hybrid**
**(55%)**

dusty, orange-colored spores. The orange spores are like dust and if you rub the leaf surface, you'll notice the spores lofting about. As symptoms progress, leaves turn yellow and dry up. Sanitation and fungicide application reduce the incidence of the disease as does choosing less susceptible cultivars. The same Cornell Fact Sheet lists the following as least susceptible: 'Age of Gold', 'All-American Hero', 'Antique Rose', 'Barbara Mitchell', 'Butterscotch Ruffles', 'Catherine Neal', 'Creole Blush', 'Dainty Designer', 'Devonshire Cream', 'Ed Brown', 'Fashion Design', 'Femme Fatale', 'Gentle Rose', 'Golden Melody', 'Happy Returns', 'Heartfelt', 'Holy Spirit', 'Joie de Vivre', 'Joleyne Nichole', 'Lavender Bonnet', 'Lilac Lady', 'Mac the Knife', 'Mae West', 'Meadow Sweet', 'Neon Pink', 'Pink Flirt', 'Prairie Blue Eyes', 'Raspberry Splash', 'Siloam Bill Monroe', 'Siloam Double Classic', 'Siloam Ury Winnifors', and 'Yangtze'. Check with your local extension office for updates.

Mites and aphids are troublesome and thrips can be damaging if allowed to proliferate. All daylilies thrive in full sun but tolerate partial shade as well. Propagate by dividing into plantlets with a single fan of leaves in early spring or fall.

Quick Reference to Hemerocallis Species

| | Height (in.) | Leaves longer than flower stalk | Flower color | Flower stalk branched |
|---|---|---|---|---|
| *H. dumortieri* | 18-24 | Yes | Yellow | No |
| *H. lilio-asphodelus* | 30-36 | No | Yellow | Yes |
| *H. middendorffii* | 24-30 | No | Yellow | No |

***-dumortieri*** (dew-mor-tee-ew′ ree) Early Daylily 18-24″/18″
Spring Yellow Siberia, Japan Zones 2-9

The leaves of this light yellow-flowered daylily are about ½″ wide and 1½′ long. The flower stalks (scapes) are a little shorter than the leaves and thus the flowers are not held high above the foliage as in the hybrids. The scapes are unbranched and carry 2-4 sessile (no pedicel) flowers per stem. The flower buds are tinged brown outside and the 2-3″ long flowers are funnel shaped and fragrant. It is a charming small daylily and the earliest to flower.

***-lilio-asphodelus*** (lil-ee′ o ass-fo-del′ us) Lemon-Lily 30-36″/30″
Late Spring Lemon Siberia, Japan, China Zones 3-9
(syn. *H. flava*)

The foliage is 18-24″ long and about ¾″ wide. The arching scape is branched and bears 5-9 lemon-yellow 4″ long flowers per stem. The flowers are sweetly fragrant and held well above the foliage. Plants are vigorous and spread rapidly. The dried flower buds were a famous aphrodisiac known as gum-jum and imported from China and Japan. Few cultivars are available but the species provides a pleasing color, lovely fragrance, and strong and sturdy growth. This plant was popular but has since been superseded by the newer hybrids.

***-middendorffii*** (mid-an-dorf' ee-eye) Middendorf Lily 24-30"/24"
Early Summer Yellow Siberia, Japan Zones 3-9

Plants are similar in habit to *H. dumortieri* and the flowers are also sessile on the scapes. The flower scapes, however, are longer than the 2' long leaves resulting in the flowers being held above the foliage. The tightly clustered 2-3" long flowers open after *H. dumortieri* but before *H. lilio-asphodelus.* They are fragrant, cup shaped and the petals are not as reflexed as those of the hybrids. Beneath each group of 2-4 flowers are conspicuous bracts. Plants are quite tolerant of shade and moisture.

**Hybrids:**

It is impossible for any one individual to walk you through all the choices, so I let the pros do the walking. In fact, if I walked you through a daylily garden, you'd never want another daylily. Every year the American Hemerocallis Society presents two major medals and numerous Awards of Merit to outstanding daylilies, and if you are not sure what to purchase, I suggest starting with one or two of these. Also I have listed some of the winners from the All America Daylily Selection Council (I don't make this up). Many of these cultivars can be found at better retailers or on the Internet. Have fun.

The President's Cup Award is presented to the hybridizer of the cultivar considered to be the most outstanding of all clumps observed by attendees of the National Convention tour gardens. The Silver Stout Award is the highest honor a cultivar may receive, and named in honor of Dr. A. B. Stout, considered by many as the Father of Modern Daylily Breeding in America.

| Year | President's Cup | Silver Stout Award |
|---|---|---|
| 2000 | 'El Desperado' | 'Elizabeth Salter' |
| 2001 | 'Mary's Gold' | 'Ida's Magic' |
| 2002 | 'Beautiful Edgings' | 'Bill Norris' |
| 2003 | 'Golden Hibiscus' | 'Primal Scream' |
| 2004 | 'Ruby Spider' | 'Moonlit Masquerade' |
| 2005 | 'In The Heat Of It All' | 'Fooled Me' |
| 2006 | 'Adorable Tiger' | 'Ed Brown' |

The Award of Merit is bestowed on 12 cultivars that are not only distinctive and beautiful, but also perform well over a wide geographic area.

| 2000 | 2001 | 2002 |
|---|---|---|
| 'Bill Norris' | 'Chance Encounter' | 'Moonlit Masquerade' |
| 'Betty Warren Woods' | 'Seminole Wind' | 'Beautiful Edgings' |
| 'Daring Dilemma' | 'Canadian Border Patrol' | 'Sherry Lane Carr' |
| 'El Desperado' | 'Fooled Me' | 'Ruby Spider' |
| 'Mask of Time' | 'King Kahuna' | 'Mary Ethel Anderson' |
| 'Primal Scream' | 'Autumn Wood' | 'Ferengi Gold' |

**2000 *(cont.)***

'Dena Marie'
'Ruffled Perfection'
'Nosferatu'
'Chris Salter'
'Indian Giver'
'Yabba Dabba Doo'

**2001 *(cont.)***

'Creative Wood'
'Jedi Dot Pierce'
'Bela Lugosi'
'Dragon King'
'Elegant Candy'
'Peggy Jeffcoat'

**2002 *(cont.)***

'Splendid Touch'
'Smuggler's Gold'
'Druid's Chant'
'Cindy's Eye'
'Fortune's Dearest'
'Something Wonderful'

**2003**

'Ed Brown'
'Desperado Love'
'Wisest of Wizards'
'America's Most Wanted'
'Larry Grace'
'Marked by Lydia'
'Black Ambrosia'
'Magic of Oz'
'Etched Eyes'
'Mister Lucky'
'David Kirchhoff'
'Rosewitha'

**2004**

'Lavender Blue Baby'
'Awesome Blossom'
'Trahlyta'
'Clothed in Glory'
'Pearl Harbor'
'Strawberry Fields Forever'
'Tune the Harp'
'All American Chief'
'Mystical Rainbow'
'Francis of Assisi'
'Buttered Popcorn'
'Starman's Quest'

**2005**

'Sabine Bauer'
'Pure and Simple'
'Skinwalker'
'Spacecoast Tiny Perfection'
'All Fired Up'
'Schnickel Fritz'
'Ram'
'Moses' Fire'
'Brookwood Lee Causy'
'Cherokee Pass'
'Spacecoast Starburst'
'Big Kiss'

**2006**

'Celebration of Angels'
'Darla Anita'
'Roses in Snow'
'Two Part Harmony'
'Wild Horses'
'Desert Icicle'
'Jerry Pata Williams'
'Mildred Mitchell'
'Swallow Tail Kite'
'Barbara Dittmer'
'Tangerine Horses'
'Lady Neva'

And if that is not enough, there is also an All American Daylily Selection Council (AADSC), which is an organization that administers a network of test sites throughout North America, and performs rigorous evaluations of daylily cultivars (www.daylilyreseach.org) . Based on over 50 criteria, the AADSC selects but two winners a year. Some of the recipients are 'Lavender Vista' (2007), 'Buttered Popcorn' (2006), 'Miss Mary Mary' (2005), 'Chorus Line' (2004), 'Plum Perfect' (2003) and 'Judith (2002).

***Hepatica*** (he-pa-ti′ ca) Liverleaf Ranunculaceae

Nature's early spring wardrobe needs no help making the garden hormones flow in most of us. With early daffodils, forsythias, redbuds and bluebells, spring can more than hold its own. But as if there weren't enough, early spring, like a gardening bully, hordes more and more wonderful plants that tease and tantalize gardeners with their ephemeral beauty and demanding conditions. As if trilliums, trout lilies and primroses weren't sufficient, the hepaticas are additional icing on the early spring cake. In fact, their earliness results in the undivided attention of every awakening gardener.

The shape of the leaves suggested the shape of the liver to early botanists and the genus is derived from the Latin *hepar*, liver. In the 16th century, according to the *Doctrine of Signatures*, the likeness to the liver led to its adoption as a cure for liver ailments by herbalists and physicians (see *Pulmonaria* for additional details).

About 10 species of hepaticas are known and some hybridization and selection have resulted in flowers of various colors, double flowers and intermediate forms. As I stumble upon more and more species and variants of this genus, I tend to agree with

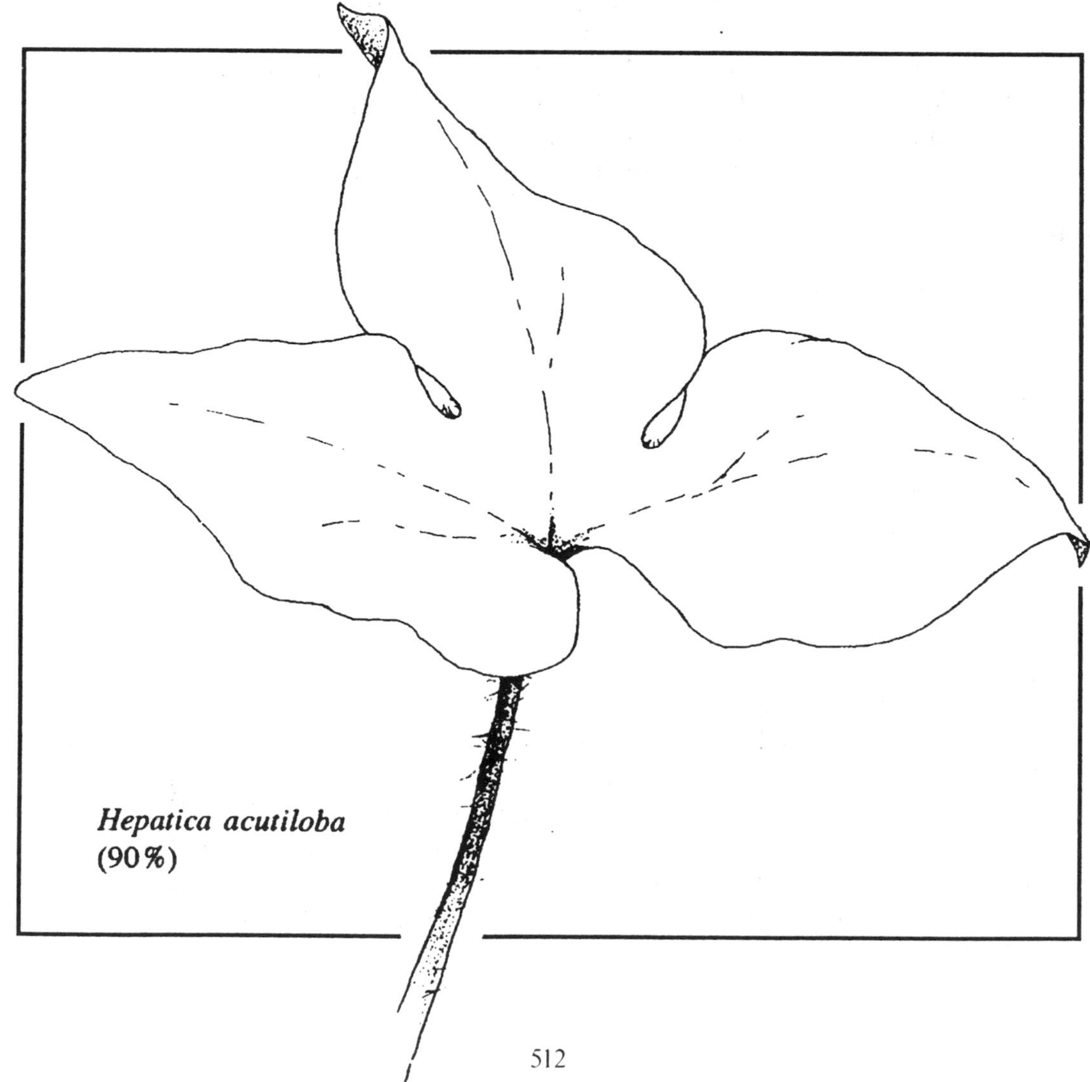

***Hepatica acutiloba***
**(90%)**

H. Lincoln Foster's suggestion that "it is possible that all hepaticas are but variants of a single circumpolar species with local variations in leaf pattern".

They may be distinguished from similar genera such as *Anemone* by having three involucre bracts found just below the colored sepals. The flowers of *Hepatica* have no petals (apetalous) and the showy parts are sepals and stamens. The leathery leaves are always basal, usually 3-5-lobed and have long petioles. Often the leaves are suffused with purple, particularly those that persist from the previous year.

All require shade, moisture, a good deal of compost and do better where competition from other plants is minimal. In the Armitage garden, they compete with oak trees, squirrels and any number of spring-flowering plants and by midsummer, I can hardly find them in the forest of foliage. I should probably get rid of the intruders, but I like them as well.

Propagation is most efficient by division, although it is a slow process at best. Seeds may be used and sometimes gathering fresh seed is the only way to influence decent germination. Seeds are shed when they are green and may be collected by placing a small bag over the senescing flowers. However, seed germination is more successful in nature than it is by gardeners, no matter how many times seeds are stratified, scarified or prayed over. Similar to *Helleborus*, nature does it better.

Quick Reference to Hepatica Species

| | Flower color | Leaf lobes |
|---|---|---|
| *H. acutiloba* | Blue, white | Pointed |
| *H. americana* | Blue, white, pink | Rounded |

**-*acutiloba*** (a-cute-i-lobe' a) Hepatica 3-9"/6"
Early Spring Lavender, White Eastern United States Zones 3-7

The leaves are 4-6" across and each of the three lobes is, in extreme forms, pointed at the tips. There is some variation in the species and subdivisions in the three lobes are not all that uncommon. Hybridization occurs between this and *H. americana*, therefore not all plants in a colony exhibit this sharply lobed characteristic. The lavender flowers are about 1" across and open before the new leaves appear in the spring. The first time the plants flower in the spring makes one wonder what all the fuss is about as they can look quite bedraggled, particularly if the old leaves have been beaten up by the winter. The contrast between the fresh lavender flowers and the dark bruised foliage is unavoidable; however, within a few days you will be in love with them.

The new foliage emerges while some flowers are still opening and continues to increase in size over many weeks. Plants provide fresh early flowers, leathery handsome foliage all season and absolute lack of maintenance. The only thing not available is a consistent source of plants for gardeners unwilling to accept plants ripped from the wild. As the demand for hepaticas and other native species increases along with the awareness of their provenance, nursery-propagated plants will be the norm rather than the exception.

**Cultivars:**

'Millstream Pink' was built up slowly by H. Lincoln Foster in his garden called Millstream, in Connecticut. These vigorous plants have large blossoms of vivid deep pink. To have 'Millstream Pink' is to have a legacy of one of the great American gardeners.

***-americana*** (a-me-ri-kah′ na) Round-Lobed Liverleaf 3-8″/6″
Early Spring Lavender, White Eastern United States Zones 3-7

Other than the morphological contrasts between them, few differences in garden worthiness, location or performance occur between this and the previous species. The leaf lobes of *H. americana* are decidedly more rounded, leaves a little more hairy, plants a little smaller and flowers are a little bigger, but it is the similarities rather than the differences that impress people. Intermediates occur when populations are grown near each other.

Both species are best planted in groups so that eventually, sizable colonies can be enjoyed. Try your hand at seed propagation, it may be the only way to obtain sufficient plants. Both species occur as far west as Missouri and Manitoba, although they are more numerous east of the Mississippi.

**Cultivars:**

I have seen plants in English gardens labeled as *H. triloba* 'Rosea' and 'Rose Form' but have not seen them offered in the United States. They produce many small pink and rosy red flowers respectively.

**Related Species:**

*H. nobilis* is one of the two European species becoming more available through specialty nurseries. Native throughout temperate European woods and into Asia, the plant is hardly distinguishable from the American species, but is somewhat intermediate between them. Flowers are generally bluer (less lavender) than the American species and a little larger. Numerous color forms have been propagated and may be found in European gardens. A Japanese variant (var. *japonica*) is also cultivated, in fact, the Royal Horticultural Society lists 99 cultivars, selections and strains of this variant. I have yet to see one. However, I have seen and admired 'Rosea', with rosy pink flowers, and 'Caerula', with sky blue blossoms. Other forms that lucky gardeners might find are 'Ada Scott' with double purple flowers, 'Alba', white flowers, and 'Marmorata', whose blue flowers are spotted with white. Double flower forms such as 'Plena', 'Rubra Plena' and 'Little Abington' are listed but not found without considerable searching. Heck, none of these is to be found without a little searching, but there are enterprising nurserymen like Barry Yinger of Asiatica Nursery who has spent considerable time building up stock, so help him out and buy a couple.

*H. transsilvanica* is native to Romania and is distinguishable by the shallow broad lobes, each of which is notched at the tips. The flowers are large (up to 2″ across) and usually deep blue. My colleague Mike Dirr and I stumbled across these at Wisley Garden in England in March and between cameras clicking and saliva flowing, we were suitably impressed. I have since seen them offered at various nurseries and growing at the Mt. Cuba Center in Delaware. Crosses between *H. transsilvanica* and *H. nobilis* are intermediate and known as *H.* x *media*. 'Ballard's Variety' ('Ballardii') is vigorous and bears large sky blue flowers.

***Heracleum*** (hay-ra-clee' um) Hogweed Apiaceae

Approximately 60 species occur, although only one, *H. mantegazzianum* (man-tee-gazz-ee-ah' num), giant hogweed, is seen, albeit occasionally, in gardens. When seen, however, it is seldom forgotten. Rising from thick roots in the spring, giant hogweed grows like Jack's beanstalk, producing large Queen Anne's lace-like flowers 10-15 feet above the ground. It must have also impressed early botanists as the genus name comes from the Greek name for Hercules, *Herakleon*. It is hard to believe that such biomass production can occur at such an incredible rate. If we were able to make fuel from such a plant, any worries about foreign oil would disappear. Plants are biennial, or occasionally perennial, and the statuesque plants bear ternately (in threes) or pinnately divided, foliage. Long, sheathed petioles arise from the hollow, ridged stems that are often reddish or purple. Plants are covered with conspicuous white hairs and have a strong resinous smell. The massive umbels of white or slightly pinkish flowers occur in spring and may be enjoyed on the plant or cut for drying.

While this plant is unforgettable, and while some people embrace it as a garden plant, it is also a dangerous noxious weed, and if you don't wish to be snatched by aliens or Richard Cheney, don't plant it at all. First of all, it is on the Federal Invasive Species List, a couple of Mr. Cheney's favorite words, and second of all, it can be a weapon of mass destruction. The dangerous parts are the furocoumins in the sap, which cause a light-sensitive reaction in the skin. Exposure to strong sunlight causes reddening, stinging and irritation of areas of the skin that have come into contact with the plant. The response generally occurs within 24 hours and painful fluid-filled blisters occur, which may end up in scarring. This is not a plant to have around children, and if plants are to be handled, protective clothing should be worn. Plants love moist areas and can reseed themselves with abandon. It is also on most states' noxious weed lists, it seems to have no conscience, and is even moving into northeast Ohio, Pennsylvania and New York State, and showing up in yards and gardens, not just woods and fields. Nobody moves into northeast Ohio.

Seed propagation is best left to nature and while plants are not nearly as aggressive in most American sites as they are in Britain, the dermatological problems are the same.

**Related Species:**

*H. sphondylium*, hogweed, is smaller (2-4' tall) with pale green-yellow flowers and entire to palmately divided foliage. Skin irritation is also a problem but not as severe.

***Hermodactylus*** (her-mo-dak' ti-lus) Snake's-Head Iris Iridaceae

Named after Hermes, the Greek name for the god Mercury, the genus is represented by only one member, *H. tuberosa*. The tubers are finger-like (thus the rest of the genus name *dactylus*) and plants are short-lived perennials. Plants are native to southern Europe and are fair performers at best, requiring moderate temperatures and limey soils to perform well. Where they do well, they bear fragrant flowers in the winter and early spring.

The leaves are gray-green and about 12-15″ long. The solitary flowers bear green and black falls and standards. The flowers are relatively small, about 2-3″ wide, and more interesting than they eye-catching. I read an account in which John Gerard, the classic herbalist in the late 1500s, described the color of these blossoms as "goose-turd green". Other common names having to do with the flower color include black iris and widow iris although snake's-head or snakeshead iris have become most commonly used. The name refers to the pointed buds that supposedly look like snaky heads with open mouths. Part of their charm is their earliness to flower (March-Apr) and their unusual tint. They are fun bulbs to grow, and reasonably available. Hardy to about zone 6.

***Herniaria*** (hern-ee′ air-ee-a) Rupturewort, Green Carpet Caryophyllaceae

Plants that are nothing but functional are gaining a strong following in our busy lives, allowing us to toss a plant in the ground that actually earns its price. Such a plant is H. glabra, a ground cover probably useful only between stones in a path or roaming gently over an otherwise ignored corner. Good for it.

Plants are in the carnation family, and if you ever saw a flower, it would look like a little white gypsophila bloom. But don't hold your breath, plants are grown for the mossy foliage. They never grow more than 3″ tall, so you won't even have to mow them. 'Sea Foam' has creamy margins. Hardy in zones 5-8.

I tried to find where the common name, rupturewort, came from. It is too scenic to ignore. It may be the way the fruit ruptures, but the term "wort" usually infers some medicinal use. I found that belief in rupturewort's efficacy is centuries old. A treatise written in 1597 recommended the herb for hernias and observed that "the powder thereof, taken with wine ... wasteth away the stones in the kidney and expelleth them." Plants are still thought to increase urination and relieve spasms, but scientists have yet to verify these effects.

***Hesperis*** (hes′ per-is) Rocket Brassicaceae

As many as 60 species of biennial or perennial plants have been described, all of which are characterized by white or purple 4-petalled flowers on long terminal racemes. Fifty-nine of them are never offered for sale and not likely to be seen except at good botanical gardens or as specimens on herbarium sheets. The favorite by far is the old-fashioned biennial, *H. matronalis*, dame's violet, which pops up everywhere from the Midwest to the Northeast and down to the Southeast.

***-matronalis*** (mah-tro-nah′ lis) Dame's Violet, Sweet Rocket 2-3′/3′
Late Spring White, Purple Central Europe, Southern Asia Zones 3-8

Although not true perennials, plants self-sow everywhere. Native to Europe and parts of Asia, they have become naturalized all over Europe as far north as Iceland, and throughout North America. The ½-¾″ wide 4-petalled flowers open in late April

*Hesperis matronalis*
(25%)

and early May until late June and are wonderfully fragrant, particularly in the evening. The name *Hesperis* is derived from the Greek *hespera* (the evening) referring to the evening fragrance. The 2-4″ long, alternate, hairy, sharp pointed leaves are sessile or borne on short petioles. Wherever I travel in the spring, from Georgia to Philadelphia to Boston, dame's violet pops up everywhere, providing lovely vigorous showpieces of white and purple that glow in the late afternoon sun. It has become so successful that people dismiss it as a weed, but we should have more weeds like this!

The white-flowered form stands out in the shady garden more than the purple and should be selected whenever possible. The old seed heads can be cut back to the basal foliage by June, if seedlings are not wanted. Plants require a consistent water supply to continue flowering, and prefer partial shade, particularly at the southern end of their range. They become woody at the base and may persist for a number of years, but should be considered a biennial. Plants often disappear after flowering, so annuals may be planted in the same area to fill the gaps. However, seeds emerge quite readily and persist in the garden for years. They are nectar sources for many butterflies and usually attract an array of colorful moths and butterflies.

I teach this plant every year to my students who initially confuse the flowers with those of *Lunaria*, money plant. In general, flowers of *Hesperis* are later, leaves are longer and more narrow and the fruit is long and skinny compared to the rounded fruit in money plant.

Perhaps people have asked you about the early purple phlox, another common mistake. Tell them you know it's dame-rocket because it only has 4 petals, whereas phlox has five. If you show them, they'll show others. This teaching stuff is great, isn't it? And why, they ask, is this plant saddled with the name dame's violet? The specific epithet, *matronalis*, of matrons, is derived from the old name "mother of the evening", again referring to the evening fragrance. Plants are not easily found in catalogs, but seeds are available through any seed house. *Hesperis* is handsome in an informal area or in the border itself. It is a charming plant whose ease of cultivation makes it well worth growing if random plants are not a problem.

**Cultivars:**

'Alba' is the white-flowered form and is particularly outstanding.

'Alba-plena' is one of a number of double-flowered forms. It has white, double flowers and is also fragrant. 'Lilacina Flore Plena' is a unusual lilac double form and 'Purpurea Plena' bears double purple flowers. The double forms must be propagated by division or basal cuttings.

**Related Species:**

*H. bicuspidata* (*H. violacea*) is only 8-12″ tall with wavy to entire basal leaves and sessile lanceolate (lance-like) stem leaves. The thin lowers are reddish with violet veins. A true perennial, but short-lived. Winter hardy to about zone 5.

## *Heterotheca* (het-er-o′ theek-a) Golden Aster Asteraceae

The main species is *H. villosa*, hairy golden aster, native from Indiana to coastal California, north to Canada and south to Texas. Plants bear 1-2″ long gray-green leaves that are narrow and quite pubescent. The stems and leaf bases are bristly-hairy. The 1-1½″ diameter golden-yellow daisy flowers occur on short flower stems in multibranched inflorescences. I have seen 4′ specimens in Georgia gardens absolutely covered with blooms from late summer until frost. When not in flower, it is a large, rather mundane green thing and even when flowering, it is more at home in an informal meadow than a formal border. When frost occurs, plants blacken like burnt toast and crumple like dirty rags.

Place in full sun and provide plenty of room. Plants are highly adaptable and are particularly drought tolerant. I recall visiting the garden of a friend who had moved two or three months before. We were in the midst of a drought, not uncommon that summer, and the garden had not been watered. Disaster greeted me; many plants had succumbed, but the 5′ tall, 4′ wide golden aster was radiant with golden flowers. Plants are hardy in zones 5-8. 'Golden Sunshine' is 3-4′ tall and produces 2″ wide yellow flowers a little later than the type. Plants are marvelous attractants of butterflies, and visitors will always be present.

As gardeners, we must follow the lead of taxonomists or growers who provide up-to-date nomenclature for the plants we grow. In some cases, such as the wholesale emptying of the *Chrysanthemum* genus, we are slammed from wall to wall while at other times name changes occur all around us with little impact. A whole group of yellow aster-like plants are so closely related that even with a microscope, differences are difficult to find. Such is the case with the two golden asters, *Chrysopsis* (which see) and *Heterotheca*, whose members play musical genera every few years. I have a terrible time trying to distinguish them, so I try to remember a few of the differences:

Ray and disc flowers are formed in both genera, however, the ray flowers in Chrysopsis are female and ray flowers in *Heterotheca* are bisexual. In *Chrysopsis*, the fruit is obovoid (like an egg, but broadest below the middle) and the basal leaves are in rosettes while the stem leaves are alternate. In *Heterotheca*, the flowers are bisexual, the fruit angled and leaves are mostly alternate. After all is said and done, however, some taxonomists put them together, others split them up and gardeners generally don't give a flip.

Propagate by divisions after 2-3 years or by seed harvested from the plants in the fall.

***Heuchera*** (hew′ ker-a) Coral Bell, Alumroot Saxifragaceae

"What coral bell did you buy, Heather?" I asked my daughter after a foray to her local garden center. "Dad, there were so many, I couldn't make up my mind, so I didn't buy any." Thus is the confusion with the buying public today. In the zeal and haste of introducing plants to the consumer, we forgot that sometimes we are doing more confusing than introducing.

A few short years ago, only *H. sanguinea*, coral bells, and hybrids, had gained significant popularity in North American gardens. While significant improvements had been made in *H. sanguinea* and *H.* x *brizoides* by European nurserymen, other lovely species had been ignored. In the 1990s and into the 21st century, plantsmen like Dick Lighty, formerly of Mt. Cuba Center, Dale Hendricks from North Creek

Nursery, Charles Oliver, The Primrose Path, Don Jacobs from Eco Gardens, Dan Hinkley, Kingston, Washington, and especially the Heuchera King, Dan Heims, from Terra Nova Nurseries in Oregon, have bred, selected and promoted heucheras so that today, we are awash in these things. What Heather needs is not more coral bells, but someone to tell her which is the best purple leaved, the best green leaved, the best silver one, etc. for her area. She doesn't have the inclination and certainly doesn't have the time to figure them out; she will buy an azalea instead.

The mostly evergreen leaves are usually basal and long petioled, and the margins are lobed, wavy, or entire. The foliage is particularly ornamental in some species. Petals are small or absent and the sepals usually provide the showy part of the bloom. Some species have showy flowers but many others are grown for their ornamental foliage alone. A number of species native to the mountains of New Mexico, Utah and California, such as *H. rubescens* and *H. versicolor* provide low-growing, compact alpine selections.

Many of the improved cultivars are intergeneric hybrids. Most species are readily raised from seed but the hybrids are generally raised from tissue culture and are usually divided in the garden. *Heuchera* does best in rich, moist well-drained soil in partial shade. Species grown for their foliage always look better in cooler times

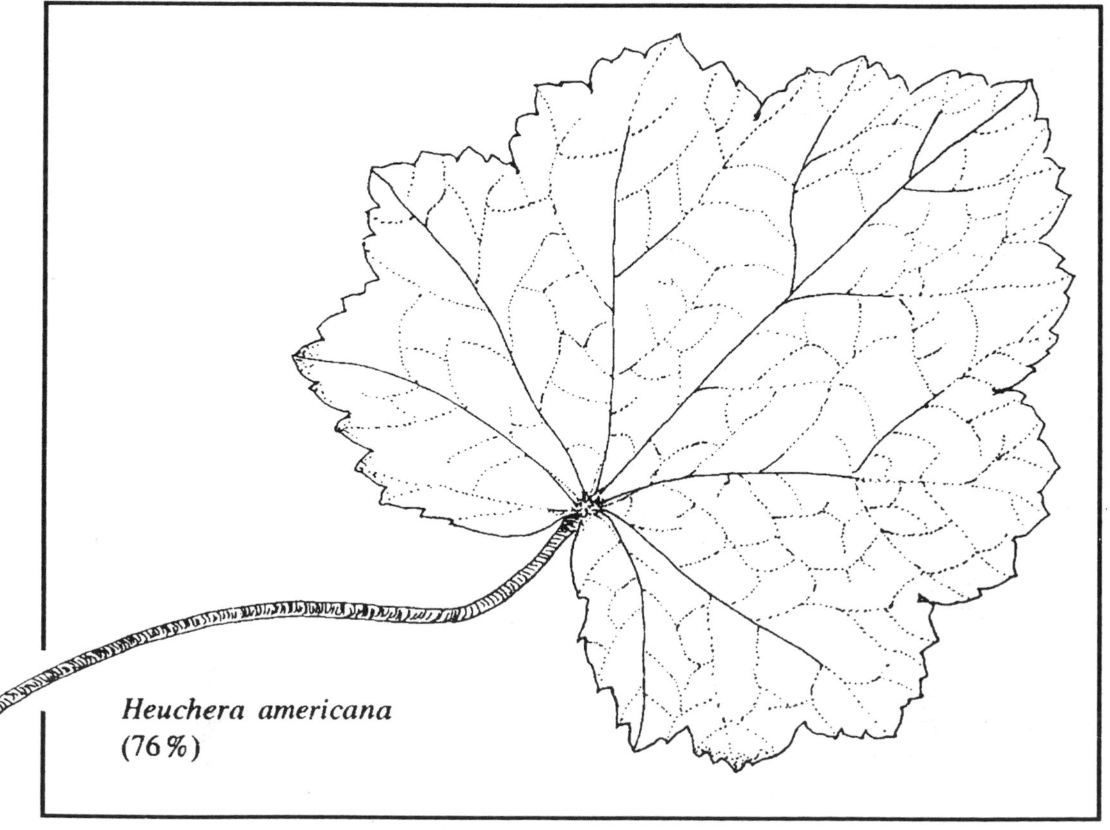

***Heuchera americana***
**(76%)**

of the year and may appear rather washed out and ratty in the heat of the summer, particularly in the southern end of the growing range. Some of the new foliage forms are much better in the heat than the older ones.

Plants in the genus *Heuchera* are fairly similar to plants of another American genus, *Tiarella*, and I often am asked "What makes them different?". This is especially vexing when plants are not in flower and even more so when people go on and on about the result of the cross between the two genera, X *Heucherella*. "How can I know *Heucherella* when I can't even tell the difference between *Heuchera* and *Tiarella*?" Here are a few hints.

| | Leaves | Stamens | Conspicuous part |
|---|---|---|---|
| *Heuchera* | Obviously lobed | 5 | Usually sepals |
| *Tiarella* | Lobed or heart-shaped | 10 | Petals, stamens |

The leaves are tough, but with a little eyeballing, the flowers can be identified. In case all else fails, count the stamens. It is not as hard as it sounds.

There are so many new hybrids each year that one tends to forget the rest of the family, the species that no longer get the respect they used to. A few choices other than hybrids await, and although finding them takes a bit more time, they are equally good garden plants in many areas.

Quick Reference to Heuchera Species

| | Height (in.) | Flower color | Leaves obviously ornamental |
|---|---|---|---|
| *H. americana* | 18-36 | Greenish white | Yes |
| *H. micrantha* | 12-24 | Yellowish white | Yes |
| *H. rubescens* | 4-12 | Pink | No |
| *H. sanguinea* | 12-18 | Reddish, white | No |
| *H. villosa* | 12-36 | Pinkish | No |

***-americana*** (a-mer-cah' na) American Alumroot 18-36″/18″
Early Summer Greenish White Eastern North America Zones 4-9

This woodland species has always been a tough, reliable performer, grown for the handsome evergreen foliage rather than the flowers. The 4-6″ long leaves are rounded to heart shaped with 5-7 lobes. Its charm comes from the mottled purple color of the young foliage, which later subsides as the leaves mature. If proper cultural conditions are provided, new leaves are produced all season, although mostly in the spring. The small, 1/8″ wide flowers are borne in 15-20″ long airy, unbranched panicles. Although they are not particularly ornamental, I enjoy them poking through the foliage and swaying in the afternoon breeze. It is one of the best heucheras for the South and is most attractive in spring and late fall. The dark, healthy, purplish foliage stands out in November, December and January while everything else has succumbed to frost or fatigue.

Plants should be grown in shade and are not tolerant of full sun, particularly if moisture is lacking. It is important that the soil remain consistently moist if foliage is to be produced throughout the season.

Alumroot can be propagated easily by division in spring or early fall. The species can also be raised from seed. Cover the small seeds thinly and place seed tray at 68-70°F with high humidity. Grow on at 60°F. Numerous cultivars have been raised recently.

**Cultivars:**

'Green Spice' has green leaves with a good deal of silver, as well as darker veins. Quite beautiful. I have also listed it under hybrids.

***-micrantha*** (mik-ran' tha) Small-Flowered Alumroot 12-24"/12"
Late Spring Yellowish White Western North America Zones 4-7

The 2-4" long foliage is gray-green and heart shaped with rounded, shallow lobes. In late spring, loose, airy spires of 1/8" wide yellowish white flowers appear. The petals are twice as long as the sepals (in most species, the petals are shorter or the same size). If well grown, which I have yet to see in much of this country, sufficient inflorescences are produced to put on a show. Usually, however, they are in the same class as those of *H. americana*. Place in partial shade, provide adequate moisture and mulch well in the winter north of zone 5. A West Coast native, it does not do well under conditions of fluctuating temperatures common to the rest of the country. It is, however, a parent of several excellent garden hybrids.

The species may be raised from seed similar to *H. americana*.

***-sanguinea*** (sang-guin' ee-a) Coral Bells 12-18"/12"
Late Spring Red New Mexico, Arizona Zones 3-8

This species has undergone intensive breeding and selection and is a common denizen of American gardens. The smallest of the garden heucheras, it is at home as an edging, tucked away in a shady corner or at the front of the border. Although the plant is small, the half-inch long, campanulate, red flowers are much larger and showier than the other species. They are held in 10-20" long, loosely branched panicles and persist for 4-8 weeks. Removing spent flower stalks results in extended flowering time. The basal foliage is heart shaped or roundish with 5-7 slightly toothed lobes.

Coral bells require excellent drainage and full sun in the North but partial shade in the South. They perform poorly in heavy clay and acid soils, therefore, coarse sand, manure and dolomitic lime must be added where necessary. The species and some cultivars may be raised from seed but division every 2-4 years is the most successful means of propagation.

**Cultivars:**

Most cultivars of *H. sanguinea* average 14-20" tall. Hybridization has resulted in improved forms but the parentage of many cultivars is confused. I have listed all the colorful hybrids separately, although they may be *H. sanguinea* or *H.* x *brizoides*. The following appear to be cultivars of *H. sanguinea*.

'Alba' has 20″ tall stems of creamy white flowers.
'Maxima' bears burgundy red flowers.
'Snow Fire' is extraordinarily beautiful, reminding me of 'Monet' (which see), but with somewhat thicker leaves. If you can grow white variegated forms, be sure to give this a try. See 'Monet' for my comments on variegated foliage.
'Splendens' is the best-known cultivar, producing rich red flowers.

**-*villosa*** (vil-lo′ sa) Hairy Alumroot 1-3′/18″
Summer White Southeastern United States Zones 6-9

The rounded to heart-shaped leaf blades are deeply 5-7 lobed, each lobe somewhat triangular. The leaves and flower stem are hairy and the ¼″ wide, small, whitish pink flowers occur in open, airy panicles up to 3′ long. This species is the latest to flower and among the tallest in the genus. Native to the Southeast, they are more at home in the heat and although not as showy as *H. sanguinea*, plants are more reliable in the hot, wet summers and make an enjoyable, if not exceptional, border plant. New hybrids (which see) that incorporate this species into the parentage should have a little better performance in warm climates. However, the hairy leaves are also a problem if afternoon rain is common, tending to trap the water, resulting in leaf spotting. Plants are excellent for moist shade.

**Cultivars:**
'Autumn Bride' was found by Richard Simon at Bluemont Nursery in Maryland. It appears to be a form of var. *macrorrhiza* (which see) with smoother and somewhat deeper green leaves. Creamy white flowers appear in the fall and continue until frost.
'Bronze Wave' is similar to 'Brownies' (which see), however this appears to be a purer form of *H. villosa*. White flowers occur in the fall.
var. *macrorrhiza* bears large pale green leaves which stand out in the garden. The small flowers are creamy white and perhaps not as exciting as the colored forms listed above, but handsome in their own right.
'Purpurea' is an excellent purple-leaved form of heuchera. The leaves are hairier and deeper purple than 'Palace Purple'.

**Related Species:**

*H.* x *brizoides* was originally designated for crosses between *H. sanguinea* and *H. americana*, however today these hybrids claim input from other species, including *H. micrantha*. So named because the smaller flowers and thin stems resembled quaking grass (*Briza maxima*). Profuse numbers of small (1/8″ wide) flowers occur with rounded, lobed foliage. Plants are generally taller than *H. sanguinea* cultivars, averaging 24-30″. The insertion of genes of *H. americana* has resulted in significant improvement in garden performance in eastern gardens, particularly in the Southeast. With the profusion of hybrids, the species designation is mostly lost.

*H. cylindrica* is native to the West Coast and produces many ¼″ wide green and cream-colored flowers on 2′ long spikelike racemes (flowers almost sessile on the flower stalk). The light green marbled foliage makes a good ground cover as plants spread out more than many other forms of *Heuchera*. They require the same conditions as *H. micrantha*. var. *glabella* is similar to the species but the lower part of the stem and leaves are smooth, not hairy. A dwarf form is also available. 'Greenfinch' is a handsome 2-2½′ tall form with greenish white flowers. 'Green Ivory', a selection of 'Greenfinch', is 2½-3′ tall and bears many white flowers with green bases. 'Green Marble' has similar flowers but also bears marbled light green leaves. 'Hyperion' is unusual for this species, bearing pink flowers with only a hint of green. All were raised by Alan Bloom of Blooms of Bressingham Nursery, England.

*H. rubescens*, alpine heuchera, is less than 6″ tall and is more at home in a rock garden situation than in a formal garden. Pink flowers are formed in the spring. Cold hardy to about zone 3, but poorly adapted to heat and humidity.

*H. versicolor* grows in southern Utah and is also more suitable for alpine conditions. Plants are a little taller than *H. rubescens* but are compact relative to the more common species. Pink buds give rise to pink flowers in the spring. *H. rubescens* and *H. versicolor* are but two of the miniature forms being more closely examined by breeders and gardeners. A few hybrids of mixed origin may be found here and there; all require excellent drainage and relatively cool temperatures. 'Constance' has handsome coral-pink flowers on 8″ tall plants. The foliage is only about 2″ tall when not in flower. 'Mayfair' bears pink flowers on 6″ tall flower stems.

**Cultivars and Hybrids**:

Most cultivars and hybrids are cold hardy to zone 4, many to zone 3. They all look better in the spring and early summer than in the fall, except perhaps for those with a good deal of *H. villosa* in the bloodline. Replant every three years to rejuvenate the clump.

So many hybrids have been bred, many quite similar in habit, but according to the breeder or the catalog, each new introduction has darker, richer, more eye-catching or simply better foliage than the last one, to say nothing of the flowers. So many forms have been raised recently that it is almost impossible to choose. I have seen dozens of cultivars in my travels and trialed dozens more in the Gardens at UGA so I now have an almost reasonable idea of plant performance. Some cultivars and hybrids are heat tolerant, but no matter what you read or hear, no heucheras tolerate full sun in the South, in fact, hardly anywhere South of zone 5. All plants flower in the spring, a few repeat bloom. I have included recent cultivars as well as some with historical value (i.e. breeding parents), and I am sure I have missed more than a few. I am often asked, "How does one tell the difference between so many?" The best response was provided by the plantsman Dan Hinkley, who eloquently replied, "Try a dart".

'Amber Waves' has bright amber, cinnamon foliage and is absolutely one of the most eye-catching plants. It is difficult not to buy it because it looks so good in the container. As beautiful as it is, its performance and vigor have been disappointing.

'Amethyst Mist' from Terra Nova Nursery has amethyst foliage and is a vigorous grower. It may not be as "sexy" as others, but comes back year after year, and is a doer. The more I see this relatively old (in heuchera years) coral bell, the more I appreciate it. If I had but one cultivar to recommend to my daughters, it would probably be this one.

'Autumn Haze' provides a potpourri of smokey colors on the leaves and reasonable pink flowers in the spring.

'Black Beauty' is as dark as 'Obsidian' and 'Licorice' (which see) and produces almost black foliage. All three can be recommended but not necessarily told apart.

'Black Bird' also has dark foliage but with a glaze of pink throughout.

'Blood Red' is about 18″ tall when in flower. The blossoms are dark red and are borne over silvery green foliage.

Bressingham hybrids are a mix of green-leaved plants with flowers in coral, pink, or white.

'Bressingham Bronze' was selected from 'Palace Purple' (which see) and has bronze, somewhat crinkled leaves.

'Bronze Wave' is similar to 'Brownies' (which see) in that they are both bronze forms of the hairy alumroot, *H. villosa*. White flowers occur in the fall.

'Brownies' is one of a number of cultivars that has incorporated *H. villosa*, hairy alum root, in its parentage. All parts of the plant are hairy, and the leaves are light brown, with a hint of green in them. Plants tolerate heat well. White flowers occur in the fall. Not sexy but a good performer.

'Café Ole' has small bronze foliage that is highly ruffled. A good choice for ruffled leaves. Plants also have abundant white flowers.

'Can Can' is a good performer with ruffled foliage and silver venation, and continues to be a fan favorite. Must be love of the cabaret.

Canyon series consists of four dwarf (less than 9″ tall) flowering hybrids originally selected by Canyon Creek Nursery in Oroville, California. They consist of 'Canyon Belle' with rosy pink sprays of flowers, 'Canyon Chimes' (rosy lavender flowers), 'Canyon Duet' (rose and white flowers),and 'Canyon Melody' (pink flowers). I think 'Canyon Duet' is the best of them all.

'Cappuccino' has wavy purple foliage topped with cream-colored flowers.

'Cascade Dawn' has purple-silver foliage with silver venation.

'Caramel' is a *H. villosa* hybrid, and bears wonderful peachy caramel foliage. Plants have been heat tolerant in our trials so far; this may be a winner.

'Cathedral Windows' has bronze to purple leaves with dark purple veins. A great name, a fair plant.

'Champagne Bubbles' is grown for the many pink flowers that cover the plant in spring. The foliage is green.

'Chantilly' has tall inflorescences of creamy white flowers over green foliage.

'Chatterbox' is a popular cultivar with large pink flowers and handsome green foliage with darker venation. This may be a cultivar of *H. sanguinea*.

'Cherries Jubilee' provides the combination of dark foliage, with a little venation, and pink to rose flowers.

'Chinook' has waxy ruffled bronze foliage and rather large pink flowers in the spring.

'Chocolate Ruffles' has intense purple leaves which are deeply cut and ruffled. The flower stems are also purple.

'Chocolate Veil' has been replaced by other darker-leafed forms, but if you can find it, it is still an excellent choice.

'Cinnabar Silver' has wonderful silver leaves with a darker venation pattern. The "cinnabar" refers to the color of the flowers.

'Citronelle' is a recent selection from Holland, bearing bright chartreuse foliage. Plants were selections from 'Caramel', therefore *H. villosa* is also part of their parentage.

'City Lights' is a deep bronze selection with white flowers.

'Crème Brulee' has bronze leaves with a touch of peach, and excellent red flowers. This is part of the Dolce™ series from Proven Winners™.

'Crème de Menthe' has silver foliage with darker venation. Part of the Dolce™ series.

'Crimson Curls' is probably, in my opinion, the best of the ruffled, curly-leafed cultivars. Bronze foliage with burgundy on the underside and rich ruffling keep people coming back for more. We have had no overwintering problems with this hybrid.

'Dale's Selection' is named for the nurseryman, Dale Hendricks, and has a great deal of *H. americana* in the bloodline. The purplish foliage is handsomely mottled with white, red and silver veins. Flowers are insignificant. This was and is an excellent performer, but has also been an important parent in the breeding of the cultivars.

'Earth Angel' produces attractive coppery bronze leaves, each with narrow green edges, and red flowers in the spring.

'Ebony and Ivory' bears ruffled bronze foliage over which arise many off-white flowers. A vigorous performer.

'Fandango' has silvery somewhat ruffled foliage and pink blooms, which if conditions are positive, will flower again.

'Fantasia' produces pink flowers over lobed silvery leaves.

'Eco-Magnifica' came from Don Jacobs of Eco-Gardens in Decatur, Georgia. The silver-hued foliage has green veins and a green edge. Quite vigorous and unique. 'Eco-Improved' is similar but with more silvering on larger leaves. Also used as a parent to provide the silver mottling in many of the modern hybrids.

'Firefly' is an old-fashioned hybrid, mostly made up of *H. sanguinea*. However, it is still popular due to colorful dark wine-red flowers.

'Frosted Violet', from The Primrose Path in Pennsylvania, bears pink purple foliage over which are formed small pink flowers. Vigorous and eye-catching. Plants have *H. villosa* in the parentage.

'Geisha's Fan' has dark leaves but with obvious silver venation. Small pink flowers accompany the foliage.

'Georgia Peach' comes from Terra Nova Nursery and is the first of their Southern Belle™ series, bred for tolerance of heat and humidity. It likely has a good deal of *H. villosa* in its bloodline. Unfortunately, I have not trialed it in Georgia, so I can't tell you if it is a "peach" or a pit.

'Ginger Ale' is a vigorous hybrid, has a combination of chartreuse bronze with a little pink. Sounds gruesome, but quite nice. The foliage has slight venation as well. Light pink flowers are formed above the foliage.

'Green Spice' has become one of my favorites. Its understated leaves are green with some silvering in the veins, and this stands out against its more riotous cousins.

Not sexy, not overbearing, just a fine-looking plant. Often listed as a cultivar of *H. americana* (which see).

'Guardian Angel' is one of the numerous selections in the Angel series, developed in Europe. This one is only about 12″ tall with small white flowers over dusky bronze foliage.

'Gypsy Dancer' produces dark veins throughout the silvery leaves, and many pink flowers. These flower as prolifically as any heuchera I have seen.

'Harmonic Convergence' has bronze and silver foliage with light pink flowers. Plants have performed well at the Gardens at UGA.

'Hearts on Fire' produces deep bronze foliage and dozens of white flowers with a hint of pink. Plants are useful in containers or rock garden situations.

'Helen Dillon' exuberantly bears loads of pink top rose flowers over green leaves with silver markings. Named for the exuberant grand dame of Irish gardening.

'Hercules' has deep red flowers over green and white variegated foliage. May be closely related to *H. sanguinea*.

'Hollywood' is another excellent flowering selection, providing large, rose-colored flowers over handsome bronze foliage. The flowers are among the largest of the recently selected cultivars.

'Jade Gloss' has glossy silvery leaves and dark green veins, the undersides of which are purple. Large pink flowers arise in spring.

'June Bride' has green leaves but bears a profusion of white flowers, each with a hint of pink. No longer common, superseded by newer forms.

'Key Lime Pie' is similar to 'Lime Rickey' in having bright chartreuse foliage. Very eye-catching in containers and in the ground.

'Licorice' is similar to 'Obsidian' in having glossy dark, almost black leaves. In our trials at the Gardens at UGA, plants were equally good in every way. Part of the Dolce™ series.

'Lime Rickey' is one of the most colorful chartreuse forms on the market. The leaves are slightly ruffled and the small flowers are white. Between this and 'Key Lime Pie', no other chartreuse choices are required.

'Mahogany' has ruffled, shiny leaves in a nice mahogany color. The foliage is the best part of the plant.

'Mardi Gras' is a weird assemblage of color on the leaves, a real raucous Mardi Gras. It definitely takes some getting used to. Not one of my favorites, but I am Canadian.

'Marmalade' is a changing kaleidoscope of colors with pink and salmon being most obvious. Red flowers occur in the spring.

'Mars' is one of the many coral bells named after planets, a series that originated from breeders in Holland, also including 'Mercury', 'Saturn' and 'Venus', selected for their leaves rather than the flowers. This one has bronze foliage, 'Mercury' is green with dark markings, 'Saturn' bears rounded purple leaves and 'Venus' has silver tinted foliage.

'Midnight Burgundy' has dark purple, almost black foliage. Stunning, as are the other almost black forms.

'Midnight Rose' has deep bronze to purple leaves that are spotted with pink dots. Not my favorite, but interesting, to be sure. Plants were a sport of 'Obsidian'.

'Mint Frost' has dark green venation through the silver foliage.

'Mocha Mint' is similar to many silvery foliage cultivars with deeper venation, such as 'Mint Frost' and 'Crème de Menthe'.

'Monet' is one of a few white variegated or spotted foliage forms. The green leaves are copiously splashed with white. Red flowers contrast well. Beautiful to be sure, but none of the white variegated forms like this have particularly good heat tolerance.

'Molly Bush' is a darker selection of 'Palace Purple' selected by Allen Bush of Louisville. In the first edition of this book (1989), I mentioned that Mr. Bush was selecting consistency from 'Palace Purple' and this plant, named for his daughter, is the result.

'Montrose Ruby' arose from a cross between 'Palace Purple' and 'Dale's Selection' in the 1990s and was named for the former Montrose Nursery in North Carolina. These breakthrough hybrids exhibited purple leaves with silver markings, and not only became popular selections but also served as the building blocks for the next generation of heucheras.

'Mystic Angel' starts out with green foliage and darker venation and turns to bronze as the season progresses.

'Obsidian' produces deep purple, almost black foliage. One of three or four cultivars that display this waxy deep dark look, and this is an excellent, popular form. Quite beautiful. Flowers are insignificant on all the black forms. I like this and 'Licorice' as my choices for a black cultivar.

'Palace Purple' was one of the finest introductions in recent years, selected as the Perennial Plant of the Year in 1991 and is still as good as any. The ivy-shaped foliage is deep purple but the color is deeper in the spring and fall, fading to bronze green under hot summer conditions. The flowers are of small consequence and add little to the plant. There is a good deal of variation in depth of color and those with the darkest reds should be propagated vegetatively. Due to the demand for this plant, a good many retailers were selling seed-propagated plants, to the great detriment of the cultivar. While mainly true from seed, green-leaf, purple-leaf forms and all hues in between were thrust at the gardening public. Today, the 'Palace Purple' name designates a plant that may be a superior garden plant or merely a mediocre one. Demand vegetatively-propagated plants or look for 'Purple Palace Select' or 'Palace Purple Improved'.

'Paris' has excellent rosy red flowers over bronze to silver leaves. Plants will rebloom, good for containers. Somewhat similar to 'Hollywood'. Makes me wonder if 'Sioux City' will be next.

'Peach Flambe' actually does have peach-colored foliage, at least in the spring. The smooth margins of the leaves allow for the color to show up well. White flowers are also formed.

'Peach Melba' has peachy to salmon foliage. A beautiful plant, not as bright as 'Amber Waves', somewhat similar to 'Peach Flambe'.

'Peachy Keen' kind of reminds of 'Mardi Gras', that is, the leaves are so busy with so many colors, it becomes tiring. Just my opinion, of course.

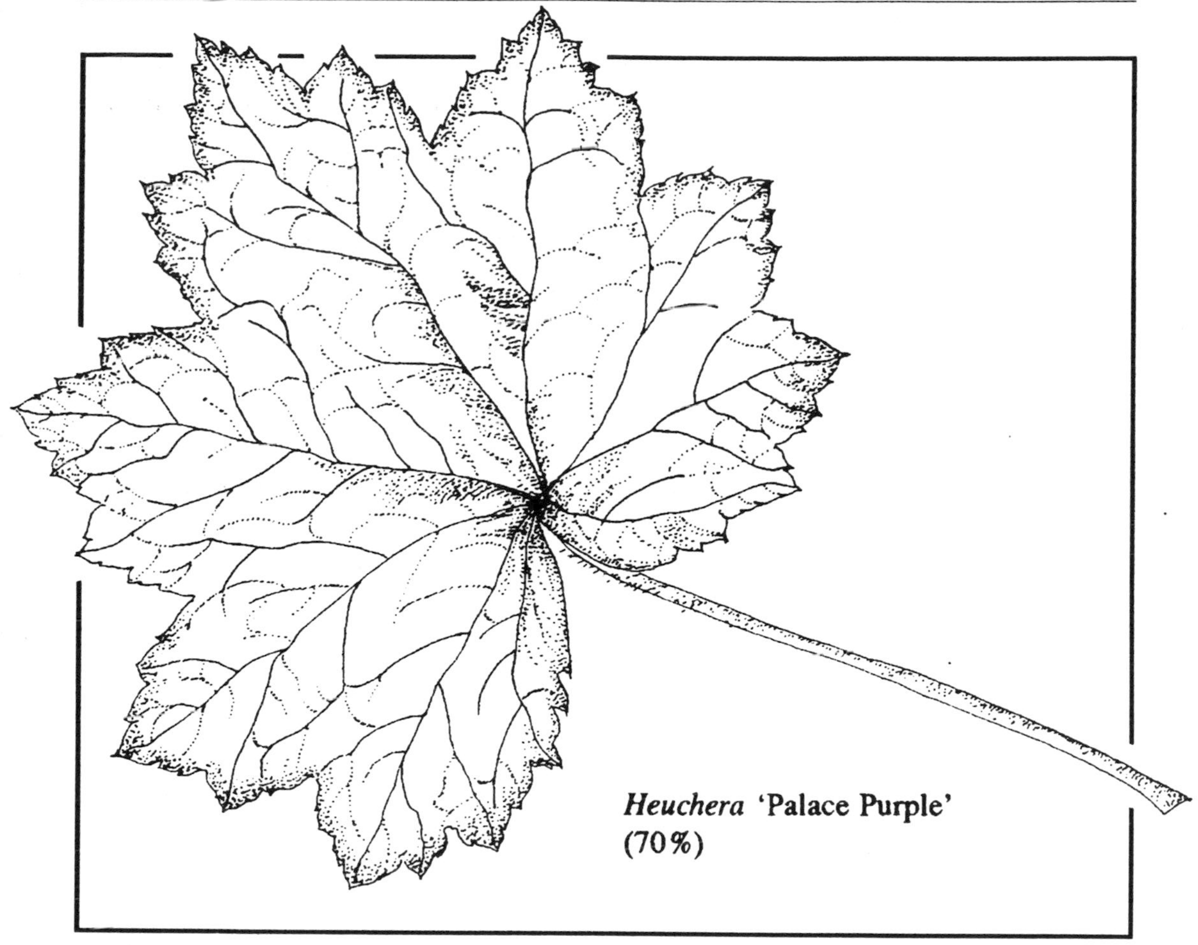

***Heuchera* 'Palace Purple'**
**(70%)**

'Peppermint Spice' has foliage somewhat resembling that of *H. americana*, however, rose-pink flowers are formed in the spring. I am a fan of all the "Spices".

'Persian Carpet' produces handsome mounds of silver foliage with greenish purple venation.

Petite series comes from Charles and Martha Oliver and consists of hybrids of alpine species, thus ensuring short compact habit, and if conditions are right, an abundance of flowers, usually pink, sometimes white. 'Petite Pearl Fairy', with purple foliage and rose-pink flowers, is one of my favorites. Excellent for small areas or rock garden settings.

'Pewter Veil' is one of the Veil series, and this one produces pewter-colored foliage. A vigorous grower.

'Pewter Moon' has pewter veins on the silver-green leaves. The backsides of the foliage are purple. Flowers are light pink.

'Plum Pudding' is more compact than many others and has shiny deep burgundy leaves.

'Pink Lipstick' is grown for the many tall pink flowers which arise over the green foliage in the spring.

'Prince of Orange' is a particularly gruesome selection with ruffled leaves in shades of orange and brown. That this a rather recent selection tells me that perhaps we can stop now.

'Purple Mountain Majesty' has consistently bright purple leaves and creamy white flowers in the spring.

'Purple Petticoats' bear dark compact foliage ruffled foliage, purple on the top and burgundy beneath.

'Rachel' produces shiny purple leaves and good pink flowers.

'Raspberry Ice' has many rose-pink flowers over handsome silvered foliage.

'Raspberry Regal' bears raspberry red flowers on tall naked flower stems. The foliage is not particularly exciting but the plant adds a robust dimension to the many cultivars. Terrific for cut flowers as well. Old cultivar, hard to locate.

'Rave On' has wonderfully deep pink flowers over small bronze silvery leaves. This has been the best flowering heuchera in our extensive trials at Georgia, bar none!

'Regina' is one of my favorite coral bells. She bears dozens of flower stems of rosy pink flowers over handsome dark bronze foliage.

'Rose Mirrors' has handsome pink flowers over consistently bronze foliage.

'Royal Velvet' produces dark bronze foliage with silver veins and light pink flowers.

'Ruby Bells' probably is a cultivar of *H. sanguinea* and bears many ruby red flowers over green foliage.

'Ruby Veil' of the Veil family, bears large ruby-bronze leaves. Quite vigorous.

'Sashay' has ruffles on the leaf ruffles, with green on the upper surfaces and bronze below. As I see this a bit more, it is growing on me.

'Shenandoah Mountain' has trialed very well in the Gardens at UGA. Plants are vigorous and produce silvery purple foliage and many creamy white flowers.

'Silver Light' is compact and probably as silvery as any of the silver heucheras we have trialed. Pink flowers are formed in late spring.

'Silver Lode' has dull bronze silver foliage over which tower sprays of white flowers.

'Silver Scrolls' has performed well and provides a lovely pink cast to the silver foliage in the spring, then gets darker as the summer progresses. White flowers with pink are formed in the spring.

'Silver Shadows' has silver leaves with a hint of pink. The leaves are thick and the plants are nicely compact.

'Snow Angel' was one of the first of the variegated forms. White spotting with rosy pink flowers. This was selected by Bluebird Nursery, Clarkson, Nebraska, and was a 2003 Plant Select® winner, a program for the Rocky Mountain and Plains states. In the East, it is beautiful, but with little staying power in the heat.

'Sparkling Burgundy' bears light burgundy foliage in the spring that darkens to a more burgundy caste in the summer. White flowers are produced in the spring.

'Starry Night' has dark foliage with pink and white bicolored flowers.

'Stormy Seas' has shown good vigor in our trials. The ruffled foliage is a mix of bronze, silver and light colors.

'Strawberry Candy' is another of the wonderful flowering cultivars that have seemed to disappear with the advent of the love affair with colorful foliage. Handsome green foliage with obvious venation is at the base of the deep pink flowers.

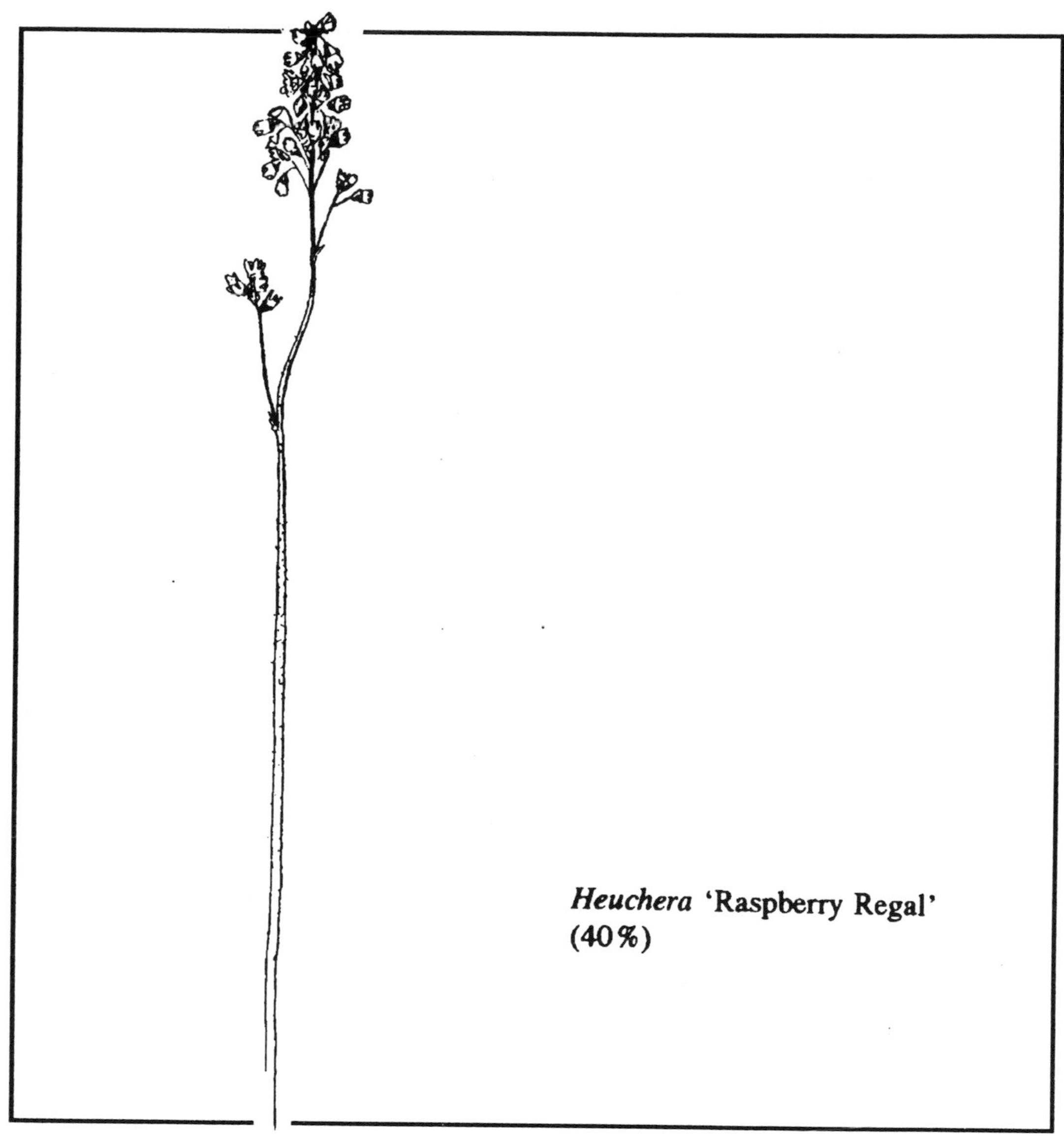

*Heuchera* **'Raspberry Regal' (40%)**

'Strawberry Swirls' bears strawberry pink flowers over ruffled light green foliage.

'Tango' has glossy burgundy leaves and deep red flowers.

'Vanilla Spice' is similar to 'Peppermint Spice'.

'Velvet Night' was probably one of the darkest heucheras when first introduced, but others have superseded it. Still a nice hybrid, with plum black leaves with metallic silver venation.

Veil is attached to the name of many excellent new cultivars raised by Dan Heims. All are 15-20″ tall. I have already mentioned 'Chocolate', 'Pewter' and 'Ruby Veil', but others such as 'Emerald Veil' with silvery foliage with a green edge and green veins and 'Silver Veil', silver netted with cerise-rose flowers, may still be available.

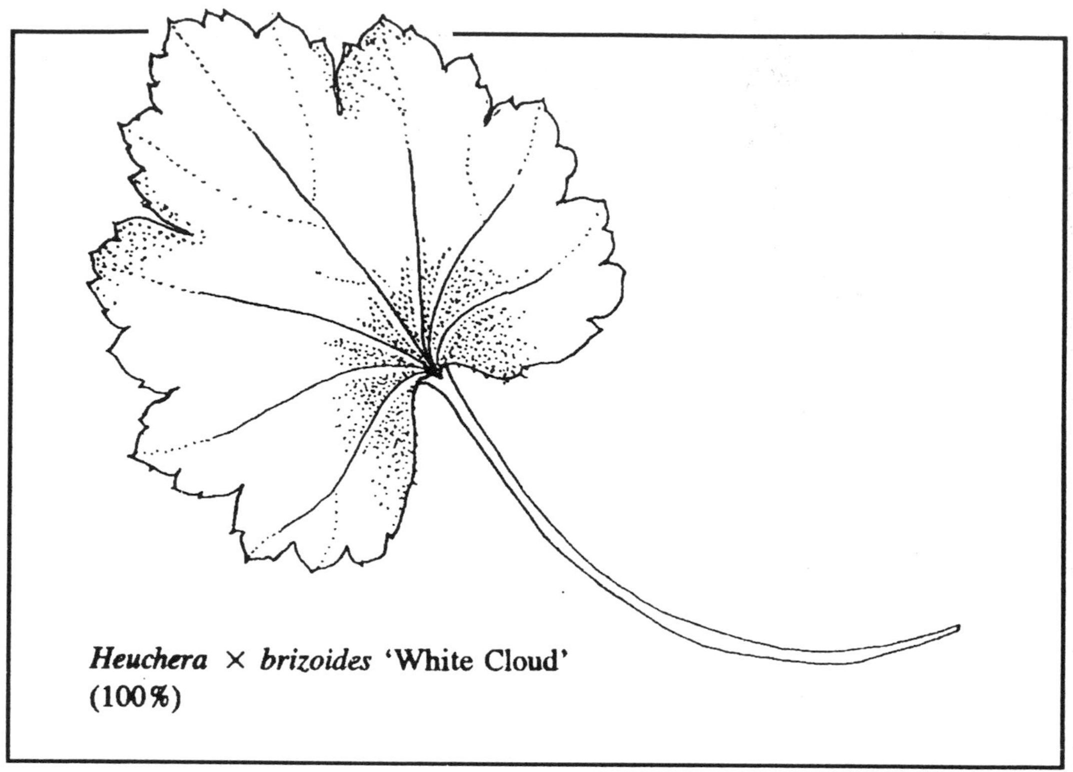

***Heuchera* × *brizoides* 'White Cloud' (100%)**

'Vesuvius' is one of the best combinations of flower power and handsome foliage I have seen. Many pink to rose flowers atop the burgundy foliage. Quite outstanding.

'White Cloud' produces dozens of flower stalks upon which hundreds of small white flowers are carried. This is an old cultivar in coral bell years but is still one of the finest cultivars and is truly a "white cloud". 'Coral Cloud' is similar in habit, but produces dense sprays of coral-red flowers.

## *X Heucherella* (hew′ ker-ell-a) Foamy Bells Saxifragaceae

Many examples of hybrids are between species within a genus (interspecific hybrids) however a few intergeneric hybrids (between genera) have also occurred. X *Heucherella* (the X denotes an intergeneric cross but is not sounded) occurred in 1912 in Nancy, France between a heuchera hybrid and *Tiarella cordifolia*. One of the early popular species (X *H. alba*) was produced in the 1950s by Alan Bloom of Blooms of Bressingham Nursery. Although heucherellas combine garden-worthy characteristics of both parents, the offspring vary a great deal in vigor and character. Some introductions in recent years grow well under nursery production conditions but do poorly under "real world" conditions. Recently, as the number of hybrids of *Heuchera* and *Tiarella* have exploded, one would expect a similar morphing of cultivars of foamy bells. However, since heucherellas are sterile, hybridization has been slower than for either parent.

Two species are recognized, X *H. alba*, and X *H. tiarelloides*, known as white foamy bells and foamy bells, respectively. The parentage is slightly different but both are somewhat stoloniferous and require similar environments of moist shade, similar to the parents. Full sun is not recommended.

**Cultivars**:

Because of the generic cross, many gardeners have a "I must have one" feeling about them, and plants have become reasonably popular. They perform well in the Northeast and Northwest, reasonably well in the Midwest, and struggle to persist for more than a few years in the South. As much as I enjoy the botany of the genus, I have yet to be thrilled with garden performance in most areas of the country for any but 2-3 of them. However, where they do well, they can be quite spectacular.

*Older cultivars (before 1995):* Most of these are no longer commercially available, but they provided some of the "bones" for the modern cultivars.

'Bridget Bloom' produces lovely shell-pink flowers, mounded habit, and flowers for at least eight weeks. Plants often take a year or two to become established. I have seen some impressive plantings in the Northeast and Midwest but in the South, it is marginal at best. Compared with the ease of its parents, it is a difficult plant to recommend. This cultivar was raised in 1955 by Alan Bloom, and was the earliest selection on the market. For no other reason, its historical value makes it important.

'Crimson Clouds' has deeper green, almost purple coloration on the leaves and dark pink flowers. Raised by Heims from tissue culture of Terra Nova.

'Pink Frost', raised by Charles and Martha Oliver (1987), bears pink starry flowers over silver-green foliage.

'Rosalie', another early Oliver introduction (1983), produces dark green leaves with purple centers. The flowers are deep pink.

'Snow White' produces probably some of the whitest flowers in this intergeneric cross.

'White Frost' has white flowers with a touch of pink.

*Modern cultivars:*

'Birthday Cake' from Terra Nova Nursery, has coppery bronze foliage and many spires of white flowers. The copper color is unique.

'Burnished Bronze' has more glossy and less cut foliage than the previous cultivar, and produces pink flowers in the spring.

'Cinnamon Bear' forms a low mound of lobed leaves of dull cinnamon brown. Creamy white flowers appear in late spring and early summer.

'Dayglow Pink' is a handsome selection bearing green lobed leaves, each with a dark center. The dozens of deep pink flowers contrast well with the foliage.

'Heart of Darkness', bred by Primrose Path Nursery, refers to the dark centers in each of the deep green leaves. Plants produce many white flowers.

'Kimono' has lovely lobed leaves with reddish venation. One of the best performers, they grow well even in areas where others do poorly. I have seen many white flowers at times, but they are not heavy flowerers.

'Party Time' is a shorter form (less than 12") producing green leaves with a hint of bronze, and many light pink flowers.

'Quicksilver' has been a hit in most gardens, because of its good looks and above average vigor. Plants did well in the Gardens at UGA compared to others at that time and I recommend it often. The dark silvery green foliage combined with the white flowers are most effective.

'Stoplight' and its cousin 'Sunspot' have brought bright foliage color to the genus. This selection bears large, rich golden leaves with red venation and a red center. White flowers are formed, but they add little to the plant. Excellent in shady areas where plants do well.

Strike it Rich series from Proven Winners™ consists of 'Pink Gem' with pink flowers over green leaves, and 'Gold' which has chartreuse leaves with red venation, similar to 'Sunspot'.

'Sunspot' is similar to 'Stoplight' but the leaves are more rounded, considerably smaller and do not bear as much red pigment. Still quite eye-popping.

'Viking Ship' is vigorous and bears cut leaves, somewhat similar to red maple foliage. The large pink to coral flowers are quite beautiful.

## *Hexastylis* — See *Asarum*

## *Hibiscus* (hi-bis' cus) — Hibiscus — Malvaceae

*Hibiscus* contains over 200 species, mainly from tropical and subtropical areas of the world. The diversity of the genus is easily seen when one passes a large shrub or small tree of rose of Sharon, *H. syriacus*, admires the huge flowers of the hardy hibiscus, *H. moscheutos*, observes the exotic flowers of the greenhouse-grown *H. rosa-sinensis*, and marvels at the reseeding tendencies of the annual flower-of-the-hour, *H. trionum*. Many of the more choice species are native to southern United States and gardeners in those areas may expect additional cultivars in the near future.

Annuals have been used in the flower trade for some time and include the aforementioned white-flowered *H. trionum*, the seed-propagated F1 hybrids such as the Southern Belle series, the marginally hardy shrubby Confederate rose, *H. mutabilis* and the red-leaved red shield, *H. acetosella*. The latter is going through some wonderful times, with new cultivars like 'Maple Sugar', 'Panama Red' and 'Panama Bronze' finding their way to American gardens. Depending on severity of the winter and amount of mulching, some of these annuals may return as far north as zone 8, but from the gardening point of view, they should be treated as annuals; anything that returns is a bonus. Few species are cold hardy north of zone 5, but flowers are so bold and useful, they are worth trying even as annuals.

Quick Reference to Hibiscus Species

| | Height (ft.) | Flower color |
|---|---|---|
| *H. coccineus* | 5-7 | Scarlet, red |
| *H. moscheutos* | 2-3 | Various |
| *H. mutabilis* | 8-10 | Pink |

***-coccineus*** (cock-sin-e′ us) | Swamp Hibiscus | 5-7′/3′
Summer | Red | Georgia, Florida | Zones 7-9

Plants are some of the showiest in June and July in the southern states, producing many solitary, 3-5″ wide, red flowers in the upper leaf axils of the tall plant. The stamens are extended from the flower making them as handsome from close up as from a distance. The leaves are palmately compound and look like those of either Japanese maple or marijuana, whichever you happen to be most familiar with. Tony Avent of Plant Delights Nursery calls it a "see through" plant because of its tall, skinny stature. While they are not as dense as many other species, they will stop traffic and

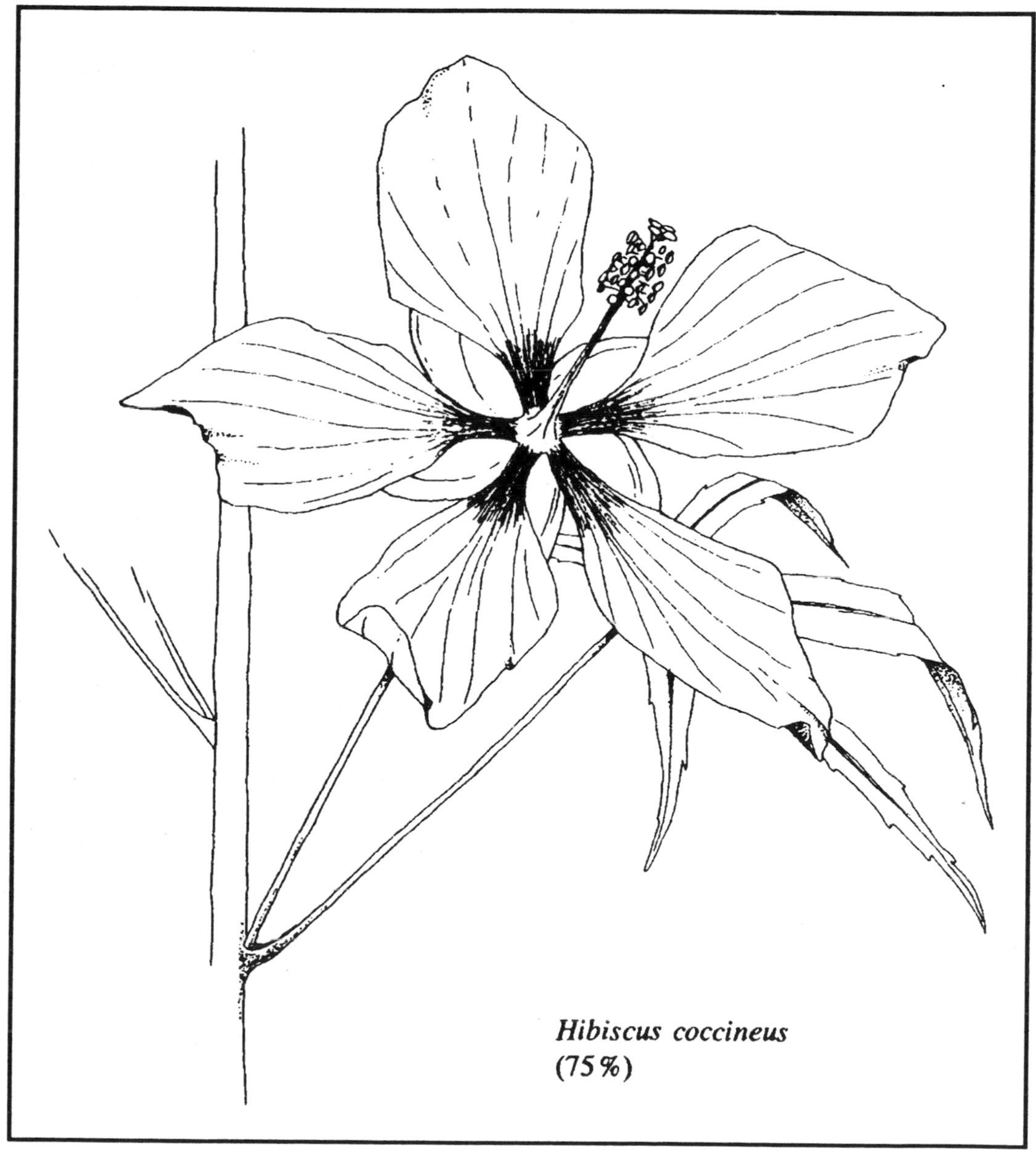

*Hibiscus coccineus*
(75%)

result in more questions from your visitors than most other plants in flower at that time. The plants become woody at the base and the stems and the ornamental seed pods can also be enjoyed over the winter.

One of the bonuses of planting this species is that plants are not attacked as vigorously by Japanese beetles whereas its more common cousin, *H. moscheutos*, often looks like a shotgun exploded through the leaves after the beetles have arrived.

They are called swamp hibiscus for good reason—they love wet areas and require a sufficient supply of water, especially as they begin to flower, to be at their best. They may even be planted in the shallow end of garden ponds. Plant in full sun for best effect. Shade results in even taller plants with a paucity of flowers. Plants are late to arise in the spring; don't give up too quickly.

**Cultivars**:

'Red Flyer' is a hybrid between *H. coccineus* and *H. grandiflorus* from Plant Delights Nursery in Raleigh, North Carolina. The 10-12′ tall plants produce three-lobed leaves and red wide open flowers similar to *H. coccineus.*

***-moscheutos*** (mos-kew′ tas) Common Mallow 3-4′/3′
Summer Various Eastern United States Zone 5-9

Vigorous and robust, these large-leaved and large-flowered plants grace gardens south to Miami and as far north as Indianapolis. Once established, many stems emerge late in the spring and flower from early to midsummer. The unlobed ovate to lance-shaped leaves range from 4″ to 10″ in length and the 4-5″ wide flowers are white, rose or pink and borne in the axils of the many stems.

Two of the biggest problem are Japanese beetles and sawflies, which are attracted to this and other members of the Malvaceae, such as hollyhocks. However, not all cultivars are abused equally, perhaps a defense mechanism may be genetically enhanced with additional selection.

Plants require full sun and good air circulation for disease suppression. Consistent soil moisture is also important but they need not be planted in swampy areas.

**Cultivars**:

Today's cultivars are likely hybrids with other vigorous members of the genus. Many breeders have left their mark on this species and we are all better for them.

Few have left a greater legacy than the Fleming Brothers—Jim, Robert and David—from Lincoln, Nebraska. They spent over 50 years creating unique hybrids, celebrated for their stunning blooms, cold hardiness and compact growth habit. Unfortunately, all three brothers have passed away, the last, Dave, in 2001. They crossed various native species of hibiscus to create their hybrids, many of which are now lost. However, their business continues to thrive today, and some of their more recent crosses have been distributed widely. Plants may be considered compact, but don't fool yourself, a single plant is sufficient. I have seen them as hedges or in smaller groups of three to five but space has not been an issue. Most are winter hardy to zone 4 or 5.

'Anne Arundel' is a pink-flowered hybrid which grows 4-5′ tall. The foliage is more deeply cut than most of the other cultivars. This cultivar has been around for many years and her popularity is undiminished.

'Blue River II' bears clear white flowers with no eye, up to 10″ across. The deep green foliage bears a hint of blue. An excellent long-flowering selection.

Carafe series from Yoder Brothers in Barberton, Ohio, consists of large-flowered plants that grow to about 3′ tall. Plants include 'Bordeaux', 'Chablis', and 'Grenache', with red, white and pink flowers, respectively. Flowers average 8″ across. Zones 5-9.

'Clown' bears enormous pink-purple flowers, each with a dark eye. Plants grow 4-5′ tall.

Cordial series is a group of upright, well-branched plants standing about 4′ tall, with dark green foliage and large, saucer-shaped flowers. At least five different colors are available.

'Cranberry Punch' has deep red flowers on 2-3′ tall plants. Developed by Dr. Carl Whitcomb of Oklahoma.

'Crimson Wonder' bears rich red ruffled flowers up to 10″ across.

'Crown Jewels' is similar to 'Kopper King' but is more compact in every way. Flowers are only about half the size but dark colors and red-eyed flowers are still the norm.

'Disco Belle', 'Disco Rosy Red', and 'Disco White' are all F1 seed-propagated strains which are popular because of their compact habits and large flowers. Excellent plants for the smaller garden, but unfortunately, similar to most others, Japanese beetles can be devastating.

'Fantasia' has big semi-double rose-red flowers, each with a darker center, on 3-4′ tall plants.

'Fireball' is another Fleming hybrid, this one with fire engine red flowers. Plants are not quite as upright or vigorous as 'Kopper King', but the flower color can be seen from at least two football fields away.

'Flare' was introduced in Texas and was named one of the Texas Superstar™ plants. The semi-glossy leaves and 10″ wide fuchsia-red flowers are borne on 5′ tall plants.

Fleming Hybrids are the result of the excellent work of the Fleming brothers. They all bear huge 8-10″ wide flowers, often pink but many with picotee edges and centered with a red eye. Great plants, great work.

'George Riegel', introduced by Carroll Gardens in Maryland, bears fine light pink flowers with a dark red eye. About 4′ tall in full sun.

'Giant Maroon' is self-explanatory.

'Kopper King' is quite outstanding. Plants grow 4′ tall and equally white and produce copper colored foliage which persists reasonably well throughout the summer. The large white flowers have a tinge of pink and sport a large red blotch in the center.

'Lady Baltimore' is an old and well established hybrid, producing 6-9″ wide deep pink slightly ruffled flowers with red centers. Plants generally grow 4-6′ tall.

'Lester Riegel' bears pink flowers with a red eye and deeper pink veins.

'Lord Baltimore' has large crimson red ruffled flowers and deeply lobed leaves. Profuse bloomer.

'Moy Grande' appears to be a hybrid between *H. moscheutos* and *H. grandiflorus* and was bred by Mr. Ying Doon Moy, formerly of the San Antonio Botanical Garden. The flowers resemble the shape of those of *H. grandiflorus* and the foliage is seldom attacked by beetles. Plants have thrived in the Gardens at UGA.

'Old Yella' tells me that someone could not spell, or there was only a partial yellow color somewhere. The flowers are white with a small red eye. The foliage is green and in fact, the plants are fair at best. The only yellow I can find is in the flower buds. This cultivar gets absolutely eaten up by Japanese beetles.

'Pink Clouds' was introduced by Bluebird Nursery in Clarkson, Nebraska. The 4-5′ tall plants produce maplelike foliage, over which are borne large 10-12″ diameter pink flowers.

'Plum Crazy' produces deep plum, ruffled 8-9″ wide flowers. The foliage is deeply cut.

'Raspberry Rose' produces dozens of 8-10″ wide raspberry-red flowers in midsummer. Not a small fellow—provide room for a 7′ tall plant in the garden.

'Royal Gems' is only 3-4′ tall and produces rose-colored flowers with a red eye. The foliage is dark green, with a hint of purple in the spring.

'Ruby Dot' has white flowers with slightly overlapping petals. Each flower has a ruby red eye. Plants grow about 4′ tall.

'Southern Belle' is a mixed strain of red, white, pink and bicolored flowers. They are larger than the other Belles such as 'Disco Belle'.

Splash series from Yoder consists of short, compact plants, about 2½′ tall at maturity, with 8-9″ diameter flowers. 'Pinot Noir' and 'Pinot Grigio' have red, and white with pink-centered flowers, respectively.

'Strawberry Swirl' has light pink flowers with clean white veins. Plants grow to about 4′ tall.

'Sweet Caroline' bears large dark-veined light pink 6-8″ wide flowers slightly ruffled at the edges. Plants grow quite large, sometimes attaining over 5′ in height.

'Turn of the Century' can grow quite tall, up to 7′ in height. The bicolored flowers are very light pink, with darker pink coloration on the edges. The center of the flower is cherry red.

| -***mutabilis*** (mew-tah′ bi-lis) | | Confederate Rose | 8-10′/5′ |
|---|---|---|---|
| Pink | Late Summer, Fall | China | Zones 7-10 |

The common name, Confederate rose, makes one think that this species is native to the South. However, plants are from China and were given the common name when introduced to Florida. This can be a large (up to 10′ tall) shrubby plant with broad fuzzy palmately lobed leaves and large pink flowers. The stems become woody by the end of the season and new growth in the spring is slow to emerge. The limits to cold tolerance are probably zone 7, perhaps zone 6b with sufficient mulching. Even as annuals, however, plants are worth the space.

The term "mutabilis" means "changing", referring to the change of flower color. In the species, flowers open white or pink but change to deep red in the evening. I think the pink flowers which do not change color are even more handsome. Plants require full sun for best performance and consistent moisture. Less susceptible to Japanese beetles than *H. moscheutos* but more tasty to them than *H. coccineus*.

**Cultivars:**

'Flore-plenum' is the most common form, bearing fully double pink blossoms which resemble large camellia flowers.

'Raspberry Rose' bears raspberry red single flowers.

'Rubrum' has more oval leaves and large scarlet single flowers. Plants can get 7-8′ tall but if cut back in early summer, a less aggressive plant will result.

**Related Species:**

*H. aculeatus*, pineland hibiscus, has wonderful yellow flowers on 2-3′ tall plants. Likely hardy in zone 7 and south.

*H. grandiflorus*, velvet mallow, is one of my favorite species. Plants can grow 4-5′ tall but the gray velvety leaves—12 inches long, three to five lobed—are stunning. They remind me of lamb's ear, *Stachys*, when I rub them and put them against my cheek. Oops, sorry, getting a little too intimate with the plants. The 5-6″ wide flowers are usually pink, often with a crimson spot at the base and don't flower until late summer. White-flowered forms are also known. Hardy in zones 7 to 9, possibly into zone 6 with sufficient winter mulching. Native to the coastal areas of the southeastern United States. Some hybrids with *H. coccineus* have occurred.

*H. lasiocarpos*, wooly mallow, has 4-6″ long, hairy leaves with 4-5″ wide pink or white flowers with red centers. Plants are about four feet tall. A handsome, relatively unknown species native from southern Illinois to Florida. Likely hardy in zones 5 to 9.

*H. palustris* has handsome large pink flowers, although they sometimes are white or purple. Plants grow up to 8′ tall with flowers up to 6″ across. Native from Massachusetts to North Carolina and to Ontario and Illinois.

## ***Hosta*** (hos′ ta) Plantain Lily, Funkia Liliaceae

Daylilies may be kings of the sun but unquestionably hostas are the emperors of the shade. I remember walking down my grandmother's path in Montreal as a child where variegated hostas had long ago been planted on either side. It was a dim, dark pathway but the light airy foliage lit the way. Nothing else would grow there and that path was a living testament to the toughness of these lovely plants that my grandmother identified as funkias. They also made my grandmother seem like a horticultural genius.

Hostas have been around for centuries but were "rediscovered" in the 1980s and there has been little letup since. The nomenclature is in a state of flux and the parentage of most hybrids is not always certain. Many times hostas are sold with a cultivar name only (i.e. no specific epithet), because there have been so many different species in the pedigree that it is far easier just to call it by a single name. Having said that, the genus *Hosta* is probably as well documented as any genus we grow. Most hostas are registered with the American Hosta Society and specific information on the breeder, plant description and parentage are available. At the time of this writing (2007), the AHS showed over 3,500 cultivars on its website. Not quite as many as *Hemerocallis* but enough to fill the back yard.

Leaf texture may be shiny, smooth or puckered, various shades of green, blue-green, white, or edged with gold, yellow or white. They may be narrow, broad and wavy, entire or even twisted. When not in flower, plants can range from 6″ to 3′ in height. Although hostas are usually grown for their foliage, the flowers can be quite magnificent. In some taxa, wonderful 3′ spires (racemes) of lilac, purple, or white flowers rise above the foliage in summer and in mature plantings are as ornamental as bright spring tulips. Where large, old green-leaved hosta clumps occur, they are usually *H. fortunei* or *H. ventricosa* whose lavender and violet flowers, respectively, overwhelm the landscape around them. I am reminded of the great old flowering clumps at Chesterwood in western Massachusetts, the Minnesota Landscape Arboretum in Chaska, the Cleveland Botanical Garden, and many other mature garden plantings. Fragrance has become an important element in the garden and hostas are not without their scented members. Using the white flowers of *H. plantaginea* as a building block, numerous plants are touted for their aromatic blossoms. These include the cultivars of *H. plantaginea* ('Honeybells', 'Grandiflora') and hybrids with names like 'Fragrant Bouquet', 'Summer Fragrance' and 'Fragrant Blue'. However, if fragrance is important, others such as *H.* 'Heaven Scent', 'Invincible', 'So Sweet' and 'Sugar and Cream' are also nicely scented. A much-heralded breakthrough in breeding in the 1990s resulted in the double white flowers of 'Aphrodite', which some gardeners fainted over, especially after they received the bill. While the flowers of hosta are in themselves handsome, they have had little to do with the increased popularity of this genus. In fact, flowers are best removed from many plants less they detract from the foliage.

There are literally hundreds of hybrids, cultivars, and species from which to choose and more become available every year. Perhaps it is time to slow down lest there develop as many cultivars of hosta as there are of petunia. There are so many hostas now that the professional breeder must make serious financial decisions concerning the payback of new cultivars and hybrids which are only marginally different from those already on the market. The amateur breeder will continue to enjoy the results of his hobby, naming clones regardless of existing similarities.

Hostas grow best in rich, well-drained soil with constant moisture and light shade. They tolerate moderately heavy shade and grow well in areas where grass dies and ferns and mosses delight. The tolerance of sun for some taxa is constantly debated, and if moisture is plentiful and constant, many can tolerate full sun. This is especially true in the Northeast and Northwest where ample moisture is available. However, why does one want hostas in full sun when there are so many choices for sunny areas and so few for the shade? Without doubt, these plants do not tolerate full sun in the South or Midwest. Moisture is important and allowing plants to dry out is the quickest way to ruin the planting. Under dry conditions, leaves are smaller, turn light brown and papery around the edges and never reach their full growth potential.

The amount of puckering on the leaves dictates usefulness under trees. Those heavily puckered catch the drippings from tree leaves complete with gums, saps and other materials. Said drippings cause plants to look particularly wretched. Glossy or smooth-leaved plants are less prone to tree droppings.

Hostas are fabulous choices for the low-maintenance garden but are in no way problem-free. Nothing is more frustrating than to discover plants ravaged by deer. Usually, the deer wait long enough to let you think that they may not be interested this year, then some silent dinner bell bongs inside the entire herd's heads, and another year is down the tubes. I am not sure what can be done, other than building a deer fence or spraying some disgusting-smelling concoction on the plants every week. I use a commercial product called Liquid Fence™ and it works well for me. This is not an endorsement, simply my preference. I live in the woods, and I have to do something. But I still love my hostas and refuse to give in to Bambi.

I have seen enough plantings of hostas in various parts of the country to realize that the love affair with these fine plants will abruptly end if the deer problem is not treated seriously by the breeders. We have enough blues, yellows and variegated forms, what we don't have is enough deer-resistant ones. I have seen partial lists of "deer resistant" cultivars in various catalogs, but that list needs to be seriously tested in a proper program, expanded and used as stock blocks for the program. I hope the breeders can tackle this problem or hostas may go the way of the American chestnut.

Then there are slugs. Slugs and snails devour the newly emerging foliage with gusto. Hostas are to slugs what chocolate is to people. Early and frequent application of slug pellets is essential to keep them at bay. Beer may also be used, but why waste good beer? Without doubt, the gardener can reduce slug problems by good maintenance of the plants. Remove old leaves, weed around the plants and use a loose, shallow mulch to keep the plants growing vigorously.

Then there are voles. These little suckers burrow underground and bump into the roots of your prize hostas only. Not being happy with the interruption of their journey, they simply eat the obstruction. One day, the plant is fine, the next day, it is leaning to portside and can easily be lifted since almost all the roots have been devoured. If you don't rescue the plants at that stage, they may simply disappear down the vole hole, as if a string puller from hell was slowly reeling it in. Gardeners claim that castor beans planted near the hostas help, others dilute castor oil with water and dump it in the holes, while those more frustrated don't even dilute it, trying to castor oil them to oblivion.

Black vine weevils have destroyed leaves of my plantings before I even knew they were there. They are about ½-1" long, black and incredibly hungry. They appear in north Georgia around mid June and stay about 2-3 weeks. With heavy infestations, they cover the plants and ravage the leaves. And let us not forget our friends the cutworms, who cut the leaves off as if with a razor, foliar nematodes, and Hosta Virus X. The latter two can be present in the plant and hardly show any symptoms, or can ravage the plant over time. And yet, we still buy these plants, verifying once again that gardeners are as crazy as ever.

Most hostas do not need dividing for many years and are, in fact, look far better as they age. Many plants often take 4-5 years before they reach maturity of form and color, and should not be judged too harshly if they are not "catalog-perfect" before then. Established clumps (greater than 5 years old) bear little resemblance to the majority of immature hostas grown in the average garden. Plants may be divided after 4-5 years and shared with your neighbor, but only if said neighbor promises you a bottle of high quality wine. Take a wedge-like slice when dividing and the division will not missed. Divide early in the spring when the tightly curled leaves are emerging. The number of crowns are easily visible at that time and damage is minimized. The price of a hosta varies with its availability and ease of propagation. Breakthroughs in tissue culture have occurred in recent years and many hostas offered today had their humble beginnings in a test tube.

Commercial production of hostas takes place throughout the country, generally in containers under shade. One of the problems with the production of any crop is that rapid turnover is correlated with relatively high fertility regimes. In areas of high temperatures, the use of nitrogen fertilizers results in loss of variegation in many cultivars. This is a lesson for both gardeners and producers, that is, hostas do not require large amounts of nitrogen fertility in the summer. This does not mean no fertilizer, simply that the best time to feed all hostas (I use a slow-release form) is early in the spring as the leaf spears just begin to emerge. Hostas are heavy feeders, but small amounts 2-3 times during the year is better than dousing them in the summer.

**Hosta Species**

While it seems that only hybrids are ever offered, the hosta world first cut its teeth on the many species of hostas that were originally propagated. Many of the species reside in collectors' gardens or botanical gardens, but seldom are many sold to the gardener. That is not to say they are without merit, quite the opposite in fact, simply they are seldom as colorful nor have such "interesting" names as many of the modern hybrids. Cultivars and variants of many species are offered (*H. sieboldiana* 'Elegans', *H. sieboldii* 'Kapitan', H. *plantaginea* 'Grandiflora', *H. fortunei* 'Albopicta' and H. *undulata* var. *univittata*.), but for all intents and purposes, rightly or wrongly, hostas are grown and sold by cultivar name only.

Some of the more popular species include *H. crispula*, curled leaf hosta, *H. decorata*, blunt hosta, *H. fortunei*, Fortune's hosta, *H. lancifolia*, lance leaf hosta, *H. plantaginea*, fragrant hosta, *H. sieboldiana*, Siebold hosta, *H. sieboldii*, seersucker hosta, *H. undulata*, wavy hosta, *H. ventricosa*, blue hosta and *H. venusta*, dwarf hosta.

Attempts have been made to key hostas into species but with so many common hybrids the exercise is difficult and quickly defeats all but the most patient plantspeople. There are, however, a number of characteristics which the observant plantsperson can use to detect differences between species and hybrids. These include foliage color, leaf texture (amount of puckering), margin, as well as the number of pairs

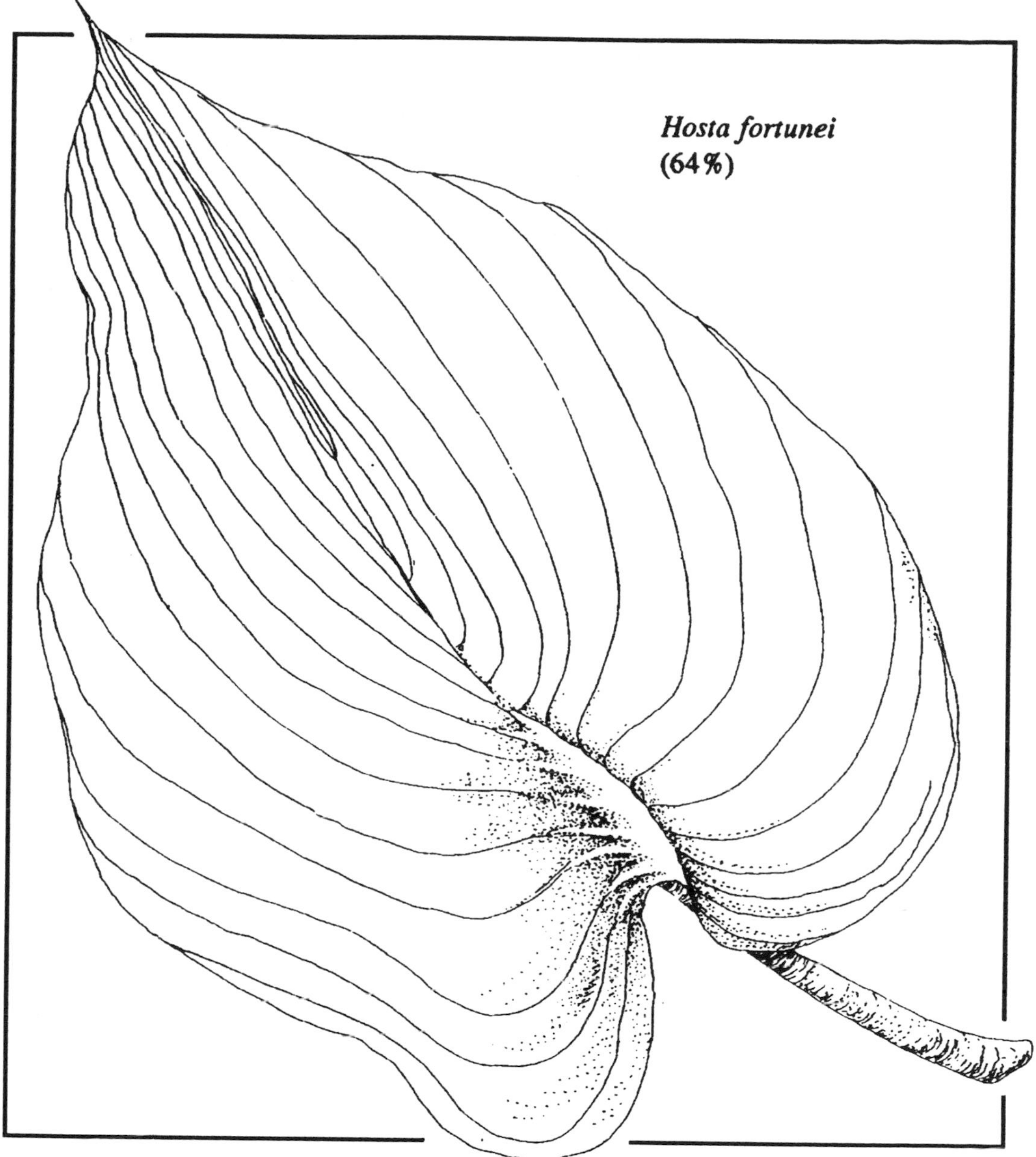

*Hosta fortunei*
**(64%)**

of veins on either side of the leaf midrib. Floral characteristics include the denseness of the inflorescence, flower color, and even the color of the anthers.

**Hosta Characteristics**

*Leaf color*: The diversity of leaf color and plant habit, not flowers, keeps the hosta desire fueled. Since the first thing everyone looks at in hostas is the foliage, hostas are classified according to foliage color (green, blue, chartreuse, variegated, etc.). Variegation patterns vary widely, from thin, white-variegated margins, to yellow and gold splashed throughout the leaf.

*Hosta plantaginea*
(60%)

*Mature size*: Further description of size is usually included to allow the gardener and landscaper to take a guess at the mature size when they are studying that 6″ pot containing a couple of leaves.

- *Dwarf* selections are less than 10″ tall. Cultivars encompass all leaf colors and patterns and are excellent for containers and rock gardens.
- *Small* hostas (10 to 15″ tall) are terrific for edging purposes, can grow together as ground covers or as background plants in the garden.
- *Medium* size taxa (15 to 22″ tall) can also be used for edging but generally are planted as ground covers, background or even as single specimens.
- *Large* taxa (over 22″ tall) are for those who prefer a more grandiose scale, and include selections that may reach 2-3′ tall and up to four feet wide when properly grown.

*Landscape use*: The use for hostas is determined by the gardener, but most cultivar descriptions include the following:

- Edger plants are used for edging, mainly small and medium hostas.
- Ground cover plants are usually quick growers, often stoloniferous and can be planted in large groups.
- Background plants are larger, and are often planted in clumps of three to five.
- Specimen plants may be any size, but are unique for fragrance, texture, color pattern, etc. They are among the most eye-catching. Often, one plant is sufficient to make a display.

*Flowering time*: Flowering time (spring, summer, fall) is sometimes included on good web sites or catalogs. Flowering time will be later in cool climates and earlier in warm.

**The Cop-Out**

In the first edition (1989) I grouped hostas by leaf color (green, white margins, etc.) and listed approximately 150 cultivars. In the second edition (1997), I spent weeks trying to gather similar information and listed over 210 cultivars. As I sat down in 2007 to try to add the last 10 years' worth of new members, I became stupefied at the challenge. After a few weeks of frustration (so many growers, descriptions so diverse, even for the same cultivar), I decided to smarten up and list a couple of sites the reader can learn all there is to know about cultivars. I hate "passing the buck" but I believe I am passing the right buck. The American Hosta Society (*www.hosta.org*) and the American Hosta Growers Association (*www.hostagrowers.org*) are two excellent organizations to provide answers. State chapters of the American Hosta Society may also be active. A number of excellent mail order nurseries specialize in hostas and they can not only sell you the hosta of your dreams but also provide quality information for hostas in your area. In short, they can do it better than I. However, I don't want to pass on every buck, so I have gathered a few lists. Here are a few interesting assemblages of hostas.

*Alex J. Summers Award* recognizes a member of the American Hosta Society for having given outstanding service to the Society, to the development of the genus *Hosta*, or both. The award winner then selects a hosta with distinguished merit.

*The Hosta of the Year* is named each year by the American Hosta Growers Association and recognizes a outstanding cultivar.

| | **Summers Award** | **Hosta of the Year** |
|---|---|---|
| 1995 | 'Sagae' | |
| 1996 | *H. laevigata* | 'So Sweet' |
| 1997 | *H. nigrescens* | 'Patriot' |
| 1998 | 'Alvatine Taylor' | 'Fragrant Bouquet' |
| 1999 | 'Breeder's Choice' | 'Paul's Glory' |
| 2000 | 'June' | 'Sagae' |
| 2001 | 'Krossa Regal' | 'June' |
| 2002 | 'American Halo' | 'Guacamole' |
| 2003 | 'Corkscrew' | 'Royal Splendor' |
| 2004 | 'Bridegroom' | 'Sum and Substance' |
| 2005 | 'Guardian Angel' | 'Striptease' |
| 2006 | 'Aphrodite' | 'Stained Glass' |
| 2007 | 'Dorothy Benedict' | 'Paradigm' |

Also, the AHS conducts popularity polls each year among its members. Here are the last three years' results; results for 2007 had not been posted as of February, 2008.

| | 2006 | 2005 | 2004 |
|---|---|---|---|
| 1 | 'Pandora's Box' | 'June' | 'Pandora's Box' |
| 2 | 'Baby Buntung' | 'Sagae' | 'Little Sunspot' |
| 3 | 'Lemon Lime' | 'Sum and Substance' | 'Lemon Lime' |
| 4 | 'Tiny Tears' | 'Striptease' | 'Blue Mouse Ears' |
| 5 | 'Popo' | 'Guacamole' | 'Medusa' |
| 6 | *H. venusta* | 'Paul's Glory' | 'Tiny Tears' |
| 7 | 'Green Eyes' | 'Krossa Regal' | *H. venusta* |
| 8 | 'Feather Boa' | 'Paradigm' | 'Twist of Lime' |
| 9 | 'Cookie Crumbs' | 'Blue Angel' | 'Popo' |
| 10 | 'Vanilla Cream' (tied) | *H. montana* 'Aureomarginata' | 'Shiny Penny' |
| 10 | 'Twist of Lime' (tied) | | |

When all is said and done, have fun and happy hunting!

***Houttuynia*** (hoo-tie′ nee-a) Chameleon Plant Saururaceae

The genus contains several species but only one, *H. cordata*, has gained favor in recent years with the multi-colored ground cover form 'Chameleon'. The green, alternate leaves of the 9-15″ tall species are approximately 2-3″ long, heart shaped, and there is a palpable love-hate relationship with this plant. Let me explain.

As for me, I have seen many plantings in this country and don't yet understand why people get excited about it. Plants require abundant moisture and are, in fact, classified as water plants. The foliage can be extremely colorful, with bright splotches of purple, pink and red. In the cooler times of the season, the leaves look like an elf has spilled paint all over them. However, there is a catch or two and one should be careful about embracing this plant too quickly. In fact, one should not embrace this plant at all. Although I have seen references to the lemony fragrance of the foliage, I use this plant to introduce my students to how bad plants can really smell. After tearing off a leaf and taking a whiff, at least two thirds of them make a face and say something unprintable about my teaching methods. Another problem is that once introduced, plants will take over. They remind me of mint in the way in which they invade, defying eradication and reveling in their obnoxious behavior. Lastly, the beauty of the variegated foliage often reverts to the plain green of the species. I can occasionally handle smelly, invasive plants if they provide sufficient beauty but this plant is history when it reneges on its promise of colorful foliage. Gardeners in the South find more reversion than those in the North, likely the result of warmer temperatures. However, stick this sucker in a sturdy container, toss it in a garden pond away from the edges, and you will be a brilliant gardener.

To be fair, I was also most pleasantly surprised when a planting at the University of Georgia filled in to make an outstanding ground cover. The plants did all they were expected to do, making a dense carpet with excellent flower power. Of course, the

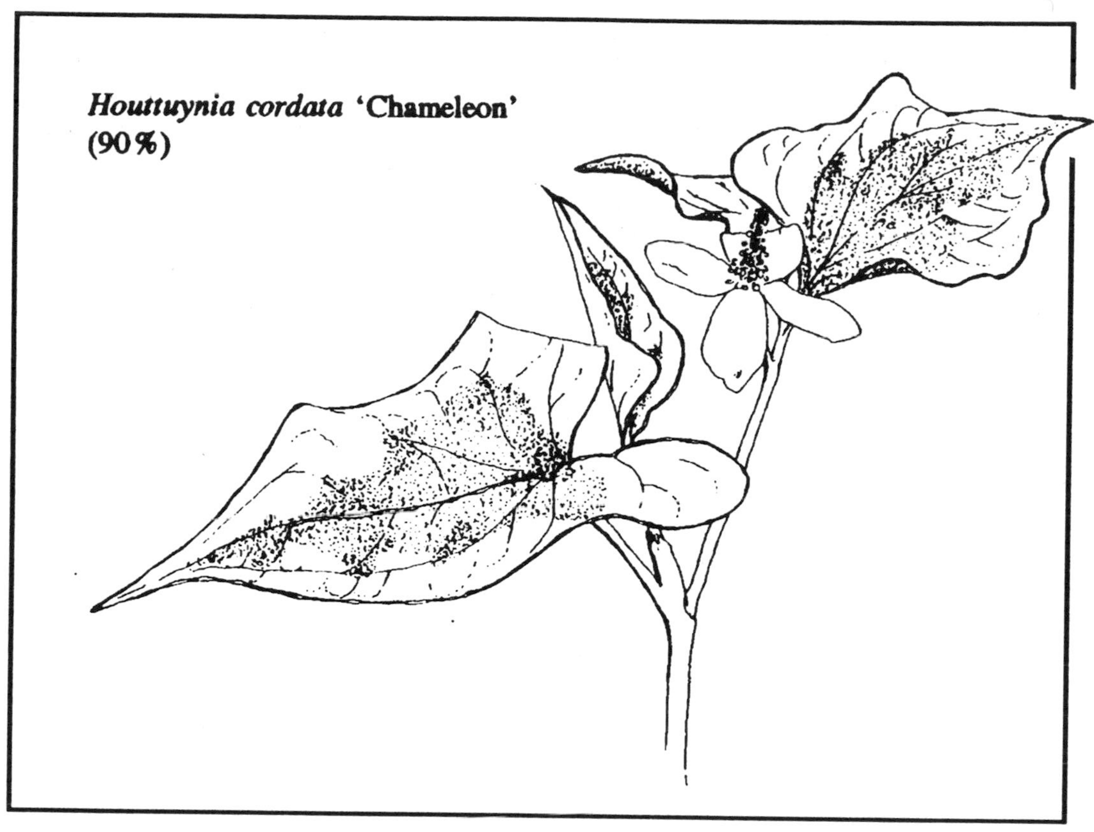
*Houttuynia cordata* 'Chameleon' (90%)

planting was surrounded on all four sides with concrete, plants reverted to green and within a year, stems appeared in the cracks of the sidewalk. But, for that difficult area, *Houttuynia* was a good choice. This plant best illustrates the Armitage axiom "There is no such thing as a bad plant, only a bad use for a good plant". Hardy in zones 3-8.

Propagate by division to multiply as needed or root 2-3″ long terminal cuttings in spring and summer.

**Cultivars:**

'Chameleon' ('Tricolor', 'Variegata') has leaves splashed with white, pink and red. The half-inch white flowers are quite lovely but of secondary interest and appear on 1-2″ spikes in May and June. Comments as to its performance have been mentioned above.

'Plena' bears purple-tinged green leaves and double white flowers. Pretty flowers, equally obnoxious.

## *Hyacinthoides* (high-a-sin′ thoid-eez) Bluebell Liliaceae

This genus consists of ten bulbous species native to western Europe, and includes the English and Spanish bluebells. In John Gerard's famous *Herbal* or *Generall Historie of Plantes* (1597), he enlightened his readers with such little-known facts as "the roots being beaten and applied with white wine, hinder or keep back the growth of hairs". At that time, the bulbs were also called sea onions and eaten by sailors (under duress, I'm sure).

Bluebells prefer moist, shady areas and are quite at home near coniferous woodlands where soils are somewhat acid. In the garden, they should be planted in groups of at least 50 (they are not expensive) where their straplike leaves will provide greenery before and after the bell-shaped, blue-purple flowers have opened.

Taxonomically, storm clouds have been brewing for a long time. People finally accepted the movement of certain species from *Scilla* into *Endymion* and were beginning to understand the botanical differences which exist between the two genera. However, the correct name for *Endymion* on the grounds of priority is now *Hyacinthoides*, a name change that has become as "official" as any.

*Hyacinthoides* was removed from *Scilla* because of botanical differences in bulb habit and flower morphology. The following table illustrates a few of the subtle differences.

| | **Hyacinthoides** | **Scilla** |
|---|---|---|
| *Bulb morphology* | Totally renewed each year | Not renewed each year |
| | Covered with tubular scales | Thin membranous cover |
| *Flower morphology* | Bracts and bracteoles | Bracts only |
| *Height* | Usually more than 12″ tall | Usually less than 12″ tall |

The two common species, *H. hispanica*, Spanish bluebell, and *H. non-scripta*, English bluebell, are similar and readily hybridize when planted near each other, resulting in many intermediate forms. They can be identified in that the former usually bears 12 or more flowers, with flared but not reflexed petals. Each individual flower stem (pedicel) is 1-1½″ long. The latter usually has 6-10 flowers in which the petals are strongly reflexed, and the flower stem is not over ½″ long.

Propagate by lifting established clumps in the fall and dividing the bulbs for planting. There will be many more bulblets around the mother bulb which can be lifted. Bluebells reseed prolifically and seed can be sown in containers in the fall. Seeds germinate readily but plants require approximately one year before they form bulbs and are ready for planting. Flowering occurs about 18 months later.

***-hispanica*** (his-pah' ni-ka) Spanish Bluebell 12-15″/12″
Spring Blue Europe, North Africa Zones 4-7

By far the more robust of the common species, the foliage consists of 5-6 shiny green linear leaves, approximately 1″ wide and convex on the back sides. Twelve or more one-inch, bell-shaped, nodding flowers are borne on each flower stem. They are held in an upright raceme and the petals are slightly flared at the base of the flower.

Plant the bulbs about 2-4″ deep in a well-drained area in the fall. Plants tolerate considerable shade and the colors and fragrance brighten a woodland garden. Unfortunately, the leaves become weatherbeaten and shabby before they disappear. These plants are tough enough, however, if the leaves are an eyesore, the foliage can be removed before it turns yellow and the sticky mess cleaned up. Bulbs should be planted in parts of the garden where leaf unsightliness will not be a problem. A number of cultivars and hybrids are readily available.

**Cultivars:**
var. *alba* has creamy white flowers but can vary from clear white to soft pink.
'Blue Giant' has deep blue flowers on 18″ tall stems.
'Blue Queen' bears bell-shaped flowers of porcelain blue.
'Dainty Maid' has rosy pink flowers.
'Danube' ('Donau') bears dense racemes of dark blue flowers.
'Excelsior' has 1-2″ diameter flowers of deep purple-blue. Probably the best known and popular cultivar in this genus.
'Queen of Pinks' has long elegant spikes of soft clear pink.
var. *rosea* has rose-pink flowers which can be quite variable in color and habit.
'Rosabella' bears soft pink flowers.
'White City' has clean white flowers.
'White Triumphator' is a beautiful clear white-flowered selection with dark stems. This is one of the best whites.

***-non-scripta*** (non-skrip′ ta) English Bluebell 12-15″/12″
Spring Blue Western Europe Zones 5-8

In England in late May or early June, the oak and beech woodlands and fields are alive with nodding bluebells. Although few communities can boast of English climate, we do just fine, thank you, where large clumps can also be established quickly. The several strap-shaped leaves are up to a foot long and a half-inch wide. The 6-12 bell-shaped fragrant flowers appear on an arching terminal raceme. The petals are flared and reflex back more than those of the previous species. Plant the bulbs 4-5″ deep and by the hundreds if possible, preferably on a wooded hillside or along the edge of a placid pond. They are not plants for the herbaceous border but are magnificent specimens for the woodland garden. Bulbs are inexpensive and will not need division for years.

The stems and bulbs exude a "slimy, glewish juyce" that were used "to set feathers upon arrows instead of glew, or to paste books with." (Gerard). In gardeners' terms, unless you are setting feathers or pasting books, these plants are a mess once they finish flowering. Also note that when removing the flowers, it is important to snap or cut the stems near the base. Do not pull them from the bulb or significant damage and loss of plant vigor will occur.

**Cultivars:**
'Alba' is a white-flowered form.
'Rosea' bears pink flowers.

## ***Hyacinthus*** (hy-a sin′ thus) Hyacinth Liliaceae

If one was to read only major bulb catalogs, one would surely believe the definition of floral perfection was the florist's hyacinth, *H. orientalis*. There is a conspicuous difference of opinion about hyacinths. As a forced flower, some people find the bright colors and sweet scent heavenly while others comment on its sickening odor. Louise Beebe Wilder, a marvelous gardener, wrote in her delightful book *Adventures with Hardy Bulbs*, 1936, that she looked at them as "obese, fat-stalked, overstuffed, overscented Leviathans." The sentiments of most people are somewhere in between. The name *Hyacinthus* was given by Homer, the flowers said to have sprung from the blood of the dead Greek youth. As you all recollect, Hyacinthus, in Greek myth, was a beautiful youth of Amyclae (an ancient city near Sparta). He was loved by both the god Apollo and by Zephyrus (the west wind), and the youth preferred Apollo. Zephyrus, out of jealousy, blew a discus thrown by Apollo so that it struck and killed Hyacinthus. From his blood sprang a flower bearing his name.

They are plants which prefer cool climates (to zone 3), performing poorly as perennials south of zone 6, although still effective as annuals. Where they are effective as perennials, they may be left in the ground for many years, but are slow to multiply. Best results occur if replaced at least every 2 years, regardless of location. Bulbs are relatively expensive and some industrious gardeners lift and dry them every spring and replant in the fall. Although this results in better longevity of the bulbs, I have never felt that energetic. If bulbs are to be removed, wait until the leaves have begun to turn yellow. Wash off the soil and store in perforated sacks at about 40°F in a well-

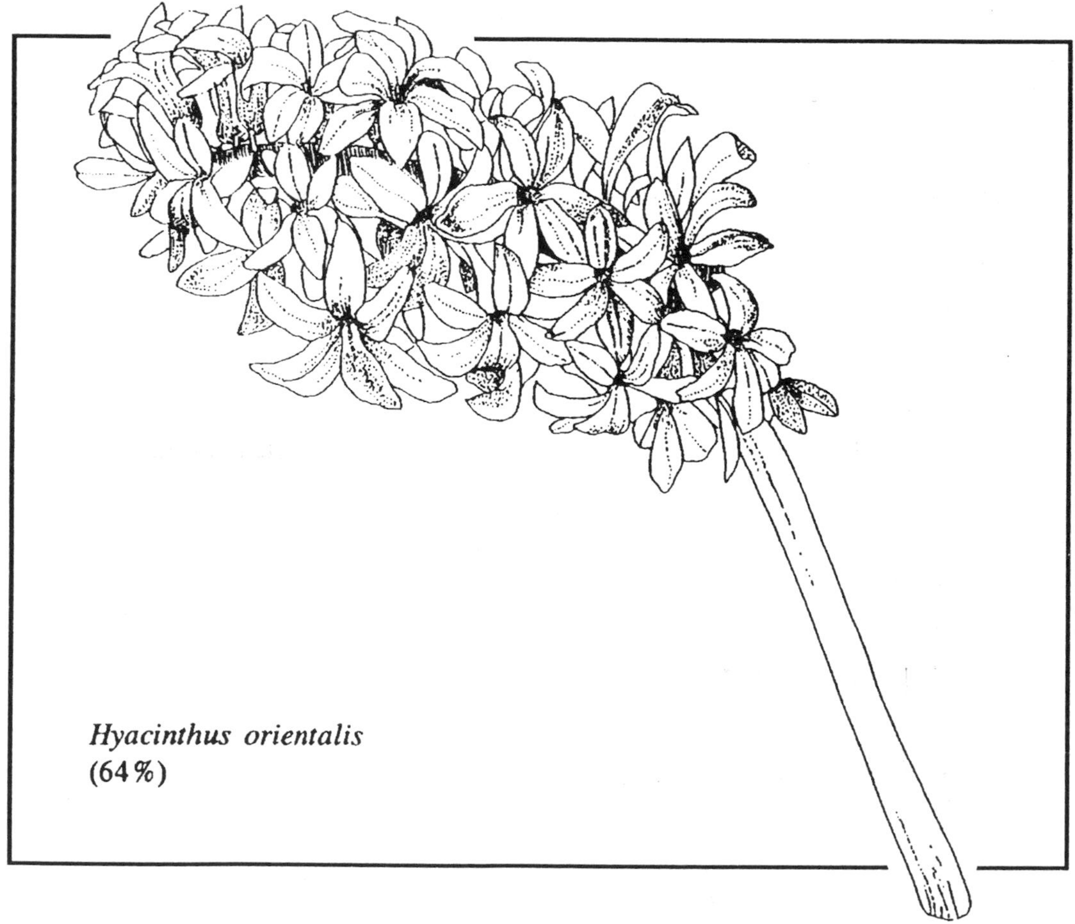

*Hyacinthus orientalis*
(64%)

ventilated area. Onion bags and unheated garages work well. Better yet, don't go to McBurger as often and save that money for a new bulb order.

It is not necessary to plant great drifts, regardless of the advertisements, as 6-12 plants nestled in a protected area or beside a pond can make a very effective display. Plant sufficient numbers, however, to be able to bring some inside to savor the fragrance, if you like it. Plant bulbs about 6″ deep in the fall, and bulb to bulb for best display.

Unfortunately, some people are allergic to the papery exterior of the bulbs and severe dermatitis can result. This is not a common occurrence and usually occurs only with people who come into contact with the bulbs every day. However, if skin irritation occurs, gloves should be used whenever bulbs are handled.

For forcing indoors, plant 3 bulbs in a 6″ wide pot and water well. Place the pots in the refrigerator (or anywhere where temperatures can be held between 30 and 40°F) for about 12 weeks. Once they are removed from the cool area, approximately 3 weeks are needed for full flowering if placed in a sunny spot at about 70°F. Therefore, if they are to be forced for a holiday such as Valentine's Day or Mothers Day or a birthday, place in the cool area about 15 weeks ahead of time.

Dozens of cultivars are available and it is a wonderful exercise in indecision to look through the gorgeous photos in the catalogs. There is nothing better than browsing through those catalogs to bring a little spring into long winter months.

**Related Genera:**

All previously recognized species of *Hyacinthus*, except *H. orientalis*, have been shuffled off to other genera. *H. amethystinus*, Spanish hyacinth, has become *Brimeura amethystinus*; *H. azureus*, azure hyacinth, has been relegated to *Muscari azureus*; and *H. candicans*, summer hyacinth, is now *Galtonia candicans*.

## *Hydrastis* (hid-ras′ tis) Goldenseal Ranunculaceae

Oh, to be able to go to the woods and find some goldenseal! Unfortunately, it is more and more difficult to enjoy this plant because of unscrupulous digging for medicinal purposes as well as reduction of habitat, sometimes due to inevitable development but sometimes due to untrammeled and unconscionable destruction by 4-wheelers. They should all be blown up.

Goldenseal, *H. canadensis,* was introduced to early settlers by Cherokee Indians who used it as a wash for skin diseases, wounds, and for sore, inflamed eyes. Goldenseal root has acquired a well-deserved reputation as a natural antibiotic and as a remedy for various gastric and genitourinary disorders. Numerous references to goldenseal appeared in medical writings as far back as 1820 as a strong tea for indigestion. Today it is used to treat symptoms of cold and flu and as an astringent, antibacterial remedy for the mucous membranes of the body. Goldenseal's long history of use among North Americans flourished after the Civil War as it was an ingredient in many patent medicines. It has been collected to the point of near extinction.

Plants grow 10-15″ tall, arising from the gnarly yellow rhizome from which it gets its common name. Plants generally produce a single long-petioled 5-8″ wide palmately lobed basal leaf. The lobes of the leaf are sharply pointed and unequally toothed. The stems which arise bear two leaves near the top, similar in shape but smaller than the basal leaf. The greenish white, half-inch wide flower occurs at the top of the stem and is rather ephemeral. In fact, the 3 sepals fall off as the flowers open and there are no petals anyway. The ornamental value of the flowers is based on the many stamens which extend from their centers. The fruits ripen into scarlet berries about two thirds of an inch long.

Plants are native in moist or low woodlands from Connecticut to Minnesota, Ontario, west to Kansas and Missouri and south to Georgia. There is no longer any need to dig plants from the wild (if you can find them) because specialty nurseries are selling plants propagated from seed and are establishing their own stock plants.

## ***Hydrophyllum*** (hi-dro-fil′ um) Waterleaf Hydrophyllaceae

About four species of this native genus are occasionally available to the American gardener. The name "waterleaf" does not mean that plants are happy in wet areas or swamps but refers to the watery or juicy leaves found in some species. My favorite species is *H. canadense*, native from Quebec to northern Georgia and west to Missouri. The foliage is palmately lobed, often with creamy "watermarks" on the tops (another explanation for the common name). The plants bear white to lavender flowers on short stalks, seldom rising above the foliage. The flowers, whose stamens project from the petals, are 5-lobed and held in 3 to 5 flowered clusters (cymes) which start coiled up and straighten out once the flowers open. It is essentially hairless and that characteristic along with the fact that the flowers are borne within the canopy make this species different from the hairy biennial, *H. appendiculatum*. Plants tolerate moderate shade and prefer moist, rich soils. I made the mistake of placing mine in deep fern shade and they performed poorly. Hardy from zone 4 to 7.

Two other eastern species with pinnately divided leaves and more visible flowers are also handsome. In *H. virginianum*, John's cabbage, the leaves consist of 3 to 7 segments and plants grow to two and a half feet tall. The white to lilac flowers are held above the foliage. Plants are cold hardy to at least zone 3 and south to zone 6. *H. macrophyllum* has 7-9 leaf segments, each coarsely toothed. The white flowers are held well above the foliage and the entire plant is "watermarked" and hairy. Plants likely have the same hardiness limits as *H. canadense*.

A western native, *H. capitatum*, cat's breeches, is sometimes seen in catalogs but is relatively rare. The 4-5″ long leaves are pinnately divided with each segment lobed at the ends. The white or lavender blue flowers are usually held in capitate (head-like) inflorescences on short flower stalks. Plants are about 9-15″ tall.

## ***Hylotelephium*** See *Sedum*

## ***Hymenocallis*** (hy-men′ o-cal-is) Spider Lily Liliaceae

These are weird-looking flowers, each tropical blossom having thin elongated petals like the legs of a spider. The petals are attached to a cuplike part of the flower, similar to that of a daffodil. White is the normal color, but yellow is not uncommon in some of the hybrids. The genus is native to a number of countries but without doubt, some of our native species such as the marsh spider lily, *H. liriosme*, the sweetly fragrant *H. caroliniana* and the nicely aggressive 12″ tall *H. traubii* are some of our finest bulbs, competing with *Zephyranthes* and native lilies for attention. The unique flowers of the genus and their rather slow multiplication rates have made them prime candidates for extinction, and plants of *H. coronaria* now appear on federal and state endangered lists. *H. caroliniana* is native from Michigan to Florida and hardiness is probably zone 5-9. This is likely what you are receiving when you order spider lilies. However, be cautious when using the common name, as spider lily is better known in nurseries as *Lycoris*, and they are not at all similar.

Specialty nurseries are also bringing in species from other lands including *H. areanifolia* from the West Indies, and *H. riparia*, with thick broad leaves and cold hardiness to zone 7. The wonderful *H. eucardifolia* from Mexico sports short, broad foliage and white flowers on a 9-12″ tall plant (probably hardy in zones 7-9). A number of beautiful hybrids are also being developed and distributed by mail order nurseries, many cold hardy to about zone 7.

Planted in full sun, mature bulbs will flower in late spring. Cut flowers persist up to a week in water.

**Hybrids**:

'Advance' consists of white flowers with a hint of yellow inside. The petals are not as "spidery" as most other selections.

'Bellum' has white flowers with creamy yellow centers.

'Carribea' has late white flowers with excessively long petals.

'Mystery' was found within an old population of bulbs in Ty Ty, Georgia and consists of large fragrant white flowers.

'Pax' is a large yellow-flowered form.

'Sulphur Queen' has soft yellow flowers with a green throat.

'Tropical Giant' was first described by Dr. Thad Howard from the San Antonio Botanical Garden and has become a popular choice for a fast-growing bulb bearing large white spiderlike flowers. Hardy to at least zone 7.

'Zwarenburg' has large white flowers and a scalloped cup.

## ***Hypericum*** (hy-per′ i-cum) St. John's-Wort Clusiaceae

With the hue and cry for low maintenance and the rush to ground covers, *Hypericum* is being used more and more in this country. The genus contains over 400 species of shrubs, sub-shrubs (partly woody) and herbaceous perennials, many of them ornamental. With so many species, the diversity of habit and flowering is difficult to generalize. However, in general, flowers are bright yellow, vary from $^1/_5$″ to 3″ in diameter and may be solitary or clustered. They have 5 petals, 5 sepals and many stamens that form a bushy center. Some species, such as *H.* x *inodorum* and *H. androsaemum*, produce ornamental fruit (capsules) used in bouquets and arrangements. Leaves of St. John's-wort are opposite or whorled and most species do best in full sun to partially shaded locations and moisture-retentive soil.

The most common species are less than 2′ tall and are suited for low borders or as ground covers, such as *H. calycinum* that spreads rapidly by underground stems. However, a number of species are shrubby and relatively large. They include the shrub-like *H. hookerianum*, which may bear 2″ wide, somewhat pendant flowers which light up the 4-5′ plant, *H. frondosum* 'Sunburst' with its large yellow flowers on a shrubby body, and *H. densiflorum*, whose flowers may be small but which makes a terrific shrubby plant tolerant of extreme heat and humidity.

The hardiness of St. John's-wort depends on the origin of the species or hybrid. With such a large genus, adaptability is variable. In general, the species discussed here are cold tolerant to about zone 4 or 5, and heat tolerant only to the northern limits of zone 7. Most will survive in hot, humid climates but disease and dieback limit their effectiveness. Those native to Europe, such as *H. calycinum*, have the most difficult time looking their best while Chinese and Japanese species have a wider climatic range. Species native to the eastern United States such as *H. densiflorum* (New Jersey to Georgia) do well throughout their range. While most are hardy perennials, a few such as the bog hypericum, *H. anagalloides*, are annuals except in coastal areas of the United States.

The healing powers were (and are) renowned. Plants of St. John's-wort (probably *H. perforatum*) were used in combination with "white wine two pintes, oile olive foure pounds, oile of turpentine two pounds..., set in the Sun eight or ten daies...." to heal wounds, particularly those "made with a venomed weapon" (Gerard). In ancient times, herbalists wrote about its use as a sedative and a treatment for malaria, as well as a balm for wounds, burns, and insect bites. Today, preparations are used for depression, anxiety, and/or sleep disorders.

Both the genus and common names likely arose from the belief in the magical healing powers of the plants. *Hypericum* comes from the Greek words, *hyper* (over) and *eikon* (picture), because it was hung above pictures to ward off evil spirits. The common name was based on the belief that the potency of its healing powers was increased by smoking it in fires kindled on the eve of St. John's Day, June 24, in rites that go back to antiquity. Lastly, the hypericums used to belong to the Hypericaceae, but most taxonomists now agree that it should be placed in the Clusiaceae, although they are still used interchangeably.

Quick Reference to Hypericum Species

| | Height (in.) | Flower diameter (in.) | Use | Flowering wood |
|---|---|---|---|---|
| *H. androsaemum* | 24-36 | ¾-1 | Tall sub-shrub | New |
| *H. buckleyi* | 9-12 | ¾-1 | Small sub-shrub | Old |
| *H. calycinum* | 15-18 | 2½-3 | Ground cover | Old |
| *H. olympicum* | 9-12 | 1½-2 | Ground cover | New |
| *H. patulum* | 18-36 | 1½-2 | Medium sub-shrub | New |

***-androsaemum*** (an-dros-aye′ mum) Tutsan 2-3′/2′
Summer Yellow Europe, North Africa Zones 5-7

Plants are grown more for their habit and fruit than for the flowers. Although the bright yellow flowers are only about 1″ wide and cannot compete with those of many other species, they are not to be ignored. The entire, sessile leaves are 3-4″ long and do not have the black glands seen in many species. Tutsan, which probably comes from the French *toute saine* (heal all), in reference to its healing powers, produces colorful fruits which change from yellowish to deep red and finally to dark brown. Plants are grown commercially for the fruits which find their way to upscale bouquets and arrangements.

The species is hardy only as far north as zone 5 (try mulching heavily in zone 4); its southern limit is probably zone 7. Plants are not particularly heat tolerant and every time I try it in the Armitage garden (zone 7), plants melt out, regardless of planting site.

Propagate by seed or terminal cuttings.

**Cultivars:**

'Albury Purple' is certainly the most handsome cultivar available. Plants differ from the species by having foliage with a burgundy hue which contrasts well with the yellow flowers. Cut back the old wood hard as the best leaf color is on the new growth.

'Excellent Flair' is propagated from seed and is more compact than the species. Plants performed well in the Horticulture Gardens at Georgia for a year, then pooped out and died. Many new "Flairs" have been produced, mostly for the cut flower trade. They are beautiful in bouquets, but a little challenging outdoors.

'Glacier' has green foliage spotted in white. It catches the eye, but it is a little too busy for my tastes. Plants are nice in the spring, but don't have the vigor of the species.

'Gladys Brabazon' also has white mottled foliage. Plants bear red fruit in late summer.

'Golden Tutsan' has a mounding habit and obvious chartreuse foliage. Beautiful in the spring.

***-buckleyi*** (buk-lee′ eye) Blue Ridge St. John's-Wort 9-12″/24″
Summer Yellow North Carolina to Georgia Zones 5-8

This little-known species should be used more often, particularly in southern gardens. The plant forms rounded low-growing mats which make an effective ground cover. The stems do not root readily and therefore plants do not spread rapidly. Some fall color is also provided as the ¾″ long, blunt, gray-green leaves turn a lovely red in September and October. The 1-1½″ diameter flowers have 3 styles, distinct exserted stamens and occur in groups of three at the end of the stems.

Although not as flamboyant as other species, it is more adaptable to conditions in the eastern and southeastern states and may be counted on to grow and flower in those areas. This species is native to the Appalachian Mountains and not commonly cultivated.

Propagate by seed or from soft basal cuttings in the summer.

***-calycinum*** (kal-i-sigh′ num) Aaron's Beard 15-18″/24″
Summer Yellow Southeast Europe, Turkey Zones 5-7

This is one of the main species offered in American horticulture, and in some cases, its popularity has diminished the importance and availability of others. The many protruding stamens suggest the name Aaron's beard and when in flower, it can be one of the finest ground covers available. I have seen it cover areas under trees, crawl over hillocks and berms, and change barren hillsides into seas of green and yellow. One of the finest plantings may be seen at The Butchart Gardens on Vancouver Island, Canada. The leaves are 3-4″ long, blue green and conspicuously fine netted beneath.

The 2-3″ wide flowers are usually solitary, consisting of hundreds of stamens with reddish anthers, and five styles. The stamens are in five bundles giving the flower a rose-like appearance. The 4-angled stems grow upright as well as along the ground.

Plants perform better in the northern end of their hardiness zone than in the southern end. In warm climates, they grow well and are evergreen under normal winters but flower sporadically. In the heat of summer, leaves can dry, turn black and fall off. In cold winters, the leaves may fall off or turn brown from desiccating winds, particularly when followed by bright sun. It is a vigorous grower and can be invasive if placed in a small garden area. Plants should be sheared back every few years to keep them in bounds. Where plants grow well, they perform best in full sun or with some afternoon shade. Finding ground covers for full sun is difficult, and this plant is often recommended to spill down sunny banks.

Propagate by cuttings, division or seed. Cuttings should be taken from vegetative shoots in late spring or early summer. A rooting hormone is useful but not essential. Seeds germinate readily but not uniformly.

**Cultivars**:
'Brigadoon' bears golden foliage and is quite outstanding in the garden.

***-olympicum*** (o-lim′ pi-kum) Olympic St. John's-Wort 9-12″/12″
Late Spring Yellow Southeast Europe, Asia Minor Zones 6-8

With delicate ½″-1″ long sessile, pointed, grayish green leaves attached to trailing stems, plants are useful at the front of the garden, tucked in and around rocks and as a ground cover. The 1½-2″ wide flowers are large relative to the size of the plants, and occur in 2-5-flowered cymes at the end of the stems. The many stamens are arranged in three bundles and the sepals are rigidly pointed, almost sharp. Hardiness is a limitation but where these plants do well, they can be spectacular. Flowers are produced mid May to early June in zone 8. The species tolerates partial shade but also grows well in full sun.

Propagate by fresh seed or by soft basal cuttings in early summer or terminal cuttings in fall.

**Cultivars:**

var. *citrinum* bears handsome pale yellow flowers but is otherwise similar to the species.

***-patulum*** (pat-ew' lum) Golden Cup St. John's-Wort 18-36″/24″
Summer Yellow China, Japan Zones 5-7

This evergreen shrub bears shoots which are somewhat purplish, spreading, and drooping. The 1½-2½″ long leaves are gray-green beneath. The flowers are held in clusters of 2-4 and bloom profusely in June and July and sporadically until frost. The rounded petals overlap on the ½-2″ diameter flowers.

Only the species can be propagated from fresh seed but cultivars may be propagated in the summer by taking 4-5″ long cuttings of non-flowering shoots, preferably with a piece from the parent plant. Insert the cuttings in a well-drained medium, keep moist and warm, and rooting should take place in 3-4 weeks.

**Cultivars:**

All varieties and cultivars of *H. patulum* flower on new wood, therefore, plants which don't die to the ground in winter should have the previous years' stems cut to a few buds of old wood in the spring.

'Sungold' is a pretty, arching 18-24″ tall sub-shrub with slightly larger flowers and greater cold hardiness than 'Hidcote'.

'Henryi' has flowers up to 3″ across and 2-3″ long leaves. It is vigorous and well worth searching out. Recently, this was placed in its own species (*H. henryi*) by some authorities.

**Related Species:**

*H. cerastoides* is also a short ground cover, growing 9-12″ tall. The star-shaped light yellow to deep yellow flowers are larger than the leaves and when they appear in late spring to summer, they cover the plant. Native to eastern Europe, likely hardy from zones 4-7.

*H.* x 'Hidcote' originated in Hidcote Manor Garden in England. Its parentage is in question but it likely arose from *H. cyathiflorum* 'Gold Cup' x *H. calycinum*. Plants grow 18″ to 3′ tall with 2-3″ diameter sterile yellow flowers. The numerous stamens, which occur in 5 bundles, are shorter than the petals. The sterility of the flowers results in persistent flowering of the hybrid, a trait which has made it one of the most popular hypericums in Europe. It is not as adaptable to vagaries of climate found in North America, however. In the colder climes of its range, it will die down in winter to reemerge next spring. In warmer areas, leaves remain evergreen and plants reach heights of three feet. It is particularly susceptible to root rot and wilt and severe losses occur in warm, humid climates.

*H.* x *moserianum* (*H. calycinum* x *H. patulum*) is 2-3′ tall with the 3″ wide flowers of *H. calycinum* and the overlapping petals of *H. patulum*. Flowers appear over several months. 'Tricolor', the most common cultivar, bears green, cream and pink leaves and red stems. I used to think plants were simply gaudy, but the more I see of it, the more I enjoy it.

*H. polyphyllum* differs by having grayer leaves, less pointed sepals often speckled with a few black dots, and the absence of a woody base. The golden yellow flowers are 1½-2″ across and occur in 4-10 flowered clusters at the end of the stems. It is likely that plants sold under this name are *H. olympicum*. 'Lemon Butterfly' is 6-8″ tall with large bright yellow flowers. 'Sulfur Pearl' is only 4″ tall and produces large bright yellow flowers. 'Sulphureum' has sulphur yellow flowers, as does 'Citrinum', which is probably the same thing.

*H. reptans* is only 6-9″ tall with narrow leaves which form dense tufts. Plants are heat tolerant to zone 8 and bear 1″ wide yellow flowers.

*H. wilsonii* is very similar to *H. calycinum* but smaller. The bright golden yellow flowers are about 2″ wide and borne on terminal stems.

***Hypoxis*** (hi-poks′ is) Star-Grass Hypoxidaceae

Even gardeners who grow this little bulbous plant in their gardens are surprised to learn that the genus consists of approximately 150 species. Most of the grassy species with small yellow star-shaped flowers are unknown and rather inconspicuous and very difficult to locate. However, *H. hirsuta*, yellow star-grass, native from Maine to Florida and west to Texas, is offered by many bulb specialists. Plants bear hairy grass-like 12″ long, 2-4″ wide leaves. The small 1″ yellow flowers are held in a 3-7 flowered inflorescence in late spring and summer. They will self-seed where they are comfortable and unless planted in groups of a dozen or so, will likely go unnoticed in the garden. Plant about 2-4″ deep and 6-8″ apart in well-drained or raised beds. They are small, terrific for the front of the garden or rock garden, not "socks-knocking-off", but interesting and well worth trying. Likely hardy in zones 4 to 8.

*Hakonochloa macra* 'Aureola'

*Hedychium gardnerianum*

*Helenium autumnale* 'Mardi Gras'

*Helenium autumnale* 'Moerheim Beauty'

*Helianthus*
'Lemon Queen'

*Helianthus salicifolius*

*Heliopsis helianthoides*
'Lorraine Sunshine'

*Helleborus argutifolius*

*Helleborus*
'Ivory Prince'

*Helleborus orientalis*
Royal Heritage strain

*Hemerocallis*
'Frans Hals'

*Hepatica transsilvanica*

*Heuchera*
'Amethyst Mist'

*Heuchera*
'Marmalade'

*Heuchera*
'Obsidian'

*Heuchera*
'Sashay'

*Heuchera*
'Tango'

*Heuchera sanguinea*
'Snow Fire'

× *Heucherella*
'Birthday Cake'

× *Heucherella*
'Stoplight'

× *Heucherella* 'Sunspot'

*Hibiscus grandiflorus*

*Hibiscus* 'Kopper King'

*Hibiscus* 'Moy Grande'

*Hosta* 'Great Expectations'

*Hosta* 'June'

*Hosta* 'Samurai'

*Hosta* 'Sun Power'

*Houttuynia cordata*
'Plena'

*Hyacinthoides hispanica*

*Hypericum calycinum*
'Brigadoon'

*Hypericum × inodorum*
'Elstead'

*Imperata cylindrica* 'Rubra'

*Inula ensifolia*

*Inula helenium*

*Ipheion uniflorum*

*Iris cristata*

*Iris ensata* 'Variegata' with *Heliopsis*

*Iris japonica* 'Nadia'

*Iris tectorum*

# I

***Iberis*** (eye-beer′ is) Candytuft Brassicaceae

Many gardens sport this popular genus in the form of *I. sempervirens*, the perennial matted candytuft, however approximately 39 other annual or perennial species are known, many of which were discovered in Spain (originally known as Iberia). Although they have been superceded by more colorful bedding plants, a number of annual species are grown, such as the delightful *I. amara*, rocket or hyacinth-flowered candytuft. The perennial species, including the aforementioned candytuft, are actually sub-shrubs whose stems are woody at the base. The leaves are alternate and usually entire while the 4-petaled flowers are often white or pink. Plants are tufted and well adapted to the front of the garden or cascading over rock walls. Full sun and well-drained soils are a necessity. All perennial forms should be cut back heavily after flowering at least once every two years to reduce fruit set and maintain quality foliage.

Quick Key to Iberis Species

| | Height (in.) | Flower color |
|---|---|---|
| *I. gibraltarica* | 9-12 | Outer pink, inner white |
| *I. saxatilis* | 3-6 | White, tinged purple |
| *I. sempervirens* | 9-12 | White |

***-gibraltarica*** (ji-brawl-tahr′ i-ca) Gibraltar Candytuft 9-12″/12″
Spring Pink and White Gibraltar Zones 7b-9

Because of limited hardiness, this is seldom seen in North American gardens. The 1″ long evergreen leaves are toothed, particularly near the ends, and produced in basal rosettes. The flowers are arranged in 1½-2″ long flattened umbel-like inflorescences. The outside flowers are pink to red while those inside the inflorescence are white or slightly tinged pink. They are worth trying as a self-sowing annual north of zone 7. Seeds germinate readily and softwood cuttings of non-flowering shoots root within 14-21 days.

| -***saxatilis*** (saks-ah′ ti-lis) | | Rock Candytuft | 3-6″/6″ |
|---|---|---|---|
| Spring | White | Southern Europe | Zones 3-7 |

The word *saxatilis* means "growing on rocks" and this compact plant is perfect in and around rocks. The evergreen, entire leaves are only about 1/8″ wide and 3/4″ long. Flowering and non-flowering stems occur. At the tips of the former appear umbel-like inflorescences of half-inch white flowers often tinged with purple, especially as they fade. Plants are very cold hardy, unusual for a species native to southern Europe.

Propagate similar to *I. gibraltarica*.

| -***sempervirens*** (sem-per-vi′ renz) | | Evergreen Candytuft | 9-12″/18″ |
|---|---|---|---|
| Spring | White | Southern Europe | Zones 3-8 |

This is certainly the most popular of the candytufts. It has been used for dozens of decades as an edging plant to bridge lawns with taller plantings in the garden. The evergreen foliage consists of numerous ¼″ wide and 1-1½″ long, entire leaves. Plants are woody at the base and should be cut back severely at least every other year to insure they do not get leggy. The flowers are usually white although there may be some variation in clearness of color in seed-propagated material. Cool nights and days also result in more pinking of the flowers. The 1½-2″ wide inflorescence is borne in the lateral axils rather than terminal as in *I. saxatilis*. Flowers open in early March in zone 7 gardens, April further north, and persist for ten weeks.

All cultivars may be propagated by cuttings while the species is readily raised from seed.

**Cultivars:**

The numerous selections offer improvements in flower color and habit but there is little real difference between many of them. For best uniformity in the garden, select those which have been propagated vegetatively.

'Alexander's White' is 10-12″ tall and very floriferous. An excellent cultivar for much of the country.

'Autumn Beauty' is about 10″ tall with white flowers in the spring, reblooming in the fall. The fall rebloomers are becoming more sought after, however, the jury is still out on their performance. Flowering in the fall is never as profuse as in the spring, however, that is not uncommon for rebloomers of any genus. The problem occurs with summer maintenance. If summers are particularly hot and dry, plants are too exhausted to put on much of a fall show. They do not appreciate being ignored as much as the non-rebloomers.

'Autumn Snow' is 8-10″ tall and has clear white flowers larger than those of the type. It blooms profusely in the spring and again in the fall. Probably the best of the fall rebloomers.

'Compacta' is only 4-6″ tall and the leaves are tightly grouped.

'Golden Candy' differs by having chartreuse foliage, particularly apparent in the spring. White flowers contrast well with the bright leaves.

'Little Gem' is 5-8″ tall and has small, clear white flowers. One of the best dwarf forms.

'October Glory' is about 8″ tall and reblooms well in the fall. See comments about 'Autumn Beauty'.

'Purity' is another white-flowered form and has lustrous, deep green leaves and an abundance of flowers. It is slightly taller than 'Little Gem' and smaller than 'Snowflake'.

'Pygmaea' is a prostrate form that hugs the ground and sends up small white blossoms in early spring. The most compact cultivar available.

'Snowflake' is 8-10″ tall and bears 2-3″ wide inflorescences of pure white flowers that shine on sunny spring days.

'Snowmantle' is more compact than 'Snowflake'.

**Related Species:**

*I. sayana*, dwarf candytuft, is a tough miniature candytuft for alpine or trough gardens, requiring excellent drainage for best success. Plants grow 1-2″ tall and spread to about 9″ in width. The white flowers cover the plant in early spring. Hardy to zone 3, south to zone 6.

***Imperata*** (im-per-ah′ ta) Blood Grass Poaceae

The only ornamental useful form of the genus is *I. cylindrica* 'Rubra', also sold as 'Red Baron', a relatively slow-growing wine-red tipped grass. However, the non-colored species itself is an aggressive weed, and is now listed as a Federal noxious weed. 'Rubra' occasionally reverts to its green-leaved parent and those shoots must be eliminated aggressively.

I have seen some handsome plantings of Japanese blood grass, particularly in the upper Midwest, most notably at Olbrich Botanical Gardens in Madison, Wisconsin and at the entrance of the spectacular Botanical Garden at the Niagara School of Horticulture. In such areas, the red leaves become even redder as the season progresses and provide some excellent red fall color. Where they are growing well, the clumps are usually about 12-18″ and provide a striking touch of red to the perennial garden.

However, plants are scrawny and color up poorly south of zone 5, and are not worth the money or time spent. They are better adapted to tubs and containers, growing with other plants, so if they look lousy, the other plants can cover them up. They are listed hardy from zones 6 to 9 but the further south this grass is planted, the less the red color is seen. I would list it zone 4b-6b Oversold and over-hyped for most gardeners.

***Incarvillea*** (in-car-vill′ ea) Hardy Gloxinia Bignoniaceae

Long before President Nixon and the U.S. table tennis team "opened" China to the West, hardy French Jesuits were active throughout the country in the 16th to 19th centuries. While I am not entirely sure about the spiritual learning they dispensed, some became excellent plantsmen. Jean D'Incarville was a French Jesuit who became a botanical correspondent to the botanist Bernard de Jussieu. In his lifetime (1506-1557), he became an avid collector and botanist and this genus honors his name. Plants are not commonly grown perhaps because of the variability of performance in different areas of the country. Plants grow from a long taproot, and are usually available through bulb supply catalogs. It is not hardy in many areas of the country but when grown in the right location, the plants can be magnificent. The flowers resemble gloxinia and the leaves are similar to Jacob's ladder (*Polemonium*). Of the six species, only *I. delavayi* is readily available in the United States.

***-delavayi*** (del-a-vay′ eye) Delavay Incarvillea 18-24″/18″
Spring Rose Purple China Zones 5-7

The 12″ long basal leaves consist of 6-11 pairs of pinnately compound leaflets (each 4-5″ long) that form a handsome mound of foliage. Five to twelve flowers are carried on a raceme held 1-2′ above the foliage. The trumpet-shaped rose purple flowers are 2-3″ long and wide and have yellow throats. Remove blossoms after flowering to extend bloom time.

Although it's often listed as hardy in zones 4-7, I have had little success over-summering plants in zone 7. They are inhabitants of rocky, mountainous areas and do well where soils are well drained and nights are cool. Certainly, gardeners on the West Coast (zone 7) do much better than those in eastern and southern zone 7. Well-drained, sandy soils and partial shade are recommended. In zones 5 and 6, mulching the plants in the fall is good practice.

The roots are handsome in a gardenesque kind of way, and every year at the Southeastern Garden Show in Atlanta, a bulb company attractively displays the roots and sells them to unsuspecting show-goers. I can't imagine how many actually grow, let alone flower. However, I can imagine how many beginning gardeners are turned off gardening after a promise of such beauty results in mush. When will we ever learn?

The specific epithet (*delavayi*) is also associated with *Osmanthus delavayi*, and honors Jean David Delavay, a French missionary and explorer in Yunnan, China. Between 1881 and 1888, he sent back more than 200,000 specimens—4000 different species—of which 1500 were new to botany.

Plants have a long taproot, making the division difficult. Seed propagation is the easiest means to increase the various species. Fresh seed sown and placed under heat and high humidity results in seedlings in 10-20 days.

**Related Species:**

*I. compacta* is 8-12″ tall and more compact than the previous species. Most of the height of the species is due to the flower stems which carry 3-7 red-purple flowers. There is little or no plant stem.

*I. olgae* grows up to 3′ tall with only 3-4 pairs of leaflets. The rosy red flowers are borne in a branched inflorescence (racemose panicle).

*I. mairei* (*I. grandiflora* var. *brevipes*) has 2-3 flowers but each may be up to 3″ across, often with a yellow throat inside the flower.

## ***Indigofera*** (in-di-gof′ er-a) Indigo Fabaceae

You would think that with over 700 species of *Indigofera* known, a few of them would be commonly grown in North America. The good news is that they are becoming better known in nurseries so obtaining some of these plants will require less sleuthing than before. Of course, since I happen to live in the Valley of Nurseries in north Georgia, I am able to find an *Indigofera* or two just down the road. However, that most nurseries have not embraced them tells us that plants are either difficult to establish, or not sufficiently garden-flashy to propagate in large numbers. If you have grown some, you know it is not the former, as plants can roam and reseed with temerity. Many are sub-shrubs (i.e. with woody stems) which usually die back or can be cut back to the ground each year. Others are true woodies, so when looking for plants, be sure to check both the perennial and shrub sections of the nursery or catalog.

The indigo dye extracted from the leaves and young stems of some species, mainly *Indigofera tinctoria*, has been traced on Egyptian mummy cloth from 2300 BC. Although plants are native to southeast Asia, indigo plantations were established by the English in India, Sumatra and most notably, the West Indies, during the colonial period and through the 19th century. The plants were also introduced to South Carolina in 1742 and grown extensively until the War of Independence, after which the importance of cotton resulted in its decline. Plants escaped from cultivation and may still be found in coastal areas of South Carolina and Georgia, south to Florida and west to Louisiana. When plants of *Indigofera* were in short supply, other "false indigos" were used (see section on *Baptisia*). The introduction of a synthetic by Bayer in 1878 resulted in the decline of the plantations.

From the garden standpoint, plants are shrubby and bear pealike flowers and pinnately compound leaves. Chinese indigofera, *I. kirilowii*, may be the most ornamental species available. Plants grow 2-4′ tall and bear densely packed axillary racemes of rose-pink flowers. The inflorescences may be up to 5″ long and remain in flower most of the season. The leaves, which are usually shorter than the inflorescences, consist of 7-11 leaflets. Plants grow from a rhizome but they are not invasive. I also like *I. pseudotinctoria* that grows 2-3′ tall. However, even better is the cultivar 'Rose Carpet', because of its tight habit and 12″ tall frame. Plants bear pink flowers in late summer and fall.

The plant that has found a home in the eastern United States is *I. decora*. The more I see of this plant, the more I enjoy it. They are only about 12-18″ tall with 9-11 leaflets. The base is woody and plants die to the ground in the winter. In the spring (mid to late May), the axillary pale pink racemes, which are almost as long as the 4-5″ leaves, nod open on the flower stems. Be warned, however, that it can be terribly invasive, colonizing by stolons and almost impossible to pull out.

The plants we often see when visiting gardens in Europe are those of *I. heterantha*, which generally grow about 4′ tall and have small (¼″ long) pale pink to rosy purple flowers held in 4-6″ long terminal racemes. The 3-4″ long leaves consist of 13-21 odd-pinnate leaflets. They do well on the West Coast, but lose much of their appeal once they cross the mountains. Similarly, another fine species is *I. potaninii*, a little shorter than *I. heterantha*, but distinguished by having lilac-pink flowers in axillary racemes and leaves of only 5-11 leaflets. Also much better in climates with cool nights.

Cut all plants back hard in late winter or early spring. *I. kirilowii* appears to be hardy to zone 6, the others to zone 7. If reseeding is a problem, cut back the flowers before fruit set.

## ***Inula*** (in′ yew-la) Inula Asteraceae

The genus consists of about 60 species, and half a dozen have outstanding ornamental properties not found in other yellow daisies abundant in the summer garden. Unfortunately, few shine in most gardens in North America. Most species are hairy and coarse, and bear alternate leaves. Plants range from 6″ dwarfs to 7′ giants and the flowers are equally varied in size. All flowers are orange-yellow and may be borne solitarily or in few-flowered inflorescences. The foliage of many species is large, bold and impressive, and in some like *I. candida*, silver-green.

In general, *Inula* is easily grown when placed in full sun and moist, well-drained soil, although most tolerate somewhat boggy conditions. The tall species may be impressive in spring and summer, but after they flower, they generally decline rapidly. For all species, good drainage is essential and success is more likely in areas with cool climates. I have seen magnificent plants in European gardens, particularly in Ireland, where inula is as common as Guinness. However, in much of the United States, more abusive climates limit the beauty, especially of the giant forms.

*I. ensifolia* and *I. royleana* are the primary species for the average garden while the impressive *I. helenium* and *I. magnifica* are bigger, coarser and more suitable for larger, less formal areas. All species may be propagated by seed or division.

It can be frustrating looking at some of the members of the aster family, scratching your head trying to figure out the genus, let alone the species. This genus is similar to *Arnica*, *Doronicum* and *Senecio* except for minor differences in flower and foliage. In the following table, some of the minor differences are noted. This stuff looks complicated and boring (and it is) but for those who must know more, here is more. The involucre bracts are the papery structures at the base of the flower head, and there may be one to many rows (series) of them. The term "clasping" means that the petiole clasps the stem like baby's fingers around your own. Other differences also occur in fruit but that is best left to reference books of a higher plane.

| | Leaf arrangement | Involucre bracts | Stem leaves |
|---|---|---|---|
| *Arnica* | Opposite | Equal, not overlapping, 2-3 series | Not clasping |
| *Inula* | Alternate | Unequal, overlapping in many series | Not clasping |
| *Doronicum* | Alternate | Equal, not overlapping, 1-3 series | Clasping |
| *Senecio* | Alternate | Equal, in one series | Not clasping |

<u>Quick Reference to Inula Species</u>

| | Height (in.) | Flowers solitary | Leaves very hairy |
|---|---|---|---|
| *I. ensifolia* | 12-24 | Yes | No |
| *I. helenium* | 48-72 | No | Yes |
| *I. royleana* | 18-24 | Yes | Yes |

**-*ensifolia*** (en-si-fo' lee-a) Swordleaf Inula 1-2′/2′
Late Spring Yellow Europe, Asia Zones 3-7

This is one of the best of the small inulas as it is self-branching, compact and produces many long-petaled, bright yellow to orange daisylike flowers. The 1-2″ wide flowers are borne singly at the end of the stems and persist for about 6 weeks. The sessile leaves are less than an inch wide and 3-4″ long. They are further distinguished from other low-growing inulas by having 3-7 parallel veins. The species name means "swordlike" and refers to the shape of the leaves.

Plants are heat tolerant to zone 7 and are a good alternative to *Doronicum orientale*, another small yellow daisy, but unlike *Doronicum*, these do not go dormant in the summer. Plants are short lived in the Southeast, persisting for 2-3 years, longer in the North.

Propagate by seed or division in the fall.

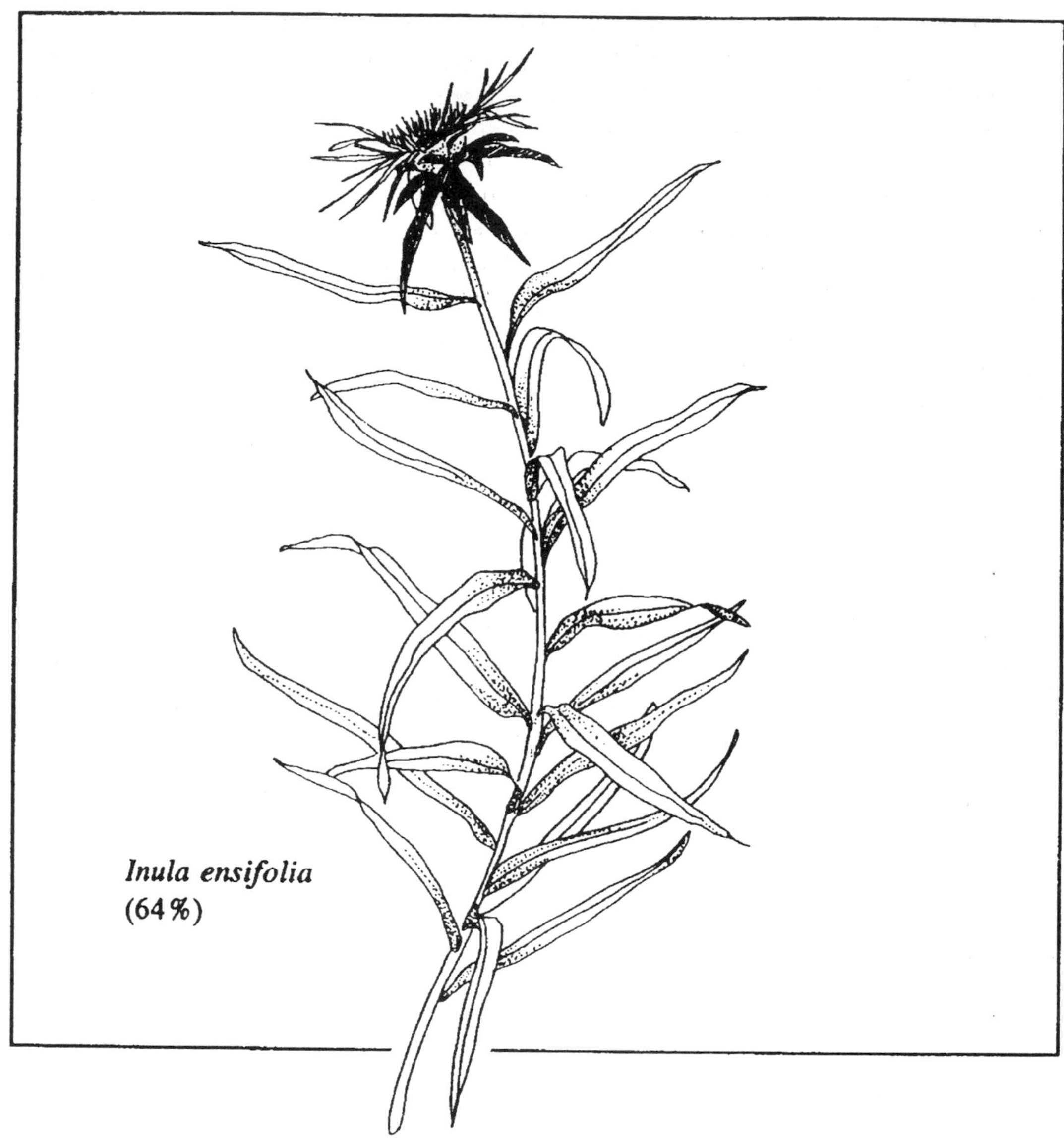

*Inula ensifolia*
(64%)

**Cultivars:**

'Compacta' is more compact and grows 8-12″ tall.

'Gold Star' forms 10-15″ tall bushes covered with yellow daisies.

'Mediterranean Sun' is similar to the above, but perhaps with more yellow flowers.

***-helenium*** (he-len′ ee-um) Elecampane 4-7′/4′
Summer Yellow Europe, Northern Asia Zones 3-7

Although native elsewhere, plants have been naturalized in eastern North America. Dried roots yield a white, starchy powder called inuline that has long been valued for medicinal uses. In fact, elecampane is a living drugstore, also yielding a volatile oil, a resin, and a bitter extract, all of which were employed by herbalists of old. If you grow this plant and don't like it, grind it up and try it on your sick dog.

It enjoys full sun but will tolerate limited shade. The basal leaves can be as long as three feet (1-2′ is a bit more common) and are held on petioles up to one foot long. They become much reduced in size, and sessile as they ascend the brownish furrowed stem. They are velvety beneath but rough-hairy above. The 2-3″ wide flowers usually occur in groups of two or three but occasionally are solitary.

Plant in well-drained moist soil in full sun. They are coarsely magnificent in flower but fade quickly after flowering, particularly if abundant water cannot be supplied. These can be big and require a lot of room to grow well: space them at least 3′ from other specimens.

Propagate by seed or divide in the fall or early spring.

| ***-royleana*** (royl-ee-ah′ na) | | Himalayan Elecampane | 1½-2′/3′ |
|---|---|---|---|
| Late Summer | Orange | Himalayas | Zones 3-7 |

The flowers are terrific but the unbranched habit does not make it an especially popular garden plant. The 6-10″ long leaves are oval, slightly toothed, and densely fuzzy underneath (tomentose). The upper leaves are clasping, the lower are 3-4″ wide on long winged petioles. The solitary orange-yellow flowers are 3-4″ across and emerge from black buds in late summer and fall. With narrow ray flowers, the daisies look like big orange spiders.

All inulas are better plants for northern climates than southern, but this one even more so. Plants tolerate moist conditions and need cool nights for best performance.

Propagate from divisions in early spring or from seed.

**Related Species:**

*I. candida* is a handsome 9-12″ plant with white hairy foliage and solitary yellow flowers. They are native to Greece and therefore require excellent drainage as found in rock gardens, containers or raised beds. Full sun is needed. Perhaps hardy in zones 5 to 7.

*I. magnifica* is also a big coarse plant, growing at least 6′ tall. It differs from elecampane, *I. helenium*, in that the flowers are nearly 6″ across and arranged in a many-flowered inflorescence (corymb). The center of each flower (disc flowers) is deep yellow, while the narrow well-spaced ray flowers are golden yellow and 2-3″ long. The stem often has purple striations. May be better garden plants than *I. helenium*; hardy in zones 3-7.

*I. orientalis* grows 2-2 ½′ tall and bears 4-6″ long entire leaves with marginal glands. The orange-yellow solitary flowers are up to 3″ wide. 'Grandiflora' was selected for even larger flowers. Native to the Caucasus, plants are cold tolerant to zone 3. A good garden plant where space is limited.

*I. salicina* is similar to *I. ensifolia* in that it grows about 2′ tall and bears many flowers with yellow rays and orange centers. A little more weather tolerant than *I. ensifolia*. Hardy in zones 4 to 7.

*I. verbascifolia* is probably the best rock garden species, growing only about 6-9″ tall. Plants have fuzzy leaves like a mullein. Sometimes listed as *I. candida* var. *verbascifolia*.

## *Ionactis* See *Aster*

## *Ipheion* (if′ ee-on) Starflower Alliaceae

The genus contains about 10 species but only *I. uniflorum*, spring starflower, is cultivated to any extent. It is a species that no genus seems to want. At one time or another, *I. uniflorum* has been classified under *Brodiaea* (where it is still often called *B. uniflora*), *Milla*, *Triteleia*, or *Tristagma*. Pertinent differences between common species of three closely related genera are given below.

| | ***Brodiaea*** | ***Ipheion*** | ***Triteleia*** |
|---|---|---|---|
| Origin | North America | South America | North America |
| Root | Corm | Bulb | Corm |
| Leaves | Rounded | Flat | Keeled beneath |
| Fertile Stamens | 3 | 6 | 6 |
| Inflorescence | Umbel | 1-2 flowered | Umbel |

***-uniflorum*** (ew-ni-flo′ rum) Spring Starflower 4-6″/8″
Spring White, Pale Blue Argentina, Uruguay Zones 5-9

One of my favorite spring bulbs—I pack them in like peas whenever space becomes available in my garden. They are lovely along paths, at the front of borders, or in rockeries where they should be planted in generous drifts. The pale green, nearly flat leaves are 1/4 to 3/8″ wide, 6 to 9″ long, and smell like garlic, although not as pungent, when crushed. This garlic-like smell seems to turn some people off, but if it bothers you, simply don't crush them. The leaves come up in the fall and can in themselves add some late winter interest to the garden if not covered with four feet of snow. The flowering stem rises about 6″ above the foliage and usually bears one but sometimes two pleasantly fragrant blossoms. The 1″ wide star-shaped flowers are about 1″ long and have a lovely whitish, porcelain blue hue. Plants enjoy well-drained soils in full sun where colonies increase rapidly. In some gardens, particularly in the South, plants can become invasive. Plants have escaped from gardens throughout the country. I see them in old homesteads from Aiken, South Carolina to the fine gardens of Williamsburg, Virginia, where this pedestrian plant grows like the ubiquitous dandelion. However, unlike the dandelion, plants go dormant and disappear from mind and eye in late spring to early summer. As for me, I welcome the invasion.

Bulbs may can also be forced in containers. Plant about 7-10 bulbs in a 4 or 6″ pot, place the pot in the refrigerator or a cooler where temperatures are around 40°F, leave for 8-10 weeks, then bring out to flower. They cannot compete with tulips but their delicacy and scent are worth the effort.

*Ipheion uniflorum*
(100%)

Offsets are readily produced and if new colonies are wanted, simply lift existing plantings after flowering, separate bulbs and offsets, and replant immediately where desired. Plants should be divided every 3-4 years to maintain vigor.

**Cultivars:**

'Album' is a terrific large white-flowered form. The main vein of the clean white flowers is purple, making a handsome contrast.

'Alberto Castello' is similar to 'Album' but has larger flowers.

'Charlotte Bishop' has lovely pink flowers with a small white center.

'Froyle Mill' has dark violet flowers.

'Jesse' is similar to 'Rolf Fiedler' but the flowers are an even deeper blue.

'Rolf Fiedler' is outstanding. He has shorter, wider leaves than the species and handsome clear blue flowers on short flower stems. Unfortunately, colonies are slower to fill in and flowers are not as numerous.

'White Star' is similar to 'Album' and may well be the same.

'Wisley Blue' is most popular and has larger (up to 2″ wide) flowers of lavender blue.

***Iridodictyum*** see *Iris*

***Iris*** (eye′ ris) Iris Iridaceae

The age-old misconception that iris is a summer-flowering plant should at once be dispelled. Few other genera provide flowers as long and as often as the iris. Even though most flowers stay open only a day or so, with reasonable selection and care, it is possible to have one kind of iris or another in flower for seven or eight months of the year. The genus took its name from the Greek goddess Iris, who was the messenger of Juno, the goddess of marriage. Iris walked between heaven and earth over a bridge made by the rainbow. Legend says that wherever she walked on earth, her footprints bore flowers with as many colors as the rainbow.

The iris was said to have first been adopted as an emblem in the sixth century by King Clovis of the Franks, the first king (about 480 AD) of a federation of tribes in northern Europe, after a clump of yellow flag iris had shown him where he could ford a stream and escape a superior force of Goths (a Germanic tribe that migrated from Sweden, flourishing in the first through fourth centuries AD). The flower was revived as an emblem, the Fleur-de-Louis, in 1147 when Louis VII of France set off on the ill-fated second crusade, and later became known as the Fleur-de-lis. The emblem has been used since 1180 as a badge of the kings of France and was probably the yellow flag iris, *Iris pseudacorus*. The iris has been adopted by many kings since and has represented the birth of Christ in classical paintings. Not to be outdone, even the Canadian province of Quebec uses the Fleur-de-lis on her provincial flag. Countries of the world seem unabashedly attached to the beauty of the iris and in any one garden, English, Spanish, Dutch, Persian, German, Californian, Japanese, Louisiana, Pacific Coast, and Siberian iris may be found.

Plants range from the tiny *I. danfordiae*, Danford iris, to large water irises such as *I. pseudacorus*, yellow flag iris. Many species such as *I. sibirica* are easily grown while others such as the exotic *I. susiana*, *I. haynei* and *I. samariae* require truly religious experiences to insure continued success. Bearded iris are most common and so many cultivars have been produced that they have been divided into miniature dwarf, standard dwarf, intermediate, miniature tall, border, and standard tall bearded groupings. The standard tall bearded irises are the most common but dozens of cultivars are available in all the bearded groups. Plenty of species, however, exist for the hardcore taxonomic gardeners.

It would take many years to visit enough gardens around the world to see all the species and much longer to collect them for your own garden. Although it's interesting to see obscure species in botanical gardens, fewer than twenty species are readily available in this country. However, there is sufficient choice of color, habit, and environmental needs within that group to satisfy all but the greediest of iris lovers.

The floral parts are in sets of three. Flowers consist of 6 segments: 3 inner standards that generally are upright and 3 outer falls which are reflexed. The standards are large and showy in many species but are reduced in *I. ensata*, Japanese iris, and are nothing but short bristles in *I. setosa*, bristly iris. Three style branches arch over the anthers and the stigma is found on the underside of the branches near the end. This combination of style, anther, and stigma lies on the inner part of the fall and essentially makes a tunnel through which insects must enter to feed on the nectar, insuring that said insect collects lots of pollen to further impregnate other unsuspecting flowers.

Some species require constantly moist soil and perform best along sides of ponds or pools, thus the ability to maintain soil moisture is an important consideration in selecting iris species. Probably only *I. laevigata*, rabbit ear iris, has an absolute requirement for water, looking particularly shabby if planted in "normal" soils. Yellow flag iris, Louisiana irises, Japanese irises and many of the beardeds will succeed wonderfully well in damp soils, but perform well in "normal" soils, that is, rich well-drained soils and full sun to partial shade. Although some species are bulbous (all of these are unbearded), most iris have underground rhizomes, a horizontally creeping stem, and may or may not be crested or bearded.

Due to the size of the genus, it continues to be stretched like the truth or squeezed like orange juice by taxonomists as more and more in-depth studies are conducted. For example, the further understanding of chromosomal differences has resulted in name or changes in relationships between taxa. Hybridization, both natural and formal, has also led to much head scratching about where to place the resultant progeny. Classifications date from 1930 (Dikes-Diels) to 1953 (Lawrence) and 1961 (Rodionenko), and all made significant changes to the genus. According to the various systems, the genus is divided into sub-genera which again subdivide into sections, sub-sections, and groups or series. Each series may have 5 to 25 species and each species may be subdivided into numerous cultivars. Did you get that?

The work of Rodionenko also removed the bulbous iris to their own genera (*Xiphium*, *Iridodictyum*, and *Juno*). In this book, the genus remains intact but I note changes where appropriate. Gardeners need not lament the changes in academia, but rejoice in this great group of plants, no matter what names they are called.

I like to cut off about half the foliage after irises have flowers in order to reduce foliar fungal and bacterial problems. Of course, that means (1) I actually have to remember and (2) do it. Suffice it to say that the advice is good, but not all of us do it. Propagation of the rhizomatous iris can be accomplished by dividing with a sharp spade or by pulling apart tangled rhizomes with garden forks. Although the latter takes more time and effort, healthier and faster flowering plants result.

The flowering times listed below illustrate the long seasonal interest (adapted from *The World of Iris*, AIS, 1978). Not all species included in this list are described. The American Iris Society is a must for enthusiasts.

| Mid to southern states | Mid to northern states | Group | Includes |
|---|---|---|---|
| L.Nov-L.Jan | Nov-Mar. | Unguicularis | *I. unguicularis* |
| M.Feb-M.Mar | M.Mar-M.Apr | Reticulatas | *I. bakerana* |
| | | | *I. danfordiae* |
| | | | *I. histrio* |
| | | | *I. histriodes* |
| | | | *I. reticulata* |

| Mid to southern states | Mid to northern states | Group | Includes |
|---|---|---|---|
| L.Feb-E.Apr | E.Apr-E.May | Min. Dw. Bearded | *I. chamaeiris*<br>*I. pumila* |
| M.Mar-M.May | L.Apr-L.May | Medians | St. Dw. Bearded<br>Int. Bearded<br>Border Bearded<br>Min. Tall Bearded |
| M.Mar-M.Apr | L.Apr-M.May | Junos | *I. bucharica*<br>*I. willmottiana* |
| E.Apr-E.May | L.Apr-E.Jun | Arils | *I. hoogiana*<br>*I. korolkowii*<br>*I. hookeriana*<br>*I. susiana* |
| E.Apr-L.May | L.Apr-M.Jun | Xiphiums | *I. xiphium*<br>*I. xiphoides*<br>Dutch hybrids |
| L.Apr-E.May | E.May-L.May | Vernae | *I. verna* |
| L.Apr-L.May | E.May-E.Jun | Evansias | *I. cristata*<br>*I. tectorum* |
| L.Apr-L.May | M.May-M.Jun | Tall Bearded | *I. pallida* |
| E.May-E.Jun | M.May-L.Jun | Louisianas | *I. fulva*<br>*I. hexagona*<br>*I. nelsonii* |
| M.May-M.Jun | E.Jun-L.Jun | Siberians | *I. sibirica*<br>*I. sanguinea* |
| M.May-M.Jun | M.Jun-M.Jul | Spurias | *I. graminea*<br>*I. spuria* |
| E.Jun-L.Jun | L.Jun-L.Jul | Apogon | *I. ensata*<br>*I. laevigata*<br>*I. pseudacorus*<br>*I. setosa*<br>*I. versicolor* |
| M.Sep-M.Nov | E.Sep-E.Oct | Rebloomers | Many species |

*Abbreviations:* E = early, M = mid, L = late, Dw = dwarf, Min = miniature, Int = intermediate, St = standard

When I teach this genus to my students, I find it easier to break it down into bulbous and non-bulbous species, then take the great group of non-bulbous taxa and divide them into those with a beard ("Pogon" or bearded iris), those with a crest ("Lophiris" or crested iris) and those with no beard or crest ("Apogon" iris). Peggy Martin, one of my former students, who, with her classmates was struggling to learn the myriad of botanical terms and species in my perennials class, simply called the apogon types the "nothing" iris. Hard to argue with Peggy's common sense.

Quick Reference to Iris Species

| | Height (in.) | Color of flowers | Bearded, crested or apogon | Bulbous or rhizome |
|---|---|---|---|---|
| I. "bearded hybrids" | 8-36 | Various | Bearded | Rhizome |
| *I. cristata* | 6-8 | Lavender | Crested | Rhizome |
| *I. danfordiae* | 2-4 | Yellow | Apogon | Bulbous |
| *I. ensata* | 24-30 | Various | Apogon | Rhizome |
| *I. foetidissima* | 18-24 | Lilac | Apogon | Rhizome |
| *I. pallida* | 24-36 | Violet | Bearded | Rhizome |
| *I. pseudacorus* | 24-36 | Yellow | Apogon | Rhizome |
| *I. reticulata* | 2-4 | Violet | Apogon | Bulbous |
| *I. sibirica* | 24-36 | Blue | Apogon | Rhizome |
| *I. tectorum* | 12-18 | Lilac | Crested | Rhizome |
| *I. unguicularis* | 9-12 | Lilac | Apogon | Rhizome |
| *I. verna* | 4-6 | Blue | Apogon | Rhizome |
| *I.* "xiphium hybrids" | 12-18 | Various | Apogon | Bulbous |

**Bearded Hybrids** Bearded Iris 8-36"/10-24"
Early Summer Various Hybrid Zones 3-10

The majority of people who first use iris in the garden try one of the bearded hybrids. When I wrote the first edition of this book in 1989, it was estimated that well over 90% of all iris used in this country were in this group and that 90% of those were the tall bearded types. Today, they are still wildly popular, but the acceptance of the Siberian, Louisiana, Spuria and Japanese forms have reduced the dependency somewhat. Market research, however, has not determined whether there was such a high demand because breeders turned out so many hybrids and cultivars, or there were so many available that it became difficult to buy anything else. Regardless of the reasons for their popularity, new cultivars continue to be produced and the demand continues.

Bearded irises are "bearded" because of the beard of hairs easily visible in the middle of the falls. I am a great believer in simplifying gardening—we make it way too complicated for beginners and veterans alike. If any group of plants has been made crazy, it is the bearded iris group. They may be classified into dwarf (less than 15"), intermediate (15-28"), and tall bearded iris (28" or taller). The American Iris Society has further divided the dwarfs into miniature (4-10") and standard categories (10-15") and the intermediates were split into intermediate, table and border iris groups. And cultivars, good grief there may be as many irises as there are daylilies. Geez Louise, this is crazy. However, for the iris lovers out there, here are the descriptions adapted from the American Iris Society. With so many cultivars to choose from, I decided that I was useless and let the award-winners have their say. So after each description you will find award winners from the AIS since 2000. If you just like to garden, find one of these cultivars and garden away.

**The Dykes Medal** is the most prestigious award and is presented by the AIS to the "best" iris each year.

2000 'Stairway to Heaven'
2001 'Yaquina Blue'
2002 'Mesmerizer'
2003 'Celebration Song'
2004 'Crowned Heads'
2005 'Splashacata'
2006 'Sea Power'
2007 'Queen's Circle'

**Miniature Dwarf Bearded**: the tiniest of bearded irises, growing up to 8″ tall. They are also the earliest to bloom.

2000 'Bugsy'
2001 'Hey There'
2002 'Scruples'
2003 'Squiggles'
2004 'Dinky Circus'
2005 'Little Drummer Boy'
2006 'African Wine'
2007 'Wise'

**Standard Dwarf Bearded**: some of the most useful garden plants, ranging in height from 8-16″. They begin their bloom as the medium dwarf beardeds are ending, still quite early in the iris season. They are best displayed in clumps. The colors are nearly unlimited since these show all the different "spot patterns" of the miniatures, as well as the plicatas and pinks seen in the tall bearded forms.

2000 'Vavoom'
2001 'Starbaby'
2002 'Little Blue Eyes'
2003 'Dot Com'
2004 'Minidragon'
2005 'Marksman'
2006 'Ruby Eruption'
2007 'Music'

**Intermediate Bearded**: stand 16-27½″ tall, with their bloom season overlapping the former two classes.

2000 'Dark Waters'
2001 'Maui Gold'
2002 'Protocol'
2003 'Bottled Sunshine'
2004 'Gnu Rayz'
2005 'Starwoman'
2006 'Midsummer Night's Dream'
2007 'Delirium'

**Border Bearded:** essentially small versions of the tall beardeds in the same height range and bloom size as the intermediates, but blooming with the tall beardeds. Good border bearded forms have round, ruffled petals that complement their small size.

2000 'Apricot Frosty'
2001 'Cranapple'
2002 'Baboon Bottom'
2003 'Lemon Up'
2004 'Orange Pop'
2005 'Christiana Baker'
2006 'Anaconda Love'
2007 'Go For Bold'

**Miniature Tall Bearded:** this class is distinguished by heights from 16 -27″. The blooms are smaller than on a border bearded and the stems are thin and wiry.

2000 'Pardner'
2001 'Bangles'
2002 'Reminiscence'
2003 'Apricot Drops'
2004 'Merit'
2005 'Ace'
2006 'Baubles and Beads'
2007 'Madam President'

**Tall Bearded:** have stalks with a height 27″ or more, with branching stems and many buds. In addition to a wide variety of colors and patterns, the tall beardeds display qualities such as ruffling and lacing more frequently than do the other classes.

2000 'Mesmerizer'
2001 'Fancy Woman'
2002 'Local Color'
2003 'Crowned Heads'
2004 'Splashacata'
2005 'Sea Power'
2006 'Queen's Circle'
2007 'Starring'

***-cristata*** (kris-tah′ ta) Crested Iris 3-9″/15″
Spring Pale Blue, Yellow Crest Eastern North America Zones 3-8

Many iris are native to the United States but this is one of the finest available. The woody, spindle-shaped shallow rhizomes creep along the surface resulting in rapid multiplication of the clump. The leaves are 4-6″ long and arise from the rhizome. One to two flowers are produced on each 2-3″ tall stem; the standards are shorter and narrower than the falls and the crest is a lovely deep yellow. Plants tolerate partial to heavy shade (although they flourish in morning sun) and look magnificent in great drifts in the woodland garden. The forest floor awash in pale blue is a sight to savor. Plants combine well with Canadian columbine, *Aquilegia canadensis*, wood poppy, *Stylophorum diphyllum* and all sorts of woodsy plants.

**Cultivars:**

var. *alba* ('Alba') is a white-flowered variety not as common or as vigorous as the type. Yellow crests contrast with the handsome flowers that contrast far more with the woodland floor than the type. I received a very vigorous form from one of our fine Southern gardeners and writers, Barrie Crawford. It grows significantly faster than the other white clumps in the Armitage garden. This demonstrates the diversity even within varieties of this species.

'Caerulea' (var. *caerulea*) has darker blue flowers than the species.

'Eco Bluebird' from Eco-Gardens in Decatur, Georgia provides light blue flowers with gold markings.

'Powder Blue Giant' provides light blue flowers.

'Tennessee White' may be the best white form available. Plants are vigorous and produce many more flowers than other comparable white cultivars I have seen. Selected by Tennessee nurseryman Don Shadow of Shadow Nursery.

'Shenandoah Sky' is a darker blue form.

***-danfordiae*** (dan-ford′ ee-eye) Danford Iris 4-6″/6″
Early Spring Bright Yellow Eastern Turkey Zones 5-9
(syn. *Iridodictyum danfordium*)

The bulbs have a netted or reticulated cover with brownish fibers, thus belonging to the group known as reticulated iris. Brilliant yellow flowers with brown spots on the falls open in early spring or late winter depending on soil temperature.

Plants are short and should be planted where they can be enjoyed close up. The leaves are square, hollow, and barely developed at time of flowering, although they grow 12″ long after flowering. The standards are less than ¾″ long and the falls have small brown or black spots. I love these plants when they flower in the spring but then I tend to forget about them. Plants like hot, dry conditions during their long summer dormancy and invariably, they break into masses of small bulbs, resulting in leaves but few flowers the next year. They should be treated as annuals or biennials and replaced every other year.

***-foetidissima*** (foy-ti-dis′ i-ma) Stinking Gladwin 18-24″/18″
Summer Lilac Europe Zones 6-9

This unusual plant is one of the few irises grown for the fruit rather than (or instead of) the flowers. The leaves are evergreen, about 18″ long and are characterized by their somewhat foul odor when broken or crushed. Another common name is roast beef plant, which may give an indication of its fragrance. With all this attention to its malodorous properties, I must say that the Armitage nose has not recoiled at the scent. That I usually have hay fever when I smell it may help. The purplish gray flowers are 2-2½″ across and rather forgettable. Not until autumn is the beauty of this plant appreciated. Then, the seed pods split open and reveal rows of scarlet seeds, which provide yet another common name, coral iris. The seeds remain attached throughout the winter if not snatched by birds or squirrels. The fruiting stem may be hung upside down to dry and used for indoor decoration.

*Iris foetidissima*
(64%)

Plants do well in partial shade and are among the most shade tolerant of iris species. Due to their evergreen nature, the foliage can look cruddy in the spring. Taking old leaves off in the spring does not hurt the plant and gets rid of a bunch of potential disease organisms. Two to three years are necessary to establish a clump of stinking gladwin. The first year in the Gardens at UGA yielded few seed capsules but six to eight fruits overflowing with colorful seeds appeared the following year.

Propagate by seed, or lift and divide in the fall.

**Cultivars:**

'Citrina' (var *citrina*) bears flowers of pale yellow and mauve. A mixed-up color scheme but not entirely without beauty.

'Fructo-alba' translates to "white fruit" and occurs very rarely. Difficult to find and not nearly as bright as the regular form anyway.

'Lutea' (var. *lutescens*) has handsome light yellow flowers.

'Variegata' has variegated leaves which add foliar appeal to an otherwise drab plant. A slow grower.

***-ensata*** (en' sata) Japanese Iris 24-30"/24"
Summer Various Northern China, Japan Zones 4-9

Occurring in east Asia to Siberia, *I. ensata* is by nature a meadow rather than a marshland plant. However, plants adapt well to afternoon shade and moist soils. The leaves are bright green and have a prominent center rib (unlike *I. laevigata*) and are about one inch wide. In its native form, plants are rather unimpressive, with ordinary red purple flowers, small standards and floppy falls. However, over the centuries the Japanese have developed large-flowered plants characterized by the virtual elimination of the standards and subsequent increase in size of the falls. The flowers may be up to 10" across and due to lack of standards, the overall appearance is that of a table top. Cultivars include singles (with 3 broad, overlapping falls), doubles (with 6 falls which are actually standards and falls lying together), and gruesome peony-style flowers with up to 12 flower parts. Japanese iris look particularly good if placed at the base of stairs so that as you descend, the tops of the flowers are in view.

Plants perform well in any organic-rich soil where moisture can be consistently provided. They are quite happy in a shallow pond or bog but can be grown in normal soils as well. Fertilize plants in early spring and summer. Acidic conditions are necessary and lime must not be added to the soil. A number of lime-tolerant cultivars were bred by the late German hybridizer Max Steiger, and released in Europe in the late 1950s and early 1960s but are found only through specialty iris growers. Plant in full sun or afternoon shade.

The name *I. kaempferi* is also commonly used for this species, however, upon study, it was found that plants were called *I. ensata* by the Swedish taxonomist, Thunberg in 1794, whereas the name *I. kaempferi* was not provided by Franz von Siebold of Holland until 1858. So, *I. ensata* it is. Actually, it is one of the few times I am pleased with a name change; I never could spell *I. kaempferi* correctly.

Plants may be divided in spring and fall.

**Cultivars:**

Cultivars that have been developed are truly magnificent and are becoming less expensive and more available every year. Some people remove the big flowers as soon as they fade, but then you will miss the large wonderful fruit. As with other popular species of iris, catalogs and websites provide the most vivid descriptions of cultivars. The pictures are also prettier. Here are the best of the best from the American Iris Society.

| | | | |
|---|---|---|---|
| 2000 | 'Bellender Blue' | 2006 | 'Sing The Blues' |
| 2001 | 'Picotee Princess' | 2007 | 'Dirigo Pink Milestone' |
| 2002 | 'Electric Glow' | | |
| 2003 | 'Lion King' | | |
| 2004 | 'Epimetheus' | | |
| 2005 | 'Blue Spritz' | | |

**Louisiana Iris** Louisiana Iris 3-4′/3′
Summer Various Southern United States Zones 4-9

Louisiana irises constitute a unique group in the iris family in that they consist of five distinct species of iris, indigenous to a limited area of south central Louisiana and the Gulf Coast marsh areas of Texas to Florida. The species that make up the Louisianas are *I. brevicaulis, I. fulva, I. giganticaerulea, I. hexagona* and *I. nelsonii,* although plant breeders have provided gardeners with many hybrids that are now more common than any of the species. They are non-bearded, non-crested iris and generally have narrow falls and drooping standards. All of the species are handsome in their own right but their hybridization, natural or otherwise, has resulted in numerous wonderful named hybrids. Guidelines for garden use include sun and lots of water. They do not require bogs but do better where copious water can be provided.

*I. brevicaulis*, Lamance iris, is the shortest species in the Louisiana complex, growing about 12-14″ tall with thick, short, often zig-zag stalks. The flowers are lilac blue to deep blue and occur within the leaves. In the Armitage garden, plants become very leafy and after flowering, must be divided before they eat more space.

*I. fulva* has 4″ flowers in brick red or copper-red and occasionally yellow. This is one of the few red-colored iris and does well in the sunny garden. *I. giganticarulea* is very similar to, and may be a variety of, *I. hexagona*. Flowers are larger (4-6″ across) and occur only in Louisiana coastal areas. Plants thrive in flooded areas and may tolerate brackish water. *I. hexagona* is the most easterly native, occurring in Florida, South Carolina and Georgia. Long, narrow, light green leaves and lilac flowers with yellow markings on the falls. Plants move about the garden freely but can not be termed as aggressive. *I. nelsonii* has 4-5″ wide bright red to purple flowers, but generally more intense than the color of *I. fulva*. They are shorter than *I. fulva* and found only in Louisiana in a limited location south of the town of Abbeville. Not discovered until 1938, they became known as "Abbeville Irises", "Abbeville Reds", or because of their similarity to *I. fulva*, "Super-Fulvas".

The hybrids that have been developed have increased the range of color and usefulness of these plants. Early hybridization of *I. fulva* x *I. brevicaulis* by the famous iris pioneer W. B. Dykes resulted in 'Fulvula' in 1910. Through the 1920s and 1930s, dozens of hybrids were registered with the American Iris Society. Many crosses between *I. fulva*, and *I. hexagona* became popular in the 1930s. The discovery of *I. nelsonii* in 1966 opened up the hybridization process to include red and terra cotta colors. Joseph Mertzweiller produced some of the first tetraploid cultivars in 1973 and tetraploids continue to evolve, although at a much slower rate than the diploids.

The northern limits of Louisiana iris continue to be expanded. Plants have been successful in Sioux Falls, South Dakota and have been described in many plains states, the Midwest and California. Plants tolerate full sun to a little afternoon shade in the South, consistent watering and fertility and soil improved with organic matter.

One of the more knowledgeable gardeners about this fine group of hybrids is Josephine Shanks of Houston, Texas. She is the Louisianas' best friend, imploring us to give the group a try, and her enthusiasm and knowledge have helped many a gardener improve his garden.

**Cultivars**:

Numerous cultivars have been bred and are available in white ('Clara Goula', 'Rokki') to lavender ('Ione', 'Ashley Michelle'), red ('Sun Chaser', 'Parade Music'), yellow ('President Hedley', 'Professor Barbara') and bicolors ('Colorific', 'Bold Pretender'). The Louisiana Iris Society of America provides cultivars and useful gardening information, including the following Louisiana iris winners.

2000 'Cajun Sunrise'
2001 'Praline Festival'
2002 'Extraordinaire'
2003 'Cajun Sunset'
2004 'Hot and Spicy'
2005 'Red Velvet Elvis'
2006 'Peaches in Wine'
2007 'My Friend Dick'

**-*pallida*** (pa' li-da) Sweet Iris 24-36"/24"
Summer Violet Northern Italy Zones 4-9

This species is an important building block in the development of the bearded iris, yet it has some lovely attributes of its own. Although the bearded flowers are fragrant, they are an unremarkable lavender-blue, and much more statuesque flowers may be found in any number of bearded hybrids. Some say the flowers smell like grape juice. My sense of smell must not be that well developed. The foliage, however, is an excellent soft gray green color that is retained throughout the year and is a good foil for dark green plants in the garden.

Like other bearded species, *I. pallida* grows best in well-drained soils and is not particularly tolerant of wet feet. Full sun is preferred but partial shade is tolerated.

**Cultivars:**

'Argentea-variegata' has flattened leaves of silvery white and green stripes. The lilac-blue flowers complement the foliage.

'Variegata' ('Zebra') has white and cream streaking on blue-green leaves. An exceptional garden plant with all-season appeal.

var. *dalmatica* is the best of the glaucous foliage plants with larger leaves and handsome foliage.

***-pseudacorus*** (sood-a′ ko-rus) Yellow Flag Iris 24-42″/24″
Early Summer Yellow Europe Zones 5-9

Yellow flag iris has been grown for centuries and all parts of the plant have been found useful, in one way or another, over the years. The rhizome acts as a powerful cathartic, the powdered roots were used as snuff and contain antidotal properties for poisons. The seeds were roasted for a coffee-like beverage while the flowers produced a yellow dye.

This is a most adaptable species. To be sure, plants are at their best where the roots are submerged in water or at least constantly moist. Heights of three to four feet are not uncommon in such situations. However, they also grow well in dryer areas as long as irrigation is provided when Mother Nature falls behind with rain. *I. pseudacorus* has grown well in my shaded garden, tucked away in a corner (as well as one can tuck a plant of this size), through two major droughts. When grown under less than ideal conditions, plants are shorter and less vigorous. This is not usually a problem as plants grown in streams and ponds are often too big for most gardens.

The 12-15″ long leaves are sword shaped, bright green and rather coarse. The 2″ long yellow flowers are not particularly large but often have brown veins with a brown blotch on the falls. The fruit capsules of all varieties are large and sought after for dried arrangements. I grow this species through plants of *Sedum* 'Autumn Joy'. The sedum grows around the foliage throughout the summer and the swordlike leaves of the iris provide additional architectural interest.

I always include this plant as one of my "no-brainers" for beginning gardeners. However, I was taken to task at one lecture for even suggesting this as a garden plant when it is so inclined to naturalize in waterways. Like *Lythrum* in the North, *I. pseudacorus* can indeed escape and cause problems in southern streams and wetlands. It has a long way to go before it becomes the nuisance of loosestrife, however, be forewarned. This baby likes it here!

Propagate by division of the rhizome every 2-4 years or raise from seeds. Seed-propagated plants are variable and take two years to flower.

**Cultivars:**

'Alba' is a good-looking white form.

'Bastardii' (var. *bastardii*) bears pale primrose flowers without the markings on the falls. The person who named this must have been having a bad day.

'Flore-pleno' is an ugly double-flowered form. Curious is a kind way of describing the flowers.

'Golden Queen' (var. *superba*) produces bright yellow flowers without the usual brown markings.

'Rising Sun' bears lovely yellow flowers, grows 3-4′ tall and is likely a hybrid with *I. ensata*.

'Variegata' has yellow stripes on the leaves and is the finest of all the water irises for spring foliage effect. The flowers are lost in the variegated effect but the leaves are so outstanding that the flowers are not missed. Unfortunately, the variegation disappears as the summer warms up and leaves revert to green. Next spring, however, leaves reappear variegated. Plants are not as tolerant of shade as the species.

***-reticulata*** (re-tik-ew′ lah-ta) Reticulated Iris 2-4″/6″
Winter, Early Spring Violet Turkey Zones 5-8
(syn. *Iridodictyum reticulatum*)

The little bulbs are among the earliest to emerge in the spring or even in late winter. In the Armitage garden, flowers appear by February 15 and persist until the first week in March, depending on the weather. Few plants surpass the richness of the purple and gold flowers, each possessing the delightful fragrance of violets. Bulbs have netted veins similar to *I. danfordiae* and should be planted 2-3″ deep. The pointed leaves are acutely four-angled and 1-3″ tall at flowering time, then elongate to 12-18″ tall after the flowers have finished. Because of their diminutive size at flowering time, bulbs must be planted in large numbers to make any kind of show. Leaves disappear by late spring or early summer and annuals may be used to fill in the gaps. All species in the reticulated iris group require dry summers for the bulbs to ripen and set buds for the next year. In areas with heavy summer rains, plantings decline in the first three years but those that adapt continue to flower in larger clumps each year. Many of my original bulbs had disappeared but those remaining are magnificent.

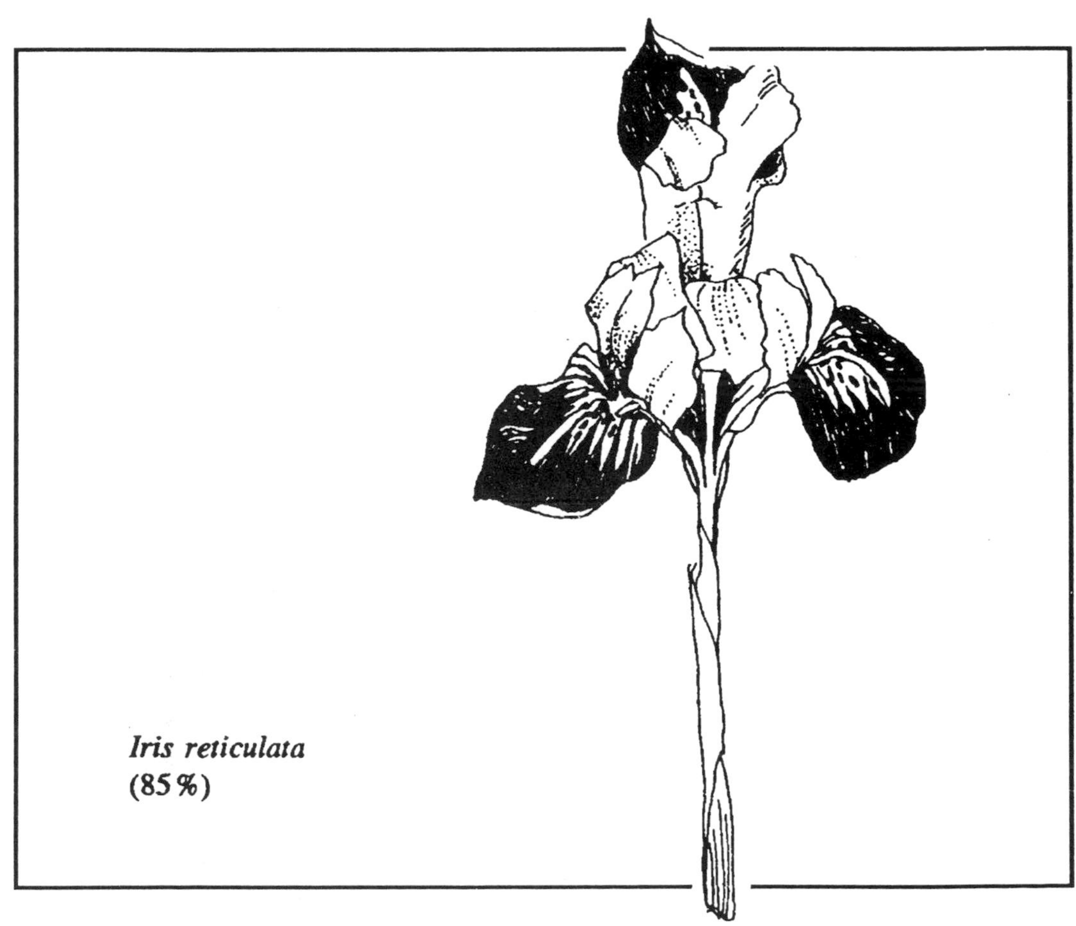

***Iris reticulata***
**(85%)**

The offsets may be divided immediately after flowering.

**Cultivars:**

Many are hybrids with other bulbous iris, but are generally listed under *I. reticulata*.

'Cantab' has pale blue flowers with violet on the falls and shows up well in the spring.
'Clairette' is sky-blue, and the blue to violet falls also have a white patch.
'Edward' bears dark blue flowers with orange on the falls.
'Gordon' is about 6″ tall with blue-violet flowers.
'Harmony' has royal blue flowers with a yellow and white blotch on the falls. This is the most common bulbous iris, and used in large numbers by the greenhouse industry for pot plant forcing. Place as many bulbs as possible in a pot, place in a cool place (35-40°F) for about 10 weeks, then bring out to room temperatures.
'Herculès' produces deep purple flowers with an orange blotch on the falls.
'Ida' bears blue flowers with a yellow blotch.
'J.S. Dijt' has purplish red flowers with a little white and yellow on the falls.
'Joyce' has handsome sky blue blossoms with white blotches on the falls.
'Marguerite' produces dark blue flowers over yellow and green variegated foliage.
'Natascha' bears creamy ivory flowers with a gold-yellow blotch.
'Pauline' produces purple to violet flowers with a white blotch on the falls.
'Purple Gem' has deep purple flowers.
'Spring Time' bears light blue and dark blue bicolored flowers.

***-sibirica*** (si-bi′ ri-ka) | Siberian Iris | 24-36″/24″
Spring | Blue | Central Europe, Russia | Zones 3-9

Native to moist meadows, Siberian iris does well in a moist or bog garden, but performs equally well in normal garden situations as long as moisture can be delivered throughout the season. They are simply smaller than when grown in your favorite bog. This lack of water response also occurs with *I. sanguinea*, an unexciting blue-flowered species, *I. pseudacorus* and *I. versicolor*.

Siberian iris has 2-5 blue-purple flowers per stem, but they may occasionally be lavender or white. The 1-2″ wide flowers are held well above the narrow lancelike foliage. Many cultivars are available, including vigorous tetraploids (twice as many chromosomes as usual), which make the species pale in comparison. The many flowers (each plant can produce 12-20 flowers) unfurl in mid May and provide a certain touch of class that is the hallmark of the Siberian iris. I prefer them to tall bearded types not only because of their smaller, more delicate flowers, but because they are less prone to soft rot or iris borer. Like many irises, however, it is not a good idea to go on holiday for more than a week, as flowering in the Siberians comes and goes quickly.

Unlike the bearded iris, they should not be disturbed until the clump is obviously producing fewer flowers than normal. Use two spading forks to divide and do not allow the divisions to dry. They resent being disturbed and may take a year or more to look their best.

*Iris sibirica*
(81%)

**Cultivars:**

Many fine cultivars of Siberian iris are available and one must give way to those ubiquitous iris catalogs and online nurseries for a proper overview of available colors and range of vigor. Here are a few winners gleaned from the website of the American Iris Society.

2000 'Over in Gloryland'
2001 'Strawberry Fair'
2002 'Lake Keuka'
2003 'Careless Sally'
2004 'Blueberry Fair'
2005 'Where Eagles Dare'
2006 'Riverdance'
2007 'Ships Are Sailing'

*Iris sibirica*
(68%)

***-tectorum*** (tek-tor′ um) Roof Iris 12-18″/18″
Summer Lilac China, Japan Zones 4-8

Because of the interesting shape of the flowers, the evergreen foliage and the increased availability, this species has gained popularity every year. It certainly has become one of my favorites. Its specific name, *tectorum*, means "growing on roofs", from the custom of being grown on the edges of thatched roofs in Japan. The powdered roots were also used by ladies in China for whitening their skin.

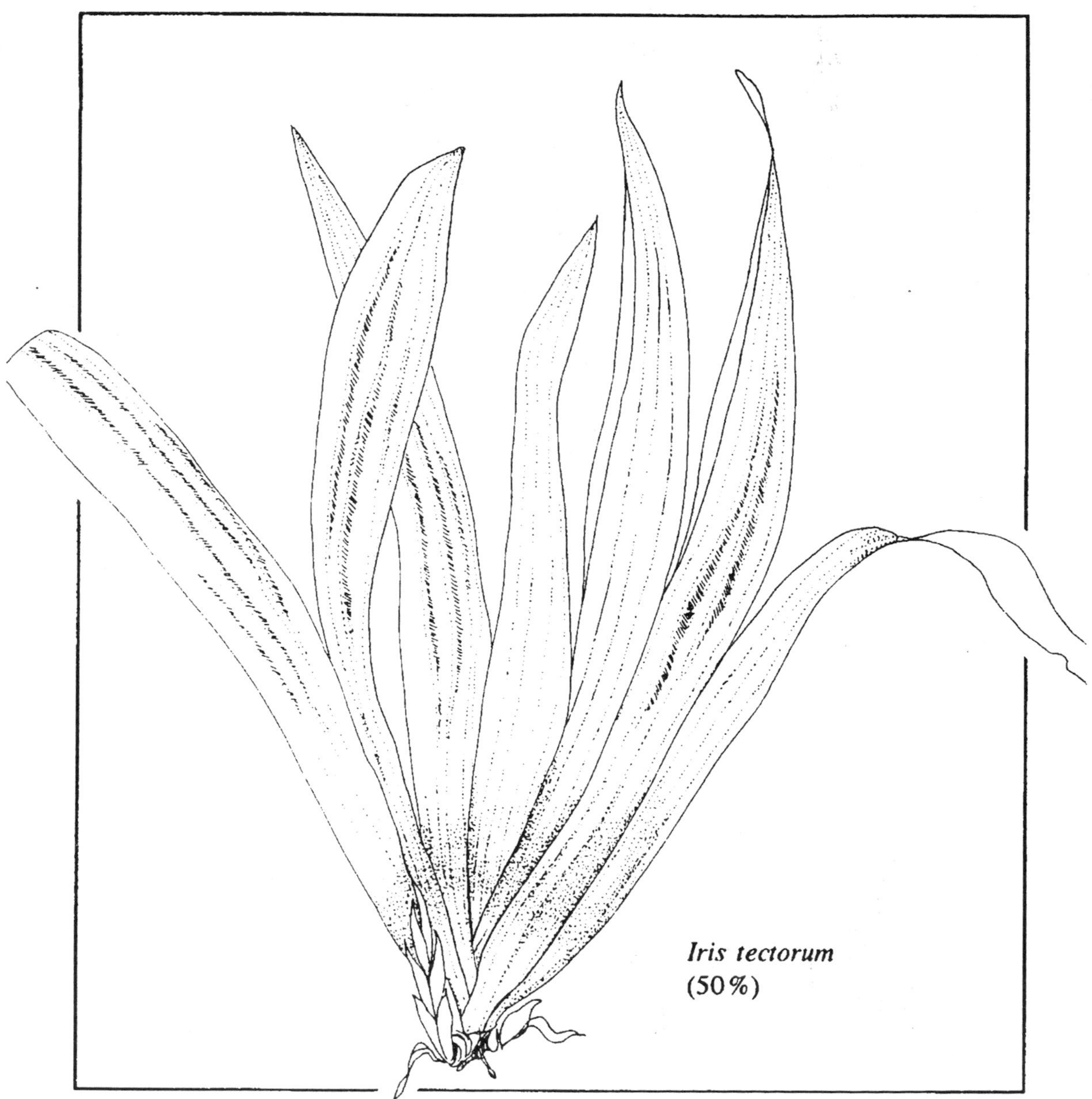

*Iris tectorum*
(50%)

The large 6″ wide lilac flowers are mottled with dark blue to black blotches. Plants belong to the crested iris group (as does *I. cristata*), because of the conspicuous whitish brown jagged crest (rather than a beard) on the flowers. The standards lie almost level with the falls, resulting in an open, wide flower. Each flower stem usually bears two flowers and the evergreen leaves are 6-8″ wide, yellow-green and somewhat floppy.

Partial shade is tolerated but roof irises prefer full sun and well-drained soils. A number of reports on culture, particularly from England, suggest that plants are heavy feeders and must be moved from site to site every other year. The reports state that without heavy fertilization, the plant quickly depletes the soil and flowering is sparse. I have not found this to be necessary in my experience. However, plants should be fed by applying 1-2 tablespoons of a complete fertilizer such as 8-8-8 around the soil at the base of the plant (take care not to allow the granules to touch the leaves or the crown) in the spring as the plant becomes active.

Propagate by division of the rhizomes immediately after flowering, just as the last flower has faded. Plants can be moved at any time of year, providing they are irrigated well.

**Cultivars:**

var. *album* is harder to find and more expensive but is no longer rare. The flowers are white with a yellow crest on the falls.

'Variegatum' has lavender blue flowers and variegated foliage.

***-unguicularis*** (un-gwik-ew-lah′ ris) Algerian Iris 9-12″/12″
Winter, Spring Lavender Algeria, Greece Zones 7-9

This useful iris is best known for its late winter bloom time and is easily identified by the almost total absence of a stem. The 18-20″ long and ½-1″ wide evergreen leaves are produced in a tuft and the flowers are cradled in the leafy center. The solitary blossoms are nicely fragrant and are usually lilac-blue to white. A wonderful plant for mild climates but it can be disappointing when frosts knock back the leaves and flowers. Plants tolerate partial shade but perform best in full sun. In the Armitage garden, I have had flowers on Christmas Day as well as on Valentine's Day. On other years, the frosts have beaten plants up to the point where no flowering has occurred at all. Plants can be recommended in the Pacific Northwest and the Gulf States.

**Cultivars:**

'Alba' bears white flowers; the falls have a central green-yellow line.

'Abington Purple' produces purple-blue flowers with a yellow stripe down the falls.

'Mary Barnard' has darker violet-blue flowers.

'Oxford Dwarf' produces deep blue flowers with white, blue-veined falls.

'Speciosa' has deep violet flowers with a central yellow stripe. The leaves are shorter and more narrow than the species.

'Walter Butt' bears large pale silver-lilac flowers. Quite handsome.

***-verna*** (ver′ na) Vernal Iris 4-6″/12″
Spring Blue Eastern United States Zones 6-10

This dwarf native plant has a creeping rootstock similar to *I. cristata*. The 1½″ long flowers are dark blue with a large orange blotch on the falls. They are similar in habit to the dwarf bearded irises, but much smaller. This species is taxonomically very close to the bearded irises and some people refer to the flower as semi-bearded. Upon inspection, the pubescence on the falls is noticeable. The shortened stems are no longer than six inches long. The narrow foliage is approximately 6″ long during flowering but elongates to 9-12″ after flowering.

Plants prefer shady, dry areas but do not grow as well as crested iris, particularly in woodland settings. They are most at home in a raised bed where good drainage can be provided. Garden in the Woods in Framingham, Massachusetts has some wonderful plantings.

Propagate by division of the rhizome after flowering.

**Xiphium Hybrids** (zi′ fee-um) English, Spanish, Dutch Iris 12-18″/12″
Spring Various Southern Europe, Northern Africa Zones 6-9

These bulbous iris are seen mainly in florists shops as cut flowers but few are sufficiently weather tolerant to be used in all but Southern gardens. As a group, they have been reclassified to the genus *Xiphium* and historically have included English and Spanish iris, but today almost wholly consist of hybrid Dutch irises. It is difficult if not impossible to find English or Spanish irises for sale, but you may find them in better botanical gardens or bulb collections. Dutch hybrids are more tolerant of inclement weather than the others and provide plants for color and cut flowers.

Historically, the English iris are the last of the group to flower and do so in June to July. They are predominantly *I. xiphoides* (X. *latifolium*) but other species have undoubtedly played a role in their development. Growing 1-2′ tall, they have the largest flowers (5″ across) of the group. Although no yellow flowers are available, white, blue, pink, or purple occur and all have a gold blotch on the falls. They are native to the French and Spanish Pyrenees but are called English iris because they reached the Low Countries from England, most probably without notice of their true habitat. They grow well in English gardens but are difficult in North America because of the requirement for constantly moist soil. Copious amounts of water and rich soils are necessary.

Spanish iris *I. xiphium* ( *X. vulgare)* is smaller in all respects than the English iris. and likely a hybrid of a number of bulbous species. Plants are 12-18″ tall with 3-4″ diameter flowers in a wide range of colors. Bright sunshine and warm, dry exposures are preferred. Seldom grown or seen in American gardens.

The Dutch iris was originally produced by the Tubergen Nurseries in Haarlem, Holland and is best described as a large and earlier-flowering strain of Spanish iris. They are the first to flower, starting in mid May and continuing through June. In zones 7 and south, the foliage appears in the winter and although the leaves may be killed back by frosts, little damage to the flower bud occurs (unless the petal color is visible at time of frost). They are hardier than the others and may be occasionally overwintered to zone 6b, but cold winters every few years will likely get them, even in zone 7. Plants are 15-24″ in height and flowers are 4-5″ in diameter. They are particularly popular as cut flowers and may be forced in greenhouses year round. When planted in groups of a dozen or so, they make lovely garden plants requiring little room, and can be enjoyed inside and out. There are dozens of cultivars in a varied range of colors from bright yellow to the darkest blue.

In general, bulbs should be planted about 6″ deep and once planted, need not be disturbed. However, all species and hybrids in the Xiphium group can be split into bulblets after the foliage has died down. Many naturally split into two larger bulbs as well as many smaller offsets. The larger bulbs may be replanted and will flower the following year, the smaller ones should be set aside and allowed to mature in a propagation bed until large enough to flower. Don't expect more than 2 years out of the bulbs; anything longer is gravy.

**Cultivars:**

These are mainly Dutch iris, although some diligent searching may yield some English and Spanish forms. All are about 18-22″ tall.

'Apollo' has yellow falls and white standards.
'Blue Magic' consists of blue flowers with a yellow blotch on the falls.
'Bronze Beauty' produces flowers with a mixture of bronze and gold colors.
'Casablanca' is all white except for the yellow markings on the falls.
'Eye of the Tiger' has deep blue standards and bronze falls.
'Golden Harvest' is easily seen, consisting of bright golden flowers.
'Oriental Beauty' produces light blue standards and bronze-yellow falls.
'Purple Moon' is just that, but also has some yellowing on the falls.
'Sapphire Beauty' bears violet standards and dark blue falls with yellow blotches.
'Sky Beauty' bears flowers with different shades of blue, including dark and light hues, on each flower.
'Symphony' has milky white standards and yellow falls.
'White Excelsior' bears clean white flowers, each with a yellow blotch on the petals.

**Related Species:**

*I. bucharica* (*Juno bucharica*), Bokhara iris, bears fragrant creamy standards and yellow on the falls on 12-18″ tall stems in April. I love this plant! I grow it for its late spring flowers and although, at least in the Armitage garden, it does not return in subsequent years, I enjoy the party while in session. The leaves are 8-12″ long, 2½″ wide, glossy above, whitish underneath and arranged like a ladder up the short stem. Very uniris-like. Foliage disappears by midsummer.

*I. chrysographes*, goldvein iris, has dark maroon flowers with gold markings on the falls. An outstanding but little-known species. Consistently moist soil is required. Numerous forms exist; the most sought after is probably 'Nigra' or 'Black Form' which is so dark purple as to appear black. Plants have been hybridized with other related forms such as *I. forrestii*.

*I. gracilipes*, slender iris, is a graceful species of the crested iris group. It is shade tolerant, 8-10″ tall, and bears beautiful lilac-pink flowers with an orange crest over narrow, arching foliage.

*I. histrio* (*Iridodictylum histrio*), Syrian iris, is distinctly bluer than *I. reticulata* with a hint of red in its makeup. Usually flowers earlier than reticulated irises.

*I. histriodes* (*Iridodictylum histriodes*), harput iris, is larger (6-9″) and flowers 1-2 weeks later than reticulated irises. Plants have a creamy white area on the falls, and produce many smaller offsets than *I. reticulata*. This has become more popular in recent years and cultivars like 'Frank Elder' (pale blue flowers with yellow), 'George' (dark purple), 'Katherine Hodgson' (light blue to gray with yellow markings) and 'Lady Beatrix Stanley' (blue with white blotches). Many more are also available.

*I. lacustris*, dwarf lake iris, is similar to crested iris but is only about 3″ tall, and has narrower leaves and a more slender rhizome. The flowers are slate blue with a whitish patch and yellow crest on the falls. It is native to the shores of the Great Lakes. Unless you live on those shores, *I. crisata* is probably a better garden plant and surely far more available.

*I. laevigata*, rabbit ear iris, is a most magnificent iris. The 2-3″ wide flowers are flattened and lavender blue. The blue-green leaves have visible black "watermarks" along the veins. Plants are easily distinguishable from *I. ensata* because of the smooth leaves compared to the raised central midrib of *I. ensata*. They are also more lime tolerant than Japanese irises. Rabbit ear iris is difficult to find in this country because of the narrow limits of adaptability. Roots must be constantly moist and it is best grown on streambanks, bogs, or other areas high in moist organic matter. The finest examples I have seen are at Longstock Water Gardens near Longstock, England. Some cultivars have been selected. 'Alba' bears pure white flowers which make it even prettier than the species; 'Rose Queen' has attractive pink flowers; 'Snowdrift' produces creamy white flowers with a hint of purple, and 'Variegata' has sharp white leaf variegations which contrast well with the blue flowers. Probably the best variegated form to hold its variegations throughout the season.

*I. mandschurica* resembles the yellow flag iris but is considerably more difficult to find and to grow. Plants don't grow quite as tall and are at home in shallow water.

*I. sanguinea* is native to Siberia as well as Japan, Korea and China. Plants are generally shorter than *I. sibirica* and the unbranched flower stems usually bear only two purple terminal flowers. 'Snow Queen' is about 2½′ tall with milky white flowers. *I. sanguinea* used to be called *I. orientalis*, which is a distinct species, resulting in all sorts of confusion.

*I. spuria*, seashore iris, requires plenty of water in spring and fall but prefers to be hot and dry during the summer. The best thing about the spurias is that they remain as a clump, not opening in the middle like Louisiana or bearded types do. It is a complex group due to its vast range, from North Africa to Denmark. Few sources can be found for this species, but countless cultivars have been bred in Europe. They are less tolerant of our harsher climate than that found in the British Isles or southern Germany, where they flourish. Hybrid forms grow to 4′ in height and almost as wide. Flowers consist of long narrow falls, usually wider at the ends, particularly in the cultivars, and narrow, upright, often frilly standards in an assortment of colors. Flowers open in June and July. Some of my favorite hybrids are 'Cambridge Blue' with lavender and yellow flowers, 'Shelford Giant' with handsome creamy white and yellow flowers and 'Orange Maid', whose bright orange-yellow flowers can be seen from "miles away". Plants resent disturbance and should not be moved unless necessary. A few great ones from the AIS follow.

2000 'Ila Remembered'
2001 'Missouri Springs'
2002 'Sunrise in Missouri'
2003 'Missouri Sunset'
2004 'Missouri Rainbows'
2005 'Missouri Iron Ore'
2006 'Adriatic Blue'
2007 'Missouri Orange'

*I. versicolor*, blueflag iris, native to North America, is similar to *I. pseudacorus* in size, habit, and tolerance to moisture. This is the common blue flag iris found in moist soils from eastern Canada to Pennsylvania. The flowers occur in shades of reddish or bluish purple. It is adaptable to most moist climates but not common in the trade. 'Karmesina' has red flowers on 3′ tall stems.

*I. winogradowii* has to be one of the most beautiful dwarf iris in existence. Although that statement is based on my limited experience, it took my breath away when I saw clumps in the rock garden at Wisley, UK. The lemon-yellow flowers have an orange stripe in the center of the falls. They are larger than the Danford iris but, no doubt, the bulbs will behave the same, requiring replacement every other year. Difficult to find, and expensive.

## ***Isopyrum*** (eye′ so-pye-rum) False Rue-Anemone Ranunculaceae

This genus has come into the gardener's eye only in the last decade, not because it has recently been discovered, but because it was mixed up with, and obscured by, other similar plants like *Anemonella*, rue-anemone. The main species available to gardeners, at least in the East, is *I. biternatum*. I have a tough time telling the two apart, even if they are side by side. However, plants in this genus have alternate leaves, those in *Anemonella* are opposite; the sepals here tend to overlap, those of *Anemonella* are thinner and seldom touch; and the leaves are more shallowly divided in *Isopyrum* than *Anemonella*.

Plants grow in moist, rich, low woodlands, often in alkaline soils, which suggests a low application of lime may be useful at home. Like *Anemonella*, these 6-8″ tall plants are spring bloomers and ephemeral, emerging as soon as temperatures warm above 40°F, and will be in flower as long as temperatures remain in the 50s.

Other species occur in the West, such as *I. stipitatum* and *I. hallii*, which may be better choices for Western gardeners.

A taxonomic movement is underfoot to change the genus to *Enemion* (*E. biternatum*), so simply be aware that the label may change but the plant does not.

***Ixia*** (iks-ee′ a) Wand Flower, Corn Lily Iridaceae

The corn lilies are native to the Cape Province of South Africa and rather uncommon in North American gardens. Flowers arise from corms planted 2-3″ deep after the last frost. Plants can survive a winter temperature in the upper 20s but really should be thought of as frost-free plants. They are winter hardy only from zone 9 but with winter protection, may survive in zone 7b. Soils with a basic pH are preferable and lime should be incorporated in acid soils prior to planting. The common name, wand flower, refers to the thin, wiry stems which wave in the wind while the other common name, corn lily, is in reference to the plants appearing in grassy fields.

About 45 species are known but the corms offered in catalogs are hybrids developed by Dutch nurserymen. The plants produce 8-12″ high wiry stems and narrow, grasslike leaves. The cup-shaped flowers are composed of six brightly colored segments, and a spike of 9-12 blooms is produced from each corm. The colors are bold and brilliant, ranging from white with a blue, red, or purple center to yellow and red forms usually with an eye of a different color.

Corms are inexpensive and the resulting flowers are gorgeous. They are worth trying, even as annuals, to add brightness to the late spring and early summer garden. They are excellent container plants, and container and all can be moved to a protected site during the winter, if necessary. Alternatively, they may be treated like gladiolus and removed in fall, stored in a cool place and replanted in the spring. At this time, the small cormels may be removed.

These are fun plants, to be placed where they can be admired, costing little and returning lots.

**Cultivars:**

'Afterglow' has orange flowers with dark red centers.
'Bluebird' produces white flowers with deep blue centers.
'Bridesmaid' bears white flowers with a red eye.
'Hogarth' has creamy yellow flowers with a purple eye.
'Marquette' consists of deep yellow flowers with purple tips.
'Rose Emperor' bears rose-pink flowers with a deeper colored eye.
'Uranus' makes dark yellow flowers with red centers.
'Venus' consists of magenta flowers with a darker center.
'Wonder' produces pink double flowers.

**Related Species:**

*I. maculata* has yellow flowers with black spots on the throat.

*I. paniculata* bears 6-12 large (1-1½″ wide) creamy white to yellow flowers.

*I. viridiflora*, green ixia, is one of the more interesting species. Plants have 1-2″ wide flowers consisting of extraordinary blue-green petals with a purple-black eye.

***Ixiolirion*** (iks-io-lir′ ee-on) Siberian Lily Amaryllidaceae

This small group of bulbous plants occurs in fields and rocky hillsides in western and central Asia at altitudes up to 8000 feet. Some authorities recognize four species while others believe that all plants are variants of *I. tataricum*. Likely, what is sold today are hybrids of the various species.

***-tataricum*** (tar-tar′ i-kum) Siberian Lily 12-20″/18″
Spring Blue Central Asia Zones 7-9

The 3-8 linear leaves give rise to a spreading inflorescence (umbel) of 4-6 sky blue, lily-like blossoms on slender rounded stems. The flowers bear segments with 3-5 dark lilac ribs. They should be lifted (like gladiolus) when planted north of zone 7, although some catalogs list them hardy to zone 6. They are hardy to 5°F but require sunny, well-drained sheltered positions. In the South, winter drainage is most important as bulbs rot if soil does not drain rapidly.

Similar to other half-hardy minor bulbs, *Ixiolirion* is inexpensive and can be used even as an annual. Many of the minor bulbs are hidden treasures that will be discovered only with a little plant exploration of our own.

# J

***Jeffersonia*** (jef-er-son′ ee-a) Twinleaf Berberidaceae

"Though an old man, I am but a young gardener." summarizes the thoughts of many of us who find that the more we learn, the more we understand how little we know. The above quote is attributed to Thomas Jefferson, one of America's best-known naturalists and gardeners who also just happened to be the third President of the United States. Twinleaf, *J. diphylla*, commemorates Mr. Jefferson, and refers to the way in which each leaf is deeply cleft into two leaf "twins". The 1″ wide white flowers grow singly on leafless stems, changing into small pear-shaped pods which come off like a lid. The leaves are small at flowering time and reach full size when the fruits mature.

Plants are native from New York and southern Ontario to Wisconsin, Iowa and south to Alabama. They naturally flower in April and May and should be placed in partial shade and moist soils. They grow best in limestone soils and benefit from the addition of lime in the spring. My friends, Norman and Doris Giles, who garden in the acid soils of north Georgia, place some calciferous stones around the plants, which provide alkalinity over time. Their plants look a great deal better than mine. Don't even think about digging these from the wild, or the President will come back to get you. Good native nurseries are producing plants from seed and they are becoming more available as demand rises. Much better in the North than South, probably most effective in zones 5-6.

**Related Species**:

*J. dubia* flowers in late spring or early summer and is native to northeast Asia. The 2-lobed leaves are rounded to kidney-shaped with pale blue to lavender flowers. They are handsome and appear to be more acid-tolerant than our native species. If you can find these, try them, as many people feel they are superior garden plants to our native. Hardy to zone 4.

***Juncus*** (junk′ us) Rush Juncaceae

The rushes are not in every gardener's vocabulary, in fact, most people look at them as some sort of aquatic weed, if they see them at all. The flowers are small and consist of 3 petals and sepals (like lilies) and the leaves are usually cylindrical, and often hollow. All of the approximately 225 species thrive in moist or wet locales and are useful in moist areas and around semi-natural ponds where they aid in providing stability to the soils. They are also useful as bird cover in aquatic areas. As we look to enhance wetlands, a number of rushes have found their way into various catalogs and nurseries and are being touted as reasonable garden plants for the boggy or pond area. They still look like aquatic weeds, functional ones anyway. However, they require sun to partial shade and should not be immersed in water more than 3″ deep.

*J. effusus*, common rush, is probably the best known and tolerates conditions from zone 4 to 9. Plants are stemless, all the leaves being basal, and they grow 18″ to 30″ tall. They turn yellowish in the fall, then brown, then disappear. The species has some ornamental value but one selection seems to have caught on. 'Spiralis' is known as corkscrew rush because each leaf looks like a green corkscrew. Although they will survive dry conditions, continuous moisture is much preferred. I have also seen a similar plant listed as 'Curly Wurly'. A recent introduction from the University of British Columbia, also with stems spiraling out of control, is 'Unicorn'. They are best planted in containers that can be constantly wet or on the edges of ponds. The growth habit is essentially prostrate and reminds me of a squirming octopus in need of euthanasia. Children, especially young boys, are said to like this plant, but they also like pulling wings off butterflies, so who can trust them? Curious is an apt description: ugly, interesting and unusual also fit. Perhaps that is enough. Hardy in zones 4-9.

*J. inflexus* is an upright rush and is represented by 'Afro', a robust corkscrew form with thick blue green stems, and 'Lovesick Blues', an introduction from Plant Delights Nursery in Raleigh, North Carolina. The latter produces a mound of long weeping blue green stems in the moist garden. Zones 4 (5)-9.

*J. patens* is native to California and has an upright habit. 'Carmen's Grey', blue rush, sends up bluish stems that grow about 12″ long. Plants provide yellow fall and evergreen winter garden interest and appear to be more tolerant of drier soils, although moist conditions are still appreciated. 'Carmen's Japanese' may be the same thing but the stems don't appear as bluish grey. Both (or the one) come from Ed Carmen of Carmen's Nursery in Los Gatos, California. Probably zones 7-9.

# K

**Kalimeris** (kal-i-mer′ is) Kalimeris Asteraceae

This group of about 10 species is from eastern Asia. Plants consists of alternate leaves and white to lavender flowers. Few differences occur between *Kalimeris, Boltonia* and *Aster*, and all can be fine flowering plants. I was asked to identify some plants that could have been any of the three genera and found that only by looking closely at the flower structures through a 10X scope could I even make an intelligent guess. It seemed to be that there must be characteristics relatively easy to distinguish, otherwise why not stick them all in one genus? None of the distinguishing details was easy to evaluate, but with the help of the scope, the bracts around the flowers (involucre bracts) and the little hairs attached to them (pappus bristles) could be seen. The term "scarious" means thin, dry and often translucent. For what it is worth, here are some of the differences.

| | |
|---|---|
| *Aster* | margins not scarious, unequal, overlapping in 2, usually many series, pappus bristles uniform |
| *Boltonia* | margins scarious, equal, overlapping in 1-3 series, pappus bristles non-uniform |
| *Kalimeris* | margins scarious, equal, overlapping in 2, usually many series, pappus bristles uniform |

Only three species of *Kalimeris* are found in cultivation.

***-pinnatifida*** (pin-a-tif′ i-da) Japanese Aster 1-2′/2′
Summer White Japan Zones 4-8

In talks I present or plant lists I make, this plant goes near the top of "no-brainers": one which can be planted without fear of failure. I have seen this double, white-flowered, sun-loving plant from Vermont to south Georgia, Washington to California, and have seldom been disappointed. Most of the leaves are pinnately lobed (pinnatifid) although upon examination, some of the leaves are entire. The double white flowers with their yellow stamens sometimes start out single, but as plants mature throughout the season the flowers are double.

Other than its remarkable adaptability, there is nothing particularly spectacular about the plants. It is their ability to be totally ignored and abused that endears them

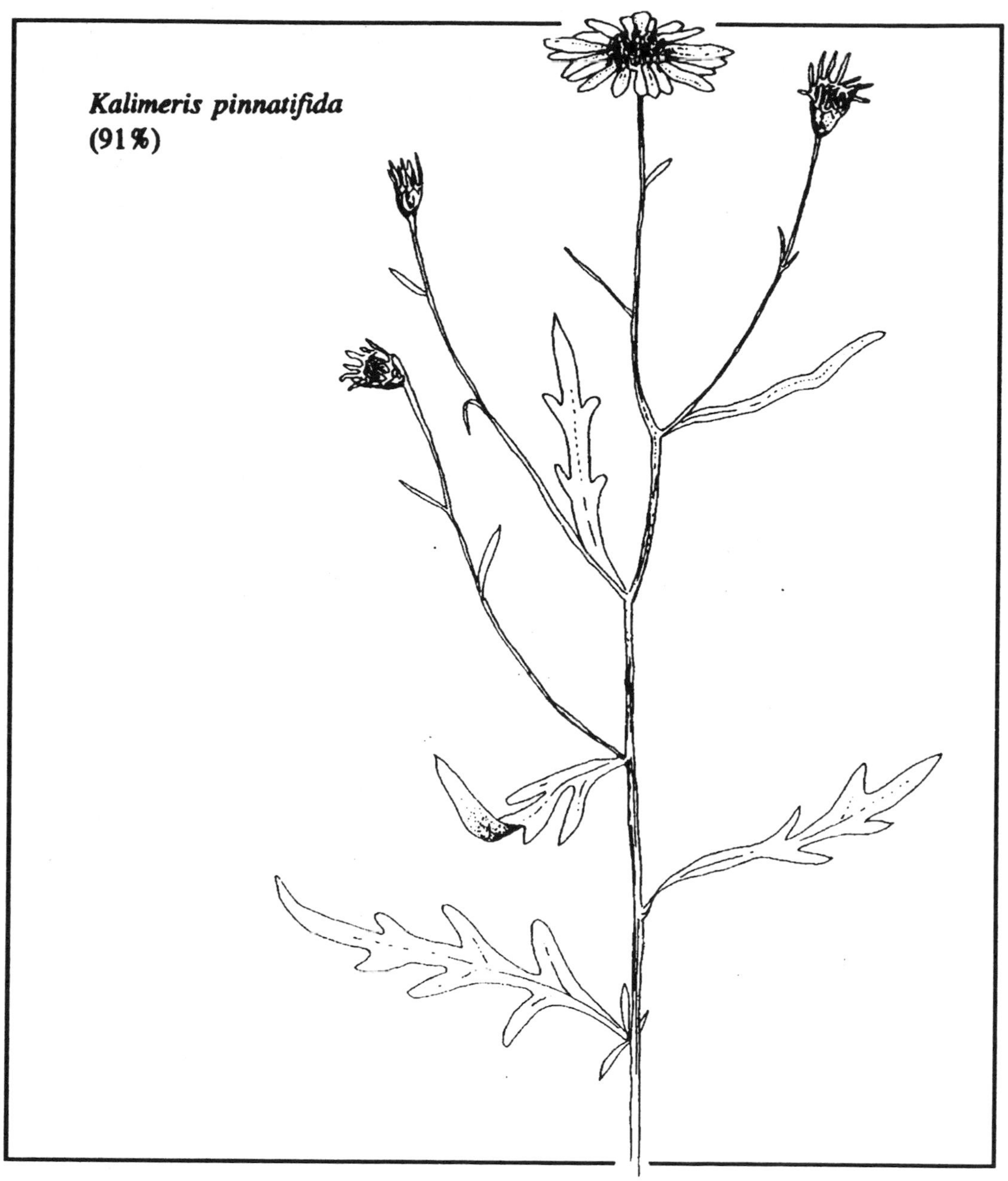


to gardeners. If gardeners are confused about what plant to begin with, I usually recommend this one.

They are best suited to sunny conditions but do well in a little shade as well.

**Related Species:**

*K. incisa* has single starry lavender flowers with yellow centers and oblong-lanceolate leaves. Plants grow about 2′ tall and are excellent garden performers. A number of wonderful cultivars have been introduced, the most common being 'Blue Star'.

Plants are only about 1′ tall and bear light blue daisy flowers. 'Jim Crockett' is an exceptionally good performer bearing darker blue flowers on a 9-12″ frame. There is confusion as to whether it belongs here or under *Boltonia*. Zones 4-8.

*K. integrifolia*, Asian aster, produces white single daisies on 2′ tall plants. The leaves are narrow and entire. Similar to others in the genus, plants are easy to grow and maintain. If plants are cut back after flowering, new flowers should appear in about 2 weeks. Zones 5-8.

*K. yomena* is native to Japan and is represented by 'Shogun', sometimes sold as 'Variegata'. Plants grow about a foot tall and produce colorful green leaves splashed with white and pink. The variegation is best in the spring. Small white flowers are produced, but the plants are grown mainly for the foliage. Zones 5-8.

## ***Kirengeshoma*** (ki-reng-ge-show′ ma) Yellow Waxbells Hydrangeaceae

Only one or two species have been described in this genus and only *K. palmata*, yellow waxbells, has been introduced to gardeners in North America. Reports on garden performance have been mixed, and those who do well with it happily extol its virtues. However, many gardeners have struggled. It is definitely a plant that should not be given up after a single failure.

***-palmata*** (pahl-may′ ta) Yellow Waxbells 3-4′/4′
Summer Yellow Japan Zone 5-7

The opposite, 7 to 10-palmately lobed leaves, carried on thinly branched stems, are hairy and toothed around the margins and are possibly the best part of this plant. The basal leaves are 6-7″ wide while those near the top are smaller and sessile and often have a purplish cast when sunlight falls upon them. The half-inch long, waxy, bell-shaped flowers may be found nodding from the axils of the topmost leaves in late summer and fall. Unfortunately, individual flowers start to turn brown at the edges in a matter of days. There are usually three flowers in each inflorescence (cyme) and the weight of the flowers and subsequent fruit causes stems to bow to the ground. Waxbells produce the "Stephen King" of fruit. Three long, pointed horns protrude from a brownish green swollen capsule; the effect is enough to cause a nightmare.

Plants are cold hardy to zone 5 but do poorly in the hot summers. I tried it in my garden and it quickly surrendered to the elements. Native to cool woodland areas, its performance is dubious further south than zone 6. Great care must be taken in choosing a site. One in semi-shade, sheltered from strong winds, in a constantly moist but not boggy area, with an abundant source of organic matter and an absence of lime, should be chosen.

*Kirengeshoma* has been called a "rarity for the connoisseur". This is a plant for those interested in experimentation, and with a willingness to fail several times before being successful. Where successful, large colonies will fill in rapidly. An unusual plant from its bowed gracefulness to its horned fruit, it adds a touch of grace to the shade garden.

Propagate by division after 3-5 years only if necessary. Allow plants to remain undisturbed for as long as possible.

**Related Species:**

*K. koreana*, native to Korea, may grow to six feet tall. The narrow petals of the soft yellow flowers turn upward at the tips.

***Knautia*** (not-ee′ a) Knautia Dipsacaceae

Well known to Europeans as a hedgerow or meadow plant, the pale purple-blue flower heads of field scabious (*K. arvensis*) attract little interest in gardening circles. However, one of its relatives in this genus of 60 or so members has attracted a considerable following as a short-lived but colorful garden plant. The flower heads of *K. macedonica* resemble pincushion flower (*Scabiosa*) but are deep purple, rather than lavender or pale yellow. The old name for the plant (*Scabiosa rumelica*) may still be found in catalogs and gardens. The leaves are entire at the base of the plant but pinnately lobed as they ascend the stem.

Plants are best grown so they grow through and among other plants in the garden. Plants start out neat and tidy in the spring, growing to a height of about 2-3′, but as hot days of July unfold, they begin to stretch, and flop around by midsummer, resulting in that neat and tidy thing to be just a rumor. This in no way precludes plants from the garden, and where appropriate, a single cutback in mid spring helps plants retain a little dignity later on. Leave 12-15″ of growth behind. I have had little success keeping plants more than 2 years, three years may be pushing it even in cool climates. They are most compact in the Northeast and coastal Northwest, and become more rambunctious in the South. Hardiness is from zones 4-7.

Plants can be propagated from seed if placed in moist containers at 70-72°F.

**Cultivars:**

'Burgundy Wine has wine red flowers on 2-2½′ stems.

'Mars Midget' produces dark red flowers on 15-18″ tall plants. A nice choice where a dwarf habit is needed.

'Molten Pastels' has flowers in red, pink and many pastel colors.

***Kniphofia*** (nee-fof′ ee-a) Red Hot Poker, Torchlily Asphodelaceae

The 60-70 species are characterized by basal tufts of long, coarse, v-shaped, sword-like leaves and spikelike inflorescences of bright, shortly stalked flowers. Although best known for orange-red flowers, species and cultivars occur with green, coral, yellow, red, scarlet, and bicolor blooms. Torchlilies may be as small as 18″ (*K. pumila*, dwarf torchlily), or as large as the 8′ giant hybrids. Many of the plants in today's gardens are *K. uvaria*, common torchlily, whose red flowers become yellowish green as they mature but most are hybrids between 2 or more species. Flowers on the upper half of the spike are still opening and bright red, while the lower ones are finished and yellow-green, and the spike is often described as two-tone. Many cultivars have been raised from seed, resulting in much variation. New Zealand is one of the finest areas in the world to see torch lilies; the bold magnificent deep orange spires of *K. uvaria* and *K. praecox* dominate roadsides, meadows and gardens in June and July.

***-uvaria*** (oo-vah′ ree-a) Common Torchlily 3-5′/4′
Late Spring Red South Africa Zones 5-8

The gray-green evergreen foliage is 18-36″ long and sharply pointed. After the flowers senesce, the leaves fall apart and plants become an eyesore. Cut the foliage about halfway back to improve appearance without injury. The flower stems must be removed after flowering to insure continued bloom, to say nothing of the dead flowers detracting from those newly emerged. In the Gardens at UGA, 20 flower stems emerged from our original clump of 3 seed-propagated plants and dominated the late spring garden. Flowers open as early as May 10 in the garden, but late May and early June are more common north of zone 7. Plants require full sun, and do not tolerate consistently wet feet. In zones 5 and 6, the foliage can be tied over the crown of the plant in the fall to exclude water, which may subsequently freeze and kill the plant.

Seeds of *K. uvaria* should be placed at 40°F temperatures for about 6 weeks. Germination will be erratic but seedlings should begin to emerge within 3 weeks. Keep soil moist and out of direct sunlight. Be patient; retain the seed tray for 3 months before discarding. Plants flower the second year. Cultivars and hybrids may also be divided in the fall.

**Cultivars:**

Occasionally a few other species are offered, but many more hybrids are now presently available to extend the choice of flowering season, height, and color. The parentage is confused but *K. uvaria*, *K. galpinii*, *K. praecox* and *K. macowanii* appear to have taken some liberties with each other. Most flower in late spring and early summer.

'Ada' has 3-4′ tall upright deep orange-yellow spikes.
'Alcazar' bears bright red flowers with a hint of salmon in early summer on 3-4′ tall stems.
'Border Ballet' is a 2′ tall mixture of plants bearing flowers of red, pink, yellow and creamy white.
'Bressingham Comet' has flowers of yellow and bright red on 2′ tall plants.
'Bressingham Sunbeam' bears soft yellow candles, the plants growing only 2′ tall.
'Candlemass' produces rush-like foliage with yellow-orange flowers. About 3′ tall.
'Cobra' grows about 3′ tall with dark bronze flower buds that give way coppery yellow flowers. From Blooms of Bressingham.
'Corallina' bears coral-red flowers in late summer and fall on 2′ tall stems.
'Dropmore Apricot' grows 2-3′ tall and bears apricot-colored flowers in summer.
'Earliest of All' blooms in early summer with orange-red and yellow flowers. Plants grow 18″ to 24″ tall.
'Express' has many orange-red flowers on 3½′ tall plants.
Fairyland Hybrids is a group of seed-propagated plants with orange flowers in late spring. About 2-3′ tall.
'First Sunrise' is an early-flowering form that grows 2′ tall with consistently orange flowers.

'Flamenco' consists of inflorescences that bear red, yellow and orange flower hues.

'Green Jade' is one of the tallest of the bunch, topping out easily at 5′. The flowers are green, then change to off-white as the flowers mature.

'Glow' ('Coral Sea') blooms with pastel coral-red flowers on 2-3′ tall plants in late summer.

'Gold Mine' is about 3′ tall and bears golden amber and yellow flowers.

'Ice Queen' is an excellent foil to stronger colors in the garden, as are all the white-flowered forms. The heads are creamy white to pastel yellow, growing about 5′ tall.

'Innocence' blends copper-orange flowers which turn pastel yellow and finally creamy yellow on narrow inflorescences. Two to three feet tall.

'Little Maid' was bred by Beth Chatto of Essex, England and opens yellow, fading to creamy white. Growing only 18-24″ tall, it looks terrific in containers as well as the garden.

'Lola' makes 'Little Maid' look like an elf. 'Lola' can easily attain heights of 5′ or more, and throw out brilliant orange-red pokers in early summer.

'Maid of Orleans' has ivory flowers on 2′ tall stems. Against a dark background, it stands out without being as garish as some of the screaming scarlet-flowered forms.

'Nancy's Red' grows about 2′ tall with bright red pokers.

'Paramentier' is a 3-4′ tall plant with dozens of reddish-orange to salmon flower stalks.

'Wayside Flame' has flaming orange-red flowers up the stem in late summer and fall.

'Primrose Beauty' grows 3′ tall with primrose yellow flowers. A stunning plant.

'Primrose Mascot' bears primrose yellow flowers in midsummer on 2-3′ tall plants.

Royal Castle hybrids are a mixture that grows 2-3′ tall with vibrant yellow-orange flowers.

'Royal Standard' bears scarlet buds that open to bright yellow flowers.

'Samuel's Sensation' produces scarlet flower heads on five-foot plants.

'Shenandoah' is one of the more cold-hardy cultivars, blooming with an orange top and yellow base in early summer.

'Shining Scepter', a Blooms of Bressingham cultivar, grows about 3′ tall with golden tangerine flowers in midsummer.

'Springtime' has upper flowers of coral red-tipped yellow, and muted yellow basal flowers. 'Royal Standard' and 'Springtime' are 3-4′ tall.

'Timothy' bears salmon-peach flowers on 3½′ tall stems.

'Toffee Nosed' is unusual as the name. The 3′ tall stems produce ivory flowers through the poker, and orange flowers at the top. An Award of Merit selection from the Royal Horticultural Society (RHS), Wisley, in 1993.

'Underway' produces apricot-orange flowers in midsummer.

'Vanilla' has grassy foliage with creamy white flowers in summer on 2-3′ tall plants.

'White Fairy' produces large creamy white flowers on robust 3′ tall plants.

**Related Species:**

*K. caulescens* is an evergreen perennial, about 3-4′ tall, with short, stout stems bearing tufts of broad-based, gray-green leaves. Fat spikes of flowers open deep coral-red, then change to light lemon-yellow. An RHS Award of Merit selection in 1993.

*K. northiae*, yucca poker, has wide blue green leaves that make the plant, when out of flower, resemble a yucca. The foliage is exceptional, and the orange flowers simply make the plant even better. This is one of my favorite pokers, looking like a fat yucca when not in flower. Native to the high mountains of South Africa, hardy to zone 6.

*K. rooperi* is a late-flowered species. blooming in September in most of the land. The fat squatty flowers are orange and yellow. Zone 7-9.

## ***Kosteletzkya*** (kos-tel-lets-kee′ a) Virginia Mallow Malvaceae

A relative newcomer to the ornamental garden that native plant enthusiasts gush over. Of course, relative is relative, as this plant was named the North Carolina Wildflower of the Year in 1989. Plants resembles *Hibiscus* but with small pink flowers. They are native from Florida to Texas and north to southern New York. *K. virginica* is the best known of the 30 or so species and its other common name, seashore mallow, reflects its common habitat.

Plants grow 3-4′ tall with hairy foliage and bear solitary pink flowers from midsummer through fall. Although tolerant of marshy conditions, plants also grow well in common garden soils.

Full sun is necessary. Propagate by seed or division.

# L

***Lamium*** (lay-mee′ um) Dead Nettle Lamiaceae

Most of the approximately 50 species are considered weeds. Related to stinging nettle, *Urtica dioica*, but lacking the stinging hairs, they are known as dead nettles. The stems are often stoloniferous and creeping at the base while the leaves are generally ovate to kidney shaped. The most popular species is *L. maculatum*, an excellent ground cover for semi-shaded locations.

Lamiums are easily propagated by cuttings throughout the season. Division may be accomplished any time as long as adequate moisture is provided to the plantlets.

***-galeobdolon*** (ga-lee-ob′ do-lon) Yellow Archangel 9-15″/18″
Spring Yellow Europe, Western Asia Zones 4-8
(syn. *Lamiastrum galeobdolon*)

This has become one of the more popular ground covers in many shade gardens because of its aggressive growth and ability to put up with adverse conditions. Plants spread by short underground stolons and are best used where allowed to roam freely as they can be difficult to control. The 1-3″ long leaves are oval, slender-pointed and serrated. During late spring, whorls of 5-6 yellow flowers, each about ¾″ long, arise from the leaf axils. Heavy to partial shade is best in the southern end of its range but some direct sun is tolerated further north. Plants are useful for filling in heavily shaded areas where little else grows. If plants become too leggy, cut back to 6-8″. When I get particularly busy, I take the old lawn mower to the planting. Works wonders.

The botanical name has changed a couple times but it seems to have resettled back into *Lamium*, although it is still listed as *Lamiastrum* in a few catalogs. Regardless of its name, it is a hard-working blue-collar type which seems not to care where the taxonomists or the gardener puts it.

Propagate by divisions or terminal cuttings.

**Cultivars:**

'Compactum' is much more compact than the species, does not grow as rapidly, but is useful for small areas.

'Herman's Pride' was found by Herman Dykhousen of Holland while traveling in Yugoslavia. Plants have smaller leaves and flowers and plants grow in upright

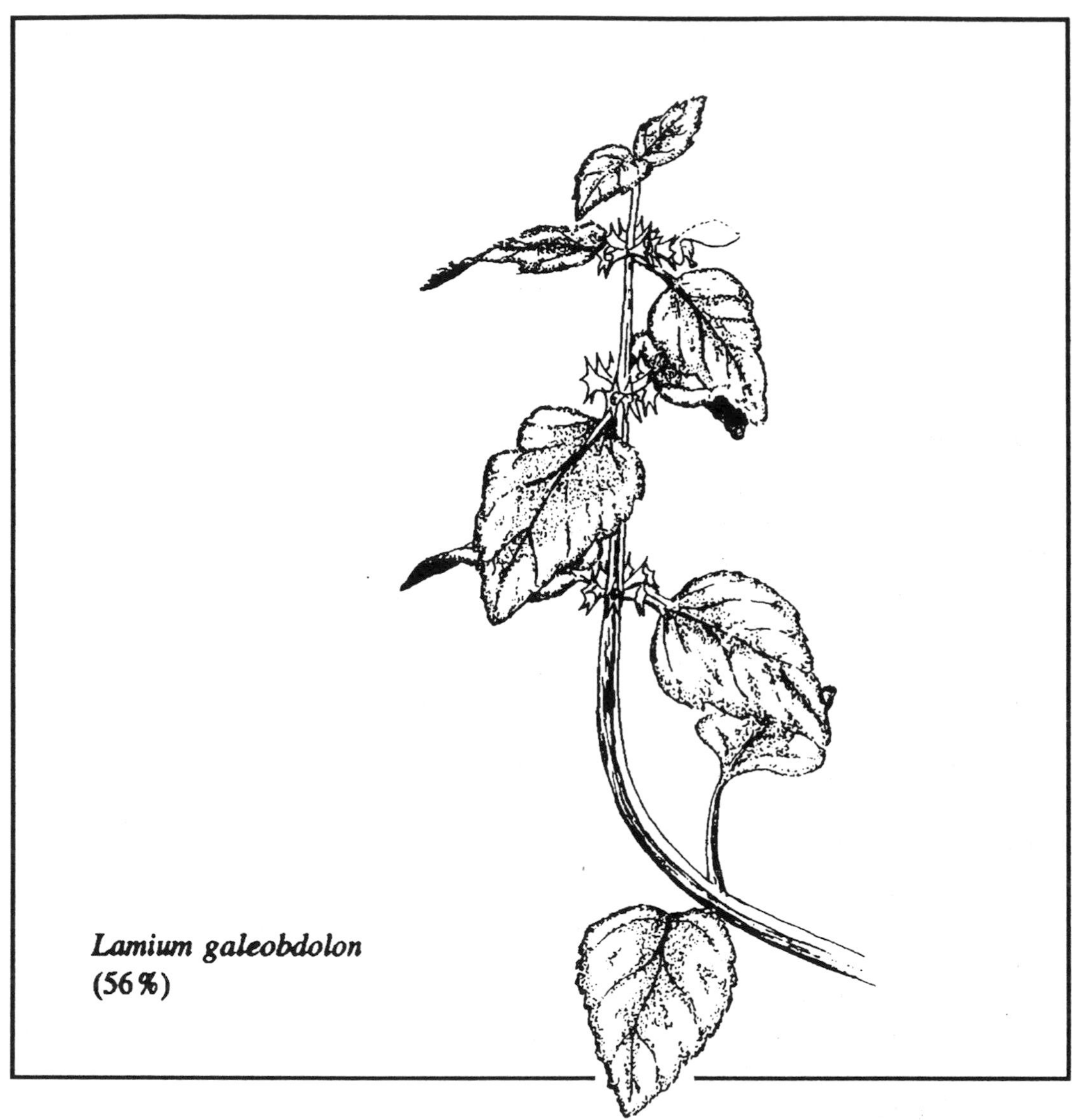
*Lamium galeobdolon*
(56%)

clumps and do not spread like the species. The foliage has beautiful silver markings between the green veins and is most handsome. This is an excellent cultivar, particularly in the spring while the plants are still compact. As the summer progresses, plants can become a little leggy but not nearly as much as the cultivars of *L. maculatum*. Under particularly warm dry conditions, plants may go summer dormant.

'Petit Point' is shorter but otherwise similar to 'Herman's Pride. Plants have more of a tendency for summer dormancy.

'Silver Carpet' has smaller, more silvery leaves than 'Variegatum' and is less aggressive.

'Silver Spangled' has long running stems with silver splashed on the green leaves. Plants are intermediate in size between 'Herman's Pride' and the species.

'Variegatum' is the most common form with silver variegation running through the leaf blade while the midrib and margins remain green. It is a terrific plant for the darkest areas of the garden. The correct name for this form may be 'Florentinum', but few nurseries use that name.

***-maculatum*** (mak-ew-lah′ tum) Spotted Nettle 8-12″/18″
Spring Red to Purple Europe, West Asia Zones 4-8

The oppositely arranged, 1-2″ long leaves usually have white stripes or blotches beside the midrib. The purplish red flowers bloom at the end of the stem all summer and are partially lost in the leaves. Although some cultivars grow well as far south as zone 9, the species performs best in areas of cooler nights that keep growth more compact. In the summer in zones 7 to 9, plants become straggly and must be cut back to maintain some semblance of order. Plants will remain evergreen in mild winters. Provide an evenly moist, well-drained soil in partial shade. If plants repeatedly dry out, bare patches appear.

**Cultivars:**

The species is seldom used, having been replaced by selections with superior foliage and flowers.

'Album' has white flowers and a silver stripe in the middle of the green leaves.

'Ann Greenaway' has been one of my favorites since it was introduced in the early 2000s. The leaves are a handsome combination of chartreuse, silver, and shades of green. The light pink flowers appear in late spring to midsummer. They brighten the garden or the container, and as long as water is applied occasionally, they do well in most locales.

'Aureum' has the same white midvein area as the species but the rest of the leaf is a soft yellow. The flowers are light pink. It is not as aggressive and will not do well in full sun, particularly in zones 7 or south.

'Beacon Silver', one of the most popular cultivars, has silver leaves surrounded by green margins. The foliage stands out well and catches the eye even in a shaded area. Flowers are pinkish purple. Occasionally the leaves are flecked with tiny purple dots, the result of a fungal infection. The fungi do little damage. Rather boring but an excellent performer.

'Beedham's White' has chartreuse foliage with handsome contrasting white flowers.

'Chequers' has a wide silver stripe in the middle of each leaf and deep pink flowers. It is similar to 'Beacon Silver' but with broader green margins. Plants are 9-12″ tall when in flower.

'Golden Anniversary' was a wonderful surprise in our trials. I did not think I would like the green and yellow variegated foliage, but plants grew rapidly and overflowed the ornamental containers all summer. Flowers were mauve-pink but actually are not needed. Very eye-catching.

'Orchid Frost' produces silver foliage, over which are found pink- to rose-colored flowers.

'Pink Chablis' has outstanding silver leaves with dark green margins. The pink flowers add additional beauty. A winner!

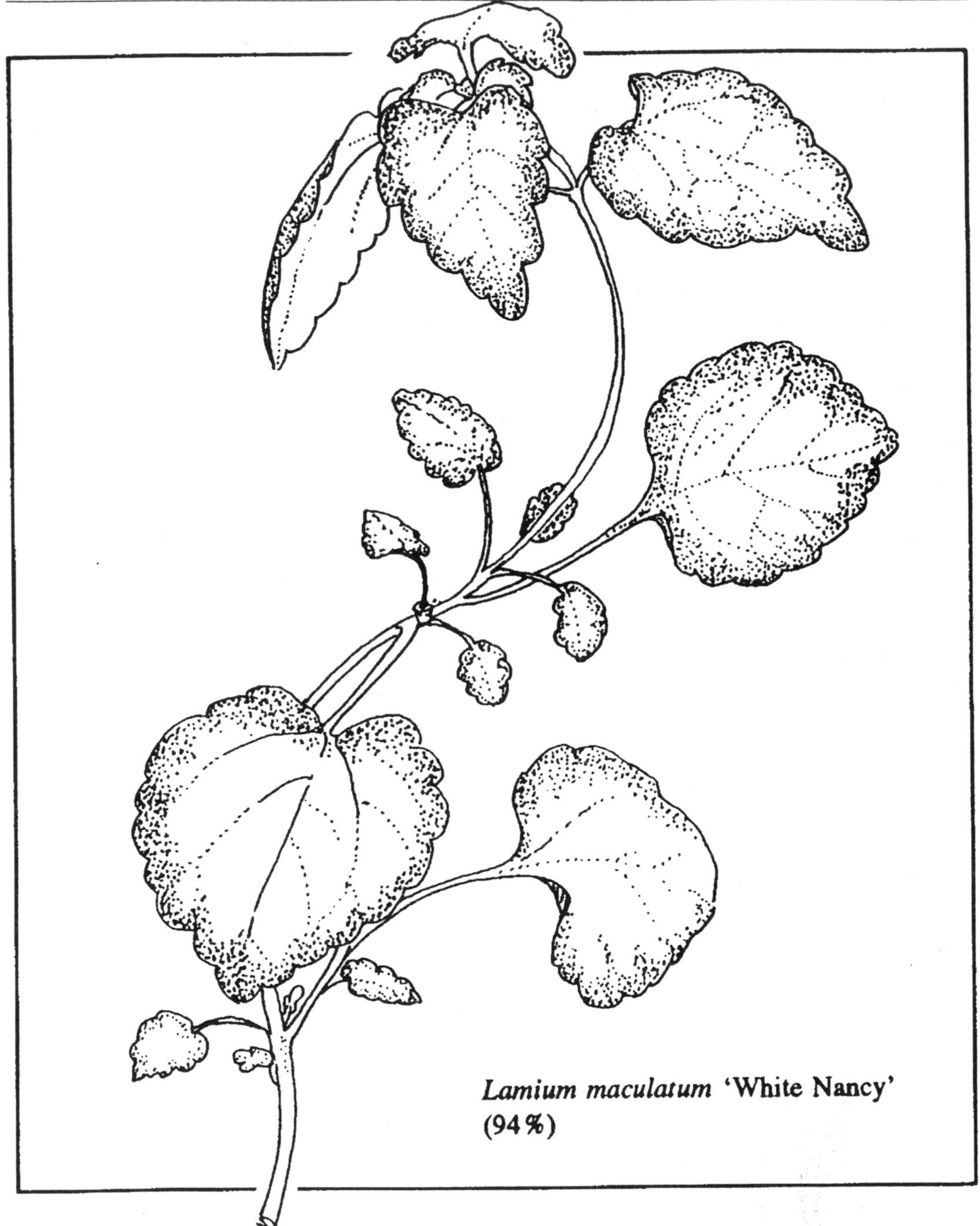

*Lamium maculatum* **'White Nancy'**
**(94%)**

'Pink Pewter' bears soft pink flowers and silvery foliage with narrow green margins.

'Purple Dragon' has rich purple flowers that sit on the silver-green foliage.

'Roseum' is similar to 'Chequers' but the leaves are wider and the flowers are paler pink.

'Red Nancy' is similar to its more famous sister, 'White Nancy', but with rosy pink flowers.

'Shell Pink' has leaves with white blotches and large light pink flowers.

'White Nancy' is 6-8″ tall and fills in rapidly. It has often been described as a white-flowering 'Beacon Silver'. The additional white of the flowers in the summer is particularly appealing. I thought this was one of the better forms but in subsequent years it loses vigor in hot summers.

**Related Species:**

*L. album*, white dead nettle, has a more upright growth than *L. maculatum*. Some botanists lump the species together, others split them off because the leaves are more pointed and sharply toothed. The green foliage contrasts well with the white flowers. Not as aggressive as *L. maculatum* but worth trying. 'Goldflake' has leaves with golden stripes, but is almost impossible to find; 'Pale Peril' produces golden shoots in the spring, then fades to lime green as the summer progresses.

*L. orvala* is a clumping species, similar in habit to, though not as handsome as 'Herman's Pride'. Plants grow in 18″ clumps and bear red to purple axillary flowers over green foliage. 'Album' produces large white flowers, 'Silva' has silver markings in the center of the leaves. Plants are native to central and southern Europe, probably hardy in zone 4-7.

## ***Lathyrus*** (lath′ i-rus) Sweet Pea Fabaceae

The genus consists of over 100 members but unless one searches for seeds from specialists, it is almost impossible to find plants of more than one or two species for the garden. The annual sweet pea, *L. odoratus*, is best known as a vigorous climbing vine bearing colorful fragrant flowers. A number of perennial species also occurs. *L. grandiflorus*, two-flowered sweet pea, has spectacular 1½″ long rose-red flowers. Many species are native to North America including the climbing purple-blue marsh pea, *L. palustris*, and *L. venosus*, showy wild pea, whose purple and white flowers are borne on stems up to six feet long. Although known by botanists from Saskatchewan, south to Texas and east to Georgia, these plants are unfamiliar to most gardeners. Not all members of the genus are climbers; a few non-viney participants are also known. *L. gmelinii* is a wonderful bushy plant, growing 12-18″ tall. The yellow to orange flowers are held in 4- to 12-flowered inflorescences (racemes) above the compound leaves. The most common and available species seems to be *L. vernus*, which bears the wretched name of spring vetchling.

Most species tolerate winter temperatures to about 5°F; the most cold hardy to about –5°F, occasionally lower with good snow cover or mulch. Heat is a nemesis, and all species look best in early spring regardless of locale.

***-vernus*** (ver′ nus) Spring Vetchling 9-12″/18″
Spring Red to Violet Europe Zones 5-7

Two to three pairs of 1½-3″ long light green leaflets per leaf are produced on sparsely branched stems. In early spring, five to eight ¾″ long, reddish violet flowers are borne on short axillary racemes. The racemes are shorter than the leaves and may be lost in the foliage without a thorough search. Plants are deep rooted and thus able to tolerate drought. It is not a rapid spreader and the foliage dies down after flowering.

Although cold tolerant to zone 5, zone 4 with mulch, plants are not particularly heat tolerant. They have not performed well in zone 7, and struggle to survive in hot summers. In partial shade, plants did little more than survive and, in full sun, death was swift. The application of lime around the base of the plants or in the planting hole helps their performance.

To propagate, carefully divide the rootstock about two weeks after flowering. Use a sharp knife and allow at least one eye to remain on each piece of separated root. Seeds should be soaked in warm water overnight prior to sowing. Transplant when seedlings reach the 3-5 leaf stage. If seeds are sown in the spring, flowering occurs one year later.

**Cultivars**:

'Albiflorus' has creamy white flowers with a hint of blue.

'Albo-roseus' bears rose and white flowers. This may occasionally be listed as 'Variegatus'.

'Cearulea' ('Cyanus') bears light blue flowers.

'Rose Fairy' has crimson-magenta flowers on 12-15′ tall plants. The shiny green foliage contrasts well with the flowers.

'Roseus' produces pink blossoms.

**Related Species**:

*L. gmelinii* var. *aureus*, golden yellow vetchling, grows 18″ tall and bears light green leaves topped with erect heads of fawn or yellowish brown flowers. It was absolutely stunning in the Royal Botanic Garden at Edinburgh, but then again, everything was. The quality of the foliage declines later in the season in all but the coolest areas of the country.

*L. latifolius*, everlasting sweet pea, produces flowers in many colors. It is native to Europe but has escaped and may sometimes be found growing wild in eastern United States. A number of nurseries offer this vine in mixed colors but if single colors are desired, look for 'Pink Pearl', 'Red Pearl' or 'White Pearl'.

## *Lavandula* (lav-an′ dew-lah) Lavender Lamiaceae

Lavender is an indispensable herb and a surprisingly useful ornamental plant. All parts of common or English lavender, *L. angustifolia*, are fragrant and provide oils for the perfume industry. The genus name comes from the Latin *lavo*, "I wash", referring to lavender water, long used as a fragrant wash. Lavender was also early recognized as a useful herb by Gerard who explained that flowers when "mixed with Cinnamon, Nutmegs, and Cloves, made into pouder, and given to drinke in the distilled water thereof, doth helpe the panting and passion of the heart, prevaileth against giddinesse, turning, or swimming of the braine, amd members subject to the palsie." (Gerard's *Herbal*). Lavender farms still operate in Europe and New Zealand for perfumes and potpourri.

The flowers are held in a terminal long-stalked spike, usually blue or purple, sometimes white or pink. In general, the native habitat is on poor soils in dry and hilly areas, thus the need for excellent drainage is preordained. Most are frost tender, although a few can be expected to be perennial if cold weather does not persist below 5°F. Winter protection should be provided in their northern limits.

***-angustifolia*** (an-gust-i-fo′ lee-a) Common Lavender 2-3′/3′
Summer Blue Mediterranean Region Zones 6-9

Two and one-half inch long, ¼″ wide opposite gray-green evergreen leaves occur on square stems. The 3-4″ long terminal flower spikes consist of 6-8 whorls of lavender flowers subtended by gray-green bracts. The fragrant flowers (and foliage) are often dried and used in potpourri. The plants are pretty enough to be included in the mainstream garden and need not be shunted off to languish in obscurity, visited only when flowers are to be sacrificed. They are superb for edgings, and the gray-green foliage calms even the harshest of leaf and flower colors.

Plants require full sun and well-drained soil. If soils are poorly drained, plants rot quickly. High humidity and lots of rain can also result in similar chaos, particularly in areas of hot summers. Pruning to 6-8″ in the spring results in vigorous new growth. For drying, pick flowers when showing color but before fully open. Hang them in a cool, dry spot.

Propagate by taking 3-4″ long cuttings of non-flowering shoots with a heel of older wood in the fall or early spring. Roots will appear in 14 days if placed in sand, under mist. Remove cuttings from mist as soon as roots appear. Seed sown and placed in 70-75°F and humid conditions will germinate rapidly, although erratically. More uniformity will result by cooling the seed flat at 40°F for 2-4 weeks prior to placement in warm temperatures. I have lost enough plants to the vagaries of weather, both summer and winter, to propagate my favorite cultivars every year.

**Cultivars:**

Selections have been based on improvements in flower color and habit. Some may be selections of lavandin, *L.* x *intermedia*, a hybrid between *L. angustifolia* and *L. latifolia*. There are literally dozens of these things; the Royal Horticultural Society lists over 100 cultivars of *L. angustifolia*, and almost the same number of *L.* x *intermedia*. However, many of these can be found only through specialty nurseries.

'Alba' produces creamy white flowers.

'Baby White' is one of the most handsome white-flowered forms. The plants are about 15″ tall, compact and free-flowering.

'Blue Cushion' has lavender blue flowers on mounded plants which grow about 15″ tall.

'Cynthia Johnson' is another blue-flowered form with gray stems and gray-green leaves. Its claim to fame is hardiness to zone 4. I'll believe it when I see it.

'Dwarf Blue' is only 12″ tall and sports dark blue flowers.

'Fred Boutin' grows 15-18″ tall with violet-purple flowers over silvery foliage.

'Goldburg' is a handsome white and gold variegated cultivar with lavender flowers. Plants stand out in the garden.

'Granny's Bonnet' has silver buds that open into deep violet flowers. Plants are about a foot and a half tall.

'Grappenhall' has long lavender-blue flowers on 2-3′ tall plants.

'Graves' bears light blue flowers.

'Grey Lady' produces lavender blue flowers and handsome silver-grey foliage.

'Grosso' bears large fat lavender flower spikes over 2-3′ tall mounded plants. A selection of *L.* x *intermedia*.

'Hidcote Blue' grows about 18″ tall and has deep purple flowers. 'Hidcote Superior' is similar but more uniform; should replace 'Hidcote Blue'.

'Hidcote Giant' is similar to 'Hidcote Blue' but grows up to 4′ tall.

'Hidcote Pink' bears very light pink, almost white flowers. The whitish buds open to show the pink flowers. Cultivars sold as 'Hidcote Pink', 'Loddon Pink' and 'Rosea' are difficult to tell apart.

The Intrigue series has been an excellent surprise. Plants stand only 12-15″ tall but the stiff upright gray-green stems and foliage provide no maintenance plants all season. Violet Intrigue™ is the best.

'Irene Doyle' is sometimes called "two seasons lavender" because of its propensity to rebloom in the fall. This will happen if summer conditions do not stress it too badly.

'Jean Davis' has pinkish white flowers, blue-green foliage and is 10-15″ tall.

'Lavender Lady' is an excellent seed-propagated cultivar which flowers the first year from seed. The lavender-blue flowers are held over compact green foliage.

'Loddon Pink' is about 15-18″ tall with soft pink flowers.

'Munstead Dwarf', which bears early lavender flowers, grows only 12″ tall.

'Provence' has lavender blue flowers, and is a cultivar of *L.* x *intermedia.*

'Rosea' is a light pink-flowered form, often used as an ingredient of eau de cologne.

'Royal Purple' bears long spikes of lavender flowers.

'Seal' can grow up to 4′ tall with long stems of pale lavender flowers.

'Sharon Roberts' has deep lavender flowers and dark blue sepals over handsome gray-green leaves.

'Silver Edge' (*L.* x *intermedia*) has green leaves with creamy silver margins. Flowers are light lavender.

'Twickle Purple' has such a great name it should be fun for you to try. The flowers are light purple and the bushy plants grow 15-18″ tall.

**Related Species:**

*L.* x *allardii* is sometimes known as hedge lavender, for its 3-5′ tall plants that are commonly grown as hedges in Europe. Plants are hybrids between *L. dentata* and *L. latifolia* and produce purple flowers and somewhat grayish foliage.

*L. latifolia*, spike lavender, is similar to common lavender but has silver-green foliage. Plants are fuller and grow 1-1½′ tall. Cold hardy to zones 6 or 7.

*L. stoechas*, French lavender, has purple flowers crowned with a cluster of ¾-1″ long, petal-like veined bracts. When well grown, these are probably the most beautiful of the lavenders. In subsp. *pedunculata*, the flower stems (peduncles) are longer than the spikes and rosy red bracts. The long purple bracts are the chief attraction of this unique flower. A number of cultivars have been introduced, most growing 18-24″ tall. A couple of recent introductions are the Ruffles series and the Lace series, both with attractive ruffled bracts. All need excellent drainage. Cold hardy to zone 7.

'Alba' is the white form; 'Otto Quast' produces fragrant, purple flowers all summer; Passione™ has deep purple flowers; 'Pastel Dreams' has long flower spikes stems and each inflorescence consists of creamy white bracts, contrasting with the lavender color of the rest of flowers; 'Snowball' has a mounding habit, growing about 18″ tall, and creamy white flowers. 'Wings of Night' bears long showy bracts and deep purple flowers. The narrow green-gray foliage is an excellent contrast. 'Willowbridge Calico' has purple and white bicolor flowers.

**Lavatera** (lah-va-te′ ra) Tree Mallow Malvaceae

The tree mallows are much more popular in Europe than in America, essentially telling us that the climate in much of this country is not to its liking. About 25 species of annuals, biennials and perennials are known, most native to the Mediterranean, Europe and California. The annual *L. trimestris* is popular in northern and western states and the perennial forms are beginning to be embraced by American gardeners. The flowers of lavatera are similar to other members of the mallow family and differences between lavatera, hollyhock (*Alcea*), *Malva* and *Sidalcea* can be found under *Alcea*.

The perennial forms are not terribly perennial, stem hardy to zone 7, perhaps root hardy to zone 6 (5 with mulch and prayers), and are small to mid size woody shrubs. In colder areas, they may die to the ground in the winter but new growth returns in the spring. Almost all the perennial forms offered are *L. thuringiaca*, or hybrids with this as an important parent.

***-thuringiaca*** (thur-inge-ee′ a-ca) Tree Mallow 5-7′/5′
Spring Pink Southeastern Europe Zones 6-9

These are big plants for big areas, not to be shoehorned into a tiny space. The 3 to 5-lobed, heart-shaped to orbicular leaves are slightly hairy and 3-4″ long. The stems become quite woody with age and the flowers are usually borne singly in the upper part of the plant. Not at all difficult to grow, the plant is undemanding as to soil and rainfall, but requires full sun and a moderately well-drained location. Japanese beetles and mealy bugs can cause havoc but tree mallow is far less disfigured than its annual cousin. The species is seldom grown, having been replaced by a number of cultivars.

**Cultivars**:

Most authorities believe that the following are probably hybrids of *L. thuringiaca* and a similar species, *L. olbia*. All flower in late spring to early summer.

'Barnsley' was introduced by Rosemary Verey of Barnsley Gardens, England in 1986 and is still one of the best forms offered. They are six- to eight-feet-tall multistemmed shrubs with beautiful fringed flowers. The 2″ wide flowers open white and fade to pink, each with a contrasting red eye. Sometimes flowers will revert to rose-red after a few years. If only a few stems revert, simply cut them off.

'Bredon Springs' has rich pink flowers with white centers borne on long spikes. Plants grow 5-6′ tall and bear softly hairy leaves.

'Burgundy Wine' is shorter (about 3-5′) and more sprawling in habit than 'Barnsley'. The flowers are vivid rose-purple to pink-purple.

'Candy Floss' has grey-green foliage and bright pink flowers on 3-4′ tall plants. The flowers have a whitish center due to the white stamens.

'Ice Cool' ('Peppermint Ice') has handsome white flowers, occasionally fading to pink. The 3-5′ tall shrubs bear light to grey-green foliage.

'Kew Rose', introduced in 1989, bears deep pink flowers with purplish stems. Plants can get big, up to 10′ in height.

'Lilac Lady' has lavender-blue flowers on a 3′ tall shrub.

'Red Rum' is interesting for the black stems in the spring and the dark red flowers later in the season. Plants grow 4-5′ tall.

'Shorty' is a good descriptive name for the plant habit, which is much shorter than other cultivars. Plants grow 18-24″ mounds consisting of many stems, with many light pink flowers.

'Wembdon Variegated' has marbled yellow and white leaves with dark pink flowers. Plants are about 6′ tall.

**Related Species:**

*L. olbia*, also known as tree mallow, differs from *L. thuringiaca* mainly by having most flowers in long leafless racemes. Plants are 4-5′ tall and native to the Mediterranean, therefore benefitting from low humidity and well-drained soils. The summer and fall flowers are normally deep red-purple but 'Aurea' has chartreuse foliage in the spring. 'Rosea' has lighter pink flowers. Zone 7b.

## *Leontopodium* (lee-on-toe-pod′ ee-um) Edelweiss Asteraceae

After being entranced by Julie Andrews and the Von Trapp family's adventures in "The Sound of Music", I was ready to be stunned by the beauty of this mystical plant. After all, a plant that so passionately stirs the hearts of the Austrians should be at least as pretty as, say, a dandelion. In its mountain habitat, edelweiss (*L. alpinum*) is quite lovely, but bringing it down to lowland gardens has done nothing for its mystique. Nurseries should refrain from offering it to anyone who is not a rock gardener or alpine plant lover.

The silvery white woolly flowers are held within the silvery green downy leaves, which surround the flowers in the shape of a 3″ star. If plants are provided with alpine conditions, cool temperatures, sunny area and rocky soils, they will be all they can be. Some gardeners have such conditions, but for the rest of us, enjoy the movie and let well enough alone.

***Leptinella*** (lep-tin′ el-a) Brass Buttons Asteraceae

Plants are generally sold as flagstone plants, step-on plants or other such names. They are ground covers, less than 2″ tall and are best used in areas where filling in cracks is an obsession. The small wavy leaves are the best part of the plant, the tiny buttonlike flowers are handsome enough but are so small as to be insignificant. The dark leaves are densely packed and where plants grow well, fill in rapidly. That they are native to New Zealand should serve as suitable warning that they will not do well in many areas of this country. Plants are similar to those of *Acaena*, New Zealand bur (which see), but are easily distinguished by the flowers: brass buttons is in the aster family, New Zealand bur is in the rose family.

Plants were forever listed under the genus *Cotula*, but now enjoy their own generic rank. The main species is *L. squalida*, and according to some observations, is hardy to zone 5, others say zone 4, and yet others claim it dies below zone 7. 'Platt's Black' has purple foliage and can look pretty, as well as pretty ratty at times. Other species include *L. gruveri*, miniature brass buttons, which appears hardy to zone 7, and *L. perpusilla*, perhaps hardy to zone 5. They all do the same thing, and only by trial will you determine which one is best for you.

***Lespedeza*** (les-pe-dee′ za) Bush Clover Fabaceae

While technically shrubs, this group of plants behaves so much like herbaceous perennials that it may be included with clear conscience. Approximately 40 species occur, all with alternate trifoliate leaves and pea-like flowers usually arranged in loose racemes. The plants used in American gardens have long pendant branches and are terrific growing on a bank, allowing the flowering stems to be better seen. Their late summer and fall flowering habit is also a bonus for tired gardens.

Propagate by divisions of the clump or from seed.

***-thunbergii*** (thun-berg′ ee-eye) Thunberg Bush Clover 3-5′/5′
Pink, White Fall Japan, China Zones 4-7

This is the real treasure of the group, having long (4-5′) pendant wiry stems that bear dozens of 6-8″ long racemes of rose-purple pea flowers. In the fall, when they are at their peak, the stems are so laden with flowers that they almost lie on the ground. In warm climates, some summer flowering may occur but the best is saved to the end. I have seen this plant in more and more gardens, from Swarthmore in Pennsylvania to lower Georgia. In the gardens of my Charlotte friend, Ann Armstrong and my colleague, Mike Dirr in Athens, the plants were outstanding. While in flower, they are spectacular but they need room and can take over a substantial area in a heartbeat. The only other serious drawback is their tendency to reseed themselves and occasionally root at stem nodes that lie on the ground. They also can be rather messy looking when not in flower. The good news is that they can be (and should be) whacked down to the ground in early spring prior to new growth. Everything occurs on new wood and the plants are better for the punishment.

**Cultivars:**

'Albiflora' bears good white flowers but the stems are not as arching as the species. More upright, less architectural.

'Avalanche' is covered with small white flowers in the fall with a cascading plant habit similar to 'Gibralter'.

'Gibraltar' has long (4-5′) arching stems with vivid rosy pink flowers in terminal clusters, causing the plant to cascade. Probably the most popular cultivar of the lot.

'Pink Fountains' has many pink flowers in late summer and fall.

'Samidare' produce pink and fuchsia flowers.

'Spilt Milk', sometimes sold as 'Variegata' has similar lavender flowers as the species but also bears intriquing white speckled leaves. It is not a clean variegation and the cultivar name is apt, however, it does provide some foliar interest, but then so do leaf miners.

'White Fountain' has brilliant white flowers and is a better choice, particularly for southern gardeners, than 'Albiflora'. More arching, better plant.

**Related Species:**

*L. bicolor* differs by having smaller, less showy flowers earlier in the season, usually mid to late summer into early fall. All in all, useful but not outstanding. However the white form, 'Alba' is quite handsome while a much more floriferous violet-pink form, 'Summer Beauty' is excellent.

*L. liukiuensis* (named for part of the Ryukyu Islands, an archipelago of 55 islands in the East China Sea) has upright rather than pendulous branches. 'Little Volcano' was introduced by Ted Stevens of Nurseries Carolinia and is characterized by small green leaves, later covered with magenta flowers in the fall. Probably cold hardy to about zone 6.

## ***Leucanthemum*** (lew-can′ the-mum) Shasta Daisy Asteraceae

Excellent plants for the sunny gardens, plants go under names like Nippon daisy, oxeye daisy and Shasta daisy. The oxyeyes and Nippon daisies are spectacular native flowers, providing white flowers along the roadside and meadows. All three used to reside in the genus *Chrysanthemum*.

x ***superbum*** (soo-per′ bum) Shasta Daisy 2-3′/2′
White Summer Zones 3-8

The Shasta daisy is one of the most popular daisies because of availability and ease of cultivation. It was hybridized in the 1890s by the American plantsman Luther Burbank (1849-1926), by crossing *L. lacustre*, Portuguese chrysanthemum, *L. vulgare*, European daisy, and *L. maximum*, Pyrenees chrysanthemum. In 1901, Burbank named his first mix for California's Mt. Shasta and continued to introduce new cultivars until 1925. An amazing botanist.

The lower leaves are up to 12″ long with short petioles while the upper leaves become shorter as they ascend the stem and are sessile. All the foliage is dark green and toothed. The 2-3″ diameter white flowers are borne singly and cultivars are available in single and double forms.

Plant in full sun with good drainage especially in areas where winter rain is common. It is a good plant for southern gardens; however, it is short lived and usually declines after 2-3 years. Remove spent flowers before they go to seed. Deadheading may allow a second bloom on some of the more vigorous cultivars. Divide or replace any time.

Plants are sometimes difficult to distinguish because of their hybrid makeup, and are often confused with the European oxeye daisy, *L. vulgare*. Some excellent work by David Brandenburg of the Dawes Arboretum in Newark, Ohio has helped make the distinction a little clearer. David tells us that in Shasta daisies, the basal leaves are longer and serrated; in oxeyes, they're shorter but with long stalks, and have scalloped margins. The stem leaves are also different: in the former they are serrated, in the latter, they are shallowly divided. Contact David for more information.

All cultivars can be propagated by divisions in spring or fall and many cultivars can be obtained from seed.

**Cultivars:**

It is interesting that this plant, bred by an American, is more popular in European gardens than here, but then again, how many do we really need?

*Singles*:

'Alaska' is one of the oldest and still one of the best cultivars. The pure white flowers have yellow centers and are 3″ in diameter and borne on 2-3′ tall stems. It is also cold hardy.

'Avondale' has yellow-splashed glossy leaves and single daisies.

'Barbara Bush' was introduced in 1994 by Walters Garden of Zeeland, Michigan to honor the former First Lady. Flowers are similar to 'T. E. Killin' but the foliage has creamy gold margins.

'Becky' is one of the best forms ever and has garnered numerous awards, not the least of which was being named the Perennial Plant of the Year in 2003. I have grown it and find it particularly good in the heat of the South. They stand upright, even after flowering and a hard rain, and flower for up to 8 weeks if the large white flowers are deadheaded. Named for Becky Stewart of Garden Designs in Decatur, Georgia.

'Brightside' is a seed strain from Jelitto Seed, and produces white flowers with a clean yellow center. Plants grow 2½ -3′ tall.

'Everest' is similar to 'Alaska', but has 3-4″ diameter flowers and is 3-4′ tall.

'Little Miss Muffet' is only 8-12″ tall with 2-3″ wide creamy white flowers and an orange center.

'Little Princess' bears large white flowers with yellow centers on 12″ tall stems.

'Majestic' has 3-4″ diameter flowers with small yellow centers borne on 3′ tall plants.

'Phyllis Smith' has single to semi-double white flowers with a yellow center. Plants stand about 2′ tall.

'Polaris' is a magnificent 3′ tall selection with 4-5″ diameter clean white flowers.

'Silver Princess' is a dwarf selection similar to 'Little Miss Muffet' and may be raised true from seed. These two cultivars can be used as bedding plants as they flower about 12 weeks from sowing and remain in flower most of the season.

'Snowcap' is a compact, bushy low-growing (15-18″) plant that is highly weather tolerant. Rainfall and high winds don't affect it as much as the taller cultivars. This is my favorite dwarf cultivar.

'Snow Lady' is a seed-propagated dwarf (12-15″ tall) Shasta daisy with 2″ wide clean white flowers. Plants flower the first year from seed and won the prestigious All-America award in 1991. This is one of the best dwarf forms in cultivation.
'Starburst' is one of the more vigorous cultivars, growing to 4′ tall. The white flowers are up to 4″ wide.
'Sunshine' opens with pale yellow flowers with gold centers. They fade to creamy white as temperatures rise. Plants are tall (at least 3′) and will topple.
'Switzerland' produces white flowers over a long period of time. Plants grow 2-3′ tall and appear to be hardier than many other white-flowered forms.
'T. E. Killen' is an old-fashioned cut flower form, with large white flowers around a crested gold center. Plants grow about 30″ tall.
'Tinkerbelle' is about 2½′ tall with stiff stems and single white daisies.
'White Knight' is also propagated from seed and bears white single flowers on 18-24″ tall plants. They are extremely floriferous, but short-lived.

*Doubles*:
'Aglaia' has fringed petals that make the flower look like it has been attacked by caterpillars.
'Cobham Gold' has flowers which are creamy outside with a raised yellow center.
'Crazy Daisy' bears 2½-3″ wide creamy white flowers, often with quilled ray flowers, with a small yellow center.
'Diener's Double' bears flowers with frilled petals on 2′ tall stems.
'Esther Read' flowers earlier than most cultivars and is only about 2′ tall.
'Highland White Dream' is a semi-double white flowering form. Plants are about 30″ tall.
'Ice Star' has fully double, clean white flowers on 2′ tall stems. The flower stems appear to be sufficiently strong so plants won't fall over in a heavy rain.
'Marconi' is a popular cultivar with 4″ diameter, clear white flowers on 3′ tall stems.
'Mount Shasta' is 2′ tall and has fully double flowers surrounding a raised center.
'Sedgewick' is one of the most cold hardy double Shastas, bearing large domes of white flowers.
'Wirral Pride' is 2-3′ tall and flowers are obviously raised in the center.

***-nipponicum*** (nip-pon-i′ cum) Nippon Daisy, Montauk Daisy 1-3′/3′
Late Fall White Japan Zones 5-9

Plants are not used to advantage in North American gardens, however, they can make excellent garden specimens. Plants produce shiny, almost succulent dark green foliage covered with 2-3″ diameter white flowers with green centers. Flowers open in September or October and bloom until frost. The bushy plants range from 3-5′ tall. The common name Montauk daisy refers to its escape in the Montauk area of Long Island where it flowers happily in late fall.

Grow in full sun and provide moist but well-drained soils. Plants may be pinched once in the spring to induce more bushy growth. This little-known plant, if provided with a little fertilizer and water, can be as rewarding as any chrysanthemum grown.

***Leucojum*** (lew-ko′ jum) Snowflake Amaryllidaceae

The snowflakes consist of 9-10 low-growing bulbous species with nodding white flowers. The predominantly white flowers are responsible for the common name. They are divided into two distinct groups based on the appearance of the leaves. The first group has shiny straplike leaves and includes the robust and larger-flowered species spring and summer snowflakes, *L. vernum* and *L. aestivum*, respectively. The second group has threadlike leaves and used to be a separate genus, *Acis*, but now shares the same roof. The only species of this group cultivated to any extent is the autumn snowflake, *L. autumnale*. The autumn snowflake tolerates dryer soils than the other species, but is also much more difficult to establish in most North American gardens.

The flowers of all species consist of 6 segments, 3 outer and 3 inner, of approximately equal size. They are white and tipped with green, yellow, or a tinge of red. Bulbs should be planted in the fall in large drifts, 3-5″ deep. Flowering begins the next spring, immediately after the snowdrops (*Galanthus*) and continues into early summer.

*Leucojum* is often confused with *Galanthus* but a number of recognizable differences separate the genera.

| | ***Leucojum*** | ***Galanthus*** |
|---|---|---|
| Flower stalk | Hollow | Solid |
| Number of leaves | Numerous | 2-3 |
| Number of flowers | 2-5 | 1 |
| Flower segments | 2 equal groups | 2 unequal groups |

Snowflakes are better plants for the South than snowdrops. They tolerate partial shade but prefer a sunny location with adequate moisture. Bulbs should be left undisturbed for at least three years to allow them to multiply, and moved when overcrowded. Plants propagated from seed take 3-4 years to attain flowering size. The bulbs are inexpensive enough that seed propagation can be left to the breeders.

Quick Reference to Leucojum Species

| | Number of flowers per flower stem | Flowering time |
|---|---|---|
| *L. aestivum* | 2-8 | Mid Spring |
| *L. autumnale* | 1-3 | Late Summer |
| *L. vernum* | 1-2 | Early Spring |

***-aestivum*** (ies′ ti-vum) Summer Snowflake 12-18″/10″
Mid Spring White Central, Southern Europe Zones 4-8

The name summer snowflake is a misnomer, for the species flowers only several weeks after *L. vernum*, spring snowflake. Three to five flowers usually occur on the hollow flower stem (scape), each about 1″ across, bell shaped and drooping. The pure white segments are tipped inside and out with jade green. The dark green leaves are about a half inch wide and 1-1½′ long.

**Cultivars:**

'Gravetye Giant' is a large-flowered cultivar useful when planting only a few bulbs in a small corner. It produces 1-1½" long flowers on taller stems and is worth the extra expense.

var. *pulchellum* blooms earlier and has smaller flowers than the species, but otherwise is almost identical.

**-*autumnale*** (ow-tum-nah' lee) Autumn Snowflake 4-6"/6"
Late Summer White Southern Europe, Mediterranean Zones 5-8

Autumn snowflake does not have a large following because it is not as easily established as other species, not as easily found in garden catalogs and more expensive when it is. On the other hand, the flowers, described as "delicately flushed lilies-of-the-valley", open when small bulbs are most welcome. Other characteristics separate the species from the common snowflakes. The nodding ½-¾" long flowers are tinged with red and open in late summer in the South or early fall in the North. The thread-like leaves appear after the flowers and remain evergreen. The foliage dies away in early summer, and at that time bulbs may be divided and moved. Bulbs are planted in the spring or early summer and are not usually available for fall planting.

Some gardeners throw their hands up in frustration trying to establish these plants while others would not have a garden without them. They are native to dry, sandy soils and excellent drainage is a must. Size precludes it from areas other than the rock garden or small containers where it can be enjoyed on the patio or deck.

**-*vernum*** (ver' num) Spring Snowflake 10-12"/10"
Early Spring White Central Europe Zones 3-9

This most accommodating snowflake seems to thrive in virtually all conditions. It overlaps the flowering time of snowdrops (*Galanthus*) in the South and flowers about two weeks later in the North. The plant is not as tall but the leaves are a little broader (up to ¾" wide) than those of the summer snowflake. The flowers are white, drooping, and usually borne one to two per flower stalk. The white segments are tipped with green similar to *L. aestivum*.

Unfortunately in the past there have been a number of instances where plants ordered as *L. vernum* turned out to be *L. aestivum*. There seems to be enough stock of both species and there need be no problem when dealing with an established bulb supplier.

**Cultivars:**

var. *carpathicum* usually bears two flowers per stem. Each flower is tipped with yellow rather than green. Most handsome.

**Related Species:**

*L. roseum* is 4-6" tall and bears pale pink to rose flowers in the fall. It is further distinguished by having a shorter flower stem and usually has only one flower per stem compared to the 2-4 flowers commonly found on the stem of *L. autumnale*. The above two species are in the "I love a challenge" class. I am confident there are many gardeners who welcome such plants.

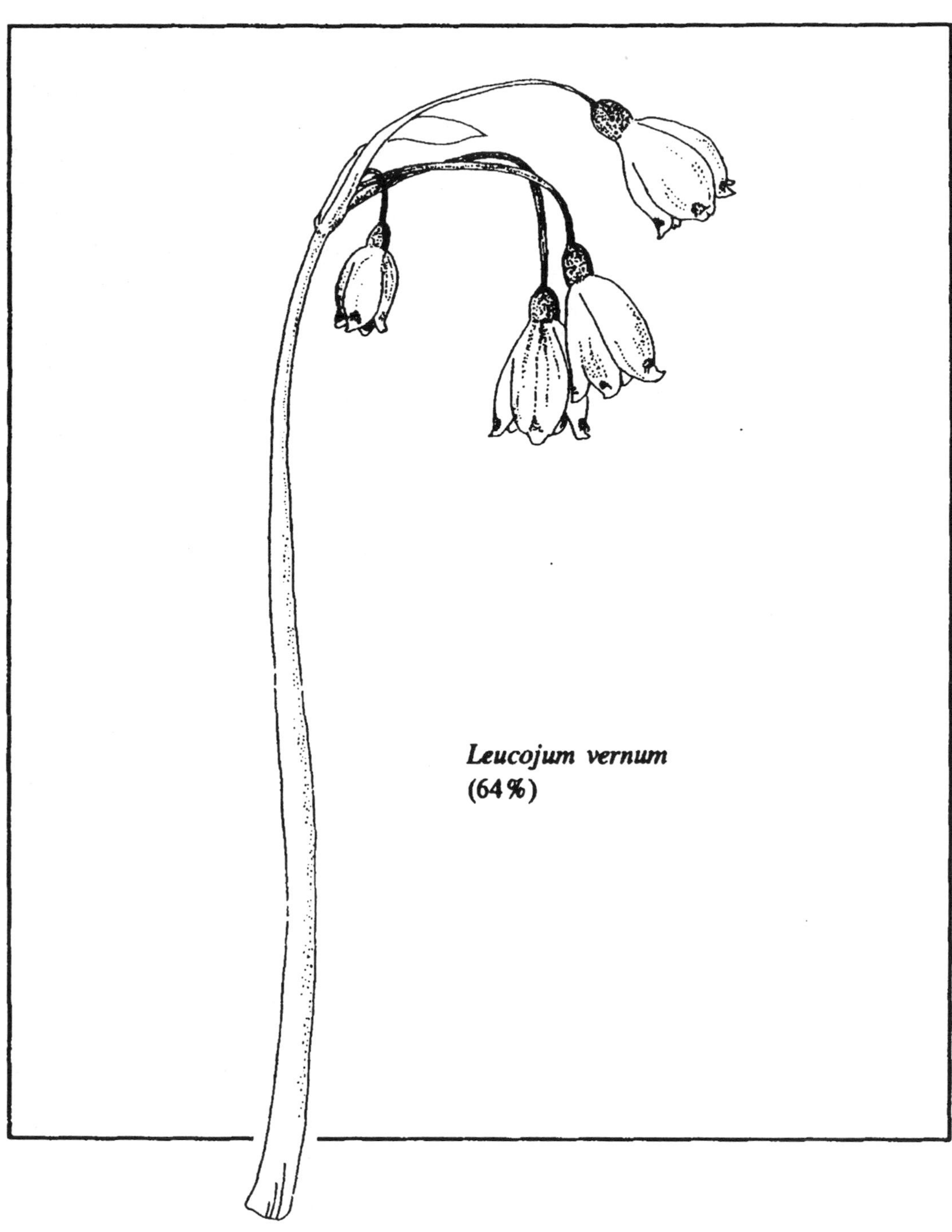

*Leucojum vernum*
(64%)

***Lewisia*** (loo-is′ ee-a) Bitterroot Portulacaceae

It is fitting that this beautiful native western genus commemorate that great explorer, Captain Meriwether Lewis who with his friend, William Clark, explored the Great Plains and beyond in the early 1800s. The common name refers to the Bitterroot Mountains of Montana where Lewis and Clark met some of their most severe challenges in their historic journey to the Pacific. The genus consists of approximately 20 species, and a few specialist nurseries, mainly in the Northwest, offer a fine selection to gardeners. However, only one (*L. cotyledon*) is commonly offered in the garden trade, the others being relegated to collectors' gardens.

Plants form tight symmetrical rosettes of spatulate (like a spatula) deep green, thick fleshy leaves. The showy flowers are usually pink-purple with dark stripes, although colors vary in any one population. Hybrids have been developed by breeders and hobbyists and gardeners can enjoy yellow, red, orange, salmon, cream or white flowers. Dozens of flowers are produced, each consisting of 7-10 petals and many stamens, and held in racemes or panicles.

Lewisias are almost unknown by gardeners in the East and when they see them, they gasp in admiration, assuming something so beautiful would be impossible to grow. The fact is that lewisia is much tougher than it first appears, but not without problems. Plants don't have a prayer of survival in heavy garden soils, no matter how well drained you think they may be. While lewisias are cold tolerant to about zone 6, they are susceptible to crown rot when moisture accumulates around the plant. A rock garden or addition of gravel to the soil or growing in gravel is one key to success in areas of summer rain and humidity. Full sun is also beneficial. Plants succeed well in stone walls, where light and drainage are optimized. My friend John Elsley of Greenwood, South Carolina was successful with lewisia in the gravel path by his house. In Garden in the Woods in Framingham, Massachusetts, plants looked wonderful in the scree garden.

*L. cotyledon* is evergreen as are plants of *L. longipetala*, and *L. columbiana*, other species sometimes offered in the trade. However, a number such as *L. brachycalyx* and *L. oppositifolia* are deciduous, which if available, are worth trying because they are dormant during wet winters.

**Cultivars and Hybrids**:

'Alba' has white flowers.

'Ashwood' strain is a mix of plants with red, apricot or yellow flowers.

'Constant Comment' has beautiful rosy pink flowers.

'Edithae' (*L. columbaria*) is 3-4″ tall and has pink flowers with darker veins.

'George Henley', a hybrid between *L. columbiana* and *L. cotyledon*, bears dozens of wonderful brick red flowers.

'Kathy Kline' bears white flowers, and Kathy Kline hybrids consist of a mix of colors.

'Little Peach' bears eye-catching yellow-orange flowers.

'Little Plum' is a selection of *L. longipetala* and has about 8 plum-colored straplike petals.

'Norma Jean' produces pink flowers on 8-10″ tall plants.

'Paula' has lavender to pale purple flowers.

'Pinkie' (*L. cotyledon* x *L. longipetala*) has flowers in various shades of pink on relatively dwarf plants.

'Praline' has semi-double flowers in many shades.

'Rainbow' is a mixture of pastel and deep flower colors.

'Rose Splendor' has pale pink to rosy flowers.
'Trevosia' resulted from crosses between *L. columbiana* and *L. cotyledon* var. *howellii*. The handsome salmon-pink flowers are produced over fleshy dark green leaves.

***Liatris*** (lie′ a-tris) Blazing Star, Gayfeather Asteraceae

Liatris sends up tall stems, at the end of which is an inflorescence of 15-45 oblong, usually purple flowers. Although belonging to the daisy family, the flowers consist of disc flowers only, and are very un-daisylike. Flowers provide not only architectural interest, but botanical interest as well. They are one of the few cultivated flowers with the unusual habit of opening from the top of the inflorescence to the base (basipetally). The straight, strong stems carry narrow, entire, alternate foliage.

With the exception of *L. spicata*, plants are often found on dry stony ground or on the edge of woods. Many are tolerant of poor dry soils but are quite happy on fertile, well-drained soils; *L. spicata* requires more moisture than others, and is also known as marsh blazing star.

Liatris experienced a meteoric rise as a cut flower in the 1980s and is still popular today. Few florists do not include gayfeather in bouquets and arrangements. Their appearance into the American floral market resulted because Dutch flower exporters included it in the "Dutch Mix" sent to American wholesalers. Soon, liatris became popular as a "Dutch" flower. The irony is that *Liatris* is native to North America, and is a wildflower in much of the United States! Today plants are produced as cut flowers in greenhouses and fields by hundreds of growers.

The tuberous roots should be planted 4-6″ deep in well-drained soil in full sun. Plants associate well with *Rudbeckia*, *Monarda*, and *Echinacea*, three other native North American species. Most species bloom in late summer and into early fall. The flowers are absolute magnets for monarch butterflies and seeds are favorites among many songbirds, particularly finches.

Liatris are easily raised from seed that flower the following year. The tuberous roots may also be lifted, cut with a sharp knife allowing at least one eye to remain, and replanted. Dust the cut ends with a fungicidal powder.

Quick Reference to Liatris Species

| | Height (ft.) | Flower color |
|---|---|---|
| *L. pycnostachya* | 3-5 | Mauve |
| *L. spicata* | 2-3 | Mauve |

***-pycnostachya*** (pik-no-stak′ ee-a) Kansas Gayfeather 3-5′/2′
Summer Mauve Wisconsin to Louisiana and Texas Zones 3-9

Largest of the cultivated species, this is the least useful for the garden. The 10-15″ long lower leaves are lancelike and about a half-inch wide and become reduced in size as they ascend the stem. The flower spike is 15-18″ long and consists of numerous

½-¾″ wide flowers along the length. Leafy bracts, often longer than the individual flowers, are produced under the flowers.

*L. pycnostachya* is too tall for most gardens and the spikes become so heavy they fall over, resulting in the growing end of the spike twisting upwards. Support is necessary, particularly in the second year. Plants should be treated as short-lived perennials, at least in the South. Experiments in Georgia indicate that two years of good performance was the norm, three years if conditions were perfect. Although problems exist, it flowers heavily and 12 flower stems per tuber are not uncommon in the second year. The species is found in moist soils of the Great Plains but does not tolerate wet feet in winter. A well-drained, moisture-retentive soil in full sun is necessary for best results.

**Cultivars:**

var. *alba* has creamy white flowers.

'Eureka' is a vigorous form with reddish-purple flowers on 1-1½′ long flower spikes in early summer. Plants were selected as a winner in 2006 by the GreatPlants® Program, a joint effort of the plant industries of Nebraska.

***-spicata*** (spi-kah′ ta) Spike Gayfeather 3-5′/2′
Summer Mauve Maine to Florida and Louisiana Zone 3-9

This is the most popular species for the garden, particularly some of the cultivars. The basal leaves are usually 10-12″ long and a half-inch wide, progressively reduced in size up the stem. The inflorescence is 6-15″ long and individual flower heads are sessile and mauve. *Liatris* should be thought of in the same way gardeners think of gladiolus. That is, the plants are "just there" until flowering, the flowers are excellent in the garden and as cut flowers, but then the plants begin to look shabby. It is not you, that's the way it is with liatris.

Plants were trialed in the cut flower program at the University of Georgia. Roots arrived under the name of *L. callilepis*, which most authorities treat as a synonym of *L. spicata*, although some European taxonomists still treat it as a separate species. In the first year, plants were the same size as 'Kobold' and no support was necessary. The flowers were darker purple, and growth and yield were excellent. In the second year, however, plants grew 3-4′ tall and required support to maintain straight spikes. Yield and quality of flowers were still excellent. It is a fine cut flower and is still produced by commercial growers home and abroad.

**Cultivars:**

'August Glory' has purple-blue flowers on 3-4′ tall plants.

'Floristan White' is 3′ tall and bears many creamy flowers. It performed well and showed no signs of decline after four years in Georgia tests.

'Floristan Violet' bears darker purple flowers than the species.

'Kobold' ('Gnome') is one of the finest selections for the garden. Plants are seldom taller than 2½′ and multiple spikes of lilac-mauve flowers are produced in early summer.

'Silvertips', introduced by Carroll Gardens, has lavender blooms with a silver sheen. Plants are 3-4′ tall.

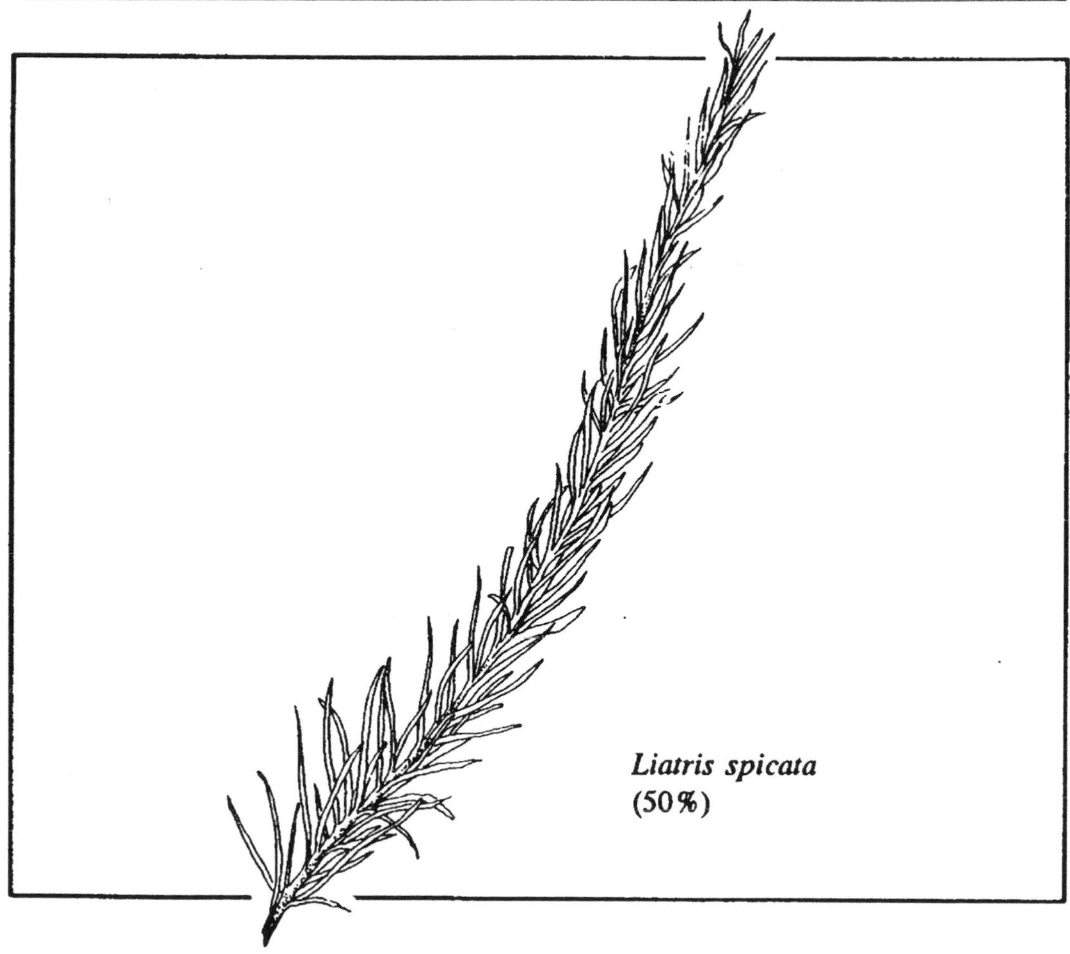

*Liatris spicata*
(50%)

var. *montana*, native to the mountains of Virginia and North Carolina, is only 10-20″ tall and bears ¾″ wide flowers on compact spikes. It can be found through wildflower specialists.

**Related Species:**

Dozens of garden-worthy species may be found through native plant specialists and in catalogs. Many are much underused.

*L. aspera*, rough gayfeather, grows 3-4′ tall with hairy leaves. Plants bear 15-40 one inch wide, rounded lavender to purple flowers, each spaced well apart. The blooms open later than other species and make excellent cut flowers, used either fresh or dried. Plants are also favorites for many birds and butterflies. The species occurs from North Dakota to Ontario and Ohio to Texas and Florida.

*L. ligulistylis*, meadow blazing star, has wonderfully large and full flower heads. They are made up of distinctly stalked rounded purple flowers borne on many branched stems. Plants are 3-5′ tall, and flower in late summer to early fall. Hardy to zone 4.

*L. microcephala* performs well in dry soils and full sun. Plants grow up to two feet tall, although ours are around 18″. The flowers are normal rose-purple but the leaves are narrow and grasslike. Usually multi-stemmed and ornamental. A terrific plant for those who find *L. spicata* too tall. Native to the southern Appalachian Mountains, hardy in zones 6-9. A white form, 'Alba', is sometimes offered.

*L. mucronata*, native to central and south Texas, bears 3-5′ tall stems with lilac mauve flowers. Plants tolerate alkaline soils better than many other species. This species is relatively unknown, however, superb specimens may be seen at the San Antonio Botanical Garden. Zones 7-9.

*L. scariosa*, tall gayfeather, is similar to rough gayfeather and material is likely mixed up in the trade. The leaves are quite smooth and the basal ones up to 2″ wide. The dense flower spikes consist of individual flower heads that are distinctly stalked. 'September Glory' bears purple flowers that open almost simultaneously. 'White Spire' is similar to 'September Glory' but has white flowers. Both are better garden plants than *L. pycnostachya*.

*L. squarrosa* (American devil's bit) grows 1-2′ and produces large, tuftlike flowers from early to late summer. Plants are native from Virginia west to Colorado and south to Florida and Texas.

*L. squarrulosa* (southern blazing star) was selected as the 1998 North Carolina Wildflower of the Year by the North Carolina Botanical Garden. Plants grow 6′ tall and withstand abuse well, and thriving in poor soils. Plants, however, are not easily available through nurseries.

## ***Libertia*** (lee-bert′ ee-a) Libertia Convallariaceae

*Libertia* is native to South America and New Zealand. Plants have short creeping rhizomes (similar to *Iris*), long fibrous roots and evergreen foliage. Unfortunately, it is still difficult to buy these plants, perhaps because they are so tender, being cold hardy only to zone 7 or 8. The flower consists of 6 segments, the three outer ones usually shorter, firmer and less showy than the inner ones. Of the eight species, *L. formosa* is most easily obtained, although occasionally a couple of others will surface.

The subject of liverworts, non-vascular plants related to mosses, is not normally discussed in mixed company, however, a Belgian woman, Marie A. Libert, did some of the best work on those nondescript flowerless plants in the early 1800s. Ironically, she is now remembered for this genus with such outstanding flowers.

*Libertia* is closely related to *Sisyrinchium* and *Diplarrhena* but the segments of the former are all equal in size while in the latter, the inner segments are shorter than the outer.

***-formosa*** (for-mo′ sa) Showy Libertia 15-20″/12″
Spring White Chile Zones 7-9

The ¾″ long white flowers are held in tapering, one-foot long inflorescences and remain effective for 3-4 weeks. The flowers are densely clustered, unlike other species whose flowers are loosely arranged. The 6-12″ long swordlike leaves are about ½″ wide and produced in a fanlike arrangement similar to leaves of *Iris*. Plants should be placed in full sun or partial shade in groups of at least a half dozen. I have admired this species in gardens throughout Europe but have not seen outstanding clumps anywhere but in the Northwest. Plants simply do not tolerate the heat and humidity during the summer, and the lack of summer vigor inhibits subsequent flowering the next spring. However, plants have escaped into California and are reasonably common there.

Division of the rhizome is the easiest method of propagation but seed may also be used. Plants require two years to flower from seed.

**Cultivars:**

'Grandiflora' has flowers significantly larger than those of the species. The plant is also more robust, resulting in a better garden display.

**Related Species:**

*L. ixioides* is native to New Zealand and bears three to eight 1″ wide white flowers, often tinged green on the outside. The flowers are less densely arranged and have longer pedicels than *L. formosa*. It is difficult to establish in North America but may be the loveliest of all the species.

*L. peregrinans* is about 12-15″ tall and quite slow growing, but can produce wonderfully colored foliage. 'Bronze Sword' has orange-bronze leaves striped with dark green. The white flowers are slow to develop and plants are most useful for the foliage color. 'Goldfinger' has a yellow vertical band on each leaf. 'Taupo Blaze' is similar in habit but with dark bronze and green leaves. Plants likely need to be brought inside during the winter in most areas of the country.

*L. pulchella* has white flowers similar to *L. formosa* but the foliage is much narrower, almost grassy. Hardy to zone 7 or 8, but does not perform well in summer heat.

## *Ligularia* (lig-yew-layer′ ee-a) Ligularia Asteraceae

These large plants may be 6′ tall in flower and equally broad, although some excellent breeding is downsizing some of the species. Some, such as *L. dentata*, bigleaf ligularia, are grown for their attractive foliage while *L. stenocephala*, narrow-spiked ligularia, has attractive rocket-like flowers. *L. siberica* and the 5-6′ tall *L. japonica* are simply impressive and best thought of as architectural features in a moist garden setting.

All species and cultivars must be grown in damp, cool areas. I have seldom seen well-grown plants south of zone 6; in fact, except for parts of New England, I have seldom seen plants of this genus look good for longer than a month anywhere east of the Rocky Mountains. In Michigan, if plants survived the cold winters, the hot summers were not to their liking. In north Georgia, plants look lovely in the spring but wilt every day during the summer and beg to put out of their misery, unless provided with consistent moisture and shade. To be fair, I have seen spectacular plants in proper sites, but those sites are not easy for the average gardener to provide. Around ponds, along stream banks, or wherever their roots can stay constantly moist, and afternoon shade can be provided are potential locations. While moisture is always welcome, its nemesis, the slug, is not. Plants can be badly disfigured if slugs are a problem in the garden.

Only a small number of the approximately 80 species are garden worthy. All have bright yellow daisy flowers held in a raceme or in a branched inflorescence just above the long-petioled leaves. Large alternately arranged leaves arise from the base and ascend the stem.

The petioles of the basal leaves completely encircle the stem with a short sheath. This encircling sheath separates *Ligularia* from the closely related genus *Senecio*. Propagation is primarily by division although seed may be sown when fresh.

Quick Reference to Ligularia Species

| | Height (ft.) | Leaf shape | Inflorescence shape |
|---|---|---|---|
| *L. dentata* | 3-4 | Kidney | Branched |
| *L. przewalskii* | 5-6 | Triangular | Raceme |
| *L. stenocephala* | 3-4 | Triangular | Raceme |
| *L. wilsoniana* | 4-6 | Kidney | Raceme |

**-*dentata*** (den-tah′ ta) Bigleaf Ligularia 3-4′/4′
Summer Bright Orange China Zones 5-8

The long-stalked leaves are the best part of the plant. They are disk shaped to kidney shaped, up to 20″ wide, and coarsely toothed. Large clumps of established plants are particularly impressive. The 2-5″ diameter, bright orange flowers are held in branched corymbs. The 10-14 ray flowers are long and straplike and appear to be wilting even in moist growing areas. Personally, I think the flowers are ugly as sin, and detract from the plant. Allow flowers to develop the first year to become familiar with the bloom, then remove the developing flower stalks in subsequent years. However, if you are lazy like me, the flowers come and go without great fanfare.

Grow plants in cool, moist conditions or not at all. Although plants recover from constant wilting, too many other lovely plants are available to allow these to tie up garden space unless the correct site is available.

**Cultivars:**

'Britt-Marie Crawford' bears shiny chocolate purple foliage with wavy margins. Plants stand 3-4′ tall when the orange flowers are in bloom. The leaves are significantly darker than those of 'Othello' and if you are successful with ligularias, this is the cultivar of choice.

'Dark Beauty' has very dark leaves with bright orange flowers.

'Desdemona' is still the most popular cultivar, bearing large deep purple foliage. Leaves are beet red upon emergence in the spring, become green on top but remain purple on the undersides as they mature. They are more compact than the species.

'Golden Queen' is similar but with bright orange flowers.

'Gregynog Gold' (*L. dentata* x *L. veitchiana*) has bright orange flowers held on an upright, conical inflorescence over richly veined heart-shaped serrated leaves.

Plants can reach 6′ tall. Developed in Wales, it is seldom seen in commercial catalogs any more.

'Moor's Blood' bears deep purple foliage and orange flowers.

'Orange Princess' has green leaves and light orange blooms.

'Othello' is similar to 'Desdemona' but not as compact and with smaller flowers. There is not, however, a great deal of difference between them.

'Sommergold' has deep orange flowers.

***-stenocephala*** (sten-o-seph′ a-la) | Narrow-Spiked Ligularia | 4-5′/5′
Summer | Yellow | Japan, North China | Zones 5-8

Unlike bigleaf ligularia, this species is better known for flowers than foliage. The purplish flower stems end in spikelike 12-18″ long racemes bearing many 1-1½″ wide bright yellow flowers. The light green leaves are triangular to heart shaped with coarse triangular teeth around the margin. The large leaves (up to a foot long and as wide) lose abundant amounts of water on warm days resulting in wilted foliage. It is one of the earliest flowering ligularias.

This popular form is a classic garden plant where moist conditions can be maintained. I have seen spectacular plants almost everywhere I travel, and they can stop traffic. That they wilt during hot days is simply something to accept, the rewards of contented plants more than make up for it. However, plants are seldom content south of zone 6. Regardless of zip code, moist soil conditions, cool nights and afternoon shade are necessary. They do not require dividing but if additional plant material is needed, division should be accomplished in early spring or late fall. Copious amounts of water must be provided for plantlets to become established.

**Cultivars:**

'Little Rocket' is a dwarf form of 'The Rocket' and grows only about 2′ tall even when in bloom. Plants are more useful for smaller gardens but are as thirsty as others.

'The Rocket' is the most common form of the species and seen everywhere. It is a little more compact, and has 18-24″ long upright racemes of smaller lemon yellow flowers, but still tops out at about four feet. The long spikes are wonderful design components in the garden. It may also be listed as a cultivar of *L. przewalskii*.

'Weihenstephan' is similar to 'The Rocket' but has larger gold flowers.

***-wilsoniana*** (wil-son-ee-ah′ na) | Giant Groundsel | 4-6′/4′
Summer | Yellow | China | Zones 5-8

One of the many species named for "Chinese Wilson", Ernest Henry Wilson, this plant bears dark green kidney-shaped basal leaves with sharp serrations. The yellow daisy flowers are held in a long raceme in July to August. It can be distinguished from other raceme-bearing plants by having circular hollow petioles. This is way underused and one of the more handsome ligularias I have seen, but it is a challenge to find them in this country.

Like other ligularias, cool weather and moist conditions are beneficial, but this little-known species deserves more use.

**Related Species:**

*L. fischeri*, Fischer's ligularia, has 8″ wide gray-green heart-shaped leaves and bears 4′ tall inflorescences of orange-yellow flowers. This is not a small plant. Collected by Dan Hinkley of Heronswood Nursery from high elevations of South Korea. Probably cold hardy to zone 4.

*L. hodgsonii*, Hodgson's ligularia, is similar to *L. dentata* but grows only 2-3′ tall. Leaves are tinged purple on the undersides, and green and hairy on top.

*L. japonica* is impressive. A 4′ tall clump consisting of large finely palmately dissected leaves makes this plant quite different than those of most other species. Add to that 6′ tall spikes of yellow-orange daisylike flowers and the impressive part becomes obvious. The other obvious part is the need for consistent moisture. Zone 4 to 7a.

*L. macrophylla* has large, wide swordlike leaves like no other. The bluish leaves are attached to the stem by obvious winged petioles. The many yellow flowers are about 1″ wide and held in dense crowded panicles. Growing 4-5′ tall, these are handsome, impressive plants.

*L.* x *palmatifolia* is a hybrid between *L. dentata* and *L. japonica*. The hybrid is intermediate with lobed rounded foliage. They are about 5′ tall and have golden yellow flowers in late summer. Hardy to about zone 6.

*L. przewalskii* (sha-val' skee-eye), Shavalski's ligularia, is named after the Russian explorer, Nicolai Przewalski. Plants are similar to *L. stenocephala* and the two species are often confused. Both are native to northern China, bear spikelike yellow flowers and dark flower stems. However, the stems of *L. przewalskii* are blacker and the leaves are palmately cut, not heart shaped. The plant is taller and usually has five ray florets in each flower compared with three in *L. stenocephala*. Plants are used like 'The Rocket' and equally effective.

*L. siberica*, as the name implies, is cold hardy to around zone 3. The numerous daisylike yellow flowers are 1-2″ wide over rounded green leaves with handsome silver-white backs. Moisture is necessary.

## ***Lilium*** (lil′ ee-um) Lily Liliaceae

Few gardeners can scour garden catalogs and then show sufficient self-discipline to refrain from ordering at least a dozen lily bulbs for the garden. They grow from 12″ to 7′ in height, flower colors cover the entire spectrum of the rainbow (except blue), plants bloom from early summer to late fall, are exceptionally hardy, can be long lived, and are relatively inexpensive. Many of the 80-90 species are still available to the gardener, but with the recent interest in commercial hybridization, the hybrids are often touted with more fanfare than the species. Magnificent additions within the genus have occurred with the work of American and European plant breeders and gardeners are the ultimate winners.

Lilies are native to three main areas of the world and their provenance somewhat determines their position in the garden. European species (*L. bulbiferum, L. candidum, L. martagon, L. monadelphum, L. pyrenaicum*) and their hybrids require rich soils well amended with organic matter. Many Asiatic species (*L. auratum, L. leichtli-*

*nii, L. henryi, L. regale, L. rubellum, L. speciosum, L. tigrinum*) and their hybrids produce roots not only at the base of the bulb but also at the stem just above the bulb. These should be planted 8-10″ deep to allow for stem-rooting. North American species (*L. canadense, L. pardalinum, L. philadelphicum, L. superbum*) and their hybrids are not stem-rooted but often have stoloniferous or rhizomatous bulbs. Well-drained soils amended with leaf mold and peat moss provide the greatest success.

General statements about lily culture are impossible to make due to our diversity of climate. While it is enjoyable to read about the ease of growing lilies in England (or elsewhere), the cultural information must be applied to North American gardens most cautiously. However, a broad rule, provided by Alan and Ester Macneil in *Garden Lilies* states that most Asiatic types do well in areas east of the Rocky Mountains, while those native to the Pacific Coast (*L. pardalinum, L. parryi, L. washingtonianum*) and to Europe often struggle there. European species do well on the West Coast, and western American species do better on the other side of the ocean than on the other side of the mountains.

Lilies usually arrive packed in moist peat moss and should not be removed until planting time. They dry out quickly if exposed to the air because they have no natural protection around the bulb to prevent desiccation. Planting depth varies with species but in general they should be planted 2-3 times deeper than their diameter. However, *L. davidii* should be planted 8″ deep while *L. candidum* requires shallow planting. All lilies look better when planted 9-12″ apart in groups of three to five. Organic matter should be spread around the emerging stems in early spring, especially those which are stem rooters. The taller lilies, particularly those with large trumpet flowers, should be staked. Insert bamboo stakes close to the stems (without piercing the bulbs) when they are about one foot tall and tie securely as they grow.

Remove flowers when they fade to reduce seed set. If flowers are to be brought inside, cut as little stem as possible. The leaves and stem manufacture food for next year's flowers and if too much is removed, performance declines in subsequent years. The stems can be removed in the fall after they have died back, although I like to leave some of the stem around all winter so bulbs can be located in spring. Most are sun-loving plants but many tolerate partial shade. The most important cultural requirement is good drainage, particularly in the winter, although abundant water is required in the summer.

A number of diseases have plagued lilies from the beginning of their cultivation and still persist today. Botrytis, a fungal disease, is known as gray mold because of the grayish residue that occurs on leaves and stem particularly after prolonged rain. Bottom leaves usually fall off and although plants are disfigured, little permanent damage occurs. Basal rot is caused by *Fusarium oxysporum* and occurs on infected bulbs. Symptoms are yellow foliage and total disintegration of the bulb. It occurs more often in warm climates than in areas with cooler summer conditions. Most lily propagators dip their bulbs in fungicide after harvesting from the field, and basal rot is not as serious today as in the past. However, it will not go away. The most serious disease is lily mosaic virus which is carried from plant to plant by aphids. Symptoms vary, but in general, irregular yellow streaks or mottling appear on the leaves and many become twisted and distorted. The most susceptible species are *L. formosanum* and *L. auratum*, although *L. canadense*, *L. japonicum* and *L. superbum* are often infected and act as carriers. It is advisable to plant these some distance from other lily species. The virus can also be spread from tulips, particularly Rembrandt types, and tulips and lilies should not be planted side by side.

While diseases of the lily are frustrating to the gardener, the bulbs were used for many medicinal purposes in medieval times. Ulcers and scurvy were diminished when treated with bulbs pounded with honey; when mixed with barley and baked, they were said to cure dropsy. Even corns were soothed with an ointment made from boiling the bulbs. Modern medicine has failed to confirm these uses, but studies are alive and well.

Lilies are propagated vegetatively or sexually. Vegetative propagules include scales, stem bulbils, or division. The advantage of vegetative propagation is to multiply hybrids or cultivars which will not come true from seed. The biggest disadvantage is the transmission of viral or fungal pathogens from mother to daughter plant. Scale propagation may be done on most species in June and July in the United States. Discard the outer scales and peel the inner scales of the bulb. Dip the cut end in a fungicide (available at a garden center) and place into clean coarse vermiculite or a mixture of sand and peat moss. Tie a polyethylene bag over the container and place in a warm area. Small scales such as those of *L. superbum* or *L. pumilum* should be almost covered while bigger ones such as those of *L. henryi* may be left protruding above the surface. Bulbils will form on the scales in 4-10 weeks and some top growth will occur. At that time place the container in a cooler for at least 6 weeks of cold temperatures (less than 40°F). Pot up in the spring and allow for additional growth or place in the garden at this time.

Stem bulbils occur on *L. henryi*, *L. tigrinum*, many of the Backhouse hybrids, and occasionally on *L. bulbiferum*. Simply remove these bulbils when ripe (usually in midsummer) and plant them in a peat medium in a propagation frame. Overwinter to provide the necessary chilling and place container and plantlet in the garden the next spring. For those so inclined, breaking off the top of the plant just when flower buds are visible will force many plants to form adventitious stem bulbils. Some species such as *L. speciosum* have rhizomatous bulbs and careful removal of the daughter bulbils is a useful method of propagation. Reproduction by seed is time-consuming for some species but surprisingly fast for others. The main advantage of seed propagation is freedom from disease. Many species germinate rapidly and top growth occurs in 2-3 weeks. Others form a bulbil prior to top growth development, and in these species, it appears as if nothing is happening and seeds are often discarded too soon.

Most lilies require a minimum of 6 weeks of cold to develop good flowering stems. Lilies raised from seed may take 4 years to flower. Others such as *L. formosanum*, Formosa lily, flower the first year after the cold treatment.

*Types of hybrids*: Just like daylilies, peonies, dahlias and irises, lilies need their own board of referees to keep the hybrids straight. This group is the North American Lily Society (www. lilies.org) and I have deferred to their expertise in matters of lily hybrids. They have classified hybrids into 8 divisions based on the parentage, the position (nodding, upright) and shape of the flower (trumpet, star, bowl). Some of these divisions can be useful for gardeners looking for certain shapes or heights, and some may also help determine if the cultivar will perform in their climate. For most gardeners, this may be a little much and you may simply want to select by catalog photos or from the list of popular and award-winning cultivars listed below. Here is the latest lineup.

*Asiatic Hybrids* (Div. 1): Cultivars are derived from numerous Asiatic species. They are among the earliest to bloom, and are the easiest of lilies to grow. The flowers can be upward facing, outfacing, or pendant, and generally are not scented.

*Martagon Hybrids* (Div. 2): Also known as Turk's cap lilies, plants are generally relatively tall, characterized by the many downward-facing flowers and whorled leaves. These are tolerant of some shade, but still perform best with at least 5 hours of sun.

*Candidum Hybrids* (Div. 3): Hybrids are derived from *L candidum*, *L chalcedonicum*, *L monadelphum*, and other related European species, but excluding *L. martagon*. Flowers are also downward facing and leaves are whorled. This division includes few cultivars, and they are not easily found in commerce.

*American Hybrids* (Div. 4): Hybrids mainly made up of western North American species such as *L. pardalinum*, *L. humboldtii*, *L. kelloggii*, and *L. parryii*. These are challenging outside of the western United States and Canada, but they are worth trying in areas where cool nights, light soil and dappled shade can be provided.

*Longiflorum Hybrids* (Div. 5): This division includes hybrids derived from *L. longiflorum* (Easter lily) and *L. formosanum* and provide large white trumpet flowers. These hybrids are some of the easiest to grow and are easily raised from seed, but not particularly long lived in the garden.

*Trumpet and Aurelian Hybrids* (Div. 6): Aurelians are hybrids that include *Lilium henryi* in their ancestry. Trumpets and Aurelians bloom in mid to late season, and their heavy flower heads may require staking. They may also require a mulch in cold winter areas, and some protection from late spring frosts.

*Oriental Hybrids* (Div. 7): Cultivars are derived from *L. auratum*, *L. speciosum*, *L. nobilissimum*, *L. rubellum*, *L. alexandrae*, and *L. japonicum*. They perform best with plenty of water, humus-rich soil that is slightly acid, and mulch for a cool root run.

*Miscellaneous Hybrids* (Div. 8): These are simply not covered by other divisions. "Orienpets" are hybrids between Division 7 (Oriental) and Division 6 (trumpet & Aurelian) which combine the flower shape and color of the Orientals with toughness of trumpets and Aurelians. They may be better suited to hot summer areas than the Orientals, and more resistant to winter cold than the trumpets.

Having written all this, it is increasingly obvious to me that confusion reigns as to how to know which is which. For beginning gardeners and students, all these divisions are way too much. Yet, with a little effort, some semblance of order in the main groups can be learned. If I focus on teaching my students the "big three"—Asiatics, Orientals and martagons—along with a few species, we can push back considerable fog. Asiatic hybrids are earliest to flower, have smaller leaves than the Orientals, generally but not always, have upward facing flowers and range from 1-3′ in height. The Asiatics, however, provide the most variability in color and habit and are available in a tremendous color range. They are least fussy about the soil and fertility requirements, adapting to almost any well-drained soil and occasional feeding. Orientals are distinguishable from Asiatics by being taller, having larger flowers (often outward facing or nodding), and with much wider, more succulent leaves along the stem. The flowers are generally more fragrant than those of Asiatics. I find the leaf size the easiest method of distinguishing them. The martagons have pendulous flowers whose petals are rolled back (reflexed). The martagon forms have whorled leaves and usually grow only about 3′ tall. They do better in alkaline soils (pH 6.5 to 7.5) and struggle a little in acidic soils. Other groups are also important (the fragrant Trumpet and Aurelian classes are also fun to grow) but there is only so much lily nomenclature I can hammer into my students' heads.

What with the thousands of cultivars out there, none of this identification nonsense is at all necessary to enjoy the plants. However, the NALS conducts popularity polls among its members and then designates cultivars to its Hall of Fame (cultivars that scored first in popularity polls for three years). So if you're confused, start with these.

*Popularity Poll Winners*

| | 2004 | 2005 | 2006 |
|---|---|---|---|
| 1. | 'Leslie Woodruff' | 'Anastacia' | 'Anastacia' |
| 2. | 'Anastacia' | 'Miss Alice' | 'Iowa Rose' |
| 3. | 'Caravan' | 'Claude Shride' | 'Pizazz' |
| 4. | 'Iowa Rose' | 'Catherine the Great' | 'Landini' |
| 5. | 'Starburst Sensation' | 'Iowa Rose' | 'Citronella' |
| 6. | 'Arabesque' | 'Caravan' | 'Easter Moon', 'Starburst Sensation' |
| 7. | 'Chianti' | 'Northern Sensation' | 'Claude Shride' |
| 8. | 'Pizzazz' | 'Pizzazz' | 'Arabesque', 'Conga d'Or' |
| 9. | 'Fangio' | 'Starburst Sensation' | 'Triumphator' |
| 10. | 'Louis XIV' | 'Ariadne' | 'Angela North' |

*Hall of Fame Winners*

1. 'Black Beauty'
2. 'Casa Blanca'
3. 'Connecticut King'
4. 'Enchantment'
5. 'Journey's End'
6. 'Leslie Woodruff'
7. 'Northern Carillon/Silk Road'
8. 'Red Velvet'
9. 'Scheherazade'
10. 'White Henryi'

*Species*: The proliferation of hybrids has left some of the species out in the cold from the viewpoint of garden appeal. The species, however, possess a charm of their own and although some are uncommon, others such as tiger lily and regal lily will always occupy a space in the summer garden.

Quick Guide to Lily Species

| | Ease of growth | Flower color | Height (ft.) | Flower shape | Flower time |
|---|---|---|---|---|---|
| *L. amabile* | MD | Red, black spots | 2-3 | Nodding | J, J |
| *L. auratum* | ME | White, yellow band | 2-4 | Bowl | A, S |
| *L. bulbiferum* | MD | Red-orange | 3-4 | Cup | J, J |
| *L. canadense* | D | Golden yellow | 2-4 | Nodding | June |
| *L. candidum* | E | White | 2-4 | Trumpet | June |
| *L. formosanum* | ME | White | 4-6 | Trumpet | Aug. |
| *L. henryi* | E | Light orange | 4-6 | Nodding | J, A |
| *L. maculatum* | ME | Orange | 2-3 | Upward | M, J |
| *L. martagon* | MD | Purple-red | 3-4 | Nodding | J, J |
| *L. monadelphum* | D | Yellow, lilac spots | 4-5 | Nodding | J, J |
| *L. philadelphicum* | D | Orange-red | 2-4 | Erect | J, J |
| *L. pumilum* | E | Coral-red | 1-2 | Nodding | J, J |
| *L. regale* | E | White | 4-6 | Trumpet | J, A |
| *L. speciosum* | E | White, red spots | 4-5 | Nodding | J, A |
| *L. superbum* | E | Orange | 4-7 | Nodding | J, A |
| *L. tigrinum* | E | Orange, spotted | 4-5 | Nodding | A, S |

*Ease of growth:* E= easy, ME= moderately easy, MD= moderately difficult, D= difficult (for gardens east of the Rocky Mountains)

*Flower time:*
In zones 4, 5: A, S = August, September; J, A = July, August; J, J = June, July
In zones 6, 7: A, S would flower in July and August; J, A in June and July; J, J in May and June

**-*auratum*** (ow-rah′ tum) Goldband Lily 2-4′/1½′
Summer White Japan Zones 4-9

*L. auratum* has often been described as "the queen of the lilies" and is well deserving of the name. The large flowers have prominent gold bands down the center of each white petal and are heavily spotted with gold and crimson. The wonderfully fragrant blooms are borne horizontally and each of the 5-15 blossoms is 6-10″ in diameter. The flowers are funnel shaped, the petals are slightly reflexed, but no long flower tube is produced as in the trumpet lilies. The red anthers contrast prominently with the white petals.

The introduction of *L. auratum* bulbs to England and North America in 1862 created a groundswell of interest in this and other lilies. Unfortunately, the wholesale propagation of bulbs in Japan was handled poorly and basal rot and lily mosaic decimated plantings. Few established plantings remain. This species and *L. formosanum*, Formosa lily, are the two most susceptible to lily mosaic and complete destruction of the entire plant, including the bulb, can occur within one year. Propagation and cultural techniques have greatly improved and although there is far less incidence of disease, the reputation still lingers.

This species is more frost tender than many others and should be mulched well in zones 4 and 5. Bulbs require a well-drained soil and do not tolerate lime. They are also particularly sensitive to winter moisture. Bulbs grow on volcanic ash and lava debris in Japan, indicating their dislike of moisture around the bulbs. The bulbs are not stem rooters and should be planted about 6″ deep. In the Armitage garden, flowers opened during the first two weeks of June for about 3 years, until other woody plants took over the area. Although not a long-lived species, often disappearing in 2 to 3 years, it is lovely enough that frequent renewal is justified.

**Cultivars:**

'Earth Angel' bears white flowers with a particularly visible yellow band. Plants are only about 2′ tall. This is also used in greenhouse production for potted plants.

'Opala' is a handsome large-flowered white form.

var. *platyphyllum* is better than the type with larger, less heavily spotted flowers. It is a vigorous grower and can reach heights 6-8′.

var. *rubro-vittatum* has a crimson rather than a yellow band through the petals. 'Crimson Beauty' and 'Red Band' are names given to selections of this variety.

var. *virginale* is an albino form of the species, with pale yellow banding and few or no spots.

**Hybrids with *L. auratum*:**

*L.* x *parkmanii*, (Oriental hybrid, Div. 7) raised in Boston in 1869 by Francis Parkman, an amateur gardener, is a cross between *L. auratum* and *L. speciosum*. The segments are crimson inside with white margins and the flat flowers are up to 12″ across. The original hybrids were lost but subsequent crosses have been made. This is considered to be one of the finest hybrids ever produced.

'Empress of China' (*L.* 'Jillian Wallace' x *L. auratum* 'Crimson Queen') has a pale green stripe in the center of the petals, and maroon spots.

'Empress of Japan' (*L. auratum* x *L. speciosum*) bears white flowers with a golden band and purple spotting on the petals.

'Excelsior' (*L. auratum* var. *platyphyllum* x *L.* 'Jillian Wallace') has rose petals with narrow white margins.

Imperial Strain, Potomac hybrids, and Jamboree Strain also are hybrids between *L. auratum* and *L. speciosum*.

***-bulbiferum*** (bul-bi′ fe-rum) Fire Lily 3-4′/1½′
Summer Orange Red Eastern and Central Europe Zones 2-7

The species is occasionally offered but is often outclassed by many of the hybrids. It is, however, hardy, vigorous and one of the easiest lilies to grow. The orange-red, cup-shaped flowers are erect or outward facing and have yellow blotching at the base. If the flowers are disbudded or if the stem is damaged, many bulbils appear in the axils of the leaves. For large-scale production, plants are cut off to induce bulbil formation from the leaf axils.

Bulbs should be planted 6-8″ deep and are not particular as to soil type. They are tolerant of shade and should be placed where they remain undisturbed.

**Cultivars:**

var. *chaixii* is a dwarf plant, seldom over 2′ tall, with orange flowers.

var. *croceum* has brilliant, deep orange flowers. In Northern Ireland, it is the symbol of the Order of the Ulster Orangemen, who celebrate the victory of William of Orange in 1691. This variety is also one of the parents of the hybrid 'Redbird', a purple-stemmed plant bearing red flowers with mahogany spots.

**Hybrids of *L. bulbiferum*:**

*L. bulbiferum* has been used extensively in hybridization resulting in erect-flowered hybrids known as *L.* x *hollandicum* or *L.* x *maculatum*.

***-candidum*** (kan′ di-dum) Madonna Lily 2-4′/1½′
Summer White Eastern Mediterranean Zones 4-9

This may be the earliest lily in cultivation, grown circa 1500 BC in Crete. The Madonna lily has always represented the good and beautiful to artists and poets. The Madonna flower is depicted in paintings and frescoes by Botticelli and Titian and is still considered by many to be the "lily of the valleys" mentioned in the Song of Solomon (2:1-2). The 10-20 funnel-shaped flowers are pure white (the name *candidum* means not just white but "of dazzling white"), 3-4″ long and equally wide. They are delicately fragrant and each waxy flower faces outward to allow full view of the lovely yellow stamens.

This is one of the few bulbs that must be planted near the surface: only 1″ of soil should cover the bulb. Basal evergreen leaves form soon after bulbs are planted in the fall. It is best placed in the company of other low-growing plants that shade the bulb but not the stem leaves. For this reason, Madonna lily does well in the mixed border where it may persist for many years.

**Hybrids with *L. candidum*:**

*L.* x *testaceum* (*L. candidum* x *L. chalcedonicum*) bears pendant fragrant ivory flowers flushed with pink and scarlet anthers. One of the oldest hybrids (early 1800s), plants are known as Nanking lilies, even though the original hybrids probably arose in Holland or Germany. Difficult to establish but worth trying an expensive bulb or two.

'Apollo' (*L.* x *testaceum* x *L. chalcedonicum* var. *maculatum*) has tan flowers with apricot shading.

'Zeus' (*L.* x *testaceum* x *L. chalcedonicum*) has deep red flowers. All hybrids bear pendulous flowers.

***-formosanum*** (for-mo-say′ num) Formosa Lily 5-6′/1½′
Late Summer White Taiwan Zones 5-8

The outward-facing flowers are funnel-shaped with reflexed petals. The 2-4″ long off-white blooms often have purplish brown markings on the outside to match the purplish hue of the stem. Five to six fragrant flowers are borne in the stem axils in late summer in the South and autumn in the North. The late-flowering characteristic is sufficient to recommend the species but in the North, too little time may be available for the bulb to ripen after flowering and bulbs may persist only a year or two. In the South, this is not a problem. One of the drawbacks (or attributes) to the species is the height, up to 4-6′ tall, often requiring support in windy areas. On the other hand, the seed capsules are among some of the most handsome in the genus and add interest to the fall garden.

Unfortunately, bulbs are susceptible to virus diseases, particularly lily mosaic. The virus causes rapid decline of the bulb and increases the potential of infection to other bulb species in the garden. To avoid infection, it is not advisable to plant Formosa lilies among other lilies. (Also see *L. auratum*).

**Cultivars:**

var. *pricei* is only 18-24″ tall and a definite improvement on the species. Plants are suitable for the front of the garden and should be planted like *L. candidum*, using other plants to provide shade for the base. Flowers open earlier, and bulbs are more cold hardy than the species. This is one of the fastest species to flower from seed, flowering the first year. Germination occurs in 3-4 weeks in warm (70-75°F), humid areas. var. *pricei* also comes true from seed.

***-henryi*** (hen′ ree-eye) Henry Lily 4-6′/2′
Late Summer Orange Central China Zones 4-7

One of the building blocks of the hybridizer, it has been a parent of many a grateful hybrid, as well as an excellent long-lived species, flowering prolifically in mid to late summer. This lily was discovered by Augustine Henry (1857-1930), an Irish plant explorer who traveled throughout China. Plants were named *L. henryi* by E. H. Wilson. The bulbs are exceptionally large (8-10″ in diameter), and relatively resistant to fungi and viruses. The length and width of the leaves vary considerably but become smaller near the top of the stem. The stem itself varies from green to dark purple. The 2″ wide nodding, light orange flowers have strongly reflexed petals and the centers have numerous raised projections called papillae.

This stem-rooting species should be planted 6-8″ deep. The major disadvantage is the inherent inability of the stems to stand upright. They start to bend long before the flower buds have reached appreciable size and can touch the ground as the flowers open. Support early in the growing season; better still, allow them to grow through shrubs in the mixed border. It is native to limestone cliff faces in China and therefore appreciative of high pH soils.

Under favorable conditions, seedlings reach flowering size in about three years. Multitudes of small bulbs forming at the base of the stem may also be detached and grown on.

**Hybrids with *L. henryi*:**

The Aurelian hybrids (Div. 6) are the most important hybrids associated with *L. henryi*. They arose from crosses with *L. sargentiae*, Sargent's lily, a trumpet lily whose white flowers sport a brown tint. The resulting crosses produced hybrids whose flowers vary in shape from trumpet, bowl-shaped, and pendant to sunburst types.

**Cultivars:**

Many clones from various strains of the Aurelian hybrids have occurred over the years; all benefitted from the added vigor and stronger garden constitution of their parents.

'Black Beauty' is a vigorous hybrid resulting from the cross between *L. henryi* and *L. speciosum*. Flowers are deep crimson with recurved petals. These normally incompatible species were hybridized using embryo culture, a powerful technique for the development of future hybrids. 'Bright Star' is a sunburst type lily (star-shaped flowers which open flat) with white flowers and an orange-gold center.

'Eureka', a bowl-shaped, outward-facing, pale orange lily also resulted through embryo culture (*L. henryi* x 'Wiltig', an Asiatic hybrid).

'First Love' has 6-8″ wide gold flowers with pink edges. The flowers are clearly bowl shaped and outward facing.

Golden Clarion Strain consists of trumpet-shaped flowers ranging from yellow to gold, usually with maroon or deep crimson on the outside.

'Heart's Desire' has bowl-shaped flowers in shades of white, cream, yellow, or orange.

'Honeydew', a trumpet form, has long, pendulous flowers which are greenish yellow outside, deep yellow inside.

'Limelight' bears funnel-shaped trumpets of chartreuse yellow. Unfortunately, it is rather sensitive to virus.

'Pink Perfection' has 6-8″ long, deep pink trumpet flowers. Plants grow 8′ high in my garden.

'Thunderbolt' bears deep apricot starburst flowers with tinges of green and purple on the outside of the petals.

***-martagon*** (mar′ ta-gon) | Martagon Lily, Turk's-Cap | 3-4′/1½′
Summer | Purple-Red | Europe, Asia | Zones 3-7

This lily has a wide distribution, ranging from Portugal to northern Mongolia and from Britain to Siberia. As would be expected, it is variable in habit and adaptable to a wide range of climates and garden environments. Plants tolerate partial shade as well as full sun, a plus for many gardens.

The word "martagon" may be derived from a Turkish word denoting a special form of turban used by sultans. This rather loose translation has evolved into the common name of this plant, the Turk's-cap lily. Many other species with the same nodding flower orientation are referred to as turk's-cap flowers. Alchemists in the 15th century held the martagon in high regard for its ability to change metals into gold, perhaps because of the golden roots.

Plants are distinguished by 3-4 whorls of leaves consisting of 6-9 leaves per node. The nodding flowers are dull purplish red and spotted dark purple throughout. The petals are strongly recurved and each stem bears 20-30 small flowers. The 1-2″ wide flowers are fragrant but the fragrance is in the nose of the smeller. I find the odor rather unpleasant. There are even those who claim it "stinks".

**Cultivars**:

'Album' is an albino form with creamy white unspotted flowers and pale green leaves. It is particularly outstanding in front of a solid green background in the garden and, unlike other albino forms, grows vigorously.

var. *cattaniae* is similar to the species but has dark maroon unspotted flowers and hairy buds and stems. I find the unspotted nature of the flowers more pleasant than the type. Crosses made in Scotland between these two varieties yielded cherry-colored flowers sold as 'Gleam' and 'Glisten' but I am not aware of any commercial source in the United States.

**Hybrids with *L. martagon***:

Backhouse hybrids (Div. 2) resulted from *L. martagon* and its varieties, particularly var. *cattaniae*, and *L. hansonii*, a nodding orange-yellow species. They were developed at the end of the last century and are still widely grown. Named clones include 'Mrs. R.O. Backhouse', with orange-yellow flowers flushed with pink, and 'Brocade' with pale, buff yellow, recurved flowers. They are vigorous, excellent garden plants.

Paisley hybrids (*L. martagon* 'Album' x *L. hansonii*) contain nodding flowers of clear white, orange and mahogany. The hybrids are occasionally listed as *L.* x *martha*. No named cultivars have yet been developed.

-***philadelphicum*** (fil-a-delf′ i-cum) Wood Lily 2-4′/1½′
Summer Orange-Red Eastern North America Zones 4-7

This North American native ranges from Nova Scotia to Ontario and from southern Quebec as far south as North Carolina. Fiery orange-red erect flowers with dark maroon spots contrast with the dark green whorled leaves. Open wooded areas and areas with partial afternoon shade are common locales to find this native. The flowers are sufficiently showy that mass plantings are not necessary, and if provided ample space, are visible from one end of the garden to the other.

Unfortunately, this is not one of the easier lilies to establish and only a small percentage persist more than two years. However, those that do become established are long lived. The rock garden serves the needs of this diminutive lily better than the mixed border, particularly when the soil is sandy and highly acidic. Given the wide distribution, it is surprising that establishment is so difficult. Sowing seed in the cold frame in fall, with subsequent planting of the seedlings next spring, reduces root disturbance and helps establish the plants.

***-pumilum*** (pew′ mi-lum) | Coral Lily | 1-2′/1½′
Summer | Coral-Red | Eastern China, Siberia | Zones 3-7

The exceptionally waxy, coral-red, nodding flowers are unlike any others. The petals are highly reflexed and practically unspotted. Each stem may bear up to twenty, 2″ wide flowers in early summer, although 10 is more common. The numerous leaves are narrow and grasslike. As coral lily is a stem-rooting species, bulbs should be planted about 4-5″ deep.

Plants are not long lived and accepting this fact makes them much less frustrating to grow. They persist 2-4 years at best in full sun. Prolific amounts of seed are produced which provide new seedlings to perpetuate the species for many years. Four years is about the maximum length of time bulbs persist, however, removing spent flowers keeps plants in place a little longer but eliminates the source of fresh seed for new plantings.

**Cultivars:**
'Golden Gleam' is a golden form of the species.
'Red Star' bears star-shaped scarlet flowers about a week later than the type.
'Yellow Bunting' is a pure yellow form that comes true from seed.

***-regale*** (re-gah′ lee) | Regal Lily | 4-6′/2′
Summer | White | China | Zones 3-8

The regal lily was discovered by the great plant explorer E. H. Wilson in western Szechuan in 1903. Imagine his thrill of gazing upon drifts of pure white lilies "not in twos and threes but in hundreds, in thousands, aye, in tens of thousands. The air in the cool of the morning and in the evening is laden with delicious perfume exhaled from each bloom." (*The Lilies of Eastern Asia*, 1925, by E. H. Wilson). While we poor modern working stiffs cannot duplicate this sight, a half dozen bulbs can still provide almost as much pleasure. The trumpet-shaped flowers are white with a canary yellow inner funnel, and usually wine colored on the outside. The stigmas are green and the anthers golden yellow. There may be up to twenty flowers per stem, 5″ wide and 6″ long, although 8-10 is more common. The air is heavy with fragrance at dusk, and an evening walk among the regals is unforgettable. When in flower, this is the dominant plant in the garden. Other plants should be chosen to complement and not compete.

Bulbs should be planted 6″ deep in well-drained soil in partial shade or full sun. One problem with regal lilies is that they appear in early spring and may be nipped by late spring frosts. Planting through low-growing plants such as *Campanula carpatica* protects the new shoots while providing color at the base. Bulbs are long-lived and multiply rapidly, however, once planted, they resent disturbance.

Seeds are produced prolifically and flowering plants can be produced in as little as two years.

-***speciosum*** (spee-cee-o′ sum) Speciosum Lily 4-5′/2′
Summer White with Red Japan Zones 4-8

Once grown in large numbers for the cut flower trade, the species has been superseded by the hybrids. It is still, however, a popular late-flowering lily for gardens with full sun and lime-free soil. The 6″ wide, white, fragrant flowers have reflexed petals flushed with pink and heavily spotted with pink or crimson. They have red fleshy bumps (papillae) in the center of the blossom, similar to *L. henryi*. A well-grown plant may have as many as 30 blossoms per stem although 15-20 is more realistic. Plant bulbs about 6″ deep. Due to their susceptibility to virus and disease, keep them away from *L. auratum* and *L. formosanum*.

**Cultivars**:
'Album' (var. *album novum*) has white flowers with a pale green band radiating from the center. Purple spots also occur on the petals.
'Roseum' bears 8″ wide soft pinkish red flowers with a white margin around the petals.
'Rubrum' produces large, 8″ wide ruby-red flowers with a broad white margin. These are commonly known as rubrum lilies.
'Uchida' may be a cultivar of var. *rubrum* or a hybrid with *L. auratum*. Nevertheless, the vigorous plants perform well and bear rich carmine-pink, spotted flowers. 'Uchida' is more virus resistant than the species.

**Hybrids with *L. speciosum***:
'Allegra' (*L. auratum* x *L. speciosum* 'Rubrum') x *L. speciosum* 'Album' has beautiful white recurved flowers with a central green star.
Other hybrids such as *L.* x *parkmanii* have been listed under *L. auratum*.

-***superbum*** (soo-perb′ um) American Turk's Cap Lily 4-7′/2′
Late Summer Orange Eastern United States Zones 4-8

The variable American turk's cap lily used to be far more abundant in eastern United States than it is today. Peter Hanson of Brooklyn, after whom *L. hansonii* was named, "once found a spot in New Jersey where there were at least 5000 plants of this noble lily in flower at once, ranging up to 2 meters high and bearing as many as 30 flowers to a stem, but out of the whole number it was difficult to find three exactly alike." (*Monograph of the Genus Lilium*, 1877-1880, by H. J. Elwes). *L. superbum* is a martagon-type lily (see *L. martagon*), with orange-red, heavily spotted reflexed flowers often with a green center at the base. The stems are usually flushed with dark purple and may bear up to 40 flowers although 20 is more common. Plants prefer damp conditions and perform better if they do not dry out during the summer, although bulbs are more tolerant of being dried out than many other species. They can be found in many wet areas in the Arnold Arboretum. The leaves are whorled like *L. martagon* and the bulbs are rhizomatous resulting in the establishment of large colonies. Seed sown in the fall will reach flowering size in two years.

**Cultivars:**

A number of cultivars were raised by Mrs. J. N. Henry, an amateur lily enthusiast from Gladwyne, Pennsylvania. This is the same remarkable lady after whom *Itea* 'Henry's Garnet' is named.

'Norman Henry' has fine unspotted butter-yellow flowers.

'Port Henry' bears clear pale orange flowers with only faint spotting. Other cultivars were also selected which bear the Henry name but unfortunately most have been lost.

***-tigrinum*** (ti-gri′ num) Tiger Lily 4-5′/2′
Summer, Fall Orange, Spotted China, Korea, Japan Zones 3-9

The few demands as to soil type, sun or shade or irrigation make the tiger lily one of the easiest to grow. The 2-4″ long flowers have strongly recurved petals and may be up to 9″ wide. Each stem bears 8-20 deep orange flowers with purplish black spots. Bulbs are stem rooters and should be planted 6″ deep and mulched around the base to allow full development of stem roots. The purplish green stem has white cobweb-like hairs and numerous black bulbils that are formed in the leaf axils.

*L. tigrinum* was used as a food plant for more than a thousand years by the Chinese, the bulbs being quite edible and said to taste like artichoke. It is interesting that *L. candidum*, Madonna lily, has been grown for an equal length of time for beauty, not the food value. Debates still rage in lily circles as to which species was first cultivated.

Unfortunately, *L. tigrinum* has a history of being infected with lily mosaic virus. In this species, however, the symptoms are almost entirely masked. Aphids spread it to other species quite readily and thus the tiger lily is seldom found in the gardens of lily enthusiasts (as for me, I love it). Established plants, however, may live for years and multiply rapidly. Vigorous efforts have been made to raise virus-free stock and it is better to pay the extra price for this material than to infect the rest of the garden.

Plants multiply readily from bulbils formed at the base of the bulbs. Abundant seed is also produced which is scattered randomly by birds and plants to germinate along roadsides and streams. Plants are regular citizens of roadsides throughout the Northeast and the Eastern Townships in Quebec, Canada.

**Cultivars:**

Many seed-propagated cultivars are available in white, yellow, pink, red, cream, orange, and gold. All are variable and flowers are heavily sprinkled with black dots.

var. *fortunei* has bright salmon-orange flowers and is distinguished by the dense woolly hairs which coat the stem. It is later flowering than the species and is particularly useful in the South where frost doesn't occur until November or December.

var. *flaviflorum* has yellow flowers but is particularly susceptible to virus and has not proven to be a good selection.

var. *flore-plena* has double flowers but, in my opinion, is rather coarse. The style and grace of a lily flower lies in its clean lines and simple architecture. Double-flowered lilies destroy such grace.

var. *splendens* has larger, brighter reddish orange flowers than the type and is one of the best varieties for the late garden.

**Hybrids with *L. tigrinum*:**

'Cardinal' (*L. tigrinum* x *L. amabile*) has nodding, orange-red flowers that bloom late in the season.

Mid-Century hybrids include some of the best-known lilies. They resulted from crosses between *L. tigrinum* and *L.* x *hollandicum*. 'Enchantment' bears bright orange, outward-facing flowers on 2′ tall stems. An excellent cut flower species. 'Cinnabar' is only 1½-2′ tall and bears bright maroon-red, erect flowers.

**Related Species:**

*L. canadense*, Canada lily, is one of the most beautiful lilies in existence, and also one of the most frustrating. I thought this was a problem limited to the South, but gardener Judy Laushman of Oberlin, Ohio states that "emergence is spotty and life is short even where summers are not particularly warm, like northeast Ohio." Plants bear whorled leaves and butter yellow flowers and have a similar growth habit to *L. superbum*. However, Canada lily differs by having dark-spotted yellowish flowers rather than orange, by less reflexed petals, and by the absence of a green spot at the base of the flower.

*L. iridollae*, pot of gold lily, was found by Mrs. J. N. Henry (see cultivars of *L. superbum*) in southern Alabama. Native to Alabama and Florida, it bears nodding pure yellow flowers on 3′ tall stems. Unfortunately, this little gem is difficult to find but if a source is discovered, it should definitely be used in southern gardens.

*L. longiflorum*, Easter lily, may also become a beautiful garden plant. If potted lilies are received as gifts, plant immediately after flowering. The pure white flowers are 4-7″ long and 1-1½″ broad. Unfortunately, bulbs are winter hardy only to zone 8 (zone 7 if well mulched). The good news is that numerous crosses with the Easter lily are now available (Longiflorum hybrids, Div. 5), expanding the color selection and the climatic adaptability. 'Aladdin' hybrids are multicolored hybrids between *L. longiflorum* and various Asiatic hybrids. They are about 2′ tall, with upward-facing, slightly fragrant flowers. 'Aladdin's Dream' is a pink-flowered form that was selected from the hybrids above. 'Longidragon' (*L. longiflorum* x 'Black Dragon') has trumpets of white flowers with chartreuse throats, but the back of the petals are purple-black.

*L. michauxii*, is similar to, but a more southerly species of, *L. superbum* and was thought to be a variety (*L. superbum* var. *carolinianum*). Native to the southeastern United States, plants are tolerant of summer heat and humidity. It is not as floriferous as *L. superbum* but bears 3-5 fragrant, nodding light orange or crimson turk's-cap flowers. The species is well worth growing in zones 8-10. Named for Andre Michaux, the famous French plant explorer, who traveled extensively through the southern United States in the 18th century.

*L. pardalinum*, leopard lily, has 9-20 whorled leaves and 2-4″ wide nodding flowers. They are yellow at the base, orange-scarlet above and spotted maroon. Native to California, they are magnificent for western gardens but perform poorly in the East.

***Limonium*** (li-mon′ ee-um) Statice, Sea-Lavender Plumbaginaceae

Well over 150 species of statice have been characterized and a number have become well established in the garden and florist trade. However, with the introduction of so many new perennials in the last 20 years, the role of statice has essentially been relegated to that of a cut flower. People who enjoy cutting flowers from their own garden may still purchase seed or plants of common annual statice, *L. sinuatum*, available in many colors. Statice enthusiasts might want to experiment with *L. sinense*, an annual with small yellow flowers and *L. perezii*, Perez statice, a 3-4′ tall stout plant with 12-15″ wide flat dark blue flowers with white centers.

Common perennials such as *L. latifolium* and *L. tataricum* bear large airy heads of tiny flowers in shades of lavender and blue and are useful fresh or dried. The flowers are composed of outer sepals (calyx) and inner petals (corolla) and may be different colors. In some species, the corolla falls early, leaving the calyx in full color.

Statice prefers late afternoon shade in the southern part of the range (zones 7, 8) but will tolerate full sun further north. Good drainage is essential as they are all susceptible to various fungal diseases prevalent in moist soils. To dry the cut flowers, harvest before they fully open. Tie the stems in bundles and hang upside down in a shady, dry, airy shed.

Propagate by root cuttings (see *Anemone*) and division in early spring or by seed. Seeds are small and should be barely covered. Germination occurs in 2-3 weeks under warm (70-75°F), humid conditions.

Quick Reference to Limonium Species

| | Height (in.) | Hairy leaves | Color of corolla |
|---|---|---|---|
| *L. latifolium* | 24-30 | Yes | Blue |
| *L. tataricum* | 10-15 | No | Ruby-red |

**-*latifolium*** (lah-tee-fo′ lee-um) Sea Lavender 24-30″/30″
Summer Lavender-Blue Bulgaria, Southern Russia Zones 3-8
(syn. *L. platyphyllum*)

Plants may reach 2½″ tall and equally wide with over a dozen flowering stems when well established. The flower stalk is slender and multi-branched, creating a flower head 18-24″ across. The 6-10″ long leaves are produced in rosettes and are often just as wide (*latifolium* means wide leaf). Small, branched hairs cover the leaves, which taper at the base into petioles nearly as long as the blades. Plants are susceptible to crown and root rot and should be spaced 18″ or more, otherwise air circulation is restricted and disease increases. Some authorities have renamed the plant *L. platyphyllum*. Others have not.

Propagate from seed in late fall or from division. Seed is the easiest and least disruptive form of propagation. The roots are long and division is difficult. Established clumps should not be disturbed.

**Cultivars:**
'Blue Cloud' has lighter blue flowers than the type.
'Blue Diamond' has sprays of blue-purple flowers on 10-15″ stems.
'Violetta' bears dark violet flowers and is an outstanding garden plant.

**Related Species:**

*L. bellidifolium* is only 4-10″ tall at flowering, and bears sprays of lilac flowers over handsome lanceolate foliage (*bellidifolium* means beautiful-leafed).

*L. gmelinii*, Siberian statice, produces 2-3′ tall spires of smoky lilac flowers in late summer. This is an extremely vigorous grower, particularly when provided with deep, rich soil and plenty of moisture.

*L. minutum* is an interesting little plant. Plants are native to the Balearic Islands and live in limey soils by the coast. They grow 3-5″ tall and bear white flowers over dark green leaves. Rock gardens only.

***Linaria*** (lyne-ah′ ree-a) Toadflax, Butter-and-Eggs Scrophulariaceae

Sometimes, one needs a plant roadmap to determine whether some plants are annuals, perennials or "perennial-annuals", those that readily self-sow, therefore, are always there. *Linaria* is the latter. The genus consists of about 100 species, one of which is the common toadflax, *L. vulgaris*, a well-known relatively handsome perennial weed found along northern roadsides. Another good-looking weed, *L. genistifolia* var. *dalmatica*, is listed as a noxious weed in the state of Washington and should be planted with caution, particularly in the West. Some of the "old-fashioned" species are being rediscovered and may be considered as perennials to zone 5, but are not happy with high temperatures, making them spring annuals (like pansies) in the southern parts of the country. Not a one of these is a surefire perennial in any garden east of the Rockies, and spending hard-earned money on them may not be the best idea. However, inveterate gardeners will surely gamble; here are a few to swipe your card for.

*L. purpurea*, purple toadflax, is native to central and south Italy and Sicily but has been naturalized in the British Isles and occasionally in the United States as well. They are closely related to snapdragons and have long, narrow racemes of small flowers, each with a single spur (like a columbine) at the base. Plants grow 2-3′ tall and flower all summer long in moderate climates. The narrow leaves are whorled at the bottom part of the stem but may be alternate at the top. Flowers are usually purple but the most popular form is 'Canon J. Went', a pink-flowered form that comes true from seed. 'Springside White' has white flowers and gray-green leaves. 'Antique Silver', a 4-6″ tall plant with pinkish silver flowers and 'Natalie', with blue flowers on 15-18″ plants, are hybrids which increase the toadflax palette. Cut back plants if they get weedy. Plants are winter hardy to about 5°F and can be perennial with a little mulch, however, self-seeding keeps plants all over the garden. South of zone 6, it should be treated as a fall-planted annual, although if plants make it through the summer, they should return. Good drainage helps.

*L. alpina*, alpine toadflax, is hardy to zone 4 or 5, and bears small violet/yellow or sometimes entirely yellow flowers. Plants grow only 4-8″ tall and are best in rock gardens with good drainage and cool summers.

*L. triornithophora* is occasionally offered as a perennial but is cold hardy only to about 23°F (zone 8, maybe), but will self-sow in temperate climates. It is an eye-catching ornamental plant with large flowers, resembling birds on the fly. Its wonderful common name is three birds flying.

## ***Linum*** (ly′ num) Flax Linaceae

Flax has been grown for centuries for oil, fiber and ornament. The perennial *L. perenne* and the annual *L. usitatissimum*, common flax, were grown for fiber to make linen, cordage and rope. During Tudor times in England, when linen tablecloths adorned the tables of abbots and kings, a royal proclamation was issued that a better source of cordage was necessary to properly equip the newly established Royal Navy. *Linum* was replaced by *Cannabis sativa* as the source of royal rope. Little did they know about the other mind-bending properties of that now infamous plant! Linseed oil is produced from the seeds of *L. usitatissimum*, and flax is still farmed aggressively in Europe; few travelers seeing rolling fields of blue flax flowers are unimpressed with the beauty. Beats the heck out of corn and soybeans.

Three or four species out of the approximately 150 are used for ornamental purposes but I am noting more nurseries offering a larger selection. The red-flowered *L. grandiflorum* is an annual, but most others are perennial. *L. lewesii*, western blue flax, is native to the Sierra Mountains and grows about 2′ tall with sky-blue flowers. *L. capitatum*, with yellow flowers, and *L. suffruticosum*, with white flowers, are less than 1′ tall and perform wonderfully well in sunny rock garden settings.

Flax plants may be short lived but can often reseed prolifically. Named cultivars may be propagated vegetatively. The flowers are 5-petaled and are blue, white, yellow, or occasionally red. Although the individual flowers last only a day, so many flowers are produced that the plant is in flower over a 4-6 week period. The leaves are alternate, narrow, and usually entire. *Linum* is easily grown in a light, well-drained soil in full sun, but other than *L. perenne*, don't expect more than a couple of years from most of them.

Propagate by divisions or stem cuttings, or from seed sown in a cool area where soil temperature is 50-60°F.

Quick Reference to Linum Species

| | Height (in.) | Flower color |
|---|---|---|
| *L. flavum* | 15-18 | Yellow |
| *L. narbonense* | 18-24 | Blue |
| *L. perenne* | 12-18 | Blue |

***-flavum*** (flay′ vum) Golden Flax 15-18″/12″
Summer Yellow Europe Zones 5-7

The fact that this species is not offered by more nurserymen is a shame, especially as some cultivars and varieties are of exceptional garden merit. The 1″ diameter golden yellow flowers consist of petals much larger than the sepals. Up to fifty flowers may be carried in a single inflorescence. The base of the stems become somewhat woody, and the narrow, lanceolate leaves have 3-5 veins and small glands on each side of the leaf base. Plants benefit from a loose mulch of pine straw, leaves or wheat straw over the winter.

**Cultivars:**

'Compactum' is superior to the type, stands 6-9″ tall, and is covered with yellow flowers.

***-narbonense*** (nar-bon-en′ see) Narbonne Flax 18-24″/18″
Summer Blue Southern Europe Zones 5-8

This long-lived blue-flowered species is one of the best for the garden. Winter protection must be provided in zone 5 and further north. The 2″ wide funnel-shaped flowers are blue with a clear white center. The white stamens contribute to the bicolor effect. The ¾″ long, narrow leaves have three veins. After flowering, cut back stems to eight inches. Similar to the other *Linum* species, well-drained soils are necessary, and plants flower well in full sun or partial shade.

**Cultivars:**

'Heavenly Blue' has ultramarine flowers on 12-18″ tall stems. More compact than the species, it does not fall over with rain and wind. Greater compactness, however, is still required and would be most welcome.

'Six Hills' bears brighter blue flowers.

***-perenne*** (pe-ren′ ee) Perennial Flax 12-18″/12″
Spring Blue Europe Zones 4-8

The flowers are more open than those of *L. narbonense*, smaller, and without the white eye. The ¾″ wide, azure blue flowers open for up to 12 weeks when planted in partial shade. In the South, the first flowers open in early April and continue into late June. Further north, plants open later but continue to flower even longer. Plants are easy to distinguish from similar species by the wiry stems (try to break them) and the many nodding flower buds. The narrow 1″ long leaves transpire little water and tolerate the heat of southern summers. As with other flax species, it abhors wet feet and will not return next spring if winter drainage is poor. When planted in a group of six or more, the plants provide a lovely display. The stems become long and leggy in the heat of the summer and require pruning after flowering.

Seed-grown plants often flower the first year. Divide in spring or early fall.

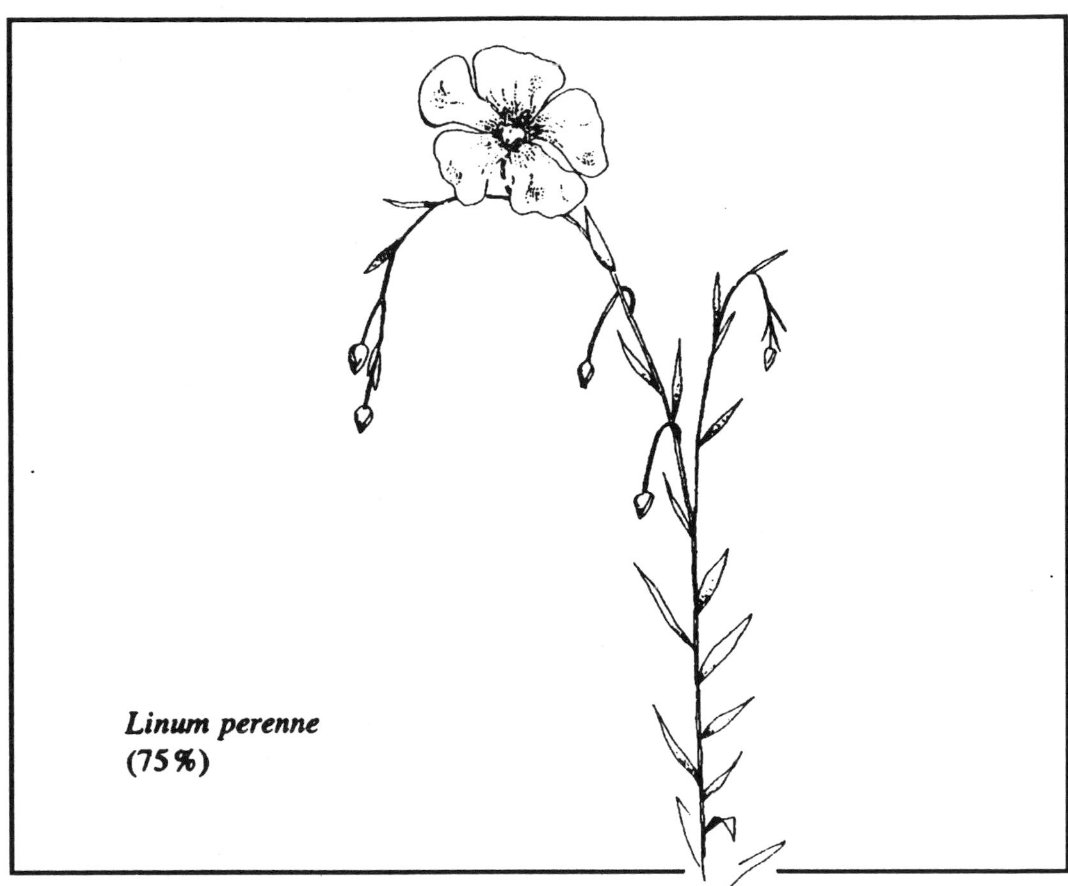


**Cultivars:**

'Album' is widely available with white flowers on upright stems. It is not a clear white, however, and appears washed out in full sun.

'Alpinum' (subsp. *alpinum*), alpine flax, grows 8-12″ tall with slender, wiry stems which carry ¾″ wide, clear blue flowers. It is not as floriferous as the species, but if given well-drained soil in full sun, lovely drifts of blue result.

'Caerulea' has clear, sky-blue flowers.

'Diamant White' grows about 15″ tall with white flowers.

'Sapphire' has blue flowers and is more compact than the species. It is an excellent garden plant, growing only 10-12″ tall.

**Related Species:**

*L. capitatum*, purging flax, is similar to golden flax but the leaves are in basal rosettes and the flowers occur in a dense inflorescence. Flower heads of *L. flavum* are much more open.

*L. lewisii*, western blue flax, is native to the high plains and essentially throughout the western half of the country. Plants are similar in flower color and habit to *L. perenne* but are more cold hardy (at least to zone 3) and better able to handle inclement weather. 'Appar' is a named cultivar that may be more uniform than the species.

*L. suffruticosum*, thistle flax, has 1″ diameter white flowers with purple veins and needlelike leaves. Plants are native to southern Europe and are more useful for gardens west of the Rocky Mountains. var. *nanum* is only 2-4″ tall and prostrate. It is handsome where low-growing white-flowered plants are needed.

***Liriope*** (lear′ree-ope, le-rye′o-pee) Lily-Turf Convallariaceae

In the *Standard Cyclopedia of Horticulture* by L. H. Bailey (written 1900, revised in 1943), *Liriope* received a minimum of space because it was "little cultivated". Today, it is one the premier and predominant landscape ground cover plants in the South. Of the five species, only *L. muscari* is commonly cultivated.

***-muscari*** (mus-cah′ ree) Blue Lily-Turf 12-18″/12″
Late Summer Lilac Eastern Asia Zones 6-9

A healthy disregard for heat, humidity, and drought, and a built-in resistance to insects and diseases make this an excellent ground cover. The straplike, dark green 1-1½″ wide evergreen leaves emerge from the crown of the plant. The lilac-purple flowers are borne on dense spikelike flower stalks in August. Dark black berries ripen in the fall and persist into the winter. Plants are not particular concerning soils, if drainage is adequate. Large clumps are formed by means of the short, thickened stoloniferous roots. When planted 8-12″ apart, *Liriope* provides an effective ground cover that is occasionally used as a substitute for grass. Plants tolerate heavy shade although they will take longer to spread and the flower stems will be more elongated compared to plants grown in full sun. In late winter, plantings may be mowed to the ground to eliminate old foliage and allow a new flush of growth in the spring. I suppose the true pinnacle of success of a plant is when it does so well as to be taken for granted. This is true for liriope in the South.

The continued popularity of liriope has seen an increase in crown and leaf rot, caused by the fungus *Phytophthora palmivora*. Initially, the symptoms include one or more mature leaves developing a pale to bright yellow color, then extending upward from the leaf base toward the tip. Immature leaves close to the growing point may also become diseased, developing tan discoloration. This will become more of a problem in wet soils. Fungicides have limited effectiveness. Avoid susceptible cultivars such as 'Evergreen Giant'.

*Liriope* is closely related to *Ophiopogon*, mondo grass, but is hardier, has broader leaves, and flowers above the foliage, while the flowers of mondo grass often flower within the foliage.

Propagation by division results in many plantlets which can be replanted or handed over the fence to a new neighbor. The seed coat is hard, and soaking seeds in warm water before sowing results in more uniform and faster germination. Tissue culture has also been successfully used to multiply slower cultivars.

**Cultivars:**

*Green-leaved forms:*

'Big Blue' bears wide dark green leaves and lavender flowers. One of the most popular forms.

'Christmas Tree' has unique lilac flowers on spikes much wider at the base which taper towards the tip, resembling a Christmas tree.

'Evergreen Giant' is 18-26″ tall with large leaves and a vigorous habit.

'Lilac Beauty' bears showy, stiff, lilac flower clusters held well above the foliage.

'Majestic' has larger, deep lilac flowers. This form is similar to 'Big Blue' but grows slightly more upright.

'Munroe's White' is the best white-flowered cultivar but is slower growing than the lilac types. The flowers stand out and provide an additional dimension to the species.

'Royal Purple' has deeper purple flowers than other selections.

'Super Green Giant' can grow up to 2′ tall, and is useful for areas where some height on ground covers is called for.

*Interesting foliage forms:* In general, variegation patterns, silvering and chartreuse foliage will be brighter in the spring than the summer, and in brighter light than in shade.

'Gold Banded' has wide arching leaves with a narrow gold band down the middle and bears lavender flowers.

'John Burch' produces attractive variegated foliage and cockscomb-shaped lilac flower spikes.

'Okina' produces mainly white leaves, with some green. Later, the white portion becomes speckled with green. By the end of the season, leaves will be totally green. The time span of whiteness is inversely proportional to the temperature. Lilac flowers occur in late summer.

'Peedee Ingot' has chartreuse leaves most of the summer and lilac-purple flowers in late summer. Plants are bright enough to lighten up shaded areas.

'Silvery Midget' grows about 8″ tall, and bears short green leaves with narrow white bands.

'Silvery Sunproof' has almost white leaves in full sun but more green or yellow-green in partial shade. Flowers are lavender.

'Variegata', the most common of all the lily-turfs used for foliar effect, bears creamy margins that brighten up any landscape. Seeds yield about 65% variegated plants. Flowers appear about 2 weeks later than the species. This variety does not spread as rapidly as the type so it is a little more expensive to purchase.

**Related Species:**

*Liriope spicata*, creeping liriope, is cold hardy to zone 4 and used as a rapidly spreading ground cover. It is only 10-15″ tall and has narrower leaves (only about ¼″ wide) than *L. muscari*. Plants, in effect, resemble feathery grass. Foliage tends to be more yellow-green during the winter than *L. muscari*. The pale lavender flowers are not as showy as those of *L. muscari*. 'Silver Dragon' has 2′ long, ¼″ wide silver leaves and is quite beautiful.

## ***Lithodora*** (lith-o-door′ a) Lithodora Boraginaceae

*Lithodora* is fairly common in European gardens and is greatly admired for the lovely blue flowers and creeping habit. Of the approximately seven species, *L. diffusa* is the best garden species. Although best suited to the climate of the Northwest, with adequate protection and a proper site, it can also be a valuable plant in other parts of the country as well.

Over the years, *Lithodora* has been both included in and separated from a closely related genus, *Lithospermum*. The two genera are now considered separate and while botanical differences are subtle, the easiest way to distinguish the two is through the flower color. In general, flowers of *Lithodora* are blue or purple, while those of *Lithospermum* are mostly yellow to orange or white. As simple as that seems, one or two cultivars and variants of *Lithodora* may have white flowers as well. The habits of both are usually prostrate, but upright forms have also been introduced.

***-diffusa*** (di-few′ sa) | Acidsoil Lithodora | 8-12″/12″
Summer | Blue | Southern Europe | Zones 5-7

This low-growing plant has ¼-1″ long, alternate, narrow, sessile leaves, hairy on both surfaces. The foliage is evergreen in mild climates. The ½″ long flowers occur at the end of lateral stems that emerge from every leaf axil. They are deep blue with reddish violet stripes and appear from midsummer to fall. Plants are not tolerant of weather extremes and suffer in the South, particularly if placed in full sun or allowed to dry out. In the partially shaded raised garden of some friends in Athens, Georgia, plants performed well for a couple of years. While they never flourished compared to Irish gardens, they were still exquisite while alive. Cold temperatures of about 5°F are tolerated and mulching is beneficial in zones 5 and 6. Trim plants back if they become weedy to maintain some semblance of compactness. Sharp drainage is a must, particularly as stress from hot summers or cold winters increases. Planting on a slope or in raised beds greatly increases the chance of success.

*Lithodora* is one plant that knocks your socks off when it is well grown, but due to temperature extremes, is a difficult plant to grow well throughout the country. The common name results from the intolerance to lime, and plants require acid soils for optimum performance. This is not true of other species of *Lithodora* or *Lithospermum*.

If propagated by soft stem cuttings in humid, warm conditions, rooting will take place in 14 to 21 days. Seeds may also be used but the seed coat is hard and germination takes a long time unless seeds are soaked in warm water for at least two days, or the seed coat is scarified with light sandpaper or other abrasive material.

**Cultivars:**

var. *alba* has white flowers but is not as showy as the species or the following cultivars. Who wants a white lithodora?

'Cambridge Blue' bears beautiful porcelain-blue flowers.

'Grace Ward' consists of silvery green mats with intense blue flowers.

'Heavenly Blue' is one of the lower-growing (3″) cultivars and an excellent plant with numerous clear blue flowers.

'White Star' has flowers with an obvious white centers surrounded by blue.

**Related Species:**

*L. oleifolia*, olive lithodora, forms mounds consisting of ascending stems loaded with pink flower buds which open to lavender blue flowers. Not as cold hardy, probably only to about zone 7b.

## *Lithospermum* (lith-o-sperm′ um) Puccoon — Boraginaceae

Although little used, a number of handsome plants native to the United States are occasionally offered. Flowers are usually orange-yellow but white is not uncommon. Plants are much more adaptable to temperature extremes than *Lithodora* and easier to grow. At the same time, many species are native to sandy soils and drainage is still important.

*L. canescens*, puccoon, is also known as red-root and Indian paint because of the red juice in the roots, used as a dye or for facial paint by native Americans from Ontario to Alabama and west to Arizona. The 9-12″ tall mounded plants bear small yellow-orange flowers in early spring. The flowers are sessile or almost so along the terminal one third of the flowering stems. *L. incisum* (syn. *L. angustifolium*) is quite showy with large handsome bright yellow flowers. The lobes of the flowers are fringed, making it easily distinguishable from other species. The genus performs well as far south as zone 7, and north to zone 5, 4 with protection.

## ***Lobelia*** (lo-bee′ lia) Lobelia Campanulaceae

Lobelia consists of over 250 species of annual and perennial herbaceous plants. Most are quite beautiful but a few species like *L. inflata*, Indian tobacco, with its curious swollen fruit, are considered weeds and quickly forgotten. That is unfortunate because Indians and early settlers routinely used this native plant for many medicinal purposes. In small doses, it helped relieve breathing, and was known as asthma weed; in large doses, it induced vomiting, not a bad course of action to relieve the oft-occurring bouts with poorly cooked or stored meats. Thus its other common name, puke weed.

One of the most popular bedding plants is the blue-flowered annual lobelia, *L. erinus*, used for edging or in hanging baskets. The perennial species, however, provide a brilliant splash of summer color and range from the deepest scarlet to the darkest blue. All have alternate leaves and tubular or star-shaped flowers on racemose inflorescences held well above the leaves.

The perennial lobelias are somewhat short lived and must be replaced or divided at least every three years. Many are native to stream banks and other areas of moist soil and prefer a rich, moist, but well-drained location in the shaded garden. In the Northeast and Northwest, plants tolerate full sun or partial shade, but in the Midwest and South, shade is essential. Regardless of where they are grown, a shallow (½-1″ deep) winter mulch is beneficial. If mulched heavily, plants die. Remove mulch early in the spring.

Lobelias are native to many parts of the world but the American species are most numerous and colorful. The cardinal flower, *L. cardinalis*, is everyone's favorite and has been used as a parent in many outstanding hybrids. However, dozens of others, while perhaps not as eye-catching, are potential gems in the garden. *L. glandulosa*, with light blue flowers, and *L. elongata*, with deeper blue flowers, have 3-4′ tall spires and, although difficult to locate, make fine garden plants.

Considerable breeding has produced many hybrid strains. They have become quite popular as many may also be raised from seed, allowing greenhouse production of large numbers. Hybrids produced by master lobelia-ists like Thurman Maness from Pittsboro, North Carolina, Wray Bowden in Ottawa, Ontario, and numerous breeders in Europe have provided an exciting assortment of goodies with dark stems and brilliant scarlet or purple flowers.

The species may be propagated from seed or division; the hybrids and named cultivars should only be divided. Seed is tiny and should be lightly covered to insure it does not dry out. Sow under warm (70-75°F), moist conditions.

Quick Reference to Lobelia Species

| | Height (ft.) | Flower color |
|---|---|---|
| *L. cardinalis* | 2-4 | Red |
| *L.* x *gerardii* | 3-5 | Purple |
| *L.* x *speciosa* | 3-5 | Red, pink |
| *L. siphilitica* | 2-3 | Blue |

**-*cardinalis*** (kar-di-nah′ lis) Cardinal Flower 2-4′/2′
Summer Red North America Zones 2-9

This species has an extensive natural range: occurring as far north as New Brunswick, south to Florida, and west to Texas. The plant is usually unbranched with 3-4″ long, dark green, irregularly toothed leaves attached either directly to the stem or by a very short petiole. Each 1½″ long flower is brilliant cardinal and the lower lip, consisting of 3 distinct lobes, is bent downward. Up to 50 flowers may be produced on a single 2′ long inflorescence. One forgets the morphology, taxonomy and everything else, however, when the hummingbirds arrive. Then, they are hummingbird flowers, and the few dollars spent for plants produces dividends unparalleled in the New York Stock Exchange. In the Armitage garden, flowering begins in early August and continues for about three weeks. Flowers open from the base to the apex (acropetally) but by the end of a month or so, the inflorescence looks "tired". Plants were honored with the prestigious Plants of Merit award from the Missouri Botanical Garden in 2006.

Soil amended with copious amounts of aged manure or peat moss, which will retain moisture during dry weather, is essential for garden performance and longevity. Growth and flowering occur in dry areas but flowers are not as persistent or dramatic. In most parts of the country, shade should be provided for part of the day, and certainly during late afternoon. Abundant seed is produced which may be sown in a greenhouse, cold frame, or allowed to self-sow.

**Cultivars:**

'Alba' has white flowers.

'Golden Torch' is truly eye-catching, with golden foliage competing for attention with the bright red late summer flowers. I really like this plant.

'Rosea' bears rose-pink flowers.

-x ***gerardii*** (ger-ard-ee′ eye) Hybrid Purple Lobelia 3-5′/2′
Summer Purple Hybrid Zones 5-7

Plants are the result of a cross between either *L. cardinalis* or *L.* x *speciosa* 'Queen Victoria', and *L. siphilitica*. To add to the confusion, they are sometimes mistakenly included under *L.* x *hybrida*. The habit of the plant is similar to *L. cardinalis*, with unbranched stems bearing many star-shaped purple flowers, with a pink tinge, on spikelike racemes. The 4-6″ long clasping leaves are dark green and elliptical. Stems are strong and seldom need staking. This hybrid appears longer-lived than the spe-

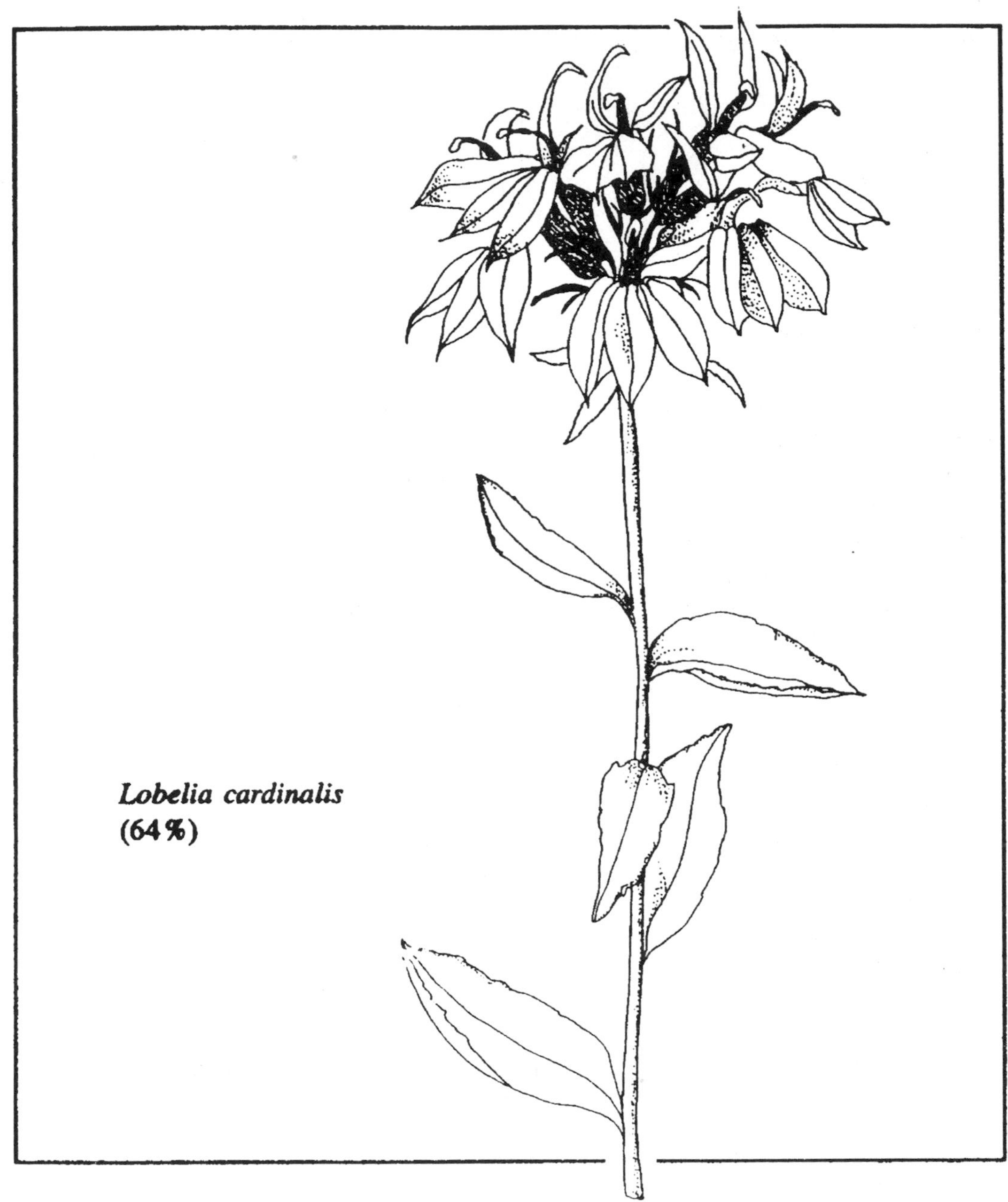

*Lobelia cardinalis*
(64%)

cies. Moist soil, partial shade and a light winter mulch are recommended. They have looked particularly outstanding in the Montreal Botanical Gardens.

Terminal cuttings or division are the common methods of propagation but *L.* x *gerardii* comes fairly true from seed.

**Cultivars:**

'Rosenkavalier' has pink flowers.

'Vedrariensis' (still listed as *L.* x *vedrariensis*) has green foliage with a red tinge and dark violet flowers.

***-siphilitica*** (si-fi-li′ ti-ka) Big Blue Lobelia 2-3′/1½′
Late Summer Blue Eastern United States Zones 4-8

The specific name arose from the supposed medicinal properties but it is now grown for ornamental value only. The one-inch long blue flowers are surrounded by leafy bracts and are "weedier" than *L. cardinalis*. The flowers, which tend to fade into the bracts, are held in dense terminal racemes above the unbranched plants. They appear later than cardinal flower and persist for about four weeks. The 3-5″ long leaves are narrowed at both ends and attached directly to the flower stem (the bottom leaves have short petioles). Constant moisture and partial shade are necessary for optimum performance but, unfortunately, plants are short lived and should be divided and moved every 2-3 years. However, the plant still has many fans, as shown by its being named the North Carolina Wildflower of the Year in 1993. With all the name changes to our favorite plants, such as chrysanthemums and asters, why don't the taxonomists get to work at changing this one?

Propagate the species by seed and cultivars by division.

**Cultivars:**

'Alba' is a white-flowered form of the species.

'Blue Peter', developed by Blooms of Bressingham in England, has light blue flowers on a three-foot plant and may prove more perennial than others.

'Grape Knee-Hi' is a hybrid but has a good deal of blue lobelia in its parentage. It grows 12-18″ tall and is sterile.

-x ***speciosa*** (spe-cee-o′ sa) Hybrid Lobelia 3-5′/3′
Summer Red, Pink Garden Hybrid Zones 5-8
(syn. *L.* x *hybrida*)

*L.* x *speciosa* is a catchall name for the numerous hybrids developed from *L. splendens*, *L. cardinalis*, and *L. siphilitica*. The addition of the other two species to *L. splendens* results in hybrids which are longer lived and more tolerant of soil types and moisture. If a perennial bronze-foliaged cardinal flower is desirable, it will be well to stay away from *L. splendens* and consider the hybrids. Unfortunately, they don't have the winter hardiness of *L. cardinalis* or *L. siphilitica*, however, some of these are most glorious plants and worth a try even if they bring but a single year of glory.

Propagate hybrids from offshoots in late summer and fall. Stem cuttings in midsummer for cultivars. Seed is available for some hybrids.

**Cultivars:**

'Bee's Flame' bears vermilion-red flowers and beet-red foliage and can reach heights of five feet. This is an absolutely magnificent plant in moist, partially shaded conditions.

Compliment series is available from seed and is a midsize group with flowers of red, pink, purple or scarlet. Not as spectacular as some of the others, but hardy and colorful.

'Cotton Candy' is one of many hybrids developed by the North Carolina plantsman Thurman Maness, whose breeding work with this genus will be his legacy.

Crossing *L. cardinalis* and *L. siphilitica*, he has provided us with numerous selections. This one is 2′ tall with large lavender to pink flowers.

Fan series is about 2-2½′ tall and occur in half a dozen colors. The best is probably 'Fan Scarlet', which seems to hold its color well and is less susceptible to the abuses of weather.

'Dark Crusader' provides dark purple foliage in combination with blood-red flowers.

'Monet Moment', another Maness creation, bears rose-pink flowers on vigorous plants.

'Pink Flamingo' has leaves similar to *L. siphilitica* and rich rosy-pink flowers in late summer. A Maness original.

'Purple Towers' has dark purple flowers on vigorous 4-5′ tall stems. Quite outstanding.

'Queen Victoria' is one of the most popular cardinal flowers, with brilliant red flowers over bronze foliage. In flower, plants grow 3-5′ tall. Hardy in zones 6 to 8.

'Rose Beacon' grows 2-3′ tall and bright rosy pink flowers. Another Maness hybrid.

'Royal Robe' may be a cultivar of *L. cardinalis* but is more likely a hybrid of *L.* x *speciosa*. Plants bear deep red flowers with maroon leaves.

'Ruby Slippers', developed by Maness, bears bright garnet-red flowers on robust plants.

'Russian Princess' has bright reddish purple flowers with purple foliage.

'Shrimp Salad' is 3-4′ tall with soft pink flowers.

'Sparkle Divine', a hybrid developed by Thurman Maness, bears purple-fuchsia flowers on long inflorescences on 3′ tall plants.

'Tania' is a Royal Horticultural Society Award of Garden Merit winner, with rosy lavender flowers over silvery green foliage in late summer. Plants grow about 3′ tall.

'Wildwood Splendor', also developed by Maness, produces large lavender flowers in late summer.

A number of tetraploids (double the usual number of chromosomes, were developed by Wray Bowden at Ottawa, Canada. Parents include *L. siphilitica*, *L. cardinalis*, 'Queen Victoria' and 'Illumination'. The plants have large flowers, thick, stiffly erect stems, thick leaf blades, and well-developed fibrous roots. The stems usually have a bronze cast and although still somewhat short lived, are winter hardy to zone 3 or 4 and appear to be excellent garden plants. Numerous cultivars have been developed but six of the best are listed. These are becoming harder to find.

'Brightness' is 3-4′ tall with bright cherry red flowers atop dark bronze foliage.

'Hamilton Dwarf' is only 2′ tall with 6″ long blood-red racemes maturing to crimson.

'Oakes Ames' bears deep scarlet flowers and bronze stems and leaves.

'Robert Landon' produces large cherry-red flowers and has proven exceptional in tests in Ottawa.

'Simcoe' also has scarlet flowers on 2′ long racemes.

'Wisley' has lighter red flowers and stem color than 'Oakes Ames'.

**Related Species:**

*L. bridgesii*, Bridges lobelia, is similar but has soft pink rather than red flowers. Stunning in habit and flower and somewhat similar to blood lobelia, but difficult to find in North America.

*L. elongata* has long, narrow leaves and bears light blue flowers on one side of the flower stem. Grows 3-4′ tall and performs well in zones 7-9.

*L. sessilifolia* is native to Korea, Taiwan and Japan and winter hardy to zone 5, zone 4 with protection. The violet-blue flowers are held in dense terminal spikes. The upper leaves are sessile (thus the name) and the plants grow 3-5′ tall. Plants appear to be more adaptable to drier soils than other species.

*L. splendens* (syn. *L. fulgens*), Mexican lobelia, is closely related to *L. cardinalis*. Plants have larger bracts beneath the flowers, are more pubescent, and usually have bronze stems and leaves. Bronze-leaf cardinal flowers, particularly if grown from seed, are very likely *L. splendens*. Although spectacular in flower, they are much less cold hardy (to zone 7 or 8), shorter lived, and not as tolerant of dry soils as *L. cardinalis*. 'Illumination' bears large spikes of deep scarlet flowers over bronze foliage.

*L. tupa*, blood lobelia, has unique wrinkled, gray-green, soft downy leaves. Plants are more branched and can easily grow 3-5′ tall. The 2-4″ long tubular scarlet red flowers are held in terminal racemes, and are as spectacular as cardinal flower when in flower, provide a lovely display in summer and early fall. Plants are native to Chile and cold hardy only to about zone 7. Another spectacular lobelia that is limited to the Northwest because of its relative lack of heat and cold tolerance.

## *Lunaria* (loon-air′ ee-a) Honesty, Money Plant Brassicaceae

Honesty has been a popular garden plant since Victorian times when it was grown for the round, papery-thin fruit (silicles). The most common species is the biennial dollar plant, *L. annua*, and the only one listed in the majority of garden catalogs. However, *L. rediviva*, perennial honesty, is more persistent where conditions are suitable.

*Lunaria* is not difficult to grow and does well in almost any garden soil if some afternoon shade is provided. The leaves are opposite, toothed and heart shaped. The purple or white flowers are held above the foliage and fruit is present while the uppermost flowers are still opening.

Quick Reference to Lunaria Species:

| | Height (ft.) | Flower color | Fruit shape |
|---|---|---|---|
| *L. annua* | 2-3 | Purple, White | Round |
| *L. rediviva* | 3-4 | Purple | Oblong |

**-*annua*** (an-yew′ a) Honesty, Dollar Plant 2-3′/2′
Spring Purple Europe Zones 4-8

While technically a biennial species, it self-sows so readily that it is always somewhere in the garden, although probably not where originally planted. The Armitage

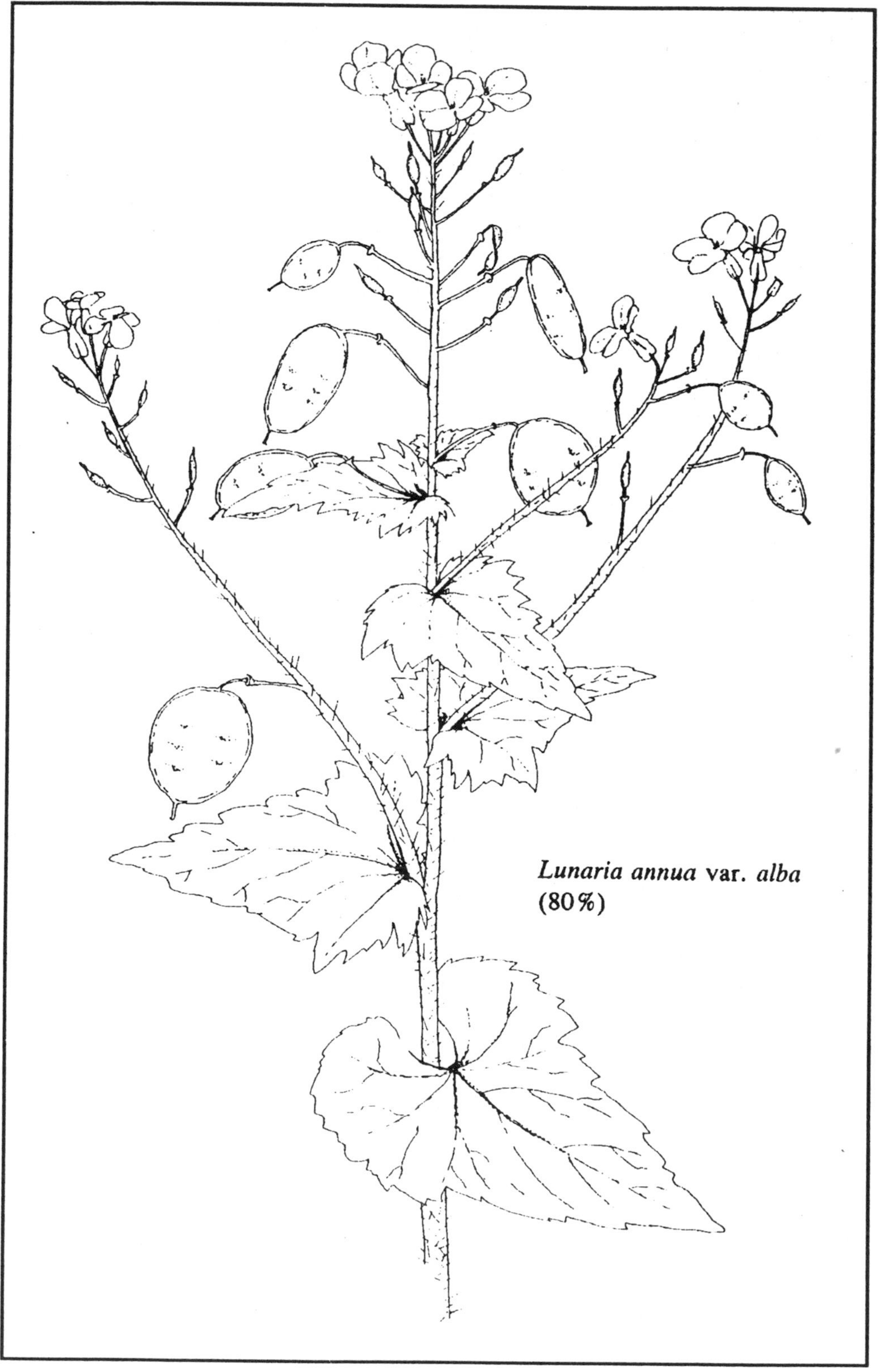

*Lunaria annua* var. *alba*
(80%)

garden is often smothered in the stuff in April, at which time flowers and fruits are all over the garden. Even though it is a weed, I love it. The heart-shaped leaves are usually alternate, coarsely toothed and the upper ones are sessile. A good deal of variation exists in the species. The flowers are usually purple but the var. *alba*, with white flowers, is just as common. In my garden, I try to maintain purple populations in the same area as the yellow daffodils. The late daffodils and the early lunarias make a wonderful combination. I leave the white-flowered ones in the shaded garden where they brighten up the area. When seed or plants are purchased, there is a good chance that both colors will be present.

The fruit is the most ornamental part of the plant and is 2″ wide, round, and papery thin. If brought inside, the stems must be cut just as the green color disappears from the fruit. Hang upside down in a cool, well-ventilated place for 3-5 weeks. They dry exceptionally well and make wonderful additions to winter bouquets. The downside of this species is that they seed everywhere so you better not get tired of them because they will be your partners in the garden for a long time. Susan is brutally honest in her evaluation of the plants in the summer and fall, wondering why I have left so many weeds around.

Plants should be placed in full sun in the North and away from afternoon sun in the South. The white-flowered forms are handsome in the spring shade garden as light reflects off the flowers and brightens the surrounding greenery. Flowering occurs in late April in north Georgia (zone 7), and mid May in Iowa (zone 5). Plants are evergreen but the late summer and winter foliage is not going to impress anyone but yourself.

The species and varieties can be raised from seed (although var. *variegata* yields variegated and green leaf forms). Seed germinates irregularly over time; placing seed at 35-40°F for 4 weeks enhances uniformity. Plants are notoriously difficult to transplant from one garden to another. Much better to collect mature seed and scatter them around.

**Cultivars:**

var. *alba* has white flowers (see text).

var. *atrococcinea* has deep red flowers, difficult to locate.

'Munstead Purple' has flowers of rich purple.

var. *variegata* bears leaves with irregular white margins resulting in a plant with handsome foliage that rivals many far more expensive variegated plants, good-looking flowers and desirable fruit. This cannot be said of many other plants.

***-rediviva*** (re-di-veev′ a) Perennial Honesty 3-4′/2½′
Spring White Europe Zones 4-8

This plant's existence is still a well-kept secret. In the first edition of this book (1989), I could find no offering of perennial honesty in the United States. By the second edition (1997), a few nurseries were listing it. Today, well—even fewer. Perhaps that says something about the plant's, rather than the industry's, performance.

Plants are larger than *L. annua*, have finely toothed, petioled leaves and smaller, lighter purple, more fragrant flowers. Other than overall size, the main difference is the 2-3″ long, 1″ broad elliptical fruit compared to the round fruit of *L. annua*. They may be dried similarly. Although not as well known as money plant, this species is worth seeking. Well-drained soil in partial shade provides optimum growing conditions, however, the soil should not be allowed to dry out.

Propagate from division in spring or by seed. Seed must be kept warm and moist for the first two weeks, then placed at freezing or just above for 4-6 weeks. Finally, expose seeds to 70-75°F until germination occurs. This system of germination is best accomplished by sowing seed in the fall and burying the seed trays in soil for the winter. In the spring, seed will germinate.

***Lupinus*** (loo-pie′ nus) Lupine Fabaceae

Flowers any more perfect as those of the lupine hybrids are difficult to imagine. One of my most vivid memories is the Lupine Garden at Chatsworth House, England. Great drifts of orange, blue, white and purple assailed my senses as I neared the walled garden. As each flower took shape, nowhere could I look without sucking in my breath in utter delight. The scene was simply too perfect to be true. However, not to be outdone, the western states threw down the "sucking breath" gauntlet and held me affixed with fields of blue lupines in Texas, Colorado and California. This utter delight stuff was killing me.

Well over 70 species are found in the central mountain and plains states: Texas claims a few dozen, the Northwest has its fair share and just when I thought I could recognize a lupine, I was introduced to the unifoliate lupines of the southeastern sandhills. It is a given that lupines are beautiful, so why aren't nurseries making lots of money off us by selling them to us? Unfortunately, many are difficult to propagate and/or produce in containers and lack garden persistence when grown away from the native habitat. Today, more choice is being offered, including the delightful *L. perennis* (which see) and *L. sulphureus*, with its small blue flowers. The northwestern species, *L. polyphyllus*, from which the hybrids obtain so much of their beauty and vigor, can also occasionally be found. Unlike other West Coast natives, plants are reasonably tolerant of cold, heat and humidity (zones 3-6). Leaves consist of 10-16 fingerlike leaflets, and flowers are normally deep blue although var. *albus* has white flowers and var. *roseus* has rose blooms. Another lovely perennial species is *L. arborescens*, the tree lupine, native to California and growing well only on the West Coast. This subshrub bears many stems with lemon-yellow flowers although occasionally violet or white are seen. Numerous handsome annuals such as *L. hartwegii*, Hartweg lupine, a 2-3′ tall plant with blue and rose spikes occur. As much as I enjoy the garden hybrids, nothing comes close to the natural beauty of the native species in their native habitat. May we be smart enough to protect them!

The best lupine by far for most gardeners in the East, even the Southeast, is our blue-flowered sundial lupine, *L. perennis*. Finally, eastern nurseries and native plant specialists have discovered this plant, a species native from Maine to Minnesota and south from Louisiana to Florida. That it is "easier to establish" than many others does not make it a no-brainer, as plants may still succumb to wet feet, heat and high humidity, but success with lupines is not measured in acreage. The wonderfully fragrant flowers are generally blue to violet, but occasionally color breaks will occur and other hues will appear. The leaves are divided into 7-11 segments. Do not be surprised if after flowering plants appear to fall apart and die: some will disappear, some will go dormant but if they are growing well, many seedlings will appear, often at a fair distance from the mother plants.

Suzy Bales, one of my good gardening friends and a superb garden writer, finds that sundial lupines do wonderfully well in her Long Island garden. She states "I planted seeds in our vegetable garden approximately ten years ago and they reseeded so abundantly, I have had more plants than I need. They love seeding in the wood chips in the paths as well as the raised beds. Some still die out each year in the formal garden probably because the soil, despite yearly additions of compost, is a clay mixture." She goes on to say "Why would anyone struggle with Russell lupines when you can grow these with so little effort?"

As smart as Suzy is and as beautiful as the native species are, they are not well known among gardeners. Without doubt, the most popular of the perennial species, however, are the various hybrids, including the most famous of them all, the Russell hybrids (perhaps because they have been the only ones easily available). When well grown, few flowers withstand close scrutiny as well as the lupine: they look even more perfect from 3 inches than from 3 feet. The multicolored spires add an aristocratic aura to the garden provided by few other species. They should be placed in the fall garden in zone 5 and south in October and success is more likely if transplanted to the garden from at least one-gallon containers. The smaller the transplant, the more time that is necessary to establish the plants before the onset of cold weather. Since few of us live in England, let's set the record straight. Lupines, at the best of times, are short-lived perennials and for gardeners who live in areas of hot summers, they are best grown as annuals, if at all. They look terrific in March and April if planted in October. Even in the Northeast and much of Canada, lupines tend to be short-lived and should routinely be replaced. Plant in full sun the fall in well-drained, acidic soil. They are relatively easy to grow if soils are rich and conditions are cool, and flowers persist for weeks in the spring garden. Often self-sown seedlings emerge, and although the progeny will not be the same colors as the parents, half the fun is guessing just what is coming next.

Propagate species and hybrids from seed. Some of the species are difficult to germinate and should be soaked in warm water overnight or placed in containers and provided with 4-6 weeks of cold, moist stratification between 30 and 40°F. Seeds of the hybrids are available as complete mixes or as single colors.

**Hybrids:**

James Kelway of Langport, England crossed *L. polyphyllus* with *L. arborescens* in the late 1890s and other English pioneers such as Downer and Harkness continued the early development of lupines by developing hybrids with many different flower colors. One of the first breakthroughs was the red 'Downer's Delight' raised about 1917 and honored by the Royal Horticultural Society in 1918. In 1911, the flowers of the various cultivars, forms and hybrids of *L. polyphyllus* caught the attention of a hobby gardener from Yorkshire, England by the name of George Russell. Continuing Kelway's work, he included other species such as *L. mutabilis* (a five-foot plant with white and blue flowers) from South America, and *L. nanus* (a lovely 1′ tall annual with blue flowers) from California. By 1937, Russell had perfected flowers of blue, purple, yellow, intense reds, deep pinks, and numerous combinations of bicolors. Many of these original breakthroughs are still available today as Russell hybrids. Some of the new hybrids from Russell's work are offered as 'Russell Hybrid Improved'. Continued development of the herbaceous lupines has continued since Russell's time and new cultivars appear every year. Some of the following cultivars are listed as Russell hybrid cultivars, others as *L. polyphyllus* hybrids, or on their own. Hybridization has merged the various cultivars and little "purity" of hybrids has been maintained.

**Cultivars and hybrids:**

'Carmine' bears tall carmine flowers.

'Chandelier' has yellow flowers on 3′ tall plants.

'Delicate Pink' bears soft pink flowers.

'Gallery Hybrids' are 15-18″ tall and occur in shades of blue, pink, red and white.

'Garden Gnome' is a dwarf (18-24″) form in many colors.

'Ivory' is a handsome form with creamy white flowers.

'Little Lulu' is available in many colors on 18-24″ tall plants.

'Manhattan Lights' has tall spires in purple and gold, about 2′ tall.

'Minarette' consists of dwarf (18-20″) plants in mixed colors.

'My Castle' is 2-3′ tall with brick-red flowers.

'Noble Maiden' bears white flowers atop 2′ tall plants.

Popsicle is a series of colors ranging from blue, pink, red, white and yellow. A popular compact series.

'Red Flame' has bright red blooms.

'The Chatelaine' produces pink and white bicolor flowers.

'The Governor' produces perfect blue and purple flowers on 2-3′ stems.

Woodfield hybrids produce flowers in nearly all colors (except for blue and green) with some interesting bicolors as well. They bear good stem strength and are less sensitive to many of the leaf and crown diseases of some of the older ones.

## *Lychnis* (lick′ nis) Campion Caryophyllaceae

Lychnis comes from the Greek *lychnos*, meaning lamp, providing an apt description of the flame-colored flowers of certain species. The name *campion* is believed to be derived from "champion" because some species were used to make garlands for victors in public games or tournaments. Much of the older literature still refers to plants in the genus as champions. About 20 species are included, although the number changes constantly. Flowers have 5 petals, plants have opposite leaves and swollen nodes, similar to other members of the family. There was so much variation in species originally placed in the genus that many have been transferred to others such as *Silene* and *Agrostemma*. Such is the imperfection of plant classification. To add to the confusion, a carmine-red flowered intergeneric hybrid arose between *Lychnis* and *Silene*; X *Lychnisilene rosea*, sometimes listed as Lychnis 'Rolly's Favorite'.

Of the twenty species, many are brilliantly colored but short-lived garden plants. Most have simple, opposite leaves and bright orange, rose, or red flowers produced singly, in twos or in many-flowered clusters. In many areas, they are like shooting stars, brilliant during their time but quickly disappearing. Further north, they persist longer but still must be replaced every few years.

All species are easily propagated from seed that may be sown directly in the garden or in containers for subsequent transplanting.

Quick Reference to Lychnis Species:

| | Height (in.) | Flower color | Inflorescence few- or many-flowered |
|---|---|---|---|
| *L.* x *arkwrightii* | 18-24 | Orange-scarlet | Few |
| *L. chalcedonica* | 24-36 | Scarlet | Many |
| *L. coronaria* | 24-36 | Rose | Few |
| *L. flos-cuculi* | 12-24 | Deep Rose | Few |
| *L.* x *haageana* | 10-18 | Orange-scarlet | Few |
| *L. viscaria* | 12-18 | Red | Many |

**-x *arkwrightii*** (ark-right′ ee-eye) Arkwright's Campion 18-24″/12″
Early Summer Orange-Scarlet Hybrid Origin Zones 6-8

This hybrid between *L. chalcedonica*, Maltese cross and *L.* x *haageana*, Haage campion, was popular due to the brilliant orange-scarlet flowers. However, as brilliant as it is, the inability to cope with cold winters and moderate heat tolerance has relegated it to a "temperennial". The 1½″ wide flowers are carried in a 3-10 flowered cyme and contrast well with the dark bronze foliage. They have notched petals and are often borne singly the first year. Garden longevity is not nearly as good as *L. chalcedonica*. In the South, longevity is 2-3 years; in the North, more than one season may be possible with adequate protection. Plants should be pinched early in the season to force additional shoots and reduce the potential legginess. In their first year in the Gardens at UGA, plants flowered from April 27-June 25. After flowering, the swollen seed pods turned from green to brown providing additional interest in the season. Shade should be provided in zones 7 and 8 but full sun is acceptable further north.

Propagate by division or stem cuttings. Little variation occurs with seed-grown plants, which flower the first year.

**Cultivars:**

'Orange Gnome' is only 8-10″ tall and bears the same spectacular flowers as 'Vesuvius'. A bit more weatherproof and still an explosion of color.

'Vesuvius' is similar but has vermilion flowers, a color one either loves or hates. Still reasonably popular, best treated as an annual or two-year plant.

**-*chalcedonica*** (chal-ce-don′ i-ka) Maltese Cross 24-36″/18″
Summer Scarlet Eastern Russia Zones 3-7

Maltese cross was a favorite in every grandmother's garden (it was in mine) and is indeed an old-fashioned flower. Evidence suggests that the plant was introduced to Europe at the time of the Crusades. It was believed to have been brought back to France by Louis IX from the Holy Land and is also known as Jerusalem cross. That it had traveled from Russia and was cultivated in Constantinople (*chalcedonica* means of the Chalcedon district, near Constantinople) at that time further suggests that it was indeed an early introduction. Ease of cultivation and rich flower color keep this species popular today. The ¾-1″ wide flowers are deep scarlet and held in dense rounded clusters of twenty to fifty and can be seen a football field away. The individual flowers are shaped like a cross, partly accounting for some of the common name. The opposite, 2-4″ long dark green leaves often clasp the stem. This is the most persistent species of the genus. Plants perform best in well-drained soil with consistent moisture and full sun.

They are easily raised from seed and divisions. Natural seed populations may yield salmon, rose, and even white-flowered offspring.

**Cultivars:**

'Alba' has white flowers.

'Carnea' produces carmine-red flowers.

'Morgenrot' is about 2′ tall with pink flowers.

'Rosea' bears rose-colored flowers.

var. *rubra-plena* (*flore-plenus*), a double red form, is even more brilliantly colored than the type. Plants are difficult to produce commercially thus difficult to locate. White, salmon, and rose forms are available but none is equal to the scarlet.

***-coronaria*** (ko-ro-nah′ ree-a) Rose Campion 24-36″/18″
Spring Rose Southern Europe Zones 4-7

Rose campion is a handsome species when well grown. The woolly, 2-4″ oblong leaves are grayish green and contrast with the 1-2″ wide, single, rose to red flowers profusely produced during the summer. This species was the first of the genus to receive the name lamp-flower, not for the glory of the flowers, but because its leaves were downy and soft "fit to make candle-wicks". "Wanting cotton, they used the downy Substance which covers its leaves for the Wicks of Lamps". The flowers almost glow, making them difficult to coordinate with other plants. There are, however, other problems associated with this species. It is not a true perennial, and although plants may survive a number of seasons, should be treated as biennials or annuals. In the South, flowering is magnificent and decline rapid. In almost all areas, second-year plants are often better than first year and may bloom profusely on 3′ high and wide bushy gray-green specimens. The heat and summer rains of the second season result in loss of much of the foliage and plants that return to life the next spring are tired from their struggle to survive. However, they seed themselves prolifically and never disappear. In the North, flower colors are brighter due to cooler night temperatures in the summer. The plants are also short lived there. For best results, place in full sun, or provide shade from afternoon sun, in well-drained soil. To overwinter plants in areas of little snow cover, plant in raised beds or place a liberal addition of gravel around the roots.

Propagation of all species can be accomplished from seed or basal cuttings taken in the spring.

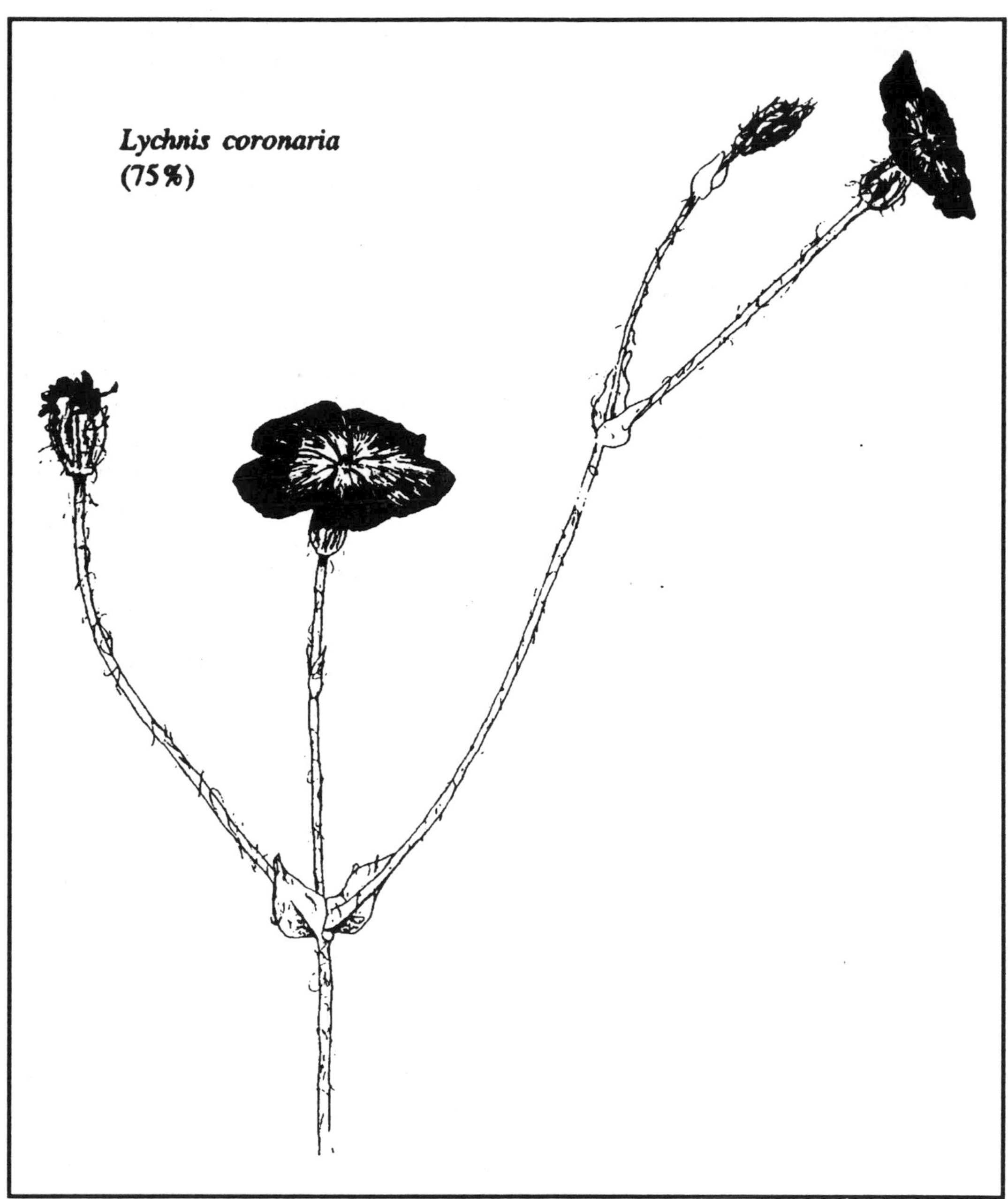


**Cultivars:**
'Alba' has white flowers.
'Angel Blush' has white flowers with a pink flush throughout.
'Atrosanguinea' bears carmine-red flowers.
'Blood Red' has flowers which are more red than magenta.
'Dancing Ladies' is a mixture of white and carmine, usually with a dark eye.
'Flore-plena' has double flowers.

'Gardener's World' bears deep crimson-red double flowers on 2′ tall gray stems. In general, double flowers set seed poorly compared to singles and this is no exception. The result is that flowers remain open longer, but populations may decline more rapidly.

'Maiden's Blush' has light pink flowers.

'Oculata' is similar to 'Angel Blush' and differs by having a pink eye rather than flushed pink.

***-flos-cuculi*** (flos-kew-kew′ lee) Ragged Robin 12-24″/12″
Summer Deep Rose Europe Zones 3-7

From the rosette of narrow, grasslike, gray-green leaves emerge many stems bearing 1-3 rose to red flowers. The petals are deeply cut into four segments, thus resembling a "ragged robin". Flowering persists for 6-8 weeks. Plants are adapted to sunny, moist areas and do well in the garden only if sufficient moisture can be provided. I saw a wonderful display in 1992 at the European Floriade where they were combined with field orchids and native European grasses. Beautiful in their simplicity. Not to be outdone, the garden of my friends, Ram and Tom Gibberson in Athens, sports ragged robins everywhere, providing a cheery laid-back look to their magnificent garden. Plants reseed prolifically.

Seed is the best means of propagation. Seed placed in warm (70-75°F), humid conditions germinates within 21 days. Otherwise, allow the seeds to fall and get out of the way.

**Cultivars:**

'Alba' has clear white flowers but is otherwise similar to the species.

'Alba Plena' bears double white flowers.

'Jenny' is my favorite, growing vigorously but not reseeding quite as prolifically.

'Nana' is less than 6″ tall.

'Rosea Plena' ('Pleniflora') is an excellent selection, bearing double flowers of pink to deep rose. This double campion was known as bachelor's buttons during Elizabethan times.

**-x *haageana*** (hah′gee -ah′ na) Haage Campion 10-18″/12″
Summer Orange-Scarlet Hybrid Origin Zones 5-7

It is interesting that this popular plant is a hybrid between two species seldom used as ornamental plants. The cross occurred between *L. fulgens*, brilliant campion, a 2-3′ tall plant with bright scarlet flowers and *L. coronata* var. *sieboldii*, crown campion, a 10-12″ tall plant with white, slightly notched petals. The result is a good garden plant with large, 2″ wide, orange-scarlet flowers. The flowers are distinctive, having petals with two lobes, each having small teeth on the margin.

Full sun and consistent moisture are keys to growing this hybrid, although partial shade is beneficial in the South. While often placed at the front of the garden because of size, the bright flowers are noticeable even in the shadow of taller neighbors. Plants may go dormant in late summer in the southern half of the country but reappear the following spring. As with other species of *Lychnis*, two to three years is the normal life span, after which replacement is necessary. Slugs enjoy dining on this delicacy and suitable slug deterrents should be used in early spring. Plants are still available, but the popularity has declined due to the various problems.

Plants come fairly true from seed.

***-viscaria*** (vis-cah′ ree-a) German Catchfly 12-18″/10″
Early Summer Magenta Europe Zones 3-7

This plant is sometimes included in a separate genus, *Viscaria*, however, similarities with other *Lychnis* species indicate it should be included here. The foliage is grasslike and grows in tufts. The 1″ wide magenta flowers appear in early summer and are sometimes difficult to weave into the overall color scheme. The flower stalk is sticky (viscous) just below the 3-5 flowered panicle, as are the internodes, thus accounting for the specific and common name.

Plants tolerate full sun in the North but partial shade is required in the South. They are more tolerant of dry conditions than many other members of the genus.

Propagate by seed or division.

**Cultivars:**

'Alba' ('Albiflora') bears white flowers.

'Splendens Plena' ('Flore-plena') has double rose-pink flowers and is the best form of the species. It is sometimes listed with creative name of Passion™.

**Related Species:**

*L. alpina* produces lavender flowers that cover the 5-9″ mat-forming plants in late spring. Best for the rock garden: cold hardy to zone 3 or 4.

*L. flos-jovis*, flower-of-Jove (Jupiter) is similar, also bearing white-woolly foliage. The plants are only 1-2′ tall, with muted scarlet flowers about ¾″ wide. The lobed flowers are carried in a loose inflorescence somewhat similar to the flower head of primrose. Plants are longer lived than those of rose campion and should be used more in this country. 'Hort's Variety' bears clear rose-pink flowers on 10″ tall plants.

*L.* x *walkeri*, a sterile hybrid between *L. coronaria* and *L. flos-jovis*, has carmine-red flowers on short flower stems. 'Abbotswood Rose' is a compact, floriferous plant covered with bright pink flowers: 'Hill Grounds' grows 2½′ tall and produces pink-red flowers over gray leaves.

*L. yunnanensis*, Yunnan campion, is 10-12″ tall with white to pink flowers. The flower stems are sticky, similar to *L. viscaria*.

## ***Lycoris*** (lie′ core-is) Resurrection Flower, Naked Ladies Amaryllidaceae

This bulbous genus consists of about eleven species with wonderful eye-catching flowers. The leaves arise in fall, winter or early spring and persist until late spring or early summer, then disappear. The unwary gardener might believe that the bulbs have died and should be removed. In late summer and fall, however, smooth straight flower stalks arise from seemingly barren ground (thus its common names) to produce umbels of small trumpet-like flowers of pink, red, yellow or white. The flowers and plant habit are remarkably similar to *Nerine sarniensis*, a cut flower species native to South Africa which also exhibits summer dormancy. In some species, the stamens are extended far beyond the petals, resulting in another common name, spider flower. Bulbs should be planted about 6″ deep in the fall in full sun or partial shade and overplanted with annuals or low-growing perennials. Plants naturally hybridize and better retailers may offer interesting hybrids of *L. radiata*, as well as more difficult to find species. These are truly magnificent plants, and if cold hardiness is not a concern, stock up and be surprised.

*Lycoris squamigera*, autumn lycoris, is the most reliably cold hardy north of zone 6. Some of the hybrids offer cold hardiness into zone 6 as well, but much further north is a crapshoot. All species spread by bulb offsets and some do a good deal of traveling by seed. Divide and replant after flowering. Offsets flower in 1-2 years.

Quick Reference to Lycoris Species

| | Height (in.) | Flower color | Flowering time |
|---|---|---|---|
| *L. aurea* | 12-24 | Yellow | Summer |
| *L. radiata* | 12-18 | Red | Fall |
| *L. squamigera* | 18-24 | Pink | Late summer |

***-aurea*** (ore-ee′ a) Golden Lycoris 1-2′/2′
Summer Yellow, Gold China Zones 7-10

In the fall, bulbs produce ¾″ wide, glaucous, sword-shaped foliage, that dies back in late spring. The 3″ long funnel-shaped golden-yellow flowers appear on 18″ long scapes in summer. The stamens and style protrude slightly from the flower (exserted). Bulbs should be planted so the neck is just below the soil surface. Since flower buds are formed during winter and spring, beds must be well drained during those seasons or flowers will not develop.

***-radiata*** (raid-ee-ah′ ta) Short Tube Lycoris, Spider Lily 12-18″/12″
Fall Red China, Japan Zones 7-10

*L. radiata* has the shortest flower tube, thus the common name, and the smallest flower among the common garden species. The 1½-2″ long flowers, however, provide brilliant splashes of deep red in September and October. The long stamens look like spider legs and spider lily is an apt common name. A good deal of variability in flowering time occurs, including some early forms which flower as early as August. The leaves, which emerge in fall and persist through the winter, are only 4-6″ long and ¼″ wide making them much less of a nuisance than those of the other species. Unfortunately, flowers persist for less than two weeks. In the Armitage garden, these are like

*Lycoris radiata*
(64%)

dandelions, groups of blood-red flowers appear everywhere in the fall. We should all have such dandelions. Plant in full sun-fewer flowers occur in partial shade.

**Cultivars:**

var. *alba* has white flowers with yellow tinges at the base of the segments. It is pretty but cannot compare to the species.

var. *pumila* is a dwarf form of the species, growing only 6-9″ tall.

**-*squamigera*** (skwah-mi′ ge-ra) Autumn Lycoris 18-24″/24″
Late Summer Rose Pink Japan Zones 5-9

Autumn lycoris is the most common because of its greater growing range. Cold hardy to zone 5, the lovely rose pink flowers may be enjoyed by more gardeners. Approximately four to seven, 3″ long fragrant flowers appear on 2′ tall scapes in mid to late summer. Although the flowers are wonderful, the spring foliage is messy as it dies down. The 9-12″ long and 1″ wide leaves are fresh in the winter, but look terrible in late spring and summer. The size and density of the foliage make it difficult to interplant annuals. Bulbs spread rapidly and make wonderful gifts to neighbors. Divide every 4-5 years.

**Cultivars:**
var. *purpurea* bears lilac to purple flowers.

**Related Species:**
*L.* x *albiflora* (*L. radiata* x *L. traubii*) bears small white flowers and narrow leaves on 12-18″ stems. Bulbs are marginally hardy in zone 5b.

*L. sanguinea*, red heart lily, bears four to six, 2″ long orange-red flowers in August and September. The stamens are not as exserted as *L. radiata*. Plants are 12-20″ tall. Like many other species, this one has been neglected by gardeners. Plants are available and hardy to zone 6.

*L. sprengeri* is similar to *L. squamigera* except that the plants are not as tall. The rosy pink flowers appear in late summer. Not as cold tolerant as *L. squamigera*.

*L. straminea* produces straw-colored flowers in late summer to early fall. Plants are about 2′ tall.

*L. traubii* is named for Dr. H.P. Traub who worked on many bulbous plants in the 1950s and 1960s. Plants bear wonderful bright yellow flowers and may be hardy to zone 6.

## ***Lygodium*** (lie-goad-e′ um) Climbing Fern Schizaeaceae

To people new to gardening, a climbing fern seems to be a contradiction in terms. People normally think of ferns as green blobs that just sit there, not as vigorous clematis-like plants. Although climbing ferns are not well known, there are about 40 species around the world, most of which are native to the tropics. Only one or two species are sufficiently hardy to be grown outdoors

The easiest of these, in my opinion, is the Japanese climbing fern, *L. japonicum*. Its native habitat is immense, extending to Japan, India, China, Indonesia, Malaysia, New Guinea and Australia. Plants introduced to this country have escaped and are fairly common in southern and West Coast gardens. Plants, which multiply by the running rootstalk, are vigorous in zones 7 to 10 and growth can be rampant. The differences between the Japanese and the American species are fairly easy to distinguish; the airy sterile fronds of this one are pinnately lobed or compound, rather than palmate. In warm climates (like the Armitage garden), plants can spread spores everywhere and become a bit of a nuisance. For me, I welcome them, but they may be cut to the ground in the fall to reduce spore production.

Vigorous, handsome, but not as aggressive is our native Hartford fern, *L. palmatum,* reported from southern New Hampshire to eastern New York, Ohio, Kentucky and south to Florida. Two types of leaves (fronds) occur on well-grown plants. The sterile fronds are palm shaped, deeply lobed into 5 to 7 blunt segments. The fertile fronds are found only on the top of the branched vine, similar in shape but much smaller and more constricted. Most of the vine is evergreen, however, the fertile fronds are deciduous. Place in moist, partially shaded areas and acidic soil. They do not do well in basic soils or those where high levels of lime occur. As I see these plants in the gardens of my friends, I marvel at the light green airy appearance and the lushness of the rampant growth. Why is it then that I can hardly get these plants to grow at all? I can't even get them to grow through a 2′ tall azalea. I will keep trying.

Propagate by division and place daughter plants in different areas in the garden.

***Lysichiton*** (lie-sik′ i-ton) Skunk Cabbage Araceae

Do plants really smell like skunks? Do they look like cabbages? If you are able to visit a colony of these plants on a still day, your nose would start twitching and your eyes would dart about looking for white-striped creatures. The smell is not oppressive but it is there, particularly if you were told the common name ahead of time. Healthy plants don't look like iceberg lettuce but the large leaves could be construed as cabbage, I guess.

Only two species occur, both of which are aquatic plants living in shallow water in moderate climates. *L. americanum* is native to the Northwest while the other species (*L. camtschatcensis*) grows in northeast Asia. Both are stemless, have upright, bold light green leaves about 2-4′ long and 1-2′ wide. The margins of the leaves are usually wavy and they smell musky particularly if bruised. After flowering, leaves remain upright but ultimately appear wilted during the summer. In the spring, the flowers emerge from the base surrounded by a cloak (spathe) of yellow or white. Neither is particularly popular in gardens because they are aquatic, have a limited growing range and they colonize readily.

*L. americanum* is native to boggy areas from San Francisco to the Santa Cruz Mountains, north to Alaska and east to Montana in boggy areas. Plants are also quite at home in the Midwest and, my goodness, they are everywhere in the Northeast as a visit to the wetter areas in the Garden in the Woods in Framingham, Massachusetts will attest. The flowers consist of a greenish spadix surrounded by a bright yellow spathe that emerges before the leaves. The spathe color is the most easily distinguishable difference between the two species.

*L. camtschatcensis* bears flowers with a white spathe that are actually rather sweetly scented. Plants are also more compact in all parts than *L. americanum.* Regardless of the species, the cold hardiness range is about zone 5, warm to about zone 7, as long as consistent moisture is maintained. Slugs can certainly be a problem.

Of course, trust Dan Hinkley, owner of the original Heronswood Nursery in Washington, to cross the two species. The resultant hybrid has large creamy yellow flowers and is even more vigorous than either species, which is rather unbelievable. Zones 5-8.

***Lysimachia*** (lie-sim-ak′ ia) Loosestrife Primulaceae

*Lysimachia* was named in honor of King Lysimachus of Thrace. Thrace, as you recall, included present-day northern Bulgaria, northeastern Greece and parts of eastern Serbia and eastern Republic of Macedonia. After the Balkan wars at the beginning of the 20th century, Thrace was divided between Bulgaria, Greece and Turkey. Such historical geography helps to explain how the genus got its name, because it was believed that this plant was used to pacify angry oxen by "appeasing the strife and unrulinesse which falleth out among oxen at the plough, if it be put about their yokes". (Gerard's *Herbal*). The origin of the legend began with King Lysimachus who, as a last resort, waved a plant of *Lysimachia* before a pursuing, maddened beast, thus tranquilizing it, all having occurred in Thrace. Hmm, great story, don't know as I would want to try it. Loosestrife is a literal translation of the Greek word *Lysimachia*.

Approximately 150 species occur with opposite or whorled leaves and small rounded or bell-shaped flowers borne either singly or in narrow racemes. In general, plants establish easily in rich, moist soil and some species travel through the garden at the speed of light. Most loosestrifes thrive in the northern part of the United States and Canada but only a few make good garden plants for the South.

Quick Reference to Lysimachia Species

| | Height (in.) | Flower color | Habit |
|---|---|---|---|
| *L. ciliata* | 24-36 | Yellow | Upright |
| *L. clethroides* | 24-36 | White | Upright |
| *L. nummularia* | 4-8 | Yellow | Creeping |
| *L. punctata* | 12-24 | Yellow | Upright |

***-atropurpurea*** (at-ro-pur-pur′ ee-a) Purple Loosestrife 2-3′/2′
Summer Purple Southern Europe Zones 6-8

When I first saw this in a garden in Ireland, I had never seen it before in America. The green leaves are similar to those of gooseneck loosestrife but the flowers are deep purple and stand more upright. It does not appear to move around nearly as much as many of the others, but I had not seen enough plantings to be sure of its garden stability. Not nearly as aggressive as most other species. Many a gardener has fallen in "pot love" with the plant and been disappointed. May have to be treated as a tem-perennial, but that's not so bad, as long as you know ahead of time.

**Cultivars**:

'Beaujolais' has a nice name and may be the name under which most of these plants are marketed.

***-ciliata*** (cil-ee-ah′ ta) Fringed Loosestrife 2-3′/2′
Summer Yellow North America Zones 4-8

Plants are distributed throughout much of the United States and are one of the few native loosestrifes useful for the garden. Plants bear shiny green leaves about 4″ long and 2″ wide. The smooth leaves are usually opposite but sometimes occur in whorls of 4, and are distinctive by their hairy petioles and margins (ciliate). The yellow flowers often have a blotch of red at their base and are borne singly or in twos in the upper portion of the plant in summer. They grow best in moist conditions but tolerate drought better than most other species. They have a running root system and plants can appear out of nowhere, multiplying quickly to become a major nuisance. Plants do well in full sun but tolerate partial shade. More flowers are formed in the sun, but produce more foliage than flowers in the shade.

Propagate by division any time.

**Cultivars:**

'Firecracker' has chocolate brown foliage and yellow flowers and has superseded 'Purpurea'. To my eye, they are not a great deal different, except for the better name. Equally aggressive as the species, it is not a plant you want to put among your more delicate flora.

'Purpurea' is usually the only form found for sale. The foliage emerges deep purple and holds the color well, except in the hottest months, when it fades to muted green. The yellow flowers contrast well with the foliage. Similar aggressive growth habit.

***-clethroides*** (kleth-roi′ deez) Gooseneck Loosestrife 2-3′/3′
Late Summer White China, Japan Zones 3-8

This was one of my favorite plants when I lived in Montreal. The fine foliage and the handsome white, arching flower spikes were not only appreciated in the garden but could also be enjoyed inside as a cut flower. Growth was vigorous but its wandering nature was not difficult to control. In Michigan, although plants were still enjoyable, I found myself wondering how plants appeared in areas where I knew they had not been planted. In Georgia, this beautiful northern plant liked it so much that it began to explore every square inch of my garden and was seriously thinking about trying out the neighbor's. Unfortunately, the flower heads were smaller and the plants rather weedy, and it was relegated to a local plant sale. I now enjoy it in other peoples' gardens. This has all the possibilities of becoming the next kudzu of the land.

Numerous half-inch wide white flowers are held in a 12-18″ long, narrow, curved raceme which resembles a goose's neck, thus the common name. The inflorescence straightens as the fruits mature. The slightly pubescent, 3-6″ long leaves are opposite and narrowed at each end. Moist, but not waterlogged soils, and full sun result in optimum growth. Due to the roaming tendencies, sufficient room must be provided. A garage on one side and pavement all around might just help. Gooseneck loosestrife is grown commercially as a cut flower in northern Europe and the United States and has found its way into florist bouquets throughout the world. Provided with floral preservative, cut flowers persist for nearly a week.

Propagation is not difficult by division or seed.

**Cultivars:**

'Geisha' is less aggressive than the species, mainly because the variegated foliage is not as efficient in feeding the roots. The handsome foliage consists of green leaves with wavy yellow margins, above which the gooseneck white flowers appear in the summer. If you are frightened of the species, give this a try. It will still spread, but not nearly as rapidly.

***-nummularia*** (num-ew-lah′ ree-a) Creeping Jenny 4-8″/24″
Early Summer Yellow Europe Zones 3-9

This European native has become naturalized in the eastern United States and is often found at the edge of wooded areas. The fragrant 1″ diameter, bright yellow flowers are borne singly in the axils of the opposite, rounded 1″ long leaves. Plants are prostrate and each long stem produces roots along the length resulting in rapid multiplication. Plants multiply quickly and large patches of creeping Jenny appear in a single season where soil is moist. Plants are used as ground covers by streams, pools, or other moist areas. Plants are certainly aggressive but are so easy to remove that they are seldom thought of as invasive.

Propagate by division in spring or fall.

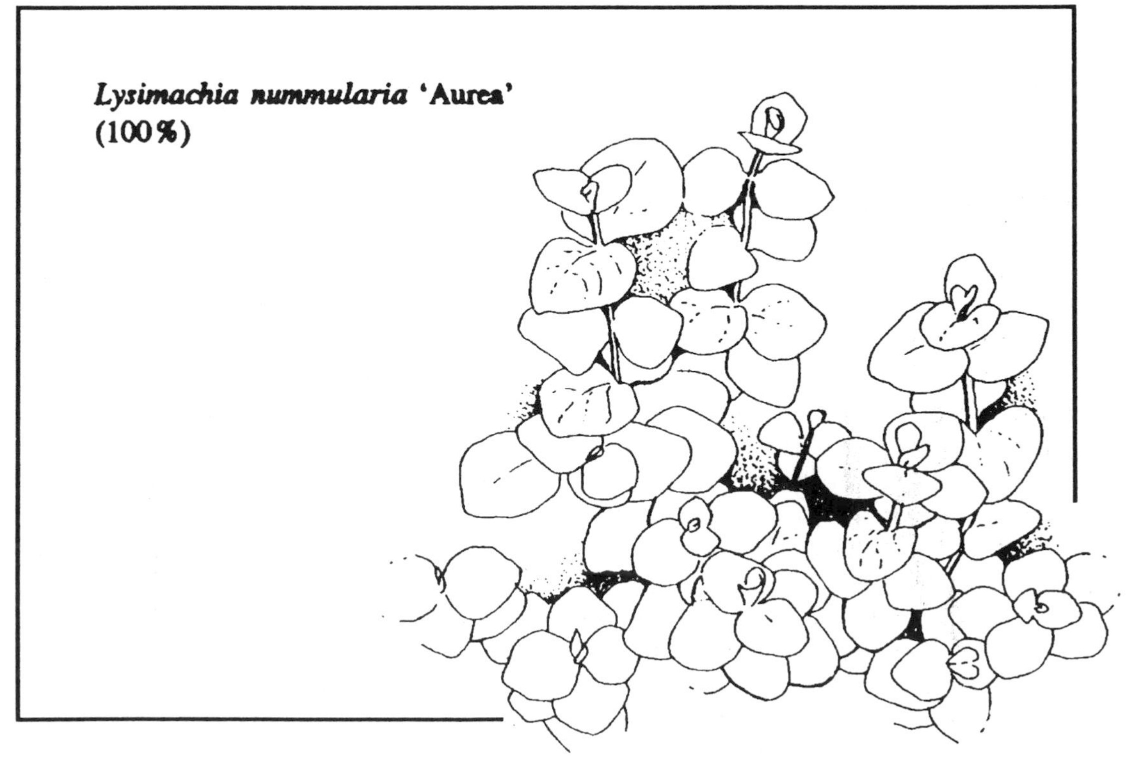

***Lysimachia nummularia* 'Aurea'**
**(100%)**

**Cultivars:**

'Aurea' is the most popular and with good reason. The lime green to yellowish leaves brighten up any shady area in which it is planted. The yellow flowers, however, are not as noticeable. In hot summers, the plant population shrinks but always return as cooler weather arrives.

***-punctata*** (punk-tah' ta) Yellow Loosestrife 1-3'/1'
Summer Yellow Europe, Western Asia Zones 4-8

This species has also found North America to its liking and is found growing in moist areas throughout the country. Particularly fond of damp, shady areas, the plant is often known as the "ditch-witch" of the countryside. The 1-3" long whorled leaves occur in groups of 3s or 4s. The ¾-1" wide flowers are also whorled and borne in the upper leaf axils from May to September. They are lemon-yellow with a small brownish circle in the throat. Plants are much better for zones 4 and 5 than for 7 and 8 where they become more weedy and the flowers lose their sparkle. This loosestrife can certainly be considered invasive, so be careful.

Propagate by cuttings or seed.

**Cultivars:**

'Alexander' has white and green variegated foliage and is handsome for the first year or two but seems to revert and decline after that.

Golden Alexander™ is a better plant, with yellow and green foliage, and similar yellow flowers. Once again, beautiful but (in my opinion) disappointing over time. Regardless, I would put them in my sunny garden if I found them at my local retailer.

**Related Species:**

*L. congestiflora*, dense-flowered loosestrife, forms dense mats of dark green stems and terminal ½-¾" wide yellow flowers. Native to China, it is cold hardy to about zone 7 if winter mulch is provided. Introduced originally by Dr. Don Jacobs of Eco-Gardens in Georgia, plants are presently offered by many nurseries. 'Eco Dark Satin' bears yellow flowers with a red throat and 'Outback Sunset' provides yellow flowers over variegated leaves. Hardy only to zone 8, perhaps 7b. Other newer cultivars with better cold hardiness (zone 6) appeared in the early 2000s. 'Persian Carpet' produces small-dark green leaves with handsome red venation. 'Persian Chocolate' produces darker foliage and is more aggressive. Both cultivars are excellent ground covers—aggressive but not invasive—and useful for difficult areas. They grow well in semi-shaded conditions and produce yellow flowers in late spring and early summer.

*L. ephemerum* produces narrow, branching 12-15" long spires of starry white flowers over several weeks. The opposite foliage is gray green, sessile, and joined at the base around the stem. The most important characteristic is the lack of invasiveness. This is a decent plant and deserves to be planted much more widely. I had high hopes for it in the Armitage garden, but heat and humidity don't seem to agree with it. Fair in Michigan, okay in New York, terrific in the Northwest. Hardy to zone 6 (perhaps 5) and well worth trying in the Northeast as well.

*L. fraseri*, a stoloniferous native to eastern North America, also produces yellow flowers in the axils of the 2′ tall plants. Plants have square stems and opposite leaves. Also known as *L. lanceolata* and *Steironema lanceolatum*. Try it in zones 5 to 8.

*L. japonica* is about 12″ tall with small yellow flowers and opposite foliage. The most interesting cultivar is the carpet-forming 'Minutissima'. Only 1-2″ tall, it is terrific between flagstones in walkways where it acts like grass and may be abused with abandon. The starry yellow flowers open in June and July. I saw some fantastic carpets in the garden of Margaret Grigg in Charlotte. Plants were everywhere, but unobtrusive when not in flower. Hardy in zones 5 to 8.

*L. vulgaris*, also known as yellow loosestrife, has similar growth habit and leaf arrangement as *L. punctata*, as well as flowers of the same color. The main difference is that most of the flowers of this species are borne at the end of the stem (terminal) whereas those of *L. punctata* are produced in the axils of the leaves along the stem. Both species are aggressive and love moist conditions.

## ***Lythrum*** (li′ thrum) Lythrum Lythraceae

*Lythrum* is one of those plants whose beauty enthralls those who don't know it well, but is an aggressive overbearing weed to those who do. The entire leaves are opposite and bear small pink or purple flowers on leafy spikelike racemes along the length of the four-angled flower stem. In general, moist soils are preferred but plants grow well in well-drained garden soils if not allowed to dry out.

Although native to Europe and Asia, plants have become naturalized in North America and have invaded the marshlands, highways and byways in the northern United States and Canada during the summer. Southern Ontario, upper New York State and the Northeast, among other places, are ablaze with this "weed" in July through September. Plants have escaped along marshes, lakes, along river margins, wet meadows, prairies, and ditches. One plant may produce 2.5 million seeds and according to the National Species Invasive Center (NSIC), it is estimated that over 400,000 acres of wetlands in the U.S. are lost annually through invasions of *L. salicaria*. They have been listed as noxious weeds in 27 states, and are illegal to sell there.

Some excellent breeding resulted in sterile cultivars, which seemed to be the answer to the wetland problem, allowing gardeners to plant loosestrife without guilt. If only the sterile cultivars are used, and they are nowhere near fertile plants, few seedlings will occur. However, research has shown that sterility occurs only when no plants of the wild species are in the neighborhood. When plants of 'Morden Pink' or 'Morden Gleam', two sterile cultivars, were planted near *L. salicaria*, the seed of the resulting hybrids was over 80% viable and germinated, thus contributing to the spread of purple loosestrife.

So, should plants even be listed in a garden book? The answer has to be no, even though gardeners in whose states plants are still sold may make a case for their use. However, in fairness to this plant and in the hope that the more education means more responsibility, here is a quick reference to telling the two main species apart. Most of the invading material is probably *L. salicaria*.

*Lythrum salicaria*
(100%)

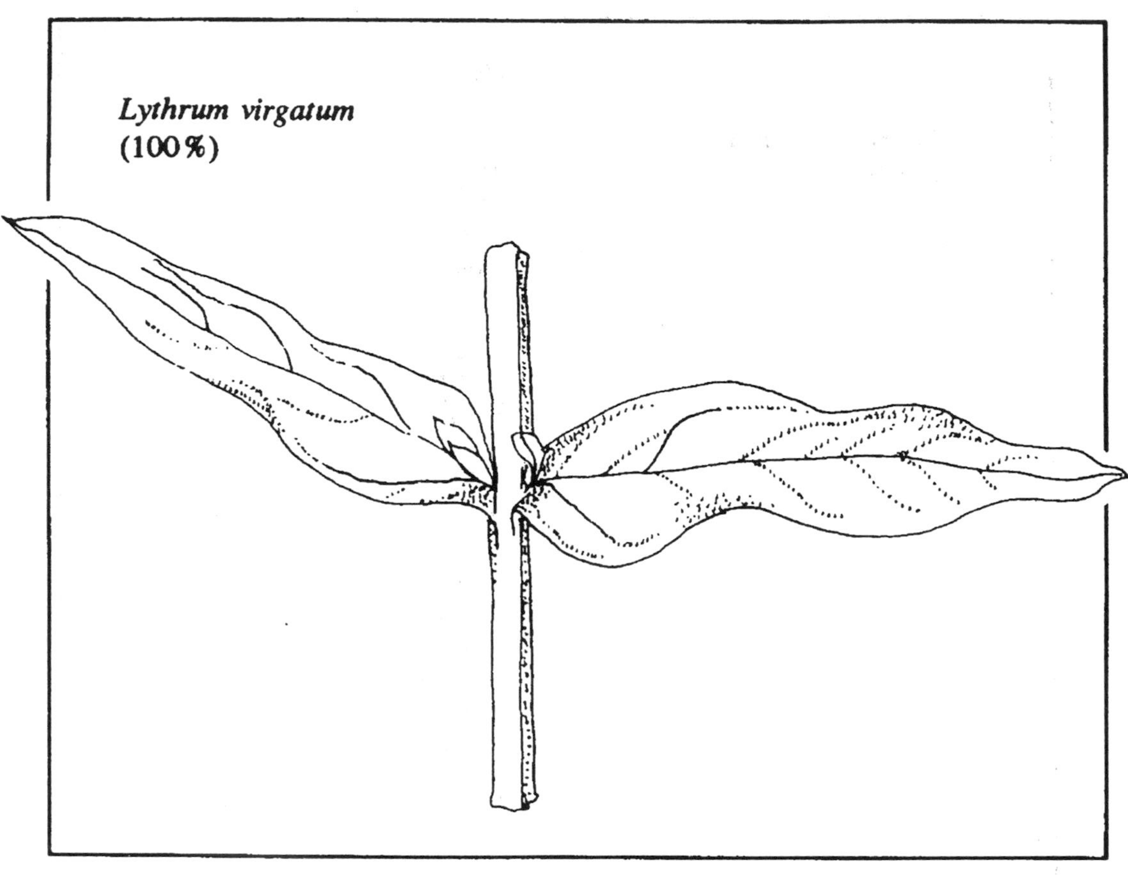


Quick Reference to Lythrum Species

| | Height (ft.) | Flowers distinctly stalked |
|---|---|---|
| *L. salicaria* | 3-5 | No |
| *L. virgatum* | 2-3 | Yes |

# M

**Macleaya** (ma-klay′ ya) Plume Poppy Papaveraceae

The genus consists of three species although hybridization has resulted in at least one intermediate form. Few people looking at the five- to eight-foot-tall plants would guess they are part of the poppy family. As poppyish as these may be, stay away from them unless you have a large area ready for poppy colonization. The main species in American gardens is *M. cordata*, although other species may occasionally surface.

***-cordata*** (kor-dah′ ta) Plume Poppy 6-10′/6′
Summer Cream China, Japan Zones 3-8

This most impressive plant towers 6-10′ in height and is topped by 10-12″ long plumes (panicles) of cream-colored flowers. Each flower is apetalous (no petals), has only two sepals, but bears 25-30 ornamental stamens. The 8″ wide heart-shaped leaves are pubescent beneath and consist of about seven lobes. As do many members of the poppy family, *Macleaya* bleeds yellow sap. Its stature relegates it to the back of the border or the middle of the island bed but it is also most impressive as a specimen plant where nothing detracts from the pleasant foliage. The gray-blue backs of the leaves are one of the most ornamental parts of the plant, and if poetry is your schtick, then you may wax poetic as you watch the young leaves fluttering in the wind. Plants are also used for cut foliage and flowers where bold, short-term celebrations are called for, although neither the flowers nor the foliage is particularly persistent in the vase.

Seldom is sufficient room provided and plants often outgrow their welcome. They spread aggressively which detracts from, rather than adds to, the beauty of the garden. Some gardeners claim with a straight face that one plant will cover one acre. Not quite, but many people who have planted this poppy are constantly trying to find unwary people to take divisions. The poetry you are waxing may wane as you watch plants colonize your peonies. To be fair, they are terrific if room is available and have often been used as a screen for trash pails or doghouses. As an alternative, they are reasonably well behaved in 3-5 gallon ornamental containers; this way they don't escape and the foliage can still be enjoyed.

Propagate by divisions in the spring or from seed. The small seed should be barely covered and placed in a warm (70-75°F), moist environment. Germination occurs within 2 weeks but is not particularly uniform.

**Cultivars:**

'Alba' has whiter flowers than the species.

'Flamingo' produces gray-green stems and small pink flowers.

'Kelway's Coral Plume' is almost as aggressive as the species but bears coral to pink flowers.

**Related Species:**

*M.* x *kewensis* is a hybrid between *M. cordata* and *M. microcarpa*. The terminal inflorescence has many lateral branches and consists of creamy white to buff flowers.

*M. microcarpa*, small fruited plume poppy, is similar in habit to *M. cordata* but bears bronze flowers consisting of 8-12 stamens. The nondescript flowers open in early summer and the fruit contains a single seed compared with the 4-6 seeded capsule of *M. cordata*. The roots are even more rhizomatous than *M. cordata*.

***Macrothelypteris*** (ma-kroh-the-lip′ ter-is) — Mariana Maiden Fern (syn. *Thelypteris torresiana*) — Thelypteridaceae

*M. torresiana* is the only one of about 9 species of these terrestrial ferns sufficiently hardy to be included in this book. Plants used to be part of the large genus known as *Thelypteris*, presently reduced to about 2 species. The *macro* part of the name refers to its size; this plant will grow 3-4′ tall and equally wide under suitable conditions. Plants grow from creeping rhizomes, allowing them to naturalize freely. The large pale green fronds are triply lobed or cut (tripinnatifid) and make a large airy display. They do have a rather musky, acrid odor when you get your nose up close and personal.

Ferns are hardy from zone 7 (7b) and south, enjoying bright light but requiring some afternoon shade and sufficient moisture to allow the rootstalks to run and run they may. They are, however, one of the more sun-tolerant ferns. Mulch well in the winter north of zone 7.

Propagate by division in the spring as new growth appears.

***Maianthemum*** (may-anth′ e-mum) — Mayflower, May Lily — Convallariaceae

The genus name comes from *maios*, the month of May, and *anthemon*, blossom, referring to its timely spring flowering. Unfortunately, just when everyone was getting comfortable with the May lilies, the genus increased dramatically with the infiltration of the former genus *Smilacina*, false Solomon's seal. In most recent floristic works, the genus *Maianthemum* has been limited to three species because of its flowers, whereas the remaining species, which bear 6-tepaled flowers more typical of the Liliaceae, were placed in the genus *Smilacina*. In 1986, J. V. LaFrankie placed all the species in a single genus, and over time, the change has slowly been incorporated into the literature. However, until taxonomists and horticulturists agree on the changes, I have elected to keep *Smilacina* separate in this book, but the plants you have forever known as *Smilacina* may now be listed under this genus.

For our purposes, *Maianthemum* consists of three species of carpet-like ground covers, one of which, *M. canadense*, Canada mayflower, is found all over the woodlands of much of North America. Plants are native as far west as British Columbia, east to Delaware and south to the Appalachian mountains of north Georgia.

In general, stands of *M. canadense* stand 3-6″ tall and produce creeping rhizomes that can clothe a shady woodland area in handsome foliage and fruit. A single leaf is produced from the underground stem that essentially disappears as the flowering stem appears. The flowering stem bears two lily-of-the-valley-like leaves, each about 3″ long followed by small white flowers, consisting of two sepals and two petals in the spring. The flowers give way to reddish berries with darker speckles. On one of our student field trips to Cape Cod, we came across what seemed like acres of mayflowers in the Heritage Plantation in Sandwich, Massachusetts. Such a small plant, such a marvelous sight! The further north, the better the plants perform and multiply. They do poorly in the South; save your money.

Purchase plants by the dozens when available, one plant does little. Moist shade in coniferous woods is excellent; deciduous woods also work but the large leaves of some oaks and maples may smother the plants. They may be easily propagated by division in the spring.

**Related Species:**

*M. dilatatum*, false lily of the valley, is a Western native which spreads by rhizomes, similar to *M. canadense* in the East. White flowers form in the spring in the axils of the shiny green leaves. Later, light green with brown mottling pea-sized berries are formed which eventually turn red in the fall. Plants are native from Alaska, the Yukon and British Columbia, and south to Washington and Oregon. Plants also are found in Russia, thus the other name, *M. kamtschaticum*.

## *Malva* (mal′ va) — Mallow — Malvaceae

Closely related to *Hibiscus* and *Alcea*, plants are equally beautiful in flower, and equally subject to attack by a host of insects and diseases. The leaves are usually lobed or dissected and the flowers, with five notched petals, are carried singly or in clusters. Many similarities occur between various genera in the family; a useful key to their differences may be found under *Alcea*, the hollyhocks. Approximately 30 species of annual, biennial and perennial species occur and all are relatively easy to grow, insects and other assorted bugs not withstanding. Two or three are particularly useful for the garden.

### -*alcea* (al-see′ a) — Hollyhock Mallow — 2-3′/18″

Summer — Rose, White — Europe — Zones 4-7

The deeply 5-parted light green leaves contrast with the 2″ deep rose to white flowers that appear in the axils. Flowering begins in early summer and continues for 6-8 weeks. The flowers are produced singly in the leaf axils near the top of the plants. The small, triangular sepals are beneath the pale red to whitish petals. All mallows enjoy full sun, well-drained soils and moderate to high pH. Garden performance is superior in the North compared to the South where spider mites, thrips, Japanese beetles, and a potpourri of foliar diseases find the plants particularly appealing.

Propagate by seed, terminal cutting in spring, or division. Seeds are available with excellent germination.

**Cultivars:**

'Fastigiata' has essentially superceded the species and is offered by most perennial specialists. Plants are upright, well branched and carry 2″ diameter pink to rose-pink flowers.

**Related Species:**

*M. moschata*, musk mallow, grows to 3′ tall and is naturalized in the northeastern United States and eastern Canada. On a recent trip to the eastern Townships in southern Quebec, it was in every garden on every road. Combined with orange daylilies and 'Annabelle' hydrangeas, those gardens were colorful. The leaves differ from the former species by being 5-parted with each part additionally 1-2 parted. Although the showy rose-colored flowers are up to 2½″ wide, garden performance is fair at best in the South, much better in zones 3-5. Plants are summer hardy to zone 8 but perform consistently well only in zones 3-5. 'Alba' has deeply cut leaves and white flowers. 'Appleblossom' has soft pink flowers on 2-2½′ tall stems. 'Rosea' bears pink flowers. Propagate from seed.

| | | | |
|---|---|---|---|
| -***sylvestris*** (sil-ves′ tris) | | Wood Mallow, Tree Mallow | 1-3′/2′ |
| Late Spring | Mauve | Europe, North Africa | Zones 6-8 |

This short-lived plant (sometimes grown as a biennial) resembles other species but has shallowly 5-7 lobed, rough, hairy leaves. The petals of the large mauve flowers are three times the length of the sepals. The flowers of some forms often have dark stripes resulting in bicolors. They occur singly or in 2-5 flowered clusters in the upper leaf axils.

Plants perform well in full sun or partial shade and well-drained soils. Easily propagated from seed in the spring.

**Cultivars:**

'Alba' grows about 2′ tall with clean white flowers.

'Brave Heart' bears large pale rose-pink flowers with a distinctive dark purple eye on upright 3′ tall plants.

'Cottenham Blue' flowers earlier than others, with pale blue flowers and darker veins on 2-3′ tall upright plants.

'Mauritiana' is taller, smoother and has more obtuse lobes. The dark rosy red flowers have dark purple stripes. This is probably a subspecies of *M. sylvestris*.

'Mystic Merlin' is variable in its flower color, starting as dark lavender and fading almost to pink.

'Primley Blue' is the best known blue-flowered cultivar. Plants are much more prostrate, usually growing only about 18-24″ tall. The flowers are a soft blue with darker veins.

'Zebrina', also known as *Alcea zebrina* and *Malva zebrina*, is 2-3′ tall with white to very pale pink flowers striped with raspberry-red veins. The flowers look like pinwheels all summer. While said to be hardy as far north as zone 5, they are persnickety in the cold as well as the heat. People love it, but it is sometimes better to think of it as an annual. Easy to propagate from seed.

***Malvaviscus*** (mal-va-vis′ kus) Sleeping Hibiscus Malvaceae

Fascinating shrubby plants from Mexico and South America, they draw crowds because of their swirling 1-2″ vibrant scarlet flowers that never fully open (thus the common name). The petals twist about the extended stamens, appearing to squeeze them tighter and tighter. The plants are big, growing grow 3-5′ tall, and bear hairy unlobed or somewhat 3-lobed leaves. The only species which is sufficiently cold hardy to be called a perennial is *M. arboreus*, also known as wax mallow and turk's cap. They are hardy to zone 7b, perhaps all of zone 7, and are certainly worth a try, even if they grow only as an annual.

The variety most offered is var. *drummondii* (also known as *M. drummondii*), with leaves almost as long as they are broad, bearing prominent hairs on the top surface of the leaves. The flowers are similar to the species. This is a plant for the more daring gardeners who want to try something "otherworldly". Plant in well-drained soil in protected areas, and among other sturdy plants so they can lean on them for support. Flowers occur on new wood and only in the fall. Plants may be cut back hard in the spring when signs of life reappear. Spider mites and Japanese beetles may visit in the summer.

Propagate by softwood cuttings or seed.

**Cultivars:**

'Pink' is a little-seen variant of *M. arboreus*. Equally handsome.

***Matteuccia*** (ma-too′ see-a) Ostrich Fern Dryopteridaceae

Although about four species occur, *M. struthiopteris* (*M. pennsylvanica*), the ostrich fern, is one of the best, biggest and most popular terrestrial ferns today. The tall, erect, gracefully arching plant grows in tufts of ostrich-plume-shaped dark green fronds. Both vegetative and fertile fronds occur, the vegetative ones emerging from the base and spreading out at the tip, like a big shuttlecock. The fronds can be up to 4′ long and 12″ wide, each one cut into 40 or so pairs of leaflets. Each leaflet is cut into about 30 pairs of subleaflets or lobes. The stiff fertile leaves arise from the base, consist of small leaflets divided to the midrib, and grow about 2′ tall. They begin green after the first flush of vegetative fronds, then turn brown with the many spore cases. The vegetative fronds wither with the first frost but the fertile ones remain "everbrown" throughout the winter. By the end of the season, the fronds become a little ragged and can be trimmed back. Plants spread by underground rhizomes, rapidly forming colonies in damp areas. They can become invasive.

Having written such a mundane description, I can say that this is simply one of the most classic of the ferns and excellent where a bold grouping is needed. Moisture is essential, and plants tolerate a good deal of sun. Plants do well in the North, but in the heat and humidity of the South (zone 7 and south) are marginal, never attaining the majesty of growth where summers are cool. In my garden in Athens (zone 7b), they struggle and are wimpy, yet in other gardens here in Athens, they are almost like weeds. How can that be? Well, here is the rub.

Apparently two separate populations have been identified, the European form, *M. s.* var. *struthiopteris,* and the American form, *M. s.* var *pennsylvanica*. The American form differs only slightly, by having scales the same color, opposed to the bicolored scales of the European variety. The fronds of the European form are lighter green and a little smaller, and the stalk of each frond is darker in the European form as well. In the North, it does not matter which form you use, they will both do well. In the South, find a gardener who is growing these successfully, and see if she will allow you to have some. This will undoubtedly be the American variety.

Some taxonomists still treat *M. struthiopteris* and *M. pennsylvanica* as separate species, the former being the European ostrich fern, the latter known as the American ostrich fern. The differences, other than native habitat, are that the fronds of the European form are lighter green and are a little smaller. Today, the two forms are lumped together by most taxonomists.

## *Mazus* (may′ zus) Mazus Scrophulariaceae

For some reason, this charming ground cover is not well known. About 30 species have been described, each with creeping stems, and many white to purple-blue flowers in the spring. The basal leaves are rosetted or opposite, the stem leaves are alternate, toothed or incised. The most cold-hardy and most useful species is *M. reptans*, native to the Himalayas. Hardy to zone 6 (perhaps 5), plants are terrific for planting among stones and in rock gardens or pathways. The small 2-lipped flowers occur in late spring and are held in few-flowered racemes. Generally, flowers are lavender-blue, but 'Alba' is probably more available and the flowers stand out well on the 2-3″ tall plants. I like these plants growing in and around my flagstone walk in the garden. Not quite as tough as turf, but you don't have to get the Lawn-Boy out either.

Some plantspeople offer *M. japonicus* from eastern Asia, in particular the white form 'Albiflorus'. Plants are about 2-4″ tall, and covered with white flowers. Some reports suggest that plants are far less cold hardy than the *M. reptans*. Since there appears to be so little difference between the two, go with the *M. reptans*.

Plants tolerate full sun or partial shade; in the South, some afternoon shade is appreciated. Consistent moisture is necessary but wet feet are a no-no. Easy to propagate by division any time in the season. Cuttings may also be used.

**Related Species:**

*M. radicans* is native to New Zealand and produces a very dense, low-growing ground cover with deep green foliage and small white flowers. It is beautiful in a pot, in a container and between stones, however, its cold hardiness is very much in dispute. Some nurseries have it listed to zone 4, my guess is closer to zone 8.

***Meconopsis*** (me-ko-nop′ sis) Himalayan Blue Poppy Papaveraceae

More than any other plant mentioned among gardeners or shown in slides on someone's talk, the Himalayan blue poppy elicits classic garden emotions of beauty, grandeur, awe and most of all, frustration and failure. The first encounter with the blue poppies, usually somewhere in the British Isles, leaves people breathless and always asking, "Where do I get them?". They seem so easy and carefree in such gardens, reseeding and hybridizing everywhere that we all feel that they should do well in our own gardens. Not a chance! Except for small pockets of MecFriendly climates on the West Coast, protected areas along the St. Lawrence River in Quebec, and here and there where summers are cool, winters are mild or the ground is consistently insulated with snow, these plants should not be used. For North American gardeners who do well with this genus, congratulations, I'll be over soon. However . . .

. . . I don't mean to rain on anyone's parade but let's get real concerning promotions of these plants. They die, usually within one year, but they may struggle through a couple of years. They won't look like the photo, which is probably why you bought the plants in the first place. There are not many plants like this in garden catalogs but promoting *Meconopsis* as a "new crop for everyone" really gets my goat; it is simply not true. A number of years ago, a respectable mail order nursery used a photo of blue poppies on their cover! They sold a lot of poppies but disappointed a lot of people.

Regardless of what I say, people want to know about these plants and a number of beautiful species and hybrids do exist. The best known are the blue forms, such as *M. betonicifolia* and *M. x sheldonii*, however red (*M. napaulensis*), yellow (*M. paniculata, M. regia*) and white species and forms also exist. *M. dhwojii* has interesting blue green, mostly basal, pinnately compound leaves. Light yellow flowers are produced on this plump 2′ tall plant, after which the plants die. All species are native to the Himalayas except the crepe-like Welsh poppy (*M. cambrica*).

The Welsh poppy is native to western Europe, including the British Isles, and produces yellow to orange flowers which look at first glance very much like California or Iceland poppies. They reseed everywhere in their native habits, springing up in sunny fields or at the base of shady walls. They are common in the Northwest, where deadheading is recommended to reduce their reseeding tendencies. The bright green hairy foliage contrasts well with the 2″ wide whimsical flowers. Double forms ('Floropleno'), deep orange ('Aurantiaca') and named cultivars such as 'Frances Perry', with scarlet flowers, may occasionally be found. This is the one species that we should be experimenting with a great deal more. In the Southeast, it might be able to be planted with the fall pansies, in the North, as a summer annual. *M. villosa*, native to Nepal, has a similar habit and flower.

The best-known blue form is the common Himalayan blue poppy, *M. betonicifolia*, which naturally grows in alpine meadows at altitudes of 9000-12,000 ft. Plants are short lived and occasionally monocarpic, meaning that they produce their 4-6 flowers in summer, then make seeds and die. *M. grandis* is similar but differs in the shape of the bottom leaves, which are tapered into a narrow stalk at the base, compared to the cordate bases of the lower leaves of *M. betonicifolia*. They are generally longer lived. The hybrid between these two species, *M.* x *sheldonii*, was raised in 1937 in Oxford, England and is sterile. A number of named cultivars have since been developed. I think of many fine United Kingdom gardens when I think about the blue poppies, but some of the finest blue poppy scenes are found in Mt. Stewart in Northern Ireland and Branklyn Gardens in Scotland. The cultivar 'Branklyn' was raised there and has a hint of mauve in the flowers. 'Slieve Donard,' raised by the famous Northern Irish nursery of the same name, has longer, more pointed petals than the original cross. They are also exceptionally beautiful in the Jardins de Metis in the Gaspe in Quebec. A must-visit garden, and a whole lot closer than Branklyn.

After all is said and done, it would be a shame never to see such marvelous plants. Since traveling to European gardens is not a realistic choice for many of us, visit a few Northwestern gardens or Canadian gardens or go to a garden talk where the speaker tells you how easy these plants are to grow. One characteristic of gardeners is to never say never. Purchase some seeds or a few plants for the challenge; the worst that will happen is they won't live and who knows, they may surprise us all.

## ***Melianthus*** (me-lee-anth′ us) Honey Flower Melianthaceae

The genus consists of about 6 species of shrubs from the lowlands of South Africa to the higher elevations of the Transvaal. The best known is honey flower, *M. major*, which looks like a large blue-green fern when young. The alternate leaves are about 1′ long, divided into 9-11 toothed leaflets. Soft to the feel and a terrific hue, these leaves are highly sought after by the discerning gardener. This handsome foliage also smells. Rubbing part of a leaf under your nose evokes fragrances of peanut butter, or as a couple of my Jewish friends exclaimed, "It smells just like halva." Wayne Winterrowd and Joe Eck used it to perfection in containers and throughout their North Hill garden in Readsboro, Vermont, knowing full well it would not overwinter. I have viewed these plants often in my travels and they generally looked good when they were about 2′ tall. However, where they perennialize, they can get quite lanky. I have also seen these as 6-8′ tall woody monsters, whose charm and usefulness disappeared at foot three.

Unfortunately, it is one of the least cold hardy members of the genus, not tolerating most winter climates well at all (perhaps hardy to zone 7 or 8). It looks great in Victoria, but in the Armitage garden, plants stayed about 2′ tall, struggled in the wet summer and perked up in the fall and winter. I lost them during the late winter, due as much to the moisture as the temperature. The foliage is so handsome that I ordered it again, and with better drainage it looked good. Then it died the next year. I think I have emerged from my *Melianthus* stage of life, but I still enjoy it where it does well. The reddish brown flowers occur in axillary and terminal racemes and are quite spectacular, if not terribly handsome.

This genus is certainly worth trying to push the garden envelope a little further. Full sun to partial shade and a location with well-drained soils protected from drying winds are recommended.

**Cultivars:**

'Antonov's Blue' has even bluer leaves than the species. Plants are 5-6′ tall when in flower.

'Purple Haze' has a more purple tinge on the bluish foliage. It is also noteworthy because it is relatively dwarf, maturing to only about 3′ tall.

**Related Species:**

*M. cosmosus* has dark green foliage which is much more dissected than *M. major*. Plants may be a little more cold hardy.

*M. pectinatus* is shorter and less robust but also has finely cut green foliage.

## *Mertensia* (mer-ten′ see-a) Bluebells Boraginaceae

Plants from this genus include those from high elevations as well as those from lowland areas. Many of the 40-45 species are native, including the outstanding blue-clustered flowers of Rocky Mountain bluebells, *M. alpina*, the western *M. lanceolata*, better known as languid ladies, the tall northern *M. paniculata*, and the best-known eastern member, Virginia bluebells, *M. virginica*. Other lesser-known and occasionally available members are native to Asia such as *M. sibirica* and the magnificent blue-leaved *M. asiatica*. All have alternate leaves with blue to pink flowers that unfold in a one-sided inflorescence.

***-asiatica*** (ayes-ee-at′ i-ca) Blue Leaf Bluebells 6-12″/15″
Spring Blue Japan Zones 4-7
(syn. *M. simplicissima*)

Here is a plant with a number of fine qualities but one serious flaw for most American gardens. It is unique in that a tight rosette of blue leaves forms that is unlike any other bluebell normally seen. The flowering stems extend from the rosette but plants remain prostrate, bearing blue flowers in the axils from spring to early summer. The flowers are not as visible against the leaves as in other species, so the foliage has to look good for the plant to look good. However, usually they don't. Therein lies the flaw; this is a difficult plant to gush over when half the leaves are turning yellow and the flowers are fair at best. I love the foliage of this plant in early spring, but other than in the Northwest, I have not seen too many outstanding specimens as the season wears on. However, don't listen to my complaints; they are certainly worth a try for the foliage alone.

Plants need excellent drainage; a rocky area is best and plants should be protected from desiccating winds.

***-virginica*** (vir-jin′ i-ka) Virginia Bluebells 1-2′/1′
Spring Lavender-Blue Eastern United States Zones 3-8

I have noticed many species of *Mertensia* now available through mail order catalogs, and that is terrific news for all of us. However, few plants are easier and less pretentious for most gardeners than Virginia bluebells, which provide so much pleasure

*Mertensia virginica*
(92%)

that they should be part of all spring gardens. I look forward with anticipation to its appearance in my garden every March and April.

From the moment the blue-green, mouse ear-shaped leaves break the soil in the spring until they disappear in summer, plants provide great pleasure. Nearly all members of this family have coarse hairy foliage, but Virginia bluebells produce 4″ long, 3-4″ wide leaves that are as smooth as a baby's bottom. Clusters of 5-20, one-inch tubular flowers are borne in nodding racemes at the end of the stems. The buds and young flowers are pink, but turn a lavender-blue as they mature. The leaves yellow as summer progresses, and completely disappear by midsummer in most parts of the country. This creates a problem if planted in large numbers or in a prominent place, however, annuals may be used to advantage to cover the empty spaces or they may be planted in shady areas where their absence will be less conspicuous. A handsome combination occurs when yellow wood poppies, *Stylophorun diphyllum*, are interplanted. The color combination is excellent and the wood poppies cover the bare ground left by the bluebells. Moist areas and partial shade are necessary, particularly in zones 6-8. Plantings should not be disturbed and given time, will slowly colonize the area.

Propagate by fresh seed, or by spring division when colonies are sufficiently large.

**Cultivars:**

'Alba' has white flowers but is not as vigorous as the species.

'Rubra' has pink flowers but is no great improvement on the species.

**Related Species:**

*M. maritima*, oyster plant, is somewhat similar to *M. asiatica* in that the foliage is blue-green. I would like to see this native plant (Montana to northern California) offered as a possible replacement for *M. asiatica*. Plants are more upright and if they could be propagated could be quite useful. Likely hardy to zone 4 or 5. Many taxonomists have merged the two species, referring to the latter as *M. maritima* subsp. *asiatica*.

*M. paniculata* is native from central and western Canada to central Idaho and western Montana. The plants are 2-4′ tall but bear flowers similar to Virginia bluebells. They do not go dormant unless under heavy stress.

*M. siberica*, Siberian bluebells, is also a lovely garden plant. Plants grow to 18″ tall, are fuller and less coarse in appearance than *M. virginica*. The foliage does not go dormant in the summer. Why it is so difficult to find remains a mystery. More plants must be grown in North America to provide additional information on garden tolerance.

## *Miscanthus* (mis-kanth' us) Eulalia Grass Poaceae

Of all the changes that have occurred in American gardening in the last 20 years, one of the most significant and persistent was the embracing of ornamental grasses in landscapes and gardens. Many people saw the beauty of native grasses, but like goldenrod, the natives could never get past the bias in peoples' minds. The acceptance of native and "wild" landscapes brought many grasses into the mainstream of the gardening public, and their low maintenance needs and classic forms found many converts. But it was the efforts of Wolfgang Oehme, James van Sweden and Kurt Bluemel, who introduced many American gardeners to the beauty of ornamental grasses and rocketed this concept forward. *Miscanthus* was their cornerstone.

This group of Chinese and Japanese plants include species and cultivars ranging from 3 feet to 12 feet tall. They are grown for their low-maintenance, handsome and sometimes quite colorful foliage. Their late summer and fall flowers also provide additional architectural interest throughout the winter, often equal to their summer charm. About three species are offered in American nurseries but by far, the most popular are the many selections of common eulalia grass, *M. sinensis*. New cultivars continue to be added to enhance the habit, provide more colorful foliage and to create even better flowers.

Recently, seedlings have been showing up where they are not supposed to be, having reseeded from domesticated garden plants. A number of states in the Northeast, Northwest and the Carolinas are considering putting the entire genus on their invasive plant list. This may be a serious problem in the future if sterile cultivars are not more rapidly developed.

Quick Reference to Miscanthus Species

| | Height (ft.) | Evergreen |
|---|---|---|
| *M.* x *giganteus* | 10-12 | No |
| *M. sinensis* | 3-8 | No |
| *M. transmorrisonensis* | 3-4 | Yes |

**-x *giganteus*** (flor-id-ewe′ lus) Giant Eulalia Grass 10-12′/4′
Fall Silver Asia Zones 5-9

The name of this plant is in limbo, it has long been recognized as *M. floridulus*, then *M. f.* 'Giganteus', and *M. giganteus*. I believe the taxonomists have split the difference and given it this hybrid designation. At the State Botanical Garden in Athens, I teach my students the difference between this species and the common *M. sinensis*. It is not hard, all one has to do is look at them side by side. The plants are similar, however, the mature size of this 10-14′ behemoth and the tall silvery plumes give it away. These robust plants produce stems that can measure up to two inches in diameter. They are big enough to be used as hedging or screen, strong enough to be a good windbreak and tolerant of salt spray. If it is so good, why don't we see more of them? Plants are generally too tall for most gardens and the green foliage, although dramatic, is not as sexy as newer cultivars of *M. sinensis*. The bottom leaves also have a tendency to fall off by late summer, leaving a rather bare bottom. However, flowers of the hybrid are sterile, a big plus for people confused about which miscanthus cultivars will reseed and which will not.

In August and September, the flowers start out as reddish-tan buds which give way to the big silvery plumes well above the foliage. Fall brings a reddish hue to the clumps. They must be planted in fertile, moist soil in full sun. Some morning shade is fine, however, the more shade, the more chance of toppling.

Propagate by seed or by chainsaw. This is not a plant one divides with a shovel.

**Cultivars:**

'Gilded Tower' is a 2007 introduction that claims the same super growth but with green and yellow striped leaves.

***-sinensis*** (si-nen′ sis) Common Eulalia Grass 3-7′/3′
Fall Silvery Asia Zones 6-9

The explosion in the use of ornamental grasses can be directly traced to the use of this grass by forward-looking architects and landscape planners, followed by the introduction of a continuous stream of new varieties. The attributes of eulalia grass are obvious in the sunny landscape; they may be used as specimen plantings and provide colorful foliage in the spring and summer. However, probably the most valuable feature is their winter habit; the clumps remain "evertan" and the flowers stay fresh looking all winter, providing something other than snow and slush to look at during the cold season.

All plants require plenty of space to be at their best, sun is necessary, although they tolerate more shade than most people admit. Rust on the leaves can be a problem, particularly in densely planted populations. They tolerate drought but irrigation is useful for best growth. Although the main selling point is the foliage, the flowers are also terrific in arrangements and are particularly pretty with coneflowers and fall salvias. The species and a few cultivars ('Gracillimus', 'Variegatus', 'Zebrinus') have been available for many years but many selections that improve the habit or flowering have recently been introduced. A variety of miscanthus, var. *condensatus* (at one time a cultivar, 'Condensatus') has much denser, larger flowers than the type and broader foliage. Flowers have a purplish tint.

**Cultivars:**

*Habit (Green foliage)*:

'Adagio' is a terrific plant because of its compact habit (only about 3′ tall) with narrow leaves and pinkish plumes which later turn white. A heavy seeder, not recommended for southern gardens.

'Andante' grows up to 7′ in height and has wonderful weeping green leaves with an obvious white stripe in the center.

'Arabesque' also has narrow foliage and is a good choice for smaller gardens. Plants are 2-3′ tall with salmon to white flowers.

'Goliath' wears its name well. A vigorous grower, up to 9′ in height, with early, very large flowers. Big and robust for the full-figured garden.

'Gracillimus' is one of the older selections, with narrow green foliage and silvery flowers. The leaves of mature specimens are less than a half-inch across. A terrific specimen plant, however, they tend to be floppy after a few years in the garden. Many of the newer "gracillimus-type" selections ('Arabesque', 'Morning Light') are improvements.

'Little Kitten' is only about 2′ tall. Cute, but hardly impressive.

'Silver Spider' is an elegant plant with narrow leaves and wide open flower heads. I first saw this in its full glory at Bluemont Nursery in Maryland, and I had to have some. They grace the Armitage garden and the University Horticulture Garden with equal aplomb.

'Yaku Jima' is a handsome, compact, fine-textured form of miscanthus. Plants grow 3-4′ tall and while they are not small, are useful for smaller gardens. Older and only slightly different than 'Nippon'. Another heavy seeder, not recommended for southern gardens.

*Variegated or Striped Foliage*:

'Cabaret' is fast becoming one of the more popular selections, although it has been difficult to find in the past. The wide green leaves bear a clean white band down the middle making this an excellent non-floppy variegated form. This is likely a cultivar of var. *condensatus*.

'Cosmopolitan' is another wide-leaved, wide white-banded selection similar in habit to 'Cabaret'. Also likely a cultivar of var. *condensatus*. A sport with silver bands rather than white, it has been called 'Cosmo Revert' by Heronswood Nursery.

'Gold Band', introduced by Terra Nova Nursery, stands only about 2′ tall without flowers and bears upright banded foliage.

'Golden Feather' has green leaves with gold margins. Slow growing and 3-5′ tall.

'Morning Light' is a variegated variety of *M. sinensis* 'Gracillimus' and is botanically known as 'Gracillimus Variegatus'. The much improved horticulture name 'Morning Light' was penned by Kurt Bluemel. Vertical bands of white run along the narrow leaf margins, making them look even more narrow. This compact grower (4-5′ tall) has handsome flowers which emerge reddish, then age to a soft tan. This has emerged from the pack as one of the most popular cultivars.

'Mysterious Maiden' has the narrow leaves of 'Gracillimus' and the gold banding of 'Zebrinus'. The vase-shaped habit is handsome; plants grow at least 5′ tall.

'Rigoletto' is a dwarf form of variegated miscanthus grass. Shorter and more upright than 'Variegatus'. Arose from Bluemel Nursery in Maryland.

'Sarabande' is becoming the narrow-leafed grass of choice in many landscapes. The fine texture, the silver plumes and the upright, non-floppy habit are great improvements.

'Silver Arrow' is a variegated type with more upright growth and a pink tint to the plumes.

'Variegatus' is one of the granddaddies of the group, with wonderful variegated foliage, which can be seen across a football field. Its drawback is that it is big and tends to flop over later in the season. Plants are being replaced by more narrow-leaved variegated forms like 'Rigoletto' and 'Morning Light'. In the Armitage garden, it is colorful and shade tolerant.

*Leaves Banded*:

'Little Nicky', aka 'Hinjo' is about 2-3′ tall with yellow bands.

'Little Zebra' is a compact form, about 3′ tall, with yellow bands and reddish flowers in the fall.

'Little Dot' is a "zebrinus-type" of grass but more compact and low growing (3′ tall) with gold bands across each leaf.

'Strictus' has been the "zebrinus-type" choice in recent years because the stripes are more visual and the plants are more upright with little tendency to fall over. The smaller and more compact habit have made it highly sought after in smaller gardens.

'Tiger Cub' is another more recent, small, compact "zebrinus-type" that has been well received in the UK but has not made its way over here (at least not under that name). The stripes show up early in the growing season and remain until frost.

'Zebrinus' is another of the founders of the miscanthus club. The horizontal yellow to golden leaf stripes made it a favorite but it is big and floppy. It is now giving way to the many new sturdier and more dwarf "zebrinus-type" selections.

*Flowers*:

'Malepartus' differs by having more bronze-green foliage and large feathery pink-purple plumes when they first appear, turning silver at maturity. Plants are 6-7′ tall.

'November Sunset' is a robust late-flowering form with large silver plumes. Plants are 6-8′ tall with copper-tan color in the winter.

'Rotsilber' bears almost red flowers in the fall over silvery green foliage. The flowers fade to the normal silver-tan as winter sets in.

'Silver Feather' is a selection with a relatively wide separation between the foliage and the flowers. Numerous, very large silver flowers separate it from the species.

*Fall Color*:

'Autumn Light' is hardy to zone 5 and produces silver plumes in early to mid September.

'Graziella' is also a "gracillimus-type" with narrow foliage but with large silvery plumes held well above the leaves. The foliage turns burgundy to bronze in the fall.

'Purpurescens' is one of the more colorful selections. The foliage starts to turn red in the summer, changing to deep purple-red as the weather gets colder. My kind of grass, colorful foliage, good flowers and compact grower. This is fabulous at the Chicago Botanic Garden.

'Nippon' is a relatively recent selection with compact (3-4′ tall) narrow leaves and good red-bronze fall and winter color.

| ***-transmorrisonensis*** (tranz-mor-ih-son-en′ sis) | | Evergreen Miscanthus | 3-4′/4′ |
|---|---|---|---|
| Fall | Tan | Taiwan | Zones 6-10 |

A relatively new species to the landscape trade, this 3-4′ plant forms dense clumps of glossy green, narrow leaves. The airy flowers are 6-8″ long and appear like long horses' tails. There are a number of selections of *M. sinensis* with similar traits, however, the evergreen foliage, at least in zone 8 south, sets this species apart. Further north, plants are not evergreen but are slower to lose the green color than other species. A handsome plant for full sun and moist conditions. All the miscanthus grasses are useful for winter interest, but this provides some greenery as well.

***Mitchella*** (mi-chel′ la) Partridge Berry Rubiaceae

Only two species are found in the genus, and one, *M. repens*, is native from Newfoundland to Minnesota and south to Florida and Texas. The genus commemorates the work of Dr. John Mitchell (1676-1768), a botanist in Virginia who corresponded with Linnaeus about many American genera. Plants are part of the acidic ground flora of rich woods and often found under conifers like hemlock and larch. Plants are evergreen and the creeping stems are covered with small shiny, rounded opposite leaves. Plants are not sufficiently showy to cause a collective intake of breath, but they are handsome ground covers on well-drained soils. The deliciously fragrant, small, off-white flowers are borne in pairs and each pair gives rise to bright scarlet-red berries in the summer and fall that often persists through the winter. The fruits are the most colorful part of the plant. Under suitable conditions, plants are heavily berried. They are edible, but hardly flavorful, unless you are a partridge.

The leaves are among the most handsome of evergreen ground covers, and plants multiply by rooting at the nodes when they touch the ground. I love it around water, such as by a small pond in the garden.

Propagate by taking pieces of the stem and pinning down the nodes into moist soil. Cuttings may be excised and easily rooted or seeds may be cleaned from the berries and sown in moist soils. Seeds may require up to two years to germinate.

***Mitella*** (my-tel′ la) Bishop's-Cap, Mitrewort Saxifragaceae

About 20 species of these modest plants with heart-shaped leaves and small whitish flowers are known. Most are native to the western United States where they flourish in moist, shady woodlands. The only easily obtainable species, however, is two-leaved bishop's-cap, *M. diphylla*, native from Quebec to Minnesota and south to Missouri and South Carolina. Plants grow about 12″ tall and produce a pair of sessile or very short-stalked leaves about halfway up the flowering stems. The basal leaves are three to five-lobed, roughly hairy on both sides, and 1-2″ long. The leaves are the best part of the plant. Many white, fringed flowers, each about 1/8″ wide, are held in a long 8-10″ raceme in spring. While not terribly colorful, a close look uncovers quite exquisite flowers that look like a bit of lace. After flowering, black shiny fruit occurs. Plants do well in zones 3 to 7.

I often confuse plants of this genus with those of *Tiarella* and *Heuchera* and have been seen scratching my head many times while looking at them. To those who are smarter than I, ignore my frustrations; to those who are similarly confused, here are a few hints to help us out. The foliage is similar in all species but first look for leaves on the flower stem, then look closely at the flowers, in particular, the petals and the stamens. Once you look at enough of them, the foliage will call out their names and even without flowers, you will have no problems.

| | Leaves on flower stems | Petals on flowers | Number of stamens |
|---|---|---|---|
| *Heuchera* | No | Entire | 5 |
| *Mitella* | Yes (2) | 3-cleft | 10 |
| *Tiarella* | No | Entire | 10 |

Use plants as ground covers in partially shaded areas where soils are consistently moist and friable. Propagate by seed or division.

**Related Species:**

*M. breweri* occurs in the Rocky Mountains of British Columbia, the Sierra Nevadas and the Olympic Range in Oregon. It is more compact and mounded than *M. diphylla* and bears small white flowers. Probably hardy in zones 4 to 7.

## *Molinia* (mo-lean′ ee-a) Moor Grass Poaceae

*Molinia* includes a small number of European grasses with showy flowers and good fall color to the foliage. The plants are entirely deciduous, disappearing in the winter and providing no winter interest. However, the stiff see-through flower stems stand well above the foliage and are handsome in summer. The best known of the moor grasses is purple moor grass, *M. caerulea*, available from most nurseries that handle ornamental grasses. The arching leaves are about ½″ wide and 12-18″ long; plants form thick tussocks that grow about 2′ tall. The flowers are yellowish to dark or light purple, and appear in late June to mid July about two feet above the tufted foliage.

Handsome leaves, airy flowers, easy culture and good fall color make it a terrific plant for massing in the landscape. Their only drawback is their relatively slow growth rate; small divisions require 2-3 years before they flower. Buy bigger divisions or don't complain. Plant in full sun and acid soils in zones 4 to 7. Afternoon shade is tolerated in the South.

Propagate by division in early fall or spring.

**Cultivars:**

ssp. *arundinacea* is the giant of the group. Plants simply take up space most of the summer, when seemingly all of the sudden, 5-7′ tall flower stems are dominating the landscape, and you wonder where it has been hiding. Quite a wonderful tall non-miscanthus grass for the garden.

'Moor Flame' is a compact cultivar with scarlet fall color.

'Skyracer' is a cultivar of subsp. *arundinacea*, tall moor grass, and is robust and much taller than moor grass. Plants are 7-8′ tall when in flower and the stiff stems dance on the slightest wind. Terrific yellow-orange fall color.

'Variegata' is the most popular cultivar of moor grass, each leaf colored with yellow-white stripes along the 15″ length. The plants are a great improvement on the species, if more colorful grasses are desired.

## *Monarda* (mo-nard′ a) Bee Balm Lamiaceae

Monarda is a plants that elicits a "love-hate" relationship in gardeners. People love it for the ease of growth, wonderful flower color and pleasant leaf fragrance; others hate it because of its well-deserved reputation of being mildew susceptible and quickly taking over large chunks of the garden. I have seen great swaths of scarlet bee balm in the Smoky Mountain National Park in North Carolina, growing in semi-shaded locations, with nary a spore of mildew. How can such beautiful plants become such an eyesore when they are brought into a more pampered garden setting? It is a fact that whenever a species that evolved in a climate over many years is taken from that climate, bad things often happen. The problem has been exacerbated by breeders who concentrate on flower color while ignoring disease tolerance. Unfortunately, most breeding and evaluation of new cultivars has taken place in Europe, where disease pressure is far different than that found in most American regions.

About 16 species are known but two are fairly common. The leaves are toothed, aromatic and usually opposite. The flowers are terminal, obviously two-lipped and often surrounded by brightly colored bracts. The most common species and the one in which significant breeding has occurred is common bee balm, *M. didyma*. Other good but not as ornamental plants include wild bergamot, *M. fistulosa*, and the annual *M. citriodora*.

*Monarda* is named for Nicholas Monardes, a Spanish botanist who authored the first book on medicinal flora of North America in 1571. His book, published when he was 78 years old, was translated to English as *Joyfull Newes* in 1578.

Quick Reference to Monarda Species

| | Height (ft.) | Flower color |
|---|---|---|
| *M. didyma* | 2-4 | Red |
| *M. fistulosa* | 2-5 | Rose, purple |

**-*didyma*** (di′ di-ma) — Bee Balm, Oswego Tea — 2-4′/3′
Summer — Red — Eastern North America — Zones 3-7

The American botanist John Bartram (1699-1777) first collected bee balm near Oswego, New York. The leaves were used to make tea and plants were routinely included in kitchen gardens for their herbal properties. Plants are also well known for the high yields of nectar for bee habitats. Growing naturally along stream banks with overhanging trees suggests its rightful place in the garden is an area where moisture can be freely provided.

The four-sided stems bear 4-6″ long, thin, scented, pointed leaves. The bright scarlet flowers are surrounded with red-tinged bracts and carried in globular terminal, whorled clusters. Removing the faded flower heads results in more than 8 weeks of flowering. If grown well and properly cared for, a planting of bee balm is a magnificent sight. Unfortunately, this is not always the case. If plants dry out, the stress results in greater susceptibility to foliar diseases such as powdery mildew. While powdery mildew can be present even in native plantings, it can be much worse in the garden, particularly if plants are crowded, or the soil is not consistently moist. Spray with a fungicide starting in early June through frost. This "mildew thing" may be overblown for gardeners who grow bee balm without a problem, however, if mildew is a problem, try some of cultivars listed as more resistant.

Bee balm multiplies by underground stems and can be invasive, taking over large areas of the garden. Clumps tend to die out in the center and must be divided every two to three years for aesthetic purposes. Provide full sun or afternoon shade.

As garden plants, they are lovely in the North but in the South are more trouble than they are worth. However, if placed in a rather wild, moist area where large clumps can form and some mildew is not as objectionable, they make wonderful plants attractive to bees, butterflies, and hummingbirds.

**Cultivars:**

There are far too many cultivars. The differences between them are often minor and all claim to be superior for garden culture. Most catalogs list mildew resistance for the cultivars they sell (if they don't, shop elsewhere) but all such claims (including mine) should be taken with a grain of salt. To paraphrase a well-known saying, "The proof is in the garden". Many of the cultivars listed are hybrids between this and *M. fistulosa*, wild bergamot.

'Alba' is the white form of the species and is often seen interspersed in the wild red populations in native habitats. Other cultivated white forms bear larger flowers.

'Adam' bears cerise flowers, is more compact, and withstands dry conditions better than other cultivars.

'Aquarius' produces light pink flowers on 2-3′ tall plants.

'Beauty of Cobham' stands about 3′ tall with pale pink flowers.

'Blue Stocking' carries violet-blue blossoms. One of my favorite blues, appears to be robust and more heat and drought tolerant than many others.

'Bryan Thompson' is said to be mildew free. Plants originated from Tyler, Texas and bear white flowers on 3-4′ tall stems.

'Cambridge Scarlet' is one of the most enduring cultivars, introduced in the early 1900s. The three-foot stems bear flaming scarlet flowers over vigorous plants. Still popular but being superseded by more mildew resistant selections.

'Cherokee' is one of a number of new hybrids bred by Piet Oudolf of the Netherlands. Selections were based on disease resistance as well as colorful flowers. Most bear Indian names. 'Cherokee' has rose-pink flowers on 3′ tall stems.

'Colrain Red' is about 3′ tall with bright red flowers.

'Comanche' bears darker pink flowers with tan centers.

'Coral Reef' has coral to pink flowers on 3′ tall stems.

'Croftway Pink' was introduced in 1932 and is still among the more popular cultivars. Plants bear rosy pink flowers that blend quietly into the garden. Not mildew resistant.

'Dark Ponticum' bears violet to purple flowers on 3′ stems.

'Donnerwolke', introduced in 1973, produces dozens of lilac flowers on 3′ plants. It was spectacular when I saw it at the Montreal Botanical Garden.

'Fireball' is less than 18″ tall, with intense red flowers in the summer.

'Gardenview Scarlet' was developed by Henry Ross at Gardenview Park in Strongsville, Ohio. Introduced as a scarlet, mildew-resistant clone, it has, for the most part, lived up to its highly mildew resistant reputation. However, monarda is monarda . . .

Grand Marshall™ comes from Morden, Manitoba (see Petite series), and produces fuchsia flowers on 2′ stems.

Grand Parade™ is from the same series and is only 15-18″ tall, with great shiny foliage and pink to magenta flowers.

'Kardinal' has deep red flowers on 3′ stems.

'Jacob Cline', from the respected plantsman Don Cline, is grown by a number of nurseries who feel it is one of the most mildew resistant of any of the available cultivars. This is probably the most popular cultivar today. The flowers are deep red.

'Little Siberia' was found at Little Siberia Perennials in Granville, Vermont. The small flowers are bright pink and produced on 2½-3′ tall plants.

'Loddon Crown' produces mahogany to purple-red flowers and purple-tinged foliage. About 3′ tall.

'Mahogany' has some of the darkest wine-red flowers of any cultivar and grows 3′ tall.

'Marshall's Delight is named for former Agriculture Canada breeder, Henry M. Marshall. It was developed in Morden, Manitoba from a cross between 'Cambridge Scarlet' and *M. fistulosa* var. *menthaefolia*. Plants bear rich pink flowers on relatively mildew-free plants.

'Melissa' is a pink-flowered selection about 3-4′ tall.

'On Parade' produces many deep maroon flowers on 30″ tall plants.

'Panorama' is a seed-propagated strain of 3′ tall plants of mixed colors.

Petite series has many followers. Bred by scientists at Agriculture Canada in Morden, Manitoba, they exhibit stunning colors, cold hardiness and dwarf habit. Plants are only 1-1½′ tall and include 'Petite Delight' (rose-pink) and 'Petite Wonder' (pink). Mildew resistance is marginal, however, they were beautiful in the Toronto Music Garden.

'Prairie Fire' has lilac-red flowers.

'Prairie Gypsy' bears raspberry pink flowers on 2-3′ tall stems.

'Prairie Night' is a handsome old (1955) cultivar with rosy red blooms.

'Raspberry Wine' bears clear wine red flowers over dark green foliage. Introduced by White Flower Farm.

'Scorpion' has violet-purple flowers on 3′ tall plants.

'Sioux' is one of the few white-flowered forms available. The flowers are slightly tinged with pink.

'Squaw' is relatively mildew resistant with deep red flowers.

'Snow Maiden' ('Snow White') provides creamy white flowers on 3′ high stems. Plants were introduced in 1955 but the cultivar is still relatively popular.

'Stone's Throw Pink' is an example of breeders running out of names. The light pink flowers are borne on 3½-4′ tall stems.

'Sunset' bears purple-red flowers on 3′ tall plants. Fairly mildew resistant.

'Twins' produces dark pink flowers.

'Vintage Wine' erupts with many red-purple flowers in midsummer.

'Violet Queen' has deep purple flowers. I have some trouble seeing significant differences between flowers described as violet-blue ('Blue Stocking'), lilac-blue ('Prairie Night'), or purple (Violet Queen'). Probably just me, but perhaps not. However, I am never ashamed to admit I can't tell the differences when faced with a bewildering display of tags that list different names, but look alike. I know I am not alone.

***-fistulosa*** (fist-ew-low′ sa) | Wild Bergamot | 2-5′/3′
Late Summer | Rose, Purple | North America | Zones 3-7

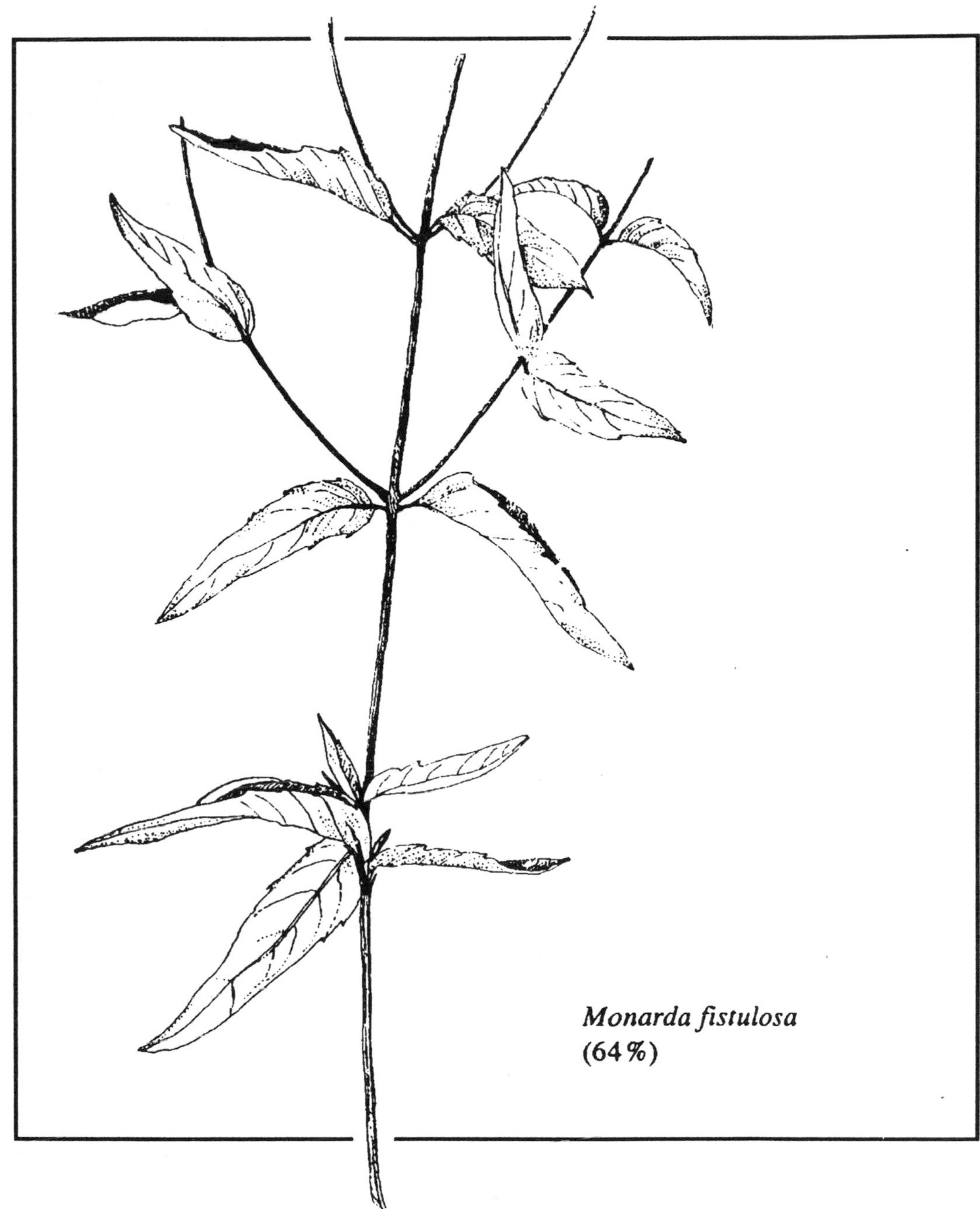

*Monarda fistulosa*
(64%)

The stem is less noticeably four-angled than *M. didyma* and the 4″ long leaves are slightly more hairy and less toothed. The flowers are also borne in tight whorls surrounded by bracts and range from light lavender to whitish pink. The throat of the sepals on each flower is densely hairy, a totally useless piece of information for gardeners, however, this characteristic helps distinguish this species from the previous. The stems grow out of the previous flower head, creating a candelabra effect. Heights of 5′ are not uncommon. Because the flowers are not as brilliantly colored as common bee balm, little interest has been shown in developing this as a garden plant. However, their greater tolerance to dry conditions and resistance to mildew has made them important in the breeding of the hybrids discussed above. Plants are better suited to a wild area rather than the cultivated garden. Plants were, and still are, used in the treatment of headaches and fevers.

Division every 2-3 years will maintain plant vigor. Seed is also available. Germination takes place in 2-3 weeks if seed is lightly covered and placed in a warm (70-75°F), moist environment.

**Cultivars:**

'Claire Grace' seems to be quite resistant to mildew. She bears lavender flowers on 3-4′ tall plants. The plants was found by Barb and Michael Bridges of the former Southern Perennials and Herbs in Tylertown, Mississippi, and named for their daughter.

**Related Species:**

*M. bartlettii*, Bartlett's bee balm, is one of the best plants I have trialed for many years. Plants travel very little, mildew is sparse or nil and the rosy pink flowers are beautiful. If you can find a source, give it a try. I highly recommend it.

*M. punctata*; spotted bee balm, bears lovely whorled yellow to cream flowers with purple spots (*punctata*). The bracts beneath the flowers range from pink to lavender. Plants are tolerant of dry soils, relatively tolerant to mildew and perform well in zones 4-8.

## ***Morina*** (mo-reen′ a) Whorlflower Morinaceae

That this group of plants is seldom seen in North American gardens abundantly demonstrates the good sense of gardeners. I believe that only one species, *M. longifolia*, is sufficiently ornamental to think about using, however, the lovely whorled shell pink flowers belie the spiny prickly nature of the entire plant. This is definitely a plant not to let your fingers do the walking on, as the rosette of leaves and the bracts subtending the flowers can draw blood. *Morina* is found only in gardens where the gardener has someone else do the work. When not in flower, it looks like a wicked thistle in need of removal. The closest garden plants displaying such wickedness I can think of are the prickly bear's breeches, *Acanthus spinosus* var. *spinosissimus* and "ornamental" members of the plume thistles, *Cirsium*.

Without the flowers, they are about 9-12″ tall, about 2′ in flower. In their defense, I must concede that the flowers are colorful, starting out white, turning to shell pink and occasionally to bright crimson. Full sun and excellent drainage are necessary. Plants are native to the Himalayas and hardy in zones 6 and 7, zone 8 on the West Coast. Heat and humidity are not appreciated.

Another species, *M. persica*, is also offered. Plants are shorter, with dark pink flowers, but are less ornamental.

## ***Muhlenbergia*** (myoo-len-ber′ jee-a) Muhly Grass Poaceae

Not so long ago, if anyone had heard of muhly grass, he or she might have thought it had something to do with mules. Today, at least in the South, the muhlys are gathering a large following. The genus contains more than 150 species from open grasslands, mostly from Mexico and southern United States, although a few are native to Asia. They are grown for the threadlike leaves and the thin stems that together create a weeping effect. Some of the more useful species are grown for their clumping bamboo look (*M. dumosa*), while others such as *M. filipes* and *M. capillaris* produce flowers like purple baby's breath. The limitation with all the muhly grasses is their relative lack of cold tolerance, most being winter hardy no further north than zone 7; some, like bamboo muhly, *M. dumosa*, probably zone 7b to 8. They all tolerate full sun to some afternoon shade and are best planted in large clumps. All can be seed propagated, however, some of the better selections are unstable from seed and vegetative propagation ensures continuation of the better selections.

-***capillaris*** (kap′ i-lair-us) Pink Muhly Grass 1-3′/3′
Pink Fall Mexico, Southern United States Zones 7-9

I admit to gushing over this grass for to me, this is the most colorful grass I know, and one of the most useful for gardens and landscapes. The thin drooping foliage is nothing memorable and in fact, throughout most of the year, it is but a filler. However, in September and October, plants are magically transformed into spectacular displays of pink fireworks, causing heads to turn and cars to crash. In Athens, the University of Georgia landscape is ablaze in the fall, outdoing even the red and black of the 93,000 football Dawgs that pour into campus every Saturday. As the flowers mature, they slowly turn to a tan color. Good drainage is needed, but plants are drought and wind tolerant.

**Cultivars:**

'White Cloud' produces clouds of white flowers in September. It also catches the eye but not as quickly as its pink sister.

**Related Species:**

*M. dumosa*, bamboo muhly, looks like clumping bamboo in every way, from its graceful hanging habit to the light airiness of the thin foliage. The small purplish flowers are insignificant compared to the evergreen foliage. Plants have done well in Raleigh, North Carolina, a solid zone 7; maybe they have more cold hardiness than at first believed. Plants grow 4-6 feet in a single season, so are also useful even if they don't survive the winter. They are also terrific in large containers, which may be brought into a protected area during the winter.

*M. lindheimeri*, blue muhly, is a favorite of those who enjoy bluish foliage. Drought and heat tolerant, this 2′ tall Texas native sports thin, soft blue leaves about 15″ long. The flowers are grayish to purple providing this species with the handsome combination of foliage and flowers. Hardy to zone 7.

***Mukdenia*** (muck-den′ ee-a) Mukdenia Saxifragaceae

Only recently has anyone ever heard of mukdenia and with that name, who can blame them? The species used in gardens, *M. rossii*, is characterized by low clumps of smooth, deeply lobed, maple-like leaves. The clusters of small white flowers appear on leafless stems in spring just as the leaves are emerging. The leaves turn bright orange to yellow in fall. This is a beautiful plant, but it has not been grown in enough of the country to provide decent garden performance data. Plants are likely hardy to at least zone 5. Full sun in the North, partial shade further south.

**Cultivars**:

'Crimson Fans' hit the garden airways big time in 2006-7 and is being sold throughout the country. It differs in that the leaves are obviously marked with burgundy, and at least in the Northwest, the color holds all season. Quite beautiful.

***Muscari*** (mus-car′ ree) Grape Hyacinth Hyacinthaceae

Grape hyacinths have graced gardens for centuries and are well known for the bright cone of urn-shaped blue flowers in the spring. However, flowers also occur in shades of pink, white and yellow. The musky odor of the yellow brown-flowered *M. racemosum*, musk hyacinth, is responsible for the name *Muscari*. It is interesting that this species, after which the genus was named, has now been placed in a totally different genus (*Muscarimia moschatum*) by some authorities. Nothing is sacred!

All species are sun lovers and need little more than well-drained soil to look their best. They are excellent plants for the rock garden, especially in large bold groupings. In Mainau, the exquisite island garden in southern Germany, grape hyacinths depicted the Sea of Constance (in which the garden resided) in a portrayal of the island's location. The "river" of *Muscari* at Keukenhof Garden in the Netherlands is even more famous. The point I am making poorly here is that grape hyacinths are not only beautiful, but functional as well.

The flowers are tightly held in a dense raceme and often consist of sterile upper flowers and fertile lower ones. Usually, but not always, the mouth of the flowers is constricted. The two most common in the garden are *M. armeniacum* and *M. botryoides* and differences are difficult for anyone but the taxonomist to unravel. Fortunately, there are no differences in garden requirements. Regardless of the name on the package, enjoy their beauty. Other lesser-known species can provide equal enjoyment.

Quick Reference to Muscari Species

| | Height (in.) | Flower color | Flower shape |
|---|---|---|---|
| *M. armeniacum* | 6-8 | Pale blue | Cone |
| *M. botryoides* | 6-8 | Pale blue | Cone |
| *M. comosum var. monstrosum* | 6-12 | Mauve | Plume |
| *M. latifolium* | 6-8 | Bi-color | Cone |

***-armeniacum*** (ar-men-ee-ah′ cum) Armenian Grape Hyacinth 6-8″/6″
Spring Pale Blue Turkey Zones 4-8

Depending on the source of bulbs, this or *M. botryoides* is the common grape hyacinth. The 6-8 leaves are about ¼″ wide and appear in the fall. In areas without significant snowfall, they can be rather messy throughout the winter and early spring but do serve a useful function. Edith Eddleman, former curator of the perennial border at the J. C. Raulston Arboretum at North Carolina State University, suggested using *Muscari* as a marker for other spring-flowering bulbs or late-emerging perennials whose leaves have not emerged at time of spring cleaning. Having a bulb or two of grape hyacinths reminds you that other plants are still sleeping and to keep the shovel away. The leaves soon fade into the background as the blue conical flower spikes begin their annual emergence. Each mature bulb will send up 1-3 flower spikes with 20-40 densely packed, ¼″ long, pale blue urn-shaped flowers.

All cultivars may be propagated by bulbils. Separate and replant in the fall. Seed is produced but offspring may not be the same as the parent.

**Cultivars:**

'Blue Spike' is one of the fullest of the grape hyacinths due to the double, soft blue flowers.

'Cantab' bears flowers of soft blue on 6″ stems.

'Christmas Pearl' is an early violet-flowering selection, about 8″ tall.

'Early Giant' has cobalt blue flowers with a white rim at the mouth of each.

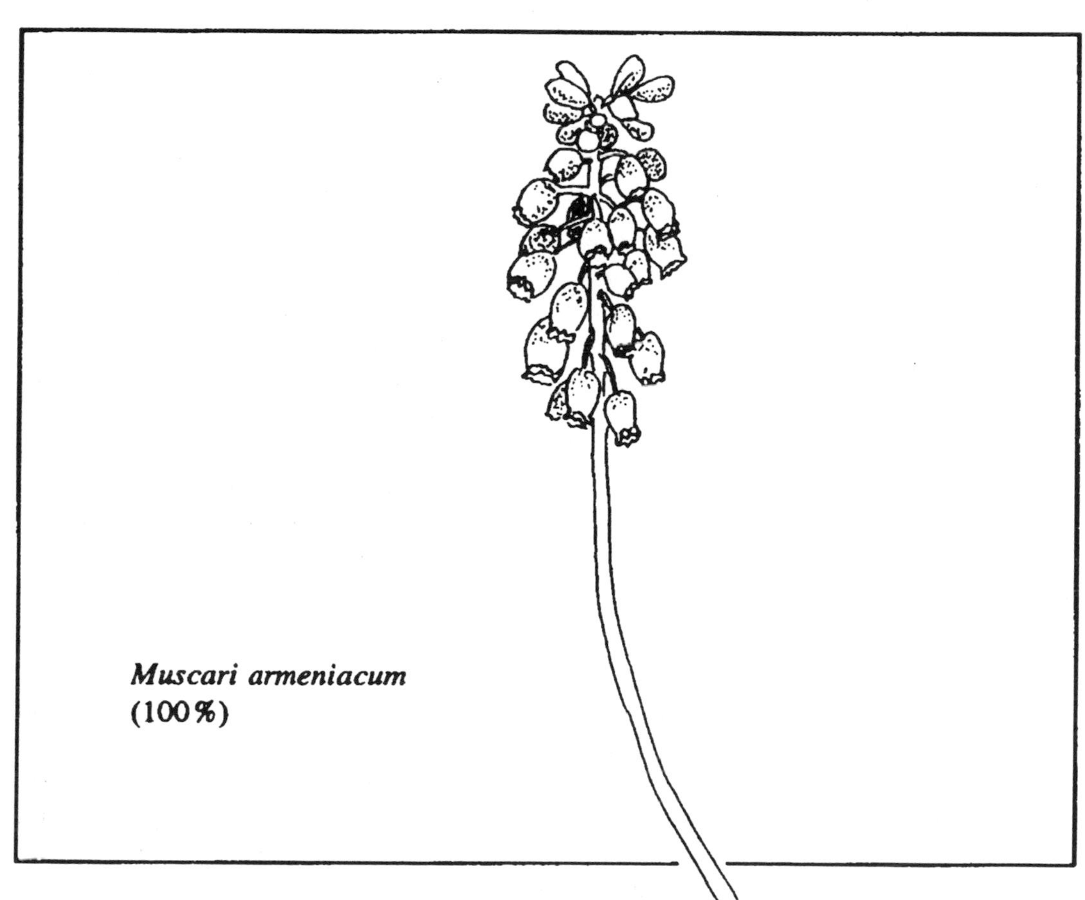

***Muscari armeniacum***
**(100%)**

'Fantasy Creation' provides double blue flowers on compact flower stems. A terrific cultivar if you like double flowers.
'Heavenly Blue' bears gentian blue flowers and multiplies rapidly.
'Saphir' has dark blue flowers with a white rim.
'Valerie Fennis', named after one of the grand dames of English gardening, is one of my favorites. Plants bear pale lavender blue flowers that are truly exquisite.

***-botryoides*** (bot-ree-oi′ deez) Common Grape Hyacinth 6-8″/6″
Early Spring Blue Italy, France Zones 2-8

The common name for the genus was based on this species because the flowers looked like a miniature bunch of blue grapes. Bulbs are common in the garden trade not only because of the lovely blue flowers but also because of the white and pink varieties available. The 2-4 leaves are usually shorter than the inflorescence and about 1/3″ wide. *M. botryoides* is more cold hardy than *M. armeniacum* and flowers earlier. Otherwise, there is not a great deal of difference.

Propagate by bulbils although the species will self-sow.

**Cultivars:**

var. *album* bears clean white flowers. This makes a good garden plant and is the white grape hyacinth of catalogs.

var. *carneum*, a pink-flowered form, fades quickly to flesh-colored flowers and is not particularly attractive.

***-comosum*** (ko-mow′ sum) Tassel Grape Hyacinth 6-12″/6″
Spring Mauve Western Asia, North Africa Zones 4-8

This species and common variety *monstrosum* have the dubious distinction of being "conversation-piece" plants. In describing this plant, Louise Beebe Wilder (*Adventures with Hardy Bulbs*) states that "The fact that the uppermost flowers . . . are gathered into a bunch, and stand wildly on end on long pedicels, while the lower flowers, that are cylindrical, droop dismally, does give the plant a somewhat distraught appearance". Louise was looking at the sterile upper flowers that have been modified into thin filaments, resulting in the interesting appearance. The 3-4 thick leaves are up to 1 1/2′ long. The species is different enough to have been renamed *Leopoldia comosa* by some authorities although I have never seen it listed as such in any trade catalogs.

Propagate by bulbils.

**Cultivars:**

var. *monstrosum* (syn. *plumosum*) is even more atypical for a grape hyacinth and well described by its varietal name. All the flowers of the inflorescence are sterile and look like slender filaments. This altogether curious plant is most attractive under sunny, pleasant skies but after a rain looks like a half-drowned puppy in need of a home. It is the kind of plant one orders in a weak moment, based on the glowing commentary of a bulb catalog. It is seldom ordered again.

***-latifolium*** (lah-tee-fo′ lee-um) One-Leaved Grape Hyacinth 9-12″/5″
Late Spring Violet/Blue Turkey Zones 3-8

This is one of my favorites, because of the lack of messy foliage (only one leaf produced) and the neat racemes of two-tone flowers. The uppermost sterile flowers are a good blue, the bottom fertile ones are violet. I had these in my garden for many years and they are as reliable as any other grape hyacinth I've planted. They are later than others, not flowering until mid to late April. They spread themselves around where they are happy. One such place is Denver, where they flower with abandon through grass, through snow and wherever the seed happens to fall.

**Related Species:**

*M. aucheri* has two thin leaves and bright azure flowers. It is best known for the variety *tubergenianum*, Tubergen's grape hyacinth, that bears many densely arranged deep blue and pale blue flowers on the same spike. Plants grow 4-8″ tall. 'Blue Magic' has dark blue flowers with white on the tips. 'Mount Hood' is really interesting, fading to white at the top, like a crown of snow, over the blue flowers below. 'Sky Blue' has soft blue flowers. 'White Magic' has clean white flowers.

*M. azureum*, azure grape hyacinth, has 2-3 thin leaves and blue campanulate flowers with a darker stripe on the lobes. The flowers are earlier, and the mouths are not as constricted as with the other species. They are also more tolerant of shade. Hardy to zone 5. 'Album' is a white form, 'Amphibolis' has pale blue larger flowers.

*M. macrocarpum* is best known for the cultivar 'Golden Fragrance' which produces wonderfully fragrant yellow flowers on 6-8″ stems. The flowers are longer and thinner than those of common grape hyacinths.

## ***Myosotis*** (my-o-so′ tis) Forget-Me-Not Boraginaceae

The forget-me-nots have always had a special appeal to gardeners of all ages. There are many stories as to the derivation of the common name but most agree that the tale of the young man collecting these flowers for his lady by the bank of the river is the most touching. He slipped and fell into the fast-moving stream and as he was being swept away, he clenched the flowers in his hand and cried "Forget me not!" to his lover on the shore. Touching, but perhaps he should have let go of the flowers and tried swimming instead.

None of the 40-50 species is particularly long lived but most are self-sowers and appear to be perennial. They grow less than a foot tall and produce inflorescences coiled like the tail of a scorpion (scorpioid cymes). The leaves are alternate and usually hairy. All species do well in partial shade but full sun may be tolerated in the North if ample moisture is available.

Quick Reference to Myosotis Species

| | Height (in.) | Habit |
|---|---|---|
| *M. scorpioides* | 6-8 | Prostrate |
| *M. sylvatica* | 6-8 | Upright |

***-scorpioides*** (skor-pee-oi' deez) | True Forget-Me-Not | 6-8″/8″
Spring | Blue | Europe, Asia | Zones 3-8

Often referred to as the water forget-me-not because they grow naturally in water; constant moisture is required if plants are to perform well in a "normal" garden. Because of the stoloniferous nature and prostrate growth habit, stems may grow to 18″ long. The lovely 1/4″ wide flowers are bright blue with a small yellow eye. Plants look particularly beautiful in a partially shaded woodland growing on the banks of a stream. They also may be grown in shallow water in a garden pond.

Propagation by seed is easiest.

**Cultivars:**

'Sapphire' has bright sapphire blue flowers.

'Semperflorens' is much more compact than the type and more floriferous.

'Thuringen' bears sky blue flowers.

***-sylvatica*** (sil-va' ti-ka) | Woodland Forget-Me-Not | 6-8″/6″
Spring | Blue | Europe | Zones 3-7

This is the common forget-me-not of the "normal" garden, where moisture may be inconsistent. Plants are usually biennial, but their reseeding nature should make them appear to be perennial, even if they move about a little. Dense cymes of fragrant, 3/8″ wide azure-blue flowers with distinctive yellow eyes are produced in April and May. The 2-3″ long hairy leaves are lance shaped, somewhat pointed and have 3 faint veins. In the North, flowers are produced prolifically in late spring and sporadically through the late summer. In the South, the dense leaves must be thinned in June to reduce the incidence of leaf rot that often occurs due to afternoon thunderstorms and hot humid weather. If not thinned, the hairy leaves hold water, creating perfect conditions for diseases. Plants seldom last more than two years in the South or three in the North. However, they self-sow abundantly and many additional plantlets emerge in the spring.

Propagate by seed or by division in the spring or fall.

**Cultivars:**

'Alba' has white flowers but why anyone would want to grow a white forget-me-not is beyond me.

'Blue Ball' bears indigo blue flowers over compact, ball-shaped plants.

'Royal Blue' is taller than the species and produces dark blue flowers.

Victoria series is offered in light blue, dark blue, lavender, pink and white. They are only about 10″ tall, compact and easy to grow from seed.

**Related Species:**

*M. alpestris* is similar to *M. sylvatica*. The differences are in the length of the flower stalk relative to the sepals (much longer in *M. sylvatica*, about equal in *M. alpestris*). Most plants sold as *M. alpestris* are probably *M. sylvatica*. Both are fine species and the only importance to the gardener in distinguishing between the two is the satisfaction of knowing what one is growing.

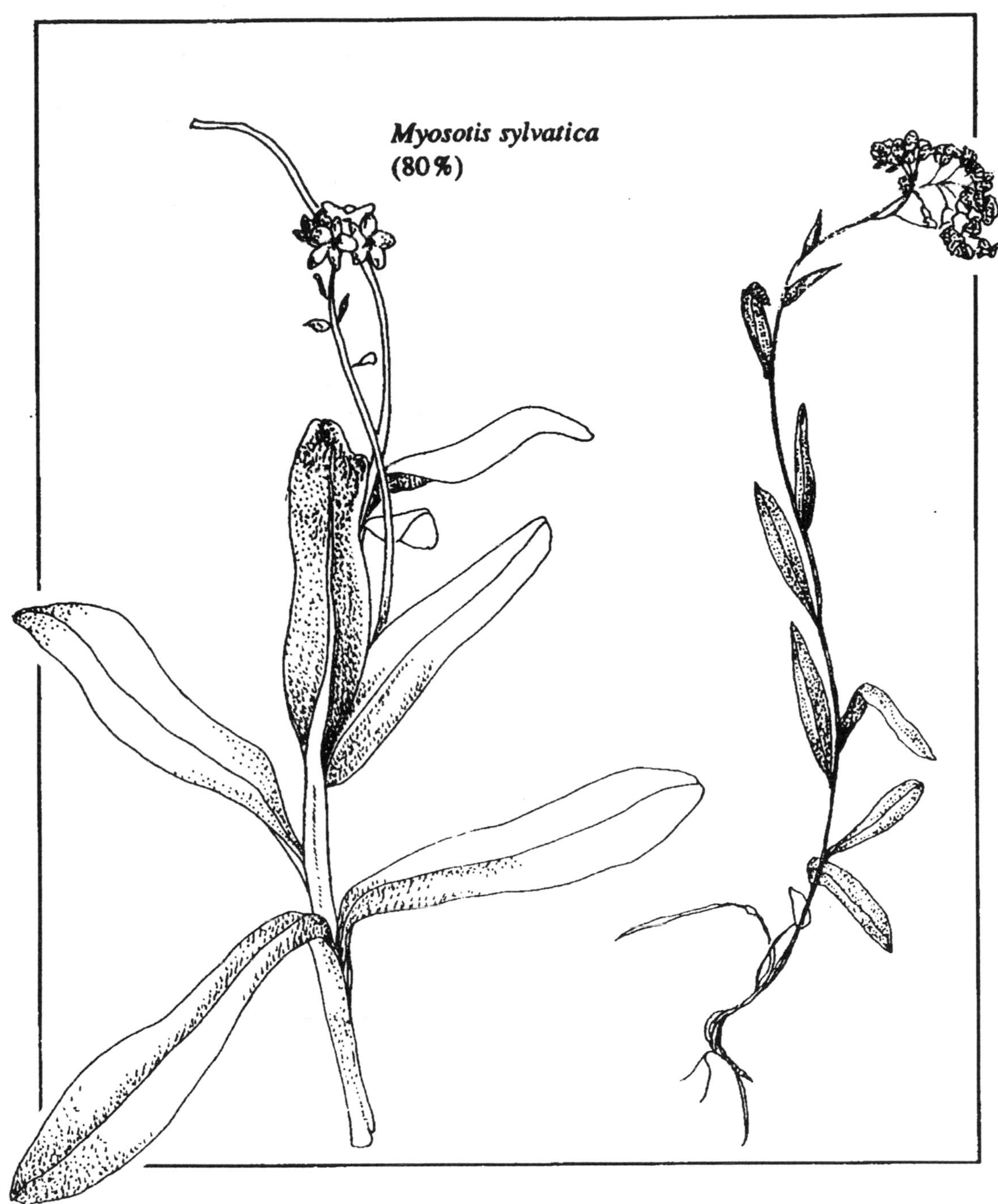
*Myosotis sylvatica*
(80%)

**Related Genus:**

*Myosotidium* is known as Chatham Island forget-me-not, and is occasionally offered from seed or as a special in a mail order catalog. They have large bergenia-like leaves and beautiful forget-me-not flowers. However, they are native to the Chatham Islands, off the coast of New Zealand, and the chances of living for more than a year (10 minutes with humidity and heat) in most North American gardens is close to nil. But what the heck-if you find seed or plants, enjoy them in containers, bring them in over the winter.

## *Myrrhis* (mi′ ris) Sweet Cicily Apiaceae

Consisting of one species of aromatic perennial herb (*M. odorata*), the 3-4′ plants are useful for multiple applications in the garden. For herb fanciers, the leaves are used fresh in salads and the unripe seeds are used for a substitute for anise. For the rest of us, sweet cicily bears umbels of clean white flowers in early summer and its fresh green foliage makes a bracing contrast to other plants in the garden. The parsley-like foliage can be cut back periodically so the freshness can be maintained. Hardy to zone 7 (zone 6 with some protection).

Propagate by seed.

# N

***Narcissus*** (nar-sis′ us) Jonquil, Daffodil Amaryllidaceae

The bright yellow, white and orange flowers splash across the dreary early spring landscape to bring the world to life. Such is the role of daffodils, the first of the major bulbs to welcome spring. The attributes of the daffodil have been praised for centuries. Homer spoke of "The Narcissus wondrously glittering, a noble sight for all, whether immortal gods or mortal men . . .". Centuries before Homer, the flowers were used by the Egyptians in funeral wreaths and have been found in crypts and tombs, preserved after 3000 years.

The origin of the word *Narcissus* is accompanied by some good stories. In Book III of Ovid's *Metamorphoses*, Narcissus was a beautiful and proud young man who rejected advances from lovers of both sexes. A rejected youth prayed to the gods that Narcissus might himself one day succumb to the pain of unrequited love. Nemesis, the goddess of vengeance, decided to answer his prayer.

Later, when Narcissus was lying on the bank of a pool, he saw a beautiful face looking back at him. He fell in love with the image, which appeared to respond to his gestures but remained unattainable. Day after day he stayed there, longing for the beautiful boy and slowly wasting away. Ovid says that, even after death, Narcissus found a pool in which to gaze at himself in the underworld. Above ground, the nymphs who went to bury his body found "only a flower with a yellow center surrounded with white petals."

Who knows how these tales arise but another story is credited to the writer Plutarch (AD 46-120). He claimed the name of the plant comes from the Greek *narke* and refers to the heavy or narcotic effects produced by it. Sure enough, the narcissus is on every list of poisonous plants. According to Pliny (AD 23-79), the Greeks believed that narcissus gave off evil emanations, their scent causing headaches, madness or even death. Accounts of the dulling properties of narcissus persisted at least until the nineteenth century! Hard to believe anyone grew the thing.

All daffodils and jonquils belong to the genus *Narcissus*. The common name, jonquil, popular in the southern United States and in England, comes from the Latin word *juncus* meaning rush, and refers to the round leaves on *N. juncifolius*, rush-leaf daffodil. The term has since been accepted to describe dwarf, small-cupped daffodils with rushlike leaves. In some people's minds, the common name, daffodil, is used only for the large trumpet-flowered forms like 'King Alfred', but for most gardeners it describes just about all species and varieties. Although the large-flowered hybrid daffodils are best known, there are many smaller species that are greatly overlooked. Some of these flower as early as January in Southern areas and as late as June in Northern gardens. For instance, *N. minimus* (syn. *N. asturiensis*), least daffodil, is a terrific early bloomer, flowering in late February in Bronxville, New York, in early February in Tidewater, Virginia, and as early the first day of the new year in Charlotte, North Carolina. Vast beauty and charm reside in these relatively undiscovered species, although finding them can be an altogether frustrating experience. However, half the fun of gardening is the hunt for something different and the discovery of something new.

A well-drained soil, deeply worked and containing humus is ideal for narcissus. Bulbs prefer neutral to slightly acid soil and lime should be incorporated into highly acidic soils. Bulbs flower abundantly in woodland soils with natural leaf mold, but should be planted away from hungry tree roots. Narcissus can be naturalized wherever bulbs may be left undisturbed, however if naturalizing in lawns, the grass cannot be cut until the narcissus leaves have yellowed. Removal of leaves too early results in poor performance in subsequent years.

Many times I am asked about how much cold daffodils require to flower. The simple answer is as much as possible: the longer the cold, the stouter and taller the flower stem. (Also see tulips). However, if bulbs cannot be planted in early fall, put them in the refrigerator. Some people see the month of March and discover a bag or two of daffodils in the garage or the back of their pickup. Don't give up, get them in the ground (assuming they are not mushy) and be patient; some leaves will appear the first spring, they will likely flower the following spring.

About 60 species of narcissus are known, many available to gardeners, although the greatest breakthroughs in garden daffodils have resulted from interspecific hybridization. Some marvelous breeding has created today's large-flowered hybrids, often resulting from an embarrassing number of parents. In the daffodil flower, the cup is known as the corona and the outer flared segments are collectively called the perianth. There has been so much breeding work in *Narcissus* that twelve categories, based on flower morphology, have been developed to classify the species and hybrids. The first four categories are the most popular but I love some of the other more subtle forms that follow. Following is a table of classification and a cultivar of each type. Dozens of additional cultivars can be found in good catalogs and in retail outlets.

*I. Trumpet Narcissus*

One flower to a stem, corona as long as, or longer than perianth segments.

The category is further classified into Ia, Yellow ('Dutch Master'); Ib, Bicolor ('Preamble'); Ic, White ('Mount Hood'); and Id, Other ('Apricot Surprise', apricot perianth, orange corona).

*II. Large-cupped Narcissus*

One flower to a stem, corona more than one-third, but not equal to the length of the perianth segments.

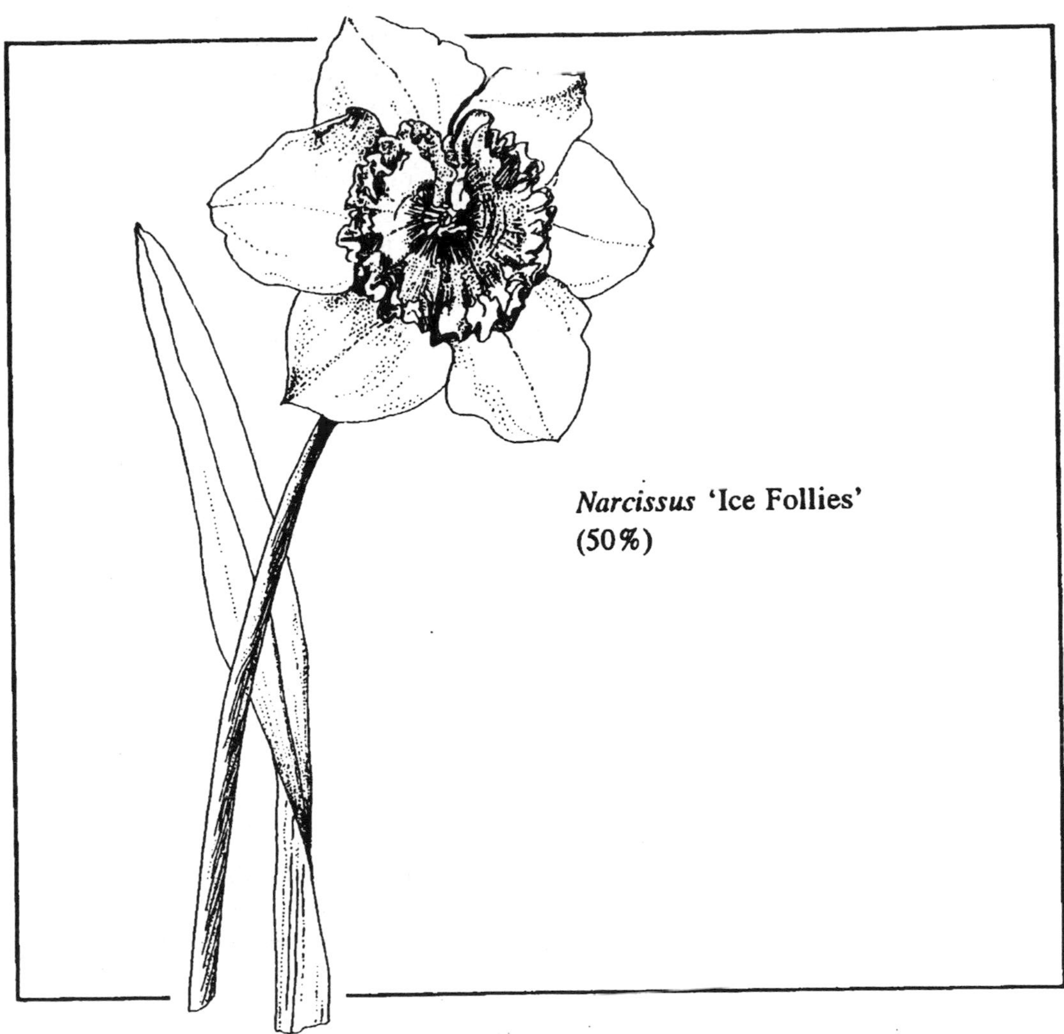

*Narcissus* **'Ice Follies'**
**(50%)**

As in the previous category, it is further classified into IIa, Yellow ('Carlton'); IIb, Bicolor ('Flower Record'); IIc, White ('Milk and Cream'); and IId, Other ('Bantam', yellow perianth, red corona).

*III. Small-cupped Narcissus*

One flower to a stem, corona not more than one-third the length of the perianth segments. IIIa, Yellow ('Jezabel'); IIIb, Bicolor ('Barrett Browning'); IIIc, White ('Angel'); IIId, Other ('Birma', deep yellow petals, small orange-red trumpet).

*IV. Double Narcissus*

Flowers double ('Flower Drift', white/yellow).

*V. Triandus Narcissus*

Obvious characteristics of *N. triandus*, the dominant parent of the hybrids: Slender round leaves, drooping white flowers borne in clusters, perianth segments bent back to reveal a globular corona, like teardrops. Often called the angel's tears daffodil. Usually 9-12″ tall. Also available as var. *alba*. Hardy in zones 4-9. This section is further classified into Va, Large Corona in which the corona is not less than two-thirds the length of perianth segments ('Hawara', soft yellow); Vb, Small Corona in which the corona is less than two-thirds the length of the perianth segments ('April Tears', yellow).

*VI. Cyclamineus Narcissus*
Obvious characteristics of *N. cyclamineus*, the dominant parent: Perianth segments turned back, long cylindrical corona, serrated at the edge, early blooming, usually 6-10″ tall. Hardy in zones 6-9. ('Jetfire', yellow/red).

*VII. Jonquilla Narcissus*
Obvious characteristics of *N.jonquilla*, the dominant parent: Rushlike channelled leaves, fragrant golden-yellow flowers borne in clusters of 3-6, with a cup-shaped corona. Usually 6-12″ tall. Hardy in zones 4-9. ('Baby Moon', pale yellow).

*VIII. Tazetta Narcissus*
Obvious characteristics of *N. tazetta*, the dominant parent of the hybrids: Four to six narrow leaves, flowers almost flat with a shallow corona, very fragrant. Flowers borne 4-8 to a 12″ tall stem, often referred to as paperwhites or bunch-flowered narcissus. Usually 12-15″ tall. Some are hardy in zones 5 to 9 ('Geranium', white with orange cup); others (generally referred to as paperwhites) are only hardy to zone 7 ('Ziva', white).

*IX. Poeticus Narcissus*
Obvious characteristics of *N. poeticus*, the dominant parent: Narrow blue-green leaves. Flowers are solitary, white with small saucer-shaped corona of pale yellow, edged red and often referred to as pheasant's eye. Sweetly fragrant and late flowering. Hardy in zones 4-9. ('Actaea', white with yellow cup edged red).

*X. Species other than those previously listed*
Some really neat species can be found in the category, and may well be worth trying out for no other reason than to have a little fun.

*XI. Split corona Narcissus*
Distinguished by the corona (cup) being split for at least one-third its length. Very showy, and also referred to as collar and papillion daffodils. These are further classified into XIa, Collars in which the corona split for at least a third of its length ('Orangery', creamy white with orange collar); XIb, Butterflies that are characterized by the sunburst of color from the center of the corona ('Papillion Blanc', white with green and yellow corona).

*XII. Miscellaneous Narcissus*
All daffodils not falling into any of the above categories. Most of these are miniatures falling into various divisions. I'm not sure why cultivars fit into this division and not remain in standard divisions, but I assume a catchall division is required ('Tete-a-Tete', yellow).

***-bulbocodium*** (bul-bow-ko′ dee-um) Hoop Petticoat Daffodil 8-12″/6″
Early Spring Yellow Southern France, Morocco Zones 6-8

Another striking but frustrating "I have to have" species. Although plants are small, they are beautiful when flowering in large masses or where they are naturalized. The petticoat daffodils always elicit interest and conversation because of their unique flower shape. Three to four rushlike leaves, up to 15″ long, emerge early in the spring. Unique, solitary, bright yellow flowers on eight-inch stems arise through the foliage. The perianth is made up of narrow segments but the cup is widely expanded and resembles a petticoat. Excellent drainage is necessary to overwinter the bulbs. You might want to plant them in containers or protected areas because inclement weather in January and February can spoil emerging blossoms. Don't expect much success as a perennial in the Southeast or Northeast. The Pacific Northwest is the best area to see the species in the garden.

**Cultivars:**
var. *citrinis* has lemon yellow blossoms.
var. *conspicuous* is the latest to bloom and produces deep golden yellow flowers.
'Primrose' describes the color of this beautiful flower.
'Tenuifolius' bears a 6-lobed wide yellow corona above thin threadlike leaves.

***-cyclamineus*** (cyk-la-min′ ee-us) Cyclamen Daffodil 4-6″/6″
Spring Yellow Spain, Portugal Zones 5-7

These are neat flowers. E.A. Bowles described them "like the ears laid back of a kicking horse". I first came across these beautiful cyclamen-like flowers on a spring trip to Wisley Gardens in England where they are naturalized along with other small bulbs in a meadow. Even my good friend, Michael Dirr, who is always looking up at this tree or that one, found himself on his hands and knees admiring without apology. Dirr and Armitage in a meadow, sounds like the beginning of a bad poem.

Unfortunately, they are more difficult to naturalize in North America for the same reasons that many southern European species are difficult. Our temperature extremes—hard unforgiving storms, heaving due to snow and ice—aren't conditions that allow the species to take over. However, even a dozen bulbs, enjoyed for a couple of years, will make your spring an unforgettable one. Put them where drainage is excellent, such as a raised bed or a rock garden and in full sun. If you have trouble with the species, select some of the cultivars with *N. cyclamineus* as the dominant parent (Group 6); they are much easier.

**Related Species:**

*N. cantabricus*, Cantabrian daffodil, bears fragrant white "petticoat" flowers in early spring. Only one leaf is formed and flowering occurs as early as January or February in North Carolina. This is sometimes offered as *N. bulbocodium* var. *monophyllus*. Likely cold hardy to zone 7.

*N. nanus*, dwarf daffodil, (sometimes sold as *N. lobularius*) is 6-8″ tall and bears small, fragrant white flowers with a rich yellow cup.

*N. obvallaris*, tenby daffodil, has 12″ long stems topped with golden yellow flowers.

*N.* x *romieuxii* is a tetraploid, probably the result of *N. bulbocodium* x *N. cantabricus*. The sulphur yellow "petticoat" flowers are the first yellow daffodils to emerge in the spring. Hardy to zone 7 with a long yellow, green-tinged cup.

*N. tazetta*, paperwhites, are usually forced for indoor use, but if the fragrance makes you gag, you may not want to force them again. They are cold hardy to about zone 7b, flowering in warm winters in December through February, and outdoors the smell is pleasant. Most are white flowered, however some yellow forms have recently been introduced. 'Canaliculatus', Chinese lily narcissus, has white petals with a yellow cup., and is cold hardy to zone 7a.

**Wister Award Winners:**

The American Daffodil Society (ADS) honors what it feels are the best daffodils for performance in a garden setting with the prestigious Wister Award. A number of criteria are used to select the cultivar, but essentially, it is based on garden performance and availability. For the befuddled among us, these cultivars are a good place to start.

The category is in parentheses; the description is from the ADS.

1995 'Salome' (II), white and pink, large-cupped, with a yellow rim on the cup.
1996 'Peeping Tom' (VI), a yellow cyclamineus hybrid.
1997 'Rapture' (VI), an all-yellow cyclamineus hybrid.
1998 'Intrigue' (VII), yellow petals, white cup, several blooms per stem.
1999 'Tripartite' (XI), a split-corona hybrid, with several blooms per stem.
2000 'Monal' (II), a yellow and red large-cupped daffodil.
2001 'Golden Aura' (II), all yellow with a large cup.
2002 'Bravoure' (I), trumpet daffodil with white petals and a yellow cup.
2003 'Tahiti' (IX), a yellow and orange double daffodil, strong stems.
2004 'Segovia' (III), a white and yellow miniature daffodil.
2005 'Fragrant Rose' (II), a later blooming pink and white daffodil.
2006 'Dainty Miss' (VII), intermediate-sized, all-white flower.
2007 'Camelot' (II), all yellow-cupped daffodil.

## *Nassella* (na-sell′ a) Hairgrass Poaceae

This is one fabulous grass, so unlike the coarse Ravenna grasses and miscanthus grasses. The thin leaves and silky flowers make you want to do silly things, like hug it, and rub it all over your body. Well, perhaps not that silly, but it does have a lambs' ear quality about it. Plants are known as *N. tenuissima* and were once classified as *Stipa tenuissima*. The bright green leaves are very thin and flexible and eddy with the wind. They are about 2′ tall, not a lot taller even when flowering. The flowers are tan to yellowish green in early summer and are particularly beautiful when they catch the late afternoon sun. To me, they are among the most engaging of any grass offered today. Plants are native to Mexico and the Southwest and unfortunately hardy only in zones 7-9. Plants can self-seed readily.

***Nectaroscordum*** (nek-ta-ro-skor′ dum) Sicilian Honey Garlic Alliaceae

The botanical name comes from *nektar* from Greek mythology ("the drink of the gods") and *scordium* ("plant smelling of garlic"). The genus, which consists of about three species, is closely related to *Allium*, which is redolently obvious when the leaves are crushed. The plants may smell like onions, but they do not look like any other onion I know. Botanically, they differ from *Allium* by having outer petals with 3-5 veins, while those of *Allium* have only one.

A truly interesting and fascinating bulb; plants grown in the garden are *N. siculum*, and grow to four feet tall and bear 20-30 pendulous, bell-shaped green flowers tinged with white and purple margins. They are held in a loose umbel from the top of the stem, opening in early summer. The weirdness of the plants must account for their popularity because they are surely not subtle or diminutive. The strap-shaped leaves emerge early in the spring, mature by flowering time, then disappear once flowering is complete. Plants are invasive where they are comfortable and can become a nuisance, but few places in North America afford such comfort. *Nectaroscordum* is native to France and Italy, and high humidity or severe winters are not well tolerated. The plants offered for sale may be hybrids and listed as *N.* x *siculum*. Plants are hardy from zones 7-9.

Bulbs should be set 2″ deep and about 18″ apart. Leave bulbs undisturbed once established.

**Cultivars:**

subsp. *bulgaricum* is similar but has white to yellow flowers which are tinged pale pink and green above, edged white and flushed green below. They are native to eastern and central Europe and a little more cold hardy (likely to zone 6).

***Nepeta*** (nep′ e-ta) Nepeta Lamiaceae

One of the better-known representatives of this genus, at least in stories and lore, is catnip (*N. cataria*), an old-fashioned, blue-flowered plant. There is nothing particularly special about it except in its perverse ability to make cats crazier than they already are. The famous French botanist and plant explorer, J. P. de Tournefort wrote in the early 1700s about the effect of this magical plant on the feline race ". . . when a Cat has smelt it (even before she has well seen it), hugg'd it and kiss'd it, wantonly running upon it and scouring away from it by turns, and has rub'd herself against it very much and long, using strange Postures and playing with it, she at last eats it up and devours it entirely." This is not a pretty picture! It is also said that catnip repels rats: whether this is because of the oils in the plant or the fact that a cat may jump on the plants at any moment, I'm not sure. Apparently cats are not fussy as to plant age; they tear up young and old plants with equal happy fervor.

The genus, however, is much more than common catnip, consisting of over 250 species. *Nepeta* has square stems, opposite leaves and white to blue flowers, although a little-known ornamental species, *N. govaniana*, Kashmir nepeta, has yellow flowers.

Many of the commonly-offered species, particularly *N.* x *faassenii* and 'Six Hills Giant' are best grown as edging plants but tend to cascade over the area they are designed to edge, either a charming sight or a terrible nuisance depending on one's degree of patience. The gray-green leaves help blend other plants together in the garden. They perform best in full sun and well-drained soil and tolerate partial shade in zones 5 and 7, but prefer full sun in northern areas. The more common species such as *N.* x *faassenii* and *N. racemosa* (*N. mussinii*) are low-growing edgers. However, some excellent taller, more upright species are starting to be more recognized. These include *N. grandiflora*, *N. nuda*, *N. subsessilis* and *N. sibirica*.

There is confusion as to the identity of species sold under the name *Nepeta*. It is easy to know *Nepeta* by its unique fragrance and the grayish leaves and purple flowers, however, the species are so closely related, it is difficult to tell them apart without a label. The most popular is the hybrid Faassen's catnip, *N.* x *faassenii*, with numerous cultivars, however, they are similar to *N. mussinii*; so similar that the some taxonomists have folded it into *N.* x *faassenii*. Other species mainly differ in their habit and vigor.

I used to think that *Nepeta* was easy to distinguish from other genera; plants were usually shorter, more floppy and always easy to tell apart by the difference in foliage smell. However, with the increased popularity of the taller, less fragrant forms (such as *N. sibirica* and *N. subsessilis*), I needed a way to distinguish *Nepeta* from blue-flowered tall salvias. To do so, tear apart a flower and find the stamens. If the plant is a *Salvia*, there will be 4 stamens, but two will be long and two will be short or rudimentary. If the plant is a *Nepeta*, the four stamens will be the same size.

Quick Reference to Nepeta Species

| | Height (ft.) | Flowers | Flower color | Leaf length |
|---|---|---|---|---|
| *N. x faassenii* | Up to 2′ | Sterile | Lavender | 1-2″ |
| *N. govaniana* | 2-3′ | Fertile | Yellow | 3-4″ |
| *N. nervosa* | Up to 2′ | Fertile | Lavender | 3-4″ |
| *N. siberica* | 3-4 | Fertile | Lavender | 2-4″ |
| *N. subsessilis* | 1-3 | Fertile | Lavender | 2-3″ |

**x *faassenii*** (fah-sen′ ee-eye) Faassen Nepeta 18-24″/18″
Early Summer Lavender-Violet Hybrid Zones 4-7

Plants were named for J.H. Faassen, a Dutch nurseryman in whose nursery the hybrid first appeared. Plant taxonomists have at one time placed these plants in *N. mussinii*, *N. racemosa*, or as hybrids of *N. racemosa* x *N. nepetella*. Don't worry about it, thwart those scientists and simply buy a cultivar. Generally growing 1-2′ tall, the bushy plants consist of upright and prostrate flowering stems. The small (1-2″ long) scalloped, grey-green leaves have short petioles and are straight across at the base (truncate). The many flowers are lavender to violet-blue and occur in elongated racemes almost always in the leaf axils. If flowers are closely studied, one can see that the sepals (calyx) are almost as long as the petals (corolla). Since plants are sterile, no seed is formed, therefore any plants raised from seed will not be *N.* x *faassenii*. Flowers appear about a week later than those of *N. racemosa* but are more persistent. This hybrid is a better garden plant, although not as cold hardy as many other species.

Propagate by spring division or by terminal cuttings. Take 3″ long cuttings in summer and root in sand or peat-perlite mix. Rooting occurs within 2 weeks.

**Cultivars:**

All cultivars should be sheared to 12-15″ after flowering for repeat blooms.

'Blue Dwarf' produces many pale blue flowers on compact plants.

'Blue Ice' produces interesting icy blue flowers which fade to creamy white on maturity.

'Blue Wonder' is 12-15″ tall, compact, and bears dark blue flowers on 6″ tall spikes. Cut back after flowering for repeat bloom in the fall.

'Dropmore' has larger leaves and flowers and is more upright than the hybrid. Bigger and more noticeable and can grow up to 2′ tall.

'Joanna Reed' is a natural hybrid between *Nepeta sibirica* and *N. faassenii*. Plants have an upright habit and bear violet-blue flowers with pink throats over gray-green foliage.

'Pool Bank' produces purple-blue to blue flowers on 3′ tall plants.

'Six Hills Giant' is the best-known catnip, and taller and sufficiently different to be classified under a horticultural (rather than taxonomic) species called *N. gigantea*. One of the finest plants I have seen, it is used extensively for edging pathways and for mass plantings. The 9-12″ tall racemes consist of dark violet flowers borne in axils and terminals atop 3′ tall erect plants. Plants are greener and flower later than the species. To distinguish it from other catnips, I pick a flowering stem and expect it to stretch from wrist to elbow. A quick and dirty test like that often helps me out; it may do the same for you.

'Snowflake' bears creamy white flowers on 12-15″ plants.

'White Wonder' is a white-flowering form of 'Blue Wonder'.

***-govaniana*** (go-van-ee′ a-na) | Yellow Catnip | 2-4′/2′
Summer | Yellow | Himalayas | Zones 4-7

A most un-nepeta-like nepeta, more curious than useful. The yellow flowers and the mild catnip odor belie its roots. The flowers are held differently than other catnips as well, borne in long, lax 2-3-flowered racemes rather than the many densely-flowered racemes seen in other species. Flowers occur in mid to late summer in the axils of the large serrated oblong-elliptical leaves.

Little seen in North America, probably a good thing.

***-nervosa*** (ner-vo′ sa) | Veined Nepeta | 1-2′/2′
Early Summer | Lavender-Blue | Iran | Zones 5-7

The term *nervosa* refers to the nerves or veins on the foliage and the most obvious characteristic is the strong veins on the entire or slightly toothed 3-4″ long leaves. The lower leaves have short petioles while the upper ones are sessile. The lavender-blue flowers are held in a dense cylindrical raceme in which the sepals of each flower are about half the length of the petals.

Plants are useful for edging, falling over the edges of beds. They form spreading mats and flower for a long time in early and midsummer. Some shade should be provided in the afternoon, particularly in the South. Plants may be sited on poor soils therefore fertilize sparingly or plants will get stringy. This is as heat tolerant a catnip as is available. Similar to other species and cultivars, they should be cut back hard when the plants look like string beans.

Propagate by cuttings or division.

**Cultivars**:
'Blue Carpet' is about 1′ tall and produces violet-blue flowers.

***-sibirica*** (si-bi′ ri-ca) Siberian Catnip 24-36″/24″
Summer Lavender Sibirica Zones 3-7

A number of characteristics distinguish this catnip from others. It is probably the most cold hardy, taller than most and more invasive. The 2-4″ long lanceolate leaves have broad, almost rounded teeth and are slightly gray on the top sides. The rich blue flowers are held in many whorls in a long raceme.

Similar to but not nearly as strong in fragrance as other nepetas, they are nonetheless one of the most handsome plants, particularly when provided a little afternoon shade. They do poorly in wet soils and overly rich soils may result in rampant plants. If they get too flippy-floppy, give them a haircut early in May or after they flower.

**Cultivars**:
'Souvenir d'André Chaudron' is one of my favorites in the nepeta world. In cool climates, plants are 2-3′ tall with impressive vigor and wonderfully dense lavender-blue flowers. In warm weather, they can flop over in late summer, requiring a cut back. But where they grow well, they are impressive. Plants will reseed.

***-subsessilis*** (sub′ ses-il-is) Japanese Catnip 1-2′/2′
Lavender Summer Japan Zones 4-7

With so many low-growing nepetas available, it is nice to have some upright forms. Plants are strong upright growers if placed in full sun and moist conditions. They originate from wet mountain slopes of Japan and if soils are too dry, will perform poorly. Similarly, hot summer temperatures result in some decline, but if plants are cut back, they will return happily. The leaves are smooth, only slightly aromatic and somewhat shiny (for a nepeta) and the flowers are held in dense whorls.

**Cultivars**:
'Blue Dreams' and 'Pink Dreams' are seed-propagated selections about 2½′ tall with blue and pink flowers respectively.
'Candy Cat', 'Cool Cat', 'Kit Kat', and 'Super Cat' have light pink to rose flowers, pale lavender flowers, blue, and violet-blue flowers, respectively. 'Cool Cat' is a little taller (up to 2½′) than 'Candy Cat', 'Kit Kat' is only about 18″ tall, and 'Super Cat' can reach 4′ in height.
'Sweet Dreams' is about 18″ tall with two-tone burgundy and pink flowers over green foliage.

*Lamium maculatum*
'Pink Chablis'

*Leucanthemum* × *superbum*
'Becky'

*Leucanthemum* × *superbum*
'Broadway Lights'

*Liatris spicata*
'Kobold'

(L) *Ligularia macrophylla*
(R) *Ligularia wilsoniana*

*Ligularia dentata*
'Britt Marie Crawford'

*Lilium*
'Black Beauty'

*Lilium*
'Pink Perfection'

*Lobelia tupa*

*Lychnis chalcedonica* 'Flore Plena'

*Lychnis flos-cuculi* 'Jenny'

*Lycoris aurea*

*Lycoris radiata*

*Lysimachia ephemerum*

*Lysimachia punctata*

*Macleaya cordata*

*Mertenisa virginica*

*Miscanthus sinensis*
'Cosmopolitan'

*Miscanthus sinensis*
'Gracillimus'

*Miscanthus sinensis*
'Malepartus'

*Molinia caerulea*
'Variegata'

*Monarda bartlettii*

*Monarda didyma*
'Raspberry Wine'

*Muhlenbergia capillaris*

*Mukdenia rossii*
'Crimson Fans'

*Nassella tenuissima*

*Nepeta racemosa*
'Snowflake'

*Nepeta*
'Six Hills Giant'

*Nepeta × faassenii*

*Oenothera biennis*

*Oenothera*
'Lemon Drop'

*Oenothera speciosa*
'Twilight'

*Onopordium acanthium*

*Origanum rotundifolium*
'Kent Beauty'

*Origanum vulgare*
'Newtown Wonder'

*Ornithogalum thyrsoides*

*Osmunda cinnamomea*

*Osmunda claytoniana*

*Oxalis deppei* (foliage)

*Oxalis regnelii*
'Purpurea'

**Related Species:**

*N. grandiflora* is also a tall catnip, growing 30-36″ on sturdy stems. The relatively large lavender-blue flowers are held in spikes (flowers with no individual flower stems) and bloom for many weeks. A good plant from zone 5 to zone 7, zone 8 in the west. 'Dawn to Dusk' has light pink flowers.

*N. nuda* is little known in the American garden trade but is a most impressive plant, if well grown. The well-branched plants are at least 3′ tall (I have seen them almost 5′ tall) with leaves up to 3″ long. The lavender-blue flowers have purplish spots and are carried in axils and terminals. Likely cold hardy to about zone 6.

*N. racemosa* produces gray, hairy, heart-shaped leaves with a rounded apex, about 1″ long and highly scented. Plants are similar to but more prostrate and shorter than *N.* x *faassenii*. The pale blue flowers consist of numerous ½″ long, lipped flowers held in loose terminal racemes. They make a pleasant, if not outstanding, plant for the garden. The species and cultivars set seed profusely. In my Georgia garden, plants did well but the flowers faded in the sun and never attained the sparkle I have seen in the North or overseas. Plants persisted for about three years before succumbing to heat, cats, dogs, and children. 'Little Titch' is only 9-12″ tall with lavender-blue flowers. The best cultivar of the bunch is 'Walker's Low', growing to about 18″ and in flower for much of the season. The 2007 PPA Plant of the Year. 'Snowflake', however, is no slouch either, as plants are covered with small white flowers most of the summer.

## *Nerine* (ner′ ene) Nerine Amaryllidaceae

This group of bulbs resembles *Lycoris* and *Amaryllis*. *Nerine* consists of about 20 autumn-flowering species, but seldom are any of them seen in North American gardens, except in some West Coast areas. The strong 2′ stems of *N. bowdenii* and *N. sarniensis* terminate in 10-15 tubular, crimson to rosy pink flowers and have been used for many years as a commercial cut flower. All species are native to South Africa, and only *N. bowdenii* is marginally hardy in zones 7-9; others can be used in containers to be removed like gladiolus. The large umbels of rosy pink flowers emerge on leafless stems in late summer or fall, then go dormant during the summer. In mild climates, the strap-like leaves are evergreen. A number of gardeners in the Southeast have been pleasantly surprised with the performance of *N. bowdenii* as a perennial in their gardens. The summer is the dormant period and in their native habitats, they prefer to be dry.

I was fortunate to live in New Zealand for a short time, and with a fine scientist, Dr. Ian Warrington, was able to study and appreciate the beauty of *N. sarniensis*, the Guernsey lily. The flowers of the species are crimson and almost iridescent. Their importance as a cut flower in that country and in the Channel Islands have resulted in greenhouse forcing protocol as well as an aggressive breeding program. Although this is not quite as hardy as *N. bowdenii*, if you are successful with that nerine, try the Guernsey lily as well.

In containers, mix in a significant amount of organic matter and plant with the necks of the bulbs slightly above the surface of the soil. Withhold water until the flower scapes appear.

Numerous hybrids such as 'Salmon Supreme' and 'Mother of Pearl', among others, have been bred and are outstanding. All you have to do is find them!

# O

**Oenanthe** (o-nanth′ ee) Flamingo Plant Apiaceae

I first saw this plant when a member of a garden audience asked me "Do you know what this is?" as a stump-the-chump type of question. The audience members sat on the edge of their seats as I, in my usual professorial manner, tugged at my chin, scratched my head and mumbled something inaudible. My best guess was a poor-looking container of bishop's weed, *Aegopodium podagraria,* but alas and alack, I was stumped once again. I remember seeing a plant similar to this one at Wisley Gardens in England but could not put a name to it. Without doubt, senility was setting in quickly.

The plant was, and is, *Oenanthe javanica* 'Flamingo', a bishop's weed lookalike with tricolored foliage. Its claim to fame is the pink hues on the leaves, particularly when young. The white flowers are produced in midsummer. Plants grow well from zones 6-8 but are not as aggressive as its lookalike. They require full sun to partial afternoon shade and prefer moist soils. In their native habitats, they are generally found in marshland, moist meadows and other damp habitats. Plants may be planted in "normal" garden soils, but growth will be slower. Plants are not common but have become easier to find in the last two to three years.

Propagate by seed, divisions, stem cuttings or layering.

**Oenothera** (ee-no-the′ ra) Evening Primrose, Sundrop Onagraceae

Of the 125 or so species of annuals, biennials, and perennials, about a half dozen are well-known garden plants. Many are native to the United States and Canada and have become well established in gardens. The leaves are alternate, and stems are often woody at the base. The 4-petaled flowers are usually yellow, although white and rose flowers occur on a number of lesser-known species. Height ranges from 4-6″ for the diminutive *O. acaulis*, dandelion sundrop, to the 4′ tall common evening primrose.

A number of species have vespartine flowers, meaning they open in the evening and accounting for one of their common names. For example, the flowering habit of the common evening primrose, *O. biennis*, now more of a roadside weed than a garden plant, fascinated the English poet Keats who was "startled by the leap of buds into ripe flowers" and for "shutting again with a loud popping noise about sunrise". However, many species do not exhibit this nocturnal manner and are referred to as sundrops. Japanese beetles find *O. biennis* particularly tasty and Harry Phillips (*Growing and Propagating Wild Flowers, 1985*) reports that their presence spares neighboring plants from attack. I want to be the neighbor.

Flowers of most species persist only for a day or so, but many buds are produced, resulting in long-flowering garden plants. As with other genera, differences of opinion occur as to what plants belong in what taxonomic niche. Many similarities occur between species and it is inevitable that shunting back and forth occurs. Changes in *O. lamarckiana* and *O. missouriensis* have occurred and *O. tetragona* has also "officially" disappeared. As gardeners, we should select the cultivars we like, and not worry too much if the nursery has it filed under the correct name.

This genus, along with *Epilobium*, *Fuchsia* and *Gaura*, belongs to the evening primrose family, Onagraceae. In general, recognizing family characteristics is difficult for most students and of little interest to others, however this is one of the easiest families to recognize. Plants of this family bear flowers with 4 or 8 petals and 4 sepals, an uncommon number. However, the telltale sign is at the base of the open flowers. There, the four translucent sepals are reflexed behind the flower like the ears of your dog when her head is hanging out the car window, and are very persistent. Once recognized in one member of the family, they are easily recognized in others.

Quick Reference to Oenothera Species

| | Height (in.) | Flower color | Flowers nocturnal |
|---|---|---|---|
| *O. caespitosa* | 4-8 | White, Pink | Yes |
| *O. fruticosa* | 18-24 | Yellow | No |
| *O. macrocarpa* | 6-12 | Yellow | No |
| *O. odorata* | 18-24 | Yellow | Yes |
| *O. perennis* | 12-24 | Yellow | No |
| *O. speciosa* | 12-24 | White | No |

**-*caespitosa*** (say-spi-to′ sa) Tufted Evening Primrose 4-8″/12″
Early Summer White, Pink Western North America Zones 4-7

The prostrate species is native from northern Mexico, north to Washington and east to the Sierras. Plants naturally grow in scrubby soils in very dry areas, at altitudes of 3000 to 8000 feet. If they are to be cultivated, they are most suitable for the front of the border or in the rock garden. Plants are stemless and the 4″ long narrow, hairy leaves are clustered in a rosette. Erect flower buds give way to 2-3″ wide fragrant flowers that open in late afternoon, continue into the night and close the next morning, often by ten o'clock or noon. When open, flowers can almost cover the plant. They open white and fade to pink with contrasting yellow stamens, persisting for 4-6 weeks. Beautiful plants for dry, sheltered, sunny locations, but lousy elsewhere. Forget them in the South. They require excellent drainage and do poorly in hot, humid climates.

Propagate by seed or division in the spring. Seeds should be lightly covered and sown in a well-drained medium. Place seed tray in warm (70-75°F), humid conditions.

**Cultivars:**

var. *eximea* is similar in flower habit but has stems, resulting in a somewhat taller plant (8-12″).

subsp. *marginata* has white flowers and is offered by a number of nurseries.

***-fruticosa*** (froo-ti-ko′ sa) Common Sundrops 18-24″/2′
Summer Yellow Eastern North America Zones 4-8

Most of the popular garden cultivars are found here. The reddish, slender, hairy stems bear 1-3″ long, hairy, entire, lance-shaped sessile leaves. The basal leaves are 2-4″ and a little over 1″ wide. Erect flower buds open to a terminal cluster of 1-2″ wide, bright yellow flowers, making this one of the prettiest species of the genus. The seed capsule is one way of distinguishing this species from other yellow-flowered forms. It is shaped like a club, tapering to a slender stalk (a shape known as clavate). Full sun is necessary for best performance and dry soils are tolerated, if not embraced. One of the mainstays of the evening primrose group was *O. tetragona*, however, it has now been classified as *O. fruticosa* subsp. *glauca*. Many of the better garden cultivars belong to this subspecies of *O. fruticosa*.

Propagate by seed or division in summer.

**Cultivars:**

Some of these may be hybrids with other species; be sure to ask for the cultivar when purchasing selections of sundrops.

'African Sun' is an example of perhaps a selection or perhaps a hybrid. Nevertheless, plants display good flower power with light yellow flowers and reasonable vigor.

'Erica Robin' produces bright yellow flowers on willowy stems. The leaves emerge yellow with red spots. Plants probably belong to subsp. *glauca*.

'Fireworks' grows about 18″ tall with red stems and buds which open to 2-3″ wide bright yellow flowers. In trials at the Gardens at UGA, flowering occurred from May 20 to mid June.

'Highlights' grows 12″ tall with 2″ wide yellow flowers.

'Illumination' has thicker, more bronzy leaves with large yellow flowers.

'Lady Brookborough' bears dozens of bright yellow flowers.

'Lemon Drop' is likely a hybrid and has been an excellent performer in the Gardens at UGA, flowering for a longer time than other sundrops. Plants have a nice mounded habit with plenty of light yellow flowers.

'Summer Solstice' is about 18-24″ tall with yellow flowers in June and July.

'Yellow River' is about 18″ tall and has 2-3″ wide deep yellow flowers. The foliage turns mahogany brown in the fall.

***-macrocarpa*** (mac-ro′ car-pa) Ozark Sundrops 6-12″/12″
Summer Yellow South-Central United States Zones 4-7

Plants used to be known as *O. missouriensis*, but recent shifts in taxonomic thought have changed it to its current name. When plants are well grown, their beauty is unrivaled. Although short in stature, their paper-thin flowers may be up to 5″ across. Solitary, bright lemon-yellow, funnel-shaped flowers persist for many days. The sepals are often spotted red in the bud stage and remain so even while the flowers are open. The fruit capsule is ellipsoid and winged, a rather curious sight. The spreading plants are deeply rooted and bear short reddish stems with upright growing tips (decumbent). The 1-4″ long leaves are petioled and entire. Plants are native to Missouri, Oklahoma and Kansas and south to Texas.

Plants can struggle in the summer heat in the South while in the North, the addition of a winter mulch is often beneficial. Plant in full sun to partial shade and allow soil to occasionally dry out. Plants are included in xeric landscape or gardening programs, so good drainage is a must.

Propagate by seed as soon as ripe or by division after flowering.

**Cultivars:**

'Comanche Campfire' bears large silvery leaves borne on ruby red petioles, and big yellow flowers. An excellent performer as shown by the fact that in 2001, plants were introduced in the GreatPlants® program, a joint effort of the Nebraska Nursery and Landscape Association and the Nebraska Statewide Arboretum. Plants grow approximately 15″ tall and 20″ wide.

'Greencourt Lemon', found in the garden of Countess von Stein Zeppelin in Germany, has gray-green leaves and pale yellow 3″ wide flowers. I love this plant, but it is short lived in many North American gardens.

'Lemon Silver' belongs to subsp. *fremontii*, characterized by grayish leaves and bright yellow flowers. This selection is only about 12″ tall, and has wonderful muted yellow flowers over obvious gray-green foliage. Plants hate wet feet, plant them high and dry.

'Silver Blade' is the name given for *O. m.* subsp. *incana*. The tern "incana" means gray or silver and this plant's claim to fame is the wonderful gray foliage. Plants were selected in 1999 for the GreatPlants® program (see 'Comanche Campfire' above).

***-odorata*** (o-do-rah′ ta) Twisted Evening Primrose 18-24″/2′
Early Summer Yellow Southern South America Zones 4-8

The fragrant, solitary yellow flowers have a red tinge, are 2-3″ wide, and open in late afternoon. The base of the plant is somewhat woody and the sessile, 4-6″ long stem leaves have conspicuous wavy edges.

This is a fair garden performer at best but other yellow-flowered species are available which are hardier, more floriferous, and provide open flowers during the day and evening.

Propagate by seed or division.

***-perennis*** (pe-ren′ is) | Nodding Sundrops | 12-24″/18″
Summer | Yellow | Eastern North America | Zones 3-8
(syn. *O. pumila*)

This common sundrop occurs over much of eastern North America and may be treated as a biennial or perennial. The 1-2″ long leaves are lancelike, slightly hairy, and entire. The plant often begins to flower when 5-9″ tall but the flower stalk continues to expand to 1½ to 2′ in height. The flower buds are nodding, thus the common name, and reveal handsome 1″ wide yellow flowers. The leafy flower stalk is often branched, and diurnal flowers (open during the day, closed at night) are carried in loose panicles or racemes. This species is commonly offered by nurserymen but is not

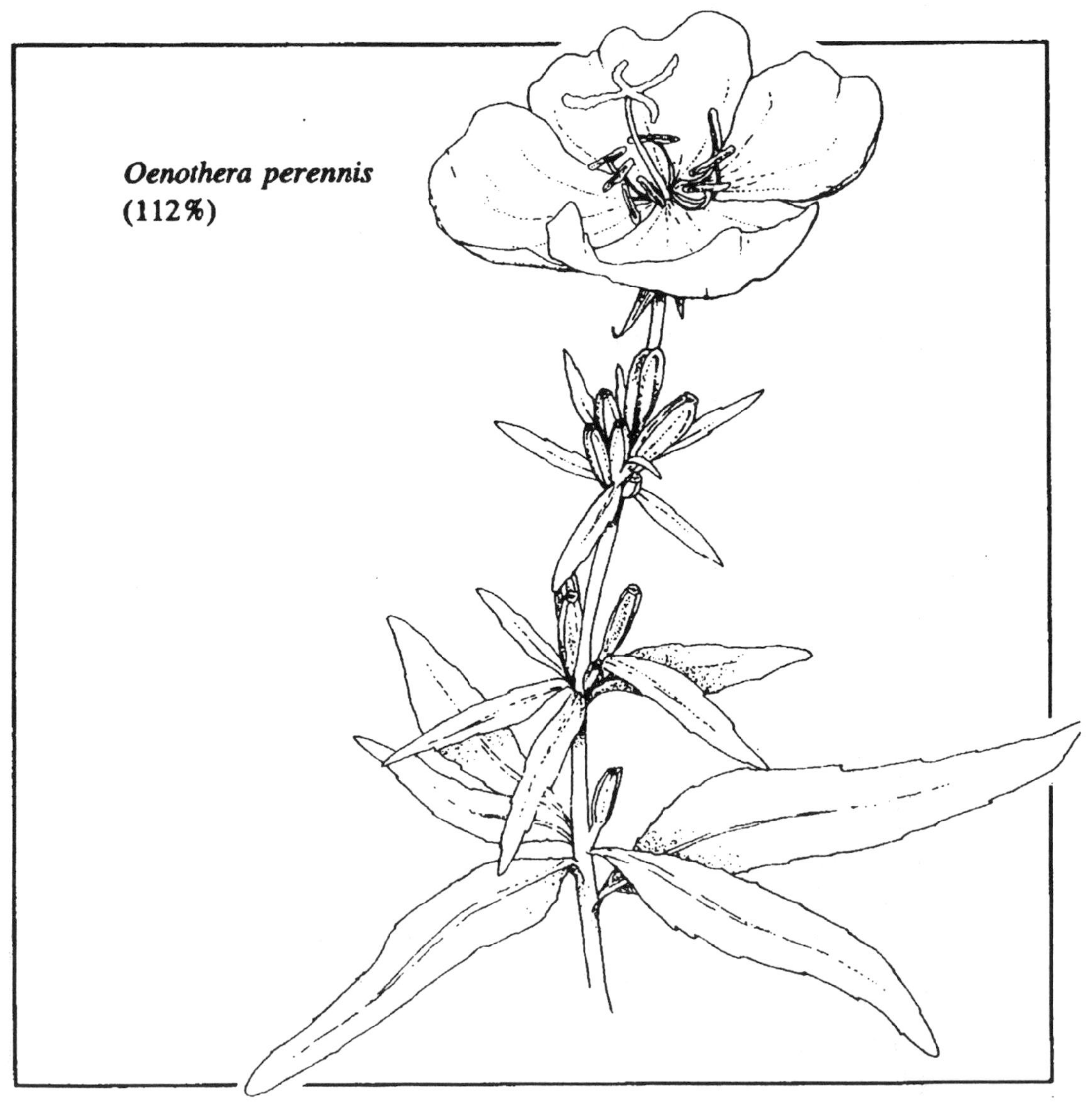

***Oenothera perennis* (112%)**

as showy as *O. fruticosa*. Perhaps it is so popular because people look at the botanical name and believe they are purchasing a long-lasting perennial plant.

Grow in full sun with decent drainage. Cut back hard after flowering when plants look bedraggled. New rosettes will form soon after.

Propagate by seed any time or by division in the spring or fall.

***-speciosa*** (spee-see-o' sa) Showy Evening Primrose 12-24"/18"
Summer White, Rose South-Central United States Zones 5-8

Due to the stoloniferous rootstock, plants tend to spread more rapidly than many other species. In fact, this is a bloody weed—a beautiful plant, but an aggressive thug. The 1-3" long linear leaves are pinnately lobed and bear a soft pubescence. The 1-2" diameter flowers, which appear in the axils of the upper leaves, start white and mature to rose, the color that is usually associated with this plant. If grown in full sun and moderately good soil, handsome, compact plants result. However, in rich soils or when heavily fertilized, plants become a rampant nuisance. Plants are naturalized along roadsides in north Georgia and may be found in dry places, fields, and prairies. High humidity is tolerated but plants do better in the Plains states and western part of the country than in the East and South.

Propagate from seed or division.

**Cultivars**:

'Alba' bears white flowers.

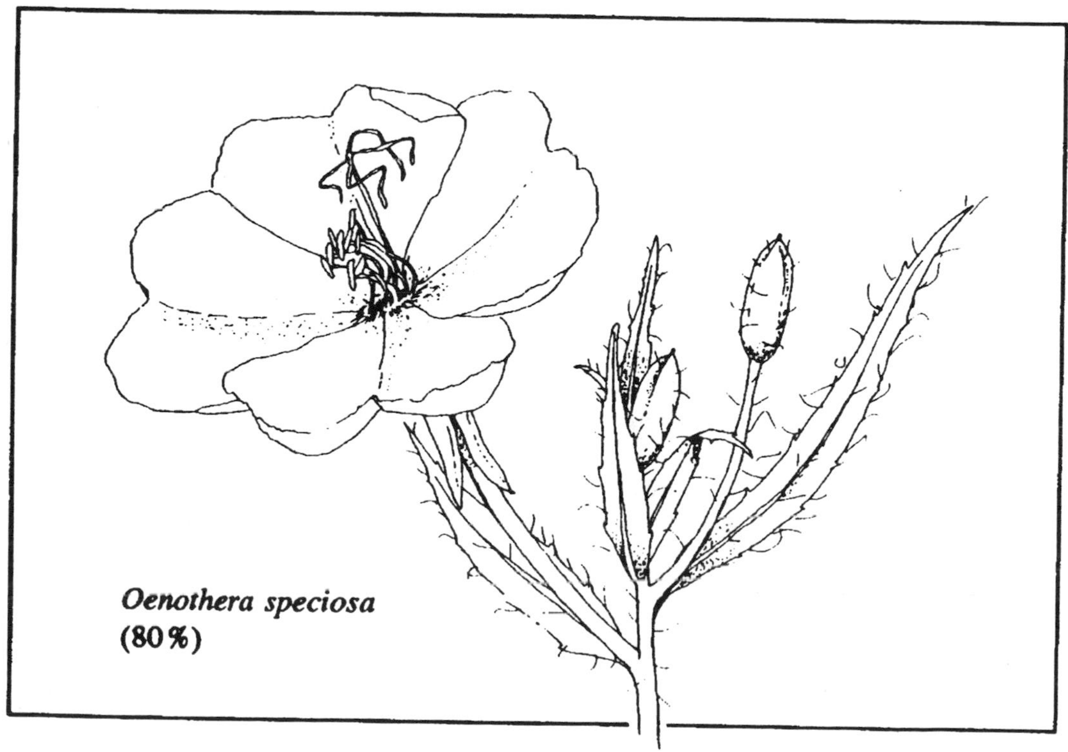

***Oenothera speciosa***
**(80%)**

**Related Species:**

*O. acaulis* has 2-3″ wide white flowers which fade to rose and open in the evening. Plants have dandelion-like leaves and grow 6-9″ tall. In fact, the leaves are so similar to dandelions they are often mistaken for weeds and pulled out in spring. Full sun and well-drained soils are needed. Probably not winter hardy north of zone 5.

*O. berlandieri*, Mexican evening primrose, is a bit of a mystery plant. It has arisen in catalogs in recent years and some of the most handsome cultivars have been paired with it. However, it is hardly ever listed in a reputable reference volume and when referenced is usually shuttled to another species. It has been listed as *O. speciosa* var. *childsii*, *O. speciosa* var. *berlandieri*, simply *O. speciosa* and more recently *Calylophus berlandieri*. Nevertheless, plants appear to be less invasive and neater than those of *O. speciosa*. Plants bear slender prostrate branches about 6-12″ tall, upon which are produced 1-2″ diameter rose-colored flowers. 'Siskiyou', from the terrific nursery of the same name, bears 2″ wide pink saucer-shaped flowers over 8″ plants. 'Woodside White' is about 15″ tall, producing large white flowers with a chartreuse eye. Performance has been excellent in zone 6-8.

*O. biennis*, common evening primrose, is a most variable species, but in general has leafy, erect branched stems and large yellow flowers which open in the evening. Plants can reach 8′ in height, but generally flower when five to six feet tall. They should be treated as annuals or perennials, but often reseed themselves. Plants are native to eastern North America but have naturalized in Europe, earning the common name German rampion.

*O. drummondii*, beach evening primrose, is native to areas on the Atlantic and Pacific coasts, down to Baja California. The spreading plants are covered with sharp, stiff hairs throughout and bear gray-green leaves and pale yellow 2-3″ wide vespartine flowers. Terrific salt-tolerant plants for sandy soils; heavy soils should be avoided. Probably hardy in zones 8-10, maybe into zone 7. I first saw this in the sandy soils near the Swan River in Perth, Western Australia. I brought some seed back, but Georgia was not exactly to their liking. Dead as a doornail in about five minutes.

*O. glazioviana*, Lamarck's sundrop, has to be one of the neatest plants around. This large-flowered evening primrose is best known for the cultivar 'Tina James', named after the gardener in Reisterstown, Maryland. All buds in a population of mature plants will open with a "pop" at the same time in the evening. Plants are often found in childrens' gardens where signs announce the opening time each night. At the marvelous childrens' garden created by Jane Taylor at Michigan State University, people literally line up to see the wonderful event. Her garden is an enchanted place; dusk with 'Tina James' is magical.

*O. rosea*, rosy evening primrose, has rose-colored flowers but the buds are erect, not nodding like those of *O. speciosa*. The flowers open pale pink and mature to rich rose. This species is becoming less difficult to locate and sometimes seed can be obtained from rare plant specialists.

## *Oligoneuron*

See *Aster*

***Omphalodes*** (om-fa-lod′ eez) Navel-Seed Boraginaceae

A few species of *Omphalodes* are occasionally grown in the United States, and like most members of the Boraginaceae, have blue flowers, alternate leaves and bear hard fruits (nutlets). The common name, navel-seed, comes from the deep groove in the nutlet, a characteristic which separates *Omphalodes* from the other members of the family. It is sometimes confused with *Myosotis* and *Cynoglossum* because of their similar size, foliage, and blue flowers. Some of the more visible differences include:

| | **Habit** | **Leaves** | **Pubescence** | **Flowers** | **Nutlet** |
|---|---|---|---|---|---|
| *Omphalodes* | Creeping* | Petioled | Sparse | Blue | Slightly hairy |
| *Cynoglossum* | Upright | Petioled | Stiff | Dark blue | Prickly |
| *Myosotis* | Upright | Sessile | Slightly | Blue with eye | Smooth, shiny |

* *O. verna*, the most common in cultivation

An annual species, *O. linifolia*, flaxleaf navel-seed, about one foot tall with fresh white flowers, is occasionally grown but the two perennials offered are *O. verna*, blue-eyed Mary, and *O. cappadocica*.

Quick Reference to Omphalodes Species

| | Height | Stoloniferous |
|---|---|---|
| *O. cappadocica* | 8-12″ | No |
| *O. verna* | 4-8″ | Yes |

***-cappadocica*** (kap-a-doe′ si-ca) Navelwort 8-12″/10″
Blue Spring Asia Minor Zones 6-8

Plants are not as vigorous or "cute' as the better-known *O. verna*, but as plants become more available, they are starting to be appreciated a little more. The 3-4″ long basal leaves are quite hairy and have prominent lateral veins. The basal leaves have long petioles but the smaller stem leaves are almost sessile as they ascend the stem. The half inch wide flowers are bright blue and held on long flower stems (pedicels) forming elongated racemes near the top of the plants. Occasionally clones will appear with white centers to the blue flowers.

A cool, shady well-drained site works best. Excellent drainage is a must. They are not particularly tolerant of high heat and humidity and are better plants for the West Coast zone 8 than the southern zone 8.

Seed is the method of choice for these plants. Although division may be used, they do not recover well when the roots are disturbed.

**Cultivars:**

'Cherry Ingram' was named after the famous plant explorer, Collingwood "Cherry" Ingram (1880-1981), a British ornithologist, traveler, botanist and expert in ornamental cherries. Plants are 12-18″ tall with blue flowers that fade to lavender-violet. Plants are a little larger than the species.

'Joy Skies' is probably a hybrid and bears small blue flowers.

'Lilac Mist' has lilac flowers in the spring on 4-8″ plants.

'Parisian Skies' bears many azure blue flowers above a nice rosette of dark green leaves.

'Starry Eyes' bears flowers with the margin of each purple petal outlined in pinkish white, resulting in a eye-catching starry effect. Quite handsome.

**-*verna*** (ver′ na) Blue-Eyed Mary 2-8″/12″
Spring Blue Southern Europe Zones 6-9

*O. verna* is well established in European gardens but only beginning to be appreciated in North America. Spreading rapidly by underground stems, it makes a useful ground cover for partially shaded locations. The 1-3″ long oval leaves are long petioled, and have a short, abrupt point at the end. They are entire, conspicuously veined and remain evergreen in the South. The long flower stems bear 2-4 deep blue, ½″ wide flowers with white throats which cover the foliage in spring and early summer. The blue-eyed flowers were a favorite of Queen Marie Antoinette, thus accounting for the popular name.

Although plants are tolerant of poor soils and dry shade, garden performance is enhanced in moist areas and partial shade, as long as soils are well drained. Full sun results in stunted plants which never attain the graceful habit seen in partial shade. Slugs tend to dine on it, as they do on many other stoloniferous species, and slug repellent should be applied in early spring.

Propagate from seed or division in spring immediately after flowering.

**Cultivars:**

var. *alba* is similar, but has white flowers.

## *Onoclea* (o-no′ clay-a) Sensitive Fern Dryopteridaceae

The genus consists of but one species, *O. sensibilis*, the sensitive fern, but what a wonderful bachelor it is. The common name was apparently given by early North American settlers who noted that plants were highly sensitive to early frosts, and one of the first ferns to collapse in the fall.

This is a un-fernlike fern, consisting of broad smooth pinnatifid leaflets. "Pinnatifid" means that the leaflets don't quite terminate at the stem, but are winged. Plants consist of two types of leaflets: the sterile green forms which are easily recognized, and the fertile brown 12″ tall stalks. The fertile stalks consist of small, hardened beadlike divisions of fertile leaflets, which turn dark brown with age. Ferns are also known as bead fern because of the appearance of the fertile stalks. The fiddleheads are pale red in the spring.

They tolerate and in fact explode in moist soils, but are less aggressive in dry soils. Plants multiply through their creeping rootstalk, forming extensive colonies over time. For some, this is one of our favorite native ferns, easily grown from southern Canada to Florida. For others, it is too aggressive.

Another fern which closely resembles sensitive fern is the native netted chain fern, *Woodwardia areolata*, and the two are often confused. *Woodwardia* is smaller and the fertile fronds are not bearded, but form puckered, narrow leaflets. The sori (spore cases) are carried in broken chainlike rows on these fertile fronds. *Woodwardia* is a far better choice if soils are not consistently moist, but they too are aggressive colonizers.

**Onopordum** (o-no-por′ dum) Scotch Thistle Asteraceae

If you found yourself staring down the massive spiny stem of this plant in Scotland or in some other northwestern European land, the last thing you would suggest is that it would actually be sold as a garden plant. James V of England chose this plant as the Scottish emblem and it became known as the Scotch thistle. Other names followed, like cotton thistle, Queen Mary's thistle or the silver thistle. The first time I saw a Scotch thistle (*O. acanthium*) was on a tea towel that somebody gave my mother upon returning from a trip to Scotland. To me, it represented nothing more than additional dishes to dry. However, as I have matured as a gardener, I have had to open my mind to the creativity of designers and the need for something impressive, regardless of garden size. Thus, I have had to accept Scottish weeds in the garden.

While they are deadly, I grudgingly admit that the large gray leaves with their deep sinuses and spiny fingers on the 6-8′ tall plants do add an exclamation mark to the garden. The leaves generally run down the side of the stems resulting in winged stems to which the leaves attach. They are biennial and produce a handsome silver rosette the first year before extending to their full height the second year. The branched silvery stems are particularly handsome set off against a background of dark shrubbery. The thistle flowers are usually purple but occasionally white-flowered forms occur. Plants may seed wildly; be careful, one plant is about all a garden can handle.

Plants differ from cardoon, *Cynara cardunculus* (which see) by being taller and having winged stems. Leaves are more hairy in cardoon than in Scotch thistle.

Propagate from seed sown in summer, planted out to form a rosette prior to hard frosts.

**Related Species:**

*O. acaule* forms handsome white-pubescent rosettes in the summer and fall and then sends up white flowers on short flower stems in late spring or summer. Since plants are essentially stemless, they are only about 12″ tall. Hardy to zone 7.

*O. bracteatum* is about 4′ tall and bears white pubescent leaves often tipped with yellowish spines. The large 6″ diameter purple flower heads are produced in late spring and summer. A little easier for mid-size gardens although hardy only to about zone 7.

**Ophiopogon** (o-fee-o-po′ gon) Mondo Grass Convallariaceae

The 5-10 species of edging and ground cover plants are often confused with *Liriope muscari*, common lily-turf. Both genera are tufted, have basal leaves, and bear bluish purple flowers in summer. However, the leaves of mondo grass are far more narrow than those of common lily-turf, the smaller flowers are hidden by the leaves, the fruits are metallic blue compared to the lustrous black fruits of *Liriope*, and the species are less cold hardy. These differences, however, do not make mondo grass any less useful or ornamental.

*Ophiopogon* is an excellent edging plant and ground cover that tolerates full sun but prefers areas of moist soils and partial shade. Numerous cultivars and species are now being offered, including *O. chingii*, Chinese mondo, and *O. kansuensis*, also from China. The most common species are *O. japonicus*, dwarf mondo grass and *O. planiscapus*.

-***japonicus*** (ja-pon′ i-kus) Dwarf Mondo Grass 8-15″/12″
Summer Lilac Japan, Korea Zones 6-9

The numerous dark green grasslike leaves are 15″ long and ¼″ wide. Light lilac flowers are held in short terminal racemes, almost hidden by the foliage. The long underground stolons and tuberous roots result in spreading, drought-tolerant plants useful as edging or ground covers.

The most common method of propagation is by division, although seeds germinate in 6 weeks if the berries are soaked for 24 hours to facilitate removal of the pulp.

**Cultivars:**

'Gyoku-Ryu', introduced by Dr. John Creech, is even shorter and more compact than 'Nippon'. Plants could easily be substituted for turf if you could afford to do so.

'Little Tabby' has handsome silver-veined evergreen leaves and white flowers in spring and early summer. Plants are very slow growers and perhaps are better used as a mixed container plant rather than a ground cover. This is a fabulous plant. Find it, buy it.

'Nippon' is only 2-4″ tall and has whitish flowers in the summer. This is similar to and may be the same thing as 'Nana'.

'Pygmaeus' ('Compactus') is one of a number of dwarf forms, growing no more than 3″ tall. A container such as a dish garden is best.

'Silver Dragon' is similar to 'Variegatus', producing white variegated foliage on 12″ tall plants.

'Seoulitary Man' came from Tony Avent of Plants Delight Nursery in Raleigh, North Carolina. This is a clumping form with narrow leaves that does not produce runners and seems to stay put.

'Sparkler' is only 4-6″ tall and produces white flowers over the shiny green leaves.

'Torafu' was first introduced by plantsman Barry Yinger of Asiatica Nursery. Leaves have cross-hatching of yellow bands, similar to zebra grass (*Miscanthus* 'Zebrina'). Interesting, to be sure.

'Variegatus' has white-margined foliage with negligible blooms. Known as silver mist plant.

**Related Species:**

*O. chingii* grows about half a foot tall and has long narrow, somewhat pendulous leaves. Small white flowers are produced in early to mid summer. Zones 5 or 6-8.

*O. jaburan* is coarser than *O. japonicus*, with light purple to white flowers. Plants grow 15-18″ tall but are not as good a ground cover as the previous species. Cold hardy to zone 8 or 9. 'Aureus' bears yellow-striped leaves which provides additional foliar interest. 'Variegatus' ('Vittatus') has white-striped leaves and is also more effective than the species. Both look particularly good in groups of 12 or more.

*O. planiscapus* is best known for its black-leaved cultivars. 'Nigrescens', known as black mondo grass, produces dark purple, almost black leaves on 6″ tall plants. The flowers are light lilac to pink and followed by black berries in the fall. Growth is slow, but the foliage provides a wonderful contrast to light-colored foliage such as the light green species of hosta, or in concert with creeping Jenny (*Lysimachia congestiflora* 'Aurea'). It is grown successfully as far north as zone 5 but zone 6 is more realistic. Partial shade in the South is recommended, full sun is best in the North. 'Arabicus' is a shorter (4-6″), perhaps darker clone.

## ***Origanum*** (o-ree-gah′ num) Oregano Lamiaceae

About 20 species are recognized, but the genus is better known for the herbs oregano and marjoram than for its ornamental value. Although sweet marjoram, *O. majorana*, is used mainly as a culinary herb, oregano has made breakthroughs into the ornamental arena. Common oregano, *O. vulgare*, is used as a bright underplanting while a number of cultivars of this and a closely related species, *O. laevigatum*, are enjoyed as a garden plant and a long-lasting cut flower. Numerous cultivars have been developed so there is no longer any doubt about the ornamental value of the genus.

The opposite leaves of all species are aromatic and the flowers are whorled like a salvia's. The majority require alkaline soils and in fact turn over and die in highly acidic or poorly drained soils. They are native to the Mediterranean and therefore do not appreciate high heat when combined with high humidity. Plants, however, have done well in the Midwest and southern Canada, and some excellent cultivars are making their way to the market.

***-laeviegatum*** (lay-vee′ ga- tum) Marjoram 1-2′/2′
Late Summer Purple Middle East Zones 5-9

Plants are becoming more and more popular as additional nurseries offer the species. Flowering occurs in mid summer to fall in most areas, and is a terrific butterfly plant. Plants are subshrubs—woody at the base but dying to the ground in the fall. Growing 18-24″ tall, they are used as striking garden plants and cut flowers. They do best in gravelly soil and are highly drought tolerant.

**Cultivars**:

'Amethyst Falls' is a hybrid of confusing origin, but certainly appears to have some of this species in it. The selection was made at Bluebird Nursery in Clarkson, Nebraska from seeds provided by gardeners Gwen and Panayoti Kelaidis. Panayoti is the curator of the rock gardens at the Denver Botanic Garden, Gwen is the gardener. Amethyst flowers, interesting grayish foliage and a nice fragrance are part of this hybrid. Zones 5-7.

'Barbara Tingley' produces small petals surrounded by rosy green papery bracts.
'Herrenhausen' has reddish purple foliage, deepening even more in the fall. The flowers are pale lilac to purple, depending on temperature. Plants grow upright in cool weather but tend to sprawl in warm days. Named after the 17th century garden near Hanover, Germany.
'Hopley's Purple' is better known as a cut flower than as a garden plant, but will be used as more material becomes available. Plants can grow over 2′ tall and produce strong pink to mauve flowers with large bracts. A knockout!
'Pilgrim' is about 2′ tall with rich lavender flowers.
'Santa Cruz' has soft pink flowers. Probably a hybrid.
'Silver Anniversary' is a handsome variegated form with pink flowers.

***-vulgare*** (vul-gah′ ree) Oregano, Pot Marjoram, Wild Marjoram 1-3½′
Summer Violet Europe Zones 3-7

This rhizomatous plant is seldom used but a number of cultivars selected for leaf color are coming out of the closet. The leaves are 1-2″ long, usually entire but sometimes slightly toothed. Each leaf has many glands which when broken result in the familiar fragrance of this herb. The violet to purple flowers are held in a loose panicle occurring in early to late summer. The bracts which surround the flowers actually provide the ornamental value, although flowers are more useful in the related species than this one.

Place in well-drained soils and provide some afternoon shade for golden forms. Propagate by cuttings or division.

**Cultivars:**

'Album' has bushy, light green leaves with white flowers. Plants are about 15″ tall.
'Aureum' is a popular form with golden foliage and purple flowers. Used as a spreading 4-6″ tall ground cover.
'Compactum' is only 2-4″ tall.
'Compactum Aureum' is even shorter and more compact than 'Aureum'. Particularly useful for growing between rocks on a pathway or a patio.
'Dark Leaf' has dark bronze foliage with strong fragrance and flavor. The foliage tends to fade in the heat.
'Newtown Wonder' has golden leaves similar to 'Aureum' and appears closely related in every way.
'Variegata' bears golden-green variegated foliage.

**Related Species:**

*O. libanoticum*, hopflower oregano, produces bracts of lavender and chartreuse. Plants are trailing and will be best if allowed to fall over banks or out of containers. In 2004, plants were included in the Plant Select® Program, administered by the Denver Botanic Gardens and Colorado State University.

*O. rotundifolium* 'Kent Beauty' is a handsome mounding plant (< 1′ tall) with lovely veined blue-green leaves and pink bracts at the end of the pendulous stems. Zone 5-8.

***Ornithogalum*** (or-nith-og′ al-um) Ornithogalum Liliaceae

Over 150 species are found in this bulbous genus and many are useful for border plants or as cut flowers. The most common species, *O. umbellatum*, star-of-Bethlehem, has been grown for centuries and is such a vigorous colonizer that many gardeners consider it a weed. Others such as *O. thyrsoides*, chincherinchee, and *O. arabicum*, Arabian star flower, are better behaved and produced throughout the world for cut flowers. With the exception of some South African species (e.g. *O. dubium*), all produce white flowers with green stripes on the petals. Those from South Africa are generally in orange-yellow-red tones and are insufficiently hardy to be considered perennial except in the most frost-free areas of North America. Hybrids are produced for commercial cut flower production although gardeners will likely not benefit. In fact, few species perform well except in mild moderate climates on the West Coast, although few situations exist that deter *O. umbellatum* from colonizing the world. As a general rule of thumb, all species are best treated similar to *Gladiolus*.

In general, plant bulbs 2-3″ deep and in bold clumps. Allow 10-12″ between larger species, about 6″ between the smaller ones. Plants go dormant soon after flowering.

Quick Reference to Ornithogalum Species

| | Height (in.) | Flower color | Flower number |
|---|---|---|---|
| *O. arabicum* | 18-24 | White, black center | 6-12 |
| *O. nutans* | 12-15 | Greenish white | 3-12 |
| *O. thyrsoides* | 12-15 | White | 12-30 |
| *O. umbellatum* | 6-9 | White | 10-20 |

***-arabicum*** (a-ra′ bi-kum) Arabian Star Flower 18-24″/18″
Summer White Mediterranean Zones 8-10

Due to lack of winter hardiness in most parts of the country, this species is not as popular as other members of the genus. The 12-18″ long leaves emerge early and generally lie on the ground. In north Georgia, leaves emerge in December and are invariably damaged by frosts. The clusters of fragrant white flowers rise 1-2′ high in early summer and have conspicuous yellow anthers and a jet black ovary. Flowers do not open all at once, but there are always enough to provide a nice show. They tend to close just before nightfall when they appear like "immense pearls clustered in some sumptuous ornament" (Wilder, *Adventures with Hardy Bulbs, 1936).* The flower heads are also popular as a cut flower because of their excellent shelf life.

Plant bulbs about 6″ deep in a well-drained area in full sun. Lift again in the fall prior to the first hard frost. Store the bulbs in peat moss in a cool, dry place and replant after the last frost date in the spring. In zones 8-10, they can remain in the ground and flowers appear in late spring to early summer, although the flower heads require staking to prevent twisting of the flower stem. They are best suited to gardens of California and the Pacific Northwest.

Propagate by removing offsets when the bulbs are lifted. The offsets usually require 2-3 years before flowering. Bulbs raised from seed will be of plantable size in 18-24 months.

**-*nutans*** (new-tanz) Drooping Star-of-Bethlehem 12-15″/12″
Early Summer Greenish White Southern Europe Zones 5-9

This species has naturalized in the Northeast but is not a particularly well-known plant in America. The narrow 3/8″ wide leaves are about 12-18″ long, and often have a white line running lengthwise down their middle. The 2″ wide greenish white flowers are star shaped, somewhat drooping, and have lovely white margins in front and green midribs in the rear. They are loosely borne on a 12-15″ tall stem in late spring and early summer, and shortly after flowering the plant withers away. Where bulbs are comfortable, they can become quite a nuisance, even a bully. I have known many a frustrated gardener to toss bulbs over her shoulder as she weeds her garden. *O. nutans* can tolerate partial shade and is often planted on the edge of woodlands or in partially shaded areas. It also may be naturalized through grass, and because the leaves disappear quickly, the grass may be cut before it gets knee high, a common problem when naturalizing other bulbs such as daffodils in grassy areas.

Propagate similar to *O. arabicum*.

**Cultivars:**
var. *boucheanum* has larger, whiter flowers than the type but is difficult to locate.

**-*thyrsoides*** (thur-soi′ deez) Chincherinchee 12-15″/12″
Summer White South Africa Zones 8-10

Like *O. arabicum*, chincherinchee is known mainly as a cut flower in the florist shop. In most areas it is not cold hardy, however, bulbs are inexpensive and can economically be treated as annuals. Alternatively, bulbs may be lifted, similar to gladiolus and tuberous begonias. They produce 5-6 broad leaves above which emerge 12-30 pure white, 3/4″ long flowers with brown centers on 12″ tall flower stems in early summer. As with *O. arabicum*, plants are best adapted to West Coast gardens.

The common name, chincherinchee, is an onomatopoeic word used to describe the sound of the south winds as they blew through the stalks and flowers in the hedgerows in Cape Province of South Africa. In North America, the species is still referred to as star-of-Bethlehem, particularly by users of cut flowers, perhaps because chincherinchee is so difficult to get your tongue around. Star-of-Bethlehem should be reserved for *O. umbellatum*.

The shelf life of the flowers is legendary and they will last for months in water or on the plant. If you can't grow them in the garden, pick some up at the florist and enjoy them at home. Plants are poisonous and should not be included in your salad. In South Africa, incidents of cattle poisoning occurred when plant parts were accidently included in the forage. Even cows are smart enough to avoid them in fields.

Propagate similarly to *O. arabicum*.

**Cultivars:**

var. *album* has dark-centered pure white flowers that are more densely arranged on the stem.

var. *aureum* bears golden yellow flowers.

'Mount Blanc' and 'Mount Everest' are white double-flowered forms developed specifically for the cut flower trade.

**Related Species:**

*O. saundersiae* is known as giant chincherinchee because of its imposing size. The clean white flowers have a large green-black eye and are borne at the top of the 3′ tall plants. It is used as a cut flower but can be used effectively if planted in groups of at least three. Plants must be lifted and stored over winter.

***-umbellatum*** (um-bel-ah′ tum) Star-of-Bethlehem 6-9″/6″
Late Spring White Mediterranean Zones 4-9

This is the best-known species due to its ability to survive where most others can not. Although native to the Mediterranean, it has become naturalized in many areas of the northeastern United States and as far south as Mississippi. Plants have been grown and enjoyed for hundreds of years; Linnaeus believed that this plant was the "dove's dung" mentioned in the Bible (2 Kings 6:25) and eaten by the Samarians during the great famine. Other accounts of the edibility of these bulbs abound through folk literature, however, in *Plants of the Bible*, H. and A. Moldenke showed the bulbs to be poisonous unless cooked. Regardless of culinary properties, this species has been and will continue to be around for quite some time.

Bulbs produce a mound of narrow, smooth leaves, each about 12″ in length, followed by a flower stem carrying 10-20 star-shaped white flowers. Each flower is about 1-2″ across and striped green on the outside of the three outer segments. The flowers are also remarkable for their consistency in opening just before noon and closing again before sunset. It is so punctual that plants are known as the eleven o'clock lady in the English, French, and Italian languages. Other common names include six o'clock flower, wake-at-noon and sleepy Dick.

This species is not fastidious as to planting site. Deep shade should be avoided but partial shade to full sun is acceptable. Once established, plants are drought tolerant. Bulbs multiply rapidly by bulbils and should be planted where they may be allowed to roam. They are aggressive thugs at times; in the Armitage garden they have mounted a quiet but sustained attack over the years. If additional plants are required, dig the bulbs after flowering, remove the offsets, and replant them in a suitable location.

## *Orontium* (o-ron′ tee-um) Golden Club Araceae

Useful for ponds, pools or swampy areas, golden club is a handsome aquatic plant when controlled. The thick rhizomes of *O. aquaticum* give rise to leathery basal leaves which are elevated or floating, depending on the depth of water. Plants can be potted up and placed in water no deeper than about one foot. Plants belong to the jack-in-

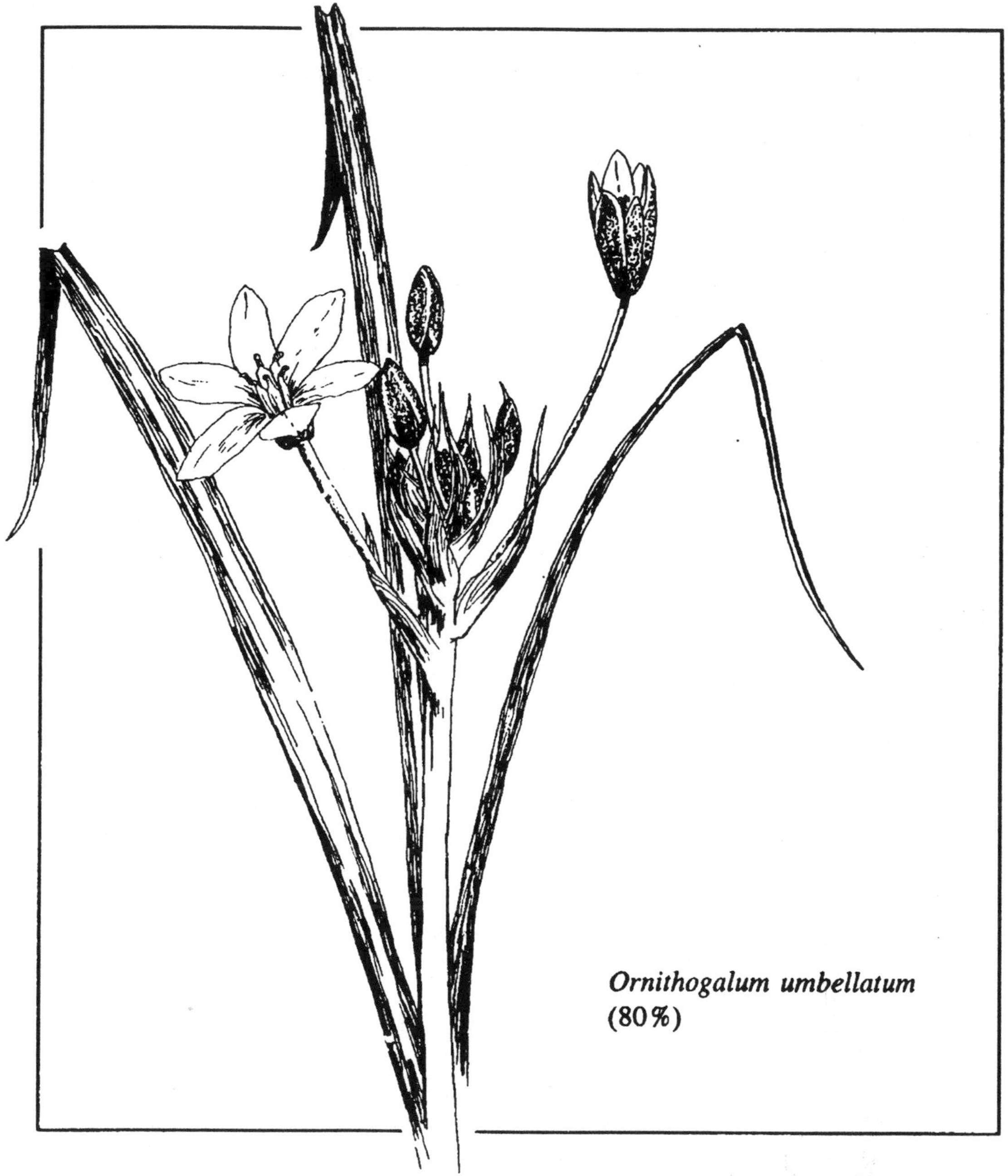

*Ornithogalum umbellatum*
(80%)

the-pulpit family, whose flowers consist of a colorful spathe (pulpit) surrounding a narrow flowering spathe (jack). Many yellow flowers are held on each long narrow spadix but the small green spathe drops off before the flowers appear. Flowers occur in spring.

Plants will spread in the margins of ponds and wet areas by self-seeding in the wet environment. Seeds are shed from the green berries that form after flowering. This is the only species in the genus and is native from Massachusetts to Kentucky and south to Florida. Plants may be considered hardy to 0-5°F.

***Osmunda*** (os-mun′ da) Flowering Fern Osmundaceae

Named for Osmunder, the Saxon god of war, some of the most vigorous garden ferns may be found in the 12 species of the genus. They are probably the largest and coarsest of our native ferns with massive rootstocks, which in mature clumps can be seen up to a foot above the base of the plant, like short tree trunks. The roots themselves are black and wiry and were aggressively harvested for osmunda fiber, widely used as a growing medium for orchids.

They differ from other genera of ferns by having large, globular spore cases (sporangia) with a short, stout stalk. The species within the genus may be distinguished by where the sporangia are found. They are held in separate areas on the leaf stem (interrupted fern), at the top of the rachis (royal fern), or on separate fertile structures (cinnamon fern).

Plants are quite happy in moist areas and if properly irrigated should do well in average garden soils. All are temperate ferns and while they are warm hardy to zone 7b, they are more vigorous when grown in cooler areas.

Quick Reference to Osmunda Species

| | Fronds | Fertile sporangia |
|---|---|---|
| *O. cinnamomea* | Pinnate | Separate stems |
| *O. claytonia* | Pinnate | Share rachis with pinna |
| *O. regalis* | Twice-pinnate | Top of rachis |

***-cinnamomea*** (sin-a mo′ mee-a) Cinnamon Fern 3-5′/3′
Eastern United States Zones 3-7

One of the classic woodland ferns, the cinnamon fern is a popular, easy-to-grow showy plant. In early spring, the fertile leaves are first to appear. The crosiers (fertile fiddleheads) are densely covered with silvery white hairs, then turn bronze as they expand. The unfolding of the fertile crosiers is probably the most ornamental phase of the fern. As they unfold, they stand stiff and erect. The sterile fronds emerge a little later and unlike the fertile ones, tend to grow outward, rather than erect. The spore cases are in clusters, start green and mature to cinnamon. The spores within are bright green. After the fertile leaves have formed, the handsome sterile fiddleheads, which are originally covered with silver-white hairs, unfurl from the clumps of above-ground roots to form the arching fronds so well known in eastern woodlands. The base of each frond bears scattered tufts of cinnamon-colored woolly fibers, thus accounting for its common name. In the fall, the fronds turn a handsome golden, then bronze before succumbing to frost. Plants are native from Labrador to Florida and west to Illinois and Minnesota. Plants also occur naturally in Central and South America, West Indies and eastern Asia.

One of the more heat-tolerant ferns, they do relatively well as far south as zone 7b, assuming sufficient and consistent moisture is available. Otherwise, they are stunted compared to their northern siblings. Shade, moisture and humus-rich soils are essential.

Spores must be sown immediately upon maturity as they do not remain viable for very long once they have been shed.

***-claytonia*** (klay-ton-ee′ a) — Interrupted Fern — 3-4′/3′
Eastern North America — Zones 3-6

Here is another fern which can eat up significant acreage where well established. This fern evokes more comments about its curious form than about its classic beauty. The sterile fronds are wider at the middle than at either end and always arch outward. When they arise in the spring, they are often covered with woolly pinkish hairs that soon disappear. The fertile stems grow upward. It is the curious arrangement of leaflets (pinnae) and spore cases (sporangia) on the same stem which makes this fern unique. Usually 3-8 fronds occur in which the leaflets are interrupted by four or more pairs of dark brown sporangia. Once the spores have been shed, the sporangia fall off, leaving the stems bare in the center for the rest of the season. The leaflets below the spore cases are smaller and more widely spaced than leaflets on the rest of the plant. The species was named for John Clayton, also well remembered for the wonderful spring wild flower, *Claytonia*.

Similar to other members of the genus, shade and rich moist soils are needed for best performance. They perform poorly in hot summers and although occasionally enjoyed as far south as zone 7, they are not nearly as striking as further north.

Propagate similar to cinnamon fern.

***-regalis*** (re-gah′ lis) — Royal Fern — 4-6′/4′
Cosmopolitan — Zones 4-7

The closer you get to this plant, the less it looks like a fern and more it looks like a member of the legume family, like locust, or even sweet pea. The leaves are twice-pinnate, meaning that the leaflets (pinnae) are divided once again into pinnate leaflets. Where they are happy, they are some of the biggest, most robust plants around, not just in the fern family, but in all herbaceous plants. Of course, in the Armitage garden, they look like my dog Hannah uses them for her bed. I was ready to dismiss this as another fern that I would have to get on a airplane to admire, until I visited my friends Donna and Ed Lambert, right here in beautiful Athens. Donna's love of ferns has made her woodland garden a mecca for fern lovers everywhere. She has transported incalculable loads of leaf litter to enrich her soils (something I have been too lazy to do, thus the difference in our gardens) and her ferns, including the royals, have responded in glorious fashion. Providing abundant organic matter is important.

The smooth fiddleheads arise in early spring from the massive wiry root tussocks of the established clump. The roots of this species were the main source of osmunda fiber mentioned above, although the other species are also used. The foliage is a translucent green, which, if the light behind it is just right, appear to be almost fluorescent. The light brown sporangia are formed on the top of the sterile leaves, thus accounting for its other common name, flowering fern.

Plants can handle more direct sun than the other members of the genus and can tolerate full sun in the North if provided with moisture throughout the season. Its natural habitat is in wetlands, along streams, bogs and low spots in pastures and meadows. It will tolerate water up to its "knees", but is equally happy at the edge of streams or in boggy settings.

Propagate similar to cinnamon fern.

## *Oxalis* (oks-ah′ lis) Wood Sorrel Oxalidaceae

To extol the beauty of wood sorrel to most gardeners elicits chuckles or outright rebuke, depending on the manners of the listeners. However, with well over 800 species, it makes little sense to dismiss the whole genus because of a few experiences with a weed or two (okay, thousands of weeds). Most of these low-growing plants arise from tubers and are often found in the bulb section of the catalog. The genus is cosmopolitan, but centers of diversity exist in North America, South America and South Africa. Some of our better natives include *O. oregana*, from the West and *O. violacea*.

Most species have palmate leaflets, generally in 3s, which usually fold down at night. The flowers occur singly or in small inflorescences, and often close in the evening. Flower color ranges from yellow to white and pink. They can produce copious amounts of seed which are ejected forcibly when the fruit is ripe, causing the weedy species to appear everywhere, although the seed of the sought-after ones never seem to germinate. There are some really obnoxious members, in particular the yellow-flowered greenhouse/houseplant weed, *O. repens*, which puts roots down to China and chuckles over attempts to remove it. I'm not sure *O. corniculata* is a great deal better. Although numerous ornamental species have been recently introduced to American gardeners, only three or four enjoy much popularity and none is seen on a regular basis.

The term *Oxalis* comes from the Greek word for sharp, referring to the sharp taste of the leaves, the result of the presence of oxalic acid. Eating too many leaves can cause severe discomfort, even death, however, the leaves of a European species, *O. acetosella*, have long been harvested for soups and salads.

Some of the more weedy species arise from long fibrous roots, while the more ornamental forms tend to come from small tubers. Propagate the former from seed, the latter from division of the clump.

Quick Reference to Oxalis Species

| | Number of leaflets | Flower color | Number of flowers |
|---|---|---|---|
| *O. adenophylla* | 9-22 | Pink | 1 |
| *O. deppei* | 4 | Red to pink | 5-12 |
| *O. regnellii* | 3 | Pale pink to white | 2-4 |
| *O. violacea* | 3 | Pink to white | 2-8 |

***-adenophylla*** (a-den-o-fil′ la) | Sauer Klee | 2-4″/6″
Pink | Late Spring | Chile, Argentina | Zones 5-8

In my opinion, this is the most beautiful member of the genus. Plants arise from a brown, ragged-looking tuber that is covered with a mass of fibers. The best parts of the plants are the smooth, silver-gray leaves consisting of around 12, but up to 22 leaflets. If conditions are to their liking, the plants form compact mounds, slowly spreading over time. The leaves are handsome enough but the flowers add yet another dimension. They are generally formed singly but there may be as many as three in one inflorescence. Each pale pink to lilac flower is about an inch across with a white center.

One of my colleagues, Linda Copeland, from Atlanta, did an experiment to force flowers on potted tubers in the greenhouse. She found that if tubers were potted and placed in a cold (40°F) area for about 10 weeks, they would flower after another 4-5 weeks. They made knockout plants that were either given as gifts or planted in the spring garden. Tubers are highly susceptible to wet feet and are best planted in a rock garden or where drainage is excellent.

They naturally occur in full sun above the tree line in the Andes, so cold weather should not deter them; however, wet feet is sure death, particularly in the winter. High temperatures are also not to their liking. I have had little success in perennializing them in the Athens area but my heavy clay soils are more suitable for pottery than for this oxalis. Let my failures not be a deterrent; they are inexpensive and are too beautiful not to at least be enjoyed as annuals. Plant the tubers in the fall and show them off next spring.

***-regnellii*** (reg-nel-lee′ eye) | Oxalis | 4-8″/12″
Summer | Pink | South America | Zones 7-9

One of the most popular and tougher species in the genus. Although leaves of the species are green, the common form 'Atropurpurea' consists of leaves that are purple to purple-green on the top side and deep purple beneath. As the plants mature the tubers multiply and significant clumps form. The pink or sometimes white flowers are about 1″ across and contrast well with the foliage. The centers of the leaves often have triangular markings. Different patterns have been selected so that today plants with purple or green leaves, with pink to white markings, may be included in containers or the garden.

Normally, a good deal of shade is recommended so I was pleasantly surprised when we had to put some mature plants in full sun in the Gardens at UGA. Within 3 days, the plants looked like they had been burned up and totally disappeared. However, within 2 weeks, the leaves re-emerged and plants thrived in that hot, sunny environment. Nevertheless, full sun does cause a good deal of plant stress.

The biggest problem I see is rust, an orangeish discoloration of the leaves caused by the fungal pustules. I have noticed this mainly on plantings of the purple-leafed form of *O. triangularis*, but have seen it on other species as well. The disease can disfigure the entire colony. Rust is much more prevalent in stressed conditions, such as lack of irrigation, very hot weather, etc. I have noticed a much higher prevalence in plants grown in full sun than those in shaded areas. I simply cut them back and allow new foliage to emerge, but I also recommend some shade if possible. Place in the front of the garden in decently drained soils.

**Cultivars**:

'Fanny' has a silver pattern in the center of the dull green leaves. The pattern disappears in the heat of the summer, but usually returns with the onset of cool nights. Flowers are pink.

'Irish Mist' bears green leaves speckled with white. The pattern fades in the heat, but is lovely in the spring and fall. White flowers top the plant in early spring.

'Jade' has dull green, often described as pewter, foliage. Subtle, best used where it can be admired easily. White flowers are formed in the spring.

'Silver Shadow' is a sport of 'Jade'. The green leaves have a large silver pattern on the top. Quite handsome, but not as pretty as 'Jade'.

***-violacea*** (vie-o-lac-ee' a) Violet Wood Sorrel 6-8"/12"
Pink, White Spring, Summer North America Zones 6-8

Native from Florida to Massachusetts and west to Minnesota and Colorado, this little gem can provide all sorts of color in partially shaded areas. The four leaflets are purple-bronze underneath and green above. Two to eight pink to rose flowers per flowering stem can smother the plants from late spring all the way through summer. Flowers often don't open until mid morning, when light gets stronger or temperatures warm up a little.

No doubt, this sorrel can look weedy, particularly when overgrown or in hot, dry weather. They may be easily cut back and always pick up when watered or when cooler weather prevails. Allow them to naturalize and they will soon become established in areas where they will be maintenance free. Plants tolerate heavy shade, but fewer flowers are formed: they perform well in full sun if watered well.

**Related Species:**

*O. crassipes* is often mistaken for *O. violacea*, however a few differences can be seen. First, plants of the former grow from rhizomes whereas those of the latter grow from bulbs. The rose-colored flowers usually have a darker purple eye. Plants often die back in the hot weather, but are cold hardy to zone 5. Native to South America, mainly Paraguay. Plants are beautiful and well behaved. A white form, 'Alba', and a pink form, 'Blush' are also offered.

*O. deppei* usually has 4 leaflets and is known as the lucky clover, good luck clover or good luck plant. Even its new botanical name, *O. tetraphylla*, reflects the plant we all want to look over. Plants arise from true bulbs and give rise to green leaves, often with a V-shaped purple band. The red to lilac-pink flowers with yellow throats are produced in 5-10 flowered umbels in late spring and summer. 'Iron Cross' has deep purple V-shaped banding which forms an "iron cross".

*O. enneaphylla*, scurvy grass, is a smaller version of *O. adenophylla*. The leaves consist of 9-20 blue-green leaflets, and large white flowers with lavender veins occur

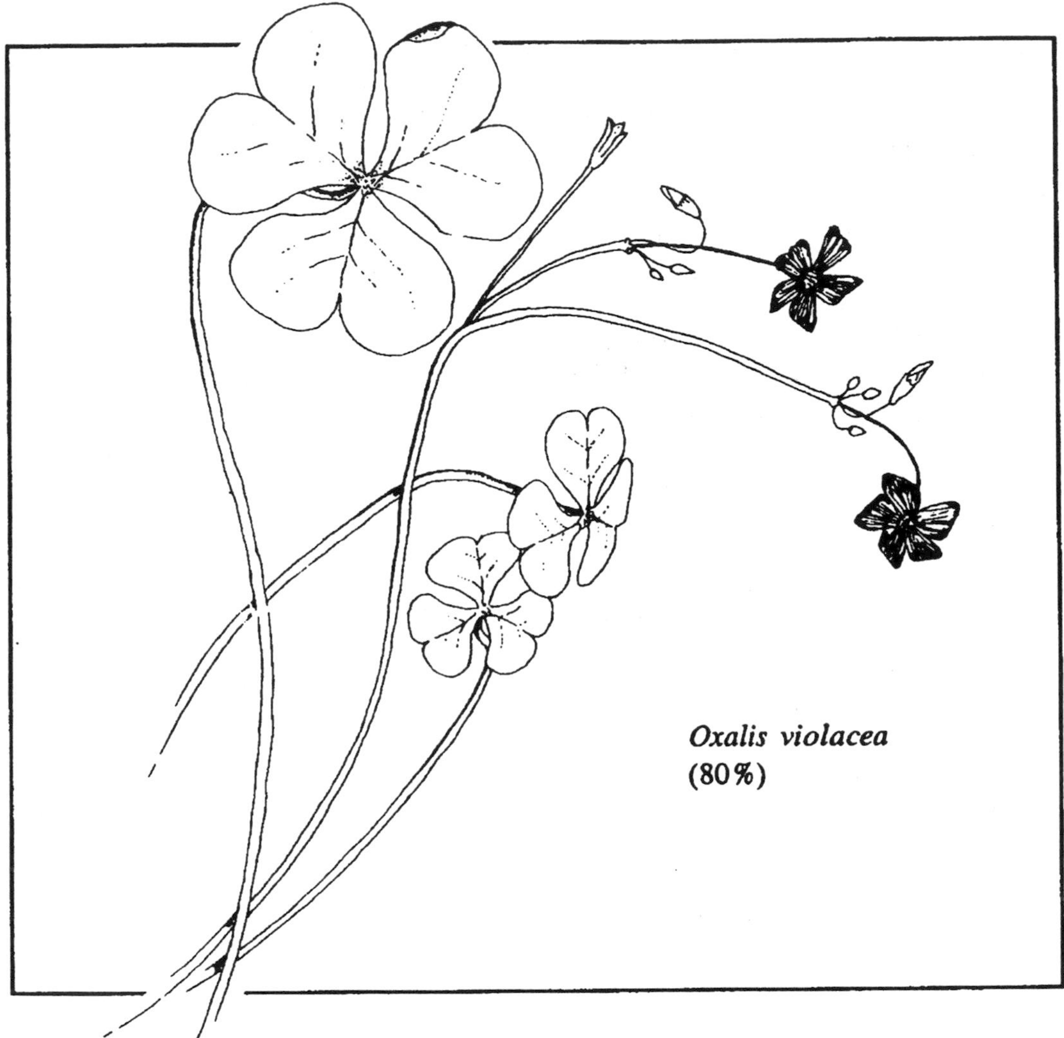

*Oxalis violacea*
**(80%)**

in late spring and summer. Cold hardy to zone 8, zone 7 with protection. 'Patagonia' has deep rose-pink flowers.

*O.* 'Lucky' has small dark leaves and yellow sterile flowers. This hybrid was introduced by the Ecke Ranch in California and has potential as an interesting accent plant. They grow only 6-8″ tall. We have tried but have had little success in getting excited about the plants at the Gardens at UGA.

*O. oregana* is a green thing from the western North America and not really worth considering. However, a variegated form with white mottling on the leaves is sometimes offered.

*O. triangularis* is listed a half dozen ways. Some nurseries list it as *O. regnellii* 'Triangularis', *O. regnellii* 'Atropurpurea', others as subsp. *triangularis*. Regardless, plants are green with a pink marking on the base, forming a triangle in the center, and bear pink flowers. The most common form is var. *atropurpurea*, also known as *O. t.* subsp. papilionacea 'Atropurpurea'. This is far too complicated for something as simple as gardening, so simply buy the one with the purple leaves.

# P

**_Pachysandra_** (pa-kis-an′ dra) Spurge Buxaceae

Although only about 5 species occur, the genus includes one of the most cultivated species in the landscape today, Japanese spurge, *P. terminalis*. The spurges' main function in life is as a ground cover, particularly under trees, where they compete well for the limited sun, nutrients and water associated with wooded areas.

Plants multiply by rhizomes and have alternate leaves, usually grouped in whorls at the end of the stems. While the plants are grown mainly for the foliage, the flowers provide some interest as well. They are unisexual and may be white or pinkish, and the long stamens of the male flowers give rise to the generic name. Pachysandra comes from *pachys*, thick, and *andros*, man; in reference to the thick stamens. Fruit is formed on female plants, however, most forms in cultivation are male.

The spurges are easily propagated by division, or by rooting softwood terminal cuttings in the summer.

Quick Reference to Pachysandra Species

| | Height (in.) | Leaf length (in.) | Inflorescence length (in.) |
|---|---|---|---|
| *P. procumbens* | 9-12 | 3-5 | 4-5 |
| *P. terminalis* | 9-12 | 1-3 | 1-2 |

**-*procumbens*** (pro-kum′ benz) Allegheny Spurge 9-12″/12″
Spring Pinkish White Southeastern United States Zones 5-9

Plants are native from West Virginia, south to Florida and west to Louisiana, but are still not seen nearly enough in southern gardens and almost never in the North. Plants are evergreen, although to be honest, the old leaves look terrible by March and should be removed, if you remember. If they are not removed, no problem, but doing so allows you to better enjoy the fresh new leaves that emerge in the spring. They are borne on long petioles and may be up to 4″ long. Each leaf is mottled with purple and is coarsely toothed towards the apex, but entire near the tapered base.

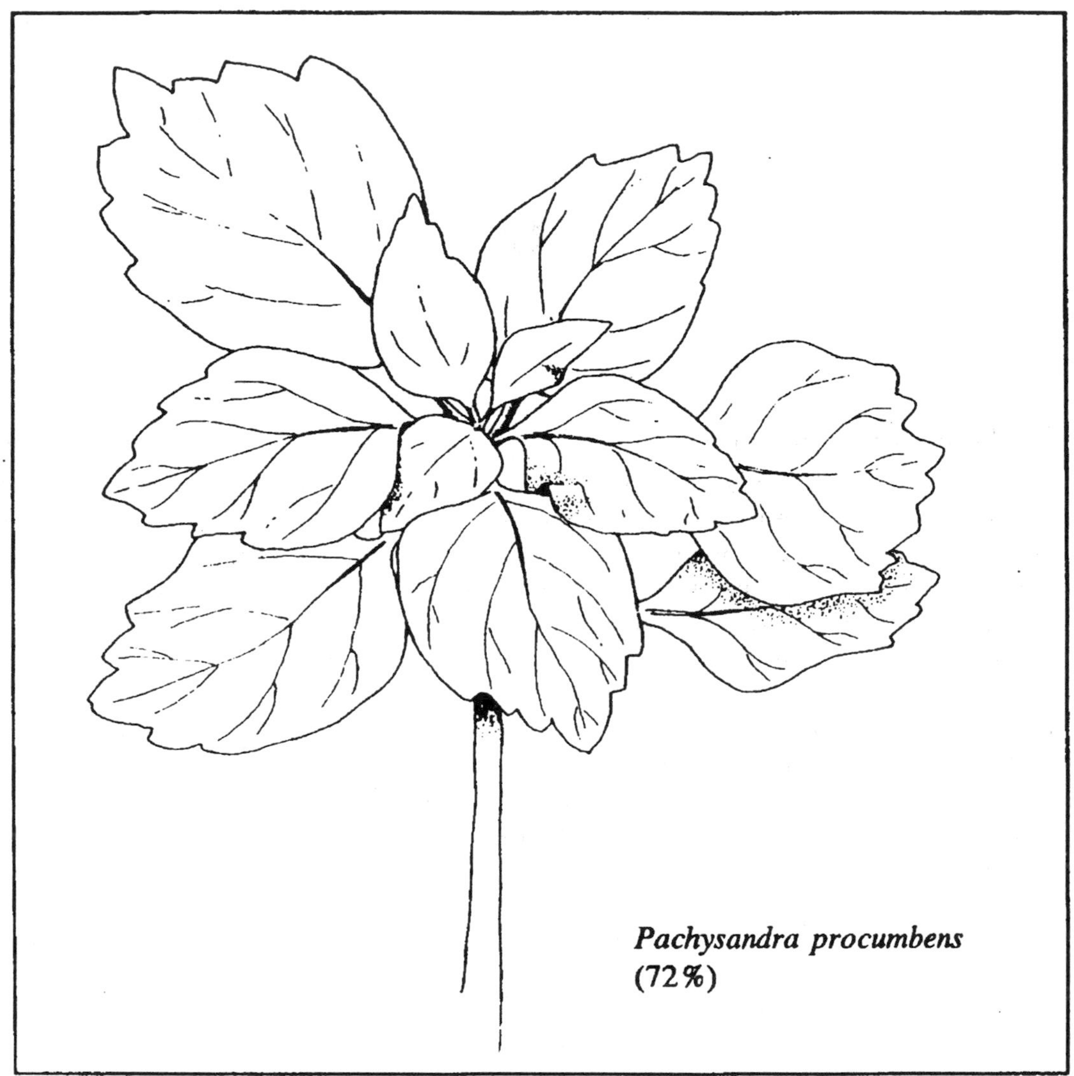

*Pachysandra procumbens*
(72%)

The white flowers have a pink tinge, particularly if the weather is cool. The flowers are borne at ground level in the axils of the leaves and are not terminal as in *P. terminalis*. Leaf litter or other mulch around the plants may have to be removed to find them. It is not nearly as vigorous a ground cover as Japanese spurge but individual clumps are far more handsome. This is a much overlooked plant and a good substitute for *P. terminalis* where only a small planting is needed. Unfortunately, problems with propagation and slow growth will always limit its appeal.

A number of years ago, I was walking around Mt. Cuba Center in Delaware with the former curator, Richard Lighty, who has forgotten about 10 times more about native Piedmont plants than any of us ever knew. He pointed out that there may be at least two strains of the species. He showed me a miniature form found in the Holden Arboretum outside Cleveland and a larger form, sometimes referred to as 'Penn State

Strain'. I hope someone will work with this species and provide more vigor so more people can take advantage of it.

**Cultivars:**

'Angola' is a recent introduction from Plant Delights Nursery in Raleigh, North Carolina, on which a pewter mottling is produced on the olive green leaves. The flowers are similar to the species. Tony Avent found the plant near the infamous Louisiana State Penitentiary in Angola. As he noted the plant and the prison he wrote "I thought . . . well, I thought I'd better get the hell out of there, but not without a piece of this attractive heat-loving clone." For Tony's duress, let's all buy some.

'Kingsville' was selected by the late Henry Hohman of Kingsville Nursery in Kingsville, Maryland. Plants have silver markings on the dull green leaves. According to world renowned plantsman Barry Yinger of Asiatica Nursery in Lewisberry, Pennsylvania, ". . . this is the most beautiful form we have seen."

***-terminalis*** (ter-mi-nah′ lis) Japanese Spurge 9-12″/18″
Late Spring White Japan Zones 4-9

Even with the hundreds of new plant introductions every year, this still remains one of the most functional plants in today's landscapes. The rhizomatous nature allows plants to colonize an area aggressively, the result of which is that this visitor from Japan has found conditions in America more to its liking than its American cousin. The dark evergreen leaves are alternate but are grouped in whorls at the top of the stems. They are toothed towards the apex, 1-3″ long and about half as wide. The creamy white flowers are borne at the top of the stems (*terminalis* is derived from the position of the flowers).

Although this is, and will likely always be, a useful and rapidly growing ground cover, a number of diseases such as rhizoctonia root rot, fusarium leaf blight, and leaf blight canker have become more prevalent. Euonymus scale can also result in significant damage to overgrown clumps. Thinning and grooming the plantings as well as application of fungicides should be practiced regularly. While it may be overused, a carpet of shining Japanese spurge under mature trees is a beautiful sight. The plantings under the copper beeches at Longwood Gardens are particularly remarkable.

**Cultivars:**

'Cutleaf' has, you guessed it, deeply cut leaves.

'Green Carpet' provides a 6-8″ tall carpet. It has darker green leaves and is more compact than the species.

'Green Sheen' has polished green leaves that are almost like a mirror. An introduction from Dr. J.C. Raulston of the North Carolina Botanical Garden, Raleigh, North Carolina.

'Silver Edge' has thin silver-white margins and is similar to 'Variegata'.

'Variegata' bears irregularly white variegated leaves. Plants are not as vigorous as the species but the leaves are more interesting. 'Variegata' and 'Silver Edge' should be located in shade because leaves scorch in full sun. Although minor differences may be seen, the two cultivars provide essentially the same look.

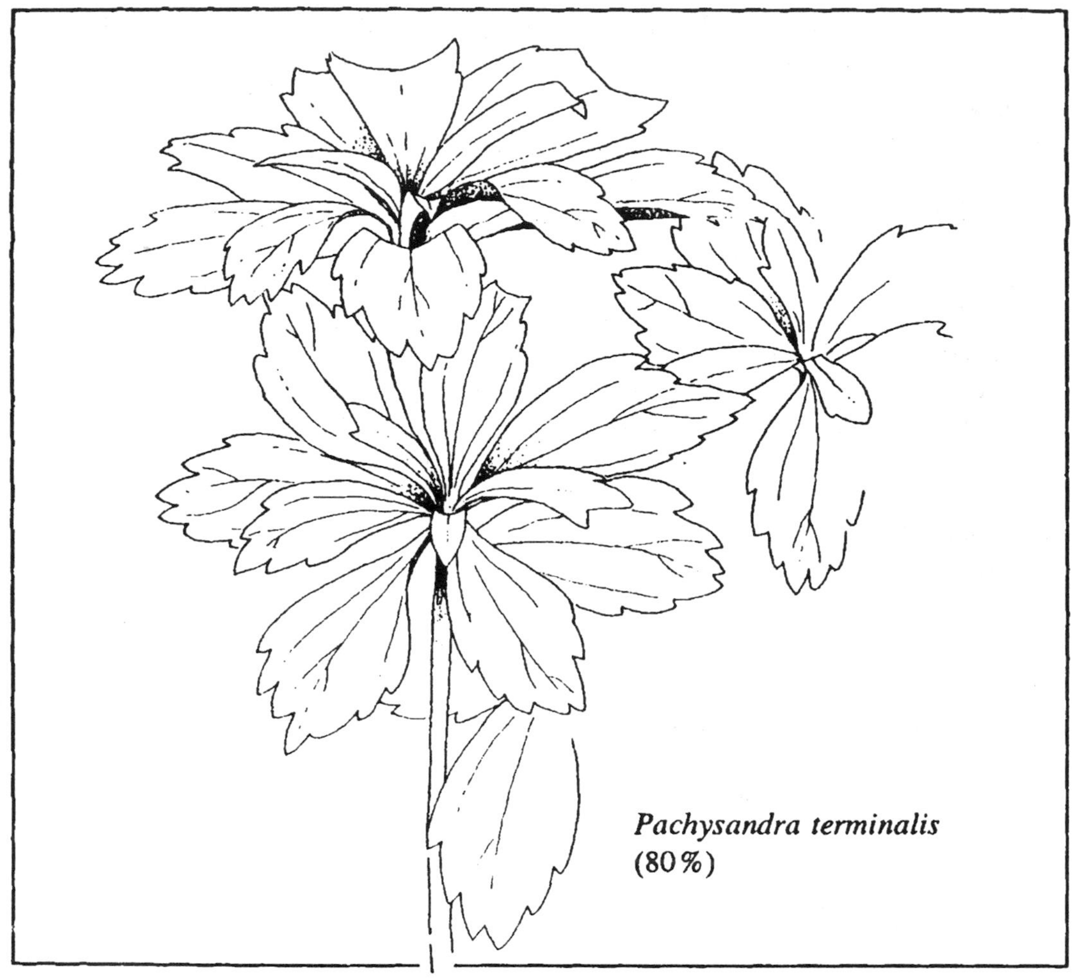

*Pachysandra terminalis* (80%)

**Related Species:**

*P. axillaris* is a Chinese species similar to *P. procumbens* in that it is slow growing. Plants are woodier at the base and a little taller, and the white flowers are also borne in the axils of the leaves. The pointed leaves are serrated and beautifully shiny. Well worth a try but may be useful only in zones 7-9.

*P. stylosa* is seldom seen and even less available. This Japanese native bears light green foliage and spreads slowly. The whitish pink flowers are produced in late winter to early spring.

## *Paeonia* (pay-on′ ee-a) Peony Ranunculaceae

The peony's great popularity rests upon cold hardiness, ease of culture, and the early blossoms. Add to that the tremendous number of flower colors, forms and plant habits and it is not surprising that the peony has attracted the interest of amateur and professional breeders, botanists, taxonomists, and horticulturists, all of whom have become enamored by the genus. The common garden peonies are classified into herbaceous species, most of which have arisen from the Chinese peony, *P. lactiflora* and the common peony, *P. officinalis*; and woody species, mainly selections of the tree peony. The herbaceous species have received the most attention and are far more important garden plants than the tree forms. This is not surprising considering the array of flower shapes and colors, to say nothing of the handsome red fruits formed after the flowers have disappeared.

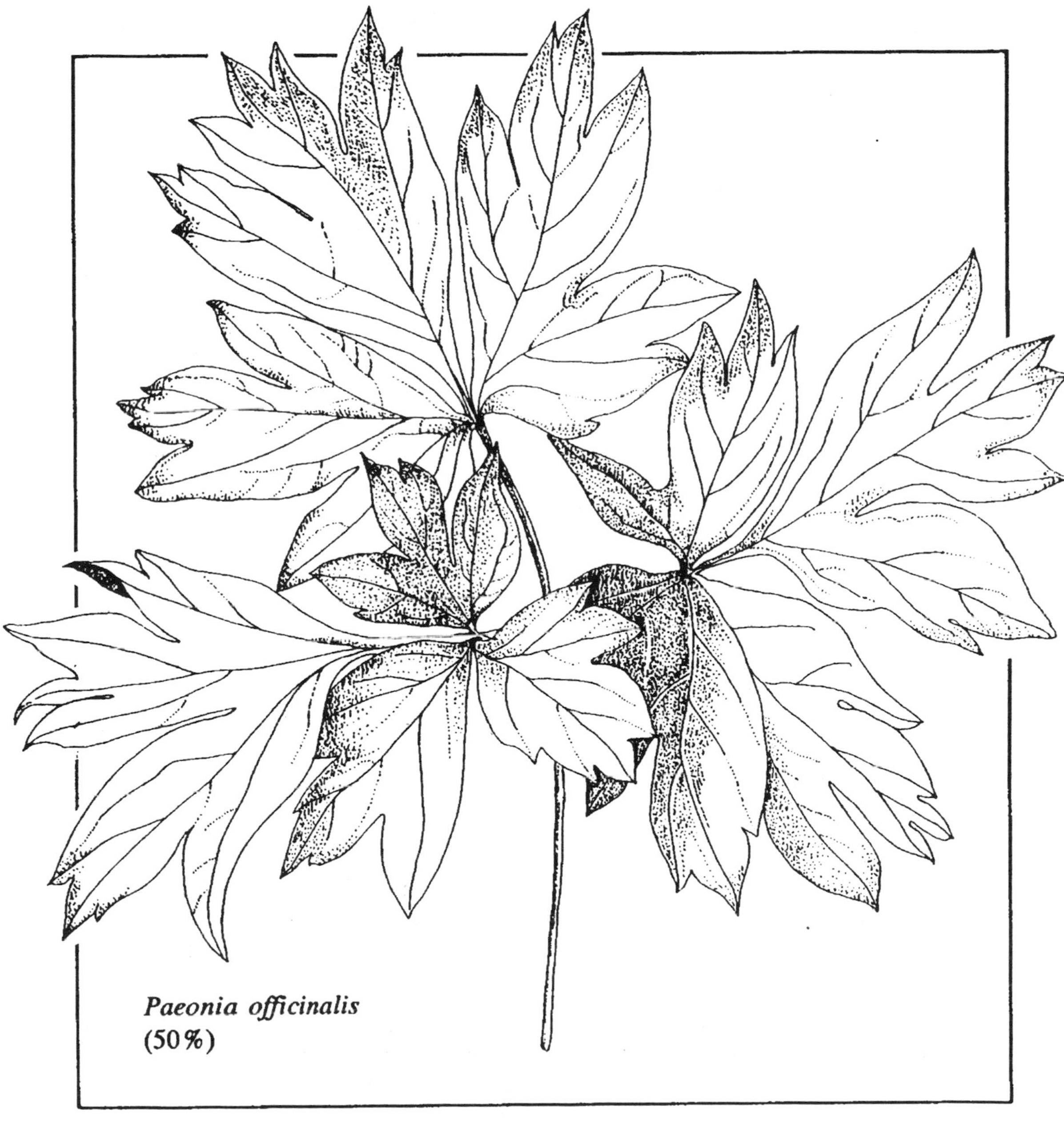

***Paeonia officinalis***
**(50%)**

The classification of the herbaceous species has been tackled by a number of wise and learned men, one being F.J. Stern, who in 1946 divided the genus into 3 sections, 4 subsections, 16 groups, 33 species, and 12 botanical varieties. All but five of the species and varieties have synonyms, twenty-six have from 1 to 10 synonyms each, seven have from 10 to 20 and one has 34! This illustrates not only the magnitude of the work of the botanists of the past but also the fact that much confusion exists as to what constitutes a species, subspecies, etc. A more useful horticultural classification based on flowering time divides the genus into three divisions, early- , mid- and late-flowering species and is a useful guide for those wishing to select garden species. The following list of species and their flowering times is based on John C. Wister's book, *The Peonies*, 1962.

**Division I.** Mostly early to late-May blooming
Very early blooming: *P. wittmanniana*, *P. w.* var. *macrophylla*, *P. mlokosewitschii*, *P. daurica*, *P. tenuifolia*.
Later flowering: *P. anomala*, *P. veitchii*.
Latest: *P. coriacea*, *P. arietina*, *P. bakeri*, *P. obovata*.

**Division II.** Mid-May blooming
*P. officinalis*, *P. humilis*, *P. mollis*, *P. peregrina*.

**Division III.** Late-May blooming
*P. lactiflora*.

Unfortunately, most true species are difficult to find in commerce, so when you find an enterprising nursery who is willing to take the chance to propagate and offer them, give them a go. The emerging buds and new leaves of some of these are incredibly handsome. That they are not easily found is a testament to their relative difficulty of production compared with common peonies. With the exception of *P. japonica*, *P. veitchii*, *P. tenuifolia*, *P. mlokosewitschii* (mlo-ko-sa-vich′ ee-eye), *P. maifleuri*, *P. obovata*, *P. emodi* and the double forms of *P. officinalis*, most are not terribly good garden plants anyway.

As far as the common herbaceous peonies, there are surely many fine choices, so many cultivars, in fact, that the American Peony Society (APS) divides the flowers of herbaceous peonies into four different forms.

*Single*: Five or more petals are arranged around a center made up of stamens with pollen-bearing anthers.

*Japanese*: This is really a double form but is characterized by five or more petals around a center made up of stamens with non-pollen bearing anthers (stamenoides). The absence of pollen distinguishes this form from the single flower form. The term "anemone flowered" is used when the stamens in the center have been transformed into narrow petal-like structures called petaloids.

*Semi-double*: Five or more outer petals are arranged around the center consisting of broad petals and stamens with pollen-bearing anthers. There may be a distinct center of stamens or they may be in rings intermixed among the petals, however, the stamens are always clearly visible and prominent.

*Double*: There are five or more outer petals but the stamens have been completely transformed into petals, making up the bulk of the flower. Often there is no trace of the stamens although in some cultivars they may be present or partially petaloids. In double types, however, stamens are not a prominent part of the flower.

**Flowering Times**:

Peony cultivars are classified not only by flower type but also by relative flowering time. Early-flowering cultivars may flower as early as late March in the South or mid April further north while the late-flowering types may be in bloom 4-6 weeks later. Those which flower in the middle are referred to as mid-season cultivars.

**Peonies in the South**:

Peonies love cold weather: the colder the winter, the better they grow. They go dormant in the fall and require a certain number of chilling hours (hours below 40°F) to break dormancy, grow and flower the next year. Therefore, it is unreasonable to expect peonies to do well in Sarasota, Florida or McAllen, Texas. However, many cultivars do fine as far south as zone 7. Many people leave the chilly climates of the Midwest or Northeast to live in the South and are convinced that peonies cannot be grown. While few peony cultivars do as well in the South as the North, there is no excuse for transplanted northerners to pine over the absence of their beloved plants. A fair number of cultivars (although only a small fraction of the total available) have been tested at the University of Georgia gardens and a few general statements may be made concerning selection of peony cultivars for southern areas.

1. Select early to mid-season cultivars. The later the flowering time, the warmer the weather and the weaker the stem strength. There is a greater chance for disease as the weather becomes warm and humid. Also, with warmer weather, doubles may not fully open.
2. Select single or Japanese flower forms. In general, semi-double or doubles should not be grown, particularly if they flower late. The more petals on the flower, the more rain will be trapped in the flower allowing disease, especially botrytis, to disfigure the blooms. This still leaves a vast selection of lovely cultivars from which to choose. For those who wish to have semi-doubles or doubles in the southern garden, select only early-flowering cultivars. However, don't let me lead you astray. Peonies will forever be a northern plant, global warming not withstanding, and will continue to be better in Quebec City than Atlantic City.

In general, peonies prefer full sun, well-drained soil and abundant water, particularly when they are vigorously growing in the spring. Plants may be fertilized with a low nitrogen fertilizer such as 8-8-8 but overfertilization can result in reduced flowering. Attention should be paid to planting depth when putting the crowns in the ground. The buds (eyes) on the rootstock should be approximately 2″ below the soil; if they are planted too deep, poor flowering will result. Some research suggested that deep planting inhibited flowering due to the absence of light on the crowns. As the soil layer increases, no light reaches the developing flowering buds and flower initiation does not take place. Perhaps this explains why older plantings do not flower particularly well.

**Failure to Flower:**

The American Peony Society has listed many reasons and possible solutions why peonies fail to flower well. They include:

*A. No buds appear:*

| Reason | Solution |
|---|---|
| 1. Plants too young and immature. | Allow them to mature. |
| 2. Planted too deep or too shallow. | Examine and if eyes are more than 3″ below ground, lift and replant. |
| 3. Clumps too large and too old. | Divide the clump if it stops flowering (after 3-10 years) leaving three eyes per division. |
| 4. Too much nitrogen. | Cut down on frequency or concentration of fertilizer. |
| 5. Moved and divided too often. | If the clump is flowering well, it should not be moved. Clumps can remain in place well over 10 years. |
| 6. Too much shade. | Move to sunny location. |

*B. Buds appear but flowers do not develop:*

| Reason | Solution |
|---|---|
| 1. Buds killed by late frost. | Better luck next year. |
| 2. Buds killed by disease. They usually turn black and die. | Plant earlier cultivars. Spray fungicide as directed for botrytis. |
| 3. Buds attacked by thrips. They open partially, turn brown and fall. | Spray as directed. |
| 4. Buds waterlogged due to excessive rain. | Plant singles or Japanese forms. Bagging buds will help. |
| 5. Plants undernourished. | Fertilize with 8-8-8 and bonemeal. |
| 6. Excessively hot weather. | Plant early flowering cultivars. |

Hybridization and selection of peonies have continued unabated and it is impossible to recommend cultivars. Many hybrids are still available today from the work of Professor A.P. Saunders (1869-1953), who created more hybrid races and varieties (more than 17,000) than all other breeders, past and present, combined. He was responsible for the breakthroughs that allowed coral to be introduced. His selections 'Coral Charm' and 'Coral Sunset' are still part of many of today's cultivars. Growing some of his hybrids is like owning a piece of peony history. Cultivars and hybrids of many other fine breeders such as Anderson, Auten, Nicholls, Kreckler, Klehm, Franklin, Lemoine, Sass, and Crosse are also available. Every year new hybrids and selections appear and it is more difficult to keep up with them all. Numerous catalogs glowingly describe hybrids and cultivars and usually provide more than adequate information. The American Peony Society also publishes a list of best cultivars, the following have won the Gold Medal Award, the highest honor given by the APS, denoting excellent performance both in garden and exhibition.

1995 'Sparkling Star'
1996 'Garden Treasure'
1997 'Old Faithful'
1998 'Myra MacRae'
1999 'Ludovica'
2000 'Pink Hawaiian Coral'
2001 'Early Scout'
2002 'Etched Salmon'
2003 'Coral Sunset'
2004 'Do Tell'
2005 'Angel Cheeks'
2006 'Bartzella'
2007 'Many Happy Returns'

***Tree Peonies:***

Tree peonies are not trees at all, but have woody stems which do not die down to the ground in the winter. They should more accurately be called shrub peonies as they seldom attain a height of more than five feet, although I have dropped my jaw on seeing the 7-8′ forms in Wales and Scotland. The most common tree peonies were derived over 1400 years ago from garden forms of the Chinese moutan peony, *P. suffruticosa*. The herbaceous peonies were valued by the Chinese for the medicinal value of their roots while the "improved" or moutan peony was treasured for its ornamental value. By the year 750, lists of over thirty named varieties, including some yellow-flowered types, had been registered in China, although it was not until the late 1700s that any plants found their way to Europe. Until 1846, although hundreds of so-called distinct varieties were imported, they were the same 5 or 6 varieties brought back by the original European explorers. At that time, Robert Fortune, a plant explorer for the Royal Horticultural Society, returned to England with 25 of the finest selections from China, from which today's garden forms have arisen. The yellow tree peony, *P. lutea*, and the maroon tree peony, *P. delavayi*, were not discovered until 1883 and 1884, respectively, and have since been used to create additional hybrids. In America, the first tree peonies were imported from England in the early 1800s and numerous references to the "almost unknown" plant which are ". . . adorned by gorgeous blossoms" appeared in the American gardening magazines as late as 1928.

The culture and care of tree peonies are shrouded in mystery but once established, they are as long lasting as many of the herbaceous types. John C. Wister in *The Peonies*, 1962, provides a list of cultural notes. I have interspersed a few of my own comments.

1. Tree peonies are native to mountainous areas and are used to cold and snow in the winter, and some heat in the summer. In the Pacific Northwest, adequate summer heat is often lacking, and a sufficiently long cold period is not available in the extreme southern states, while winter protection may be needed in the Northeast.

   The southern limit of tree peonies has not been defined and in Atlanta, Georgia, some gardeners have had some success while others cannot produce plants with more than one flower per year. Plants are presently being tested at the University of Georgia to provide a few answers for southern gardens. Two cultivars, 'Jade Plant White' and 'Change Hong' (red flowers), have been selected for heat and humidity.

2. A slightly basic soil is preferable; good drainage is essential.
3. Plant in the fall. Plant grafted plants 6-12″ below the graft union to encourage formation of roots on scion wood.
4. Plant in partial shade. This is particularly true south of zone 6.
5. Winter protection by covering or wrapping with straw or other material is desirable north of New York City.
6. Pruning should be accomplished occasionally if needed. There is seldom a good reason to cut plants back hard, however, this can be done if necessary. Cutting back to 8-12″ high may be beneficial at times to encourage the formation of new shoots. All pruning, trimming and cutting should be accomplished in early fall.
7. Remove all suckers originating from the rootstock. Production of suckers is greatest the first two years after planting.

Commercial propagation of tree peonies has been accomplished for over 900 years by grafting the desired cultivar on an herbaceous peony root stock, and is still practiced today. Research has been conducted on grafting to stocks of *P. suffruticosa* but suckering is too heavy. In all grafted plants, regardless of rootstock, the plants should be set deep enough to encourage the scion to form its own roots. Cuttings of *P. suffruticosa*, if taken in September, root at about a 40% rate, which may be practical for the amateur but not the commercial propagator. Little success has been reported with softwood cuttings taken in April. They may also be propagated by layering, that is, pegging some of the branches in March to root into the ground. At least two years is needed for sufficient root production.

Many fine cultivars of tree peonies are available and a list of the best of best is difficult to put together. If I had to have but one cultivar, I would select 'Joseph Rock', one of the finest forms to be introduced. Not only that, but it commemorates one of the great American plant explorers, who was commissioned by David Fairchild of the United States Department of Agriculture to explore areas of India, Burma and Indo-China in the 1920, and then by Charles Sprague Sargent of the Arnold Arboretum in 1922 to investigate the Yunnan area of China. He remained in China for 27 years, collecting over 80,000 plant specimens. Not only is 'Joseph Rock' beautiful, but it adds to the excitement of gardening.

Many hybrids with *P. suffruticosa* and *P. lutea* are also being introduced, as well as crosses between herbaceous and tree forms such as the 3′ tall 'Bartzella'. Terrific plantings may be seen around the country, and should be visited to be appreciated. Consult the American Peony Society, a specialist peony producer, or your favorite nurseryman.

## *Packera* see *Senecio*

## *Panax* (pan′ ax) Ginseng Araliaceae

There are only two reasons to grow *Panax*. One is that you have discovered how much money this crummy little plant is worth and you have decided to be a ginseng entrepreneur. Good luck with that! The other is that you discovered—once you went broke trying to sell ginseng—that the plant tolerates, even prefers, deep shade.

The only species available is *P. quinquefolius*, American ginseng, a poor substitute for the real thing, *P. ginseng*, which is from Korea and northeast China. Plants produce a single whorl of three leaves, each leaf divided into 3-7 leaflets. The greenish white flowers are formed in a small umbel in late spring or summer and later give way to bright red fruit. They are good plants for heavy shade and rich, moisture-retentive soils. Plants are moderately ornamental at best but most certainly are excellent objects of conversation.

Propagate by division.

***Panicum*** (pah′ ni-cum) Switch Grass Poaceae

Long ignored as an ornamental grass, switch grass has been a constant in the American landscape. Plants were early colonizers and part of the immense tallgrass prairie, so familiar years ago in the interior United States. The movement to ornamental grasses has stimulated vast interest in *Panicum* and breeding for better selections of *P. virgatum* has been going full bore. Part of the interest in panicums is the acceptance of all things native, and the other is that there is significant noise afoot that some states may put *Miscanthus* on their invasive plant lists, a move which will undoubtedly result in far fewer miscanthus cultivars being used.

The ½ to ¾″ wide, flat-bladed upright leaves are green to gray-green in the species and form relatively tight clumps in full sun. The panicles of airy flowers emerge in the early fall and are useful as cut flowers for both fresh and dried arrangements. Plants persist through the winter and some selections provide stunning fall color, turning a muted beige during the winter. Many cultivars, however, turn the color of dried hay, handsome but hardly stunning.

They are best planted in clumps of at least three, thereby allowing them to present their foliage and flowers *en masse*. On the University of Georgia campus, they are used in large numbers to provide low-maintenance islands of color and form. They are easy to grow, needing nothing more than sun and a little water. At the Chicago Botanic Garden and the Olbrich Botanical Gardens in Madison, Wisconsin, grasses are used everywhere, and none to better advantage than the panicums.

Propagate by division after 3-4 years. Seedlings can be a nuisance and if the area is well suited to switch grass, the species can become a nightmare. Select sterile forms whenever possible.

**Cultivars:**

'Cloud Nine' was one of the earlier cultivars introduced. Plants bear beige flowers in late summer and fall and blue-green foliage in the warm season. Their drawback is their 7-8′ height, and if planted in warm climates, some support may be necessary.

'Dallas Blues' can also get big and at the Chicago Botanic Garden, walking through the 'Dallas Blues' planting can be a wee bit claustrophobic. The foliage significantly bluer than others and the flowers are darker brown. Plants grow about 6′ tall and can be quite vigorous, but I find them more ornamental in containers than in the ground.

'Haense Herms' is one of the oldest cultivars, but still useful. Plants are similar to the species but are a little more compact and have a red-orange tint in the fall. The whitish flowers and red foliage in the fall make a marvelous combination.

'Heavy Metal' from Kurt Bluemel of Baldwin, Maryland, has metallic blue leaves on upright compact plants. The foliage turns an amber yellow in the fall, turning to beige in the winter. Plants grow 6-7′ tall.

'Northwind' is most impressive in that it is a stiff and upright grower, not needing support. Plants bear green foliage with a hint of blue and flower wonderfully in the fall. An excellent large landscape plant where maintenance is low on the list. My #1 choice.

'Prairie Fire' has blue-green foliage that turns red in early summer. Flowers are rosy red in late summer and fall. It appears to be an improvement over 'Shenandoah'.

'Prairie Sky' is a terrific choice for a lower-growing cultivar, topping out at 3-5′. It is planted all over the UGA campus and needs no maintenance except a little trimming every now and then.

'Prairie Wind' is 6-7′ tall, and has been tested with success on the windy prairies of Nebraska and Kansas.

'Rehbraun' was a favorite before the advent of better, newer selections. The plants are about 3-4′ tall and are a lovely reddish brown in the fall.

'Rotstrahlbusch' is about 3′ tall without flowers, up to 4′ when the airy amber flowers emerge in summer. The foliage turns a handsome red in autumn.

'Shenandoah' works in some areas but not many. Its claim to fame is the red coloration on the leaves, even in the summer. I have been disappointed in most plantings I have seen in that the foliage has little obvious red color and the vigor is poor. Save your money. Plants grow about 3′ tall.

'Squaw' is 3-4′ tall with good red fall color. An introduction from Kurt Bluemel, the grass specialist in Maryland.

'Strictum' is one of the older cultivars, producing narrow upright clumps of bluish green foliage. Its main attribute is its usefulness in smaller gardens.

'Trailblazer' is 4-5′ tall with open airy flowers. The foliage turns orange-yellow in the winter.

'Warrior' is particularly vigorous and striking, growing 4-5′ tall with good red fall color. Also from Bluemel.

**Related Species:**

*P. amarum*, bitter panic grass, is native up and down the East Coast and into the Gulf States. It is threatened or endangered in Connecticut and Pennsylvania. Plants are low growers and not particularly striking. However, 'Dewey Blue', introduced by Rick Darke of Pennsylvania, has handsome blue foliage on 2-3′ tall plants. They perform best in sandy to loamy soils and do poorly in clay. Compared to *P. virgatum*, this is a slow grower. Tan flowers occur in the fall.

## ***Papaver*** (pa-pah′ ver) Poppy Papaveraceae

The poppies are usually represented in American gardens by the Oriental poppy, *P. orientale*. However, about 40 species of poppies are known and I am hard pressed to find an ugly one among them, except when they are dying in my garden. There are some terrific plants in this genus, unfortunately, many look terrible in the South, and few are commonly available. One of the most northerly species in the plant kingdom, *P. radicatum*, is found on the north coast of Greenland.

The most famous species is the annual red poppy, *P. rhoeas*, immortalized by the Canadian Army surgeon John McCrae in the hauntingly beautiful poem "In Flanders Field". I bore my students to death with the story of the red poppy partly because it is an interesting part of horticultural sociology and partly because I feel very close to the two main figures in the story. John McCrae lived in the college town of Guelph, Ontario (where I went to school), and his small house on Water Street is marked with an inscription of his poetic accomplishments. The person who really made the red poppy famous, however, was the "poppy lady", Moina Michael, an unassuming schoolteacher who lived in the countryside around Athens, Georgia. She was so inspired by John McCrae's poem that appeared in *The Saturday Evening Post* that with nothing but determination and spirit, she single-handedly transformed the poppy into the Veterans Day flower, sold to raise money in the United States, England and Canada on every Veterans Day since 1925.

This is the same species that was selected and reselected by the Reverend W. Wilks of Shirley, England and became known as the Shirley poppy. Other annuals or biennials include mission poppy, *P. californicum*, tulip poppy, *P. glaucum*, the stunning but infamous opium poppy, *P. somniferum* and the subtly beautiful biennial *P. triniifolium*. For garden purposes, few poppies are long lived; the Oriental poppy and *P. bracteatum*, great scarlet poppy, are the only true perennials available through most nurseries. Iceland poppy and alpine poppy may persist for a couple of years. Many self-sow prolifically and new plants can be counted on year after year.

Poppies are characterized by nodding flower buds, solitary flowers on long flower stalks, milky juice, and leaves that are lobed or dissected. The seed capsule is hard, oval, and usually quite decorative.

Quick Refcrence to Papaver Species

| | Height (in.) | Flower diameter (in.) | Plants go dormant |
|---|---|---|---|
| *P. alpinum* | 8-10 | 1-2 | No |
| *P. nudicaule* | 12-18 | 3-6 | No |
| *P. orientale* | 18-36 | 5-7 | Yes |
| *P. somniferum* | 24-36 | 3-4 | No |

***-alpinum*** (al-pine′ um) Alpine Poppy 8-10″/8″
Summer Multicolored European Alps Zones 4-6

A dwarf species, it is most suited for the rock garden or front of the border. Plants are not heat tolerant and seldom survive the summer south of zone 6. Regardless of geographic location, well-drained soil is absolutely essential. Plants are tufted (i.e. all leaves emerging from same place) with 2-6″ long gray-green leaves. The 1″ wide silky flowers are held on bristly-hairy 4-10″ long flower stalks. Although not particularly long lived, plants can self-sow prolifically.

Seed sown in January will be ready for planting in March. Plants flower the first year from seed.

**Cultivars:**

var. *burseri* bears white flowers. Some authorities believe *P. burseri* is the correct name for plants grown as *P. alpinum*.

**-*nudicaule*** (new di-kaw′ lee) Iceland Poppy 12-18″/12″
Spring Multicolored Subarctic Regions Zones 2-7

This northern species is becoming more and more popular in, of all places, the South. They tolerate low winter temperatures, and fall plantings produce spectacular drifts of vibrant flowers in the spring. Plants are becoming more visible in public and private gardens every year. Although unable to survive hot summers in the South, Iceland poppies are perennial in the North, living 2-3 years and flowering from early spring to early summer. Plants are rosetted, stemless, and produce 4-6″ long, gray-green pinnately lobed leaves. The silky flowers are up to 6″ wide and are borne on 12″ high leafless flower stems. Most are seed propagated and mixtures are most common. The selections from the species also make a wonderful potted plant for indoor use and more plants are seen in florists' displays and mass market outlets. It is also the only species suitable for cut flowers.

Seed-propagated plants flower the first year. Seeds collected from F1 hybrids, however, result in plants dissimilar from the parent plant. In areas where they are perennial, division may be accomplished after a few years, but the need for division is highly unlikely.

**Cultivars:**

A number of cultivated forms offer specific colors and heights. It seems each new cultivar provides larger and more vibrant flowers than the previous. Most are propagated from seed and some variation inevitably results.

Breeze series is only about 18″ tall and available in orange and yellow.

'Champagne Bubbles' is an F1 hybrid with 3″ diameter flowers in mixed colors.

'Coonara Pink' has 2″ wide flowers in pastel pink shades.

Gnome series comes in many colors but all the flowers top 9-12″ tall plants. Good weather tolerance.

Kelmscott Strain is 12-18″ tall and consists of mostly pastel colors.

Monarch Mix bears flowers up to 2″ wide in many bright colors.

'Popsicle' has 3-4″ wide flowers in an assortment of colors.

'Summer Promise' contains both solid and bicolor 2-3″ diameter flowers on 2′ tall stems.

Wonderland Mix is more compact than the type and bears 2-3″ diameter flowers. Bright orange 3″ wide flowers are available as 'Wonderland Orange'. This is the best selection for windy areas and has proven resilient even in the windswept beds of Auckland Botanic Gardens.

***-orientale*** (o-ree-en-tah′ lee) Oriental Poppy 18-36″/24″
Early Summer Scarlet Southwest Asia Zones 2-7

This is certainly the most conspicuous and popular poppy in North America. Few sights are more arresting than the vibrant orange-red flowers of two or three plants massed in the garden. The leaves are pinnately lobed and sharply toothed although they appear sharper and more bristly than they feel. The flowers of the species are 3½-4″ across, scarlet with a black blotch on the base of each petal forming a black eye. And the cultivars-even more outstanding! However, there are a couple of problems. The first is that flowers are like fireworks, spectacular one day, gone the next. Flowers are short lived and if temperatures warm up prematurely, they disappear even more rapidly. Add to this the unfortunate habit of going summer dormant and totally disappearing by mid to late summer and one can see why the use of Oriental poppy has declined. Plants such as *Mertensia virginica*, Virginia bluebells, also go summer dormant but can easily be replaced by a few annuals. With big plants such as Oriental poppies, more planning is necessary. Large filler plants such as *Gypsophila*, *Perovskia*, and *Boltonia* will cover much of the space vacated by the poppies and flower later.

In areas south of zone 6b, Oriental poppies perform poorly and are seldom used. The only success I have seen in the South is with seed-grown plants planted in the fall. Dormant plants ordered from catalogs invariably break dormancy within 2-3 weeks of fall planting and are killed or badly damaged by winter weather. Some mail order firms will ship in the spring and if the plants can be obtained early enough, they do much better in zones 7 and 8 than those fall shipped. Nevertheless, Oriental poppies are cold climate plants and nothing can be done to change that fact.

Propagate by root cuttings and division. Root cuttings are taken in the spring by dividing the roots into 3-4″ lengths, inserting upright in sandy soil, and barely covering. If the root sections are harvested early in the spring or immediately after flowering, the plant may be replaced without damage. Division may be necessary every 3-5 years and should be done after flowering when dormant. This allows root recovery and growth in the fall so plants may flower the next year. Dividing in spring results in poor flowering that year.

**Cultivars:**

Many cultivars are available; some are hybrids with other species, particularly *P. bracteatum*, great scarlet poppy. New cultivars are being bred mainly in Europe, and seem to double every five years.

*Bicolored:*

'Carousel' has lovely white flowers with orange margins.

'China Boy' has ruffled orange flowers with a creamy white center.

'Maiden's Blush' produces large ruffled white flowers with a soft pink edge. About 2-3′ tall.

'Picotee' was an early picotee (bicolor) form with white flowers and deep salmon edges.

'Pinnacle' bears bicolored flowers of white and red. Subtle but handsome.

'Showgirl' has ruffled pink flowers with white centers.

*Lavender:*

'Lavender Glory' is about 30″ tall with lavender flowers.

'Patty's Plum' is beautiful. Deep lavender to plum flowers stand 2-3′ tall.

*Orange:*

'Beauty Queen' has light bronze apricot flowers, about 3-4′ tall.

'Dubloon' flowers earlier than most cultivars and bears orange, fully double blossoms.

'Fireball' produces double orange flowers on 2′ tall plants.

'Harvest Moon' bears marvelous large, double, golden yellow flowers.

'Prince of Orange' has orange flowers, as its name suggests, but is not all that princely.

'Salmon Glow' bears double flowers of salmon-orange.

*Pink, Salmon:*

'Betty Ann' is about 30″ tall with handsome pink petals with crinkled margins.

'Carneum' has light salmon flowers on 3′ tall plants.

'Cedar Hill' produces light rose flowers on 3′ tall plants.

'Cedric Morris' bears large pink flowers with frilled petals and a black center.

'Degas' is only about 2′ tall and bears salmon flowers with dark spots. Plants bloom later than most others.

'Fatima' provides ruffled light salmon petals with pink edges.

'Glowing Rose' has watermelon pink flowers on stout 2-3′ tall plants.

'Helen Elizabeth' bears salmon-pink flowers without the blotching found in 'Barr's White'. This is a classic.

'Juliane' ('Julianna') has no basal blotches but is a brilliant pink throughout.

'Karine' is relatively short with clear pink flowers and small red spots at the base.

'Lighthouse' bears large light pink flowers with a wide dark center. Stunningly handsome.

'Little Dancing Girl' produces large soft pink flowers, each with a distinctive dark blotch.

'Mrs. Perry' has pale salmon pink flowers with black blotches over 3′ tall plants. This cultivar and 'Marcus Perry' were raised at the famous Enfield Nursery in England, owned by Mr. Amos Perry.

'Pink Ruffles' has pink flowers with fringed petals.

'Prinzessin (Princess) Victoria Louise' produces flowers of light pink with prominent black spots.

'Queen Alexander' is a common salmon-pink form with a black center.

'Raspberry Queen' is large, vigorous and sports dark rose-pink flowers.

'Turkenlouis' ('Turkish Delight') is one of the mainstays of the showstopper crowd. Beautiful salmon-pink flowers with dark centers.

'Watermelon' is aptly named, producing watermelon-pink flowers.

*Red:*

'Allegro' is an excellent dwarf form, growing less than 20″ tall with large scarlet flowers.

'Avebury Crimson' has single brilliant red flowers on 3′ tall plants.

'Beauty of Livermere', from Little Livermere village in Sussex, England, is one of the finest reds I have seen.

'Big Jim' is big, up to 3′ tall, and bears deep red flowers with crinkled margins.

'Bonfire' has fire red flowers.

'Brilliant' also produces fiery red flowers.

'Carmen' bears deep red flowers on strong 2-3′ tall plants.

'Claret' bears burgundy red flowers.

'Curlilocks' produces deeply serrated red-orange flower with black center spots. This can be an absolute knockout.

'Flamenco Dancer', from Walters Garden, Zeeland, Michigan, has bright red flowers with fringed petals. A sport of 'Turkenlouis' (above).

'G.I. Joe', originally included at the request of my then 8-year-old son, has deep red flowers and is quite lovely despite the name. It was nice to show him that not all G.I. Joes throw grenades and major in hand-to-hand combat.

'Glowing Embers' bears ruffled scarlet flowers on 2′ plants.

'Goliath' grows nearly 4′ tall with orange-red flowers and a black eye.

'Ladybird' produces dozens and dozens of small deep red flowers with black spots. I first saw these at Falkland Garden in Scotland and they were some of the smallest poppies I had seen but also some of the most floriferous.

'Marcus Perry' has brilliant scarlet-red flowers.

'Surprise' bears dozens of vermillion red flowers with black spots on 3-4′ tall plants.

'Warlord' has large deep red flowers.

*White:*

'Arwide' bears 3″ wide white flowers with orange venation and black centers.

'Barr's White' has pure white flowers and blackish spots at the base of the petals.

'Black and White' is, as the name suggests, white with black spots at the base of the petals.

'Fatima' is a compact plant with white flowers and pink margins.

'Perry's White' is not new but is still a beautiful cultivar. Off-white flowers with a black eye make the flowers appealing.

'Royal Wedding' produces large clean white flowers with dark centers.

'Snow Queen' produces large white flowers with black basal spots.

'Springtime' is another white-flowered form with pink margins.

'White King' has large white flowers with black spots at the base.

| **-*somniferum*** (som-ni′ fe-rum) | | Opium Poppy | 2-3′/3′ |
|---|---|---|---|
| Late Spring | Multicolored | Greece, Orient | Zones 8-10 |

In northern areas of the country, this species should be treated as an annual but it self-sows prolifically in zones 6-7, and often overwinters with protection in more southerly regions. It is the oldest poppy in cultivation and has been used not only for narcotics, but for the edible seeds, often sold as birdseed under the name of "maw-seed". The narcotic properties of the species have long been recognized, in fact,

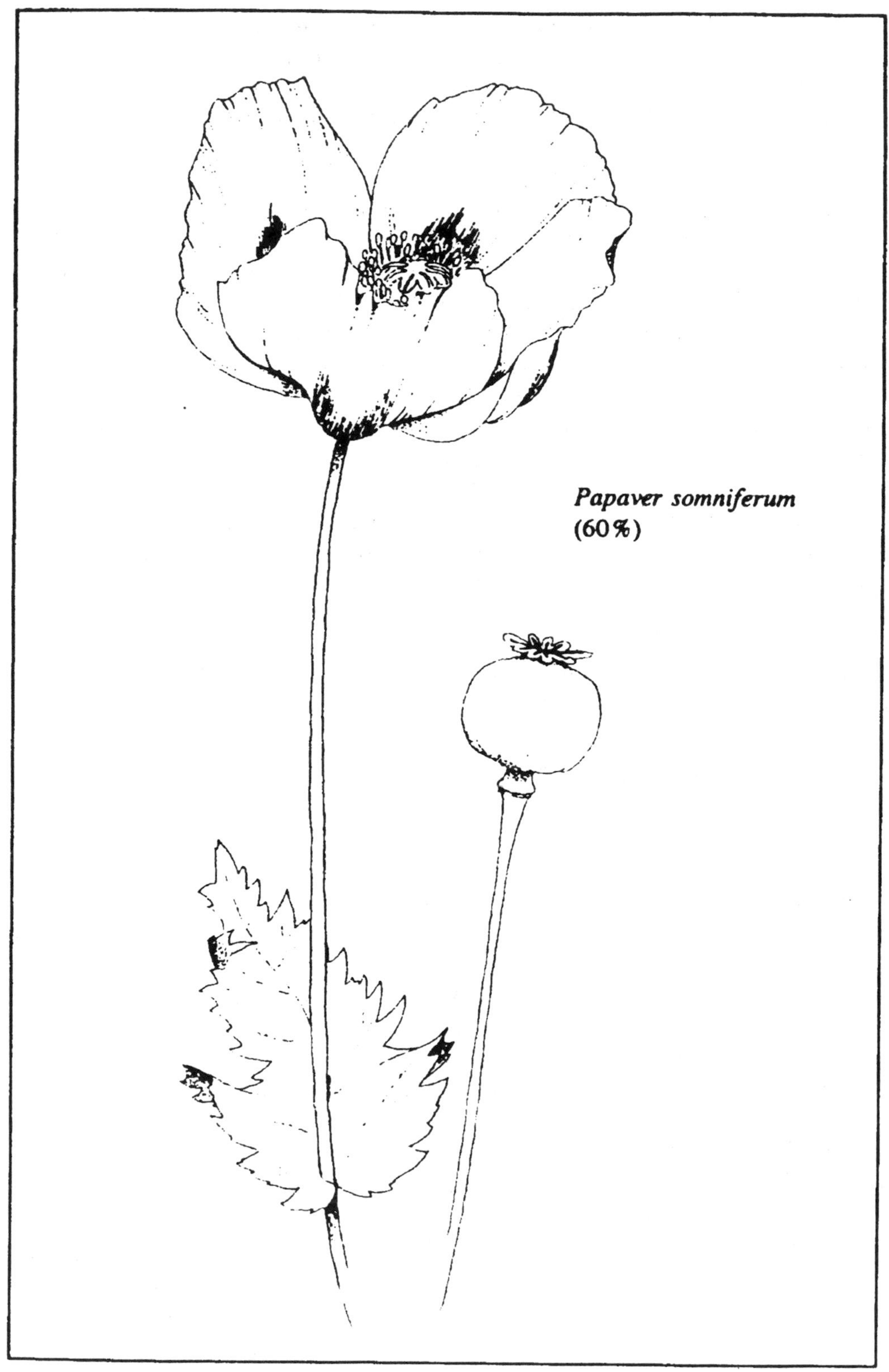
*Papaver somniferum*
(60%)

poppy juice was at one time mixed with baby food to make babies sleep. Opium is made from the sap of the green seed capsules and was known by the Greeks and Egyptians several centuries before the birth of Christ. The plants are tall and the lack of branching further accentuates the height. The gray-green leaves are unequally toothed at the base and clasp the stem. The plants are not particularly attractive but the flowers more than compensate. They are 4-5″ across and range from white through pink, red to purple, although no yellow or blue flowers yet exist. In most flowers, showy black blotches are found at the base of the petals, providing additional beauty. Unfortunately the flowers drop their petals quickly and make poor cut flowers. Two common flower forms are found in gardens today: the carnation-flowered and the peony-flowered strains. The former has fringed petals, the latter does not. The peony-flowered strain is sometimes listed as *P. paeoniaeflorum* and the flowers resemble those of double peonies.

*P. somniferum* is a short-lived plant but the seed is viable, particularly after being chilled in the winter. Every spring, southern gardens are alive with seedlings of opium poppies, many in different places than the year before. Those allowed to remain flower profusely. I used to take my students to the beautiful spring garden of Mrs. Laura Ann Segrest in Athens, Georgia. We stood in awe of the symphony of color provided by this magnificent plant now better known for its ability to cause pain rather than its potential for beauty.

Laws are changing in the United States about growing this plant. Many cut flower growers have been producing opium poppy for the decorative pods, which were once a common item in floral shops and in dried arrangements. There is as much chance of getting high on these things as seeing the man on the moon. However, many states aggressively prohibit the growing of plants, period. Give me a break, go catch serial killers and leave my garden alone. However, if you are a serious athlete, one thing is well known. The ingestion of poppy seeds on poppy seed buns will result in a positive drug test. Since most of us need not worry about random drug tests, let's enjoy them for their beauty and be done with all this legal mumbo-jumbo.

**Cultivars:**

var. *album* has white flowers and whitish seeds.

**Related Species:**

*P. atlanticum* has gray-green foliage and peach to pale pink flowers on 12-18″ tall plants in late spring or early summer. Quite handsome.

*P. bracteatum*, great scarlet poppy, grows 2-2½′ tall and bears large blood-red flowers. It differs from *P. orientale* in having 2 large leafy bracts at the base of the flowers and lacks the black blotch at the base.

*P. kerneri* has ½″ wide yellow flowers and is closely related to *P. alpinum*.

*P. pilosum* is reputed to grow up to 3′ tall, but I have not seen it much taller than about 18″. Flowers are orangey yellow with whitish spots at the base of the petals. Likely hardy to about zone 6.

*P. pyrenaicum*, Pyrenees poppy, has green rather than gray-green leaves. The plants are 4-6″ tall and the 1″ wide flowers are yellow to orange.

***Paradisea*** (pa-ra-dees′ ee-a) St. Bruno's Lily Liliaceae

A genus consisting of only two species, both of which resemble a cross between a tuberose and *Anthericum*, the St. Bernard lily. They are grown from tubers, from which emerge 6-8 basal leaves about 1″ across. The white, almost transparent flowers are held in a 15-20 flowered spike well above the foliage. The flowers are held on one side of the raceme, rather than all around it. The characteristic of holding the flowers so high above the foliage, along with their one-sided position, are two of the main differences between this and *Anthericum*, whose flowers barely emerge above the leaves. The most common species is *P. liliastrum*, which in flower is about 2′ tall. The flowers are subtly fragrant and the tips of the petals are often tinged with green. The other species occasionally offered is *P. lusitanica*. It differs by being more vigorous, taller (up to 5′ tall) and bearing flowers on 2 sides of the raceme.

This species is seldom grown in American gardens mainly because of lack of availability. Cold hardiness is not well established but plants tolerate sustained temperatures of at least 5°F, probably much more. Heat tolerance is unknown, but since plants are native to alpine meadows of southern Europe, I don't hold out much hope for success in southern gardens.

Propagate by removal of small tubers in the spring. Seed is also viable.

***Pardancanda*** (par-dan′ kan-da) Candy Lily Liliaceae

The genus should be written X *Pardancanda norrisii* because plants resulted from an intergeneric cross between *Belamcanda chinensis*, blackberry lily, and *Pardanthopsis dichotoma*, the vesper iris, however the X is silent. The flowers resemble blackberry lilies but the range of colors is far greater and much more ornamental. Much of the original breeding work was conducted in South Carolina by Dr. Jim Alston of Wayside Gardens, and by breeders at Bluebird Nursery in Clarkson, Nebraska, as well as independent work in Eurasia. Most of the selections are cold hardy to at least zone 5.

*P. norrisii* provides a wide range of colors on 2-3′ tall plants, and is often most available. However, the Dazzler series, from Bluebird Nursery, brings plants only 15-18″ in height with the same dramatic colors. Other series have been developed with mixed colors such as Jungle series and Sunset Tones from this program. Individual colors are less common but 'Sangria' has plum-colored flowers with blue-green leaves and grows only about 18″ tall.

The vesper iris itself is occasionally offered as well. Flowers occur mostly in pastel colors on 2½′ tall iris-like plants. The flowers open only in late afternoon and evening. Hardy to zone 3.

***Paris*** (par′ is) Paris Liliaceae

At the time of the last edition, this was an almost unknown genus and although it is slowly emerging from obscurity, it is not yet ready to be the next daylily. Closely related to *Trillium*, these interesting plants will never be common because of difficulties of propagation. However, as I leaf through my catalogs, I come across more each year. There are well over 50 species and related varieties, but perhaps three or four will ever see the light of commerce. Not until I saw a clump of *P. tetraphylla* in Sissinghurst and then in Scotland did I begin to appreciate why they are so sought after. Plants are native to Japan and should be reasonably hardy in zones 5-8.

In *P. tetraphylla*, the foliage is in two to three whorls of four sessile leaflets, each whorl about 8″ above the one below it. The single flower sits atop the terminal whorl and consists of 4-6 greenish sepals. Poisonous blue-black berries can occur in late fall. Three other species are known but are even more unavailable than the one described. The name *Paris* has nothing to do with the city, but comes from the Latin *par*, meaning equal, and refers to the regularity of the leaves and flowers.

If you can find some plants, give them a try. Plant them in a rich soil in dappled shade.

## ***Parthenium*** (par-then-ee′ um) Wild Quinine Asteraceae

An absolutely wonderful native, *P. integrifolium* bears bold leaves and large flat clusters of buttonlike creamy white flowers. I first discovered this in the plantings at Powell Gardens, Kingsville, Missouri, just outside Kansas City. Upright and stately with course aromatic foliage and growing 2-3′ tall, it was fascinating and covered with butterflies. I later stumbled upon some equally wonderful plants in the Perimeter College Gardens in Decatur, Georgia and knew then we had a winner. This Midwest native can stand alone but is probably used best as part of a "wild" garden or meadow.

With such a common name, one would expect that plants have been used medicinally. The tops of the plant have a medicinal "quinine-like" bitterness and are used to treat intermittent fevers. It has traditionally been used in alternative medicine to treat debility, fatigue, respiratory infection, gastrointestinal infection, and venereal disease. According to some web sites, wild quinine is currently being used with great success by many herbalists throughout the United States and Europe for diseases such as lymphatic congestion, colds, ear infections, sore throats, fevers, infections, and Epstein-Barr virus. *Parthenium* has been studied in scientific laboratories and clinics across Europe. Findings from these studies indicate that this medicinal herb stimulates the immune system. Pharmacopoeia in the garden!

## ***Patrinia*** (pa-trin′ ee-a) Patrinia Valerianaceae

*Patrinia* consists of about 15 species that enjoyed a meteoric rise in popularity in the 90s. One of the explanations for this rise is that they look good with many other garden plants and are excellent companions for almost everything. When I first saw some of the yellow-flowering species, I thought they just looked like overgrown mustard plants, and wondered what all the fuss was. The leaves are opposite, often pinnately cut or lobed, and provide a coarse presence in the garden. The small individual flowers are usually yellow, sometimes white, and are held in airy corymbose panicles well above the foliage. The flowers are persistent, lasting well into the fall in most gardens.

Patrinia has been determined to be a host for daylily rust, caused by *Puccinia hemerocallidis*. The fungus requires two hosts to complete its life cycle, *Hemerocallis* being one and patrinia often cited as another. Its role is still unknown and no symptoms of daylily rust appear on patrinia.

Quick Reference to Patrinia Species

| | Height (in.) | Flower color |
|---|---|---|
| *P. gibbosa* | 12-18 | Yellow |
| *P. scabiosifolia* | 36-72 | Yellow |
| *P. villosa* | 24-30 | White |

**-*gibbosa*** (jib-bos′ a) 12-18″/18″
Yellow Summer Japan Zones 5-8

A small version of the more common forms sold, *P. gibbosa* is handsome if not particularly showy. The 4-6″ long leaves are pinnately cut and coarsely serrated and almost appear to be blistered. The soft yellow flowers are held in a 4″ wide loose inflorescence (cyme) in early summer and persist for at least 6 weeks. Plants are effective in the front to mid position in the garden. They need full sun, although some afternoon shade in the South does not hurt, and decent drainage.

Propagate by seed.

**-*scabiosifolia*** (skab-ee-o′ si-fo-lee-a) Scabious Patrinia 3-6′/2′
Yellow Summer Japan, Korea Zones 5-8

The leaves at first glance look like those of common scabious, *Scabiosa*. The oblong to ovate basal leaves are hairy and deeply toothed and the pinnately cleft, coarsely toothed stem leaves are borne on short petioles or almost sessile. The yellow flowers are produced the second year and are held in many inflorescences well above the foliage. I enjoy Tony Avent's description on his Plant Delights web site, in which he uses the common name golden lace. Sounds a whole lot better than scabious patrinia, doesn't it? Flowers may be cut and brought inside for persistent color in arrangements.

For many years, there was confusion when plants were placed in the garden; some were 5-6′ tall while others were only about 3′ tall. Apparently two forms exist in the horticulture trade, the tall one referred to the Korean form, the smaller referred to the Japanese or compact form. Both are heat tolerant and excellent plants for hot, humid summers. Plants can reseed prolifically, so be prepared to have them around for awhile.

Propagate by seed.

**Cultivars:**

'Nagoya' is the name under which the shorter "Japanese" form is marketed. Plants are more suited to the smaller garden, but at 3′ in height, this is not a tiny plant. They have done very well in the heat and humidity including gardens in Tallahassee, Florida and in the Gardens at UGA.

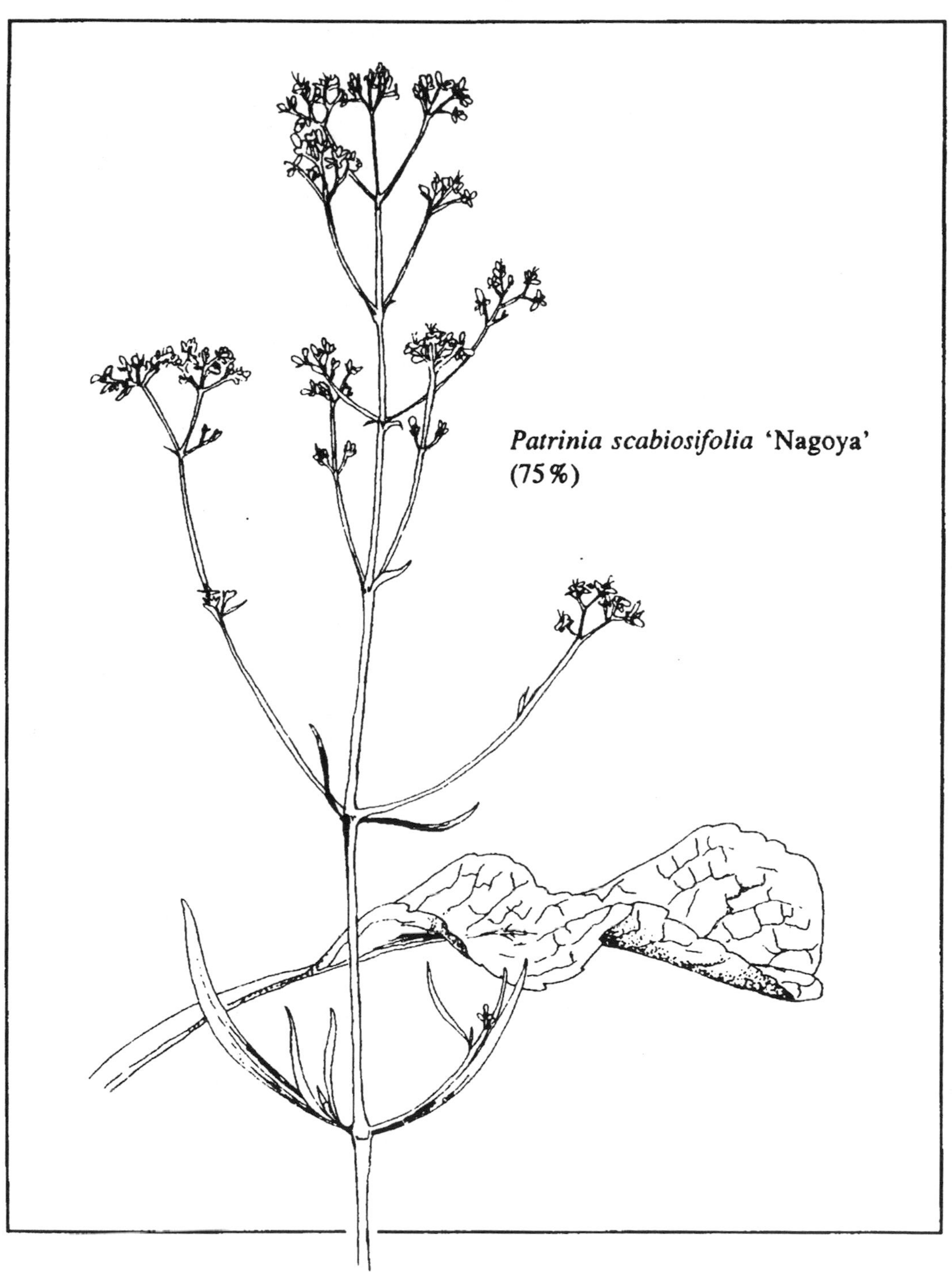

*Patrinia scabiosifolia* 'Nagoya' (75%)

***-villosa*** (vil′ losa) White Patrinia 2-3′/2′
White Fall Japan Zones 5-8

Plants are somewhat stoloniferous and the 2-3′ height make useful clumps in the late summer and fall garden. The off-white flowers are held in flat heads just above the foliage, which resembles the leaves in the other species. The flowers blend with and accentuate other plants in the fall. Introduced by Heronswood Nursery.

Propagate by seed.

**Related Species:**

*P. triloba* is a stoloniferous, slow-growing 12″ tall ground cover with small sulphur-yellow flowers, each with a small spur at the base. They are produced in late spring and early summer on short flat inflorescences. The red stems bear palmately parted and irregularly serrated leaves. Excellent for rock gardens where it flowers later than many other rock plants. Prefers a lightly shaded area in consistently moist soil. Best in zones 5-7.

## *Peltiphyllum* see ***Darmera***

## *Peltoboykinia* (pel-to-boy′ kin-ee-à) Saxigragaceae

Taxonomic confusion reigns in the saxifrage family, but probably no more than in the group of water-loving plants found within. Species of the genus *Boykinia* are found in the southeastern United States (*B. aconitifolia*) and the West (*B. rotundifolia*, *B. jamesii*) but are seldom seen in gardens.

A Japanese member, *B. tellimoides*, is more common (although still relatively unknown), in public and collectors' gardens. This species (and only this one) was recently changed to *Peltoboykinia*. I justify the name change and remember it because the leaves are essentially peltate (meaning that the petiole attaches near the middle of the leaf, rather than the base). Plants are about 2′ tall and have rounded leaves with 7-9 lobes. Plants prefer moist soils but do not require wet feet to do well. The thick creeping rhizomes will spread, and although invasive, it is less so than other similar plants used around water, such as *Darmera*. The flowers appear in terminal inflorescences (cymes) and are a rather nondescript greenish yellow. This is one of the finest foliage plants for the moist area. If provided with moist conditions, plants perform in zones 6-7 in the East, to zone 8 in the West. They do far better in cool summers than hot ones. Plants may be divided at any time, however, find a strong back and a hefty shovel.

I find that many people, including myself, get confused with all these big, leafy water lovers, so I have outlined some of the main differences among them. Because *Petasites* belongs to the Asteraceae, the flower structure is totally different (like an aster) and is easy to distinguish when in flower.

| | **Family** | **Flowering time** | **Flower color** | **Number of stamens** |
|---|---|---|---|---|
| *Boykinia* | Saxifragaceae | With leaves | White | 5-10 |
| *Darmera* | Saxifragaceae | With emerging leaves | Pink | 10 |
| *Peltoboykinia* | Saxifragaceae | With leaves | Greenish-yellow | 10 |
| *Petasites* | Asteraceae | With emerging leaves | Pink, white | Many |

*Peltoboykinia* is much smaller, and better behaved than *Darmera* or *Petasites*, and will not eat your house.

**Related Species:**

*P. watanabei*, also from Japan, is similar in habit and culture as the above. Leaves are more deeply divided and plants are shorter.

## ***Pennisetum*** (pen-i-see′ tum) Fountain Grass Poaceae

This genus consists of about 80 species of annual and perennial grasses, two or three of which have gained in popularity. They are loosely tufted plants with flat leaf blades and dense, spikelike panicles of flowers. The many plumose (meaning feathery) inflorescences make them different from most other species. Examining the spikes, you may see that the upper flowers are perfect (male and female parts together) while the lower ones are male or sterile. This arrangement of flowers helps to distinguish *Pennisetum* from other genera. But who wants to look at individual flowers when the feathery spikes are so beautiful? Some of the most handsome species are annuals, including *P. setaceum*, particularly the purple-leaved cultivar 'Burgundy Giant' with its wide purple leaves and purple-red flowers, and *P. villosum*, called feathertop because of the feathery plumes covering the plants. The most common perennial grass is *P. alopecuroides*, whose many cultivars have become mainstream plants throughout the country.

***-alopecuroides*** (a-lo-pek-ew-roi′ deez) Perennial Feather Grass 24-30″/24″
Silver-Bronze Late Summer East Asia, West Australia Zones 5-9

The leaves are about ½″ wide and 20-24″ long. The leaves turn yellowish to brown in the fall and persist in the winter. The feathery bottlebrush flowers arise in late summer to fall and range from coppery bronze to deep purple. Plants grow well on almost any site, but require full sun to be at their best. The species may self-sow and become a nuisance, however, most of the named cultivars are easily propagated by division. *P. caudatum*, with silvery early flowers, is sometimes offered but is so similar to *P. alopecuroides* that they have now been lumped together.

**Cultivars:**

'Cassian' has golden-tinged foliage with excellent color in the fall. The creamy inflorescences are held well above the foliage and tipped with silver. Plants grow about 30″ tall. A little less cold hardy than most others, supposedly hardy only to zone 6.

'Foxtrot', from Bluemel Nursery in Maryland, is 3-4′ tall and one of the largest and strongest growing fountain grasses. They produce four-inch long bottlebrush plumes and lovely gold fall color.

'Hameln' is the most popular cultivar due to its compact 24-30″ tall growth. Essentially, it is similar to the species, but more compact. The flowers are silvery white in late summer and fall, and it does not reseed much at all.

'Little Bunny' is the shortest of the available cultivars. It is great for small gardens, growing less than 12″ tall, with the silvery plumes just peeking above the foliage. Useful for the smallest gardens or the rock garden.

'Little Honey' is a white variegated sport of 'Little Bunny'.

'Moudry' is said by many to be the most handsome form, often referred to as black fountain grass. Plants grow to about 30″ with deep green leaves and long black plumes of flowers in the fall. Can reseed vigorously!

'National Arboretum' comes from the U.S. National Arboretum and carries fountains of deep purple to brown flowers above the 2-3′ tall plants. Also a vigorous reseeder.

'Weserbergland' is similar to 'Hameln' but taller and more spreading in habit.

**Related Species:**

*P. orientale*, oriental fountain grass, is occasionally offered and differs by having foliage which is more blue-green, and silvery pink flowers on 2-3′ tall plants. The plants are not as covered with flowers as other species but it is one of the most persistent flowering grasses, blooming from May to September. Plants are hardy from zones 6-9 (zone 6 with protection) and should be used more often in southern climates. Some interesting cultivars have been introduced. 'Shogun' grows about 3′ tall and is topped with deep pink flowers. 'Tall Tails' is really neat. This is not a small grass; plants can be 4-5′ tall but arch over making a handsome pendulous display. The beige flowers may have a touch of pink in them and are 7-9″ long. 'Red Head' produces red fountains of flowers earlier than other forms. Plants are about 4′ tall.

## ***Penstemon*** (pen-stay′ mon) Bearded Tongue Scrophulariaceae

Penstemon seems to have sufficient members for almost everybody's garden, but their popularity in North America has not mirrored its popularity overseas. Of the 250 species, many are native to western North America and Mexico and often require rather specific environmental conditions to do well. Originally, the eastern United States was fertile ground for early plant explorers and *P. hirsutus*, native from Quebec to Kentucky, and *P. laevigatus*, from Pennsylvania to Florida, went to England to become gentrified. It was not until the 1800s that David Douglas went west and discovered and named 18 new species including *P. ovatus*, *P. heterophyllus* and *P. venustus*.

Numerous hybrids have been introduced from Europe and their popularity is on the rise. All species are relatively drought tolerant and in fact, the biggest limitation to many of the hybrids doing well in the United States is the amount of winter moisture in many regions. Except for a few of the eastern U.S. species, plants demand sunny, dry locations.

All have opposite leaves, and showy flowers with long corolla tubes that open to five petals. Most species have red, pink, or lavender flowers although *P. confertus* bears many whorls of sulphur-yellow blooms. Flowers have five stamens, the characteristic upon which the genus name is based, but one of them is sterile (stamenoid) and lacks a well-developed anther. Tearing open the petals and seeing the four plus one stamens helps to determine that the flower you are mutilating is actually a penstemon.

Height ranges from six inches up to three feet. A number of low-growers such as *P. caespitosa*, mat penstemon, *P. pinifolius*, pine leaf penstemon, with its needlelike leaves, *P. crandallii*, Crandall's penstemon, and large-flowered species such as the pink-flowered *P. davidsonii* and *P. newberryi* occur. One or two of the eastern plants has been introduced into cultivation. The pink-purple flowered *P. smallii* is one of the finest wild flowers I have grown and *P. laevigatus*, smooth bearded tongue, and *P. australis*, southern penstemon, are being slowly adopted by gardeners. In the last 10 years, *P. digitalis* has enjoyed a meteoric rise because of the popularity of the dark-leaved cultivar 'Husker Red'.

The lack of consistent winter hardiness and the aversion to wet feet have created problems cultivating many of the showier hybrids. They are marginally hardy in the northern states and in the South; significant improvements in soil and drainage are required to provide longevity. Even the most recent cultivars have not stopped people in their tracks, as do penstemons overseas or on the West Coast. Where rainfall is low, drainage is excellent, and sun is available, however, there are many beautiful forms from which to chose.

To be on the safe side, cuttings should be taken in the fall or seed started in winter. All others, such as the showy *P. x gloxinioides*, should be well mulched after cuttings have been taken.

Quick Reference to Penstemon Species

| | Height (in.) | Flower color |
|---|---|---|
| *P. barbatus* | 18-36 | Pink, rose |
| *P. digitalis* | 24-36 | White |
| *P. campanulatus* | 18-24 | Various |
| *P.* x *gloxinioides* | 18-24 | Red, scarlet |
| *P. pinifolius* | 10-20 | Scarlet |
| *P. smallii* | 18-24 | Lavender, purple |

***-barbatus*** (bar-bah′ tus) Common Bearded Tongue 18-36″/18″
Spring Pink, Rose Southwestern United States, Mexico Zones 2-8

The tubular flowers are borne in thin spires and are lipped like flowers of *Salvia*. The lower lip has short bristly hairs that extend into the throat, thus providing the common name, bearded tongue. The leaves and stems are glaucous (covered with a whitish substance, an epicuticular wax, that rubs off), and the leaves are lance shaped to linear. The flowers are 1-2″ long and usually occur in long narrow, 2-3-flowered racemes that open from the bottom and persist 2 to 3 weeks. Each flower is strongly 2-lipped and varies from light pink to carmine. Plants are quite winter hardy and also tolerate the heat of the South. In the University of Georgia Horticulture Gardens, flowers opened from early May to mid June. Plants persisted for about three years before division became necessary.

Plants are presently available in a mixture of colors only. Propagation of the named cultivars is by terminal cuttings taken in early to late summer. Some of the named introductions such as Hyacinth Mix and 'Twilight' can be propagated by seed as can the species and subsp. *torreyi*.

**Cultivars:**

'Albus' is the white version of the species. A good choice for a tough white penstemon.

'Bashful' has orange flowers on 12-24″ tall plants.

'Coccineus' grows 2½-3′ tall with scarlet flowers.

'Crystal' is similar to 'Bashful' but bears white flowers.

Hyacinth Mix is a popular seed-propagated series that bears mixed colors of red, pink, and scarlet.

'Iron Maiden', at least in the southern half of the country, is one of the finest performers I have come across. Dozens of skinny, eye-catching orange-red flowers are borne on tall spikes in late spring to mid summer. The tubular flowers are much narrower than most other cultivars and appear more refined. The foliage is unblemished, and as healthy as any penstemon I have trialed.

Navigator series includes 18″ tall plants with flowers ranging from rose to pink to lavender.

'Praecox' flowers earlier than the species; 'Praecox Nanus' is earlier and shorter. Plants are available in pink, red and violet. Sometimes sold as 'Rondo Mix'.

'Skylight Mix' is another excellent seed-propagated selection. The large tubular flowers are violet to cherry red and often, although not always, white inside the tube. Short-lived but beautiful.

subsp. *torreyi* is a scarlet form of the species with little or no beard on the lower lip. It is often sold as 'Torre'.

'Twilight' is a seed-propagated cultivar bearing 2-3″ long flowers.

***-campanulatus*** (kam-pahn′ ew-lay-tus) Harebell Penstemon 18-24″/24″
Summer Various Mexico, Guatemala Zones 7-8

Plants are not often seen in American gardens but appear to be the dominant parent of a number of hybrid strains making their way into this country. Hardiness in North American gardens is marginal, as the hybrids are not tolerant of winter temperatures below 25°F, or hot summer temperatures of the South. *P. campanulatus* has narrow, lance-shaped, sharply toothed leaves and 3″ long tubular flowers. The stamenoid (see introduction above), if one takes the time to look, is bearded and a good identifying characteristic for the species. The flowers are pink, dark purple, or violet and borne in a long, narrow inflorescence in midsummer.

**Cultivars:**

'Pulchellus' has violet to lilac flowers.

'Purpureus' bears purple flowers.

***-digitalis*** (di-gi-tah′ lis) Smooth White Penstemon 2-3′/18″
Summer White Eastern United States Zones 4-8

This fine native plant can't compete with the color of some of the hybrids, however the 4-5″ long oblong-lanceolate leaves are dark green throughout the summer. The white flowers, which are occasionally flushed with light pink, are held in a panicle well above the leaves in early to midsummer. This is one of the finest species for hot summers and has thrived in the Armitage garden for years. Plants are native from Maine, west to South Dakota and south to Texas.

**Cultivars:**

'Pink Dawn' is a hybrid of dubious parentage, but *P. digitalis* is certainly one of them. Plants grow about 2′ tall and have handsome pink flowers. They are more compact than 'Husker Red'.

'Husker Red' was developed by Dale Lindgren at the University of Nebraska. They bear the same white flowers as the species but the leaves are a deep maroon. The foliage remains colorful throughout the summer except in southern climates. Plants need full sun to maintain their color. In the shaded Armitage garden, it reverts to close to the species once the heat hits. The cultivar was designated the 1996 Perennial Plant of the Year by the Perennial Plant Association.

'Woodville White' has cleaner white flowers than the species.

**-x *gloxinioides*** (gloks-in-oi′ deez) Gloxinia Penstemon 18-24″/20″
Summer Various Hybrid Zones 5-7

The specific epithet has no official botanical standing but refers to hybrids between *P. hartwegii* and *P. cobaea*. *P. hartwegii* has drooping scarlet or blood-red flowers and entire leaves, while *P. cobaea* has large reddish purple to whitish flowers and sharply toothed leaves. The hybrids have inherited the large flowers from *P. cobaea* and are often referred to as gloxinia penstemons. The flowers are about 2″ wide, equally long and borne on tall, open racemes.

None of the hybrids is particularly hardy except on the West Coast and all must be well mulched regardless of location.

**Cultivars:**

'Midnight' has dark green leaves, stands about 18″ tall and bears deep purple bell flowers. Performs well in hot, humid climates.

***-pinifolius*** (pie-ni-fo′ lee-us) Pine-Leaf Penstemon 10-20″/15″
Summer Scarlet Southwest United States Zones 7-8

The woody base and the needlelike leaves, many crowded at the top of the stem, provide the unique characteristics of this native penstemon. The tubular flowers are scarlet to coral-red and cover the plant in the summer. Plants require excellent drainage and are terrific in hot, dry rocky areas or rock gardens where they perform well.

**Cultivars:**

'Magdalena Sunshine', from the Magdalena Mountains of New Mexico, bears bright yellow flowers. It is said to be more compact and an improvement on other yellow forms, but it is a little too early to tell. Found by Jay and Ann Lund of Portland, Oregon.

'Mersea Yellow' is about 12″ tall with bright yellow flowers.

***-smallii*** (small-ee′ eye) Small's Penstemon 18-24″/2′
Late Spring Lavender Eastern United States Zones 6-8

The flowers of this wonderful native plant are pink-purple on the outside and striped with white inside. The 4-6″ long leaves are smooth on the bottom and sometimes slightly pubescent above. Plants tolerate shade but do better in at least 6 hours of full sun. A good choice for eastern and southern gardeners who love penstemon but have trouble with the fancier kinds.

**Related Species:**

*P. grandiflorus*, shell-leaf penstemon, grows about 3′ in height and throws up long spikes with mostly light pink flowers. 'Prairie Snow' has large white flowers, 'War Axe' provides many different flower colors. Both cultivars were chosen for the GreatPlants® Program, a cooperative venture between the Nebraska Nursery and Landscape Association and the Nebraska Statewide Arboretum. Zones 5-8.

*P. heterophyllus* is best known commercially by the cultivar 'Blue Spring', which grows 18-24″ tall and bears gentian-blue flowers. Zones 5-8.

*P. strictus* is 2-3′ tall and provides rosy lavender flowers. Zones 4-8.

**Hybrids:**

Many of the more commonly offered cultivars are hybrids with mixed parentage, but certainly include *P. barbatus*, *P. campanulatus* and *P. x gloxinioides*, among others. I tried to figure out which cultivars belonged to which species, but it is better to lump them all together. The main thing to remember is that your garden is not in England and they will likely not be long-lived. Provide full sun and good drainage.

'Alice Hindley' is a hybrid of *P. campanulatus* and bears large (2½-3″ long), pale mauve, wide-mouthed tubular flowers with white interiors. Plants are about 2′ tall and late flowering. This is a magnificent plant when well grown.

'Apple Blossom' bears white flowers with a pink blush.

'Blackbird' has relatively small but deep purple flowers. These received a highly favorable rating as part of the Great Plant Picks program, which chooses outstanding plants for Pacific Northwest Gardens.

'Blue Midnight' produces late spring purple flowers on 2′ tall plants.

'Blue Robin has handsome azure blue flowers on the outside and pink centers.

'Catherine de la Mare' has bluish flowers that fade to purple. Plants are about 18″ tall.

'Charles Rudd' bears large tubular cherry-red flowers with a white interior.

'Chester Scarlet' is about as scarlet as I have seen. Growing a little over 2′ tall, plants are showstoppers.

'Crushed Grapes' has dark purple trumpet-shaped flowers in summer. About 4-5′ tall.

'Edithae' is a low grower with large pink-purple flowers.

'Elfin Pink' is about 12″ tall with clear pink tubular flowers. Probably a *P. barbatus* hybrid.

'Evelyn' is about 18″ tall with many 1″ long flowers of pale pink borne over very bushy plants. It is hardier than most of the penstemons, probably having *P. barbatus* in its parentage.

'Firebird' is one of the best-known selections due to the exceptionally deep red flowers.

'Garnet' has dozens of large, 1½-2″ long wine-colored flowers which open in late summer and fall. The thin, lanceolate leaves are bright green but this hybrid is only moderately hardy in the United States, likely having *P. hartwegii* or *P. campanulatus* in its parentage. Originally introduced as 'Andenken an Friedrich Hahn'.

'Hewell's Pink' bears large tubular flowers of pink with a white spotted interior.

'Hidcote Pink' is a light pink form with many nodding flowers on 3-4′ tall stems.

'Hopley's Variegated' is an interesting variegated penstemon with lavender flowers. Grows about 2′ tall and hardy to zone 6.

'Mother of Pearl' bears many pearly white (white with shades of pink) flowers in midsummer.

'Papal Purple' is only 12-15″ tall with pale purple tubular flowers. From Washfield Nursery in Kent, England.

'Party Dress' has pink flowers on 2′ tall stems. Recommended as a good cut flower.

'Pike's Peak Purple' is a selection from *P.* x *mexicali*, crosses made from Mexican and southwest American taxa. The 15-18″ tall plants have dark purple flowers and dark green leaves. In 1999, this was named a winner by the Plant Select® organization, a cooperative program between the Denver Botanic Garden and Colorado State University.

'Pink Chablis' was introduced in 2005 and produces handsome rosy pink flowers on 15-20″ tall stems.

'Pink Endurance' bears tubular flowers that are cherry pink on the outside and white inside.

'Port Wine' really does have flowers of a port wine color. Plants grow about 18″ tall.

'Prairie Dawn', bred by Glenn Viehmeyer at the University of Nebraska, produces pale pink flowers.

'Prairie Dusk' provides clear purple flowers on 18″ tall plants.

'Prairie Fire', part of the wonderful Prairie series, bears lilac-red flowers mottled with white inside.

'Prairie Splendor' was introduced by Dale Lindgren from the University of Nebraska. Plants are about 20″ tall and carry flowers in red and pink. A GreatPlants® introduction in 2005. Zones 4-8. All of the Prairie series are evergreen in southern climates.

'Pretty Petticoat' has dense flowers of purple, each with a white center. About 2′ tall.

'Purple Bedder' consists of 2′ tall plants with deep purple flowers.

'Radjah' produces bright scarlet red flowers on 2-3′ tall plants.

'Raven' bears dark purple to almost red flowers on 2′ plants.

'Red Rocks' has rosy magenta flowers with a white throat. Highly rated by the Great Plant Picks trials at Joy Creek Nursery in 2002, as well as being a Plant Select® favorite (see 'Pike's Peak Purple' above) in 1999.

'Rose Elf' is a prolific flowering plant with shell-pink flowers. A *P. barbatus* hybrid.

'Rubicundus' has wide tubular scarlet flowers with white centers.

'Ruby' is similar to 'Firebird' with 2½-2″ long, rich ruby red flowers on 3′ tall plants.

'Ruby Candle' produces ruby red flowers on 2′ tall stems.

'Schooley's Yellow', bred by Dale Lindgren at the University of Nebraska, has bright yellow flowers on 2′ tall plants. A good deal of *P. barbatus* appears to be in this hybrid.

'Sissinghurst Pink' bears light pink flowers.

'Snowstorm' is one of the better white-flowered forms I have seen. Large white flowers with purple stamens are produced are on 2-3′ tall plants.

'Southgate Gem' produces many large deep scarlet red flowers.

'Sour Grapes' was raised by Margery Fish of England and the flowers are bunched as the name suggests. The indigo blue buds swell to form flowers in shades of amethyst and blue. This beautiful plant is likely a hybrid with *P. hirsutus*, hairy penstemon, native to the northeastern states.

'Sweet Grapes' is only about 18″ tall, and bears deep purple trumpet flowers. Stands up well to wind and rain.

'Stapleford Gem' is confused with 'Sour Grapes' but is distinct because of its lighter color and taller and more robust habit.

'Thorn' has handsome pink and white bicolored flowers.

'White Bedder' is a dwarf (12-15″) form with tubular white flowers.

'Windsor Red' has deep red flowers.

## ***Perovskia*** (pe-rof′ skee-a) Perovskia Lamiaceae

Although approximately seven species occur, the most popular is *P. atriplicifolia*. The stems are square in cross section and the flowers are borne in terminal racemes or panicles.

***-atriplicifolia*** (a-tri-pli-ki-fo′ lee-a) Russian Sage 4-5′/4′
Summer Light Blue Afghanistan to Tibet Zone 5-9

As a garden plant, *Perovskia* provides beauty and a strong fragrance. The odor from the plant is pungent, but only when the leaves are bruised or crushed. Way back when, during the Cold War when we at least knew who had nuclear weapons, we used to joke that the common name came from the odor (like the feet of Russian soldiers): now we are smarter, we know it was named for General V.A. Perovski (1794-1857).

The tubular light blue flowers are two-lipped and arranged in whorls along many-branched 12-15″ tall panicles. The coarsely toothed gray-green leaves are 1-2½″ long and 1″ wide. The loose flowers and small foliage provide a feeling of lightness and airiness to the garden. The flowers appear in mid to late summer and are particularly stunning when combined with a white-flowered plant such as *Boltonia*. Flowers persist for up to 15 weeks; lasting from early July to mid September in most gardens, including mine. Plants lean toward the light and tend to flop over as they mature.

Full sun and adequate drainage must be provided to survive wet winters. Late frosts will knock plants back badly, but in most cases they recover and grow rapidly.

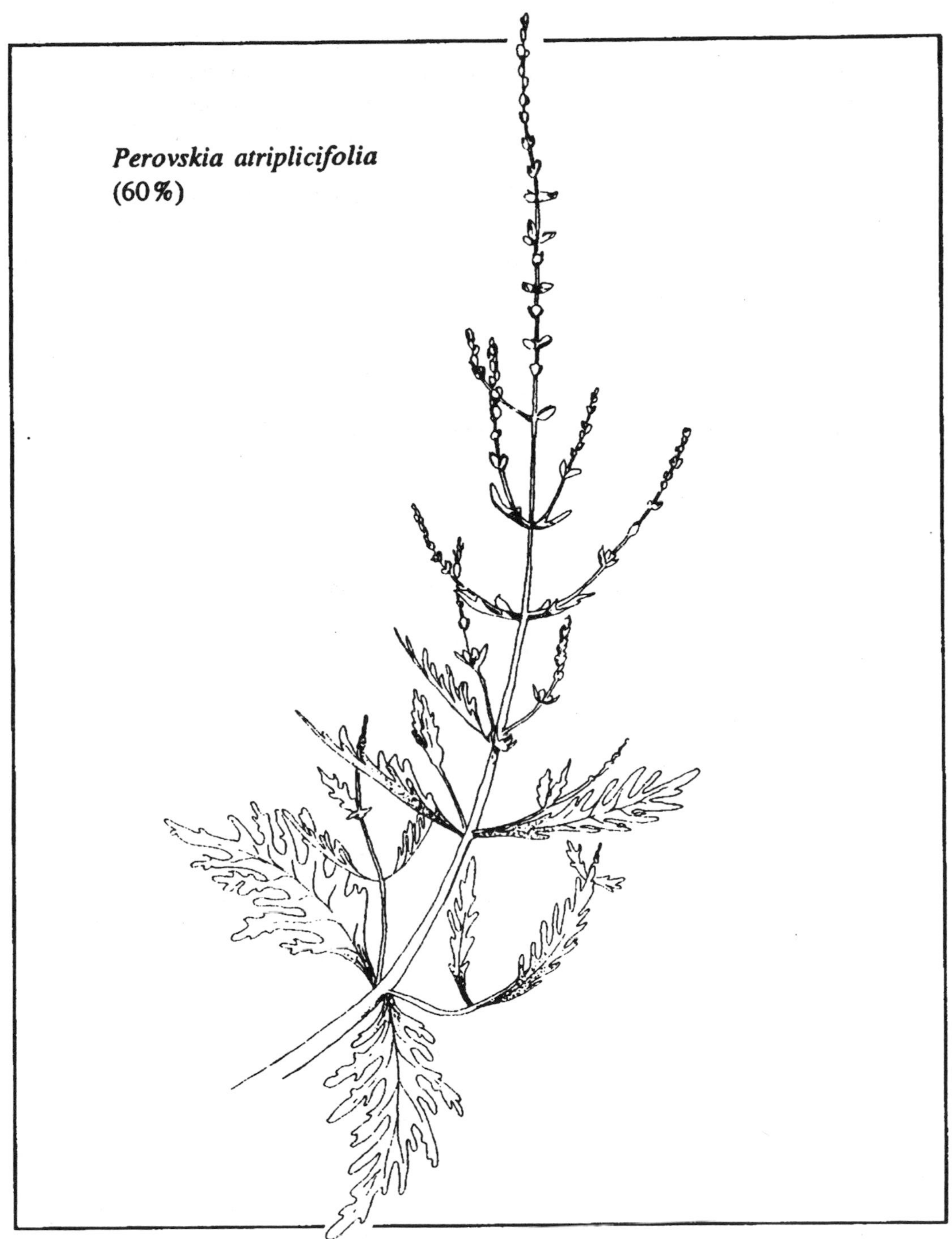

*Perovskia atriplicifolia* (60%)

Cut back to 12-18″ after the first hard frost in the fall. Leave some of the stem buds as these provide next year's growing points.

Two problems plague this plant. The first is its tendency to flop even in the brightest sun. It is simply difficult to make this plant sit up straight. The other is that it is only a mediocre plant in areas of high heat and humidity. The floppiness combined with the poor color in hot summers does little to enamor it to many Southern gardeners. However, it was sufficiently inspirational in other parts of the country, as it was voted the Perennial Plant of the Year by the Perennial Plant Association in 1995.

Propagate by offshoots that occasionally arise after 2-3 years or take softwood cuttings in the summer. Take a 3″ long shoot, including stem and leaves, dip in root hormone, place in sand, and cover to maintain humidity. Use of plastic to maintain humidity is better than a mist system, as excessive moisture in the rooting bench results in loss of cuttings. Roots appear in 14-21 days. Do not cut back hard until new growth has started in the spring.

**Cultivars:**

'Blue Mist' flowers earlier and has lighter flowers than the species.

'Blue Spire' has deep violet flowers and deeply cut foliage.

'Filigran' has filigreed foliage with light blue flowers. The upright plants have a more delicate appearance than the species and are probably a little bluer than others in hot climates.

'Little Spire' is shorter and not quite as floppy as the species. This may be a hybrid between this and *P. abrotanoides*, and I have seen it listed as belonging to both. It has been a good performer at the Gardens at UGA but still not as colorful as in Northern gardens.

'Longin' looks the same as 'Blue Spire' but perhaps has narrower foliage.

**Related Species:**

*P. abrotanoides*, Caspian perovskia, is more branched, taller, and bears darker blue flowers than *P. atriplicifolia*. The gray-green linear-oblong leaves are 1-2″ long and deeply cut. Plants are less compact than Russian sage.

## ***Persicaria*** (per-si-kar′ ee-a) Smartweed, Knotweed Polygonaceae
(syn. *Polygonum*)

In the last edition, I fretted and waffled on the name change from *Polygonum* to *Persicaria*. At that time (1997) I stated that "many taxonomists have sliced up the entire genus and placed nearly all of it into *Persicaria*, and a few into *Fallopia*. However, many other taxonomists disagree and have retained *Polygonum* pretty much intact. Rather than change something that may be changed right back again, I have retained everything in *Polygonum*." I am still waffling, as the Integrated Taxonomic Information System, the USDA Plants database, the RHS database and others still cannot agree. However, it seems horticulturists have embraced the change, so as I write this in 2007, *Persicaria* it is.

Although most of the approximately 150 species are not ornamental, a few could make welcome additions but are generally overlooked. In this country, knotweeds have been colored with a "weedy" crayon, due to the persistence of such unwelcome guests as *P. aviculare*, the common knotgrass of lawns and patios, *P. pensylvanicum*, Pennsylvania smartweed, and the most common of all our weeds, *P. persicaria*, lady's thumb (most taxonomists have left these weeds in *Polygonum*). Unfortunately, these intruders have blinded gardeners and nurserymen alike to the beauty of some of the cultivated species. Certainly many ornamental species are also aggressive, some to the point of being invasive, however numerous wonderful choices are still available to the discerning gardener.

All species have alternate leaves and many have somewhat swollen leaf nodes. Its original name has the same roots as that of *Polygonatum* (which see), but *gonu* refers to the jointed stems rather than jointed rhizomes in this genus. Some species may attain heights of 5-7′ and require ample space. The big, stoloniferous forms have received a lot of press about their aggressive nature, however, our ignorance about where to site them or how to take advantage of their obvious attributes should reflect on the gardener, not the plant. Obviously, they need a lot of room. So be it—give them room and enjoy them or leave them be.

*P. amplexicaulis*, mountain fleeceflower, can be a noble, beautiful plant and magnificent cultivars have been introduced. Thugs such as *P. mollis* are handsome and look wonderful in a large shady setting but space can not be a concern. If it is, they should be left to others. On the other hand, the leaves of *P. vacciniifolia* are less than one inch long and plants are less than one foot tall. Long pink flower spikes rise above the spreading plants. People tend to run from many of the more vigorous forms not because they aren't ornamental (in some cases, they are showstoppers), but because of their tendency to colonize huge areas. Once established, they do not go gently into that good night—small land mines are needed to eradicate them. However, with the selection of clumping forms of the taller species, they are beginning to creep into commerce once again.

Plants known as magic carpet, *P. capitata*, must be mentioned here although they are annuals in most of the country. Some references list it as cold hardy to zone 6 but it dies in zone 7. However, plants reseed themselves religiously and this low-growing specimen with gorgeous foliage and pretty pink, dense, globular flowers is well worth planting in shady or sunny locations.

Most species are comfortable in full sun to semi-shade with constant moisture. While they are not bog plants, dry soil inhibits establishment. Once established, they are persistent. Unfortunately, the more ornamental species are not particularly heat tolerant and perform poorly south of zone 6. However, heat tolerance is improved if consistent moisture is available.

All species are easily propagated from division and most may be raised from seed.

Quick Reference to Persicaria Species

| | Height (in.) | Flower color |
|---|---|---|
| *P. affinis* | 6-9 | Rose-red |
| *P. amplexicaulis* | 36-60 | Red |
| *P. bistorta* | 18-30 | Pink |
| *P. polymorpha* | 48-72 | White |
| *P. vacciniifolia* | 6-12 | Rose-pink |
| *P. virginiana* | 12-24 | Pink, red |

***-affinis*** (a-fee′ nis) Himalayan Fleeceflower 6-9″/12″
Summer, Fall Rose-Red Himalayas Zone 3-7
(syn. *Polygonum affine*)

Plants are most effective as front of the border subjects or ground covers, bearing erect, mostly basal leaves (2½-4″ long) which taper to the petiole. The deep green 4″ long leaves turn bronze in fall. Numerous deep rose-red flowers are arranged in dense 2-3″ long terminal spikes and turn whitish as they mature. Plants are most effective in cool, moist areas and provide stability and beauty to a troublesome bank, or carpet stones in a rock garden. It is not as invasive as many of the other species and may be controlled with selective pruning. Some shade is tolerated but full sun and moisture are necessary for dense plantings.

I have seen marvelous plantings on the West Coast and in the Northeast. The South has not been a friendly place.

The easiest method of propagation is division in the spring or fall. Terminal cuttings (3-4″ long) and seed propagation are also effective. Seeds require stratification (place in moist sand or peat moss at 40°F for 6-8 weeks).

**Cultivars:**

'Border Jewel' is 8-12″ tall and bears pink flowers over deep green foliage. As the flowers mature, they change to a much deeper red. The foliage also turns red in the fall.

'Darjeeling Red' has deep pink flowers and is a vigorous selection.

'Dimity' is smaller and more refined (if a persicaria can be called refined) than other selections. Pink upright flowers on 4-6″ tall plants.

'Donald Lowndes' is about 8-10″ tall and carries double salmon-pink flowers. Probably the best selection for North American gardens.

'Superba' is more vigorous than other cultivars and the pink flowers turn crimson as they mature.

***-amplexicaulis*** (am-pleks-i-kaw′ lis) Mountain Fleeceflower 4-6′/3′
Summer Red Himalayas, China Zones 4-7
(syn. *Polygonum amplexicaule*)

A plant that, regardless of what the catalogs say, requires significant space in the garden. Plants can be big, bold and bodacious, although well-behaved cultivars have been introduced. It is a stout, clumping species that can flower from summer until the first frost. The alternate leaves are longer than wide and somewhat pointed at the tips. A characteristic to this species is the obvious manner in which the leaves clasp the stem (*amplexicaulis* means leaves clasping stems). The flowers, which may be pink, red or white, arise in short spikes at the ends of the stems in summer and fall.

The plants do not spread as rapidly as some of the other stoloniferous forms but they still form dense large clumps that get denser and larger with time. Pickaxe or backhoe is needed if removal becomes necessary. Full sun and consistently moist soils are needed for best performance.

In 2002, some of the plant gurus of the state of Washington discussed the pros and cons of persicarias. Two of the most knowledgeable plantspeople, Marietta and Ernie O'Byrne, felt that *P. amplexicaulis* was too leafy and potentially floppy for most of the season. Having that said, I have seen some marvelous plantings of persicaria in the equally marvelous gardens at Wave Hill on the Hudson River in New York.

Propagate by division of the clump; be careful of your back.

**Cultivars:**

'Atrosanguineum' is as big as the species but bears deep crimson-red flowers.

'Firetail' is an excellent selection. Plants are not invasive but do need a lot of room. They can grow to 4′ tall and produce large, clasping, heart-shaped leaves. The crimson flower spikes, if grown well, can be 6″ long. Known as 'Speciosa' in Europe.

'Golden Arrow' brings golden foliage to the species. Plants bear bright red flowers on 2′ tall plants. Quite a nice combination.

'Inverleith' bears dark crimson flowers on short spikes on 3-4′ tall plants.

'Rosea' has dark rosy red flowers.

'Taurus', introduced by Blooms of Bressingham, features dark red flowers on 2½-3′ tall plants.

***-bistorta*** (bis-tor′ ta) | Snakeweed | 18-30″/30″
Early Summer | Pink | Europe, Asia | Zones 3-7
(syn. *Polygonum bistortum*)

This clump-forming plant has 4-6″ long, wavy, medium green leaves with a striking white midrib. Most leaves arise from the base of the plant and form handsome clumps even when not in flower. The flowers, however, are held well above the foliage and are made up of 4-5″ long dense spikes of soft pink. The stamens of the individual flowers protrude, resulting in a bottle brush appearance. The flowers are long lasting and are used as a cut flower in the florist trade. They look terrific in Chicago Botanical Garden and throughout the Midwest and North. Lousy in the Southeast.

Propagate similar to *P. affinis*.

**Cultivars:**

'Carnea' has cherry red flowers with contrasting white stamens. Plants are actually a subspecies (subsp. *carnea*) but may also be incorrectly labeled as a species (*P. carnea*).

'Superba' is larger with bigger flowers than the species and is superior to the species. This cultivar is easier to find than other persicarias mentioned here.

***-polymorpha*** (poli-more′ fa) | Giant Fleeceflower | 4-6′/4′
White | Late Spring | Himalayas | Zones 4-8

This is a relatively new plant for North American gardeners and as it is planted more, it is gaining more converts. A number of good characteristics are worth noting. Plants are big but not aggressive, flowering continues for many weeks, even months, and little maintenance, other than dividing it when needed, is required. Flower buds resembling fat broccoli spears occur at the ends of the vigorous stems. Soon the buds elongate into plumes of creamy white fleece flowers, which turn pinkish over time. Caterpillars and other chewing insects are occasionally a problem, but few serious insects and diseases have been reported. However, this is a large plant and it must have sufficient room to spread its wings. In the North, this is a more spectacular plant than in the South, but even as far south as Raleigh, North Carolina, plants have done well. I saw spectacular specimens in Pennsylvania and especially in the Niagara School of Horticulture gardens in Niagara-on-the-Lake, Ontario.

My friend and crazyman, Wolfgang Oehme, of Maryland is in love with this plant. Every time I see him, he extols its virtues. And of course, when one of horticulture's superstars feels this strongly, we should all pay attention and take notice. Propagate by division.

***-vacciniifolia*** (va-seen-ee-i-fo′ lee-a) Vaccinium Fleece Flower 6-12″/18″
Late Spring Rose-Pink Himalayas Zones 5-7

The antithesis of the large bullying species must be this rock-covering, ground-hugging species. The elliptical leaves are ½ to ¾″ long, smooth, entire and acute at both ends (somewhat like a cranberry). The long woody stems may be 3′ long and the 2″ long spikes of rosy pink flowers arise from the dense foliage in late spring and early summer.

I first saw this plant in Christchurch Botanic Garden in Christchurch, New Zealand. It took on the shape of the large rock beneath it and was absolutely covered with flowers, to the point that leaves were not visible. We should all be so lucky.

Terrific for cooler summers and well-drained soils. An excellent rock garden plant.

***-virginiana*** (vir-gin-ee- aye′ na) Tovara 1-2½′
Summer Pink to Red Eastern North America Zones 4-8

The plant continues to flip-flop between genera. Plants originally started out in the genus *Polygonum*, then switched to *Tovara* because of obvious differences in habit and flower structure, then back to *Polygonum* and who knows, may now be in *Persicaria*. What the heck, if I am getting rid of *Polygonum*, I might as well dump the genus *Tovara* as well. Plants have long been confused as to their identity, so perhaps this is the right time. However, you have to feel bad for Simon Tovar, the Spanish physician for whom the genus was named.

*Tovara* can become a nuisance within a few years of planting. The pure green-leaved species is seldom seen but the green and white variegated form, 'Variegata', is handsome. The elliptical 4-10″ long leaves are slow to emerge in the spring but clothe the plants in dense green and white by early summer. The tiny pink to red flowers, formed in late summer and fall, are held in slender terminal and axillary spikes. Seeds are viable and hundreds of little tovaras may appear in the summer and spring, quickly making you curse the person from whom you received an innocent-looking beginning. I really don't recommend the species or cultivar to anyone. My plant came from

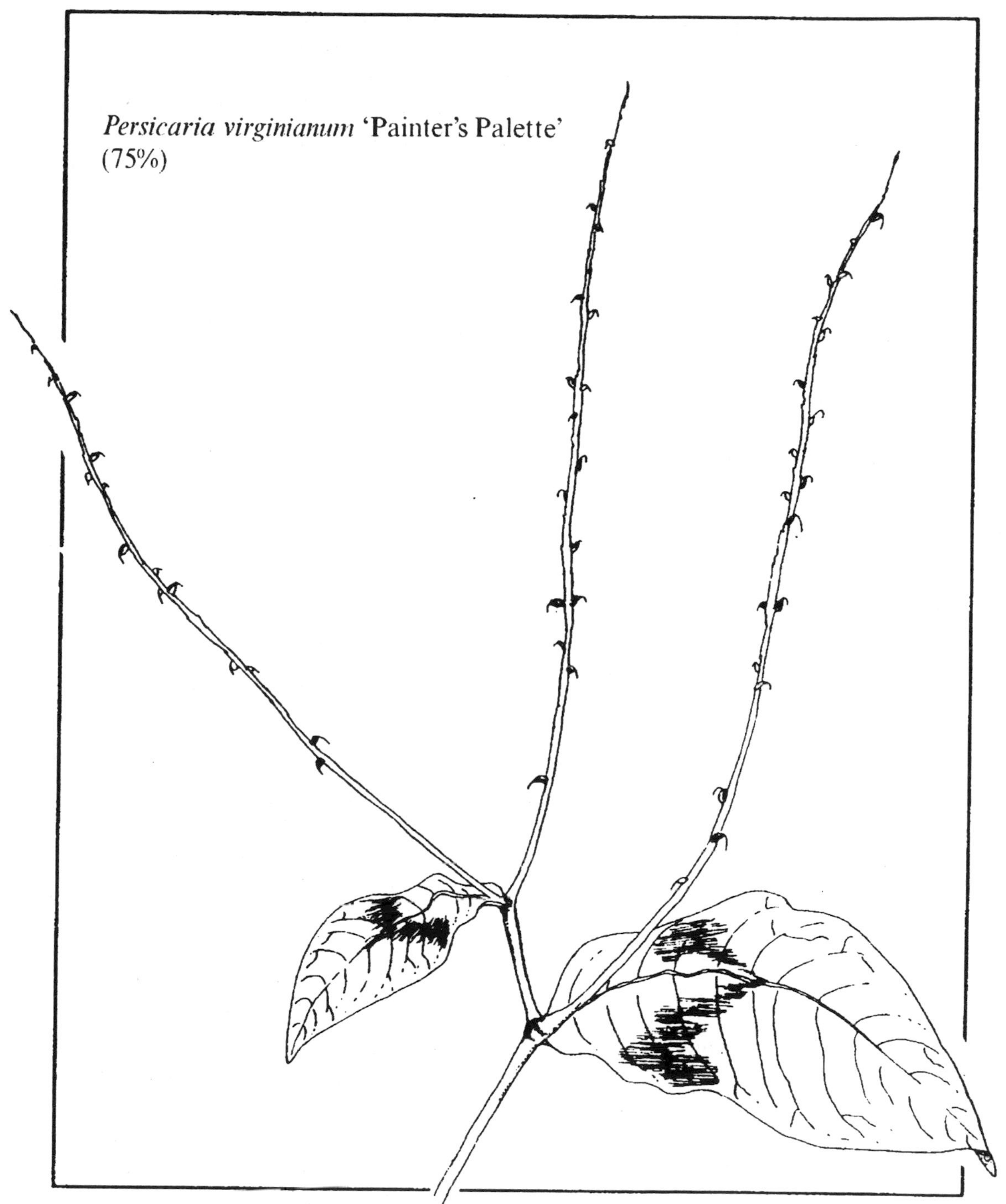
*Persicaria virginianum* 'Painter's Palette' (75%)

one of my favorite nursery people, Robyn Duback, Robyn's Nest Nursery, Vancouver, Washington. I think she delighted in sending me this obnoxious weed to pay back for her bent shovel and pick (see *Aruncus*).

Plants should be protected from the wind as leaves are damaged easily. In most soils and surely in rich, moist ones, and partial shade, tovara spreads rapidly from seeds and quickly becomes a nuisance. This is far more a problem in warm climes than in the North.

Propagate by division in spring or fall, or from seed.

**Cultivars:**

'Brushstrokes' has large green leaves with purple chevrons in the middle. Small red flowers are formed in late fall. The late flowering tendency may result in flowers being frostbitten before seeds form.

'Compton's Form' is much more beautiful and perhaps less aggressive. Use with caution, but worth another look.

'Lance Corporal' has chartreuse green leaves with a red chevron. Tends to reseed in warm climates.

'Painter's Palette' is similar to 'Variegata' but has a V-shaped reddish-pink blotch in the center of each leaf. The new leaves are creamy white and touched with light green and pink. A superior cultivar, but no less aggressive.

**Related Species and Hybrids:**

*P. campanulatum*, lesser knotweed, is a creeping, stoloniferous species that grows 3-5′ tall, and bears white or pink-red flowers in dense panicles. The narrow leaves generally have purple midribs. Look out! They can roam.

*P. microcephala* is included here only because of a number of fine cultivars, the best known being 'Red Dragon'. These 3′ tall plants have burgundy leaves with a blue-gray chevron in the middle. Small white flowers are also formed. This is a clumping plant that gets bigger over time but does not run. In areas of warm nights, the color fades somewhat in the summer. Originated at Crystal Palace Perennials, St. Johns, Indiana. Other recent introductions include 'Chocolate Dragon', with darker foliage but otherwise similar to 'Red Dragon', and 'Silver Dragon' a 3′ tall clumper with silvery leaves that include an olive-green border and central red vein. The new growth is reddish but that disappears as the leaves mature. Similar white flowers occur. 'Dragon's Eye' has a wider, more distinctive silver chevron. All are excellent, non-aggressive forms for the garden and all are hardy in zones 6-8 (perhaps a little colder).

*P. japonica* (*P. cuspidatum*, *Fallopia japonica*, *Reynoutria japonica*), Japanese knotweed, is a creeping, clumping form that can get out of hand. Plants grow about 6′ tall and bear creamy white flowers. Avoid the species; 'Compactum' is only about 18″ tall and bears pink flowers in the summer. 'Crimson Beauty' has gorgeous crimson flowers in late summer and fall and although the stems are a bamboo-like 7′ tall, plants are not too rampant, 'Spectabilis' ('Variegata') is big but at least it has unique leaves splashed with white, yellow and pink. I didn't say it was pretty, only unique. It will also colonize your neighbor's place.

***Petasites*** (pet-a-see′ tees) Butterbur Asteraceae

An axiom my students frequently hear from me is "There is no such thing as a bad plant, just a bad use for a good one." This lesson could be given every time one talks about an aggressive thug, like fleeceflower or butterbur. Plants (*P. japonica*) are fabulous for covering acres of boggy soil with large kidney-shaped leaves on 3′ petioles, anywhere moist, shady, cool conditions are present. The light mauve to deep rose flowers with their protruding stamens occur in short clusters and appear before or just as the leaves are reappearing in early spring.

They are best in cooler climes such as the Northwest or areas of the Midwest and Northeast. In hot, humid areas, they flop and stagger, falter and die.

These plants are not for the faint of heart. If you are a little frightened of such plants, put them in sunken tubs or other such restricting containers. That will help until you .realize you are crazy for planting it in the first place, and can then give it as a house-warming present to that nice young couple who just moved in down the street. Hardy in zones 6-8.

For those who are confused between large bog plants like *Petasites*, *Peltoboykinia*, and *Darmera*, see the section on *Peltoboykinia*.

**Cultivars:**

var. *giganteus* is large and particularly wonderful. The "giganteus" part refers to the thin rounded leaves, easily 2′ across on plants 5-6′ tall. 'Nishiki-buki' is a selection with green leaves containing large creamy white sections. This may also go under the name *P. giganteus* 'Variegatus'.

'Purpureus' is similar to the species, with more purple pigment in the leaves.

'Variegatus' is a variegated form with a heavy splashing of cream and gold.

**Related Species:**

*P. frigidus* var. *palmatus*, sweet coltsfoot, is native to the Northwest and into the northeastern states and Canada. Plants have palmately divided leaves and early spring white flowers and are usually no more than 2′ tall. Plants are threatened or endangered in five northeastern states. This is a plant for northern gardens, and prefers moist soils. 'Golden Palms' has beautiful chartreuse leaves in the spring.

***Petrorhagia*** (pet-ro-rah′ gee-a) Tunic Flower Caryophyllaceae

The genus was recently called *Tunica* but neither name is well-known beyond the rock garden enthusiasts. Although 25-30 species occur, only *P. saxifraga* appears to have any significant following. The plants resemble creeping baby's breath (*Gypsophila repens*) and are used to clamber over rocks or onto pathways. They are native to high elevations and rocky or sandy soils, therefore telling us that drainage is most important to success. It is undemanding in its cultural needs, as long as it hangs from walls or is in raised beds. Heat results in long internodes and plants should be cut back hard in early to midsummer in the South.

The flowers are pale pink, often with darker veins, and the combination of small leaves and tiny flowers provide a delicate picture. Numerous cultivars have been selected. Double forms such as 'Alba Plena' and 'Pleniflora Rosea' are covered with white and rosy flowers respectively. 'Lady Mary' ('Lady Marie') has double soft pink flowers and 'Rosette' is a compact form with double pink blooms.

Plants are hardy from zones 5-7, although they also do well in zone 8 on the West Coast. In the South, the foliage is evergreen and performs in hot weather only if drainage is outstanding and plants are trimmed occasionally.

***Phalaris*** (fa-lah′ ris) Canary Grass, Ribbon Grass Poaceae

Approximately 20 species occur, with many narrow flat blades and narrow spiky panicles, only a few of which are ornamental. They grow in normal garden soils in full sun or partial shade. The main selection grown is *P. arundinacea* 'Picta', known as gardener's garters, and grown for the white-striped variegated foliage. Their stoloniferous nature make plants effective as a ground cover; however these same attributes result in such aggressive growth that they can become invasive. It can be a thug!

The plants grow about 18″ tall but flop over time. While it is a useful ground cover, it never seems to cover the ground particularly well, leaving patches here and there. Plants are evergreen in mild climates, but should not be thought of as an ornamental winter grass. All selections of ribbon grass grow well in boggy soils and can also be submerged a few inches in a garden pond. Propagate all selections by division only.

**Cultivars**:

A number of improved taxa have been selected, each with a better habit or cleaner variegation, and may be less invasive.

'Dwarf Garters' is a dwarf form of 'Picta', growing only 10-15″ tall and spreading more slowly. The variegation is similar to 'Picta', but it is a better garden plant than ground cover.

'Feesey's Form' is much improved over 'Picta', having much less green and more white on each leaf. The leaves are tinged pink in spring. It is about the same size as 'Picta' but spreads slowly. I have also seen a similar plant referred to as 'Strawberries and Cream', and I can't tell much difference between them.

'Luteo-picta' bears gold and green variegated foliage and also spreads rapidly. The variegation is beautiful in early spring but tends to fade in the heat of the summer.

***Phegopteris*** (feg-op-ter′ is) Beech Fern Thelypteridaceae

Ferns in this group were always grown under the *Thelypteris* label, but were recently reclassified. There are many beech ferns but two are good old-fashioned, tough green ferns. They include the narrow beech fern *P. connectilis*, and the broad beech fern, *P. hexagonoptera*. They both have triangular-shaped fronds which droop about 45 degrees, making urn-shaped plants.

The favored habitats of the narrow beech fern are wet pockets near running water, in nature they are often found under small waterfalls. In the garden, moisture is necessary for best performance. They are usually light green and are easily distinguished from the broad beech fern by the lowest pair of leaflets which droop downward and outward, and are distinctly spaced from the next upper pair.

The broad beech fern has much broader fronds and is larger and more erect than its cousin, the narrow one. This is normally found in open, rather sunny spots and does not perform well near running water. The beech ferns have sori that are uncovered (no indusia) and these distinguish them from members of *Thelypteris*. Both ferns are best in zones 3-6, will be satisfactory in zone 7, but will not be as aggressive. Perhaps that is not a bad thing, as they can flow like lava.

## ***Phlomis*** (flo′ mis) Phlomis Lamiaceae

These plants are finally finding garden homes in North America as more species are being offered by nurserymen. Naturally, they are found mainly in the temperate regions around the Mediterranean basin and east into Asia. The leaves and stems are often whitish gray (from small hairs) and the flowers are in whorls, like salvia. They consist of two-lipped corollas (petals) with sepals that may be somewhat sharp. Given the proper conditions of soil, sun, and moisture, they can be outstanding, and I have seen more good-looking plants in my recent travels through the United States than I did ten years ago. They are particularly good in Mediterranean climes, such as southern California. They do not tolerate extremes in temperatures so the East sometimes can be a challenge. However, if grown well, the gray-green foliage and yellow or lavender flowers allow these coarse plants to look good even in bud, and incredible in bloom.

Quick Reference to Phlomis Species

| | Leaf color | Leaf shape | Flower color |
|---|---|---|---|
| *P. fruticosa* | Gray-green | Elliptical to lanceolate | Deep yellow |
| *P. italica* | Gray-green | Oblong to lanceolate | Pink-mauve |
| *P. longifolia* | Green | Lanceolate | Orange-yellow |
| *P. russeliana* | Green | Ovate | Sulphur yellow |

***-fruticosa*** (froo-ti-ko′ sa) Jerusalem Sage 2-4′/3′
Spring Yellow Mediterranean Zones 4-8

This may be the best choice for most gardens because of the late summer flowers and gray-green foliage. The 2-4″ long leaves are coarse, wrinkled and white-woolly beneath. The stems have woolly hairs, and are slightly yellowish. The leaves are evergreen in milder climates and the gray color is retained all winter. The most arresting features (as well as the prettiest) are the flower buds, tightly whorled in the axils of the uppermost leaves. Twenty to thirty tightly closed flower buds occur in tiered whorls, so the flower stems are like light green candelabra. The butter yellow flowers open in late spring and provide a pleasing contrast to the gray-green foliage. Plants flower in the summer in the North, but during the late winter in southern California.

Full sun is required in the North and partial shade in the South. They are fairly drought resistant and salt tolerant. In the South, leaves remain evergreen in the winter but plants die to the ground north of zone 7.

Propagate by division in the fall or spring, or sow seed. Shoot cuttings, taken in the fall, may also be used. Treat with rooting hormone, place in a loose medium, and cover with clear plastic to maintain humidity. Rooting occurs in 7-14 days. Place sown seed at about 70°F, keep moist but not wet.

**Cultivars:**

'Miss Grace' has the same bright yellow flowers and gray foliage that are so wonderful on the species. At 3′ tall, she is large but not ungainly.

| ***-italica*** (ee-tal′ i-ca) | | Italian Sage | 1-2′/2′ |
|---|---|---|---|
| Summer | Pink-Mauve | Balearic Islands | Zones 6-8 |

Having been under the false impression that all plants of the genus had yellowish flowers, I soon learned once again how little I knew. Happens all the time! This is one of the many species with pink to mauve flowers and is a well-kept secret in North America. Plants cannot be called tidy, producing a branched shrublike growth. The green leaves are covered in whitish felt, particularly on the underside, and soften the plant considerably. The flowers are held in distinct whorls, each consisting of 5-6 flowers.

Plants do well in dry areas, disliking the combination of high humidity and heat. Place in full sun and well-drained soil.

| ***-russeliana*** (ru-sel-ee′ ane-a) | | Jerusalem Sage | 3-4′/3′ |
|---|---|---|---|
| Summer | Sulphur Yellow | Syria | Zones 5-8 |

Plants are bigger, coarser and greener than *P. fruticosa* and require more room in the garden. The ovate (like an egg) dull green leaves are 5-6″ across and 6-7″ long and the 3-5 whorls of flowers are a soft yellow. Not as hardy as *P. fruticosa* or as easy to establish.

**Cultivars:**

'E.A. Bowles' ('Edward Bowles') is not a cultivar but a hybrid between *P. fruticosa* and *P. russeliana*. The size and color of the leaves are intermediate between the two and the pale yellow flowers are less butter yellow than *P. fruticosa* but not as soft as *P. russeliana*. Plants originated in 1965 at Hillier's Nursery in England from seed supposedly sent by the late E.A. Bowles. It is a terrific robust plant; my first choice when I can find it.

**Related Species:**

*P. cashmeriana*, Kashmir sage, is more robust than *P. italica*, growing to 3′ in height and bearing many more pale lilac flowers. A better plant if a pink-flowered phlomis is wanted.

*P. chrysophylla*, goldleaf Jerusalem sage, is 24-30″ tall with whorls of golden-yellow flowers. It is a low-growing evergreen subshrub (woody stems) whose leaves are more heart shaped than those of *P. fruticosa*. It has not been available long enough to know the hardiness constraints, but probably to zone 6.

*P. longifolia* has long (4-6″) leaves and whorls consisting of 12-20 butter yellow flowers. The leaves are green on the upperside and gray-green below. One of the most handsome of the yellow phlomis. The leaves are longer and not as gray as those of *P. fruticosa* and are easy ways to tell the two apart. 'Bailanica' simply differs in the leaf shape, having ovate leaves rather than lanceolate leaves.

*P. samia* has gone through some confusing times lately. The flowers are pink to purple and the plant bears oval to lance-shaped leaves that end in a tapered point (acuminate). The confusing part is that it has sometimes been offered with yellow flowers, but that is either a misprint or a misunderstanding of the catalog maker. Grows up to 3′ tall and hardy in zones 7-9.

*P. tuberosa* is so called because of the small tubers that arise from the roots. Plants produce large green leaves and lilac flowers, and often have reddish stems.

## ***Phlox*** (floks) Phlox Polemoniaceae

*Phlox* has enough marvelous members that at least one plant should reside in everyone's garden. Although the best-known is *P. paniculata*, garden phlox, many others can be grown that are more disease resistant, lower growing, and easier to cultivate. In fact, the genus is represented by species ranging from 6″ to 3′ in height. The annual phlox, *P. drummondii*, has undergone significant improvements through breeding and is easily grown from seed. One of the most common perennial phlox is moss phlox, *P. subulata*, whose magnificent mantles of fluorescent pink, white and blue radiate from hills, roadsides, and gardens everywhere in this country. The first specimen of this plant was sent to England by John Bartram in 1745 and was termed a "fine creeping Spring Lychnis". In 1919, the intrepid plant explorer Reginald Farrer enthusiastically wrote that "the day that saw the introduction, more than a century since, of *P. subulata*, ought indeed to be kept as a horticultural festival."

All species are native to North America. They all have five-petaled flowers and opposite leaves. One of the easy ways to determine if the plant is indeed a phlox (and not a dianthus, or something otherwise confusing) is to hold the sepals in one hand while pulling the petals with the other. The corolla (petals) will come away easily and you can see the long corolla tube. People often confuse phlox with dame's rocket (*Hesperis*); refer to *Hesperis* for a little help.

In general, many low-growing phlox prefer shade whereas taller species do best in full sun. They require well-drained soils to remain in the garden for any length of time, yet are often the first plants to show signs of drought. Fall planting is best although early spring planting is almost as safe. One of the finest breeders of phlox, particularly the low-growing forms, was H. Lincoln Foster, whose Connecticut garden was called Millstream House. Many of our finest cultivars and hybrids bear the Millstream name and attest to his foresight.

Two major pests of phlox can result in serious damage. Spider mites attack all species with equal fervor and are particularly damaging in hot, dry weather. If chemicals are your thing, use miticides, not insecticides, at the first sign of infestation. If the weather stays particularly warm and dry, continue application every week. Powdery mildew is a fungal disease characterized by white, feltlike growth on the leaves and stems in midsummer. It is particularly offensive on garden phlox, *P. paniculata*. Some cultivars are so susceptible to mildew they are impossible to grow without application of fungicides, so why bother? However, many new cultivars have been bred for mildew resistance. If necessary, fungicides may be sprayed around June 15 and then applied every 10 to 14 days thereafter. *P. maculata*, spotted phlox, has become more popular in recent years because of the relative resistance to mildew.

Most low-growing phlox are propagated by seed or terminal cuttings. Root cuttings may be used with all species, a practice common for *P. paniculata* cultivars and other upright species. Two-inch pieces of larger diameter roots are cut and placed upright, with the base end down, and covered with 1″ of sand or peat-perlite mix. The mix must be kept moist and the environment humid.

Quick Reference to Phlox Species

| | Height (in.) | Flower color | Petals notched |
|---|---|---|---|
| *P. divaricata* | 12-15 | Blue | Slightly |
| *P. maculata* | 24-36 | Various | Slightly |
| *P. paniculata* | 36-48 | Mauve | Slightly |
| *P. stolonifera* | 6-12 | Lavender | No |
| *P. subulata* | 6-9 | Various | Slightly |

***-divaricata*** (di-vah-ri-kah′ ta) Woodland Phlox 12-15″/12″
Spring Blue Eastern North America Zones 3-8

This is one of the most useful and still overlooked phlox for today's gardens. The leaves are dark green, oblong, and 1½-2″ long. Plants spread slowly by creeping rhizomes above which 12-15″ tall flower stems ascend in the spring. Shoots that do not bear flowers (sterile) don't ascend, but root at the nodes. The somewhat fragrant 1½″ wide flowers are usually light blue but vary to lighter or darker shades. The ends of the petals are slightly lobed and the flowers are loosely held in panicles. This species makes a wonderful edging plant for partially shaded, moist well-drained areas. Most of the cultivars and species can be trimmed or cut back after flowering to encourage additional growth.

Woodland phlox may be propagated from seed. The cultivars and hybrids are best multiplied from terminal shoot cuttings or root cuttings.

**Cultivars:**

'Blue Dreams' is an excellent selection with blue-lilac flowers on 8-10″ long stems. Plants are also more robust than the species.

'Blue Elf' is only 4-5″ tall and best in a rock garden or area where it will not be outcompeted. The small leaves form a dense, low-growing mat covered in April with fragrant, light blue flowers.

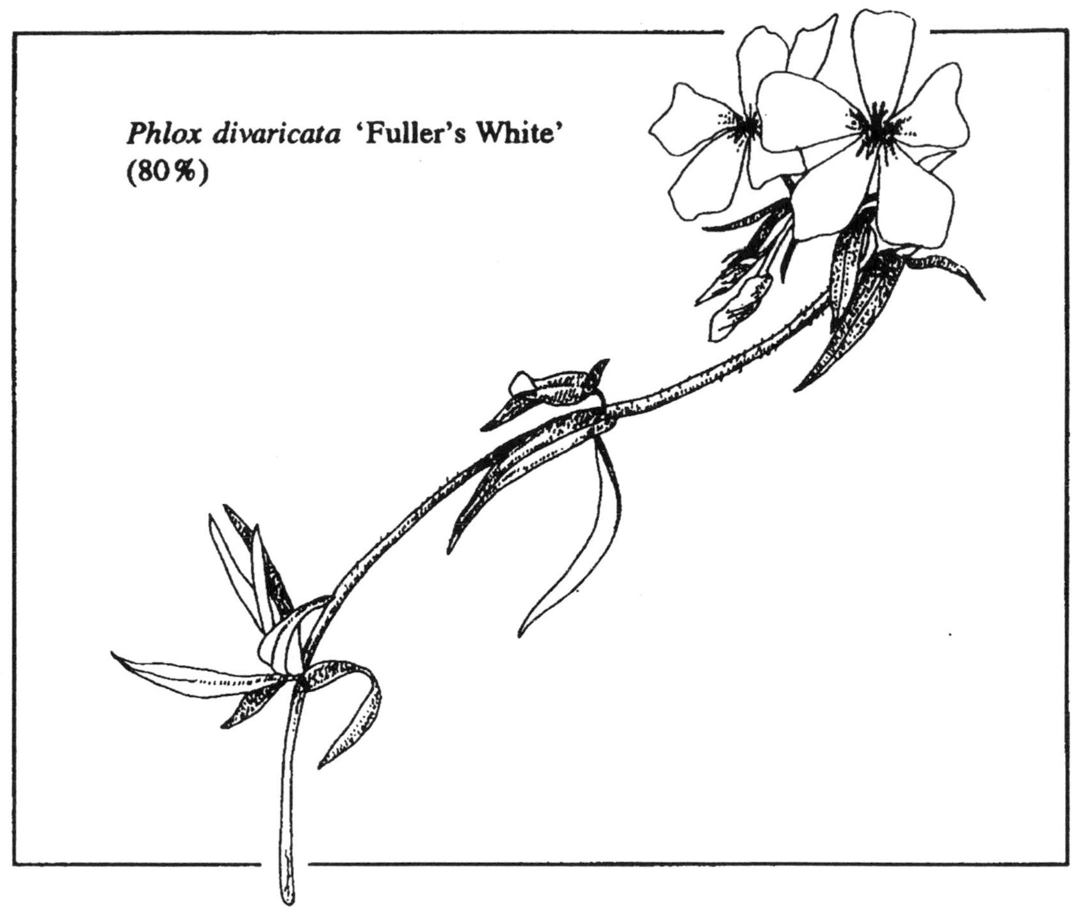

***Phlox divaricata* 'Fuller's White' (80%)**

'Blue Moon' bears large, overlapping violet-blue petals. Plants were introduced by the New England Wildflower Society in Framingham, Massachusetts.

'Charles Ricardo' has star-shaped blue flowers with a hint of fragrance.

'Clouds of Perfume' (what a great name) has pale blue flowers with narrow petals. They have more fragrance than normally associated with other selections. An excellent performer in the trials in the Gardens at UGA.

'Dirigo Ice' is 8-12″ tall and bears icy blue flowers with slightly notched petals. This is a mainstay in the Armitage garden and always draws second looks.

'Fuller's White' is more dwarf (8-12″) and is so completely covered with clear, white flowers in the spring that it looks like a snowbank. The leaves are slightly smaller than those of the species and the flowers are definitely notched at the end of the petals. It is also more sun tolerant than the species. Although the species is an excellent garden plant, it cannot hold a candle to this cultivar. Flowering starts in early April and persists for 4-5 weeks in my garden. Found by Henry and Sally Fuller of Easton, Connecticut.

var. *laphamii* is native to the western United States and bears dark blue flowers with entire petals on 18″ stems. Cut back hard after flowering.

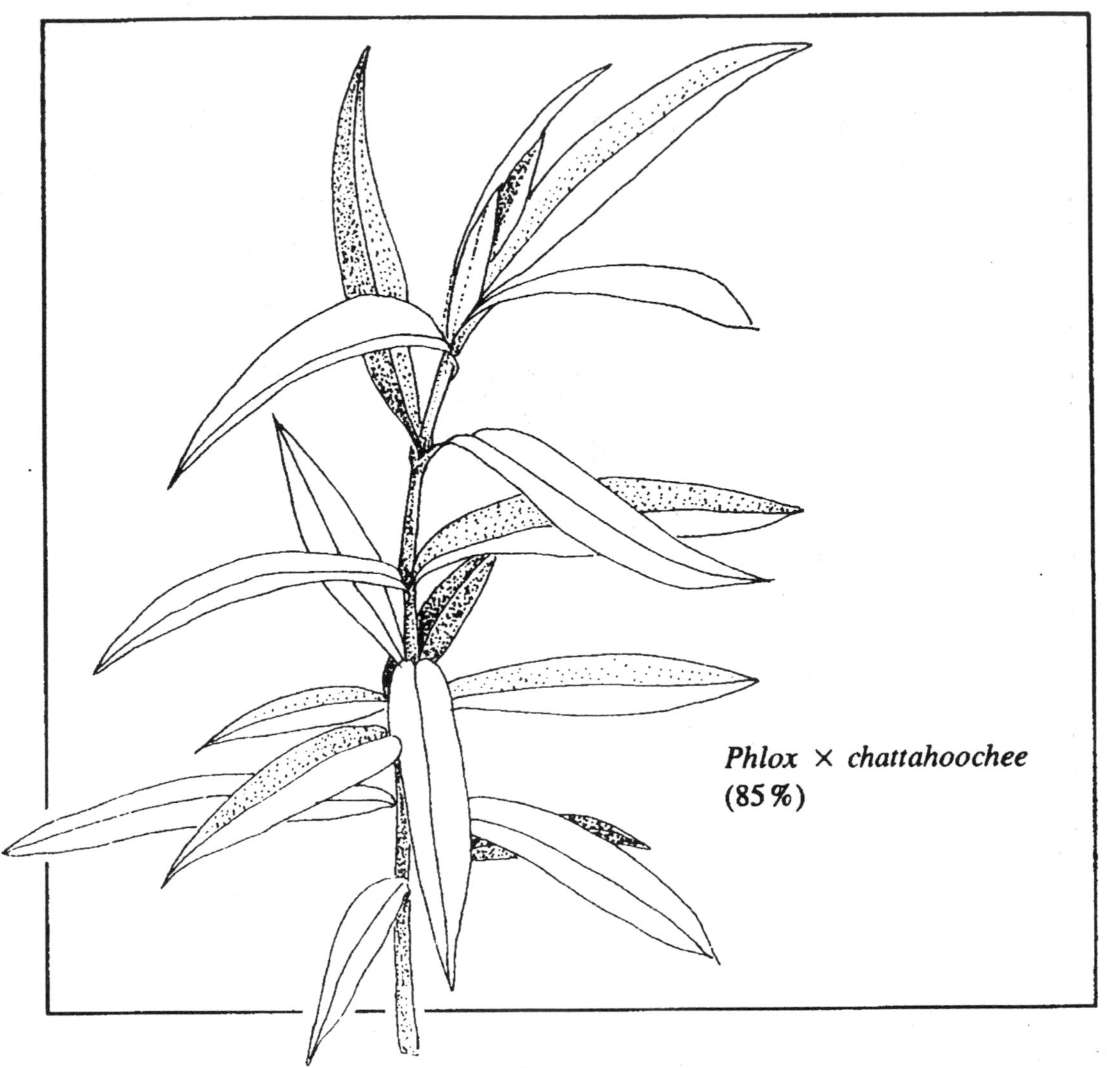

*Phlox* × *chattahoochee*
(85%)

'London Grove Blue' has deep blue fragrant flowers on compact plants.
'Louisiana' bears purple-blue flowers with a magenta eye.
'Mary Helen' produces deep blue flowers with a distinct red eye.
'May Breeze' is similar to 'Dirigo Ice' but with a little more pink.
'Opelousas' bears violet-red flowers on 12-15″ stalks.
'Parksville Beach' arose from the travels and mind of Tony Avent, Plant Delights Nursery, Raleigh, North Carolina. Plants are 4-6″ tall with pink flowers. Plants were found near Parksville Beach (1500′ elevation) in Polk County, Tennessee.
'Plum Perfect' has pink-lavender flowers with a violet eye.
'Twilight' is most unusual, producing many light lavender star-shaped flowers. The petals are much more narrow than those of other selections.
'White Perfume' has fragrant clean white flowers.

***-maculata*** (mak-ew-lah′ ta) Wild Sweet William 24-36″/24″
Early Summer Mauve-Pink Eastern North America Zones 3-8

This species is coming into its own now that additional cultivars have entered the market. The mauve-pink flower color did little to inspire excitement and the species labored in relative obscurity. The leaves are 2-4″ long, linear to lancelike and arranged up the stem like the steps of a ladder. They are also thick, glossy dark green and slightly pointed. The stems are hairy and usually, but not always, mottled red. The main differences between this species and *P. paniculata* are darker green leaves, conical panicles and earlier flowering. Some cultivars have much better mildew resistance. All can be cut back after flowering and in many cases a second bloom will occur.

Propagate by division of offshoots, from root cuttings, and occasionally from terminal cuttings.

**Cultivars:**

'Alpha' bears rose-pink flowers with a hint of a darker eye.

'Delta' has long panicles of white flowers with rose-colored eyes.

'Flower Power' is about 3½′ tall with 8″ flower stalks of fragrant white flowers, each with small flecks of pink. The flower stems are also spotted. They are vigorous and relatively disdainful of mildew.

'Magnificence' is likely a hybrid or cultivar of *P. carolina*. The 3′ tall plants are relatively mildew resistant and bear rosy pink flowers.

'Miss Lingard' brought the species out of obscurity. She is an excellent pure white cultivar which flowers earlier and is much more mildew resistant than the popular summer phlox. (The parentage of 'Miss Lingard' is confusing. She has also been attributed to *P. carolina*, Carolina phlox, and may well be a hybrid between the two species).

'Natascha' has pink and white flowers, like a pinwheel, and grows about 2′ tall. We have trialed this plant for many years and it has proven to be quite exceptional. The plant was discovered by Luc Klinkhamer at the Central Botanical Gardens of Belarus, and named after the garden curator.

'Omega' produces white blossoms with a small lilac eye and is more floriferous than 'Miss Lingard'.

'Rosalinde' has dark pink flowers.

***-paniculata*** (pa-nic-ew-lah′ ta) Garden Phlox 3-4′/2′
Summer Magenta Eastern North America Zones 4-8

This species is surely the most magnificent of upright phlox and more cultivars and colors have been advertised in catalogs than all others put together. This has resulted in a most popular plant, which if placed in the right location will flower spectacularly. Sites in full sun with good air movement are necessary for best performance. Plants perform better in the North than in the deep South as they are not particularly heat tolerant. Under prolonged hot summer conditions, plant vigor diminishes and susceptibility to root rot organisms increases.

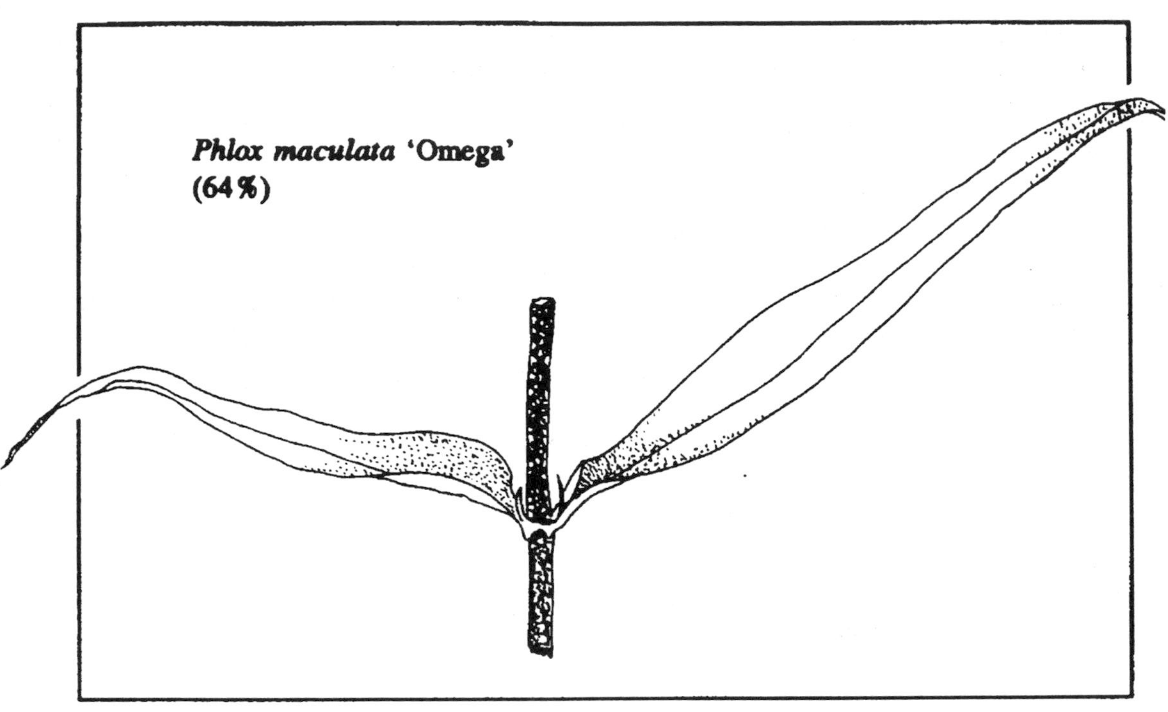


Unfortunately, some cultivars are highly susceptible to powdery mildew, regardless of location. To reduce the incidence of disease, thin clumps to four or five strong shoots in the spring, and always apply water to the base of the plant and not the foliage. If overhead watering is necessary, water in the morning to allow the leaves to dry during the day. Watering at night results in rapid mildew infestation, a reason plants struggle where late afternoon and evening summer thundershowers are common. Mildew is less of a problem in dry seasons and windy locations. Fungicide application should begin in most areas by early June and continue every 10 days to two weeks. If you think this is more trouble than these plants are worth, you are probably right. Take advantage of less mildew-susceptible cultivars or species such as *P. maculata*.

The leaves are 2-5″ long, and have slender points at the end but are not as thick as those of *P. maculata* or *P. carolina*. The flowers are held in a large, dense pyramidal panicle, up to 8″ across, each tubular flower averages one inch across, often lavender or in shades of pink or lilac. The stamens and style are often equal to or longer than the corolla tube.

Most garden phlox cultivars are propagated from root cuttings. Offshoots, which often arise at a considerable distance from the parent plant, may be divided in the spring.

**Cultivars:**

The species itself is seldom seen in gardens. This is unfortunate as it is the most mildew resistant of all. Today, tremendous numbers of cultivars are offered and the best way to choose is to consult one of the many garden catalogs. Some of the newer cultivars are definitely more resistant than older ones. Have fun!

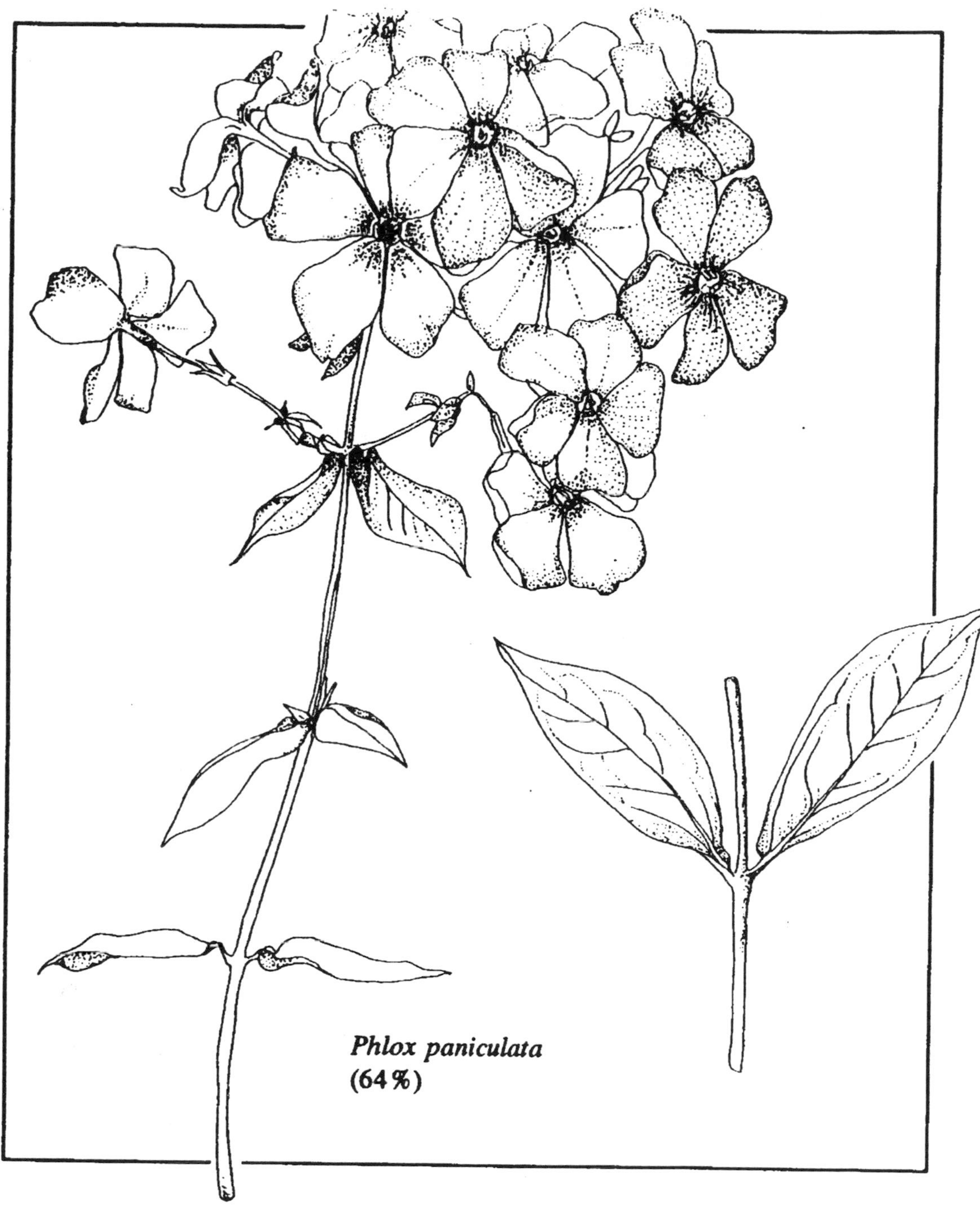

*Phlox paniculata*
**(64%)**

*Orange*: There are no true oranges, but the breeders are closing in.

'Orange Perfection' is a vigorous selection with salmon-orange flowers with a small red eye early in the summer.

'Prince of Orange' has orange-salmon flowers, each with a small red eye. Plants are about 3′ in height.

*Pink/Salmon:*

'Bright Eyes' has pale pink blossoms with a crimson eye. One of the best performers and surely one of the most popular.

'Dodo Hanbury Forbes' has pink to rosy flowers borne in large trusses.

'Dorffreude' bears deep pink flowers with a red eye on 3′ tall plants.

'Dresden China' produces pastel pink flowers with a deeper rose-pink eye.

'Elizabeth Arden' is a beautiful pink-flowered selection with a red eye.

'Eva Cullum' has large heads of clear pink flowers with a dark red eye. Plants are 2-2½′ tall and do not require staking. Eva Cullum, the woman, was in charge of the retail department of Blooms of Bressingham Nursery in the 1970s and was honored with the introduction of this plant by Alan Bloom.

'Evangeline' has pink-salmon flowers with a hint of white in the center.

'Fairest One' has salmon pink blooms with a dark red eye.

'Fesselballon' is about 2′ tall and produces pink flowers with a dark eye. Nice fragrance.

'Sir John Falstaff' bears large flowers of salmon pink on 2-3′ tall plants.

'Fairy's Petticoat' has large heads of pale pink with darker eyes.

'Flamingo' is about 2′ tall with flaming pink flowers and a white eye.

'H.B. May' produces large bright pink flower heads on 3-4′ tall plants.

'Juliet' has pale pink flowers with a white eye on 2′ plants.

'Junior Dance' is part of the series of Juniors, this one is about 18″ tall and bears bright coral-pink flowers.

'Little Princess' is part of the Little series, this one shorter than some of the others, maturing at less than 2′ tall. Flowers are pink, with wide white eyes.

'Miss Ellie' has bicolored flowers with dozens of light rose petals with dark rose centers. Plants grow up to 4′ tall.

'Miss Pepper' has pale pink flowers with a darker eye. Plants are 2-2½′ tall.

'Otley Choice' was bred in the 1940s but is still available today. The flowers are similar to 'Bright Eyes'.

'Pinafore Pink' also bears flowers similar to 'Bright Eyes' but on dwarf 12-15″ tall plants.

'Pink Gown' is compact, only 24-30″ tall, with rosy pink flowers in late summer.

'Pixie Twinkle', 18-20″ tall, has light pink flowers, each with a white eye.

'Salmon Beauty' is an early-flowering form with salmon-pink flowers with a white eye.

'Shortwood' has bright pink flowers on 3½′ tall plants. Found by Stephanie Cohen of Temple University, who, when asked why she chose that name replied "Longwood was already taken."

'Tracy's Treasure' is 4-5′ tall, with soft pink flowers.

*Purple, Lavender:*

'Amethyst' has deep lilac flowers.

'Ann' is a late bloomer with large lavender flower heads.

'Blue Boy' bears lavender blue flowers on 3′ tall plants. Plants flower in late summer.

'Blue Paradise' has violet-blue flowers with an even deeper blue eye. About 3-4′ tall.

'Caroline van den Berg' bears flowers of deep purple.

'David's Lavender' is a sport of 'David' which emerged with much fanfare. A good plant, with lavender flowers, but does not have the vigor of its parent.
'Franz Schubert' has lilac blooms with a star-shaped darker eye. In recognition of the great composer, the plant was raised and named by Blooms of Bressingham.
'Junior Dream' has short stems and produces deep purple flowers.
'Katherine' has lavender flowers on 2-3′ tall plants. Good mildew resistance has been reported in the Midwest.
'Laura' bears deep purple flowers, each with a starry white center. Flowers are mildly fragrant.
'Lavender' is, for all intents and purposes, the species. It is tough, vigorous, absolutely foolproof and mildew resistant. Its only drawback is the lack of sexy flowers.
'Lilac Time' produces large heads of lilac blue flowers.
'Little Boy' is not little, about 2½′ tall. Plants bear lavender flowers in the summer.
'Nicky' has deep, velvet magenta flowers on 3-4′ tall plants. Truly eye-catching. From Niche Gardens, Chapel Hill, North Carolina.
'Pixie Miracle Grace' is part of the relatively new Pixie series of short (about 20″) plants. This one has lavender petals with white centers.
'Progress' has pale violet blossoms with a darker eye.
'Robert Poore' is exceptional. We tested some of the first plants in the Gardens at UGA and were astounded by the deep rich lavender flowers and disdain for mildew. Named for landscape designer Robert Poore of Flora, Mississippi.
'Russian Violet' bears purple-violet flowers in large trusses. Plants are 3-4′ tall.
'Starlight' produces deep violet flowers.
'Sternhimmel' has light lavender flowers on 2-3′ tall plants.
'The King' bears purple-lavender flowers on 2-3′ tall plants.

*Scarlet, Red:*
'Barnwell' bears rose-red flowers with a deeper red eye.
'Brigadier' grows nearly three feet tall with deep red flowers.
'Leo Schlageter' has bright red to scarlet flowers on 30″ plants. An old cultivar from Arends nursery in Germany that continues to stay around.
'Othello' sports deep red flowers with 6-7 week long blooming period.
'Sandra' produces bright scarlet flowers on 2′ tall plants.
'Red Feelings' is part of the Feeling series, which are quite different and will not appeal to everybody. Some of the Feelings plants produce very small flowers, but have colorful bract-like appendages around the flowers. 'Red Feelings' produces tiny sterile flowers hidden inside modified ruby-red petals. 'Fancy Feelings' and 'Natural Feelings' have small flowers with narrow bright pink petals and curly pink petals with green streaks respectively. These are fascinating, sort of like a train wreck. Others in the series have essentially no flowers at all and include 'Empty Feelings', with persistent russet-beige "bracts" and 'Midnight Feelings', a mahogany-black variety with the same form. The latter are exceedingly ugly, but certainly interesting to look at, and useful as cut flowers. Bred by cut flower breeder René van Gaalen of the Netherlands.
'Red Riding Hood' has cherry red flowers over a compact 2′ tall plant.

'Spitfire' is an old cultivar from Germany, introduced in the 1930s as 'Frau Alfred von Malthner', but is still an excellent salmon-red form.
'Starfire' has striking cherry red flowers that immediately catch the eye, even from a distance. Probably the truest red.
'Tenor' is an early bloomer, bearing rosy scarlet flowers on 2′ tall plants.
'Windsor' bears pale rose flowers with a salmon eye.

*Variegated Leaves*: All do poorly in heat and humidity.
'Becky Towe' has green and yellow variegated leaves with deep rose flowers.
'Harlequin' was produced by Alan Bloom of England and has variegated foliage with violet blue flowers. Plants appear to have lost vigor as they are difficult to produce.
'Nora Leigh' bears creamy white leaves with a center line of green. The foliage is far more remarkable than the rather common pink-lavender flowers. It makes a wonderful accent for the front or middle of the garden. Afternoon shade is required.

*White:*
'Bartwentynine' is such an unbelievable name it leaves no doubt as to where the breeders were when it was named. Regardless, clean white flowers top a plant less than 2′ tall. A little mildew, but too early to tell if it is as free as they say.
'Blue Ice' bears white flowers with a pinkish-blue eye.
'David' may still be one of the best whites today. Plants are as mildew resident as any *paniculata* selection in cultivation. The original plant was first spotted in the Conservancy Garden at the Brandywine Museum by Richard Simon of Bluemont Nursery. Excited as only Richard could be, he rushed in to see the director, Mrs. F.M. Moobury. Hardly able to contain himself, Richard politely asked for a few cuttings to propagate in his nursery, and to his and everyone else's great delight, the plants were even better in cultivation than in the wild garden whence they originated. The plants were named for David, Mrs. Moobury's late husband.
'Mia Ruys' is a compact plant, growing less than 2′ tall.
'Mt. Fuji' ('Mt. Fujiyama') was the most popular white for years but is not seen much anymore as newer and better selections of white-flowering phlox are superseding it. If mildew is not a problem, plants are still very nice, bearing dense 12-15″ long flower heads. It shines from a distance.
'Prime Minister' is white with a hint of pink and a red eye.
'Shorty White' is a low grower (12-15″ tall) with clean white flowers.
'White Admiral' has clear white large flower heads. Plants bloom 1-2 weeks later than 'Mt. Fuji'.
'World Peace' blooms late in the season with pure white flowers over handsome glossy green leaves.

***-stolonifera*** (sto-lo-ni′ fe-ra) | Creeping Phlox | 6-12″/12″
Spring | Violet, Lavender | Eastern North America | Zones 2-8

This species is possibly the most shade tolerant of the phlox and forms a dense cover under quite shady conditions. Creeping phlox is low growing and, similar to woodland phlox, produces both flowering and sterile shoots. The leaves on the sterile shoots are 1-3″ long and narrowed at the base while those on the flowering shoots are oval, no more than 1″ long, and not as narrow at the base. The petals are usually unnotched, and the lavender ¾″ wide flowers are held in a 2-3 flowered inflorescence called a cyme. Plants spread by stolons and by rooting at the nodes of the sterile stems. An excellent species, it is not as brilliant or as vigorous a garden performer as other low growers species but its classiness and subtlety make it a long-time favorite. The entire species is so good that it was denoted as the 1990 Perennial Plant of the Year by the Perennial Plant Association. Plants tolerate partial shade and consistent moisture.

Propagate by division any time of year. Terminal cuttings of sterile shoots may also be used.

**Cultivars:**

'Ariane' bears loose heads of white flowers with a yellow eye.
'Blue Ridge' has blue-lilac flowers. Good performer, very popular.
'Bruce's White' is characterized by white flowers with a yellow eye.
'Fran's Purple' has starry lilac and purple flowers over 8-10″ stems.
'Homefires' bears showy rich pink flowers.
'Iridescens' produces somewhat iridescent blue-mauve flowers.
'Melrose' has large pink flowers.
'Pink Ridge' forms 6″ tall mats with dark mauve pink flowers.
'Sherwood Purple' bears purple-blue, highly fragrant flowers over 6″ stems and is the most popular cultivar.

***-subulata*** (sub-ew′ lah-ta) Moss Phlox 6-9″/12″
Early Spring Various Eastern North America Zones 2-8

It is difficult to drive or walk any distance in the spring and not see these plants carpeting a bank and providing spring color to an otherwise drab and dreary residential landscape. Plants may be found in blue, white, and purple, but the overwhelming majority in landscapes are pink with a darker eye, thus accounting for one of its common names, moss pink. Plants make few demands, but full sun and well-drained soils result in best performance. They are so abundant and so successful that they have to put up with names like "gas station plant" and "trailer park plant". Success is measured in many ways.

The narrow linear leaves are only about one half inch long, close together, and quite stiff, almost to the point of being prickly. Three to five flowers are borne in a loose panicle just above the matted foliage. The petals are slightly notched to entire, and open flat. The stamens protrude from the flower and the style is up to one half inch long. Differences between *P. subulata* and *P. nivalis* (the two are often confused) can be found under *P. nivalis*. All taxa require relatively well-drained soils and full hot sun for best flowering.

Propagate by division or layering. To layer, place a section of non-flowering shoot on the ground and cover lightly with soil. Keep the area moist and the stem will root into the soil. Cuttings may also be taken, preferably in late fall for best rooting.

**Cultivars**:

There is little difference among selections within any color and the same plant may be masquerading under two or three different names. Some of these definitely are sections or hybrids with other low growers such as *P. ovata*, *P.bifida*, *P. douglasii* and *P. nivalis*. They may also be listed under *P.* x *frondosa* (*P. subulata* x *P. nivalis*) and *P.lilacina* (*P. subulata* x *P. bifida*), but that is way too complicated.

*Blue, Purple:*

'Atropurpurea' bears wine-red flowers.

'Blue Hills' has notched flowers of deep blue.

'Blue Emerald' has medium blue flowers.

'Emerald Cushion Blue' produces many blue flowers on vigorous plants.

'Hillview Pink' discovered at the Washington nursery, Hillview Gardens, bears dozens of rosy pink flowers.

'Keryl' has lavender-blue flowers with more rounded petals than the norm.

'Millstream Jupiter' is an outstanding selection from Lincoln Foster of Millstream Garden. The flowers are deep blue with a yellow eye.

*Pink:*

'Apple Blossom' has pale pink lilac flowers with a darker eye.

'Drummond Pink' was introduced in 2007 and produces much larger flowers than most other cultivars. Flower color is more towards magenta than pink, but maybe that is just my eyes getting old. Looks to be a winner.

'Emerald Cushion Pink' produces light pink flowers on a plant of mounding habit.

'Encore' has light pink flowers and will rebloom if cut back hard after flowering.

'Fort Hill' produces deep pink flowers with a darker red center.

'Maiden's Blush' produces pink flowers with a red eye.

'Millstream Daphne' has deep pink flowers with a dark eye. Compact and vigorous.

'Millstream Laura' bears pastel pink flowers on compact plants.

'Morning Star' produces flowers of pale pink.

'Perfection' has pinkish flowers.

'Sunrise' produces peach-pink flowers on compact plants.

'Venus' bears pink flowers.

'Vivid' has strong red-pink blossoms.

*Red:*

'Beauty of Ronsdorf' is probably a selection of *P. douglasii* and bears bright rosy red flowers on mounded compact plants.

'Crackerjack' is a showstopper with brilliant crimson red flowers on compact plants.

'Crimson Beauty' produces rose-red flowers.

'Fort Hill' bears fragrant rosy pink flowers which are deeply cut on the petals.

'Mars' has very intense red blooms.

'Red Wing' grows vigorously and bears rose-red flowers all spring.

'Scarlet Flame' is a deep scarlet red with an even darker eye.

*White:*

'Candy Stripe' was originally introduced as 'Tamanonagalei' so it is no surprise that the name was changed. The white flowers are striped with pink. Outstanding.

'Coral Eye' is another Foster creation and bears beautiful pink-white flowers with a deep coral eye.

'Snowflake' is the showiest white I have seen. Incredibly compact and absolutely covered with starry clean white flowers; in the spring, it is a mound of snow.

'Snow White' has small white flowers on miniature plants.

'White Delight' is more open than the above but bears good white flowers.

**Related Species:**

*P.* x *arendsii*, Arend's phlox, is the result of crosses between *P. divaricata* and *P. paniculata*, and arose in the Arends nursery in Germany in 1912. It is intermediate in height and can be quite floriferous. We tried some of the initial forms ('Anja', 'Hilda', 'Suzanne') at the Gardens at UGA and as beautiful as the flowers were, they were covered in mildew in no time flat. However, new selections such as 'Babyface' (pink with red eye), 'Eye Catcher' (light pink with dark center), 'Ping-Pong' (light pink), 'Pink Attraction' (dark pink), and 'Purple Star' (purple with dark eye), have become available and may be better.

*P. bifida*, sand phlox, is a low-growing plant with short linear leaves and deeply notched violet-purple to white petals appearing in early spring. It is tough and views poor soils and drought with contempt. Absolutely beautiful but not long lived in "normal" garden soils. One of the finest we ever trialed was 'Eco Lavender' from Don Jacobs of Eco-Gardens, Decatur, Georgia. Best used in rock garden situations. 'Colvin's White' is a pure white form bearing deeply cut flowers in spring. Snowmass™ is a recent Plant Select® selection, a program administered by the Denver Botanic Garden and Colorado State University. Plants grow about 20″ tall and are covered with white star-like flowers in the spring. The species has been used in creating *P.* x *lilacina* hybrids (see *P. subulata*) and is hardy from zone 4 to zone 8.

*P.* x *chattahoochee*, Chattahoochee phlox, (often mistakenly offered as a cultivar) is a cross between *P. divaricata* var. *laphamii* and the pale purple-flowered downy phlox, *P. pilosa*. The flowers have entire petals with a striking purple eye and the foliage consists of longer, wider, dark green leaves. It is short-lived, flowering itself to oblivion as well as being mildew and fungus susceptible. But when it is alive, it is outstanding. Flowering occurs from early April to early June. Found by the grand dame of American gardening, Mary Gibson Henry of Gladwyne, Pennsylvania.

*P. glaberrima*, smooth phlox, is an excellent stoloniferous species with baby bottom smooth stems. Plants bear rosy pink flowers and growing 2-3′ tall. 'Interior' has been selected with deeper purple-red flowers. 'Morris Berd' grows to 18-24″ tall and has rose-pink flowers and dark green leaves. The best form is 'Triflorum' which grows only 8-12″ tall and produces many pink flowers in groups of three ("triflorum"). Eats up heat and humidity.

*P. nivalis* is similar in habit, appearance, and flowering time to *P. subulata*, and has been overlooked by breeders and gardeners alike. All make excellent plants for the rock garden or front of the border. The 1″ wide flowers are usually entire but may be slightly notched and range from purple to pink or white. Plants differ from moss phlox in that the petals are normally entire (notched in *P. subulata*), and the stamens and style are much shorter (up to one half inch long in *P. subulata*, less than one-eighth inch long in *P. nivalis*). Full sun and well-drained soils are necessary for success. 'Camia' is a lovely pink form with flowers a little larger than the species. Other hybrids with *P. nivalis* include 'Eco Brilliant' and 'Eco Flirtie Eyes', with mauve and white-eyed flowers, respectively. Both were selected by Don Jacobs.

*P.* 'Minnie Pearl' was found in Mississippi by Karen Partlow and is likely a natural hybrid between *P. maculata* and *P. glaberrima*. Plants are vigorous, but less than 2′ tall and covered with white flowers long before the summer phlox open. Little mildew reported to this point.

*P. pilosa* tolerates full sun and flowers between *P. divaricata* and *P. paniculata*. Plants grow 1-1½′ tall and are covered with short hairs. Plants are stoloniferous and multiply rapidly. They perform well in the South. A number of good selections are available. 'Eco Happy Traveler', from Don Jacobs at Eco-Gardens, bears fragrant deep rose flowers. 'Ozarkiana' has light pink blooms with white centers and 'Slim Jim' has narrow leaves and light lavender flowers.

*P.* x *procumbens* is a cross between *P. stolonifera* and *P. subulata*. It combines some of the vigor of *P. subulata* with the larger flowers of *P. stolonifera*. The plants grow 1′ tall and bear ¾″ wide purple flowers. Numerous cultivars have been bred. 'Millstream Variety' is a trailing form with rose-pink flowers spoked with darker stripes. Flowering plants are 9-12″ tall. "Variegata', one of the finest varieties I have seen, has dark green leaves edged in white. It produces mauve-pink flowers. The foliage is better than the flowers.

*P.* 'Spring Delight' is reported to be a cross between *P. paniculata* and *P. stolonifera*. It grows 15-20″ tall and produces dozens of rose-pink flowers. Exceptionally good in trials at the Gardens at UGA.

## ***Phormium*** (for-mee′ um) Flax Lily Agavaceae

I originally included this genus at the request of my West Coast friends, particularly Stephanie Shelton, who had been such a help in preparing the second edition of the book. Today, designers and landscapers absolutely desire these plants. Although the West Coast is still the only area where the genus thrives, they are being used more and more as accents in large containers, to be moved indoors in the winter. When plants were originally brought to America they found success in San Francisco and other California locations.

The two species of large leafy plants, both native to New Zealand, are *P. colensoi* (syn. *P cookianum*) and the better known *P. tenax*. The leaves, which are all basal, yield an incredibly tough fiber, thus the common name. When we lived in New Zealand, we marveled at the colors, forms and toughness of these plants, used everywhere from highway medians to brilliant town squares. I wish we could use more of these dramatic plants in landscape beds and containers in North America, but the long production time, expense of plants, and the relatively poor winter hardiness (zone 8 or 9) have resulted in poor availability for professionals. Regardless, if as a gardener, you can find them, go for it, they are definitely worth trying.

The best form for smaller plants is *P. colensoi*. It generally grows 3′ tall and bears pendulous flowers, a distinguishing feature from the erect flowers of *P. tenax*. However, most of us won't see flowers at all. Numerous cultivars have been developed, some of which are hybrids.

*P. tenax* is the best known, due to its magnificent habit and large erect flowers. The leaves often attain lengths of 6-9′ and are 2-5″ wide, although it is doubtful they will ever attain that size in your 16″ containers. The flowers may then grow up to 15″ above the basal foliage. They are usually dull red but may vary to almost pure yellow.

Plants may be divided (with saw or very strong shovel) or raised from seed with a great deal of patience.

**Cultivars and Hybrids**:

Descriptions of many of these hybrids (*P. tenax*, *P. colensoi*) came from my time in Australia and New Zealand. Since they are annuals in most of North America, heights and flowers descriptions may not exactly be realistic.

'Apricot Queen' is 3′ tall with pale yellow and apricot on the leaves.
'Aurora' produces leaves striped in red, salmon pink and yellow.
'Bronze Baby' grows 3′ tall with reddish bronze foliage.
'Bronze Elf' has 2′ tall bronze foliage.
'Burgundy' bears deep claret leaves.
'Cream Delight' has soft creamy variegation, growing about 3′ tall.
'Chocolate' is dark brown and 4′ tall.
'Dazzler' bears deep bronze and scarlet 4′ long leaves.
'Duet' has light yellow to chartreuse edges on the 2′ tall leaves.
'Firebird' is about 5′ tall with bright scarlet leaves that fade to bronzy purple as they age.
'Flamingo' has many colors on the 2′ leaves, including orange, rose and yellow.
'Goldspike' grows about 5′ tall and bears yellow striped leaves.
'Guardsman' is erect, grows 5′ tall and has bronze leaves striped with red and deep pink.
'Jack Spratt' is a dwarf, upright form with pale bronze leaves.
Lancer series was introduced in 2006 by Bodger Botanicals in Lompoc, California and includes 'Lancer Bright Green', 'Lancer Green with Red Edge' and 'Lancer Green with White Edge'. Plants are excellent for containers.
'Maori Chief' and others in the Maori series ('Maori Maiden', 'Maori Queen') have bronze leaves striped with pink and red in various patterns.
'Radiance' is 5-6′ tall with red and gold banding.
'Sundowner' grows 5-6′ tall with bronze foliage edged in deep rose.
'Tom Thumb' is only 2′ tall with narrow green leaves edged in red.
'Thumbelina' is only about 12″ tall, and provides bronzy purple leaves.
'Tricolor' is dark green with white edges.
'Yellow Wave', growing up to 4′ in height, has leaves strongly variegated with yellow.

***Phuopsis*** (foo-op′ sis) Phuopsis Rubiaceae

Only one species (*P. stylosa*) occurs in the genus. It is one of those plants you can pass by without seeing, but once having stopped to view it, is not easily forgotten. It is a mat former with long stems of tiny sticky whorled leaves that get all over you, and many small pink flowers at the tips. It must be grown in well-drained soils and is best for rock gardens or hanging off walls.

The flowers and foliage have a peculiar smell; some people find it pleasant, others recoil in horror. Once flowering has occurred in the spring, cut the plants back hard to reduce weediness. I truly like this plant but it is best grown in cooler summer climates and maintained with a stern hand to ensure flowering. Plants melt out in high humidity-high heat summers. It is short-lived regardless but may reseed vigorously if conditions are to its liking. Cutting back reduces both problems. Plants are perennial to about zone 6 (with protection) but may reseed anywhere.

Propagate from seed, division or cuttings.

***Phygelius*** (fye-geal-ee′ us) Cape Fuchsia Scrophulariaceae

Phygelius is seldom grown as a perennial in gardens except on the West Coast, although with new cultivars being developed, gardeners in the Midwest and Southeast are giving them a try one more time. These native South African plants are sufficiently cold hardy to about zone 7, but, at least with older cultivars, they grow and flower poorly in heat and humidity. I have read of instances of plants surviving Michigan winters, but that does not occur consistently. I have also read glowing reports on their performance in Florida, and I too enjoy a little fiction.

I love the plants when I see them well grown but my experiences in my garden have ended in disappointing long, leggy weedy things. However, all sorts of weird things happen in the Armitage garden, so perhaps I should not be so negative.

Plants are generally semi-evergreen sub-shrubs with a woody base. The lower leaves are opposite but often alternate as they ascend the stem. The tubular flowers are usually one-sided and pendulous, with 5 lobes and pink to orange in color. In mild winters, plants are evergreen to semi-evergreen but in cold winters, they may be killed to the soil line. Cut back any old growth in the spring just above ground level anyway, to induce new vigorous growth. Suckering occurs so plants may spread rather quickly in good sites. All should be planted in full sun and in a well-drained area. Using the lee of a wall is common practice to provide a little more protection from wind and cold. Protective siting and winter mulching may allow plants to survive into zone 6.

Only two species are found: *P. aequalis* with 2-3′ tall plants bearing dusty pink flowers, and *P. capensis*, with 4-6′ tall shrubby growth and red and yellow flowers. The hybrid between them (*P.* x *rectus*), originally produced pale red pendulous flowers but has been selected to yield some excellent colors and many branched flower stems. Plants flower in summer and can persist into the fall.

Propagate by the suckers or by stem cuttings.

**Cultivars and Hybrids:**

'African Queen' has scarlet flowers that are a lighter tone inside.

'Caborn Flame' bears orange flowers with variegated foliage.

'Coccineus' is a cultivar of *P. capensis* with long narrow scarlet red flowers.

'Devil's Tears' bears beautifully vivid scarlet flowers.

'Moonraker' is a popular plant with soft pastel yellow flowers. It is a cross between 'Yellow Trumpet' and 'Winchester Fanfare' and the flower color is similar to the former. The flowers are borne all around the stem rather than on one side as in 'Yellow Trumpet'.

'New Sensation' has rose-pink flowers with pink throats. Plants are 3′ tall.

'Pink Elf' is probably the most distinct form of this group. Plants are more compact than others and bear rosy pink flowers all around the flowering stem.

'Pink Trumpet' produces salmon-pink flowers on 3′ tall plants.

'Salmon Leap' has bright rosy salmon flowers.

'Sunshine' has pink flowers and chartreuse leaves. Interesting but not for the heat.

'Trewidden Pink' bears soft pink flowers with bright yellow throats.

'Winchester Fanfare' produces one-sided inflorescences of dull red flowers, similar to but not as pendulous as 'African Queen'.

'Yellow Trumpet' is a cultivar of *P. aequalis* and has pale yellow flowers with deeper yellow lobes. The plants are compact and vigorous. It has also been offered as 'Cream' and 'Cream Delight'.

***Physalis*** (fi-sal-is) Chinese Lantern Solanaceae

Of the 80-100 species, only the common Chinese lantern, *P. alkekengi*, is found in North American gardens. The name comes from the Greek *physa* meaning bladder, and plants are grown mainly for their decorative orange fruit that resembles a bladder. It was believed that all members of this genus were edible and of great medicinal value. Sufferers of gout were said to have relieved the disorder by ". . . taking eight of these berries at each change of the moon." (Miller, P., *The Gardener's Dictionary*, 1805). It became discredited as a medicinal plant by the end of the eighteenth century and all that can now be said is that if some person ". . . foolishly be invited to taste of the fruit, they will not surely die: for if not their medical virtues, their innocency has been abundantly proved." (Thornton, R. J., *A Family Herbal*, 1814). The annual *P. ixocarpa*, however, is quite edible. It is native to Mexico and the southern United States, and has wonderful names such as jamberberry, tomatillo, and tomatillo ground cherry.

***-alkekengi*** (al-ke-ken′ jee) Chinese Lantern 18-24″/24″
Summer White Japan Zones 3-9

Plants spread by underground stems and, where they do well, can become a nuisance, creating a definite glut of lanterns in the neighborhood. The opposite leaves are deltoid-ovate (shaped like a fat arrowhead) and up to 5″ long. One inch wide white flowers with yellow stamens are carried singly in the upper leaf axils. The actual fruit is small and cherry-like, but is surrounded by the dark orange-red inflated husk, which arises from the mature calyx. The entire fruit is 2-3″ long and up to 6″ in circumference. Harvest them by late summer because if left on the plant, they become skeletonized.

Plant in full sun and provide constant moisture, particularly when the lanterns are developing. Allowing plants to dry out results in weedy-looking specimens with small fruit. Fertilize in the spring with a side dressing of complete fertilizer; excessive applications may result in luxurious foliar growth with little fruit production.

Seeds should be chilled for 4-6 weeks at 40°F. Germination is slow and may require up to 8 months. Division in early spring or fall is possible.

**Cultivars:**

'Gigantea' has larger flowers and fruit (up to 8″ wide) than the type.

'Pygmaea' grows only 12-15″ tall.

## ***Physostegia*** (fie-so′ stee gee-a) Obedient Plant Lamiaceae

Twelve species are known; all tall and erect with square stems, and lancelike opposite leaves. The only species cultivated to any extent is *P. virginiana*, known as obedient plant or false dragonhead. It took me forever to figure out this "obedient" thing. I pushed flowers up, then down and they would stubbornly spring right back . However in a rare lucid moment, I pushed the flower sideways, and voilà, there it stayed. You can do all sorts of weird and wonderful things with the many flowers.

***-virginiana*** (vir-jin-ee-ah′ na) Obedient Plant 3-4′/3′
Late Summer Pink Eastern United States Zones 2-9

Plants grew for many years in our cut flower trials at the University of Georgia and have been adopted as cut flowers because of the straight stems, classic spikelike flower heads, and outstanding flowering. Large clumps are formed that spread vigorously in good soil. If soils are rich or temperatures exceedingly warm, plants may flop over. This is not a plant for the "nice-guy" gardener, as merciless rogueing is needed to keep plants contained. As for its reckless forays through the garden, obedient it is not! The 1″ long flowers are normally pinkish and sessile on 12-18″ tall spikes. This is a long-day plant and begins to flower in August and continues until late September.

Plants are not fussy as to soil but perform better in acid pH. They are heavy feeders but if too much fertilizer is applied, growth is even more rampant than normal. Plant in well-drained soils in full sun.

**Cultivars:**

'Alba' has white flowers and blooms earlier than the species or cultivars; about three weeks earlier than 'Pink Bouquet' in north Georgia. Plants are shorter than the species.

'Eyeful Tower' from Plant Delights, Raleigh, North Carolina, is a 6-7′ giant with pink flowers.

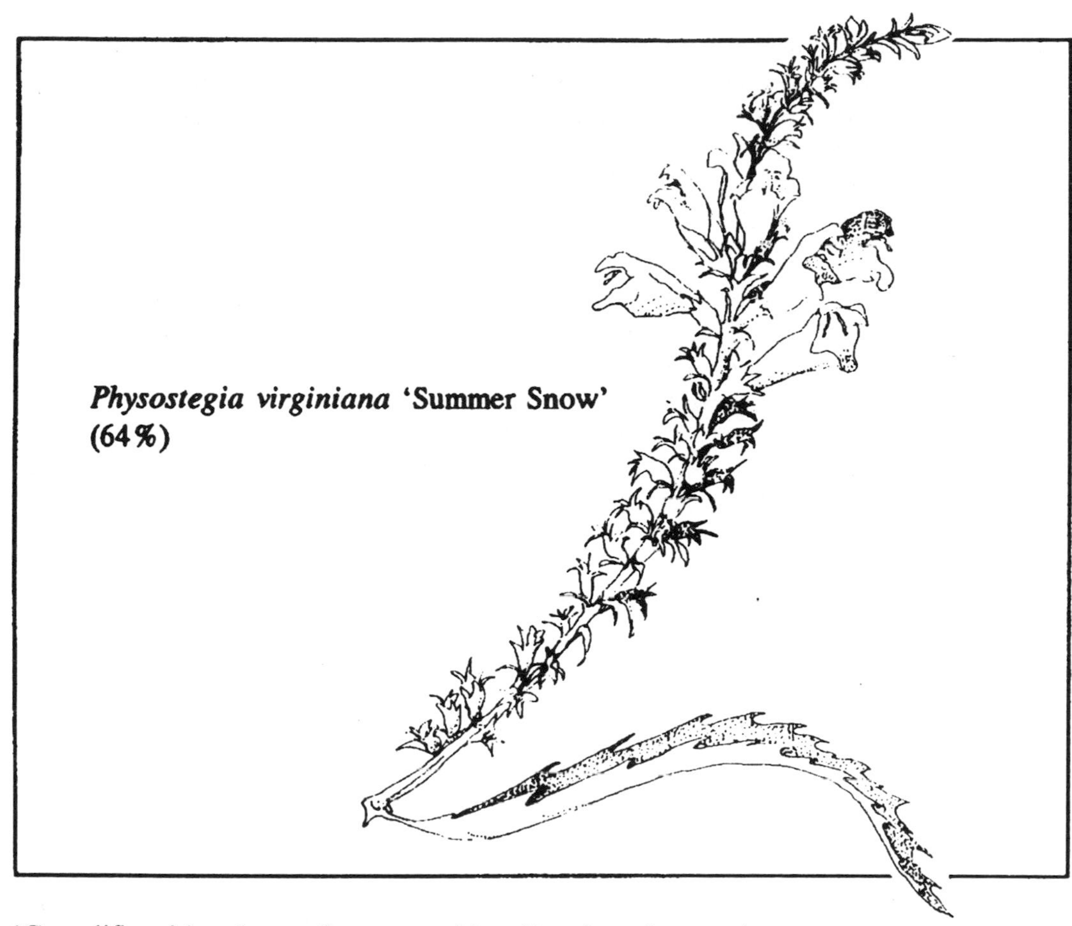

***Physostegia virginiana* 'Summer Snow' (64%)**

'Grandiflora' has larger flowers and is taller than the species.

'Miss Manners' is a great selection, with lovely white flowers on 2-3′ tall plants. However, the best thing about the plants is that they don't flop and they are not aggressive. Far better than other white cultivars on the market.

'Nana' is only 12-18″ tall. 'Alba Nana' is a similar-sized white form.

'Pink Bouquet' is a bright pink cultivar that grows 3-4′ tall. Plants are beautiful but not self-supporting.

'Red Beauty' is not red, but deep pink, at best. However, the plants are vigorous and a little closer to the elusive true red cultivar, which will likely occur some day.

'Summer Snow' has clean white flowers and is a little less invasive than the species.

'Variegata' is a pleasing form in which the leaves are edged white. It reminds me of *Phlox paniculata* 'Nora Leigh' in that the foliage is even better than the flowers.

'Vivid' is 2-3′ tall with vibrant pink flowers. It is the most compact and upright of any form.

## *Phyteuma* (fie-tew′ ma) Rampion Campanulaceae

Few people know about this diverse genus, consisting of approximately 40 species with violet to blue flowers. They are not exactly commonly available; however, some of the more adventurous nurseries have begun to offer them. The leaves are alternate, but often arranged so closely together as to resemble a mound. The flowers are generally arranged in a dense head-like inflorescence (like clustered bellflower, *Campanula glomerata*) and sit just above the foliage. All species prefer full sun and do not like wet feet. The species I prefer is *P. scheuchzeri*, sometimes called the weakstem rampion, due to its almost total lack of stem, and tufted growth. The clustered blue-mauve flowers reside 6-12″ above the leaves. Plants do better on limed soils and need to have decent drainage, particularly in the winter. Hardy in zones 6 (5 with protection) to 8. Rampion (from *rapa*, turnip) was once regularly cultivated in English kitchen gardens, and much valued as a wholesome esculent vegetable, but is seldom grown for use now.

A few other species may also be offered. The spiked rampion, *P. spicata*, is a 2-3′ tall plant with heart-shaped basal leaves and large creamy white flower heads. The variety *coeruleum* has blue flowers. *P. orbiculare*, roundheaded rampion, grows 1-2′ with rounded violet-blue flower heads in the summer. All are worth trying in zones 5 to 8, if rampions are in your future.

## ***Phytolacca*** (fi-to-la′ ca) Pokeweed Phytolaccaceae

To recommend pokeweed as a garden plant invites laughter and derision from almost all gardeners, particularly those in the South who often curse its very existence. Poke salad, which includes the young leaves of pokeweed, boiled twice to remove toxins, and seasoned well, has historically been used as a southern green. The roots, older leaves and the berries, however, can be poisonous. Regardless of your taste, it is not often included within garden boundaries. The perceived enemy among us is our native American pokeweed, *P. americana*, and not even I will try to talk anyone into its ornamental value. However, just because I won't doesn't mean somebody else won't. A few breeders have selected cultivars; the one that is most fascinating is 'Silberstein', speckled poke, with creamy and chartreuse flecks on the green foliage. The leaves are even more fascinating against the red stems and purple berries.

However, the genus consists of over 30 species and a few of them are very handsome. Some of the more civilized species like Indian poke, *P. acinosa*, are intriguing, with tall racemes of creamy flowers and fabulous purple fruit, but only marginally hardy in zone 8. The species with perhaps the most potential may be Chinese poke, *P. clavigera*, that makes dense plantings of ovate green leaves with white midribs, over which arise cylindrical racemes of pink flowers, followed by purple fruit. They are leafy, to be sure, but they are not as untidy or invasive as our native. Plants have not been tested extensively but should be hardy to about zone 6. All species produce fleshy purple berries, which can make one seriously ill. Keep little kids away.

The leaves are just as tasty to slugs and other critters as our native species. I planted *P. acinosa* in my garden and while it was neater and more decorative than the native, it was chewed badly by caterpillars. It also reseeded at the base but was eventually removed.

**_Pimpinella_** (pim-pen-el′la) Pimpinella Apiaceae

A relative of the ubiquitous Queen Anne's lace, it has not caught on in the hearts and wallets of gardeners. Two species were grown for medicinal purposes, *P. major* and *P. saxifraga* while *P. anisum*, anise seed, is used for cooking. Only *P. major* is used as an ornamental and is generally seen as part of the "wild" border or meadow. The leaves are pinnately compound with 3-9 segments and each segment is toothed. The finely cut leaves provide a lacy look to the border. The white flowers consist of flattened compound umbels and look like large obedient roadside weeds.

Plants are native to the British Isles, and south to Portugal in open meadows and hedges. Provide full sun and place in an area where they will not detract from the garden when they decline after flowering. They perform well on the West Coast and are hardy in zones 5-7 elsewhere.

**Cultivars:**

'Rosea' is the best cultivar and the only one worth spending money on. The soft pink flowers rise well above the finely divided foliage.

**_Pinellia_** (pie-nel-lee-a) Pinellia Araceae

The genus is related to Jack-in-the-pulpit and calla lily but is less familiar to most gardeners. The woodland plants are natives to China and Japan and grow from a small tuber. Some species have simple heart-shaped leaves, others bear compound leaves, that are generally divided into 3-7 segments and attached to the stems by long petioles. The flowers consist of a rolled-up spathe and a long narrow spadix, often with a long "tail". They are not as interesting or spectacular as the Jacks, but they are still great fun for the woodland gardener. However, beware—they can become a little too much fun and plants, especially *P. ternata* and sometimes *P. pedatisecta*, have been known to romp through the woodland. I happen to be a fan of the family and enjoy experimenting with many of the species.

*P. cordata* is one of my favorite forms. It is small, only about 6″ tall, and consists of cordate green leaves with handsome silver venation. I place mine among rocks by the pond. Zones 5-7.

*P. pedatisecta*, green dragon, is probably the most common with its compound leaves and long green tail wiggling out of the spathe. This has one of the largest flowers in the genus. All pinellias grow well in partially shaded woodland areas in which adequate water is available. Plants are hardy in zones 6-8. Look out, this can be a big time nuisance.

*P.* x 'Polly Spout' is likely a hybrid between *P. pedatisecta* and *P. tripartita* 'Atropurpurea'. Plants came from Dick Weaver, formerly of We-Du Nursery on Polly Spout Lane, in Marion, North Carolina. They appear to be intermediate between the two taxa.

*P. tripartita* has broad trifoliate (in three parts) leaves and narrow spathes, creamy outside and purple inside. This is an upright strong grower, and reseeds a little, but seldom is a nuisance. The 8-10″ long spadix stands at attention as it emerges from the green spathe. 'Atropurpurea' is about a foot tall and is characterized with spathes that are deep purple inside. 'Dragon Tails' could just as well be called 'Variegata'. I received a plant from Ozzie Johnson of Atlanta and have enjoyed the green and chartreuse coloring of the leaves. Even the flowers, which are similar in form to the species, may be variegated. I really enjoy this plant. 'Golden Dragon' has beautiful golden foliage in the spring, but loses the color in the summer. 'Silver Dragon' has silvery foliage.

Propagate by breaking up the tubers or grow from seed.

## ***Plantago*** (plan-tag′ o) Plantain Plantaginaceae

Two hundred plus species exist in this genus and at least 190 of them are in my lawn. They are tough, impossible to eradicate and obnoxious weeds. So why are they in this book about ornamental plants? For every dumpster there is a gold mine. For every weed, there is a treasure. Between pulling and cultivating plantain, life is confusing. *P. major* carries a number of reasonably ornamental cultivars.

'Rubrifolia' is effective when combined with the light green foliage or white-flowered short-statured plants like *Campanula carpatica* 'White Clips'. As the name suggests, the leaves are purplish but the foliage is large and the flower stems are also dark. They are something I would not want too many of, but they make an effective spot of purple color. The foliage does not fade significantly in the heat of the summer. 'Atropurpurea' is more greenish purple than 'Rubrifolia' but they are sold interchangeably. A singularly monstrous form is 'Rosularis', in which a bundle of tangled globular green leaves replaces the flower on the scape. A curiosity at best, and sure to spark heated debate on the meaning of "ornamental plant". A variegated form ('Variegata') with cream and green leaves is also cultivated. This is sometimes listed as *P. asiatica* 'Variegata'. All cultivars are hardy in zones 4-9.

## ***Platycodon*** (pla-tee-ko′ don) Balloon Flower Campanulaceae

The genus is related to *Campanula*, *Adenophora*, and *Codonopsis* but is characterized by the inflated flower bud that looks like it will burst as it matures. The only available species, *P. grandiflorus*, is one of the best plants for a child's garden as kids are truly fascinated by killing off the balloons with random sharp objects. The flowers are also distinguished by opening at the top rather than on the sides or at the base.

***-grandiflorus*** (grand-i-flor′ us) Balloon Flower 2½-3′/2′
Summer Blue China, Japan Zones 3-7

I am always treated to a beautiful garden when I visit my friend Suzy Bales on Long Island. Roses, containers, bouquets of fresh flowers and perennials are all included. On one summer day, a potpourri of white, blue and pink balloons caught my eye, all ready to transform themselves into handsome flowers. Unlike mine, the plants stood tall and required no support. Must be those Long Island Sound breezes.

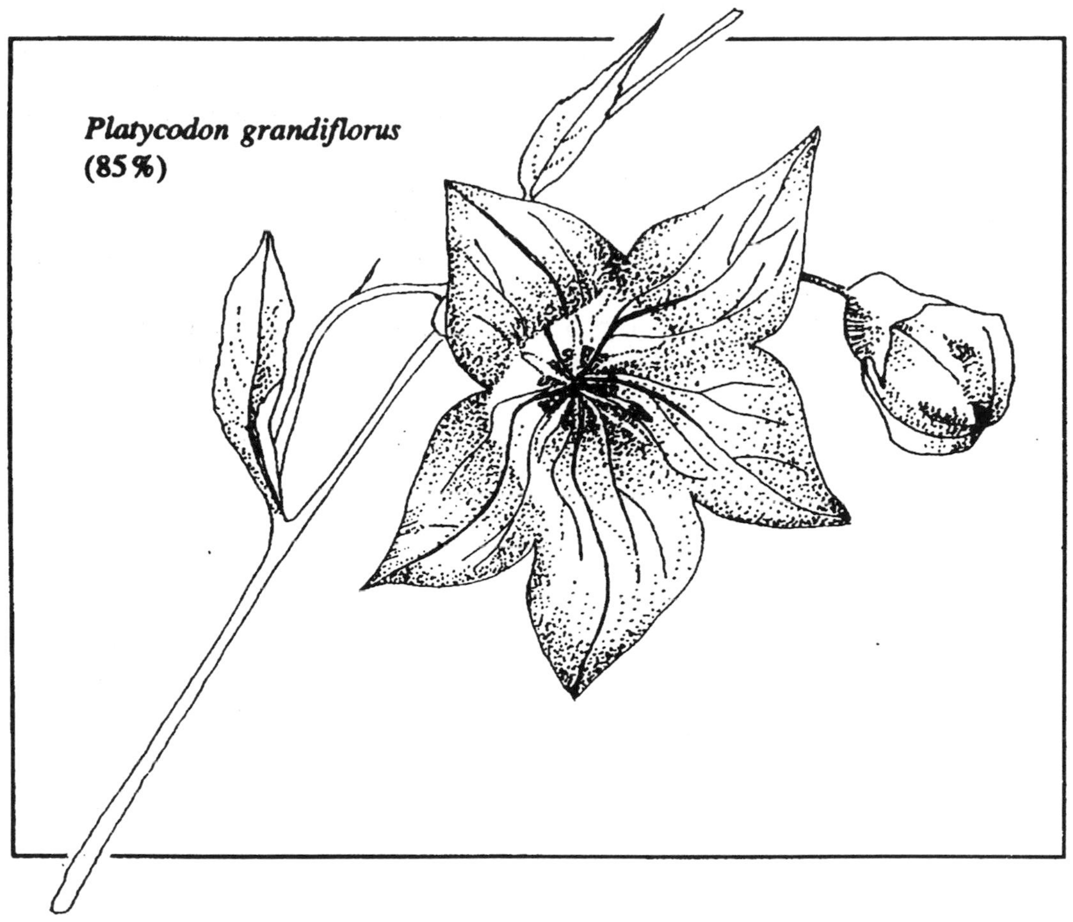

***Platycodon grandiflorus* (85%)**

The leaves, unequally spaced on the upper part of the stem and often whorled at the base, are sharply serrated, ovate and about 1-3″ long. The flowers are usually solitary, 2-3″ across and bluish purple. When the "balloon finally pops", it reveals a five-lobed blossom with rich purple veins and yellow-white stamens. Flowers look particularly good with 'Coronation Gold' yarrow or some of the yellow lysimachias. *Platycodon* is one of the latest perennials to emerge in spring so care must be taken not to plant over or dig it out accidentally during spring cleaning. This is not a problem if, like me, you never get around to cleaning anyway.

Full sun is necessary in the North but plants appreciate some protection from the afternoon sun (i.e. partial shade) in the South. Plants are long lived and ten-year-old plants are not uncommon. They seldom need dividing, and have few insect or disease pests, making this a truly low-maintenance species. However, plants of the species, particularly in hot summers, may grow too tall and flop over if support is not provided. This is alleviated by proper cultivar selection.

Seed germinates readily with warm temperature and moisture. Some literature states that balloon flower does not divide well. I have divided and moved clumps in the spring when shoots were 2-4″ tall without damage.

**Cultivars:**

'Albus' has white flowers with yellow or bluish veins.

'Apoyama' produces violet flowers on 10-15″ tall plants. An excellent dwarf upright form.

'Apoyama Fairy Snow' is a dwarf white-flowered form.

Astra series is only 8-10″ tall with double blue and pink flowers.

'Hakone Double Blue' bears double bright blue flowers on 15-24″ tall plants. The flowers are fuller than those of var. *plenus*.

'Freckles' has white flowers spotted with blue. An introduction from Hillview Gardens in Washington. I have not seen this but I hope it is not the same as the next item.

'Florovariegata' has white flowers streaked with blue. Unfortunately, the variegation is not stable and after a few years, leaves revert to a milky white. Plants are rather tall and weak as well.

Fuji series, a seed strain from Japan, with blossoms of pink, white and blue, grow 2-3′ tall. They are most suitable for cut flowers.

'Komachi' is 12-24″ tall with clear blue flowers. The bud swells to about 2″ in diameter but never opens. Interesting but kind of like holding your breath too long.

'Mariesii' is shorter (1-2′ tall) and more compact than the species with 2″ diameter flowers. This has always been a reasonably good cultivar but with the advent of more dwarf selections, others have superseded it.

'Misato Purple' grows 15-18″ tall and bears violet-purple flowers.

'Plenus, a double-flowering form, is interesting but not particularly handsome.

'Sentimental Blue' is an outstanding dwarf selection with large 2″ diameter flowers on 6-9″ tall plants. 'Sentimental White' can sometimes be found but seed availability has been a problem. Flowers from seed the first year.

'Shell Pink' is a seed-propagated selection with 2″ wide pink flowers on 18-24″ tall stems.

## *Podophyllum* (pod-o-fil-um) May Apple Berberidaceae

Everyone who has ventured into the eastern woods in the spring must have noticed the clumps of big shiny green umbrella-like leaves. The trend to more natural gardens and the aging of our urban woodlands have increased the need for shady native plants, and may apple fits the bill. There are few more delightful sights than new leaves of our *P. peltatum* freshly emerged from the soil, still pulled tight around the stem like an unopened umbrella. They open slowly to form dark green, palmately lobed umbrellas, sometimes in patches so thick that the ground beneath them must be experiencing a drought even during torrential rain. The white nodding flowers are formed only on the axil where the leaves form a "V" and can be seen through rather than from above the plants. Plants with only a single leaf will not flower. The fruit start off green and ripen to yellow.

In order to appreciate the flowers of may apples and other plants whose blooms occur beneath the foliage, it may be a good idea to plant them on a bank or ledge, so

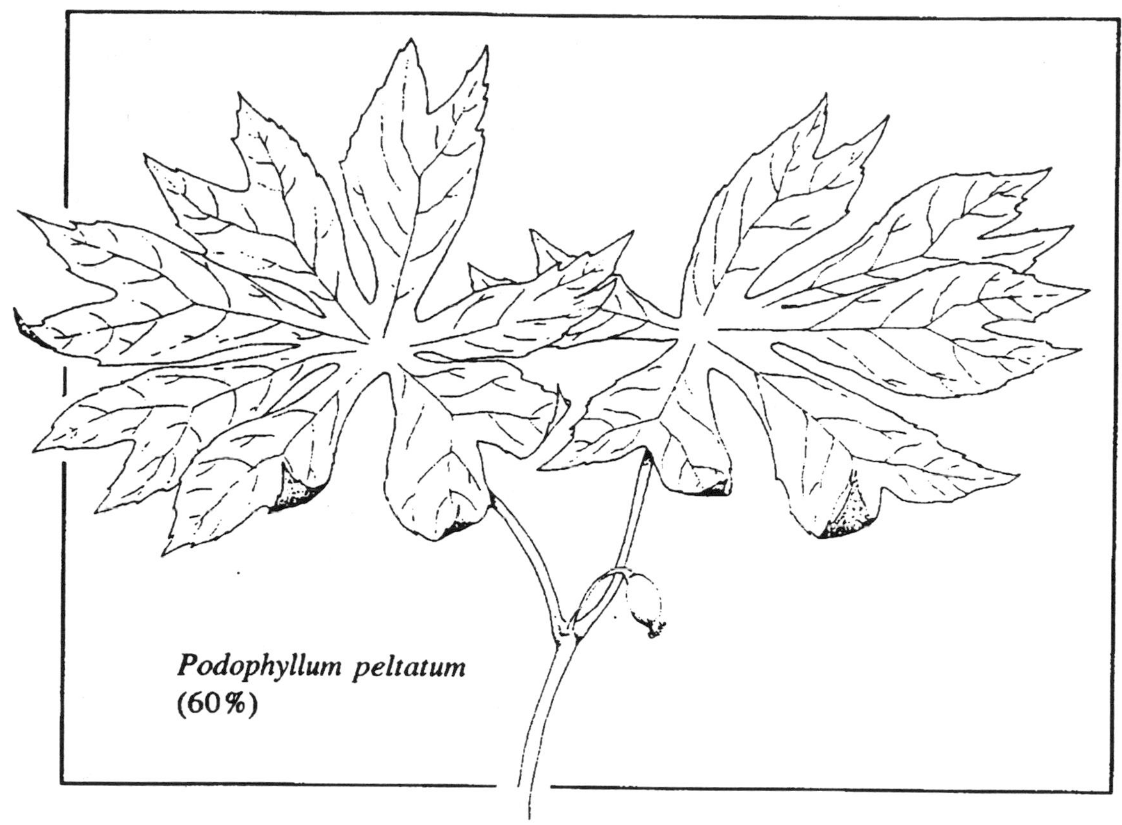

*Podophyllum peltatum*
(60%)

that they are not at shoe level. In the gardens at Mt. Cuba Center in Delaware, they are planted on a bank above a path, so that as you walk by, the flowers are close to eye level.

May apple has been a useful medicine for some time. Doses of tea made from the roots eased liver ailments, rheumatism, arthritis and acted as an antidote for poisons and snake bites. It was also used by North American Indians to treat tumors and growths of various sorts while resin from the plant was used in the removal of benign warts and skin growths. Reports also showed that the addition of Jacob's ladder, *Polemonium reptans*, to the tea increased its potency.

When teaching plants to my students, I try to have them understand terms like "peltate", "axillary" or "palmately compound". The leaves of this plant illustrates "peltate" so well that anybody could explain it. However, it all falls apart when someone asks "How can this plant be in the same family as barberry? They don't remotely resemble each other!". I am left muttering about single ovaries with numerous ovules on a thickened placenta and the fruit a berry. Then I remember than other native woodlanders such as *Jeffersonia*, blue cohosh and epimedium are also in this family. It is good to know that the taxonomists are as confused as we are. Enjoy the plants, ignore the family. Our native does not have a lock on the genus, however, as the Asian species have definitely arrived.

**Related Species:**

*P. hexandrum* (*P. emodi*) has rosy white upward-facing flowers that appear before the leaves emerge or just as they are emerging. Hardy in zone 6-8.

*P. pleianthum* has gained a significant following, especially in my garden. Each 3-5 lobed leaf is about 10″ across, each one so shiny green it looks like leaf wax was applied. The flowers occur beneath the leaves but are fire engine red, and large. The large red fruit occurs in midsummer. I can't get enough of it. Plants are stoloniferous and I have seen a small population starting in the shade on the oaks. Can a drift be far behind?

*P. versipelle*, with its huge 15″ wide peltate leaves deeply divided into 5-8 lobes, is also handsome. The flowers are borne in umbels, approximately 6-10 per inflorescence, and are usually concealed by the tallest leaf. The flowers are crimson red and can smell pretty bad. The leaves, however, are wonderful and make the trouble of finding these plants well worthwhile. Hardy to about zone 6.

*P. veitchii* (*P. delavayi*) is also quite unbelievable; the margins of the large leaves are cut and divided so much as to look like fuzzy umbrellas. Flowers are usually red, but may also be white or pink.

**Additional Hybrids:**

'Kaleidoscope', from Terra Nova Nursery is almost impossible to describe. The 15-18″ wide leaf is a kaleidoscope of colors including green, silver surrounded by black rings. Large red flowers are formed beneath the leaves. Quite remarkable.

'Spotty Dotty' has large chartreuse leaves with brownish spotting here and there. Red to garnet clusters of flowers occur beneath the foliage. Equally indescribable. Both grow in zones 6-8.

## ***Polemonium*** (po-lee-mo′ nee-um) Jacob's Ladder Polemoniaceae

Many of the 20-30 species are similar in habit and appearance, and are excellent garden plants. The alternate leaflets are arranged ladder-like along the long leaves. The flowers are usually a shade of blue, but pink, white, and yellow blossoms also occur. Plants range in height from about 3′ (*P. foliosissimum*) to about 8″ (*P. viscosum*). Many are native to Europe and the western United States and are not particularly long-lived in the eastern half of the country (*P. reptans* is an exception). The foliage is handsome on most species and plants are ornamental, even when not in flower. In general, little success has been seen with the genus south of zone 7a, particularly *P. caeruleum* and *P. foliosissimum*. They are good plants in cooler climates and require full sun to partial shade, and well-drained soil.

Quick Reference to Polemonium Species

| | Height (in.) | Flower color |
|---|---|---|
| *P. caeruleum* | 18-24 | Blue |
| *P. carneum* | 18-24 | Pink |
| *P. pulcherrimum* | 8-12 | Blue, yellow throat |
| *P. reptans* | 8-18 | Light blue |

***-caeruleum*** (se-ru′ lee-um) | Jacob's Ladder | 18-24″/18″
Summer | Blue | Europe | Zones 2-7

The leaves bear up to 20 leaflets that supposedly represent the ladder of which Jacob dreamed and the angels climbed. The 3-5″ long basal leaves form dense tufts and are attached to the base of the stem by 4-6″ long petioles. The stem leaves are much smaller and the petiole diminishes until the leaves are sessile at the top of the stem. The leaflets are mostly entire and taper to a long point. The 1″ wide, light to deep blue flowers sport yellow stamens and occur in drooping terminal cymes.

Plant in full sun to partial shade in well-drained soils. In general, this species is intolerant of hot, humid conditions and does not do well south of zone 7, although it will produce many evergreen leaves for a few years. Further north and west, it is a much better plant where flowers will be produced for weeks. Plants have tons of cold hardiness and perform well over a wide geographic range. I have seen excellent stands in zone 6 and in southern Ontario, zone 4.

Propagate by seed or division. Sow seed in a humid, 70-75°F environment. Germination occurs in 2-3 weeks. Remove seedlings from warm, humid environment as soon as first true leaves are visible.

**Cultivars:**

'Album' has white flowers that are a pleasant contrast with the dark green leaves.

'Bressingham Purple' is a hybrid with a good deal of *P. caeruleum* in it. We trialed this plant for many years in the Gardens at UGA and it has been an outstanding performer. The dark green foliage arises from dark, almost purple stems, followed by lavender blue flowers. A nice upright habit as well.

'Brize D'Anjou' was also introduced from Blooms of Bressingham and has clean variegated leaves of green and white. While plants are unique and not easy to overlook, they have fared poorly in much of the country, disappearing rather quickly.

'Dawn Light' bears clean white flowers on 18″ plants.

'Himalayanum' has larger (up to 1½″ across), deeper blue flowers than the species. This variety was considered to be a separate species (*P. himalayanum*) and may still be offered as such.

'Primadonna' produces lovely light blue flowers on 12-15″ plants.

'Snow and Sapphires' is an upright white and green variegated form that has better vigor than 'Brize D'Anjou'. Blue flowers occur in late spring to early summer.

***-carneum*** (kar-nee′ um) | Salmon Polemonium | 18-24″/18″
Summer | Pink to Salmon | Western United States | Zones 6-8

I include this species for purely selfish reasons. It is a lovely plant but, unfortunately, not as easy to grow as it is beautiful. Generally, the 3-8″ long leaf consists of 12 to 21 leaflets. The 1½″ long pink flowers fade to purplish and are held in lax, few-flowered cymes. Rather fussy about the environment, it does not tolerate heat or full sun and is less cold hardy than other species. Consistent moisture is required but plants decline rapidly if drainage is poor. However, when sited properly, it is a wonderful plant and if you find a nursery carrying the plant, don't hesitate to try it; just don't spend a lot.

**Cultivars**:
'Apricot Delight' has pink to apricot flowers on 18″ plants.

***-pulcherrimum*** (pul-cher′ i-mum) Skunkleaf Polemonium 8-12″/12″
Summer Blue with Yellow Throat Western United States Zones 3-7

This low-growing species is particularly suited to a dry rock garden or stone wall in full sun or partial shade. The leaves are 4-6″ long and consist of up to 30 leaflets, although usually fewer than 25. Small (¼″ long) flowers are held in dense cymes and are usually blue with a yellow throat but vary to violet on the petals with white interiors.

Propagate by seed or division.

***-reptans*** (rep′ tanz) Creeping Polemonium 8-18″/12′
Spring Light Blue Eastern North America Zones 2-7

This is a wild flower through much of the eastern woodlands and the Midwest plains. They are excellent foliage plants and provide fresh greenery all season. Plants are seldom over one foot high. The common name is a misnomer as the plant has a shallow rhizome and is not stoloniferous. The stems are weak and diffuse, but the plant doesn't creep nearly as fast as it reseeds. The 7-15 leaflets are about 1″ long and topped by light blue, half-inch long flowers borne in loose drooping clusters (corymbs). After flowering, the plants are covered with tan-colored fruit, another wonderful attribute of this little-appreciated plant. If placed in partial shade and kept moist, plants are easy to grow, and may seed vigorously.

**Cultivars:**
'Alba' bears white flowers.
'Blue Pearl' grows 8-10″ tall with bright blue flowers.
'Stairway to Heaven' is a yellow and green variegated form that is the best choice for a variegated ladder. Leaf tips are pink in the cool weather of spring. In the East and Midwest, plants keep their variegation until temperatures get consistently warm, then colors sort of melt together. Introduced by Bill Cullina of Garden in the Woods, Framingham, Massachusetts.

**Related Species and Hybrids:**

*P. boreale*, arctic polemonium, grows 9″ tall with ½″ diameter blue-purple flowers and 13-23 leaflets per leaf. This species was extolled for years by L.H. Bailey and admired by the English plantsman Graham Stuart Thomas. Its nomenclature is in great need of study. It has been described as a hybrid with *P. reptans*, or as a variety of *P. caeruleum*. Regardless of the location in the taxonomic cupboard, it should be sought out and tried in North American gardens. 'Heavenly Habit' has larger flowers with a little yellow. Hardy at least to zone 3.

*P. foliosissimum*, leafy polemonium, is the best of the upright blue species, if properly grown. It is stouter, stronger, and has larger flowers than *P. caeruleum*. The flowers have bright yellow stamens and plants are exceptionally vigorous. It is longer lived than *P. caeruleum* and produces little seed. The species does not tolerate heat and high humidity. Unfortunately, although native to western United States, it is seldom offered in North America.

*P. pauciflorum* is sometimes called yellow Jacob's ladder due to the pale yellow tubular flowers hanging near the ends of the 18″ tall stems. Flowers have a bluish to reddish blush and appear during the summer. Likely hardy to zone 7, maybe 6.

*P.* x *richardsonii* is the name given to hybrids between *P. caeruleum* and *P. reptans*. Plants are about 10-12″ tall and are intermediate in their stoloniferous habit. The 1″ wide flowers are sky blue and massed at the end of the stems. Flowers appear in early summer but plants are good rebloomers. 'Album' has white flowers. Almost impossible to find without serious searching.

## ***Polianthes*** (po-lee′ anth-eez) Tuberose Agavaceae

This genus consists of over 10 species, however only *P. tuberosa*, the highly fragrant tuberose, is available to gardeners. The name *Polianthes* may have been derived from *poly*, many and *anthos*, flower, referring to the many-flowered stalks. Others have suggested that it was derived from *polios*, shining, white, and *anthos*, flower, referring to the shiny flowers. Only Linnaeus knows for sure.

In the early 1900s, North Carolina was one of the major producers of tuberose tubers for export, producing over six million tubers within a 25-mile radius of the town of Magnolia. Today there is little tuber production in the United States, most of it having moved to countries where labor is less expensive. Cut flower production, however, is alive and well in the southern United States, California and the Midwest.

***-tuberosa*** (tew-ber-o′ sa) Tuberose 3-4′/3′
Late Summer, Fall White Mexico Zones 7-10

Best known for its fragrance and glistening white blossoms, the flowers appear to have been recently waxed. The fragrance is delicious to some and overbearing to others. Flowers are still used for weddings and the scent of one or two stems is all that is needed to fill the entire chapel. The plant is derived from a tuberous rootstock, thus the name. The leaves are linear, channeled, and spotted with brown on the underside. The 2-2½″ long white, funnel-shaped flowers appear on a 2-3′ raceme between August and October.

Tuberose is a heat-loving species and tubers must be started in the house or greenhouse in the spring before soils are warm. Plant in the ground after the threat of frost. After the first fall frost, lift the tubers and hang them in a warm (45-50°F ), dry place. In the Carolinas, Georgia, parts of Tennessee, Florida, the Gulf Coast states and much of California, plants are perennial under most winters if mulch is provided. The best mulch is the layer of dead leaves that carpets the ground after the first hard frost.

Tuberose may be propagated from offshoots removed in the fall when tubers are dug and replanted the following spring.

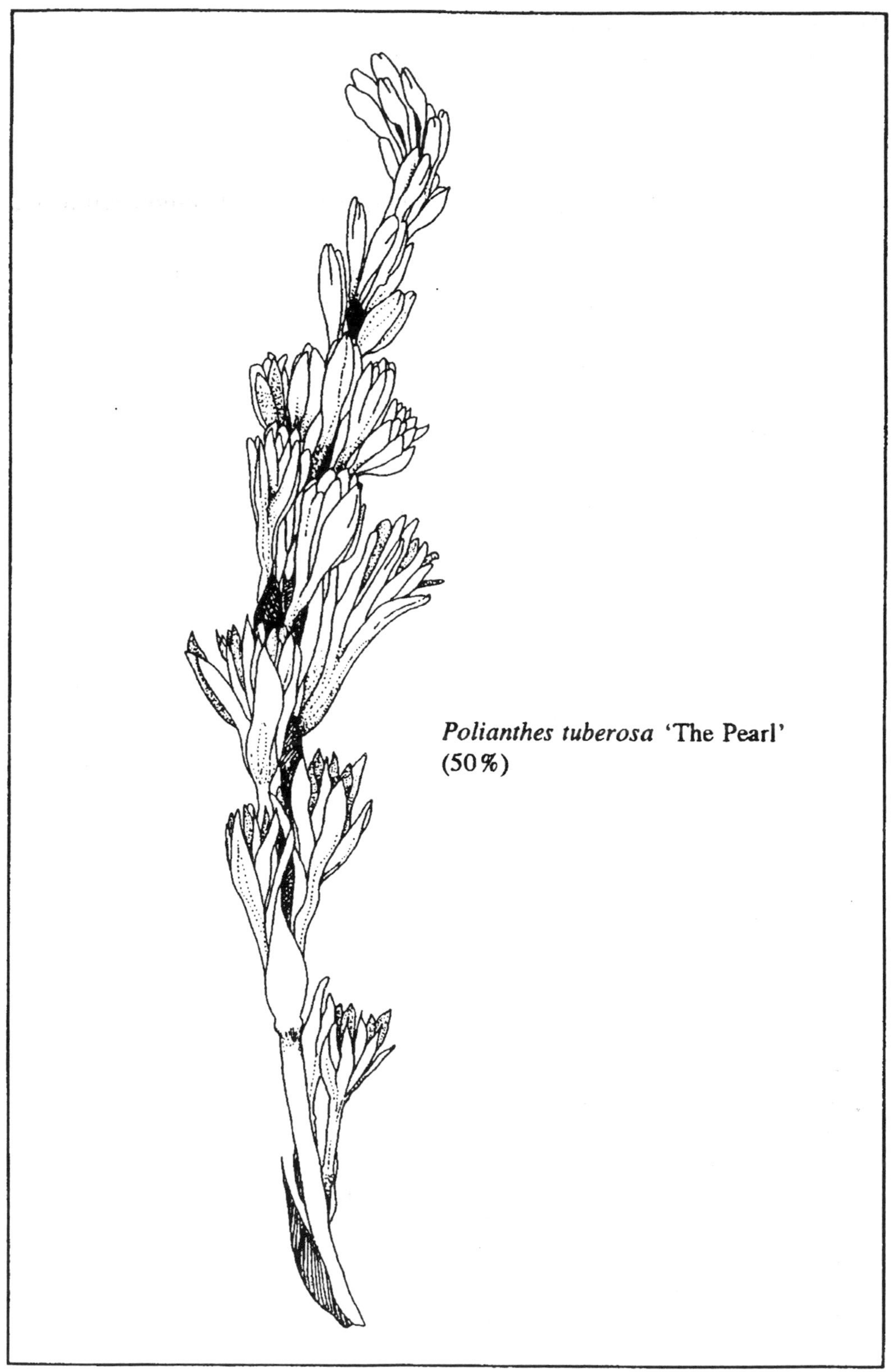

*Polianthes tuberosa* 'The Pearl'
(50%)

**Cultivars:**

'Gracilis' has narrower leaves and flowers with longer tubes.

'Marginata' is a variegated form of the tuberose, with white margins on the narrow leaves. Growing only 8-12″ tall, this miniature is more of a collector's item than a plant grown for the fragrant flowers. It is difficult to locate.

'Mexican Single' is a better cultivar with flowers more closely spaced on the stalk.

'The Pearl', a double-flowered form, has been around for ages and is the best cultivar for the garden. This is one of the unusual instances where doubling the flower petals is a definite improvement based on garden performance. However as a cut flower, it is not as good as the single forms because the extra petals decline more rapidly.

## ***Polygonatum*** (po-lig-o-nay′ tum) Solomon's Seal Convallariaceae

Of the approximately 60 species, a number have left the realm of wild flowers and joined the mainstream of garden plants. The botanical name comes from *poly*, many and *gonu*, knee joints, referring to the many-jointed rhizome from which the leaves rise. The common name Solomon's seal may have been derived from the circular sunken scars that remain on the rootstock after the leaf stalks die and fall off; the scar somewhat resembles a seal impressed on wax on official documents or letters in former times. Gerard, the English plantsman, believed the powdered roots were an excellent remedy for broken bones. He wrote in the late 1590s that roots pulverized and drunk in ale, "soddereth and gleweth together the bones in a very short space . . .". He believed that this property of sealing wounds was why the plant received the name Solomon's seal.

Most species are comprised of long, graceful, unbranched shoots bearing alternate leaves and whitish, pendulous flowers hanging from the leaf nodes. They range in height from the 6″ *P. humile*, dwarf Solomon's seal, to the great Solomon's seal, *P. commutatum*, whose stems may grow to 8′ in length. The main reason for including these plants in the garden is their architectural qualities. The leaf orientation is delightful and the variegated forms are particularly showy. Leaves persist until frost and turn a lovely tan yellow in the fall. The 1-3″ diameter blue-black fruit is interesting if not spectacular and adds to the charm. An indispensable genus for the landscape architect.

Plants tolerate heavy shade and grow well in shady, moist areas. All are readily propagated in the fall by division of the rootstock. It is necessary to leave at least one bud on the divisions. Seed should be stratified at 40°F for 6 weeks before sowing.

Quick Reference to Polygonatum Species

| | Height (in.) | Flower color | Flowers per axil |
|---|---|---|---|
| *P. biflorum* | 12-36 | White | 1-3 |
| *P. commutatum* | 36-72 | White | 3-8 |
| *P. humile* | 6-9 | White | 1-2 |
| *P. odoratum* | 18-24 | White | 1-2 |

***-biflorum*** (bi-flo′ rum) Small Solomon's Seal 1-3′/2′
Spring White-Green Eastern North America Zones 3-8

This North American species extends as far north as New Brunswick, south to Florida, and west to the Mississippi Valley in shady, cool, woodland areas. The 4-4½″ long, alternate leaves are nearly sessile, and have 2-5 main nerves running down the leaves, although only the midrib is prominent toward the leaf tip. The ½ to ¾″ flowers are greenish white and occur in pairs beneath the arching stems. There is significant variation in the species and flowers may be bunched in 3s and 4s, although 2 flowers per leaf axil is the most common.

Plants require shade and moisture and are easily propagated by division of the rhizome.

***-commutatum*** (kom-mew-tay′ tum) Great Solomon's Seal 3-7′/4′
Late Spring White-Green United States to Mexico Zones 3-7
(syn. *P. giganteum*, *P. canaliculatum*)

A plant that truly needs space, it will gobble up significant acreage as its wings expand. Plants have been known to reach 7′ in height (although 4-5′ is more reasonable) and may form colonies equally wide, so it may not be a good subject for the average suburban garden. Plants are not invasive; in fact in my garden, I wish they were more so, they are simply large plants. However, few plants are more outstanding on the edge of moist woodland areas, where the 3-7″ long leaves can be displayed to advantage. Approximately 10 prominent nerves extend the full length of the leaves. The ¾″ long yellowish green to whitish green flowers are held in a 3-8 flowered umbel in the leaf axils. Deep purple berries and golden foliage are the norms for the fall season, providing additional reasons to include these plants for the garden. Some authorities have lumped this species with *P. biflorum* causing considerable confusion. It is bigger in every way, and if it is to be lumped, it at least deserves a variety or subspecies designation. Let's leave it here until the dust settles.

***-humile*** (hum-e′ lee) Dwarf Solomon's Seal 5-9″/3″
Spring White-Green China, Japan, Korea Zones 5-8

After seeing the grand pendulous species of great Solomon's seal, the appearance of this little guy is surprising, but equally delightful. Early in the spring, they pop out of the ground with flowers already formed and rise straight up—no bent backs here—to a sturdy five to nine inches. Generally one, sometimes two, whitish flowers are formed at the axil but many of the new stems may have none at all. Plants spread nicely, forming a dense clump in 2-3 years. I received some plants from the great plantsman Charles Cresson of Swarthmore, Pennsylvania, and they have thrived in the Armitage garden under conditions of moderate shade and minimal maintenance. A great plant.

Other relatively small species are out there as well. *P. hookeri* is only 3-5″ tall but bears lilac to purplish flowers. *P. hirsutum* is also relatively small but usually bears 3-5 flowers at each axil.

***-odoratum*** (o-do-rah′ tum) Fragrant Solomon's Seal 18-24″/2′
Spring White-Green Europe, Asia Zones 3-8

The one inch long white flowers are constricted at the base and wear a skirt of yellow green. They occur in pairs, occasionally singly, dangling from the leaf axils underneath the leaves. On quiet spring evenings, the flowers exude a lovely lily-like fragrance, although a tuberose this is not. The stems are somewhat angular and carry 8-12 lancelike leaves along their 18″ length.

**Cultivars:**

'Fireworks', from Barry Yinger of Asiatica Nursery, combines white margins and yellow markings on each leaf. Beautiful, rare and still pricey, but worth a try.

'Flora Plenum' is an unusual double-flowered form. You won't see the doubleness unless they are planted on a slope or wall or you get down on your knees.

'Thunbergii' is bigger and stouter in every way than the species. Shoots grow 3′ tall, leaves are up to 6″ long and flowers are 1-1½″ long.

'Variegatum', with its soft green leaves edged in a broad strip of creamy white, is, without doubt, the best form of this species. The variegation makes the plant jump out, and it is a bright addition to dull shade. However, they tolerate almost full sun and if so planted, the colony will be denser and shorter, and in my opinion, much more eye-catching. Flowers appear in mid April in the South, a few weeks later to the North, and persist for 2-3 weeks. They make excellent cut stems whose clean lines add beauty to any arrangement. I am often asked to speak on native plants and enjoy talking about our native species, but I cannot leave this one out; I use it to remind everyone that gardens are apolitical.

**Related Species:**

*P. falcatum* is a handsome species, growing 2-3′ tall. The leaves are somewhat sickle shaped but not always. Pairs of white flowers occur at each axil in the spring. 'Nippon Sunbeam' appears to be lightly brushed in white lines, resulted in a subtle variegation. 'Silver Lining' has bold white midribs. Zones 4-8.

*P. filipies* has two-foot long stems, with greenish flowers hanging at each axil. The somewhat pendulous nature of the stems makes the plants' mature height only about a foot. Cold hardy to zone 6.

*P.* x *hybridum* is a hybrid between *P. multiflorum*, Eurasian Solomon's seal, and *P. odoratum* and is intermediate between the parents. 'Flore-pleno' has double, more persistent flowers. 'Striatum' is also known as 'Grace Barker' and has leaves that are striped creamy white, and not just on the edges as in *P. odoratum* 'Variegatum'. The differences between the two variegated forms are minor and it is likely that plants are mixed up in the trade.

*P. kingianum* will make everyone look twice, wondering if they are looking at a Solomon seal or something on which to hang Christmas ornaments. Long, narrow conifer-like leaves ascend the stem, and at each node hang small rosy orange flowers. Plants grow 4-5′ tall in partial shade. Likely cold hardy to zone 6.

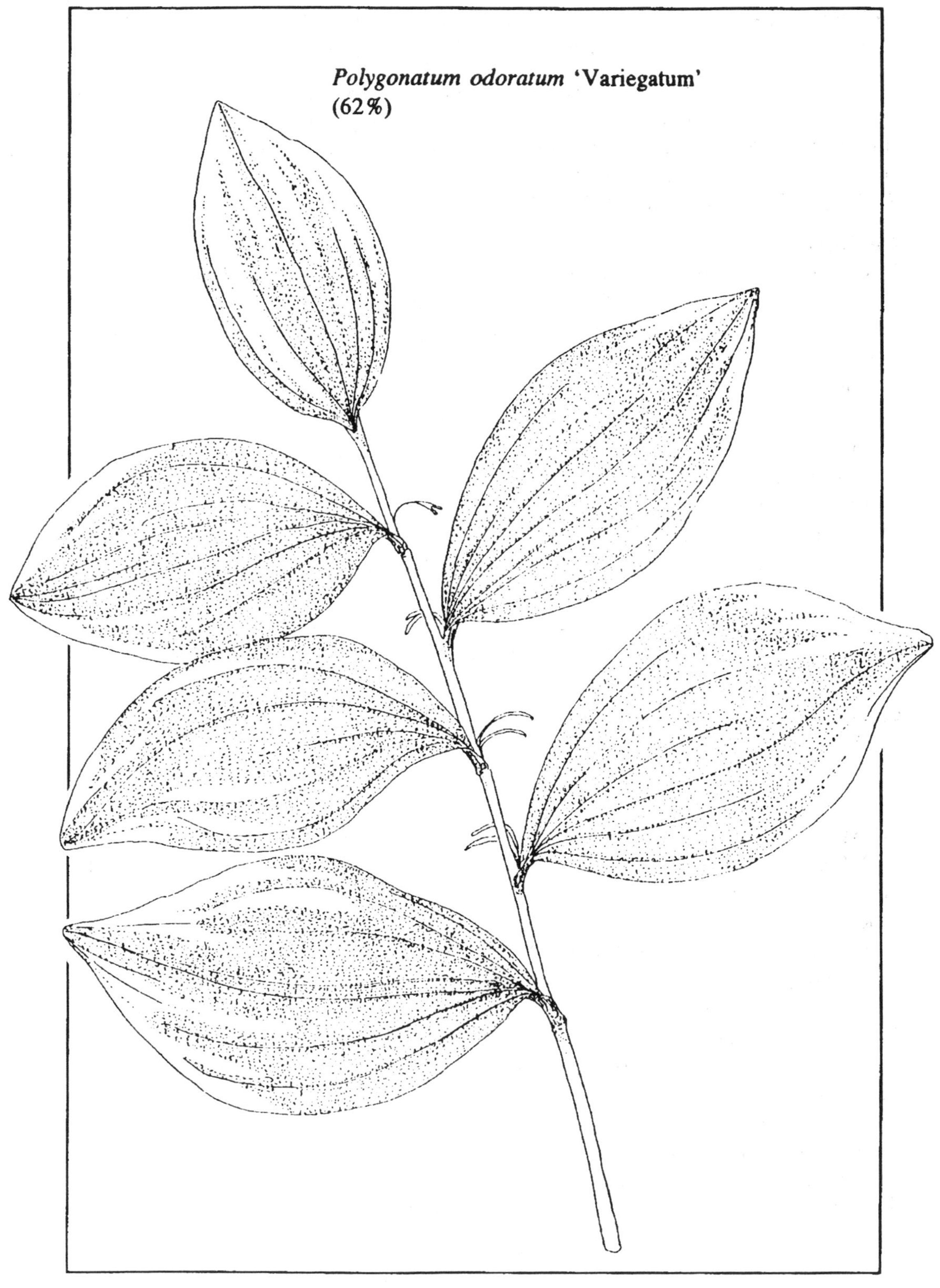

*Polygonatum odoratum* 'Variegatum' (62%)

***Polystichum*** (po-lis′ ti-kum) Holly Fern, Shield Fern Dryopteridaceae

Over 200 species belong to this large genus of ferns, some native to wide areas of North America, others to Europe and the Far East. Most are coarse, rigid ferns and many are evergreen. They are small to medium in size and a few are quite popular in American gardens. The stipe (portion of stem beneath the leaflets) is highly scaled and the spores are contained in rows of round indusia (spore cases) on the underside of the fronds. They do not occur on separate stems (like cinnamon fern). Partial shade and moist soils are necessary for best performance. Many of these ferns perform better in slightly alkaline soils, and an application of limestone every spring may make a difference. Although many are evergreen, removing the old fronds early in the spring allows the new highly ornamental fiddleheads to be far more visible.

Quick Reference to Polystichum Species

| | Times pinnate | Color of stipe |
|---|---|---|
| *P. acrostichoides* | 1 | rusty |
| *P. polyblepharum* | 1 | rusty |
| *P. setiferum* | 2 | rusty |
| *P. tsus-sinense* | 2 | black |

***-acrostichoides*** (a-kro-sti-koi′ deez) Christmas Fern 12-18″/12″
North America Zones 4-8

A very common woods fern, particularly in the East, and the easiest species to establish. The common name came from the fact that the fern is green at Christmas although it is mainly the sterile fronds that remain green, the fertile ones tend to wither. Spores are borne on sharply reduced pinnae (leaflets) on the top one-third of the fertile fronds. The fronds are wider in the middle than at either end, and each pinna has a "toe" on one side. I love to pull off a leaflet, hang it with the toe facing down, and imagine that "Twas the night before Christmas . . . and the stockings were hung by the chimney with care." I know, schmaltzy, but my jaw-dropping students don't soon forget the Christmas fern. I also point out that the characteristic of the bottom two pinnae pointed down, but that is not nearly as much fun.

Describing fern morphology can be tedious. I can think of a dozen reasons to include ferns in my garden, and not one of them requires my knowing a frond from a pinna but bear with me nevertheless. Christmas fern has a classic fern shape and its ease of growth and evergreen nature are wonderfully rewarding. It does not compete with other larger, more colorful ferns, but it is tough and undemanding. In the Armitage garden, ferns cohabit with hostas and wild flowers and make the shade that much more pleasant.

***-polyblepharum*** (pol-lee-bleph-a′ rum) Tassel Fern 15-24″/20″
Japan, Korea Zones 6-8

Every time I visit the shady garden of my good friends Donna and Ed Lambert in Athens, I marvel at the fern lady's ability to grow almost every fern on the planet.

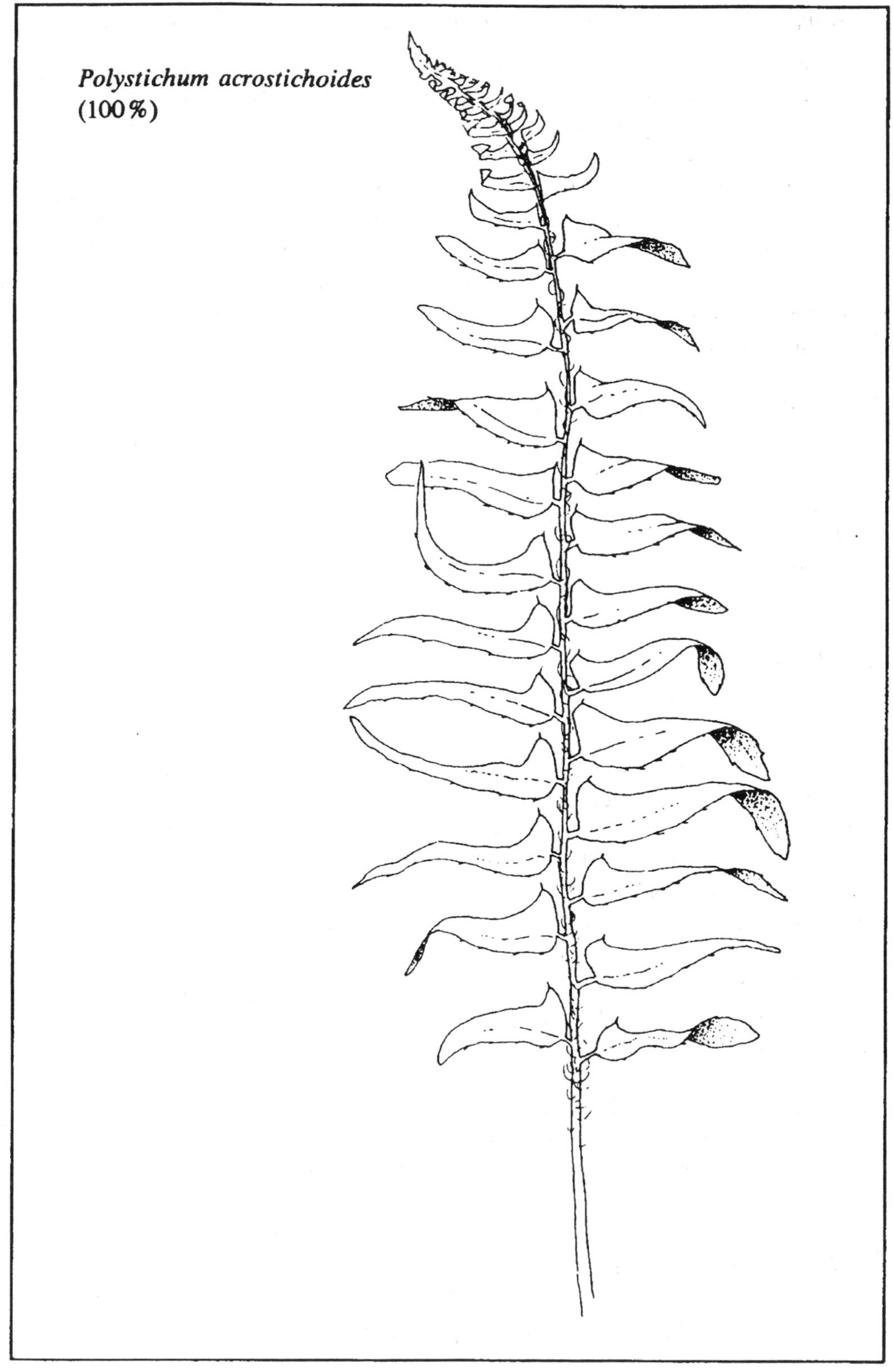
*Polystichum acrostichoides*
(100%)

In my garden, the tassel fern struggles and usually succumbs in a few years, but in Donna's, it is always spectacular. The spectacular part comes from the evergreen glossy green fronds that make this one of the most handsome ferns available. The bases of the stipes are heavily tufted with membranous brown scales and the glossy fronds are 12-20″ long and about 10″ wide. Although evergreen, the foliage looks pretty awful by winter's end.

Not as easy to establish as Christmas fern, nor as vigorous, but well-grown specimens are unbeatable, shimmering in the shaded garden unlike any other.

| ***-setiferum*** (say-ti′ fe-rum) | Soft Shield Fern | 1-2′/18″ |
| --- | --- | --- |
| | Europe | Zones 5-7 |

These ferns are not seen as much as other species probably because American gardens tend to be hotter and more humid than their native habitat. The other reason it is not seen as much is simply that it is seldom offered, certainly relative to more popular cinnamon and Christmas ferns. Plants form rosettes that are handsomely dissected and usually soft to the touch. The light green fronds unfurl over a long time and look like a tight knot at the top of each one. The knot is often a softer, more cinnamon color than the fronds. Soft shield fern is immensely popular in Europe and the West Coast and over 300 cultivars have been selected by fernites. As for me, I'll stick with the species.

**Cultivars:**

'Acutilobum' has sharply pointed leaflets (pinnae) on the narrow fronds.

'Congestum' is shorter and more compact than the species and carries dense fronds with overlapping leaflets.

'Cristatum' has the ends of the fronds crested. Awful thing. Its crested fronds make this particularly hideous.

'Divisilobum' has arching, greatly dissected fronds.

'Herrenhausen' has finely divided fronds on a 10-12″ plant.

'Proliferum' is known as Alaska fern and is more cold hardy than the other selections. Fronds are finely divided and plants are 12-18″ tall.

'Rotundatum' produces almost round leaflets (pinnae) on the upright fronds. There is also a crested form ('Rotundatum Cristatum').

| ***-tsus-sinense*** (tsoo-see-men′ see) | Korean Rock Fern | 1-2′/2′ |
| --- | --- | --- |
| | Japan | Zones 6-8 |

Handsome ferns for well-drained location, they are characterized by the contrast of the black stems with the green fronds. They are not dwarf but they seldom grow more than a foot tall. Well-grown plants may attain two feet in diameter.

In the Armitage garden, plants do not thrive (of course, in the Lambert garden, they are exceptional), but nor do they struggle badly. They grow slowly and one has to look hard to be overwhelmed. However, in small groups or set against a natural rock background, they are impressive.

**Related Species:**

*P. aculeatum* has glossy stiff fronds, and is sometimes called the hard shield fern. Plants may attain widths of 3′ and grow 2′ tall. One of its attributes is its cold tolerance, hardy to zone 4.

*P. braunii*, Braun's holly fern, is a slower growing fern more common in northern states than in the South. The leaflets (pinnae) are cut into about a dozen subleaflets, giving this semi-evergreen plant a much finer feel than Christmas fern. The stems are covered with long tanned scales, and the new fronds often have a silvery flush to them and as they mature, turn glossy green. Easily grown. Zones 4-7.

*P. munitum* is the Western equivalent to the Christmas fern. It differs by having more pointed and longer fronds. Evergreen, smaller and hardy to zone 5.

## *Potentilla* (po-ten-till′ a) Cinquefoil Rosaceae

Most of the 500 species of cinquefoil are herbaceous, although the best known and probably the most useful species in North American gardens is the woody bush cinquefoil, *P. fruticosa*. Cinquefoils prefer cool soils and cool nights to look their best; there are few areas where plants are as pretty as the catalog photo, and they are essentially useless south of zone 6, although I surely have not seen them all. Many herbaceous species are offered in the trade (more than this genus warrants) and some are seed propagated, resulting in significant variation.

The name comes from *potens*, meaning powerful, in reference to the supposed usefulness of the genus in medicine and magic. In particular, common cinquefoil, *P. reptans*, was considered most effective against ague (chills, fever). The number of leaves a man needed was immaterial as long as "Jupiter is in the ascendant and the Moon applying to him" (Culpepper, 1649). Early dentists also provided their unsuspecting patients with a root concoction because "the decoction of the roots held in the mouth doth mitigate the paine of the teeth." (Gerard, 1597).

Most cinquefoils have palmate leaves that people may mistake for strawberries, and are seldom more than 2′ tall. The 5-petaled flowers may be yellow, red, rose, or white. Many species, useful for the rock garden, form mats of 4-12″ tall foliage.

Quick Reference to Potentilla Species

| | Height (in.) | Flower color | Leaves in 3s or 5s |
|---|---|---|---|
| *P. atrosanguinea* | 18-30 | Red | 3 |
| *P. nepalensis* | 12-24 | Purple | 5 |
| *P. neumanniana* | 6-9 | Yellow | 5 |
| *P. recta* | 12-30 | Yellow | 5 |
| *P. tridentata* | 6-12 | White | 3 |

***-atrosanguinea*** (at-ro-sang-guin′ ee-a) Himalayan Cinquefoil 18-30″/24″
Summer Red Himalayas Zones 5-7

Having seen plants in numerous places around the world, I can confidently state that its main contribution to gardening is as a parent for a number of named hybrids, and not for its own beauty and performance. The silky-hairy leaves are three-parted with toothed margins. The 5-8″ long petioles make the plant look stretched by early summer. The 1″ wide flowers are deep red but plants are not particularly floriferous. Full sun, cool nights and good drainage are prerequisites for good performance.

Propagate the species by seed and the hybrids by division.

**Hybrids with *P. atrosanguinea*:**

'Firedance' grows only 12″ tall and is more compact than the species. Deep coral flowers are produced.

'Flamenco' has blood red flowers with a dark eye. Plants can stretch to 2′ tall.

'Gibson's Scarlet' was highly touted as a tough, brilliantly colored plant but has not lived up to expectations in much of the United States. The flowers are deep scarlet and plants are more compact than *P. atrosanguinea*.

'Gold Kugel' is an orange-golden-flowered selection that tends to get a little weedy.

'Glory of Nancy' is an old hybrid with large, 2″ wide double flowers of red and gold. It also has lovely gray-green leaves and is one of the better hybrids.

'Hamlet' is a scarlet double-flowered form.

'Monsieur Rouillard' bears double orange-red flowers.

'Reyneur' also has scarlet semi-double flowers with a very small black center.

'Vulcan' has deep red double flowers, growing only about 12″ tall.

'William Rollisson' has semi-double vermilion flowers with yellow backs. Plants grow about 15″ tall.

'Yellow Queen' has bright yellow single flowers over silvery foliage and attains but 12″ in height.

| ***-nepalensis*** (ne-pa-len′ sis) | | Nepal Cinquefoil | 12-24″/20″ |
|---|---|---|---|
| Summer | Crimson | Nepal | Zones 4-7 |

This single-flowered species produces many strawberry-like purple to crimson flowers in early summer and continues to flower sporadically throughout the summer. Although flowering continues for a relatively long time, plants persist for only 2-3 years in most settings. The basal leaves are long stalked, up to 1′ long, and the 2″ long leaflets are coarsely toothed. The 1″ wide flowers are rose-red and held in loose, branching panicles. The plant is compact until the long leafy stems rise up to 2′ or more in the summer, at which time severe pruning is necessary.

The species and cultivars arise fairly true from seed.

**Cultivars:**

'Miss Willmott' (var. *willmottiae*) is 10-12″ tall and produces carmine flowers with a darker base. It is a better choice than the species.

'Melton Fire' has strawberry red flowers with a flush of lemon yellow and purple centers.

'Ron McBeth' has quite lovely carmine red flowers, an improvement to the older 'Miss Willmott'. Plants are about 12″ tall.

'Shogran' also has red flowers but grows only 6-8″ tall.

'Roxana' bears orange-scarlet flowers on 18″ stems.

***-neumanniana*** (new-man′-e ann-a) Spring Cinquefoil 6-9″/12″
Spring Yellow Western Europe Zones 4-7

The name keeps changing on this dwarf plant, darting in and out of *P. tabernaemontani*, *P. verna* and now *P. neumanniana*. However, if you can find them, they work well in well-drained sunny areas regardless of the name. The mat-producing species has numerous decumbent 2-5″ long rooting stems. The long-petioled leaves are 5-7 palmate, wedge shaped and serrated near the apex. The ½″ wide golden yellow flowers are held in 3-5 flowered cymes at the end of 6-8″ long ascending stems.

**Cultivars:**

'Nana' is only about 4″ tall and covered with golden yellow flowers almost the same size as the species. The best of the species.

***-recta*** (rek′ ta) Sulphur Cinquefoil 12-30″/15″
Summer Yellow Southern Europe Zones 3-7

Introduced from Europe, plants can be troublesome weeds, particularly in the limestone areas of the Midwest and Northeast. Plants are tufted with leaves consisting of 5-9 toothed, densely hairy leaflets about 2-4″ long. Three-quarter inch diameter yellow flowers are carried on terminal compact corymbs.

All are easily seed propagated under warm (70-75°F) moist conditions. Plants may also be divided after 2-3 years.

**Cultivars:**

var. *sulphurea* is similar to the species but has sulphur-yellow flowers.

'Macrantha' (var. *warrenii*) has 1″ diameter bright yellow flowers in loose terminal clusters. It is not as weedy as the species and flowers for a longer time. This is the best form of the species for the garden.

***-tridentata*** (tri-den′ ta-tah) Three-Toothed Cinquefoil 4-10″/12″
Summer White Northeastern North America Zones 2-8

Plants are native from Greenland to North Georgia and are included because of their tenacious growing habit. They grow on rock outcroppings and fill in areas thought to be unuseable, and are particularly useful for acid soils. The basal leaves consist of 3 leaflets with 3 prominent teeth at the apex (thus the common name). The stem leaves, however, are often entire. The small, ¼″ wide white flowers cover the plants in early summer and although many plants are more ornamental, they can be lovely when properly sited and are particularly useful on dry banks and rocky areas.

Propagate by seed or division of the runners.

**Cultivars:**

'Minima' is a dwarf, more compact form of the species.

**Related Species:**

*P. alba*, white cinquefoil, is a handsome 3-5″ tall ground cover well suited for the rock garden or other sunny, well-drained area. Plants have glossy leaves with 5 palmate leaflets and pure white flowers in early spring.

var. *argyrophylla*, undersnow cinquefoil, is similar to Himalayan cinquefoil except that the flowers are yellow rather than red. Formerly known as *P. argyrophylla*.

*P. aurea*, golden cinquefoil, is also a low-growing potentilla (8-10″) with yellow flowers. The stems of *P. neumanniana* root much like runners and thus the plant becomes a mat, whereas those of *P. aurea* ascend, resulting in clumps. It is a useful, colorful ground cover for full sun.

*P.* x *hopwoodiana*, a cross between *P. nepalensis* and *P. recta*, the weedlike sulphur cinquefoil, is about 18″ tall with pink flowers, rosy red at the base and edged white on the margins.

*P. megalantha*, native to Japan, has a fuzzy, cuddly rosette of leaves consisting of 3 leaflets. The plants are 6-8″ tall and bear solitary 1-2″ wide bright yellow flowers in the spring.

*P. reptans*, common cinquefoil, is a 4-6″ ground cover, bearing many yellow flowers. 'Pleniflora' has double yellow flowers.

*P. thurberi*, thurber cinquefoil, is native to New Mexico and California. It is shorter than *P. nepalensis* and commonly has 7 leaflets rather than 5. The flowers are a rich dark brown to purple and are held in an open inflorescence. In *P. nepalensis*, the petals are nearly twice as long as the sepals but are about the same size in *P. thurberi*. From the garden viewpoint, there is little difference between them, although *P. thurberi* may be longer lived and more heat tolerant. 'Monarch's Velvet' has deep red flowers.

*P.* x *tonguei*, a cross between *P. anglica* and *P. nepalensis*, is offered by many nurserymen. It has lovely salmon, single flowers with a pinkish center. Plants are only 3-8″ tall and make a pretty ground cover for sunny areas. Cold hardy to zone 5, it has problems with heat above zone 7.

## ***Primula*** (prim′ eu-la) Primrose Primulaceae

Primroses are nature's way of welcoming spring, and their absence from the garden is excusable only if climate does not allow successful culture. Most garden species are not long lived but their beauty makes them well worth growing, even as annuals. There are over 400 species, many of which are more at home in the moist cool climate of the British Isles, New Zealand, Canada, and the Pacific Coast than in areas of the United States where summer droughts and temperature extremes are common. However, many primroses are perfectly cold hardy to zone 3 and nearly all are cold hardy to zone 5. Only a few do well in the South (as far south as zone 8), although it is often assumed, incorrectly in many cases, that they will not survive hot, dry summers. One should never assume anything without trialing, and within this genus, numerous highly adaptable species exist. However, having said that, almost without exception, primroses thrive in relatively cool summers, adequate levels of moisture and well-drained soils that allow moisture to drain freely away from roots in the winter. While one can see many species growing in full sun in England the great majority of this country is not even close to the English climate. Shade is necessary for the majority of available primroses, however the water lovers tolerate more sun as long as their love is fulfilled.

The majority of primulas are native to northern temperate zones and species occur in bogs, meadows, woodlands, and rockeries. They range in size from the tiny 1″ tall

*P. minima*, least primrose, to tall, stately candelabra primroses such as *P. japonica*. The unique *P. vialii*, has violet-blue flowers held in a short, dense spike, completely atypical of primrose. Many of the common garden primroses are hybrids of *P. veris*, common cowslip, *P. vulgaris*, English primrose, and *P. juliae*, Julia primrose, and are known as polyantha primroses or "polys" for short. Breeders have increased the size of the flowers while making the plants more compact. They are popular as potted plants in Europe and have gained some following as bedding and potted plants in North America. *P. malacoides*, another pot plant species, is used extensively in winter gardens of Australia and New Zealand but is not sufficiently weather tolerant to be used here. Great drifts of white, pink, and burgundy brighten the winter landscape at every corner.

The meadowland species of Europe such as *P. veris*, *P. elatior* and *P. vulgaris* are most common in the United States, but species from China (*P. pulverulenta*), Japan (*P. japonica*, *P. sieboldii*), the Himalayas (*P. denticulata*, *P. florindae*), and mountainous regions of Europe (*P. auricula*, *P. allionii*) are also available to the primrose lover. All require consistently moist soil and partial shade. Winters seldom result in plant losses, but fluctuations of soil moisture during the hot summer months can be devastating.

There are so many species that one can become as much a primula collector (or at least an admirer) as a hosta or daylily collector. In my case, since north Georgia is not the most amenable area for primrose culture, I must use my camera and eyes more than my soil and trowel. A number of primula I have admired won't make it into this book, due to lack of space and availability, however I love *P. burmanica*, with its stout flower stems rising 2′ in the air and covered with purple-red flowers, *P. capitata* with its rich blue-violet buttonlike heads of flowers and *P. glomerata*, whose flowers remind me of *Scabiosa*. If you can find some of these, send me a few. I love that some of the northern nurseries like Evermay Nursery in Old Town, Maine, offer dozens upon dozens of primroses. Go visit online and support their efforts.

The taxonomy of this diverse genus has long occupied the minds of botanists and is presently divided into thirty sections. The most valuable sections horticulturally are Auricula, that contains *P. auricula* and other low-growing species for cool climates and the cool greenhouse; Candelabra, containing a vast array of species with whorls of flowers in tiers on long flower stems; Denticulata, the home of the drumstick primrose, *P. denticulata*; and Vernales, where the ever-popular cowslips, oxslips, and polyanthas reside. I have probably covered way too many plants in this tome (probably why the damn thing is so heavy), but I will have barely touched on the diversity in this genus.

Quick Reference to Primula Species

| | Height (in.) | Type of inflorescence | Need for moisture |
|---|---|---|---|
| *P. auricula* | 2-8 | Umbel | Moderate |
| *P. denticulata* | 8-10 | Globe | Moderate |
| *P. florindae* | 24-30 | Umbel | Critical |
| *P. japonica* | 12-24 | Umbels in tiers | Critical |
| *P.* x *polyantha* | 8-12 | Umbel | Low |
| *P. sieboldii* | 4-8 | Umbel | Moderate |
| *P. vialii* | 12-15 | Spike | Moderate |
| *P. vulgaris* | 6-9 | Solitary | Low |

***-auricula*** (ow-rik′ ew-la) | Auricula Primrose | 2-8″/8″
Spring | Yellow | European Alps | Zones 3-7

Although the flower color of the ancient species is bright yellow, many color forms are common in cultivation. The 1″ wide flowers are bell shaped and usually fragrant. The thick leaves are 2-3″ long and equally wide. Two main forms of *P. auricula* occur, those with flowers and stems densely coated with a white mealy substance (farina), and those that are smooth and not powdery. Both types contain flowers of a single color (i.e. no eye) as well as those with a white or yellow eye. Plants are shallow rooted and should have winter protection to reduce heaving from alternate freezing and thawing. The species is not difficult to grow, but unfortunately, is difficult to locate. Although some cultivars are beautiful, there is something wonderful about growing the species that people have been trying to "improve" for over 350 years.

Auricula enthusiasts have developed dozens of cultivars which are often found in the homes and gardens of collectors, much like African violets. They are classified as show, alpine, double and border auriculas, and remind me of delicate Hummel figurines. I bought a couple of plants of Barnhaven hybrids recently but they succumbed within a year to the wonderful southeastern summer. Beautiful but not particularly rugged.

The species and some named cultivars are best propagated from seed. Divisions or 1-2″ long stem cuttings may be taken from established plants after flowering or in the fall. Root in a moist mixture of clean peat and sand. When plants are large enough, they can be placed in the garden. Most auriculas are purchased as collections, providing a number of colors for containers.

***-denticulata*** (den-tik-ew-lah′ ta) | Drumstick Primrose | 8-10″/12″
Spring | Lilac, White | Himalayas | Zones 4-7

Globular flower heads atop thin stems make this species easy to recognize. The leaves are spatulate (look like spatulas), and sharply toothed. They are 4-6″ long at flowering time, and later expand to a foot after flowering. Flowers appear when leaves are just emerging, and both leaves and flower stems expand at the same time. Drumstick primroses are some of the earliest to flower, opening in March and April.

In North Georgia, my plants were wonderfully green all winter, until temperatures of 10°F settled in for several nights. Without snow cover, those temperatures were particularly devastating and plants were badly damaged. Many plants recovered and flowered well but flower stems were thin and weak. The use of winter mulch in all climes where snow cover is minimal is highly recommended. Evergreen boughs or loose pine straw should be placed over the plants during the winter. Leaves or other materials that become heavy and smother the plants should be avoided. If plants are grown in a warm greenhouse during the winter and planted in the spring, they may not receive sufficient cold to flower. Fall planting is best because plants receive natural cold treatment in the fall and winter and flowering is improved. Moist, partially shaded areas are necessary for best garden performance.

All are best propagated by seed. Sow seed in May to June for fall planting or September to October for spring planting. Division is also a useful method of propagation.

**Cultivars:**
'Alba' is a popular white-flowered form.
'Cashmeriana' is a large purple-flowered form with yellow powdery farina beneath the foliage.
'Cashmeriana Rubin' ('Rubins') has carmine-red flowers.
'Karryann' has creamy yellow variegation on the leaf margins. Flowers are light mauve.
Ronsdorf Strain is a seed-propagated mixture of white, purple, bluish, or rose flowers held about a foot above the foliage.

***-florindae*** (flo-rin′ day) Florinda Primrose 2-3′/2′
Late Spring, Summer Yellow Tibet Zones 6-8

If you have read anything about the early plant explorers who suffered immense hardships and adventures in China, you will want to obtain some of these plants, found by Frank Kingdom-Ward and named for his wife, Florinda. If you enjoy high escapade combined with plant lore and horticulture history, you will relish the true stories.

Plants enjoy damp locations and look their best in moist soils beside a stream or pond. The broad glossy leaves are ovate and have a heart-shaped base, and are attached to the stem by reddish winged petioles. At the top of the strong stems are borne yellow, farinose flowers. The term "farinose' means having a mealy, granular texture, which often can be rubbed off. There may be up to 40 such flowers, each about 1″ across and with a strong fragrance. I haven't seen too many good plantings of this species in the United States but a sunny area with rich, consistently moist soils will please both the gardener and the plant.

Propagate by seed or division.

**Cultivars:**
Keilour Hybrids have flowers in shades of yellow.

***-japonica*** (ja-pon′ i-ka) Japanese Primrose 12-24″/24″
Late Spring Various Japan Zones 5-7

This and many related species have been placed in the division Candelabra due to the many whorls of flowers superimposed on the flower stem. *P. japonica*, which is probably the least temperamental of the candelabra types, bears 2-6 whorls of purple flowers; each whorl consists of 8-12 flowers nearly an inch across and held at right angles to the stem on ¾″ long pedicels. To round a corner and see a display of these plants in full bloom is a marvelous experience. The leaves are 6-12″ long, 2-4″ wide and have irregularly shaped dentations on the margins. As with all the candelabra types, proper conditions for success are critical. Moist soil and a boggy area that does not dry out in the summer are ideal. Place where there is some water movement as plants languish under stagnant conditions. Roots require cool, moist conditions and the tops should be in a shady area. One of the finest displays I have seen in this country is at Winterthur Gardens, Delaware (zone 6), although lovely plantings also occur at Sky Hook in Vermont (zone 4). The grandest planting must be at Longstock Park Water Garden in England, where hundreds of stately candelabras vie for attention with the gunneras, *Iris laevigata*, hosta, mimulas, ferns and other moisture-loving species. A trip in early summer to any of these gardens is worth the effort. I have even had success in the Armitage garden by placing some at the side of a small water feature, where the plants are consistently misted and moist.

Significant natural hybridization occurs among cultivars and species in the Candelabra group and it is best to locate taxa some distance from each other. Self-sown seedlings develop into lovely, but differently colored plants than the parents.

Most candelabra primroses can be raised from seed. Sow seed as soon as ripe or as soon as received. Seeds sown in June or July may be large enough to plant out the same year. If sowing is delayed until the fall, plants will not be large enough to transplant until the following spring. *P. japonica* and *P. pulverulenta* are effectively propagated by division but others of the candelabra group may also be carefully divided.

**Cultivars:**

'Album' produces white flowers.

'Jim Saunders' arose from Longstock Park Water Garden and is named after one of the former head gardeners there. The flowers are a rich cherry red.

'Miller's Crimson' has bright red flowers.

'Postford White' is one of the finest cultivars to date. It has large white flowers, each with a yellow eye. Better than 'Album'.

'Rosea' has pink to rose blooms. 'Miller's Crimson and 'Rosea' come true from seed.

Redfield hybrids arose from seedlings in the Redfield garden in Hampton, Connecticut.

Rowallane hybrids arose from Rowallane Garden in Northern Ireland. Vigorous and beautiful.

-x ***polyantha*** (pah-lee-anth' a) Polyantha Primrose 8-12″/9″
Spring Various Hybrid Zone 3-8

This is the most common and popular group of primroses in American gardens. It is a mixture of *P. veris*, the fragrant, deep yellow cowslip primrose, *P. vulgaris*, the sulphur yellow English primrose, and probably *P. juliae*, the bright purple-flowered Julian primrose. The parents are lovely species, and some such as *P. juliae* have also been hybridized to yield such excellent cultivars as 'Wanda', a dark purple-red flower, and the most interesting 'Garryarde Guinevere', with purple-tinted foliage and shell pink flowers.

The many years of hybridizing *P.* x *polyantha* have resulted in a glorious array of flower colors, some with large eyes and others clear faced. The small leaves are dark green and heavily veined. The flowers may be up to 1½″ across in single or bicolor shades and arranged in umbels on 4-6″ tall stems. The polys belong to the Vernales group and although members do not appreciate dry soils, the requirement for constant moisture is not as critical as for other groups of primrose. Natural fertilizer, such as composted cow manure, applied generously once a year is most helpful.

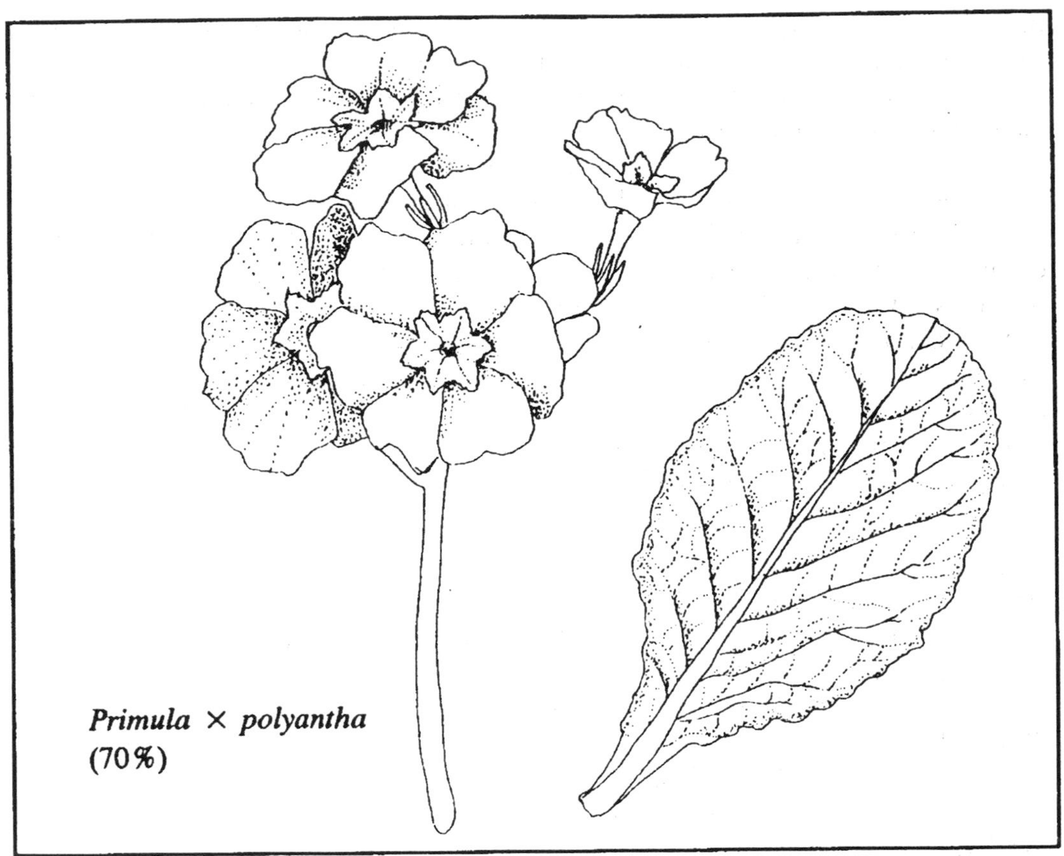

*Primula* × *polyantha*
(70%)

The polyantha hybrids have received tremendous attention from plant breeders, particularly those in the greenhouse trade. The florist primrose has long been a staple in the pot plant market in Europe and Japan but still has not caught on in North America. If a potted primrose is purchased as a gift, enjoy it indoors and then plant outside when weather permits. Primroses are an important bedding plant in the Northwest where conditions are ideal. Slugs and spider mites are the principal pests of polys. We have trialed many cultivars of polys as fall-planted landscape plants in the Gardens at UGA but they can't yet compete with pansies. The cold weather and lack of snow cover results in a good deal of leaf disfiguration and death, and plants struggle. However, we keep looking for more uses in the East for these beautiful hybrids.

Propagate by division or fresh seed.

**Cultivars:**

Many strains and hybrids are available from nurseries, additional colors and names are being developed by American, European, and Japanese breeders every year.

Barnhaven hybrids have large vibrant flowers borne on diminutive foliage. One of the finest hybrids developed.

Danova series is a mix of colors and has been the best performer in all our trials.

'Giant Bouquet' is similar to 'Monarch' and bears 2-2½" diameter flowers.

Monarch strain has 2″ diameter flowers of mixed colors but is also available in single colors.
'Pacific Giant' is a seed mixture of large-flowered plants in shades of blue, yellow, red, pink, or white.
'Tie Dye' has wonderful blue and yellow bicolor flowers. They were more heat tolerant than I suspected and persisted for 3 years in the Armitage garden.

***-sieboldii*** (see-bold′ ee-eye) Siebold Primrose 4-8″/8″
Late Spring Various Japan Zones 4-8

Plants are pubescent everywhere but the flower. The 2-4″ long ovate leaves are heart shaped at the base and have scalloped margins. The petioles are often longer than the leaf blades. The 1-1½″ wide flowers are held well above the foliage in 6-10 flowered umbels. They are usually purple with a white eye but may be white or rose. It is a wonderfully showy species and needs to be tried more often. In North American gardens, the foliage often goes dormant in late summer.

The species is somewhere between *P. japonica* and *P.* x *polyantha* in its requirement for moisture. Plants must not be allowed to dry out repeatedly but do not have to be planted in a bog-like setting. They have been used successfully in moist woodland plantings.

Propagation by seed but cuttings may be taken similar to *P. auricula*.

**Cultivars:**
'Akatonbo' has dark rose, lacy flowers.
'Isotaka' bears 8-10 flowered umbels of beautiful white blooms backed in purple-pink hues.
'Pago-Pago' provides reddish to pink flowers.
var. *purpurea* bears masses of purple red flowers.
'Shi-un' has large lavender flowers.
'Snowflake' produces large white flowers.
'Sumina' bears large blooms of wisteria blue.

***-vialii*** (vee-ahl′ ee-eye) Vial's Primrose 12-15″/12″
Spring Violet-Purple China Zones 5-7

The first time people see a well-grown clump of plants, they guess anything but a primrose. The leafless flower stems emerge from the large rosette and bear spikes of violet-purple flowers. The flowers are red in bud, turn violet and then fade to pink. They are plants to be enjoyed on the West Coast or in overseas travels; I have not seen many successful plantings in the East, and none in the South. Of course, half the fun is trying. Provide moisture-retentive alkaline soils and partial shade.

Propagate from seed or division.

***-vulgaris*** (vul-gah′ ris) English Primrose 6-9″/9″
Spring Yellow Europe Zones 5-8

This is one of the easier primroses to grow, tolerating drier soil conditions and more heat than many others. The leaves are tufted, often wrinkled, and downy beneath resulting in a soft pubescent feel. They are about 2-3″ long at flowering time but, like *P. denticulata*, continue to expand and within a month of flowering, double in size. The tubular, 1″ wide flowers are sulphur yellow, often with a dark yellow blotch near the eye, and are borne singly. The flowers do not have the "take-your-breath-away" quality of other primroses but a group of a dozen in full spring finery helps provide that elusive, relaxing feel of the English garden. This species and *P. kisoana* are the most rewarding for Southern gardeners.

This species has also been an important parent of the *P.* x *polyantha* hybrids and so many crosses, self-crosses, and back crosses have occurred that the Vernales group is becoming a taxonomic free-for-all.

Propagate by seed or division.

**Cultivars:**

'Jack-in-the-Green' is an old cultivar whose curious charm has stayed the test of time. The flowers are pale yellow and are surrounded by large greenish sepals which look like a loose-fitting collar.

'Katie McSparron' is a cultivar of *P. veris*, and provides handsome double yellow flowers in the spring. In the Gardens at UGA, they were exceptional for three years, then succumbed. One of my favorite primroses.

'Quaker's Bonnet' is only one of numerous double forms of *P. vulgaris*. Double deep rose flowers occur in spring.

'Rubra' has rose-colored flowers.

subsp. *sibthorpii* has early-emerging pink flowers, although some may be nearly white. Doubles and hose-in-hose variants sometimes occur. The earliest of the early primroses; undemanding and handsome, highly recommended.

**Related Species:**

*P.* x *bullesiana* is a cross between *P. bulleyana* and *P. beesiana*, a species with fragrant rose flowers with yellow eyes named for Bee's Nursery in Chester, UK. Flowers occur in rich shades of violet, wine, and yellow.

*P. bulleyana*, named for A.K. Bulley, the founder of the aforementioned Bee's Nursery, has flowers of deep reddish orange and has been hybridized with a number of other candelabra species to produce an array of interesting flower shades.

*P. chungensis* bears whorls of fragrant red tubular flowers with orange petals.

*P. heladoxa* has large, golden yellow flowers with deeply notched petals. Six, 12-20 flowered whorls may occur on 24″ tall plants. Plants are particularly showy in moist, open places.

*P. kisoana* is one of the best primroses for gardeners who don't have primrose-friendly garden spots. Heat tolerant and with a low degree of difficulty in normal soils. The rounded leaves are wrinkled and the stoloniferous nature allows colonies to increase. The pink flowers are only 4-6″ tall but they make a pleasant mat in the spring. A white form is also available.

*P. latifolia*, sticky primrose, has sticky foliage and ½″ wide rose-red flowers arranged in 10-25 flowered umbels. Plants require limey soils to perform well. They are sometimes listed as *P. viscosa*.

*P.* x *pubescens*, a cross between *P. auricula* and *P. rubra*, bears rose-purple flowers with a white eye. Probably the oldest hybrid primrose in cultivation, it is represented by many forms and cultivars. 'Bewerley White' has creamy white flowers on 6-8″ long flower stems. 'Mrs. J. H. Wilson' bears 1-2″ diameter rose-purple flowers with white eyes.

*P. pulverulenta* has deep red flowers with a deeper red or purple eye. The scape is mealy and carries many whorls of flowers. The best cultivar is 'Bartley's Strain', with lovely soft pink flowers. The species is an important parent in many hybrid candelabra primroses.

*P. sikkimensis*, Sikkim primula, is similar to the former species, but is usually shorter. The glossy, wrinkled leaves are oblong and the flowers are yellow or creamy white. Plants need consistent moisture.

## ***Prunella*** (pru-nell′ a) Self-Heal Lamiaceae

Of the approximately 12 species, the most common is *P. vulgaris*, the familiar self-heal that is an invader of lawns. However, a few species have wonderful ornamental features as well. All have opposite leaves, terminal spikes of whorled flowers and self-sow vigorously. The main species used in gardens is *P. grandiflora*, often offered as *P.* x *webbiana*.

**-*grandiflora*** (grand-i-flor′ a) Self-Heal 9-12″/12″
Summer Purple Europe Zone 5-7

The opposite leaves are 3-4″ long and 1-2″ wide, usually dark green with entire margins. The purple flowers are held on short compact inflorescences, each flower subtended by a small bract. Consistently moist soil and full sun to partial shade are preferable. In areas of cool summers, they can be quite aggressive and have been known to escape and roam freely throughout the garden. Moisture is important since plants that consistently dry out quickly die. Growth is better in zone 5 than in zone 7.

**Cultivars:**

'Alba' has pale pink to white flowers.

'Little Red Riding Hood' has crimson red spikes and is about six inches tall.

'Loveliness' has pale lavender flowers. The "Loveliness" group may well be hybrids (*P.* x *webbiana*).

'Pink Loveliness' bears pink flowers. I was pleasantly surprised with the performance of this cultivar in my Georgia garden, but their longevity under such warm environments is marginal at best.

'Red Cap' has rosy red flowers.

'Summer Daze' is a dwarf compact form with many pink flowers, slightly flared at the ends.

'White Loveliness' produces large white flowers and is the best white form. 'Blue Loveliness' is mentioned here and there, but I have never seen it.

**Related Species:**

*P.* x *webbiana* likely resulted from the crossing of *P. grandiflora* and *P. g.* var. *pyrenaica* (*P. hastaefolia*) and is often also listed as *P. grandiflora.* The only differences between *P. grandiflora* and *P.* x *webbiana* are that *P.* x *webbiana* has shorter blunter leaves, more compact flower spikes, and is shorter. Both have dark purple flowers and similar growth habits. The cultivars above may also appear under the hybrid listing.

***Pteridium*** (ter-id-ee′ um) Bracken Fern Polypodiaceae

A fern which one either loves or hates, depending on whether it colonizes the entire homestead. *P. aquilinum* is the dandelion of roadsides on the West Coast, and anyone who has traveled in northern Europe can not help but comment on these aggressive weeds along the roadways. The ferns are 2-3 times pinnate, one of the terrestrial ferns with compound fronds. The fronds look like big wings, and the genus name comes from the Greek word *pteron*, meaning wing.

Plants are large, 2-4′, and extremely aggressive in well-drained soils. They are northern ferns and do poorly in areas of high heat and humidity. Interestingly, although ferns can be incredibly aggressive, this is a difficult fern to transplant, especially if given a piece from your neighbor. The best bet is to gather the rhizome with a newly developing frond, transplant to rich soil, then once established, plant it out. A few ornamental cultivars have been selected, including 'Cristatum' with crested fronds. 'Grandiceps' is much less aggressive and is a curious plant with reduced fronds.

Bracken ferns are beautiful to those who can't grow them, they are miserable for those who can't get rid of it. Perhaps I can trade with someone for a few pieces of kudzu?

***Pulmonaria*** (pul-mon-air′ ee-a) Lungwort Boraginaceae

Lungworts have been around forever, and there always seems to be a new one to look at. So many additional lungworts are now available even since the second edition (1997) that they are getting out of control. Of the 12-14 species, four are particularly attractive for the shade garden. All produce blue or pink flowers in the spring, generally opening one color-usually pink-then turning blue before falling. This charming habit has given rise to the common name of soldiers and sailors. Flowers open before the foliage emerges or at the same time, often as early as early March in the South and a few weeks later in the Midwest and North. The alternate stem leaves are often spotted and sometimes provide better identification characteristics than the basal leaves.

The breeding efforts of Dan Heims of Terra Nova Nursery have repainted the palette of pulmonarias. On the one hand, we have much more choice, on the other hand, it is difficult to tell one from the other or to know if all cultivars perform well. This is one of the best genera for partially shaded gardens and will only receive more attention as gardens become more shaded over time.

In the sixteenth and seventeenth centuries, the "Doctrine of Signatures" was practiced by herbalists of that time. This doctrine, based on a treatise by Theoprastus Bombast von Hohenheim (1493-1541), better known as Paracelsus, suggested that the outward appearance of plants dictated their virtues. Thus the perforated leaves of common St. John's-wort indicated that it was useful remedy for cuts and wounds; the convoluted shell of the walnut was specific for troubles of the brain, and the spotted leaf of *Pulmonaria*, which so resembled a diseased lung, was an obvious cure for ailments of that organ. The ancient study of herbalism had fallen to some of its lowest depths of irrationality during those times but is finally recovering. Today, herbal medicine is alive and robust, counting many gardeners and non-gardeners among the converts. Fortunately, those who understand the curative properties of our garden plants also understand that they don't need an outward appearance for inward contentment.

All the lungworts should be planted in partial shade and provided with adequate moisture. However, one of the quickest ways to lose them is to have wet soils, particularly in the winter. I am an expert in killing these plants, however, I am getting the hang of this drainage thing. They spread by creeping rootstocks, but not to the point of being invasive. They can look really lousy in the summer if allowed to dry out or if drowned. Lousiness is compounded by hot weather. If leaf margins look tattered, they may be cut back in the summer, fertilized lightly and will return fresh.

A drawback to the genus is its susceptibility to powdery mildew. I have seen plants turn white with the fungus, particularly if air circulation is poor, the air is wet and temperatures remain cool. A fungal spray (mildicide) may be applied in early spring. If planted in morning sun, mildew is much less of a problem. Cutting back and discarding infected leaves also helps reduce the incidence.

Presence or absence of obvious leaf spotting is a fairly easy beginning point to separate species from each other. Cultivars of *P. officinalis*, *P. longifolia* and *P. saccharata* are almost always spotted: *P. angustifolia* and *P. rubra* seldom are. This is how I begin teaching students the difference between them, however, as breeders do more hybridization, this distinction blurs.

Quick Reference to Pulmonaria Species

| | Height (in.) | Spotted leaves | Flower color |
|---|---|---|---|
| *P. angustifolia* | 9-12 | No | Bright blue |
| *P. longifolia* | 9-12 | Yes | Purple blue |
| *P. rubra* | 12-24 | No | Coral red |
| *P. saccharata* | 9-18 | Yes | Blue |

***-angustifolia*** (ang-gus-ti-fo′ lee-a) Blue Lungwort 9-12″/24″
Spring Bright Blue Central Europe Zones 2-7

Unspotted, bristly, lanceolate leaves emerge with the first flowers. Tight pink buds open into deep blue, drooping, funnel-shaped flowers. The flowers are among the bluest and most ornamental in the genus. It makes an excellent ground cover under shrubs and competes well with trees for water and nutrients. It performs better in the North than in the South (below zone 6) because the foliage tends to wilt under the warmer temperatures. Spring flowering is not affected. The leaves are sort of "just there" and these plants should be placed where the flowers can be enjoyed, then allow them to be overgrown with more colorful partners.

Propagate by division after flowering.

**Cultivars:**

'Azurea' sports lovely gentian blue flowers, tinted red in bud.

'Blaues Meer' has larger, brighter blue flowers than the species.

'Johnson's Blue' is a smaller form (only about 8-10″ tall and wide) with narrower leaves.

'Mawson's Variety' bears bright violet-blue flowers.

'Munstead Blue' has rich blue flowers and is similar to the previous cultivar.

'Rubra' bears light red flowers. As far as I know, this is the only pinkish open flower in the species.

***-longifolia*** (long-gi-fo′ lee-a) Long-Leafed Lungwort 9-12″/24″
Spring Purple-Blue Western Europe Zones 3-8

The name *longifolia* describes the long, narrow foliage (at least six times as long as wide). The dark green leaves are gray spotted and pointed, becoming narrower and smaller up the stem. Crowded terminal racemes of purple-blue flowers vie for attention in the spring, a little later than other species. It is a good plant for use as a ground cover or in the front of the garden and is the most adaptable to warm, humid conditions.

Propagate by division after flowering.

**Cultivars:**

'Bertram Anderson' has violet-blue flowers and dark green leaves spotted with silvery green.

'Cevennensis' is a naturally occurring variety from the Cevennes in France. Plants have long (up to 2′ long) narrow, silver-spotted leaves with dark violet-blue flowers. Stunning in containers and the garden. Supposedly more sun and drought tolerant; I have not noticed that.

'Coral Springs' has coral-pink flowers.

'Diana Clare' provides violet-blue flowers over narrow silvery foliage that is a little wider than the typical "longifolia" form. May be a hybrid.

'Golden Haze' is 'Bertram Anderson' but with gold margins. Interesting, but not as wonderful as 'Bertram' himself.

'Little Blue' bears spotted leaves with small blue flowers.

***-rubra*** (rew′ bra) Red Lungwort 12-24″/30″
Early Spring Bright Red Southeastern Europe Zones 4-7

This species is unique in a number of ways. Specifically, the flowers open early in the spring, one of the earliest of the lungworts to flower, and the coral red blooms are a marked departure from the usual blue hues. In fact, this color is not at all common in plants of the Boraginaceae. The light green foliage is evergreen in milder climates and has soft hairs that produce a velvety texture. The oblong leaves narrow abruptly into the stem and are virtually sessile. It is a pretty plant that makes an interesting splash in spring and then disappears into the summer landscape. Plants do better in the North than the South and are outstanding on the West Coast.

**Cultivars:**
'Albocorollata' has handsome white flowers that open later than the species.
'Barfield Pink' has soft unspotted foliage and red flowers with white margins.
'Bowle's Red' has deeper red flowers and lime-green slightly spotted leaves.
'Redstart' has dark red flowers and is more compact than the species.
'Salmon Glow' has showy salmon flowers.

| ***-saccharata*** (sa-ka-rah′ ta) | | Bethlehem Sage | 9-18″/24″ |
|---|---|---|---|
| Spring | Blue | Italy, France | Zones 3-7 |

By far, the most popular species of pulmonaria because of the availability of good cultivars and the highly prized spotted foliage. Leaves are more spotted than *P. longifolia* and appear to have had sugar dusted over the green leaves, thus the specific name. Leaves are about three times as long as broad and the white blotches tend to coalesce. The pink flower buds open into funnel-shaped flowers that turn blue with age. It is a useful addition as a foliage accent, even if plants do not flower.

Plants require sufficient moisture if leaves are to remain ornamental throughout the season. The spotted leaves show up well in the garden but few things look worse than wilted, ratty, spotted leaves. Although not as water loving as *Ligularia* or *Primula japonica*, adequate moisture- but well-drained soils- must be provided during the warm days and nights of summer.

Propagate from division after flowering.

**Cultivars and Hybrids:**

Many of the following are hybrids, with *P. saccharata*, *P. angustifolia* and occasionally *P. longifolia*. Trying to discriminate one from the other requires faith and guesswork. If ever too many cultivars existed, it is with this genus. I am not too sure if the explosion of hybrids is the gardener's gain, or just adds to the gardener's confusion.

'Alba' has white flowers and can be raised from seed.
'Apple Frost' is a compact grower with silver spotting over apple green leaves.
'Argentea' bears white flowers and almost solid silver leaves.
'Benediction', named for the Seattle gardener, Loie Benedict, bears deep blue flowers in early March and large silver-spotted leaves.
'Berries and Cream' has silvery leaves and rosy pink flowers that mature to lavender blue.
'Blue Ensign' has wide unspotted dark green leaves, likely from *P. angustifolia*, and large blue flowers.

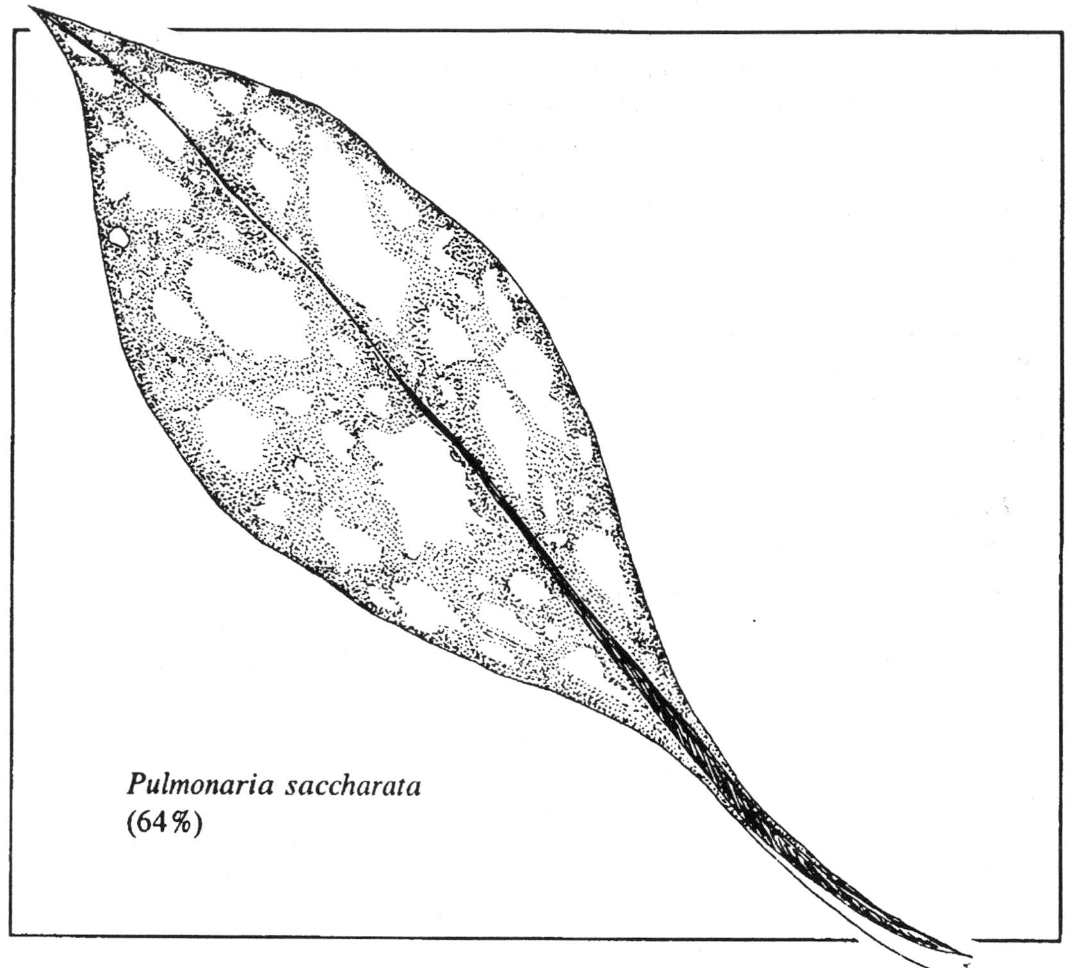

*Pulmonaria saccharata*
(64%)

'Blue Mist' has small leaves with many small white spots and flowers of the lightest blue.

'Boughton Blue' has silvery gray blotches randomly throughout the long, narrow leaves. The flowers are clear blue.

'British Sterling' is one of my favorites, although it is not as vigorous as I would like it to be. Magenta flower buds open to blue flowers over shiny leaves with silvery white spots that coalesce nicely. Most of the green is around the margin. Sounds awful, but quite beautiful.

'Cotton Cool' has handsome silver leaves and deep blue flowers.

'Dark Vader' (what was he smoking?) from Terra Nova Nursery is characterized by silver spotting on the leaves and blue flowers.

'David Ward' was supposed to take the gardening world by storm. The leaves are essentially variegated, with thin white margins around dull green blades. I first saw this plant at Butterstream Gardens outside Dublin, Ireland. Everyone there did a double take. Unfortunately, we are not in Dublin, Toto, and they have been a big disappointment on this side of the ocean.

'Dora Bielefeld' has lighter green foliage than many other cultivars. Plants have moderate silver spotting and persistent pink flowers.

'Excalibur' is quickly becoming popular due to the leaves being almost totally silvery white with a green margin and midrib. Absolutely brightens up the shade. Rosy flowers are secondary. Another terrific selection from Dan Heims.

'Glacier' has rounded green leaves with a good deal of silver spotting. The round leaves are different from most of the others. Light blue flowers in early spring.

'High Contrast' has narrow wavy foliage, speckled with white, and pink to blue flowers.

'Highdown' is taller than the species. Dangling rich blue flowers are produced very early in the spring.

'Janet Fisk' is one of the best I've tried, with heavily marbled foliage and pink flowers which fade to lavender. Vigorous and heat tolerant.

'Kingswood' has a random pattern of white throughout the dark green leaves. Blue flowers.

'Leopard' bears green foliage marked with silver blotches, and red-purple flowers.

'Lewis Palmer' has long, narrow silver-spotted foliage, the spots sometimes running together. Flowers open deep blue and fade to pink.

'Little Star' from Dan Heims has narrow leaves with silver spots. Deep blue flowers emerge early in the spring. Compact and neat.

'Majeste' comes from France and provides some of the most handsome silver foliage I have seen. Blue to pink flowers occur in the spring.

'Margery Fish', named after the noted English horticulturist, is more vigorous than the species and is a favorite in Europe. She varies from heavy spots to almost entirely silver. Although still grown here and there, she has been superseded by others.

'Merlin' comes from Europe and has both pink and blue flowers on the same plant in the spring. The leaves are short and moderately spotted.

'Milky Way' rapidly makes large clumps due its vigor. The heavily spotted leaves are long and narrow (like 'Roy Davidson') with deep blue flowers.

'Moonshine' has obvious silvering throughout the leaves in the spring, which changes to spotted as the season progresses. Small pale blue flowers occur in the spring.

'Mrs. Kittle' has clean white spots on dark green foliage. Not a big plant, but she looks good in the Armitage mix. Light rosy flowers.

'Mrs. Moon' is an old favorite with large silver-spotted leaves and pink flowers which turn blue. She is probably a hybrid with *P. officinalis*.

'Northern Lights' has silver foliage and large blue flowers.

'Nuernberg', from Germany, has pink and blue flowers together and leaves heavily spotted with silver.

'Pierre's Pure Pink' is named for Pierre Bennerup of Sunny Border Nursery, one of our more colorful confreres. The pink salmon flowers remain that color without fading; the leaves are moderately spotted.

'Pink Dawn' has striking spotted leaves with sprays of pink flowers.

'Raspberry Ice' has white margins in the spring that disappear with time. The flowers are deep pink to rose.

'Raspberry Flash' has similar rosy pink flowers as the previous cultivar but the leaves are splashed with white.
'Regal Ruffles' is quite different in flower than most other lungworts. The flowers are ruffled and tucked in the rosette of leaves.
'Roy Davidson' is a hybrid with *P. longifolia* and *P. saccharata*. The spotted leaves are longer than they are wide, but not to the extent of *P. longifolia*. They are heat tolerant and do well in hot, humid climes. The pink flowers turn blue with maturity.
'Samurai' is a hybrid for sure, probably with *P. longifolia* as one parent. Handsome silver foliage with dark margins are the norm, although the margins fade later in the season.
'Silver Lance' provides spotted, narrow foliage, suggesting some *P. longifolia* in the parentage, and coral red flowers.
'Silver Shimmers' has some of the largest blue flowers in the bunch, with silver to spotted leaves.
'Silver Streamers' has ruffled, almost pure silver foliage.
'Sissinghurst White' has large white flowers and silver-white spotted leaves. The flowers are most handsome but the foliage is not as striking as the species.
'Spangled Gentian', from Don Jacobs of Eco-Gardens, has long narrow leaves and gentian blue flowers.
'Smokey Blue' produces silvery spotted foliage and pink flowers which turn blue over time.
'Spilled Milk', again from the indomitable Mr. Heims, has broad foliage which is mostly silver, although spots of green are found here and there. Pink flowers.
'Trevi Fountain' is a hybrid with *P. longifolia*, thus having longer narrower leaves, each with silver spotting. The flowers are deep blue.
'Victorian Brooch' has blue, lavender and rose flowers on the same plant. Spotted white to silver foliage is also produced.

**Related Species:**

*P. officinalis*, Jerusalem cowslip, has rough, heart-shaped leaves usually spotted with white. They are not particularly showy, but the early blue and pink flowers are cheerful in the late winter and early spring. Flowers differ from *P. saccharata* by being smaller, while the leaves are more elliptical, sharp-pointed and rougher to the touch. 'Cambridge Blue' has darker blue flowers and 'White Wings' bears clean white blooms.

## ***Pulsatilla*** (pul-sa-til′ a) Pasque Flower Ranunculaceae

As I started rewriting this chapter, it seemed nobody but crazy rock gardeners or alpine enthusiasts grew pasque flower anymore. I know the genus is the state flower of South Dakota, so the people in Rapid City and Yankton must be awash in these plants, but where is everyone else? Was I alone among non-South Dakotans in thinking that this was one the greatest groups of plants for colorful early spring flowers and some of the most ornamental fruit in the entire plant kingdom? But then there it was in the Bluebird Nursery of Clarson, Nebraska's catalog: "The genus *Pulsatilla* was named 2006 Great Plants® Perennial of the Year!" This program is

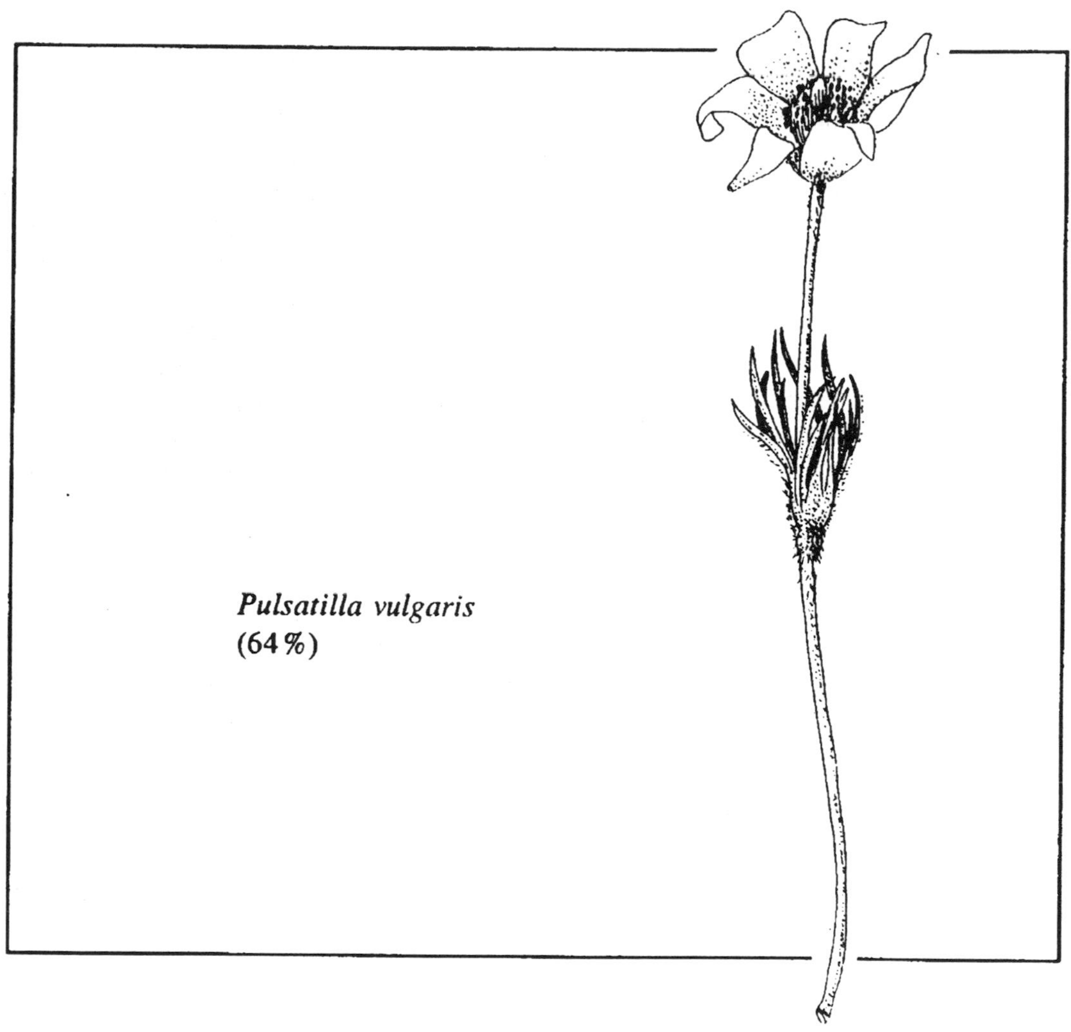
*Pulsatilla vulgaris*
(64%)

a cooperative venture between the Nebraska Nursery and Landscape Association and the Nebraska Statewide Arboretum. Yes, Virginia, there are great plantspeople in this country after all.

The lack of mainstream acceptance has to do with relatively scarcity of plant material (which will now change), poor tolerance of weather extremes, and the need for great drainage and cool temperatures. Sounds like a rock/alpine gardener's dream, doesn't it? However, as the Nebraska program points out, there is no reason why plants can't be placed in a mixed bed, as long as the environment suits it.

About a dozen species are known and all were once included with *Anemone*. Although some taxonomists still retain this marriage, the presence of feathery elongated styles on the fruit resulted in the separate genus. Flowers are apetalous (no petals) and wrapped in furry, pointed involucral leaves that unfurl as the satiny flowers open. Flower colors include the darkest violet (*P. pratensis*), forget-me-not blue (*P. halleri* 'Budapest'), yellow (*P. sylvestris*), and white (the North American *P. occidentalis*). Blossoms are borne singly in the axils of feathery, tufted foliage. The fruits, which are as ornamental as the flowers, double the garden value. The foliage dies back in mid to late summer.

In my first edition (1989), there was nobody trying anything but *P. vulgaris*, the common pasque flower. Today, few growers are offering plants of any species, the aforementioned program and affiliated growers not withstanding. Maybe more people need to visit the Denver Botanic Garden in early spring and see the various forms and species of pasque flower spilling everywhere in their rock garden. They reseed themselves, flower through the snow and act like a darn weed.

While the common pasque flower is certainly worth growing, so is *P. alpina*, alpine pasque flower, with its much divided foliage, white flowers (yellow in var. *sulphurea*) and huge feathery seed heads. Nor do we enjoy the considerable charm of *P. nuttalliana*, lion's beard, native of the western United States, whose large blossoms appear even before the leaves unfurl. Perhaps the loveliest of dwarf pasque flowers is *P. vernalis*, vernal pasque flower, whose light purple campanulate flowers open even before the snow disappears. But I waffle on the pasques, as I believe *P. halleri*, either with its pinkish flowers (subsp. *slavica*) or darker flowers (subsp. *styricha*) may be my favorite today. Tomorrow is yet another day. A rock garden enthusiast or a local specialty grower can assist in locating some of the difficult to obtain species.

*Pulsatilla* should be planted in full sun in the North and full sun to partial shade in the South. Many species are terrific rock garden plants and all require excellent drainage. They are not long lived at the best of times but if drainage is poor, plants seldom survive the season. All pasque flowers are better suited to climates with moderate summer temperatures and low humidity.

***-vulgaris*** (vul-gah′ ris) Pasque Flower 9-12″/12″
Early Spring Purple Europe Zones 5-7

The emergence of the plants alone is a good enough reason to grow them. The silky hairy leaves pushing out of the ground in late winter or early spring are themselves exceptionally ornamental. The wine purple, urn-shaped flowers appear before the foliage has fully emerged and consist of six pointed sepals (no petals) that encircle egg-yolk yellow stamens. Soon after the flower has closed for the last time, the feathery seed head rises 12-15″ above the foliage. The basal leaves are 4-6″ long, pinnately dissected, and silky hairy when young. Plants will seed themselves all over, if you are lucky, then go summer dormant.

Propagate by fresh seed because seeds go dormant soon after maturity (See *Actaea*). Plants may be carefully divided after they have been well established but in general, do not transplant well.

**Cultivars:**

'Alba' has pretty, creamy white flowers that offer better contrast to the leaves than the purple flowers of the species. We had success with this plant in the Gardens at UGA, flowering in early April and persisting for two weeks. The silky flower heads lasted well into May.

subsp. *grandis* is the same as the species but is more vigorous, bigger and more suitable for the border.

Heiler hybrids encompass a wide range of flower colors from cream to dark red. Plants are about 12″ tall.

'Papegano' differs by having fringed semi-double flowers, in a range of colors.

'Rubra' has flowers that some call red but are really more of an intense purple. I have also seen this listed as 'Red Clock'.

**Related Species:**

*P. patens*, spreading pasque flower, is only 4-8″ tall and bears lavender flowers in early spring.

## ***Puschkinia*** (push-kin′ ee-a) Striped Squill Liliaceae

This small genus is closely related to *Scilla* and *Chionodoxa* but differs botanically in minor ways. They are less ornamental than those two genera but sufficiently pleasing if planted where they can be admired "up close and personal". Only one species is common in cultivation, *P. scilloides*.

***-scilloides*** (skil-loi′ deez) Striped Squill 4-6″/6″
Early Spring Pale Blue Orient Zones 4-8

This is similar to *Scilla*, the specific epithet meaning "like Scilla". Two to four linear leaves arise in the spring, followed by a leafless flower stalk with 2-6 nodding pale blue, bell-shaped flowers. The petals of each flower have a deep blue stripe running down their centers. This stripe plus the paleness of the flowers are good identification features. Plant in hundreds if possible but plant at least a dozen where they may be admired close up. Not the least of its charms is the pleasant fragrance, which smells like a spice cabinet whose contents were removed, so just a faint reminder remains.

*Puschkinia* tolerates full sun or partial shade. Plant bulbs about 4″ deep in mid to late September. Flowering occurs as early as mid February in the South and a month or so later in the North. They seldom need division but if flowering is sporadic, the offsets may be removed and replanted.

**Cultivars:**

'Alba' is a white form.

'Compacta' has flowers closer together on the scape, and more flowers than the species. It is not easy to locate.

'Libanotica' has pale blue flowers with darker blue stripes.

## ***Pycnanthemum*** (pink-nan-the′ mum) Mountain Mint Lamiaceae

The mountain mints consist of about 21 species with highly aromatic foliage. Some are not particularly showy but the strong minty fragrance of the leaves, particularly when crushed, may be reason enough to include a few in the garden. The flowers, which are white or purplish, distinctly two-lipped and mixed with conspicuous bracts, are produced at the tips and often in the axils as well. The common name is a bit of a misnomer, as most of the species are more common in lowlands than in the mountains. I had the common mountain mint, *P. incanum*, in my garden for years and every spring, as it emerged and grew into a tight little ball, I would walk by and break off a few leaves for a whiff of mint. Kept the plant pruned, I must say. Unfortunately, as the garden became shadier, the plants became leggier and toppled by midsummer, creating a green hairball of absolutely no value. I now go to the north Georgia mountains and see it there. This species is much happier in full sun and cool nights than in my shaded garden.

However, clustered mountain mint, *P. muticum,* with ovate leaves and silvery bracts, has become a great favorite with designers. Plants are about 3′ tall and when the bracts color up, they are beautiful. The small pink flowers are also great attractions for butterflies. Plant *en masse*, and in mid to late summer, they give the appearance that a fine dusting of snow has covered the garden. If you have a chance to visit the Chicago Botanic Garden, the mountain mints and grasses, along with goldenrods and cone flowers, are alone worth the price of admission.

Other species finding favor are those with narrower, more refined foliage, such as *P. tenuifolium*, a plant that grows in a compact clump and consists of leaves at least 4 times longer than wide. The creamy white bracts are held on the ends of the stems. *P. virginianum*, native to moist meadows of the Southeast, grows 2-3′ tall with white flowers and small bracts in the summer. The glossy narrow leaves make it a useful addition.

All mountain mints can roam freely. They are better behaved in full sun and moist but not wet soils. An early haircut does wonders for their disposition; cut back in late spring. Most grow well from zone 3 to 7.

*Pachysandra procumbens*

*Pachysandra terminalis*

*Paeonia veitchii*

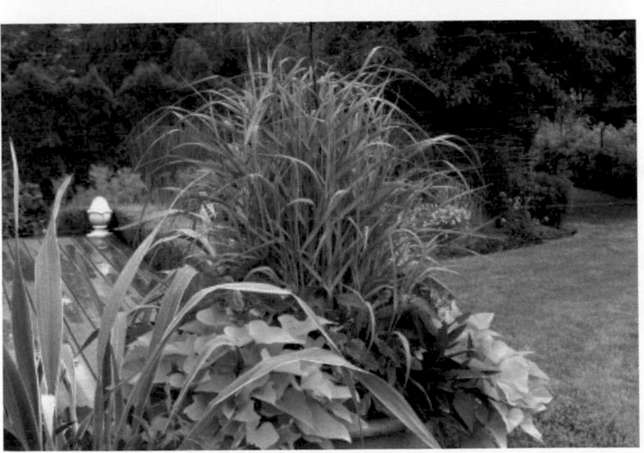

*Panicum virgatum* 'Dallas Blues' with *Ipomoea batatas* 'Margarita'

*Panicum virgatum* 'Heavy Metal' with *Rudbeckia* 'Goldsturm'

*Panicum virgatum* 'Northwind'

*Panicum virgatum* 'Shenandoah'

*Papaver orientale* 'Fireball'

*Papaver orientale*
'Turkish Delight'

*Papaver somniferum*

*Paris tetraphylla*

*Pennisetum alopecuroides*
'Hameln'

*Pennisetum* 'Prince'

*Pennisetum orientalis* 'Karley Rose'

*Penstemon barbarus* 'Hyacinth Mix'

*Penstemon* 'Firebird'

*Penstemon* 'Ruby'

*Penstemon* × *mexicali*
'Sunburst Ruby'

*Persicaria affinis*
'Superbum'

*Persicaria amplexicaule*
'Fire Tail'

*Persicaria polymorpha*

*Phlomis fruticosa*

*Phlomis tuberosa*

*Phlox divaricata*
'Fuller's White'

*Phlox douglasii*
'Firecracker'

*Phlox paniculata*
'David'

*Phlox paniculata*
'Delta Snow'

*Phlox paniculata*
'Eva Cullum'

*Phlox paniculata*
'Nora Leigh'

*Physostegia virginiana*
'Variegata'

*Phytolacca acinosa*

*Platycodon grandiflorus*
'Hakone White'

*Podophyllum* 'Kaleidescope'

*Podophyllum peltatum* (flowers)

*Podophyllum pleianthum*

*Polemonium caeruleum* 'Bressingham Purple'

*Polemonium reptans*
'Stairway to Heaven'

*Polygonatum odoratum*
'Variegatum'

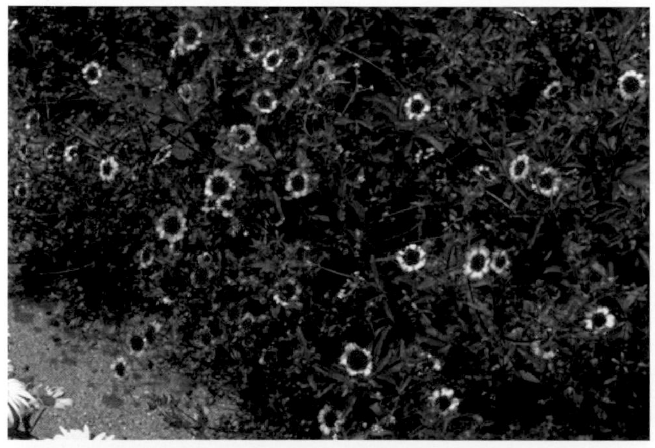

*Potentilla nepalensis*
'Miss Willmott'

*Primula bulleyana*

*Primula denticulata*
'Alba'

*Primula japonica*

*Primula vialii*

*Pulmonaria longifolia*
'Ceevennensis'

*Pulmonaria saccharata*
'Moonshine'

*Pulmonaria saccharata*
'Silver Shimmers'

*Pulsatilla halleri*

*Pulsatilla vulgaris*

# R

***Ranunculus*** (rah-nun′ kew-lus) Buttercup Ranunculaceae

The genus is somewhat similar to *Anemone* in its diversity. Plants with tuberous roots (classified as bulb species in the commercial trade) and those with fibrous roots are grown. About 250 species occur, but only a few are worthy of inclusion in the garden, and in fact most are awful pests. The tuberous-rooted species, *R. asiaticus*, was a popular florist plant and cut flower early in this century and is undergoing a renaissance as new cultivars are developed. It can be grown as a garden plant, but tubers must be lifted in the fall in most parts of the country. The small yellow buttercup that children put under their chins to see their skin turn yellow is *R. acris*, tall buttercup, and double forms of this diminutive wild flower have been developed for the garden. One species that has received much attention is an indestructible ground cover. The lesser celandine, *R. ficaria*, has bright yellow flowers and forms tight mats of round, crisp leaves which advance though the neighborhood like lava from Mount St. Helens. This tuberous-rooted species is about 2-3″ tall and its "pleasant face" so impressed William Wordsworth that it became the subject of his long poem "To the Lesser Celandine" and two more "To the Same Flower". Appreciate it where useful, but keep it out of your garden. Several other species should be treated the same way. *R. repens*, creeping buttercup, jogs more than creeps and, as pretty as the flower is—particularly the equally invasive double form, 'Flore-pleno'—it can take over an area within a couple of years. Plants may be admired along the Riverwalk in San Antonio where they smother banks with glossy green leaves and double yellow flowers. I like this plant more in my neighbor's garden than in mine.

The flowers of buttercups are usually yellow, but *R. aconitifolius* has white flowers and those of *R. asiaticus* are offered in a rainbow of colors. The leaves are often basal and then alternate up the stem. Leaf shape ranges from compound to lobed to scalloped and are even grasslike in *R. gramineus*. The flowers generally have five petals and sepals in single-flowered species.

I was asked how to tell "yellow buttercups" from the marsh marigold, *Caltha palustris*. Numerous differences occur, but *Caltha* has no petals compared to the five in *Ranunculus*. The petals also have a small nectary at their base, a good identification characteristic which also serves to separate this genus from *Adonis*, a closely related genus. A few species such as *R. ficaria* and its selections go summer dormant.

Others, like the European water buttercup, *R. aquatilis*, and the native swamp buttercup, *R. septentrionalis*, thrive in wet places, thus the name *Ranunculus*, derived from *rana*, a frog.

Quick Reference to Ranunculus Species

| | Height (in.) | Flower color | Root type |
|---|---|---|---|
| *R. aconitifolius* | 24-36 | White | Fibrous |
| *R. acris* | 24-36 | Yellow | Fibrous |
| *R. asiaticus* | 12-30 | Various | Tuberous |
| *R. montanus* | 3-6 | Yellow | Creeping |

**-*aconitifolius*** (a-kon-ee-ti-fo′ lee-us) Aconite Buttercup 24-36″/30″
Spring White France Zones 5-8

The name *aconitifolius* refers to the similarity of the foliage to that of species of *Aconitum*, in that the glossy green leaves are palmately parted into 3-5 sections. The similarities end there, however, as the flower of this plant is single, about 1″ across, and white. The upper leaves are sessile and flowers are held many to a stem, producing loose sprays in late spring and early summer. The species itself is seldom seen except in botanical gardens and available only from specialty seedsmen. In fact, it seems we don't much care for this plant here, as I can find more offerings from British nurseries than North American ones. Plants are best placed in full sun to partial shade and benefit from consistently moist soil. Propagate from seed or division in fall or early spring.

**Cultivars:**

'Flore-pleno', with its double white flowers was introduced to Britain by Huguenot refugees and became known as fair maids of France. It is also known as white bachelors' button being "very suggestive of buttons, but only remotely so of bachelors" (Sutherland, W., *Handbook of Hardy and Herbaceous Plants*, 1871). It is a better garden plant than the species and does not spread as rapidly as other members of this genus. Plants garnered an Award of Merit from the Royal Horticultural Society, Wisley, in 1993.

'Grandiflorus' (var. *platanifolius*) has larger flowers than the species and if the single form is to be grown, this is the variety of choice.

'Luteus-plenus' is an obscure double, yellow-flowered form seldom seen and even more difficult to locate. The flowers are similar to those of the double meadow buttercup, *R. acris*, but the plant is not hairy.

**-*acris*** (ah′ kris) Meadow Buttercup 18-36″/30″
Spring Yellow Europe Zones 3-7

Although native to Europe, the species has found conditions in Canada, the Atlantic states and as far south as Virginia to its liking, and has naturalized in those areas. The golden yellow flowers are about 1″ across, have spreading sepals and are hairy beneath. The flower buds are also hairy. Leaves are palmately divided into 3-7 sections, five being most common, and are often marked with black spots. The plant is much branched and bears many flowers. It is a wonderful weed with fleshy roots, and although a few better behaved forms are available, they are still ranunculus.

All forms may be propagated by division or seed.

**Cultivars:**

'Flore-pleno', yellow bachelor's button, is sold under names such as 'Plenus', 'Plena', and 'Multiplex' but all have the same double yellow buttonlike flowers. Plants are handsome but if moisture is available and soil is rich, they may spread rather quickly. Plants combine well with *Crocus tomasinianus*.

'Hedgehog' has dark brown markings on the leaves and pale yellow flowers.

var. *stevenii* is much less invasive and has single and semi-double flowers. Heights of 3-4′ are not uncommon, however, and plants are more prone to topple than the lower-growing forms.

***-asiaticus*** (ah-see-ah′ ti-kus) Persian Buttercup 12-30″/24″
Spring Various Asia, Crete Zones 8-10

This is a magnificent plant when grown well. In California, I have seen great rows of ranunculus cultivars in pastel shades, each flower fully double and seemingly perfect. I had to remind myself that I was in the rarified growing area of the Salinas Valley and would not have the same success on the East Coast. And a visit to southern California would not be complete without a trip to the famous Flower Fields in Carlsbad, where acre upon acre of flowers provide a quite unbelievable spectacle.

The history of the species is like a roller coaster. Few flowers have risen so high, to fall so low. In 1665, there were 20 types listed in the catalog of the Royal Gardens of Paris, and in 1775, a nurseryman named James Maddock listed nearly 800 kinds, and fifty thousand seedlings were raised annually in his nursery alone. By 1820, the number listed by nurserymen had dropped to 400 and in 1898, Shirley Hibberd wrote in her book *Familiar Garden Flowers*, that the named varieties were reduced to "a few dozen only, or perhaps less than a score". Today it is difficult to find more than "mixed colors". One of the main reasons for the decline was the difficulty of cultivation. Tubers do not tolerate frost and must be lifted after the leaves have turned yellow, and cool spring temperatures are necessary for best quality flowers. They also must have excellent drainage; successful gardeners use raised beds. As annuals, they can be dazzling, but success is not always consistent. They can be grown as perennials (perhaps two years) in zones 7 and south. If tubers are planted in early spring and mulched, those plants that do flower are worth the extra effort. Seed-propagated plants should be transplanted early in spring after danger of frost.

The leaves are two or three parted and the plant is erect. The flowers are about 3″ across and almost always double. Flower color is quite variable but tubers may be ordered in separate shades of red, yellow, etc.

Tubers can be divided after digging in the fall. Seed of newer hybrid forms may be sown approximately 5 months prior to planting out. Seed should be sown at 60-62°F but no chilling requirement is needed. Germination occurs over 6-8 weeks.

**Cultivars:**

A number of horticultural divisions of this species have resulted from the many years of breeding and selection. The florists' section, called Persian ranunculus, are variable in form and color and the most highly cultivated members of the genus. The gardeners' section, called Turban ranunculus, thought to be var. *africanus*, have larger, broader leaves that are less cut than those of the species. The petals are curved inward forming a spherical flower very much like a double peony.

Bloomingdale Strain was the first hybrid from seed and this low-growing series has become popular with greenhouse growers as a pot plant. It is more heat tolerant and flowers earlier than previous selections. The large flowers occur in vibrant mixed colors and are enjoyed as an indoor plant or as a garden specimen.

'Color Carnival' is a mixed bag of colorful 18-24" tall plants, usually available only from seed. The double flowers are camellia shaped.

'Superbissima' is a vigorous tall form with large semi-double flowers, available in mixed colors from red to white.

Tecolote Strain ('Tecolote Giants') includes plants that are taller than the previous strain and better for cutting. This strain has been around for a long time and is available in separate shades. New cultivars are being introduced, primarily by Japanese breeders, and ones such as Early Dwarf Strain appear easier to grow than many of the previous types.

***-montanus*** (mon-tah' nus) Mountain Buttercup 3-6"/12"
Late Spring Yellow Europe Zones 5-8

The leaves are 3-5-lobed and the flowers are borne singly. The leaves, which emerge from the base, are petioled but those on the stems are sessile. The yellow flowers possess the classic buttercup shape and color and are borne singly or up to three per inflorescence. The creeping rootstock results in rapid spread in good soils, making it a good ground cover, but not as invasive as *R. ficaria* or *R. repens*.

Propagate from division or seed.

**Cultivars:**

'Molten Gold' is similar to the species but has larger, golden yellow flowers. It does well in well-drained soils and full sun to partial shade.

**Related Species:**

*R. bulbosus* is one of the many yellow-flowered species which all kind of look the same. The plants arise from bulb-like roots and bear 3-lobed leaves and single yellow flowers. The most common form, however, is the double 'Flore-pleno'. These plants can gallop around the garden: full sun and moist soils invite an invasion. I have a good deal of trouble telling all these buttercups apart, and pulling up the plants to check for swollen roots is hardly good etiquette, particularly at someone else's garden. I have included a table after Related Species for those who can't stand not knowing what it is. For the remaining smart people, a yellow buttercup is a yellow buttercup.

*R. ficaria*, lesser celandine, has a rosette of dark green, heart-shaped or scalloped basal leaves often with brown or silver markings. Native to Europe, they have become naturalized in the United States and can become very invasive. It is everywhere in the fine garden at Planting Fields in Long Island. I was asked to lecture there, and had prepared to talk about some of the cultivars listed below, but as the director Vinnie Simeone led me through colony after colony of lesser celandine on the property, I realized that people probably hated the stuff, and the last thing they wanted to hear was how wonderful my ranunculus were. I expected to be shouted out of the place. Fortunately, the audience was polite, after all, this was New York. In fact, some cultivars are far less invasive than their parents. 'Aurantiaca' has brown (sometimes a little silver) mottled leaves and shiny orange-yellow flowers. It is also aggressive. One of my favorite little plants in the Armitage garden is 'Brazen Hussy', given to me by Pam Harper of Virginia, one of this country's treasured writers and gardeners. The 6″ tall plants have bright yellow flowers over chocolate brown leaves. They are in flower before most everything but the earliest daffodils. Great fun plant with a wonderful name; multiplies by root bulblets. Both selections go summer dormant. 'Double Mud' produces double burnt yellow flowers, the outside row of petals has muddy purpling. 'Green Petal' is a particularly gruesome double-flowered plant with green petals bearing a hint of yellow.

*R. repens*, creeping buttercup, is similar to *R. acris* but differs in a number of subtle ways. Creeping buttercup is shorter and can be equally invasive. It is similar to meadow buttercup but the basal leaves are divided into three leaflets and the flowers are usually borne singly while the leaves of *R. acris* are not divided, but are 3-7-lobed and the flowers are generally borne several together in an inflorescence. The most common form is the double 'Flore-pleno', but the most handsome form of creeping buttercup, without any doubt, is 'Joe's Golden', otherwise known as 'Buttered Popcorn' and 'Susan's Song'. The leaves are chartreuse with margins of dark green. Terrific in foliage, the flowers are the typical yellow. This is a stunning plant, but make no mistake, it will take over the garden. Here is a note from a former friend in Ohio. "I rue the day you sent me this plant. It has survived a sharp hoe, Round-Up, weekly mowing, and living directly in the path of the mailman's daily route to the porch. It is indestructable."

*R. yakuschimanus* is only 2-3″ tall and bears ½″ wide waxy yellow flowers over yellow-veined leaves. It is a wonderful undiscovered little ground cover gem.

The differences between a number of these look-alike yellow buttercups may be useful for identification. The following table may help.

To Too Many Yellow Buttercups

| | **Leaves** | **Root** | **Height** |
|---|---|---|---|
| *R. acris* | 3-7 (usually 5) deeply lobed | Fibrous | 24-36″ |
| *R. bulbosus* | 3 leaflets, each segment deeply divided | Bulb-like corm | 12-24″ |
| *R. ficaria* | Entire, heart-shaped | Tuberous | 9-24″ |
| *R. repens* | 3 leaflets, each segment shallowly divided | Stoloniferous | 10-24″ |

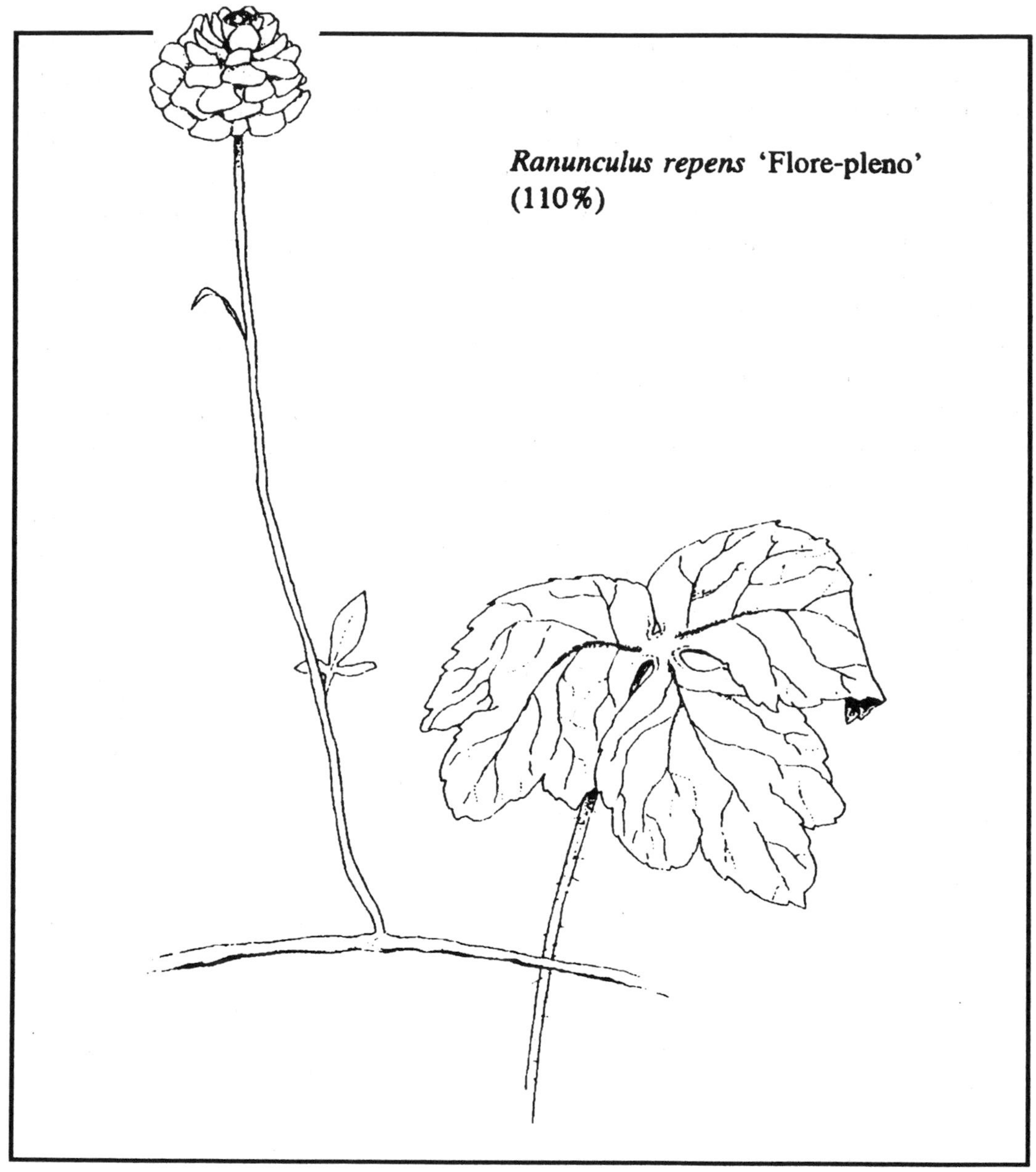

*Ranunculus repens* 'Flore-pleno' (110%)

***Ratibida*** (rah-ti-bid′ a) Ratibida, Mexican Hat Plant Asteraceae

One of our native prairie coneflowers, ratibida is distinguished from other coneflowers mostly by the tan brown to black, tall cylindrical receptacle (disc) and pinnately divided leaves. A couple of taxa of *Rudbeckia* are quite similar, such as *R. laciniata* and *R. nitida* (which see), but in those plants the discs are greenish and the leaves are simple (not divided or deeply lobed). General differences between coneflowers are discussed under *Rudbeckia*. Mexican hat plant is a tough daisy, and is spectacular in meadows.

Two species are occasionally offered to gardeners, differing in rather subtle characteristics. The most distinctive feature of *R. columnifera* flowers is the 2" long, narrow cone, at the base of which are attached 3-7 drooping, yellow ray flowers. Plants grow 2-3′ tall. While the species is handsome in its own right, two cultivars are making forays into American gardens. 'Buttons and Bows' has double the number of ray flowers, each rust colored and attached to the elongated cone. A particularly handsome form is var. *pulcherrima*, with mahogany red flowers hanging from the tawny brown cone. Plants perform in full sun and any reasonable soil. Cool climes are more to their liking than warm ones, and if comfortable they will flower 4-6 weeks. They grow well in zones 3-7.

*R. pinnata* is the classic prairie plant, with drooping yellow ray flowers and a prominent cone. It differs mainly in having leaves with three to seven narrow segments and ray flowers longer than the raised disc. This is much more available than the former. Plants generally grow 3-5′ tall. Hardy in zones 3-7.

Propagate from seed.

***Rehmannia*** (ray-mahn′ ee- a) Chinese Foxglove Scrophulariaceae

I have been both impressed and disappointed with the performance of *R. elata*, Chinese foxglove, in the sunny Georgia garden. When it grows well, it is a conversation piece and a lovely addition, however, it seems to be persnickety from year to year. Sometimes plants simply stop growing, or appear here and there in a ratty column rather than a dense population.

The entire plant is hairy. The alternate leaves are up to 10" long and have 3-6 lobes. The flowering stems arise all season (except in my garden), although late spring is the most floriferous time. The large bright rose flowers have a yellow throat and are obviously two-lipped. They resemble *Mimulus* or foxgloves. Plants reseed freely and a few small plants can quickly provide many plants. The main limitation is its cold hardiness. Zone 7 is not a problem, however, I suspect they may do fine to about zone 6.

Other species which may be found are *R. glutinosa*, with reddish brown to yellow flowers and *R. angulata*, similar to the above but with sessile leaves.

Propagation is easy from fresh seed or divisions from the colony.

***Rhazya*** see *Amsonia*

***Rheum*** (ray′ um) Rhubarb Polygonaceae

Telling non-gardeners that rhubarb can be used as an ornamental plant is like telling them to grow goldenrod as a cut flower. In both cases, however, it is simply a matter of selecting the right form and not closing your mind before opening your eyes. The tall fresh panicles of edible rhubarb, *R. rhabarbarum* (*R.* x *cultorum*), provide a dimension of height and leaf texture to the spring garden. Who says we have to have the vegetable garden in the back forty, let's plant ornamental veggies in the garden itself. Other rhubarbs may have more pizzazz, but good old common rhubarb adds leaf texture, decent flowers and a tasty petiole to boot. Of course, if the petioles

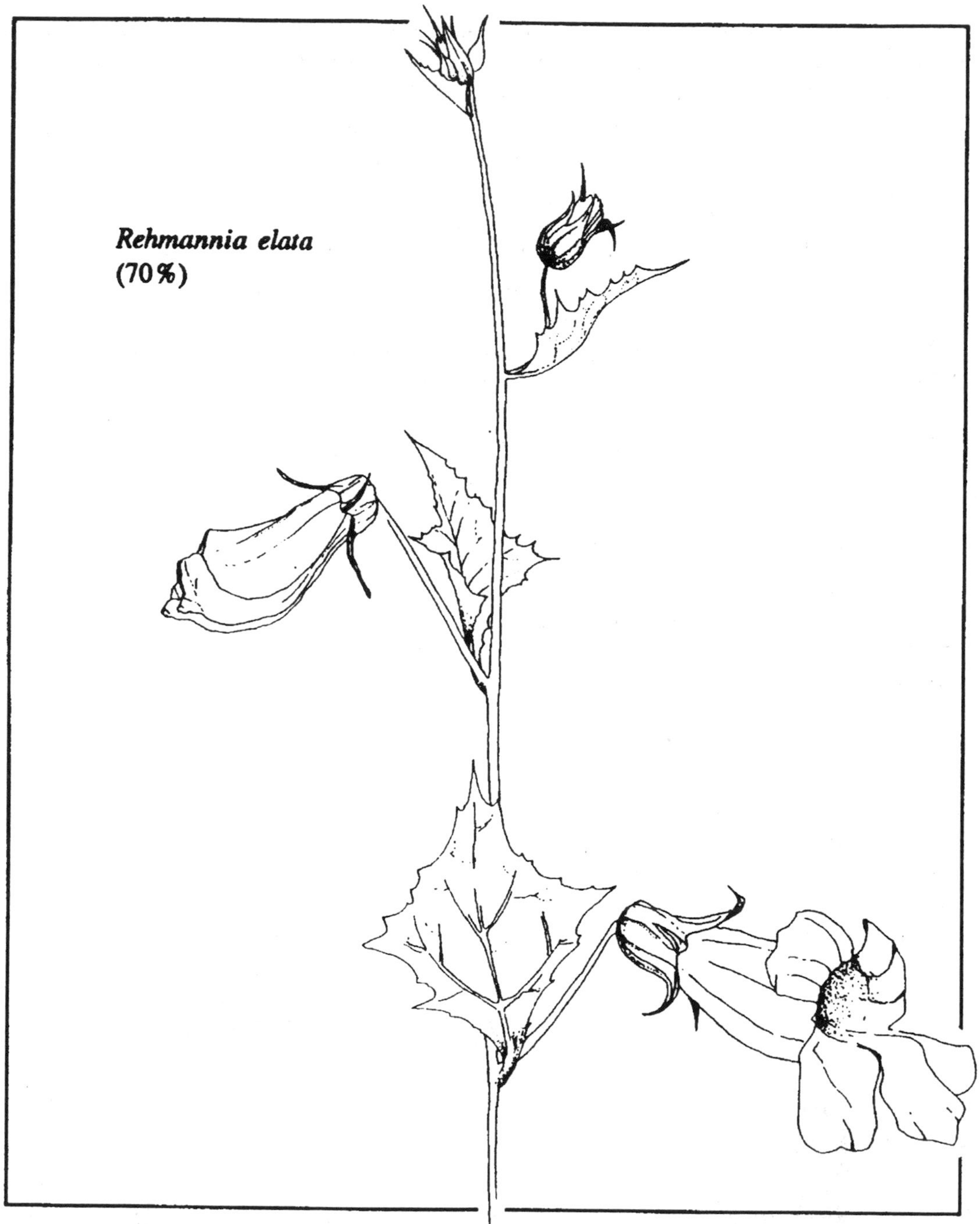
*Rehmannia elata*
(70%)

are eaten, there is little left of the plant to consider anyway. However, a number of species are wonderfully ornamental and commercially available in North America. They taste terrible, but are magnificent garden specimens.

***-compactum*** (com-pak′ tum) | Dwarf Rhubarb | 2-3′/3′
Summer | White | China | Zone 5-7

One of the smaller ornamental rhubarbs, it requires far less space than the bigger specimens. The glossy, heart-shaped leaves are 12-18″ wide with wavy margins, and in the summer creamy white flowers give rise to a wide panicle with many drooping branches. A handsome plant for flower and foliage.

Full sun and well-drained soils work well.

***-palmatum*** (pahl-mah′ tum) | Ornamental Rhubarb | 5-7′/6′
Summer | Red, White | China | Zone 5-7

This most imposing specimen makes one forget that rhubarb is a vegetable. A constant supply of moisture, well-drained soils, partial shade, copious fertilizer in the spring and lots of room are prerequisites. The dark green, 2-3′ wide basal leaves are deeply and sharply palmately lobed (thus the species name). Deep red 2′ long panicles reach to the sky. In combination with red peonies or variegated Solomon's seal, the plant is unforgettable. Unfortunately, plants are not as easy to grow as garden rhubarb and are more sensitive to drought and heat; they succumbed rather quickly after a couple of lean years in my garden but so do most rhubarbs. Without doubt, they are meant for cooler climates. However, if constant moisture is maintained, success is more likely if temperatures are warm. Fall planting is best. Once established, plants persist for many years.

Propagation of cultivars is best accomplished by division, making sure that each division has a dormant crown bud. The species and varieties may also be raised from seed.

**Cultivars:**

'Atrosanguineum' is the best form. Leaves emerge in the spring with a dark purple hue that persists, at least on the reverse, into summer. The flowers are deep cherry red followed by attractive fruit. This may be the same as the plant I see listed as 'Red Select'.

'Bowles' Variety' is similar to the previous cultivar but has rose-red flowers.

var. *tanguticum* bears dark purple leaves which are less deeply cut than the species. The flowers appear on erect side shoots rather than terminal as in the previous forms and may be white, pink, or red. Often raised from seed, considerable variation occurs.

**Related Species:**

*R. alexandrae* is 3-4′ tall and bears undivided foliage that resembles overgrown plantain leaves. The pale greenish yellow flowers are borne in a narrow panicle in spring.

*R. kialense* is a difficult-to-locate but charming find. Plants are stoloniferous and can create a dense ground cover. The pleated leaves are reddish green and the greenish red flowers are held in open panicles. Hardy in zones 5-7.

*R. tibeticum* is only about 2′ tall but has unusually puckered, pleated foliage. The large rounded leaves are spectacular enough, but the red to pink early spring flowers form an equally wonderful display. Zones 5-8.

***Rhodohypoxis*** (row-do-hi-poks′ is) Red Star Hypoxidaceae

Including this bulbous plant may be pushing the perennial envelope a little far, as plants are native to South Africa. However, they naturally occur at 7000-8000′ elevations in the Drakensberg Mountains, providing winter hardiness to around 25-28°F. They are so beautiful, with six tepals colored in various shades of pure white to pale pinks to deep reds, that they are well worth trying, if only for a season. The flowering plants are only 3-6″ tall and are perfectly suited to nooks and crannies of the rock garden. They enjoy plenty of moisture in the spring and early summer but abhor wetness in the winter, a problem in all but the best well-drained, water-retentive soils (there is an oxymoron, for sure).

The only species commonly available is *R. baurii*, which produces keeled, narrow leaves and flowers in ones or twos on 5-6″ tall scapes. In the wild, three distinct forms are found: *R. baurii* var. *baurii*, with deep pink to red flowers, var. *platypetala* with white flowers and var. *confecta*, with bicolored flowers. Hybridization and selection have occurred and named cultivars have arisen but today most catalogs offer a mixture of white, pink and red-flowered forms. They are sometimes found in flower in florist shops, having been produced as a pot plant for sale on Valentine's or Mother's Day. One way to enjoy them more than one year is to grow the bulbs in pots and plunge them in the garden in the early spring. Bring them out before winter sets in and store them cool but not freezing. One of my favorite places to visit is the garden of Ernie and Marietta O'Byrne in Eugene, Oregon. They have fabulous everythings, but some of the most stunning rhodohypoxis you'll ever see. Gardeners on the Pacific Coast and those with protected locations might be pleasantly surprised by leaving them in the garden over the winter. Nothing ventured, nothing gained!

**Cultivars**:
'Albrighton' has deep red flowers.
'Dawn' opens pale pink and fades to white.
'Eva Kate' is a vigorous selection with deep pink flowers.
'Fred Broome' consists of light pink and rosy pink flowers.
'Harlequin' has flowers which change from pink to white.
'Helen' bears white flowers with smudges of pink on the edges of the tepals.
'Pictus' is a vigorous white, with pink blushing on the tepals.
'Ruth' provides clean white flowers.
'Tetra Red' has intense red blossoms.

**Related Species:**

*R. milloides* is more vigorous and has flowers in which the tepals are in two layers of three, separated by a noticeable gap. No such gap occurs in *R. baurii*. They are also more tolerant of wet feet and drainage is less of a problem. Several colors exist, although 'Claret' with deep red flowers is beautiful.

***Rhodophiala*** (row-do-fee′ al-a) Oxblood Lily Amaryllidaceae

A wonderfully colorful small bulb, closely related to amaryllis, but far more subtle. I suppose their garden habit is actually more closely related to *Lycoris*, as these too go summer dormant, then in late summer or early fall produce marvelous deep red flowers. The only species cultivated is *R. bifida*, cold hardy to about zone 7. Thanks to Becky and Brent Heath of Brent and Becky's Bulbs in Gloucester, Virginia, I have a number of them in my garden; I wish I had many more. var. *spathacea* is magenta pink. Full sun is best, but plants tolerate some shade as well.

***Rodgersia*** (rod-jerz′ ee-a) Rodgersia Saxifragaceae

The rodgersias contain at least five wonderfully coarse, bodacious species, native to China and Japan. The genus commemorates the American navy commander, Admiral John Rodgers (1812-1882), who was in charge of the expedition during which *R. podophylla* was discovered. It is ironic that, although discovered by an American, so few are grown in America. However, as more American nurseries are now offering these plants, this is beginning to change, and plants are not uncommon in the Northeast and southern Canada.

They survive in ordinary soil but perform best in rich, moist soils and partial shade. The flowers are borne in large panicles (like those of *Astilbe*) on tall stems and may be white, yellow, or shades of red. All species are apetalous (no petals) and the flower color is provided by the sepals and stamens. Leaves of most species are compound, basal and dark green. Plants spread to 5′ and sufficient room is needed to look their best. One or two plants is all that is needed to provide unique architectural detail along a stream, lake, or water feature. They are best naturalized along a waterside or large pond.

One of the neatest old-time species, *R. tabularis*, has been reclassified as *Astilboides tabularis* (which see).

Quick Reference to Rodgersia Species

| | Height (ft.) | Flower color | Leaf arrangement |
|---|---|---|---|
| *R. aesculifolia* | 3-6 | White | Palmate |
| *R. pinnata* | 3-4 | Rose-red | Pinnate |

***-aesculifolia*** (ees-skew-li-fo′ lee-a) Fingerleaf Rodgersia 3-6′/6′
Late Spring White China Zones 5-6

The large basal leaves are usually composed of seven, 4-10″ long leaflets that are coarsely toothed and narrowed at the base. They are palmately compound and resemble the leaves of the horse-chestnut, *Aesculus*. The 1½-2′ long panicle consists of flat clusters of creamy white flowers which open later than the other species. One of the characteristics of this species is the shaggy brown hair that covers the petioles, flower stalks and principal leaf veins. Flowers are not as spectacular as other species but plants are beautiful when sited properly.

Propagate by division or seed. Sow the tiny seeds on the surface and sub-irrigate so seeds and seedlings are not washed away. Germinate at 70-75°F; after seedlings have emerged, place at 50-60°F.

***-pinnata*** (pi-nah′ ta) Featherleaf Rodgersia 3-4′/4′
Late Spring Rose-Red China Zones 5-7

The foliage is often bronzed, particularly in the spring when temperatures are still cool. The leaves are pinnately compound but on some plants the leaflets are so closely attached that the leaves look palmate. It is necessary to closely inspect a number of leaves to be sure. The term for this confusing arrangement is pseudo-pinnate, which has a certain romantic ring to it. In fact, hybrids between *R. aesculifolia*, *R. pinnata* and others have resulted in the blurring of leaf arrangement among species. I was pleasantly surprised to see this plant in the excellent gardens at Michigan State University. They leaves were a little crispy by the beginning of August but were doing relatively well. Usually, there are five to nine 6-8″ long leaflets, widest in the middle and narrowed at both ends. The rose-red flowers are borne in branched panicles but considerable variation in flower color occurs. The branching habit of the inflorescence results in a terrific show of flowers.

Propagate similarly to *R. aesculifolia*.

**Cultivars:**

var. *alba* has a long, loose inflorescence composed of creamy white flowers. In some cases the flowers are almost yellow. A beautiful form.

'Chocolate Wings' is interesting. The foliage of most rodgersias emerges dark, but this one stays dark longer.

var. *elegans* bears rose-pink flowers.

var. *rosea* has rose flowers.

var. *rubra* has dark red flowers.

var. *superba* has bronze-purple leaves not as coarse as the type and a longer inflorescence of persistent rose-red flowers. This is the best garden specimen.

**Related Species**:

*R. henrici* is so similar to *R. aesculifolia* that some authorities consider them the same. The difference is that the leaflets are more sharply pointed (acuminate) and the flowers are red-purple.

*R. podophylla*, bronzeleaf rodgersia, is also similar to *R. aesculifolia*, but the leaves consist of five glossy green leaflets, each with 3-5 shallow lobes towards the tips. The foliage turns bronze in the summer. The yellowish white flowers are held in 1′ long, dense, attractively nodding panicles. The flowers differ by having pointed sepals and shorter panicles.

*R. sambucifolia*, elderberry rodgersia, is so named because of the obvious resemblance of the leaves to those of *Sambucus*, elderberry. Plants are about 3′ tall, with 7-11 pinnately arranged leaves. The flat-topped panicles consist of many densely held white or pink flowers. 'Rothaut' ('Red Skin') has bronze leaves.

## ***Rohdea*** (row-dee′ a) Sacred Lily Convallariaceae

Many years ago I saw some plants (*R. japonica*), but only because someone pointed them out to me. They are offered by many nurseries as an "evergreen addition to the winter garden", or as "a tough complement to more colorful plants" or even as "glossy green specimen plants". I kept looking at these things and obviously, I was missing something. To me, they just looked like upright green foliage plants, like an old *Aspidistra*, which is not all bad, but I must admit that looking like an aspidistra is no great shakes either. They were tough, but so was a rock. They could be darlings of the homogenous and low-maintenance set, but to me, it was a waste of good garden space. Of course, the fact that these are so expensive and that people buy them means that I may be dumb as that rock.

However, I was taken by the ear by a number of brilliant gardeners, including Ozzie Johnson of Atlanta, Barry Yinger of Pennsylvania, and a few others, and I have seen the light. Variegated leaves, good flowers, handsome fruit, no maintenance—okay, okay, they are madonna-esque. I think the problem may have been that I could only afford two plants and in my designing fervor, I stuck them far from each other. A drift it was not, but I am coming around . . . slowly. With the trend towards do-nothing gardening, I expect them to be even more popular in years to come.

The thick green basal leaves are about 15″ long and 2-3″ wide and in the summer, a short spike of inconspicuous yellow-green flowers is produced, themselves giving way to red berries. They do well under difficult circumstances like dry shade and gardeners in zones 5-9 can be successful with sacred lily. Numerous cultivars from Japan with exotic Japanese names are available to the rhodeaphile, each about the cost of a New York dinner. Money well spent if they turn you on. Some taxonomists have recently reclassified *Rohdea* to the family Ruscaceae.

**Cultivars**:

'Aureo-striata' has leaves with yellow stripes.

'Galle' has more narrow foliage than the species. That it is from the great late plantsman Fred Galle of Callaway Gardens may be the only valid reason to pay good money for it.

'Herbie' produces dark green leaves with distinct white margins. Plants are 8-10″ tall.

'Nobori Ryu' is less than a foot tall and characterized by the raised veins on the dark green leaves.

'Striata' has leaves striped in white.

'Talbot Manor' produces thick leaves that bear white margins, but often look as if they have been haphazardly brushed with white paint.

***Romneya*** (rom-knee′ ya) Matilija Poppy, California Tree Poppy Papaveraceae

Barely cold hardy in most of the country, this plant is nevertheless an impressive perennial where it thrives. The impressive part comes from the large stature (plants grow to 8′ tall), the smooth blue-green foliage and the 4-5″ wide fragrant silky white flowers. The leaves are about 6″ long, consisting of 3-4 spreading lobes, one always terminal. Flowers consist of 3 sepals, six petals (in 2 whorls of 3) and many yellow stamens. They open in late summer and fall.

Only one species occurs (*R. coulteri*) but var. *trichocalyx* has more finely divided leaves and is a little slower growing. Native to southwest California, they tolerate temperatures to about 15°F if grown in soils with excellent drainage and planted in protected areas. The stems become woody at the base but the entire plant generally dies down to the roots in the winter. Plants may be pinched back in the spring or early summer to allow branching and maintain a bit more dwarfness. Flowering occurs on the current season's growth. Under optimum conditions, plants will spread aggressively by underground runners, with plantlets appearing many feet away, so be prepared to pull up unwanted plants. This is a truly beautiful plant where it is hardy and certainly useful, if at times a little too rambunctious, on the Gulf and West Coasts. For the rest of us, it is toast.

The suckers which are often sent up from the roots may be separated and used for propagation or use root cuttings or seed. Germinate seed at 65-70°F.

## ***Roscoea*** (ros-ko′ ee-a) Roscoea Zingiberaceae

*Roscoea* belongs in the "almost-impossible-to-grow-but-I-must-have-one" group of plants, such as *Meconopsis*. Travelers come back from West Coast and European gardens with tales of beauty and a need to try such exotics. *Roscoea* belongs to the ginger family, which is a pretty good hint that it won't be happy in Peoria. Many gingers can be grown, but where winter exists, the only member of that group most of us can grow is the ginger lily, *Hedychium*, and its range doesn't extend terribly far. However, in the spirit of adventuresome gardening, *Roscoea* is certainly worth a try, if you can locate some. I notice that gardeners in Victoria, British Columbia have great success with these plants—hardly fair, they get both Victoria and roscoeas.

The main species is *R. cautleoides*, whose leaves and flowers resemble the cattleya orchid. The leaves are about 6″ long and an inch wide although not always fully expanded at flowering. The 6-7 pale yellow flowers are carried well above the upright foliage and look like a cross between an iris and an orchid. 'Kew Beauty' has pale yellow, larger, more orchid-like flowers. Plants are more winter hardy than most think, perhaps to zone 7, however heat and humidity are not at all to their liking. If roscoeas are your thing, try the fabulously pink to purple flowers in *R. alpina*, *R. humeana* and *R. purpurea*. In the latter, the flowers are bicolored pink and white. Quite extraordinary. All of the species are outstanding, but if they were as good here as in European gardens, we would see them offered by many more nurseries. Maintain even soil moisture in partial shade.

Propagate from divisions or seed.

## ***Rosmarinus*** (rose-ma-reen′ us) Rosemary Lamiaceae

*R. officinalis* is the ultimate ornamental herb, providing beauty, fragrance and persistence. Rosemary is familiar to everyone because of the aromatic leaves used for potpourri, perfumes and seasoning. These gray-green Mediterranean plants are woody shrubs, and can easily grow 4-6′ tall over time. The flowers are usually light blue to white and occur in late winter to early spring and attract bees from miles away. Numerous cultivars have arisen with different habits and leaf and flower colors. They are grown by herb specialists as culinary companions to thyme, oregano and lavender or as ornamental standards (small potted trees). Plants are hardy to zone 7 (to zone 6, with protection). The roots are more cold tolerant than the tops and so winters may cause top death, however, new growth will occur in the spring. The biggest threat to winter persistence is poorly-drained soils.

Place in full sun, and if a sheltered dry area is available, rosemary can even be pruned and groomed as a hedge. Both acidic and basic soils are appropriate.

**Cultivars:**

'Albus' has white flowers.

'Arp' is a well-known cultivar, originally found by Madalene Hill in Arp, Texas. It has some of the best cold hardiness (zone 6) and consists of 3′ tall upright plants with light blue flowers.

'Athens Blue Spires' is an upright, vigorous and hardy form whose light blue flowers absolutely cover the erect branches in late winter or early spring. Good cold tolerance (zone 6).

'Aureus' bears leaves speckled with yellow.

'Blue Boy' is a dwarf form with small leaves.

'Furneaux Hardy', named for Lane Furneaux, a fine Texas plantswoman, grows upright to 4′ and bears dark blue flowers in the winter.

'Golden Rain' has yellow variegated foliage.

'Huntington Carpet' is a compact, prostrate form with sky blue flowers in the winter.

Irene™ is a prostrate form with dense, gray-green narrow leaves and violet-blue flowers. A great plant to cascade down a wall or container.

'Lockwood de Forest' is a procumbent form, otherwise very similar to 'Tuscan Blue'.

'Majorca' is 3-4′ tall with dark blue flowers, 'Majorca Pink' bears pink flowers.

'Maltese White' is 3′ tall with small clusters of white flowers and silver-green stems.

'Prostratus' is a common low-growing form.

'Roman Beauty' is a cascading selection with blue flowers and gray-green foliage. Excellent for containers or the edges of walls.

'Tuscan Blue' has dark blue flowers and narrow leaves.

'Silver Spires' may be the same silver-leaved plant grown in 1654 in Europe, and then lost to cultivation. The plant has pale green leaves with white margins, and in full sun can appear almost white.

## ***Rubus*** (rub′ us) Brambles Rosaceae

*Rubus* is best known for the tasty blackberries and raspberries, or for the pain inflicted by the prickles and thorns that attack when we try to get rid of them. Of the 250 species, a number are quite ornamental, however, finding more than a half dozen in catalogs is a challenge. One of my more memorable encounters with the genus was with a group of friends wandering around the grounds of the Chesterwood Estate, in Stockbridge, Massachusetts, the former home of the famed American sculptor, Daniel Chester French. In the wooded area, we reveled in the colonies of interrupted ferns intermingled with thimbleberry, *R. odoratus*, now commonly available to gardeners. On returning home to my garden, the beauty was quickly forgotten amidst the curses of pulling out the ragged canes of yet more brambles.

Some of these brambles, however, can be incredibly ornamental. The silver fronds of *R. thibeticus* 'Silver Fern' are such a lovely departure from the common bramble that you catch yourself thinking the unthinkable "Should I actually buy a bramble for the garden?" Most of the species are shrubs and extremely variable, and it is difficult to tell one from another in many cases. If plants are successful, they can become invasive, requiring far more time to remove than to plant.

Quick Reference to Rubus Species

| | Spines | Flower | Habit |
|---|---|---|---|
| *R. calycinoides* | Sparsely | White | Prostrate |
| *R. odoratus* | None | Pink-purple | Arching |

**-*calycinoides*** (kal-e-si-noid-eez) Ornamental Raspberry 6-12″/2′
Summer White Taiwan Zones 6-8

The prickly, hairy stems root as they crawl along the ground. The wrinkled simple leaves are ovate to almost rounded. Each leaf has 3-5 lobes with sharp serrations and the insignificant white flowers are borne singly, but plants should not be grown for the flowers. For partially shaded situations, this is an excellent ground cover that will not take over the entire garden.

Propagate by cutting away the rooted stems.

**Cultivars:**

'Emerald Carpet' is an aggressive ground cover, laden with handsome puckered leaves. In the fall, a fine red color evolves. Few flowers, little fruit. This is often listed under *R. calycinoides*, *R. pentalobus* and *R. rolfei*. The last is probably correct.

**-*odoratus*** (o-do-rah′ tus) Thimbleberry 2-3′/3′
Summer Pink-Purple Eastern North America Zones 3-7

The most common and easiest to grow ornamental bramble, this vigorous deciduous shrub inhabits shady woodlands throughout the Northeast up into Canada. The simple leaves are 5-lobed, serrated and pubescent beneath. These 'brambles for borders" produce stems that are light brown, peeling and hairy, and grow up and out, arching over and over. The best news about the stems is that they have few or no spines. The term *odoratus* means fragrant, and the pink-purple 2″ wide flowers have a pleasant, if not overbearing fragrance. About 7-10 five-petaled flowers are held in each inflorescence above the leaves in June to August. The fruits are red to orange and produced in late summer and fall.

Plants are aggressive tall ground covers in moist, shady areas and should not be planted in a small area. They are terrific for shaded woodlands and the combination of bright flowers, deep green leaves and lack of spines makes them useful. However, many a gardener has become frustrated with the aggressive nature and vowed "never again".

**Cultivars:**
'Albus' is similar to the species but has lighter green leaves and white flowers.

**Related Species:**

*R. microphylla* also has rounded, shallowly 3-lobed leaves but many more white flowers with maroon sepals. Small red fruit is formed in the summer. 'Variegatus' has marbled pink and white foliage. Hardy to zone 7b.

*R. spectabilis*, salmonberry, is a reasonably nice western weed, but 'Golden Ruby' bears golden chartreuse leaves and pretty rosy red flowers. Zones 5-8.

*R. tricolor* is a prostrate grower with 4-sided stems and deep glossy green leaves which are white-tomentose beneath. The stems are not spiny, but bristly. The 1″ wide white flowers are produced singly or as a few flowers together. Hardy in zones 7 (perhaps 6) to 8.

## *Rudbeckia* (rud-bek′ ee-a) Coneflower Asteraceae

If one had been tramping about Sweden in the early 1700s, one may have met a physician with a keen botanical interest. His name was Olaus Olai Rudbeck, and the genus that bears his name is one of the best known in gardens throughout the world. That all species of *Rudbeckia* are native to North America didn't stop Linnaeus from commemorating his former teacher in 1753.

*Rudbeckia* consists of about 30 North American species of annuals, biennials, and perennials. The best-known wild flowers, such as the annual black-eyed Susan, *R. hirta*, are included. In the Armitage garden, *R. hirta* reseeds prolifically every year and flowers for 2-3 months beginning the first week of June. This just happens to be my wife Susan's favorite flower. One of our favorite trips is to the Smoky Mountains in North Carolina where the wild black-eyed Susans compete with mountain mints, lobelias and monardas in openings alongside hiking trails in the summer and early fall. Life is good. Hybridization and selection have yielded magnificent cultivars such as 'Prairie Sun', 'Irish Eyes', 'Toto' and the outstanding 'Indian Summer'; regardless of claims to the contrary, they should be treated as annuals.

Several genera are buried under the name coneflower, including purple coneflower, *Echinacea*, and *Ratibida*, prairie coneflower. Numerous specific morphological differences occur which are the final word in separating some of the genera (such as disc scales being persistent on *Rudbeckia*, deciduous in *Ratibida*). A few horticultural clues may be useful:

| | ***Coreopsis*** | ***Echinacea*** | ***Ratibida*** | ***Rudbeckia*** |
|---|---|---|---|---|
| Leaf arrangement | Opposite | Alternate | Alternate | Alternate |
| Ray flowers | Yellow | Purple[1] | Yellow | Yellow |
| Shape of disc | Flattened | Raised | Columnar | Raised[2] |

[1]cream colored in *E. pallida*
[2]columnar in *R. laciniata*

The perennial species all have yellow to gold ray flowers and brown to black centers. The size and shape of the center (cone) and the height of the plant are distinctive. Of the useful coneflowers, the ubiquitous 'Goldsturm' is about 2′ tall while selections of *R. laciniata* and *R. maxima* can reach 7-10 feet. The foliage may be entire or deeply cut and is almost always alternate. Growing coneflowers is not at all difficult—they thrive in full sun to partial shade in ordinary garden soil. Some species, such as *R. laciniata*, benefit from moist soils, while *R. hirta* tolerates dry conditions. Once coneflowers start flowering, color is provided until frost. *R. laciniata* starts flowering in my garden in mid June, *R. triloba* in late June, *R. fulgida* and *R. maxima* in late July. All flower about 3 weeks later in the Northeast and Midwest.

Quick Reference to Rudbeckia Species

| | Height (in.) | Color of disc |
|---|---|---|
| *R. fulgida* | 18-30 | Brown-purple |
| *R. laciniata* | 30-72 | Greenish |
| *R. maxima* | 48-72 | Black |
| *R. nitida* | 36-48 | Greenish |
| *R. triloba* | 24-36 | Black |

***-fulgida*** (ful-gi′ da) Orange Coneflower 18-30″/24″
Summer Yellow Southeastern United States Zones 3-8

This species has entire, slightly hairy foliage. The 3-veined basal leaves are twice as long as broad (oblong to lanceolate) and carried on much-branched stems. The 2-2½″ wide flowers consist of up of 12-14 yellow ray flowers surrounding a brownish purple disc. Plants are rhizomatous and form large clumps after 2-3 years. Although not invasive, colonies form rapidly in rich loose soil. Several varieties and cultivars are popular but the species is becoming more common because of its higher tolerance to heat and humidity.

Propagate by seed, division or terminal cuttings.

**Cultivars:**

The varieties and cultivars may be separated by shape and size of foliage. Differences are slight, but all are excellent garden plants.

var. *deamii* grows about 2′ tall, has larger basal leaves and is more floriferous than the species. The basal leaves are not as wide as the species (3/8 to half as broad as long), while the upper stem leaves are about as large as the basal leaves and have small, well-spaced teeth. Stems are not as branched. Plants are slightly better than the species.

'Goldsturm' is a selection of var. *sullivantii*, found in a Czechoslovakian nursery in 1937. Plants have dark green foliage that contrasts beautifully with the 3-4″ wide deep yellow flowers. The center consists of a nearly black cone. Full sun and moist soils are necessary for best performance. Plants are magnificent from late July well

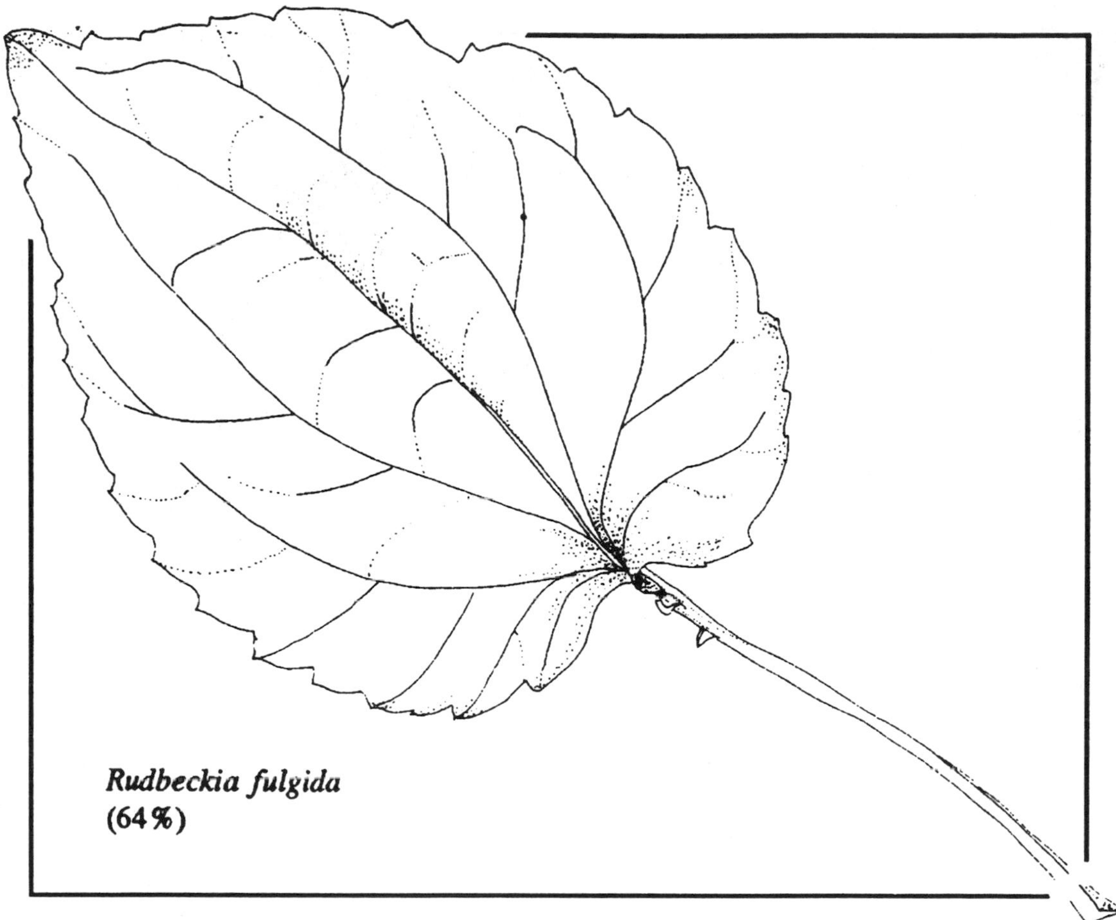

***Rudbeckia fulgida***
**(64%)**

into September. Plants were so good they were designated a Perennial Plant of the Year for 1999 and are still one of the most popular perennials used today. Unfortunately, its popularity resulted in demands that could not be met by vegetatively-propagated means. In response to the demand, growers resorted to seed propagation. Today I deal only with nurseries who can assure me they have the real thing. From seed, most plants are var. *sullivantii*, which, fortunately, are almost as good. This messing up of vegetative clones has also occurred in 'Coronation Gold' yarrow, *Heuchera* 'Palace Purple' and *Sedum* 'Autumn Joy', with far worse results.

var. *speciosa* has basal leaves which are entire or shallowly lobed. The stem leaves are coarsely toothed. Plants are about 24-30″ tall and the flowers are 2-3″ across with deep orange ray petals.

var. *sullivantii* is much like var. *deamii* but the stem leaves are successively reduced in size until the uppermost are merely large bracts. The name refers to botanist William Starling Sullivant (1803-1873), born in Ohio, who was among the first to describe many plants of central Ohio.

***Rudbeckia* 'Goldsturm'**
**(64%)**

***-laciniata*** (la-sin-ee-ah′ ta) Cutleaf Coneflower 5-7′/4′
Summer Yellow North America Zones 3-9

Plants are native from Quebec west to Montana and south to Florida, Texas and Arizona, growing in moist fields and grassy roadsides. The dull green lower leaves are deeply 3-7 lobed while the upper leaves are sessile and less deeply cut into 3 lobes.

The stems, which branch only near the top, have short stiff hairs that feel like sandpaper when handled. The 2-3½″ wide blooms are made up of drooping yellow ray flowers surrounding a green cylindrical disc. Plants do best in moist soils but drier soils may be tolerated as long as irrigation is provided during drought. Place in full sun to partial shade. Plants are long lived and 10 years of good garden performance are not uncommon. Cutting spent flowers after that first flush results in additional flowering in the fall. These are big plants, not suitable for a small garden, but spectacular where well grown. Some of the finest specimens can be seen in the great Cantigny Park in Wheaton, Illinois.

Propagate the species from seed, division, or terminal cutting. Cultivars must be propagated vegetatively by division or cuttings.

**Cultivars:**

'Golden Glow' propelled this species from an overlooked wild flower to a garden staple. Introduced to the garden trade in 1894 as var. *hortensia*, it has been popular ever since. Unlike most others in this species, it can be quite aggressive. Plants grow 3-5′ tall and are covered with large, fully double lemon yellow flowers. Unfortunately, they are also often covered with aphids, to which this cultivar is most prone. 'Golden Glow' has been replaced by newer cultivars that are shorter and a little less attractive to aphids.

'Goldquelle' ('Gold Fountain', 'Gold Drop') bears double yellow flowers and a is clump-former, growing 2½-4′ tall. In full sun, stems are sufficiently strong to support the heavy flowers; in shady areas, they fall like cooked spaghetti. Likely a hybrid with *R. nitida.*

'Herbstsonne' ('Autumn Sun') grows up to 7′ tall and is one of the finest coneflowers in cultivation. Arguments arise as to whether it belongs here or with *R. nitida*, but for me, it belongs here. Dozens of long, drooping sulphur yellow petals surround a green cylindrical disc producing a glorious scene in late August through October. Towering over red dahlias, blue asters and purple coneflowers, it is the king of the sunny fall garden. In the North, the stems usually don't require staking, however, they may need some support in the South. Cold hardy to about zone 5.

'Soleil D'or' ('Golden Sun') bears single flowers consisting of wide golden ray flowers.

***-maxima*** (max-i′ ma) | Giant Coneflower | 5-8′/3′
Summer | Yellow | United States | Zones 5-9

The common name is particularly fitting as these plants look down on most others in the garden. They are like a seven-foot basketball player who weighs 150 pounds. The bold 2′ long and 8-10″ wide basal leaves are blue-green and as they ascend the stem, they clasp the stem. The distinctive leaves, along with the handsome yellow flowers, have made this plant a favorite of garden designers. However, garden designers are often clueless and plants are at best fair garden specimens, unless put in groups of at least five, where the skinny-minis can fill out as a family. As a contrast to fine-textured species or simply to raise the ceiling of the garden room, these have become more and more common since their introduction to commercial production in the

*Rudbeckia maxima*
(75%)

late 1980s. The leaves tend to be more evergreen the further south one travels. The yellow drooping ray flowers are attached to black cylindrical cones and although the flowers may be up to 5″ in diameter, they always look small because of the immense size of the plant. In full sun, plants are upright and do not need support. Don't put in shade.

Propagate by root cuttings (see *Anemone*).

***-triloba*** (tri-lo′ ba) Three-Lobed Coneflower 24-36″/18″
Summer Yellow United States Zones 3-10

These plants are some of my favorites in the sunny summer garden. The much-branched plants carry many small (1½″ across) yellow flowers with purplish black, raised central discs. Flowers appear about the same time as 'Goldsturm' and persist nearly as long. The basal leaves are obviously 3-lobed and the stem leaves less so. Plants are seldom listed in perennial catalogs, perhaps because *R. triloba* is technically a biennial (although that does not stop the common foxglove from being listed as a perennial everywhere). This is unfortunate because it is more persistent than many biennials and will reseed with abandon. Plants perform best in open areas but can tolerate a little shade. In that case, support may be necessary to keep plants upright. This overlooked native should be included in more gardens. This is such a good plant that it was designated a Georgia Gold Medal Winner in 1996 and actively promoted to gardeners throughout the southeastern United States.

Propagate the species by division, seed, or cuttings; var. *nana* is best propagated by division. Plants propagated from seed in the spring flower the first year.

**Related Species:**

*R. missouriensis*, Missouri coneflower, usually grows 2-3′ tall and bears yellow flowers with black discs on branched stems. The leaves and stems are conspicuously hairy. Flowers appear in mid to late summer and continue to fall. Zones 5-8.

*R. nitida* is similar to *R. laciniata* in that the yellow ray flowers droop and the disc is greenish and quite columnar. However, plants are shorter with rounded, sparsely toothed, almost entire leaves. They are native to the South and winter hardy to zone 6 or 7. Various cultivars have been assigned to the species over the years, including the well-known 'Herbstsonne' (see *R. laciniata*). Plants can't read, so except for taxonomists, sleep should not be lost as to where they belong.

*R. subtomentosa*, sweet coneflower, grows about 4′ tall and differs from *R. triloba* in having all the leaves with obvious petioles and a dull purple-brown disc rather than the black seen in the former species. The stems are also covered with soft down. Smell the flowers and you may pick up the scent of anise, accounting for its common name. Although plants sometimes open up in the middle, particularly after a hard rain, they are showy for areas of full sun and way underused; hardy to zone 5 (4 with a little protection). 'Henry Eilers' is making a splash in gardening circles because of the 4-5′ tall upright habit and light yellow, narrow, quilled ray flowers with brown cones in late summer and fall.

Rudbeckia triloba
(80%)

***Ruellia*** (rue-ell-ee′ a) Mexican Petunia, Texas Petunia Acanthaceae

I did not include ruellias in earlier editions of this book because I always considered them annuals. Species such as the red *R. elegans* and the beautiful creeping ruellia, *R. squarrosa* should be considered annuals except in the most southerly locales. Of course, living conditions in Madison, Georgia are certainly different than Madison, Wisconsin, and some of the ruellias are perennials in the southern third of the country. The most common and toughest of them all is *R. brittoniana*, whose 4-5′ tall stature, combined with petunia-like flowers and black stems, has made the plant popular throughout the country, although cold hardy only to zone 7. In areas where they are perennial, they will root to China and spread by stolons, making their removal a major challenge. Add to that its reseeding tendencies, and one can see why not being hardy may be an advantage. However, this is one tough plant: heat, humidity, drought, and bugs do not faze it.

**Cultivars**:

'Alba' has white flowers but is not as floriferous or vigorous as the species.

'Chi-Chi' is about half the height of the species but much better branched, thus making a wider plant. The flowers are a soft pink. Quite beautiful.

'Katie's Dwarf', named for Katie Ferguson of Odessa, Texas, is less than 6″ tall and where conditions are to its liking, will be covered with lavender-blue flowers for much of the summer. In marginal areas, few flowers are produced. 'Katie's Pink' and 'Katie's White' have been produced as well, but the original is the best of the three.

**Related Species**:

*R. humilis* is cold hardy to zone 5, and in mild winters to zone 4. They reseed everywhere and the small light lavender flowers occur most of the summer. Plants are about a foot tall.

***Ruta*** (rue′ ta) Rue Rutaceae

Many herbs are considered highly decorative and rue surely belongs in that category. A number of plants travel under the common name rue, including rue anemone (*Anemonella thalictroides*), goat's rue (*Galega officinalis*), wall rue (*Asplenium ruta-muraria*), and the various species of *Thalictrum* which make up the meadow-rues. The alternate, pinnately compound leaves of rue are particularly pungent and dotted with purple glands. The yellow flowers, consisting of four sepals and four petals (occasionally five of each) and 8-10 stamens, are usually borne in corymbs. Plants may be propagated by seed or cuttings. Of the 40 species, only *R. graveolens* is used to any extent outside the herb garden.

**-*graveolens*** (gra-vee′ o-lenz) Rue, Herb of Grace 12-36″/30″
Summer Pale Yellow Southern Europe Zones 4-8

This species was well established in European monastery gardens in the 1100s because its aromatic odor suggested medicinal value. If one could swallow the concoction of leaves and stems without gagging, it was supposed to help one stay young. In fact, the original Greek name was rute, from *ruomai*, to preserve, a reference to the plant's effect on longevity. It is a sub-shrub, meaning that the base of the plant becomes woody but the plant dies back almost to the ground in the winter. The ¾″ diameter flowers are a rather dull yellow. The flowers are all right, but compared to the blue foliage of some of the cultivars, they take a back seat. The reason for its popularity as an ornamental plant is because of the lovely glaucous blue, delicately cut foliage, particularly on some cultivars. It should also be mentioned that handling of the foliage can cause dermatitis (like poison ivy) in susceptible individuals when the skin is exposed to sunlight. This happens more in nurseries handling large quantities of material but can occur with gardeners as well. Plant in full sun and well-drained soil. Wet feet result in doomed plants.

Propagate the cultivars from terminal cuttings in late summer and early fall.

**Cultivars:**

'Blue Beauty', a mounding plant, bears excellent blue-green foliage and is an asset to the front of the border.

'Blue Mound' is a mounding form about 15″ tall, with blue-green foliage. This is similar to 'Blue Beauty'; I cannot tell the difference.

'Curly Girl' has curly lacy blue foliage that is bushy and compact.

'Jackman's Blue' is about 30″ tall. The foliage is glaucous blue and topped by the same pale yellow flowers found in the species. The cultivars help soften some of the screaming reds and yellows in the summer and fall garden.

'Variegata' has dissected leaves edged with creamy white.

# S

***Saccharum*** (sack-car′ um) Plume Grass, Ravenna Grass Poaceae

Sugar cane, *S. officinarum*, is the best-known and most economically important species in the genus. Sugar cane may not be a garden plant but hardy sugar cane, *S. arundinaceum*, native to China, is hardy to zone 6 and produces wide, white-striped leaves and handsome pink flowers in the fall, forming at the top of the tall clump. This is not a small plant, nor are most of the species. In the past, many of these garden plants were listed under *Erianthus*, but that genus has been superseded with *Saccharum*. Most plants are native to tropical and temperate areas and are adaptable to many areas of the garden, but are particularly reliable in moist areas and well-drained sandy sites. In general, plants are large (up to 12′ tall), erect, tufted, perennial grasses with flat leaf blades, and dense silky panicles of flowers in late summer and fall. Most are warm-season grasses, and have handsome, if not overwhelming, fall color.

The most common form is the massive 10-12′ tall ravenna grass, *S. ravennae*, native to southern Europe but escaped to the United States. The gray-green leaves are about 1″ wide and 3-4′ long. The 4-5′ wide clumps make dramatic specimens for the large landscape, useful for screens, highways and golf courses. They perform best in moist areas, but they don't require bogs to be at their best. They are simply too large for many small landscapes and flowers can break off in heavy winds. The fall color can be orange and the tan and purple winter costume is outstanding where sufficient room is allowed. Plants perform well in zones 6-9.

*S. giganteus*, sugarcane plume grass, equally large and wide, is also used as a large backdrop for screening or specimen plants. Plants are native to the southeastern United States, west to Texas and north to Ohio. Not as cold hardy or as tough as ravenna grass.

Another useful species includes a southeastern native, *S. brevibarbe* var. *contortum* (*S. contortum*), bent awn plume grass, which is about 2′ tall in leaf and up to 4′ tall in flower. The red fall color is one of the most handsome aspects of this species. Plants do well in wet soils. Probably hardy in zones 7 to 10.

***Sagina*** (sa-geen′ a) Pearlwort Caryophyllaceae

Who could believe that this tiny plant is related to such bouquet favorites as carnations and baby's breath? Yet a quick study of the small white flowers shows the similarities, and an even quicker study of the short stems with their swollen nodes shows they belong in the same family. The mat-forming, ground-hugging plants are becoming more popular in patio containers, around flagstones or as ground covers in the rock garden. The main species offered is *S. subulata*, pearlwort, whose tight compact growth habit makes it the best one for gardens. The narrow ½-1″ long leaves are bright lime green and form a mossy carpet when planted in partial sun and gritty, well-drained soils. Abundant summer rain is a problem, because water droplets become trapped in the leaves, resulting in rotting and melting out of various parts of the mat. Division and an occasional shearing help alleviate the problem. High humidity is also not much to its liking, particularly if grown on heavy soils. The small white flowers consist of 5 petals and sepals and are usually borne singly on short stalks in the spring. I originally thought plants were winter hardy to about zone 6, but when I saw beautiful carpets in the outstanding garden of Raymond Bilodeau and Louise Nadeau in Quebec City (zone 3), I knew this was a much tougher plant than most people assume. Of course, their garden was not only beautiful in summer, it was covered with insulating snow in the winter.

The best use for pearlwort is in containers or at the edge of a bed where watering and drainage can be better controlled. They are neat plants when the green mats ooze over the sides of containers, they are sad when they melt out in the garden. Propagate from division or seed, the cultivar from division only.

**Cultivars:**

'Aurea' is a golden yellow-leaved form. Not as common, but handsome. Requires more shade than the species.

***Salvia*** (sal′ vee-a) Sage Lamiaceae

One of my fondest memories as a young boy was drinking the nectar from the red salvia flowers that my friend's dad planted in his garden every summer. Plucking out the center of the flower (I had no idea it was called the corolla) and squeezing out the "honey" was a favorite summer pastime. Yes, we were pretty boring kids, but it is an activity I have not yet outgrown. Seems that my students think I am a complete nutcase when I demonstrate this lost art in class, but I know they quietly show their friends their newly acquired salvia-sucking skills when I am not around.

Those who know *Salvia* only as an annual bedding plant are surprised to learn that this is a vast genus, consisting of over 700 species. Salvia is a collector's dream! And collectors there are. Most plantspeople go through their "salvia stage of life" at some time in their garden careers, collecting dozens of sages with unpronounceable names, falling in love with all of them, and then like a teenager, coming around to the real world. Been there, done that. Unfortunately, nurseries feed this habit by introducing new ones every year, most of which are admired briefly before they die.

To collect them all is impossible but the trying is not. Enough ornamental species are available today that the collector can enjoy this hobby for a lifetime. My good friend Jan Waltemath in Portland, Oregon has collected dozens and will never get them all. But what fun. In this respect, *Salvia* is much like *Campanula*, and zealots of both will constantly drag you over to see their newest find. With so many sages from which to choose, however, it should not be surprising that a few new ones do "hit the ground running". Since the last edition, salvia fever has peaked, and now we can concentrate on those that have stood at least a short test of time.

In general, members have 4-sided stems, opposite leaves and whorled flowers. The tubular, two-lipped flowers are produced in terminal and axillary whorls. Blue and red are the predominant flower colors but those with red flowers are almost always annuals or short-lived perennials. Yellow, white pink and bicolors are also available. Plants range in height from less than 1′ (*S. chamaedryoides*) to immense 4-5′ tall hulks such as *S. involucrata* and 'Indigo Spires'. Many emit interesting scents when the foliage is bruised, and it is always fun to play the game of "What is this smell?" with your friends. *S. rutilans* smells of pineapple, *S. microphylla* resembles currants and *S. officinalis* smells of sage. The scents seem obvious but 9 times out of 10, another person will smell something totally different. My wife, Susan, is convinced that pineapple sage should be changed to carrot cake sage. Still others are steeped in tradition and folklore and possible new medicinal uses. *S. officinalis* comes complete with culinary and medicinal histories, as does the relatively recently discovered *S. divinorum*, of the Sierra Mazateca region of Mexico, where it is held in high esteem by the native people, and in low esteem by law enforcement who have seen the effects of the hallucinatory properties too often on the streets.

Many species are native to Mexico, the southwestern United States, California or Central America and winter hardiness in much of the country is an issue. In California alone, there are at least 15 native sages, the majority of which are highly drought tolerant. These include *S. apiana*, *S. clevelandii*, *S. dorrii*, *S. leucophylla*, *S. mellifera*, and hybrids between them. As beautiful as some of these are, they arc seldom seen east of the Rockies. Gardeners in California and the Southwest, get with the program; these are plants to be embraced and included in the garden.

Several of our more common species were sent to England in the late 1700s and early 1800s. John Ruskin wrote in *Proserpina* in 1879 that "the exotic sages have no moderation in their hues", and was particularly unhappy with the brilliant blue of *S. patens*, stating that "there's no color that gives me such an idea of violence—a sort of rough, angry scream—as that shade of blue, ungradated". Regardless of Ruskin's hysteria, some of these "exotic" sages are available in various catalogs and nurseries. As gardeners, we have our own breeders who continue to introduce and popularize this genus. Mr. Salvia, John Dufresne of Greensboro, North Carolina, has provided outstanding hybrids, and John Fairey and Carl Schoenfeld, formerly of Yucca Do in Waller, Texas have explored Mexico and the Southwest to add to and feed our *Salvia* habit. Just get online, you may be stuck there for many an hour. Plant collecting and hybridization are alive and well, you simply have to know where to look.

Many of the species we read about are annuals or half hardy perennials that overwinter only during exceptionally mild winters. I have had my "salvia binge" as I have grown or studied most of those on the following list. That I survived says something of the toughness of a gardener.

A relative hardiness guide to several salvias is provided below. Few of the "hardy" salvias survive north of zone 4 and those designated as "half hardy" over winter in zones 7 to 10, occasionally zone 6. Biennials will die after flowering regardless of location, although they may reseed readily. Of course, even the most tender half hardy forms may overwinter for a few years proving the age old truism that plants can't read. The hardiness zones are guidelines at best.

| | **Hardy, half hardy, annual, biennial**[z] | **Flower color** |
|---|---|---|
| *aethiopis* | Biennial | Dull white |
| *argentea* | Biennial | Whitish, yellow |
| *arizonica* | Half hardy | Sky blue |
| *azurea* | Hardy | Azure blue |
| *blepharophylla* | Half hardy | Scarlet red |
| *bulleyana* | Hardy | Pale yellow, black |
| *cacaliifolia* | Half hardy | Dark blue |
| *candelabrum* | Half hardy | Violet blue |
| *chamaedryoides* | Hardy | Blue |
| *clevelandii* | Half hardy | Blue |
| *coccinea* | Annual | Bright red |
| *confertiflora* | Half hardy | Red |
| *darcyi* | Half hardy | Bright red |
| *discolor* | Half hardy | Blue black |
| *farinacea* | Half hardy | Light blue |
| *forskaohlei* | Hardy | Violet blue |
| *glechomifolia* | Half hardy | Blue |
| *greggii* | Half hardy | Red |
| *guaranitica* | Half hardy | Violet blue |
| *haematodes* | Half hardy | Bluish violet |
| *hians* | Hardy | Bluish |
| *horminum* | Annual | Lilac |
| *indica* | Annual | Lavender |
| *interrupta* | Half hardy | Blue |
| *involucrata* | Half hardy | Pink |
| *jurisicii* | Hardy | Deep blue |
| *koyamae* | Hardy | Yellow |
| *lavandulifolia* | Hardy | Violet-blue |
| *leucantha* | Half hardy | Blue and white |
| *madrensis* | Half hardy | Yellow |

| | **Hardy, half hardy, annual, biennial**[z] | **Flower color** |
|---|---|---|
| *mexicana* | Half hardy | Blue |
| *microphylla* | Half hardy | Red |
| *miniata* | Half hardy | Red |
| *nipponica* | Hardy | Yellow |
| *officinalis* | Hardy | Purple |
| *patens* | Half hardy | Gentian blue |
| *penstemonoides* | Hardy | Red |
| *pratensis* | Hardy | Blue |
| *prunelloides* | Annual | Blue |
| *puberula* | Half hardy | Pink |
| *regla* | Half hardy | Orange-scarlet |
| *rutilans* | Half hardy | Bright red |
| *sclarea* | Biennial | Whitish blue |
| *sinaloensis* | Half hardy | Deep blue |
| *splendens* | Annual | Red |
| x *superba* | Hardy | Purple |
| *transsylvanica* | Hardy | Dark blue |
| *uliginosa* | Hardy | Sky blue |
| *van houttei* | Annual | Wine red |
| *verticillata* | Hardy | Lilac blue |

[z]*Hardy*: survive north of zone 7; *half hardy*: survive in zones 7 to 10, occasionally zone 6; *annual*: too cold north of zone 8; *biennial*: survive 2 years.

Looking at the above list, the choice of perennial ornamental sages is somewhat limited depending on where you live. However, incorporating several half hardy species such as pineapple sage, *S. rutilans* (usually sold as *S. elegans*, the foliage really does smell of pineapple) and its wonderful chartreuse cultivar 'Golden Delicious' (zone 7b, 8) gives fragrance and beauty. *S. mexicana* 'Limelight' and 'Lollie Jackson' are "eye candy", they are so beautiful. Numerous half hardy hybrids are also available, such as the most attractive 'Maraschino' and 'Cherry Queen'.

A potential drawback to some of the sages is that they are fall-flowerers only. But to condemn a plant because of that is to condemn plants that enjoy the shade. Fall-flowering salvias can rejuvenate a tired garden and add an entirely new dimension. Some of these include velvet sage, Hidalgo sage and wine sage. Many of half hardy sages grow so rapidly that it really doesn't matter if they return or not. Take a few cuttings inside over the winter or buy new ones in the spring. *S. elegans* var. *van houttei*, wine sage, is 3′ tall with claret red flowers that start blooming in midsummer and continue until frost. Probably the most wonderful flower color is found with the orange-scarlet Hidalgo sage, *S. regla*, which stops people in their tracks. Unfortunately, it does not flower until late October, already too late for many northern gardens. They should all be raised from cuttings that root easily throughout the growing season.

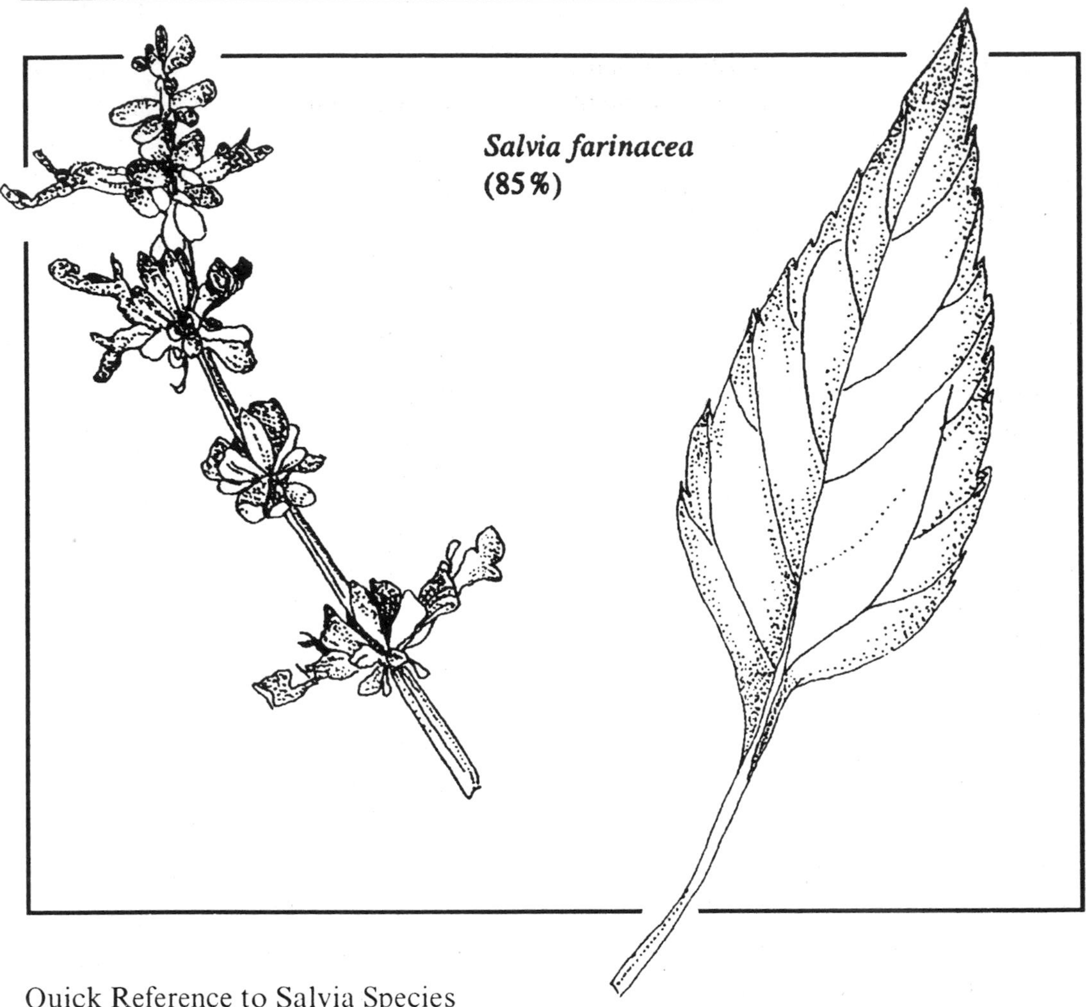

*Salvia farinacea*
(85%)

Quick Reference to Salvia Species

| | Height (in.) | Flower color |
|---|---|---|
| *S. argentea* | 24-48 | White with yellow |
| *S. azurea* | 36-48 | Azure blue |
| *S. greggii* | 20-30 | Red |
| *S. guaranitica* | 36-40 | Deep blue |
| *S. koyamae* | 20-30 | Yellow |
| *S. officinalis* | 12-20 | Purple |
| *S. pratensis* | 12-36 | Bright blue |
| *S. sclarea* | 30-48 | White/lilac |
| *S.* x *sylvestris* | 18-48 | Blue violet |

***-argentea*** (ar-gen-tee′ a) Silver Sage 24-48″/3′
Summer Whitish Southern Europe Zones 6-8

Grown for the large white-woolly foliage, plants make a wonderful contrast to green-leaved plants in the garden. The wedge-shaped, wrinkled, and irregularly toothed stem leaves are sessile and about 6-8″ long. The flowers appear the second year on seed-propagated plants but are not particularly exceptional. They appear in a slightly branched large panicle, each whorl consisting of 6-10 whitish yellow flowers. The inside part of the flower, the corolla, is about three times longer than the calyx. Having given the details of this flower's structure, I now recommend the removal of said flowers as soon as possible. This allows the foliage to remain the dominant feature of the plant and insures the plant produces leaves rather than marginally attractive flowers.

In late summer, plants often look the worse for wear, particularly if the summer has been hot and rainy. Hairy-leaved plants such as this tend to retain moisture, allowing leaf diseases to become established. It is short lived and responds like a biennial in most areas of the country. This is a terrific plant for containers and baskets as it requires well-drained gritty soils to do well. In the North, plants do well down to zone 5; in the South, they perform well north to zone 7a, struggle in 7b and quickly melt out further south. A 1997 Plant Select® winner, a program administered by the Denver Botanic Garden and Colorado State University.

Propagate by seed or self-rooting lateral offshoots that may be detached in the spring and replanted.

***-azurea*** (a-zur′ ree-a) — Azure Sage — 3-4′/4′
Fall — Azure Blue — Southeastern United States — Zones 5-9

This large plant attains 3-4 feet in height when the long slender spikes of azure-blue flowers appear. The lance-shaped basal leaves are about 3″ long but become smaller and narrower as they ascend the stem. Flowers are borne in the upper leaf axils in spikelike whorled inflorescences. The pedicels (the individual flower stalks) are short, resulting in flowers densely arranged on the stalk. A native of the Southeast, it is much more tolerant of heat and humidity than many other species. Two or three plants placed about the garden dominate the fall scene. Some of the finest specimens I have encountered were in the Horticulture Gardens at Massey University in Palmerston North, New Zealand.

Propagate from seed, division, or terminal cuttings.

**Cultivars:**

var. *grandiflora* (syn. subsp. *pitcheri, S. pitcheri*), pitcher sage, has paler green, hairier leaves and larger, paler blue flowers than the species. It is more available but no better than the type. 'Nekan' was found in the Lincoln, Nebraska area and the name is an abbreviation of Nebraska and Kansas. Plants bear azure blue flowers on 4′ tall stems, with gray-green leaves. 'September Snow' is a white-flowered form of the pitcher sage.

***-greggii*** (greg-ee′ eye) — Texas Sage — 2-3′/3′
Summer — Red — Texas, Mexico — Zones 7-10

This fine Texas native has found its way into mainstream perennial gardens, and provides more winter hardiness than most other red forms. The 1-2″ long ovate leaves have entire margins and produce a heavy sage fragrance when rubbed. The typical form has scarlet flowers and was found near Saltillo, Mexico by a Mexican trader, Josiah Gregg, in 1870. The two-lipped flowers, which may be red, pink, violet or white, are held in whorls of two or threes and have a wide lower lip and smaller upper lip. Flowers occur in early to midsummer, slow down significantly in the heat of summer, but perk up in the fall. The plants are a bit unruly and get rather messy as the season progresses. Cutting back after a month in the garden helps keep it more compact. Texas sage has become popular because of heat, humidity and drought tolerance, and is a hummingbird magnet. Most hybrids are cold hardy to zone 7, a few to zone 6, and occasionally to 5.

**Cultivars and hybrids:**

Most of the following are cultivars of *S. greggii*, but some are hybrids, often with *S. microphylla*.

'Alba' is a 2′ tall plant with white flowers with a green calyx. Plants are quite cold hardy, at least to zone 6.

'Big Pink' produces shiny green leaves on an upright 3-4′ tall plant. Handsome violet-pink petals with dark sepals occur most of the season, except in the hottest months.

'Desert Blaze' has variegated leaves with narrow white edges. Plants are only about 18″ tall and bear red flowers in spring and fall.

'Cienego D'Oro' has pale yellow flowers, growing 15-18″ tall.

'Dark Dancer' grows 4′ tall and bears maroon-red flowers. Plants bloom well through the summer and even better in the fall.

'Flame' is about 2′ tall with deep red flowers.

'Furman's Red' grows much more upright than the previous cultivars, stretching up to 3′ in height. The bright red flowers occur throughout the season, but are heavier in late spring and fall. Hardy to zone 6b. A 2005 Plant Select® winner, a program administered by the Denver Botanic Garden and Colorado State University.

'Hot Lips' is the best of them all, growing 3′ tall and equally wide in a couple of years. The flowers are bicolor red and white and can cover the plants in spring and early summer. Plants are often listed under *S. microphylla*.

'Lipstick' bears flowers with lipstick red petals with a small white throat and deeper maroon sepals. Plants are 2½-3′ tall.

'Pink Preference' is an excellent drought-tolerant cultivar with dark calyces and rosy red petals. Plants are about 3′ tall and equally wide.

'Teresa' produces many white flowers with bits of purple spotting and streaking on the petals. Different and beautiful.

'Wild Thing' is about 2′ tall and equally wide with awesome coral-pink flowers. Plants are vigorous and cold hardy perhaps to zone 5. Another 2005 Plant Select® winner.

***-guaranitica*** (gar-an-it′ i-ca) | Blue Anise Sage | 4-6′/4′
Summer | Deep Blue | Brazil, Argentina | Zones 7-10

This outstanding sage, with long deep blue flowers, begins to flower in early to midsummer and continues all season. The dark green leaves are 4-6″ long, and sparsely

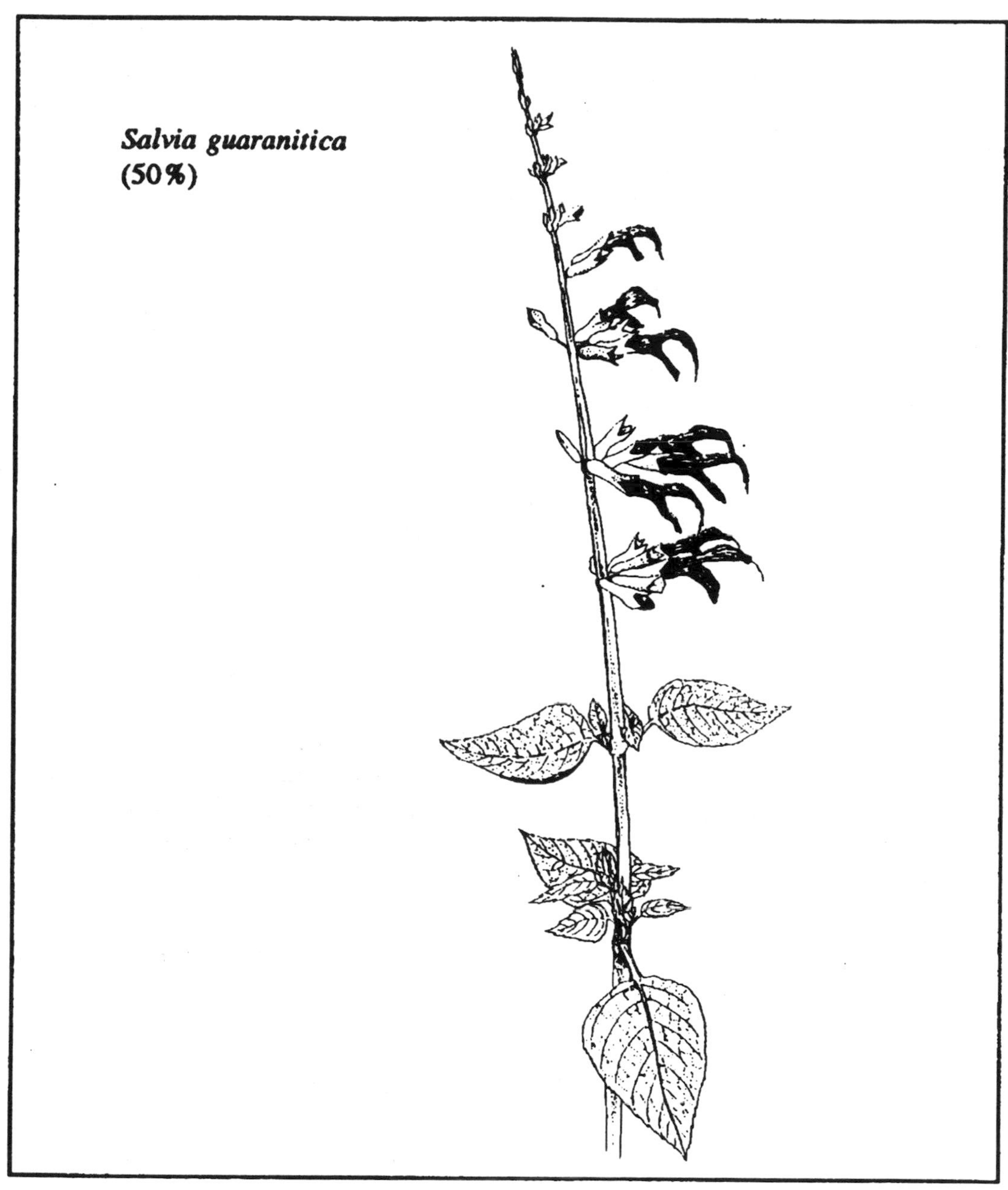

*Salvia guaranitica* (50%)

hairy. They don't have much smell when crushed and do not smell like anise. Flowers are held in whorls of 3-8, the corolla (petals) can be up to 3″ long, and the calyx (sepals) may be a different color. The lower lip is shorter than the upper one.

This is a full sun plant, growing in partial shade simply makes the plants taller and in need of support. Plants may be cut back early in the season to promote more compactness and to control height. Good drainage helps a good deal, particularly in the winter. Divide or take cuttings every third year to maintain vigor.

In Georgia, we think so highly of this species that it was awarded the prestigious Georgia Gold Award in 1995.

**Cultivars:**

'Argentina Skies' was shared with me many years ago by Charles Cresson of Swarthmore, Pennsylvania. The flowers are pastel blue, a much more muted color than that of the species. Beautiful, although not as floriferous.

'Blue Ensign' has large Cambridge blue petals with green sepals.

'Black and Blue' has large dark blue flowers with almost black sepals. Plants often reach 5-6′ in height in the South, more like 3′ in the upper Midwest.

'Costa Rica Blue' may be the same as 'Black and Blue'. They are both big, flower later than the species and have darker calyces than the corollas.

'Purple Splendor' is smaller than the former but also has dark violet blue sepals, however, the leaves are smooth.

***-leucantha*** (loo-kan′ tha) | Velvet Sage, Mexican Bush Sage | 4-5′/4′
Fall | Purple, White | South America | Zones 7-9

I had always considered this an annual, and it is for gardeners north of zone 7; but it has been such a trouper in the Gardens at UGA, as well as other gardens in the Southeast, that I have included it here.

Plants are large and tidy, with few insects or diseases ever disfiguring the wonderful velvety leaves. The foliage is dull green on the upper sides and gray green beneath. In September to November, or until the frost hits, long spires of flowers made up of purple sepals and white petals are formed, making this a dominant plant in the fall garden. Its late flowering tendencies may rule it out even as an annual in the Northeast because of early frosts, but elsewhere, this plant should not be overlooked, regardless of garden locale.

**Cultivars**:

'Midnight' flowers are entirely purple and I believe it to be even more handsome than the species.

'Santa Barbara' is a welcome dwarf form, only growing about 2′ tall and 3′ wide. Flowers are lighter purple than 'Midnight'. Unfortunately, plants do not appear to be as cold hardy as the species or 'Midnight', perhaps into zone 8.

***-jurisicii*** (jur-i-sic′ ee-eye) | Jurisici's Sage | 12-18″/12″
Early Summer | Lilac | Yugoslavia | Zones 4-8

This species has labored in obscurity for many years but has some excellent attributes. Plants are relatively small and in some cases less than a foot tall, eliminating the problem of staking—a major headache with other species, particularly in zones 6 and south. Thus it may be grown either as a rock garden plant or placed in the front of the border. Stems have long spreading white hairs but the foliage is smooth except around the margins. The branched flower spikes of deep lilac are 8″ long and consist of 3-7 whorls of upside-down flowers. This curious habit of inverted flowers

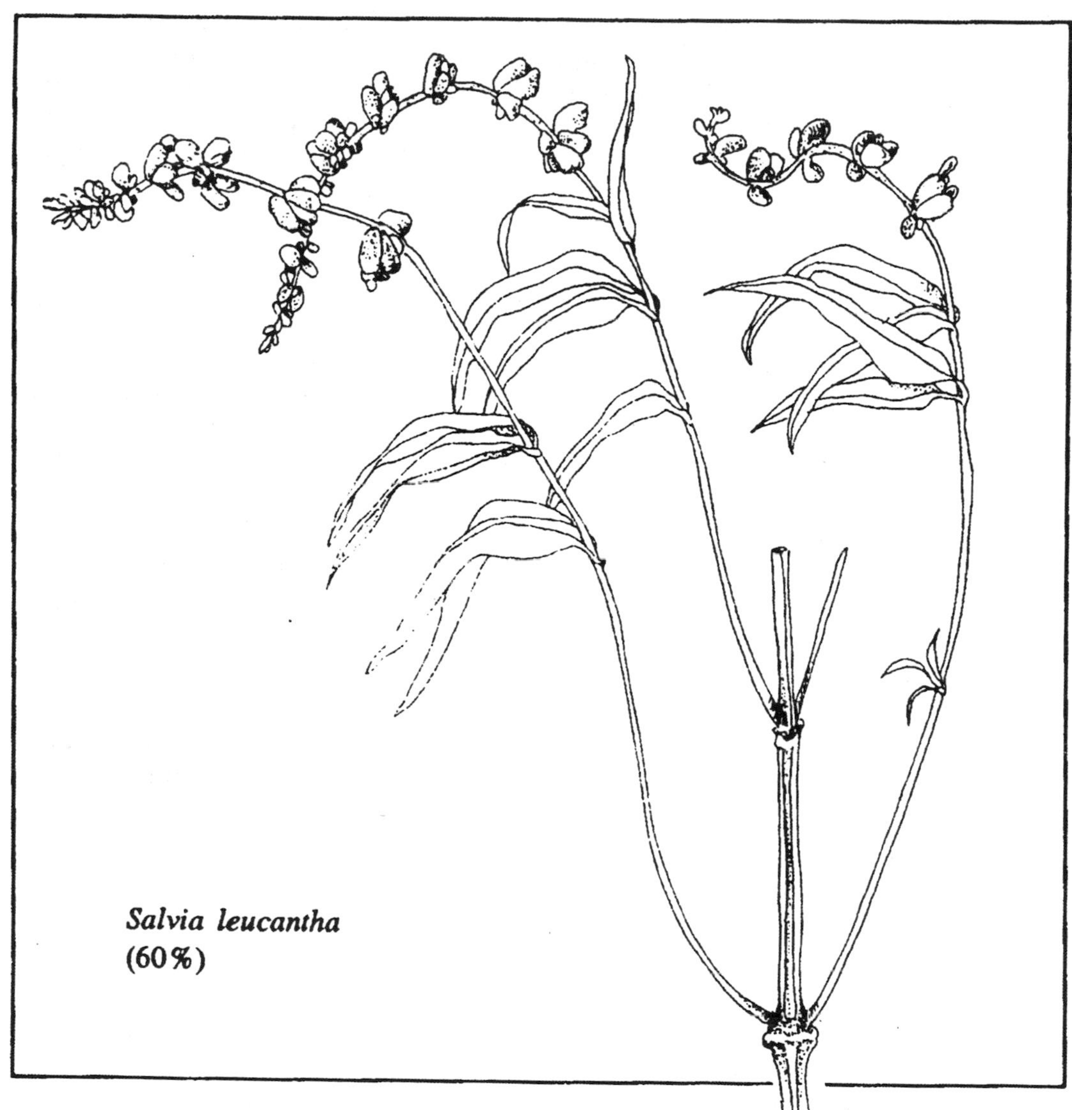

***Salvia leucantha***
**(60%)**

combined with the fact that most of the foliage is deeply lobed into pinnate sections (pinnatisect) make this species unique among the garden sages.

Plants tolerate a wide range of soils, accept a lack of rainfall, and, given a sunny location, generally behave.

Propagate from division or seed.

***-koyamae*** (ko-yam′ aye) Yellow Sage 20-30″/18″
Late Summer, Fall Yellow Japan Zones 6-8

Few of the yellow-flowered sages have become popular, mainly because of lack of hardiness or simply for not being as good as they sound. This species is hardier than most and if properly sited, is an attractive, if not a "jaw-dropper" plant. The hairy, large green leaves are as handsome as the flowers, and quickly cover the ground. They are not invasive, but can certainly be aggressive. Plants are prone to stress-related leaf spotting, particularly in times of drought. In late summer and fall, the pale yellow flowers occur on 20-30″ tall flowering stems. Worth trying in a partially shaded environment, but I have yet to be impressed. Full sun and dry soils should be avoided.

| **-*officinalis*** (o-fish-i-nah′ lis) | | Common Sage | 12-20″/15″ |
|---|---|---|---|
| Summer | Purple | Mediterranean | Zones 4-7 |

Parsley, sage, rosemary and thyme is more than a recipe for flavor or a song title. Culinary sage, *S. officinalis*, has been used to flavor food throughout history, often masking the smell and taste of the food itself. However, the species has been used as an ornamental garden plant for many years, providing more than just fragrance, but handsome foliage and flowers too. They make terrific companion plants in mixed containers, as well as for more dominant plants like roses. One of the best treatments I have seen is the wonderful rose garden at Mottisfont Abbey in England where many colorful herbs including lavenders and sages of all kinds were interplanted with the roses. One need not travel to England to take advantage of such combinations. Surprisingly simple and effective.

Plants require full sun and excellent drainage; they will not do well in heavy, poorly-drained soils. Excellent for containers or raised beds where soils and drainage can be controlled. In areas of high humidity and lots of summer rain, they can look pretty sad and ragged.

**Cultivars:**

'Albiflora' has long narrow leaves and white flowers.

'Aurea' is grown for its golden yellow foliage.

'Berggarten' is the best blue-flowered form, with wide handsome gray-green leaves and deep blue flowers over compact plants.

'Icterina' is sometimes sold as 'Tricolor' but differs in having light green leaves with wavy yellow margins, not the many colors of 'Tricolor'.

'Purpurescens' has purplish leaves, holds the color well in the summer. Looks terrific with lime green to yellow-leaved material, such as *Acorus* 'Ogon' or yellow hostas.

'Rubrifolia' has long narrow leaves and purple-red flowers.

'Salicifolia' has even narrower leaves than others. The leaves are generally 6 to 7 times longer than wide.

'Tricolor' bears leaves flecked and streaked with purple, yellow, pink, violet and white. Looks almost as odious as it sounds.

| **-*pratensis*** (prah-ten′ sis) | | Meadow Sage | 12-36″/36″ |
|---|---|---|---|
| Summer | Lavender-Blue | Europe | Zones 3-7 |

The few stem leaves are small and sessile but the 3-6″ long basal leaves are oblong, with wavy margins and long petioles. The many flowering stems rise from the basal leaves and normally bear lavender-blue flowers. Variability in flower color and size is evident in seed-grown plants. If spent blooms are removed, another flush usually results. Plants tolerate a wide range of garden soils but the leaves deteriorate if plants dry out too many times.

The debate as to whether *S. pratensis* is a separate species from *S. haematodes* is essentially passé; today the latter is considered to be a synonym of, or a grouping of *S. pratensis*.

The species and varieties may be propagated from cuttings, division or seed but cultivars should be propagated from division or terminal cuttings only. The rootstock is quite woody and care must be taken during division to avoid damage. Cuttings are more reliable than division.

**Cultivars:**

'Alba' is a white-flowered form.

'Atroviolacea' has dark violet flowers.

'Baumgartenii' is similar to 'Atroviolacea' but bears lighter violet flowers.

'Eveline' is a hybrid and has upright flowers with light pink petals and darker pink sepals.

'Haematodes' is what some taxonomists have reduced the true *S. haematodes* to. Plants are floriferous with lilac-blue flowers. If you buy *S. haematodes*, this is what you will obtain.

'Rosea' has rose-purple flowers.

'Rubicundra' bears rose-red blossoms.

'Tenorii' is probably the best of the plants listed under this species and has lovely, very deep blue flowers.

'Variegata' produces handsome light blue flowers streaked with white.

| ***-sclarea*** (sklah' ree-a) | | Clary Sage | 30-48"/3' |
|---|---|---|---|
| Summer | White, Lilac | Southern Europe | Zones 4-7 |

Plants are considered short-lived perennials or more often than not, biennials. They are used for their coarse look, large stature when in flower, and good foliage. Clary sage produces a large basal rosette consisting of many 8-10" long, broad, hairy, wrinkled leaves, rough to the touch. The many-branched flowering stems, which emerge the second year, are four-sided, rough and sticky. They bear small white to lilac flowers but it is the pink, lilac or white bracts surrounding the flowers which provide the ornamental value. They are particularly pretty in bud when the bracts are tight around the emerging inflorescences. They soon explode into hundreds of flowers (and bracts) in late spring, filling the garden with bees and butterflies. I have seen wonderful plantings in Long Island where they were combined with purple Japancse iris and red valerian (*Centranthus*).

This is an interesting plant but not one to become too enamored with. Its history of curing ailments of the eyes is fascinating (the seeds and leaves were used for eye ointments) and the bracts are numerous, however, it is short-lived, messy after flowering and it stinks. Smell is a subjective sense, but to me, the odor of the leaves and stems varies from musky (it is sometimes called muscatel sage) to disgusting. Generally, the smell is not too apparent unless you rub the stems, but on a warm, still day, you know the clary is in flower. Plants produce huge numbers of seeds that can be a problem if they self-sow.

Excellent drainage is necessary and they may need the support of other large plants around them, or staking. They are better where humidity is not too high; in the Southeast the explosion of growth is even quicker, and the mess that follows even worse. Propagate from seeds.

**Cultivars:**

'Turkestanica' is more robust, grows taller and has prettier pink to lilac flowers. Recommended over the species if available. Where nights are hot, the bracts fade to whitish.

**-x *sylvestris*** (sill-vest′ ris) Hybrid Sage 18-48″/36″
Summer Violet Blue Hybrid Zones 4-7
(syn. *S. nemorosa*)

A quick glance at the list of synonyms shows that most people, myself included, are confused as to the parentage of the numerous selections that attach themselves to the name. These include the specific epithets *nemorosa, superba* or *sylvestris*. There is sufficient difference in foliage and flower, I believe, to separate cultivars such as 'Lubecca' and 'May Night' from ones like 'Caradonna' and 'Marcus'. The former should be listed under *S.*x *sylvestris* (*S. pratensis* x *S. nemorosa*) and the latter under *S. nemorosa*. The former are sterile and cannot be raised from seed whereas the latter are mostly seed propagated. Seems a pretty obvious difference to me. Differences in habit and color exist between cultivars, as well as garden performance. However, I am going to lump them all together and let the taxonomists fight it out.

Given cool nights and good moisture, the cultivars can be truly spectacular. Numerous dense flower spikes ranging from lavender to deep rich violet-blue rise from basal leaves in May and June to make a wonderful show. Unfortunately, I have been disappointed with the hybrids in zone 7; while they survive and flower adequately, they lose their upright habit, flop over, and fade rapidly. They certainly do well, however, north of zone 7. If grown in the South, a low-growing cultivar is much preferred. They are drought tolerant and survive where many plants succumb.

**Cultivars:**

'Adrian' is a form of *S. nemorosa* with white flowers on 2′ tall plants.

'Blue Hill' has true blue flowers with a long season of bloom. Parentage close to *S.* x *sylvestris*.

'Blue Queen' has violet-blue flowers on 18-24″ tall stems with good heat and drought tolerance. Raised from seed and often forced in greenhouses, plants are becoming more and more available. Parentage close to *S.* x *sylvestris*.

'Caradonna' is about 2′ tall with dark, almost purple stems and many violet-colored flowers. They flower for weeks on end in late spring and early summer. Parentage close to *S. nemorosa*. This cultivar was named the Outstanding Perennial in 2000 by the International Hardy Plant Union.

'East Friesland' ('Ostfriesland') has deep purple flowers and is only 18″ tall. It is better than the type where summers are hot, as it does not require support. Sterile, raised vegetatively. Parentage close to *S. nemorosa*.

'Lubecca' is similar to 'East Friesland' but is about 30″ tall. Both have violet-blue flowers. Parentage close to *S.* x *sylvestris*.

Marcus™ is only 8-10″ tall and bears deep violet flowers for a long time in late spring and summer.

'May Night' ('Mainacht') has larger deep indigo flowers which are larger than 'Lubecca'. Plants grow approximately 18″ high. A 1997 PPA Perennial Plant of the Year selection. Parentage close to *S.* x *sylvestris*. This 'Lubecca' and 'East Friesland' are quite similar and are outstanding when grown in full sun, cool nights and well-drained soil.

'Montrose Best' came from the fine, albeit sadly out of business, Montrose Nursery, in Hillsborough, North Carolina. It was a chance seedling with deep blue-purple corollas and reddish calyces. Occasionally offered by mail order nurseries.

'Plumosa' has rose-purple plumelike flowers on 15-20″ tall plants. Quite different and interesting.

'Rose Queen' is the rose-flowered counterpoint to 'Blue Queen'. Floriferous and handsome.

'Rose Wine' has rosy red flowers on 2′ tall plants.

'Rugen' has gained popularity for its deep blue flowers and compact habit. Parentage close to *S.* x *sylvestris*.

Sensation Rose™ provides many upright stems of rose-pink flowers. Plants are only 12-15″ tall. This could be an excellent new salvia.

'Snow Hill' is similar to 'Blue Hill' but with clean white flowers.

'Viola Klose' has dark blue flowers.

**Related Species and Hybrids:**

*S. aethiopis*, African sage, is a biennial with basal rosettes of large, toothed leaves. The leaves are dull green but have long white hairs (tomenta) in the center in the winter and early spring. The flowers are dull white. More spectacular in leaf than in flower.

*S. bulleyana*, native to China, bears branched stems with yellow flowers often with a purple-black lower lip. Plants grow 2-3′ tall and may be hardy in zones 7-9. Very unusual and fascinating.

*S. chamaedryoides*, blue oak sage, is also a low form, growing about 12″ tall and 15″ wide. The silvery gray-green foliage is topped with racemes of sky blue flowers. A nice change from the 3-4′ tall salvias. Cut plants back in early to midsummer if necessary to maintain compactness. They are intolerant of poorly drained soils and do best in raised beds or containers. Zones 6b-8.

'Cherry Chief' has red flowers poking out of dark calyces. A fine hybrid, growing only about 18″ tall.

'Cherry Queen' is one of the many hybrids produced by Richard Dufresne. This hybrid is the result of crossing *S. greggii* and *S. blepharophylla*, eyelash sage. We have had this 3-4′ tall sage in the Gardens at UGA for 10 years and every year it starts flowering in May and continues until frost. An absolutely outstanding plant for southern gardens.

*S. darcyi*, brought to the United States from Mexico by Yucca Do Nursery, grows 3-4′ tall with orangey red flowers and light green heart-shaped foliage. Plants are likely hardy from zone 7 to 10.

*S. forskaohlei* (for-ska′ oh-lie) is about as tough a salvia as I have tried to kill. In the Armitage garden, it sat in a shaded corner, where it was crowded out by its neighbors, yet its bold green leaves and violet-blue flowers still tried to look good. People should have such an attitude! In more sun, this is a fine plant.

'Indigo Spires' is also a tall growing blue-flowering sage. It is one of the most vigorous and floriferous hybrids (*S. farinacea* x *S. longispicata*) I have grown. In flower, plants easily grow 3-4′ tall and bloom for many months. As fall settles in, the flower color becomes more intense and the spires live up to their name. Unfortunately for Northern gardeners, it is hardy only to about zone 7b, but for those who grow it, the best advice is to give it plenty of room. Cut the stems back occasionally for repeat bloom.

*S.* x *jamensis* is the name given by James Compton to the naturally occurring yellow-flowered hybrid between *S. greggii* and *S. microphylla* found at an elevation around 2000-3000′ in a Mexican mountain pass in 1991. 'California Sunset' has an unusual peach-salmon flower color. Other colors also occurred and names have been published. 'La Luna' has creamy yellow flowers, 'El Doranzo' bears peach-colored flowers. Likely hardy in zones 7-10.

*S. lyrata*, lyre-leaf sage, is one of our finest under-appreciated native sages. They may not be popular at the retail level because they are so common along roadsides and meadows. The leaves are shaped like an old-fashioned lyre and the upright flowers are purple to lavender. This would likely not be mentioned except for three purple-leaved cultivars, 'Burgundy Bliss', 'Purple Volcano' and 'Purple Knockout'. I have grown only 'Purple Knockout' and found it to be excellent, bearing deep purple foliage in the spring and fall, fading slightly in the heat of summer.

'Maraschino', a hybrid with *S. greggii* and *S. microphylla*, or *S. grahamii*, is an excellent maraschino-cherry-red sage. Hardy to zone 6.

*S. madrensis*, forsythia sage, is without doubt one of the most wonderful sages. These are big plants, at least 5′ tall and often hitting the 7′ mark. The flowers are large and butter yellow, stopping people in their tracks. Unfortunately, they don't flower until October or later, not a good deal for Pierre or Bismarck. I have not seen 'Red Neck Girl' but am pleased it is a plant and not my son's fiancee. It is supposed to flower significantly earlier and have darker stems and leaves. Zone 7b.

'Mystic Spires' is one of the best new (2005) plants to emerge in recent years. Plants are similar to 'Indigo Spires' in flower color and performance but are half the height and far more civilized. Introduced by Ball FloraPlant.

*S. nipponica* 'Fuji Snow' is a low-growing plant that never gets more than a foot tall. Plants have been thriving in the Armitage garden for many years, and are always admired by visitors. White and green variegated leaves emerge in the spring (but fade to green in the summer), after which pale yellow flowers are formed in the fall. Certainly best in the spring, and more or less ignored in late summer. The species itself, with non-variegated leaves, is also offered, but if both are available, snap up the cultivar.

'Phyllis Fancy' is about the biggest sage I have come across, rising up to at least 6′, and it can go to 8′. Height is one thing, but support is often necessary. The light lavender flowers occur in late fall, probably too late to even be used as an annual in the North if flowers were expected. Zone 7b.

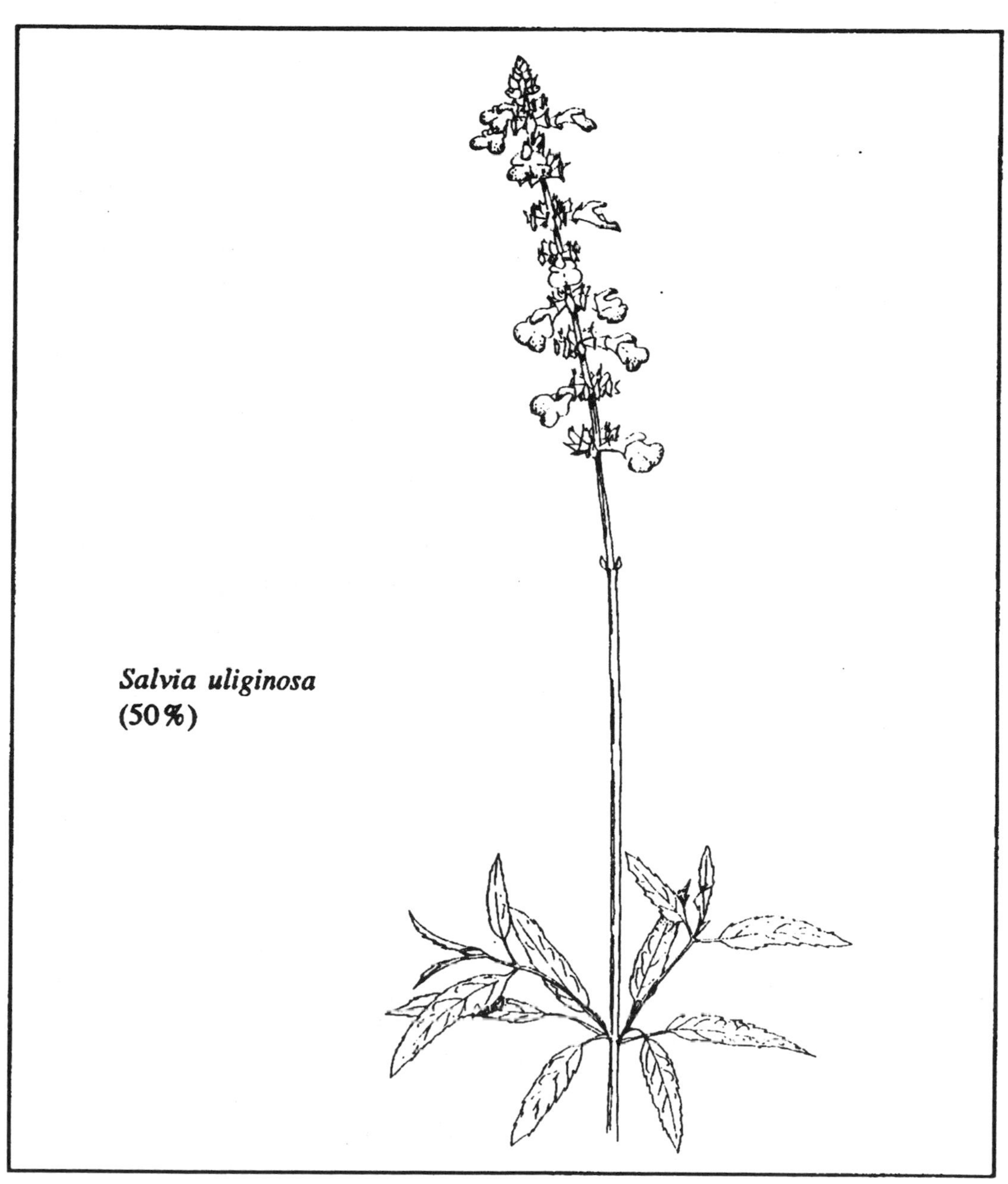

***Salvia uliginosa* (50%)**

'Purple Majesty' is a hybrid between *S. guaranitica* and *S. gesneriiflora*, a Mexican red-flowered species. The resultant hybrid is at least 5′ tall and 3′ wide with deep purple flowers. Hardy to zone 7b.

'Red Velvet' (*S. greggii* x *S. microphylla*) is about 3′ tall and has velvet red flowers.

'Raspberry Royale' (*S. greggii* x *S. microphylla*) bears magenta flowers in late summer and fall. Similar to 'Red Velvet'.

'Silkes' Dream' has been one of the nicest surprises in the Gardens at UGA. The flowers are an eye-catching orange red and are produced for months on end on 2′ tall plants. A hybrid between *S. darcyi* and *S. microphylla.*

*S. transsylvanica* is similar to *S. pratensis* and *S.* x *sylvestris* in that the plants can grow to 3′ tall. They carry large masses of lavender-blue flowers on branched flowering stems held well above the dull green leaves. They were particularly handsome in August at the University of Minnesota Botanic Garden where they had a carpet of white zinnias at their feet.

*S. uliginosa*, bog sage, grows 4-5′ tall and bears Cambridge blue flowers with small white throats in late summer and fall. However, in the Gardens at UGA, they also bloom in early June, slump in the summer and perk up again in the fall. The flowers are densely arranged in 7-20 flowered whorls and occur until frost in the North and through October in the South. Hardy from zones 6 (occasionally 5) to 9. They can be quite invasive, particularly in moist soils. Plants need support in areas of hot summers.

*S. verticillata* came on strong a number of years ago, particularly the selection 'Purple Rain'. I was impressed with its performance in the gardens at Michigan State University, and in gardens and nurseries in the Northeast but it seems to be an on-again, off-again plant in many places and somewhat disappointing. However, when grown well, it has many branched inflorescences of dark purple flowers over coarse arrow-shaped leaves, on 2′ tall plants. Plants perform well in zones 5-7.

## ***Sanguinaria*** (san-gwi-nah′ ree-a) Bloodroot Papaveraceae

Plants of this monotypic genus have always been in demand, but their availability to the gardener has always been poor. Bloodroot is a good example of the continued blurring of the distinction between wild flowers and garden plants. Although best used in shady woodland settings, it is adaptable to more formal shade gardens as well. The common name is most appropriate, as it has a red sap that becomes obvious upon division of the rootstock. The sap was used by Indians as a dye for coloring and paint. This is a terrific plant for demonstrating that garden color is not only on the outside.

***-canadensis*** (kan-a-den′ sis) Bloodroot, Puccoon 3-6″/8″
Early Spring White Eastern North America Zones 3-8

Walking down a meandering woodland path through a drift of these clean white flowers reaffirms one's faith in this crazy world. The solitary, 3″ wide flowers appear on 6″ flower stalks before the blue-green leaves have fully matured. The individual flowers, which remain closed on cloudy days, fall apart in a few days but additional

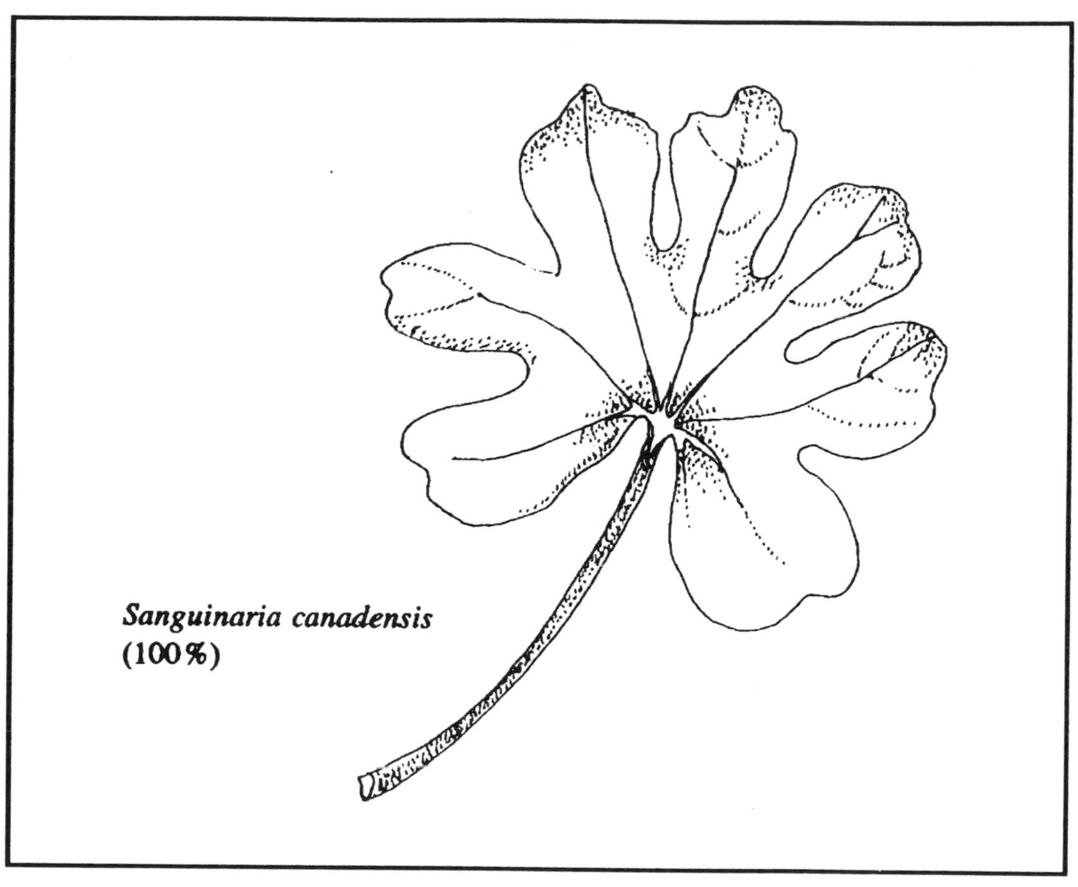
*Sanguinaria canadensis*
(100%)

flowers arise over a 2-week period. The ephemeral bloom of bloodroot was bemoaned even by Thomas Jefferson, who wrote in 1776 that on "April 6, Narcissus and Puckoon open; April 13, Puckoon flowers fallen". Jefferson notwithstanding, this is a wonderful plant to demonstrate beauty, history, and the fun of gardening. In my classes and when people visit in the spring, inevitably I will have people join me on hands and knees and dig up some roots. A quick snap of the tuber, the oozing of blood red sap, a little history and a swish of the sap across my face always leaves bloodroot in the minds of my visitors, and has proven to be a great demonstration for children.

In north Georgia, the bloodroots are at their peak in mid March through early April. In the North, they may flower as late as early May. The wavy, lobed, kidney-shaped leaves continue to expand once the flowers have finished and are almost as pretty as the flowers. The foliage persists until mid to late summer before disappearing. Lack of rain results in more rapid disappearance. They combine well with early spring flowers such as *Mertensia virginica* (Virginia bluebells), *Chrysogonum virginianum* (green and gold), and *Aquilegia canadensis* (Canadian columbine).

Propagate the species from seed but it is easier to divide the clumps of plants immediately after flowering. Seed must be sown in moist peat moss, warmed to 68°F for 2-4 weeks, cooled 4-6 weeks at 40°F and then slowly raised to 50-55°F. 'Multiplex' should be vegetatively propagated by division.

**Cultivars:**

'Multiplex' is the best cultivar for the garden. The sterile, clean white double flowers consist of approximately 50 petals. Flowers persist twice as long as the single-flowered species.

***Sanguisorba*** (san-gwi-sor′ ba) Burnet Rosaceae

The genus contains about 30 species but few nurseries offer them to the public. While it does not offer the splashy color of salvia or black-eyed Susan, there are, nevertheless, a number of beautiful species. Plants have handsome pinnate leaves, similar to those of *Melianthus*, another little-known garden plant, and bottlebrush flowers in summer. In some species, separate male and female flowers occur on the same plant, and in others the flowers are perfect (both male and female parts are present in the same flower). All flowers are apetalous and consist of small sepals and long stamens. They look good with fall-flowering plants like monkshood and *Sedum* 'Autumn Joy'. In general, plants prefer a cool, damp soil but tolerate dry conditions if irrigation is provided. The new leaves are still used to flavor soups, drinks and salads.

The name *Sanguisorba* comes from *sanguis*, blood and *sorbere*, soaking up, in reference to its reputed ability to stop bleeding. The young leaves of *S. officinalis* were, and still are, occasionally used to flavor salads.

Quick Reference to Sanguisorba Species

| | Height (ft.) | Flower color |
|---|---|---|
| *S. canadensis* | 4-5 | White |
| *S. obtusa* | 3-4 | Reddish pink |

***-canadensis*** (kan-a-den′ sis) Canadian Burnet 4-5′/4′
Summer White Eastern North America Zones 3-7
(syn. *Poterium canadense*)

The 12″ long pinnately compound leaves consist of 7-15, oblong, sharply toothed leaflets. Two- to six-inch long, rounded spikes of whitish, perfect flowers appear at the end of each stem. The stamens are exserted (stick out) and give the flowers a bottlebrush appearance. The individual flowers are up to 1½″ wide and the inflorescence extends six to eight inches. Flowering begins in early summer and lasts well into midsummer, particularly if flowers are removed as they fade. Plants are native to eastern Canada and United States and have endangered status in many of the states. Planted in combination with the orange spikes of *Kniphofia*, the whites of burnet seem whiter and the oranges of the torch lily brighter.

Plant in full sun in the North, but partial shade and a cooling soil mulch are useful in the South. Plants are vigorous and adequate room for expansion must be provided. They enjoy boggy soil, however, and if planted by the waterside, may become somewhat of a pest. Plants are still sold as *Poterium*, and taxonomists still can't seem to agree on the correct name.

Propagate by seed (similar to *Sanguinaria*) or division in the spring.

**Cultivars:**

'Red Thunder' grows about 3½' tall and produces dark red bottlebrush flowers above ferny green foliage. Probably a hybrid.

***-obtusa*** (ob-tew' sa) Japanese Burnet 3-4'/3'
Summer Pink, Red Japan Zones 4-7

This is the most ornamental burnet as it combines gray-green leaves with reddish pink flowers. The 18" long pinnate leaves consist of 13-17 leaflets with a gray-green underside. The flowers have long stamens, at least four times as long as the sepals, resulting in an airy, 4' long inflorescence. Conditions necessary for optimal growth are similar to the previous species, however, because plants are not as leafy or vigorous they are more appropriate for the border than *S. canadensis*. They are later than *S. canadensis* and fare well with late-flowering plants.

Propagate by seed or division in the spring similar to *S. canadensis*.

**Cultivars:**

'Alba' is similar but has white flowers.

**Related Species:**

*S. menziesii*, Menzie's burnet, is native to the Northwest and does best in cool climates. Deep red flowers stand over the fernlike gray-green leaves. A handsome variegated form is 'Dali Marble', characterized by clean white margins and the same maroon flowers.

*S. officinalis*, great burnet, is also a large plant, with erect, often reddish stems. The basal leaves consist of 13-25 leaflets while the stem leaves are small and sessile. The dark purple flowers are held in short inflorescences during the late summer and are much shorter than either *S. canadensis* or *S. obtusa*. 'Lemon Splash' bears leaves splashed with yellow. 'Tanna' is only about 18" tall and is more suited for the smaller garden. Flowers consist of bottlebrush-like burgundy spires. 'Pink Tanna' has pink flowers. Hardy in zones 4 to 7.

*S. tenuifolia* has some of the most ornamental leaves of the genus. The dark green cutleaf foliage stands out even when not in flower, but the red pendant spikes make a wonderful contrast. Some say the foliage smells like cucumbers. Zone 4-7.

## ***Santolina*** (san-to-leen' a) Lavender Cotton Asteraceae

Used mainly as low border or edging plants, the gray-green to bright green color shows off the foliage and flowers of plants associated with them. The flowers are yellow and the leaves are aromatic, alternate and finely divided. Of the 8 species, only a couple are grown to any extent. Regardless of choice, all require exceptionally good drainage.

***-chamaecyparissus*** (ka-mie-sip-pa-ris′ is) Lavender Cotton 1-2′/2′
Summer Yellow Mediterranean Zones 6-8

Plants are often used for edging because of the evergreen, aromatic gray-green leaves, which in sandy soils and bright light develop a white sheen. The 1½″ long alternate leaves are crowded on the stem and white woolly underneath. The flowers are comprised of disc flowers only, resulting in a globular head of marginal attractiveness. The gray leaves combine particularly well in floral designs with red leaf plants such as calico plant, *Alternanthera*.

Although some people feel the flowers look like "bright yellow lollipops in midsummer", I feel they detract from the foliage and serve no useful function. The shrubby plants become rather woody at the base and require a hard pruning immediately after flowering to keep tidy. They may be trimmed at any time until September, and are used as small hedging and in knot gardens in warm, dry parts of the country. In late fall and winter, give them a haircut to tidy them up, but do not cut back hard until new growth appears in the spring. Hard winter pruning often results in death.

Plants are tolerant of a wide range of summer temperatures, but not summer humidity. Hot, wet summers cause fungal problems and plants that open up in the middle. Drier climates are more to their liking. Winter hardiness north of zone 6 and summer hardiness south of zone 7, except in the Northwest, are questionable. The aromatic nature of the plant caught the attention of herbalists many years ago and it was an antidote against the bites of "all serpents and venomous beasts" (Gerard's *Herbal*, 1597).

Propagate any time from terminal cuttings. Seed germination is irregular and placing sown seed at 40°F for 2-4 weeks may enhance uniformity.

**Cultivars:**

'Lambrook Silver', from Lambrook Nursery in England, has more silvery leaves than the species.

'Lemon Queen' is dwarf and mound forming.

'Nana' is a name given to dwarf variants in general, which may include 'Weston' and 'Little Ness'.

'Pretty Carroll' originated from Carroll Gardens in Westminster, Maryland and is a hybrid between the species and *S. chamaecyparissus* 'Nana'. Plants are short with finer cut foliage, and an improvement on the species.

'Plumosus' bears finely cut lacy, silver-tinted foliage.

***-rosmarinifolia*** (rose-mah-rin′ i-fo-lee-a) Green Lavender Cotton, Rosemary Lavender 1-2′/3′
Summer Yellow Italy, France Zones 7-8

Green lavender cotton, long known as *S. virens*, is now also known as rosemary lavender cotton. The leaves have the look of rosemary but not the fragrance. They do smell like a sanitized santolina; that is, the fragrance is there but not nearly as obvious as the common species. Plants have narrow bright green leaves and solitary bright yellow flowers on 2′ tall stems. They are wonderful plants and while they are

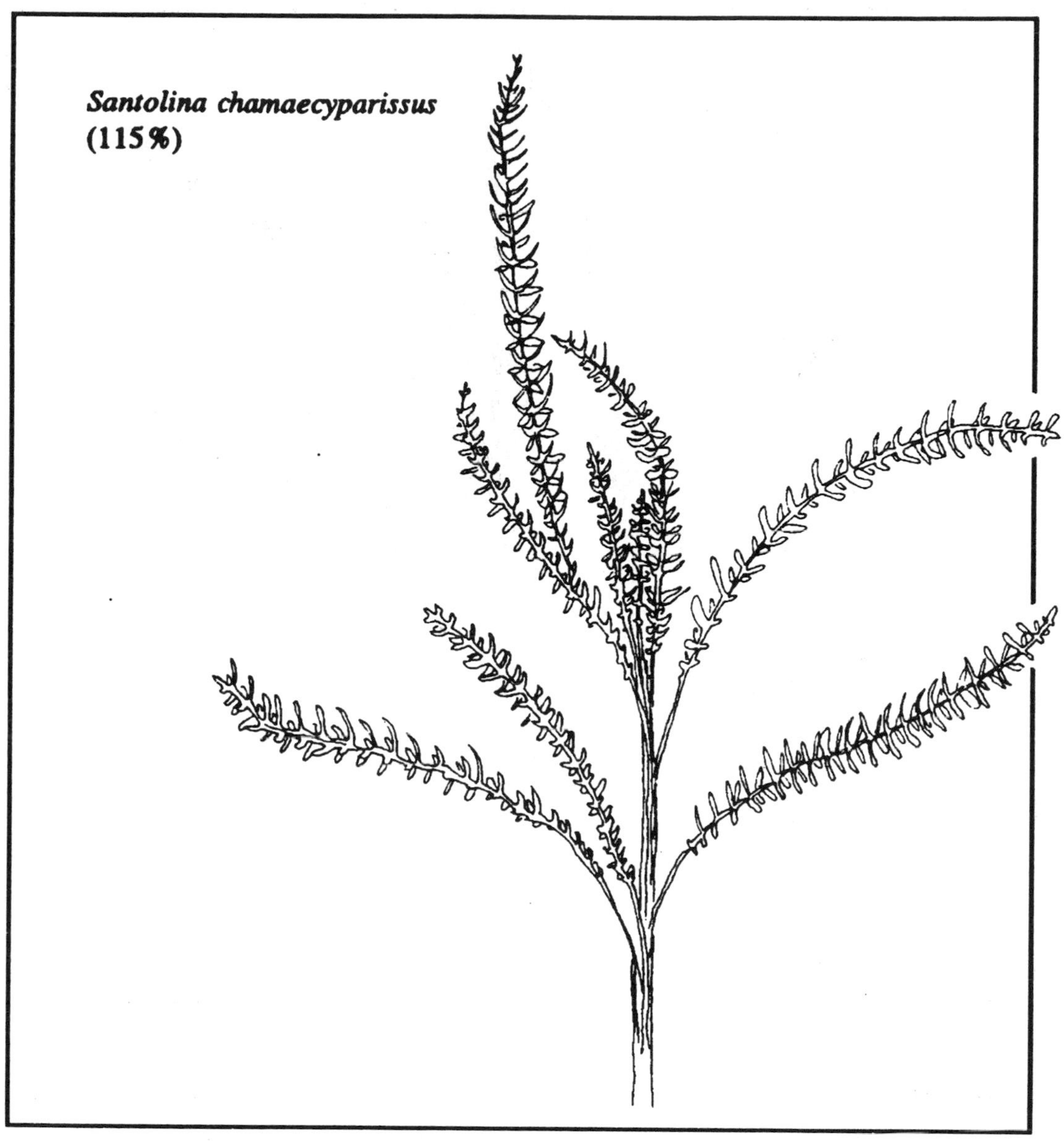


much brighter in leaf than *S. chamaecyparissus*, they still blend and unite other plants as well. Native to the Mediterranean area, plants are winter hardy only to zone 7.

**Cultivars:**
'Primrose Gem' has threadlike leaves and pale yellow flowers.

**Related Species:**
*S. pinnata* has narrow pinnate leaves and off-white flowers. Plants make large gray-green mounds. Also Mediterranean, hardy in zones 6-8. 'Edward Bowles' has gray-green, highly dissected leaves and pretty sulphur yellow flowers.

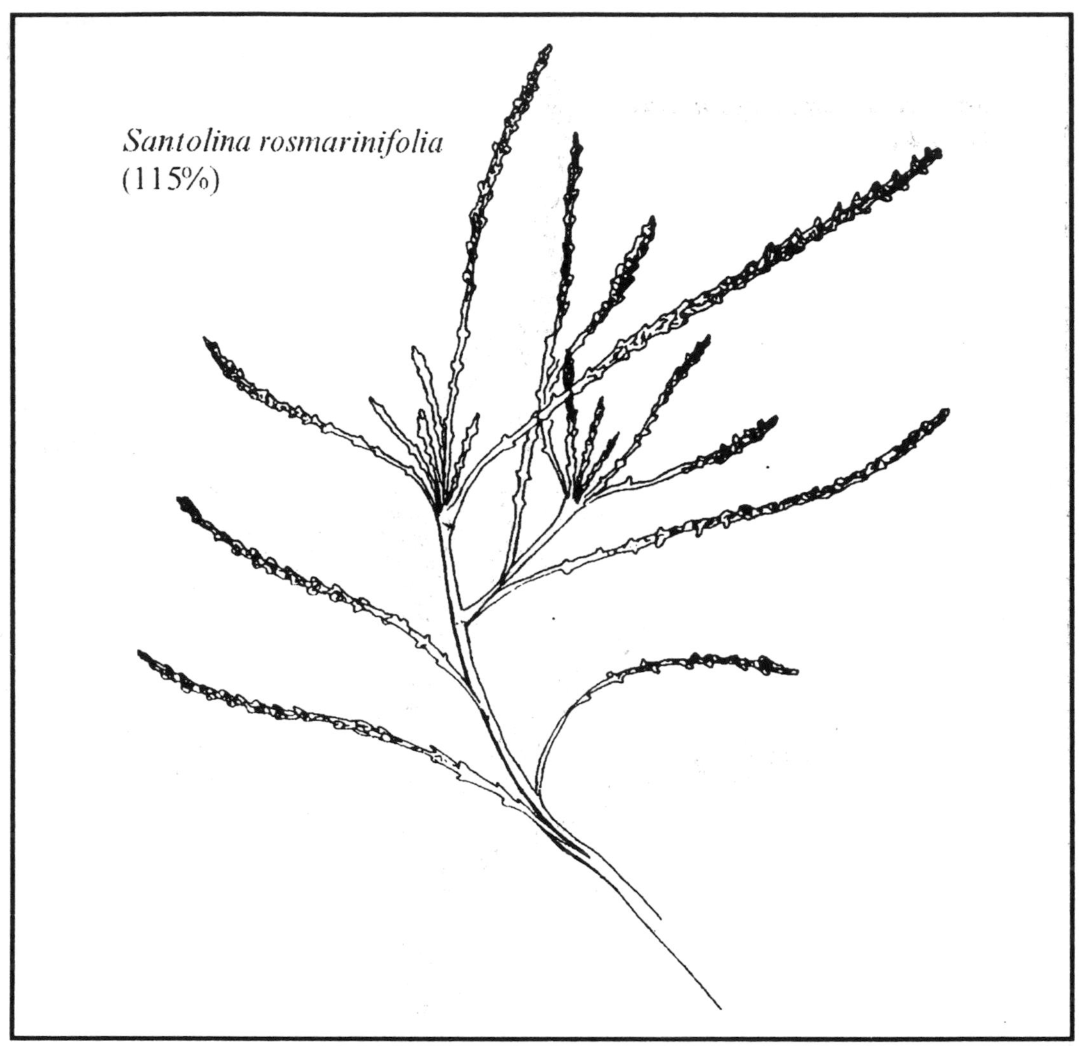
*Santolina rosmarinifolia*
(115%)

***Saponaria*** (sa-po-nah′ ree-a) Soapwort Caryophyllaceae

A number of common annual and perennial species, suitable for the low border or rockery, are found in the genus. The Midwestern roadside weed, bouncing bet, *S. officinalis*, is responsible for the common name. In Gerard's *Herbal*, 1597, the author points out that the leaves "yeelde out of themselves a certain juice when they are bruised, which scoureth almost as well as soap". If you have read the great books in the *Clan of the Cave Bear* series by Jean Auel, you will remember that the protagonists, Ayla and Jondalar, often refer to the plant used for making soap. Actually, the "soap" is rather gooey and is a poor substitute for Dial. The leaves are opposite and entire and the flowers usually have five petals. In general, plants tolerate full sun but require well-drained soil.

Quick Reference to Saponaria Species

| | Height (in.) | Habit | Flower color |
|---|---|---|---|
| *S. lutea* | 3-6 | Mat forming | Yellow |
| *S. ocymoides* | 6-9 | Trailing | Pink |
| *S. officinalis* | 12-30 | Upright | Pink |

***-lutea*** (lew-tee′ a) Yellow Soapwort 3-4″/6″
Summer Yellow Western Alps Zones 5-7

Although different from the common soapworts and more challenging to grow, this species makes a lovely rock garden plant. The ½″ wide leaves are pale green and form a mat that seldom grows taller than 4″. Clusters of small yellow flowers with violet stamens rise from the mat in early summer and continue for 3-4 weeks. It is not as cold tolerant as other soapworts and requires mulch north of zone 5. Unfortunately it is similar to other species in its intolerance to heat and poor drainage.

***-ocymoides*** (o-kim-oi′ dees) Rock Soapwort 6-9″/9″
Early Summer Pink European Alps Zones 2-7

Ease of growth and fresh pink flowers in May and June make the species the most popular garden plant of the genus. The flowers are held in loose sprays at the ends of the many branches. It climbs and clambers over rocks and is a particularly valuable trailing plant for walls or raised stonework. The 1″ long leaves are flat and olive green. The lower ones have a short petiole while the uppermost are sessile. Plants should be pruned hard after flowering to force new shoots and restrain growth. Once established, they also reseed themselves with abandon, providing a most soapworted garden. Plants are highly tolerant of cold temperatures, but are not at all happy in hot summers or in soils that are poorly drained. Although a zone 8 summer rating is often recommended, I would not grow plants above zone 7a as they tend to die out due to winter rains and summer humidity.

The species and most of the varieties may be propagated from seed. Germination is more rapid and uniform if the seed is stratified for 4-6 weeks at around 40°F. Plants may be divided and terminal cuttings may also be taken any time of year.

**Cultivars:**

'Alba' ('Albiflora') is a white-flowered form of the species, difficult to locate. The flowers are pure white. This is a good plant where a white trailer is needed.

'Carnea' has flesh pink flowers but is otherwise similar to the species.

'Floribunda' is more floriferous than other selections. The flowers are soft pink and similar to the species.

'Rubra Compacta' is a non-trailing compact form of the species with crimson flowers. It is a terrific little plant for the front of the border.

'Splendens' has large intense rose flowers and is the best garden selection.

'Splendissima' apparently has larger flowers than 'Splendens' but I have not seen much difference between them.

'Versicolor' is interesting but rather ugly. The flowers open white, then turn rose. To each her own. This is likely a cross between 'Alba' and 'Splendens'.

'White Tips' has clean white flowers over 10-12″ tall plants. May be the same as 'Alba'.

***-officinalis*** (o-fish-i-nah′ lis) Bouncing Bet 12-30″/18″
Summer Pink Southern Europe Zones 2-8

Naturalized in much of the eastern and areas of the country, it gets little respect and is often considered little more than a pretty weed. Bouncing bet has thrown off the comfort and safety of the garden to become an inhabitant of the open road. She is also known as lady-by-the-gate and few cottage gardens would be without the old lady or the gate. Bouncing bet is also the origin of the soap-making roots, although some people who used the soap also came down with dermatitis.

Plants are more upright than other species although they sprawl when planted in rich soil. The leaves are 2-4″ long, about 2″ wide, and somewhat elliptical. They are also conspicuously three-nerved and usually dark green. The individual flowers are 1-1½″ across, have five notched petals and are held in terminal and axillary cymes. Full sun is necessary; if too much shade is provided, plants become leggy and tall and flowers fade to almost white. Pinching in late spring helps to clean up this coarse and untidy plant as well as force additional flower formation. Plants bloom throughout the summer and spread by underground stolons, thus a few plants can result in a significant colony in a few years. It is interesting that bouncing bet, particularly the double forms, is now being grown commercially as a cut flower for some of the "uptown" florists. There is hope that this Rodney Dangerfield of the plant kingdom can be associated with more than the "characteristic odour of American sidewalk ends, where the pavement peters out and the shacks and junked cars begin" (Peattie, D.C., *Flowering Earth*, 1991). The double forms are far more common than the single-flowered species.

Stolons are easily divided at any time. Cuttings and seed may also be used. Seed should be stratified as mentioned under the previous species. Not all seed-propagated plants of the double varieties will be double, in some cases up to 40% of the offspring may be single.

**Cultivars:**

'Alba-plena' bears white double flowers. All double forms produce 1-1½″ diameter double flowers which resemble shaggy carnations.

'Dazzler' ('Variegata') has pink single flowers and green and creamy white variegated leaves. The variegation is stronger in cool weather and fades in the heat.

'Rosea-plena' has double flowers in shades of rose to pink. This is the most common form in cultivation.

'Rubra-plena' produces red double blooms.

**Related Species:**

*S. caespitosa* is a densely tufted hairy plant with short linear leaves, growing 4-8″ tall. The light pink flowers are about 1″ across and held on short stems over the lime green foliage in mid to late summer.

*S.* x *lempergii* is a hybrid originated by Dr. Fritz Lemberg in Styria, Austria. The only cultivar available is 'Max Frei' with soft, hairy leaves and many 1″ pink flowers. They are not as tolerant of heat or poorly drained soils as other species. These are best grown in a rock garden situation, or in a raised bed where water can be quickly drained away. We have killed a good number of these hybrids in our trials at the University of Georgia. Probably hardy in zones 3-7a.

*S.* x *olivana* is a hybrid between *S. caespitosa* and a short species, *S. pumila*. Plants are best in rock gardens where sharp drainage is the norm. Plants produce dozens of rose-red flowers in spring and early summer. Hardy to zone 4.

## ***Sarracenia*** (sar-a-sen′ ee-a) Pitcher Plant Sarraceniaceae

I did not include the genus in the first two editions and although I will never have a bog, nor do I consider these plants anything other than curiosities, the increased availability of nursery-grown plants shows how little my opinion matters. Somebody must be buying them.

All species and cultivars (and there are many) require constantly moist highly acidic soils, that is, a bog, and full sun. Let your kids feed them with fire ants if that gets them excited about gardening; soon all the kids will be visiting. Plants are as cold hardy to zone 5 and summer hardy to zone 8. An amazing number of cultivars has been selected and while there are not dozens of nurseries offering them, there are enough.

Get a little water, kill a few fire ants, have fun!

## ***Saruma*** (sa-rum′ a) Yellow Ginger Aristolochiaceae

This monotypic genus *(S. henryi)* was discovered in China in the early 1900s and is finally gaining some traction in North American gardens. I have seen plantings throughout Ireland, England and Europe but it took many more years to find it here. Obviously, I was simply looking in the wrong places, as I now see it for sale and hear wonderful things about it.

Related to, and behaving like gingers (*Asarum*), these ground covers are bigger than most gingers and bear 5″ wide, fuzzy, light-green, heart-shaped leaves. They are also more upright than gingers, growing about 2′ tall. Their foliage is enough reason to include them in the woodland garden, but the ½-¾″ yellow flowers that bloom for months on short stems above the leaves seal the deal. Zones 4-7.

The name is an anagram of *Asarum*, another useless piece of information unless you are playing plant trivia. The plants will self-sow if you are lucky or plants may be divided carefully.

**Sasa** (sa'sa) Dwarf Bamboo Poaceae

This Japanese dwarf bamboo genus has about 150 species, and one or two have become reasonably common. They are shorter than many bamboos, usually growing about 3-4′ tall and rapidly multiplying by underground rhizomes. They are being pushed as understudy plants to choke out weeds, however, they soon become as weedy as the ones they choke out, and a lot more difficult to eradicate. They are best in a woodland area where they can ramble undisturbed and unmolested. A couple of species are offered. *S. palmata* grows 3-5′ tall with wide evergreen leaves clustered at the tips of the stems (thus the term "palmata"). The leaves are bright green with rough margins which are often brown and dry in the autumn. The other species offered is the equally invasive *S. veitchii.* The leaves are held along the stem and not clustered at the ends. The whitish dry margins are even more conspicuous and as hard as I try, I find nothing ornamental about this tendency to look half dead. People try to write about the beauty of the papery tanned margins, but I don't buy it.

However, both species can fill in difficult areas of dry shade and I suppose they're better than looking at bare weedy ground. The fact that they are a bamboo should be warning enough that they should be used close enough to walk to but far enough away that you get tired getting there. Hardy in zones 6-8.

**Sauromatum** (sour-o-may' tum) Voodoo Lily Araceae

Another unique member of the aroid family that brings us the spathe and spadix arrangement of flowers revered in calla lilies and demanded by gardeners on the edge. It is closely related to *Amorphophallus* and *Dracontium.* I have outlined their differences under the former. The only species generally available is *S. venosum* whose large corms can sometimes be purchased as indoor forcing plants.

In the garden, the spathe is long and pointed, finally unpeeling like a banana into a flattened organ. The 3′ long spadix is purple and skinny and sticks straight up from the spathe. The religious right might complain about the suggestive flowers, but they want to ban Harry Potter, so who listens to them? They are suggestive to be sure, but I don't think they will contribute to the delinquency of minors.

Similar to other genera mentioned in this group, the flowers are malodorous, particularly when the sun hits them. The spadix has an internal mechanism for self-heating in order to disperse the pungent compounds more efficiently to attract bugs and such. If you can get near enough, feel the spadix once the spathe has peeled back, it will be significantly warmer than the air or the rest of the plant. It is also interesting that in heat-releasing plants like *Arum* and *Sauromatum*, salicylic acid levels (the active ingredient in aspirin) in the spadix are also elevated. That the raised acid causes production of the heat or vice versa is not yet understood, but to think we understand much about plants is being optimistic indeed. After flowering, the spotted stems and the single sickle-shaped leaf emerge. If conditions are right (partial shade, well-drained soils), seed heads may arise from the spent flowers. They will also multiply fairly rapidly, forming a colony in a few years.

Winter hardiness has always been in question. With a little winter protection, they should make it to zone 7 (perhaps even 6b), although many texts call them zone 8-10 plants. Who cares, try a plant or two, you may be happily offended.

***Saururus*** (sough′ rur-us) Lizard's Tail Saururaceae

Although I do enjoy this plant, I must be looking at the wrong lizards. The name comes from *saura*, lizard and *oura*, tail, but to my poorly trained eye, the flowers look more like fish hooks or swans' necks than lizards' tails. The only species sold in this country is *S. cernuus*, the specific name meaning nodding. The 12″ long inflorescences are interesting to look at in bloom as the white flower is comprised of the white stalks of the stamens, the flowers being totally bereft of petals or sepals. Plants thrive in a rich wet lowland area, and look dreadful under dry land conditions. The heart-shaped leaves alternate their way up the erect stem and flowers occur in early summer in the South, late summer in the North. One of the best plantings I have seen is at the native Gardens of Georgia Perimeter College in Decatur, Georgia, where the moist, shady conditions allow the creeping stems to fill in, resulting in hundreds of lizard tails all wagging at once. This is one of the country's best—and least-known—native plant gardens; if you find yourself in the Atlanta area, the gardens are well worth a visit.

Plants are native to shallow water and swamps from New England and southwestern Quebec to Minnesota and south to Florida. Hardy in zones 5 (4) to 8.

***Saxifraga*** (saks-if′ rag-a) Saxifrage Saxifragaceae

Exceptionally large and enormously diverse, this genus contains more than 300 species and 200 additional natural hybrids and varieties. The name is derived from the Latin *saxum*, rock, and *frangere*, to break, in reference to the fact that the dust-like seeds find their way into minute crevices to germinate. Along with other plants that were swept into the *Doctrine of Signatures* (see *Pulmonaria*), saxifrages' supposed ability to break rocks elevated it to the medicinal purpose of shattering kidney stones. Some species such as *S. granulata*, meadow saxifrage, are also well established in song and verse. The double form of this European meadow saxifrage is known as pretty maids; and a row of them was memorialized in the verse about Mary, Mary, quite Contrary's garden.

The genus consists of small plants, most dwarf, and none more than moderate size; all best suited for the rock garden. An exception is our native *S. pennsylvanica*, Pennsylvania saxifrage, which grows up to 3′ in height. Species are predominantly perennial although a few such as *S. sibthorpii*, Sibthorp's saxifrage, are annuals. Many form rosettes of leaves in cushions that may be hard and encrusted, in others moss-like. Most of the species are evergreen, especially the rosette formers, however, a few have alternate, deciduous leaves. The flowers are arranged singly or more often in floriferous panicles and racemes. Flower color is predominantly white but yellow, pink or red are also found. Flowers consist of 5 petals and sepals, and 10 stamens.

They are mainly alpine plants and, in their native habitats, wonderfully resistant to adverse weather. They rejoice in sharp drainage and cool climes. Hot summers are not to their liking and, in general, the further north one gardens, the more chances of success. Few species tolerate full sun and moderate shade is recommended for most locales in the United States. Fall sun is tolerated in most of Canada. Excellent drainage is essential.

Botanists have classified *Saxifraga* into 15 sections, each clearly distinguished by visible characteristics. However, even within a section, there are numerous morphological differences between species. Although a great number of saxifrages are garden worthy, only a few sections contain species that are of special value to the garden.

The mossy saxifrages (Dactyloides) form cushions of soft-leaved evergreen rosettes. This includes species such as *S. caespitosa*, tufted saxifrage, the magnificent white-flowered *S. trifurcata*, threefork saxifage, and the popular *S.* x *arendsii* hybrids. A popular section is the encrusted saxifrages (Euaizoonia), in which plants have rosettes with stiff, spade-shaped lime-encrusted leaves that provide a silvery effect. The rosettes die after flowering but underground runners give rise to new ones in the fall. They superficially resemble hens and chicks until their open sprays of summer flowers give them away. This section includes the variable *S. paniculata*, aizoon saxifrage, with many varieties and cultivars.

Another section of importance is the Kabschia saxifages (Porophyllum), characterized by firm, dense green cushions of evergreen rosettes. The leaves are small, stiff, and often needle sharp. The section Robertsoniana contains species which form dense, dark green cushions of evergreen rosettes. It is represented in the garden by the ever-present London pride, *S.* x *urbium*, found in garden centers throughout Europe and now in North America. For the southern gardener, the section Diptera contains the useful and popular strawberry geranium, *S. stolonifera*. It is hardy in zones 7-10 but can be enjoyed as a houseplant further north. Intersectional hybridization has occurred and a number of useful hybrids such as *S.* x *andrewsii*, Andrew's saxifrage, have arisen. Much of the interest and breeding of the genus has occurred in Germany, Czechoslovakia and other European countries.

However, let us not forget the tremendous efforts of Lincoln Foster from Connecticut, who hybridized a whole group of saxifrages under the catch-all series of Millstream Hybrids. Look for constellation names, mythological figures ('Aladdin', 'Demeter', 'Midas'); figures from Shakespeare ('Falstaff', 'Prince Hal'); friends and family members ('Timmy Foster', 'Wendy') and of course those with the famous garden prelude ('Millstream').

In general, however, except for a small handful of plants, saxifrages are little used and poorly understood in the United States. Although our climate is not as forgiving as that of England, Germany and the Netherlands, they are plants that, once established, provide years of graceful, maintenance-free beauty. A frequent problem is that the early spring flowers of some hybrids and species are damaged by late spring frosts. This does not mean this group of plants does not have a significant following, and if you would like to be one of the followers, checking out the North American Rock Garden Society (www.nargs.org) would be most useful.

Propagation is usually by seed, but division, cuttings, and rooted offsets are also used to multiply hybrids and cultivars. The fine seed needs exposure to low temperatures to germinate. Placing the seed flat at 32-40°F for 6 weeks results in more uniform germination. Seedlings are very slow to develop and it may take 2-3 years before plants reach flowering size. For best results, seedlings should not be exposed to temperatures greater than 60°F.

The following is but a handful of the saxifrages that may be found through specialty nurseries. The list includes the more available and easy to grow species.

Quick Reference to Saxifraga Species

| | Height (in.) | Flowering season | Flower color | Section |
|---|---|---|---|---|
| *S.* x *arendsii* | 6-9 | Spring | Various | Dactyloides |
| *S. cochlearis* | 6-12 | Spring | White | Euaizoonia |
| *S. cotyledon* | 18-24 | Summer | White | Euaizoonia |
| *S. paniculata* | 6-24 | Summer | Yellow | Euaizoonia |
| *S. stolonifera* | 3-8 | Summer | White | Diptera |
| *S. trifurcata* | 6-12 | Spring | White | Dactyloides |
| *S.* x *urbium* | 9-12 | Spring | White | Robertsoniana |

**-x *arendsii*** (ah-rendz′ ee-eye) Arend's Saxifrage 6-9″/12″
Spring Various Hybrid Zones 5-7

Developed by the Arends Nursery in Ronsdorf, Germany, the hybrid is a relatively recent addition to the saxifrage family. Plants are mossy-leaved carpet formers and, if proper conditions are provided, will cover a large area in a season. The rosettes remain evergreen and attractive throughout the year. Dozens of thin flower stalks rise over this mossy covering, each bearing a single 5-petaled flower in white, rose, pink or red shades. Semi-shaded conditions and moist soil are preferred. The sunnier the site, the more moisture retentive must be the soil. A problem in growing the mossy saxifrages in warm areas is that they often "melt out", that is, the centers of the plants rot and disappear. This is a particularly severe problem in areas of high humidity. Adding some fine soil or sand to the center of the plant helps reduce the loss.

**Cultivars**:

'Blood Carpet' is one of the many cultivars in the Carpet series of hybrid saxifrages, most of which are available from seed. It is 4-8″ tall with dark carmine-red flowers. There is very little, if any, difference between this and 'Scarlet Carpet'.

'Flower Carpet' is similar to 'Blood Carpet' but the flowers are pinker. It is a reliable, free-flowering cultivar that can be raised from seed.

'Flowers of Sulphur' stands about 4″ tall and has pale sulphur yellow flowers. It is vigorous with firm tight cushions of foliage.

'Gaiety' is an early-flowering hybrid with deep pink flowers on 4-6″ long flower stems. One of the best hybrids with pink flowers.

'Purple Carpet' is 3-4″ tall with deep purple flowers.

'Rosea' has rose-pink flowers on 6″ tall plants. They have done surprisingly well in the heat of a Georgia summer, however, they were on raised beds with excellent drainage.

'Snow Carpet' has masses of relatively large, clear white flowers, and is about 5-7″ tall. It is an old standard cultivar but still one of the best for white flowers.

'Triumph' is one of the best hybrids. The firm lacy green 6-8″ long cushions are handsome and the dark red flowers are brilliant. Remove the flower stems after fading. Self-sown plants are interesting but flower colors and habits are not true. Divide pieces of carpet after flowering but prior to the heat of summer.

**-*cochlearis*** (kok-lee-ah′ ris) Snail Saxifrage 6-12″/10″
Spring White Alps Zones 5-7

Numerous small hemispherical rosettes, comprised of many spoon-shaped entire leaves thickly encrusted with lime (leaves exude calcium carbonate), characterize the species. Rosettes are 1-2″ across, but so closely packed they form small mounds from which 10-12″ tall reddish scapes arise. The ¾″ diameter star-shaped white flowers are held in loose, one-sided panicles. Some direct sun is tolerated but partial shade is preferable. Lime should be added regularly for best performance, particularly in areas of acid soils.

Seedlings require 2-3 years to reach flowering size; vegetative propagation is faster and more reliable. Division of the rosettes in early spring or late fall is possible. Propagate in spring by lifting the mother plant and gently tearing down on the outer rosettes. Pieces of root must be removed with the offset which can be immediately planted.

**Cultivars**:

var. *major* has rosettes 1½ times larger than the species. The flowers are a little larger but not significantly so. var. *minor* has smaller flowers on 4″ long scapes and grows 6″ wide.

**-*cotyledon*** (kot-i-lee′ don) Jungfrau Saxifrage 18-24″/10″
Summer White Pyrenees, Alps to Greenland Zones 3-7

Masses of flat rosettes are produced, each 5-6″ in diameter. The 3″ long leaves are strap shaped, finely toothed and broader towards the apex. Although the flowering rosettes die after flowering, the central crown sends out new ones so that the plant forms a small colony. The branched flower stems rise 18-24″ and bear ¾″ wide white flowers with red veins or red dots on the petals. This is one of the encrusted saxifrages that is not obviously encrusted with lime. In fact, this species should be grown in lime-free soils in partial or deep shade.

Propagation is similar to *S. cochlearis*.

**Cultivars**:

var. *caterhamensis* is one of the prettiest because of the conspicuous red spotting on the petals. It also is more vigorous than the species.

var. *icelandica* has large rosettes of iron-gray leaves with 4′ tall flower stems.
var. *minor* is a dwarf version of the species and smaller in every way, bearing flowers on 6″ tall inflorescences.

***-paniculata*** (pa-nik-ew-lah′ ta) Aizoon Saxifrage 6-24″/15″
Summer Yellowish White Europe, North America Zone 2-6

This species occurs in most of the alpine and boreal parts of Europe and Asia, in North America from Greenland and Labrador to Saskatchewan, south to Nova Scotia, New Brunswick, the mountains of Vermont, and Lake Superior. With such an extensive range, it is not surprising there are many forms and subspecies. Plants form cushions and mats of small rosettes, 3″ in diameter or less, consisting of spatulate leaves with forward-pointing teeth and silvery encrustations on the margins. The flowers vary tremendously but are borne in a loose 6-18″ tall panicle. The half-inch diameter flowers are yellowish white to white, often spotted purple.

Although tolerant of lime-free situations, lime should be added to the garden site for best performance. Areas of rocky outcrops and partial shade are preferred.

Propagate similar to *S. cochlearis*.

**Cultivars:**

var. *baldensis* has small rosettes (approximately 2″ across) with reddish flower scapes.
var. *globrata* has very short flower stalks.
var. *lutea* has pale yellow flowers and is 6-10″ tall in flower.
var. *major* is the largest form of the species and sends up 15-18″ high inflorescences. The flower stems are reddish and the large leaves (1-2″ long) have a reddish tinge, which deepens in winter.
var. *rosea* has pale pink flowers with yellowish green rosettes.

***-stolonifera*** (sto-loni′ fer-a) Strawberry Begonia 4-6″/12″
Summer White Eastern Asia Zones 7-9

Also known as strawberry geranium and mother-of-thousands, plants colonize an area with threadlike runners, called stolons, similar to strawberries. The rounded leaves are silver veined above and reddish beneath. The flowering stems branch into 15-18″ tall loose racemes of many 1″ wide white flowers whose two lower petals are 3-4 times longer than the other three. Plants are useful as shade-tolerant ground covers, particularly in the South, quickly making large colonies after a few years. They are also used in hanging baskets for patio and deck. Plants are cold hardy to zone 7.

**Cultivars:**

'Harvest Moon' originated from Terra Nova Nursery and offers conspicuous chartreuse leaves. They form a handsome clump before the runners start foraging for new ground. Probably best with some afternoon shade. Beautiful but wimpy; I have killed every one I have tried.
'Maroon Beauty' has similar rounded leaves and silvery veins. The leaves have reddish tones and red pubescence on the stems.

'Stephanie' was named for my long-suffering assistant, Stephanie Anderson of Athens, Georgia. This one of the best ground cover choices because of the thick dark green leaves with silver marbling on the top and pink coloration on the underside. The stems and runners are bright red. We have grown this in the trials in the Gardens at UGA since 1995 and found it to be as tough as nails. Other similar variants include 'Calle' that is not as deeply colored and recently one called 'Kinki Purple'. What kind of a name is that?

'Tricolor' has variegated leaves of green white and pink, also known as 'Variegata'.

-***trifurcata*** (tri-fur-cah′ ta) Threefork Saxifrage 6-12″/36″
Spring White Spain, Austria Zones 5-7

This is one of the prettiest plants in this group. A massive mat in flower, with clouds of clear white flowers flowing through and clambering over rocks, is a magnificent sight. The stems are somewhat woody and the leathery, gray-green leaves are three lobed and divided into numerous triangular sections. The branched, reddish racemes are held 6-12″ above the mossy foliage and flower for 3-4 weeks in spring.

One of the most sun-tolerant saxifrages, it can be planted in full sun if sufficient moisture is provided. However, afternoon shade is beneficial.

Propagate by division similar to *S.* x *arendsii*.

-x ***urbium*** (ur-bee′ um) London Pride Saxifrage 9-12″/20″
Spring White, Pink Hybrid Zones 5-7

Although often sold as *S. umbrosa*, that species is seldom found in gardens today. *S.* x *urbium* is a hybrid between *S. spathularis*, a white-flowered species from Portugal and northwest Spain, and *S. umbrosa*, native to the Pyrenees Mountains. Plants bear loose evergreen rosettes that form dense dark green carpets from which arise the foot high, wiry, sticky flower stems. The length of these stems is one of the main characteristics which distinguishes this hybrid from *S. umbrosa*. The ¼″ wide white flowers are starry with a red tinge in the middle. The stamens are longer than the petals and provide an airy look to the sea of bloom. Soil pH is not as critical and it will grow in acid or alkaline soils as long as moisture can be provided. Shady, moist areas are preferred and plants are particularly appealing among ferns.

Easily propagated by division of the mat at any time, but preferably after flowering or in early spring prior to the formation of flower buds.

**Cultivars:**

The following may be selections of *S.umbrosa* or *S.* x *urbium*, depending on whom you believe. If you believe me, you are not to be trusted.

'Aureopunctata' ('Variegata') has golden variegated leaves and provides a lovely splash of color even when not in bloom. It is more sun tolerant than the other forms of the species.

'Chambers Pink Pride' is similar to the type but has soft pink flowers on 9″ tall flower stems. One of my favorites.

'Clarence Elliott' ('Elliott's Variety') bears compact foliage with tiny rose flowers on red 6″ tall stems.
'Primuloides' is short, with small primrose-like leaves and bright pink flowers. 'Clarence Elliott' and 'Walter Ingwersen' were derived from this selection.
'Walter Ingwersen' ('Ingwersen's Variety') bears bronze foliage and deep red flowers on 4″ tall stems.

**Related Species:**

*S. fortunei* is a clump-forming species with large glossy green leaves. The white flowers rise about 18″ above the leaves in late summer or early fall. A number of quite spectacular cultivars have been developed, although their garden worthiness seems limited to the Pacific Northwest coast or in containers anywhere. 'Rubrifolia' has rosy red flowers; 'Silver Velvet' has dark bronze leaves with wide silver veins. White flowers occur in the fall. Quite beautiful. 'Wada's Variety' is particularly good with sprays of white flowers. Better for cooler climates, but tolerates heat if given some shade.

*S. veitchiana*, also in the Diptera group, is a useful ground cover with leaves somewhat similar to 'Maroon Beauty' above, and bearing white flowers. It is slower growing than *S. stolonifera* but a good saxifrage for cold and heat, useful in zones 6-8.

***Scabiosa*** (skab-ee-o′ sa) Pincushion Flower Dipsacaceae

The pincushion plant was named for the dark purple flower heads of the annual *S. atropurpurea*, whose tufted appearance was said to resemble a velvet pincushion. Talking about pincushions and pinking shears (*Dianthus*) to my students today generally results in blank stares and a need to explain what they are, once again proving how fast times change. The dark color of that flower also signified death and accounted for one of its other common names, mournful widow (the dark purple *Geranium phaeum* is known as mourning widow, also in reference to the color). Many of the 60 species are perennial but only 2 or 3 are used to any extent in gardens today. *S. atropurpurea* and the perennial *S. caucasica* are popular cut flowers and *S. graminifolia* and *S. lucida* are shorter and more suited to the front of the border. Other scabiosa-looking species may be found in the genus *Knautia* and *Cephalaria*.

Quick Reference to Scabiosa Species

| | Height (in.) | Flower color |
|---|---|---|
| *S. caucasica* | 18-24 | Lavender |
| *S. graminifolia* | 10-18 | Pink |
| *S. ochroleuca* | 24-36 | Yellow |

***-caucasica*** (kaw-ka′ si-ca) Scabious 18-24″/18″
Summer Bluish Caucasus Mountains Zones 3-7

Up until the early 1990s, this was by far the most popular of the perennial scabiosa, providing warm lavender to blue shades in late summer to complement the yellow daisies flowering at that time. At that time, two cultivars of *S. columbaria* (see Related Species) emerged to great promotion and fanfare and have proven to be even more popular. The basal leaves are lanceolate, entire and covered with a whitish bloom giving the leaves a gray-green appearance. The stem leaves are pinnately lobed and opposite. The 3-4″ wide inflorescences are flat, and the petals shallowly 3-5 lobed. The petals are pale blue and surround a white to pale yellow center.

Plant in full sun in enriched loamy soil. They should be planted in groups of 3 or more near the front of the garden for best effect. This species does well in cool climates, especially the Northwest, but is not as vigorous during hot summers. It is not a highly recommended plant for the Southeast and even in the Northeast, plants grow rather slowly, but are popular nevertheless. Plants can be divided every 3-4 years.

The species has emerged as an important cut flower, grown in California and the Midwest. Flowers persist for about a week after cutting.

Seed sown in warm conditions (70-75°F) and high humidity should emerge in 2 weeks. Transplant to containers and grow until planting size. Two-inch basal cuttings may be taken in spring, rooted and grown on during the summer, and planted in the garden in the fall. Plants may also be divided every 3-4 years.

**Cultivars**:

'Alba' is a white-flowered form which comes true from seed but is otherwise similar to the species. 'Perfecta Alba' has larger cream-white flowers with fringed petals.

'Blue Diamonds' is a dwarf form of the species, growing only 6-8″ tall, and producing lilac-blue flowers.

'Blue Perfection' ('Perfecta Blue') has fringed, lavender-blue flowers and stands 2′ tall. It was selected from var. *perfecta* which has large fringed flowers in shades of blue.

'Bressingham White' has 3-4″ diameter flowers of clear white on 3′ tall stems and has effectively replaced an older white cultivar, 'Miss Willmott'.

'Denise' bears large lavender flowers on 2′ tall plants.

'Compliment' ('Kompliment') is 20-24″ tall with dark lavender flowers.

'Fama' has large dark, lavender-blue flowers with silver centers on 18″ tall stems. The flower color and plant habit are excellent. Popular as a cut flower.

'House Hybrids' ('Isaac House Hybrids') are a mixture of blue and white shades. They arose from selections from Isaac House in Bristol, England and have been a parent in many of the more recent selections.

'Loddon White' bears large creamy white flowers not too unlike 'Bressingham White'.

'Moerheim Blue' has large, darker blue flowers than the species.

'Moonstone' has lighter, almost pastel blue, flowers.

'Rumor' has lavender-blue flowers on 18-24″ tall stems.

'Ultraviolet', from Terra Nova Nursery, has large deep violet flowers on 2′ tall plants.

'Vivid Violet' is a hybrid with flowers that are well described by the name. More similar in form and size to *S. columbaria* than *S. caucasica*.

***-graminifolia*** (grah-mi-ni-fo' lee-a) | Grassleaf Scabious | 10-18"/18"
Summer | Pink to Lilac | Southern Europe | Zones 5-7

One of the smaller scabious, plants are best suited to the front of the garden. It has a woody rootstock and entire grasslike leaves that form loose mats of ascending stems. The foliage, silvery white due to a whitish pubescence on the leaves, forms a pleasant backdrop for the 1½-2" wide pale pink flower heads which bloom for about 6 weeks in midsummer. Plants struggle in hot humid summers. A sunny well-drained location is best.

Propagation is easiest by division but seed sown in December will provide sufficiently large plants for the garden by May.

***-ochroleuca*** (ok-ro-loo' ka) | Cream Scabious | 24-36"/24"
Summer | Cream to Yellow | Southeastern Europe | Zones 5-7

This short-lived species has branched pubescent stems with a whitish pubescence on both sides of the leaves. The bottom leaves are slightly lobed and taper down to form a petiole, while the stem leaves are pinnately dissected into 11-13 linear lobes. The flowers are formed at the end of long scapes resulting in a wiry mass of stems. The 1-2" wide primrose yellow flowers are more globular than the previous species. This is an outstanding plant when grown in full sun and well-drained soil. Plants closely resemble *Cephalaria gigantea* in flower and *S. columbaria* in habit (it is also called *S. columbaria* var. *ochroleuca*).

I have problems telling this species apart from another plant with very similar flowers, *Cephalaria gigantea*. You would think that if plants are in a different genus, they should be easy to tell apart. Not for me. Obviously, plants of *Cephalaria* are taller, but depending on height alone to discriminate differences is always a crapshoot. If you see them side by side, the differences are obvious, however, seeing them one at a time can leave you guessing. The stems of *Cephalaria* are erect, robust and strongly ridged, those of *Scabiosa* are more branched, less erect, and ridges in the stem are much less obvious. The leaf segments are much narrower in *Scabiosa* than in *Cephalaria*. For the small to medium-size garden, *Scabiosa* is much easier to use than the giant *Cephalaria*.

**Cultivars:**

var. *webbiana* is a dwarf variant which does not exceed 10" in height. It has round-toothed wrinkled leaves and flower heads that are creamier white than the species. The best selection of this variety is 'Lemon Sorbet'. Propagate by seed, division, or basal cutting similar to *S. caucasica*.

**Related Species:**

*S. columbaria* differs from *S. caucasica* by being hairier and having oblanceolate basal leaves rather than lanceolate basal leaves as in *S. caucasica*. Differences may also be seen in flower structure if placed under magnification. However, from the gardening standpoint, the main differences are its being more compact and shorter, as well as producing more flowers over a longer period of time. Two cultivars, 'Butterfly

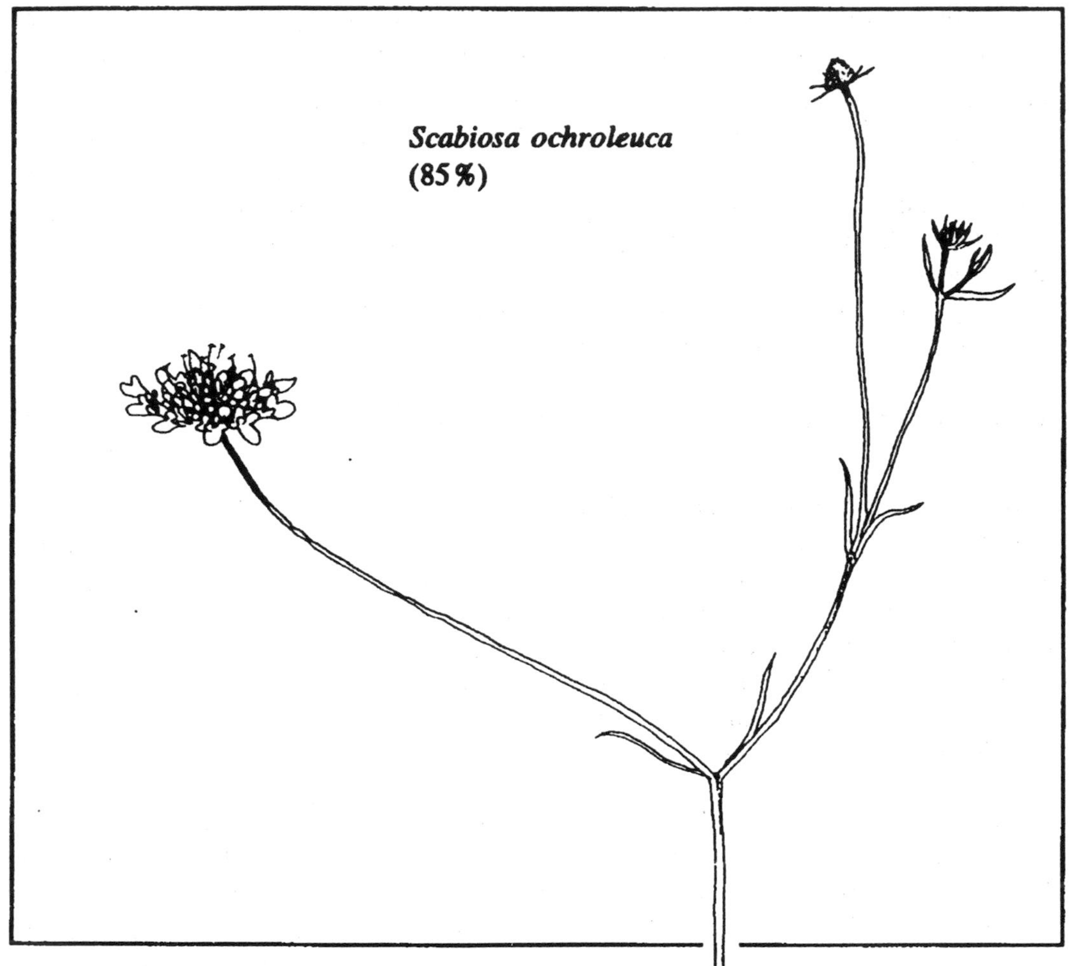


Blue' and 'Pink Mist', with lavender-blue and lavender-pink flowers respectively, were introduced in the late 1990s. 'Butterfly Blue' is exceptional; it was the 2000 Perennial Plant of the Year and is far superior to 'Pink Mist'. Since the success of 'Butterfly Blue', other selections have come to the market. 'Pink Lemonade' is a sport of 'Butterfly Blue' and enjoys yellow margins on the leaves. 'Pincushion Pink' is only 10-12″ tall and bears soft pink flowers. 'Samantha's Pink' has been outstanding, sporting many double pink flowers on 15″ tall stems. Zones 5-8.

*S. drakensbergensis*, from the Drakensberg Mountains in South Africa, has white flowers on 2′ tall plants. They may be sold as 'Snow Flake'. Once known as *S. africana*. Zones 4-7.

*S. japonica* var. *alpina* is about 9-12″ tall with finely cut, somewhat hairy foliage. The lavender-blue 2″ wide flowers appear most of the summer. I have seen a cultivar called 'Ritz Blue'; may be the same or slightly more compact.

*S. lucida* is only 1-2′ tall and is an excellent choice for the front of the garden. The leaves and stems are smoother than the other species. The 1-1½″ wide flowers are rosy lilac, and appear in late spring and flower for 6-8 weeks.

***Schizachyrium*** (shys-a-char′ ee-um) Little Blue Stem Poaceae

The unpronounceable grass has found new life in native and low-maintenance plantings, the plant of choice being *S. scoparium*. Plants are upright, producing green leaf blades and barely ornamental flowers. I have seen this used all over the place in low-maintenance settings, and it is at best useful and at worse an eyesore. Plants are about 3′ tall and in warm summers, will fall over with rain and wind, and simply look weedy. The flowers are fine, but not particularly stunning. Without doubt, its best time is in the fall and winter when the plants take on a bronze hue and little else is out there to compete with it. Having said that, I can now eat my words with a couple of excellent cultivars. 'Blaze' is similar to the species but shorter and with reddish foliage in the fall. 'The Blues' is yet a much better choice, growing sturdier, shorter and having more colorful bluish green leaves. This is one of the finest grasses in the last 5 years.

Plants are sturdier in the northern limit of its hardiness range. Zones 5-8.

***Schizostylis*** (shys-o-sty′ lus) Kaffir Lily Iridaceae

The common name hints at the fact that the genus, and its only species, *S. coccineus*, is native to South Africa, which in turn suggests cold hardiness to about zone 7 or 8. Plants have leaves and swollen rhizomes similar to Siberian iris. The scarlet flowers, whose flower spike resembles a miniature gladiolus, are about 2½″ wide and occur on one side of the flower stem only. The flower stem may reach about 20″ in length and bear four to ten, 6-petaled flattened flowers in late summer.

Plants are a little finicky due to their lack of cold tolerance, their dislike for high heat and humidity and their need for consistent moisture. Moisture is necessary, and if provided, plants perform reasonably well in full sun or partial shade. I have yet to see a "write-home-to mother" planting east of the Rockies, although the Mercer Botanical Garden in Houston, Texas has some showy specimens. As a plant, they are fair even at their best, being better as cut flowers than garden plants anyway, regardless of their location. They share this characteristic with many plants, gladiolus being the best example. Plant in groups of at least three in the garden or put in containers that can be protected during the winter.

Propagate by lifting and dividing after at least three years of growth. Dividing too early can result in significant loss of plants.

**Cultivars:**

'Alba' has white flowers.

'Major' is larger in every way than the species, also having larger and more plentiful scarlet flowers.

'Mrs. Hegarty' is a fall flowerer, with clear pink flowers.

'November Cheer' has clear pink flowers. They don't open until late fall.

'Oregon Sunset' bears coral flowers.

'Salmon Charm' has rose-salmon flowers.

'Sunrise' has large deep pink flowers.

'Viscountess Bing' is also late to flower, not opening until late September or October. The starry flowers are shell pink.

***Scilla*** (skil′ la) Squill Liliaceae

*Scilla* is a large genus, consisting of 80-100 bulbous species native to Europe, Asia and Africa. A thin covering (tunic) envelops the bulbs, from which arise straplike leaves and bell-shaped flowers. The garden species are generally less than 12″ tall, however, species such as *S. natalensis*, Natal squill, and *S. hyacinthoides*, hyacinth squill, have blue flowers on 18-36″ tall racemes. Several species have been taxonomically rearranged. The taller woodland plants, *S. hispanica*, Spanish bluebell, and *S. non-scripta*, English bluebell, are found under *Endymion*. Genera such as *Scilla*, *Puschkinia*, and *Chionodoxa* are easily confused so I have listed a few differences under *Chionodoxa*.

The garden squills should be planted in the fall in full sun or partial shade in any well-drained soil. Most flower early in the spring or late winter starting with *S. tubergeniana*, followed closely by *S. bifolia*, *S. siberica*, and finally *S. peruviana* in late spring or early summer. Bulbs combine well with other early spring flowerers such as daffodils, chionodoxas, winter aconites, and grape hyacinths. They are inexpensive, long lasting, and should be planted in large drifts, preferably 50 or more. Several late summer and fall-flowering squills, such as *S. hyacinthoides*, *S. natalensis*, and *S. autumnale* either lack hardiness or are not sufficiently showy to be worth the time or expense.

All the squills may be lifted and divided every 4-5 years. Separate the bulbs and bulblets by size, replant the largest, and grow on the smaller sizes in a nursery bed for another year before placing them in their final location. Four to five years are required for squills to reach flowering size from seed. Seeds should be shallowly sown and placed at 60-65°F under humid conditions.

Quick Reference to Scilla Species

| | Height (in.) | Flower color | Number of flowers/stem |
|---|---|---|---|
| *S. bifolia* | 4-6 | Mauve | 3-12 |
| *S. peruviana* | 8-12 | Lilac | 20-50 |
| *S. siberica* | 3-6 | Dark blue | 1-3 |
| *S. tubergeniana* | 4-6 | Pale blue | 2-4 |

***-bifolia*** (bi-fo′ lee-a) Two-Leaved Squill 3-6″/3″
Spring Mauve-Blue Southern Europe to Asia Minor Zones 4-8

This early spring bulb is excellent for naturalizing as it multiplies rapidly by offsets. The deep mauve-blue flowers are almost as rich as those of *S. siberica*, although a great deal of variability occurs. The foliage usually consists of 2 narrow (1/3 to 1/2″ wide), bronze green, channeled leaves about 6″ long, although up to 4 leaves may be present. Plants bear 6-8 starry flowers, each about 3/4″ in diameter on a 4-6″ high raceme. They flower early (in February and March) or as soon as the snow starts to melt, and are held on long thin pedicels that dance in the spring breeze. Plants reseed all over the place where comfortable.

**Cultivars**:

var. *alba* has creamy white flowers.

var. *praecox* flowers about a week earlier than the other varieties and is more robust. It has more flowers than the species.

var. *rosea* has blooms of soft shell pink.

var. *rubra* bears rosy salmon flowers.

var. *taurica* has 3-5 leaves and bears deep blue flowers on long pedicels. It is an excellent plant but difficult to locate. In the trade, it is confused with *S. siberica* var. *taurica* which has lighter blue flowers.

***-mischtschenkoana*** (mist-cheng-ko-ah′ na) Tubergen Squill 4-6″/6″
Late Winter, Early Spring Pale Blue Iran, Afghanistan Zones 4-8

The species was long known as *S. tubergeniana*, from the van Tubergen nursery in Holland from which it was introduced. Unfortunately this little thing has one of the longest tongue-tying names among garden plants, which tends to somewhat limit Mrs. Smith asking for it by name. Plants are similar to *S. siberica* var. *taurica* in habit and leaf color but the 3-4 basal leaves are up to 1″ wide. The yellow bulb is also about twice as large. They are among the earliest flowering of any of the squills. Flower spikes appear in early February in the Armitage garden and about 3 weeks later further north. Flowers break through the ground before the leaves and each spike bears 3-4 light blue flowers with a stripe down the middle of the segments. The flower color is similar to that of the later flowering *Puschkinia*. This is a great plant, and should be more common.

**Cultivars**:

'Alba' is white with a hint of lilac.

'Zwanenburg' is even better than the species. It has larger flowers and darker stripes on the petals. It is better because the species can get lost in old leaves or garden debris in late winter and early spring; this is showier.

***-peruviana*** (pe-roo-vee-ah′ na) Cuban Lily 6-10″/6″
Late Spring Lilac Mediterranean Area Zones 7-9

Both the common name and the specific epithet are misnomers, as the plant has nothing to do with Cuba or Peru, but is native to southern Europe and North African regions around the Mediterranean Sea. The name is thought to have come from the ship, the Peru, which brought the bulbs to England.

Unlike other species, plants bear 6-9 leaves in a dense basal rosette and a 6-10″ long raceme with up to 50 bright blue, starry flowers. The straplike light green leaves are 6-12″ long and 1-1½″ across with sparsely bristly margins. They are evergreen, at least in zones 7 and 8. This is a later flowering species than most of the common squills, opening in mid to late spring in the South, late spring to early summer in the North. When the flowers begin to open, they appear to rest on the leaves but as flowering continues, the scape elongates. The raceme is about 6″ across when it begins to open and consists of 50-100 blue flowers with a hint of lilac. As the flowers fully open, they reveal the yellow stamens within.

Bulbs are quite large and should be planted so the neck is at soil level, or with the base about 4″ deep. Although bulbs are not common in the trade, they should be tried more frequently as they become available. It is the showiest of the squills and does well if placed in raised beds in a warm, sunny location. Unfortunately, they don't seem to be as garden beautiful after about two years. They may survive the winters, but like many bulbs (e.g. tulips) conditions are not sufficiently favorable to replenish the bulb and allow for good successive flowers. They are not as cold hardy as some of the smaller squills, but they're not the wimps that some writers claim them to be.

**Cultivars:**

var. *alba* has white flowers.

var. *elegans* bears rosy red flowers.

var. *glabra* has lilac flowers but the leaves are not hairy. This is a common form and often sold as the species.

***-siberica*** (si-bi′ ri-ka) | Siberian Squill | 3-6″/4″

Spring | Deep Blue | Eastern Russia, Siberia | Zones 2-7

This most popular species has many attributes. It is exceedingly tough and cold hardy, reveling in arctic chills, and has the most penetrating blue color of any species, heightened even more by the blueness of the anthers. Although only 1-3 nodding flowers appear on the reddish scape (flowering stem), there are often 3-4 scapes on mature bulbs which more than make up for the paucity of flowers per stem. The individual ¼″ wide flowers often point in the same direction and usually have a darker blue stripe on the on the tepals (sepals and petals together). Bulblets are produced readily and self-sown seedlings are abundant. A small planting spreads rapidly.

Three to four straplike leaves, 6″ long and about ½″ wide, are produced in early spring. The flowers and the foliage appear a little later than snowdrops (*Galanthus*) to continue nature's gift of spring cheer. As with most small bulbs, planting 3 or 4 leads to disappointment. Plant at least 25 or preferably hundreds. The few dollars paid for 100 bulbs will be enjoyed much longer and with far less indigestion than the same amount paid for dinner at the local Burger Doodle. They may be planted under trees in a woodland or as a spring wake-up in the front of the borders. Be sure to plant them where they are allowed to ramble.

They are among the most cold hardy of spring bulbs, but do not appreciate heat and humidity. Even though plants go dormant in the spring, soil temperatures stay too warm in the South to allow them to catch their breath, and they don't do particularly well south of zone 7a.

**Cultivars:**

'Alba' makes a pretty show in the woodland setting with its white flowers against the backdrop of green.

'Azurea' has flowers of light blue.

'Spring Beauty' (var. *atrocoerulea*) is a popular form of the species and has large flowers in a lovely shade of deep blue with bright blue anthers. It is robust but produces a minimum of seed. This results in the longer-lasting flowers but clumps do not multiply as rapidly as the species.

var. *taurica* produces light blue flowers with a dark blue stripe in the center of each segment. They are usually earlier than the species.

**Related Genera:**

*Scilla bifolia* has been crossed with *Chionodoxa luciliae* and the resulting progeny are known as X *Chionoscilla* (which see).

*Scilla litardieri* bears 3-6 leaves and narrow racemes of lilac blue flowers. About 10 campanula-like flowers are produced in early spring.

*Scilla scilloides* differs from most of the squills in that it flowers in the fall. A good deal of diversity occurs in the species: some with bright pink, mauve-pink or pale blue flowers. Three to seven grasslike leaves give rise to a dense raceme of flowers. Difficult to locate, but a gem. Hardy in zones 6-8.

## *Scrophularia* (skro-few-lah′ ree-a) Figwort Scrophulariaceae

A widely distributed, highly variable genus of about 200 species, only one or two of which ever finds their way into North American gardens. The roots from plants of this genus were said to heal swelling of the lymph glands in the neck, the disease known as scrofula. The only plant I have seen in gardens is one which I wish was more available, *S. aquatica* 'Variegata'. This has an interesting leaf pattern, boldly marked with dark green and cream. It reminds me of some of the sharply variegated forms of *Brunnera* and *Symphytum*, equally difficult to find because of their difficulty in propagation.

The specific epithet helps to site the proper place in the garden for the plant, however while consistency of moisture is most helpful, it does not want to be immersed in water. I grew this plant for a couple of years in my garden until it became overgrown with more vigorous plants. It is native to western Europe suggesting that heat and humidity are not particularly to its liking, however, it should be cold hardy to about zone 5 or 6.

The leaves are about 8″ long, opposite and borne on stems that reach 2-3′ in height. The small reddish brown flowers are inconsequential but are interesting if not ornamental. I highly recommend the plant for its leaf variegation, but do not expect it to be long-lived. In the South, it can get leggy: in the North it maintains a reasonable habit.

Propagate from division only, although an occasional terminal cutting might be successful. Often, cuttings either fail to root or revert back to the all-green form.

## *Scutellaria* (sku-te-lah′ ree-a) Skullcap Lamiaceae

The skullcaps (from the shape of the fruit) comprise a large genus but few species have yet to gain widespread popularity. The reason for this is that few species are particularly garden worthy. Many times, plants are only short lived, have very tight regional preferences or are difficult to propagate, thus few are offered. In the case of *Scutellaria*, more attention has recently been paid to it, and it is starting to be picked up by more nurseries.

Plants resemble *Salvia*, having square stems and opposite leaves, particularly if comparing some of the red or rose-flowered forms. They do not have the obvious smell of sage, but the smell of all salvias is not necessary pungent. The easiest way to discern *Scutellaria* from *Salvia* is to open the flower and examine the stamens. In *Scutellaria*, there are four similar stamens; in *Salvia*, only two are fertile and normal size, the other two are rudimentary or lacking altogether. Many of the skullcaps are low-growing spreading plants and often quite woody at the base. One or two, such as *S. altissima*, are upright. Grow in well-drained soils and provide some afternoon shade in the South, full sun in the North. They are favorites for rock gardens and many species may be found by consulting rock garden enthusiasts. The Scutellaria Group website may be of interest to those who want to know more.

| ***-alpina*** (al-pine' a) | | Alpine Skullcap | 4-6"/12" |
|---|---|---|---|
| Spring | Purple | Europe | Zones 4-7 |

One of the finest scutellarias, alpine skullcap, is native to mountainous area of southern Europe, Russia and Turkestan. These low growers have many stems with small (1-1½" long) leaves and purple flowers crowded together in a short terminal raceme. The flowers have two lips; the bottom is occasionally yellow. The bracts beneath the flowers are larger than the 4-6" long flower stems themselves. They are handsome rock garden plants whose native habitat is on rocky limey soil, thus the addition of limestone to acid soils often promotes growth and flowering. In areas of high heat and humidity, the stems become leggy, and benefit from cutting back either early in the spring or immediately after flowering.

**Cultivars**:
'Alba' has white flowers.
'Arcobeleno' is about 10" tall with pink flowers above the foliage.
'Bicolor' bears purple and white blooms.
'Greencourt' produces fresh green leaves and mauve flowers over 10" tall plants.
'Moonbeam' has small, scalloped, dull green leaves and light yellow flowers.

**Related Species:**

*S. resinosa*, prairie skullcap, provides a mound of upright 8-10" tall stems and is covered with deep lavender-blue flowers in late spring. If fertilized and deadheaded, plants will flower on and off throughout the season. Native to the shortgrass prairie, plants are tough. 'Smokey Hills' has grayer foliage and purple flowers on 1' tall plants. Zones 4-7.

*S. suffrutescens*, Texas skullcap, produces small snapdragon-like rose-red to pink flowers often from late spring until early fall. Plants have a reasonably dense habit but do even better if sheared occasionally. Excellent for dry conditions as well. They have performed well in the Gardens at UGA. A 2004 Plant Select® winner, a program administered by the Denver Botanic Garden and Colorado State University.

*S. supina* is a low grower with scalloped ovate leaves and purple flowers. 'Lambert's Blue', from the garden of Ed and Donna Lambert in Athens, Georgia, is a rapidly growing 6" tall ground cover that flowers profusely in the spring. Outstanding.

***Sedum*** (sed′ um) Stonecrop Crassulaceae

The movement to embrace this large and diverse genus began in the late 1990s and continues into the 2000s. Although many species are not particularly decorative, there is a wealth of plants useful for the border and rock garden as a result of excellent selection and breeding. Most of the embracing has been done with upright forms similar in habit to the famous 'Autumn Joy', and in truth, there are far too many of these upright look-alikes. Unfortunately, the low-growing forms are still somewhat ignored. That the low-growers are not used more may be because many are rock garden plants and rock gardens have not been in vogue for many years in America. The other sad truth is that they "all sort of look alike", at least within the rock garden or border species. However, they are embraced by some with gusto, from topiaries to mosaiculture, from floral clocks to living grave sites. And certainly, with the revolution in the "green roof" concept, these little buggers will be everywhere.

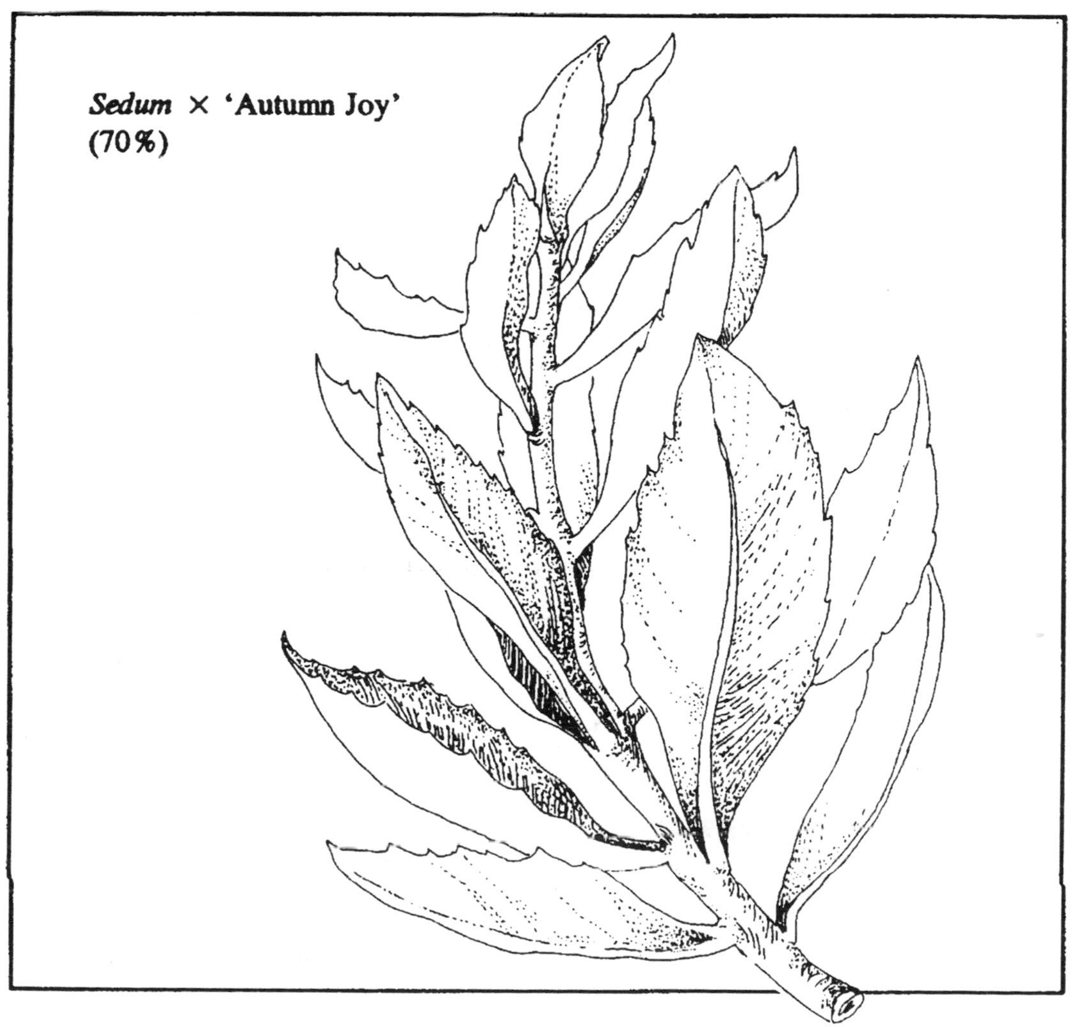

***Sedum* × 'Autumn Joy'**
**(70%)**

Finding the correct name for a stonecrop is an adventure in frustration; even the great plant hunters came back from expeditions with bags of rare plants, suitably given their botanical names and "some kind of stonecrop". A number of species are native to North America such as *S. nevii*, a lovely white-flowered, low-growing rosette former, and *S. ternatum*, whose starlike white flowers are effective in the spring garden. As other "wimpy" plants expire and leave barren ground as their tombstone, the sedums continue to provide color and vigor.

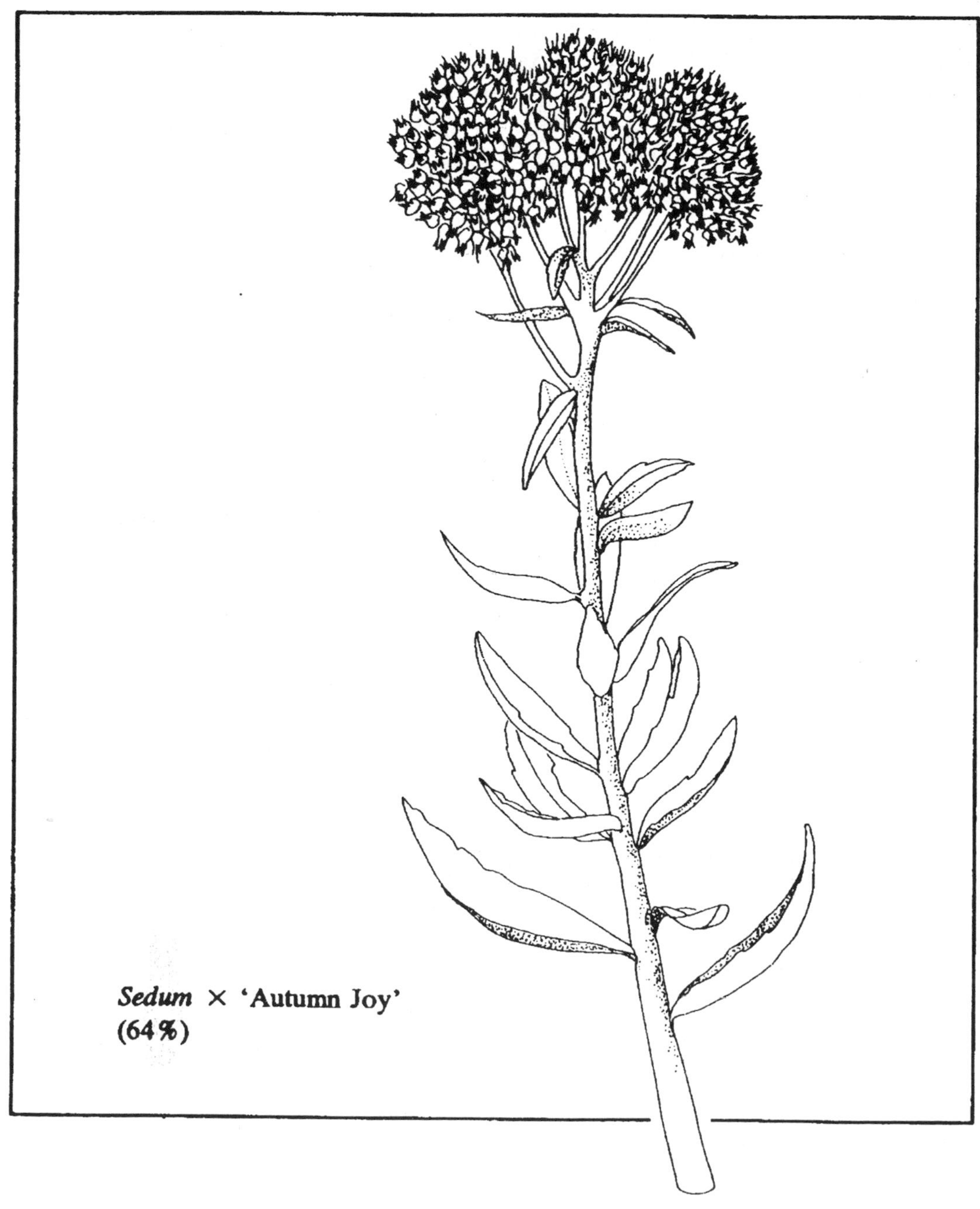

***Sedum*** **× 'Autumn Joy' (64%)**

The basic botanical definition of *Sedum* is a flowering plant with 5 petals, 5 sepals and 10 stamens. The petals are seldom attached to each other and the sepals are often fleshy and leaflike. Leaves are also fleshy and usually alternate or whorled. There is, however, so much confusion in taxonomic circles as to what does or does not constitute a species of *Sedum* that the number rose from 29 during Linnaeus's time, to 88 in 1828, 228 in 1885, 470 by the botanist Berger in 1930, but only 350 by Froderstrom in the same year, and 340 species listed by Jacobson in 1960. Since then, approximately 160 new names have been published in *Index Kewensis*, placing the number between 500 and 650. However, just to keep us honest, recent changes in nomenclature have taken many of our common upright forms such as *S. alboroseum*, *S. spectabile* and *S. telephium* and assigned them to the genus *Hylotelephium*, reducing the number once again. Do not lament if you're unsure of the botanical name of a stonecrop in the garden, you are in good company.

In general, plants prefer well-drained soils and full sun. In the South, a number of rock garden species are at their finest during the cool fall, winter, and spring months and barely hang on during the summer. Partial shade is beneficial south of zone 6. All tolerate drought and require little maintenance. Their relative ease of production means that there is no end to the choices of sedums for sedum lovers. Bluebird Nursery in Clarkson, Nebraska lists 56 in their catalog, Sunny Border Nursery in Connecticut posts 114 on their web site, and on and on.

Most stonecrops are easily propagated by 1-3″ long terminal cuttings in spring and throughout the summer. They generally root within 2 weeks. Too much water in the propagation phase results in root rots and severe decline. Seed may also be sown and plants will reach flowering size in 2 years. For many rock garden species, division is easy and the method of choice.

Quick Reference to Sedum Species

| | Height (in.) | Flower color | Flowering time |
|---|---|---|---|
| *S. acre* | 2-3 | Yellow | Late Spring |
| *S. aizoon* | 12-15 | Yellow | Summer |
| *S. kamtschaticum* | 4-9 | Yellow | Summer |
| *S. spectabile* | 12-24 | Pink | Late Summer |
| *S. spurium* | 2-6 | Rose | Late Summer |
| *S. ternatum* | 2-6 | White | Late Spring |

***-acre*** (a′ ker) Goldmoss Stonecrop 2-3″/18″
Spring Yellow Europe, North Africa, West Asia Zones 3-8

The small stature and minute leaves of this common mat-former make it excellent for planting between stepping stones, on walls and ledges, or as a filler in areas where few plants grow. The stems are decumbent (grow along the ground with their tips sticking up) and bear crowded alternate leaves. Each light green, pointed, ¼″ long leaf overlaps the one above it like shingles on a roof so that the stems appear scaly.

The golden yellow ½″ wide flowers are produced in terminal cymes. Flowering commences in late spring and continues well into summer. In North Georgia (zone 7b), it is at its best in late May, in upper New York (zone 5), mid-June.

Vigorous growers, plants obediently fill in any miserable area in the garden. They can grow so fast as to become weedy, but if provided full sun, reasonable soil, and a little moisture, plants are very showy. They should be thinned every 2-4 years to keep them in check, otherwise they can take over the world. If that is done, little other maintenance is required.

Division may be accomplished any time of year, and even pieces of plant accidentally broken will root where they fall. Seed should be covered lightly and watered gently or from the bottom so it is not washed away. Provide consistent moisture and place the seed flat at 70-75°F. Two years are necessary to reach flowering size.

**Cultivars:**

'Aureum' is a lovely plant with young leaves and shoot tips edged with a golden tint in the spring. Unfortunately, the tint is lost in the summer. The flowers are lighter yellow than the species.

'Elegans' is similar to 'Aureum' but the leaves and shoot tips are silvery. It does not lose the tint as rapidly but is not as showy as 'Aureum'. Neither of these cultivars is as vigorous as the species.

var. *majus* is larger than the species and has paler green leaves with flowers up to ¾″ across. The stems are not as densely packed as the species and are more prone to breakage in winter.

var. *minus* is the opposite of *majus* and seldom grows over 1″ tall. All parts are smaller than the species, making a compact, neat carpet.

'Oktoberfest' has creamy white flowers.

***-aizoon*** (aye′ zoon) | Aizoon Stonecrop | 12-15″/18″
Summer | Yellow | Siberia, China, Japan | Zones 4-8

The leaves are alternate and sessile, scattered along the unbranched stem and bent somewhat backwards (reflexed). The flat leaves are about 2″ long and ½″ wide, the margins sharply and irregularly toothed. The terminal yellow flowers are held on a short scape and sit literally on top of the plant. The individual flowers are about ½″ across and the flat inflorescence (cyme) is 3-4″ wide. Unlike the previous species, plants die to the ground in late fall.

Although not the most ornamental sedum, the flowers are showy for a few weeks in midsummer. It is tall enough to compete with *S. spectabile* cultivars (e.g. 'Meteor') but too tall to be used for the carpeting effect provided by *S. acre*.

Propagate by division after flowering.

**Cultivars:**

var. *aurantiacum* is showier than the species due to its red stems, dark green leaves, deep orange to yellow flowers and red fruit. Plants grow 10-18″ tall.

'Euphorboides' is more compact than the species and has larger (up to 4″ across) deep yellow flower heads.

***-spectabile*** (speck-tab′ i-lee) Showy Stonecrop 12-24″/12″
Late Summer, Fall China, Korea Zones 4-8
(syn. *Hylotelephium spectabile)*

The upright forms of sedums have generated enormous interest in the last 20 years, in fact, ever since the hybrid 'Autumn Joy' was bred in 1955. However, in the last 10 years, many more upright forms have been developed, some for the colorful foliage and others for the flowers. The species itself is similar to, mixed up with, and a breeding partner of, *S. telephium*, witch's moneybags. Plants of showy stonecrop are upright, bear pink flowers in summer and have alternate leaves. Few differences occur between it and *S. telephium*: the easiest differences to spot are the opposite leaves. Although neither species is used very much, cultivars and hybrids have multiplied like popcorn. Regardless of what plant is selected, most require full sun, but those with dark purple foliage benefit from some afternoon shade in areas of hot summers. The nomenclature of *Sedum* still remains in flux, with some authorities accepting *Hyloptelephium* for some of the upright sedums, but an equal number still maintaining *Sedum* as the "correct" name. I suspect *Hylotelephium* will eventually be accepted internationally, and in nursery catalogs in the near future.

Propagate by cuttings any time.

**Cultivars and Hybrids**:

Wow, there are a lot of upright selections, perhaps giving the heucheras and tiarellas a run for the money. I am as confused as the rest of you as to the parentage of many of the new hybrids, however, all of these are upright and similar in habit to *S. spectabile* and *S. telephium*. All are probably consistently hardy in zones 5-8, some a little more cold tolerant than others. Also, they are all better performers in areas where night temperatures are not consistently above 70°F.

'Abby Dore' provides light pink flower buds that open to rose-red flowers. Plants are 15-18″ tall.

'African Pearl' has purple foliage on red stems, and red flowers in midsummer and fall. Plants are about 2′ tall.

'Arthur Branch' is an improved form of 'Atropurpureum' and much better than 'Mohrchen', because of better upright stems and consistently purple foliage. Probably a cultivar of *S. telephium*.

'Atropurpureum' is a hybrid between *S. caucasicum* and *S. telephium*. It has been, and arguably still is, the best purple form with dark bronze foliage and rose-red flowers.

'Autumn Fire' has looked very good in many areas, including in the heat of the summer gardens at UGA. The plants are shorter than 'Autumn Joy' and the flowers brighter. This has been a winner for us.

Autumn Charm™ is a variegated green and creamy white sport of 'Autumn Joy' It appears to be stable, but time will tell.

'Autumn Joy' ('Herbstfreude') has been one of the most popular garden plants in the last 20 years. When my kids were young, they liked to gently part the upper and lower base of a leaf and blow it up like a balloon. To do this, one must have great patience and a plant tough enough to survive the rigors of being unclothed by hordes of little children. The upper leaves are smaller with more rounded bases than the lower leaves and all have a prominent midrib. Green shoots are always just below the surface and by early March, mounds of light green foliage freshen the garden. The flower buds appear whitish, slowly turn shell-pink, and age to a deep bronze red. Many flowers are supported by the flat-topped 6″ diameter corymbs. They bloom well into the fall and dry on the stem. To some gardeners, these dried flowers are picturesque and provide lovely decoration to the winter garden. To me, however, they simply look like dead flowers and I remove them after they turn brown. A problem today is that many plants are flowering in early summer, rather than the fall. A major problem that occurs with very popular plants like this one is that demand outstrips supply. Thus plants are propagated from seed, rather than cuttings, and the resulting plants are simply not 'Autumn Joy', they are one of the parents or a different hybrid. See comments with *Rudbeckia* 'Goldsturm'.

'Black Jack' is a sport from 'Mohrchen' with darker leaves and perhaps a bit more compact and a better performer. Reversion back to 'Mohrchen' can be a persistent headache. However, if you like 'Mohrchen', you'll like this one more. From Walters Gardens, Zeeland, Michigan.

'Blade Runner' has obviously serrated leaves and green foliage. It was touted as the next great sedum (as all cultivars are), but so far, it has failed to impress. Plants are slow and although I can see the blade, I can't see the running. Heck, I haven't even seen much growing.

'Brilliant' has deep pink flowers and has been a popular plant for years.

'Carl' has been a good performer in the Gardens at UGA. The compact plants are less than 18″ tall, with gray green foliage and large pink to rose flowers in midsummer.

'Carmen' bears many carmine-pink flowers on 18-24″ stems.

'Class Act' provides dark green leaves and intense red flowers on 12-15″ tall plants.

'Cloud Walker' has dark green leaves with large clusters of mauve to pink flowers.

'Frosty Morn' was introduced by Barry Yinger of Asiatica Nursery, and sports a white border around the leaves and light pink flowers in late summer and fall. This looks good every now and then, particularly in cooler temperatures, but has been disappointing in many gardens as well.

'Garnet Brocade' has lots of rose red flowers over 2′ tall plants. The garnet refers to the purple-red stripes in the gray-green foliage. From Proven Winners.

'Green Expectations' is about 18″ tall with gray-green leaves and yellowish green flowers.

'Hab Gray' impressed me in the wonderful garden of Liz and Gerald Klose in Niagara on the Lake, Ontario. Liz grows dozens of sedums and this is the one she felt deserved even more space in her garden. The handsome gray-blue leaves make it special but the pink flowers in early summer are not half bad either.

'Hot Stuff' brings the habit of 'Brilliant' but is significantly shorter (12-15″) and with bright pink flowers.

'Iceberg' is a cousin of 'Autumn Joy' with white flower heads in the fall.

'Indian Chief' has reddish flowers which fade to rosy pink. An old but still excellent selection.

'Maestro' is a sport from 'Matrona', with large pink flower clusters. Its claim to fame is its 18″ height and more compact habit, welcome characteristics to the 'Matrona' line.

'Matrona' is loved or hated with equal passion. The purple stems are handsome and the pinkish flowers are pretty enough, but regardless of where I travel in the East and Midwest, I see rather lousy-looking plants with a tendency to flop more than others. I must be looking at the wrong time and the wrong place. Plants are about 2′ tall.

'Meteor' is essentially indistinguishable from 'Autumn Joy'. According to some authors, plants are not as compact and flowering is not as long lasting. I can see no difference.

'Mohrchen' is a dark-leaved introduction from Germany which I also find way overrated. Plants look a lot better in Germany than they do in most of this country. The stems are floppy and plants resent heat and humidity. Other than that, they are fine. Red flowers appear in late summer. Probably a selection of *S. telephium*.

'Mr. Goodbud' from Terra Nova Nursery is one of my favorites. The plants are not too short (20-24″ tall) and the large flowers almost cover the plant in midsummer and early fall. The buds are a lighter color than the deep red flowers.

'Munstead Red' is a hybrid with the same parentage as 'Atropurpureum' but with deeper red flowers.

'Neon' is about 18″ tall but provides neon rose flowers. We have been pleased in the Gardens at UGA with this sport from 'Brilliant'.

'Pink Chablis' is another sport of 'Brilliant' and similar to 'Frosty Morn'. The leaves are variegated green and white and the flowers are light pink. Some claim it to be better than 'Frosty Morn', which would be a good thing indeed.

'Postman's Pride' was supposedly bred by a Belgian mailman. Plants are similar to, but smaller than, 'Purple Emperor' and are rather awful-looking purple-leaved things. The flowers are rosy red and plants grow to almost two feet. Zone 4.

'Purple Emperor' has dark purple, fleshy leaves and small pink-purple flowers in 3-6″ wide flattened heads. This has significant following in Europe as shown by the fact it was given the prestigious Outstanding Perennial Plant Award from the International Hardy Plant Union in 2002.

'Samuel Oliphant' comes from 'Matrona', but has tricolored (yellow, pink, green) leaves and small light pink flowers. I have yet to see a great-looking plant in my travels, but I am sure they are out there somewhere. Zones 4-7.

'Stardust' has whitish to silvery pink flowers on 18″ tall stems.

'Strawberries and Cream' produces dark green leaves and domed inflorescences that start off as pink buds and open to white.

'Xenox' gives us another fine descriptive name. Plants are about 15″ tall with scalloped burgundy foliage. Rose flowers open in summer. If you can stand the name, enjoy the plants. They are among the best of the purple-leaved forms.

***-kamtschaticum*** (kamt-sha′ ti-cum) Kamschatka Stonecrop 4-9″/15″
Summer Yellow Kamchatka, Korea, Japan Zones 3-8

The normally unbranched pale green stems give rise to flat, terminal inflorescences of 6-10 yellow flowers. The leaves are alternate, about 1½″ long and ½″ wide, and sharply toothed above the middle but entire near the base. The flowers are showy, about ½″ across, but seldom is the plant a mat of yellow as in *S. acre*. The flowers often give way to red seed pods. There is a good deal of variability in the species and plants that were originally given species or subspecies status (*S. ellacombianum*) are sufficiently similar that some authorities lump them together under *S. kamtschaticum*. Plants spread well if provided good drainage and full sun, and although too tall and open for a ground cover, are excellent for hillsides and banks. A tangled mass of stems occurs in the summer, and after flowering, small rosettes of leaves appear at the base of the plant which are next year's foliage. Most of the rest of the plant dies away by late fall.

**Cultivars**:
'Diffusum' bears dozens of yellow flowers which arise from dark purple buds.
'Takahira Dake' is more compact and erect than the species with reddish stems and more flowering branches. The flowers are similar to the type.
'Variegatum' has a broad white band on the leaf margins, and flowers more orange than the species. It is not as vigorous as the species and remains more compact. The leaves revert to green readily and any such growth should be removed to the base.
'Weihenstephaner Gold' is a tongue-twisting name for a marvelous college in Southern Germany. Dozens of golden yellow flowers cover this ground- hugging plant. Highly recommended. Plants are sometimes listed under *S. k.* var. *floriferum* or *S. floriferum*.

***-spurium*** (spur′ ee-um) Two Row Stonecrop 2-6″/18″
Summer White to Rose Caucasus Zones 3-7

Plants provide some of the tougher and showier stonecrops for a ground cover or rock garden. Many evergreen shoots arise from branches which root at the nodes, making a vigorous and rapidly spreading plant. The leaves are opposite, about 1″ long with shallow teeth or scallops on the upper parts of the leaves. In leaf, it is straggly, coarse, uninteresting and invasive. Ronald Evans (*Handbook of Cultivated Sedums*, 1984), in describing *S. spurium*, states that "No plant should be called completely useless, however, and from its vegetative aspect, it could be recommended for quickly covering a heap of rubble." In spite of Mr. Evans' opinion, plants have become popular because of the showy flowers. The flowering stems are about 4″ long and give rise to terminal, four-branched inflorescences consisting of many ¾″ diameter flowers. The anthers are orange-red, the petals rosy red and flowers persist for 3-4 weeks, and can be a brilliant blaze of color. The opposite leaves are bright green with a reddish margin and the leaves near the end of the stems turn redder in the fall and remain evergreen. Plants are not as vigorous in the South as in the North and as with most sedums, look terrible in midsummer.

Native to moist alpine meadows, it is not tolerant of wet feet and should be grown where drainage is excellent.

All forms of this species may be divided any time during the season.

**Cultivars:**

Many of the cultivars have been selected for the bronze-purple foliage. In general, the color is better in the spring and fall and in many cases, leaves fade badly in areas of high heat and humidity. They all require excellent drainage to maintain permanence.

'Album' is a white-flowered form of 'Dragon's Blood'.

'Atropurpureum' has burgundy leaves and rose-red flowers.

'Bronze Carpet' has a distinct bronzing of the leaves and is similar to 'Dragon's Blood'. The leaves are less permanently bronzed than 'Dragon's Blood' and some reversion to green stems occurs.

'Coccineum' is similar to the species but has scarlet flowers.

'Dragon's Blood' is the most popular cultivar with foliage strongly and permanently suffused with purplish bronze. During the spring and summer, plants are covered with dark red starry flowers. It is not as vigorous as the species. In the South, plants often melt out in the summer, particularly if drainage is not improved.

'Fulda Glow' is similar to 'Dragon's Blood' but keeps its color a little longer into the season.

'Green Mantle' produces fresh green leaves but essentially no flowers are produced.

'Leningrad White' came from the Leningrad Botanic Garden, and has many clean white flowers, potentially the best white form in the species.

'Purple Carpet' is a compact grower with dark purple leaves.

'Red Carpet' has red flowers over bronze foliage and grows 3-4″ tall. Similar to 'Bronze Carpet'.

'Ruby Mantle' has deep pink to red flowers over consistently dark burgundy leaves.

'Tricolor' produces stripes of pink, white and green on the leaves.

'Variegatum' has green leaves surrounded by creamy pink margins. Some leaves are entirely pinkish red but reversion to green shoots is common.

'Voodoo' is another purple, low-growing sedum, with pink flowers in the spring.

***-ternatum*** (ter-na′ tum) Whorled Stonecrop 2-6″/18″
Late Spring White Eastern United States Zones 4-8

The common name comes from the arrangement of leaves in whorls of three. Rounded pale green stems root from the nodes. After flowering, stems die in the fall but offshoots remain, resulting in evergreen plants. The ¾″ long, roundish leaves are borne in rosettes crowded at the ends while the lower stem is barren. The pure white starry flowers are effective for 2 to 4 weeks in April and May. Plants tolerate shady moist conditions better than most other species. For rocky slopes, few species are better. Unfortunately, *Botrytis* infections can be serious and plants are lost in wet winters in areas of little or no snow.

Reproduce vegetatively from stems which root and break away from the mother plant. These remain small during the winter and begin to grow the next spring. Plants may also be divided in early spring or fall.

**Cultivars**:

'Larinem Park' is compact, and produces multitudes of white flowers in the spring and early summer. The finest plantings I have seen are in the Southern Heritage Park above Lake Toxaway, North Carolina.

'Minus' is similar but smaller in all parts with a mature height of 2-3″, and bears leaves only at the end of the stems. The flower is smaller but otherwise similar to the type.

**Related Species and Hybrids:**

*S. alboroseum* (*Hylotelephium erythrostictum*) grows about 2′ tall and has opposite fleshy leaves and greenish white flowers in dense inflorescences (cymes). The species is seldom grown but 'Medio-variegatum' is quite popular. The succulent leaves are patterned with broad green margins around the central creamy white interiors. Interesting, and outstanding in zones 3-6. Hardy to zone 3.

*S. album* forms evergreen mats of green to bronze roundish leaves, and produces dense inflorescences of small whitish flowers. 'Murale' has bronze foliage to complement the white flowers. Perhaps zones 5-8.

*S. caucasicum* (*Hylotelephium caucasicum*), great stonecrop, is 2′ tall with opposite succulent leaves and flat flower heads of greenish yellow stars. Plants hybridize readily, often with *S. telephium*.

*S. dasyphyllum* is a ground-hugging plant with gray-green foliage. Starry white flowers emerge in June and July. Best to provide afternoon shade. Hardy in zones 4-7.

*S. ellacombianum* is sometimes classified as a subspecies of *S. kamtschaticum* but the stems are not branched, the leaves are opposite and have scalloped rather than toothed margins. It is shorter (4-6″) and more compact. Beautiful star-shaped flowers on lime-green foliage can be seen in the spring and summer. However, after all is said and done, there is little difference from the garden point of view.

*S. floriferum*, as the name suggests, produces many flowers. They are formed along the whole length of the stem. Similar to *S. kamtschaticum*, it is often listed as a variety (*S. kamtschaticum* var. *floriferum*). The flowers are smaller and paler yellow, but overall, plants put on a better show than the Kamschatka form.

*S.* 'John Creech' bears the name of an extraordinary horticulturist. It is a wonderful specimen for a place where a 2-3″ tall plant can be viewed. It is vigorous and produced rose pink flowers, given sharp drainage and sun. Tom Kimmel, of Twixwood Nursery in Berrien Springs, Michigan claims this to be the best sedum he has ever grown, bar none. The flowers occur in late May and June.

*S. maximowiczii* is considered by some authors to be synonymous with *S. aizoon*, others feel that the red, taller stems, and broader leaves make it a subspecies of *S. aizoon*, while others consider it a separate species. Regardless, plants with a *maximowiczii* label are often more showy in leaf and flower than *S. aizoon* and more useful for the garden.

*S. middendorffianum*, Middendorf stonecrop, has unbranched stems and narrower leaves (about 1/10″ wide). Plants are more upright than Kamschatka sedum. The leaves also have a sunken median groove making them somewhat V-shaped. The flowers of all three species are similar.

*S. nevii* is an Eastern native species and badly ignored. Its tufted growth is only about 3-4″ tall but consists of blue-green foliage, and reminds some people of hens and chicks (*Sempervivum*). The white flowers have dark purple anthers and are quite handsome. A terrific plant for partial shade.

*S. rupestre* (syn. *S. reflexum*), stone orpine, has bright yellow flowers over a loose mat of creeping, rooting stems. The linear, bluish green leaves are rounded in cross section (terete) and densely arranged on the stems. Plants flower in midsummer and grow 6-10″ tall. These are some of the best sedums for warm climates. 'Angelina' is outstanding, with golden foliage on long vigorous stems. Probably the best new sedum in many years; garnering awards from Texas, Georgia and the Garden Writers of America. As wonderful as it it, I think the flowers detract from its beauty. 'Blue Spruce' is a wonderful blue needle-leafed selection which fills in rapidly. Yellow flowers appear in summer. 'Cristata' is a curious little anomaly with fasciated foliage (leaves flattened looking like crests) and all in all resembling a cockscomb. The young leaves have been used in salads and soups. Some people think the term curious is far too kind, but what the heck, gardening is supposed to be fun.

'Ruby Glow' (*S. cauticola* x *S. telephium*) is about 12″ tall and bears iridescent dark ruby flowers. It is an excellent front-of-the-border plant and is particularly colorful in late summer and fall. It is now listed as *Hylotelephium* x 'Ruby Glow'.

'Sea Stars' may be a cultivar of *S. bithynicum*, *S. dasyphyllum* or none of the above. Regardless, these dense mats of bright green foliage are perfect for a small ledge where they can fill in and topple over or around rocks. Small white flowers are produced on and off during the season. Not quite as nice as 'Angelina' (see *S. rupestre*) but still a favorite of mine where a mat former is needed.

*S. spathulifolium* is native to the West Coast and bears 3/4″ wide yellow flowers and short trailing stems of blue-green spatulate leaves. 'Atropurpureum' has dark purple leaves. 'Cape Blanco' has silvery leaves with a purplish red margin and dozens of yellow flowers. Handsome in the North and West, does poorly in hot, humid summers.

'Sunset Cloud' (*S.* x 'Atropurpureum' x 'Ruby Glow') bears blue-green leaves and wine-colored flowers. The leaves are an excellent addition to the garden.

*S. tetractinum* is a low grower with rounded leaves and small yellow starry flowers. Vigorous, easy, and highly recommended. Zones 4-8.

'Vera Jameson' is short (9-12″ tall) with bronze leaves and 2-4″ wide flower heads of 1/2″ wide pink flowers. A great dark leaf selection. Vera Jameson was an avid gardener who lived in Gloucestershire, England. Mrs. Jameson loved to garden, pulling weeds until she died in 1989 at the age of 90.

## *Selaginella* (sel-ag-in′ ell-a) Spike Moss Selaginellaceae

Selaginella is simply an outstanding group of plants. They are referred to as fernlike or mosslike plants, but they really are in a world of their own. They produce no flowers, rather they reproduce by spores. These fern allies have simple, scale-like leaves on branching stems from which roots also arise. The spike mosses are grown for their interesting and often beautiful foliage, occurring in a range of vibrant greens, golden or variegated. They generally need a good deal of moisture but plants native to desert areas such as resurrection plant, *S. lepidophylla*, just curl up and wait for some rain. Others, such as *S. uncinata*, peacock-moss, have iridescent leaves, and yet others even climb *(S. willdenovi)*. Most prefer acidic soils and some shade but morning sun is not a problem.

Over 700 species are known but only three or four can easily be found. All are cold hardy to zone 7, and many have no problems as far north as zone 6. *S. braunii* is probably the most functional, providing vigorous colonies of green foliage. Nothing sexy, but simply a good plant. *S. kraussiana* may be the most popular and easiest to find. Plants are about 15″ tall and equally wide and have soft divided leaves. They form significant colonies if given a few years. The form 'Aurea' has golden foliage, at least in the spring. Zones 6-9.

I have been surprised with the performance of the unkempt but fantastic Chinese spikemoss, *S. moellendorfii*. Plants have light green foliage on 6-9″ tall plants all summer and turn a handsome bronze color in the fall. Small plantlets fall off and reproduce, so keeping them going should not be a problem. Zones 7-9.

Probably my favorite is the truly iridescent peacock fern, *S. uncinata*. Otherwise known as rainbow moss, the foliage on the 6-8″ tall plants is blue and green and if they are planted in moist conditions, can gallop through the garden. In the outstanding garden of Willis Hardin in Commerce, Georgia, the woods are alive with peacock fern, and I mean alive! I am so impressed with the ability of the plants to grow that I am using them for turf in a deeply shaded, moist area in my garden where I simply cannot grow grass. So far, so good. Zones 6-9.

## ***Selinum*** (se-leen′ um) Selinum Apiaceae

Another difficult-to-distinguish member of the carrot family, whose flowers look like so many of those wonderful roadside Queen Anne's lace-type weeds The six species are native to the Himalayas and seldom have they found their way to North American gardens. However, *S. tenuifolium* is really quite wonderful with her white flowers on top of bronze flower stems. But it is the feathery, fresh green asparagus-like foliage that makes the plant special, providing height, color and texture to the garden. It is a little wild looking, but a little wilderness among formality is not so bad.

Probably hardy in zones 4-7. Propagate by collecting and sowing the seeds.

## ***Semiaquilegia*** (sem-ee′ a-kwi-lee′ gee-a) Semiaquilegia Ranunculaceae

When I first read about this plant, I thought the name had to be a joke. Once I realized the name was authentic, I thought of ways a plant could be half a columbine: half as tall, half as pretty, half as colorful? It was definitely a slow day. It turns out that it was just a spurless columbine but when I saw the plant, I realized that it was just as tall, just as pretty and just as colorful as many columbines, and its name was so intriguing that I had to grow it. I scoured catalogs and the Internet and soon the Armitage garden was awash in half-columbines.

The main difference between this and most columbines is the lack of spurs and that the sepals are spread apart, almost starlike. Flowers are always pale rose to wine red. They differ from the spurless forms of *A. vulgaris* (which see) in color and the spreading of the sepals. Regardless of taxonomic and morphological differences, they are handsome 1-2′ tall plants with pendulous flowers and will fit in wherever columbines would be grown. The main species available is *S. ecalcarata,* whose wine-red flowers were extraordinary for the three years it graced my place. Alas, I am awash no longer. The other species sometimes sold is *S. adoxoides* which is similar but with pale rose flowers.

They persist like other columbines, lasting 2-3 years, and prefer partial shade and moist soils. Hardy in zones 4-7.

***Sempervivum*** (sem-per-veev′ um) Hens and Chicks, Houseleek Crassulaceae

If there was but a single plant my grandparents remembered, it would likely be hens and chicks. Used everywhere from small side gardens to plantings on grave sites, few gardens were complete without them. One of the reasons for the popularity was the ease of growth and adaptability to any and all conditions. The name comes from the Latin *semper*, always, and *vivo*, live, and live forever it does. Hens and chicks belong to the same family as *Sedum* but differ in having floral parts in multiples of 6 or more, while those of *Sedum* are in fives. All of the approximately 25 species appear similar and all are known as hens and chicks.

Plants are characterized by thick, fleshy, alternate leaves and flowers which rise from the rosettes in coarse inflorescences. The flowers are often rosy red but may be white, green, yellow, or purple. Young plants are formed around the base of the plant and after flowering, the flowering rosettes—"hens"—often die, leaving the "chicks" to carry on for another year.

Several species are offered by specialists including the cobwebbed houseleek, *S. arachnoideum*, which weaves gray threads from leaf to leaf and forms dense webbing, particularly in full sun. Rose-red flowers appear in midsummer on stout flower stems. 'Cobweb' is even more spidery. *S. soboliferum* produces dense mats of small green rosettes. The many offsets are attached to the mother plant by thin weak stolons and detach easily. Due to the ease with which offsets were formed and allowed to leave home, this species was the original hens and chicks. Pale yellow flowers are formed. Some nurseries offer excellent choices: in 1995, Sunny Border Nursery in Kensington, Connecticut sold over 50 taxa, and in 2006, 98 were listed on their web site. Hard to believe when all we ever see is the common houseleek, *S. tectorum*, but differences in foliage color, foliage shape and flowers distinguish one from the other. Get hold of a good catalog and give a few others a try.

Removing the offsets and planting elsewhere is the easiest method of propagation. Seed may also be obtained but three years are necessary before plants flower.

-***tectorum*** (tek-to′ rum) | Common Houseleek | 8-12″/9″
Summer | Purple-Red | Pyrenees, Alps, Apennines | Zones 3-7

The 3-4″ diameter rosettes consist of 50-60 leaves, often tinged purple on the margins. The plant is stoloniferous and the new offsets are densely crowded around the parent. The leaves are flat on the face, rounded on the back and often reddened at the base. The hairy 12″ long flower stem is clothed with hairy lancelike leaves. The flowers are 12-parted, purple red, and about 1″ across. The offsets are strong and produced on thick stolons. It is evergreen in all parts of the country. Drainage is more critical in the South than in the North.

**Cultivars and hybrids**:
var. *calcareum* has smooth leaves with brown-purple tips.
var. *cupreum* produces larger rosettes which turn rosy in cool seasons.
'Pilioseum' has large rosettes of dark green leaves. Vigorous.
'Purple Beauty' bears rosettes with purple tips.

**Related Species**:
*S. tectorum* has hybridized with many species, in nature as well as in gardens, producing numerous named forms and hybrids. *S.* x *pomellii*, Pomel's houseleek, and *S.* x *thompsonii*, Thompson's houseleek, are hybrids between *S. arachnoideum* and *S. tectorum* while *S.* x *schottii*, Schott's houseleek, is the union of *S. montanum* and *S. tectorum*. Cultivars with names like 'Oddity', 'Mrs. Giuseppi' and 'Classic' are all worth trying.

## ***Senecio*** (se-ne′ see-o) | Senecio | Asteraceae

This is an enormous genus, containing about 1000 species from the tropics of Africa and Madagascar, New Zealand, North and South America, to Japan and China. Many are annuals, including one of most useful gray-leaved plants, dusty miller, *S. cineraria*, and its even more beautiful relative, *S. viraviva*. Some are vines (*S. confusus*) and many are persistent weeds like common groundsel (*S. vulgaris*). In general, the daisylike flowers are yellow to orange but a number, including the handsome *S. smithii* also have white flowers. When I take gardeners to the British Isles, we come across what has to be one of the toughest, most salt-tolerant plants ever, the shrubby *S. grayii*, with its white-margined leaves and abundant yellow daisies. In the American garden, however, most senecios are best suited to the meadow area as they often look particularly wretched after flowering.

Only a few perennial forms are offered to gardeners (with good reason). I have found a couple of native species and one from western Asia to be reasonable plants for the marginal tracts of the garden, but with the diversity of forms, habitats and adaptability in the genus, there are likely some hidden gems just waiting to be discovered. A number of taxonomists have removed many of the species, including some of those below, to the genus *Packera*. There is still a good deal of disagreement.

Quick Reference to Senecio Species

| | Height | Flower color | Season |
|---|---|---|---|
| *S. aureus* | 6-12″ | Yellow | Spring |
| *S. doria* | 3-5′ | Yellow | Summer |
| *S. tomentosus* | 2-3′ | Yellow | Summer |

***-aureus*** (ore-e′ us) Golden Ragwort, Squaw-weed 6-12″/12″
Spring Yellow Eastern, Central United States Zones 3-8
(syn. *Packera aurea*)

I love this little plant because it does its thing with no fuss or mess. Its thing is to emerge early in the spring, send up purple flower buds that open to starry yellow flowers a few weeks later. The heart-shaped blunt-toothed basal leaves form rosettes and the stem leaves are finely and pinnately divided. The 1″ wide flowers persist for about 4 weeks in the landscape. They self-seed; one year there may be only a small group and the next year there may be a whole carpet. If you are looking for native woodland plants, these simply work. In the Armitage garden, they come and go along a shaded path, welcome in the spring, forgotten in the summer.

A solid movement has occurred to place this under the genus *Packera*. This is reflected in some newer catalogs and literature, but I will wait a little longer for the dust to settle to embrace the change.

***-doria*** (dor-i′ a) Senecio 3-5′/3′
Summer Yellow Western Asia Zones 4-7

Plants have bright green ovate to linear leaves that may be 12″ long and 4″ wide. The yellow flowers are only about an inch wide but dozens of them occur at the tops of the stems. This is a heat-tolerant senecio that enjoys poor soils and hot sun. Flowering late in the summer, it makes a useful companion to late blues and purples at that time. Cut back after flowering as it can look particularly bad late in the year.

**Related Species:**

*S. tomentosus* (*Packera tomentosa*) is a large plant, growing to 2-2½′ tall. The young leaves, which are long and slender, are covered with a whitish woolly substance. The yellow flowers with orange centers are borne on long flower stems, also with the same woolliness. Full sun is necessary.

## ***Shortia*** (short′ ee-a) Oconee Bells Diapensiaceae

Two slow-growing species from Japan and one from North America make up this woodland group. The genus, named after Dr. Charles Short, a Kentucky botanist, was the subject of a plant hunt equal to any manhunt seen on America's Most Wanted. The French plant explorer André Micheaux discovered the plant in 1788 in the mountains of South Carolina, but the specimen was in fruit rather than flower, thus was not described in his *Flora Boreali-Americana*. Asa Gray reexamined the specimen, preserved with many of Micheaux's collections in Paris, and named the plant *Shortia* in 1842. However, no other living plants could be found and great hunts and searches were all for naught until it was finally rediscovered in 1877 in Oconee County, South Carolina, thus the common name. The leaves resembled those of the closely related genus, *Galax*, thus its specific epithet, *galacifolia*.

The basal, rounded deep evergreen leaves have shallow, almost wavy margins and are borne on long petioles. Plants are 4-8" tall when in flower. The slightly nodding white flowers are borne singly and slightly nod down. The plant is considered rare, but it is less rare than local. Plants are still not common in nurseries but to dig from the wild is immoral, unethical and stupid, to say nothing that the plants will die when moved. If you can find nursery-grown plants, they are still a bit of challenge to grow in the garden, but the addition of humus and leaf mold appears to be useful. Thus planting in an area naturally rich in such materials, or the ability to add them consistently, is best. To place these plants in ordinary garden soil is like planting water lilies in a rock garden. Partial shade is also necessary. Plants are hardy in zones 6-8.

**Related Species:**

*S.* x *intertexta* is the name given to the intergeneric hybrid between *S. galacifolia* x *S. uniflora*, originally described in 1951. Plants are seldom seen except in botanical gardens and they are a little more vigorous than, but not significantly different from either parent. Plants go under the name 'Wimborne'.

*S. soldanelloides*, fringed galax, is native to Japan, and has coarsely toothed leaves and up to six flowers in a loose raceme. Flowers are deep rose at the center fading to white as they age.

*S. uniflora*, Nippon bells, is much more similar to *S. galacifolia*, and differs by having heart-shaped leaves with more deeply toothed leaves. Also native to Japan.

## ***Sidalcea*** (see-dal' see-a) Checker-Mallow Malvaceae

*Sidalcea* is related closely to the genus *Sida*, a little-known group of plants native to North America, and to *Alcea*, the hollyhock. It bears mallow-like flowers but is not as tall as hollyhock. In recent years, improvements have occurred in flower and habit. About 20 species, all native to western North America, are known. They range in natural habitat from open forest glades (*S. malviflora*) to mountainside streams (*S. candida*). Most have rose to pink flowers but one species, *S. candida*, has small white flowers with bluish anthers. Most of the improvements in the genus have occurred with *S. malviflora*, checkerbloom. Plants thrive in climates with relatively cool summers and mild winters; warm, humid summers stress plants result in higher susceptibility to diseases and insects. Cut back after flowering for additional blooms.

*Sidalcea* is often confused with other members of the Malvaceae such as hollyhocks (*Alcea*), mallows (*Malva*) and *Lavatera*; see *Alcea* for ways of telling them apart.

***-malviflora*** (mal-vi-flor′ a) Checkerbloom 2-5′/3′
Summer Rose, Pink, Purple California Zones 5-7

The 2″ wide lilac flowers are borne in terminal racemes. The basal leaves are rounded and lobed while the stem leaves are deeply cut into 5-7 smooth segments. *Sidalcea* thrives in cool, dry climates and performs poorly in the heat and humidity of the Midwestern and Southeastern states. Misery was its middle name in the Armitage garden. Plant in full sun to partial shade in well-drained soil.

Seldom is the species seen in cultivation as it is too variable and tall to be of ornamental value. Improvements in flower color and plant habit resulted from crosses between *S. candida*, white checker-mallow, and *S. malviflora*.

Propagate by lifting the clump in the fall, using vigorous sections from the outside of the plant and discarding the center. Divide every 3-4 years. The species and a number of named forms (e.g. 'Stark's Hybrids') may be raised from seed in April and planted in the fall.

**Cultivars:**

'Brilliant' is 2-2½′ tall and carries carmine-red flowers.

'Elsie Heugh' is offered by most nurserymen and bears lovely pale pink, fringed flowers on a 2-3′ tall plant. Quite beautiful and recommended.

'Loveliness' is characterized by the shell pink flowers and compact habit. Plants stand 2½′ tall and seldom need support.

'Mr. Lindbergh' has rosy red flowers and grows 2′ tall.

'Mrs. Alderson' is 3-4′ tall and bears spikes of large rose-pink flowers. This was the parent from which the dwarf cultivars 'Oberon' and 'Puck' arose .

'Oberon' has deep rose-pink flowers and is 2-2½′ tall.

'Party Girl' is more compact, growing 2-3′ tall, and bearing shell pink flowers in late summer.

'Puck' is the dwarfest of the cultivars and attains a height of 2′ and bears clear pink flowers. This cultivar and 'Oberon' are worth trying where other cultivars grow too tall, particularly in warm climates. These excellent cultivars were bred by Bloom's Nursery in England.

'Rosanna' is about 3′ tall with rose-red flowers.

'Rose Queen' has rose-pink flowers on 3-4′ tall stems. One of the oldest cultivars, it is becoming more difficult to find.

Stark's Hybrids is a seed-propagated mix bearing pale pink to deep rose flowers that range in height from 2-3′.

'Sussex Beauty' grows 3-4′ tall and has bright, satiny pink flowers.

'William Smith' has salmon-rose flowers and grows to 3′ tall.

**Related Species:**

*S. candida*, white prairie-mallow, is native to Wyoming, Colorado, Washington and Oregon. The white or cream flowers are held on dense terminal racemes on top of 2-3′ tall plants. 'Bianca' is 3′ tall with clean single blooms.

***Silene*** (si-lee′ nee) Campion Caryophyllaceae

Of the approximately 300 species, a few have found their way into widespread cultivation, particularly those suitable for the front of the garden or for the rock garden. The leaves are entire and the flowers are borne singly or on 1-sided spikes. The tips of the petals may be entire (*S. caroliniana*) but more often are notched (*S. virginica*) or fringed (*S. polypetala*). The calyx (the group of sepals) is often inflated giving the flowers a bladder-like appearance.

*Silene* is closely related to *Lychnis* and the rose-red hybrid between the two genera is called X *Lychnisilene rosea,* sometimes listed as Rolly's Favorite'. Plants are also closely related to *Viscaria,* and the genera are often used interchangeably.

| | **Number of styles** | **Number of cells in seed capsule** | **Number of stamens** | **Number of species** |
|---|---|---|---|---|
| *Lychnis* | 5 | 1 | 10 | 10 |
| *Silene* | 3 | 3 | 10 | 300 |
| *Viscaria* | 5 | 5 | 10 | 4 |

Another genus, *Melandrium*, comes and goes in and out of *Silene*, depending on who is tweaking the genus. It supposedly differs from *Silene* by having one cell in the seed capsule rather than the three found in *Silene*. However, enough authorities keep the genus together that I am happy to do the same. *Viscaria vulgaris,* catchfly, is an interesting plant whose common name comes from the fact that flies stick to its sticky stem.

A number of striking species are grown for the rock garden such as *S. acaulis*, moss campion, *S. hookeri*, Hooker's campion, and *S. argaea*, but these can be difficult and disappointing for many gardeners, requiring cool climates and exceptional drainage. One of the native flowers to the British Isles, *S. dioica*, red campion, is on every roadside over there and is occasionally grown on the West Coast. 'Graham's Delight' has variegated foliage and deep pink flowers. Two species which are also useful and much less demanding for the front of border or in the rock garden are *S. polypetala*, fringed campion, and *S. schafta*, schafta campion.

| | **Height** | **Color** | **Petal tips** |
|---|---|---|---|
| *S. acaulis* | 2-4 | Pink | Shallow notch |
| *S. caroliniana* | 4-8 | Pink | Entire |
| *S. polypetala* | 4-6 | Pink | Fringed |
| *S. schafta* | 3-6 | Magenta-pink | Entire |
| *S. virginica* | 10-20 | Scarlet | Deep notch |

***-acaulis*** (a-kaw′ lis) Moss Campion 2-4″/6″
Spring Pink, Lavender Europe Zones 2-6

The plant is referred to as being "circumpolar", inhabiting high northern or southern areas around the world. The term *acaulis* means "stemless" and these tiny plants form cushions of densely packed narrow leaves less than ½″ long. The solitary pinkish to red, sometimes lavender, flowers have shallowly notched petals and sit on top of the matted growth. Unfortunately, many plants tend to be shy flowerers.

Plants are exceptionally pretty with their smooth matted plant habit, but only if grown in cool climates. They prefer mountain ranges but if your garden is not on top of a mountain, fret not. Be sure, however, that plants are essentially grown on rocks so that drainage is as exceptional as the flowers.

**Cultivars:**
'Cenisia' has double flowers.
'Floribunda' is a good selection that appears to flower more prolifically than others.

***-caroliniana*** (car-o-lin-ee-aye′ na) Carolina Campion 4-8″/6″
Spring Pink Southeastern United States Zones 5-8

One of our lesser-known native campions, plants make ideal rock garden specimens and provide a wide range of colors. The linear leaves are bunched at the base with a central darker green midrib. The flowers are arranged in a corymb and consist of five petals, usually unnotched or just slightly notched. The tubular calyces are not inflated. Colors range from a creamy white through pale pink to carmine.

Plants require full sun to afternoon shade and excellent drainage. In their native habitat, plants are often found on limey soils, but drainage is much more important than soil pH. Plants are short-lived in general, but particularly tricky in poor conditions. Propagate by seeds or root division.

**Cultivars:**
'Bubblegum' bears pink phlox-like flowers. Kind of reminds me of Bazooka bubblegum.
'Millstream Select' was found by H. Lincoln Foster in a group of seedlings. Deep colors of pink and carmine come from seeds collected in his garden, Millstream, and are still occasionally found in alpine seed lists.

***-polypetala*** (pah-lee′ pet-a-la) Fringed Campion 4-6″/18″
Late Spring Pink Southeastern United States Zones 6-8

This wild flower is one of our most beautiful plants. Unfortunately, it is on the endangered species list for a number of states. However, collections reside happily in botanical gardens in the Southeast and tissue culture techniques have increased numbers substantially. The evergreen foliage is dark green and contrasts well with the light lavender-pink, fringed petals which emerge in late spring. The flowers are 1¼″ in diameter and produced for 3-4 weeks. If placed in full sun, the foliage yellows and becomes sparse, therefore, partial to heavy shade is recommended. Plants require well-drained moist soil. If planted in the front of the border, be sure soil is porous enough to reduce water retention around the crown.

'Longwood' is a hybrid between *S. caroliniana* and *S. polypetala,* the result of breeding research by Dr. Jim Ault while at Longwood Gardens in Pennsylvania. The resulting hybrid has beautiful deep pink, fringed petals, earlier than *S. polypetala,* but is

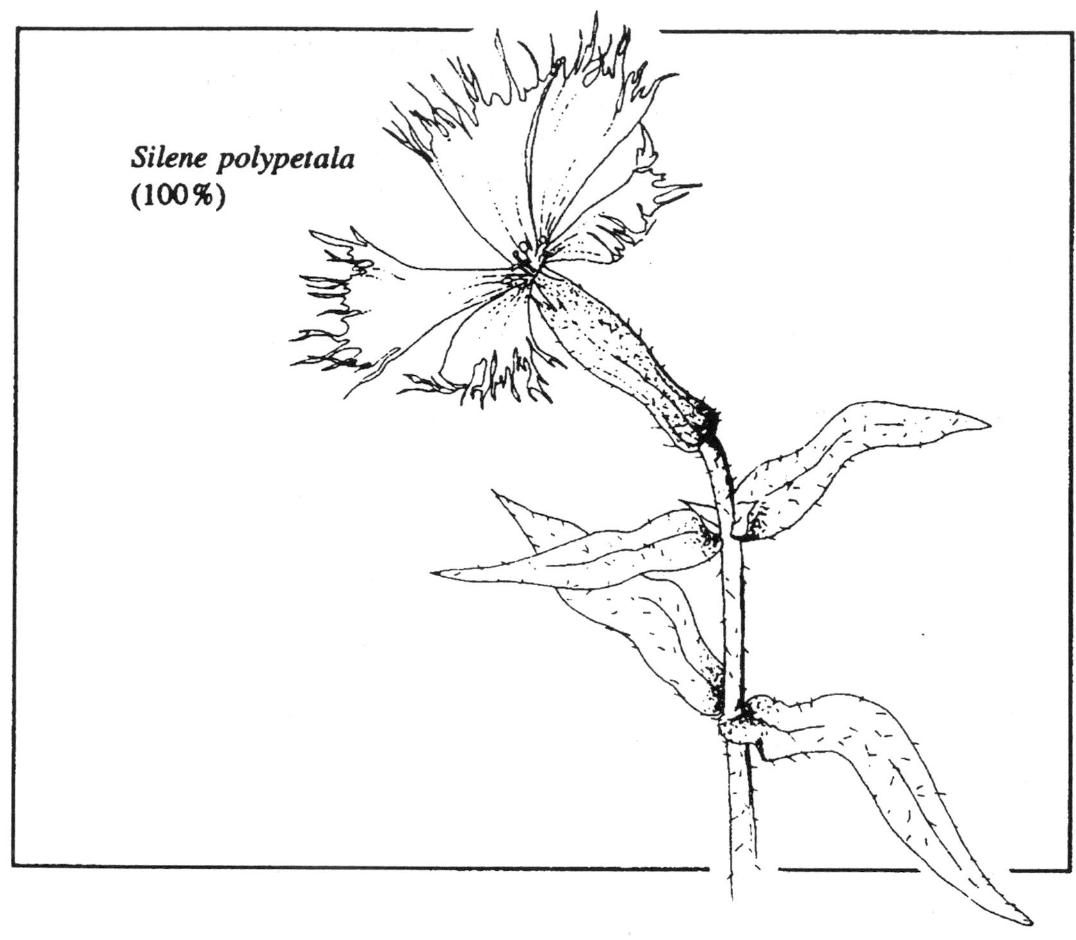


short-lived, at least where I have tried it. Dr. Ault has since been responsible for some of the finest breeding work on *Echinacea* and *Baptisia* at the Chicago Botanic Garden.

Division may be accomplished in spring or fall.

***-schafta*** (shaf′ ta) Schafta Campion 3-6″/12″
Summer Magenta-Pink Caucasus Zones 4-8

Many unbranched stems ascend laterally from a woody rootstock to form tufted mats of light green foliage. One or two pinwheel-shaped flowers (¾″ diameter) are produced at the end of each stem during midsummer to late summer and continue for 3-4 weeks. The 1″ long calyx is not inflated and is light green with 10 veins. The magenta-pink petals are notched. Full sun and coarse, gritty soil are preferable. Plants are valuable not only because of their colorful blooms but also because of late flowering.

Propagate by seed, division, or terminal cutting.

**Cultivars**:
'Shelly Pink' has pale pink flowers.
'Splendens' has rose-colored flowers on 8-10″ tall plants.

***-virginica*** (vir-gin′-i-ca) Fire Pink 10-20″/12″
Spring Scarlet Southeastern United States Zones 4-7

I love seeing this plant glowing like embers when I travel through the mountains of Georgia and North Carolina, however they are native from western New York to southern Ontario and Minnesota and south to Georgia and Oklahoma. About 2-4 opposite smooth leaves are produced which are opposite, up to a foot long and wider in the middle than at either end. The flowers are brilliant. The thin petals are deep red and cleft at the tips and the sepals are sticky.

As beautiful as they are in their native habitat, they are best left there. Plants don't do nearly as well in the lowlands as they do at home. They are short lived, although they may self-sow if placed in a well-drained sunny area where night temperatures fall in the 60s in the summer. They are seed-propagated by many nurseries and are available without guilt.

'Rockin Robin' is the result of an *S. virginica* x *S. polypetala* cross. The fringed flowers are a handsome salmon pink and keep flowering for the longest time of any campion.

**Related Species:**

*S. alpestris*, alpine campion, is another rock garden plant, needing excellent drainage and morning sun. White flowers with fringed petals are carried over 4-8″ tall plants in late spring and early summer. The narrow, glossy leaves are evergreen in zones 5-7.

*S. dioica*, red campion, is a common European weed, providing red to pink flowers during the spring and early summer. 'Clifford Moor' has lovely variegated green and yellow foliage, at least in the spring and early summer. Pink flowers occur in late spring. Like other members of this species, warm humid summers are not to its liking. 'Valley High' is a variegated form with creamy white margins and rose-pink flowers. Zones 5-7.

*S. regia*, wild pink, is even more eye-catching as *S. virginica*. Plants are taller (up to 4′) and bear 10-20 pairs of downy (finely hairy) leaves and stunning scarlet flowers. Native west to Missouri and Ohio and south to Georgia. I was fortunate to see some wonderful plantings in the Holden Arboretum in Ohio. I don't see these commonly offered as I do *S. virginica* but they are available from seed. 'Prairie Fire' was selected by Neil Diboll of Prairie Nursery in Wisconsin. Plants can grow to 4′ in height with bright orange-red starlike flowers. Zones 4-8.

*S. uniflora* is similar in that it is also one of the smooth-leaved species in the genus and is also alpine, happy to zone 3 at least. The flowering stems rise 6-8″ tall and bear 1-4 white split (bifid) flowers with an inflated calyx in summer. 'Robin Whitebreast' is a common name for the double form, whose large flowers resemble a carnation. At the Georgia trial gardens, we have thoroughly enjoyed 'Swan Lake' with milky white double carnation flowers. They also look good dripping out of mixed containers.

## *Silphium* (sil-fee′ um) Rosin-Weed Asteraceae

These tall, coarse relatives of the sunflower are native to the prairies, east to Georgia and south to Florida. In the flower heads of *Silphium*, only the ray flowers are fertile, forming the seeds around the disc, which, unlike the sunflower, yields no fruit.

Generally, flowers are yellow with black centers and the leaves are opposite (sometimes alternate). Plants yield a great deal of resin ("rosin") and thus their common name. They are tough plants, putting up with winds, cold winters and hot summers without complaint. They are not used more often in gardens mainly because they are so big (some growing 7-8′ tall) and rather weedy looking. They look much better with a prairie sky in the background than a two-story bungalow, anyway.

However, what is too big and tall to one person is bold and impressive to another, and this group of plants provides a structural specimen to the designer. Of the twenty or so species, two are fairly available and can provide fun as well as long-lived beauty. However, there is untold potential for the genus and more attention than ever is being paid to these daisies.

*S. laciniatum* is called compass plant because the coarse leaves align themselves in a north-south direction to minimize exposure to the midday sun. It is the leaves which make this plant interesting, not only because of their peek-a-boo habits with the sun but also because they are deeply cut (pinnatifid) like a pin oak, and may expand to 15″ in length. The yellow flowers open in the summer on plants 5-8′ tall.

*S. perfoliatum* also has interesting foliage, the older leaves being connate-perfoliate (the opposite leaves are joined around the stem) resulting in a cuplike attachment. Its common name is cup plant and plants were apparently used to collect rainwater by the prairie Indians. It may be put to better use as a living bird bath. The 3-5′ tall plants have 4-angled stems with light yellow flowers consisting of 20-30 ray flowers in July to August. The closely-related *S. connatum* (*S. p.* var. *connatum*) is a little shorter, has purple stems and is probably a better garden plant.

*Silphium terebinthinaceum*, prairie dock, is a plant only people who grew up in the prairies can love. The broad, coarse leaves resemble those of burdock and, you know, they're not half bad. The sunflower-like flowers are also pretty enough but they are borne on naked stems about 5′ above the leaves. It looks like a radar tower gone bad. Good conversation piece, though.

Other species which need little more than full sun are the eastern native, *S. dentatum*, with narrow light yellow petals, *S. integrifolium*, a 4-6′ tall plant with sulphur yellow flowers and *S. simpsonii*, with bright yellow flowers on 3-4′ plants. Pinch out the terminal bud in late spring to force branching and more compact growth.

All species benefit from full sun, poor soil and being ignored. Too much TLC, such as adding nitrogen fertilizers, results in lanky weak plants. Put them in the back forty and enjoy them on their terms, not yours, and you will be most pleased. Hardy in zones 3-7.

## ***Silybum*** (si′ lee-bum) Silybum Asteraceae

The genus is represented in gardens by only one species (*S. marianum*), known as holy thistle, blessed thistle or St. Mary's thistle. It is quite a stretch to include this genus in a book about perennials, because at best it is a biennial, in some cases an annual. However, it is cold hardy to about zone 7 or 7b and quite useful in southern, Californian or Northwestern gardens. They are especially wonderful in eastern Virginia, and are usually found in Colonial Williamsburg gardens. They can be treated like digitalis or dame's rocket in climates where they overwinter. In cooler climates, plants can be treated as an annual.

The reason that they are worth a try, even though they are so short lived, is because of the handsome, white marbled, thistle-like basal leaves. They are 1-2′ long and 8-12″ wide and have wavy or deeply cut margins and vicious spines. The foliage is much more pleasant to look at than to work with. The flowers are held in rosy purple heads and are surrounded by spiny bracts. They rise 3-4′ above the rosettes in early summer and although they are slightly fragrant, they are secondary to the foliage.

Plants are native to the Mediterranean area, therefore excellent drainage and full sun are required. In the South, grow in raised beds. Plants are hardy to about 5°F. Propagate by seed.

***Sisyrinchium*** (si-see-ring′ kee-um) Blue-Eyed Grass Iridaceae

Although many of the 90 species are native to North America, only a few have found their way into our gardens. The common name came from *S. angustifolium*, with grasslike leaves and starry blue flowers, native from southern Canada into much of the eastern United States. In general, plants have linear to sword-shaped leaves in the form of a fan. The stems are flattened or winged and usually bear a 2-8 flowered cluster of small flowers, enclosed in a pair of bract-like structures called a spathe, similar to jack-in-the-pulpit. These spathes are really rather useless unless you want to know what makes one seemingly identical species different than another. The similarity and size of the individual spathes are some of the characteristics that help distinguish species. It is a complex genus and species are quite difficult to tell apart and are often sold under the wrong name. But we gardeners are used to that.

Some of the more handsome plants are *S. bellum*, similar to *S. angustifolium*, but having blue flowers with yellow throats and unequal spathes. One of the finest species is *S. douglasii*, (also known as *Olsynium douglasii*), western grass-widow, which bears large satiny purple, nodding flowers among rushlike foliage. Some of the blue-eyed grasses, however, bear yellow flowers, such as the 4-6″ tall *S. brachypus*, or white flowers (*S. arenarium*). One of the larger and more ornamental forms is *S. striatum*, Argentine blue-eyed grass. The genus went through a bit of a renaissance in the 1990s and the number of species and hybrids available has increased. They have since cooled off, but are still fun to try.

***-angustifolium*** (ang-gus-ti-fo′ lee-um) Narrow-Leaf Blue-Eyed Grass 10-14″/12″
Spring Blue Eastern United States Zones 3-8

The narrow foliage and the branching stems are characteristic of the species. The stems are broadly winged and the leaves are usually shorter than the flower stems. Two to three clusters of blue flowers, usually with yellow eyes, about ¾″-1″ wide are produced in the spring.

They are terrific little plants that require no care and just blend in with the rest of the group. Obviously, they cannot be buried in the back of the garden, but by a path or in the partial shade of high pines, they do just fine. In some gardens, plants can self-sow and may become weedy. Plants tolerate full sun as well and good drainage certainly helps.

***-striatum*** (stry-aye' tum) | Argentine Blue-Eyed Grass | 12-24"/18"
Early Summer | Cream | Argentina, Chile | Zones 5-8

This lovely plant bears 9-12 creamy yellow flowers on an upright spike, similar to a gladiolus. The ¾-1" wide flowers are darker in the center and striped with purple on their backsides (thus the name *striatum*). The foliage is wider than most species (up to 1" across) and can be mistaken for an iris when not in flower. Plants have creeping rootstocks and form large clumps but are not at all invasive. After flowering, plants become messy and should be fertilized to reduce the number of leaves which naturally turn yellow, or cut back to six inches. Full sun and well-drained but moist soils are ideal. It is not as floriferous in the South as further north but worth trying regardless of locale.

Propagate by division or seed. Plants should be divided at least every 2-3 years. The small seeds should be barely covered and placed at 70-75°F and high humidity. Germination is erratic but seedlings should emerge within 3-4 weeks.

**Cultivars:**

'Aunt May' ('Variegatum') is particularly attractive with creamy white margins of the gray foliage providing additional interest after flowering. This is by far the most impressive yellow blue-eyed grass in the garden, if grown well. In the Armitage garden, however, they perished quickly.

**Related Species:**

*S. atlanticum* is also native to the eastern United States and Canada, from Nova Scotia south to Florida and west to Missouri. They may grow up to 2' tall, with 1" wide violet flowers and narrow leaves.

*S. bellum* is the western equivalent to *S. angustifolium*, native to California. The stems are more narrowly winged and the flower clusters are enveloped with shorter spathes. Flowers are similar to *S. angustifolium*, but plants are not as cold or heat tolerant. Plants are sometimes placed with *S. idahoense*, which shows how much taxonomic confusion exists. 'Album' has milky white flowers. 'Wayne's Dwarf' is a dwarf plant (3-5" tall) with blue flowers.

*S. bermudianum*, native to you know where, bears surprisingly large violet blue flowers with yellow centers. Plants are about 1' tall and persist as far north as zone 7. They are confused with other species, especially *S. idahoense* and *S. bellum*.

*S. brachypus* is aligned closely with *S. californicum* and may be the same thing. Native to the western United States, plants grow 8-12" tall and produce relatively wide (¼" wide) gray-green leaves. Star-shaped yellow flowers are produced in summer. Hardy in zones 8 (maybe 7) to 9.

*S. convolutum* is native to Central America and appears to be hardy to about zone 7b. The yellow flowers have brown veins and the leaves are sickle-shaped (falcate) and appear somewhat pleated. The starry flowers are held well above the grassy foliage in late spring and summer. Plants spread out, and grow 8-12' tall.

*S. idahoense* is very confused. I have seen plants labeled as such with small *S. angustifolia* like flowers as well as with large magnificent blue flowers. Some authorities place *S. idahoense* separately from other species, others throw in *S. macounii* and *S. bellum* as part of a *S. idahoense* complex. Plants sold as *S. idahoense* are worth trying; they may provide 1″ wide beautifully lavender blue flowers with a dark violet throat. 'California Skies' is particularly wonderful. 'Album' is a white form with yellow stamens. Excellent drainage, low humidity and cool nights are beneficial and confusion is a given.

*S. macrocephalum* produces many branched flower stems with butter-yellow flowers, each with brown venation on the undersides. Plants grow over 2′ tall. Native to South America, likely hardy to zone 7.

**Hybrids:**

A number of hybrids have been selected whose parentage is poorly known. The lack of parental guidance is unfortunate as one is always taking a chance in the East with species native to the far West and vice-versa. Regardless, there are some interesting plants out there.

'Biscutellum' has grassy leaves, grows about 12-15′ tall and produces yellowish flowers with a hint of purple.

'Devon Skies' appears to have *S. angustifolia* in it and differs by having pale sky blue flowers.

'E.K. Balls' ('Ball's Mauve) is about 8″ tall with mauve flowers and fan-shaped grey-green foliage. Plants require sharp drainage.

'Lucerne' has wonderfully large blue flowers bred by plantsman Robert Herman while in Lucerne, Switzerland. Hardy to zone 5.

'Mrs. Spivey' bears lots of small star-shaped white flowers over grassy leaves in the spring and early summer. She is only about 6″ tall. One of my favorites.

'Pole Star' ('North Star') also has white flowers which are a little less numerous but larger than those of 'Mrs. Spivey'.

'Quaint and Queer' has probably been sold more because of the name than the plant itself. It is certainly more queer than quaint. The flowers on this 8-12″ tall plant are said to be yellow and dull purple, but they are really kind of brownish. To each his own.

'Suwannee' is about 8″ tall and bears many blue flowers in spring. Plants do not reseed and make handsome clumps within a couple of years. Hardy only to zone 7b.

## ***Smilacina*** (smy-lass-ee′ na) False Solomon's-Seal Convallariaceae

Approximately 25 species of this native wild flower are known and all are found in moist shady areas. It is similar to Solomon's seal, *Polygonatum biflorum*, with alternate leaves on arching stems, berries in the fall, and golden fall color. Plants of both genera may be found side by side at the edge of humus-rich woods. There the similarities end. Many small flowers are borne in dense terminal inflorescences in *Smilacina* whereas those of *Polygonatum* are rather inconspicuous and bell shaped, borne in the leaf axils beneath the arching stems. Fruit is red in *Smilacina* and blue-black in *Polygonatum*. Plants of false Solomon's seal are best used for naturalizing in a wild flower garden or near the woods' edge.

***-racemosa*** (ray-se-moe′ sa) False Solomon's-Seal 2-3′/4′
Spring Cream North America Zones 3-7

This wild flower is native from Quebec, south to Tennessee, east to Virginia and west to Arizona. Regardless of where plants are grown, if happy, the flowering panicles can be seen 50 yards away. The arching stems bear 10-15 slender-pointed lanceolate leaves, each about 5-9″ long. The rootstock is long and thick and over the years produces an ever-widening clump. Hundreds of flowers are borne in a somewhat pyramidal panicle at the end of each stem. The individual flowers are small (1/6″ wide), fragrant, and composed of 6 spreading, equal segments. After flowering, numerous red berries with small purple spots develop. They are a favorite food for many small animals and seldom persist.

Plants thrive in shaded, moist areas such as the edge of a wooded area or near a pond or stream. The soil should be lime free, rich in humus and deep enough to allow easy penetration of the rootstock. Plants should not be disturbed for at least 3 years to allow establishment of the spreading root system. It is not tolerant of hot weather and does much better in cool climates. Although plants grow and survive south of zone 7, they are not particularly ornamental unless copious amounts of water are supplied.

Seed must be stratified and germination can take up to a year. Careful division of mature plants in the spring or fall is the most common method of propagation.

**Cultivars:**

var. *cylindrica* has shorter leaves and is smaller than the type. The panicle is more cylindrical than pyramidal but there are few obvious differences between this variety and the species. Its native range extends south to Georgia, therefore is a little more heat tolerant.

**Related Species:**

*S. stellata*, starry Solomon's-seal, is also known as star-flowered lily-of-the-valley because of the similarity of the leaves to those of *Convallaria*. It is 1-2′ tall, has light green linear leaves and starry white flowers in an open raceme. Although the flowers are a little larger, the inflorescence is much smaller than *S. racemosa* and not as ornamental.

## ***Solanum*** (so-lah′ num) Potato vine Solanaceae

Over 1400 species of plants occur in this mainly tropical genus, and none of the ornamental forms is consistently hardy north of zone 7. Of course, the genus is probably known by anyone who has ever eaten a potato (*S. tuberosum*) or eggplant (*S. melongena*), and even ornamental eggplants are being sold. Gardeners in the East also know the prickly horse-nettles, mainly *S. carolinense*, found from New England to Florida, while those in the West have unfortunately come to recognize buffalo bur (*S. rostratum*). Without doubt, with so many species out there, there are probably some extraordinary cold-hardy taxa just waiting to become the next 'Autumn Joy' sedum. However, until that time, I include only the potato vine, *S. jasminoides*.

The vine grows about 6-8′ tall with many 3-5 parted leaves on many branched stems. The flowers are held in short racemes of white flowers, tinged with blue. They are stellate (starlike) and the yellow stamens stick out from the centers. The cultivar 'Album' is better known and has darker green leaves and pure white flowers and 'Variegatum' produces handsome yellow and green foliage. Hardiness appears to be zone 7b (maybe to 6b) to 10.

We need to help other vines find their way out of obscurity in North American gardens, even though they may not be cold hardy. *S. crispum*, better known by well-traveled gardeners for the cultivar 'Glasnevin', bears lilac blue flowers with golden yellow stamens clustered on the 6-12′ tall woody plants. My favorite vine is *S. wendlandii*, whose wonderfully large blue flowers are formed all summer. They are vigorous, growing 12′ in a summer, but unfortunately also bear short thorns. Regardless, both species are terrific, find them, enjoy them, even if only for a season. Full sun is necessary.

## ***Solidago*** (so-li-dah′ go) Goldenrod Asteraceae

Considered a nuisance weed by some, or a handsome wild flower by others, the genus was all but ignored as a garden flower in the United States a decade ago. Perhaps because goldenrods have been unfairly accused of causing hay fever (ragweed is the bad guy), or because they are common roadside fixtures, few found their way into cultivation. Today, with the interest in wildlife and native plants, goldenrods have been rediscovered. Of course in Europe, hybrids, often using our natives as parents, have been developed and used for late summer flowering. We still are not hybridizing goldenrods as the Europeans are, but at least we are using them more. Hallelujah!

*Solidago virgaurea*, European goldenrod, was highly valued for healing wounds, either externally or internally applied. However, even in England, where everything seems to grow so well, our native *S. canadensis* was not particularly popular. William Robinson wrote in 1883 that these "North American Composites in borders exterminate valuable plants, and give a coarse, ragged aspect to the garden". Sounds like us talking about those awful "aliens", doesn't it? However, today's compact and colorful hybrids would make even Mr. Robinson sit up and look twice. The taller hybrids resulted from *S. canadensis* and *S. virgaurea* while the shorter ones originated from X *Solidaster luteus* (a intergeneric cross thought to be descended from *S. missouriensis* and *Aster ptarmicoides*) and *S. brachystachys*, a 6-9″ miniature goldenrod. Only the smaller forms can be recommended as they do not dominate the garden or require support. Except for a few cultivars like *S. rugosa* 'Fireworks', I still do not find them particularly attractive. I prefer the taller goldenrods by the roadside rather than in my garden. All do best in humusy soils and full sun.

The biggest problems with goldenrod, other than their poor reputations, are their height (which may be overcome with shorter, stronger hybrids) and their susceptibility to rust, a fungal disease. Rust is characterized by bronze pustules on the stems and lower sides of the leaves, and can be reduced by good air movement, bright light and well-drained soils.

Divide or use stem cuttings for the hybrids while the species may be raised from seed. The seeds germinate readily if placed under warm, humid conditions.

**Hybrid Cultivars**:

'Baby Gold' stands 2-2½′ tall with large racemes of bright yellow flowers.

'Cloth of Gold' is a dwarf but vigorous grower with dense, deep yellow flowers and grows 18-24″ tall.

'Crown of Rays' ('Strahlenkrone') has to be one of the best goldenrods I've trialed. I received this many years ago as a cultivar for use as a cut flower. The plants grow 2-3′ tall without falling over, and are covered with bright yellow plumes of flowers in mid to late summer.

'Golden Baby' grows 2′ tall with golden yellow plumes. An excellent selection.

'Goldengate' has bright lemon-yellow flowers atop 2′ tall compact plants.

'Goldenmosa' has yellow-green foliage and bears yellow flowers in early August on 2½′ tall stems.

'Golden Wings' is 5-6′ tall, too tall for most gardens. Although a lovely deep yellow, it is too close in habit to *S. canadensis* to be of value.

'Golden Thumb' ('Tom Thumb', 'Queenie') grows about 1′ tall with yellow flowers and yellowish green foliage. My choice as the most ornamental and useful cultivars.

'Little Lemon' is another short, compact perennial bred for efficient production and shipping. Plants have light yellow flowers on 8-12″ stems.

'Peter Pan' has canary yellow flowers and stands 2-3′ tall. Plants associate well with red flowers of *Lobelia cardinalis* and *Crocosmia* hybrids. Flowering continues through early September and October.

'Super' bears wonderful sulphur-yellow flowers in midsummer.

**Related Species**:

Although the hybrids may be a little easier to use in the civilized garden, those who like to incorporate wild flowers in a meadow or in a sunny wilder area might consider other useful North American species.

*S. caesia*, wreath goldenrod, has distinctive wavy, yellow flower spikes and bluish purple, wiry stems. Flowers form along the whole length of the arching stems, not just at the top. Plants grow 2-3′ tall and flower in late August and September. This is one of the more unusual goldenrods and an excellent cut stem.

*S. odora*, sweet goldenrod, is an excellent plant for the fragrant garden. The narrow leaves smell like anise when crushed. It stands 3-4′ tall and bears yellow flowers on small, spreading, one-sided panicles. Hardy from zones 3 to 9.

*S. rugosa*, rough stemmed goldenrod, is 4-5′ tall and has conspicuously hairy stems. The arching stems form a large panicle of golden yellow flowers in late September and October. Not as stoloniferous as some other native goldenrods, it can be used without fear of invasion. Ken Moore of the North Carolina Botanical Garden introduced 'Fireworks', a popular, more compact plant. This has become one of the most popular goldenrods ever, and seeing the great swaths at the Chicago Botanic Garden, I became a believer. What a treat. They look particularly good in combination with fruit of *Callicarpa americana*, our native beautyberry.

*S. sempervirens*, seaside goldenrod, is 4-6′ tall and flowers on one side only, forming a dense one-sided raceme in September and October. A useful plant for saline and sandy areas, the roots also retard sand erosion.

*S. speciosa*, showy goldenrod, has become a favorite of Midwestern gardeners due to the one-foot inflorescences of bright yellow flowers in the fall. Hardy to zone 4.

*S. sphacelata* 'Golden Fleece', was introduced by Dick Lighty of Mt. Cuba Gardens in Delaware and has become a hot item for the late summer and fall garden. The 15-18″ tall plants produce small rounded leaves and many sprays of golden yellow flowers. 'Wichita Mountains' was collected by Steve Bieberich of Sunshine Nursery in Clinton, Oklahoma. Plants grow about 30″ in height and have gold flowers in late summer. Being a rather ignorant Eastern boy, I did not even know there were mountains in Wichita, however, it was pointed out to me that not only are there mountains, they are part of the Wichita Mountains Wildlife Refuge and they are in Oklahoma, not Kansas. Little did I know that it consisted of over 59,000 square miles of unspoiled land acting as a refuge for American bison, Rocky Mountain elk, white-tailed deer, and Texas longhorn cattle, to say nothing of the hundreds of plant species. Good grief, why go to Europe when this is in our own back yard? This cultivar was included in the 2005 Great Plants® Program in Nebraska. Both cultivars are better than the species and well worth a try. Zones 4-8

## *X Solidaster* (so-li-das′ ter) Golden Aster Asteraceae

The interspecific hybrid (X *S. luteus*) is intermediate between the parents (probably *S. missouriensis* and *Aster ptarmicoides*) and arose as a natural hybrid in the nurseries of Leonard Lille, in Lyons, France. The flowers are much flatter than those of goldenrod and the plants make exceptionally good cut flowers. They are, in general, shorter than goldenrod and flower much earlier.

Grow in full sun, in areas of good air movement to reduce rust and in well-drained soils.

**Cultivars**:

'Lemore' is the original hybrid with yellow flowers on 2-2½′ tall plants.

'Yellow Submarine' bears wonderful deep yellow flowers massed together in summer. Some catalogs list it as a cultivar of *Solidago* but it appears much more like a golden aster than a goldenrod to me. Regardless, it is terrific.

## *Sorghastrum* (sore-gas′ trum) Indian Grass Poaceae

Of the 15 species, only *S. nutans*, Indian grass, is in cultivation. This native grass may be found from Canada to Mexico, from Maine to Florida and throughout the prairie states. It is a clump former, therefore will not move around everywhere. The blue-green leaves are about a half inch wide and 8-12″ long, and plants grow 2-3′ tall. The narrow, feathery 8-12′ long panicles of tan-yellow flowers are held well above the foliage in late summer, resulting in plants 5-6′ tall. As fall approaches, the flowers become more bronze and then turn an attractive burnt orange. They are excellent for fresh or dried cut flowers.

Plants are sufficiently large to be used as a specimen in the border, but if room allows, they are even more attractive as mass plantings. Provide full sun and moisture-retentive soils for best performance. They will reseed. Plants are hardy in zones 4-9.

Propagate from seed, move seedlings or divide immediately after flowering or in the spring.

**Cultivars:**

'Sioux Blue' has wonderful blue-gray foliage and is much more in demand than the species. Selected at Longwood Gardens.

***Sparaxis*** (spa-raks′ is) Wandflower Iridaceae

This colorful bulbous genus is winter hardy only in the warmest parts of the country but may be grown for late spring color and handled in the same manner as *Gladiolus* and *Ixia*. Of the four species, the most colorful is *S. tricolor*.

***-tricolor*** (tri′ ko-lor) Wandflower 9-12″/12″
Spring Orange-Red South Africa Zones 9-11

The lance-shaped leaves arise early in the spring and give rise to short spikes bearing 3 to 6 flowers of intense orange-red with yellow throats. The 1½-2″ diameter flowers have 6 equal and flared segments but due to the great variability in the species, flowers range from pure white to yellow or red. However, the yellow throat is consistent in all flowers.

Bulbs should be planted as soon as the threat of frost has passed, and lifted and separated in the fall. They are best placed in containers in the fall in a cold frame and planted out, pot and all, in the spring. Fortunately, the corms are inexpensive and mistakes in culture are affordable. This species is too lovely not to try at least once. I grow it in Georgia where corms last only one year, but a wonderful show it is.

Plants do well in California where the warm days, cool nights, and dry summers resemble its native habitat, however, they do equally well in Houston, Texas. Although single colors have been named, wandflower is generally available only as a mix of colors.

***Spartina*** (spar-tee′ na) Prairie Cord Grass Poaceae

A native prairie grass, whose toughness has allowed it to be used for planting on hills and banks for soil erosion. It seldom grows more than 2′ tall and is an aggressive, rhizomatous spreader. The flowers are not particularly showy but the ½″ wide, glossy green leaves are wonderful planted *en masse*. Do be careful, the leaves are rather sharp-sided and can be painful. They turn a golden yellow in the fall, providing a nice autumn tint. The grass is aggressive and should be planted with caution. A 1999 Plant Select® winner, a program administered by the Denver Botanic Garden and Colorado State University. Plants may be grown in zones 4-9.

'Aureomarginata' is perhaps more ornamental because of the thin gold margin on the leaves. Propagate the species by seed or division, the cultivar by division only.

***Spigelia*** (spy-geel′ ee-a) Spigelia Loganiaceae

Thirty species are native from the southeastern United States to South America. Plants bear opposite, entire leaves and tubular upright flowers. They grow in full sun although a little afternoon shade is helpful in their southern range.

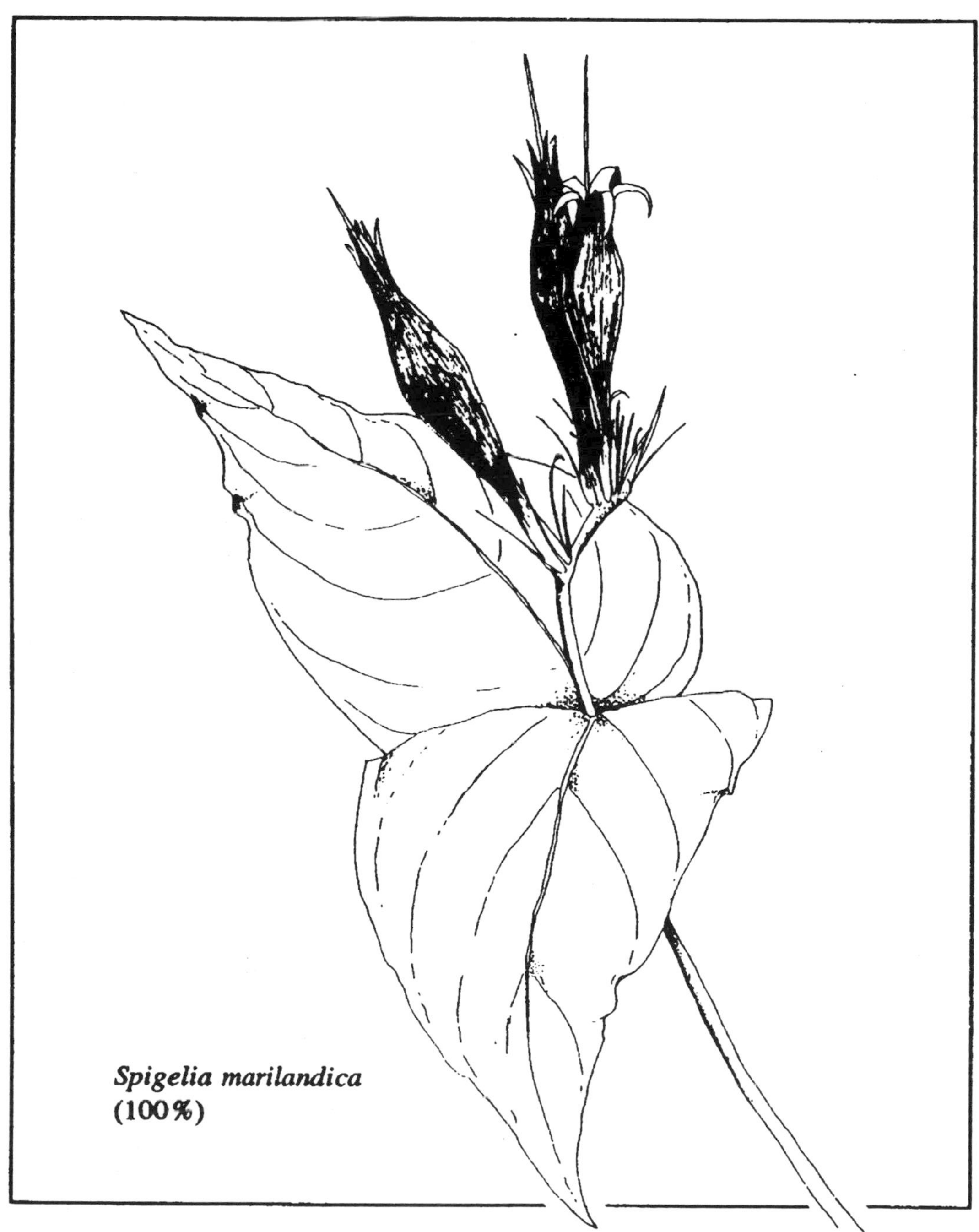

***Spigelia marilandica* (100%)**

***-marilandica*** (mar-i-land-i′ ca) Indian Pink, Pinkroot 1-2′/2′
Early Summer Red Southeastern United States Zones 6-9

In late spring and early summer, the most wonderful red flowers with yellow throats are produced from rather nondescript plants. Actually, "wonderful" doesn't nearly do the flowers justice. A grouping of plants showing off their upright tubular flowers, each 2″ long, 1″ wide and sharply lobed, can stop people dead in their tracks. They are borne on a one-sided cyme above the 4-7 pairs of 4″ long, ovate, sessile, dark green leaves. And the best news is that great breakthroughs in propagation and distribution occurred in the early 2000s, and plants are easy to locate and becoming less expensive. Place in the front of the garden or in wild flower areas in full sun to partial shade and reasonably moist soils. *En masse*, they are a striking, beautiful addition to any garden.

**Cultivars:**

'Little Redhead' is a compact form, originating from plantspeople Bob McCartney of Woodlander's Nursery, and Pam Harper from Virginia. Plants are only about a foot tall, but no matter the height, this is a great plant.

## ***Spiranthes*** (spy-rant′ eez) Ladies' Tresses Orchidaceae

This large group of plants ranges throughout all the continents, except Africa, and many are native to the United States. That they are not commonly offered for sale may be due to their difficulty of propagation, the lack of large flowers, or the lack of demand. However, similar to *Spigelia*, interest in native plants has resulted in much more reliable distribution. In general, the flowers are relatively small (usually less than ½″ long) and often spiral around the flower stem (thus the genus name). Some of the most intriguing natives are *S. gracilis*, slender ladies' tresses, and *S. grayii*, little pearl-twist, both with obvious spirals of white flowers on 2′ tall plants. One of the more common species is *S. cernua*, nodding ladies' tresses, with slightly nodding white flowers in a spiral spike. Zones 4-7.

The one I usually see for sale is another native, *S. odorata*, with bigger flowers, and not as obviously spiraled. The fragrant flowers are held in two rows forming a rather dense spike, white and often marked with green. Plants grow about 2′ tall and are best planted in moist soils in sunny to partially shaded conditions. 'Chadds Ford' is taller with larger flowers than the species.

I have seen this listed hardy to zone 3, but zone 5 may be a little more realistic. Heat tolerant to about zone 8 if proper conditions can be provided.

## ***Stachys*** (sta′ kis) Betony Lamiaceae

Over 300 species occur but only a handful are ornamental. Leaves are opposite and flowers are generally purple, although some species bear white, yellow, or red flowers. Most are perennial, though a number of annuals like the hybrid 'Hidalgo', with its beautiful salmon flowers and dull green leaves with silvery white undersides, are well worth a try. However, the genus is represented in American gardens mainly by the ubiquitous lamb's ears, *S. byzantina*, and we have been lamb-eared to death.

The flowers are not particularly handsome and in one case, plant breeders produced a non-flowering garden cultivar. Other species, however, are spectacular in flower and if you are sick of yucky lamb's ears, try one or two of the others. Most species do well in well-drained garden soils in partial shade to full sun. Good drainage is necessary.

Quick Reference to Stachys Species

| | Height (in.) | Foliage color | Flower color |
|---|---|---|---|
| *S. byzantina* | 12-15 | Gray | Purple |
| *S. macrantha* | 12-24 | Green | Purple |
| *S. officinalis* | 18-24 | Green | Red-purple |

-***byzantina*** (bi-zan-teen′ a) Lamb's-Ears 12-15″/12″
Spring Purple Caucasus to Iran Zones 4-7

Mats of velvety, white woolly leaves have made this a popular species for edging and design work. The foliage provides an excllent demonstration of the term "tomentose"—a covering of dense matted, short, woolly hairs. Plants look best in spring when the foliage is fresh but tend to decline by mid-August in humid, wet sum-

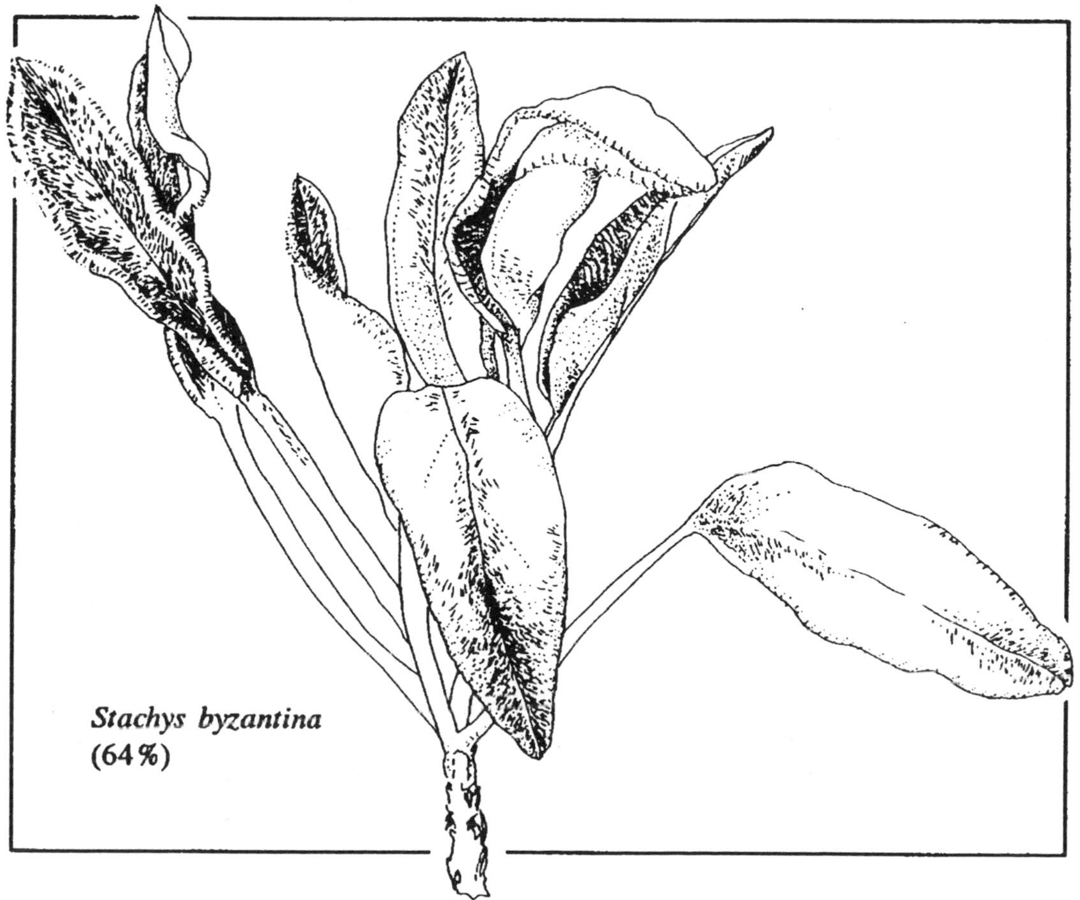

***Stachys byzantina***
**(64%)**

mers. The hairy foliage traps moisture and dew, and if summers are hot, particularly at night, significant leaf disease occurs resulting in dead patches. In my garden, it looks fresh in the spring but usually melts out by late summer. I can't begin to tell you how many of these I have killed. Zone 7b seems to be the marginal zone of heat tolerance, doing fine in many gardens, melting in many more. If the decaying foliage is cut back in late summer, plants may recover in the fall.

The purple flowers are held in whorls on a 4-6″ densely hairy spike. The corolla tube is less than ½″ long and barely protrudes from the calyx. In most perennials, the onset of flowering is anticipated, but in this case the blooms detract from the foliage. Not only do they take the eye from the handsome foliage to the mundane flower, but look worse once they have faded. Flowers should be removed as they develop.

Moist but well-drained soils are ideal. In the North, full sun is tolerated, in the South some afternoon shade is definitely appreciated. Too much shade should be avoided because leaves don't dry off. Sub-irrigation is better than overhead watering and all irrigation should be accomplished in the morning to allow foliage to dry out.

Cultivars are propagated by division and the species may be raised from seed. Germination is erratic but not difficult at warm temperatures (70-72°F) and humid conditions.

**Cultivars**:

'Cotton Boll' certainly has an interesting flower spike. The spikes appear normal but the flowers have been modified into fuzzy clusters of woolliness. Worth keeping on the plant for the double takes.

'Countess Helene von Stein' ('Big Ears') was named for the Countess von Zeppelin of Germany and is the best cultivar by far, bar none. Plants are characterized by having leaves twice the size of the species. Plants are significantly more heat and humidity tolerant than others although not quite as gray. Very shy to flower.

'Primrose Heron' has primrose yellow foliage in the spring that reverts to gray-green as summer progresses. As pretty as they are, plants lack vigor and are difficult to keep alive.

'Sheila McQueen' is about 1′ tall and is more compact than the type. The leaves are slightly larger and less woolly.

'Silver Carpet' is useful for low-maintenance gardening. No flowers are produced and carpets of silvery foliage spread rapidly.

***-macrantha*** (ma-kranth' a) Big Betony 12-24″/12″
Late Spring Purple Caucasus Zones 2-8

While the flowers of the previous species are not particularly revered, a flowering mass of this one makes a magnificent sight. The broadly ovate, dark green leaves are wrinkled and roughly hairy (scabrous). All leaves have scalloped edges and the uppermost leaves are much smaller than those toward the base. Plants spread rapidly to form mats in rich moist soils. The violet flowers are held in 2-3 distinct whorls of 10-20 flowers each about 8″ above the foliage. The corolla tube is about 1″ long and 3-4 times longer than the calyx. They can be seen from a football field away, particularly if paired with a chartreuse plant like *Alchemilla*.

At first sight, these plants are often mistaken for blue salvias, however, they don't have the herbal smell of salvia and the flowers have 4 stamens, whereas *Salvia* has only two normal ones. Plants are seen everywhere in European gardens, but their relative absence in this country suggests their dislike of summer heat and humidity found in so many American states. When people accompanying us to the British Isles see these plants, everyone from east of the Pacific Northwest wants to know what it is and why they can't find it. Plants don't look like the woolly stuff they know as *Stachys*. Full sun and well-drained soils are preferable in the North but partial shade is necessary in the South. More flowers are produced in cooler areas of the country but if moisture is applied consistently, plants tolerate heat.

Although many forms come true from seed, division is the fastest and best means of propagation.

**Cultivars:**

'Robusta' ('Superba') is the most common form, grows 24″ tall and bears spikes of 4-5 whorls of rosy-pink flowers. This is the best form for the garden.

'Rosea' is similar to the species but produces rose-red flowers.

'Violacea' has deep violet flowers.

***-officinalis*** (o-fi-shi-nah′ lis) Wood Betony 18-24″/24″
Late Spring Violet-Pink Europe Zones 4-8

Few differences exist between this and the previous species. The 4-5″ long, ovate lower leaves have long petioles and scalloped margins while the upper leaves are lanceolate and sessile. About 15-20 half-inch flowers are held in a dense spike. They are usually violet-pink, occasionally pink or white. Cultural requirements are similar to *S. macrantha* but it will not tolerate as much shade.

Propagate similar to *S. macrantha*.

**Cultivars:**

'Alba' has creamy white flowers.

'Grandiflora' produces larger flowers than the species and are soft pink.

'Hummelo' has basal rosettes of glossy, dark green leaves and small rose-lavender flowers in dense inflorescences 1½-2′ above the foliage in summer. A excellent cultivar when massed. Originally sold as a selection of *S. monieri*.

'Rosea Superba' bears rose-pink flowers and corrugated leaves.

**Related Species:**

*S. coccinea*, Texas betony, hedge nettle, has appeared in ornamental catalogs only in the last 10 years, producing scarlet flowers most of the season, similar to those of *Salvia coccinea*, and growing about 2′ tall. 'Chinook' has coral-red flowers, 'Coral Pink' produces coral blossoms, 'Hot Spot Coral' from the great High Country Gardens in New Mexico has bright red to coral flowers. Zones 6-8.

*S. germanica*, downy woundwort, also bears gray, tomentose leaves. The basal leaves have long petioles, the stem leaves are nearly sessile. The flowers are rosy pink to purple and densely hairy.

*S. monieri* is a little-known but attractive stoloniferous plant with pink to rose, densely clustered flowers. Plants are about 2′ tall and form good-sized clumps with ovate-oblong leaves. Native to the Alps and Pyrenees in southern Europe. Hardy in zone 5-8.

**Stenanthium** (sten-an-the′ um) Stenanthium Liliaceae

Unknown, unused and unloved, but an interesting group of bulbous plants native to the United States and Russia. The botanical name comes from *stenos* (narrow) and *anthos* (flower) describing the narrow flower segments. The best species for eastern gardeners is *S. gramineum*, with 2′ long broad grasslike leaves and a tall panicle of small white, greenish or purple flowers. Plants are native from Pennsylvania to Missouri, south to Florida and west to Texas. Flowers occur in mid to late summer, followed by drooping fruit in the fall. An excellent form is var. *robusta*, whose flowers are more numerous and held much more densely on the panicle resulting in a more ornamental display. In the West, gardeners might want to try *S. occidentale*, native to the coastal ranges in northern California through the Cascades to Canada. Plants are 1-2′ tall with basal, grassy leaves and drooping greenish to white flowers with reflexed petals. The flowers are larger but not as numerous as *S. gramineum*.

Place in full sun in a sheltered location. Plants are difficult to find though definitely worth a try, likely cold hardy to zone 6. Propagate by seed or division.

**Stipa** (sty′ pa) Feather Grass Poaceae

Approximately 150 species of this temperate grass occur, with twisted leaf blades and narrow panicles of flowers. The flowers are characterized by long, pointed awns (leaflike structures at the base of each flower) that catch the light and sway lithely in the breeze. In full bloom, they provide a richness of movement and color that can be found only in nature.

The only species used is *S. gigantea*, giant feather grass, and it is one of the biggest and showiest of the ornamental grasses. They are hardly gigantic when not in flower, the rolled leaves are 1½-2′ long and plants are only about 2′ tall. Flowering stems arise in late spring or early summer and top out at 5-6′. Combined with gold stamens, the 4-5″ long golden awns make a wonderful display in any bit of breeze. Plants are native to southern Europe and perform well in zones 7-10.

Another species with terrific ornamental value used to be known as *S. tenuissima*, Mexican feather grass, but it has been reclassified under *Nassella* (which see).

**Stokesia** (stoks′ ee-a) Stokes' Aster Asteraceae

The only species, *S. laevis*, occurs from South Carolina to Florida and Louisiana. This wild flower has undergone a series of breeding "operations" resulting in larger and more colorful flowers than the species. It has adapted itself so well to formal gardens that it is seldom thought of as a wild flower anymore. Plants are a cut flower crop, persisting for a week after cutting.

***-laevis*** (lay′ vis) Stokes' Aster 12-24″/18″
Summer Blue Southeastern United States Zones 5-9

The evergreen dark green, entire leaves, which often have a pronounced white midrib, are 6-8″ long, alternate and provide pleasant greenery in the winter when not covered by snow. Leaves at the base have a long petiole but become sessile toward the top of the plant. Soft spiny projections can be observed at the base of the leaves and subtending the flower buds. Two to four flowers are borne on a single stalk but open one or two at a time. Many flower stalks are present and flowering continues for about 4 weeks. The individual flowers are 4″ across and consist of two series of ray flowers. The outer are much larger than the inner set and have 4-5 deeply cut lobes. Plants are best placed at the front of the border in filtered sunlight and well-drained soil as they do not tolerate wet feet in the winter. If planted in zone 5, a winter mulch may be beneficial.

Propagate by divisions in the spring. The species may also be raised from seed. Germination is irregular; seeds should be placed at 40°F for 6 weeks prior to sowing at 70°F.

**Cultivars:**

'Alba' has white flowers and although not as floriferous as the blue cultivars, the flowers contrast well against the foliage.

'Blue Moon' has dark blue flowers on 2′ tall plants.

'Blue Danube' produces lavender-blue flowers up to 4″ in diameter. This has been the most popular of the named forms, but newer selections are better.

'Blue Star' has a little less lavender in the flowers and is almost a Spode blue.

'Colorwheel', introduced by ItSaul Nursery in Atlanta, produces different colored flowers on the 2′ tall plant. Although hardy to zone 5, results in the Gardens at UGA have been less than stellar.

'Honeysong Purple' produces large, dark purple flowers around an interesting reddish center. Plants are only about 2′ tall.

'Klaus Jelitto', named for the great German seedsman, bears lavender flowers that are a little larger than the species.

'Mary Gregory' was introduced by Niche Gardens in Chapel Hill, North Carolina and named for gardener Mary Gregory of Columbia, South Carolina. The flowers are light yellow rather than lavender and persist for a long time. An interesting plant, but not one that captures the eye very long.

'Omega Skyrocket' was discovered by Ron and Susan Dieterman of the Atlanta Botanical Garden. Seeds were grown on and plants then introduced by ItSaul Nursery in Atlanta. It is unique in that plants grow 3-4′ tall and bear white to pale blue flowers. It is a most robust stokesia: plants do not require support and are occasionally used for cut flowers. However, there are far better cut flower forms of this species, and perhaps the best than can be said is that it is interesting.

'Peachie's Pick' is the best of the new selections, bearing large lavender blue flowers over compact 2′ tall plants. They flower for a long time and are simply the best,

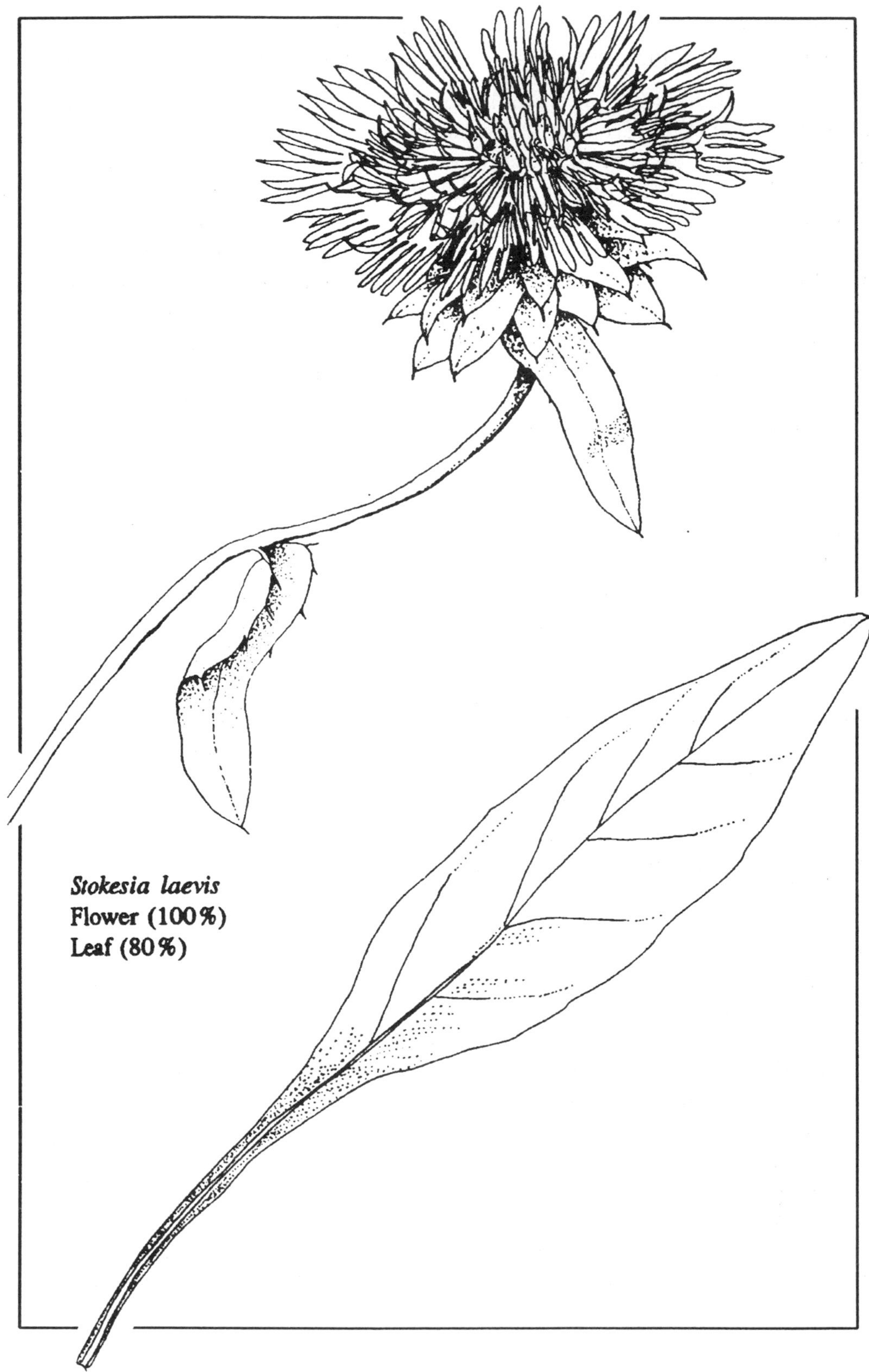

*Stokesia laevis*
Flower (100%)
Leaf (80%)

including our trials at the Gardens at UGA. Named for its discover, Peachie Saxon of Meridian, Mississippi.

'Purple Parasols' has flowers ranging from light blue to deep purple. Plants are about 18″ tall and hardy to zone 4.

'Silver Moon' bears creamy white flowers. They are larger than those of 'Alba' and equally handsome.

'Wyoming' bears many flowers of rich deep blue.

***Streptopus*** (strep-toe′ pus) Twisted Stalk, Rose Mandarin Convallariaceae

I scratched my head, I tugged at my chin, I walked in circles: I could not figure these plants out when I was looking at them in eastern Canada. They looked like a cross between *Disporum* and *Polygonatum* but they had the fattest reddest berries I had ever seen. It turns out I had not forgotten (at my age, that is always a kind revelation), I simply never knew that the plants belonged to the genus *Streptopus*, in this case *S. roseus*.

As mentioned, the foliage is common enough looking, but the 1″ wide solitary fairy bell-like flowers are flared and pink, an unusual color for a woodland plant. They are held on long stalks, which are really interesting. They arise from the stem itself and at about halfway along the stalk, it takes a sharp bend, directing the flower downward. Weird, but fun to look at. The flowers may not jump out at you immediately, but the large red fruit that occurs in July will, and it is as pretty and more noticeable than the flowers. This is a plant for northern gardeners, perhaps useful as far south as the southern Appalachians and in areas of the Northwest where heat is seldom an issue.. Howvere, you can count on them performing better in zones 3-5 than in 6-8. They are best in shaded, moist, cool soils.

Plants are native from Labrador to Ontario and Minnesota, south to the mountains of New Jersey, Kentucky and down into Georgia. Zones 3-6.

Divide or propagate from seed. Seeds can be gathered when the fruit is red. They germinate after a cold treatment but are very slow to grow after germination. Care must be taken that seedlings not succumb to overwatering or animal browsing.

**Related Species:**

*S. amplexicaulis*, white mandarin, is similar but with leaves that clasp the stem and greenish flowers with white veins. Similar fruit Zones 2-6.

***Stylophorum*** (sty-lah′ for-um) Wood Poppy Papaveraceae

The genus consists of three species but only the native species, *S. diphyllum*, is common in American gardens. An outstanding plant for the no-maintenance gardener, who will rejoice in the reseeding habit and vigor of the plants year after year.

***-diphyllum*** (di-fil′ lum) Wood Poppy 12-18″/12″
Spring Yellow Eastern North America Zones 4-8

Native to woodlands from Pennsylvania to Tennessee, and from Wisconsin to Missouri, plants emerge early in the spring and produce 8-12 basal light green leaves,

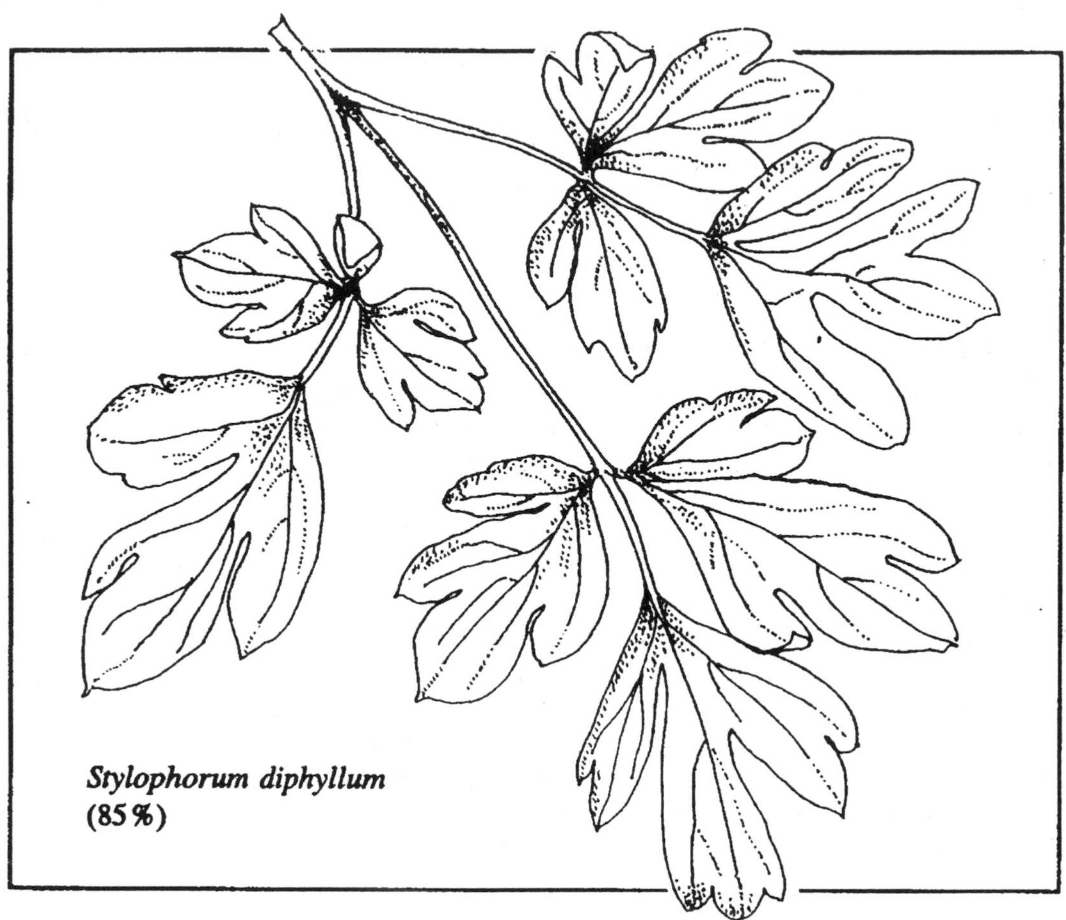
*Stylophorum diphyllum* (85%)

10-15″ long and deeply cut into 5-7 lobed divisions. The 1½-2″ bright yellow flowers consist of four petals and many stamens and open in March and April. Three to five flowers open in each terminal inflorescence.

A beautiful plant for the shaded, moist wild flower garden, and in most gardens, plants reseed everywhere. It is wonderful growing with Labrador violets, where the purple leaves and violet flowers seem tailor-made for the yellow flowers of the celandines. I received my first few plants from my friends, Ed and Donna Lambert, whose woodland is a mecca for shade gardeners. In their garden, the wood poppies are everywhere, and in the spring cover the ground with sunshine. If left undisturbed, plants colonize large areas. Foliage may disappear by late summer in normal garden conditions, however, if grown in consistently moist soils, foliage persists into fall. People are inevitably drawn towards the plants regardless of other plants in flower at the time.

Cut stems exude a yellow sap once used by native Americans for dye. Since they cohabit with bloodroot, you can have a veritable finger-painting festival, marking up all sorts of unsuspecting faces. One of the finest and most enjoyable wild flowers for bright, persistent spring color.

Seed is not difficult to germinate if sown in moist a medium at 68-72°F. Since they reseed prolifically, sit back and let nature do it. Plants should be left undisturbed

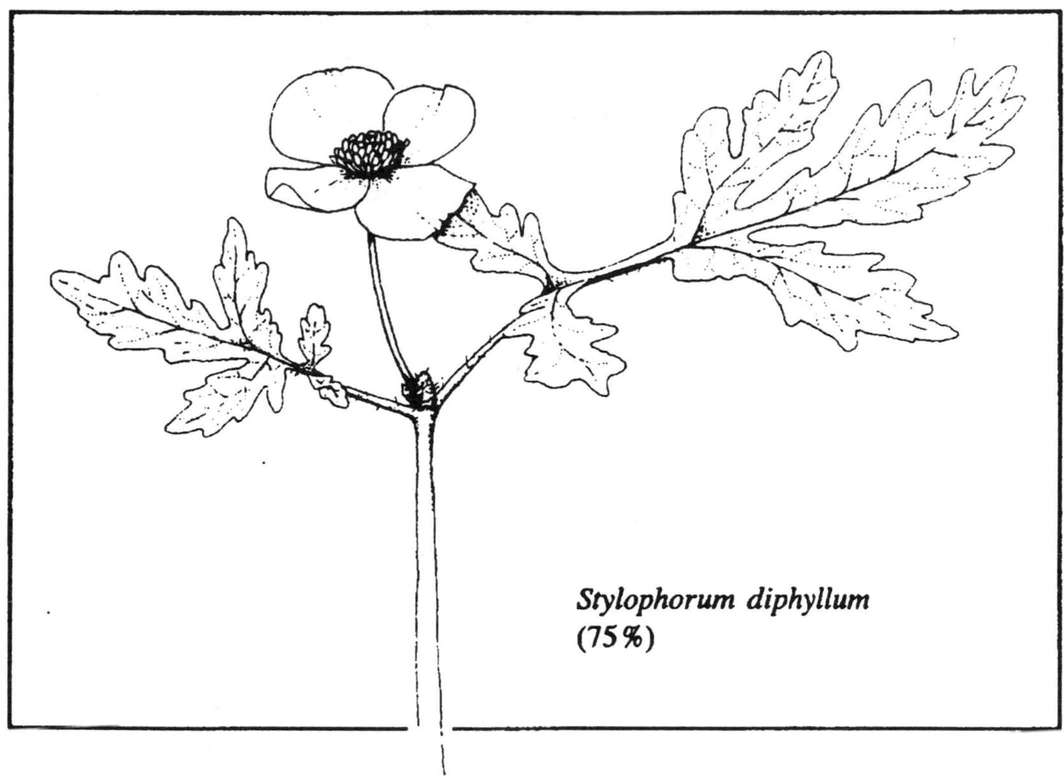

*Stylophorum diphyllum*
(75%)

but may be divided successfully if care is taken not to damage the long thick roots. Divide in early spring or fall.

**Related Species:**

*S. lasiocarpum* is native to central and eastern China but is being seen more and more in North America. They have flowers similar to *S. diphyllum* but the leaves are bigger and with more deeply cut margins. The sap is red, rather than yellow.

## *Symphyotrichum* (sim-fee-o′ tri-cum) See *Aster*

## *Symphytum* (sim′ fi-tum) Comfrey Boraginaceae

I was never a big fan of these plants and had to be talked into their virtues. Only a few of the 35 species are enjoyable additions to the flower garden. However, medicine took to these plants rapidly; *S. officinale* was used in European monastery gardens in the twelfth century and is still found in herbal gardens. It was used as a poultice to help the healing of broken bones and became known as boneset (also see *Eupatorium perfoliatum*). Go to any Internet site and type in comfrey, and you will be amazed at the medicinal value advertised today. Some gardeners grow *S. officinale* or *S. asperum*, a 5-6′ tall species, in a shaded wild flower area.

Most species are upright and 2-4′ tall, although *S. grandiflorum*, a rapidly spreading ground cover with yellow-white flowers, and *S. rubrum*, a red-flowered form, are less than 18″. Some of the clearest and prettiest blue flowers in the plant kingdom occur in this genus. The tubular flowers are often blue or purple and held in scorpioid cymes, similar to those of forget-me-nots and Virginia bluebells. The leaves are alternate and often hispid (raspy like sandpaper). All species are most suitable for moist areas in sun or dappled shade.

Divide the fleshy roots in the spring and replant immediately.

Quick Reference to Symphytum Species

| | Height (in.) | Flower color |
|---|---|---|
| *S. caucasicum* | 18-24 | Blue |
| *S. grandiflorum* | 12-15 | Yellow |
| *S. rubrum* | 15-18 | Red |
| *S.* x *uplandicum* | 36-48 | Blue |

**-*caucasicum*** (kaw-ka′ si-cum) Caucasian Comfrey 18-24″/24″
Spring Blue Caucasus Zones 3-7

The softly hairy foliage consists of 8″ long basal leaves and 6″ long upper leaves. The base of the leaves runs along the stem for a short distance (decurrent). The drooping, ¾″ long, bell-shaped flowers open pink, then turn azure blue with maturity. The corolla (petals) is 2-3 times longer than the calyx (sepals) and flowers are borne in terminal, paired, scorpioid cymes.

Partial shade and moist soils are necessary for best performance. The coarse-textured plants are excellent subjects for the wild flower area but are also useful in the border or as short specimen plants in the garden.

**-*grandiflorum*** (grand-i-flo′ rum) Large-Flowered Comfrey 12-15″/18″
Spring Pale Yellow, Cream Caucasus Zones 3-8

Rhizomes give rise to many unbranched stems resulting in rapidly spreading colonies. The stem is roughly hairy (scabrous) and bears shiny, ovate leaves of different sizes. Those on flowering stems are only about 1½″ long while those on non-flowering (sterile) stems are up to 7″. The sterile stems lie on the ground with the ends pointing up (decumbent) and are characteristic of the species. Tubular, creamy yellow, almost white, ¾″ long flowers are produced in many terminal few-flowered cymes for about 3-4 weeks. A vigorous grower that competes well against weeds, it is shade and drought tolerant. Although tolerant of dry conditions, growth is superior in moist soils.

**Cultivars**:

'Goldsmith' is about 1′ tall and bears green leaves edged and splashed with gold and cream. Flowers are pink to blue in spring. Excellent!

'Variegatum' is an outstanding cultivar bearing creamy white margins around the light green leaves. The plant is much brighter than the species, particularly when planted in shady corner of the garden.

-***officinale*** (o-fish′ i-nal) | Comfrey | 3-4′/4′
Spring | Purple | Europe | Zones 4-7

The largest of the bonesets and reasonably handsome when in flower. The large leaves are ovate to lanceolate (wider in middle than at either end) and densely pubescent. The upper and middle leaves are obviously decurrent (the leaves run down the stem) and sessile. The strong stems are winged erect and heavily branched.

The inflorescences are many flowered and are white, pink or purple-violet. Plants are big and require "fencing in" or they fall over in rains and winds and forlornly lie on the ground. Full sun helps the strength, partial shade is tolerated.

**Related Species**:

*S. asperum*, prickly comfrey, has dark green prickly-hairy leaves on plants which grow 3-4′ tall. The flowers are at first reddish, then fad to blue. Also big, coarse and raspy.

-x ***rubrum*** (ru′ brum) | Red-Flowered Comfrey | 15-18″/18″
Early Summer | Red | Hybrid | Zone 3-7

This may be used as a ground cover because of its tendency to spread, although not as rapidly as one of its parents, *S. grandiflorum*. The foliage is dark green and not as hairy as many of the other species. Dark red, tubular flowers bequeathed by *S. officinale* 'Coccineum' occur in terminal cymes. The drooping red flowers, however, do not contrast well with the hairy dark leaves. Full sun may be provided in the North but partial shade is best in the South. Provide even moisture in times of dry weather.

-x ***uplandicum*** (up-land′ i-kum) | Russian Comfrey | 36-48″/36″
Late Spring | Blue | Hybrid | Zones 4-7

This upright plant is the result of a cross between *S. asperum*, a 5′ tall bristly plant, and *S. officinale*. The stems are highly branched and bear 8-10″ long basal leaves and 2-3″ long upper leaves. The basal leaves are decurrent (see *S. caucasicum*), and all foliage is softly hairy. The 1″ long, tubular flowers appear in various shades of purple and blue in forked cymes in the upper axils of the plant. Far better in the North than the South.

**Cultivars**:

'Axminster Gold' is as large as the hybrid but is far more interesting, bearing wonderful yellow and green leaves. Plants are more mounding and better behaved than the hybrid.

'Variegatum' has leaves with broad creamy white margins and lilac blue flowers. This is a fabulous plant but can be propagated only by division or root cuttings, therefore it is difficult to build up any numbers, thus will always have greater demand than supply.

**Other Hybrids**:

A few named hybrids are out there, but it is almost impossible to tell what name belongs to what species, and are most likely all hybrids.

'Gold in Spring' is from the original Heronswood Nursery and produces early pink and white flowers and yellow foliage as it emerges.
'Hidcote Blue' is a vigorous spreader with soft blue and white flowers on 1-2′ tall plants.
'Hidcote Pink' is similar but with pink and white flowers.
'Langthorn's Pink' grows up to 3′ tall with pink flowers in early summer.
'Pink Robins' is about 2′ tall with dark green leaves and deep pink narrow flowers.

***Symplocarpus*** (sim-plo-kar′ pus) Skunk Cabbage Araceae

Like many members of the Araceae, plants can maintain higher temperatures than the surrounding air or water, and ensure that no damage occurs to the developing flowers from freezing weather. Skunk cabbage is often the earliest plant to flower in its native habitat. The only species, *S. foetidus*, is native to swampy areas in Quebec to Manitoba, south to Georgia, Tennessee, Illinois and Iowa. The mottled brown spathe is strongly incurved and bloated and totally surrounds the narrow spadix. The cabbage-like leaves arise after flowering and although the common name suggests a rugged smell, an unpleasant odor occurs only if leaves are crushed or plants are disturbed. Its sister, *Lysichiton*, with the same common name, is far smellier.

Plants will proliferate only in bogs, swamps or in stagnant water. Where they are happy, there they shall stay, produce offspring and multiply rapidly. More of a curiosity than of great ornamental beauty.

***Syneilesis*** (sine-il-lee′ sis) Shredded Umbrella Plant Asteraceae

I love this plant. It is about as un-asterish as a plant in the family can be but what fun to include this weird, wonderful thing in the garden. The leaves emerge and unfold as hairy silver umbrellas, each divided into many thin segments. Under good conditions, the leaves will stretch to almost 10″ in width and the colony will multiply. In midsummer, tall flower stems bearing small, forgettable flowers arise. Native to Japan and Korea, these 15-18″ tall plants perform better in a zone 5 garden than an eastern zone 8 garden.

Regardless, give these a try. If you are successful, you will have the most wonderful colony of weird wonderful plants in the neighborhood. Zones 5-7.

***Synthyris*** (sin-thi′ ris) Synthyris Scrophulariaceae

Native to the Plains states and west to California, these small blue-flowered plants are slowly (very slowly) becoming better known. The best performer is probably *S. missurica*, native to southeastern Washington and Idaho to northeastern California. The plant is 18-24″ tall, and consists of 2-3″ wide rounded basal leaves that are

*Ranunculus ficaria* 'Brazen Hussy' with *Acorus* 'Ogon'

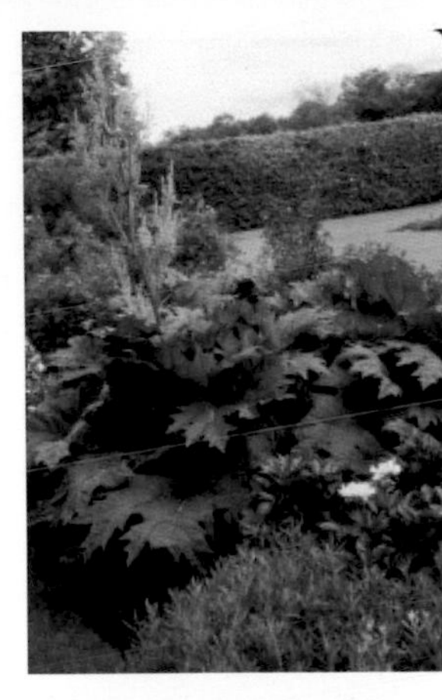

(L) *Rehmannia angulata*
(R) *Rheum palmatum* 'Bowle's Red'

*Rodgersia aesculifolia*

(L) *Rodgersia pinnata* var. *alba*
(R) *Rodgersia pinnata* var. *superba*

*Rohdea japonica* 'Seiki-No-Homare' with *Narcissus* 'February Gold'

*Romneya coulteri*

*Rubus microphyllus* 'Variegatus'

*Rudbeckia fulgida* 'Goldsturm'

*Rudbeckia subtomentosa* with *Liatris*

*Rudbeckia triloba*

*Sagina subulata*

*Salvia* 'Cherry Queen'

*Salvia* 'Indigo Spires' with *Caryopteris* 'Snow Fairy'

*Salvia* 'Mystic Spires'

*Salvia* 'Silke's Dream'

*Salvia leucantha* 'Midnight'

*Salvia lyrata*
'Purple Knockout'

*Salvia microphylla*
'Hot Lips'

*Salvia nipponica*
'Fuji Snow'

*Salvia sclarea*

*Sanguinea canadensis*

*Santolina virens*

*Schizachyrium scoparium*
'The Blues'

*Sedum*
'Iceberg'

*Sedum*
'Mr. Goodbud'

*Sedum*
'Neon'

*Sedum*
'Purple Emperor'

*Sedum rupestre*
'Angelina'

*Senecio aureus*

*Sidalcea malviflora* 'Elsie Heugh'

*Silene dioica* 'Valley High'

*Silphium gracile*

*Silphium integrifolium*

*Silphium perfoliatum*

*Spigelia marilandica*

*Stachys byzantina* 'Cotton Ball' with *Malva*

*Stachys* 'Hummelo'

*Stipa gigantea*

*Stokesia laevis* 'Peachies Pick'

*Stokesia laevis* 'Silver Moon'

coarsely toothed and held on long petioles. The small individual blue flowers, which consist of a 4-lobed corolla (petals), 4 distinct sepals and only 2 stamens, are held in a narrow raceme.

In my garden it has performed reasonably well, neither capturing one's fancy with its flavor nor disappointing people with its demise. It flowers for me in April, 2-3 weeks later in the North. Light afternoon shade and well-drained soils are all that is necessary. Plants are tough, being winter hardy to zone 3 and tolerating zone 7 summers.

**Cultivars:**

'Major' is bigger in every way.

**Related Species:**

*S. pinnatifida* has deeply cleft basal leaves and grows only 6-8″ tall. Native in Montana and Utah.

# T

***Talinum*** (tah-line′ um)  Rock Pink, Flame Flower  Portulacaceae

The only talinum I was ever familiar with was the rambunctious self-seeding annual, jewels of Opar (*T. paniculatum*). Talk about being secluded: I had missed an entire genus of hardy plants, native to the United States, many to the Great Plains of Nebraska, Missouri and Kansas. They are characterized by having succulent leaves like *Lewisia* and flowers closely resembling those of purslane, usually in shades of rose and pink. None of these are likely to be mainstreamed throughout the country, but people looking for xeric material and plants for small bright areas may want to look at the rock pinks a little closer. All tolerate dry, sharply drained soil conditions; they do poorly if "mothered" too much. All are cold hardy to zone 4, but do poorly in areas of significant rainfall and humidity.

The biggest and most common is *T. calycinum*, whose 1′ tall stems rise up to carry a loose collection of wide purplish rosy flowers, about a foot wide. Plants are available through many outlets. A tiny western form is *T. sediforme*, growing less than 6″ tall with gray-green cushions of small leaves. *T. parviflorum* is also a dwarf, but produces lovely pink flowers on wiry stems. 'Wyo', collected in southeast Wyoming by Ron Ackerman, has light pink flowers.

The taxonomists have been taking a turn at this genus as well, and moves are afoot to reclassify most of the species into the genus *Phemeranthus*. Good grief, where will it stop!

Propagate by seed.

***Tanacetum*** (tan-a-see′ tum)  Tansy  Asteraceae

This genus has been in a state of flux, with various additions and deletions over the years. The problem with all these name changes is more than simply confusion; but also trying to understand why they were done. One of the few linkages among species is that they all have scented foliage; sometimes highly aromatic, like tansy, other times, far more subtle. They also all have alternate leaves and single or double daisy flowers. A couple of relatively new additions came from *Chrysanthemum coccineum*, painted daisy and *Chrysanthemum parthenium*, feverfew.

The old-fashioned *Tanacetum* still includes some fine garden plants. Some handsome species are low growing mound-formers with attractive, white, hairy, finely divided leaves, such as *T. densum* ('Beth Chatto' is exceptional) and *T. haradjanii*. They require full sun and exceptionally well-drained soils to be at their best. Lots of these small, downy-leaved species (*T. compactum* and *T. nutallii*) are reasonably cold hardy, but cringe at the onset of wet winters and hot, humid summers. I enjoy the dwarf forms as well as the hefty feverfew species like *T. corymbosum*, whose white daisy flowers with yellow centers so handsomely combine with their coarse dark green foliage, and large leaf tansy, *T. macrophyllum*, whose deeply cut large leaves set off the white yarrow-like flowers effectively. However, I seldom see any of these plants, short, hefty or otherwise, look good by late summer in the eastern or midwestern United States and seldom do I ever see them offered for sale to the gardening public other than through the Internet. They are usually more successful in the Pacific Northwest than in the rest of the country, but what else is new?

***-coccineum*** (kok-sin' ee-um) Pyrethrum, Painted Daisy 2-3'/2'
Early Summer Various Western Asia Zones 3-7

This is not only a fine garden plant in cool areas of the country, but also the source of pyrethrum, an insecticide widely used for control of whiteflies and other sucking insects. The finely divided leaves are a vivid green; the lower ones about 10" long and attached to the stem by a long petiole while the upper are sessile. Above the foliage rise wiry stems supporting solitary 3" wide flowers. Most of the flowers are in shades of red or white with yellow centers and occur as singles or doubles.

Plants can be placed in full sun in the North but should be protected from afternoon sun in the South. Painted daisies do not tolerate heat particularly well and, unfortunately, are not good garden plants south of zone 7. In fact, one of the common complaints of gardeners is that plants look beautiful the first year and decline rapidly the second. Another problem is that they often require support, but with the advent of good dwarf cultivars, this problem is largely overcome. Flowering persists 2-4 weeks but plants are not long lived, requiring replanting or dividing every 2 years to maintain vigor. Some excellent dwarf cultivars have been introduced which should result in many more painted daisies in gardens.

Seed germinates readily in warm (70-75°F), humid conditions or divisions or cuttings may be taken in early spring or fall.

**Cultivars:**

'Atrosanguineum' bears single, dark red flowers and is the darkest red of any of the cultivars.

'Duro' produces bright, purple-red flowers about 2-3' tall. A good form for the cutting garden.

'Eileen May Robinson' has single pink flowers.

'Evenglow' is one of the best selections, producing rich salmon-red single flowers.

'James Kelway' produces single, dark red flowers.

'Pink Bouquet' produces double pink flowers.

'Robinson's Hybrids' bear double flowers, available in mixed colors and in pink, rose and crimson.
'Sensation' has double, red flowers.

***-parthenium*** (par-then′ ee-um) Feverfew, Matricaria 1-3′/2′
Late Summer White, Yellow Caucasus Zones 5-7

This cut flower is highly branched and often covered with ¾″ diameter, buttonlike flowers. The pinnately lobed foliage is strongly scented which may explain why few insects bother it and why many people don't embrace it. Each leaf is 2-3″ long, slightly hairy, and toothed. This is one of those "old-fashioned" plants that has undergone a renaissance as a cut flower and a bedding plant. Medicinally, it has always been a star. In 1597, Gerard's *Herbal* listed feverfew as a plant that was very good for "them that are giddie in the head". References to feverfew for headaches are more than a passing historical footnote. In the last 20 years, feverfew has been trumpeted for the treatment of headaches, particularly helping to prevent migraines. Since as many as one in eight people experience migraines, it is a potential welcome addition for migraine sufferers.

Roman legend states that it saved the life of a man who fell from the Parthenon during its construction, thus accounting for the specific name *parthenium*. (I don't believe it either). The foliage is also supposed to be very good fried with eggs. Please let me know.

Plants are not fussy as to soil but should be placed in full sun. The dwarf forms can be used as an edging while the larger forms are excellent border plants. In hot summers, dwarf forms tend to melt out, particularly if allowed to dry out, and cannot be recommended in the South. Even when cut back, the new growth declines in the heat and humidity. However, when kept well watered, an excellent crop has been produced in the flower trials at the University of Georgia.

Propagate similarly to *T. coccineum*. Seed may also be used.

**Cultivars:**

'Album' has single white flowers on 2′ stems.
'Aureum' has yellow foliage that turns green with the advent of flowers. It grows 8-12″ tall and is known as golden feather.
'Crispum' is a uniquely foul form with foliage curled like parsley.
'Flore Pleno' has white double flowers on 2′ stems.
'Golden Ball' is an 18″ tall yellow, double-flowering cultivar.
'Rowallane' has dozens of tennis ball-shaped white flower heads.
'Roya' bears white daisies atop 2′ tall plants.
'Santana' is only 10-12″ tall with creamy white flowers. Performance has been erratic in our garden (zone 7b), growing poorly in some years and well in others. It has done well in more northerly areas.
'Snowball' is 1-2′ tall with white double flowers.
Tetra series has fully double flowers; 'Tetra White' is probably the most common. Zone 6b to 7 at best.
'White Stars' bears clean white flowers with somewhat of a star shape.

**-*vulgare*** (vul′ gare) Tansy, Golden Buttons 3-4′/2′
Late Summer Yellow Asia Zones 5-7

The species that seems to be most adaptable to most gardens, is *T. vulgare*, common tansy or golden buttons. The fresh green, coarse leaves of tansy are highly aromatic to the touch (they make me sneeze) and are often harvested, dried, and used as potpourri. The mainly basal leaves are cut into 7-10 pairs of narrow segments, each one pinnately lobed, resulting in the appearance of a cutleaf fern. Plants can grow 3′ tall but generally peak out about 2′. The buttonlike yellow flowers are formed in late summer. Plants are hardy in zones 5-7 and should be placed in full sun or afternoon shade.

**Cultivars:**

'Crispum' is referred to as curly tansy, and while I find most of the "crispums" of the horticulture world ugly as sin, I like this one. The leaves are larger, appear lighter green, and are more deeply cut than the species, and flowering occurs sparsely if at all.

'Isla Gold' provides finely cut golden leaves throughout most of the season on 2′ tall plants.

**Related Species:**

*T. niveum*, silver tansy, provides handsome, gray cut-leaved foliage and dozens of small white daisy flowers, each with a yellow center. 'Jackpot' is touted as being more floriferous, but to me, it is not a great deal different than the species.

## ***Telekia*** (tel-ee-kee- a) Telekia Asteraceae

Telekia is one of those coarse-leaved yellow summer daisies that nobody grows, similar to other sunflower-looking things like *Inula* and *Bupthalmum* that nobody grows. In fact, they are so similar to *Bupthalmum* that two species of *Telekia* were only recently removed from that genus. For those who are curious as to why such divorces take place, oftentimes the irreconcilable differences are indeed subtle, at least to the non-taxonomist. For those who really don't care, proceed to the next paragraph. If sleep is needed, read on while I explain. Some characteristics that separate this species from *Bupthalmum* are doubly serrated highly aromatic leaves (entire margins to singly serrate in *Bupthalmum*), flowers held in racemes (usually solitary in *Bupthalmum*), and plants are taller and larger in *Telekia* than in *Bupthalmum*. The scent and large size are the most visible characteristics which differentiate them from each other.

The most common species is *T. speciosa*. Plants produce large basal leaves (14″ long and 10″ wide) on 6-8″ petioles and sessile upper stem leaves, reduced in size and rounded at the base. The stems are branched near the top of the 6′ tall plant. They are not often seen in gardens because of their coarse, gangly, large habit. The large leaves are pubescent, sessile, double toothed, and strongly aromatic. It is a vigorous grower and spreads rapidly. The yellow flowers are about 2″ across, held in a loose raceme and bloom in mid to late summer. For some gardeners and designers they are excellent as accents or back of the border plants and provide a pleasing effect for a few months, however, they decline rapidly after flowering and should be cut back before they turn crispy.

*T. speciossisma* is similar but grows only about 2′ tall on unbranched stems. Flowers are smaller but similar to the previous species.

Plants are hardy from zones 2-7a, marginal at best in 7b, and do reasonably well in zones 7 and 8 on the West Coast.

## ***Tellima*** (tel′ li-ma) Fringe-cup Saxifragaceae

The genus has been reduced to a single species, *T. grandiflora*, fringe-cup, native to western North America. *T. odorata* and *T. breviflora* are considered synonyms of *T. grandiflora* and the pink-flowered *T. parviflora* has been placed in the genus *Lithophragma*.

The scalloped 3-4″ wide leaves are heart shaped, hairy, and evergreen. They are mostly basal and have 5-7 lobes. The half-inch long flowers are greenish to creamy white and as many as 30 may occur on a single scape. As the flowers mature, they change to rose-red. The sepals are united into an inflated calyx tube and the petals are pinnately cut into threadlike segments pulled back, resulting in a "fringed cup".

Plants should be grown in ample shade and moist soil rich in organic matter. Incorporate plenty of peat or other water-holding material to maintain moisture around the roots. After blooming, the flowers become messy and should be removed unless seeds are to be collected. Plants perform well in zones 4-7. Plants are native to cool moist coniferous woods and are not particularly happy in hot climates. 'Odorata' has fragrant flowers, 'Purpurea' ('Rubra') is about 1-1½′ tall with redder stems and foliage and flowers also tinged pink.

*Tellima* is often confused with *Tiarella* and *Mitella* and, in fact, is an anagram of *Mitella* (What other genera are anagrams of each other? Check under S for the answer.). *Tellima* differs from both genera in having an inflated calyx (similar to, but not as obvious as that found in *Silene*). The fruit of all three is a capsule, but in *Tellima*, the capsule has 2 beak-like projections, whereas *Mitella* and *Tiarella* have none. It also gets confused with *Tolmeia*, piggyback plant, but I think that is only because they start with the same letter. All have similar shade and moisture requirements, all are pseudo ground covers, however, if we put the confusion behind us and concentrate on garden performance, most people would agree that *Tiarella* is better than the others.

**Cultivars**:

'Forest Frost' has flowers that turn rose pink as they mature and green leaves with silver venation that turn burgundy later in the season. A nice addition to this Western native.

## ***Teucrium*** (tewk′ ree-um) Germander Lamiaceae

These herbs have been used medicinally for hundreds of years. The name was derived from King Teucer, the first king of Troy, who used germander to relieve stomach pain and gout. The plants, somewhat woody at the base and technically subshrubs, are usually grown for their attractive, opposite leaves rather than the small purplish mint-like flowers. Of the 300 or so species, only a handful are particularly decorative and even fewer are easily available, although additional species are finding their way out of obscurity.

A tall form is our very own *T. canadense*, wild germander, native to southern Canada and the United States. Three feet tall in moist soil, it bears purple- to cream-colored flowers in a loose unbranched spike. I really think bush germander, *T. fruticans*, with its white tomentose stems, handsome foliage and large lavender flowers is the cat's pajamas. Unfortunately, it is an annual in all but the mildest climates. In a bad mood? Then you will enjoy the sharp spiny foliage of *T. subspinosum*, fortunately another annual that will inflict pain only for a single season. A species commanding a loyal following in Europe is *T. scorodonia* 'Crispum', crispy wood germander. The wavy, crested green leaves are tinged purple in winter and very decorative particularly in the cooler months. It is winter hardy to zone 6 with protection. Another crinkled leaf species is *T. massilense*, scented germander, whose gray-green foliage is accentuated by rose-colored flowers on 18″ plants. The foliage is particularly aromatic. The most common germander is wall germander, *T. chamaedrys*. All species are aromatic and neighborhood cats will reward your plant selection with their never-ending presence.

| -***chamaedrys*** (sha-mie′ dris) | | Wall Germander | 10-12″/12″ |
|---|---|---|---|
| Summer | Pink, Purple | Europe | Zones 4-9 |

This small evergreen subshrub is popular because of the compact habit and shiny green leaves. It tolerates a particularly cruel form of abuse called "edge hedging" where it is sheared into formidable evergreen globs. When allowed to grow naturally, plants are far more decorative. The scalloped, lustrous green, ovate leaves are about 1″ long and borne on branched ascending stems. Two to six rosy-purple flowers are produced in a single whorl in late summer and continue for approximately 3-4 weeks. Individual flowers are ½-¾″ long and the long lower lip is usually spotted white and red. Plants can be cut back hard—almost to the ground—in the fall or early spring.

When planted as a hedge, invariably some plants will be less vigorous than others, perhaps because of more shade or poorer soil. Doubtless a cat will love a portion of it to death, or a particularly cold winter will kill a few plants. The result is a spotty planting that pleases no one. Plants should be grown in full sun (although tolerant of partial shade) and not be allowed to dry out.

Propagate by seed or by 1-2″ terminal cuttings in May and root in a peat-perlite mixture. Excessive moisture in the rooting bench should be avoided. Rooting takes place in 3-4 weeks and plants may be grown on in pots and placed in the garden in the fall or subsequent spring. Divisions may be taken in the spring.

**Cultivars:**

'Prostratum' ('Nanum') is 6-10″ tall with rose-pink flowers in summer.

'Summer Sunshine' has pale chartreuse leaves on 6-8″ mounding plants. Short pink inflorescences occur in spring.

'Variegatum' has leaves with green and creamy variegation. Interesting but not vigorous.

**Related Species:**

*Teucrium hyrcanicum*, Caspian germander, is exceptional and should be discovered by more retailers and gardeners. Plants grow 2-2½′ tall with dozens of upright lavender flower stems in late spring, resembling those of veronica. This has been one of the finest plants in the Gardens at UGA; totally unknown to us until I planted it, now one of our favorites. 'Paradise Delight' is a bit shorter, but not a great deal different from the species. Native to western Asia.

## *Thalictrum* (tha-lik′ trum) Meadow-Rue Ranunculaceae

The exceptional diversity of the genus has been known by landscapers and gardeners for some time. The meadow-rues consist of some excellent species for the garden and, as discovered as they may be, they are still underused. In Europe, leaves of *Thalictrum* were used as a cure for the plague and jaundice, but few recoveries were recorded. The Romans also believed that to lay a newborn baby on a pillow stuffed with thalictrum flowers was to ensure riches throughout life. I gave some to my grandsons this year, just in case.

Many species have fernlike foliage and great puffs of airy flowers. The apetalous (no petals) flowers are ornamental because of the colored sepals and stamens. In some cases, male and female flowers occur on separate plants, such as the dainty early meadow-rue, *T. dioicum*, but others are bisexual. In general, they should be planted in partial shade with adequate moisture. Many are tall and most suited for the middle or back of the border, however, *T. alpinum*, alpine meadow-rue, *T. ichangense*, and *T. kiusianum*, Kyushu meadow-rue, grow less than 9″ tall. Many authorities now lump *Anemonella thalictroides*, rue-anemone, into this genus as *T. thalictroides*. I have chosen to leave it under its old name (which see).

Some of the more ornamental species are native to Japan, Europe and China but North America is no slouch either. *T. dasycarpum* has bright green leaves and flower heads of lavender and white, *T. dioicum*, early meadow-rue, provides dull green leaves and handsome small whitish flowers and gray green leaves, *T. polygamum* is 6-8′ tall and bears creamy white panicles of flowers. All are shade tolerant and should be used more.

Quick Reference to Thalictrum Species

| | Height (ft.) | Flower color | Leaflet color |
|---|---|---|---|
| *T. aquilegifolium* | 2-3 | Lilac | Blue-green |
| *T. delavayi* | 2-4 | Lilac | Green |
| *T. flavum* | 3-5 | Yellow | Blue-green |
| *T. kiusianum* | 6-9″ | Lavender | Green |
| *T. minus* | 1-2 | Yellow | Green |
| *T. rochebrunianum* | 3-6 | Lavender | Green |

***-aquilegifolium*** (a-kwi-leeg′ i-fo-lee-um) Columbine Meadow-Rue 2-3′/3′
Late Spring Lilac Europe, Northern Asia Zones 5-7

This is one of the prettiest and showiest of the meadow-rues. The lovely blue-tinted leaves are similar to columbine, thus the specific name. There are many leaflets, each about 1½″ wide and 3-5 lobed. The flowers are ornamental because of the conspicuous ½″ long lilac stamens. The sepals are greenish or white and abscise rapidly. The lilac flowers are held in a 6-8″ wide, many-flowered inflorescence, and look like big purple powder puffs. This is the earliest meadow-rue to flower and opens as early as late April in the Armitage garden, 2-3 weeks later in the Midwest. Unfortunately flowers persist for only about 2 weeks. However, the drooping, somewhat inflated fruit are interesting with their 3 small wings and persist throughout the growing season. Plants can grow up to 5′ tall but generally top out at about three feet.

These perform well throughout most of the country. The leaves, flowers, and seeds are ornamental and the plant is heat tolerant. It should be planted in a rich moist soil in partial shade. Direct sun results in less vigorous plants and later flowering.

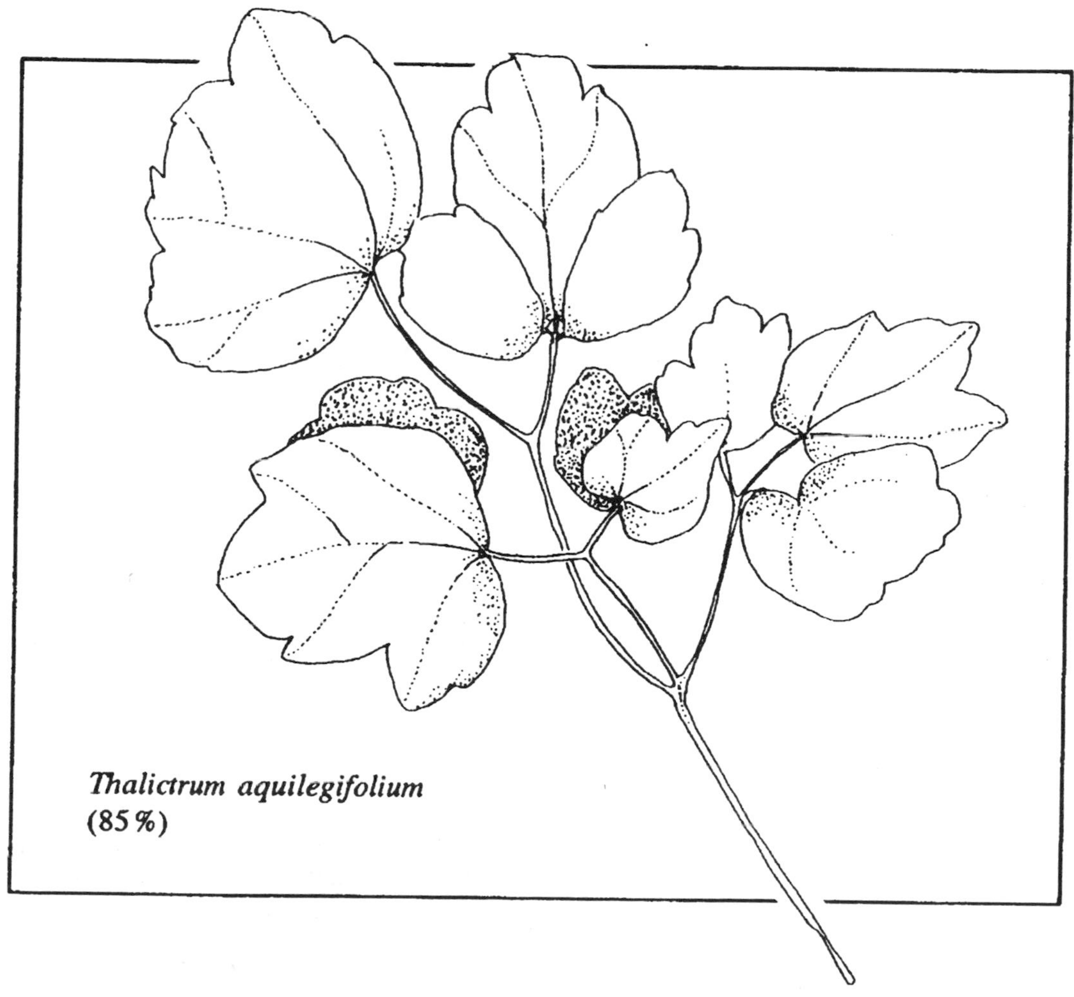

*Thalictrum aquilegifolium*
(85%)

Seed germinates readily and is the best method of propagation for the species and varieties. Cultivars may be divided in early spring or early fall. Divisions are slow to recover and must be handled carefully. Although divisions may be used to increase stock, division of the clump is not necessary for at least five years.

**Cultivars:**

'Album' has white flowers atop a 3-4′ tall plant. The white flowers contrast well with the blue-green foliage. The plant is otherwise similar to the species.

'Atropurpureum' has dark purple stems and stamens. The variety listed as 'Purpureum' is likely the same, however, the stems are not as highly colored.

'Dwarf Purple' stands about 2½′ tall, has lilac flowers and is otherwise similar to the species.

'Roseum' bears handsome light pink to pale rose flowers.

'Thundercloud' has deep purple flowers and larger flower heads than the type.

'White Cloud' is the best of the white-flowered forms with larger, whiter flowers than 'Album'.

-***delavayi*** (de-la-vay′ ee) Yunnan Meadow-Rue 24-48″/36″
Summer Lilac Western China Zones 4-7

The foliage is divided in 2-3 sections, each with three, half-inch wide leaflets providing a more fernlike and graceful look than that of *T. aquilegifolium*. Lilac sepals and creamy yellow stamens characterize flowers held in an airy, open, pyramidal panicle. The flowers are excellent for cutting but if the plants are grown too close together, the flowering stems get terribly tangled and are almost impossible to extract intact. Although often listed summer hardy to zone 8, performance has been very disappointing in my garden. Plants survive, but are not particularly effective south of zone 7a. Regardless of geographic location, plants require support to keep the slender stems erect when in flower. Similar to other meadow-rues, rich, moist soil and partial shade are beneficial.

Propagate the species from seed or division and the cultivars from division. 'Hewitt's Double' is commercially propagated by tissue culture.

**Cultivars:**

'Album' has white sepals but is not as vigorous as the type.

'Hewitt's Double' has double lilac flowers which last longer than flowers of the type. The stamens are petal-like (petaloid) resulting in the fuller flowers. An excellent garden plant.

-***flavum*** (flay′ vum) Yellow Meadow-Rue 3-5′/4′
Summer Yellow Southern Europe Zones 5-8

One of the more vigorous species, plants burst through the ground in spring with stems as thick as the necks of New Zealand All-Blacks rugby players. The species has large, green, 2-3 compound leaflets but the most common and more handsome form, 'Glaucum' has glaucous blue foliage. Good-sized clumps form within 2-3 years as a result of the vigorous deep-seated roots. The 1½" wide leaflets and leaves are useful in floral decorations and plants are worth growing for the foliage alone. The flowers are perfect (male and female parts on the same flower), consisting of pale yellow sepals and bright yellow, slender protruding stamens, and are held in an upright compact 2-4" wide pyramidal panicle and have a faint but pleasant odor. Plants are often sold under the name of *T. glaucum* because of the foliage. The species is more heat tolerant than others and also well worth growing anywhere. Plant in rich, moist soil in partial shade.

Divide the plant when needed or raise from seed.

**Cultivars:**

'Illuminator' is similar to the species once mature, but the young growth emerges pale gold and with highlights of bronze and pink. Sounds better than it is. Similar robust habit and yellow flowers are formed.

| | | | |
|---|---|---|---|
| ***-kiusianum*** (kee-oo-see-a' num) | | Kyoshu Meadow-Rue | 4-6"/12" |
| Summer | Lavender | Japan | Zones 6-8 |

This is simply a great plant. Plants occupy the opposite end of the height spectrum from *T. rochebrunianum* but are equally handsome. This stoloniferous species produces mats of green foliage with a bronze tinge. They get lost in the border situation but are wonderful growing over rocks or hanging down walls. The flowers are lilac and are borne on 4-6" tall stems in summer.

| | | | |
|---|---|---|---|
| ***-minus*** (my' nus) | | Lesser Meadow-Rue | 12-24"/24" |
| Summer | Yellow | Europe, Asia | Zones 3-7 |

This species is particularly variable and consists of many races (a group of plants from the same species but with slightly different properties; a race comes true from seed) to which over 200 different specific names have been given. In the past, names such as *T. foetidum*, *T. majus*, and most commonly *T. adiantifolium* have been applied to this species.

In general, the leaflets are three lobed and look like those of the maidenhair fern, *Adiantum pedatum*. The ½" wide perfect flowers are borne in a loose panicle with spreading branches. The greenish sepals abscise rapidly and the yellow color of the flower is the result of the slender stamens. The roots are stoloniferous but plants are not invasive. The plant is best grown for the elegant foliage, not the rather inconspicuous flowers.

Propagate good forms vegetatively by division. Seed-propagated plants will vary.

**Cultivars:**

'Adiantifolium' (var. *adiantifolium*) is the best form. Because of the variability within the species, the foliage can range from minute to the size of a half dollar. Plants using this name will at least have maidenhair-like foliage.

***-rochebrunianum*** (rosh-broon-ee′ aye-num) Lavender Mist 4-5′/3′
Summer Lavender Japan Zones 4-7

To me, this is the finest upright species in the genus. The Japanese native combines handsome foliage and wonderful lavender flowers in late spring and summer. It is an excellent background plant, able to rise 5-6′ tall, but its tall, skinny habit looks better in groups of three than as a single specimen. The leaves are 3-4 ternate (meaning leaves are three to four times divided into threes) providing a airy delicate look that inspired some writers to call them "see-through" plants. The pendulous flowers consist of small lavender sepals with threadlike stamens much shorter than the sepals. The plant grows 3-5′ tall and bears pale purple flowers. The purplish black stems are also colorful and thicker than *T. delavayi*. Plants are self-supporting.

The only downside I have found with this plant is its lack of longevity. Perhaps this occurs more in the South than in the North, but I have been mystified by the sudden death in summer or poor regrowth in the spring after about three years.

**Cultivars**:

'Lavender Mist' is the common name of the species as well as the most common cultivar available to gardeners. The cultivar differs from seedlings by having more violet flowers with gold stamens. This is the most popular of the tall lavender-flowered species, others like *T. delavayi* and *T. dipterocarpum* are not offered as often.

**Related Species**:

'Black Stockings', a hybrid from Terra Nova Nurseries in Oregon, is available through most retailers around the country. When in flower, plants can be up to six feet in height, topped with lavender to purple flowers somewhat between those of lavender mist and the columbine meadow-rue. The black part refers to the long black stems. Be careful when you Google this one, more than plants may come up. Full sun to partial shade. Zones 5-8.

*T. dipterocarpum* differs so little from *T. delavayi* that, from the gardener's viewpoint, it is the same. Most plants sold under one name may in fact be the other. The fruits are keys to separating the two species. The fruit of *T. delavayi* have 1 or 2 inconspicuous wings whereas those of *T. dipterocarpum* have three distinct wings. For gardeners with curiosity and patience, a 10X magnification lens is useful. Garden culture and performance are similar.

'Elin' may be a hybrid between *T. flavum* var. *glaucum* and *T. rochebrunianum* and grows 8-10′ tall with bronze flower buds that give way to bicolored pale yellow and lavender flowers. In cool climes, plants do not need staking. Flowers earlier than *T. rochebrunianum*. A most impressive plant! Full sun to partial shade, hardy to zone 5.

*T. ichangense* is also short, growing 6-9″ tall when in flower. The biternate leaves consist of rounded leaflets, often peltate. The mauve to pink flowers are borne in late spring to summer. Full sun or partial shade. Hardy in zones 5-7.

*T. speciosissimum*, yellow meadow-rue, has been blended into *T. flavum*, and has essentially disappeared. However, I don't buy it. Plants that have more delicate bi- or tri-ternately compound leaves, consisting of smaller leaflets, are properly found under the *T. speciosissimum* banner. The leaves are not at all glaucous. Plants bear similar yellow flowers.

*T. virgatum*, twiggy rue, is another low grower (9-12″ tall) and provides airy inflorescences of white flowers. Native to China, hardy to zone 6.

**Thelypteris** (thel-ip-ter′ is) Marsh Fern Thelypteridaceae

The genus has been sliced and diced by taxonomists and perhaps now some agreement has been reached as to where the various species actually belong. Presently, only about 3 species remain. They are small to medium-sized plants and always deciduous. They spread by creeping rootstalks and arise with slightly scaly, not chaffy, stems. The sterile and the fertile fronds are similar, unlike other ferns that have distinct fertile structures. The sori (spore cases) are generally found in widely spaced rows near the margins. Ferns are mainly found in the North and in fact can be rather unruly, taking over large areas of the garden. The beech ferns used to be here but are now classified as *Phegopteris* and the Mariana fern is now *Macrothelypteris torresiana* (which see).

One of the best performers goes under Southern shield fern, widespread maiden fern, abundant maiden fern and Kunth's maiden fern. Its botanical name is *T. kunthii* but it is also sold as *T. normalis*. No wonder we are all so confused. Nevertheless, the arching forms, the vigorous but non-invasive habit, and the bronze color in the fall makes this a winner for most gardeners.

The marsh fern, *T. palustris*, has upright, narrow, oblong fronds in a somewhat twisted habit. The leaflets are opposite and almost perpendicular to the stem. They enjoy sunny moist areas, where their delicate lacy fronds seem to dance in the breeze. Easily grown by streams, lakes and garden ponds. Hardy to about –20°F.

The New York fern, *T. noveboracensis* (may be reclassified as *Parathelypteris novae-boracacensis*) also has oblong fronds that are much broader in the middle than at either end. Usually, plants have about 3 fronds, but the creeping rootstalks result in large clumps. The fronds are never opposite, always slightly alternate. Easy to grow in the North in moist but not wet areas. A little more difficult south of zone 6.

**Thermopsis** (the-mop′ sis) False Lupine Fabaceae

The genus was well named, coming from *thermos*, lupin, and *opsis*, like. The flowers in all but one or two of the 23 species are yellow and similar in shape to the lupine. The compound leaves consist of 3 palmately arranged leaflets and 2 smaller leaflike stipules (like baptisias). Occasionally they may be confused with *Baptisia*; however, they usually emerge and flower much sooner than *Baptisia*, the foliage of most *Baptisia* species is blue green and the seed pods are inflated. In *Thermopsis*, the foliage is green and the seed pods flat. Most of the thirty or so species have opposite or whorled flowers on the flower stem. While they are related and cosmetically resemble lupines and false indigos, they are ornamental plants on their own, providing early color almost as early as the spring flowering bulbs.

A number of species are native to the United States, the most common being *T. villosa* in the East and *T. montana* in the West. Plants may be used to provide lupine-like flowers where an upright, yellow early flowering plant is desired.

Quick Reference to Thermopsis Species

| | Height (in.) | Flower color |
|---|---|---|
| *T. lanceolata* | 9-12 | Yellow |
| *T. montana* | 12-24 | Yellow |
| *T. villosa* | 30-48 | Yellow |

***-lanceolata*** (lan-see′ o-lah-ta) Golden Banner, Lanceleaf Thermopsis 9-12″/18″
Spring Yellow Alaska, Siberia Zones 2-7

Small stature and sessile, narrow leaves differentiate this species from *T. villosa*. Plants form 1-2′ wide clumps but are not at all invasive. The bright yellow flowers appear whorled and are held in a terminal upright raceme well above the foliage. The strongly recurved pods are unique and provide one of the identifying characteristics of the species. Plants may still be found under the old name *T. lupinoides*.

Place in full sun or partial shade, particularly if planted south of zone 6. Native to northern locales, it is not as tolerant of heat as the previous species. This is a good, if not spectacular, plant in the right climate.

Propagate by seed or by division. Although division is possible, months are necessary for the plants to recover.

***-villosa*** (vill-o′ sa) Aaron's Rod, Southern Lupine 30-48″/48″
Spring Yellow Eastern United States Zones 3-9

This is surely one of the most overlooked garden plants. The leaves are divided into 3 obovate (fat at the top) leaflets, each 2-3″ long and finely hairy beneath. The bright yellow, pealike flowers emerge in April in the South, 2-3 weeks later in the North, and remain colorful for 3-4 weeks. They are held in compact, erect 6-12″ long racemes. The undersides of the leaves are barely pubescent to almost glabrous, but the hollow stems are quite hairy and are responsible for the botanical name, *T. villosa*, which has superceded *T. caroliniana* as the proper botanical name. The pods are also hairy. More than 30 flower stems were produced on a three-year-old clump at the University of Georgia.

Plant in partial shade in the South, full sun in the North. The flower stalks are a little longer under shade and plants may require support. The foliage should be cut back about a month after flowering as it declines rapidly, particularly in dry situations.

Seed propagation is the best means of increasing numbers and fresh seed germinates well. Older seed requires a scarification treatment for uniform germination. Treatment with sulphuric acid is effective but should be undertaken only by trained personnel (i.e. someone with experience in a seed laboratory). Division is more difficult as plantlets do not transplant well.

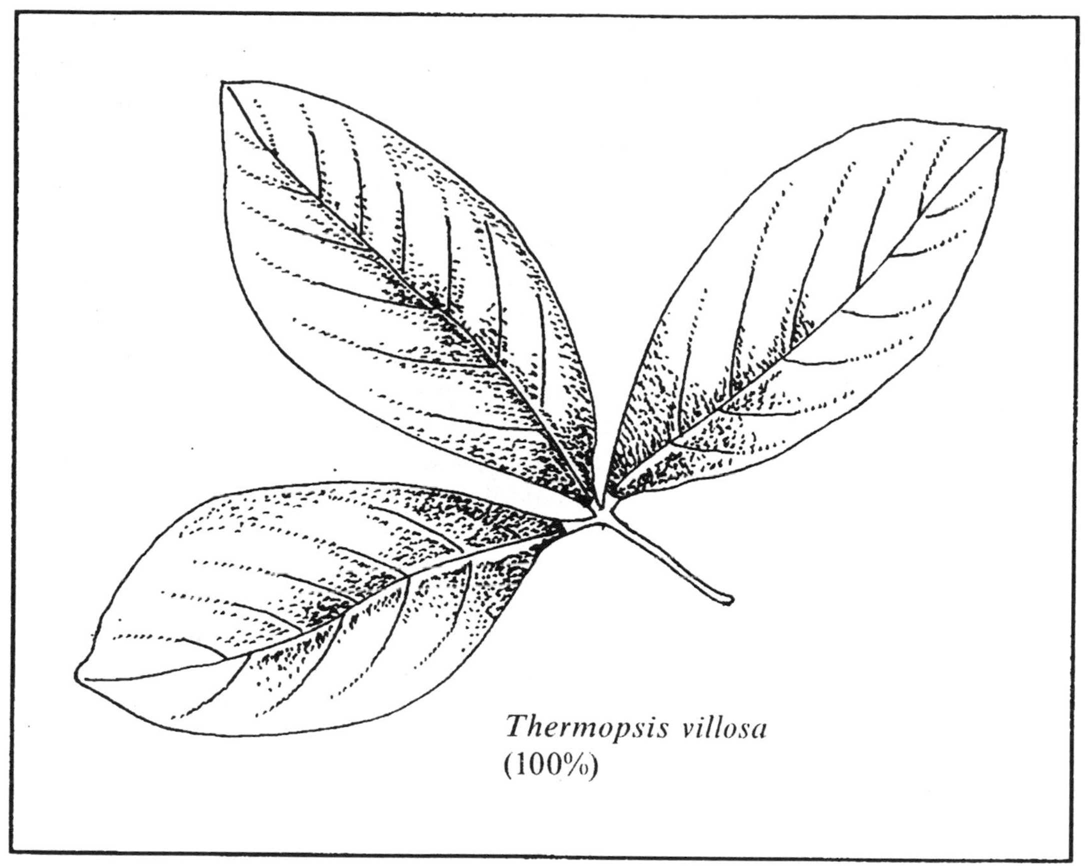

*Thermopsis villosa*
(100%)

**Related Species:**

*T. chinensis*, Chinese thermopsis, is not at all common in this country, but can be distinguished by having alternate flowers up the flowering stem. Now, thanks to North Creek Nurseries in Landenberg, Pennsylvania, and to Becky Long, one of their finest plantspeople, we have the lovely 'Sophia', with early, soft yellow flowers on 18″ tall plants. The beautiful plant was named for Becky's beautiful daughter. Zones 5-9.

*T. fabacea* grows up to 3′ tall and also bears bright yellow flowers and rather large leaflets. The axils of the plant often have short spines and the erect flowers are also found in the axils. They spread more rapidly than *T. caroliniana*.

*T. montana*, mountain thermopsis, is the western cousin of *T. villosa*. It is 12-24″ tall, has a shorter (up to 8″ long), less dense raceme, and bears linear-lanceolate leaflets compared with obovate leaflets of *T. villosa*. Very closely related; its main difference is its different provenance. Some authors claim it is invasive in rich soils but I have not noticed a problem. Hardy in zones 3-7.

**Cultivars:**

'Album' is a more compact (2½′ tall), beautiful, but rare cultivar with creamy white flowers.

**Thymus** (time′ us) Thyme Lamiaceae

"I know a bank where the wild thyme grows." stated Oberon, king of the fairies in Shakespeare's "A Midsummer Night's Dream", and "Where the heck is the thyme?" muttered my mother when she was cooking. With a genus steeped in history and steeping in the stew, it is hard not to connect the past with the present when we think about this group of plants. Common thyme, *T. vulgaris*, grows on the hillsides throughout the Mediterranean and the British Isles and was long used for its fragrance, flavoring and its many curative properties. As early as 3000 BC, thyme was used to prevent nightmares and also helped in the mummification process by the ancient Egyptians. Traditionally, thyme has been used to relieve spasms and coughing, and studies have borne out the benefit as an antispasmodic and antitussive.

A few of the approximately 350 species are used as ornamental plants, including cultivars of *T. serphyllum*, wild thyme, *T. citriodorus*, lemon.thyme and *T. pseudolanuginous*, woolly thyme. It would seem that all you have to do is smell the leaves of various thymes and separate them with your nose. Only up to a point, depending on the sensitivity of your snout. The cultivar 'Lemon-scented' smells like lemons, but even common thyme has a superficial lemon scent. However, caraway thyme, *T. herba-barona*, smells obviously of caraway, and is so tough that it is sometimes used as a "thyme" lawn. Speaking of lawns, thymes have long been used between rocks on a pathway or in areas of moderate foot traffic. One of the most creative companies I know, called Stepables™, markets "foot-traffic plants", and thymes are among their most popular.

All prefer full sun, and outstanding drainage; they rot quickly in wet areas. Hot summers and high humidity result in "melt-down" but if cut back, plants usually recover well. Thyme is often better in the North than the South, but the lure of thyme in gardens has no boundaries. Rocky outcrops where drainage is sharp and soil is gritty are best. Although native to Europe, wild thyme has escaped in the eastern United States and can be seen in meadows and hillsides in New England.

Leaves are opposite, usually less than ½" long and oval to oblong. The stems tend to creep along the ground and become woody with age. The lavender to pink flowers are crowded together in dense terminal heads, and sometimes arise from the leaf axils as well. They are extremely rich in nectar and bees are always hovering around flowering plants.

All plants, regardless of cultivar and species, should be cut back often to rejuvenate the plants and avoid rot. The further south, the more pruning is necessary.

Quick Reference to Thymus Species

| | Fragrance | Habit |
|---|---|---|
| *T. citriodorus* | Lemon | Upright |
| *T. pseudolanuginosus* | Slight thyme | Prostrate |
| *T. serphyllum* | Thyme | Prostrate |
| *T. vulgaris* | Thyme | Prostrate |

**-*citriodorus*** (cit-ree-o-dor′ us) | Lemon Thyme | 9-12″/12″
Fall | Pale lilac | Garden Hybrid | Zones 5-8

Lemon thyme is one of the more popular garden hybrids, having thought to be arisen from *T. pulegoides* and *T. vulgaris*. However, recent literature (2002) suggests that the hybrid appellation is incorrect and that the hybrid should be given specific status once again. The fragrance from the ¼″ wide oval to lancelike leaves is remarkably lemon-like. The stems are erect and can grow up to a foot tall. The oblong inflorescence usually consists of pale lilac to pink flowers. Many cultivars have been offered, some of which may be prostrate, many of which have golden or have variegated foliage. Most of the golden thymes have been reclassified under *T. pulegiodes* (which see).

**Cultivars:**

'Anderson's Gold' is a dwarf, carpeting form with golden foliage in the winter.
'Argenteus' bears silver-green leaves.
'Argenteus Variegatus' has silver variegated foliage.
'Golden Queen' bears pale green leaves with light golden variegation.
'Silver Queen' has variegations of cream to dull silver on the green leaves.

**-*pseudolanuginosus*** (soo-doe-lah-new-gi-no′ sus) | Woolly Thyme | 3-4″/12″
Summer | Pink | Unknown | Zones 5-8

The common name comes from the long hairs on the prostrate stems. The stems are somewhat 4-sided with elliptical gray leaves. The pale pink flowers are borne in early summer but plants are not as floriferous as other species. The plants are best known for their fuzziness and are terrific rock garden plants, but should be used only where drainage is spectacular. In areas of copious rain and hot, humid weather, woolly thyme often self-destructs by midsummer.

This is spectacularly used at the Niagara Parks School of Horticulture in Niagara Falls, Canada; a garden destination not to be missed.

**Cultivars:**

'Hall's Variety' ('Hall's Woolly') is 3-4″ tall and bears lavender-pink flowers over soft woolly foliage. This is likely a hybrid (*T.* 'Hall's Variety').

**-*serphyllum*** (ser-pil′ um) | Wild Thyme | 4-6″/12″
Summer, Fall | Pink, Purple | Europe | Zones 5-8

The best known of the prostrate forms, which if given cool nights, full sun and good drainage multiplies rapidly. Plants have escaped throughout New England and clothe hillsides in the Berkshires in late summer and fall. The oval leaves are pubescent with short petioles, to almost sessile. The pink to purple flowers are held in a dense rounded inflorescence, usually terminal but also axillary. More than 40 cultivars have been described and more are becoming available, ranging from creeping to upright habits, with white, pink, red or purple flowers, and with foliage from deep green to gold and variegated forms.

**Cultivars:**

'Annie Hall' has pale pink flowers on prostrate stems.

'Coccineus' has deep green leaves and dark red flowers. The incredible muddle with the names of the dark-flowered thymes has led taxonomists to suggest they all should be lumped as *T. coccineus* group. This is a sensible approach and I laud the lumping.

'Goldstream' produces lilac flowers on creeping stems with yellow and green variegated foliage.

'Elfin' bears gray-green tight foliage and lavender pink flowers.

'Magic Carpet' clings to the ground with tight, green leaves which exude some lemon fragrance. Dark pink flowers occur in the spring.

'Pink Chintz' has dark green woolly leaves and salmon-pink flowers.

'Snowdrift' bears white flowers on creeping stems.

**Related Species:**

*T. praecox*, creeping thyme, is a mat-forming, creeping species with 2-3″ tall stems and mauve to purple flowers. The lanceolate leaves are slightly hairy. 'Albus' is an unusual white-flowered form, 'Doretta Klaber' is a dense grower with dark pink flowers, 'Highland Cream' has variegated yellow and green foliage with white to light pink flowers, 'Porlock' bears rounded leaves and pink flowers, 'Rainbow Falls' has dark green leaves splashed with yellow and lilac pink flowers, 'Reiter's Red' forms tight green mats with crimson flowers.

*T. pulegoides* is native to the U.K. and bears small flowers over small, broad leaves. Many of the golden-leaf thymes have been reassigned to this species. 'Archer's Gold' is a compact upright form with golden leaves. 'Aureus' is a small (6-9″) bush with green leaves dappled with yellow. 'Bertram Anderson' is a 4″ mat-former with golden leaves that remain colorful all winter. Light pink flowers occur in summer. 'Elliott's Gold' bears golden leaves with a creeping habit.

*T. vulgaris*, common thyme, is the culinary thyme most often used in cooking but ornamental cultivars are also available. Stems are about 12″ tall, often branching and with woody stems. The leaves are sessile and about ¼″ long. 'Argenteus' has silver-edged leaves, 'Aureus' bears golden yellow leaves and rosy flowers, 'Compactus' is only 4″ tall with pale gray-green leaves, 'Silver Posie' has mauve flowers and silver-variegated foliage.

## ***Tiarella*** (tee-a-rel′ la) Foam Flower Saxifragaceae

Foam flower has become civilized in the last 10 years, its evolution from a cute wildflower to a mainstay shade-lover almost complete. To accomplish such a task, a number of things had to occur. People must write and talk about the plants, breeders must produce and hybridize new cultivars so there is something to write and talk about and plants must perform well throughout a large portion of the country. Mission accomplished: today there are dozens of cultivars and it is difficult not to trip over foam flowers in almost any garden.

Approximately 5 species occur, 4 native to North America and 1 to Asia. They all have basal leaves with long petioles and white to pink flowers in upright inflorescences (racemes). There are generally 10 stamens, often alternately long and short, with 5 sepals and 5 petals. Foam flower is an ideal ground cover and can be spectacular in mass plantings. Choice in foliage pattern, shape and size, excellent white to pink flowers and low maintenance put these plants on the A list for shady areas.

Quick Reference to Tiarella Species

| | Height (in.) | Leave shape | Stoloniferous (Y or N) |
|---|---|---|---|
| *T. cordifolia* | 6-12 | Simple | Yes |
| *T. c.* var. *collina* | 6-12 | Simple | No |
| *T. trifoliata* | 9-20 | Trifoliate | No |

-***cordifolia*** (kor-di-fo' lee-a) Allegheny Foamflower 6-12"/36"
Spring White Eastern North America Zones 3-8

Plants are native from Nova Scotia to Michigan and south to Georgia and Alabama. Each 3-4" wide, heart-shaped leaf consists of 3 to 5 lobes. The evergreen foliage has some burgundy variegation along the veins most noticeable in the spring and

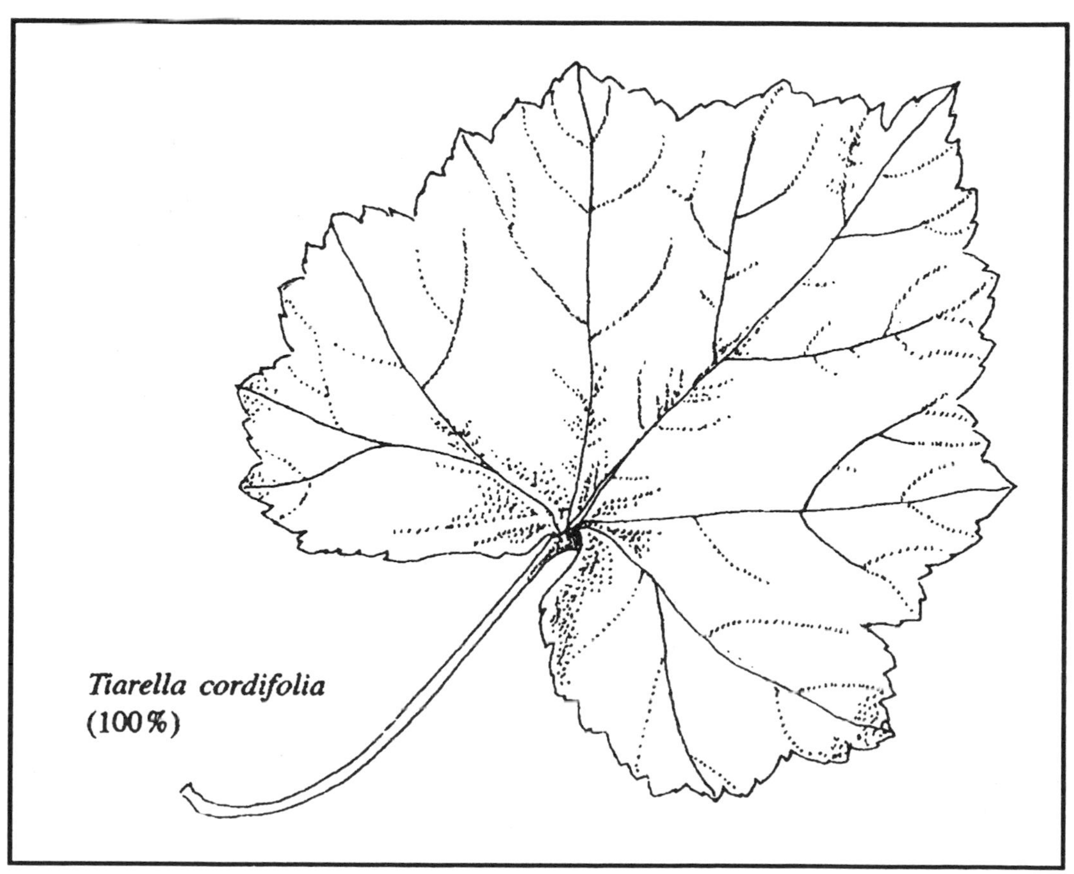

***Tiarella cordifolia* (100%)**

fall, and may be completely bronze during the winter. Foliage is similar to *Heuchera americana*, American alumroot, in this respect although significant differences in flowers occur. Delicate pink-tinged flower buds gracefully evolve into starry, creamy white flowers on 3-4″ long racemes. The ¼″ wide flowers consist of sepals about half as long as the petals, 10 stamens with brown anthers, and remain in bloom for about 6 weeks. Plants are stoloniferous and rapidly form large masses. Plants are effective with other shade- and moisture-tolerant species such as trilliums, woodland phlox, false Solomon's seal, or Christmas fern.

*Tiarella* requires moisture retentive, highly organic soils in medium to heavy shade. They will romp about but don't pretend to compete with *Vinca* or *Pachysandra* in covering the ground. Dry soils or exposure to full sun results in anemic, scrawny plants that never fill out. Soils may be enriched with organic matter such as well-rotted leaves. Wet feet, particularly in the winter, also result in significant losses.

var. *collina* (*T. wherryi*), Wherry's foam flower, differs in subtle ways. The plant is taller and, unlike the stoloniferous *T. cordifolia*, is a clump-forming species. Upon close inspection, one notices that the anthers are yellowish orange rather than brown as in *T. cordifolia*. It is equally attractive and ornamental.

Propagate from seed or division. Seed should be shallowly sown in early spring in a protected area such as a cold frame. Transplant seedlings to 3-4″ containers in 6-8 weeks.

**Cultivars and Hybrids**:

Some terrific work by breeders such as Dan Heims (Oregon), Don Jacobs (Georgia), Dan Hinkley (Washington), and Sinclair Adams and Charles Oliver (Pennsylvania) has resulted in significant improvements, but also many, many look-alikes. I enjoy them all and trialed most but if the labels were removed, I would have a very difficult time telling one from the other. In fact, I suspect even the breeders would be similarly challenged. However, some selections are certainly better garden performers than others and many have some bronze fall color as well. The trick is to find a retailer you can trust; ask for a couple of recommendations and have fun.

'Arpeggio', from Charles Oliver, produces light pink flowers over maple-leafed leaves, each with some maroon color in the center. Clump former, not a spreader.

'Black Snowflake' has deeply cut leaves and each thin segment is almost purple. White flowers with a little pink tinge are produced.

'Black Velvet' produces moderately cut foliage with dark centers.

'Brandywine' is a large-leaved form (3-4″ wide) with light green heart-shaped leaves, each one with bold red venation.

'Candy Striper' is even more finely cut than 'Black Snowflake' and bears a purple stripe down each segment. Pink buds, white flowers.

'Crow Feather' produces brighter green leaves than many others, not as finely cut but also with lots of purple coloration.

'Cygnet' bears light pink flowers over mostly green leaves.

'Dark Eye' from Terra Nova is a vigorous grower and fills in rapidly. The burgundy center of the heart-shaped leaves accounts for its name.

'Dunvegan' is an old cultivar but still excellent and a selection of var. *collina*. These clump-forming plants produce dissected 5-lobed leaves and wonderful pinkish flowers. Plants were originally developed at the Brandywine Conservancy, Chadds Ford, Pennsylvania and introduced by Dunvegan Nursery.

'Eco Red Heart', from Don Jacobs, has deep red centers in the leaves and pink to white flowers.

'Elizabeth Oliver' produces deeply lobed leaves with deep burgundy and light pink flowers. Named for the daughter of the breeder (Charles Oliver).

'Filigree Lace' is a hybrid with 'Tiger Stripe' and *T. trifoliata* var. *laciniata* and has lacy cut foliage.

'Freckles' is a medium-sized foam flower with reddish spotting, giving the leaves a freckled appearance. From Terra Nova.

'Heronswood Mist' has been a favorite of mine with its light gray-green foliage sprinkled with subtle cream and pink coloration. Probably a var. *collina* selection.

'Ink Blot' is a medium to small selection with dark green leaves and blotches of red, particularly near the center.

'Iron Butterfly' bears red-marked cut-leaf foliage with handsome white flowers.

'Jeepers Creepers' has large leaves with purple markings and large white flowers.

'Laird of Skye' has little marking on the dark green leaves but they are handsomely scalloped. The white flowers contrast well with the yellow stamens. From Dunvegan Nursery.

'Mint Chocolate' bears light green flowers with a long primary lobe, each leaf overlain with purple.

'Neon Lights' are shallowly cut and have a good deal of purple markings on the shiny leaves. Early to flower.

'Oakleaf' (var. *collina*) was the first of the cultivated forms available to the American gardener and one which spurred the interest in the genus. The leaves somewhat resemble dark green oak leaves (fortunately, oak leaves are highly diverse). The buds and flowers are pink, later fading to white. A Dunvegan Nursery introduction.

'Pink Bouquet' is a selection that is worth talking about, because of the many pink flowers in the spring. Foliage is fine, but a good flowering plant to boot.

'Pink Skyrocket' provides a good combination of cut-leaf foliage, each leaf with a purple line down the center. The many pink flowers stand straight in the air above the leaves in the spring.

'Pinwheel' appears to be vigorous and has starry white flowers with narrow petals.

'Pirate's Patch' produces rounded, slightly cut leaves with a central purple patch. Many white to pink flowers are formed in the spring.

'Running Tapestry' has 2-3″ wide heart-shaped leaves with red venation, less obvious than the venation in 'Brandywine'. The white flowers appear above the 10-12″ flowering stems.

'Seafoam' forms dozens of white flowers over the deeply cut green and purple foliage.

'Slick Rock' is a vigorous running plant with small 2″ wide leaves with 5 lobes, the uppermost leaf being longer than the others. Plants were originally found by Jim Plyer near Slickrock Creek, North Carolina.

'Spring Symphony' has been in the Gardens at UGA for years. Even though there has been an explosion of newer cultivars, this is still the one I recommend to my daughters. Plants produce many white flowers, handsome green and bronze leaves, and perform better than any others in warm climates.
'Star Fish' has light green leaves with purple centers and light pink flowers.
'Sugar and Spice' produces shiny leaves marked in purple, and white flowers, each with a pink tinge.
'Tiger Stripe' has light green foliage with red veins. The flowers are white in early spring. Plants are vigorous.
'Winterglow' has large leaves flecked with red throughout and white flowers. The fall color is golden yellow, better than most others at that time of year.

***-trifoliata*** (tri-fo′ lee-ah-ta) Three Leaved Foam Flower 9-20″/24″
Spring White Western North America Zones 4-7

This species is almost unknown in gardens in the eastern United States, better so in the West because it is native to the Pacific Coast. Instead of entire lobed leaves, the foliage consists of three leaflets (trifoliate). The middle one has three lobes and the laterals two. The leaflets provide a more delicate appearance than the previous species, but the lovely bronze tint found in the others is not present in *T. trifoliata*. The flowers are minute, consisting of threadlike petals held in long, narrow panicles. Plants are less tolerant of heat and humidity than previous species and less suitable to gardens east of the Rockies.

Seed is the best means of propagation. Propagate similar to *T. cordifolia*.

**Related Species:**

*T. polyphylla* is native to China, Japan and the Himalayas and resembles *T. cordifolia*. The white flowers are more nodding than our native species and racemes are more branched. They are likely cold hardy only to zone 6, but insufficient data are available to be sure. In the Armitage garden, it was badly out-competed and out-performed by *T. cordifolia* and its cultivars.

## ***Tigridia*** (ti-gri′ dee-a) Tiger Flower Iridaceae

The botanical name is derived from the Latin *tigris* ("tiger") in reference to the spotted flowers. All 30 species of this colorful genus are native to South and Central America but only the showiest species, *T. pavonia*, is commonly offered for sale. Bulbs are consistently winter hardy only south of zone 8, and must be treated similar to gladiolus in the rest of the country. Plants are a fascinating addition to the garden and it always surprises me that so few people try them. Perhaps that individual flowers remain open for only a single day and that they clash with just about everything account for their absence. More than likely, you are like me—we simply forget to order them.

Plants are 20-24″ tall with a fan of basal leaves and 2-3 stem leaves. Flowers are 4-6″ wide and their riot of color and shape is almost impossible to describe. They are red, orange, yellow, or white and variously blotched with red or yellow in the center. The flower, which opens in early July in the South and as late as early September in the North, consists of 3 large outer segments and 3 smaller inner segments surrounding the speckled cuplike center. The flowers persist but a day (another common name is one-day lily), but the succession of bloom lasts for 2-4 weeks.

Plant 3-4″ deep in rich well-drained soils in full sun. The best cultural method is to treat them as annuals, replacing the bulbs each year. Although the foliage may return each year in zones 7 and 8, few flowers appear. Digging bulbs every fall and separating the bulbils is possible, but their relatively low cost justifies spring replacement.

**Cultivars:**

Generally they are available only as a mixture of colors but a few varieties may be obtained from specialists.

var. *alba immaculata* bears white flowers with centers free of spots. A number of cultivars are available without the spots in the center and all bear the "immaculata" name. *Tigridia* produces such exotic flowers; growing an unspotted form is like raising a spotless leopard.

***Tolmiea*** (toll-mee- a) Piggy Back Plant Saxifragaceae

I am so far behind the times that I look at this plant (*T. menziesii*) and still see a green nondescript houseplant, whose only reason for being is the neat-looking plantlets it's piggybacking. However with the coming out of houseplants everywhere (begonias, wandering Jews, etc.) it is no surprise to see these listed in the toniest of garden catalogs. That they are native to the western United States and Canada has also made them more palatable. Plants are said to be hardy to zone 6. That means it is hardy to –5°F, which for this old houseplant hound, is hard to believe. (I opt for zone 8 at best.)

Piggyback plants have heart-shaped green leaves and are usually seen in hanging baskets, but in today's gardens, they will be most often stuffed into outdoor containers. The flowers are small and of no ornamental interest. Plantlets will form under warm conditions by midsummer.

The genus is named after Dr. William Fraser Tolmie, 1830-1886, a Scottish physician and botanist. To propagate, remove one of the many plantlets and place in a small pot. Keep moist and humid.

**Cultivars:**

'Cool Gold', from Terra Nova Nursery, Oregon, has lovely clean chartreuse foliage which, I am told, will remain as such even in the heat of a southeastern summer. And even if they croak over the winter, they are easily propagated and certainly worth a try.

'Taffs Gold', found by Englishman Stephen Taffler, has pale green leaves with a slight golden hue. Somewhat golden, but not near as golden as the previous cultivar.

***Tovara*** (to-vah′ ra) See *Persicaria*

***Trachystemon*** (tra-kee-stay′ mon) Trachystemon Boraginaceae

What a plant this is. Given the right conditions, it may well take over the world, but in most gardens in North America, it simply produces big bold leaves and early blue flowers. Two species have been described but only *T. orientalis* is occasionally offered. It loves moist soils and spreads rapidly with wet feet and cool climes. Truthfully, the main reason to recommend it is because of its toughness. The roughly hairy 6-8″ long and 5-6″ wide leaves are ovate to cordate and look like burdock. I can grow burdock without having to buy it. Of course, I did buy it and placed in my shaded back section. I now have my own patch of $6.95 burdock.

However, the blue flowers, which resemble borage, are really quite beautiful and arise very early in the spring prior to the foliage. This plant looks like an aggressive weed. In cooler, moister climates and a sunnier location than where it camps in the Armitage garden, it can become a nuisance.

Propagate by seed or division after flowering.

***Tradescantia*** (tra-des-kant′ ee-a) Spiderwort Commelinaceae

Approximately 70 species of tender and hardy plants are named after John Tradescant, the English horticulturist and botanist. He received a plant from a friend in Virginia that was subsequently named *Tradescantia virginiana* by Linneaus. The genus commemorates both father and son, Tradescant the Younger, who traveled to Virginia in 1637 and brought back to England such staples as Virginia creeper and Michaelmas daisies. Tradescant the Elder became gardener to Charles I in 1629 and was followed by his son, after the Elder's death in 1638.

Many medicinal attributes are given to the plants. The Cherokee used spiderwort for female and kidney problems, as well as for digestive ailments. Others suggest rubbing the leaves on spider and insect bites.

Several ornamental species are native to the United States. *T. hirsuticaulis* is a compact species (18-24″ tall) with dark purple flowers somewhat hidden in the light green, straplike foliage. *T. ohiensis* has 3′ tall stems which bear light blue flowers about 1″ across. Although these species are occasionally seen in gardens, it is the hybrids of *T. virginiana*, often offered under the invalid name of *T.* x *andersoniana* that are commonly available.

-***sillamontana*** (sill-a-mon′ tan-a) Hairy Spiderwort 6-9″/24″
Summer Pink Mexico Zones 7b-9

I have been so impressed with the species in the Gardens at UGA that I wanted to include it, even though some may argue its perenniality. Okay, so this is North Georgia, not North Platte, and I expect it to die there, but every spring, plants came back with vigor for us. The small green foliage is covered with thin white hairs, and the flowers are pink. Plants tolerate some afternoon shade but unless you drown them, they are as tough as nails. I am not sure of the hardiness, perhaps to 7a, probably not to North Platte. They are wonderful ground covers, could certainly be used as basket and container plants as well.

**Cultivars**:

'White Velvet' has grayer leaves and is more densely covered in cobwebs. It is even more ornamental than the species.

***-virginiana*** (an-der-son-ee-aye′ na) Spiderwort 1-2′/3′
Summer Variable Eastern United States Zones 5-9

Plants of Virginia spiderwort are characterized by dense, dull green, 18″ long linear foliage that declines after flowering. Many flower buds are formed in terminal umbels and although each flower opens for one day, flowering continues for 8 weeks. The flower parts occur in threes: 3 sepals, 3 petals, and 6 stamens form the 1-3″ diameter flower. They usually occur in blue to purple hues but pink-, white-, and red-flowered cultivars are available. These are easy plants to recognize as they are one of the few low-growing plants with 3 petals found in the garden.

*T.* x *andersoniana* was proposed by Anderson and Woodson in 1935 who were puzzled by the variation within the hardy species of the American genus. The name was proposed for the cross between *T. ohiensis*, *T. subaspera*, and *T. virginiana*. Apparently, at the time, the name was invalid due to a lack of description. However, there is little doubt that the dozens of cultivars offered are far more complex than simply being selections of the species. Today, most cultivars have been accepted under the moniker of Andersoniana Group. I think this makes sense.

From the garden point of view, essentially all cultivars are hybrids, whether the tag says so or not. Plant in full sun in any well-drained garden soil. Plants grow well, but produce fewer flowers, in partial shade in well-drained moist soil. Divide to rejuvenate the clump every 2 to 3 years. When the foliage declines, cut back to 8-12″. New foliage reappears in the fall. Plants can reseed and become a pest.

Propagate all cultivars by division in spring or fall.

**Cultivars and Hybrids**:

Most are hardy in zones 5-8.

*Blue or purple flowers*:

'Barbel' is about 2′ tall, with large (1-1½″ wide) flowers in late summer.

'Blue Denim' is really a fine choice, bearing lavender blue flowers over 24-30″ long gray-green leaves.

'Bluestone' bears mid blue flowers.

var. *caerulea plena* is a variety of *T. virginiana* and has double dark blue flowers.

'Concord Grape' is a hybrid from Dr. Kevin Vaughn at USDA and bears grape-colored flowers in mid to late summer. An excellent compact form.

'Isis' has Oxford blue 3″ diameter flowers. This is one of the best blue selections.

'J.C. Weguelin' is an excellent, vigorous cultivar with 2½″ wide China blue flowers.

'Leonora' has violet-blue flowers on 18″ tall plants.

'Little Doll' is a compact plant with light blue flowers for 4-6 weeks.

'Pauline' bears lilac flowers about 2-2½″ wide.

'Purple Dome' stands about 2′ tall and is laden with flowers of rich purple.

'Purple Profusion' has more narrow foliage and purple flowers on a compact habit.

'Sweet Kate', originally known as 'Blue and Gold', is one of the better-known forms because of the chartreuse foliage. In the spring, the leaves are shimmering yellow and make an eye-popping contrast with the purple flowers. The foliage color declines in the summer. Discovered in the garden of Mrs. H.J. Stevens of Kent Co., UK and named after her daughter Kate. Plants were first introduced by Hillier Nurseries in England. This is not for people with pacemakers; in fact it is gaudy as a velvet Elvis painting. Nothing personal, Kate.

'Valor' is 18-24″ tall and bears crimson-purple flowers.

'Zwanenburg Blue' bears 3″ wide, deep blue flowers.

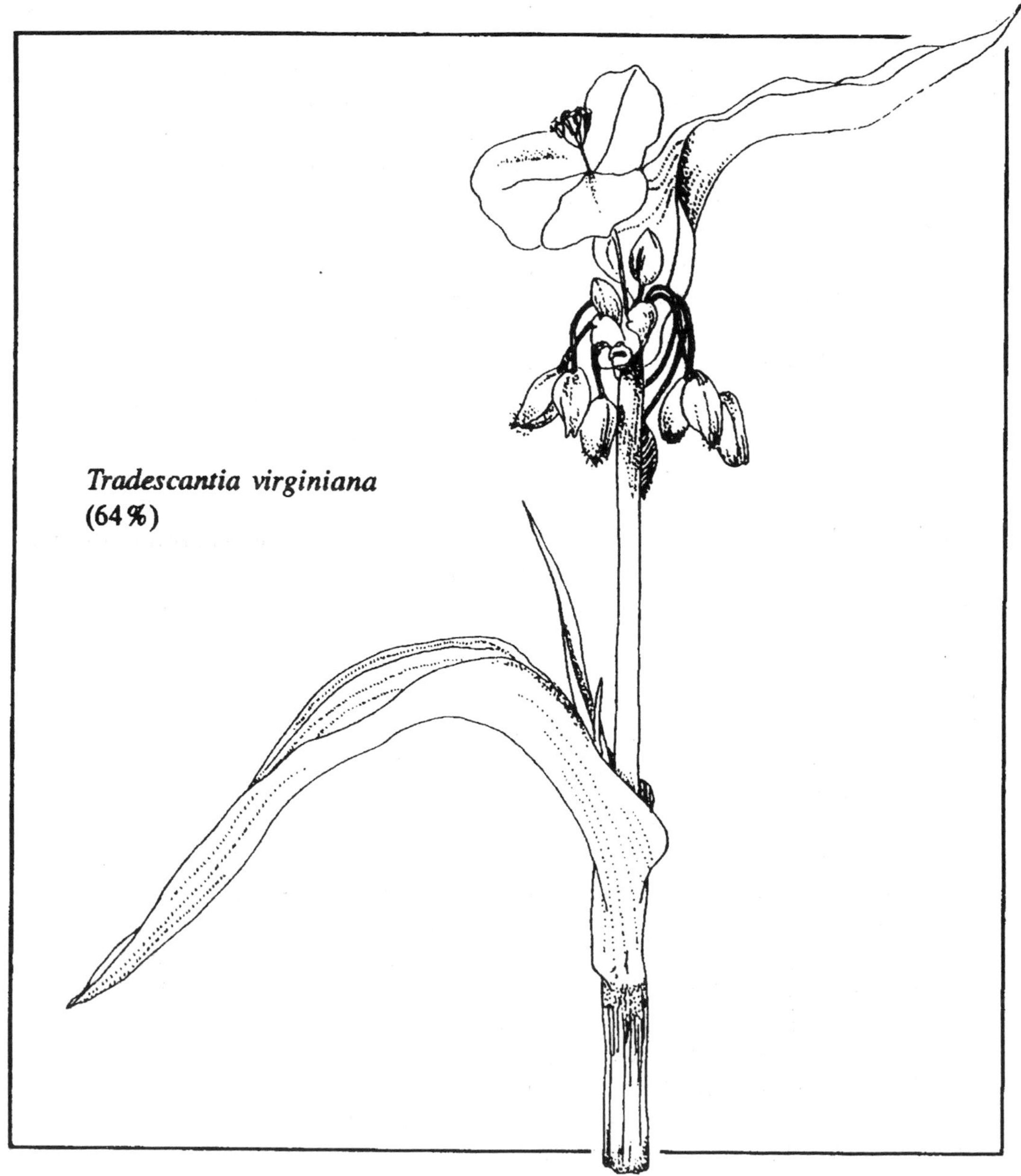

*Tradescantia virginiana*
**(64%)**

*Carmine, pink or red flowers*:
'Carmine Glow' has deep carmine flowers.
'Hawaiian Punch' bears many pink to purple flowers and good green foliage. Similar to 'Red Cloud'.
'Pauline' offers flowers described as orchid pink.
'Perrine's Pink' is about 18″ tall with clear pink flowers.
'Purewell Giant' bears flowers between deep rose and purple.
'Red Cloud' has rosy red blooms on 2′ tall plants. One of the best cultivars available.
'Red Grape' provides small red flowers on 18″ tall plants.
'Rosi' produces lilac-rose flowers and grows about 20″ tall.
'Rubra' is a variety of *T. virginiana* and bears red flowers.
'Satin Doll' bears pink flowers and obvious yellow anthers.

*White flowers*:
'Bilberry Ice' has white flowers with a blue tint on the margins and a dark purple stripe along the center of the petal.
'Innocence' has large creamy white flowers.
'Iris Pritchard' bears pure white flowers suffused with violet.
'Osprey' has large blue feathery stamens that contrast well with the large white flowers.
'Snowcap' is probably the purest white form with 2½-3″ wide flowers.

**Additional Species:**

*T. bracteata* is native to the Midwest and forms clumps with narrow foliage. The flowers are usually rose but may be white or blue. 'Angel Eyes' has blush white flowers with obvious purple centers and yellow stamens.

*T. hirsuticaulis* is only about a foot tall with deep purple flowers and contrasting yellow stamens. A wonderful native form.

*T. ohiensis* is native to meadows, edges of woods and from Massachusetts to Minnesota, south to Florida to Texas. Plants produce blue-gray leaves with blue or purple flowers in late spring and summer. Plants are more sun tolerant than some of the other species or hybrids. One of the finest spiderworts we have grown at UGA is 'Mrs. Loewer', from the brilliant folks at North Creek Nurseries in Pennsylvania. This plant provide gray-green grassy leaves, about 2′ tall, and hundreds of pale blue flowers. It looks awful at times, but fabulous most of the time. Zones 4-8.

*T. tharpii*, Tharp's spiderwort, is native to Kansas and produces low (8″ tall) mounds with deep pink to lavender flowers. Plants are tolerant of full sun and dry conditions. A 2003 introduction in the Great Plants® Program in Nebraska. Zones 4-8.

## ***Tricyrtis*** (tri-ser′ tis) Toad-Lily Convallariaceae

Let's dispense with seriousness here, and get to the spirit of gardeners. Sure, these plants are good for shade, bloom in the fall, and have a cute common name, but to talk openly, with pride, about toad-lilies is the sign of a gardener out of the closet. They are purple, for goodness sake, and not even a great purple at that. That they have a particular personality is difficult to explain, and they are often grown because they are unusual rather than showy. The flowers, however, never fail to elicit conversation and their curious beauty should be admired close up. If you're pointing out a toad-lily, I can almost guarantee that you will be asked the origin of the common name; a name like toad-lily doesn't easily slip through the conversation unnoticed. So here is where the fun begins.

Ask those gathered around the toad lilies (stash a bottle of Merlot in the clump to get them there, may be the only way) what their mothers (grandmothers) told them about handling toads. Yes, the tale is still passed down: nearly everyone will say "warts". Now take a flower and turn it over, there you will see the three warts! I can almost guarantee that the group will smile, exclaim and drink more Merlot than ever before. They will also never remember *Tricyrtis* or toad-lily, but will remember the "wart flower". Be a teacher, have fun.

Actually, the name probably came from their spotted flowers, however, with the discovery of *T. imeldae*, (named after the shoe lady of the Philippines), on Mindanao in the Philippines, a more descriptive account was provided. The area where this species was found is occupied by the Tasaday tribe, who rub the juice from the flowers and leaves on their hands before setting out to collect frogs: apparently it is considered attractive to frogs and makes them less slippery. Perhaps they should be called frog-lilies. I still like wart flower better.

Several species form compact clumps, although some are stoloniferous and form large patches. They grow from 6″ up to 3′ tall, usually with arching stems. The flowers are terminal or, more often, occur in the axils of the leaves, and consist of 6 tepals (sepals and petals look alike) and 6 stamens. Most selections open in the fall when few other plants are in flower and continue for at least 6 weeks, however, a few species such as the yellow-green flowered *T. latifolia* bloom as early as June.

One of our finest plant breeders, Darrell Probst, of Hubbardston, Massachusetts (see *Epimedium* as well), set his sights on the genus and has produced a ton of excellent new hybrids. Similarly, plant explorer Barry Yinger's numerous trips to Asia have resulted in many new offerings. Flowers of most species are shades of purple but yellow, tricolors and white can be found.

Plants of this genus, along with many other favorites like *Maianthemum*, *Polygonatum* and *Smilacina* have been removed from the lily family and placed in Convallariaceae. The only constant change is change itself.

Quick Reference to Tricyrtis Species

| | Height (ft.) | Roots stoloniferous | Base of leaves clasping the stems | Flower color |
|---|---|---|---|---|
| *T. formosana* | 1-2 | Yes | No | Crimson spots |
| *T. hirta* | 2-3 | No | Yes | White, crimson spots |
| *T. macranthopsis* | 1-2 | Yes | Yes | Yellow |
| *T. macropoda* | 2-3 | Yes | No | White, purple spots |

***-formosana*** (for-mo′ sah-na) Formosa Toad-Lily 1-2′/2′
Late Summer Lilac Taiwan Zones 4-9

This species itself is not as well known as the next but is an important parent in many of the hybrids. Often listed as *T. stolonifera*, recent studies have shown that *T. formosana* and *T. stolonifera* are closely related, and often combined as *T. formosana* Stolonifera Group.

The lower leaves are 4-5″ long and the upper are about 1″ wide with widely spaced internodes. The leaves are hairy on the undersides, particularly along the veins. The flowers are held in terminal cymes and open over a long period. Although borne in the terminals first, flowers subsequently appear in the top 4 to 6 leaf axils. They are funnel shaped, about an inch long and a half inch wide. The background color is white to slightly pinkish and the interior is prominently spotted with crimson and with a small yellow eye in the center. The filaments and styles are spotted crimson. They are impossible to describe, but really interesting to look at. In northern Georgia (zone 7b), flowers open the second week of September and persist until frost. The roots are stoloniferous and if grown in moist, semi-shady conditions, a large colony develops in 3-5 years. It is not, however, invasive. This is the best garden species because of the flower size, color, and longevity.

Division is the propagation method of choice, accomplished in early spring. Seed may also be sown in a cold frame in the fall or early spring. Plants require about 6 months to reach transplantable size.

**Cultivars:**

According to breeders and distributors, these are probably selections of this species, but I would not be surprised if some were hybrids as well.

'Alba' has clean white flowers with crimson spots. Contrasts better with the foliage than the more common pink flowers.

'Amethystina' has bluish purple flowers with a white throat spotted with red. It opens earlier than the species, flowering from late July until frost. Introduced by John Elsley, formerly of Wayside Gardens, it is spectacular. One of my all-time favorites.

'Autumn Glow' bears leaves with thin yellow margins and purple flowers in the fall.

'Emperor' is stoloniferous and was selected by Plant Delights Nursery in North Carolina. The plant produces golden leaves, each one surrounded by a creamy white edge. Plants bear orchid-like flowers.

***-hirta*** (hir′ ta) Common Toad-Lily 2-3′/2′
Late Summer Lilac Japan Zones 4-8

The common species has 2-3′ long gracefully arching stems. The stems carry many closely-set, clasping, soft-hairy pointed leaves about 3-6″ long and 1-2″ wide. In each leaf axil, one to three 1″ diameter flowers, which typically have a whitish or pale purple background covered with darker purple spots and blotches, are carried on short stalks (pedicels). Flowers also occur at the end of the stems.

Flowering begins in mid September in the South, a week or two later in the North, but is not as persistent as *T. formosana*. In our gardens, flowering was completed by mid October whereas the flowers of *T. formosana* continued for an additional 3 weeks. The roots are not stoloniferous and large clumps do not form, however, there has been some hybridization between this and *T. formosana*. Moist, fertile soil in partial shade is ideal.

***Tricyrtis hirta***
**(64%)**

Divide in the early spring while plants are still dormant. Seed propagation is similar to *T. formosana*. Seeds collected from garden plants may not be true if other species are grown nearby.

**Cultivars:**

As with the listing of *T. formosana*, many of these may well be hybrids.

'Alba' has greenish white flowers with pink stamens.

var. *albescens* has cleaner white flowers than 'Alba'.

'Guilty Pleasure' bears golden foliage and light lilac flowers. Not as vigorous as green-leaved plants, but quite lovely.

'Lilac Towers' bears flowers in the axils on long arching stems. The flowers have a white background with lilac spotting. 'Lilac Towers' and 'White Towers' may be hybrids between *T. hirta* and *T. affinis*, a short, white-flowered species.

var. *masamunei* has leaves without hairs but otherwise is similar to the species. It is seldom seen in gardens.

'Miyazaki' appears to be a hybrid between *T. hirta* and *T. formosana* with graceful arching stems and lovely pink to white axillary flowers with crimson spots that open in early fall. An exceptionally good plant.

'Miyazaki Gold' is similar to the above but with gold-edged leaves.

'Moonlight' came from Bluebird Nursery in Nebraska and bears golden leaves and lilac flowers. Plants are 15-18″ tall and were selected from *T. hirta* 'Variegata'.

'Raspberry Mousse' comes from Sunny Border Nursery in Connecticut and is about 2′ tall and 18″ wide. Flowers begin to open in late summer and are a dark chocolate-purple (I have no idea what raspberry mousse looks like, so maybe my description is close).

'Variegata' bears lavender flowers and gold-edged leaves. This is still one of the best and most vigorous variegated forms.

'White Towers' has 3′ long arching to almost horizontal stems with pure white flowers along the axils. More vigorous than the other white forms, but that may not be saying much.

***-macranthopsis*** (ma-kranth-op′ sis) Yellow Toad-Lily 1-2′/2′
Late Summer Yellow Japan Zones 6-8

This is a wonderful, little-known form of the genus, which tolerates rather heavy shade and bears 1-4 yellow flowers from the axils of arching 1-3′ long stems. I first saw this plant in the fine garden of Willis Hardin of Homeplace Nursery in Commerce, Georgia. He is one of the best gardeners in the state and tries, usually successfully, plants that "should not grow". In his garden, *T. macranthopsis* was everywhere, obviously enjoying the pine shade, moist conditions and woodland soils. In the Armitage garden, they were not quite as happy. Leaves are 3-5″ long and 1-2″ wide and pointed at the apices. The base of each leaf tends to clasp the stem. The flowers are about 1½″ long and have subtle brown spots within. Some authorities reclassify this as *T. macrantha* var. *macranthopsis*.

***-macropoda*** (ma-kro′ po-da) Toad-Lily 2-3′/2′
Late Summer Lavender China Zones 5-8

The stems do not arch over but are upright, similar to the growth habit of *T. formosana*. The oblong to ovate leaves, which measure about 4″ long and 2″ wide, are sessile or with a very short stalk and do not clasp the stem. Flowers are held mostly terminally but some are also borne in the leaf axils. They are erect, lavender or white with small purple spots and the outer petals are reflexed.

**Related Species:**

*T. affinis* is rather boring, with green leaves and small purplish flowers. However, Probst has introduced 'Key Lime Pie' with interesting bicolor (dark green in the middle, lighter green on the edges) foliage on 2-3′ tall plants. His 'Lunar Landing' is also beautiful, at least in the container, as it provides silvery foliage. The breeding is outstanding; the garden performance has yet to be intensely evaluated. Zones 5-8.

*T. lasiocarpa* has somewhat mottled growth in the spring, and is characterized by light lilac flowers, late in the fall.

*T. latifolia* has terminal primrose-yellow flowers with brown spots within. The 3′ tall plants flower as early as June, but usually in July to early August.

*T. macrantha* is similar in habit, flowering tine and flower color to *T. macanthopsis* but the leaves do not clasp the stem. Both basal lobes are on the upper side of the stem. The yellow flowers have red markings inside. This is a more difficult species to find than other yellow-flowered forms.

*T. nana*, crow leaf toad-lily is a dwarf species that has yellow flowers in the axils of green leaves on plants less than 8″ in height. 'Karasuba' has darker green leaves. Hardy to zone 4.

*T. ohsumiensis* produces compact clumps of light green leaves with creamy white markings. Plants bear bright yellow flowers in early fall. Hardy in zones 4-8. 'Nakatsugawa' is offered by Plant Delights Nursery and bears variegated leaves much like those of hosta. Similar foliage description has also been made with 'Imperial Banner', a hybrid with *T. hirta* and *T. formosana*.

**Hybrids:**

Hybrids have become popular recently. However, the parentage of many is puzzling and the new ones have not been grown for sufficient lengths of time to ascertain hardiness or performance in many areas. These hybrids come and go like snowflakes, so what is available yesterday might not be available today.

'Blue Wonder' is not blue, but rather lilac with light purple spots on the flowers. Wishful thinking is good, but the plant forgot to listen. Plants are 14-18″ tall.

'Empress' is relatively tall (24-32″) and bears large flowers that have a white background and many purple spots. An excellent performer.

'Gilt Edge' can be a stunning plant and has looked particularly good in the Gardens at UGA. The light green leaves have gold margins and orchid flowers. Handsome and different from most other cultivars.

'Golden Gleam' ('Golden Form') is as handsome in leaf as it is in flower. The leaves on the 18-20″ long stems are lime green, although they fade somewhat in hot summers, and the dark purple flowers occur in early fall. None of the gold forms tolerates high heat and humidity at all well.

'Imperial Banner' has the cleanest variegated leaves of all selections I have seen, almost looking like variegated hosta leaves. The white and green foliage contrast with lilac flowers in the fall. Highly variegated cultivars have historically lacked vigor, but perhaps this will prove to be better.

'Jasmin' is a hybrid between *T. hirta* and *T. formosana* and the flowers (which are mainly axillary) are white with dark purple spots. Closer to the latter species than the former.

'Kohaku' is a hybrid of *T. macranthopsis* and *T. hirta*. Plants bear arching 18″ long stems and large cream-white flowers with brown spots along the axils. The arching stems result in a plant less than 12″ tall.

'Lemon Lime' has green-yellow foliage with light bands of green on 18″ stems. The flowers are lilac.

'Lemon Twist', one of the many fine hybrids from Darrell Probst, has large green leaves speckled with yellow markings and light yellow flowers in the fall. About a foot tall and equally wide. A hybrid between *T. flava* and *T. ohsumiensis*.

'Lightning Strike' has interesting gold-striped leaves that are lighter in the middle and dark green along the edges. Lavender flowers occur in the fall. Terrific in the spring.

'Moonlight Treasure' is 10-12″ tall. The large, light yellow flowers are formed in the axils of the thick leaves, each spotted with silver markings. Perhaps a hybrid of *T. ohsumiensis* and *T. nana*.

'Samurai' is a vigorous grower with white margins on the leaves and lilac flowers (not as spotted purple). One of the best for variegated foliage.

'Seiryu' is similar to *T. formosana* 'Amethystina' but is more stoloniferous and forms clumps within a couple of years. The flowers open in early fall.

'Shining Light' produces yellow leaves with green margins. Compact and beautiful in the spring, but not sufficiently vigorous to do well in inclement summer climates.

'Sinonome' produces white flowers with purple speckling. Plants multiply by stolons to produce a good-sized clump. This old selection is still among the best, performing well throughout the country.

'Taipei Silk' stood out in the Gardens at UGA from the dozens of others we were trialing, and that is not an easy thing to do. The silky lilac flowers opened in mid to late summer and positively glowed. Nothing fancy about the foliage, just an exceptionally good flowering form.

'Taiwan Adbane' is vigorous and although the name is less than attractive, this thing just grows. I was not going to include it until I found a couple of nurseries selling it. A good thing, too, as the purple flowers occur from late August through October. Its only drawback is that it needs dividing a little too often.

'Togen' has some of the largest leaves in the genus (about 3 times larger than most others) on 2-3′ long stems. The lavender flowers are mostly terminal. A great selection for the impressive foliage.

'Tricolor' appears to be a selection of *T. affinis* but lacks vigor. The leaves are yellow, white and flushed with a little pink in the spring. Very slow grower.

'White Flame' has white leaves with green variegations. The spotted lavender flowers are borne in late summer and fall. Plants grow 18-24″ tall.

***Trillium*** (tril-lee′ um) Trillium Liliaceae

Although many trilliums occur in Asia, they are the epitome of the American wild flower. Trilliums have never been part of the European flora, nor have they occupied the Southern Hemisphere. They are represented in East Asia and temperate North America, and nowhere else, the largest number by far existing in the southern Appalachian Mountains . There are about 45 species and many are similar, making accurate identification difficult.

The species are divided by the presence (pedunculate) or absence of a flower stalk (sessile) and there are about an equal number of species in each. Most people find the pedunculate species more ornamental but I love both groups. I still laugh at myself when I read my comments in the first edition, in which I dismissed most of the sessile species as "unexceptional". I am a born-again trillite.

All trilliums are cherished in woodlands and gardens and people's passion for them has resulted in many trilliums being dug indiscriminately from the wild to end up dead in suburbia. The issue of digging wild flowers is no more relevant than when it comes to trilliums. Digging from a native stand when the plants are visible, that is, when they are in leaf or in flower, is not smart ecologically but even dumber horticulturally. Plants will die—end of story! One person digging five plants for her garden is probably not going to have a major impact on the population; wholesale suppliers digging illegally, on the other hand, can. Many people contend that digging a few plants helps the population by spreading them around to other areas where they can multiply. This is a valid statement if plants are in danger from construction, flooding or other potential problems. I know many people who have saved many wild flowers from destruction and I know a few who use that reason to explain away their robberies. Let's face it, people will dig some plants, but hopefully the hue and cry against digging is having an effect. Certainly, if plants must be dug, wait until they are dormant, otherwise you are committing wild flower murder. Nurseries are now propagating trilliums and other wild flowers. Nursery-grown plants may be expensive but they have an excellent chance of survival and are not disrupting any stands. Enough said!

I cannot imagine the Armitage garden without trilliums, and numerous species vie for attention with epimediums and Virginia bluebells. The expense for the plants is negligible compared to the pleasure they bring me every spring.

All species bear single stems with 3 whorled leaves and a solitary flower, each flower with 3 leaflike outer sepals and 3 petals and 6 stamens. The color and shape of the flower, leaf shape, and amount of leaf mottling are distinguishing characteristics between species, but some species are very difficult to tell apart.

I highly recommend a couple of excellent books for trillium lovers, both available online or at good bookstores: *American Treasures*, by Dan and Rob Jacobs, and *Trilliums*, by Frederick and Roberta Case, both published in 1997.

Quick Reference to Trillium Species

| | Flowers with peduncle | Flower color |
|---|---|---|
| *T. catesbaei* | Yes | Pink |
| *T. cernuum* | Yes | White |
| *T. cuneatum* | No | Maroon, purple |
| *T. erectum* | Yes | Maroon |
| *T. flexipes* | Yes | White |
| *T. grandiflorum* | Yes | White |
| *T. luteum* | No | Yellow |
| *T. sessile* | No | Maroon |
| *T. stamineum* | No | Maroon |

***-catesbaei*** (kats-be′ eye) Rose Trillium 10-12″/10″
Spring White Southeast United States Zones 7-9

The rose trillium is one of the more common Southern trilliums and is easily recognized by the wavy margins of the leaves that turn upward, and the rose-colored flower beneath the canopy of leaves. The flower is declined, meaning that is seldom erect, and often hugs the plant stem beneath the leaves. The petals often emerge white but later turn rose to pink. All parts of the flower (petals, sepals and mature stamens) are reflexed (turned up). A beautiful pedunculate trillium, but one that requires a lot of bending and lying down to appreciate.

***-grandiflorum*** (grand-i-flor′ um) Great White Trillium 18-24″/2′
Spring White, Pink Eastern North America Zones 3-7

Every time I read about the species, I find another common name listed. It is known as wake-robin, showy trillium, snow trillium, wood lily, great white trillium, and trinity flower. Plants occur as far northeast as Quebec, west to Minnesota, southwest to Missouri and south to northern Georgia, and have the widest range of any species. The sessile leaves are often wavy and may be up to 6″ long, although 3-4″ is more common. The pedunculate flowers consist of 3 large flaring petals with wavy edges, subtended by 3 smaller greenish sepals. The 2-3″ wide flower usually opens white then fades to a soft pink. About 6-8 weeks after flowering, white berries are produced. Foliage persists only to late summer, particularly if plants are allowed to dry out regularly.

Rhizomes should be planted approximately 4″ deep in highly organic, moist, well-drained soils in partial to heavy shade. Soils should be neutral to slightly acidic. The addition of well-rotted compost such as aged manure or crumbled leaves results in more rapid growth and larger plants. Interplant with other species of trilliums or with hepaticas, wild gingers, bloodroot or native ferns. If plants are stressed due to poor soil or lack of shade, they will rapidly perish.

This is probably the most ornamental and the most abused trillium of the woods. More plants have been dug—the majority dying—than all other wild flowers combined. This may have made some sense at one time when few nurseries propagated wild flowers, but today plants are offered by many mail order and local nurseries for reasonable prices. Unfortunately a few disreputable nurseries still dig from the wild. Nature takes years to build up a colony but man requires only five minutes and a shovel to destroy it.

Propagation of the plant was studied by Dr. Harry Phillips of the University of North Carolina. He demonstrated that propagation by seed is a long process, generally taking up to 8-12 months for germination and 2 to 3 years to produce a flowering plant. The seeds should be inspected as the berries ripen (about 5-6 weeks after flowers open). Seeds are mature when they are a dark russet color and should be sown immediately. Sow in a moist medium and allow the seed flat to overwinter in a protected area. Germination occurs the next spring. If seeds are purchased they will be dormant and much slower to germinate. Eight years for germination have been reported. Removing the soil around the base of the plant and cutting a V-shaped groove along the length of the rhizome causes the production of bulblets which may be removed one year later. The wound should be dusted with fungicide prior to replanting.

**Cultivars:**

var. *roseum* is an absolutely magnificent pink-flowered form. I remember first seeing in the garden of Mrs. Gertrude Wister in Swarthmore, Pennsylvania, one of the finest shade gardens anywhere, here or abroad. Colonies of pink trilliums shone like rosy beacons from the beds of green throughout the garden. Some authorities feel this form is simply a variation of natural flower color and should not be treated as a separate variety.

'Flore-pleno', a double form, is beloved or disliked with equal fervor. Some find the flowers unobtrusive and charming while others feel the doubleness reduces the natural charm of the plant and replaces it with artificiality. I happen to agree with the latter opinion.

| ***-cuneatum*** (coon-ee′ aye-tum) | | Toad Trillium | 6-12″/9″ |
|---|---|---|---|
| Spring | Maroon | Eastern United States | Zones 4-7 |

Of the many sessile-flowered trilliums, the toad trillium is appreciated as much for the wonderfully mottled leaves as for the rather difficult-to-love maroon flowers squatting atop the leafy throne. There appears to be more variability in this species than in other sessile-flowered forms. Usually strongly mottled, the maroon to bronze flower petals may be 1-3″ long and leaves may be broadly ovate to slightly so. For me, trying to distinguish between the numerous maroon sessile-flowered species is an exercise in frustration. They all really are similar in appearance, so I simply enjoy them and have long given up worrying what they are. Few of these species will be available as nursery-grown plants and wandering with a guide through the woods on a Saturday morning may be the closest you will come to seeing more than a few of these plants at a time. If you can find nursery-grown plants, forget about their name (it will likely be incorrect anyway), plant them and enjoy them in your garden.

**Related Species:**

*Sessile forms:*

*T. lancifolium* has leaves much more narrow than they are long and flowers have long, narrow petals.

*T. luteum*, yellow trillium, has long narrow petals which are generally light yellow or bronze-green. The flowers are also sweetly scented. Hardy to zone 5.

*T. recurvatum* has recurved sepals that hug the stem, and the tips of the petals that curve inward and often touch each other.

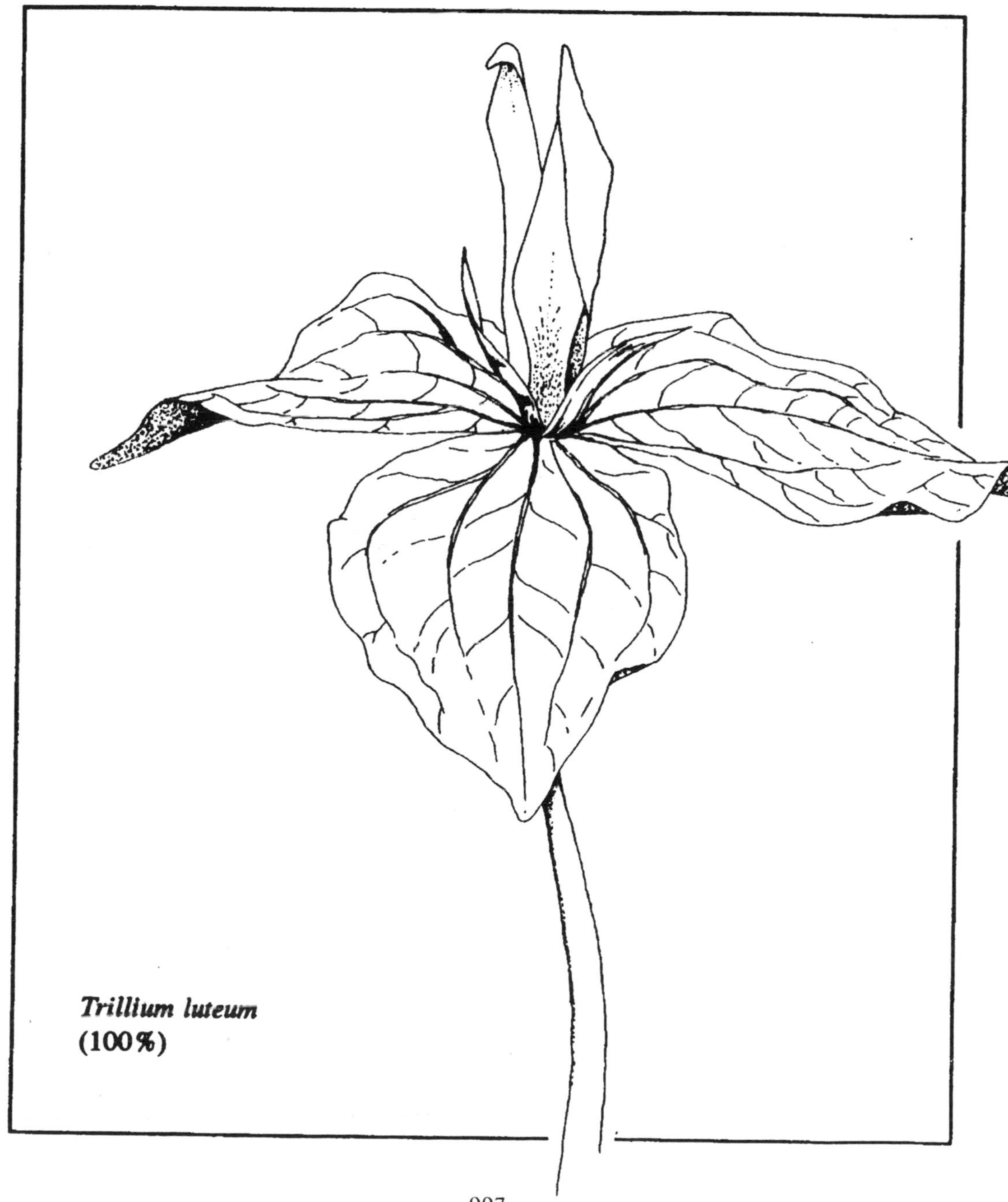

***Trillium luteum***
**(100%)**

*T. reliquum* is one of the largest, and certainly one of the most noble of the mottled purple-flowered sessile trilliums.

*T. sessile* is similar but shorter and with shorter petals, broader leaves and essentially no mottling (at least when in flower) compared to *T. cuneatum*. When the plants emerge from the ground, they may be mottled but this disappears as they mature.

*T. stamineum* is easy to distinguish by the twisted purple petals.

*T. underwoodii* is one of the first sessile forms to emerge and flower in my garden. The foliage is remarkably mottled with dark green, light green and silver, impossible to describe, but spectacular. The purple flowers resemble those of the toad trilliums and are handsome in their own right. Native to the Southeast to Florida, it tolerates heat well, and stands up in Southern gardens.

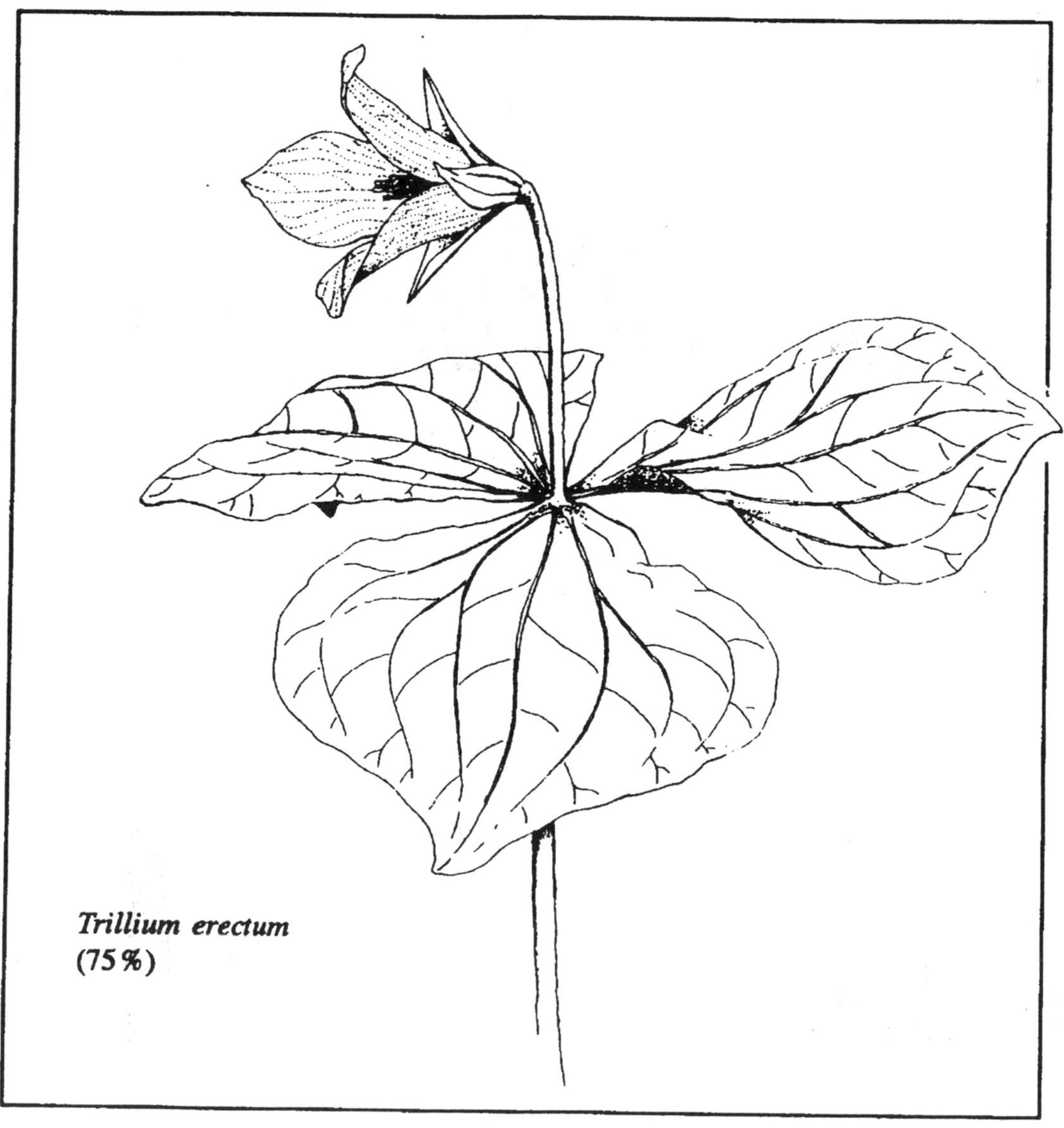

***Trillium erectum***
**(75%)**

*Pedunculate forms:*

*T. cernuum*, nodding trillium, is another pedunculate plant whose flower is tucked beneath the leaves and seldom raises its head to be seen. The flowers are white with purple anthers and the leaves have short petioles. The petals flare back exposing the anthers like shooting arrows. Plants are native from Newfoundland across Canada, down through Illinois, Iowa and south to the mountains of Georgia.

*T. erectum*, stinking Benjamin, bcars much more erect flowers and rhomboidal leaves (leaves wider in center, pointed at both ends). The flowers are usually purple but white (f. *albiflorum*) and light yellow (forma *luteum*) forms also occur. The purple flowers are malodorous but the non-purple forms lack the disagreeable smell.

*T. flexipes* has pure white flowers on long pedicels, held horizontally or level with the leaves. The petals are spreading to give the flower a somewhat flattened appearance

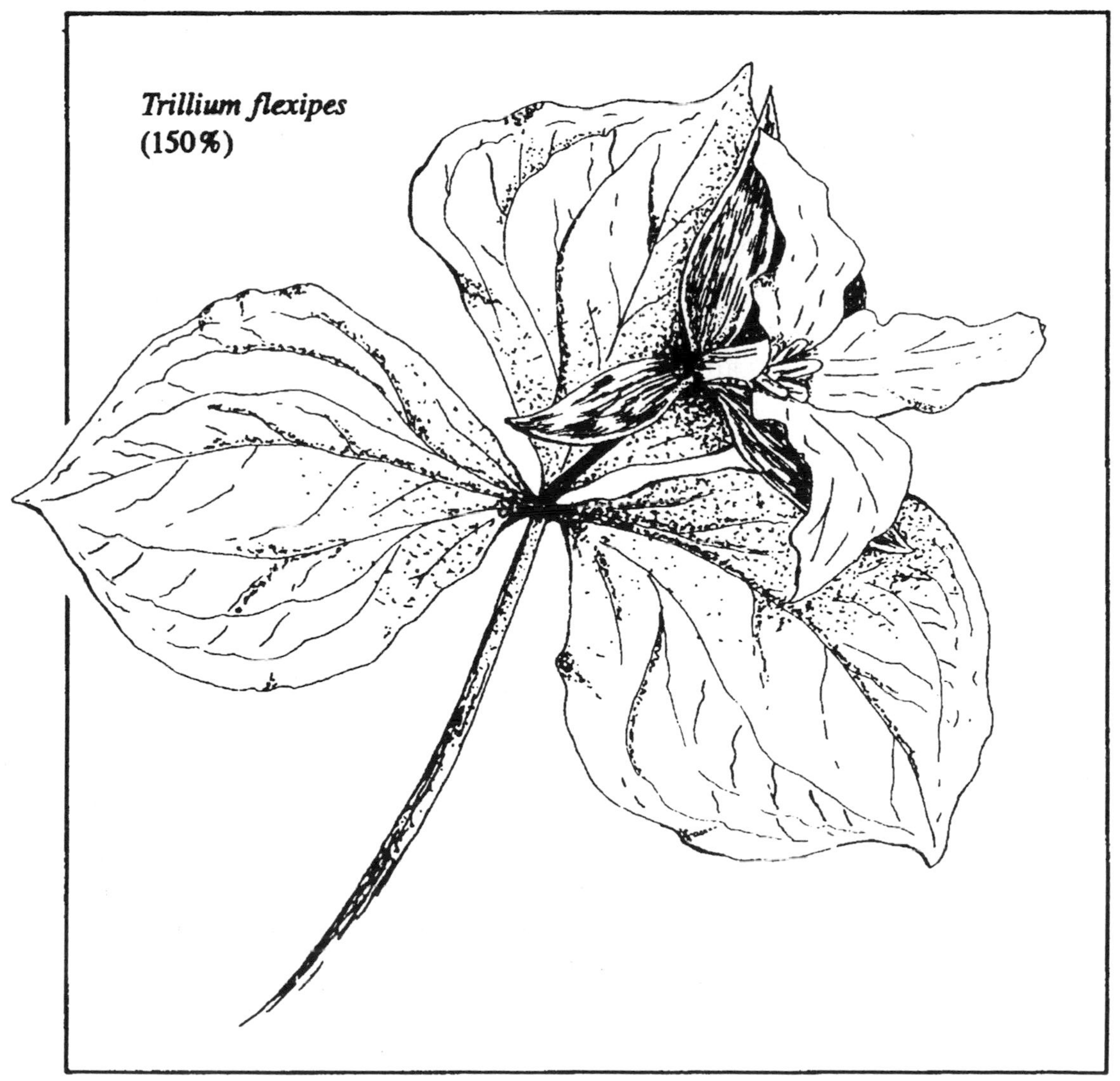
**Trillium flexipes (150%)**

and are occasionally flushed with pink. The leaves are more ovate than rhomboid. The lack of a maroon center and the erect flower are the most obvious characteristics of the species. I think this is my favorite of all the pedunculate forms.

*T. pusilum* is a dwarf (4-8″) species with narrow leaves and rosy red flower. var. *pusilum* is even shorter.

*T. rugelii* is the Southern equivalent to *T. cernuum*. The plants and flowers are bigger, and flowering occurs earlier, at least in the Armitage garden. Occasionally, plants will bear flowers with red on the petals, but this is not common.

## ***Trollius*** (tro′ lee-us) Globeflower Ranunculaceae

About 20 species are native to Europe, Asia, and North America and all are suited to moist, heavy soils. They are not tolerant of heat or drought and perform poorly south of zone 6. However, where cool, moist soils exist, *Trollius* is not difficult to grow in sun or partial shade. If this condition is fulfilled, plants may succeed as far south as zone 7a. The dark green foliage is palmately divided or lobed and often declines by mid to late summer. The foliage of most species should be pruned at that time. The orange to yellow solitary flowers consist of showy sepals. The small petals are found in the midst of the stamens and their size relative to the stamens is a useful identification characteristic.

Propagate by division in late fall or early spring; a year is necessary for plants to recover and flowering is reduced the first year after division. Fresh, ripe seed obtained from flowering plants requires approximately 3 weeks to germinate although germination will probably be less than 40%. Purchased or old seeds require over a year to germinate, if they germinate at all, and 5% germination is not uncommon.

Quick Reference to Trollius Species

| | Height (in.) | Flower color | Sepals spreading or rolled in |
|---|---|---|---|
| *T.* x *cultorum* | 24-36 | Orange, yellow | Rolled in |
| *T. europaeus* | 20-24 | Yellow | Rolled in |
| *T. ledebourii* | 24-36 | Orange | Spreading |
| *T. pumilus* | 9-12 | Yellow | Spreading |

**-x *cultorum*** (kul-to′ rum) Hybrid Globeflower 2-3′/3′
Late Spring Orange to Yellow Hybrid Origin Zones 3-6

Plants grown under this name are hybrids among *T. europaeus*, *T. asiaticus*, and *T. chinensis*. All cultivars have showy globular, buttercup-yellow flowers consisting of layers of incurved petal-like sepals that eventually open to expose the dozens of stamens. The leaves consist of 5-6 deeply cut lobes and are also ornamental. Cut back foliage in mid to late summer.

**Cultivars:**

'Alabaster' is one of the more unusual globeflowers, having cream-tinged flowers rather than the common yellow or orange. It is not as vigorous (2′ tall) and flowers tend to lose their globe shape early. However, it is worth trying.

'Canary Bird' bears tight, globe-shaped, light yellow flowers with a tinge of green.

'Commander-in-Chief' has deep orange, 3″ wide flowers.

'Earliest of All' is one of the earliest of this group and flowers in early May. The flowers are pale orange-yellow.

'Etna' is vigorous, growing 3′ tall with dark orange flowers.

'Fire Globe' bears some of the deepest orange flowers.

'Golden Queen' is probably a cultivar of *T. chinensis*, producing orange flowers later than many others.

'Goldquelle' is one of the most popular cultivars and produces 2½″ wide pure yellow flowers. The many blossoms are long lasting and useful for cut flowers.

'May Gold' stands about 2′ tall with 2½″ diameter lemon yellow flowers in early spring. This is one of the earliest cultivars to flower.

'Orange Globe' bears golden orange flower globes in midsummer.

'Orange Princess' is an excellent choice for cut flowers. It has 2½-3″ wide, deep orange flowers and grows only 2′ tall.

'Pritchard's Giant' commonly reaches 3′ in height. The medium yellow flowers are long lasting and retain their globe shape. This is also an excellent cut flower cultivar.

'Salamander' is similar to 'Fire Globe' with 2½″ wide fiery orange flowers.

***-europaeus*** (u-ro′ pay-us) Common Globeflower 20-24″/24″
Early Spring Yellow Northern Europe Zones 4-6

The 1-2″ diameter lemon yellow globular flowers are usually borne singly or occasionally in twos. Ten to fifteen sepals enclose the many stamens and the 5 small spatulate petals. The leaves are 5-parted and the leaflets are lobed and toothed. The lower leaves are petioled while those higher on the stem are sessile. This is a common garden plant in Europe and being planted more in the United States. Plants are more tolerant of dry soil than most others, although performance is still mediocre if soils dry out.

**Cultivars:**

'Superbus' is similar to the species but flowers more prolifically. It is more difficult to find the species in commerce than this cultivar.

***-ledebourii*** (led-e-boor′ ee-eye) Ledebour Globeflower 2-3′/2½′
Spring Orange Siberia Zones 3-6

Plants are vigorous and heights of 3′ are not uncommon in well-grown specimens where soils are consistently moist. The leaves are deeply cut to the base and the leaflets lobed and toothed. The deep orange, cup-shaped flowers consist of 5 spreading sepals that readily display the many stamens and narrow, upright petals. The petals are more visible than those in the previous species and are about the same length as the stamens. It flowers approximately one week later than *T. europaeus*. These are magnificent plants for the shaded bog garden or other suitably moist area.

***-pumilus*** (pew′ mi-lus) Dwarf Globeflower 9-12″/12″
Spring Yellow Himalayas Zones 4-6

This species is particularly suited to the rock garden or the front of the moist border. The stems are almost leafless and the 1-2″ wide basal leaves are 5-parted. Each leaflet is 3-lobed and attached to the stem by a petiole. The 1″ wide flowers consist of 5-6 notched stamens and 10-12 narrow petals about the same size as the stamens. Rich, moist well-drained soils and afternoon shade are ideal. A lovely plant for small niches in the garden.

**Related Species:**

*T. acaulis* is about 6″ tall and is also known as dwarf globeflower. It differs from *T. pumilus* by having stem leaves as well as basal leaves. The solitary 1½ to 2″ wide flowers are golden yellow and consist of 12-16 petals. Hardy in zones 5-7.

*T. chinensis* is closely related to *T. ledebourii* but much later flowering. It grows up to 3′ tall with 5-lobed basal and stem leaves, and bowl-shaped, 2 to 2½″ wide, golden yellow to orange flowers in summer. Native to China and Russia, hardy in zones 5(4)-7. 'Golden Queen' is about 2′ tall.

*T. laxus* is native from New Hampshire to British Columbia, and easier to establish in the shady, moist garden than many of the foreigners. The leaves are deeply cut and the 9-12″ tall plants bear solitary 1-2″ diameter yellow flowers (white to cream in var. *albiflorus*) with prominent stamens in early spring. Excellent plantings may be found in the Garden in the Woods in Framingham, Massachusetts and the Denver Botanic Garden.

## ***Tulbaghia*** (tul-bay-gee′ a) Society Garlic Amaryllidaceae

All of the twenty or so species are native to South Africa and can be included as perennials only in frost-free areas. However, the main species, *T. violacea*, can tolerate some temperatures as low as 20°F. *T. violacea* is grown from tuberous rootstocks and produces 5-9 strap-shaped basal leaves, and umbels with up to twenty pink flowers (usually with a yellow eye) in early summer. They are sometimes called pink agapanthus due to their lilac-pink flower color and the "garlic" in its common name comes from the garlicky smell of the leaves. The flowers seem to evoke different senses from different names. To some, they are sweet; to others, they are sickly sweet.

Plants don't compete with many of the more colorful bulbous plants often offered, however, it is a charming plant in a container (to be brought in the winter) or as a garden annual for those who are better at replacing than redigging. Plants require consistent watering and full sun.

**Cultivars**:

'Silver Lace' has larger flowers than the species.

'Variegata' produces leaves with creamy stripes running down the leaves. This is the best form because the foliage is handsome even without flowers.

***Tulipa*** (tew′ li-pa) Tulip Liliaceae

Few plants herald spring like the tulip. Although gardeners are deluged with advertisements in newspapers and garden centers for hybrid tulips each fall, it is well worth remembering that over 100 species are known and many are excellent garden plants. Some of the easiest and most ornamental include *T. batalinii*, *T. clusiana* and *T. tarda*. Hybrid tulips range in height from the 6″ tall Duc von Toc type to the stately 3′ tall stems of the Darwins, and flower from late March to late May.

The garden tulip was introduced to Europe in 1572 by Ogier Ghiselin de Busbecq, Ambassador of the Holy Roman Empire to Suleiman the Magnificent of Turkey. At that time, great numbers of tulips existed in Turkey and in 1715 a list of 1,323 varieties appeared in a paper by Sheik Mohammed Lalizare in the reign of Ahmed III. In 1948, *The Classified List of Tulip Names*, published by a joint committee of the Tulip Nomenclature Committee in England and the General Dutch Bulb-Growers' Society included well over 4300 names. There are many more today.

All hybrid tulips and most species should be treated as annuals, biennials or short-lived perennials. While this is not a particularly popular opinion, it is nevertheless true. Most tulips perform poorly the second year, worse the next year, and seldom "strut their stuff" by the fourth spring. Unfortunately, this is difficult for many gardeners to understand. Many of my friends consider a bulb a perennial, which once planted, should return year after year. In their zeal for tulip perenniality, they tell me that their tulips look as good the third year as the first. I know that the quality of the tulip has not gone up, rather their standards have gone down.

In the South, it is even more difficult to find tulips performing well for more than two years. Insufficient cold is available to force the flower stalk to its potential height, high night temperatures reduce stored food in the bulb, and warm summer soils promote pests and diseases. The depth of planting should be three times the diameter of the bulb, except in heavy clay soils, where shallow planting is more beneficial. In general, the depth of planting for most cultivars in average soils is about 5″. Plant in full sun in mid-September in zones 2-4, as late as early November in zones 7-8. Don't line the bulbs up like tin soldiers all in a row. Plant in bunches of at least 30, no more than 6″ apart, preferably bulb to bulb.

If plants are left in the garden, the spent flowers must be removed before seed develops, and leaves should be allowed to yellow prior to removal, regardless of where one gardens. Since the leaves provide food to the developing bulb, it makes little sense to tie the leaves up in elastic bands or string to "get them out of the way". To propagate, bulbs should be removed, cleaned and graded by size. The largest bulbs may be replanted and bulblets placed in a propagation bed where they can grow and mature.

Three years are required to produce a mature bulb from a small bulblet. In my opinion, treat the tulips as a one- or two-year plant, then put them into the compost pile.

The most recent reorganization of the genus provides 23 different classes of tulips, many of minor importance and some almost impossible to find. The following is a summary of some of the classifications used for garden tulips and a few corresponding cultivars. There are literally thousands of cultivars; those mentioned are typical of their classification.

| **Classification** | **Comments** |
|---|---|
| Single Early | This small group of short-stemmed tulips flower in late March and early April, usually growing 12-14″ tall, often fragrant. 'Apricot Beauty', 'Flair', 'Red Beauty'. |
| Double Early | 14-16″ tall, flower late April and early May, double flowers. 'Abba', 'Monte Carlo', 'Montreau'. |
| Triumph | Derived from single early and Darwin tulips. About 2′ tall, bloom in mid-May. 'Arabian Mystery', 'Couleur Cardinal', 'Gabriella'. |
| Darwin | Short, rounded petals, flower almost rectangular in outline. Up to 2-3′ tall, have largest flowers of all classes, bloom late April to mid-May. 'Apeldoorn', 'Day Dream', 'Golden Parade'. |
| Single Late | Similar to division 1, but flower in late April and May. 'Blushing Lady', 'Hocus Pocus', 'Maureen'. |
| Lily-Flowered | Derived from *T. retroflexa* and cottage tulips. Flowers have pointed, reflexed petals. About 2′ tall, May flowering. 'Ballerina', 'Mona Lisa', 'West Point'. |
| Fringed | Originally grouped with the Parrots but classified separately in 1981. The flowers boast fringed petals in either the same or a contrasting color of the flower. 'Blue Heron', 'Fringed Elegance', 'Swan Wings'. |
| Viridiflora | Characterized by green-streaked flowers. Plants grow 2-3′ tall and flower in May. 'China Town', 'Deirdre', 'Spring Green'. |
| Parrot | Have feather-like petals, usually in colorings of red orange, blue, and green. Flower with Darwins. 'Black Parrot', 'Flaming Parrot', 'Madonna'. |
| Double Late | Produce peony-like flowers in May. Grow 16-24″ tall. Blooms are up to 4″ across and long lasting. 'Angelique', 'Miranda', 'Orange Princess'. |
| Fosteriana | Derived mainly from *T. fosteriana*, hybrids have broad gray-green leaves and 4″ wide flowers on 12″ tall stems in April. 'Easter Moon', 'Orange Emperor', 'Sweetheart'. |

| | |
|---|---|
| Greigii hybrids | Leaves heavily mottled and striped with purple. Bears large flowers, with black base on 9″ stems in May. Useful for foliage effect alone. 'Oratorio', 'Quebec', 'Red Riding Hood'. |
| Kaufmanniana | Known as the water-lily tulip, hybrids are among the earliest to bloom. Short (4-8″) stems useful for rock gardens or exposed positions. 'Heart's Delight', 'Scarlet Baby', 'Stressa'. |
| *Other divisions:* | |
| Bouquet | Multi-flowered tulips, each 2′ stem bears 3-5 flowers. Derived mainly from *T. praestans.* |
| Cottage | Have egg-shaped blooms, grow 20 to 30″ tall. Late, single tulips. |
| Rembrandt | Darwin tulips with streaks on petals. Turns out the streaks were viruses, and actually are longer available commercially. |

**Other Species:**

The species tulips have been lost in the hundreds of hybrids, but have re-emerged in the last 10 years as worthy and quite beautiful garden plants.

*T. acuminata* is known as the horned tulip because of the narrow pointed petals. Plants flower in May. 'Fireflame'.

*T. bakeri* is only about 6″ tall and is among the earliest to flower. Plants are excellent for an open rock garden setting. 'Lilac Wonder'.

*T. batalinii* is as handsome a flower as found in any of the hybrids. The flowers are usually bright yellow, often with a red tinge. This is a "must-try" group, one of my favorite species. 'Apricot Jewel', 'Bright Gem', Bronze Charm'.

*T. clusiana* is known as lady tulip and grows 9-12″ tall. The flowers are red and white striped and open in April. One of the most perennial species for Southern gardeners; plants came back for 5 years in my zone 7b garden. 'Candycane', 'Cynthia', var. *chrysantha.*

*T. praestans* is a multi-flowered tulip, growing 12-18″ tall. The flowers are in shades of red and open late April to early May. 'Fusilier' , 'Tubergen's Var.', 'Zwanenburg'.

*T. tarda* is 6-9″ tall and bears up to 5 white flowers with yellow eye per stem. Excellent for rock gardens. Blooms in March.

## *Tunica* see *Petrorhagia*

## *Tussilago* (tuss-i-lag′ o) Coltsfoot Asteraceae

The name comes from *tussis*, cough, referring to the medicinal use of the leaves. Numerous medicinal benefits have been attributed to the plant, including the relief of diarrhea, coughs and congestion. That the plant has some function must explain its occasional appearance in gardens as it has little ornamental value.

A number of species occur in the genus but only *T. fafara*, coltsfoot, is grown, although it seems to be offered only through nurseries involved in organics and medicinals. This is probably good, as the flowers are almost identical to dandelions, and I don't know many gardeners who want to pay good money for more dandelions. The flowers emerge before the leaves and are borne on 4-6″ scapes with numerous purple scales. They open about the same time or a little earlier than dandelions. When the blooms begin to decline, orbicular to heart-shaped leaves appear, and become more angular as they mature. The leaves have a soft cottony matting early in the season, which diminishes with age.

Plants grow in moist areas and are hardy to zone 6. Why anyone would want to pay for this plant is somewhat beyond me, but then I've always contended that a field of dandelions can be beautiful, as long as it is not my field. A variegated form ('Variegata') also exists, allowing for a field of variegated dandelions.

# U

**_Umbilicus_** (um-bill′ i-cus) Navelwort, Wall Pennywort Crassulaceae

Every now and then a plant comes along that tickles your fancy, and for me, a few years ago, it was *Umbilicus*. The succulent leaves of the plant were glued all over walls in the UK, and the craziest looking greenish tan spikes of flowers protruded from the middle. When someone told me it was the bellybutton plant (his idea of a joke), I was tickled. Still am. Although I had never seen it over here, I am happy to report that a few crazy plantspeople are now selling the plant, properly known as *U. rupestris*.

To be successful, you need a wall, preferably dripping limestone and about 2000 years old, a hole in said wall to insert the umbilicus, lots of cool morning dew, no heat, no cold and little humidity. That leaves an island in the Straits of Juan de Fuca, but what the heck, why not help those nursery people out and have a ball? The worst you will have is a sagging umbilicus.

**_Uniola_** see *Chasmanthium*

**_Urospermum_** (your-o-sperm′ um) Urospermum Asteraceae

Two species occur in this little-known genus, both of which are native to the Mediterranean. Only *U. dalechampii* seems to be grown, and generally grown only if seed is collected from the parent plant. The plants form 2-3′ tall pubescent (softly hairy) stems and many gray-green hairy leaves. The bottom ones are about 6″ long and 2″ wide with winged petioles, the upper ones are thinner and the base of the leaves clasp the stem. The soft yellow daisy flowers occur in the summer.

We seldom see these plants in North America and perhaps there is no overwhelming reason to rush out to try to find seed. However, the flower color is easy to work into the garden and plants are reasonably easy to grow. The drawbacks are that they are Mediterranean, therefore do not care for heat and humidity. They act as biennials in most of the country but are more perennial in West Coast gardens.

Propagate by seed or division.

***Uvularia*** (oo-vew-lah′ ree-a) Bellwort, Merry Bells Liliaceae

Understated woodland native plants fill the genus; plants that are easy to overlook but once noticed, are must-haves for the garden. The botanical name comes from *uvula*, hanging down from the soft palate near the back of the throat, and refers to the hanging flowers. All five species are native to the eastern United States and are graceful woodland plants that are showy only to those who love and appreciate subtle flowers and form. I started with a few plants of the sessile bellwort, *U. sessilifolia*, which continue to spread out beneath an old dogwood in the back garden. Lots of people pass them by without so much as a second glance, until I wrestle them down and make them tell me how much they enjoy their subtle beauty.

Plants are about 9-18″ tall with thin forked stems bearing light green leaves and bell-shaped, drooping yellow flowers. The flowers are twisted in bud and slightly so in flower. A little fertilizer in the spring does wonders for the plants, making them much more vigorous than seen in the woodlands. They spread by rhizomes in forest soils, thriving in moist, shady areas. They do well under the shade of oaks and beeches and other deciduous trees. After flowering, a three-lobed fruit is formed, which rest on the leaves through the summer. For differences between this genus and similar *Disporum* and *Polygonatum*, see *Disporum*.

Quick Reference for Uvularia Species

| | Leaves | Height (in.) |
|---|---|---|
| *U. grandiflora* | Perfoliate | 12-24 |
| *U. perfoliata* | Perfoliate | 12-18 |
| *U. sessilifolia* | Sessile | 12-18 |

**-*grandiflora*** (grand-flo′ ra) Large-Flowered Bellwort 12-18″/12″
Spring Yellow East, Central North America Zones 3-9

The leaves are perfoliate (the stems appear to go right through them) and are finely hairy beneath. The stems fork about 8″ above the soil with 1 or 2 leaves beneath the fork. The pale yellow flowers are a little larger than other species, measuring about 1-1½″ long, and in each one, you can see the obvious delicate stamens, shorter than the styles (female part of the flower). The fruit, which is a capsule, is three-sided and delicately handsome in its own right. Sounds terribly technical; grow them because you like them, it is doubtful you will impress anyone else.

**Cultivars:**

'Sunbonnet' is a form that is much more vigorous, taller and more ornamental than the species.

**Related Species:**

*U. perfoliata* is similar to the above but the pale yellow flowers are only about an inch long and the stamens are shorter than the styles. The leaves are not hairy beneath. Equally terrific.

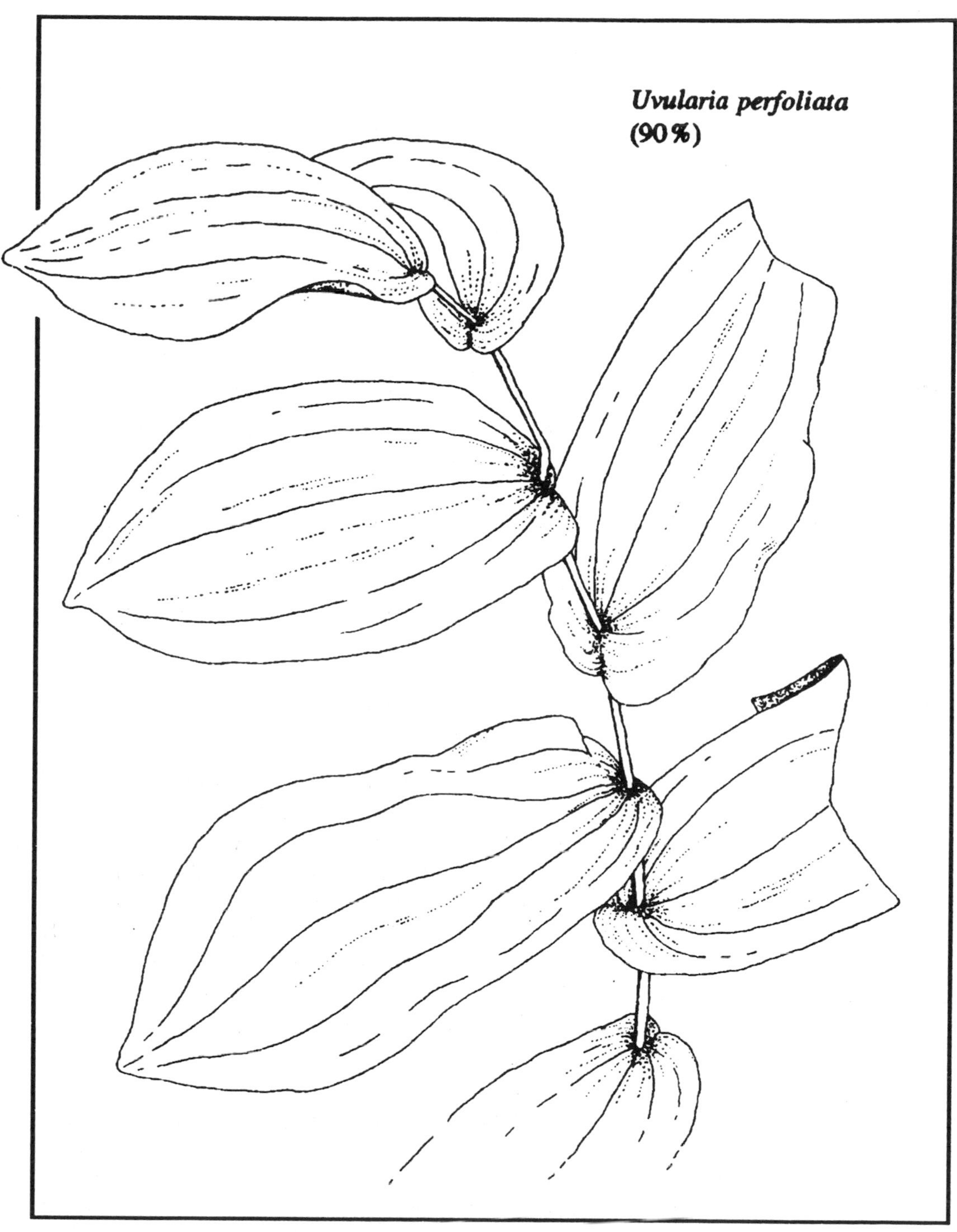


*U. sessilifolia* is less "bulky" than the others, with thinner stems and smaller, lighter yellow flowers. The name refers to the sessile (no petiole) leaves on stems that terminate in small but handsome pale yellow flowers. *U. peberula* is similar but has stems with minute coarse hairs. No difference from the garden point of view.

# V

***Valeriana*** (va-le-ree-ah′ na) Valerian, Garden Heliotrope Apiaceae

Well over 200 species occur in the genus, but I wager that no one has become tired of seeing it all over the place. The botanical name was derived from *valeo*, strong, in reference to its supposed medicinal uses. Plants are characterized by thickened tap roots and being strongly scented throughout. The basal leaves are often rosetted and the stem leaves are usually pinnately compound. The flowers, which are generally white, are held in a terminal inflorescence. Both upright and low-growing spreading species occur but generally only one or two species will be available through mail order specialists.

***-officinalis*** (o-fish′ i-nah-lis) Common Valerian 3-6′/3′
White Late Spring Europe Zones 4-7

This the most familiar valerian, native to Europe and Asia but widely naturalized elsewhere, including Canada and the United States. The roots have and continue to enjoy medical scrutiny. Valerian root has been used for anxiety, restlessness and insomnia. Although their preferred location is along streams and other wet areas, they tolerate the drier soils typical of most gardens. Plants grow up to 6′ tall and with lots of sun; they stand without support. The stem leaves are odd-pinnate, usually with 15-21 segments (7-10 pairs plus the terminal). The flowers appear in early to mid summer and are sweetly fragrant. They are generally whitish, but light lavender or pink flowers may occur. The rhizomes bear short stolons, resulting in quick multiplication. This is one of the "old fashioned" garden plants, prized for that fragrance. Such a dry description does not do well-grown plants justice.

I have to tell you that this can make one marvelous and impressive planting. This became obvious when I came across a towering robust specimen at Powell Gardens, the public garden in Kingsville, Missouri. Large clean white flowers, deep green divided foliage on a 6′ plant had me scratching my head as to what it was. I closed my eyes and let my incredible brain function take over as I silently went through the three or four plants I knew, one after the other. Upon rejecting one after the other, my brain kicked in with the solution. "Find the label, you doofus", it said. I did and it was valerian. As I walked away, I mumbled that I would have eventually got it, yeah, right. Cultivars include 'Alba' with whiter flowers, 'Coccinea', with blood-red flowers and 'Rubra', with bright red flowers. Plants are also on the no-no list in some states because they are potentially invasive.

**Related Species:**

*V. arizonica* grows only about 6″ tall. The plants are well suited for dry climates or rock garden well-drained situations, producing an evergreen mat of green foliage and rather unremarkable pink flowers. Hardy to zone 7 at best.

*V. phu* is similar in habit but not as tall as common valerian (only 1-1½′). The stem leaves are also pinnately parted but have only 3-4 pairs of segments plus the terminal one. Flowers are pinkish white but not nearly as ornamental as *V. officinalis*. 'Aurea' is a handsome cultivar that emerges with yellow stems and leaves. They remain yellow until the heat of the summer makes them fade to light green.

## ***Vancouveria*** (vang-koo-ve′ ree-a) Vancouveria Berberidaceae

Three species of ground-hugging plants are native to woodlands of the northwest United States and Canada. They are similar to *Epimedium* but have 6 stamens and petals rather than 4. If cool, moist conditions can be provided, they are useful ground covers for areas with light shade.

***-hexandra*** (heks-an′ dra) American Barrenwort 10-12″/12″
Early Summer White Washington to California Zones 5-7

Each 2-3″ long leaf is 2 or 3 times ternately (in threes) compound resulting in carpets of fernlike foliage that die to the ground in the fall. The half-inch long white flowers have reflexed sepals and petals and are held in 10-20-flowered panicles at the end of a leafless stem. When well grown, plants remind me of a white barrenwort; when poorly grown, remind me that I should not have planted it.

Plants spread by slender, underground rhizomes in cool, moist, acidic, organic soils. They are difficult to establish in areas of hot, dry summers. Although the flowers are showier, it is not as tough as *Epimedium*.

Propagate by dividing the rhizome in spring or fall.

**Related Species:**

*V. chrysantha*, golden vancouveria, has half-inch yellow flowers held in a few-flowered panicle on 12″ tall plants. Native to southern Oregon and northern California.

*V. planipetala*, redwood ivy, has white flowers sometimes tinged lavender. This species and the previous are evergreen, prefer a pH around 5.0, and are more difficult to establish than *V. hexandra*.

## ***Veratrum*** (vay-rah′ trum) False Hellebore Liliaceae

This genus contains 18 species and includes some of my absolute favorite plants. Even though many are native to the United States, it is difficult to find anyone selling them. None is commonly listed, but *V. viride* can be found with a little looking. That they are not offered by nurseries is frustrating but the fact that the leaves, seeds and roots are highly poisonous may also account for the lack of commercial zeal.

The wide, pleated leaves are particularly showy in the spring and are followed by tall panicles in the summer. *V. viride*, Indian poke, has yellowish green flowers and is reasonably common in the mountains of Georgia and North Carolina. Other marvelous forms are more common in the West, particularly *V. album*, white false hellebore, and *V. californicum* with whitish green flowers. *V. nigrum*, black false hellebore, produces dark purple flowers but is seldom available. The botanical name comes from *vere atrum*, truly black, in reference to the color of the roots; *veratrum* was the ancient name for hellebore, thus the common name.

| **-viride** (vi′ ri-dee) | | Indian Poke | 2-6′/2′ |
|---|---|---|---|
| Summer | Yellow-Green | North America | Zones 4-7a |

Native from New Brunswick to Georgia, and west to Oregon and Alaska, this wild flower is most impressive. The pleated, light green leaves are reminiscent of hosta foliage as they emerge to form large arching mounds. The leaves are alternate and as the stem emerges, the distances between the leaves become more obvious. The oval lower leaves are about 12″ long, 3″ wide, and clasp the stem with a long narrow sheath while the upper stem leaves become progressively smaller. The 18-24″ long flower stalks of broad yellow green flowers are reminiscent of a tall, green verbascum.

This species is both interesting and ornamental. It is best in the spring as the fresh foliage emerges. Even though I have trouble getting excited about green flowers, the large skinny panicles certainly bring many comments. Each individual flower is bell shaped with 6 nearly equal segments. Moist soils are necessary; if allowed to dry out, the edges of the foliage turn brown. Protection from afternoon sun is helpful to maintain freshness of the foliage. *Veratrum* performs poorly under the stress of high heat and humidity and is more suited for zones 4-6 than zones 7 and 8. Leaves of veratrum and hosta are gourmet treats for slugs and in the spring, slug pellets or other deterrents keep the foliage fresh. Partial shade is best, leaves scorch in full sun and windy conditions. A warning: patience is a must if flowers are important. Buying 1-2 year old nursery-grown plants is best, but flowering may not occur for 2-3 years. Do not dig from the wild-they will die and I will hunt you down.

Seedlings require a year before they can be transplanted, and reach flowering size in three years. Seeds must be subjected to a warm-cold-warm stratification period. Sow seed in the fall and allow it to remain under snow cover or mulch until spring. See seed treatment for *Actaea*. Division in the fall or early spring is a more effective and faster means of propagation.

**Related Species:**

*V. album* is similar, bearing flowers slightly tinted white outside and green inside. All the specimens I have seen have a lot more green than white. Plants are shorter, growing 2-3′ tall.

*V. californicum* is common in high areas of the West, usually restricted to altitudes above 5000 ft. in the mountains of western North America. Plants grow 4-6′ tall and generally have whitish flowers.

*V. nigrum* has wide basal leaves although the upper stem leaves are more lanceolate in shape. The flowers, which are purple-black, are earlier than *V. viride* but held in similar narrow panicles. Plants are 2-4′ tall.

***Verbascum*** (ver-bas′ cum) Mullein Scrophulariaceae

When mullein is mentioned, most people think of the large, hairy roadside weed with small yellow flowers, *V. thapsus*. This European species has become naturalized everywhere and was widely used for candles (stems), shoe lining (leaves), narcotic (seeds) and additional medicinal virtues. Other common names like beggar's blanket and old man's flannel suit the plants well. As interesting as the history and the names are, the roadside weed is not enough to invite the plants from the road to our gardens, but many others are.

Few realize that the genus contains many more civilized garden brethren, in fact over 300 species are known and many hybridize readily. They range in height from the 8″ tall *V. dumulosum*, a vivid yellow-flowering plant that cascades over rocks (as well as its hybrid with the dwarf *V. pestalozzae*) to the 6-8′ tall Olympic mullein, *V. olympicum*, whose branched yellow racemes look down on the rest of the garden members. *V. densiflorum* also has handsome large yellow flowers and is highly variable in height, ranging from 2 to 4 feet. Probably the most impressive of all is the broussa mullein, *V. bombyciferum*, a spectacular biennial with rosettes of 12-18″ long downy silvery-white leaves. With foliage like that, the rather ordinary yellow flowers are redundant and irrelevant. Hybridization within the genus has resulted in named selections, and availability of useful *Verbascum* hybrids is rapidly increasing.

Garden plants are more or less tomentose (hairy), with soft alternate leaves on stems arising from a rosette of basal leaves. Flowers are generally yellow but occasionally purple or white-flowered species occur. Verbascum tolerates a wide range of soils and conditions. Most do best in full sun and in poor soils.

Quick Reference to Verbascum Species

| | Height (in.) | Flower color | Leaves gray-green |
|---|---|---|---|
| *V. chaixii* | 2-3 | Yellow | Yes |
| *V. olympicum* | 3-5 | Yellow | Yes |
| *V. phoenicium* | 2-4 | Purple | No |

-***chaixii*** (shay′ zee-eye) Nettle-Leaved Mullein 2-3′/3′
Late Spring Yellow Southern Europe Zones 5-8

The stalked 3-6″ long basal foliage is wedge shaped at the base with round-toothed (crenate) margins. The upper leaves are sessile with rounded bases. Leaves are green or slightly whitish green and hairy. The 1″ diameter yellow flowers are held in tall racemes, each blossom bearing purple, woolly stamens. The inflorescences are unbranched the first 2 years but are many-branched as plants age.

Some authorities refer to this species as biennial, but it is perennial (although short lived) in most gardens. Well-drained soils in full sun are necessary for optimum

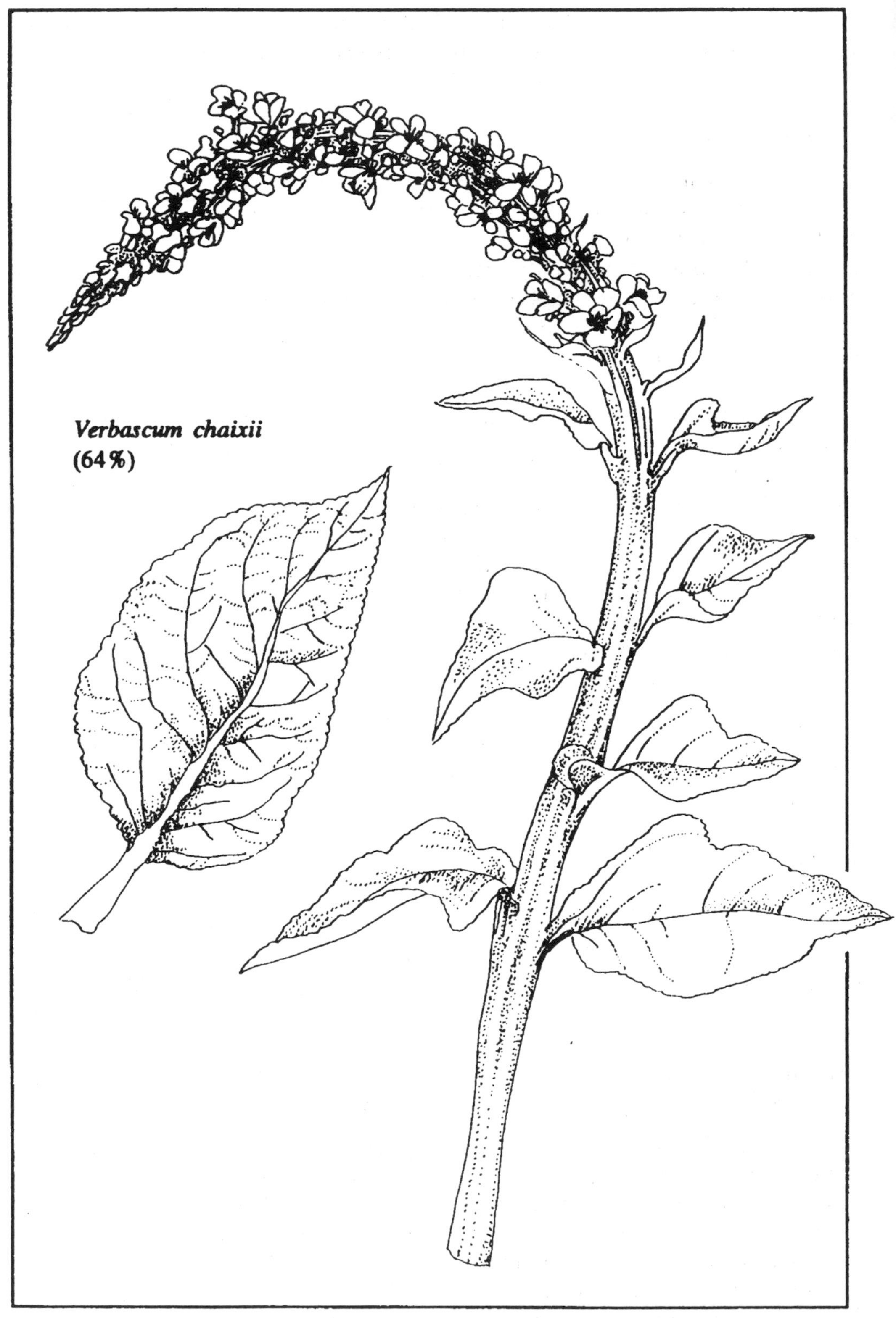
*Verbascum chaixii*
(64 %)

performance. Spider mites find all verbascums particularly appealing and if they bother you, plants should be treated with miticides during the summer, and if chemicals bother you, don't plant it.

Seed germinates quickly under warm, moist conditions. Root cuttings may also be used for propagation. Take 3″ long root cuttings in late winter or early spring and insert them upright in equal parts of moist sand and peat. Place them at 50-70°F and transplant when 3 to 4 leaves have developed.

**Cultivars:**

var. *album* has white flowers but is otherwise similar to the species. The rose to purple stamens on the white backdrop of the petals give the flowers an attractive wine-pink hue. Flowers open about June 1 in zone 8 and open for about 4 weeks.

***-olympicum*** (o-lim′ pi-cum) Olympic Mullein 3-5′/4′
Summer Yellow Greece Zones 6-8

This imposing, long-lived perennial requires good drainage, full sun and lots of space. Part of its appeal are the entire, white, woolly 6-8″ long leaves that are attractive even when the plant is not in flower. They are arranged in basal rosettes up to 3′ across. The 1″ diameter flowers are bright yellow with white-bearded stamens and held in branched 2-3′ tall panicles. Plants remain in flower for 6-8 weeks and if spent inflorescences are removed, they can reflower in the fall.

The more I see this species, the more I appreciate it. It is too tall and gangly to be called beautiful but is more than just interesting. Plants are constantly changing and if provided with basic needs of moisture and sun, they will return for years and years. Fertilizer should be applied sparingly: plants grown in rich soils and treated too kindly reach heights of 7-8 feet.

Propagate by seed or root cuttings similar to *V. chaixii.*

***-phoenicium*** (foy-nee′ see-um) Purple Mullein 2-4′/2′
Spring Purple, White Southern Europe, Northern Asia Zones 6-8

Dark green 18″ diameter rosettes of crinkled, shallowly lobed foliage give rise to 8-10 unbranched racemes, each bearing 1″ diameter flowers, in colors varying from rose-pink to purple, although 'Violetta' has deep violet flowers. Flowers are borne about one month earlier than those of *V. chaixii.* The leaves are smooth above and pubescent beneath. Plants can be quite variable and seedlings may yield flowers of purple, red, rose or white. Full sun and well-drained soils are best but plants tolerate afternoon shade, particularly in zone 8. If over-fertilized, it can grow to 5′ feet.

This is a fair garden plant but is terribly susceptible to spider mites. Although tolerant of drought, it has never been outstanding in my garden for the 5 years I have grown it. Flowers are fleeting, blooming for about two weeks, and then the plants disappear into anonymity.

Seed propagation is easy under moist, warm (70-75°F) conditions. Flower color will vary. Propagate hybrids by root cuttings similar to *V. chaixii.*

**Related Species**

*V. bombyciferum* grows 5′ tall, the entire plant being densely felted, especially the flowering spike. The sulphur yellow flowers are small (about 1″ across) but numerous in the tall spikes. A few cultivars are offered, but 'Arctic Summer' is reasonably common-shorter and more compact, but otherwise similar to the species. Plants are biennial.

*V.* x *hybridum* resulted from crosses between various vigorous species such as *V. pulverulentum*, *V. sinuatum*, *V. olympicum*, and *V. phoenicium*. Many forms have large sterile flowers and only a little hairiness on the green leaves. Flowers occur in late spring to early summer, and cutting back the spent flowers may induce secondary inflorescences. Unfortunately, due to the biennial nature of many of the parents, they are short lived and survive only 2-3 years. Generally hardy in zones 5-7. West Coast (zone 8) is perfect but East Coast zone 8 is quick death.

*V. leianthum* is a stately and incredibly impressive 6-8′ tall plant with dozens of yellow flowers in summer. Probably hardy only to zone 7.

*V. nigrum*, dark mullein, has purple stamens, long pedicels and yellow flowers. The plants are barely pubescent. The flowers are only about ½″ across and the inflorescence is unbranched. It is one of the parents (with *V. spinosum*, spiny mullein) of 'Golden Bush', an upright 2-3′ tall, yellow-flowered mullein which sends up multitudes of stems and flowers for 4-6 weeks.

*V. widemannianum* grows to a flowering height of well over 4′ but it is the wonderful white-hairy rosettes which give plants their beauty. The basal leaves are about 12″ long and 4-5″ wide. The stem leaves are less tomentose and smaller and bear branches of many 1-2″ wide salmon to purplish flowers. A biennial: enjoy the explosion, then remove.

**Hybrids**:

There are far too many, considering they are short lived (often biennial in habit) and marginal in many gardens anyway. Most of these are American bred, but there is an equal number from Holland and the UK as well. However, their beauty cannot be denied, and although they may be short lived; enjoy the craziness—just don't expect them to be around more than a couple of years.

'Banana Custard' has grayer, hairier leaves than many others and produces large yellow flowers on 4-5′ tall plants.

'Blushing Bride' has pale lavender and pink blooms. 18-22″ tall.

'Caribbean Crush' grows about 1½′ tall, and bears beautiful salmon-pink flowers in late spring to early summer.

'Cotswold Gem' is 3-4′ tall and bears racemes of rosy flowers with purple centers. A number of other 'Cotswold' cultivars have appeared including 'Cotswold Beauty', dull yellow with lilac stamens, and 'Cotswold Queen', which produces terra cotta flowers with maroon stamens.

'Dark Eyes' is only about a foot tall and has large, handsome, creamy white flowers with dark centers.

'Domino' is a popular plant in the United States and produces 1-1½″ diameter rose-pink flowers on 3-3½′ long stalks.

'Gainsborough' has pale sulphur yellow flowers and gray-green leaves. It is about 3-4′ tall but can reach 5′ in rich soils.

'Golden Bush' grows about 2′ tall with pure yellow flowers on upright spikes.

'Hartleyi' sends up many shoots of large canary yellow flowers suffused with plum. A magnificent plant.

'Helen Johnson' bears dull green leaves and salmon-peach flowers with a darker eye, on 3-4′ tall stems. 'Cherry Helen' has dark rose flowers.

'Honey Dijon' is a most ornamental cultivar from Terra Nova Nurseries. Flowers are a wonderful shade of peach and gold, each with a dark red eye.

'Jackie' is 16-18″ tall and produces peachy flowers with magenta markings. Quite lovely, but the flowers tend to fade rapidly.

'Jackie in Pink' is, well . . . 'Jackie', in pink.

'Lavender Lass' has somewhat pleated foliage and grows nearly 2′ in height. Lavender flowers with a slightly darker eye occur in early summer.

'Lemon Sorbet' has large yellow flowers with a red eye. About 20″ tall.

'Letitia' is only 1′ tall with dozens and dozens of clear yellow flowers. Terrific for well-drained sunny locations.

'Mt. Blanc' has foliage similar to 'Gainsborough' but bears white flowers.

'Pink Petticoat' has thin spikes of pink flowers.

'Plum Smokey' bears many plum-colored flower spikes about 1½′ above the green rosette.

'Raspberry Ripple' is fun, producing 2′ tall flower spikes of light pink flowers, each with a raspberry red center.

'Royal Highland' has dense spikes of apricot yellow flowers on 3′ tall stems.

'Royalty' grows 12-14″ tall and produces many rose-pink flowers.

'Sierra Sunset' takes direct aim at 'Jackie', producing many orange peach flowers on sturdy 18″ plants.

'Silver Candelabra' bears 4-6′ tall spikes of bright yellow flowers with silver woolly foliage.

'Southern Charm' has become a popular cultivar because the pink flowers have large purple centers that get larger as the flowers mature. Plants are 2-3′ tall. Plants perform better in the South than in the North.

'Sugar Plum' has many dark plum flowers on its 12″ frame.

'Summer Sorbet' produces rosy pink flowers with darker centers.

'Sunshine Spires' bears many dark yellow flowers on a substantial 22-26″ tall plant.

'White Candles' has clean white flowers.

## ***Verbena*** (ver-been′ a) Vervain, Verbena Verbenaceae

Verbena consists of approximately 250 species, and about a half dozen are in cultivation, but about a bazillion hybrids have recently been bred. They are sold mainly as bedding plants, which to some gardeners are dirty words. They are planned crosses between species like *V. canadensis*, *V. peruviana*, *V. incisa*, *V. phlogifolia*, *V. platensis* and Lord knows what other *V.*, or they may have been selected by individual plantspeople or stumbled across in an old homestead every now and then. However, after all is said and done, the hybrids should be considered annuals as they are not consistently hardy north of zone 7, and even there, it is a bit of a crapshoot. At the Gardens at UGA, we have trialed close to 200 different hybrids in the last 4 years alone! Nothing wrong with annuals, but perhaps there is enough in this book already without adding another 100 or so annuals. However, the annual hybrids so dominated the market that the perennial species have not been developed as much, although perhaps that is not such a bad thing.

The perennial species are generally rose-purple, persistent bloomers, and hardy south of zone 6. Plants generally have opposite, dentate foliage, four-sided stems and terminal flowers. They perform best in well-drained soils in full sun.

Verbena has numerous historical references. *V. officinalis* was the classical name for certain sacred branches and supposedly was used to staunch Christ's wounds on Calvary. Plants were also used medicinally; the term vervain is rooted in the Celtic words *fer*, to remove and *faen*, stone, referring to its use in treating bladder stones.

Taxonomists have reclassified most of the low-growing species into the genus *Glandularia*. This has not been widely accepted by either academics or practitioners; however, you will be seeing this genus much more.

Quick Reference to Verbena Species

| | Height (in.) | Flower color | Upright or spreading |
|---|---|---|---|
| *V. bonariensis* | 36-48 | Violet | Upright |
| *V. canadensis* | 8-18 | Red, Pink | Spreading |
| *V. rigida* | 12-24 | Violet | Upright |
| *V. tenuisecta* | 8-12 | Purple | Spreading |

***-bonariensis*** (bo-nah-ree-en' sis) South American Verbena, Tall Verbena 3-4'/3'
Summer Rose-Violet South America Zones 6b-9

This is the tallest garden verbena and particularly effective in the middle of the border. It was named for the city of Buenos Aires, where first discovered. It has since become naturalized in the United States from South Carolina to Texas. The 4" long elliptical leaves are sessile and clasp the stem. They are sharply serrated above the middle and entire towards the base. The wiry stems are roughly hairy and conspicuously 4-angled. The flowers consist of 5 petals and a corolla tube nearly twice as long as the calyx. The individual flowers measure only about ¼" across but the entire panicle is 2-4" wide.

It is an excellent plant for gardens but needs to be massed in groups. If grown in rich soil or over fertilized, it can easily reach 5' and require severe pruning. Cutting back the plant results in a many-branched specimen that takes on a shrublike habit.

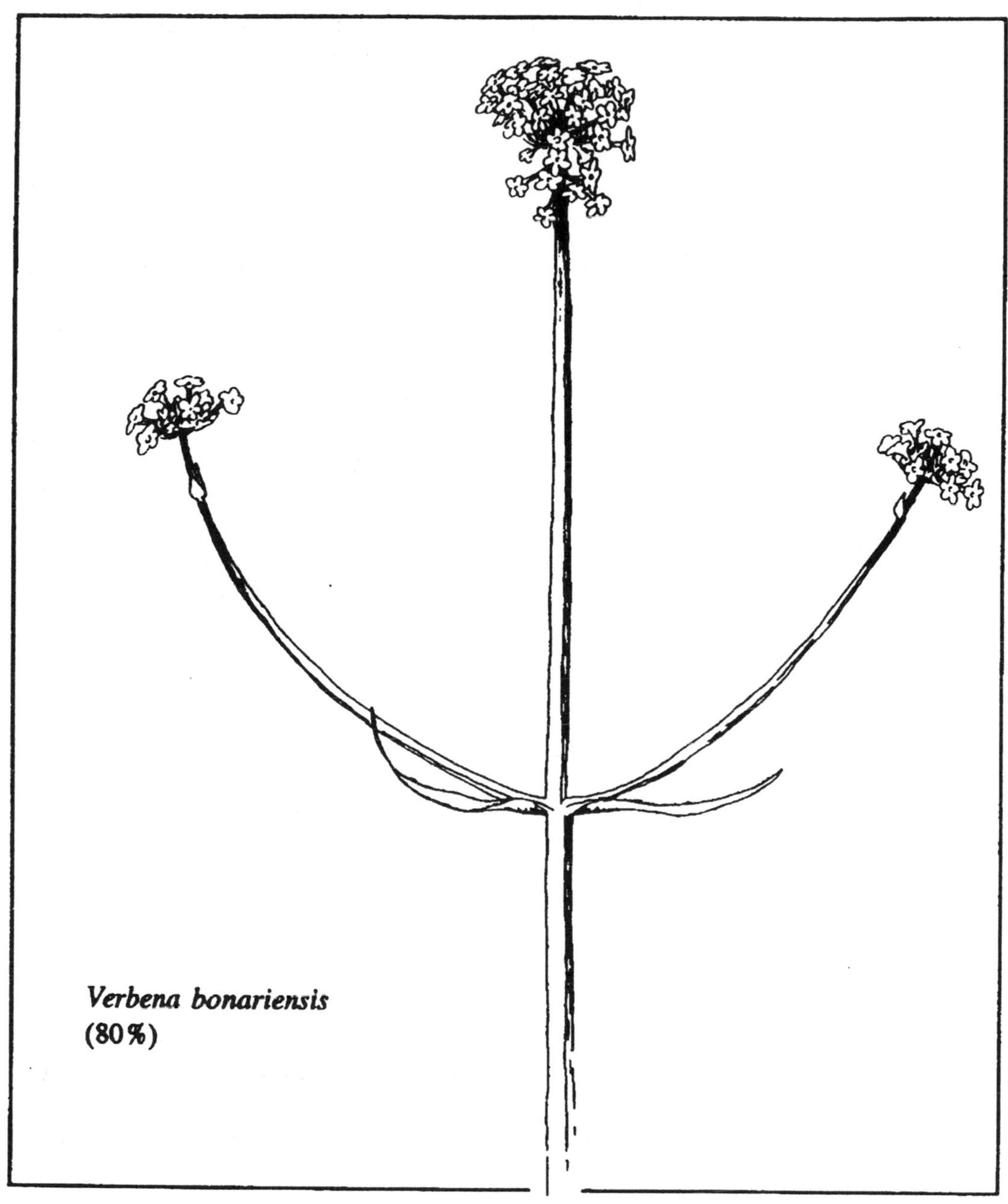

*Verbena bonariensis*
(80%)

Once in flower, it remains in bloom until frost. A drawback, however, is the susceptibility to powdery mildew, which should be treated with appropriate chemicals beginning in June. Personally, I prefer not to spray for mildew and although the white spots are unsightly, the disease does not appear to reduce vigor. North of zone 6b, this is an annual, but will reseed without conscience.

Propagate from root cuttings in the spring similarly to *Anemone* x *hybrida*. Seed sown in moist media should be placed at 40°F for 3-4 weeks, after which time the tray may be moved to 60-70°F temperatures. Germination is erratic and seedlings appear over a 3-5 week period. Two- to three-inch terminal cuttings of new spring growth may also be rooted and transplanted 3-5 weeks later.

***-canadensis*** (kan-a-den′ sis) Clump Verbena, Rose Verbena 8-18″/36″
Summer Red, Pink North America Zones 6b-10
(syn. *Glandularia canadensis*)

This species is usually treated as a annual in most of the country but is native from Virginia to Florida and west to Colorado and Mexico. The many-branched pubescent stems lie on the ground with the ends ascending (decumbent), and rooting occurs where the lower stems touch the soil. The deeply lobed ovate leaves are 1-3″ long and about 1″ wide with a triangular to wedge-shaped base. The rose-red to pink corolla tube is about twice as long as the calyx but each flower is only about ½″ wide. Up to 20 flowers may be present on each of the stalked spikes.

This species has an excellent clumping habit and may be cut back severely if the stems lose leaves or become too long. A sunny place in the border with excellent drainage is necessary. If drainage is poor, plant vigor declines rapidly and no amount of corrective surgery will improve its demeanor. Like other members of the genus, susceptibility to mildew and spider mites are problems. Many hybrids have been developed; most are annuals although 'Homestead Purple' is still the standard by which all those hybrids are judged.

**Cultivars**:

This is where those bazillion hybrids mentioned in the introduction belong, and here is where I draw the line in the sand. In the first edition (1989), I listed 2 cultivars, in the 2nd edition, 22 cultivars, and today, as I look at my travel notes and research data, I could easily list 50 or 60. I did not want to kill another tree by listing 50 or 60 cultivars that are not perennial for most of you and you can't even find in the retail store because the label only says "Four-inch red annual"?

I hate to shamelessly mention one of my books, but in *Manual of Annuals, Biennials and Half Hardy Perennials*, (Timber Press, 2001), I listed about half of those bazillion, and if you are curious, go there, or if you want to save some money, check the web for verbena hybrids.

***-rigida*** (ri′ gi-da) Sandpaper Verbena, Rigid Verbena 12-24″/18″
Summer Purple Brazil, Argentina Zones 7-10

This South American species has become naturalized from North Carolina to Florida, and gardeners are taking advantage of the heat and drought tolerance and persistent flowering, continuing through mid October in my garden. Tuberous roots are formed, which if mulched in the fall, survive as far north as zone 7. The 4-angled stems, similar to those of *V. bonariensis*, bear oblong, rigid, sessile leaves. Each 2-4″ long leaf is roughly pubescent and has wide spreading teeth. The intense purple flowers about ½″ wide and consist of a ½″ long corolla tube 2-3 times longer than the calyx. In general, this plant looks like a miniature *V. bonariensis* with similar cultural and propagation requirements. Plants are in flower all spring and early sum-

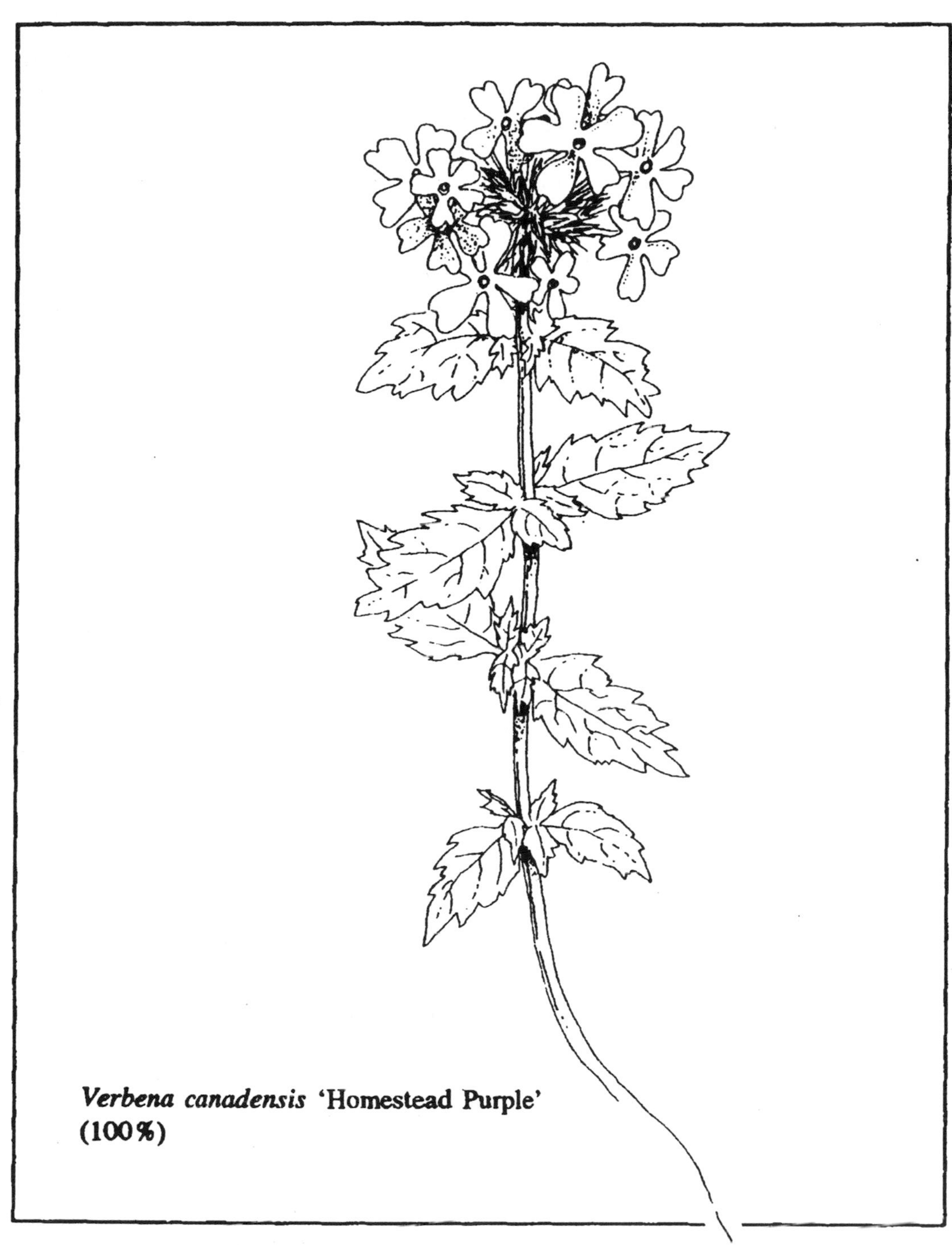

***Verbena canadensis*** **'Homestead Purple' (100%)**

mer in the South, and my trips to Macon and Augusta to see my Laura and Heather and grandkids are a little easier when the verbena colors the roadsides. An excellent front-of-the-border species, it requires no pruning to maintain vigor or habit.

Propagate similar to *V. bonariensis*.

**Cultivars:**

'Flame' stands only 6″ tall and produces an abundance of scarlet flowers. It is more vigorous than the species and spreads more rapidly. It is likely a hybrid between *V. rigida* and another low-growing species such as *V. canadensis.*

'Lilacina' has purple-blue flowers.

'Polaris' bears lavender-blue flowers on compact 12-15″ tall plants. They are quite handsome but can reseed everywhere.

***-tenuisecta*** (ten-you-i-sec′ ta) Moss Verbena 8-12″/spreader
Spring Lavender Southern South America Zones 7-10
(syn. *Glandularia pulchella*)

This plant should be as common in the South as bedstraw in the North. Naturalized from southern Georgia to Louisiana and south to Florida, it flourishes by roadsides and in fields. Many decumbent stems bear triangular leaves about 1-1½″ long which are divided into linear segments. The spikes are terminal, solitary and composed of 5-15 small (½″ wide ) lavender flowers. The flowers are about 1″ long and compactly arranged when they first open but elongate to 1½″ or more as the flowers mature. They differ from *V. canadensis* by growing lower to the ground, have deeply cut, almost lacy leaves and flower throughout the summer.

I first obtained terminal cuttings from south Georgia. Plants rooted in less than 2 weeks and 8 cuttings carpeted 20-30 square feet in the first 6 weeks. It overwinters in zone 7b two years out of five and thus I take cuttings in the fall and overwinter them. Given sufficient protection, it may be considered hardy in zone 8. If plants become leggy, they may be sheared with a lawnmower to 2″ tall and they return as fresh as ever. If sheared too close to the ground it will take a long time to fill in. For gardeners further north, it makes an excellent annual. Although not as colorful as the annual hybrids, it requires far less maintenance and provides better garden performance. Many of the hybrid cultivars mentioned above have deeply dissected leaves, and this species is obviously a significant parent.

Propagation is easy from 2-3″ terminal cuttings taken any time in the season. Rooting occurs in 5-8 days if cuttings are placed in a moist, warm area.

**Cultivars:**

The cutleaf forms resulted from *V. tenuisecta*, *V. canadensis*, *V. tenera* (*Glandularia tenera*) and hybrids between them. They are all part of the bazillion group mentioned above. Just as I wussed out with hybrids of *V. canadensis*, I do the same here. They are consistently cold hardy to zone 8, although gardeners in zone 7 may be occasionally be pleasantly surprised.

**Related Species:**

*V. hastata*, swamp verbena, is a 1-1½′ tall native plant with thin linear leaves at the base and branched, thin flower stems, each with lavender purple flowers. The flowers open at the base of the inflorescence and continue opening up the spike, while closing at the bottom. More people need to be growing this wonderful American plant. Zones 3-8.

**Verbena tenuisecta**
**(64%)**

*V. stricta* is native to the plains and produces short stiff 2′ tall plants bearing light lavender flowers in mid to late summer. "Prairie Candles' is a white-flowering form. Zones 3-7.

*V. peruviana*, (*Glandularia peruviana*), Peruvian verbena, hugs the ground and bears bright scarlet flowers. The leaves are not as incised or deeply cut as *V. canadensis*, nor are plants as tall or as winter hardy (zones 7-10).

***Vernonia*** (ver-non' ee-a) Ironweed Asteraceae

The ironweeds are native to the tropics and to a broad swath of North America. Most plants in this huge genus, consisting of approximately 1000 species, have been left to their own devices in the wild, and only a handful have graced gardens. The plants are often large, being small trees, shrubs or robust perennials characterized by alternate, usually simple, leaves with clusters of rose or purple flowers in the fall. The flowers are all tubular, consisting of disc flowers only and surrounded by bracts. The flower color takes on rusty shades that account for its common name. The species I have tried are reasonably ornamental, very vigorous and provide some good fall color in a garden that may be tired out from the summer. All require full sun; plants grow well in moist soils or in drought conditions.

The most popular species is *V. noveboracensis*, New York ironweed. The plants have pointed lanceolate leaves, entire or slightly toothed. Each flower head may be 6-8″ across and consist of 30-50 flowers. *V. glauca* is similar but has a pale undersurface to the leaves. Plants are impressive but they are big and gangly, and are often relegated to 'wilder" areas of the garden, similar to Joe Pye weed. Unlike Joe Pye, little hybridization to civilize the species has been accomplished. However, let's not get too carried away with this height thing; if the mature height is too tall, use the Armitage technique (patent pending) for height control—whack them back, hard, about a month after emergence.

Interest in ironweeds has accompanied the growing enthusiasm for native plants in this country, and additional species are being offered and lauded. Gardeners might want to try a naturally shorter species, the 3′ tall *V. fasciculata*, although two-foot plants have occasionally been touted. They are native to prairies and moist woodlands from North Dakota to Oklahoma, plants are resilient and long lived. The reddish purple flower heads are smaller than the previous species and consist of about 30 small flowers per head. There is a white selection (var. *alba*) as well. *V. altissima* (*V. gigantea*) grows 4-6′ tall in gardens and has finely toothed narrow leaves and small purple flower heads. All are cold hardy to at least zone 5, many into zone 3 and south to zone 8.

My favorite new plant is *V. lettermannii*, slimleaf ironweed, native to Arkansas and Oklahoma. Plants look very much like the better-known *Amsonia hubrichtii*, that is, with skinny, feathery leaves. Even when not in flower, plants are handsome, well behaved and only about 3′ tall. In the fall, small purple ironweed flowers occur. A wonderful new cultivar, 'Iron Butterfly,' was recently introduced by North Creek Nursery, Pennsulvania. Hardy to zone 6.

***Veronica*** (ve-ron' i-ca) Speedwell Scrophulariaceae

About 250 species, including a dozen herbaceous members, are suitable for the garden. The name Veronica is thought to have arisen because markings on the flowers of some species resemble the markings on the sacred veil of St. Veronica. St.

Veronica was one of the holy women who accompanied Jesus to Calvary, and offered Him her veil, upon which he left the imprint of His face.

*V. officinalis*, common gypsyweed, is native in many areas of the world. It can be found in Canada, all the Northern states and south to Georgia. In Europe, it was substituted for tea until the nineteenth century. Plants were used to treat coughs, stomach and urinary disorders, rheumatism and as a general tonic.

Most species have opposite leaves, and flowers are usually held in racemes. They vary from the prostrate *V. repens*, creeping speedwell, to the 4′ tall *V. longifolia*, long leaf speedwell. Veronicas differ from other members of the family by having only 2 stamens, both of which are longer than the petals. Identification between some species is difficult and ideally the label will actually be correct. However, if you have the inclination, the length of the pedicel (individual flower stalk) in relation to the length of the sepals is a useful identification characteristic. Noting if the flowers are borne terminally or in the leaf axils will also help determine.

Full sun and well-drained soils are the only demands; otherwise they are relatively easy to grow. Significant variability occurs in some species, particularly Hungarian speedwell, *V. austriaca* subsp. *teucrium* (long known as *V. teucrium*). Nursery catalogs may list the same cultivar under 2 or 3 different species. Plants attract butterflies by the hundreds. The genus is undergoing continued taxonomic scrutiny so be patient with the names.

Quick Reference to Veronica Species

| | Height (in.) | Flower color | Inflorescence terminal or axillary |
|---|---|---|---|
| *V. alpina* | 4-8 | Blue | Terminal |
| *V. austriaca* subsp. *teucrium* | 6-20 | Deep Blue | Axillary |
| *V. gentianoides* | 6-20 | Pale Blue | Terminal |
| *V. incana* | 12-18 | Blue | Terminal |
| *V. longifolia* | 24-48 | Lilac | Terminal |
| *V. pectinata* | 3-6 | Deep Blue | Axillary |
| *V. prostrata* | 3-8 | Blue | Axillary |
| *V. spicata* | 10-36 | Blue | Terminal |

***-alpina*** (al-pine′ a) Alpine Speedwell 4-8″/12″
Spring Blue Europe, Asia Zones 3-7

This small undemanding plant bears shiny green entire leaves about 1-1½″ long. The upper leaves are larger than the lower and all are elliptical to oblong. Plants spread by a creeping rootstock but are not rampant. The flowers are up to ¼″ across and held in a dense spikelike raceme. Each raceme persists for at least one week.

This is one of the many veronicas often listed under "alpines", because of their low stature and cold tolerance. However, alpine speedwell performs almost as well in the heat of zone 7 as in the cool of zone 3. The flowers are borne in the spring and continue off and on again in September and October in the South. Plants are evergreen in the South but die back in the North. It is an excellent plant for the front of the border or for the rock garden.

Propagate by division in the spring or fall. Seed germinates quickly when sown in moist media and placed in warm humid conditions.

**Cultivars:**

'Alba' is a white-flowered form that has essentially replaced the species in cultivation. It is vigorous and free flowering.

***-austriaca*** (aus-stry-ah′ ca) Austrian Speedwell 2-3′/2′
Summer Blue Mainland Europe Zones 4-7

Recent taxonomic reshuffling has forced me to include this species, although it is seldom, if ever, found in commerce. The stems are usually erect, although they may be somewhat drooping to procumbent (on the ground). The lavender flowers always arise from the leaf axils and are never terminal.

The form found in catalogs and gardens is a subspecies, subsp. *teucrium* (long known as *V. teucrium*). All the named cultivars are less than 2′ tall with blue flowers, but it is such a variable group that some botanists divide it into 5 sub-groups. For our purposes, they are low-growing, prostrate plants with both ascending sterile stems and flowering stems. The 1½″ long leaves are ovate to oblong and more or less toothed, or sometimes slightly lobed. They resemble the leaves of germander, *Teucrium*, thus its specific epithet. The ½″ wide flowers arise in elongated axillary racemes only (i.e. no terminal inflorescences) from the upper 2-3 nodes, and when in flower, plants are a sea of blue. In zone 7, flowers open in early May and persist for about 4 weeks. In Philadelphia (zone 6), flowering begins about 2 weeks later. In warm climates, cut back hard after flowering. Plants perform best in full sun but will also tolerate some afternoon shade.

Propagate by division as well as by terminal cuttings of sterile branches. Seed may be treated similar to *V. alpina*.

**Cultivars:**

Most but not all are cultivars of subsp. *teucrium*.

'Blue Fountain' is more erect and one of the tallest selections of this species. It has dense bright blue racemes on 20-24″ tall plants.

'Crater Lake Blue' is an outstanding 12-15″ selection with short racemes of intense blue flowers. It is one of the best cultivars for filling in a sunny area in the front of the garden.

'Royal Blue' bears deep blue flowers on 12-18″ tall bushy plants.

'Shirley Blue' is only about 8″ tall with short, dense racemes of mid to dark blue flowers.

'True Blue' is an excellent 12″ tall, free-flowering cultivar with deep blue flowers.

***-gentianoides*** (gen-tee-a-noi′ deez) Gentian Speedwell 6-20″/18″
Spring Pale Blue Caucasus Zones 4-7

For some reason I do not comprehend, plants are seldom seen in North American gardens. Flowering stems with small bract-like leaves rise above rosettes consisting of many entire 1-3″ long leaves. The half-inch wide, pale blue to almost white flowers (not at all gentian) are held in loose 10″ long racemes. It differs from most upright garden species in that the pedicel (the connecting stem between the flower and the raceme) is much longer than the sepals. Usually the pedicel is about the same size or shorter. When not in flower, the creeping rootstock forms dense mats of glossy foliage. This useful plant suits the front to mid-border and is useful for the rock garden because of its mat-forming tendencies.

Full sun and well-drained soil should be provided. It is more tolerant of moist soils than other species and should not be allowed to dry out.

Propagate similar to *V. alpina.*

**Cultivars:**

'Barbara Sherwood' has light lavender-white flowers, lightly striped with pale blue in late spring. Plants are only about a foot tall.

'Variegata' has white-margined foliage but flowers are similar to the species. Splashes of white appear on the basal leaves and are not particularly obvious. The variegation is best on the small stem leaves where each margin is dressed in pure white. Much more interesting than the species.

***-incana*** (in-kah′ na) Woolly Speedwell 12-18″/18″
Summer Blue Russia Zones 3-7

Without getting into the discussion, let it be known that many taxonomists—and indeed growers—treat this as a subspecies of *S. spicata* (*S. spicata* subsp. *incana*). Therefore, if you're trying to find some of the cultivars listed here, be sure to check under *V. spicata* as well. For me, there are enough garden differences that I have left well enough alone.

This is one of the few veronicas grown for the foliage as well as the flowers. The 1-3″ long toothed leaves have many long white hairs, resulting in an overall silvery-gray appearance. The lower leaves are matted and oblong while the uppermost are lanceolate; all are narrowed at the base. Small blue flowers (¼″ across) are borne on short pedicels in 3-6″ long terminal racemes and persist for about 4 weeks. This is a popular edging plant that also provides good foliage contrast. Plants perform poorly in high heat and high rainfall areas because the hairy leaves trap moisture, resulting in foliar disease. Provide full sun to partial shade in well-drained soils. Plants particularly dislike wet, cold soils.

Divide the plants in spring or take 2″ long terminal cuttings from the sterile basal branches during the summer. Sow the fine seed in a well-drained medium at 70-72°F and barely cover. If seed is covered too deeply, germination is poor. After germination, reduce the temperature to approximately 60°F.

**Cultivars**:
'Candidissima' has 6″ long leaves that are not as tomentose as the species. Otherwise, plants are similar.
'Glauca' bears more silvery foliage and deeper blue flowers than the species.
'Rosea' has a pink tinge to the flowers.
'Saraband' is about 18″ tall with compact gray-green leaves over which are produced dense racemes of violet-blue flowers.
'Silver Carpet' bears gray-green foliage and erect purple flowers. Plants are about 12″ tall.
'Silver Slippers' is an interesting if not colorful selection. The gray lancelike leaves form a dense low-growing mat but no flowers are produced. Good for rock gardens where drainage is excellent.
'Wendy' bears grayish foliage, lavender-blue flowers and grows 2′ tall.

***-longifolia*** (long-gi-fo′ lee-a) Long-Leaf Veronica 2-4′/2′
Summer Lilac Europe, Asia Zones 4(5)-8

Heights of 2½′ are average but 3½ to 4′ tall plants occur in rich soils and moderate climates. The stem is hairless or nearly so and the 2½-4″ long leaves are sharply toothed and pointed. Leaves are oblong to lanceolate with slightly hairy undersides. The lower leaves are opposite but the uppermost are often arranged in whorls. The ¼″ wide flowers are arranged in dense 12″ long racemes.

This is by far the best veronica if cut flowers from the garden are wanted. They persist for 5-7 days in water and provide a full upright spike of flowers in blues, lavenders and whites. In the garden, flowering persists for 6-8 weeks, and for the entire time, butterflies are constant companions. This tall lanky plant is most effective in groups of 3 or more. If placed in too much shade or fed too generously, staking is required. This is more of a problem in the South than in the North. The species is native to moist areas and does poorly if soil is allowed to dry out.

Propagate by division in the spring or sow seed similar to *V. incana*.

**Cultivars**:
var. *alba* is 1½′ tall and bears white flowers.
'Blauriesen' is an excellent old-fashioned blue upright form that is especially suitable for cut flowers. Often sold as 'Foerster's Blue' but they are not the same.
'Blue Giant' is 3-3½′ tall with lavender-blue flowers.
'Eveline' is compact, well branched and produces many spikes of lavender-purple flowers.
'Foerster's Blue' stands 1-2′ tall and produces deep blue flowers for 8 weeks in the summer.
var. *glauca* has deep purple flowers and blue-green foliage.
'Icicle' is one of the finest white-flowered veronicas and is probably a hybrid with *V. longiflora* var. *subsessilis* and *V. spicata*. It grows 18-24″ tall and flowers from June to September.

'Iglo' comes from Plant Delights Nursery in Raleigh, North Carolina, and provides well-branched plants with light lavender flowers, that appear whitish at a distance. They are about 3′ tall.

'Joseph's Coat' has tricolored (pink, green and cream) leaves and upright lavender blue flowers.

'Lavender Flame' is about 18″ tall with dark lavender flowers.

'Lilac Fantasy' has strong lilac-lavender flowering stems on 18-22″ plants.

'Midnight' produces dark purple flowers on 18″ tall plants.

'Pink Damask' is one of the better forms with many upright lilac-pink flowers on 2½-3′ tall plants.

'Rosea' is well branched and has rose-pink flowers. Plants can attain heights of three feet.

'Schneeriesen' bears good white flowers on 18-20″ tall plants. Similar in habit to 'Blauriesen' and also a fine cut flower form.

var. *subsessilis* is one of the best and most popular forms. It is 2-3′ tall, much more branched and compact with longer inflorescences and larger flowers than the species. Flowering occurs about 2 weeks later than the species.

***-pectinata*** (pek-ti-nah′ ta) Comb Speedwell 3-6″/spreading
Spring Deep Blue Asia Minor Zones 2-7

This prostrate species is particularly useful for edging or for dry areas in the rock garden. The base of the plant is woody and the foliage forms a dense evergreen mat. The sessile, oval leaves are ½ to ¾″ long and covered with long white hairs. They are bluntly toothed and somewhat resemble the teeth of a comb, thus earning the plant's common name. It spreads by rooting at the nodes of the prostrate stems. The axils of the ascending stems bear 3-5″ long, many-flowered, elongated racemes consisting of ¼″ diameter blue flowers with white centers.

Native to dry, shady areas, plants are more tolerant of drier conditions than other species. Good drainage and full sun to partial shade are ideal.

Propagate by division in early spring or treat seed similar to *V. alpina*.

**Cultivars:**

var. *rosea* has numerous racemes of rose-pink flowers. The racemes are a little shorter (2-4″ long) than the type but otherwise few differences are obvious.

***-prostrata*** (pros-trah′ ta) Harebell Speedwell 3-8″/spreading
Summer Blue Europe, Northern Asia Zones 5-8

Plants produce both sterile and flowering stems. The sterile stems remain prostrate and form mats of grayish green, slightly hairy foliage. The ascending flowering stems grow to 8″ tall. The serrated, ovate to linear leaves are wedge shaped at the base and ½ to 1″ long. The plants can be completely covered in flowers in the spring. Short, dense racemes of pale to deep blue, ⅓″ diameter starry flowers are formed in the axils of the ascending stems.

This is a fine plant for front of the garden, rockeries or edging. When the flowers cover the foliage, they provide brief (2-4 weeks) but brilliant spots of color throughout the garden. If the mats of foliage become too vigorous, they may be pruned to desirable proportions. Provide full sun and well-drained soil. These are tough plants, able to withstand significant abuse and persist for many years if properly sited. It is brilliant at the Denver Botanic Garden, often blooming through late snowfalls.

Propagate by division or by seed similar to *V. alpina*.

**Cultivars**:

'Alba' produces white flowers.

'Aztec Gold' is one of the best new forms in many years. The flowers are similar to the species but the golden foliage makes an eye-popping contrast, and does not significantly fade in the summer. Full sun, however, is needed for the brightest leaves.

'Blue Sheen' has small racemes of wisteria-blue flowers on 2-3″ tall plants.

'Heavenly Blue' has gained immense popularity. It bears sapphire blue flowers and creeps along at a height of about 2-4″.

'Loddon Blue' has rich deep blue flowers and is about 4″ tall.

'Mrs. Holt' has bright pink flowers in the summer and grows about 6″ tall. It is not as vigorous as the type.

'Spode Blue' bears light blue flowers.

'Purpurea' produces deep violet flowers.

'Trehane' has bright yellow-green foliage from which arise short racemes of deep blue flowers. The plants are 6-8″ tall.

| | | | |
|---|---|---|---|
| ***-spicata*** (spee-kah′ ta) | | Spiked Speedwell | 10-36″/24″ |
| Summer | Blue | Europe, Northern Asia | Zones 4-7 |

One of the most popular veronicas, it is also the parent of many hybrids. The 2″ long glossy leaves are lanceolate and toothed, except at the base and tip. The blue flowers are only about 1/4″ in diameter but have long purple stamens. They are held in dense 1-3′ long spikelike racemes at the end of the stems (terminal). Their upright form and the terminal flower stems differentiate this from many of the lower-growing species whose flowers occur only in the leaf axils.

Bloom color ranges from deep blue to white with an occasional light pink. Flowers are produced for 4-7 weeks and provide excellent color for the front and middle of the garden. Plants require sunny well-drained conditions. In the South, winter drainage is particularly important because plants succumb to many root rot organisms that proliferate in wet, cool soils.

Propagation of the species and varieties from seed is similar to *V. alpina*. Terminal cuttings and divisions, however, are the best means to propagate cultivars.

**Cultivars**:

'Alba' is similar to the species but with white flowers.

'Barcarolle' is one of a number of hybrids between *V. incana* and *V. spicata*. It has rose-pink flowers, stands 12-15″ tall and has leaves which are somewhat gray-green, due to the influence of *V. incana*.

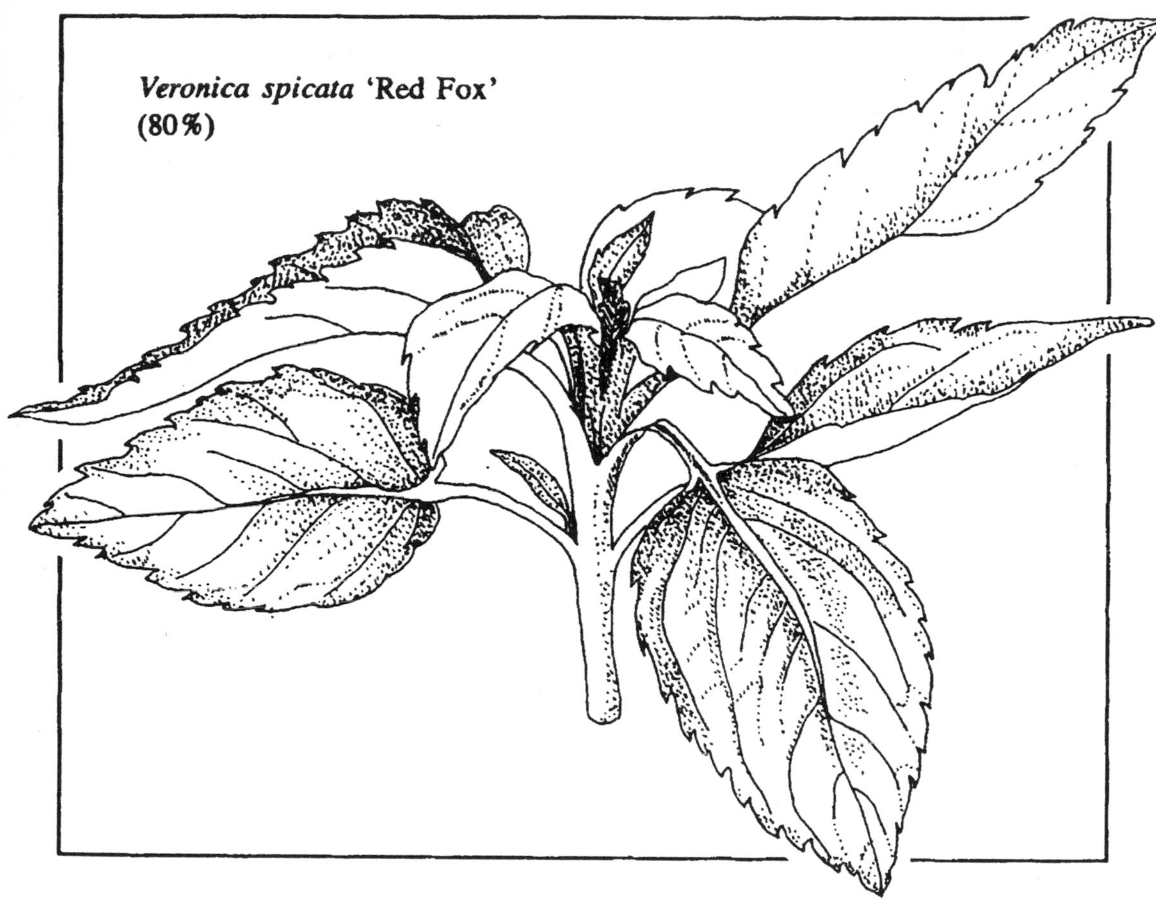
*Veronica spicata* 'Red Fox' (80%)

'Blue Charm' is one of the taller members of the group. Plants grow nearly 3′ tall and produce lavender-blue flowers in early to midsummer.

'Blue Fox' has bright lavender blue flowers on 15-20″ tall stems.

'Blue Peter' grows 24″ tall and produces dark blue flowers on 12″ spikes.

'Blue Spires' has glossy green leaves and many deep blue flower spikes on 12-18″ tall plants. Plants flower for about 4 weeks in late June and July in the Gardens at UGA.

'Erika' grows nearly 18″ tall and bears rose-pink flowers in early summer.

'Giles van Hees' is one of the best dwarf forms, growing 5-8″ tall and providing pink flowers in mid to late summer.

'Heidekind' is 8-10″ tall with compact rose pink spikes in late spring. It is not as cold hardy as the species and does poorly below zone 5, but conversely is one of the better performers in trials in the Southeast.

'Icicle' bears good white flowers on 2′ tall plants. One of the better whites.

'Minuet' has a similar parentage to 'Barcarolle' and grows 12-18″ tall. The foliage is grayer than that of 'Barcarolle'.

var. *nana* is similar to the species but only about 8″ tall.

'Noah Williams' is a variegated form with white margins and creamy white flowers.

'Purple Panther' grows less than 2′ tall with lilac spikes in early summer.

'Purpleicious' is similar to the previous cultivar but with darker purple flowers. Another example of watching too much Barney.

'Red Fox' has deep rosy-red flowers and glossy leaves. It stands about 15″ tall, is free flowering and blooms for over 5 weeks.

var. *rosea* is similar to 'Red Fox' but has pinker flowers.

Sightseeing Mix is a seed-propagated mixture of blues, pinks and lavenders on 18″ tall plants. Vigorous and a good performer.

'Snow White' has branching spikes of white flowers on 18″ tall stems.

'Tickled Pink' is 18-22″ tall with many lavender-pink flowers. May be a hybrid as it appears to be less cold hardy than others.

'Twilight' is about a foot tall and nears many lavender-blue flowers.

**Related Species and Hybrids:**

'Bergen's Blue' is an alpine form, growing about 6″ tall, with clear blue flowers. Good for stone walkways and rock gardens. Zones 3-7.

*V. bombycina*, cotton speedwell, native from Turkey to Lebanon, forms dense cushions of densely white-hairy leaves. Beautiful in leaf and even nicer when the silver-blue flowers appear. Better in cooler climate and low humidity.

*V. cinerea*, ashen speedwell, has mounds of thyme-like silvery leaves and pale blue flowers.

'Crystal River' is a 3′ tall ground cover with vigor and heat tolerance. Plants produce blue flowers in the spring. A 2003 Plant Select® winner, a program administered by the Denver Botanic Garden and Colorado State University.

'Darwin's Blue' is 15-18″ tall with dark green foliage and neat spikes of blue-purple flowers.

*V. exaltata* is closely related to *V. longifolia* and considered a synonym by many taxonomists. It blooms in mid to late summer and bears light blue ¼″ diameter flowers in dense terminal racemes. Plants grow 4′ tall but little or no staking is required.

'Georgia Blue' produces hundreds of gentian blue flowers on 6-9″ mounds. The flowers are among the earliest in the garden, often flowering with the daffodils. An exceptional plant, one I recommend to everyone. Originally labeled as *V. peduncularis*, the plant is now considered to be a cultivar of *V. umbrosa*. There are a number of differences between them, the most obvious one being flower color. *V. peduncularis* is white with pinkish veins, while *V. umbrosa* is deep blue.

'Goodness Grows' is an outstanding long-flowering hybrid that likely arose from *V. alpina* 'Alba' and *V. spicata* at Goodness Grows Nursery in Lexington, Georgia. It has the low-growing habit (10-12″) of the former and the long blue racemes of the latter.

*V. liwanensis*, Turkish speedwell, is highly recommended for Western gardeners craving a sunny ground cover. Plants are only about 2″ tall but spread rapidly, and produce blue flowers later in the spring. A 1997 Plant Select® winner.

'New Century' appears to be a hybrid, growing 8-12″ tall, and covered with light blue flowers in late spring.

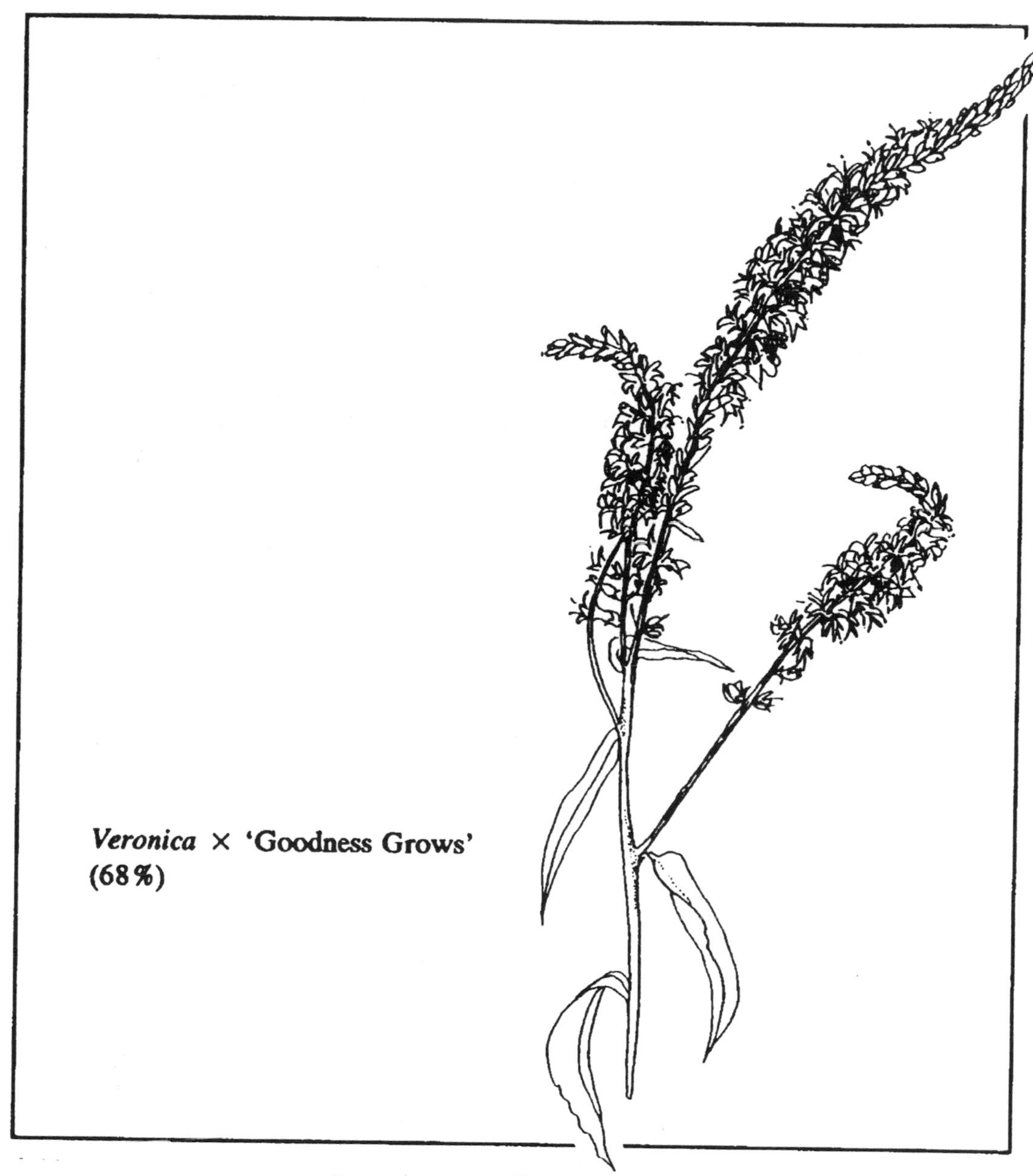

***Veronica* × 'Goodness Grows' (68%)**

*V. pinnata* is 8-12″ tall with numerous finely divided 2½″ long leaves. The flowers are dark blue on branched racemes. 'Blue Eyes' has lighter blue flowers than the species and is only about 10″ tall.

*V. repens*, creeping speedwell, is a prostrate species that loves to scramble over rocks or walls in full sun and well-drained conditions. The light blue to almost white flowers, held in terminal racemes, appear in late summer. 'Sunshine' is a golden-leaved form grown for the bright golden foliage. Very bright and handsome. Introduced by Pine Knot Farms in Clarksville, Virginia.

'Royal Candles' is one of the finest forms developed in the last 10 years. Plants are compact and bear deep blue flowers on rigid flower stems. Their parentage involves a number of taxa, including the famous 'Sunny Border Blue'. Plants are 15-18″ tall and grow from zones 3-8.

'Sonja' is similar in habit to cultivars of *V. spicata* and *V. longifolia*. Plants are upright, 2-2½′ tall, and produce lilac rose flowers. Zones 5-7.

'Sunny Border Blue' is 18-24″ tall with violet-blue flowers in mid summer to fall. Introduced into the trade in 1946 by Robert Bennerup of Sunny Border Nurseries, Kensington, Connecticut. Plants are a little lanky and perform inconsistently but their popularity went through the roof when they were designated the Perennial Plant Association's Plant of the Year in 1993.

'Waterperry' may be a hybrid, probably involving *V. peduncularis* and others. It is a wonderful 4-6″ tall plant with dozens of light blue flowers in the spring or early summer. Great in open rocky areas where it can be allowed to spread. A little later than 'Georgia Blue' and lighter flower color.

***Veronicastrum*** (ve-ro-ni-kas′ trum) Culver's Root Scrophulariaceae

Two species are cultivated, the most common being culver's root, *V. virginicum*. The plant has been tossed back and forth between this genus and *Veronica*, and although they're similar, the easiest way to tell them apart is to look at the leaves. Those of *Veronica* are usually opposite, occasionally alternate, the leaves of *Veronicastrum* are whorled.

-***virginicum*** (vir-jin′ i-cum) Culver's Root 4-6′/4′
Late Summer Pale Blue, White Eastern United States Zones 4-8

The lanceolate leaves are arranged in whorls of 3-6 around the unbranched stems. Each pointed leaf is 2-4″ long, sharply toothed, smooth above and somewhat pubescent below. The pinkish white ¼″ long flowers are arranged in dense, terminal, 6-9″ long racemes and are one of nature's butterfly magnets. After flowering, lateral racemes take over, resulting in a 4-6 week flowering period. Plants make excellent cut flowers; a good trick to obtain fuller stems is to remove the terminal flower bud as soon as it can be handled, resulting in a half dozen lateral flowers opening together.

This is an imposing plant if grown in full sun, watered well and fertilized 2-3 times a year. If placed in partial shade, plants need support and are rather unattractive.

Propagate by seed similar to *Veronica alpina*, but germination requires 4-6 weeks. Terminal cuttings (remove flowers) and divisions are also used.

**Cultivars**:

None of the cultivars is an improvement on the species, but they provide a some lavender flower colors.

'Album' is the most popular form of the species. However, there is no doubt that some purchased plants have cleaner whiter flowers than others. White is the most commonly purchased color.

'Apollo' is about 3′ tall with lilac flowers.
'Erica' provides purple-pink flowers on 3½′ tall plants.
'Fascination' bears lilac-rose flowers on 3-4′ tall plants.
'Lavender Towers' is 4-5′ tall and characterized by light purple spires. This has become quite popular because of the flower color, but is still not as good a performer as 'Album'.
'Roseum' bears pink flowers.
'Temptation' is about 3½′ tall with lavender flowers.

**Related Species:**

*V. sibiricum* is the Russian representative and is similar in habit and size. The leaves are larger, coarser and the flowers are deeper blue. Plants may be a little more cold hardy as well.

***Vinca*** (ving- ka) Vinca, Myrtle, Periwinkle Apocynaceae

Of the 12 species, 2 are incredibly popular ground covers. In some parts of the country, oceans of periwinkle may be found around every corner. All species have opposite leaves and solitary flowers borne in the upper leaf axils. The annual bedding plant, Madagascar periwinkle, formally called *Vinca rosea*, is correctly known as *Catharanthus roseus*.

***-major*** (may′ jor) Large Periwinkle 12-18″/24″
Spring Blue Europe Zones 7-9

Due to the lack of winter hardiness, *V. major* is seldom used as an outdoor ground cover north of zone 6, and even there, catalogs suggest that some winter protection may be necessary (how do you protect a ground cover, anyway?). All stems bear 2-3″ long glossy, ovate, evergreen leaves with small hairs on the margins (ciliate), but the non-flowering stems are prostrate while the flowering stems ascend. The blue, funnel-shaped flowers are 1-2″ in diameter with sepals almost as long as the corolla tube. They are borne in abundance in early spring and sporadically throughout the summer. The non-flowering stems root at the tips where they touch the ground. If provided with moist soils in partial shade, plants fill in vigorously. It is also an excellent plant for trailing over banks, or cascading from window boxes or planters. My daughters use them as "spillers" in their mixed containers. As many variegated plants are probably sold for containers and clay pots than for ground covers in both South and North.

Propagate by terminal cuttings of non-flowering stems in late spring or divide throughout the season.

**Cultivars:**

'Alba' has white flowers.
'Aureomaculata' ('Maculata', 'Oxford') has leaves with dark green margins and lighter yellowish green centers. Arose from a sport of 'Variegata'.
'Aureomarginata' bears green leaves with bright yellow margins. The yellow color is deepest in the spring and tends to fade in the summer.

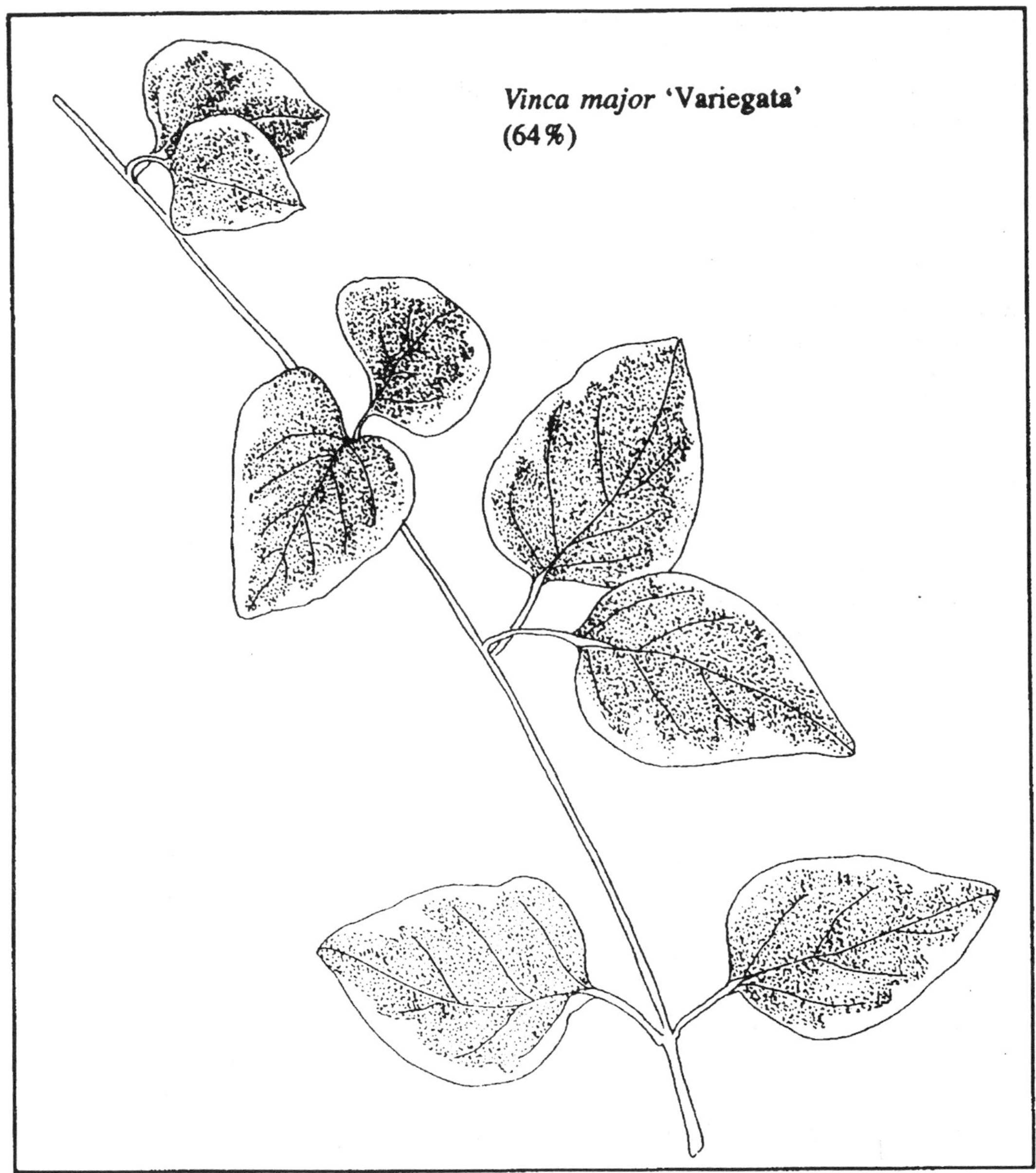

*Vinca major* **'Variegata'**
**(64%)**

'Hirsuta' ('Pubescens') bears more pubescent leaves than the species and red-purple flowers with narrow petals. The petals of the purple flowers are narrower than the species. It is similar in flower to 'Oxyloba' but is more hairy on the petioles and the corolla tube.

'Oxyloba' produces leaves more lanceolate than the species. The deep purple flowers are much more narrow than the species and even more narrow than 'Hirsuta'.

'Reticulata' has foliage netted with yellow lines.

'Variegata' ('Elegantissima') is popular in hanging baskets and window boxes. Plants have dark green leaves with irregular yellow-white margins and blue flowers.

'Wojo's Jem' is wonderfully handsome, with variegated leaves that consist of large, creamy yellow-white centers edged with deep green. Violet blue flowers contrast well. Extraordinary for mixed containers. Plants arose from Wojo's Greenhouse in Ortonville, Michigan; the "Jem" being the initials of Jessica, Emily and Beth Marie, the daughters of the owner.

***-minor*** (mine′ or) Common Periwinkle 6-12″/spreading
Spring Blue Europe Zones 4-9

That this species is so widely used in North America testifies to its toughness and ability to tolerate a wide range of climatic conditions. Such a lovely plant has a rather gruesome history. In the Middle Ages, it adorned the heads of criminals on their way to execution, and was called *fiore di morte* in Italy because it was placed on the bodies of dead infants. However, not everyone shared such gloom and plants soon became known as "joy of the ground", a name occasionally used today.

*V. minor* produces tubular bluish purple flowers ¾-1″ across and the sepals are about ⅓ as long as the corolla tube. Flowers open in the spring and, like large periwinkle, appear sporadically all season. They are such good ground covers because they also produce non-flowering stems which root at all nodes, with elliptical 1½″ long evergreen leaves with smooth, entire margins. Plants are vigorous and prefer shade and moist areas. An excellent species for a ground cover and erosion control.

Propagate by division throughout the season. Terminal cuttings of non-flowering stems may also be used.

**Cultivars**:

'Alba' has white flowers which make a nice contrast with the dark green foliage.

'Alboplena' bears white double flowers.

'Argenteovariegata' has white variegated foliage.

'Atropurpurea' produces dark purple flowers.

'Aureovariegata' has leaves variegated with deep yellow. The variegation may be on the margins or the entire leaf may be yellow.

'Blue and Gold' has gold margins on the leaves and lilac-blue flowers.

'Bowles Variety' (var. *bowlesii*) bears light blue 1-1¼″ diameter flowers and is less vigorous than the species. This is also known as 'La Graveana' ('La Grave'). 'Golden Bowles' has yellow leaf margins.

'Honeydew' produces chartreuse leaves with pale blue flowers.

'Dart's Blue' has more blue and less purple in the flowers. The stems are purple to black.

'Emily Joy' has lovely large white flowers. Plants were selected from 'Alba' by North Creek Nursery.

'Illumination' became widely available and therefore quite popular. The yellow leaves are surrounded with a green margin and are handsomely striking. The blue flowers are secondary. This cultivar and many of the variegated forms have been used more to advantage in baskets and containers than as ground covers.

'Multiplex' has double, plum-purple flowers. Also sold as 'Double Purple'.

'Fieldstone Splash' comes from Fieldstone Gardens in Vassalboro, Maine, and has dark green margins around a chartreuse center. A great introduction from a great nursery.

'Jekyll's White' ('Miss Jekyll') has single white flowers but the stems are weaker and leaves are smaller that other white flowering forms.

'Ralph Shugert' honors the noted Michigan plantsman by the same name, and his namesake vinca has many believers. Plants produce leaves with thin white margins and dark blue flowers. According to Tom Kemmel of Twixwood Nursery in Berrien Springs, Michigan, this is by far the best variegated vinca on the market today.

'Sterling Silver' bears dark blue flowers and foliage with white margins.

'Valley Glow' has light green to almost chartreuse foliage. The foliage stands out in the shade but the white flowers are somewhat lost in the leaves.

'Variegata' produces yellow variegated leaves and pale blue flowers.

## *Viola* (vie′ o-la) Violet Violaceae

Some of the oldest plants on record, violets were cultivated for their medicinal properties as early as 400 BC by the Greeks. They were raised in monastery gardens in the Middle Ages and were important items in the cut flower markets of Europe in the 19th century and well into the 20th. Over 500 species of violets are distributed in the north and south temperate zones. However, as lovely as some species are, many are equally terrible weeds, reseeding everywhere. This thuglike characteristic has made many gardeners wary of planting any of the perennial violets at all. For garden purposes, violets may be divided into two large groups. The first is the true violets, such as *V. cornuta*, tufted violet, and *V. odorata,* sweet violet, which are treated as perennials and flower in late fall and early spring. The second group is the true pansies such as *V. tricolor*, heartsease, *V. lutea* and *V. altaica.*

Hybridization of these species and others has given rise to the myriad of modern garden pansies and violas, collectively known as *V.* x *wittrockiana.* Although sufficiently cold hardy in much of the country, they have poor heat tolerance and are generally used as annuals for early spring flowering.

Two kinds of flowers are produced by most true violets. In the spring, the large, showy, infertile flowers open. They consist of a flat lower petal (a landing strip for insects), two side petals or "wings" and two upper petals. The lower petal bears a spur, similar to columbine. In the summer, flowers with rudimentary or no petals are formed at the base of the plant. These never open but self-pollinate within the closed calyx and are known as cleistogamous flowers. Seed capsules are formed which spew out small seeds to distances of up to 9 feet. Many of the non-stoloniferous species appear like magic because of this quarterback-like property. The dried, open seed capsules can easily be seen if the leaves are pushed aside in late summer and fall.

The foliage of all cultivated violets is evergreen. Garden species of violets are low growing and suitable for the front of the border or for a wildflower garden. Most tolerate full sun but prefer shaded, moist conditions. A number of native wild flowers such as confederate violet, *V. sororia*, bird's-foot violet, *V. pedata*, and Canada violet, *V. canadensis*, are ornamental but little selection or hybridization has been undertaken to introduce them as garden subjects. Their potential for improvement is great but to find more than a half dozen of the cultivars I list is frustrating work at best.

Species hybridize readily making identification difficult. In fact, L.H. Bailey stated in *The Standard Cyclopedia of Horticulture* (Vol. III, 1943) that there were more natural hybrids than there were species. Taxonomic differences among species are subtle and for those inclined to use a 10X hand lens, one of the best structures to study is the shape of the style. It is one of the few morphological factors that distinguish violet species.

Quick Reference to Viola Species

| | Height (in.) | Stems (yes or no) | Stoloniferous (yes or no) | Color of seeds |
|---|---|---|---|---|
| *V. cornuta* | 4-12 | Yes | No | Black |
| *V. cucullata* | 3-6 | No | No | Black |
| *V. labradorica* | 1-4 | Yes | No | Brown |
| *V. odorata* | 2-8 | No | Yes | Cream |
| *V. pedata* | 2-6 | No | No | Copper |
| *V. pubescens* | 8-12 | Yes | No | Brown |
| *V. rotundifolia* | 3-6 | No | No | White |

***-cornuta*** (kor-new′ ta) Horned Violet, Tufted Violet 4-12″/12″
Spring Violet Pyrenees Zones 6-9

The stems are more or less prostrate at the base before ascending and the whole plant appears tufted, thus accounting for its common name. A vigorous grower, it is often used as a ground cover and an accent plant. The evergreen leaves are ovate, 1-2″ long, less than 1″ wide and are hairy beneath. The nodes of the stem bear opposite leafy stipules about the same length as the petiole.

The 1-1½″ diameter flowers are borne on 2-4″ long stems that arise from the leaf axils. The petals are spread apart, resulting in star-like flowers on some varieties. They are slightly fragrant with a long slender spur, thus accounting for the other common name.

Flowers occur in spring and, if the plant is cut back in the summer, again in the fall. In the South, plants are heat tolerant and although some stress-related damage may occur during July and August, they do not perish like annual pansies.

Propagate by division in the fall or early spring. Terminal cuttings, approximately 2″ long, taken in spring or summer will root in 10-15 days if placed under moist, warm conditions. Seed germinates quickly if lightly covered and placed at about 70°F under high humidity. After germination, move the seedlings to a 55-60°F location.

**Cultivars**:

'Alba' has clean, pure white flowers.

'Black Magic' has flowers so deeply purple than they are almost black.

'Blue Perfection' is 6-8″ tall and produces sky blue flowers in early spring and again in the fall.

'Broughton Blue' bears many attractive pale blue flowers with darker blue veins in the center.
'Chantreyland' is similar to the above cultivar but has apricot flowers.
'Jersey Gem' has broad petals of rich blue purple.
var. *lilacina* is one of my favorite violas as it bears abundant pale lilac-blue flowers with spreading petals. It is relatively heat tolerant and is a good performer in much of the country.
'Lord Nelson' is one of the most durable selections of the species and produces small (¾″ across) violet flowers with a tiny yellow eye.
'Painted Porcelain' has pastel-colored flowers with lavender and deep purple centers.
'Rosea' bears large rose-pink flowers.
'Scottish Yellow' has pure yellow 1-1½″ wide flowers.
'White Perfection' has clean white flowers on 6-8″ tall plants.

***-cucullata*** (kuk-eh-lah′ ta) Marsh Blue Violet 3-6″/12″
Spring Violet Eastern North America Zones 4-9

The leaves and flower stems arise from the rootstock, making this a stemless species. The pale green foliage is broadly ovate to heart shaped, 3-4″ wide, and held on 3-5″ long petioles. The margins are somewhat wavy and the whole leaf is essentially hairless. Each ½-1″ diameter flower has purple veins on the lower petal while the lateral ones have dense beard-like hairs. Plants are distinguished from other native blue violets by the long flower stems which help to carry the flowers well above the foliage. Scaly rhizomes result in large clumps but plants are not stoloniferous though they can throw seed everywhere.

Plants are particularly aggressive in moist shady places. The foliage is produced throughout the year resulting in an effective ground cover. It self-sows everywhere, however, and can soon become an awful nuisance. I would not knowingly plant any of the native blue violets like *V. papillionacea* and *V. sororia* (see Related Species) in my garden due to their self-seeding habit. Plants are still sold under the old name *V. obliqua*.

**Cultivars:**
'Red Giant' has rose-red flowers.
'Royal Robe' bears deep blue flowers on 4-6″ tall flower stems.
'White Czar' has lovely white flowers with a yellow center and dark netted markings in the throat. Plants grow vigorously and tolerate more sun than the species. It is possibly a hybrid with *V. odorata* 'Czar'.

***-labradorica*** (lab-ra-do′ ri-ka) Labrador Violet 1-4″/12″
Spring Violet Northern United States, Greenland Zones 3-8

One of the shortest and one of the best garden violets in the entire genus. They are wonderful plants which if allowed to do their own thing, will make fine combinations with other early spring flowerers. Plants are native to northeastern states, parts of Canada, and as far north as Greenland, but it is one of the best little plants in the Armitage garden (zone 7b). Plants were unknown for many years but they are now

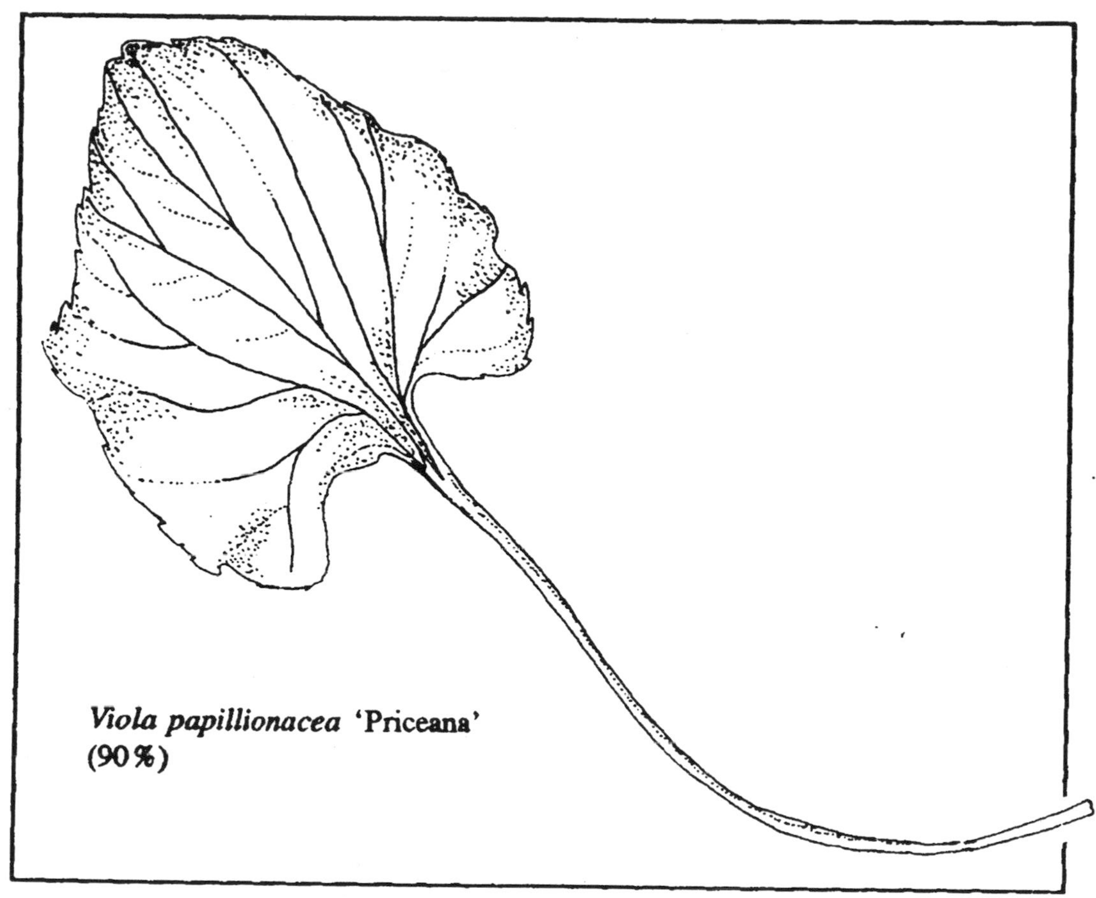

***Viola papillionacea* 'Priceana' (90%)**

more available for gardeners throughout the country. The 1″ wide, broadly ovate foliage is shallowly toothed, almost purple, and arises from a short stem. The leaves are very dark in the spring, but remain purple even in warm weather. The ¾″ mauve flowers are suffused with dark purple and appear in early spring, then sporadically the rest of the season.

The slender creeping rhizomes and hundreds of seed thrown about allow plants to fill in areas rapidly, including cracks in the sidewalks and between stones in the walkway. They are terrific companions with foamflowers, wood poppies and may apples. Provide shade and moisture and sit back and enjoy.

Divide every 2-3 years if it starts to ramble too aggressively. Seed may be treated similarly to *V. cornuta*.

***-odorata*** (o-do-rah′ ta) | Sweet Violet | 2-8″/15″
Spring | Violet | Europe, Asia | Zones 6-8

Whenever this species is planted in a garden, centuries of history are planted with it. Plants have been cultivated as long as there have been gardens, and they are mentioned frequently in Greek and Latin classics. The flower market in Athens, Greece

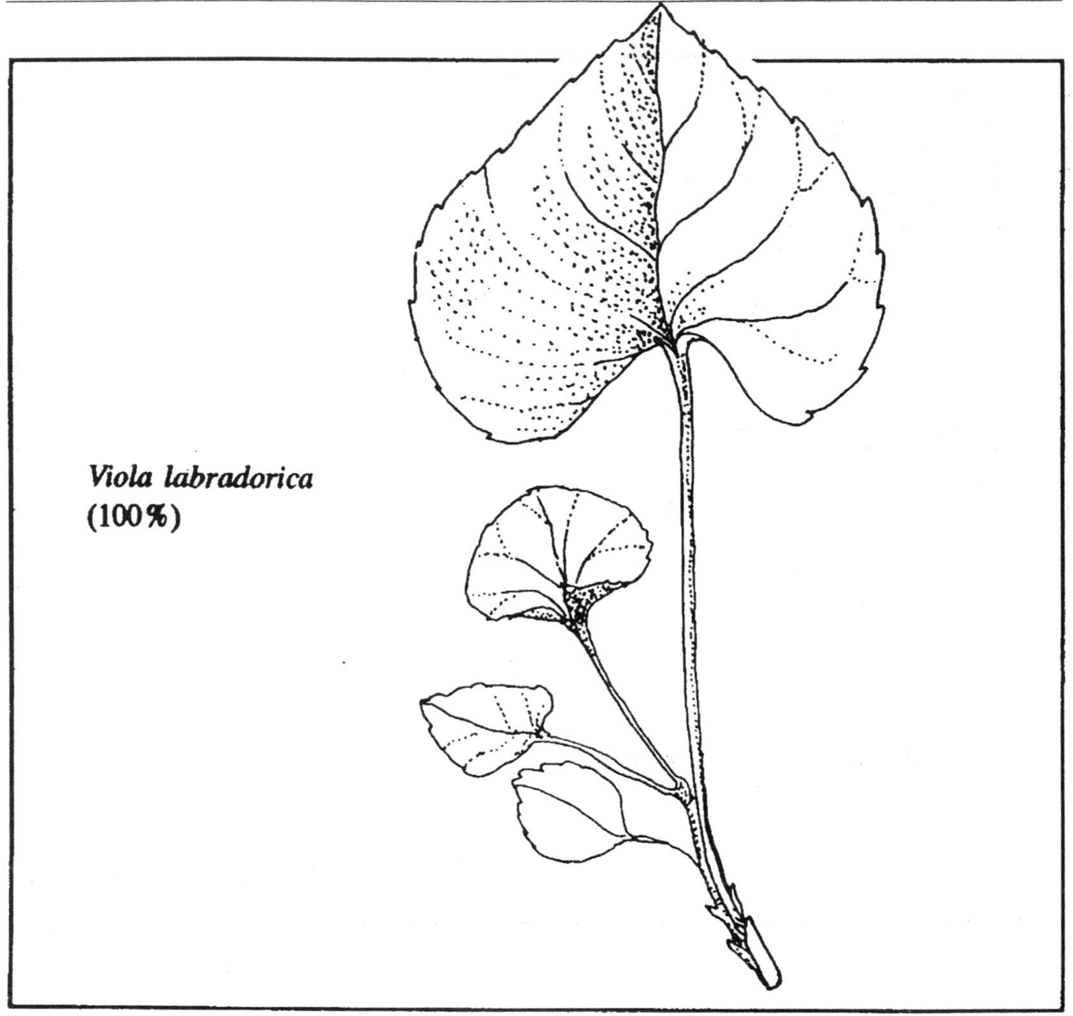


handled violets as early as 400 BC and the sweet violet became the symbol of Athens. As F.E. Dillistone writes (*Violet Culture for Pleasure and Profit, 1926*) violets were "as proud a device of the Ionic Athenians as the rose of England or the lilies of France". It was also adopted as the symbol and password of Napoleon's supporters after he was exiled to Elba; he always presented sweet violets to Josephine on their wedding anniversary. The medicinal and chemical uses are also well documented but the fragrance distinguishes it from others. The substance that provides the fragrance is ionine, which is ephemeral, meaning that the nose perceives the odor but for a short time. Thus the scent of violets is sweet, but not long lasting. This characteristic spawned huge acreage of violets for the perfume industry, particularly in France and England in 1900s. The use of violets for perfume continued into the 1940s and 1950s until chemists found a way to manufacture ionine synthetically, and little natural "fragrance of violet" is found in today's perfumes. Sweet violets, however, are still sold as cut flowers but are useful only for local markets due to the transitory nature of the fragrance.

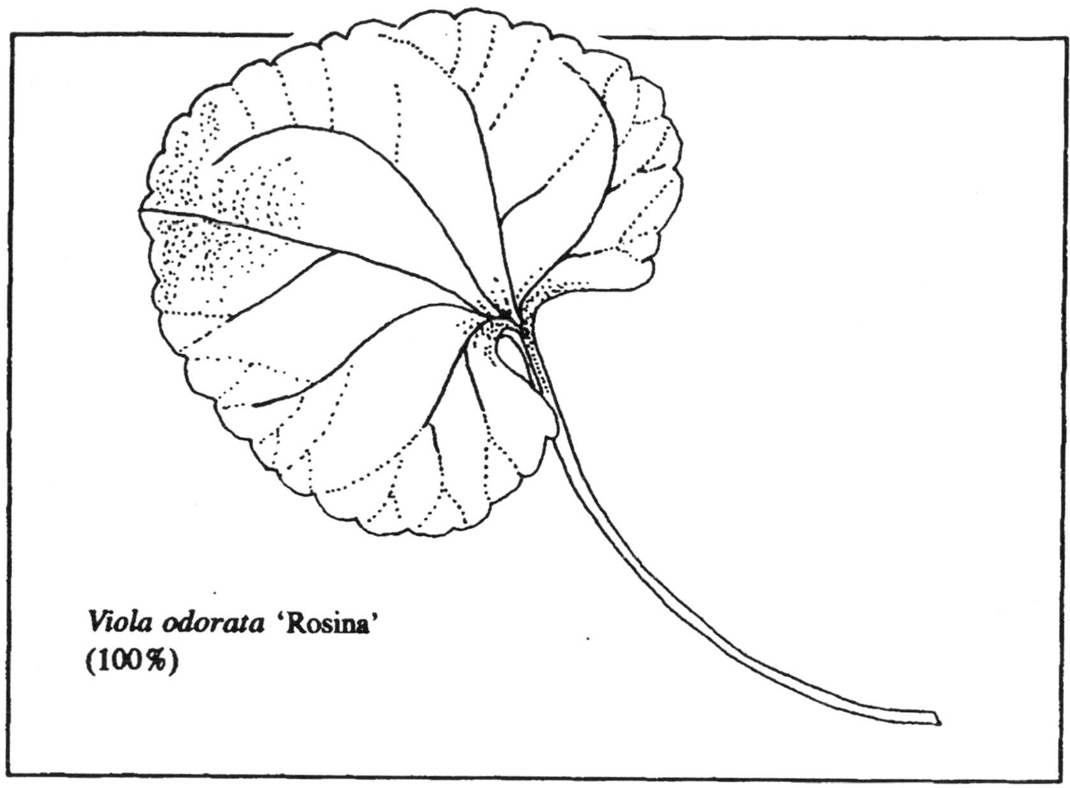

*Viola odorata* **'Rosina'**
**(100%)**

The tufted foliage is broadly ovate to kidney shaped and arises from the rootstock. Each finely pubescent leaf is 2-3" wide and has blunt shallow serrations on the margin. The ¾" long flowers are usually violet, but rose and white forms also exist. Flowers occur in the fall and appear throughout the winter in mild climates and into the spring. Prostrate runners root at the tips and allow it to spread rapidly. Flowering occurs the second year from rooting. Large-flowered double types arose in the late 1800s and became known as Neapolitan or Parma violets. They are fragrant but their ancestry is rather obscure, perhaps being derived from *V. alba* rather than *V. odorata.*

Plants grow best in the cool times of the year (this is true for all violets), but are not winter hardy below zone 6 without protection. Full sun is tolerated as long as adequate soil moisture is provided, otherwise partial shade is necessary. Every gardener should have one or two plants if for no other reason than to occasionally feel like Josephine. I would not have a garden without them.

Division of the plantlets resulting from the stoloniferous runners is practiced in the fall. Seed of the species and varieties should be handled similar to *V. cornuta.*

**Cultivars:**

'Czar' was one of the earliest selections and bears single, deep violet flowers on narrow stems. 'White Czar' may also belong here.

'Duchesse de Parme' bears double lavender-violet flowers, 'Lady Hume Campbell' has double lavender flowers, and 'Marie Louise' produces deep double violet-mauve flowers. These cultivars carry flowers on long stems which are suitable for cutting. These are but 3 of the group of plants referred to as Parma violets, an important cut flower crop in Europe in recent years. They are not particularly easy to find in North America.

'Fair Oaks' produces fragrant rosy lavender flowers.

'L'Arne' bears purple flowers.

'Queen Charlotte' has dark blue to purple flowers on 6-8″ tall stems.

'Rosina' has rose-pink flowers with a dark center.

'White Queen' has small white flowers on 6″ tall plants.

***-pedata*** (pe-dah′ ta) Bird's-Foot Violet 2-6″/12″
Spring Violet Eastern North America Zones 4-8

One of our prettiest native flowers, *V. pedata* is easy to identify because the leaves are said to look like a bird's foot. This particular bird has feet palmately divided into 3-5 narrow segments. Plants are stemless and flowers are ¾-1½″ across, borne on 2-6″ long peduncles. The upper two petals are dark violet while the lower three are pale lilac with dark veins. Five orange stamens are clustered in the center. It is certainly not the easiest violet to cultivate and demands excellent drainage and partial shade. Planting in soil over a layer of coarse gravel helps establishment. The rhizome must be kept free of standing water or rot will develop.

There are enough commercial sources of this violet available that no one need remove them from the wild. Transplanting from the wild is likely to be unsuccessful anyway, so why even bother being stupid?

Seed must be refrigerated for 5-6 weeks at 35-40°F to insure germination. If seed is sown directly in the garden, seedlings will appear the following spring. Leaf-bud cuttings (a leaf blade, petiole, with a piece of rhizome attached) may be placed in sand in late fall and winter. Rooting will occur in 3-5 weeks. Division of the rhizome may also be accomplished in late fall and winter.

**Cultivars**:

var. *alba* has white flowers that contrast well with the palmate foliage.

'Artist Palette' is a handsome blue and white bicolor from Don Jacobs of Eco-Gardens in Decatur, Georgia.

var. *concolor* is a southern variant of the species and bears larger (1½″) violet flowers with a white spot at the base of the lower petal. It is particularly suited to southern gardens.

***-pubescens*** (pew′ bes-cens) Downy Yellow Violet 8-12″/12″
Spring Yellow Eastern North America Zones 3-7

The stem and triangular to kidney-shaped foliage are softly pubescent to the touch, thus the common name. The round, toothed, round leaves are 3-4″ across and usually occur on short petioles at the top of the stem. The lower stem is often bare of leaves for 2-3″ and the upper is often branched. The large stipules (about ½″ wide) are lanceolate and entire. The bright yellow ½″ wide flowers are borne in the leaf axils and consist of lower petals veined with purple, providing a nice contrast to the yellow.

Plants are native to dry, rich, shaded areas and should be placed in a well-drained shady area in the garden. They are not as heat tolerant as many violets and perform better in zones 4-6 than in zone 7.

Propagate from seed similar to *V. cornuta*. If seedlings fail to germinate within 6 weeks, place in refrigerator for 4-6 weeks and treat like *V. pedata*. Divide the short rhizome in late fall or early spring.

***-rotundifolia*** (ro-tund-i-foe' lee-a) Roundleaf Violet 3-6″/9″
Spring Yellow Maine to North Georgia Zones 3-7

This native species' oval to circular 2-4″ wide foliage rises directly from the rootstock. Plants produce sprawling purplish stems after flowering that result in a matlike habit. The lower 3 petals of the 2″ wide yellow flowers are brown veined and quite eye-catching. Flowers are borne on 2-4″ long stalks in early spring. Plants perform particularly well in cool climates but simply open up and look sad where summers are hot.

Propagate by seed similar to *V. cornuta* or by division in spring or fall.

**Hybrid Violets:**

There are many fine violets in commerce today that don't fit any particular species, and are the result of some wonderful selection and hybridization. Many are old-fashioned selections, with a slight sweet fragrance. They are best used in containers or on a patio table where they can truly be enjoyed. Here a few of my favorites.

'Etain' has wonderful pale yellow flowers with light lavender margins. They are fragrant and quite exceptional.

'Fiona' bears beautiful light blue tinged flowers.

'Helen Mount' is an old fashioned "Johnny jump-up" but one of the best. She has purple upper petals and orange-yellow lower ones.

'Irish Molly' has flowers the size of garden violas which are bronze orange with darker centers.

'Maggie Mott' has mauve flowers with a lovely silver tinge. The centers are cream colored.

'Mars' has large green leaves with obvious purple centers. The foliage is as or more handsome than the nondescript lavender flowers.

'Molly Sanderson' bears small dark purple to black flowers with yellow centers.

'Purple Showers' has shiny foliage with dark purple flowers.

'Rebecca' has white flowers with ruffled purple margins. Quite beautiful.

'Silver Samurai' is gorgeous, providing large silvery ruffled leaves and lavender flowers in spring. Best to plant in containers to maintain the beauty of the plant.

'Syletta' is sometimes called the cyclamen viola because the silver-veined leaves resemble those of cyclamen. Plants grow as rosettes and produce forgettable pinkish flowers in the spring. They will reseed.

'Thalia' is compact with lower petals cream and upper ones purple.

**Related Species:**

*V. corsica*, Corsican violet, is touted as being perennial even in Santa Fe, New Mexico and Clarkson, Nebraska. The white-whiskered purple flowers are held above the foliage on strong stems. A 2003 Plant Select® winner, a program administered by the Denver Botanic Garden and Colorado State University.

*V. dissecta*, cut leaf violet, is a wonderful violet. It is similar to bird's-foot in that the leaves are divided. They are divided into three segments, each segment deeply divided again. The pale rose flowers are about 1″ across and are nicely fragrant. The foliage is the best part of the plant. Plants reseed with abandon.

*V. nuttallii*, Nuttall violet, also has downy foliage (but only underneath) and yellow flowers. The leaves are present at the base of the plant (lacking in *V. pubescens*) and narrower. Native to the North American prairie states.

*V. sororia* is perhaps the most common violet in the East. Heart-shaped leaves with blunt teeth and smooth stalks occur. The flowers vary from dark violet to blue, and occasionally white. Can be a big-time weed. 'Freckles' produces a unique flower with a light blue background liberally sprinkled with purple flecks, 'Priceana', the confederate violet, has white flowers with a large purple center and a small yellow eye.

*V. striata*, cream violet, is another of my favorite small native violets. Plants have creamy yellow flowers with black striations on the lower petal. Native from New York to Georgia, plants are easy to grow and self-seed with abundance but are not obnoxious.

*V. tricolor* is the old-fashioned Johnny jump-up because of their tendency to throw seeds everywhere. The small stature and wonderful three-toned flowers provide an old-fashioned look.

*Teucrium hyrcanicum*

*Teucrium chamedrys*
'Summer Sunshine'

*Thalictrum*
'Black Stockings'

*Thymus praecox*
'Coccineus'

*Tiarella cordifolia*

*Tiarella cordifolia*
'Spring Symphony'

*Tradescantia*
'Sweet Kate'

*Tricyrtis*
'Gilt Edge'

*Tricyrtis*
'Guilty Pleasure'

*Trillium discolor*

*Trillium luteum*

*Trillium underwoodii*

*Umbilicus rupestris* with *Corydalis*

*Vancouveria hexandra*

*Veratrum album*

(L) *Veratrum nigrum*
(R) *Veratrum viride*

(L) *Verbascum chaixii*

(R) *Verbascum chaixii* 'Cotswold Queen'

*Verbascum dumulosum*

*Verbascum* × *hybridum* 'Southern Charm'

*Verbena bonariensis*

*Verbena tenuisecta*

*Vernonia lettermannii*
'Iron Butterfly'

*Veronica longifolia*
'Blauriesen'

*Veronica prostrata*
'Aztec Gold'

*Veronica spicata*
'Giles van Hees'

*Veronicastrum virginicum*

*Viola cornuta*
'Jersey Gem'

(L) *Yucca gloriosa*
'Variegata'

(R) *Zantedeschia aethiopica*
'Green Dragon'

*Zephyranthes candida*

*Zephryanthes rosea*

*Zizia aptera*

*Zizia aurea* with
*Matteuccia struthiopteris*

**Waldsteinia** (wald-stein′ ee-a) Barren-Strawberry Rosaceae

Such a wonderful group of plants, yet still so little known. Approximately five species of this strawberry-like genus occur and two are occasionally seen in American gardens. Both bear trifoliate leaves, yellow flowers, and small inedible fruits. *Waldsteinia* is far more ornamental than, but not as vigorous as, another insidious strawberry relative, mock strawberry, *Duchesnea indica*. *Waldsteinia* differs by having short surface runners, smaller fruit and 2-5 pistils (*Duchesnea* has 15 or more). *Waldsteinia* is a favored guest, *Duchesnea* an uninvited party crasher.

***-fragarioides*** (fra-gah-ree-oi′ deez) Barren-Strawberry 4-6″/24″
Spring Yellow Eastern United States Zones 4-7

The strawberry-like glossy, evergreen leaves are slightly hairy and are divided into three 1-2″ long, wedge-shaped, toothed leaflets. The yellow flowers, about ½″ across, are carried in 3-8 flowered inflorescences on 4″ long flower stems. Full sun or partial shade is tolerated. Plants form a pretty mat particularly useful for edging or filling in areas along a path. Unfortunately, the flowers do not emerge through the mat but push out the sides so there are never lots of flowers to admire. Performance is poor in wet climates and although native as far south as North Georgia, it may survive but does not thrive under cultivated conditions in zone 8.

Propagate by division in spring or fall or sow seed in warm, moist conditions. It germinates erratically. After germination, place the plants at 60-65°F.

**Related Species:**

*W. geoides* is native to Hungary, with leaves and flowers bigger than those of our natives. The 3-5 lobed, sharply toothed leaves are similar to *Geum* (thus *geoides*), and the yellow flowers occur in early summer. Plants are good ground covers in the Midwest. Zones 4-7.

*W. lobata* is native from North Carolina to Georgia and is the best plant for warm climates. It differs from *W. fragarioides* by having lobed rather than divided leaves. Perform well in zones 7-9.

*W. parviflora* has 3-lobed leaves and yellow flowers on longer scapes, each flower nodding and hairy. Native from Virginia to Georgia, also good for warm gardens. Useful in zones 6-8.

*W. ternata*, Siberian barren-strawberry, is native to Siberia and is a better ground cover than *W. fragarioides*. The leaves occur in rosettes and are borne on short petioles resulting in more compact plants. Cool climates are also necessary for best growth. A winner in the Pacific Northwest.

## *Woodsia* Woodsia Fern Dryopteridaceae

These small ferns are native to temperate and tropical regions. Approximately 25 species occur, a few are evergreen, but many are deciduous, seldom growing taller than 12″. Their dwarf habit and "greenness" seem to have kept them out of mainstream gardening. As a group, the woodsias can be distinguished from other genera by the star-shaped or fringed spore cases found on the underside of the fronds. Most of the woodsias are better plants for the North than the South, and are cold hardy to at least zone 5, many to zone 3.

*Woodsia ilvensis*, rusty woodsia, is native to the northern United States, Canada, and Asia and forms a small clump of fronds that are green above and silvery white beneath. They are similar to resurrection ferns (*Polypodium*, which see), in that they turn rusty brown in times of drought but become green again after rain. They are only about 6″ tall with about 12 opposite pairs of leaflets. The most common woodsia is *W. obtusa*, blunt-lobed woodsia, which can be up to 16″ tall and is often evergreen in northern climes. About 8 pairs of leaflets occur, the lowest pair having blunt lobes. The plants naturally grow in limestone areas and lime should be added in most garden situations. Full sun to partial shade is tolerated. The interlopers to the native species are *W. polystichoides* and *W. subcordata*, native to China, Japan and Korea. The former is about a foot tall, and cold hardy to zone 4; the latter is only about half that size, and forms handsome tight clumps, cold tolerant to zone 5. Both are deciduous and best sited in rock garden areas. All woodsias tolerate full sun in the North and afternoon shade in the Midwest and further south.

## *Woodwardia* Chain Fern Blechnaceae

About ten species of chain fern occur, named for Thomas J. Woodward, a British botanist (1745-1820). Two species are fairly common garden plants. The chain ferns can be distinguished from other ferns by the way the spore cases are arranged on the fertile parts of the plant. They are in rows arranged parallel to the midrib, like links of sausages. The veins closest to the midrib are obviously netted or chained. Both garden ferns are extensively creeping and forking, moving around the soil with ease. All are deciduous. Moisture and partial shade are needed.

***-areolata*** (ar-e′ o-lah′ta) Netted Chain Fern 18-24″/12″
Summer United States Zones 4-8

The chain fern creeps and crawls throughout the Armitage garden, and is a welcome weed. Plants multiple by underground rhizomes and a sizable colony occurs within three years. The fertile fronds look much different from the sterile ones. The sterile fronds are about 2′ tall and 6″ wide with about 10 pairs of nearly opposite leaflets. Usually, the third pair is the longest. The leaflets (pinnae) are slightly wavy and the veins are raised and netted. The fertile frond is similar in shape to the sterile one but all leaflets are greatly contracted and often curved over the sausage-like fruit dots, which occupy nearly the entire width of the leaflet.

The foliage and habit are similar to the sensitive fern, *Onoclea sensibilis*, but plants are not as big and the sterile fronds are more glossy. The habit differs in that the netted chain fern is quite at home in dry soils, while the sensitive fern requires moist areas to be at its best. However, I still get them confused unless they are side by side so I thought some of you might as well. The following table may help keep them straight.

| | ***Woodwardia areolata*** | ***Onoclea sensibilis*** |
|---|---|---|
| Fertile frond | Long, thin, contracted leaflets | Beaded structure, lacking long leaflets |
| Sterile frond | Nearly opposite leaflets | Opposite leaflets |
| Leaflets | Entire to wavy | Margins obviously indented |
| Habit | "Normal" soils | Moist soils |

**Related Species:**

*W. fimbriata*, giant chain fern, is native to the West Coast from British Columbia to northern California. Plants form large clumps, each frond is often 6′ long, and even longer in constantly moist soils. Fabulous, but cold hardy only to zone 8.

*W. orientalis* should likely be considered an annual in most parts of the country (zone 7b maybe) but it is so much fun that it's worth trying and then bringing inside later. The large fronds form tiny plantlets all over, which drop to the ground, or can be plucked off and put in containers for next year's plants. Don't spend too much money on these; fun, and potentially dead fun, is worth only so much.

*W. virginica*, Virginia chain fern, has a similar sausage-like arrangement of fruit dots but they are borne on the main fronds, not on separate sterile ones. It has a similar creeping rootstalk, resulting in good-sized colonies, but is not at all invasive. The fronds are cut into about 15 pairs of almost opposite leaflets. When not fruiting, it can be confused with the cinnamon fern, *Osmunda cinnamomea*, but it does not have those cinnamon tufts of hair at the base of the stalks, and cinnamon fern is a clump former rather than a creeper. Zones 4-9.

# Y

***Yucca*** (yu′ ka) | Yucca | Agavaceae

Most of the 40 species of yucca are native to southwestern United States, although a few are also found in the West Indies. They are evergreen and grown mainly for their architectural form and dramatic flair in the landscape, at least where they are relatively novel. In the Southwest, they are put in new landscapes like junipers of the North, and every subdivision sees a couple of green yuccas standing like sentinels guarding against stray dogs and stray boys. They are tough, withstanding the abuse of anyone foolish enough to mess with them. The leaves of most species are unusually sharply pointed, which while somewhat dangerous, are not all bad. Around Palm Sunday, the landscapes may take on a special look as small children impale colored plastic eggs on the pointy tips, culminating in kaleidoscopic Easter egg trees. Who says creativity is a thing of the past?

The well-known spiny leaves have resulted in names like Adam's needle, dagger plant, Spanish bayonet, Spanish dagger and needle palm, so I need not tell you that these plants are not something that should be near where kids are playing. If kids were as smart as dogs, they would know to avoid them and play elsewhere, but they will get hurt, given time. I love these tough plants, and had some planted a fair distance from the house. But when the grandkids learned to walk, the yuccas were history.

A number of species can be grown as far north as zone 5 (even zone 4) and nearly all of the cultivated forms are cold hardy to at least zone 7. A number of variegated cultivars have been selected from a couple of species, such as *Y. filamentosa* and *Y. filifera*. The habit of yucca ranges from small trees like *Y. elata*, (soap tree), *Y. schottii* (Schott's yucca) and *Y. thompsoniana* (Thompson's yucca) that grow 7-12′ tall, to the stemless forms with their bold rosettes. A number of nurseries have discovered the appeal of these fine plants and species and cultivars are easily available through mail order sources, if your local nursery does not carry them. The main species available is still *Y. filamentosa*, Adam's needle.

***-filamentosa*** (fee-lah-men-to′ sa) | Adam's Needle | 2-3′/5′
White | Summer | Eastern United States | Zones 5-9

The rough, thick leaves are often concave or spoon-shaped, resulting in the name of spoonleaf yucca. The margins of the leaves end in narrow threadlike filaments.

The erect plants are almost stemless and form handsome clumps after a few years. The plants themselves grow 2-3 feet tall but the flower stems may rise 6-8 feet in height. The inflorescence consists of creamy white pendant flowers in the summer and persists for many weeks. The variegated forms are excellent plants for the garden, where their bright yellow or white banded leaves always draw the eye.

Full sun and good drainage are necessary. Many selections are cold hardy to about zone 6, however, plants in protected areas have been successful as far north as zone 5.

**Cultivars:**

'Bright Edge' bears leaves with wide yellow margins. Plants are smaller and work well in tighter spaces. Flower stems rise to about 3′ and carry creamy white bell-shaped flowers.

'Color Guard' is similar to 'Golden Sword' but with gold-centered leaves. Plants are about 4′ tall when not in flower; 6′ in flower.

'Elegantissima' has blue-green leaves with bright white flowers and stiffer symmetry.

'Gold Heart' produces leaves with creamy yellow centers. Plants grow about 30″ tall.

'Hairy' is a great name for a plant with blue-green leaves and at least twice the number of filaments dangling all over. Plants are about 18″ tall and have white flowers in summer.

'Polar Bear' ('Eisbar') has branched inflorescences that grow 4-5′ tall. Plants flower after about three years from seed, significantly earlier than most cultivars.

'Rosenglocken' produces flowers with pink-tinged flowers but is not as vigorous as the species.

'Variegata' bears white-margined foliage.

**Related Species:**

*Y. aloifolia*, Spanish bayonet, is native to the southeastern United States. Plants produce a large trunk which, over time, can grow up to 8′ in height. The common name provides a hint about the murderous leaves. Three foot tall spires of white flowers occur in midsummer. 'Variegata' has a leaf margin of lighter green and pale yellow. Cold hardy to zone 6.

*Y. baccata*, banana yucca, grows about 5′ tall with stiff blue-green leaves and 2′ tall flower spikes. The ivory white flowers are about 2″ across and may be tinged with some purple. The large, swollen fruits give the species its common name. Hardy from zones 5-8.

*Y. flaccida* is similar but has smaller, more flexible leaves than *Y. filamentosa*. 'Garland Gold' has leaves with wide gold bands down the centers. 'Golden Sword' has bright yellow centers particularly in the cool seasons. Flower stems can rise to 6′ in height. 'Ivory' bears creamy white flowers which are held more horizontally than pendant. Equally cold hardy as *Y. filamentosa*.

*Y. recurvifolia*, weeping yucca, is native to the southeastern United States. These stemmed plants have blue-green leaves that bend towards the ground (i.e. recurved). Probably cold hardy to zones 6 or 6b. 'Gold Ribbons', from the great Cistus Nursery on Sauvie Island, Oregon, has yellow-green leaves with thin green margins. A wonderful architectural plant, growing about 6′ tall. 'Variegata' has weeping blue-green leaves like the species but edged in yellow.

*Y. rostrata*, blue yucca, comes from Mexico and has obviously blue-green foliage throughout the year. Plants are trunk-formers and grow to 4-6′ tall. Likely hardy in zones 5b-10.

**Other Hybrids**:

A number of variegated forms are out there, and their parentage has caused a good deal of head scratching. *Y. filamentosa*, *Y. filifera*, *Y. gloriosa* and *Y. aloifolia* are probably involved. Unless they are lined up one after another, it is tough to see a lot of differences between them.

'Bell Tree' is at least 6′ tall with a large inflorescence of white flowers, usually tinged brown on the outside.

'Bright Star' has wide yellow margins around the light green leaves. White flowers occur in the summer. Cold hardy to zone 6b.

'Fountain' is dwarf (3′ tall) with creamy white flowers and wide leaves.

'Giant Bell' is over 6′ tall with stiff leaves and creamy white flowers, often slightly tinged brown on the outside.

'Gold Edge' is similar to 'Bright Edge' but has thinner leaves and clear yellow margins. Equally cold tolerant as 'Color Guard'.

'Snow Spruce' and 'Snow Fir' are both about 6′ tall with starry white flowers and yellow-white flowers respectively. Resulted from work at Foerster's Nursery in Germany.

# Z

**_Zantedeschia_** (zan-te-desh′ ee-a) Calla Lily Araceae

Approximately 8 species are native to South Africa and all have been promoted as commercial cut flower crops, although some cultivars are also offered as garden plants. The well-known flowers consist of the large ornamental spathe enclosing the erect spadix. Plants must be dug and stored through the winter (similar to a gladiolus) in all but the warmest areas of the country. The flowers, particularly of the white calla, *Z. aethiopica*, are used by florists but unfortunately are also associated with funerals, making some people hesitant to use them as garden plants. Placed in containers or in the garden, they provide a classical air to the patio, porch, or border. In the garden, they prefer partial shade but tolerate full sun. The flower stems are longer on plants grown in the shade. Callas are also excellent water plants and may be planted in a bog or beside a pond or pool.

Two problems can plague the genus. The first is an infectious bacterium (*Erwinia*), causing soft rot of the rhizomes. It occurs more in heavy soils, particularly if waterlogged for a significant period of time. The disease is easy to diagnose: the leaves begin to turn yellow, then black and the entire plant collapses in a matter of 7-10 days. Also the crown and roots smell awful. To avoid this problem, place in well-drained soils and take care if digging them in the fall to bring in or divide. Avoid cutting or injuring the rhizome and be sure they are well sun dried ("curing the rhizomes") prior to storing. If the rhizomes are divided, be sure they are dusted with a fungicide and cured before storing or placing back in the ground. The other problem is those monsters, Japanese beetles. They love to descend to the depths of the flower and scratch and chew their way through it. Usually you find them on the day you wish to cut the flower and bring it in the house.

Quick Reference to Zantedeschia Species

| | Height (in.) | Flower color | Leaf shape |
|---|---|---|---|
| *Z. aethiopica* | 24-30 | White | Arrow |
| *Z. albo-maculata* | 24-30 | Greenish white | Arrow |
| *Z. rehmannii* | 9-15 | Pink | Lanceolate |

***-aethiopica*** (aye-thee-o′ pi-ka) White Calla 24-30″/24″
Summer White South Africa Zones 7b-10

In my garden travels around the world, I cannot help but associate certain plants with certain countries. Calla lilies are to New Zealand as tulips are to Holland. Naturalized throughout the country in paddocks and low-lying moist areas, they share space with hundreds of sheep and brighten up dark and dismal winter days. Hundreds of white callas in drifts around a pond is indeed a magnificent sight. The plants are stemless; all parts arise from the broad rootstock. The dark green leaves are twice as long as broad, and carried on long petioles. The pure white spathe flares outward and is 6-10″ long. The spadix is prominent but only about 1/3 the length of the spathe.

Breeding has resulted in dwarf 18″ to 2′ tall compact forms as well as those with cream and green tints in the spathe. I love to see callas growing in the landscape, and special places like Sea Island, Georgia use special plants like white calla at the base of trees or in container plantings. The cut flower industry in this country has planted thousands of callas, both white and colored forms, in Oregon, California, Georgia and Florida. I have grown numerous callas in my zone 7b garden, but every third winter or so will wipe them out. Gardeners and cut flower growers, beware.

Propagate by cormels that readily form after the first year's growth. Lift the plants and separate from the main corm. Seed collected from plants may be sown in pots in the fall and will germinate within 1-3 months. Grow in pots until sufficiently established for placement in the final location.

**Cultivars**:

var. *childsiana* ('Child's Perfection') is dwarfer, more compact and more floriferous than the type. They are particularly useful as potted plants for the greenhouse industry.

'Crowborough' was developed in Crowborough, England and is more winter hardy and sun tolerant than the species. Otherwise, few differences exist.

'Green Dragon' is a terrible-looking thing. Torn by indecision to be green or white, the flowers are a feeble green/white blend. Plants are vigorous and grow 4-5′ tall.

'Little Gem' is 12-18″ tall and suitable for patio containers or indoors. It is more fragrant than the type.

'Whipped Cream' has the same flowers as the species but the green leaves are speckled with white.

'White Giant' is the antithesis of var. *childsiana*. Plants are large, topping out under perfect conditions at over 6′ in height. Everything is big; have fun, enjoy this monster.

***-albo-maculata*** (al-bo-mak-ew-lah′ ta) Spotted Calla 24-30″/24″
Summer Creamy White South Africa Zones 7-10

The leaf blades are 12-18″ long, 3-4″ wide and spotted with white. The creamy white spathe is trumpet shaped (not flaring as in the previous species), 4-5″ long, and has a purple blotch at the base. The main value is increased cold tolerance, compared to other species, which occasionally permits overwintering in zone 7 with protection. It has been used extensively in hybridization to take advantage of cold hardiness genes.

Propagation is similar to *Z. aethiopica*.

***-rehmannii*** (ray-mahn′ ee-aye) Pink Calla 9-15″/20″
Summer Pink, Rose South Africa Zones 8-10

This dwarfer species has 7-15″ long lanceolate leaves covered with small greenish or white spots. The 4″ long spathe is trumpet shaped and varies from pink to rose to white with a pink tint. Its size makes it particularly suitable for pot culture.

Propagate similar to *Z. aethiopica*.

**Related species and hybrids:**

Many hybrids are available which are commercially used as cut flowers or pot plants. Some of the finest cultivars are emerging from nurseries in New Zealand and California. These plants sport red, pink, yellow, gold and green spathes mostly with spotted leaves. Many of the hybrids have the purple blotch in the bottom of the spathe associated with *Z. albo-maculata*. Zone 7b at best.

'Black Magic' is an old-fashioned form that bears yellow flowers, each with a prominent black blotch in the spathe. One of the best, if still available.

'Black Pearl' has waxy, dark maroon flowers, with a thin red margin around the spathe. Plants grow up to 3′ tall.

'Captain Chelsea' bears eye-catching rose-purple and yellow flowers, with the darker color on the inside, the yellow on the outside of the spathe.

'Edge of Night', from Terra Nova Nursery, produces dark purple to almost black flowers.

*Z. elliotiana*, Elliot's calla, has silvery white spots on the foliage and produces 4-5″ long bright yellow spathes in summer. Spathes do not have a purple blotch on the back. Plants are hardy to about zone 8.

'Galaxy' has red and yellow flowers.

'Hercules' is huge; at 5-6′ tall, it is one of the largest selections for the garden. Plants produce large white flowers.

## ***Zauschneria*** see *Epilobium*

## ***Zephyranthes*** (ze-fi-ranth′ eez) Zephyr Lily Liliaceae

The zephyr lily takes its name from *zephyros*, west wind, a reference to the New World (being in the west), from where the genus arrived in Europe. Thus it also became known as the flower of the west wind. Individual species also have their common names. Flowers of *Z. grandiflora*, rosepink zephyr lily, open after every rain and are known as rain lilies. The largest member of the genus, native to the southern states, is the atamasco lily, *Z. atamasco*.

All have narrow leaves and funnel-shaped flowers borne singly on a hollow scape. In general, they prefer moist conditions in full sun or partial shade and are rather tender, usually winter hardy only to zone 8, zone 7 with protection. However, they make excellent potted plants for the deck or patio, and 10-12 bulbs of *Z. grandiflora* in a 6-8″ container makes a glorious display. If the bulbs are stored over winter, place in moist sand or peat moss in a cool (50°F) area. If pot-grown, simply keep the soil moist, not wet, and store in the same area.

Most of the approximately 35 species are spring and summer flowering, however *Z. candida* and *Z. rosea* flower in late summer and fall. There are few obvious differences among species based on botanical characteristics, and the easiest way to separate them is by flower color and season of bloom.

Quick Reference to Zephyranthes Species

| | Height (in.) | Flower color | Bloom season |
|---|---|---|---|
| *Z. atamasco* | 18-36 | White | Spring |
| *Z. candida* | 9-15 | White | Fall |
| *Z. grandiflora* | 9-15 | Rose | Summer |
| *Z. rosea* | 9-15 | Rose | Fall |

***-atamasco*** (a-ta-mas′ ko) Atamasco Lily 18-36″/18″
Spring White Southeastern United States Zones 7-10

The earliest flowering and most robust zephyr lily, it produces 4-6 bright green, channeled evergreen leaves about 18″ long and ¼″ wide. The pure white fragrant flowers emerge as pointed, pink striped buds and open flat and starlike. The perianth (petals) may be up to 4″ long. Flowers open in April and May and continue for 4-6 weeks. This species is native to damp, acid, meadowlands; dry conditions result in small, fleeting flowers. If planted in protected areas and provided with mulch, bulbs may overwinter as far north as New York. If bulbs are removed in the fall, dig before the first hard frost and store in peat moss in an area that does not freeze. Replant in the spring after the last frost. var. *treatiae* is native to Florida and blooms 2-4 weeks earlier than atamasco lily. The dull gray-green foliage is less than 1/10″ wide and red flower buds open to blossoms of pure white. Hardy only in zones 8-10.

Propagate by removal of the small bulblets in the fall or by seed. Seeds sown in a warm (70-75°F), moist area germinate within four weeks. Flowering occurs the second or third year.

***-grandiflora*** (grand-i-flo′ ra) Rosepink Zephyr Lily 9-15″/18″
Summer Rose Guatemala Zones 9-10

The foliage is 10-15″ long, narrowly strap-shaped and spreads out over the ground. The rose-red flowers are 3-4″ long and emerge from a maroon-red flower bud atop a 7″ tall scape. My great-uncle Peter in Mansonville, Quebec beams over his pots of lilies that flower like magic on his porch after every summer rain. The same excitement

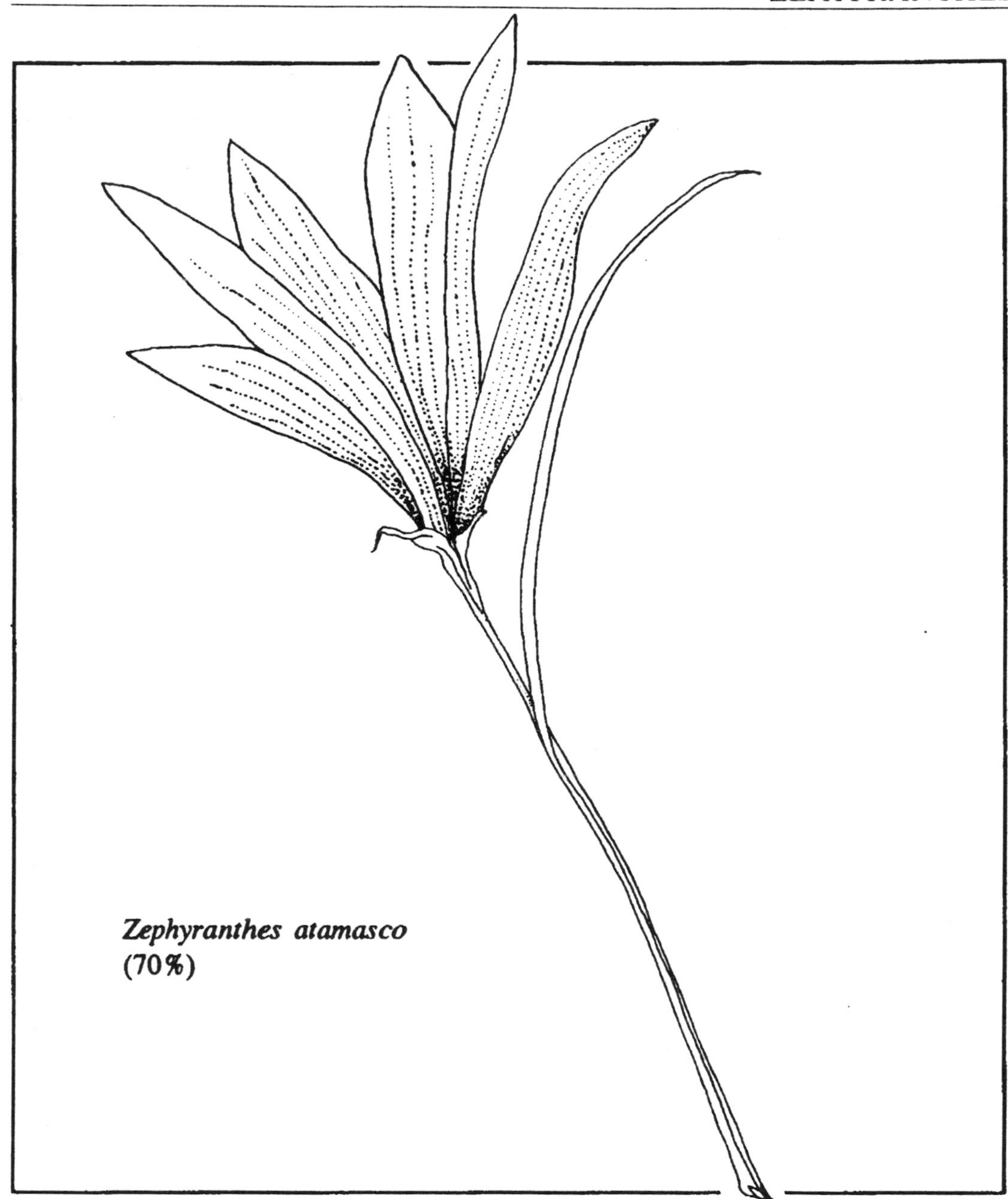

***Zephyranthes atamasco***
**(70%)**

and enthusiasm comes from Mark Krause, one of the outstanding horticulturists at Disney World in Orlando, Florida. It is little wonder that this is the most popular species of zephyr lily. Bulbs look wonderful in containers and bring rave reviews from guests.

Propagate similar to *Z. atamasco.*

**Related Species and Hybrids:**

Boy oh boy, it has taken us a long time to discover these plants, but now discovered, we have many species and hybrids from which to choose. The fabulous Yucca Do

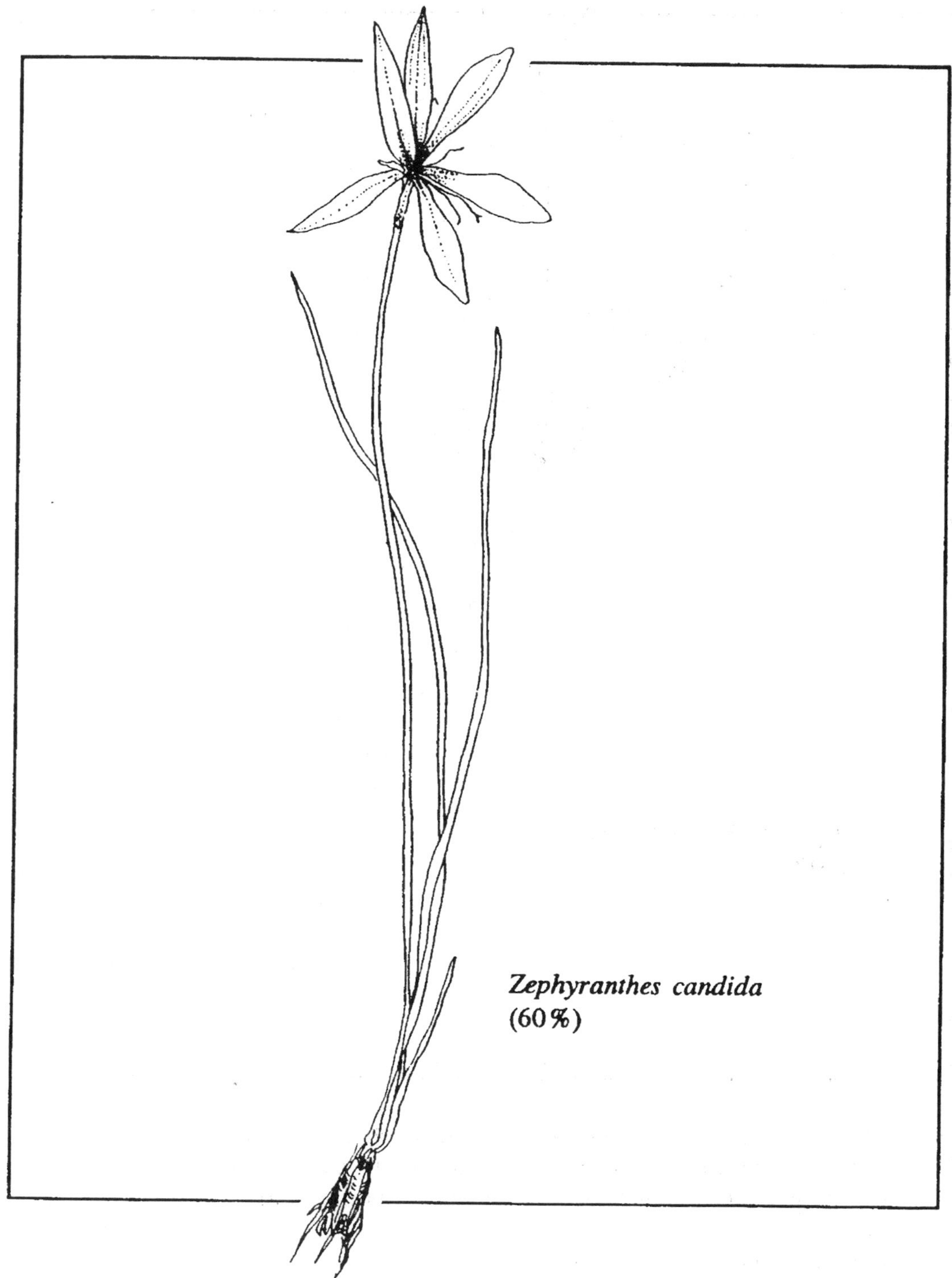

*Zephyranthes candida*
(60%)

Nursery in Hempstead, Texas, offers 20 choices; Plant Delights Nursery in Raleigh, North Carolina has 27 of these things. All are wonderful, here is a handful I know.

'Apricot Queen' is a treasure. Its shiny green leaves and salmon-peach flowers are really quite wonderful. Introduced by Thad M. Howard, the leading authority on Texas bulbs.

'Ajax' is a hybrid between *Z. candida* and *Z. citrina*, a lemon-colored crocus-like species. The leaf shape is similar to *Z. candida* and the primrose-yellow flowers resemble *Z. citrina*. Hardy to zone 8.

*Z. candida* is known as La Plata lily because of the abundance of these silvery flowers around an unnamed river in Argentina. The presence of such beauty led the discoverer, Diaz de Solis, to name it Rio de La Plata (River of Silver). Plants produce grassy leaves and silvery white crocus-like flowers with rich orange stamens that open in late May. A terrific plant.

*Z. citrina*, gold cup, has golden flowers in the fall. Zone 7.

*Z. drummondii*, Drummond's rain lily, is an early-flowering species with handsome clean white, fragrant flowers. The leaves are narrow and grasslike. Zones 7-9.

*Z. flavissima*, yellow rain lily, is about a foot tall with star-shaped golden yellow flowers. Zones 6-8.

'Grandjax' is a hybrid between *Z. grandiflora* and the hybrid 'Ajax'. Plants bear many light pink flowers with white centers. Wonderfully aggressive, and quick to fill a lonely area.

'Labuffarosea' was introduced by Yucca Do Nursery from plants growing around 4,000′ elevation in Mexico. Plants have an abundance of 2-3′ wide white flowers usually with pink on the margins. Yucca Do has subsequently released two other sports: 'Itsy Bitsy' has narrow leaves and shiny white flowers and 'Lily Pies' has rose-pink and white colors that blend on rounded overlapping petals. Spectacular.

'Pink Panther' arose from a 'Labuffarosea' seedling at Plant Delights and is similar to 'Lily Pies', but with a little more rose in the flowers.

*Z. rosea*, Cuban zephyr lily, has flowers of similar color to *Z. grandiflora* but less than half the size and which appear 3-4 weeks later. Leaves are about 8″ long and ¼″ wide. It is also a good container plant but not as long lived in the ground as *Z. grandiflora*.

## ***Zigadenus*** (zi-ga-den′ nus) Death Camas, Zygadene Liliaceae

Most of these native North American bulb species are unknown to gardeners, however, since a number of the 16 or so species are poisonous to livestock, they have become infamous to ranchers in the Midwest and Plains states. All species of *Zigadenus* (also incorrectly spelled *Zygadenus*) contain a toxic alkaloid that can cause vomiting and result in comas in humans. The most poisonous, and the species that accounts for the common name, is *Z. nuttallii*, native from Tennessee and west to Texas and Kansas. *Z. venenosus* also goes by the same common name and is found on the West Coast from California to British Columbia. Both have white flowers and arguably should not be used as garden plants. The latter, in fact, is not particularly ornamental anyway. One of the taller species is *Z. glaberrimus*, which can grow to 3′ tall with creamy white flowers.

The only species for gardens, and this can be debated, is the least toxic and probably the most ornamental of the group, *Z. elegans*. I saw this plant in all its glory at Smith College in western Massachusetts on a clear August day, where it was blooming its head off in 90 degree heat. Plants are native to Colorado, Nevada, Oregon and north to Alaska, and have also escaped into Arizona, Texas and parts of New Mexico. Plants grow about 12″ tall with 6-12″ long and ½″ wide grassy foliage. The flowers, which consist of six tepals, are greenish on the outside and creamy white on the inside and open wide in a saucer shape. They are attached to stiff 1″ long flower stem, allowing the flowers to face upward. They also have an obvious gland at the base of the tepals (the botanical name comes from *zygion*, yoke and *Aden*, gland), a characteristic useful to distinguish it from *Tofieldia*, a genus with similar flowers. Not a bad little plant, just don't put it anywhere where kids or animals might want to chew on it. Propagate by division.

***Zizia*** (ziz-e′ a) Golden Alexanders Apiaceae

About four North American species occur, and a couple are well-known plants in the Northeast, Mid-Atlantic, and Midwest. *Zizia* has yellow umbels of flowers over 2-2½′ tall plants and differs from other yellow umbelliferus species in that the central flower has no pedicel (flower stalk). Also, for those attentive souls, you will also notice that the fruit is ribbed but not winged.

Two species are occasionally offered. In my opinion, neither is much to get excited about but can be useful in the right spot (so can a billboard when you are looking for a hotel in the middle of the night). However, there is hope for me yet and I admit that the more I see the plant, the more I am coming around.

The basal and stem leaves of *Z. aurea*, golden Alexanders, are biternate (divided into three and then redivided into three again) and sharply toothed. The umbel consists of up to twenty flowers on short flower stems all approximately the same length, except for the sessile center one. They flower in April to June and are fairly common in the Atlantic states. The other familiar species, mainly in the Midwest, is *Z. aptera*. This zizzy differs from the other by having entire basal leaves that are bluntly toothed on the margins. The inflorescences are similar, although they usually consist of fewer flowers.

Propagate by seed or division.

# Glossary of Terms Employed in Text

## A

**a** prefix meaning not or without. eg. apetalous, without petals
**acaulis** stemless or with short stems only
**acephalus** headless
**acerifolius** maple leaved
**acicularis** needle like
**acuminatum** usually referring to a leaf blade whose sides are somewhat concave and taper to a point
**affinus** related to another species
**africanus** african
**alatus** winged
**albidus** white
**alternate** arrangement of leaves where one leaf occurs at each node
**alternifolius** alternate leaved
**amethystinus** violet colored
**amplexicaulis** stem clasping
**annuus** annual
**antiquorum** of the ancients
**apetalus** without petals
**apex** the tip or terminal end
**aphyllus** leafless
**aquaticus** aquatic
**aquilinus** eagle like
**arachnoides** spider like, cobweb like
**arboreus** tree like
**argentatus** silvery
**argenteoguttatus** silver spotted
**argutus** sharp toothed, notched
**aromaticus** obviously aromatic, at least if broken or crushed
**arundinaceus** reed like
**ascendens** ascending
**assimilis** similar or like
**atrococcineus** dark scarlet
**atropurpureus** dark purple
**auratus** golden
**australis** southern

## B

**baccatus** berried
**basal** pertaining to leaves which arise from the base of the plant
**bearded** having long hairs
**bellus** handsome
**biennial** of two season's growth, flowers and fruit are produced the second season from seed germination. Plants die after fruiting
**biennis** biennial
**biflorus** two flowered
**bilobus** two lobed
**biternate** twice divided into threes. Eg. leaves of Aquilegia whose primary divisions are again divided into three
**borealis** northern
**bract** a much reduced leaf, usually scale-like and associated with flowering. Eg. flowers of Eryngium are subtended by bracts
**brachycalyx** short calyx
**bulb** a fleshy underground stem with a short central axis surrounded by fleshy scale-like leaves. Eg. Lilium
**bulbil** small bulb arising around the parent bulb
**bulblet** small bulb arising in the leaf axils
**bulbosus** bulbous

## C

**caeruleus** dark blue
**calyx** the sepals as a group, directly below petals
**campanularia** bellflowered
**canadensis** Canada, but used to cover Northeastern United States
**candicans** shining
**caninus** pertaining to a dog
**cannabinus** like hemp
**cardinalis** cardinal red
**carduaceus** thistle like
**carolinianus** of North Carolina or South Carolina
**caulescens** having a stem
**cernuus** drooping
**cespitose** growing in tufts or dense clumps
**chiloensis** of the island of Chiloe off the Chilean coat, belonging to Chile
**chinensis** chinese
**chrysophyllus** golden leaved
**citratus** citrus like
**citriodorus** lemon scented
**clasping** leaf without petiole, with the base partly surrounding the stem
**clustered** leaves tightly arranged, but not opposite or alternate. Also in reference to flowers

**cochlearis** spoon like
**comans** hair like
**compactus** compact or dense
**composite** a member of the Asteraceae
**compositus** compound
**confusus** confused, uncertain, apt to be taken for another species
**cordate** heart-shaped.
**cordatus** heart shaped
**corm** solid bulb-like underground stem, not differentiated into scales. Eg. Crocus
**cormel** small corm arising from parent corm
**corniculatus** horned
**corolla** the petals as a group
**corona** an extrusion of tissue that stands between the corolla and the stamens, or on the corolla. Eg. the cup of Narcissus
**coronarius** used for or pertaining to garlands
**corymb** More or less flat-topped indeterminate inflorescence, the outer flowers open first
**crassifolius** thick leaved
**crenate** rounded teeth on margin.
**crown** the central growing point beneath or near the surface of the ground
**cymbiformis** boat shaped
**cyme** more or less flat-topped determinate inflorescence, the outer flowers open last

# D

**decoratus** decorative
**decumbent** reclining or lying on the ground, but with ends ascending
**decurrent** extending down the stem, as the leaf of Verbascum
**deflexus** bent abruptly downward
**deliciosus** delicious
**deltoid** triangular
**dentate** having teeth perpendicular to the margin, do not point forward
**dentatus** toothed
**determinate** refers to an inflorescence whose center flower opens first and axis elongation is thereby arrested
**dichotomus** forked in pairs
**didymus** in pairs
**dioeciou** male and female flowers on separate plants
**diphyllus** two leaved
**disk flower** tubular flower at the center of composites. Eg. sunflower
**diurnal** flowers open only during the day
**downy** having soft hairs.
**dulcis** sweet

## E

**edulis** edible
**elatus** tall
**emarginated** with a shallow notch at the apex
**ensifolius** sword shaped leaves
**erectus** erect or upright
**exaltatus** very tall
**excelsus** tall
**exoticus** exotic
**exserted** projecting beyond, as in stamens beyond a corolla

## F

**fallax** deceptive
**farinaceous** having a powdery or mealy coating, as in some species of Salvia
**farinosus** powdery
**ferox** very thorny
**fertilis** fruitful
**filament** the stalk of the stamen
**fimbriatus** fingered
**flaccidus** flaccid or soft
**flavus** yellow
**flexuosus** tortuous, zig zag
**florepleno** double flowers
**floribundus** blooming profusely
**foetidus** bad smelling
**fragilis** fragile or brittle
**fragrans** fragrant
**frigidus** cold regions
**fulgens** shiny

## G

**giganteus** gigantic or very large
**glaber** smooth
**gland** a general term for oil-secreting organs, sometimes a projection at the base of a structure
**glaucous** covered with a waxy bloom or whitish substance that rubs off easily
**globose** round or spherical shape
**glossy** shining, lustrous
**glutinosus** gluey or sticky
**grandiflorus** large flowered
**grandifolius** large leaved
**grandis** large
**graveloens** heavy scented
**guttatus** spotted or speckled

## H

**habit** the general outline or shape of a plant
**haemanthus** blood red flowered
**hairy** pubescent with long hairs
**hastate** in the shape of an arrowhead; the basal lobes are pointed and nearly at right angles
**head** a short dense inflorescence; the inflorescence of a composite consisting of ray and disc flowers
**helodoxa** marsh beauty
**herbaceus** herbaceous
**hexapetalus** six petaled
**hibernicus** of Ireland
**hirsutus** hairy
**hispid** having stiff or bristly hairs
**horizontalis** horizontal
**horridus** very prickly or thorny
**hortensis** of or pertaining to gardens
**humilis** low growing
**hiemalis** of winter

## I

**ibericus** of Iberia
**illustris** bright or lustrous
**imperfect** a flower that lacks either stamens or pistils
**imperialis** imperial or kingly
**incised** sharp incisions, between toothed and lobed
**incisifolius** cut leaved
**incisus** cut or incised
**incomplete** a flower that lacks either calyx, corolla, stamens or pistils
**indeterminate** inflorescence whose center flowers open last, the growth and elongation of the main axis is not arrested with the opening of the first flowers
**inermis** unarmed without thorns
**inflatus** swollen
**infundibuliformis** trumpet shaped
**inodorus** without odor
**integrifolius** entire leaved
**italicus** of Italy

## J

**japonicus** of Japan
**jubatus** crested

## K

**koreanus** of Korea

## L

**labiatus** lipped
**lacustris** pertaining to lakes
**laevigatus** smooth
**laevis** smooth
**lanceolatus** lanceolate
**lanicaulis** wooly stemmed
**latera** borne at or on the side, as in the flower bud borne in a leaf axil
**latifolius** broad leaved
**laxus** open or loose
**leianthus** smooth flowered
**lepthophyllus** thin leaved
**leucanthus** white flowered
**lilifolius** lily leaved
**linear** long and very narrow, as in leaves
**linearis** linear
**lobe** usually a division of leaf, calyx, or petals cut to about the middle
**longifolius** long leaved
**luteus** yellow

## M

**macranthus** large flowered
**macropetalus** large petaled
**macrophyllus** large leaved
**macrorrhizus** large rooted
**maculatus** spotted
**majalis** May flowering, but often used as spring flowering
**maritimus** of the sea
**marmoratus** marbled
**masculus** male
**maximus** largest
**mealy** a granular appearance
**meleagris** speckled, spotted
**meridionalis** noonday, blooming at noon
**micranthus** small flowered
**monstrosus** abnormal, monstrous
**multicaulis** many stemmed
**multiflorus** many flowered

## N

**nanus** dwarf
**natans** floating or swimming
**native** inherent or original to an area
**nitidus** shining

**niveus** snowy
**node** a joint on a stem from which leaves arise.
**nudicaulis** naked stemmed, no stem leaves
**nudiflorus** naked flowers, flowers before the leaves
**nutans** nodding

## O

**obesus** obese or fat
**oblong** longer than broad, the sides nearly parallel
**oblongifolius** oblong leaved
**obovate** broadest above the middle
**oculatus** eyed
**odoratus** fragrant
**odoratissimus** highly fragrant
**officinalis** with real or supposed medicinal value
**oleifera** oil bearing
**oppositifolius** opposite leaved
**ovalifolius** oval leaved
**ovate** egg-shaped in outline, broadest below the middle
**oxypetalus** sharp petaled
**oxysepalus** sharp sepaled

## P

**pachyphyllus** thick leaved
**paired** occurring in two's
**palmate** fan-like from a common point
**palmatus** palmately cut, like a hand with outstretched fingers
**panicle** an indeterminate inflorescence whose primary axis bears branches of pedicelled flowers, a compound inflorescence
**papilionaceus** butterfly like
**parviflorus** small flowered
**patens** spreading
**parallel** running side to side from base to tip, as in monocot leaves
**parted** cut deeply but not quite to base
**pauciflorus** few flowered
**pedatus** bird footed
**pedicel** the stalk of a flower or fruit
**peduncle** the stalk of a flower cluster or of a single flower when flower is solitary
**peltate** the petiole attached inside the margin
**perfect** a flower: having both functional stamens and pistils
**perfoliate** the leaf-blade surrounding the stem
**perianth** the calyx and corolla together. Often used when calyx and corolla are indistinguisible
**petaloid** structure resembling, but not, a petal

**petiole** leaf stalk
**petraeus** rock loving
**pleniflorus** double flowered
**plumose** feather-like
**procerus** tall
**procumbent** lying flat but stems not rooting at the nodes or tips
**prostrate** lying flat on the ground
**pubescens** pubescent or downy
**pubescent** covered with short, soft hairs
**pumilus** dwarf
**punctuate** with translucent or covered dots, depressions, or pits

## Q

**quinquefolius** five leaved

## R

**raceme** a simple indeterminate inflorescence with pedicelled flowers
**racemose** having flowers in racemes
**rachis** the axis bearing leaflets or the primary flowers of an inflorescence
**radicans** rooting
**rectus** straight, upright
**reflexed** bent abruptly backward or downward
**regalis** royal
**repens** creeping
**reptans** creeping
**revolute** rolled toward the back, as in a revolute margin
**rigens** rigid or stiff
**ringens** gaping, as in the mouth of an open flower or spathe
**rosette** a crown of leaves, at or close to the surface of the ground
**rotate** wheel-shaped with inconspicuous corolla tube, usually refers to flowers
**rubens** ruby
**ruber** red
**rupestris** rock loving

## S

**saccharum** sugared or sugary, sweet tasting or looking like sprinkled with sugar
**sagittatus** arrow leaved
**sanguineus** blood red
**saponarius** soapy
**sarmentose** having long, flexuous runners
**saxatilis** found among rocks
**scandens** climbing

**scape** a leafless peduncle arising from a basal rosette. Occasionally bract-like leaves may be present
**schizopetalus** with cut petals
**semperflorens** ever flowering
**sempervirens** evergreen
**sericeus** silky
**serratus** serate
**sessile** without a petiole or stalk
**sessilis** sessile, stalkless
**similis** similar
**simple** a leaf not compounded into leaflets, an unbranched inflorescence
**speciosus** showy
**spectabilis** remarkable, showy
**spike** an unbranched indeterminate inflorescence with sessile flowers
**spikelet** a secondary spike.
**stellate** star-like
**sterile** barren, not able to produce seed
**stolon** a horizontal stem that roots at the tip and gives rise to a new plant
**stolonifera** runners that take root
**stoloniferous** bearing slender stems just on or under the ground which root at the tips
**suaveolens** sweet scented
**sylvaticus** growing in the woods, wild
**sylvestris** growing in the woods, wild

## T

**tardiflorus** late flowered
**tectorum** of roofs of houses, pertaining to various plants that were growing on thatched roofs in Sweden and named by Linnaeus
**tenax** strong, tough
**tenuis** slender
**tepal** a segment of perianth not differentiated into calyx and corolla. Often used when sepals and petals are indistinguishible as in bulbous plants like tulips
**terminal** at the end.
**terminalis** terminal
**ternate** in threes.
**titanius** very large
**tomentose** densely woolly, hairs soft and matted
**tortuosus** much twisted
**trailing** prostrate but not rooting
**trifoliate** three-leaved. Eg. Trillium
**tuber** a short, thickened organ, usually an underground stem

## U

**umbel** an indeterminate inflorescence usually flat-topped with pedicels arising from a single point, like an umbrella
**umbellatus** with umbels
**umbrosus** shade loving
**undulate** wavy, as a leaf margin
**uniflorus** one flowered
**utilis** useful

## V X Y Z

**versicolor** variously colored
**verticillate** arranged in whorls
**virgatus** twiggy
**virginiansis** of Virginia
**viridis** green
**viscid** sticky
**vulgaris** common
**xanthinus** yellow
**yedoensis** of Yedo, now Tokyo, Japan
**zebrinus** zebra striped
**zonatus** banded with a distinct color, zonal

# Index to Scientific Names

## B

## D

## E

## H

## I

## R

## T

## U



## V

## W



## X



## Y



## Z

# Index to Common Names

## C

## G

## H



## I



## J

## M

## T

## U



## V



## W

# *Credits*

*Illustrations by Bonnie Dirr:* 9, 10, 12,15, 16, 28, 29, 30, 31, 34, 59, 70, 82, 88, 89, 92, 94, 108, 109, 113, 119, 130, 143, 147, 150, 151, 157, 161, 163, 168, 169, 192, 200, 207, 252, 263, 264, 267, 282, 289, 307, 345, 369, 383, 396, 408, 411, 433, 440, 452, 456, 461, 466, 467, 468, 492, 495, 497, 500, 503, 508, 520, 529, 532, 543, 544, 550, 566, 569, 577, 582, 585, 586, 606, 619, 623, 649, 654, 669, 677, 688, 699, 703, 707, 711, 747, 789, 790, 792, 805, 809, 816, 820, 832, 840, 843, 865, 866, 878, 883, 891, 917, 918, 949, 954 (leaf), 956, 969, 975, 979, 986, 990, 1014, 1023, 1031, 1033, 1036, 1041, 1042, 1043, 1057, 1058

*Illustrations by Dr. David Sandrock:* 37, 41, 48, 52, 64, 72, 98, 94, 123, 125, 126, 136, 140, 174, 178, 190, 197, 205, 209, 225, 246, 258, 273, 287, 310, 321, 327, 337, 352, 361, 392, 401, 428, 438, 493, 512, 517, 531, 535, 547, 561, 584, 597, 604, 647, 658, 665, 674, 678, 724, 725, 736, 742, 744, 746, 760, 765, 775, 811, 822, 852, 854, 868, 870, 881, 889, 895, 896, 910, 936, 947, 954 (flower), 957, 997, 998, 999, 1009, 1019, 1021

*All photographs by:* Allan M. Armitage except *Geranium maculatum, Podophyllum peltatum* (flowers), *Zizia aptera,* and *Zizia aurea* by Natalia K. Hamill.